Tools for Design

Using
AutoCAD 2027 and Autodesk Inventor 2027

Randy H. Shih
Oregon Institute of Technology

SDC PUBLICATIONS

SDC Publications
P.O. Box 1334
Mission, KS 66222
913-262-2664
www.SDCpublications.com
Publisher: Stephen Schroff

ISBN-13: 978-1-63057-806-0
ISBN-10: 1-63057-806-1

Printed and bound in the United States of America.

Preface

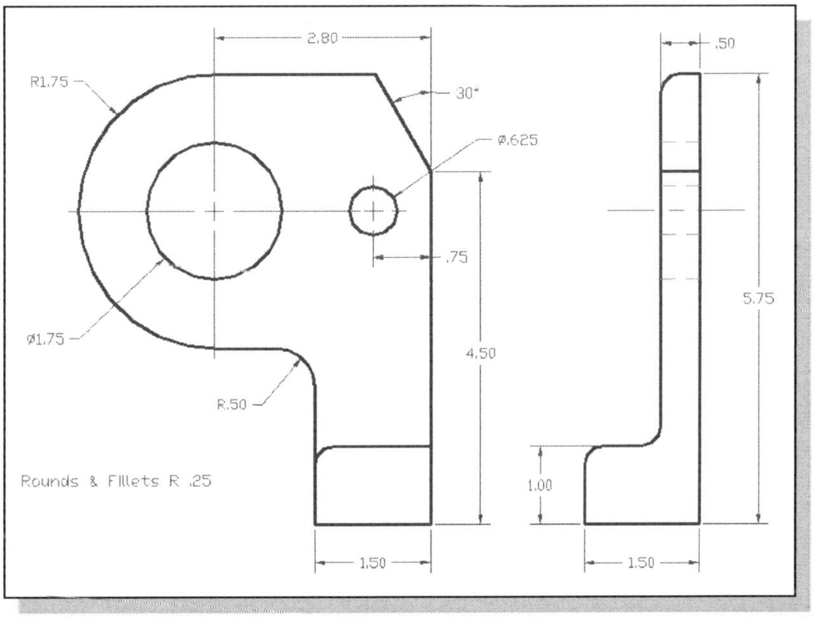

The primary goal of **Tools for Design Using AutoCAD and Autodesk Inventor** is to introduce the aspects of designing using computer aided design tools, which include both **2D** and **3D Modeling**. This text is intended to be used as a practical training guide for students and professionals. This text uses **AutoCAD® 2027** and **Autodesk Inventor® 2027** as the computer modeling tools and the chapters proceed in a pedagogical fashion to guide you from constructing basic geometry to multiview drawings, to solid models, to building intelligent mechanical designs and to creating assembly models. This text takes a hands-on, exercise-intensive approach to all the important *Computer Aided Design* techniques and concepts. This textbook contains a series of fifteen tutorial style lessons designed to introduce beginning CAD users to **AutoCAD** and **Autodesk Inventor**. This text is also helpful to AutoCAD and Autodesk Inventor users upgrading from a previous release of the software. The computer modeling techniques and concepts discussed in this text are also applicable to other parametric feature-based CAD packages. The basic premise of this book is that the more designs you create using AutoCAD and Autodesk Inventor, the better you learn the software. With this in mind, each lesson introduces a new set of commands and concepts, building on previous lessons. This book does not attempt to cover all of the AutoCAD and Autodesk Inventor features, only to provide an introduction to the software. It is intended to help you establish a good basis for exploring and growing in the exciting field of **Computer Aided Engineering**.

Acknowledgments

This book would not have been possible without a great deal of support. First, special thanks to two great teachers, Professor George R. Schade of University of Nebraska-Lincoln and Mr. Denwu Lee from Taiwan, who showed me the fundamentals, the intrigue, and the sheer fun of Computer Aided Design and Computer Aided Engineering.

The effort and support of the staff of SDC Publications is gratefully acknowledged. I would especially like to thank Stephen Schroff for his support.

I am also grateful that the Department of Mechanical and Manufacturing Engineering and Technology at Oregon Institute of Technology has provided me with an excellent environment in which to pursue my passions in teaching and research.

Finally, truly unbounded thanks are due to my wife Hsiu-Ling and our daughter Casandra for their understanding and encouragement throughout this project.

Randy H. Shih
Klamath Falls, Oregon
Spring, 2026

Table of Contents

Preface i
Acknowledgments ii

Introduction
Getting Started

Introduction Intro-2
Development of Computer Aided Design Intro-2
Why Use AutoCAD 2027? Intro-5
Why Use Autodesk Inventor 2027? Intro-6
Tutorial Style Lessons Intro-7

Section I – AutoCAD

Chapter 1
Fundamentals of AutoCAD

Getting Started with AutoCAD 2027 1-2
AutoCAD 2027 Screen Layout 1-3
Application Menu 1-4
Quick Access Toolbar 1-4
AutoCAD Menu Bar 1-4
Layout Tabs 1-4
Drawing Area 1-5
Graphics Cursor or Crosshairs 1-5
Command Prompt Area 1-5
Cursor Coordinates 1-5
Status Toolbar 1-5
Ribbon Tabs and Panels 1-6
Draw and Modify Toolbar Panels 1-6
Layers Control Toolbar Panel 1-6
Viewport/View/Display Controls 1-6
Mouse Buttons 1-7
[Esc] – Canceling Commands 1-7
Online Help 1-8
Leaving AutoCAD 2027 1-9
Creating a CAD File Folder 1-9
Drawing in AutoCAD 1-10
Starting Up AutoCAD 2027 1-10
Drawing Units Setup 1-12
Drawing Area Setup 1-13
Drawing Lines with the Line Command 1-15
Visual Reference 1-17

GRID ON 1-18
SNAP MODE ON 1-19
Using the Erase Command 1-20
Repeat the Last Command 1-21
The CAD Database and the User Coordinate System 1-22
Changing to the 2D UCS Icon Display 1-23
Cartesian and Polar Coordinate Systems 1-24
Absolute and Relative Coordinates 1-24
Defining Positions 1-25
Grid Style Setup 1-25
The Guide Plate 1-26
Creating Circles 1-30
Saving the CAD Design 1-32
Close the Current Drawing 1-33
The Spacer Design 1-34
Start a New Drawing 1-34
Drawing Units Setup 1-35
Drawing Area Setup 1-36
Using the Line Command 1-38
Using the Erase Command 1-40
Using the Arc Command 1-40
Using the Circle Command 1-42
Saving the CAD Design 1-43
Exit AutoCAD 2027 1-43
Review Questions 1-44
Exercises 1-45

Chapter 2
Basic Object Construction and Dynamic Input - AutoCAD

Introduction 2-2
Starting Up AutoCAD 2027 2-2
Dynamic Input 2-3
The Rocker-Arm Design 2-6
Activate the Startup Option 2-7
Drawing Units Display Setup 2-8
Grid and Snap Intervals Setup 2-9
Drawing Area Setup 2-10
Referencing the World Coordinate System 2-11
Creating Circles 2-12
Object Snap Toolbar 2-13
Using the Line Command 2-14
Creating TTR Circles 2-16
Using the Trim Command 2-18
Using the Polygon Command 2-20
Creating a Concentric Circle 2-22

Using the QuickCalc Calculator to Measure Distance and Angle 2-23
Saving the CAD File 2-27
Exit AutoCAD 2-27
AutoCAD Quick Keys 2-28
Review Questions 2-29
Exercises 2-30

Chapter 3
Geometric Construction and Editing Tools - AutoCAD

Geometric Constructions 3-2
Starting Up AutoCAD 2027 3-3
Geometric Construction - CAD Method 3-4
Bisection of a Line or Arc 3-4
Bisection of an Angle 3-7
Transfer of an Angle 3-9
Dividing a Given Line into a Number of Equal Parts 3-12
Circle through Three Points 3-14
Line Tangent to a Circle from a Given Point 3-15
Circle of a Given Radius Tangent to Two Given Lines 3-16
The Gasket Design 3-19
Drawing Units Display Setup 3-20
Grid and Snap Intervals Setup 3-21
Using the Line Command with ORTHO Option 3-22
Object Snap Toolbar 3-24
Using the Extend Command 3-27
Using the Trim Command 3-28
Creating a TTR Circle 3-29
Using the Fillet Command 3-30
Converting Objects into a Polyline 3-31
Using the Offset Command 3-32
Using the Area Inquiry Tool to Measure Area and Perimeter 3-33
Using the Explode Command 3-35
Create another Fillet 3-35
Saving the CAD File 3-36
Exit AutoCAD 3-36
Review Questions 3-37
Exercises 3-38

Chapter 4
Orthographic Views in Multiview Drawings - AutoCAD

Introduction 4-2
The Locator Design 4-2
The Locator Part 4-3
Starting Up AutoCAD 2027 4-3

Layers Setup 4-4
Drawing Construction Lines 4-5
Using the Offset Command 4-5
Set Layer Object as the Current Layer 4-7
Using the Running Object Snaps 4-7
Creating Object Lines 4-9
Turn Off the Construction Lines Layer 4-10
Adding More Objects in the Front View 4-10
AutoCAD's AutoSnap™ and AutoTrack™ Features 4-11
Adding More Objects in the Top View 4-13
Drawing Using the Miter Line Method 4-17
More Layers Setup 4-19
Top View to Side View Projection 4-20
Completing the Front View 4-22
Object Information Using the List Command 4-24
Object Information Using the Properties Command 4-25
Review Questions 4-26
Exercises 4-27

Chapter 5
Basic Dimensioning and Notes - AutoCAD

Introduction 5-2
The Bracket Design 5-2
Starting Up AutoCAD 2027 5-3
Layers Setup 5-4
The P-Bracket Design 5-5
LineWeight Display Control 5-5
Drawing Construction Lines 5-6
Using the Offset Command 5-6
Set Layer Object_Lines as the Current Layer 5-8
Creating Object Lines 5-8
Creating Hidden Lines 5-9
Creating Center Lines 5-10
Turn Off the Construction Lines 5-10
Using the Fillet Command 5-11
Saving the Completed CAD Design 5-12
Accessing the Dimensioning Commands 5-13
The Dimension Toolbar 5-14
Using the Dimension Style Manager 5-14
Dimensions Nomenclature and Basics 5-15
Using the Center Mark Command 5-18
Adding Linear Dimensions 5-19
Adding Linear Dimensions Using the Object Option 5-20
Adding Radius and Diameter Dimensions 5-22
Using the Multiline Text Command 5-23

Adding Special Characters 5-24
Saving the Design 5-25
A Special Note on Layers Containing Dimensions 5-25
Review Questions 5-26
Exercises 5-27

Chapter 6
Pictorials and Sketching

Engineering Drawings, Pictorials and Sketching 6-2
Isometric Sketching 6-7
Chapter 6 - Isometric Sketching Exercises 6-9
Oblique Sketching 6-19
Chapter 6 - Oblique Sketching Exercises 6-20
Perspective Sketching 6-26
One-point Perspective 6-27
Two-point Perspective 6-28
Chapter 6 - Perspective Sketching Exercises 6-29
Review Questions 6-35
Exercises 6-36

Section II – Autodesk Inventor

Chapter 7
Parametric Modeling Fundamentals – Autodesk Inventor

Getting Started with Autodesk Inventor 7-2
The Screen Layout and Getting Started 7-3
The New File Dialog Box and Units Setup 7-4
The Default Autodesk Inventor Screen Layout 7-5
File Menu 7-6
Quick Access Toolbar 7-6
Ribbon Tabs and Tool Panels 7-6
Online Help Panel 7-6
3D Model Toolbar 7-7
Graphics Window 7-7
Message and Status Bar 7-7
Mouse Buttons 7-8
[Esc] – Canceling Commands 7-8
Autodesk Inventor Help System 7-9
Data Management Using Inventor Project Files 7-10
Setting up a New Inventor Project 7-11
The Content of the Inventor Project File 7-14
Leaving Autodesk Inventor 7-14
Feature-Based Parametric Modeling 7-15

The Adjuster Design 7-16
Starting Autodesk Inventor 7-16
The Default Autodesk Inventor Screen Layout 7-18
Sketch Plane – It is an XY Monitor, but an XYZ World 7-19
Creating Rough Sketches 7-21
Step 1: Creating a Rough Sketch 7-22
Graphics Cursors 7-22
Geometric Constraint Symbols 7-23
Step 2: Apply/Modify Constraints and Dimensions 7-24
Dynamic Viewing Functions – Zoom and Pan 7-27
Modifying the Dimensions of the Sketch 7-27
Step 3: Completing the Base Solid Feature 7-28
Isometric View 7-29
Dynamic Rotation of the 3D Block – Free Orbit 7-30
Dynamic Viewing – Quick Keys 7-32
Viewing Tools – Standard Toolbar 7-33
Display Modes 7-37
Orthographic vs. Perspective 7-37
Disable the Heads-Up Display Option 7-38
Step 4-1: Adding an Extruded Feature 7-39
Step 4-2: Adding a Cut Feature 7-43
Step 4-3: Adding another Cut Feature 7-46
Save the Model 7-48
Review Questions 7-50
Exercises 7-51

Chapter 8
Constructive Solid Geometry Concepts – Autodesk Inventor

Introduction 8-2
Binary Tree 8-3
The Locator Design 8-4
Modeling Strategy – CSG Binary Tree 8-5
Starting Autodesk Inventor 8-6
Base Feature 8-7
Grid Display Setup 8-8
Model Dimensions Format 8-11
Modifying the Dimensions of the Sketch 8-11
Repositioning Dimensions 8-12
Using the Measure Tools 8-13
Completing the Base Solid Feature 8-16
Creating the Next Solid Feature 8-17
Creating a Cut Feature 8-21
Sketched Features vs. Placed Features 8-24
Creating a Placed Hole Feature 8-25
Creating a Rectangular Cut Feature 8-27

Save the Model 8-29
Review Questions 8-30
Exercises 8-31

Chapter 9
Model History Tree – Autodesk Inventor

Introduction 9-2
The Saddle Bracket Design 9-3
Starting Autodesk Inventor 9-3
Modeling Strategy 9-4
The Autodesk Inventor Browser 9-5
Creating the Base Feature 9-5
Adding the Second Solid Feature 9-8
Creating a 2D Sketch 9-9
Renaming the Part Features 9-11
Adjusting the Width of the Base Feature 9-12
Adding a Placed Feature 9-13
Creating a Rectangular Cut Feature 9-15
History-Based Part Modifications 9-16
A Design Change 9-17
Assigning and Calculating the Associated Physical Properties 9-20
Review Questions 9-22
Exercises 9-23

Chapter 10
Parametric Constraints Fundamentals - Autodesk Inventor

Constraints and Relations 10-2
Create a Simple Triangular Plate Design 10-2
Fully Constrained Geometry 10-3
Starting Autodesk Inventor 10-3
Displaying Existing Constraints 10-4
Applying Geometric/Dimensional Constraints 10-6
Over-Constraining and Driven Dimensions 10-10
Deleting Existing Constraints 10-11
Using the Auto Dimension Command 10-12
Constraint and Sketch Settings 10-17
Parametric Relations 10-18
Dimensional Values and Dimensional Variables 10-20
Parametric Equations 10-21
Viewing the Established Parameters and Relations 10-23
Saving the Model File 10-24
Using the Measure Tools 10-25
Review Questions 10-29
Exercises 10-30

Chapter 11
Geometric Construction Tools - Autodesk Inventor

Introduction 11-2
The Gasket Design 11-2
Modeling Strategy 11-3
Starting Autodesk Inventor 11-4
Create a 2D Sketch 11-5
Edit the Sketch by Dragging the Sketched Entities 11-7
Add Additional Constraints 11-9
Use the Trim and Extend Commands 11-10
The Auto Dimension Command 11-12
Create Fillets and Completing the Sketch 11-14
Fully Constrained Geometry 11-15
Profile Sketch 11-17
Redefine the Sketch and Profile 11-18
Create an Offset Cut Feature 11-22
Review Questions 11-25
Exercises 11-26

Chapter 12
Parent/Child Relationships and the BORN Technique - Autodesk Inventor

Introduction 12-2
The BORN Technique 12-2
The U-Bracket Design 12-3
Sketch Plane Settings 12-4
Apply the BORN Technique 12-5
Create a 2D Sketch for the Base Feature 12-7
Create the First Extrude Feature 12-10
The Implied Parent/Child Relationships 12-11
Create the Second Solid Feature 12-11
Create a Cut Feature 12-15
The Second Cut Feature 12-16
Examine the Parent/Child Relationships 12-18
Modify a Parent Dimension 12-19
A Design Change 12-20
Feature Suppression 12-21
A Different Approach to the Center_Drill Feature 12-22
Suppress the Rect_Cut Feature 12-24
Create a Circular Cut Feature 12-25
A Flexible Design Approach 12-27
View and Edit Material Properties 12-28
Review Questions 12-30
Exercises 12-31

Chapter 13
Part Drawings and 3D Model-Based Definition - Autodesk Inventor

Drawings from Parts and Associative Functionality 13-2
3D Model-Based Definition 13-3
Starting Autodesk Inventor 13-4
Drawing Mode – 2D Paper Space 13-4
Drawing Sheet Format 13-6
Using the Pre-defined Drawing Sheet Formats 13-8
Activate, Delete, and Edit Drawing Sheets 13-9
Add a Base View 13-10
Create Projected Views 13-11
Adjust the View Scale 13-12
Repositioning Views 13-13
Display Feature Dimensions 13-14
Repositioning and Hiding Feature Dimensions 13-16
Add Additional Dimensions – Reference Dimensions 13-18
Add Center Marks and Center Lines 13-19
Complete the Drawing Sheet 13-22
Associative Functionality – Modifying Feature Dimensions 13-23
3D Model-Based Definition 13-26
Review Questions 13-34
Exercises 13-35

Chapter 14
Symmetrical Features in Designs - Autodesk Inventor

Introduction 14-2
A Revolved Design: Pulley 14-2
Modeling Strategy – A Revolved Design 14-3
Starting Autodesk Inventor 14-4
Set Up the Display of the Sketch Plane 14-4
Creating a 2D Sketch for the Base Feature 14-5
Create the Revolved Feature 14-9
Mirroring Features 14-10
Create a Pattern Leader Using Construction Geometry 14-12
Circular Pattern 14-17
Examine the Design Parameters 14-19
Drawing Mode – Defining a New Border and Title Block 14-19
Create a Drawing Template 14-23
Create the Necessary Views 14-24
Retrieve Model Annotations – Features Option 14-27
Associative Functionality – A Design Change 14-29
Add Centerlines to the Pattern Feature 14-31
Complete the Drawing 14-32

Additional Title Blocks 14-35
Review Questions 14-37
Exercises 14-38

AutoCAD and Autodesk Inventor

Chapter 15
Design Reuse Using AutoCAD and Autodesk Inventor

Introduction 15-2
The Geneva Wheel Design 15-3
Internet Download the Geneva-Wheel DWG File 15-3
Opening AutoCAD DWG File in Inventor 15-4
Switch to the AutoCAD DWG Layout 15-5
2D Design Reuse 15-7
Complete the Imported Sketch 15-11
Create the First Solid Feature 15-13
Create a Mirrored Feature 15-14
Circular Pattern 15-15
Complete the Geneva Wheel Design 15-16
Export an Inventor 2D Sketch as an AutoCAD Drawing 15-20
Design Reuse – Sketch Insert Option 15-21
Review Questions 15-26
Exercises 15-27

Chapter 16
Assembly Modeling - Putting It All Together - Autodesk Inventor

Introduction 16-2
Assembly Modeling Methodology 16-3
The Shaft Support Assembly 16-4
Additional Parts 16-4
(1) Collar 16-4
(2) Bearing 16-5
(3) Base-Plate 16-5
(4) Cap-Screw 16-6
Starting Autodesk Inventor 16-7
Placing the First Component 16-8
Placing the Second Component 16-9
Degrees of Freedom and Constraints 16-10
Assembly Constraints 16-11
Apply the First Assembly Constraint 16-14
Apply a Second Mate Constraint 16-15
Constrained Move 16-16
Apply a Flush Constraint 16-17

Placing the Third Component 16-19
Applying an Insert Constraint 16-20
Assemble the Cap-Screws 16-21
Exploded View of the Assembly 16-22
Editing the Components 16-24
Adaptive Design Approach 16-25
Delete and Re-apply Assembly Constraints 16-29
Set Up a Drawing of the Assembly Model 16-31
Creating a Parts List 16-33
Edit the Parts List 16-34
Change the Material Type 16-36
Add the Balloon Callouts 16-38
Completing the Title Block Using the iProperties Option 16-38
Bill of Materials 16-40
(a) BOM from Parts List 16-40
(b) BOM from Assembly Model 16-41
Review Questions 16-42
Exercises 16-43

Chapter 17
Design Analysis - Autodesk Inventor Stress Analysis Module

Introduction 17-2
Problem Statement 17-4
Preliminary Analysis 17-4
Maximum Displacement 17-5
Finite Element Analysis Procedure 17-6
Create the Autodesk Inventor Part 17-7
Create the 2D Sketch for the Plate 17-7
Assigning the Material Properties 17-10
Switch to the Stress Analysis Module 17-11
Apply Constraints and Loads 17-14
Create a Mesh and Run the Solver 17-16
Refinement of the FEA Mesh – Global Element Size 17-18
Refinement of the FEA Mesh – Local Element Size 17-20
Comparison of Results 17-23
Create an HTML Report 17-24
Geometric Considerations of Finite Elements 17-25
Conclusion 17-26
Summary of Modeling Considerations 17-26
Review Questions 17-27
Exercises 17-28

Index

Bonus Chapters Available at:
www.SDCpublications.com

Chapter 18
Assembly Modeling with the LEGO MINDSTORMS NXT Set – Autodesk Inventor

Introduction 18-2
The Basic Car Assembly 18-2
Modeling Strategy 18-3
Starting Autodesk Inventor 18-4
Creating a Subassembly 18-5
Placing the Next Component 18-6
Degrees of Freedom Display 18-7
Apply the Assembly Constraints 18-8
Assemble the Next Components 18-13
Assembling Bushing and Axle 18-15
Completing the Motor-Right Subassembly 18-18
Starting the Main Assembly 18-20
Assemble the Frame and Motors 18-23
Assemble the Motor Assemblies 18-25
Adding the Motor-Right Subassembly to the Main Assembly 18-30
Assemble the Rear Swivel Assembly and Wheels 18-31
Assemble the NXT Micro-controller 18-37
Assemble the Sensors 18-40

Chapter 19
Assembly Modeling with the TETRIX by Pitsco Building System – Autodesk Inventor

Introduction 19-2
The ST1 Assembly 19-2
Modeling Strategy 19-3
Starting Autodesk Inventor 19-4
Creating a Subassembly 19-5
Placing the Next Component 19-6
Degrees of Freedom Display 19-7
Apply Assembly Constraints 19-8
Starting the Main Assembly 19-18
Adjusting the Orientation of a Grounded Part 19-20
Adjusting the Orientation of Parts 19-22
Assemble the DC Motor Controller 19-25
Assemble the Servo Controller 19-27
Completing the Chassis 19-29
Assemble the Front-Wheel Assembly 19-30

Assemble the Motor-Wheel Assembly 19-33
Assemble the NXT Micro-controller 19-38
Assemble the NXT Touch-Sensor 19-39
Conclusion 19-41

Chapter 20
Assembly Model with Vex Robot Kit - Autodesk Inventor

Introduction 20-2
The Tumbler Assembly 20-2
Starting Autodesk Inventor 20-3
Creating a Subassembly 20-4
Placing the Second Component 20-5
Degrees of Freedom Display 20-6
Adjusting the Component's Orientation 20-7
Apply Assembly Constraints 20-8
Assemble the Next Component 20-11
Assembling Bearing Rivets and Screws 20-13
Assembling Shaft Collars, Shafts and Motors 20-16
Assemble the Wheels 20-23
Modifying the Wheel Directions 20-27
Starting the Tumbler Assembly 20-30
Assemble the Chassis 20-33
Assemble the Chassis Plate 20-37
Adding the Battery Pack under the Chassis Plate 20-39
Adding the RF Receiver on the Rear Chassis Bumper 20-40
Assemble the VEX Microcontroller 20-43
Assemble the Antenna 20-46
Conclusion 20-47
Review Questions 20-48
Exercise 20-49

Notes:

Getting Started

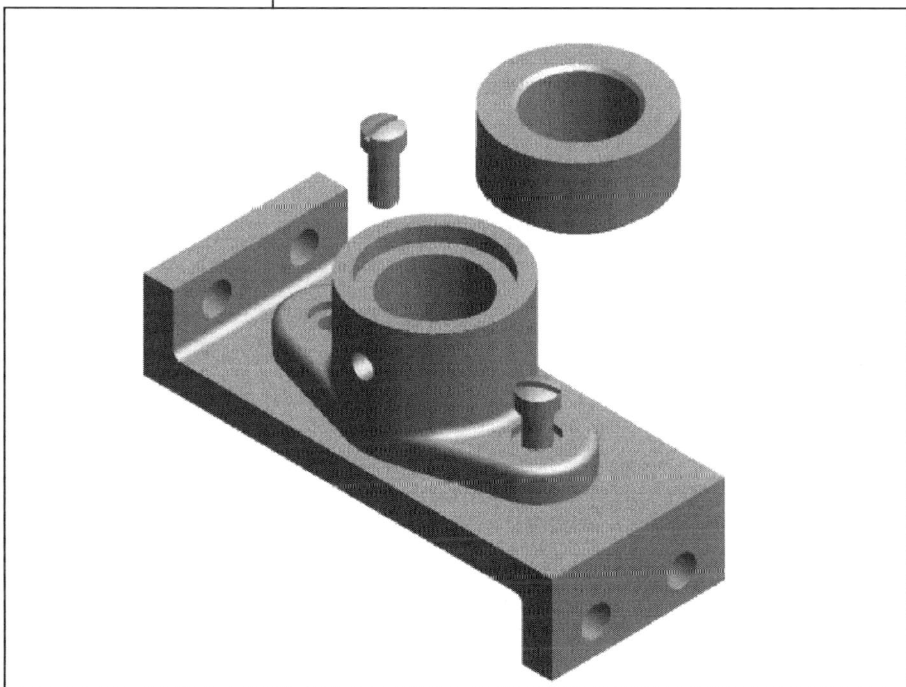

Learning Objectives

- **Basic Computer Aided Design and Computer Aided Engineering Terminology**
- **Development of Computer Aided Design**
- **Why Use AutoCAD?**
- **Why Use Autodesk Inventor?**
- **Feature Based Parametric Modeling**

Introduction

Computer Aided Design (CAD) is the process of creating designs with the aid of computers. This includes the generation of computer models, analysis of design data, and the creation of drawings. **AutoCAD®** and **Autodesk Inventor®** are both computer aided design software developed by *Autodesk, Inc*. The **AutoCAD** software is a tool that can be used for design and drafting activities. The two-dimensional and three-dimensional models created in **AutoCAD** can be transferred to other computer programs for further analysis and testing. **Autodesk Inventor** is an integrated package of mechanical computer aided engineering software. **Autodesk Inventor** is a tool that facilitates a concurrent engineering approach to the design and stress-analysis of mechanical engineering products. The computer models can also be used by manufacturing equipment such as machining centers, lathes, mills, or rapid prototyping machines to manufacture the product.

The rapid changes in the field of **computer aided engineering** (CAE) have brought exciting advances in industry. Recent advances have made the long-sought after goal of reducing design time, producing prototypes faster, and achieving higher product quality closer to a reality.

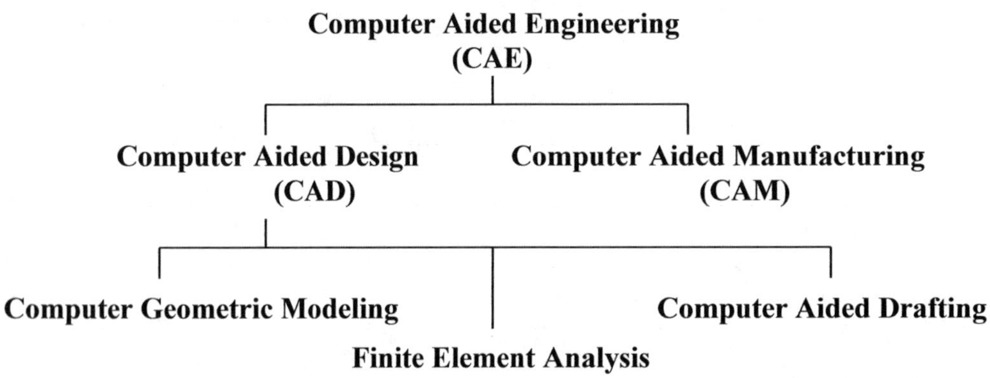

Development of Computer Aided Design

Computer Aided Design is a relatively new technology, and its rapid expansion in the last fifty years is truly amazing. Computer modeling technology has advanced along with the development of computer hardware. The first-generation CAD programs, developed in the 1950s, were mostly non-interactive; CAD users were required to create program codes to generate the desired two-dimensional (2D) geometric shapes. Initially, the development of CAD technology occurred mostly in academic research facilities. The Massachusetts Institute of Technology, Carnegie-Mellon University, and Cambridge University were the leading pioneers at that time. The interest in CAD technology spread quickly and several major industry companies, such as General Motors, Lockheed, McDonnell, IBM, and Ford Motor Co., participated in the development of interactive CAD programs in the 1960s. Usage of CAD systems was primarily in the automotive industry, aerospace industry, and government agencies that developed their own programs for their specific needs. The 1960s also marked the beginning of the development of finite element analysis methods for computer stress analysis and computer aided manufacturing for generating machine toolpaths.

The 1970s are generally viewed as the years of the most significant progress in the development of computer hardware, namely the invention and development of **microprocessors**. With the improvement in computing power, new types of 3D CAD programs that were user-friendly and interactive became reality. CAD technology quickly expanded from very simple **computer aided drafting** to very complex **computer aided design**. The use of 2D and 3D wireframe modelers was accepted as the leading-edge technology that could increase productivity in industry. The developments of surface modeling and solid modeling technologies were taking shape by the late 1970s; but the high cost of computer hardware and programming slowed the development of such technology. During this time period, the available CAD systems all required extremely expensive room-sized mainframe computers.

In the 1980s, improvements in computer hardware brought the power of mainframes to the desktop at less cost and with more accessibility to the general public. By the mid-1980s, CAD technology had become the main focus of a variety of manufacturing industries and was very competitive with traditional design/drafting methods. It was during this period of time that 3D solid modeling technology had major advancements, which boosted the usage of CAE technology in industry.

In the 1990s, CAD programs evolved into powerful design/manufacturing/management tools. CAD technology has come a long way, and during these years of development, modeling schemes progressed from two-dimensional (2D) wireframe to three-dimensional (3D) wireframe, to surface modeling, to solid modeling and, finally, to feature-based parametric solid modeling.

The first-generation CAD packages were simply 2D **computer aided drafting** programs, basically the electronic equivalents of the drafting board. For typical models, the use of this type of program would require that several to many views of the objects be created individually as they would be on the drafting board. The 3D designs remained in the designer's mind, not in the computer database. The mental translation of 3D objects to 2D views is required throughout the use of these packages. Although such systems have some advantages over traditional board drafting, they are still tedious and labor intensive. The need for the development of 3D modelers came quite naturally, given the limitations of the 2D drafting packages.

The development of the 3D wireframe modeler was a major leap in the area of computer modeling. The computer database in the 3D wireframe modeler contains the locations of all the points in space coordinates, and it is typically sufficient to create just one model rather than multiple views of the same model. This single 3D model can then be viewed from any direction as needed. The 3D wireframe modelers require the least computer power and achieve reasonably good representations of 3D models. However, because surface definition is not part of a wireframe model, all wireframe images have the inherent problem of ambiguity. Two examples of such ambiguity are illustrated.

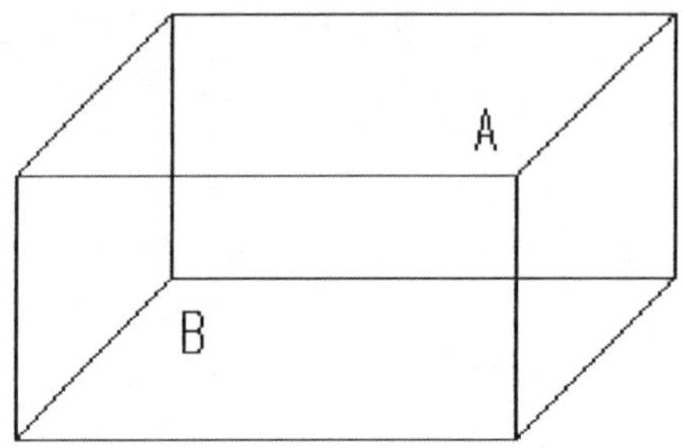

Wireframe Ambiguity: Which corner is in front, A or B?

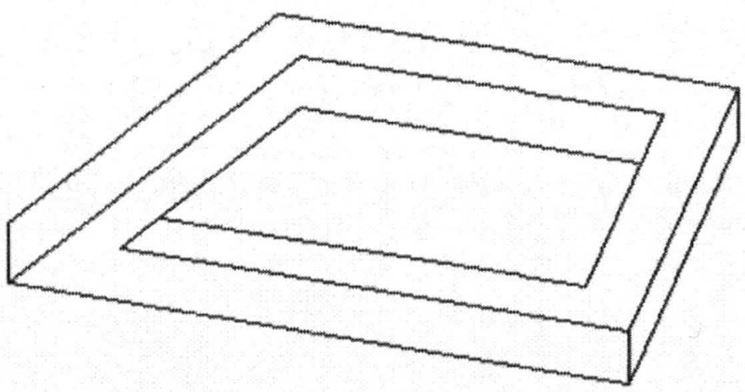

A non-realizable object: Wireframe models contain no surface definitions.

Surface modeling is the logical development in computer geometry modeling to follow the 3D wireframe modeling scheme by organizing and grouping edges that define polygonal surfaces. Surface modeling describes the part's surfaces but not its interiors. Designers are still required to interactively examine surface models to ensure that the various surfaces on a model are contiguous throughout. Many of the concepts used in 3D wireframe and surface modelers are incorporated in the solid modeling scheme, but it is solid modeling that offers the most advantages as a design tool.

In the solid modeling presentation scheme, the solid definitions include nodes, edges, and surfaces, and it is a complete and unambiguous mathematical representation of a precisely enclosed and filled volume. Unlike the surface modeling method, solid modelers start with a solid or use topology rules to guarantee that all of the surfaces are stitched together properly. Two predominant methods for representing solid models are **constructive solid geometry** (CSG) representation and **boundary representation** (B-rep).

The CSG representation method can be defined as the combination of 3D solid primitives. What constitutes a "primitive" varies somewhat with the software but typically includes a rectangular prism, a cylinder, a cone, a wedge, and a sphere. Most solid modelers also allow the user to define additional primitives, which can be very complex.

In the B-rep representation method, objects are represented in terms of their spatial boundaries. This method defines the points, edges, and surfaces of a volume, and/or issues commands that sweep or rotate a defined face into a third dimension to form a solid. The object is then made up of the unions of these surfaces that completely and precisely enclose a volume.

By the end of the 1980s, a new paradigm called *concurrent engineering* had emerged. With concurrent engineering, designers, design engineers, analysts, manufacturing engineers, and management engineers all work together closely right from the initial stages of the design. In this way, all aspects of the design can be evaluated, and any potential problems can be identified right from the start and throughout the design process. Using the principles of concurrent engineering, a new type of computer modeling technique appeared. The technique is known as the *feature-based parametric modeling technique*. The key advantage of the *feature-based parametric modeling technique* is its capability to produce very flexible designs. Changes can be made easily, and design alternatives can be evaluated with minimum effort. Various software packages offer different approaches to feature-based parametric modeling, yet the end result is a flexible design defined by its design variables and parametric features.

Why Use AutoCAD 2027?

AutoCAD was first introduced to the public in late 1982 and was one of the first CAD software products available for personal computers. Since 1984, **AutoCAD** has established a reputation for being the most widely used PC-based CAD software around the world. By 2020, it was estimated that there were over 6 million **AutoCAD** users in more than 150 countries worldwide. **AutoCAD 2027** is the forty-first release, with many added features and enhancements, of the original **AutoCAD** software produced by *Autodesk, Inc.*

CAD provides us with a wide range of benefits; in most cases, the result of using CAD is increased accuracy and productivity. First of all, the computer offers much higher accuracy than the traditional methods of drafting and design. Traditionally, drafting and detailing are the most expensive cost elements in a project and the biggest bottleneck. With CAD systems, such as **AutoCAD 2027**, the tedious drafting and detailing tasks are simplified through the use of many of the CAD geometric construction tools, such as *grids*, *snap*, *trim*, and *auto-dimensioning*. Dimensions and notes are always legible in CAD drawings, and in most cases, CAD systems can produce higher quality prints compared to traditional hand drawings.

CAD also offers much-needed flexibility in design and drafting. A CAD model generated on a computer consists of numeric data that describe the geometry of the object. This allows the designers and clients to see something tangible and to interpret the ramifications of the design. In many cases, it is also possible to simulate operating conditions on the computer and observe the results. Any kind of geometric shape stored in the database can be easily duplicated. For large and complex designs and drawings, particularly those involving similar shapes and repetitive operations, CAD approaches are very efficient and effective. Because computer designs and models can be altered easily, a multitude of design options can be examined and presented to a client before any construction or manufacturing actually takes place. Making changes to a CAD model is generally much faster than making changes to a traditional hand drawing. Only the affected components of the design need to be modified, and the drawings can be plotted again. In addition, the greatest benefit is that once the CAD model is created it can be used over and over again. The CAD models can also be transferred into manufacturing equipment such as machining centers, lathes, mills, or rapid prototyping machines to manufacture the product directly.

CAD, however, does not replace every design activity. CAD may help, but it does not replace the designer's experience with geometry and graphical conventions and standards for the specific field. CAD is a powerful tool, but the use of this tool does not guarantee correct results; the designer is still responsible for using good design practice and applying good judgment. CAD will supplement these skills to ensure that the best design is obtained.

CAD designs and drawings are stored in binary form, usually as CAD files, to magnetic devices such as diskettes and hard disks. The information stored in CAD files usually requires much less physical space in comparison to traditional hand drawings. However, the information stored inside the computer is not indestructible. On the contrary, the electronic format of information is very fragile and sensitive to the environment. Heat or cold can damage the information stored on magnetic storage devices. A power failure while you are creating a design could wipe out the many hours you spent working in front of the computer monitor. It is a good habit to save your work periodically, just in case something might go wrong while you are working on your design. In general, one should save one's work onto a storage device at an interval of every 15 to 20 minutes. You should also save your work before you make any major modifications to the design. It is also a good habit to periodically make backup copies of your work and put them in a safe place.

Why Use Autodesk Inventor 2027?

Autodesk Inventor is a 3D solid modeling software. One of the key elements in the Autodesk Inventor solid modeling software is its use of the **feature-based parametric modeling technique**. The feature-based parametric modeling approach has elevated solid modeling technology to the level of a very powerful design tool. Parametric modeling automates the design and revision procedures by the use of parametric features. Parametric features control the model geometry by the use of design variables. The word ***parametric*** means that the geometric definitions of the design, such as dimensions, can be varied at any time during the design process. Features are predefined parts or construction tools for which users define the key parameters. A part is described as a sequence of engineering features, which can be modified and/or changed at any time. The concept of parametric features makes modeling more closely match the actual design-manufacturing process than the mathematics of a solid modeling program. In parametric modeling, models and drawings are updated automatically when the design is refined.

Parametric modeling offers many benefits:

- **We begin with simple, conceptual models with minimal detail; this approach conforms to the design philosophy of "shape before size."**
- **Geometric constraints, dimensional constraints, and relational parametric equations can be used to capture design intent.**
- **The ability to update an entire system, including parts, assemblies and drawings after changing one parameter of complex designs.**
- **We can quickly explore and evaluate different design variations and alternatives to determine the best design.**
- **Existing design data can be reused to create new designs.**
- **Quick design turn-around.**

One of the key features of Autodesk Inventor is the use of an assembly-centric paradigm, which enables users to concentrate on the design without depending on the associated parameters or constraints. Users can specify how parts fit together and the Autodesk Inventor *assembly-based fit function* automatically determines the parts' sizes and positions. This unique approach is known as the **Direct Adaptive Assembly approach**, which defines part relationships directly with no order dependency.

The *Adaptive Assembly approach* is a unique design methodology that can only be found in Autodesk Inventor. The goal of this methodology is to improve the design process and allows you, the designer, to **Design the Way You Think**.

Tutorial Style Lessons

In this text, the coverage of **AutoCAD 2027** and **Autodesk Inventor 2027** are done using the task-based approach. In the first section, Chapter 1 through Chapter 5, we will first go over using **AutoCAD** to create two-dimensional multiview drawings. Chapter 6 covers the concepts and procedures of creating 3D hand sketches. The rest of the book will concentrate on using **Autodesk Inventor** to perform parametric modeling tasks. The fundamental concepts and use of different geometric construction techniques, as well as using **AutoCAD** and **Autodesk Inventor** commands, are presented using **step-by-step tutorials**. We will begin with creating simple geometric entities and then move toward creating solid models, detailed working drawings and assembly models. The basic concepts and procedures of ***design reuse***, transferring data in between **AutoCAD** and **Autodesk Inventor**, are also covered throughout the text.

Notes:

Chapter 1
Fundamentals of AutoCAD

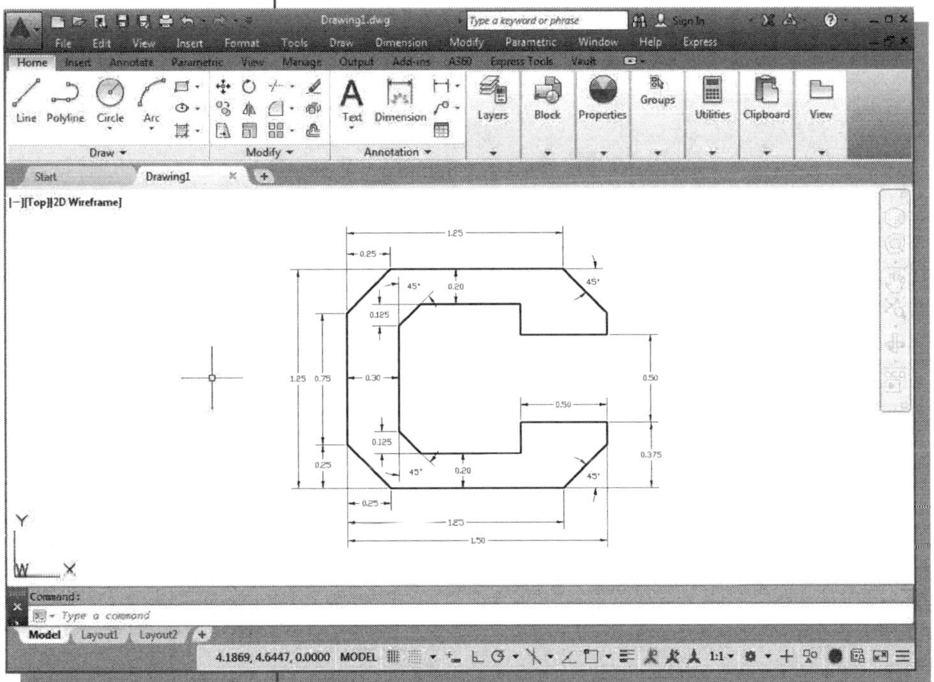

Learning Objectives

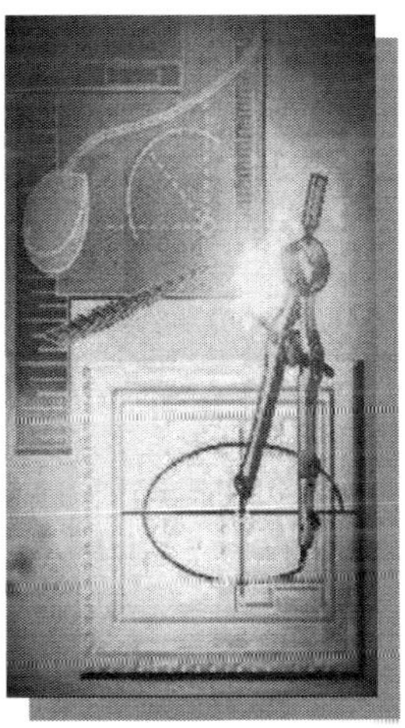

- Create and Save AutoCAD drawing files
- Use the AutoCAD visual reference commands
- Draw using the Line and Circle commands
- Use the Erase command
- Define Positions using the Basic Entry methods
- Use the AutoCAD Pan Realtime option

Getting Started with AutoCAD 2027

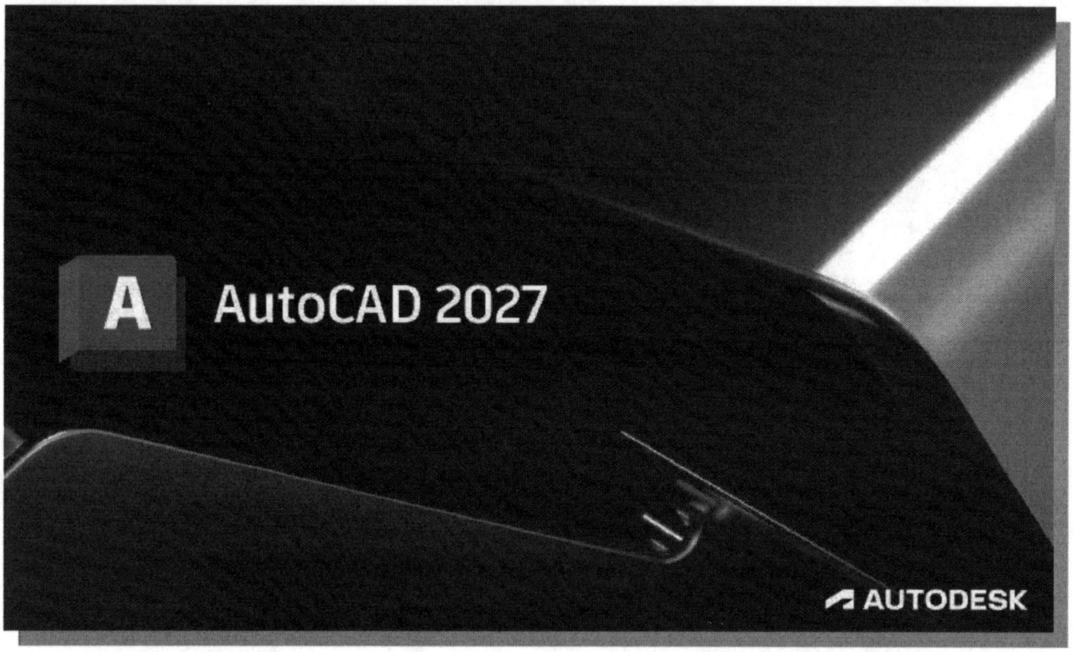

How to start **AutoCAD 2027** depends on the type of workstation and the particular software configuration you are using. With most *Windows* systems, you may select the **AutoCAD 2027** option on the *Start* menu or select the **AutoCAD 2027** icon on the *Desktop*. Consult with your instructor or technical support personnel if you have difficulty starting the software.

The program takes a while to load, so be patient. Eventually the **AutoCAD 2027** main *drawing screen* will appear on the screen. Click **Start Drawing** as shown in the below figure. The tutorials in this text are based on the assumption that you are using **AutoCAD 2027**'s default settings. If your system has been customized, some of the settings may not work with the step-by-step instructions in the tutorials. Contact your instructor and technical support to restore the default software configuration.

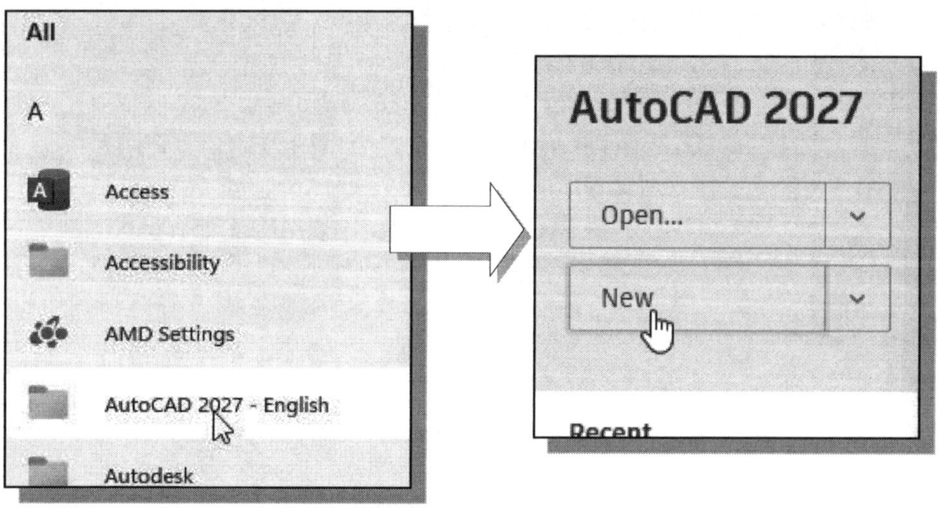

AutoCAD 2027 Screen Layout

The default **AutoCAD 2027** *drawing screen* contains the *pull-down* menus, the *Standard* toolbar, the *InfoCenter Help system,* the *scrollbars,* the *command prompt area*, the *Status Bar*, and the *Ribbon Tabs* and *Panels* that contain several *control panels* such as the *Draw and Modify* panel and the *Annotation* panel. You may resize the **AutoCAD 2027** drawing window by clicking and dragging at the edges of the window, or relocate the window by clicking and dragging at the window title area.

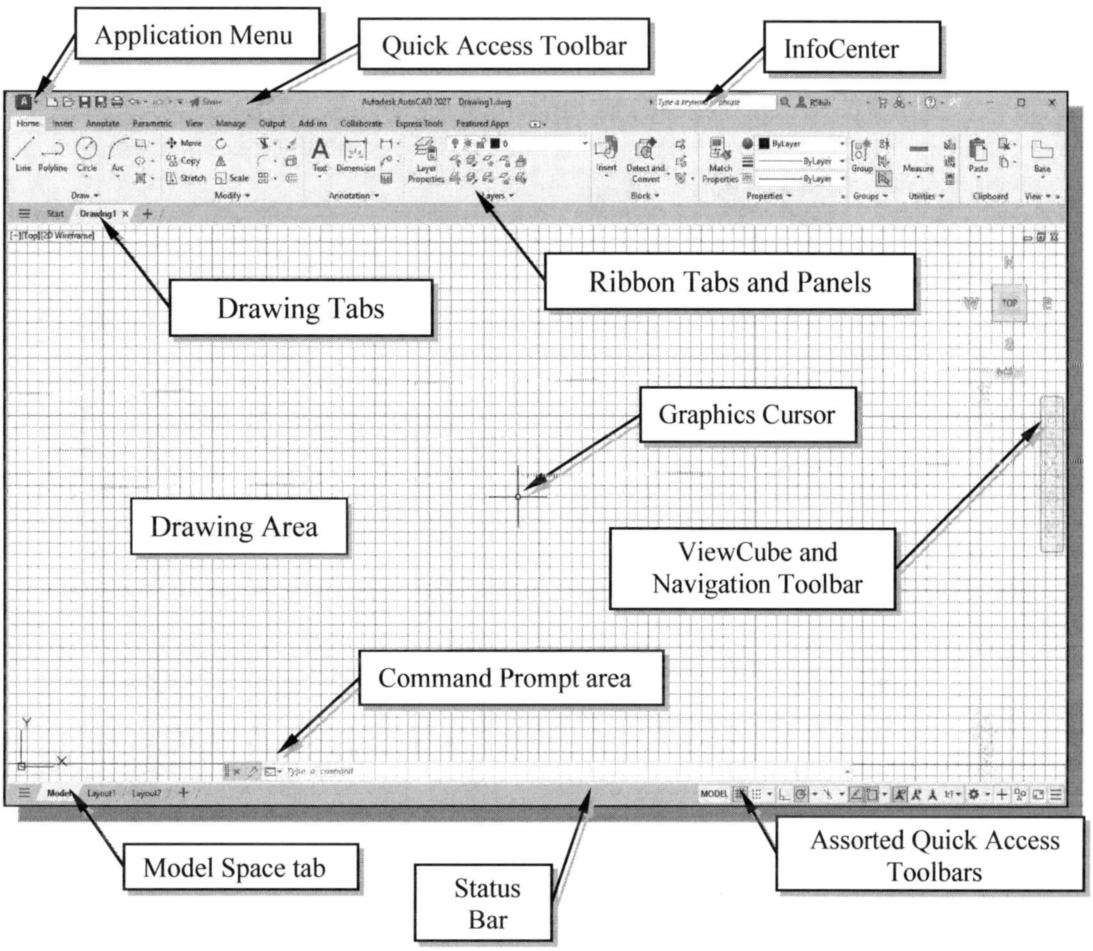

❖ Click on the down-arrow in the *Quick Access* bar and select **Show Menu Bar** to display the **AutoCAD *Menu*** bar. Note that the menu bar provides access to all of the AutoCAD commands.

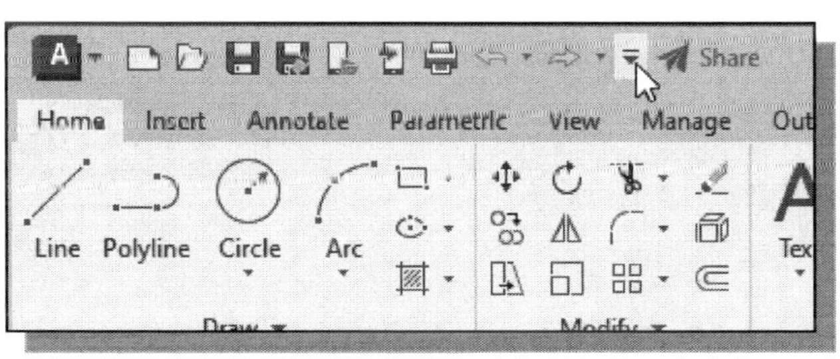

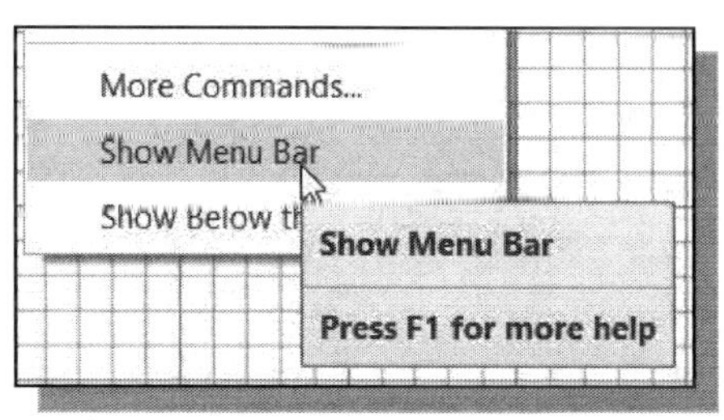

- **Application Menu**

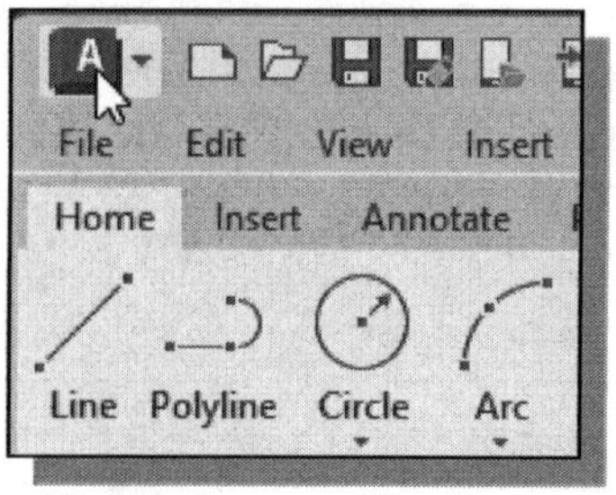

The *Application Menu* at the top of the main window contains commonly used file operations.

- **Quick Access Toolbar**
  The *Quick Access* toolbar at the top of the *AutoCAD* window allows us quick access to frequently used commands, such as **Qnew, Open, Save** and also the **Undo** command. Note that we can customize the quick access toolbar by adding and removing sets of options or individual commands.

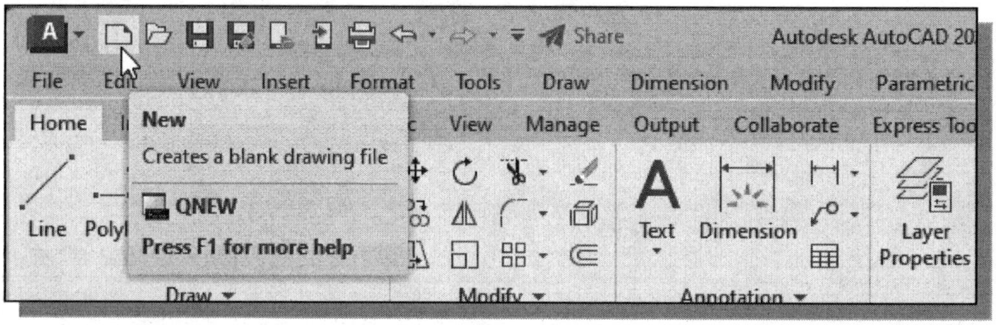

- **AutoCAD Menu Bar**
  The *Menu* bar is the pull-down menu where all operations of AutoCAD can be accessed.

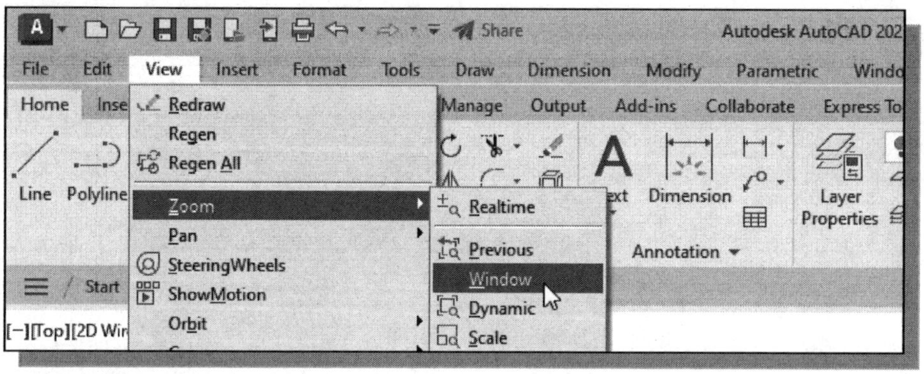

- **Layout tabs**

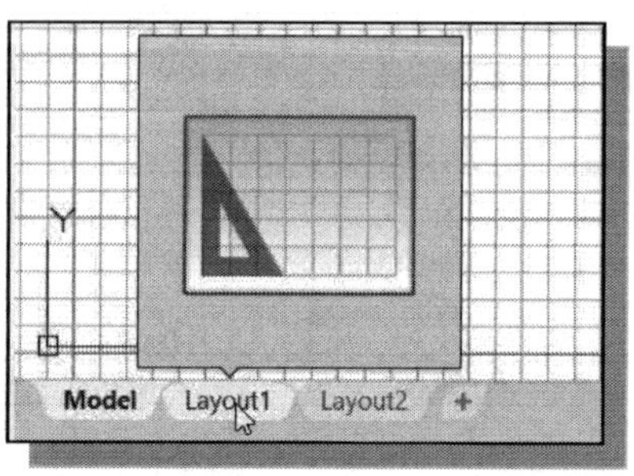

The Model/Layout tabs allow us to switch/create between different **model space** and **paper space**.

- **Drawing Area**
  The *Drawing Area* is the area where models and drawings are displayed.

- **Graphics Cursor or Crosshairs**

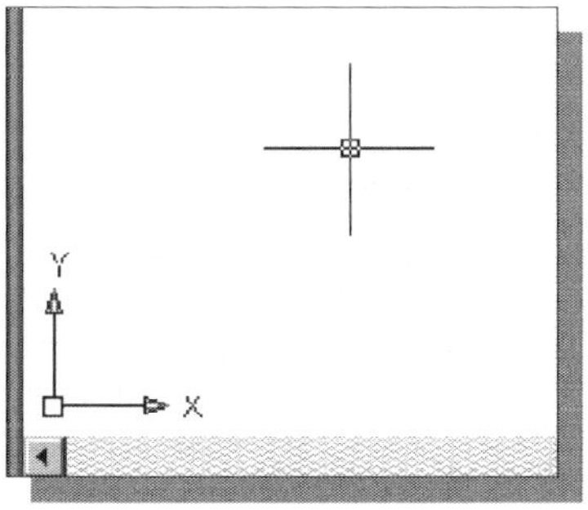

The *graphics cursor*, or *crosshairs*, shows the location of the pointing device in the Drawing Area. The coordinates of the cursor are displayed at the bottom of the screen layout. The cursor's appearance depends on the selected command or option.

- **Command Prompt Area**

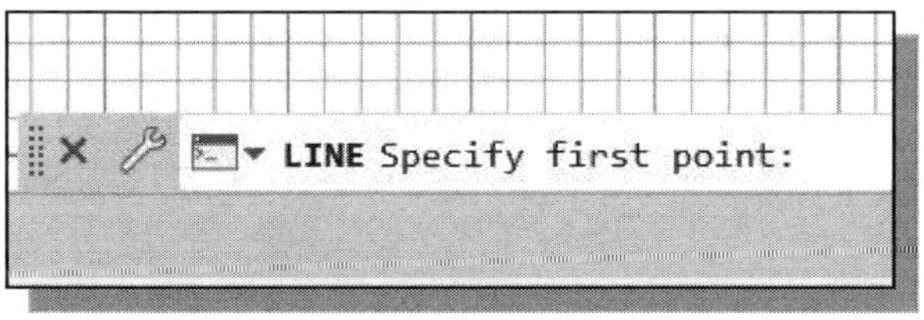

The *Command Prompt Area* provides status information for an operation and it is also the area for data input. Note that the *Command Prompt* can be docked below the drawing area as shown.

- **Cursor Coordinates**

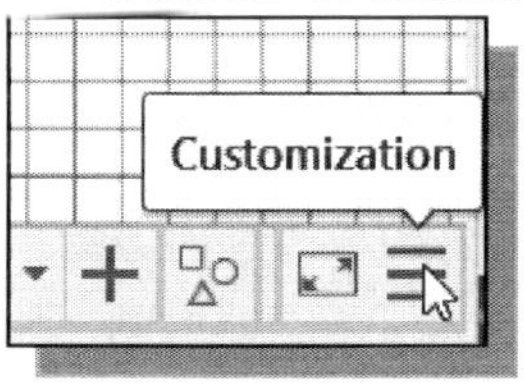

To switch on the **AutoCAD Coordinates Display**, use the *Customization option* at the bottom right corner.

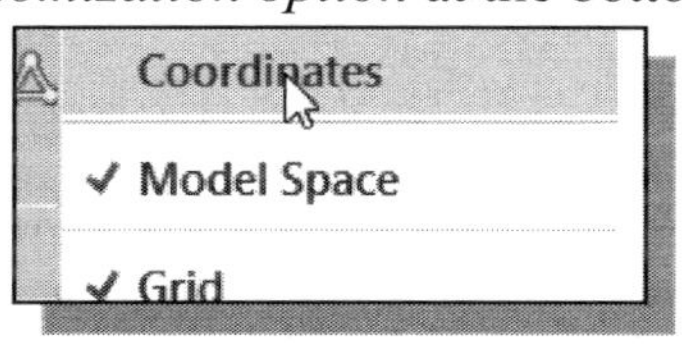

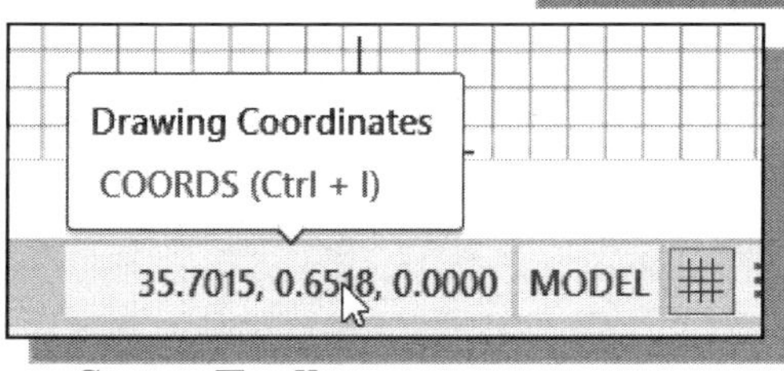

The bottom section of the screen layout displays the coordinate information of the cursor. Note that the quick-key option, [Ctrl+I], can be used to toggle the behavior of the displayed coordinates.

- **Status Toolbar**
  Next to the cursor coordinate display is the *Status* toolbar, showing the status of many commonly used display and construction options.

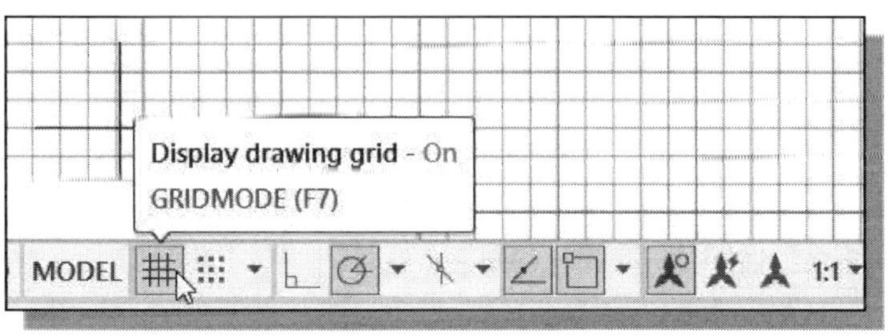

- **Ribbon Tabs and Panels**
  The top section of the screen layout contains customizable icon panels, which contain groups of buttons that allow us to pick commands quickly, without searching through a menu structure. These panels allow us to quickly access the commonly used commands available in AutoCAD.

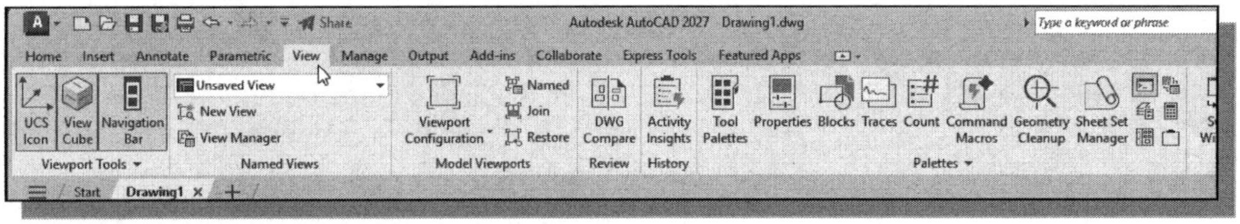

- **Draw and Modify Toolbar Panels**
  The *Draw* and *Modify* toolbar panels are the two main panels for creating drawings; the toolbars contain icons for basic draw and modify commands.

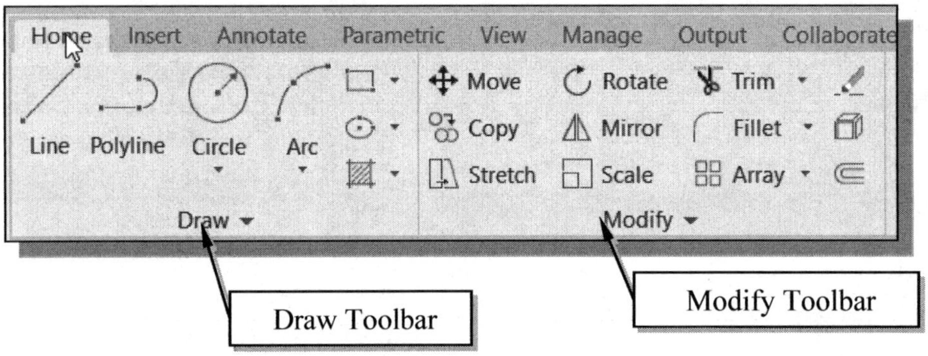

- **Layers Control Toolbar Panel**

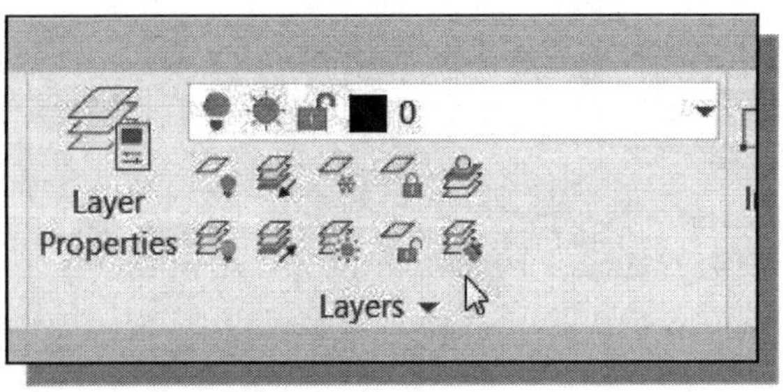

The *Layers Control* toolbar panel contains tools to help manipulate the properties of graphical objects.

- **Viewport/View/Display Controls**

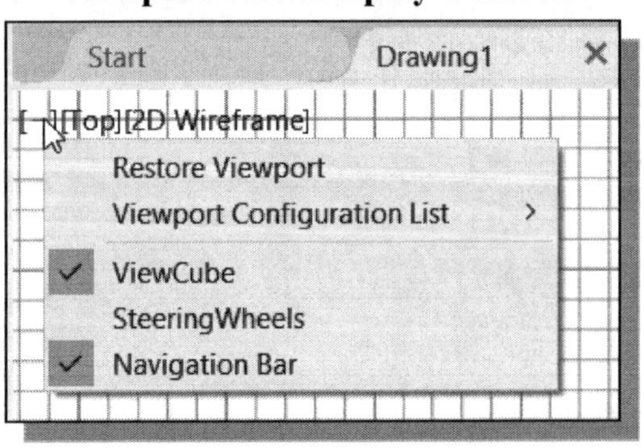

The *Viewport/View/Display controls panel* is located at the upper left corner of the graphics area and it can be used to quickly access viewing related commands, such as Viewport and Display style.

Mouse Buttons

AutoCAD 2027 utilizes the mouse buttons extensively. In learning **AutoCAD 2027**'s interactive environment, it is important to understand the basic functions of the mouse buttons. It is highly recommended that you use a mouse or a tablet with **AutoCAD 2027** since the package uses the buttons for various functions.

- **Left mouse button**
  The **left-mouse-button** is used for most operations, such as selecting menus and icons or picking graphic entities. One click of the button is used to select icons, menus and form entries and to pick graphic items.

- **Right mouse button**
  The **right-mouse-button** is used to bring up additional available options. The software also utilizes the **right-mouse-button** the same as the **ENTER** key and is often used to accept the default setting to a prompt or to end a process.

- **Middle mouse button/wheel**
  The middle mouse button/wheel can be used to Pan (hold down the wheel button and drag the mouse) or Zoom (rotate the wheel) real time.

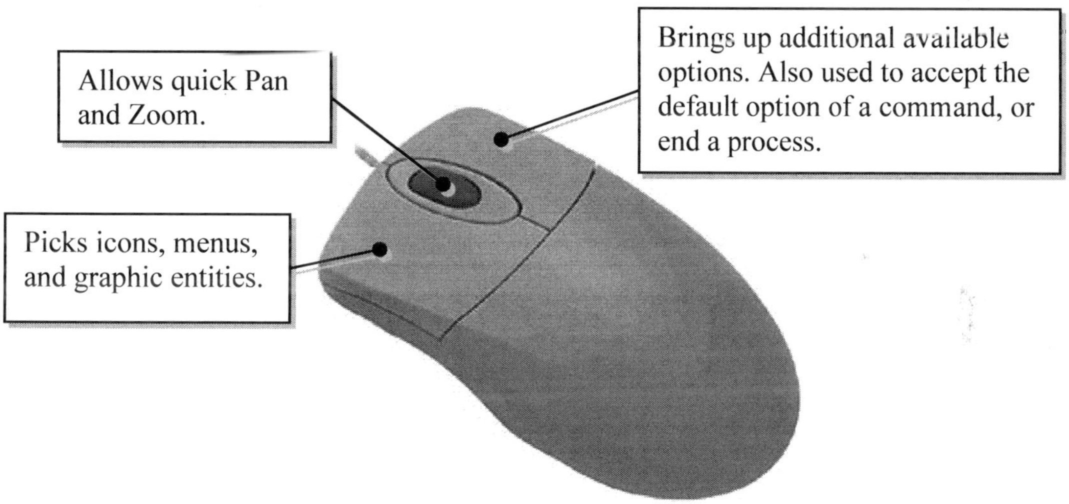

[Esc] – Canceling commands

The [**Esc**] key is used to cancel a command in **AutoCAD 2027**. The [**Esc**] key is located near the top-left corner of the keyboard. Sometimes, it may be necessary to press the [**Esc**] key twice to cancel a command; it depends on where we are in the command sequence. For some commands, the [**Esc**] key is used to exit the command.

Online Help

Several types of online help are available at any time during an **AutoCAD 2027** session. The **AutoCAD 2027** software provides many online help options:

- **Autodesk Exchange**:
  Autodesk Exchange is a central portal in AutoCAD 2027; AutoCAD Exchange provides a user interface for Help, learning aids, tips and tricks, videos, and downloadable apps. By default, *Autodesk Exchange* is displayed at **startup**. This allows access to a dynamic selection of tools from the *Autodesk community*; note that an internet connection is required to use this option.

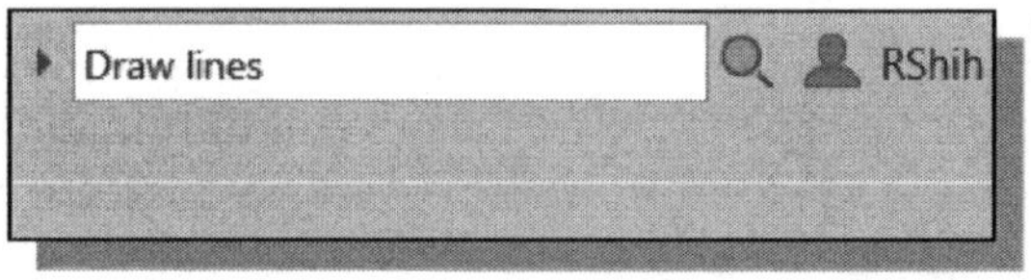

- To use *Autodesk Exchange*, simply type a question in the *input box* to search through the Autodesk's *Help* system as shown.

- A list of the search results appears in the *Autodesk Help* window, and we can also determine the level and type of searches of the associated information.

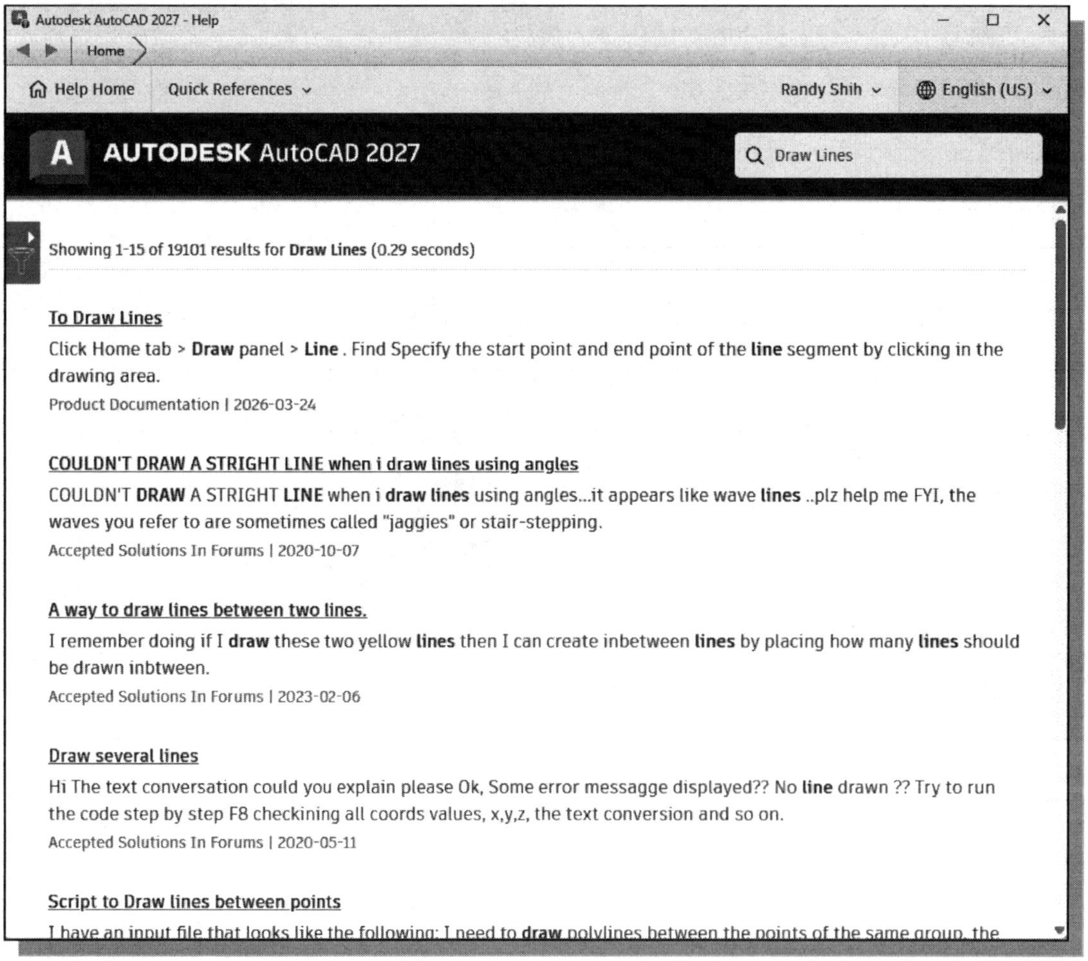

Leaving AutoCAD 2027

To leave **AutoCAD 2027**, use the left-mouse-button and click the **Application Menu** button at the top left corner of the **AutoCAD 2027** screen window, then choose **Exit AutoCAD** from the pull-down menu or type ***QUIT*** in the command prompt area.

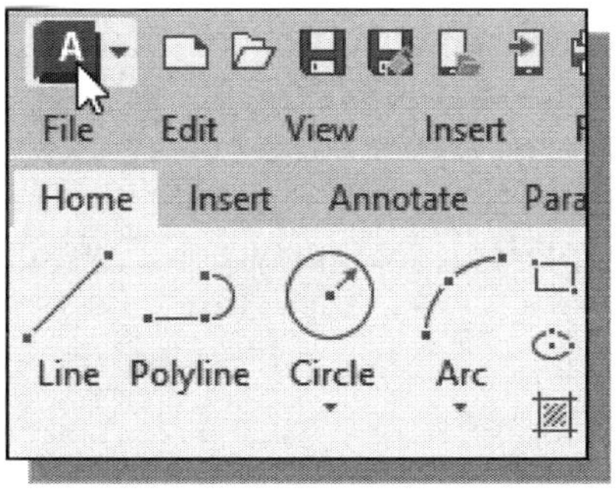

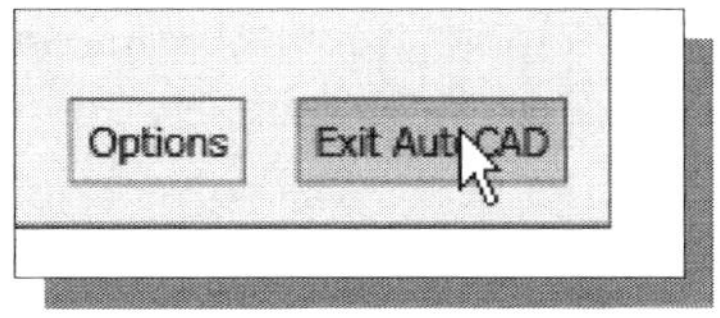

Creating a CAD File Folder

It is good practice to create a separate folder to store your CAD files. You should not save your CAD files in the same folder where the **AutoCAD 2027** application is located. It is much easier to organize and back up your project files if they are in a separate folder. Making folders within this folder for different types of projects will help you organize your CAD files even further.

➢ To create a new folder in the *Microsoft Windows* environment:

1. On the *desktop* or under the *My Documents* folder in which you want to create a new folder.

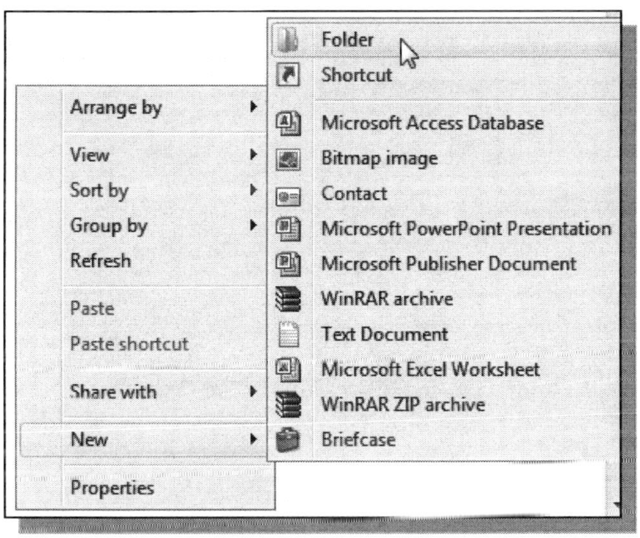

2. Right-mouse-click once to bring up the option menu, then select New→ Folder.

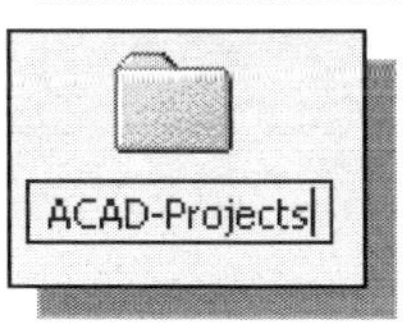

3. Type a name for the new folder, and then press **ENTER**.

Drawing in AutoCAD

Learning to use a CAD system is similar to learning a new language. It is necessary to begin with the basic alphabet and learn how to use it correctly and effectively through practice. This will require learning some new concepts and skills as well as learning a different vocabulary. All CAD systems create designs using basic geometric entities, and many of the constructions used in technical designs are based upon two-dimensional planar geometry. The method and number of operations that are required to accomplish the constructions are different from one system to another.

In order to become effective and efficient in using a CAD system, we must learn to create geometric entities quickly and accurately. In learning to use a CAD system, **lines** and **circles** are the first two, and perhaps the most important two, geometric entities that one should master the skills of creating and modifying. Straight lines and circles are used in almost all technical designs. In examining the different types of planar geometric entities, the importance of lines and circles becomes obvious. Triangles and polygons are planar figures bounded by straight lines. Ellipses and splines can be constructed by connecting arcs with different radii. As one gains some experience in creating lines and circles, similar procedures can be applied to create other geometric entities. In this chapter, the different ways of creating lines and circles in **AutoCAD® 2027** are examined.

Starting Up AutoCAD 2027

1. Select the **AutoCAD 2027** option on the *Program* menu or select the **AutoCAD 2027** icon on the *Desktop*. Click **Start Drawing** to start a new drawing.

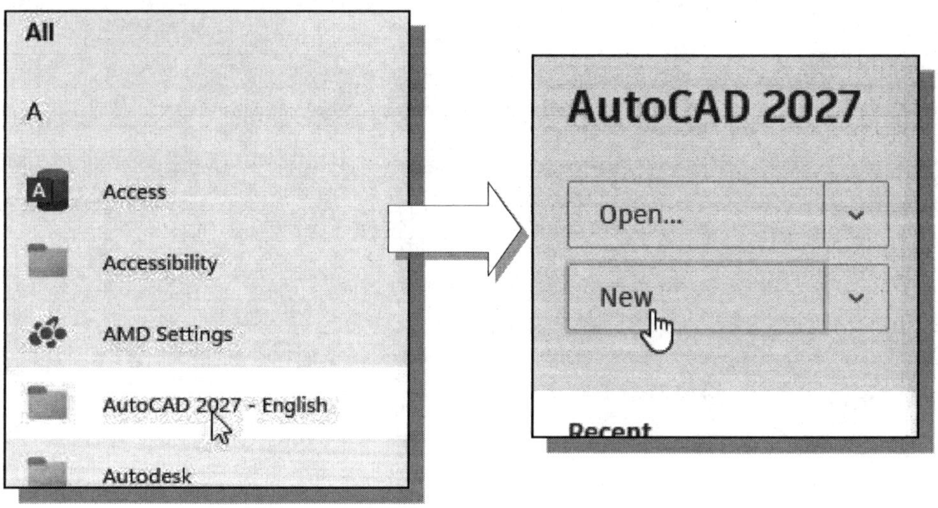

❖ Once the program is loaded into memory, the **AutoCAD 2027** main drawing screen will appear on the screen.

➢ Note that AutoCAD automatically assigns generic names, *Drawing X*, as new drawings are created. In our example, AutoCAD opened the graphics window using the default system units and assigned the drawing name *Drawing1*.

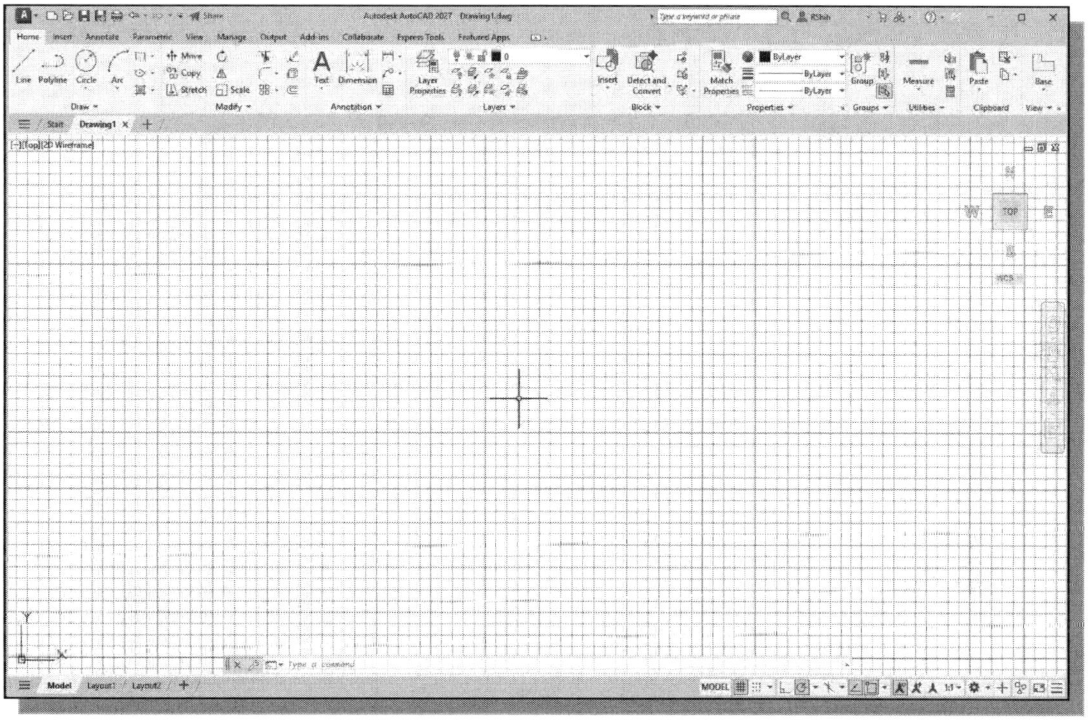

2. If necessary, click on the down-arrow in the *Quick Access* bar and select **Show Menu Bar** to display the **AutoCAD *Menu Bar***. The *Menu Bar* provides access to all AutoCAD commands.

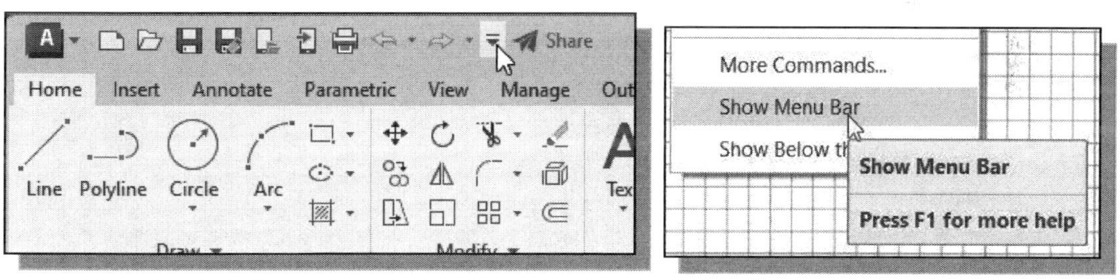

3. To switch on the **AutoCAD Coordinates Display**, use the *Customization option* at the bottom right corner.

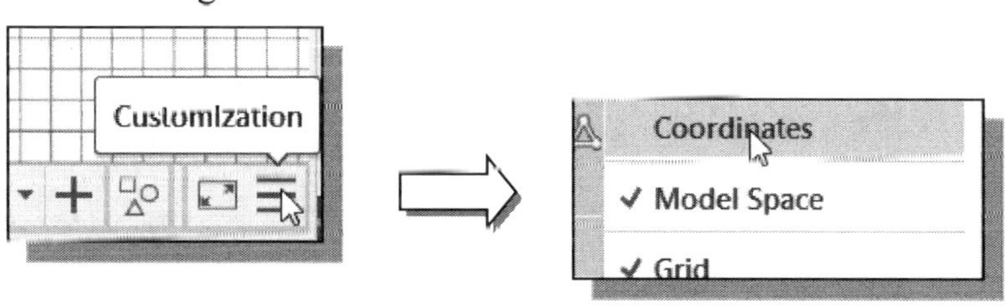

Drawing Units Setup

Every object we construct in a CAD system is measured in **units**. We should determine the system of units within the CAD system before creating the first geometric entities.

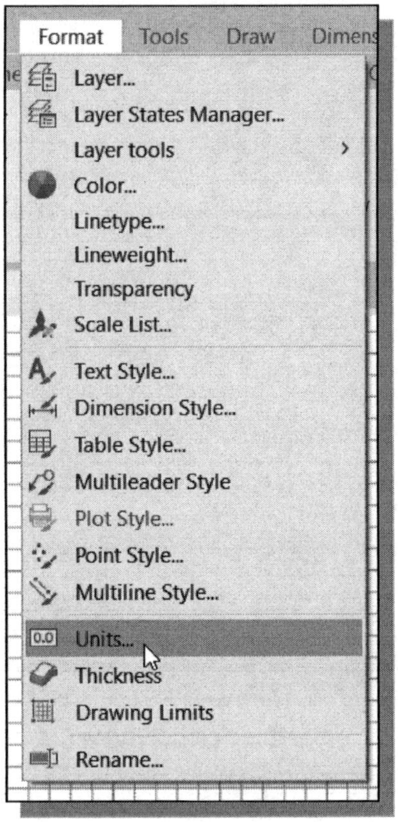

1. In the *Menu Bar* select:
   [Format] → [Units]

- The AutoCAD *Menu Bar* contains multiple pull-down menus where all of the AutoCAD commands can be accessed. Note that many of the menu items listed in the pull-down menus can also be accessed through the *Quick Access* toolbar and/or *Ribbon* panels.

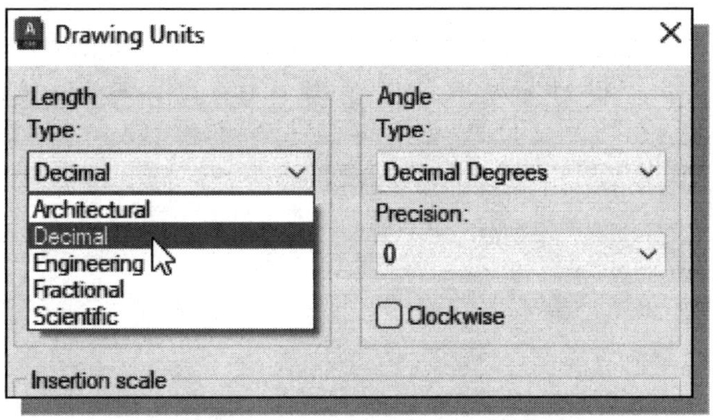

2. Click on the *Length Type* option to display the different types of length units available. Confirm the *Length Type* is set to **Decimal**.

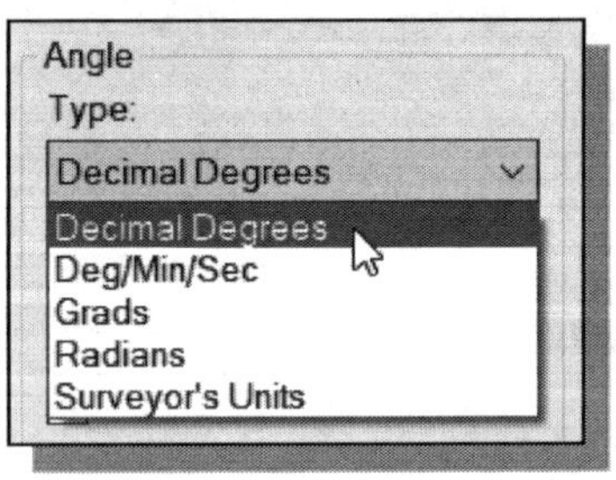

3. On your own, examine the other settings that are available.

- Also note the Insertion Scale section will show the default measurement system, such as the *English* units, inches.

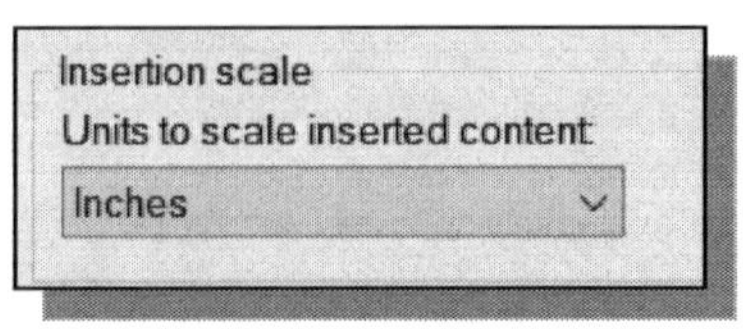

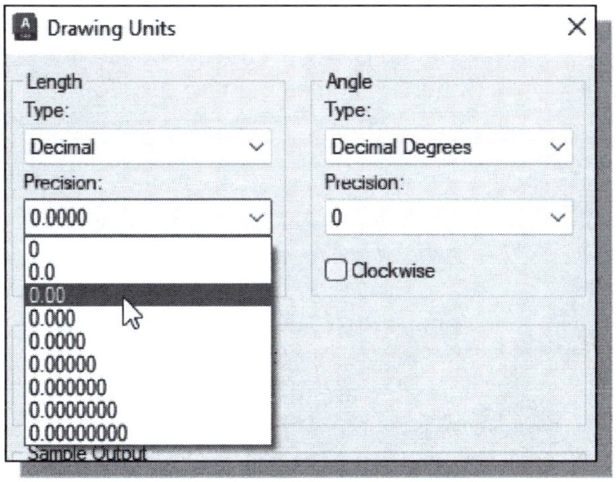

4. Set the *Precision* to **two digits** after the decimal point as shown in the above figure.

5. Pick **OK** to exit the *Drawing Units* dialog box.

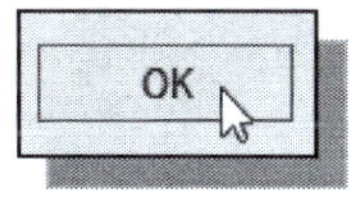

Drawing Area Setup

Next, we will set up the **Drawing Limits** by entering a command in the command prompt area. Setting the Drawing Limits controls the extents of the display of the *grid*. It also serves as a visual reference that marks the working area. It can also be used to prevent construction outside the grid limits and as a plot option that defines an area to be plotted and/or printed. Note that this setting does not limit the region for geometry construction.

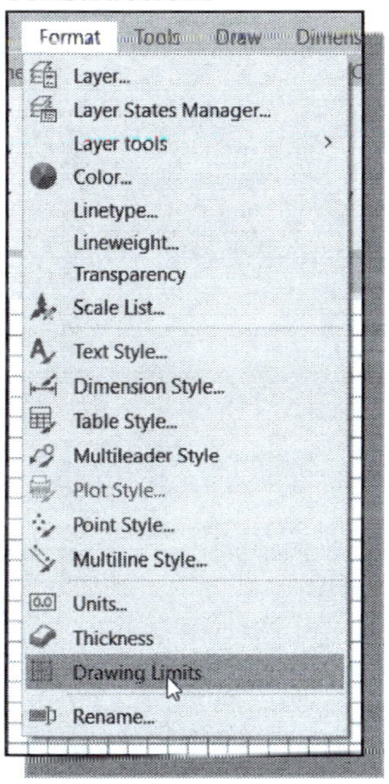

1. In the *Menu Bar* select:
   [Format] → [Drawing Limits]

2. In the command prompt area, the message "*Reset Model Space Limits: Specify lower left corner or [On/Off] <0.00,0.00>:*" is displayed. Press the **ENTER** key once to accept the default coordinates <**0.00,0.00**>.

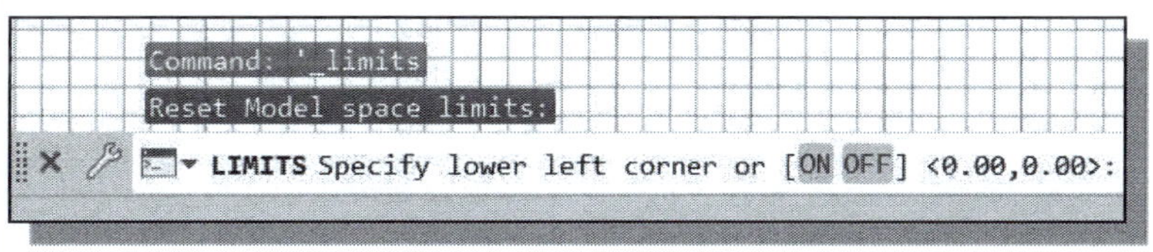

3. In the command prompt area, the message "*Specify upper right corner <12.00,9.00>:*" is displayed. Press the **ENTER** key again to accept the default coordinates <**12.00,9.00**>.

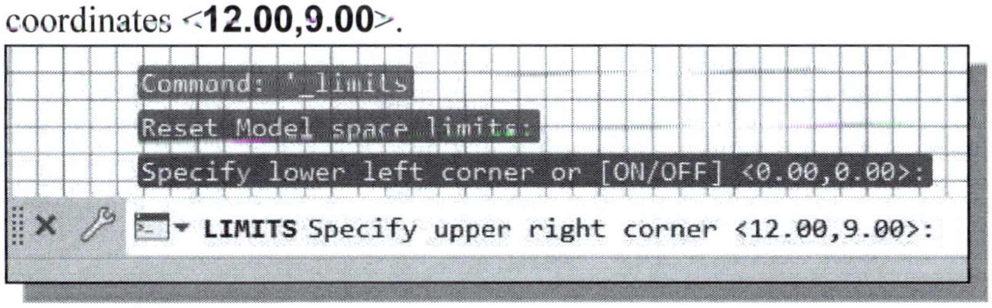

4. On your own, move the graphics cursor near the upper-right corner inside the drawing area and note that the drawing area is unchanged. (The **Drawing Limits** command is used to set the drawing area, but the display will not be adjusted until a display command is used.)

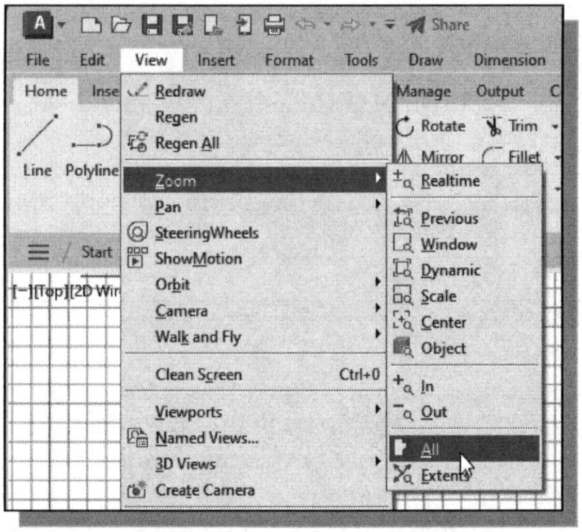

5. Inside the *Menu Bar* area select: **[View] → [Zoom] → [All]**

❖ The **Zoom All** command will adjust the display so that all objects in the drawing are displayed to be as large as possible. If no objects are constructed, the **Drawing Limits** are used to adjust the current viewport.

6. Move the graphics cursor near the upper-right corner inside the drawing area and note that the display area is updated.

7. Hit the function key [**F7**] once to turn **off** the display of the *Grid* lines.

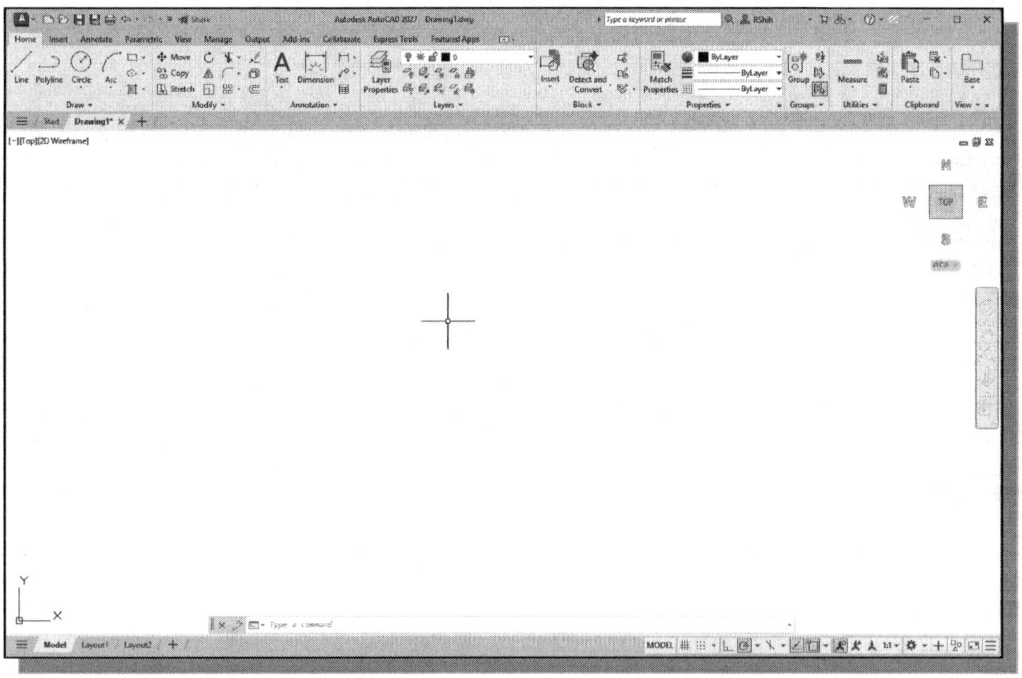

- Note that function key [**F7**] is a quick key, which can be used to quickly toggle on/off the grid display. Also, note the *command prompt area* can be positioned to dock below the drawing area or float inside the drawing area as shown.

Drawing Lines with the Line Command

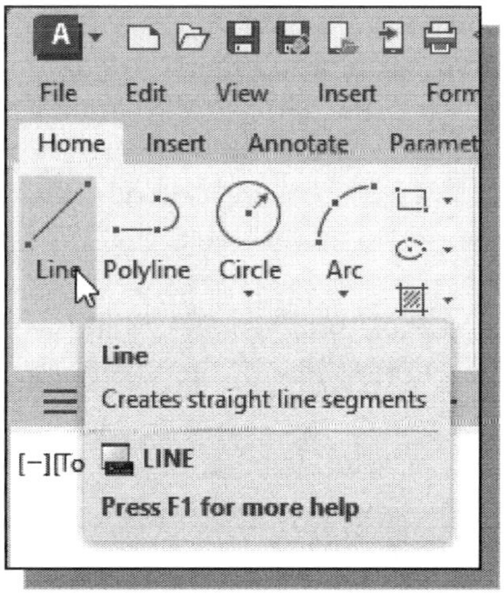

1. Move the graphics cursor to the first icon in the *Draw* panel. This icon is the **Line** icon. Note that a brief description of the Line command appears next to the cursor.

2. Select the icon by clicking once with the **left-mouse-button**, which will activate the Line command.

3. In the command prompt area, near the bottom of the AutoCAD drawing screen, the message "*_line Specify first point:*" is displayed. AutoCAD expects us to identify the starting location of a straight line. Move the graphics cursor inside the graphics window and watch the display of the coordinates of the graphics cursor at the bottom of the AutoCAD drawing screen. The three numbers represent the location of the cursor in the X, Y, and Z directions. We can treat the graphics window as if it was a piece of paper, and we are using the graphics cursor as if it was a pencil with which to draw.

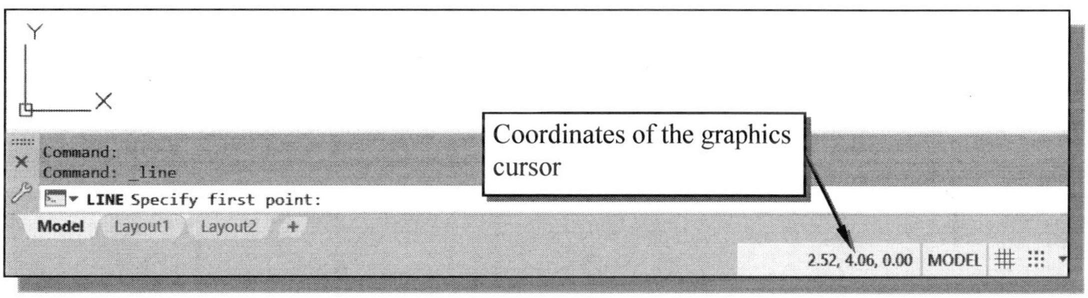

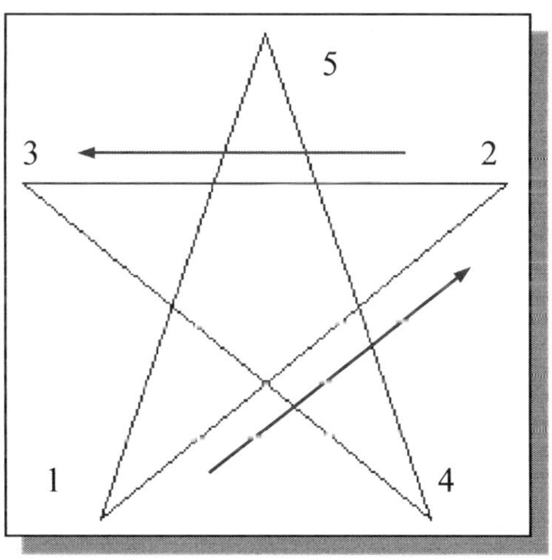

❖ We will create a freehand sketch of a five-point star using the Line command. Do not be overly concerned with the actual size or accuracy of your freehand sketch. This exercise is to give you a feel for the **AutoCAD 2027** user interface.

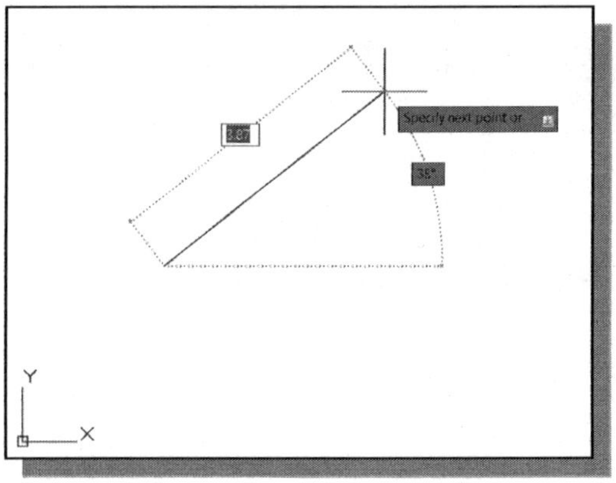

4. We will start at a location about one-third from the bottom of the graphics window. Left-click once to position the starting point of our first line. This will be *point 1* of our sketch. Next, move the cursor upward and toward the right side of *point 1*. Notice the rubber-band line that follows the graphics cursor in the graphics window. Left-click again (*point 2*) and we have created the first line of our sketch.

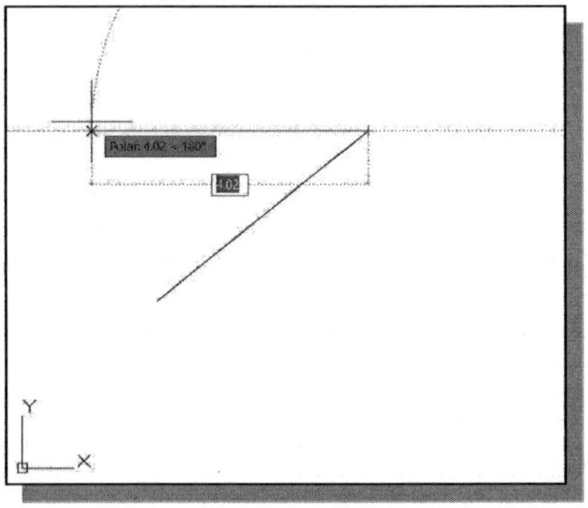

5. Move the cursor to the left of *point 2* and create a horizontal line about the same length as the first line on the screen.

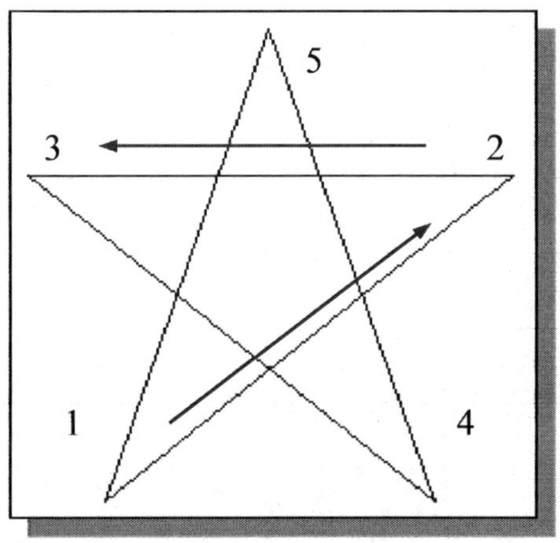

6. Repeat the above steps and complete the freehand sketch by adding three more lines (from *point 3* to *point 4*, *point 4* to *point 5*, and then connect to *point 5* back to *point 1*).

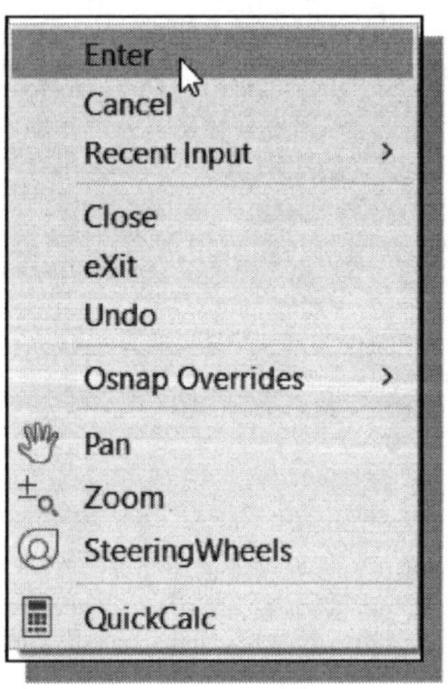

7. Notice that the **Line** command remains activated even after we connected the last segment of the line to the starting point *(point 1)* of our sketch. Inside the graphics window, **click once** with the **right-mouse-button** and a pop-up menu appears on the screen.

8. Select **Enter** with the left-mouse-button to end the **Line** command. (This is equivalent to hitting the [**ENTER**] key on the keyboard.)

9. Move the cursor near *point 2* and *point 3*, and estimate the length of the horizontal line by watching the displayed coordinates for each point.

Visual Reference

The method we just used to create the freehand sketch is known as the **interactive method**, where we use the cursor to specify locations on the screen. This method is perhaps the fastest way to specify locations on the screen. However, it is rather difficult to try to create a line of a specific length by watching the displayed coordinates. It would be helpful to know what one inch or one meter looks like on the screen while we are creating entities. **AutoCAD 2027** provides us with many tools to aid the construction of our designs. For example, the ***GRID*** and ***SNAP MODE*** options can be used to get a visual reference as to the size of objects and learn to restrict the movement of the cursor to a set increment on the screen.

The ***GRID*** and ***SNAP MODE*** options can be turned *ON* or *OFF* through the *Status Bar*. The *Status Bar* area is located at the bottom left of the AutoCAD drawing screen, next to the cursor coordinates.

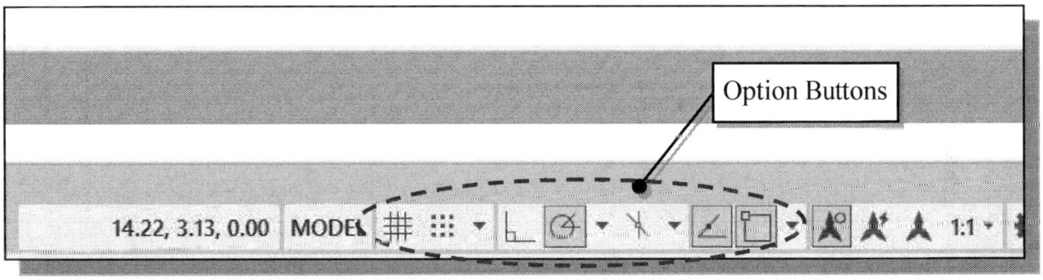

The second button in the *Status Bar* is the *SNAP MODE* option and the third button is the *GRID DISPLAY* option. Note that the buttons in the *Status Bar* area serve two functions: (1) the status of the specific option, and (2) as toggle switches that can be used to turn these special options *ON* and *OFF*. When the corresponding button is *highlighted*, the specific option is turned *ON*. Using the buttons is a quick and easy way to make changes to these *drawing aid* options. The buttons in the *Status Bar* can also be switched on and off in the middle of another command.

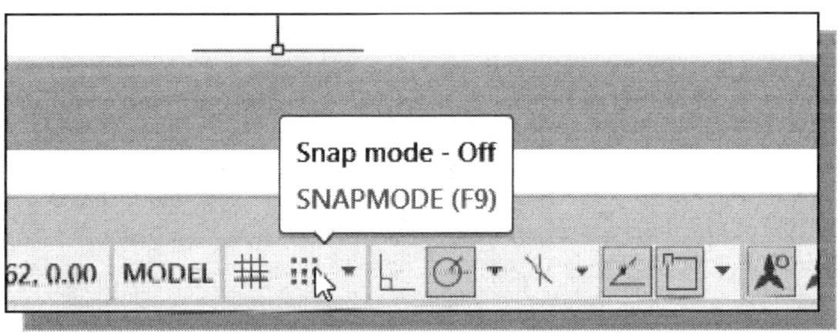

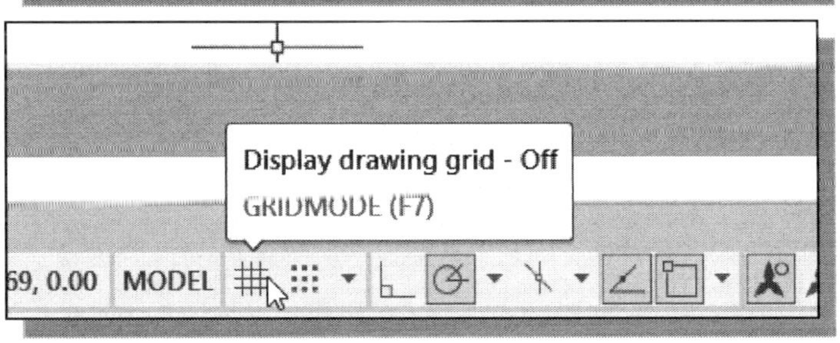

GRID ON

1. Left-click the ***GRID*** button in the *Status Bar* to turn ***ON*** the *GRID DISPLAY* option. (Notice in the command prompt area, the message *"<Grid on>"* is also displayed.)

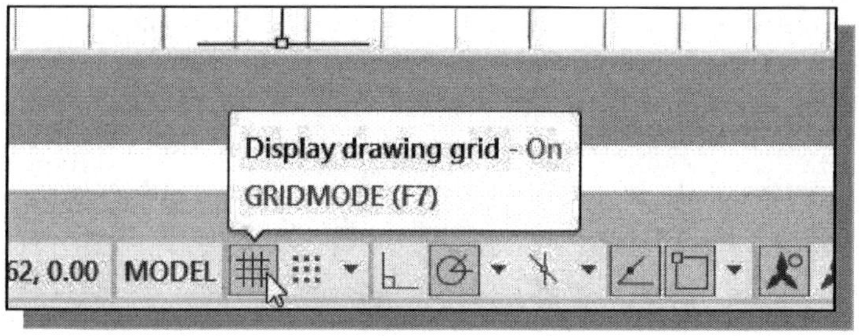

2. Move the cursor inside the graphics window, and estimate the distance in between the grid lines by watching the coordinates displayed at the bottom of the screen.

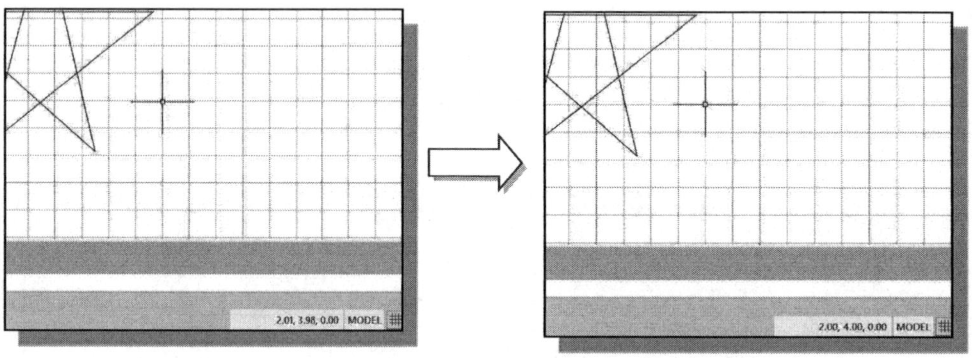

➢ The *GRID* option creates a pattern of lines that extends over an area on the screen. Using the grid is similar to placing a sheet of grid paper under a drawing. The grid helps you align objects and visualize the distance between them. The grid is not displayed in the plotted drawing. The default grid spacing, which means the distance in between two lines on the screen, is 0.5 inches. We can see that the sketched horizontal line in the sketch is about 4 inches long.

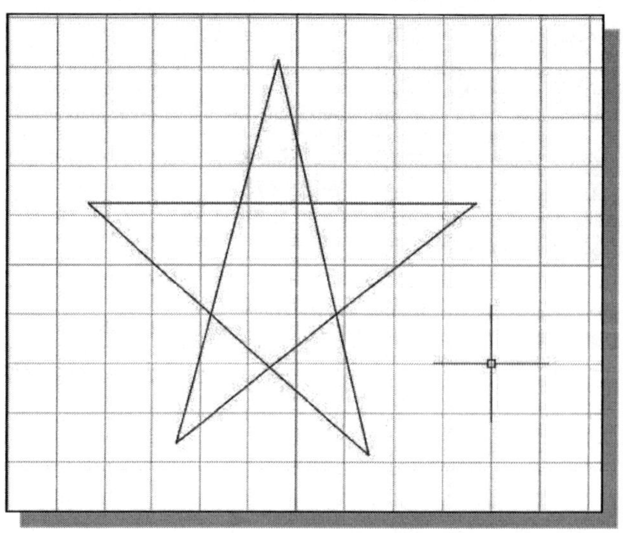

SNAP MODE ON

1. Left-click the ***SNAP MODE*** button in the *Status Bar* to turn ***ON*** the *SNAP* option.

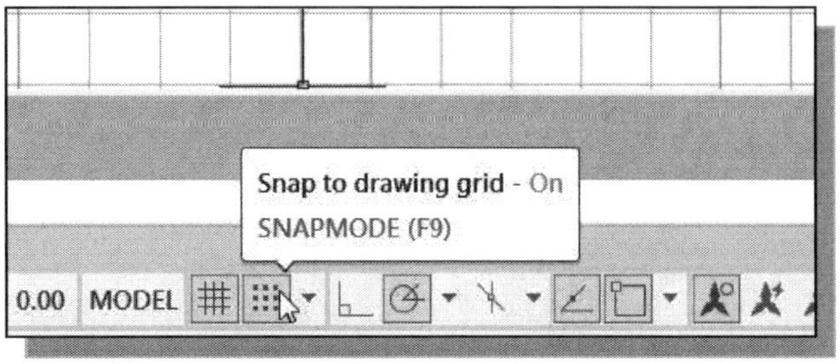

2. Move the cursor inside the graphics window, and move the cursor diagonally on the screen. Observe the movement of the cursor and watch the *coordinates display* at the bottom of the screen.

➢ The *SNAP* option controls an invisible rectangular grid that restricts cursor movement to specified intervals. When *SNAP* mode is on, the screen cursor and all input coordinates are snapped to the nearest point on the grid. The default snap interval is 0.5 inches and aligned to the grid points on the screen.

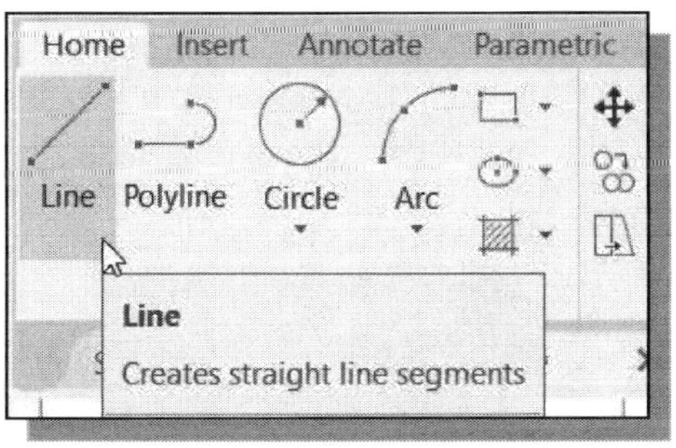

3. Click on the **Line** icon in the *Draw* toolbar. In the command prompt area, the message "*_line Specify first point:*" is displayed.

4. On your own, create another sketch of the five-point star with the *GRID* and *SNAP* options switched *ON*.

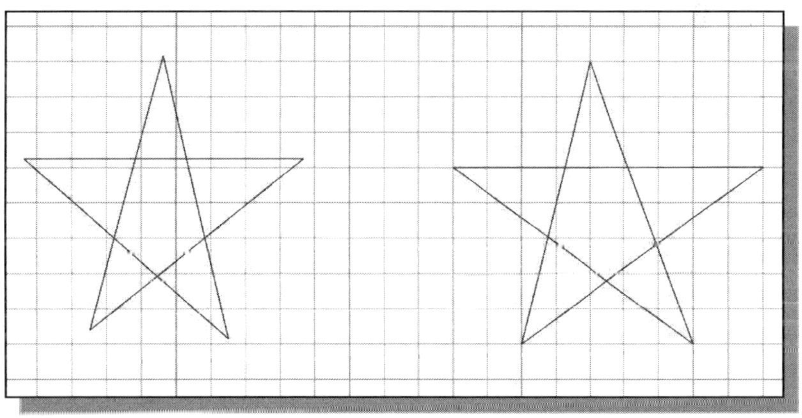

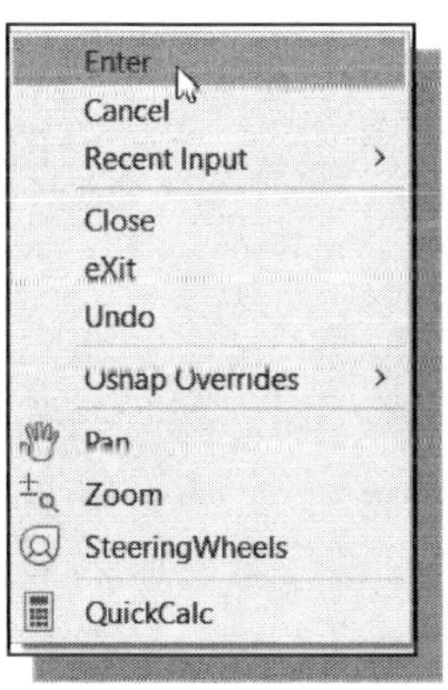

5. Use the **right-mouse-button** and select **Enter** in the pop-up menu to end the **Line** command if you have not done so.

Using the Erase Command

One of the advantages of using a CAD system is the ability to remove entities without leaving any marks. We will erase two of the lines using the **Erase** command.

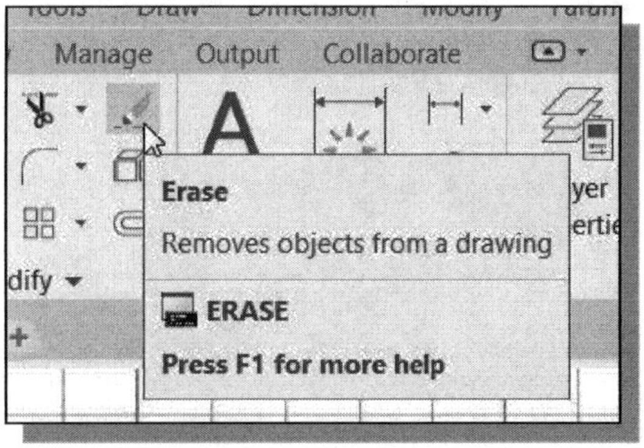

1. Pick **Erase** in the *Modify* toolbar. (The icon is a picture of an eraser at the end of a pencil.) The message "*Select objects*" is displayed in the command prompt area and AutoCAD awaits us to select the objects to erase.

2. Left-click the ***SNAP MODE*** button on the *Status Bar* to turn ***OFF*** the *SNAP MODE* option. We can toggle the *Status Bar* options *ON* or *OFF* in the middle of another command.

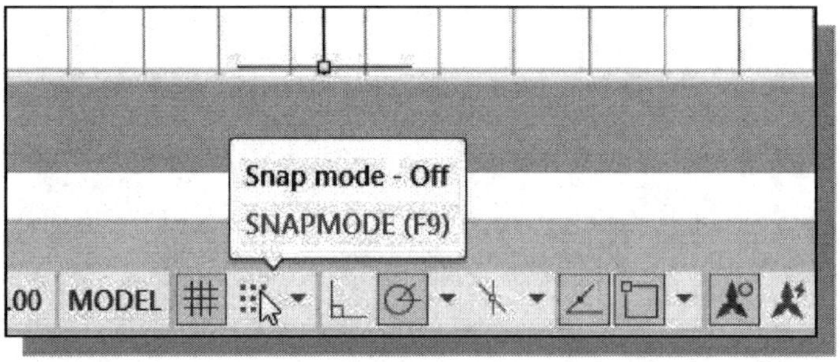

3. Select any two lines on the screen; the selected lines are highlighted as shown in the figure below.

➢ To **deselect** an object from the selection set, hold down the [**SHIFT**] key and select the object again.

4. **Right-mouse-click** once to accept the selections. The selected two lines are erased.

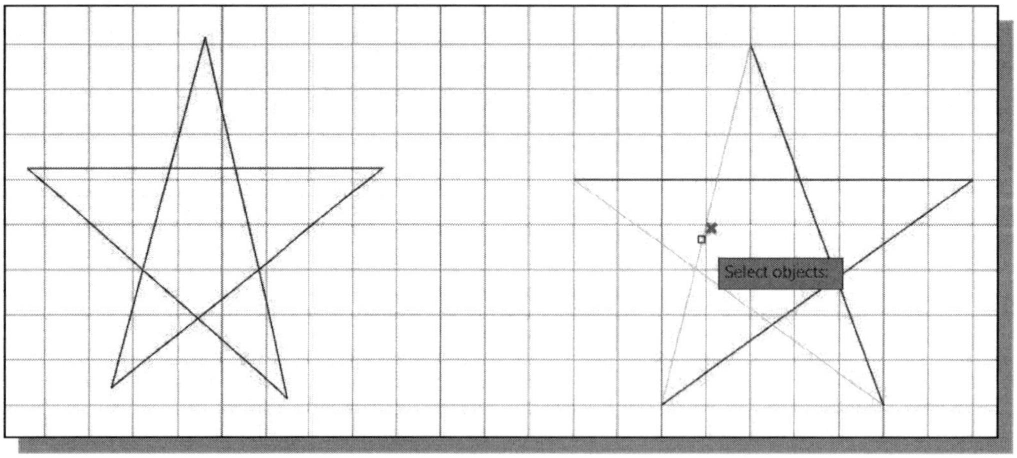

Repeat the Last Command

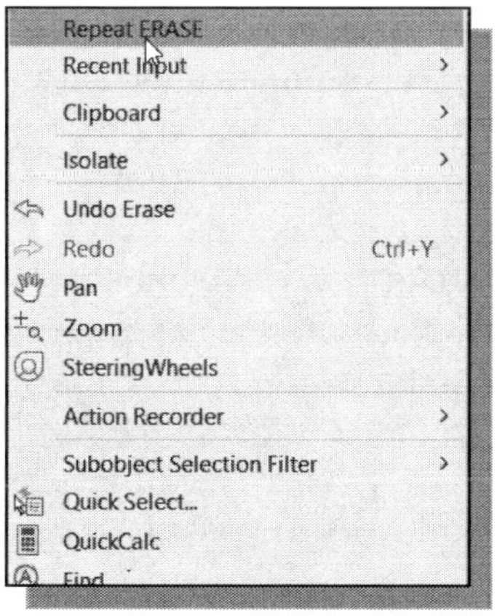

1. Inside the graphics window, click once with the **right-mouse-button** to bring up the pop-up option menu.

2. Pick **Repeat Erase**, with the left-mouse-button, in the pop-up menu to repeat the last command. Notice the other options available in the pop-up menu.

➢ **AutoCAD 2027** offers many options to accomplish the same task. Throughout this text, we will emphasize the use of the **AutoCAD Heads-up Design™** interface, which means we focus on the screen, not on the keyboard.

3. Move the cursor to a location that is above and toward the left side of the entities on the screen. Left-mouse-click once to start a corner of a rubber-band window.

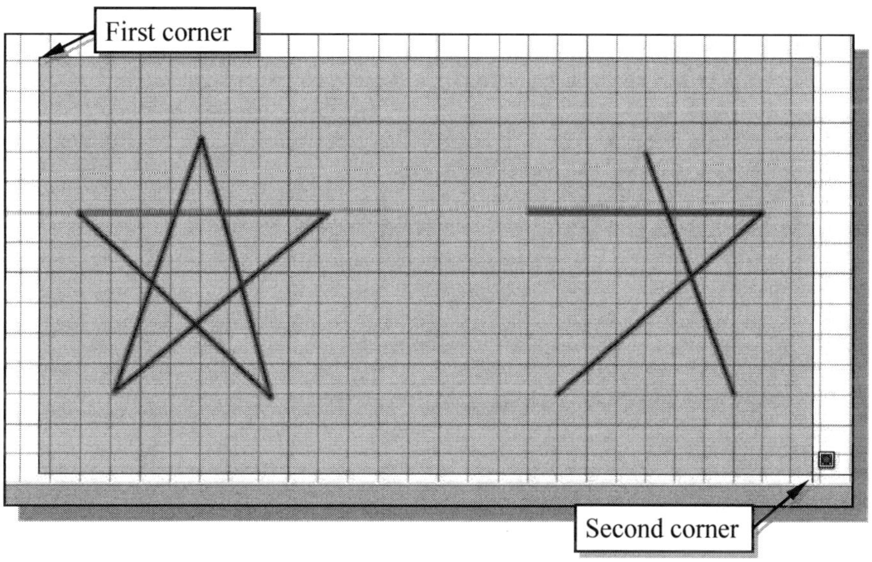

4. Move the cursor toward the right and below the entities, and then left-mouse-click to enclose all the entities inside the **selection window**. Notice all entities that are inside the window are selected. (Note the ***enclosed window selection*** direction is from **top left** to **bottom right**.)

5. Inside the graphics window, **right-mouse-click** once to proceed with erasing the selected entities.

➢ On your own, create a free-hand sketch of your choice using the **Line** command. Experiment with using the different commands we have discussed so far. Reset the status buttons so that **only** the ***GRID DISPLAY*** option is turned ***ON*** as shown.

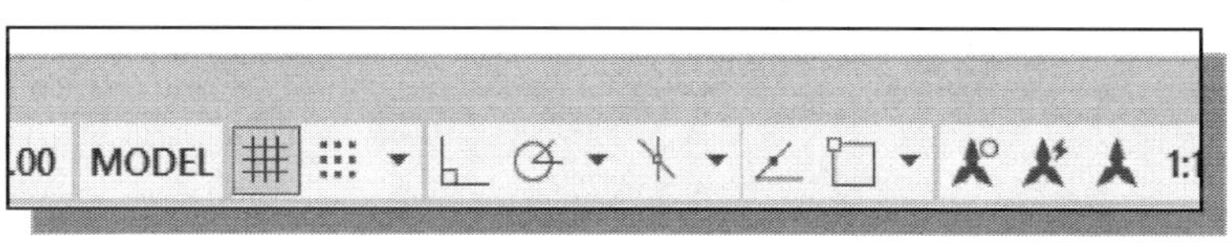

The CAD Database and the User Coordinate System

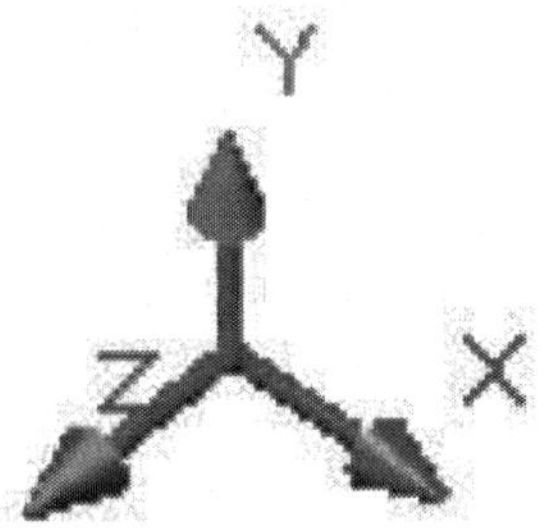

Designs and drawings created in a CAD system are usually defined and stored using sets of points in what is called **world space**. In most CAD systems, the world space is defined using a three-dimensional *Cartesian coordinate system*. Three mutually perpendicular axes, usually referred to as the X-, Y-, and Z-axes, define this system. The intersection of the three coordinate axes forms a point called the **origin**. Any point in world space can then be defined as the distance from the origin in the X-, Y- and Z- directions. In most CAD systems, the directions of the arrows shown on the axes identify the positive sides of the coordinates.

A CAD file, which is the electronic version of the design, contains data that describes the entities created in the CAD system. Information such as the coordinate values in world space for all endpoints, center points, etc., along with the descriptions of the types of entities, are all stored in the file. Knowing that AutoCAD stores designs by keeping coordinate data helps us understand the inputs required to create entities.

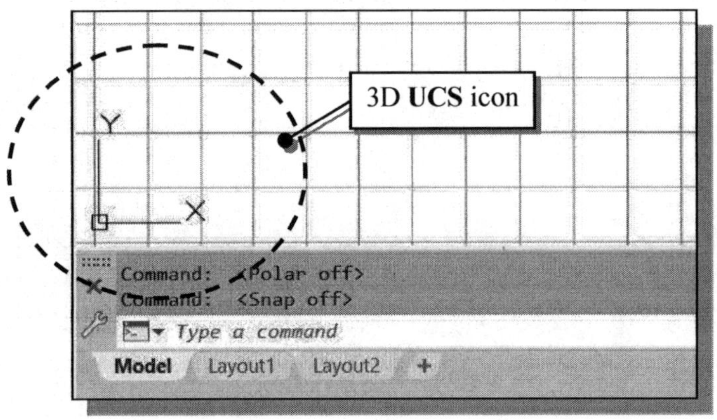

The icon near the bottom left corner of the default AutoCAD graphics window shows the positive X-direction and positive Y-direction of the coordinate system that is active. In AutoCAD, the coordinate system that is used to create entities is called the **user coordinate system** (UCS). By default, the **user coordinate system** is aligned to the **world coordinate system (WCS)**. The **world coordinate system** is a coordinate system used by AutoCAD as the basis for defining all objects and other coordinate systems defined by the users. We can think of the **origin** of the **world coordinate system** as a fixed point being used as a reference for all measurements. The default orientation of the Z-axis can be considered as positive values in front of the monitor and negative values inside the monitor.

Changing to the 2D UCS Icon Display

In **AutoCAD 2027**, the **UCS** icon is displayed in various ways to help us visualize the orientation of the drawing plane.

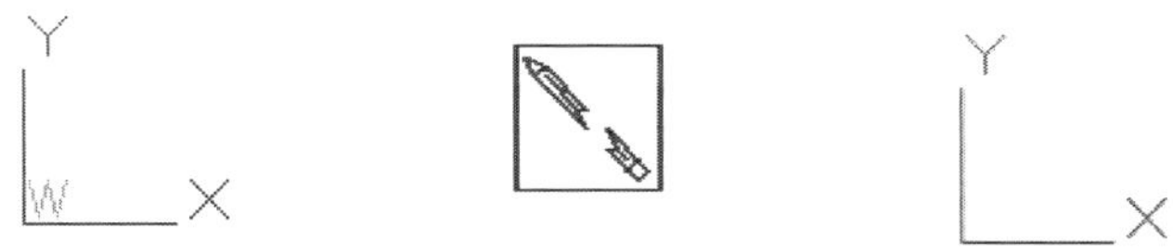

2D UCS at WCS | 2D UCS broken pencil | right side view of 2D UCS

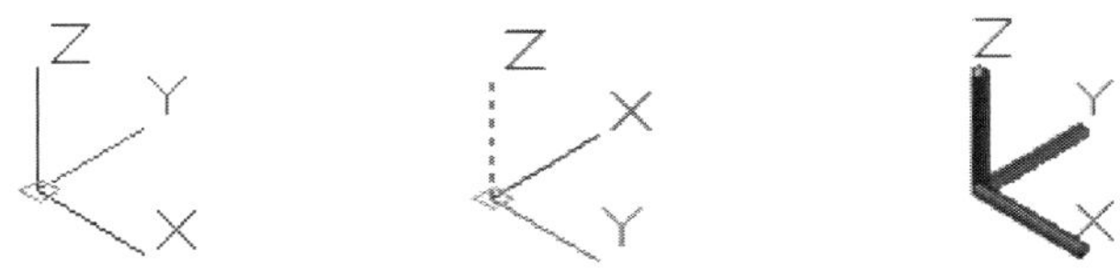

3D UCS at WCS | 3D UCS viewed from below | Shaded UCS icon

1. Click on the **View** pull-down menu and select

   [Display] → [UCS Icon] → [Properties…]

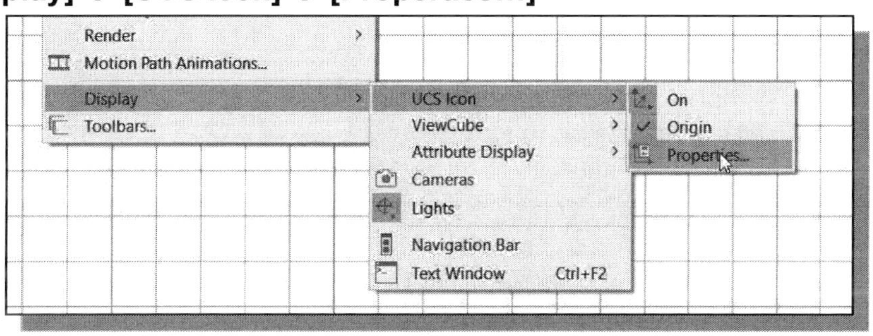

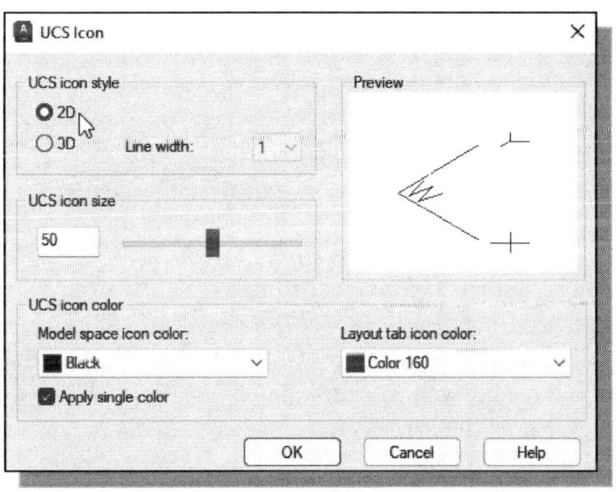

2. In the ***UCS icon style*** section, switch to the **2D** option as shown.

3. Click **OK** to accept the settings.

❖ Note the W symbol in the UCS icon indicates that the UCS is aligned to the **world coordinate system**.

Cartesian and Polar Coordinate Systems

In a two-dimensional space, a point can be represented using different coordinate systems. The point can be located, using a *Cartesian coordinate system*, as X and Y units away from the origin. The same point can also be located using the *polar coordinate system*, as r and θ units away from the origin.

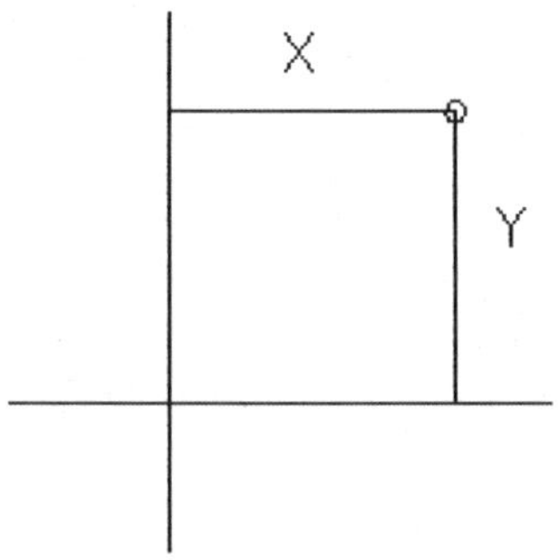

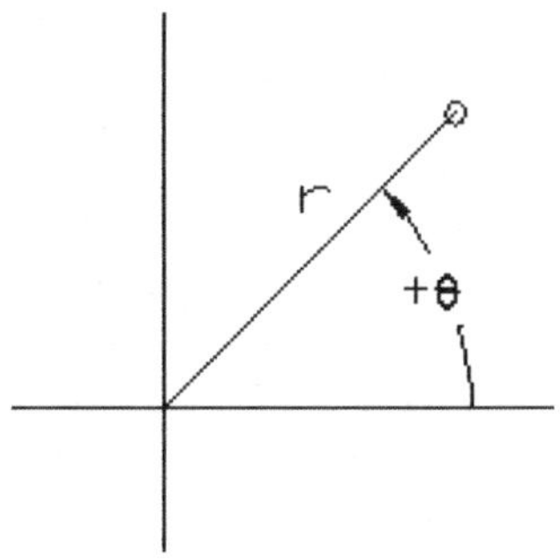

For planar geometry, the polar coordinate system is very useful for certain applications. In the polar coordinate system, points are defined in terms of a radial distance, r, from the origin and an angle θ between the direction of r and the positive X axis. The default system for measuring angles in **AutoCAD 2027** defines positive angular values as counterclockwise from the positive X-axis.

Absolute and Relative Coordinates

AutoCAD 2027 also allows us to use *absolute* and *relative coordinates* to quickly construct objects. **Absolute coordinate values** are measured from the current coordinate system's origin point. **Relative coordinate values** are specified in relation to previous coordinates.

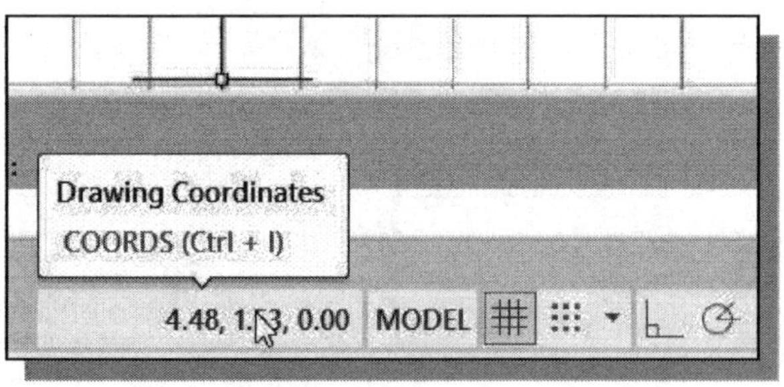

- Note that the *coordinate display area* can also be used as a toggle switch; each left-mouse-click will toggle the coordinate display *on* or *off.*

In **AutoCAD 2027**, the *absolute* coordinates and the *relative* coordinates can be used in conjunction with the *Cartesian* and *polar* coordinate systems. By default, AutoCAD expects us to enter values in *absolute Cartesian coordinates*, distances measured from the current coordinate system's origin point. We can switch to using the *relative coordinates* by using the **@** symbol. The **@** symbol is used as the *relative coordinates specifier*, which means that we can specify the position of a point in relation to the previous point.

Defining Positions

In AutoCAD, there are five methods for specifying the locations of points when we create planar geometric entities.

- **Interactive method**: Use the cursor to select on the screen.
- **Absolute coordinates (Format: X,Y)**: Type the X and Y coordinates to locate the point on the current coordinate system relative to the origin.
- **Relative rectangular coordinates (Format: @X,Y)**: Type the X and Y coordinates relative to the last point.
- **Relative polar coordinates (Format: @Distance<angle)**: Type a distance and angle relative to the last point.
- **Direct Distance entry technique**: Specify a second point by first moving the cursor to indicate direction and then entering a distance.

GRID Style Setup

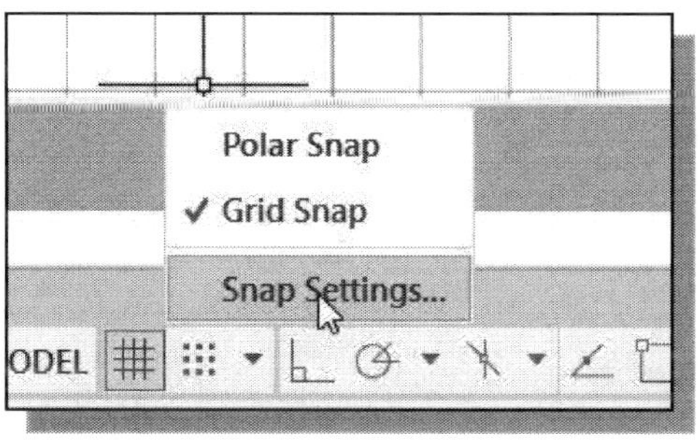

1. In the *Status Bar* area, **right-mouse-click** on ***Snap Mode*** and choose **[Snap settings]**.
2. In the *Drafting Settings* dialog box, select the **Snap and Grid** tab if it is not the page on top.
3. Change *Grid Style* to ***Display dotted grid in 2D model Space*** as shown in the below figure.

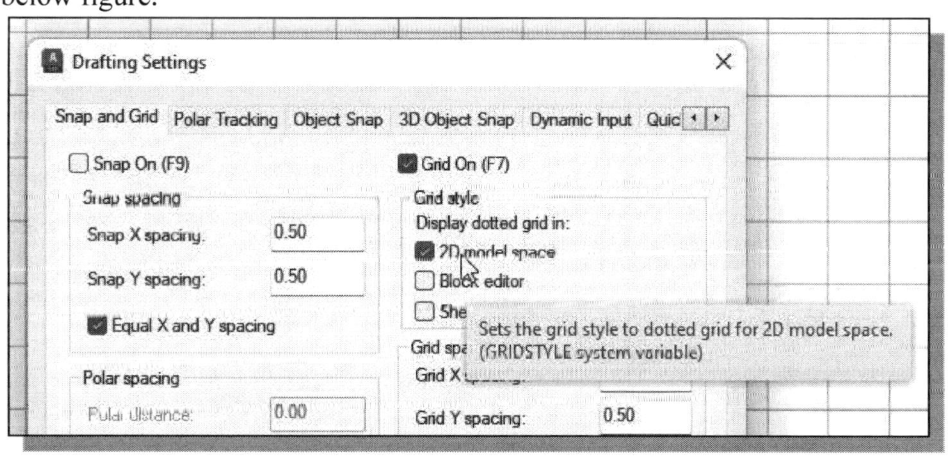

4. Pick **OK** to exit the *Drafting Settings* dialog box.

The Guide Plate

We will next create a mechanical design using the different coordinate entry methods.

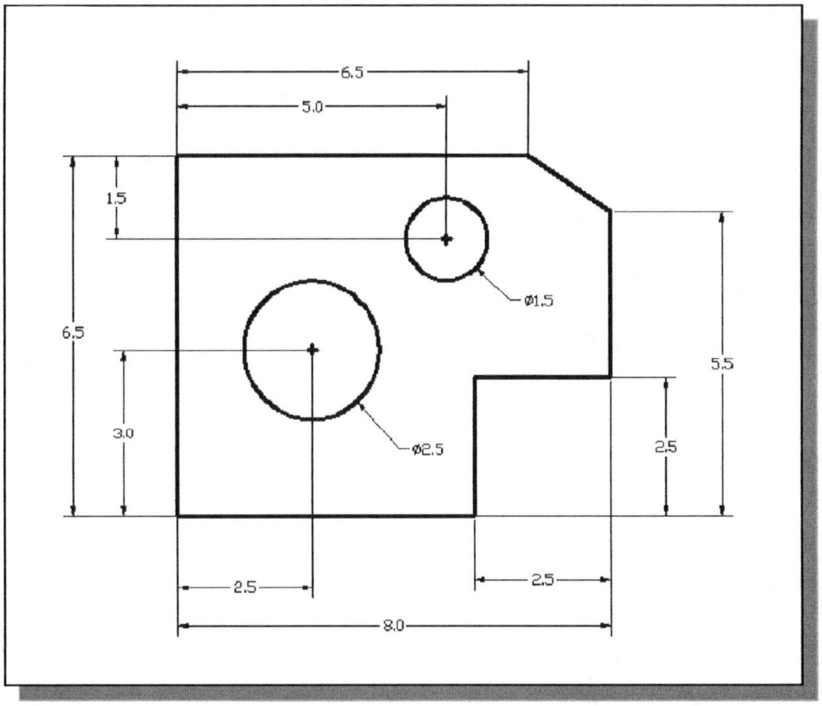

❖ The rule for creating CAD designs and drawings is that they should be created at **full size** using real-world units. The CAD database contains all the definitions of the geometric entities and the design is considered as a virtual, full-sized object. Only when a printer or plotter transfers the CAD design to paper is the design scaled to fit on a sheet. The tedious task of determining a scale factor so that the design will fit on a sheet of paper is taken care of by the CAD system. This allows the designers and CAD operators to concentrate their attention on the more important issues – the design.

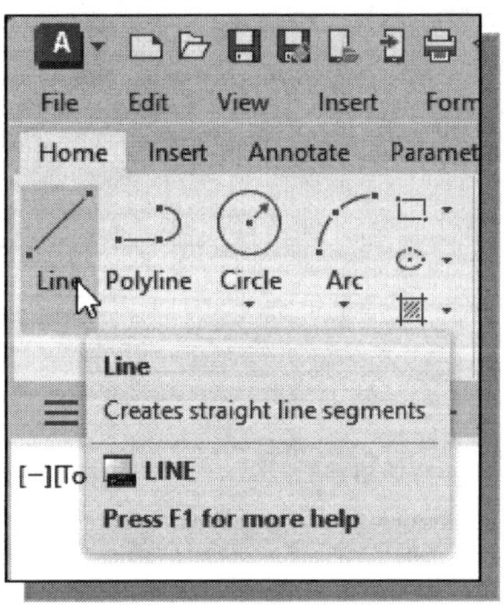

1. Select the **Line** command icon in the *Draw* toolbar. In the command prompt area, near the bottom of the AutoCAD graphics window, the message "*_line Specify first point:*" is displayed. AutoCAD expects us to identify the starting location of a straight line.

2. We will locate the starting point of our design at the origin of the *world coordinate system.*

   Command: _line Specify first point: **0,0**
   (Type ***0,0*** and press the [**ENTER**] key once.)

3. We will create a horizontal line by entering the absolute coordinates of the second point.
   Specify next point or [Undo]: **5.5,0 [ENTER]**

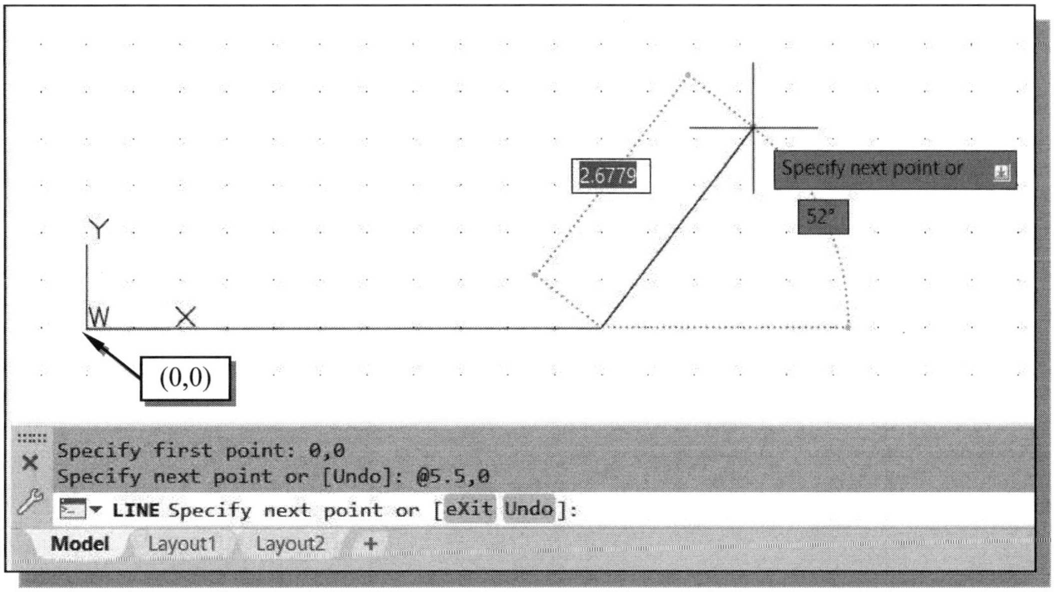

- Note that the line we created is aligned to the bottom edge of the drawing window. Let us adjust the view of the line by using the Pan Realtime command.

4. In the *Menu Bar* area select: **[View] → [Pan] → [Realtime]**

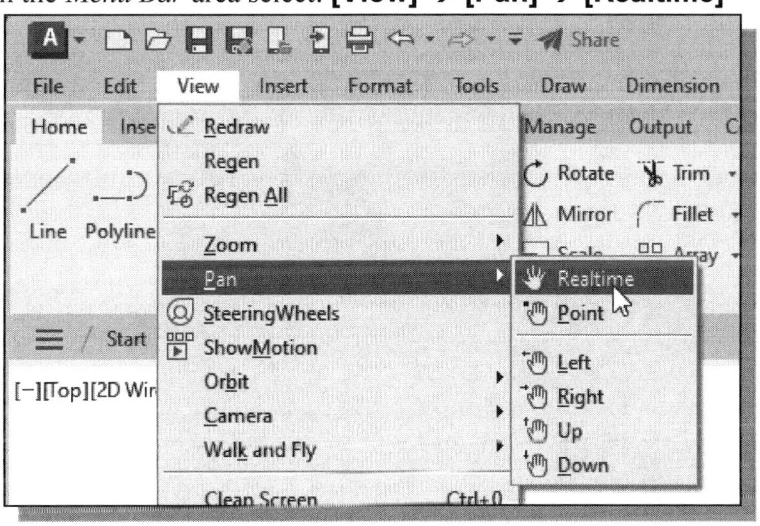

❖ The available **Pan** commands enable us to move the view to a different position. The *Pan-Realtime* function acts as if you are using a video camera.

5. Move the cursor, which appears as a hand inside the graphics window, near the center of the drawing window, then push down the **left-mouse-button** and drag the display toward the right and top side until we can see the sketched line. (Notice the scroll bars can also be used to adjust viewing of the display.)

6. Press the **[Esc]** key to exit the *Pan-Realtime* command. Notice that AutoCAD goes back to the **Line** command.

7. We will create a vertical line by using the *relative rectangular coordinates entry method*, relative to the last point we specified:
   Specify next point or [Close/Undo]: **@0,2.5 [ENTER]**

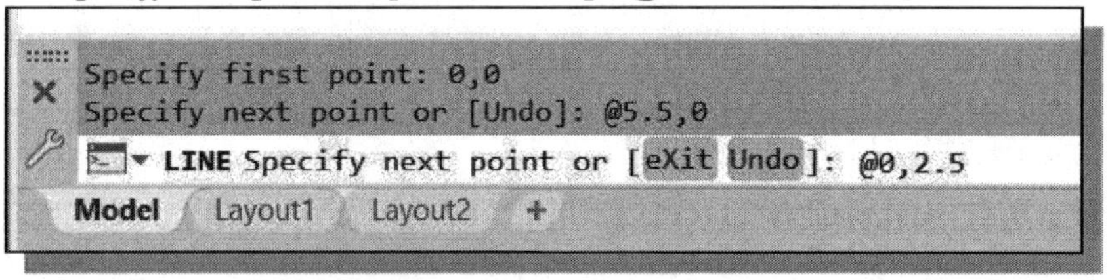

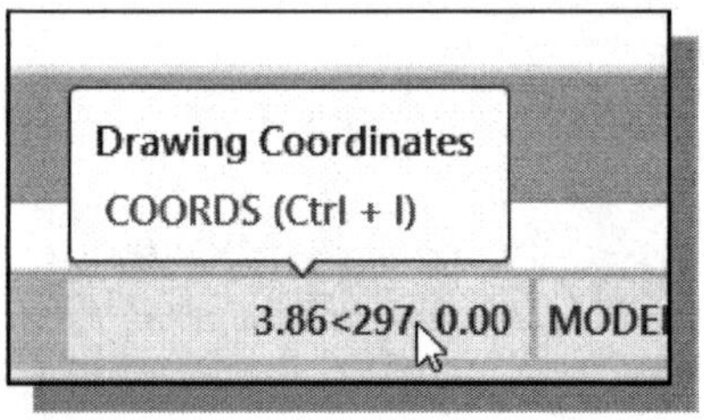

8. Left-click once on the *coordinates display area* to switch to a different coordinate display option. Click again to see the other option. Note the coordinates display has changed to show the length of the new line and its angle. Each click will change the display format of the cursor coordinates.

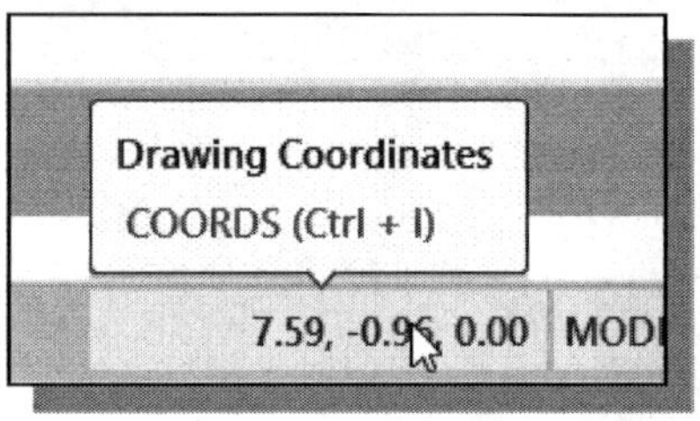

9. On your own, left-click on the coordinates display area to observe the switching of the coordinate display; set the display back to using the world coordinate system.

10. We can mix any of the entry methods in positioning the locations of the endpoints. Move the cursor to the *Status Bar* area, and turn ***ON*** the *SNAP MODE* option.

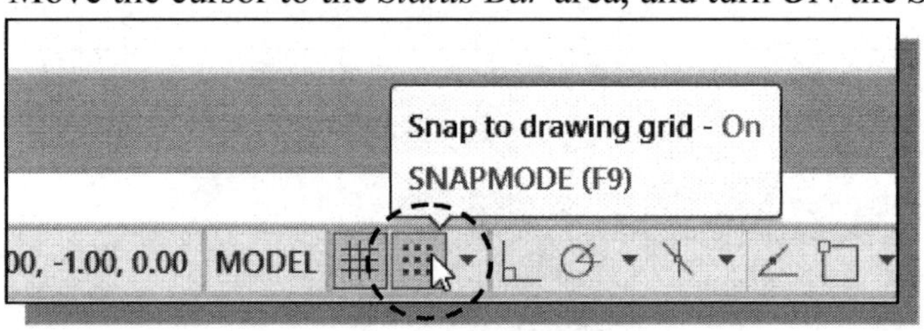

❖ Note that the **Line** command is resumed as the settings are adjusted.

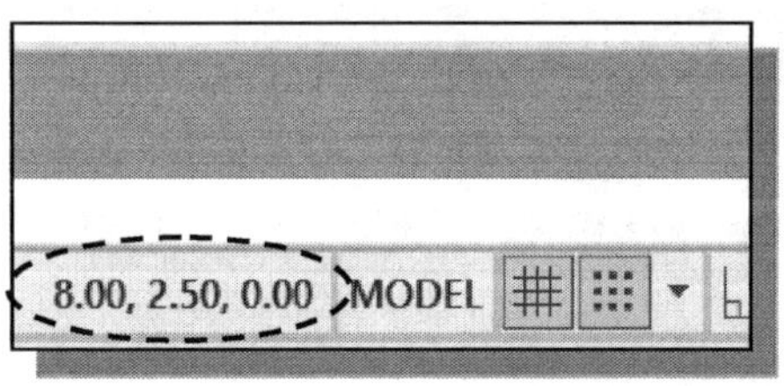

11. Create the next line by picking the location, world coordinates ***(8,2.5)***, on the screen.

12. We will next use the *relative polar coordinates entry method*; distance is ***3*** inches with an angle of ***90*** degrees, relative to the last point we specified:
    Specify next point or [Close/Undo]: **@3<90 [ENTER]**

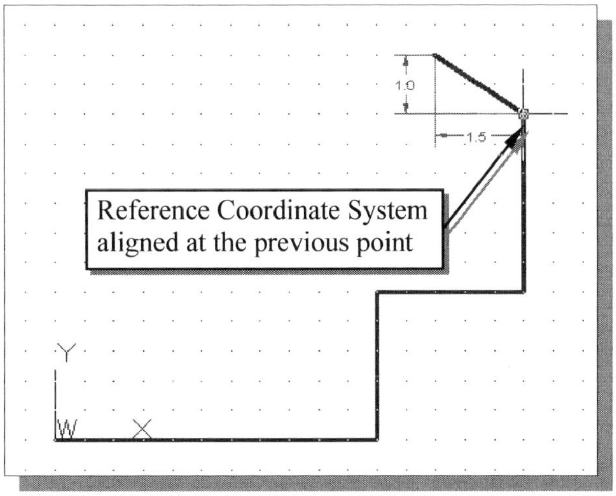

13. Using the *relative rectangular coordinates entry method* to create the next line, we can imagine a *reference coordinate system* aligned at the previous point. Coordinates are measured along the two reference axes.

Specify next point or [Close/Undo]:
@-1.5,1 [ENTER]

(***-1.5*** and ***1*** inches are measured relative to the reference point.)

14. Move the cursor directly to the left of the last point and use the *direct distance entry technique* by entering ***6.5*** **[ENTER]**.

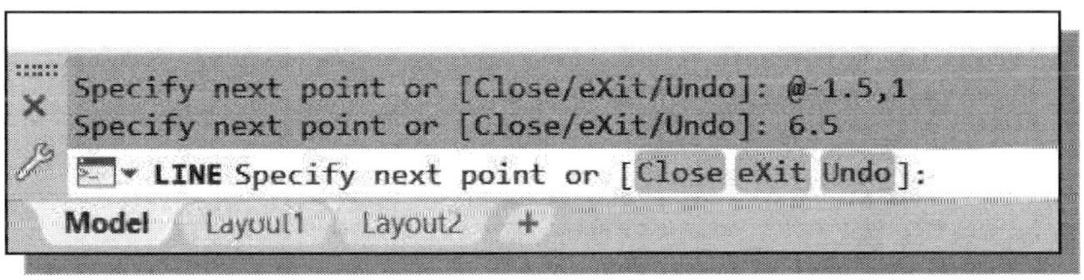

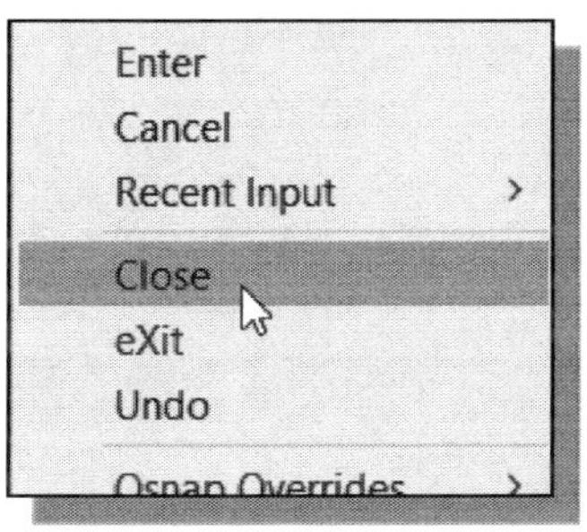

15. For the last segment of the sketch, we can use the **Close** option to connect back to the starting point. Inside the graphics window, **right-mouse-click** and a *pop-up menu* appears on the screen.

16. Select **Close** with the left-mouse-button to connect back to the starting point and end the Line command.

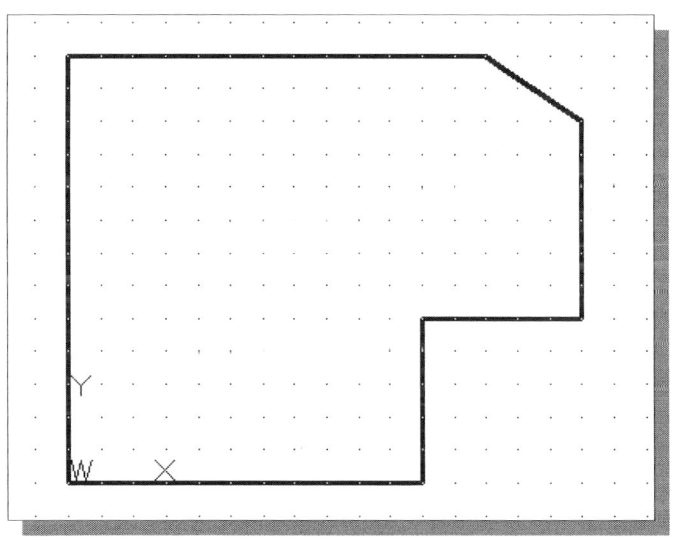

Creating Circles

The menus and toolbars in **AutoCAD 2027** are designed to allow the CAD operator to quickly activate the desired commands.

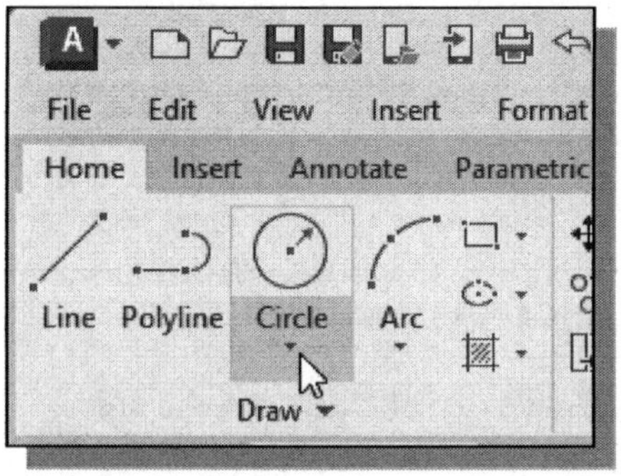

1. In the *Draw* toolbar, click on the little triangle below the circle icon. Note that the little triangle indicates additional options are available.

2. In the option list, select: **[Center, Diameter]**

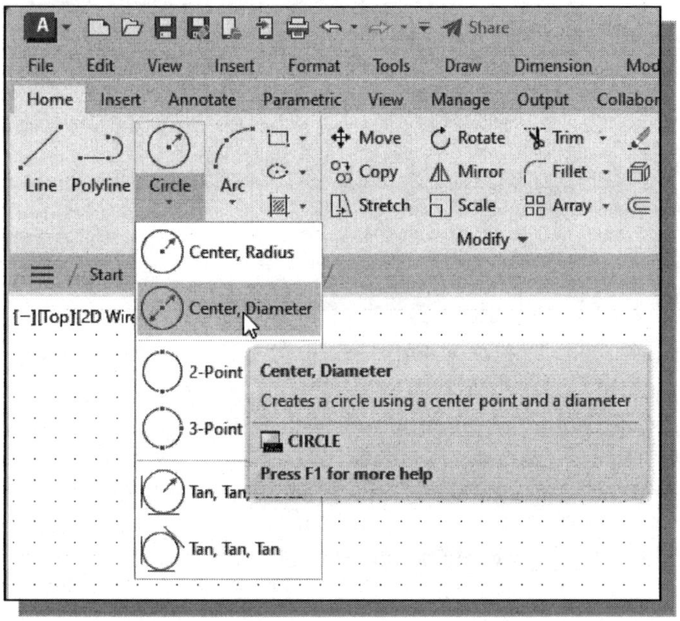

Notice the different options available under the circle submenu:

- **Center, Radius**: Draws a circle based on a center point and a radius.
- **Center, Diameter**: Draws a circle based on a center point and a diameter.
- **2 Points**: Draws a circle based on two endpoints of the diameter.
- **3 Points**: Draws a circle based on three points on the circumference.
- **TTR–Tangent, Tangent**, **Radius**: Draws a circle with a specified radius tangent to two objects.
- **TTT–Tangent, Tangent, Tangent**: Draws a circle tangent to three objects.

3. In the command prompt area, the message "*Specify center point for circle or [3P/2P/Ttr (tan tan radius)]:*" is displayed. AutoCAD expects us to identify the location of a point or enter an option. We can use any of the four coordinate entry methods to identify the desired location. We will enter the **world coordinates (*2.5,3*)** as the center point for the first circle.

   Specify center point for circle or [3P/2P/Ttr (tan tan radius)]: **2.5,3 [ENTER]**

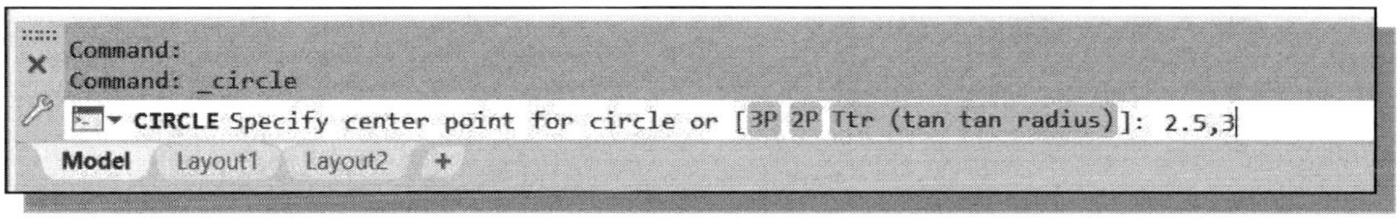

4. In the command prompt area, the message "*Specify diameter of circle:*" is displayed.
   Specify diameter of circle: **2.5 [ENTER]**

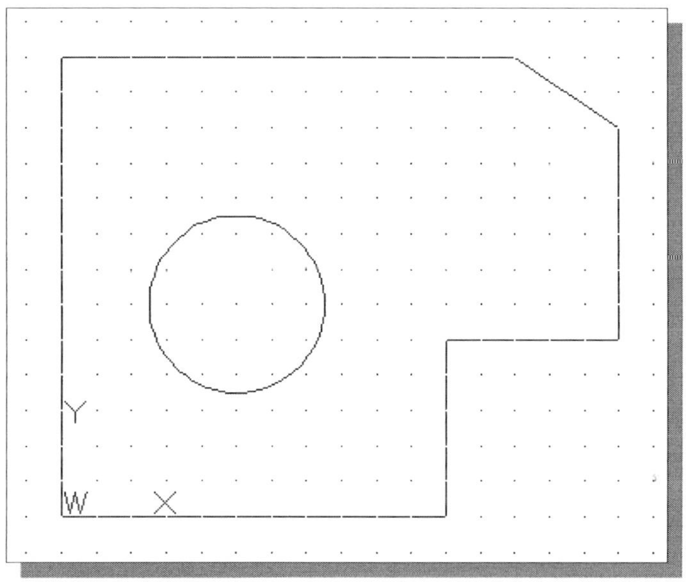

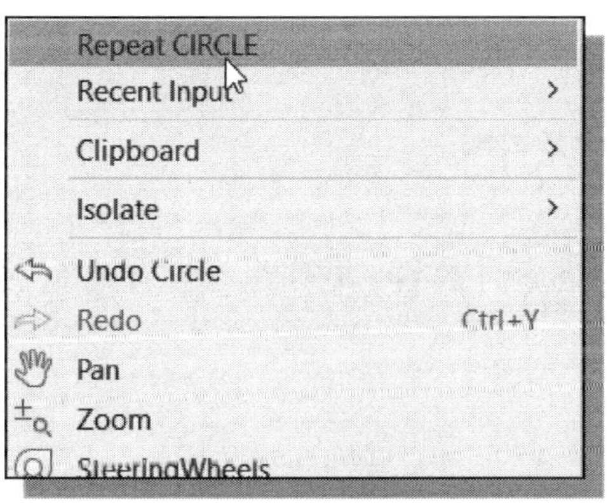

5. Inside the graphics window, right-mouse-click to bring up the pop-up option menu.

6. Pick **Repeat CIRCLE** with the left-mouse-button in the pop-up menu to repeat the last command.

7. Using the *relative rectangular coordinates entry method*, relative to the center-point coordinates of the first circle, we specify the relative location as **(@*2.5,2*)**.

Specify center point for circle or [3P/2P/Ttr (tan tan radius)]: **@2.5,2 [ENTER]**

8. In the command prompt area, the message "*Specify Radius of circle: <2.50>*" is displayed. The default option for the **Circle** command in AutoCAD is to specify the *radius* and the last radius used is also displayed in brackets.

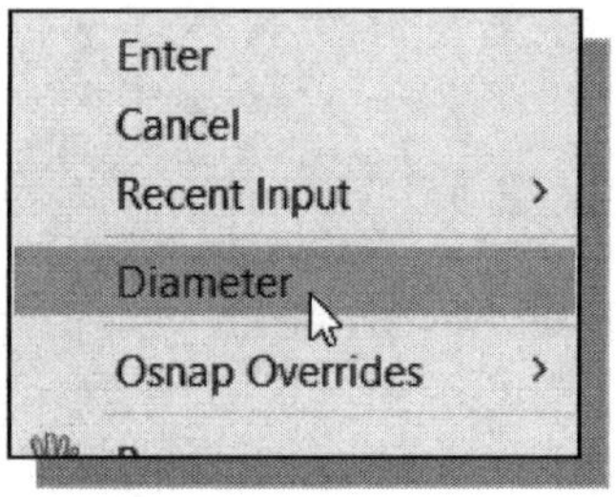

9. Inside the graphics window, **right-mouse-click** to bring up the pop-up option menu and select **Diameter** as shown.

10. In the command prompt area, enter ***1.5*** as the diameter.

    Specify Diameter of circle<2.50>: **1.5 [ENTER]**

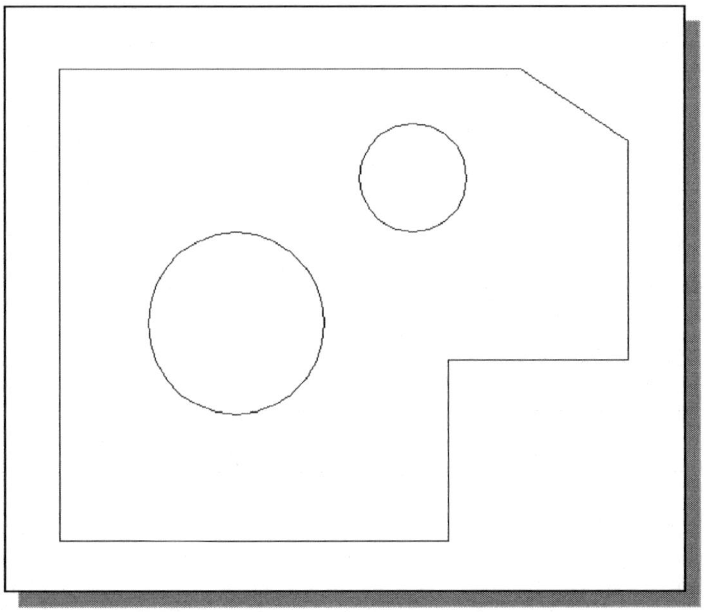

Saving the CAD Design

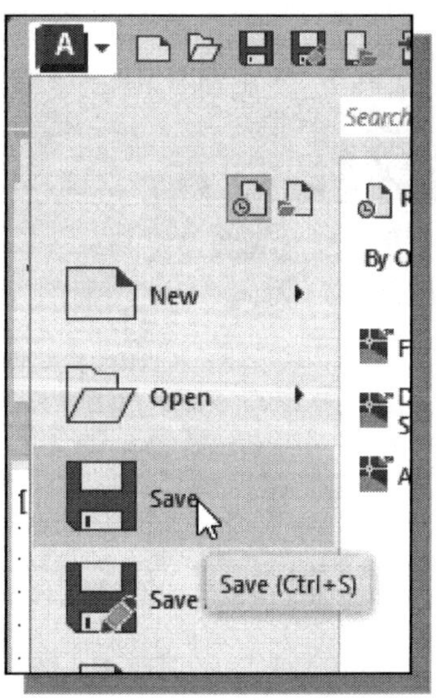

1. In the *Application Menu*, select:

   [Application] → [Save]

❖ Note the command can also be activated with the quick-key combination of **[Ctrl]+[S]**.

2. In the *Save Drawing As* dialog box, select the folder in which you want to store the CAD file and enter ***GuidePlate*** in the *File name* box.

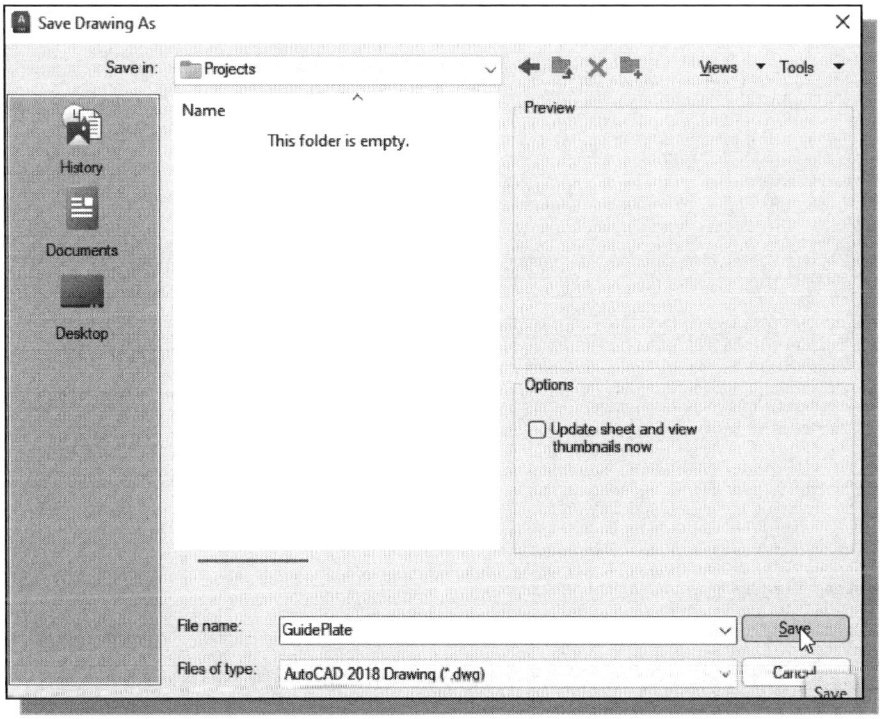

3. Click **Save** in the *Save Drawing As* dialog box to accept the selections and save the file. Note the default file type is DWG, which is the standard AutoCAD drawing format.

Close the Current Drawing

Several options are available to close the current drawing:

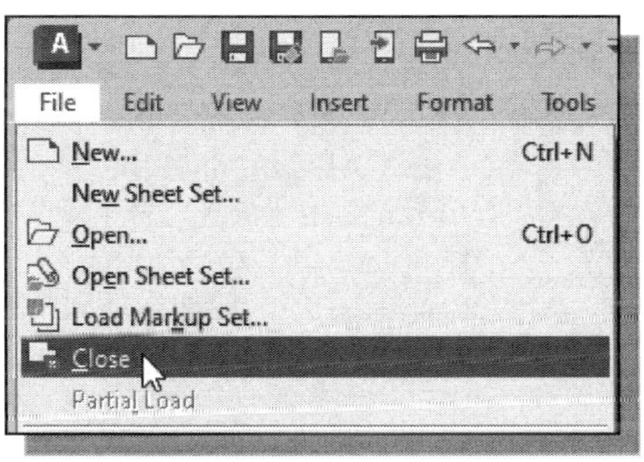

➢ Select **[Close] → [Current Drawing]** in the *Application Menu Bar* as shown.

➢ Enter **Close** at the command prompt.

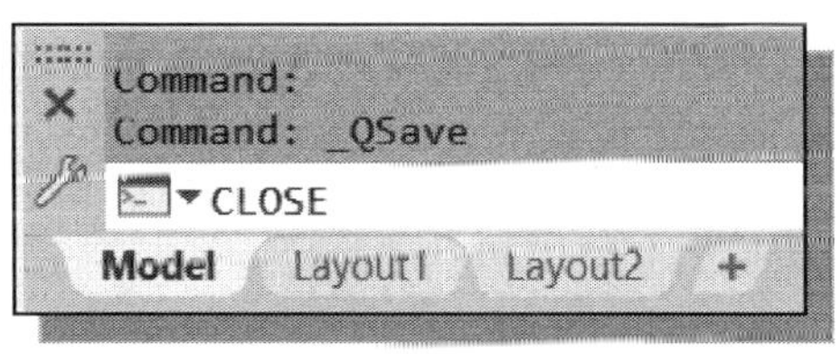

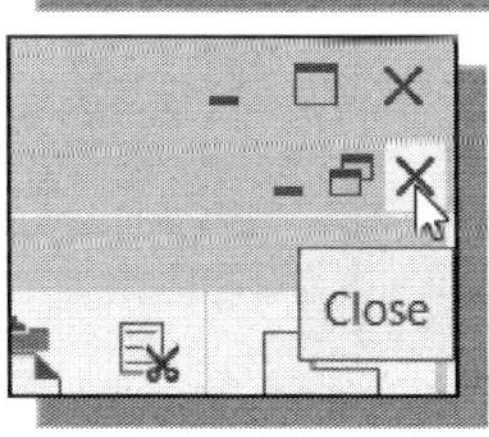

➢ The third option is to click on the **[Close]** icon located at the upper-right-hand corner of the drawing window.

The Spacer Design

We will next create the spacer design using more of AutoCAD's drawing tools.

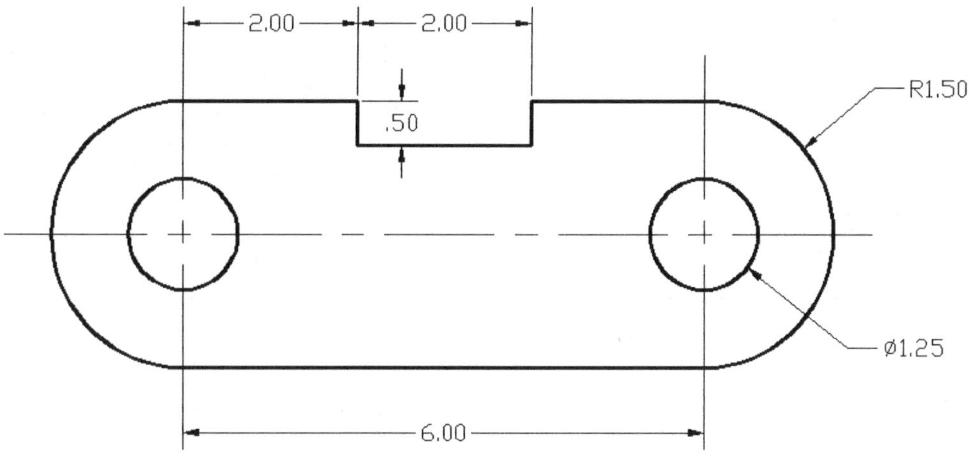

Start a New Drawing

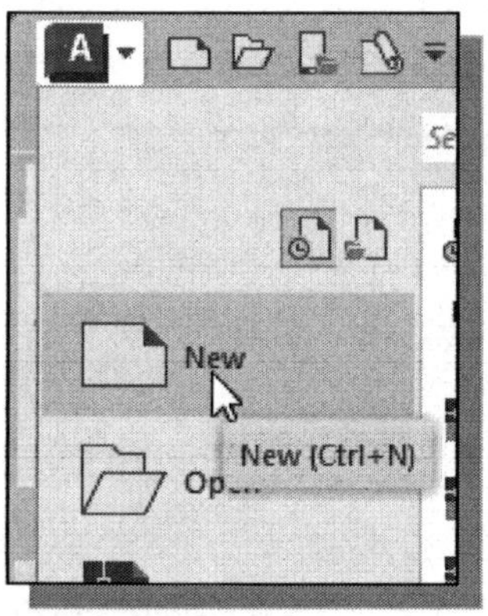

1. In the *Application Menu*, select **[New]** to start a new drawing.

2. The **Select Template** dialog box appears on the screen. Click Open to accept the default **acad.dwt** as the template to open.

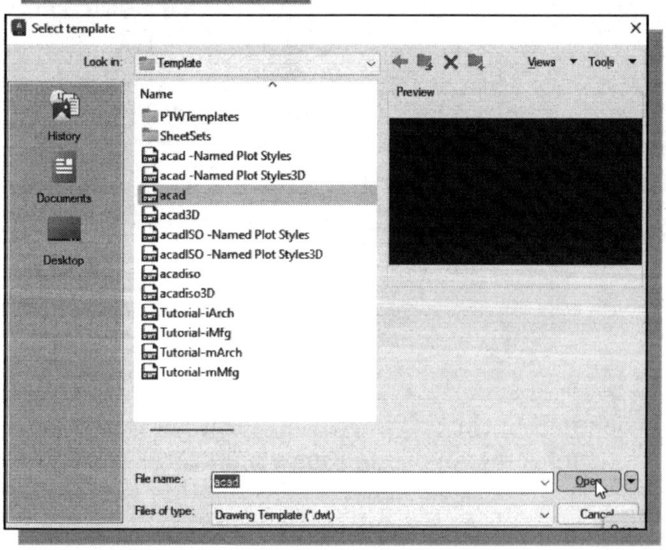

➢ The dwt file type is the AutoCAD template file format. An AutoCAD template file contains pre-defined settings to reduce the amount of tedious repetitions.

Drawing Units Setup

Every object we construct in a CAD system is measured in **units**. We should determine the system of units within the CAD system before creating the first geometric entities.

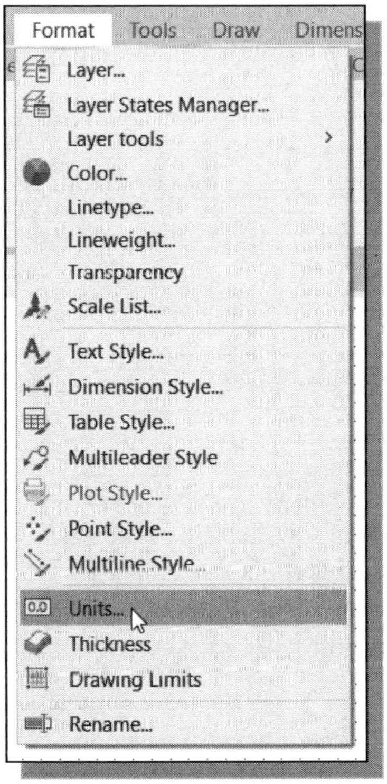

1. In the *Menu Bar* select:
   [Format] → [Units]

- The AutoCAD *Menu Bar* contains multiple pull-down menus where all of the AutoCAD commands can be accessed. Note that many of the menu items listed in the pull-down menus can also be accessed through the *Quick Access* toolbar and/or *Ribbon* panels.

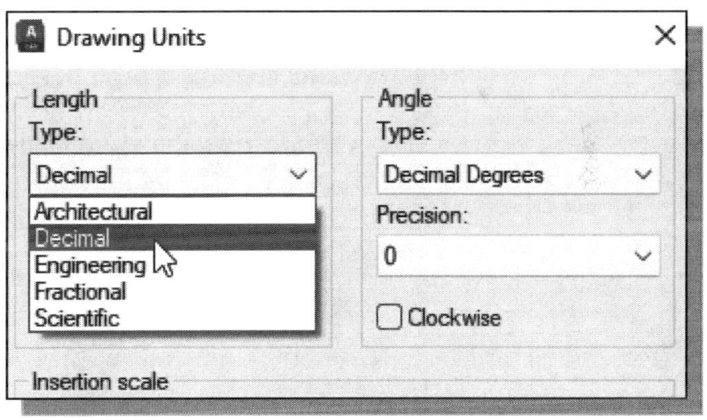

2. Click on the *Length Type* option to display the different types of length units available. Confirm the *Length Type* is set to **Decimal**.

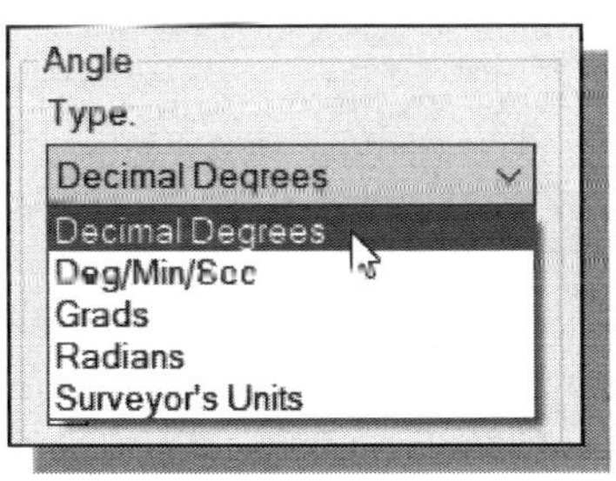

3. On your own, examine the other settings that are available.

4. In the *Drawing Units* dialog box, set the *Length Type* to **Decimal**. This will set the measurement to the default *English* units, inches.

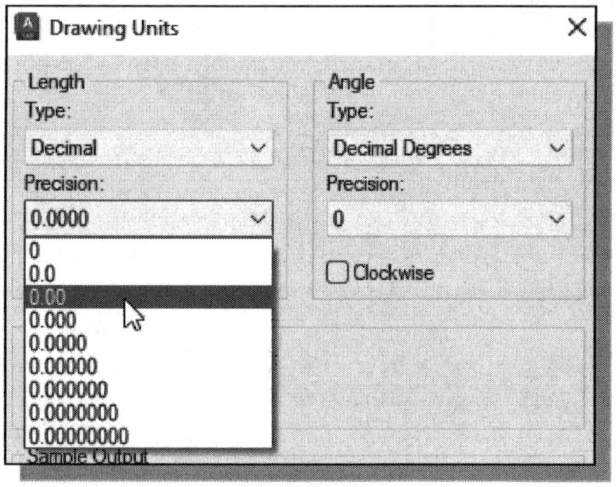

5. Set the *Precision* to **two digits** after the decimal point as shown in the above figure.

6. Pick **OK** to exit the *Drawing Units* dialog box.

Drawing Area Setup

Next, we will set up the **Drawing Limits** by entering a command in the command prompt area. Setting the Drawing Limits controls the extents of the display of the *grid*. It also serves as a visual reference that marks the working area. It can also be used to prevent construction outside the grid limits and as a plot option that defines an area to be plotted/printed. Note that this setting does not limit the region for geometry construction.

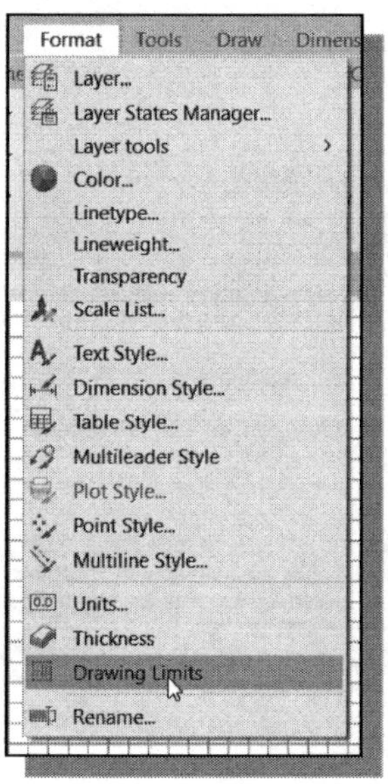

1. In the *Menu Bar* select:
[Format] → [Drawing Limits]

2. In the command prompt area, the message "*Reset Model Space Limits: Specify lower left corner or [On/Off] <0.00,0.00>:*" is displayed. Press the **ENTER** key once to accept the default coordinates <**0.00,0.00**>.

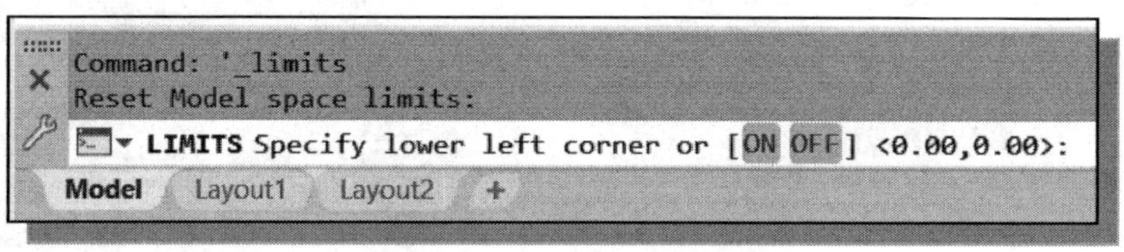

3. In the command prompt area, the message "*Specify upper right corner <12.00,9.00>:*" is displayed. Press the **ENTER** key again to accept the default coordinates <**12.00,9.00**>.

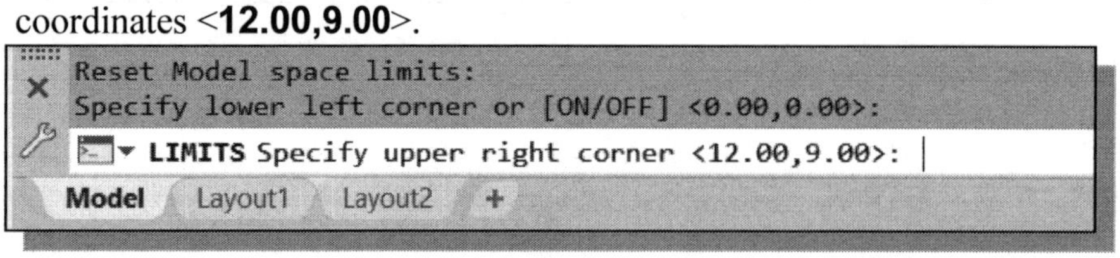

4. On your own, move the graphics cursor near the upper-right corner inside the drawing area and note that the drawing area is unchanged. (The **Drawing Limits** command is used to set the drawing area, but the display will not be adjusted until a display command is used.)

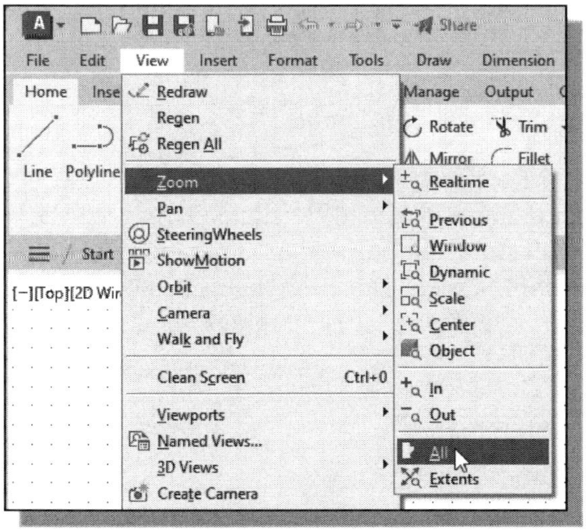

5. Inside the *Menu Bar* area select:
[View] → [Zoom] → [All]

❖ The **Zoom All** command will adjust the display so that all objects in the drawing are displayed to be as large as possible. If no objects are constructed, the **Drawing Limits** are used to adjust the current viewport.

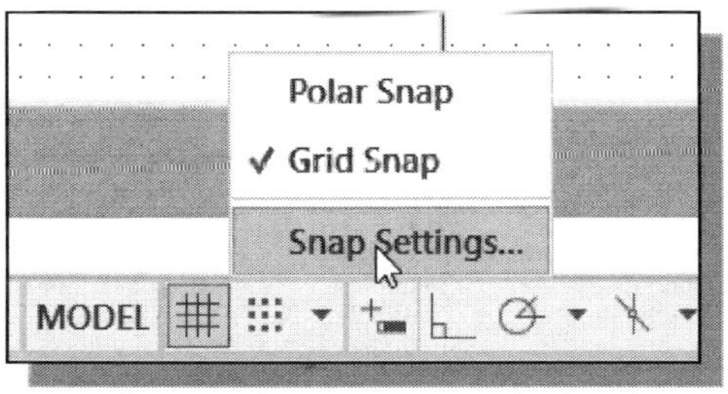

6. Move the graphics cursor near the upper-right corner inside the drawing area, and note that the display area is updated.

7. In the *Status Bar* area, **right-mouse-click** on ***SnapMode*** and choose **[Snap Settings]**.

8. In the *Drafting Settings dialog box*, switch **on** the **Snap** and **Grid** options as shown.

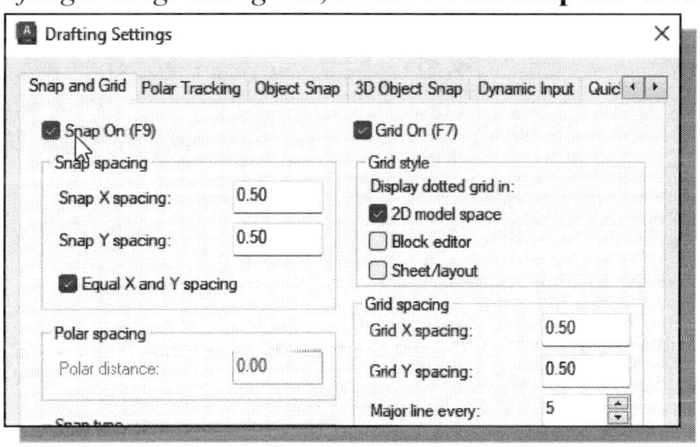

➢ On your own, exit the *Drafting Settings dialog box* and reset the status buttons so that only ***GRID DISPLAY*** and ***SNAP MODE*** are turned ***ON*** as shown.

Use the Line Command

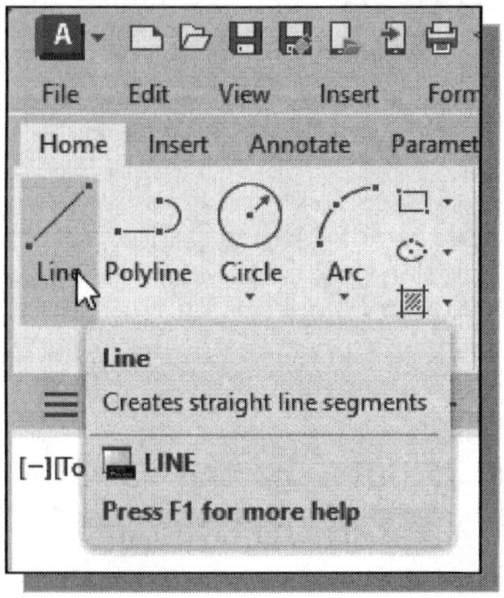

1. Select the **Line** command icon in the *Draw* toolbar. In the command prompt area, near the bottom of the AutoCAD graphics window, the message "*_line Specify first point:*" is displayed. AutoCAD expects us to identify the starting location of a straight line.

2. To further illustrate the usage of the different input methods and tools available in AutoCAD, we will **start the line segments at an arbitrary location**. Start at a location that is somewhere in the lower left side of the graphics window.

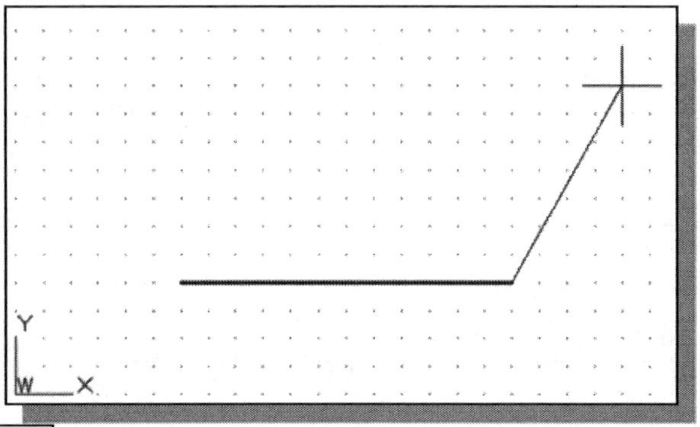

3. We will create a horizontal line by using the *relative rectangular coordinates entry method*, relative to the last point we specified:
   @6,0 [ENTER]

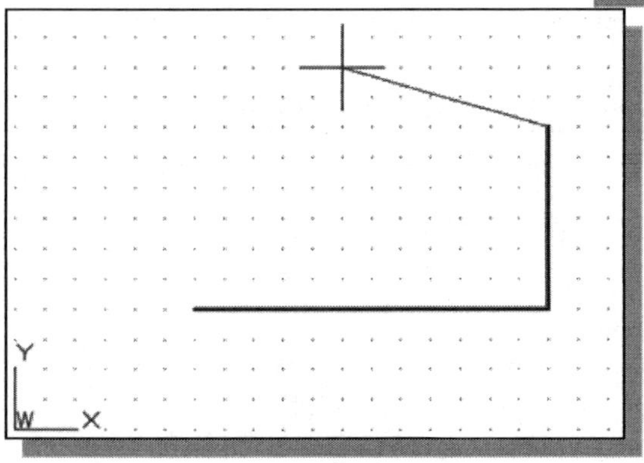

4. Next, create a vertical line by using the *relative polar coordinates entry method*, relative to the last point we specified: **@3<90 [ENTER]**

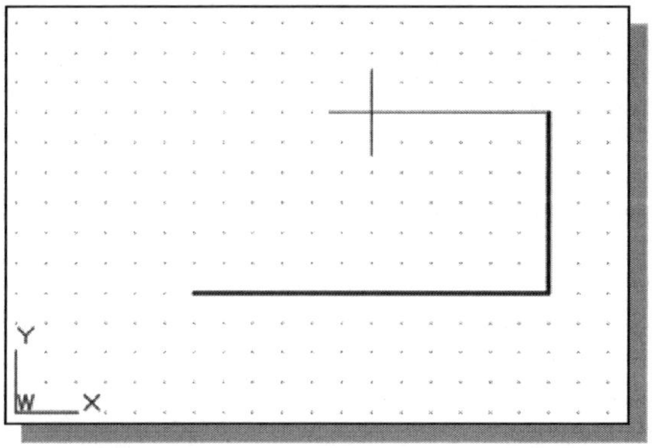

5. Next, we will use the direct input method. First, move the cursor directly to the left of the last endpoint of the line segments.

6. On your own, turn the mouse wheel to zoom in and drag with the middle mouse to reposition the display.

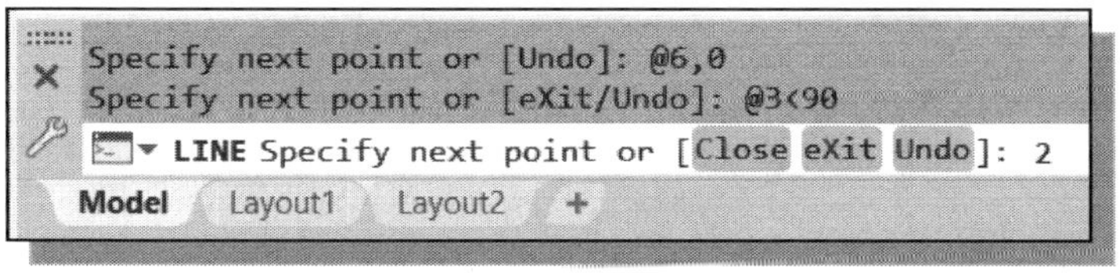

7. Use the *direct distance entry technique* by entering **2** **[ENTER]**.

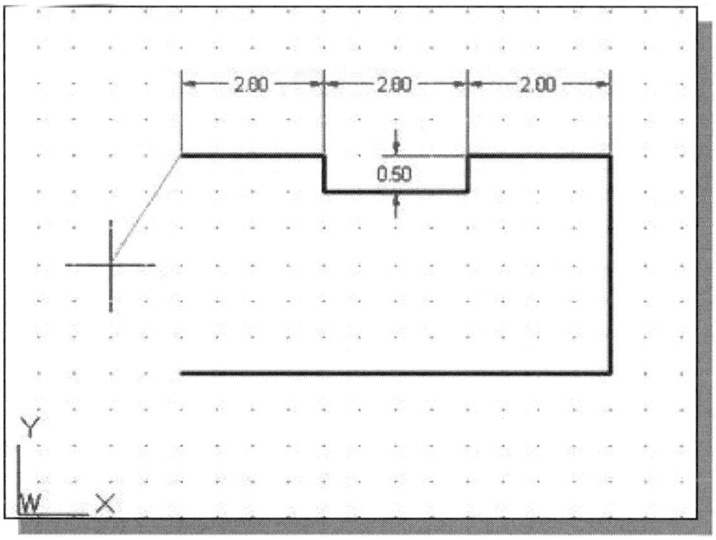

8. On your own, repeat the above steps and create the four additional line segments, using the dimensions as shown.

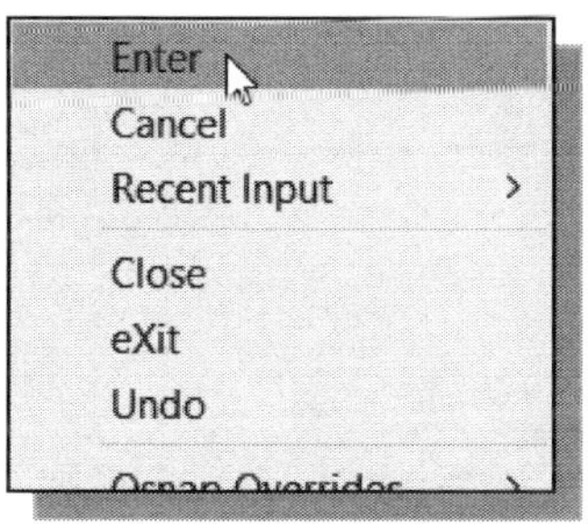

9. To end the line command, we can either hit the [Enter] key on the keyboard or use the **Enter** option, **right-mouse-click** and a *pop-up menu* appears on the screen.

10. Select **Enter** with the left-mouse-button to end the Line command.

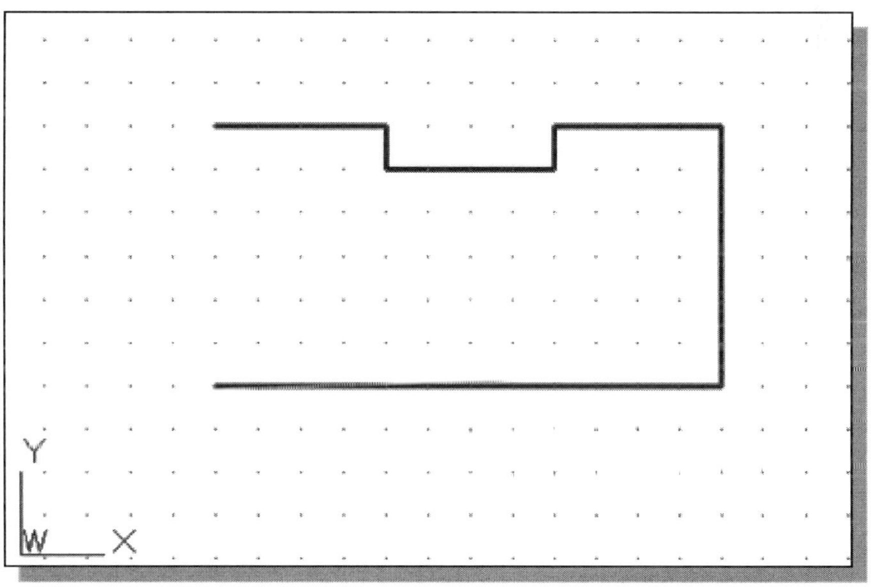

Use the Erase Command

The vertical line on the right was created as a construction line to aid the construction of the rest of the lines for the design. We will use the **Erase** command to remove it.

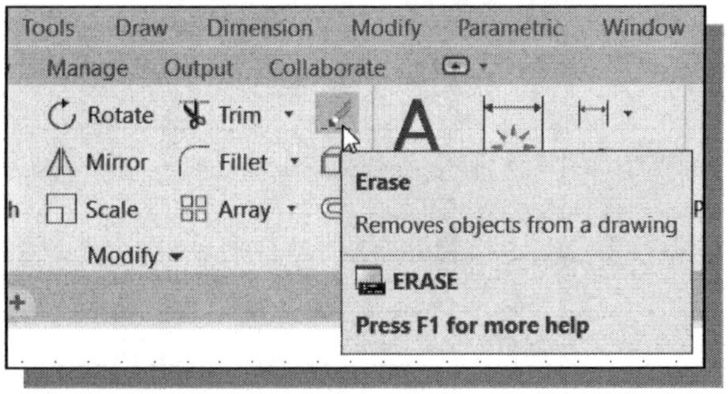

1. Pick **Erase** in the *Modify* toolbar. The message "*Select objects*" is displayed in the command prompt area and AutoCAD awaits us to select the objects to erase.

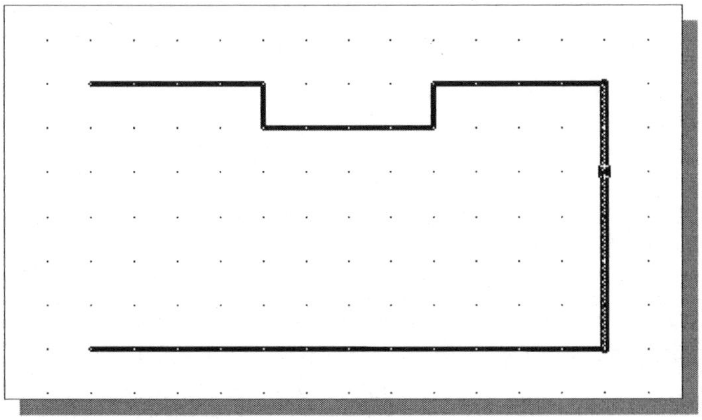

2. Select the vertical line as shown.

3. Click once with the **right-mouse-button** to accept the selection and delete the line.

Using the Arc Command

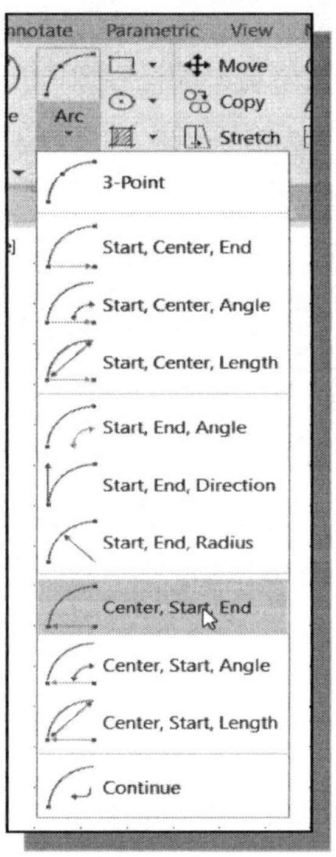

1. Click the down-arrow icon of the **Arc** command in the *Draw* toolbar to display the different Arc construction options.

➢ AutoCAD provides eleven different ways to create arcs. Note that the different options are used based on the geometry conditions of the design. The more commonly used options are the **3-Points** option and the **Center-Start-End** option.

2. Select the **Center-Start-End** option as shown. This option requires the selection of the center point, start point and end point location, in that order, of the arc.

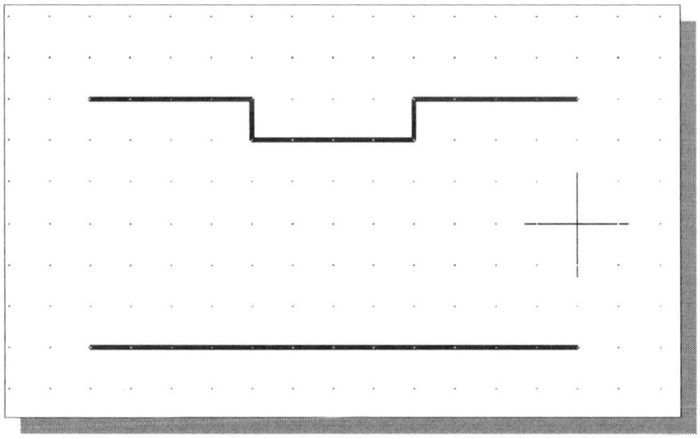

3. Move the cursor to thc middle of the two horizontal lines and align the cursor to the two endpoints as shown. Click once with the **right-mouse-button** to select the location as the center point of the new arc.

4. Move the cursor downward and select the right endpoint of the bottom horizontal line as the start point of the arc.

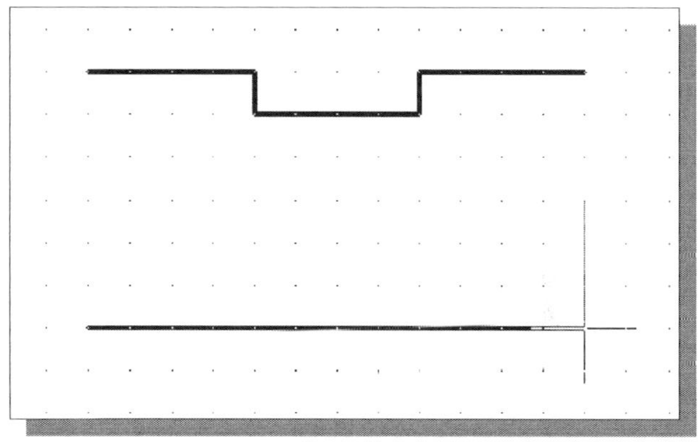

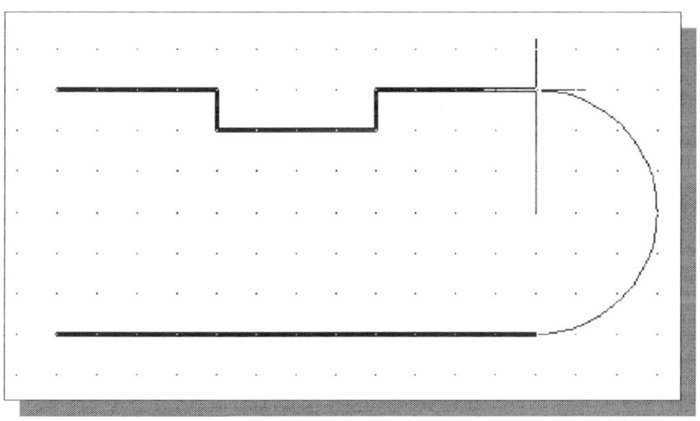

5. Move the cursor to the right endpoint of the top horizontal line as shown. Pick this point as the endpoint of the new arc.

6. On your own, repeat the above steps and create the other arc as shown. Note that in most CAD packages, positive angles are defined as going counterclockwise; therefore, the starting point of the second arc should be at the endpoint on top.

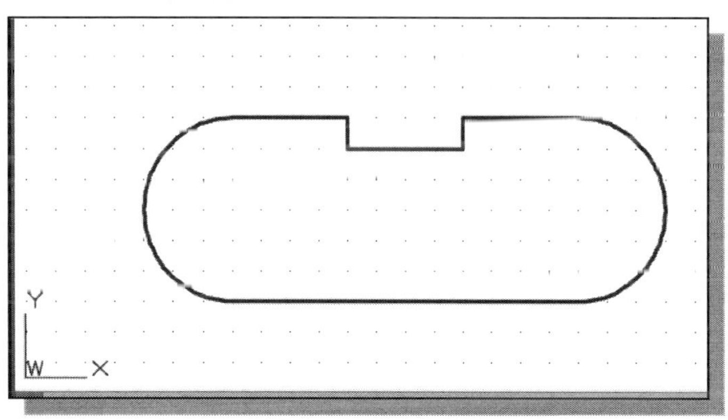

Using the Circle Command

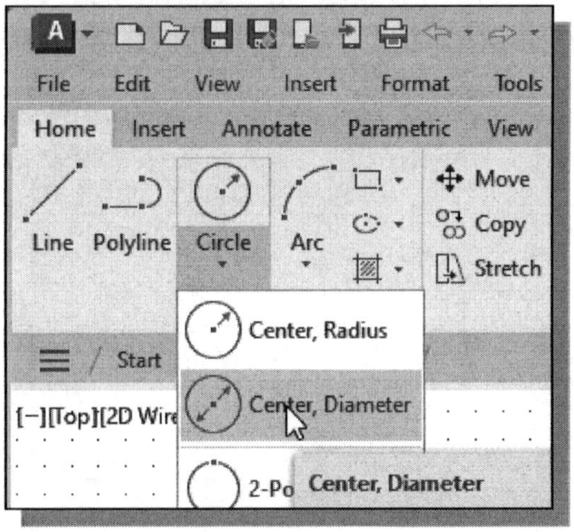

1. Select the **[Circle] → [Center, Diameter]** option as shown.

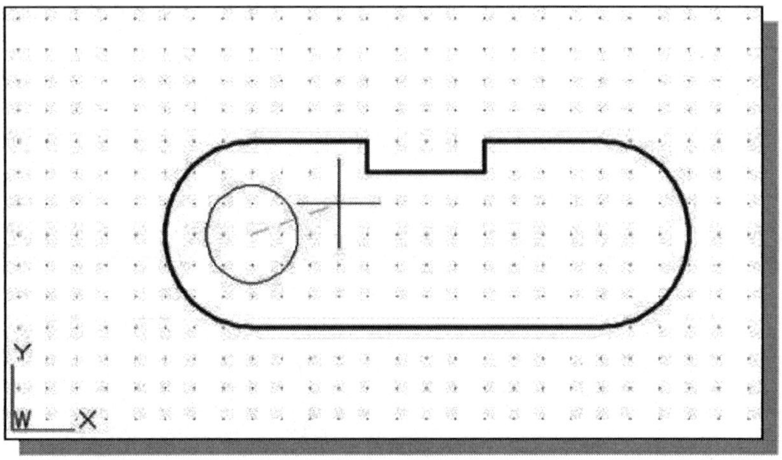

2. Select the same location for the arc center as the center point for the new circle.

3. In the command prompt area, the message "*Specify diameter of circle:*" is displayed. *Specify diameter of circle:* **1.25 [ENTER]**

4. On your own, create the other circle and complete the drawing as shown.

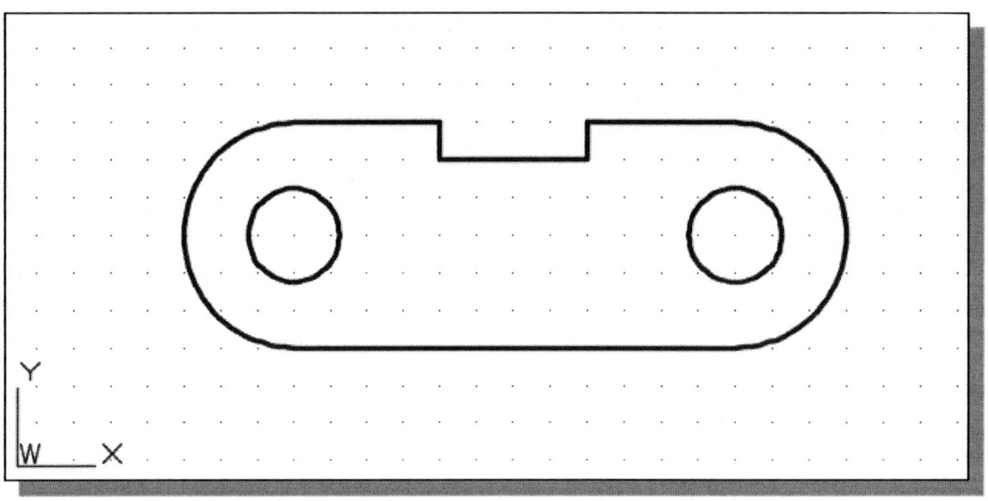

Saving the CAD Design

1. In the *Quick Access Toolbar*, select **[Save]**.

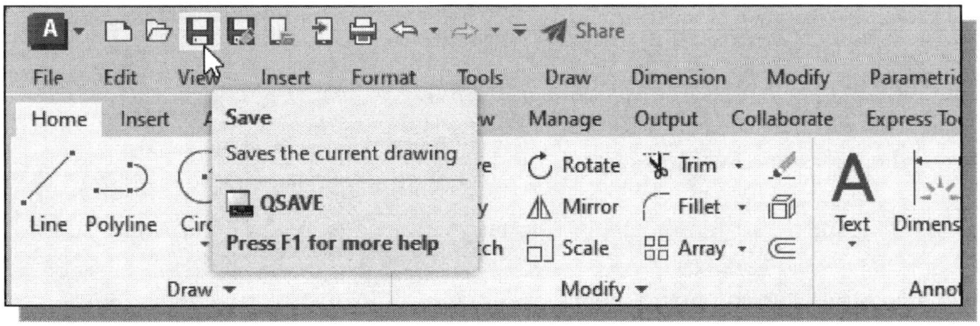

❖ Note the command can also be activated with the quick-key combination of **[Ctrl]+[S]**.

2. In the *Save Drawing As* dialog box, select the folder in which you want to store the CAD file and enter ***Spacer*** in the *File name* box.

3. Click **Save** in the *Save Drawing As* dialog box to accept the selections and save the file. Note the default file type is DWG, which is the standard AutoCAD drawing format.

Exit AutoCAD 2027

❖ To exit **AutoCAD 2027**, select **Exit AutoCAD** in the *Menu Bar* or type ***QUIT*** at the command prompt. Note the command can also be activated with the quick-key combination of **[Ctrl]+[Q]**.

Review Questions:

1. What are the advantages and disadvantages of using CAD systems to create engineering drawings?

2. What is the default AutoCAD filename extension?

3. How do the ***GRID*** and ***SNAP*** options assist us in sketching?

4. List and describe the different **coordinate entry methods** available in AutoCAD.

5. When using the Line command, which option allows us to quickly create a line-segment connecting back to the starting point?

6. List and describe the two types of coordinate systems commonly used for planar geometry.

7. Which key do you use to quickly cancel a command?

8. When you use the Pan command, do the coordinates of objects get changed?

9. Find information on how to draw ellipses in AutoCAD through the AutoCAD Help System and create the following arc. If it is desired to position the center of the ellipse to a specific location, which ellipse command is more suitable?

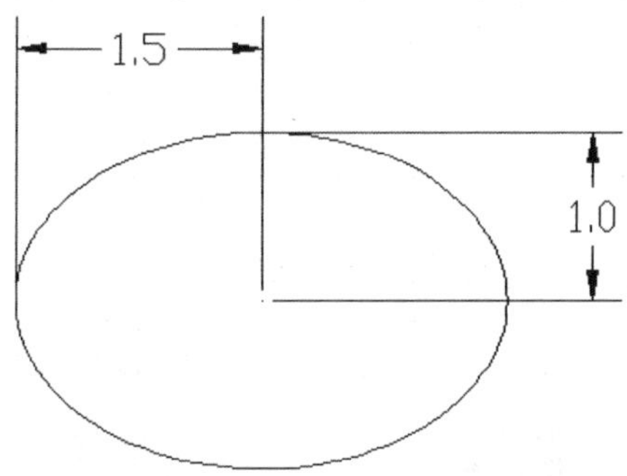

10. Find information on how to draw arcs in AutoCAD through the *Autodesk Exchange* and create the following arc. List and describe two methods to create arcs in AutoCAD.

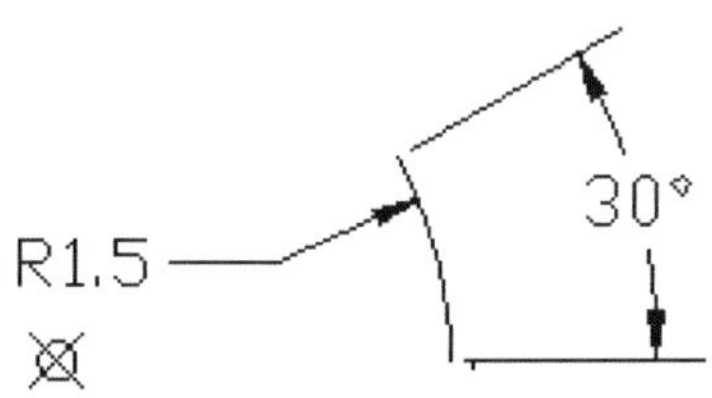

Exercises:

(All dimensions are in inches.)

1. **Angle Spacer**

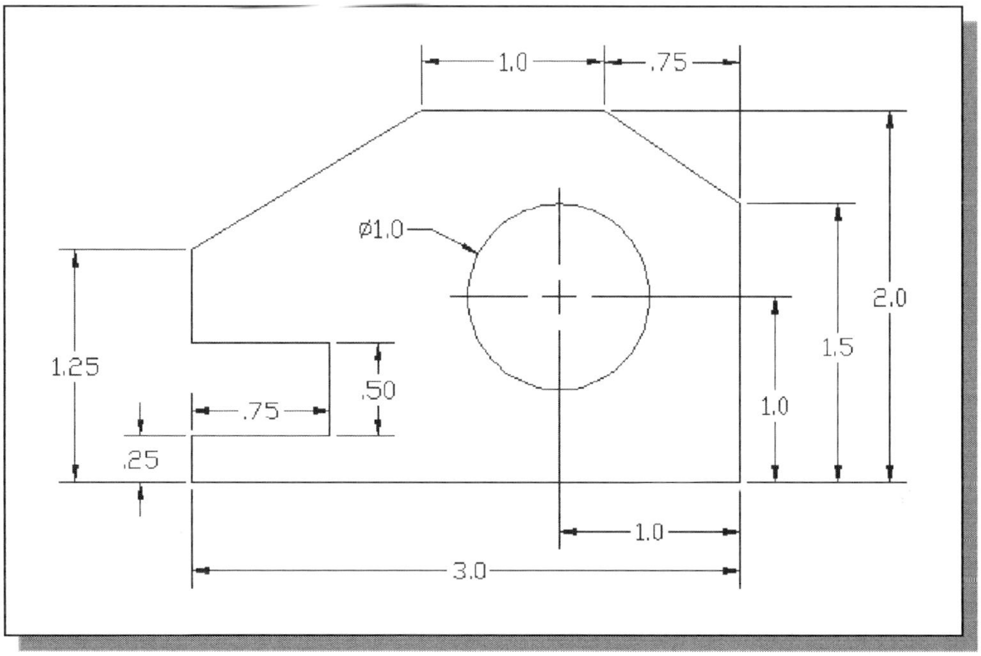

2. **Base Plate**

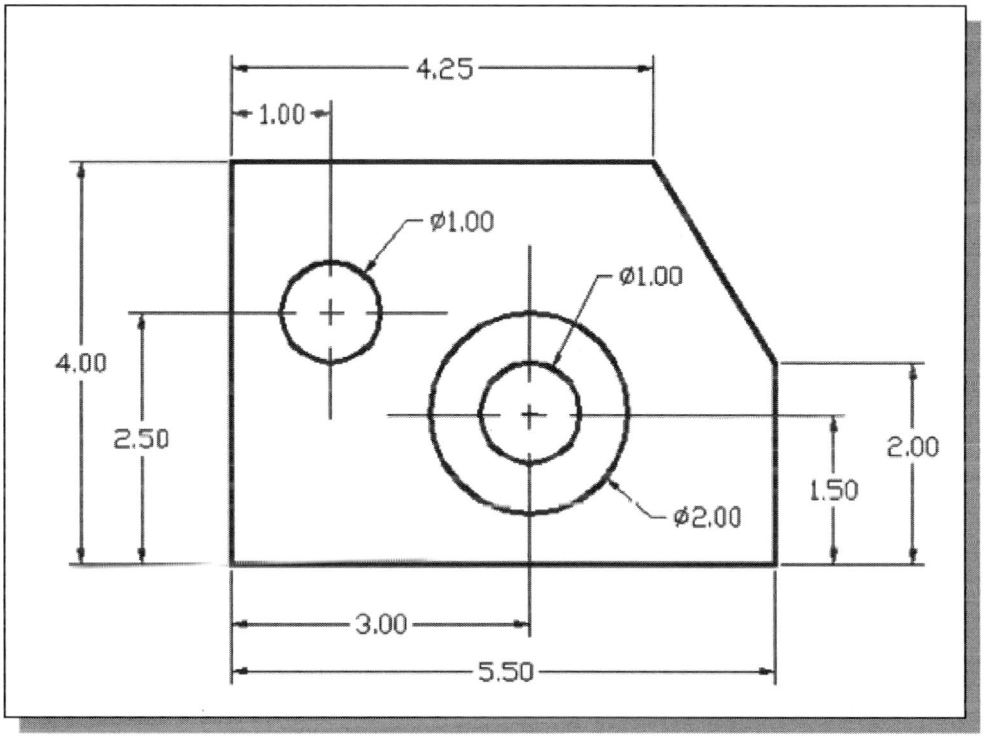

3. **T-Clip**

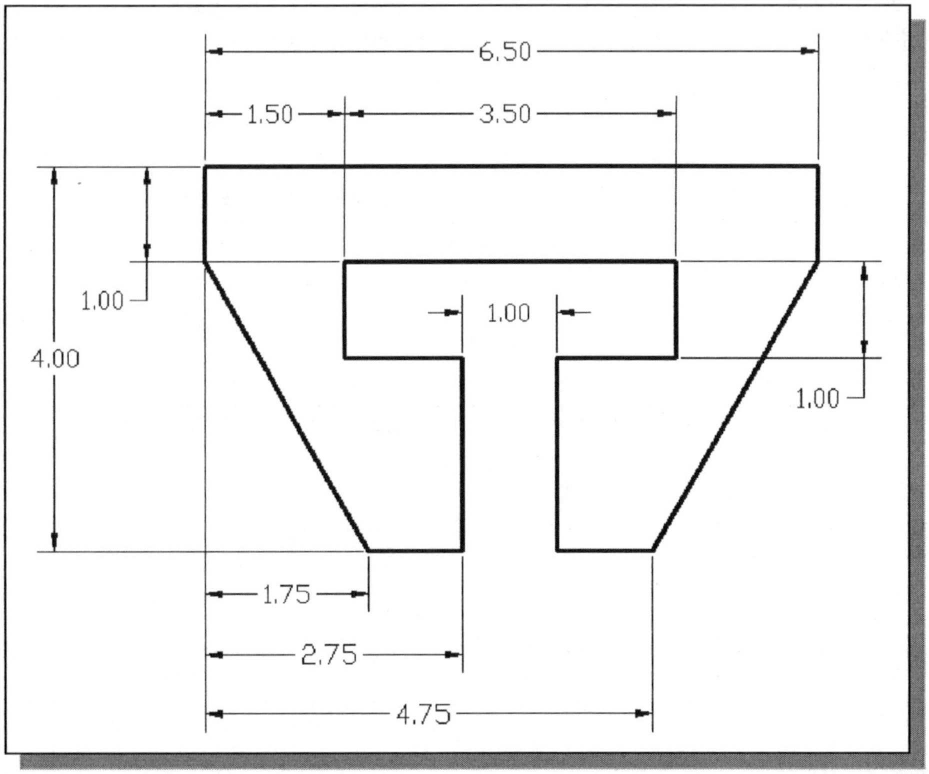

4. **Channel Plate**

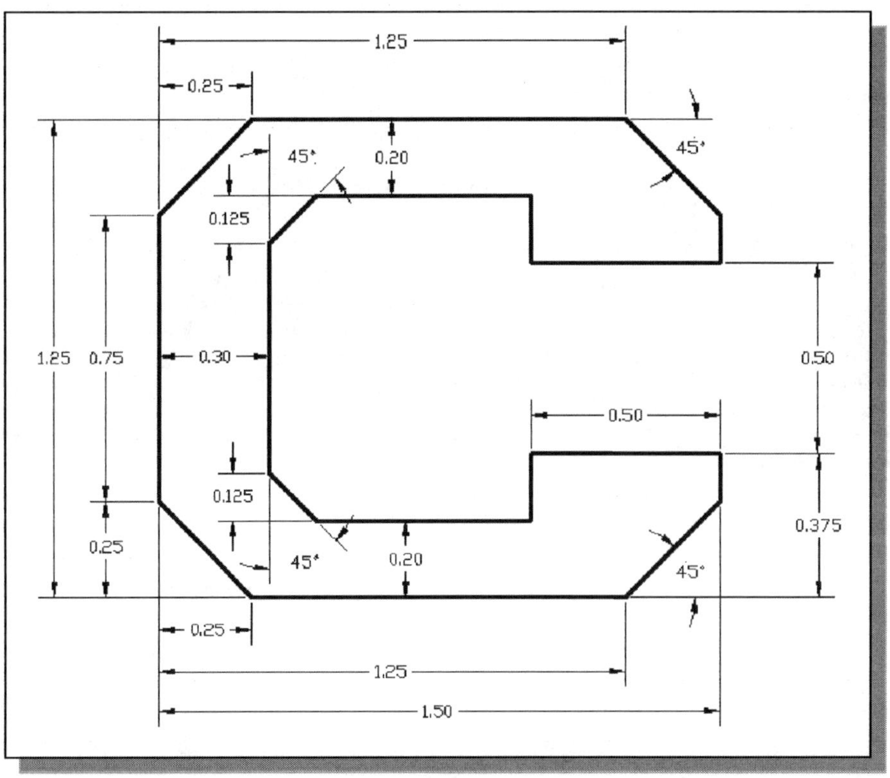

5. **Slider Block**

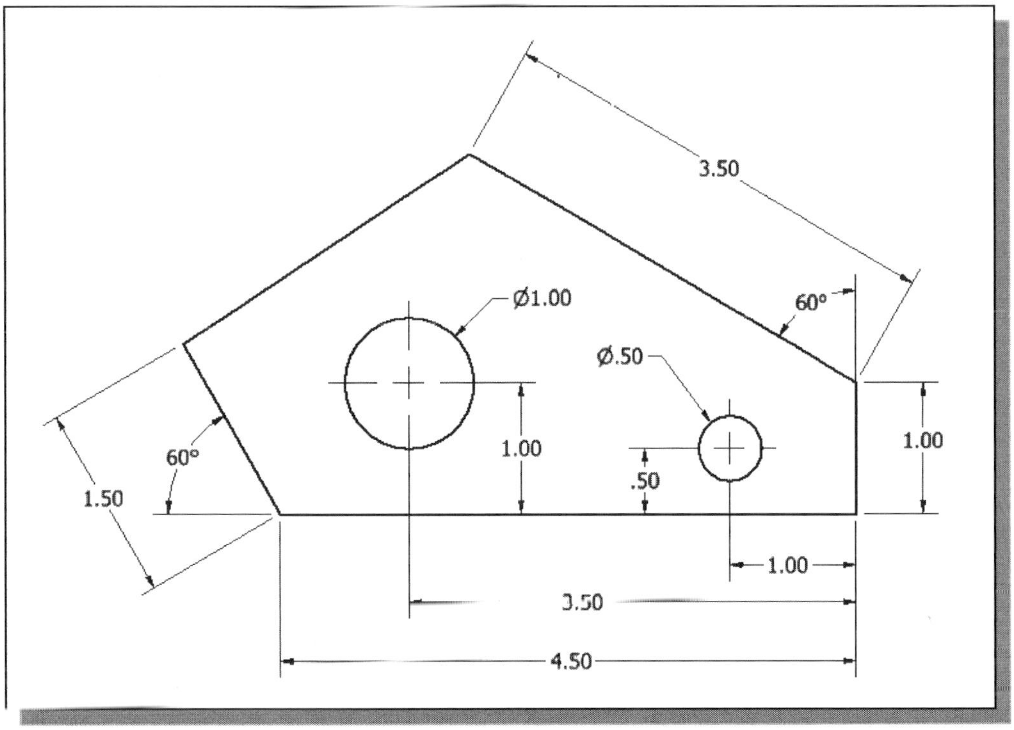

6. **Circular Spacer**

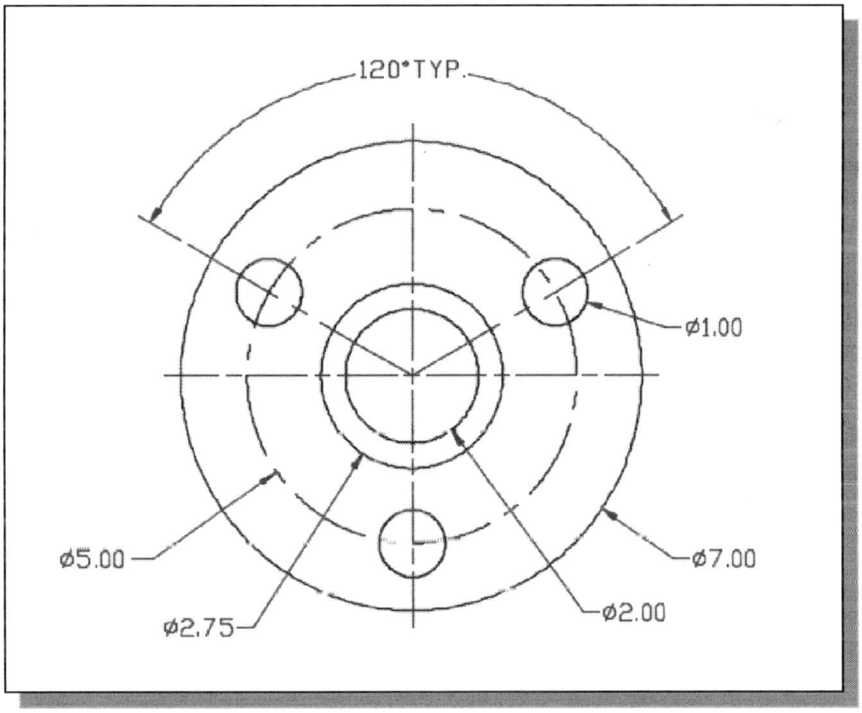

7. **Angle Base**

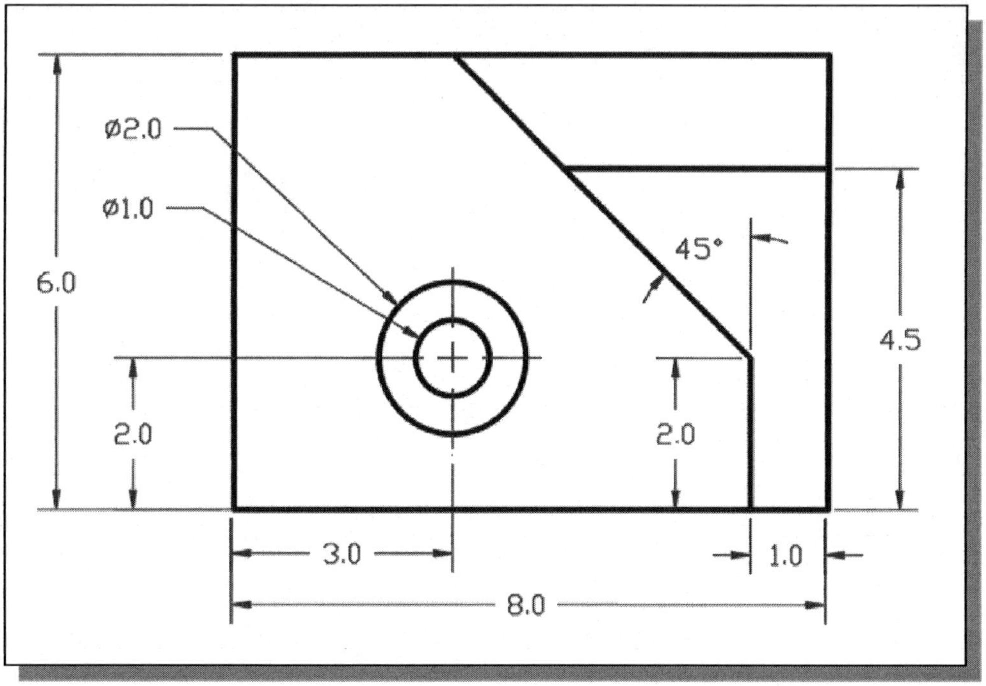

8. **Index Key**

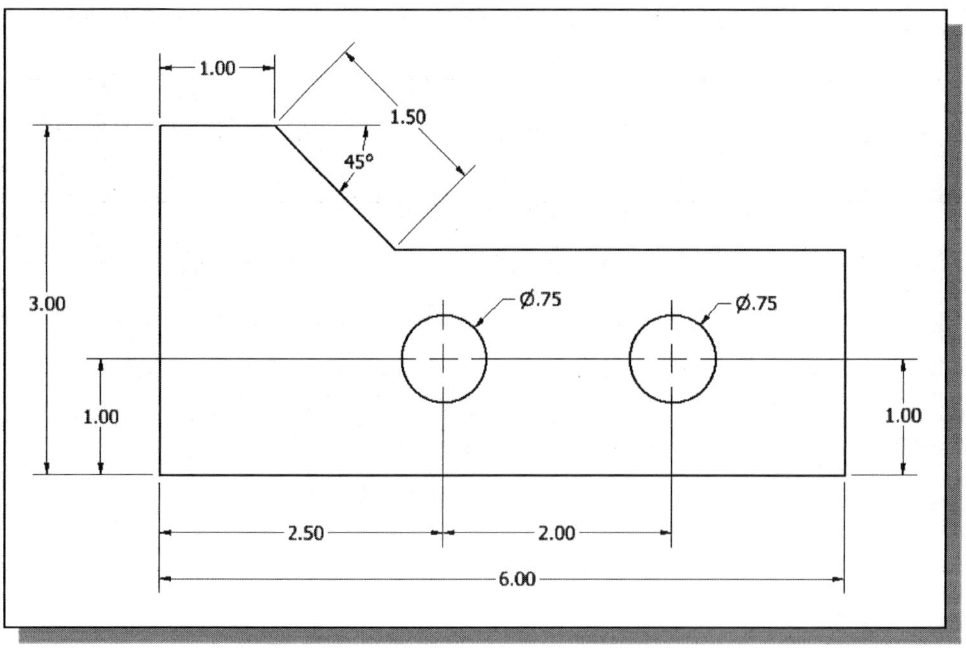

9. **Guide Block**

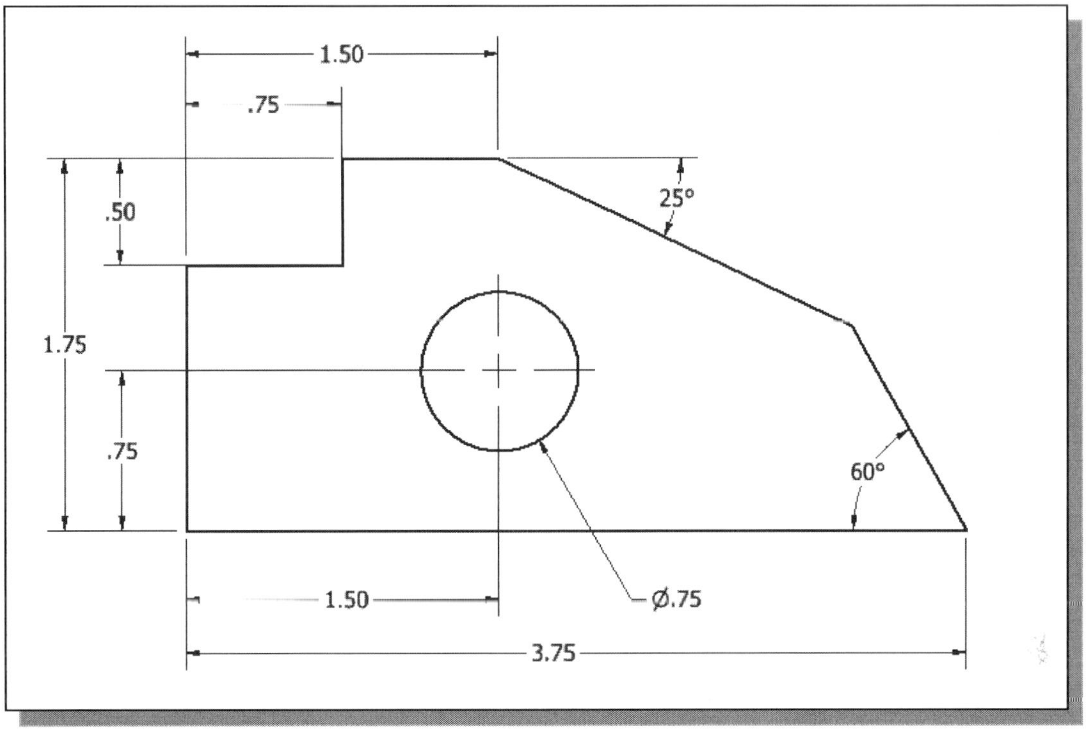

10. **Positioning Key**

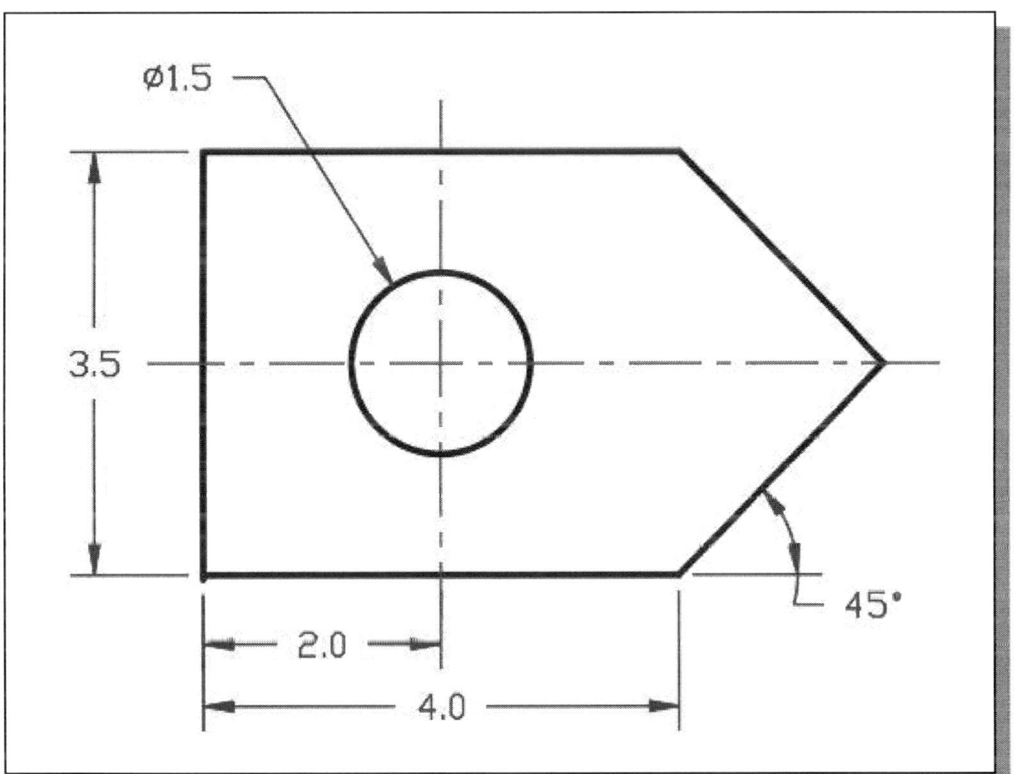

Notes:

Chapter 2
Basic Object Construction and Dynamic Input – AutoCAD

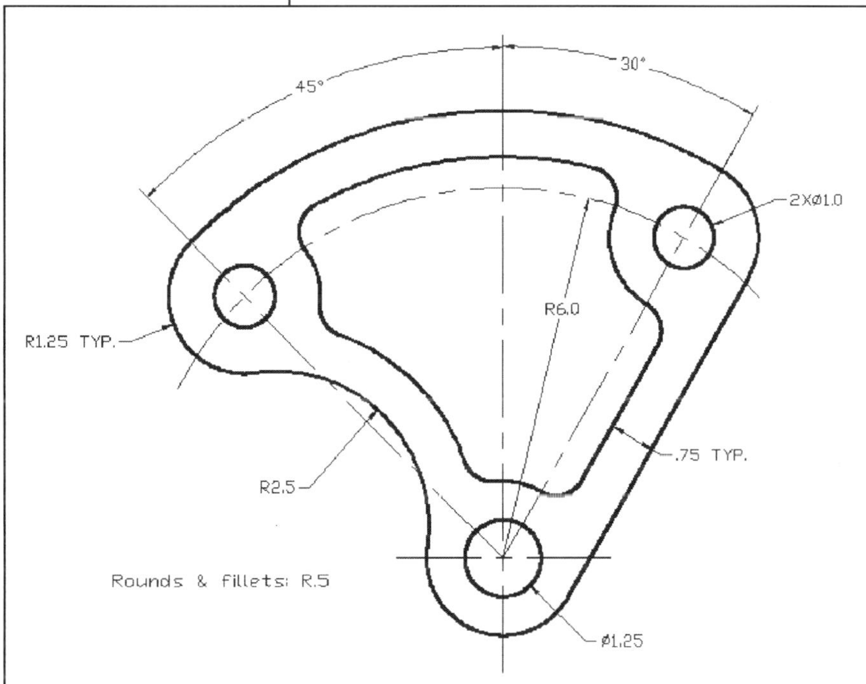

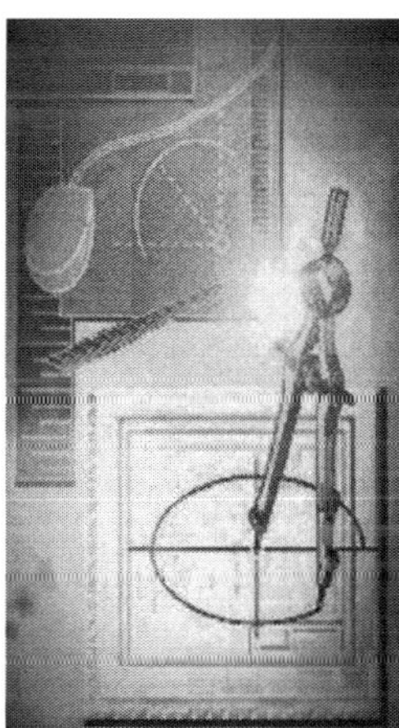

Learning Objectives

- Referencing the WCS
- Use the Startup dialog box
- Set up Grid & Snap intervals
- Display AutoCAD's toolbars
- Set up and use Object Snaps
- Edit using the Trim command
- Use the Polygon command
- Create TTR circles
- Create Tangent lines

Introduction

The main characteristic of any CAD system is its ability to create and modify 2D/3D geometric entities quickly and accurately. Most CAD systems provide a variety of object construction and editing tools to relieve the designer of the tedious drudgery of this task, so that the designer can concentrate more on design content. It is important to note that CAD systems can be used to replace traditional drafting with pencil and paper, but the CAD user must have a good understanding of the basic geometric construction techniques to fully utilize the capability of the CAD systems.

One of the major enhancements of AutoCAD 2006 was the introduction of the *Dynamic Input* feature. This addition, which is also available in AutoCAD 2027, greatly enhanced the **AutoCAD Heads-up Design** interface.

The use of the **User Coordinate System (UCS)** and the **World Coordinate System (WCS)** is further discussed in this chapter. In working CAD, one simple approach to creating designs in CAD systems is to create geometry by referencing the **World Coordinate System**. The general procedure of this approach is illustrated in this chapter.

In this chapter, we will examine the *Dynamic Input* options, the basic geometric construction and editing tools provided by **AutoCAD 2027**. We will first look at the *Dynamic Input* options, and tools such as *UNITS*, *GRID*, *SNAP MODE* intervals setup and the *OSNAP* option, followed by construction tools such as circles and polygons; we will also look at the basic Trim command.

Starting Up AutoCAD 2027

1. Start **AutoCAD 2027** by selecting the *Autodesk* folder in the **Start** menu as shown. Once the program is loaded into the memory, click **Start Drawing** to start a new drawing.

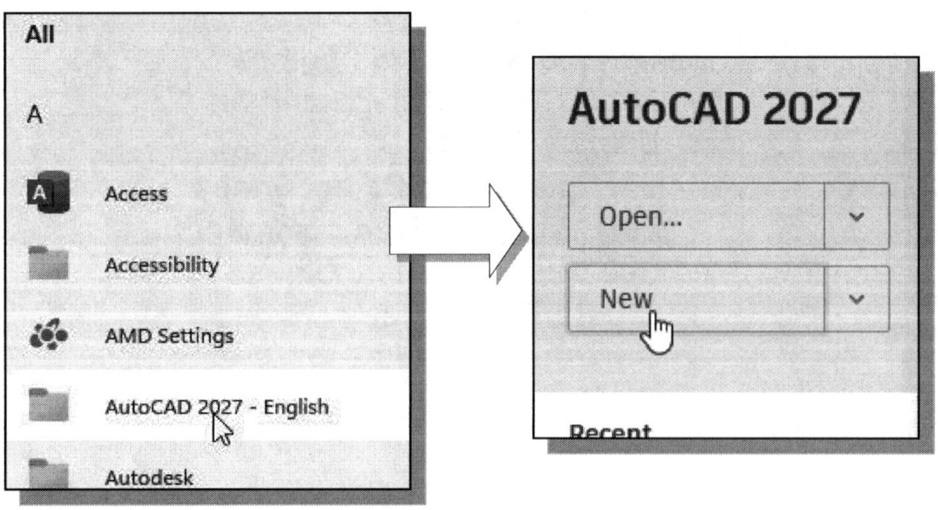

Dynamic Input

In AutoCAD 2027, the ***Dynamic Input*** feature provides the user with **visual tooltips** and **entry options** right on the screen.

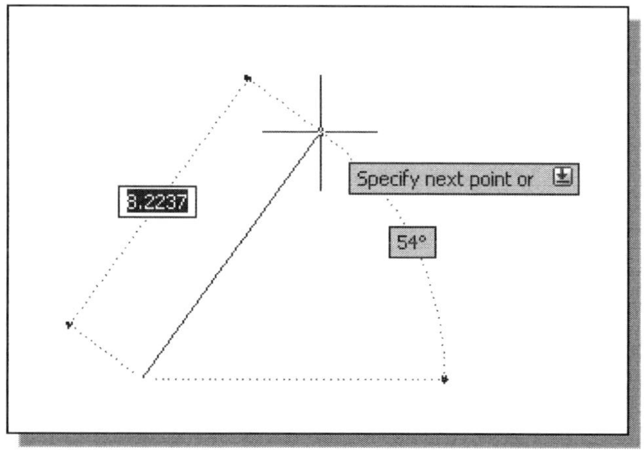

Dynamic Input provides a convenient command interface near the cursor to help the user focus in the graphics area. When *Dynamic Input* is *ON*, tooltips display information near the cursor that is dynamically updated as the cursor moves.

The tooltips also provide a place for user entry when a command is activated. The actions required to complete a command remain the same as those for the command line. Note that ***Dynamic Input*** is **not** designed to replace the *command line*. The main advantage of using the *Dynamic Input* options is to keep our attention near the cursor.

The *Dynamic Input* features can be used to enhance the **five methods** for specifying the locations of points as described in the *Defining Positions* section of Chapter 1.

1. To switch on the **AutoCAD Dynamic Input option**, use the *Customization option* at the bottom right corner.

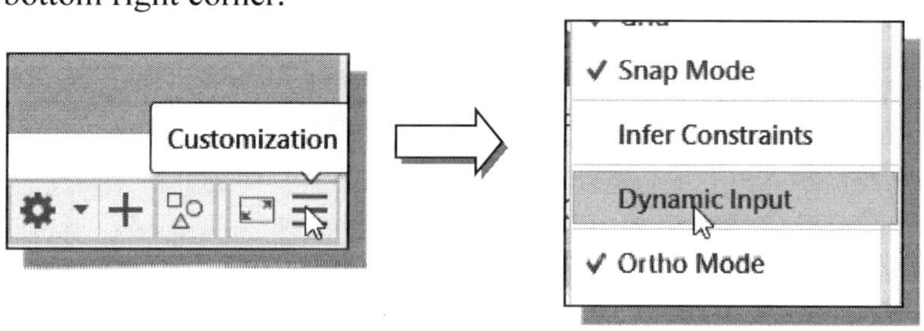

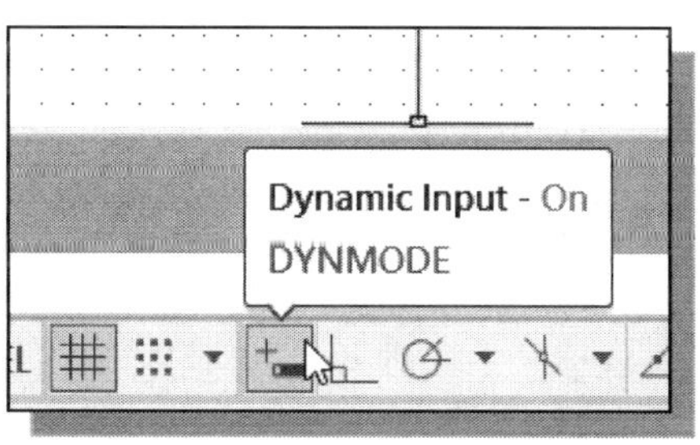

2. The *Dynamic Input* option can be toggled on/off by clicking on the button in the *Status Bar* area as shown. Confirm the *Dynamic Input* option is switched **ON** before proceeding to the next section.

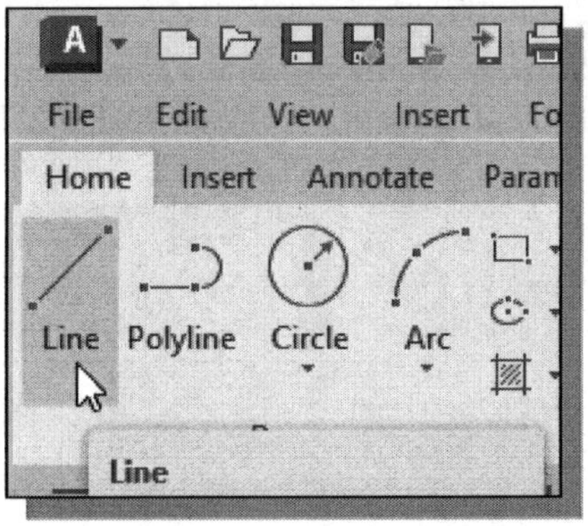

3. Click on the **Line** icon in the *Draw* toolbar. In the command prompt area, the message "*_line Specify first point:*" is displayed.

4. Move the cursor inside the *Drawing Area* and notice the displayed tooltip, which shows the coordinates of the cursor position.

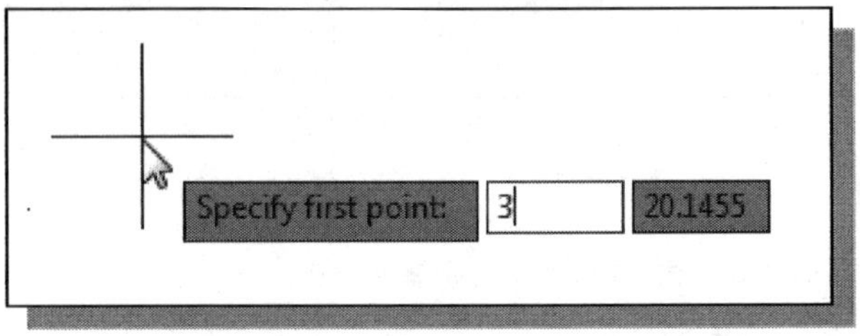

5. Type ***3*** and notice the input is entered in the first entry box.

6. Hit the **TAB** key once to move the input focus to the second entry box.

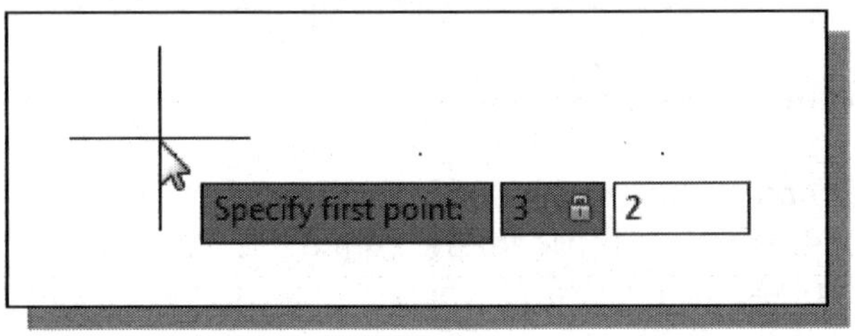

7. Type ***2*** and notice the input is displayed in the second entry box.

8. Hit the **ENTER** key once to accept the inputs. Note that the point is placed using the world coordinates.

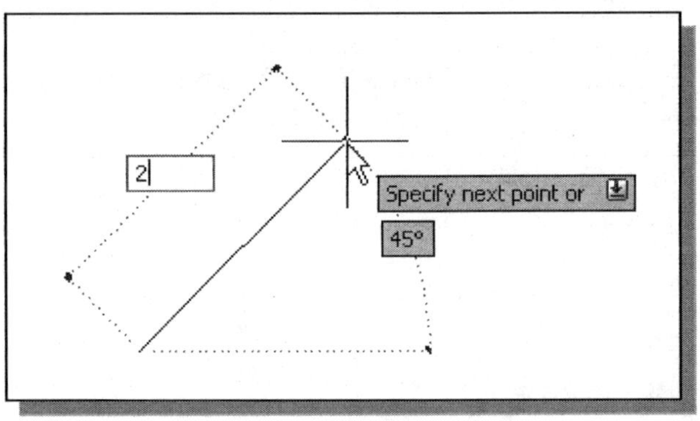

9. Move the cursor upward and toward the right side of the screen. Notice the tooltip is set to use polar coordinates by default.

10. Type ***2*** and notice the input is displayed in the entry box as shown.

11. Hit the **TAB** key once to move the input focus to the second entry box.

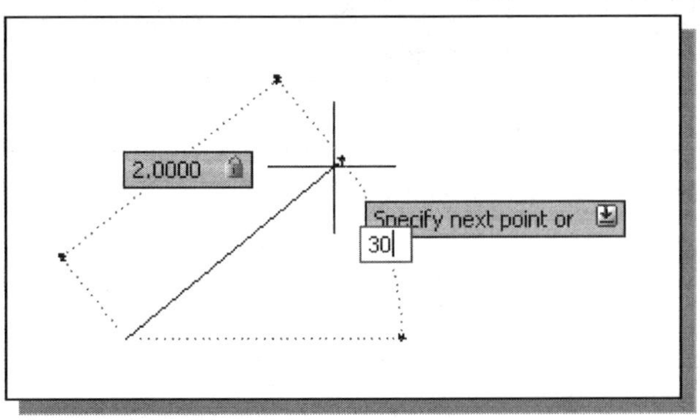

12. Type ***30*** and notice the input is displayed in the angle entry box.

13. Hit the **ENTER** key once to create the line that is 2 units long and at an angle of 30 degrees.

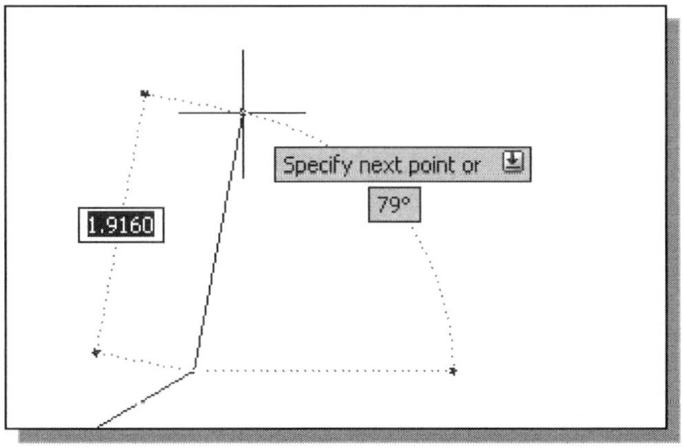

14. Move the cursor upward and toward the right side of the screen. Notice the tooltip is still set to using polar coordinates.

➢ To switch to using the Relative Cartesian coordinates input method, use a **comma** as the **specifier** after entering the first number.

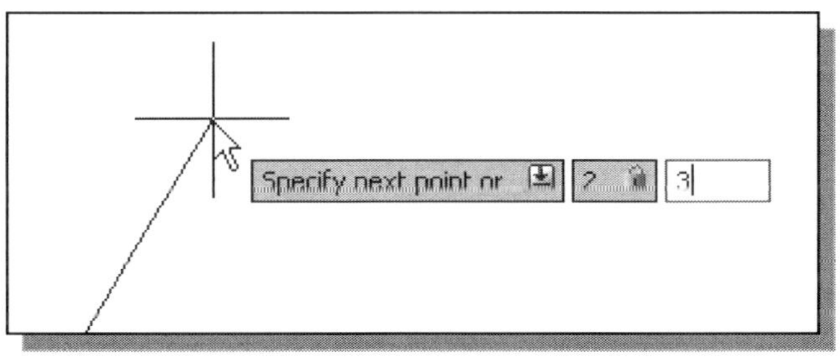

15. Type ***2,3*** and notice the input option is now set to using Relative Cartesian coordinates as shown.

16. Hit the **ENTER** key once to accept the inputs.

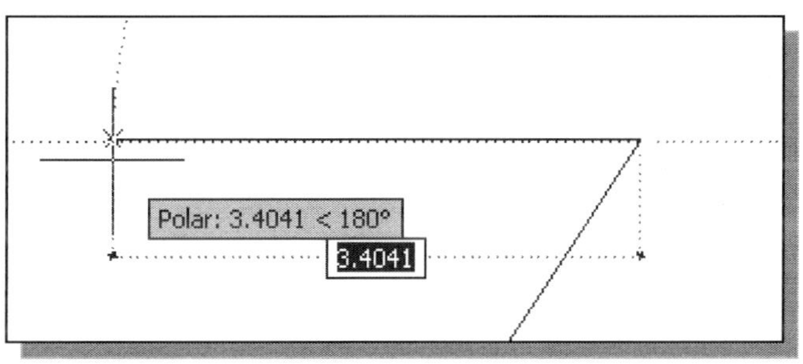

17. Move the cursor toward the left side of the last position until the angle is near 180 degrees as shown.

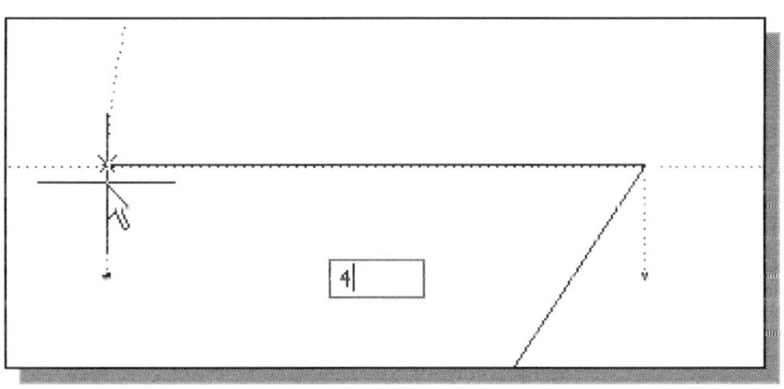

18. Type ***4*** and notice the input is displayed on the screen.

19. Hit the **ENTER** key once to accept the input and note a horizontal line is created.

➢ In effect, we just created a line using the ***Direct Distance*** option.

20. Hit the **[Esc]** key once to exit the Line command.

21. In the *Status Bar* area, **right-click** on ***Dynamic Input*** and choose **Settings**.

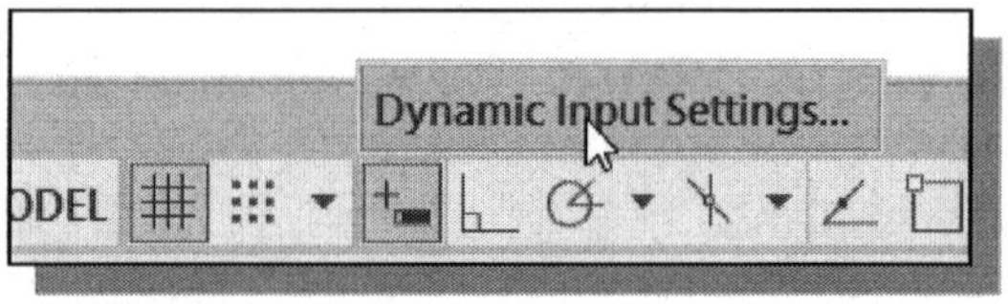

❖ The *Settings* dialog box provides different controls to what is displayed when *Dynamic Input* is on.

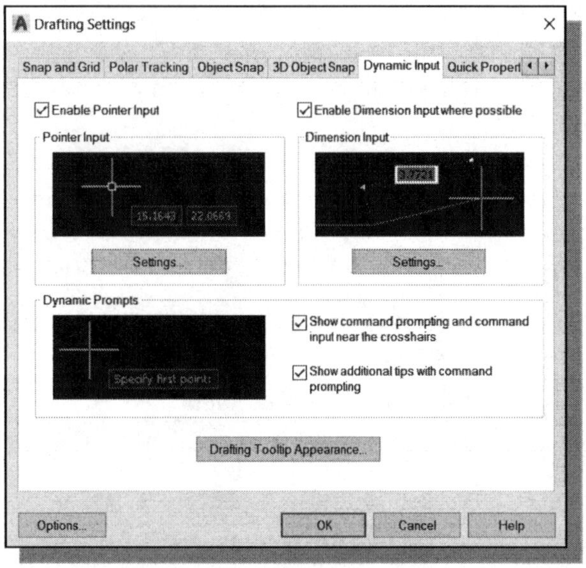

➢ Note that the *Dynamic Input* feature has three components: ***Pointer Input***, ***Dimensional Input***, and ***Dynamic Prompts***.

22. On your own, toggle *ON/OFF* the three options and create additional line segments to see the different effects of the settings.

The Rocker-Arm Design

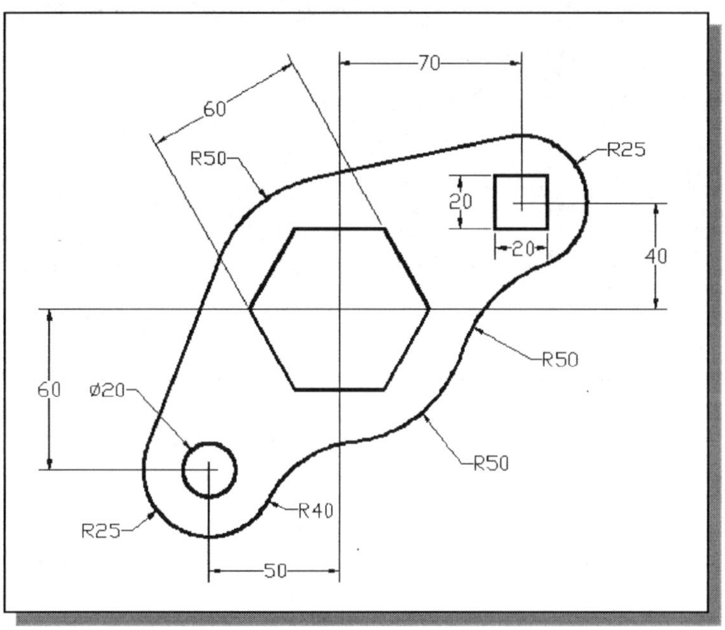

❖ Before continuing to the next page, on your own make a rough freehand sketch on a piece of paper to show the steps that you plan to use in creating the design. Be aware that there are many different approaches to accomplishing the same task.

Activate the Startup Option

In **AutoCAD 2027**, we can use the *Startup* dialog box to establish different types of drawing settings. The startup dialog box can be activated through the use of the **STARTUP** system variable.

The STARTUP system variable can be set to 0, 1, 2 or 3:

- 0: Starts a drawing without defined settings.
- 1: Displays the ***Create New Drawing*** dialog box.
- 2: Displays a ***New Tab*** with options; a custom dialog box can be used.
- 3: Displays a ***New Tab*** with options (default).

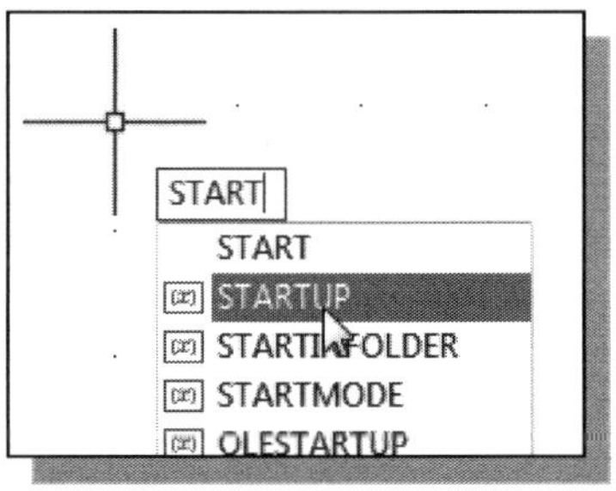

1. In the *command prompt area*, activate the **Startup** option by entering or choose the system variable name: ***STARTUP*** **[ENTER]**

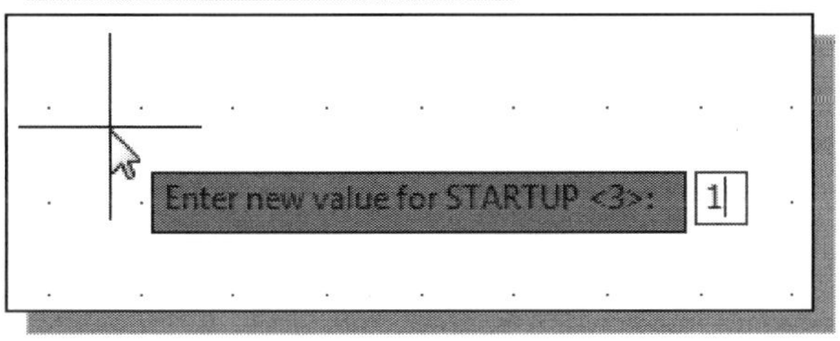

2. Enter ***1*** as the new value for the *Startup* system variable.

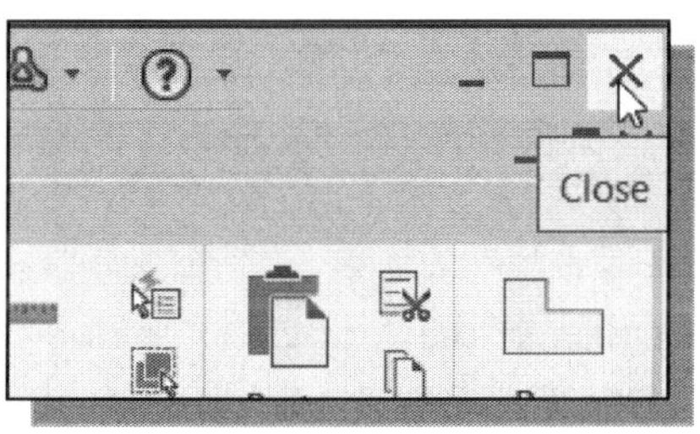

3. To show the effect of the *Startup* option, **exit** AutoCAD by clicking on the **Close** icon as shown.

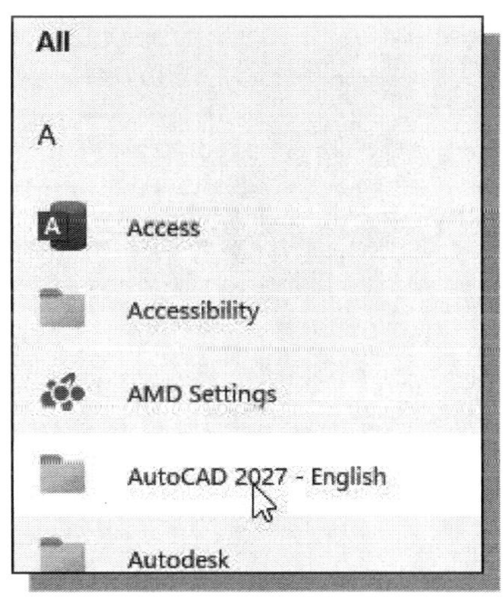

4. Restart AutoCAD by selecting the **AutoCAD 2027** option through the *Start* menu.

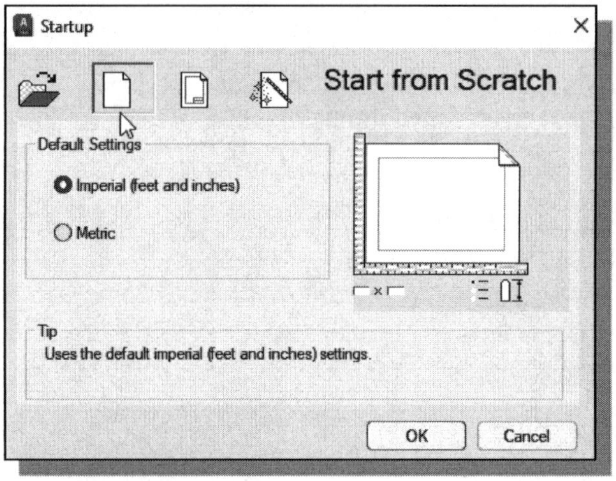

5. The *Startup* dialog box appears on the screen with different options to assist in the creation of drawings. Move the cursor on top of the four icons and notice the different options available:
(1) **Open a drawing**
(2) **Start from Scratch**
(3) **Use a Template**
(4) **Use a Setup Wizard**

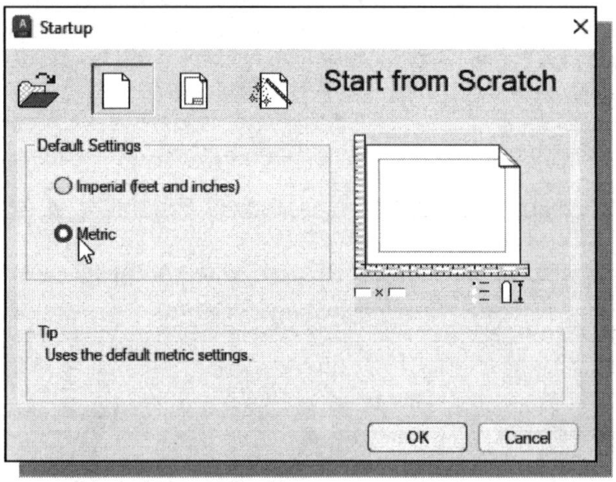

6. In the *Startup* dialog box, select the **Start from Scratch** option as shown in the figure.

7. Choose **Metric** to use the metric settings.

8. Click **OK** to accept the setting.

Drawing Units Display Setup

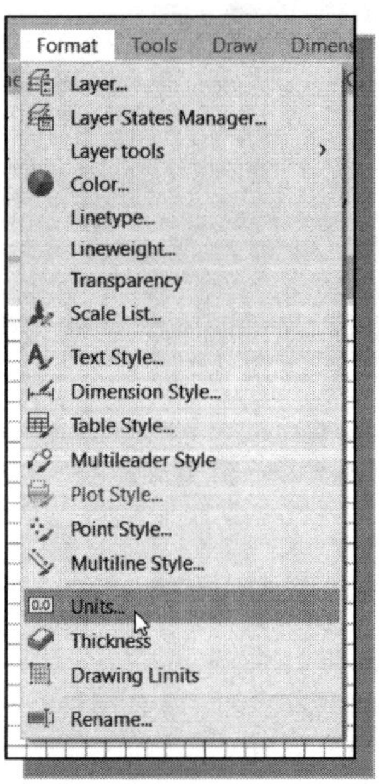

1. On your own, activate the display of the AutoCAD *Menu Bar* if it is not displayed. (Refer to page 1-4 for the procedure.)

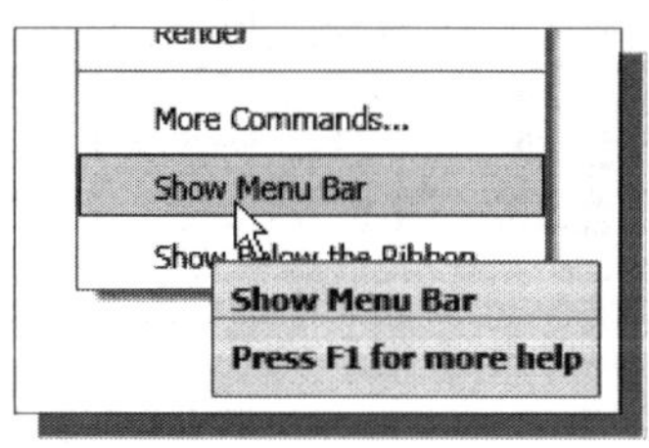

2. Click the *Menu Bar* area and select **[Format] → [Units]**.

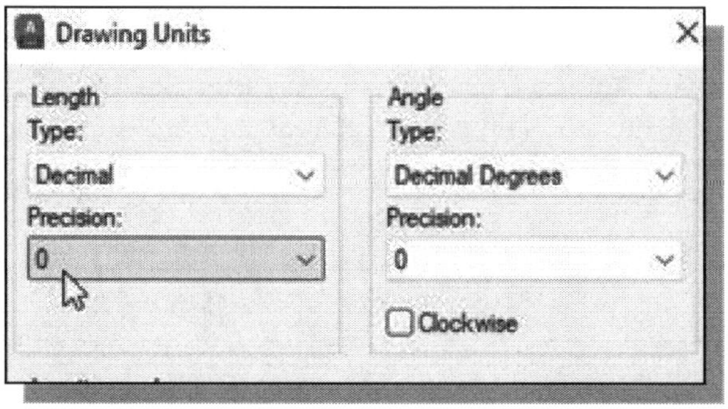

3. Set the *Precision* to **no digits** after the decimal point.

4. Click **OK** to exit the *Drawing Units* dialog box.

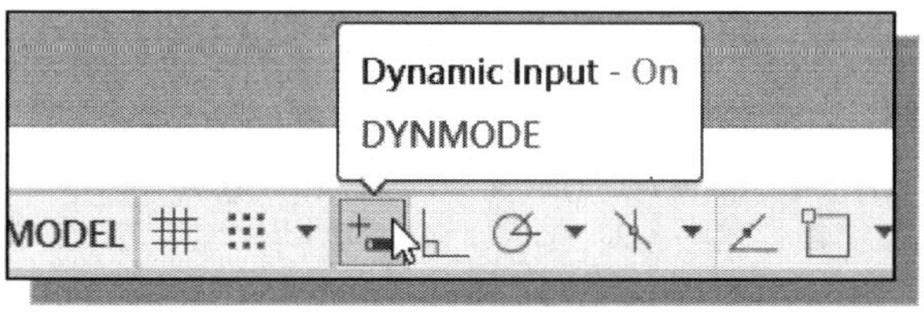

5. On your own, adjust the option settings so that only the **Dynamic Input** option is turned ***ON*** in the *Status Bar* area.

GRID and SNAP Intervals Setup

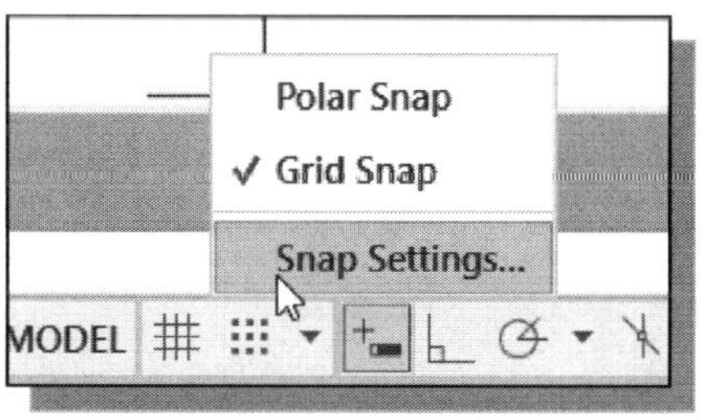

1. In the *Status Bar* area, **right-click** on ***Snap Mode*** and choose **[Snap Settings]**.

2. In the *Drafting Settings* dialog box, select the **Snap and Grid** tab if it is not the page on top.

3. Change *Grid Spacing* and *Snap Spacing* to **10** for both X and Y directions.

4. Switch ***ON*** the *Display dotted grid in 2D model Space* option as shown.

5. Switch ***ON*** the *Grid On* and *Snap On* options as shown.

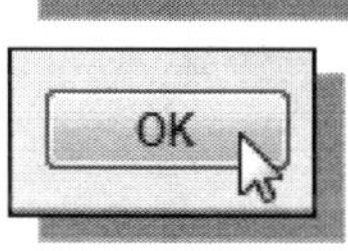

6. Click **OK** to exit the *Drawing Units* dialog box.

Drawing Area Setup

Next, we will set up the **Drawing Limits**. Setting the Drawing Limits controls the extents of the display of the *grid*. It also serves as a visual reference that marks the working area. Note that this setting can also be adjusted through the use of the command prompt area.

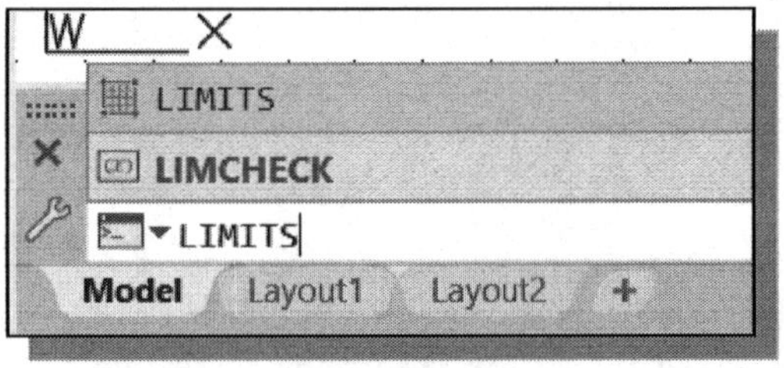

1. Click inside the *command prompt* area.

2. Inside the *command prompt area*, enter ***Limits*** and press the **[Enter]** key.

3. In the command prompt area, near the bottom of the AutoCAD drawing screen, the message "*Reset Model Space Limits: Specify lower left corner or [On/Off] <0,0>:*" is displayed. Enter ***-200,-150*** through the *Dynamic Input* entry boxes.

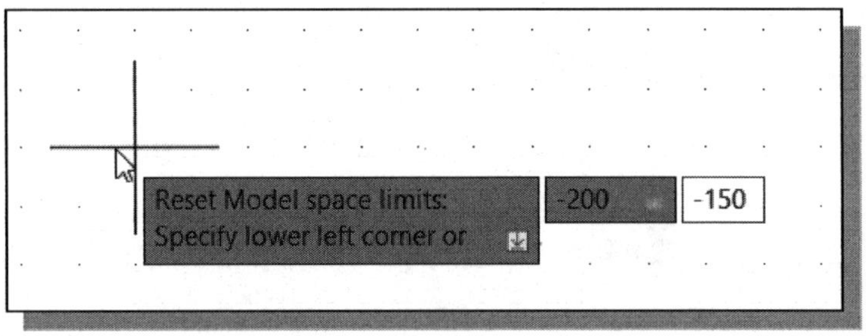

4. In the command prompt area, the message "*Specify upper right corner <420,297>:*" is displayed. Enter ***200,150*** as the new upper right coordinates as shown.

5. On your own, use the *Menu Bar* and confirm the **[View] → [Display] → [UCS Icon] → [Origin]** option is switched *ON* as shown. (The little checked icon next to the option indicates it is switched *ON*.)

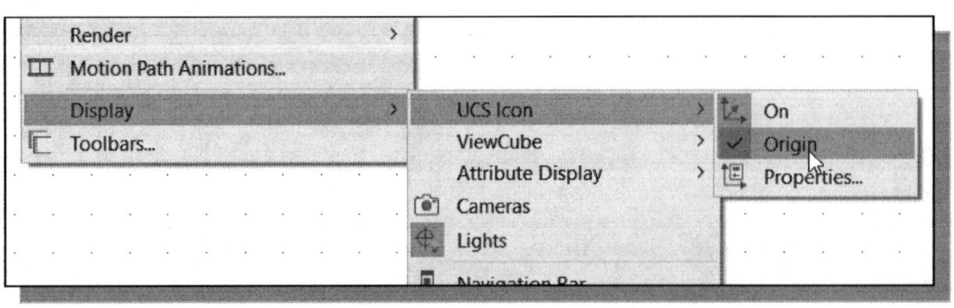

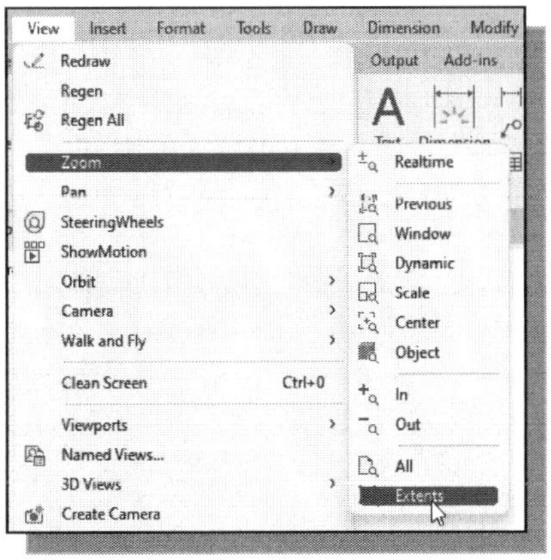

6. On your own, use the **Zoom Extents** command, under the **View** pull-down menu, to reset the display.

❖ Notice the *UCS Icon*, which is aligned to the origin, is displayed near the center of the Drawing Area.

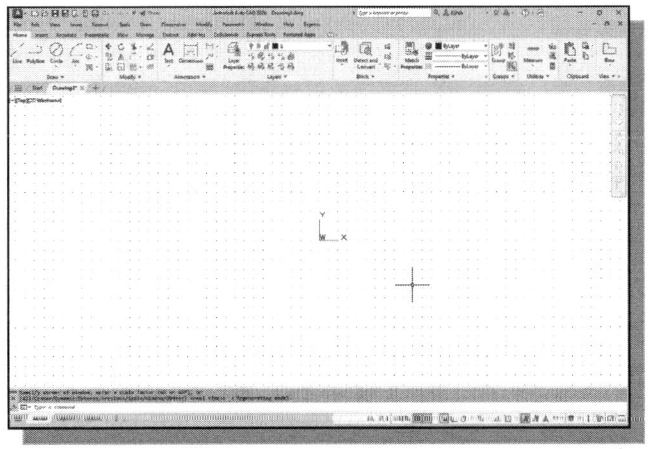

Referencing the World Coordinate System

Design modeling software is becoming more powerful and user friendly, yet the system still does only what the user tells it to do. When using a geometric modeler, we therefore need to have a good understanding of what the inherent limitations are. We should also have a good understanding of what we want to do and what to expect, as the results are based on what is available.

In most geometric modelers, objects are located and defined in what is usually called **world space** or **global space**. Although a number of different coordinate systems can be used to create and manipulate objects in a 3D modeling system, the objects are typically defined and stored using the *world space*. The *world space* is usually a **3D Cartesian coordinate system** that the user cannot change or manipulate.

In most engineering designs, models can be very complex, and it would be tedious and confusing if only one coordinate system were available in CAD systems. Practical CAD systems provide the user with definable **Local Coordinate Systems (LCS)** or **User Coordinate Systems** (UCS), which are measured relative to the world coordinate system. Once a local coordinate system is defined, we can then create geometry in terms of this more convenient system. For most CAD systems, the default construction coordinate system is initially aligned to the world coordinate system.

In AutoCAD, the default **User Coordinate System (UCS)** is initially aligned to the XY plane of the **World Coordinate System (WCS)**. One simple approach to creating designs in CAD systems is to create geometry by referencing the **World Coordinate System**. The general procedure of this approach is illustrated in the following sections.

Creating Circles

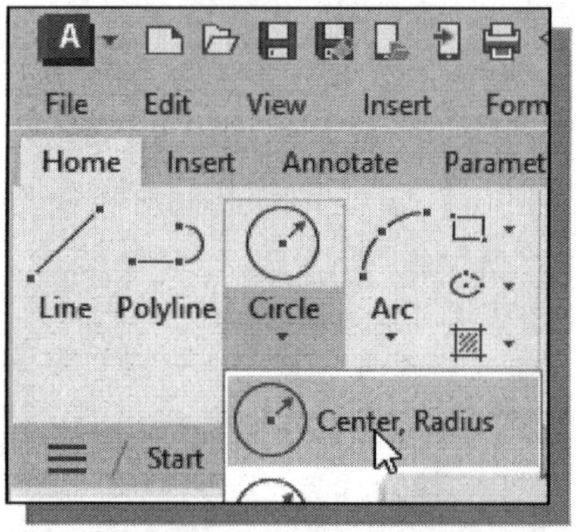

1. Select the **Circle – Center, Radius** command icon in the *Draw* toolbar.

2. On your own, dock the command prompt dialog box to the lower left of the graphics window. Note that you can adjust the size of the box by dragging the edge of the box.

3. In the *command prompt area*, the message "*Circle Specify center point for the circle or [3P/2P/Ttr (tan tan radius)]:*" is displayed. Select the **origin** of the world coordinate system as the center point.

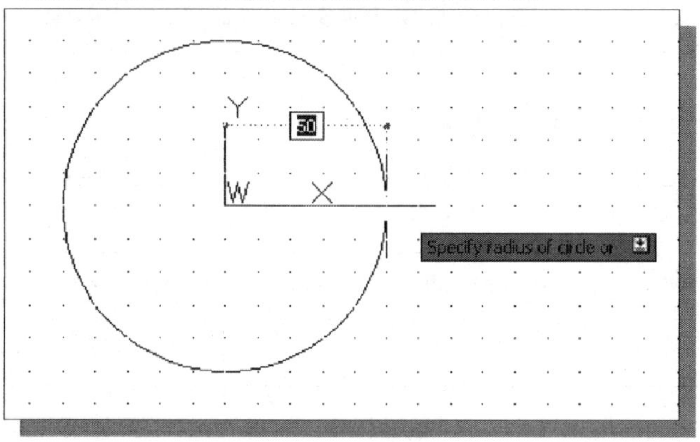

4. In the command prompt area, the message "*Specify radius of circle or [Diameter]:*" is displayed. AutoCAD expects us to identify the radius of the circle. Set the radius to ***50*** by observing the tooltips as shown.

5. Hit the **[SPACE BAR]** once to repeat the circle command.

6. On your own, select ***70,40*** as the absolute coordinate values of the center point coordinates of the second circle.

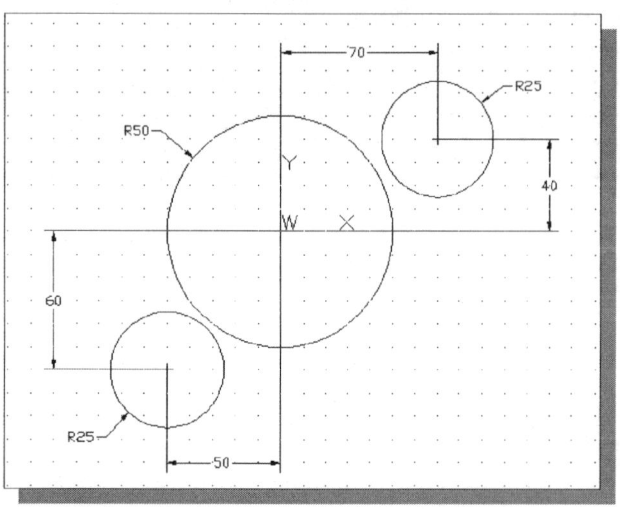

7. Set the value of the radius to ***25***.

8. On your own, repeat the above procedure and create another circle (radius ***25***) at absolute coordinates of ***-50,-60*** as shown in the figure.

Object Snap Toolbar

1. Move the cursor to the *Menu Bar* area and choose **[Tools] → [Toolbars] → [AutoCAD]**.

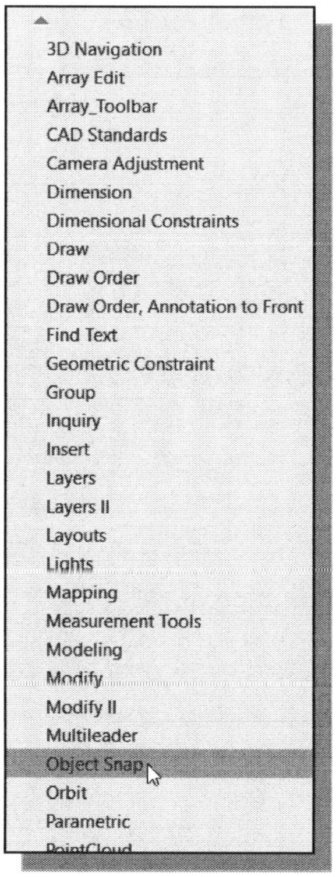

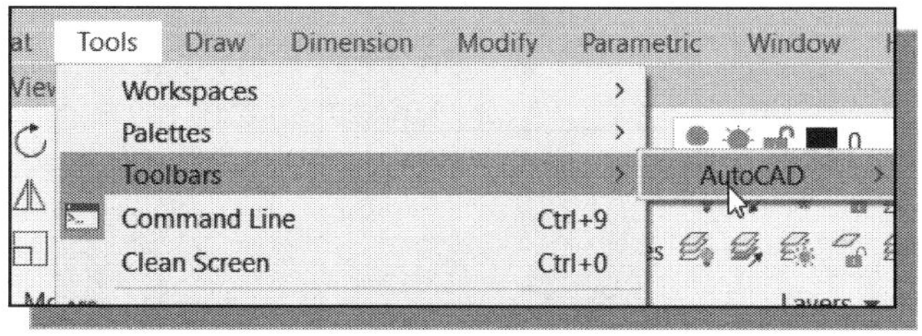

❖ AutoCAD provides 50+ predefined toolbars for access to frequently used commands, settings, and modes. A *checkmark* (next to the item) in the list identifies the toolbars that are currently displayed on the screen.

2. Select **Object Snap**, with the left-mouse-button, to display the *Object Snap* toolbar on the screen.

❖ **Object Snap** is an extremely powerful construction tool available on most CAD systems. During an entity's creation operations, we can snap the cursor to points on objects such as endpoints, midpoints, centers, and intersections. For example, we can turn on **Object Snap** and quickly draw a line to the center of a circle, the midpoint of a line segment, or the intersection of two lines.

3. Move the cursor over the icons in the *Object Snap* toolbar and read the description of each icon.

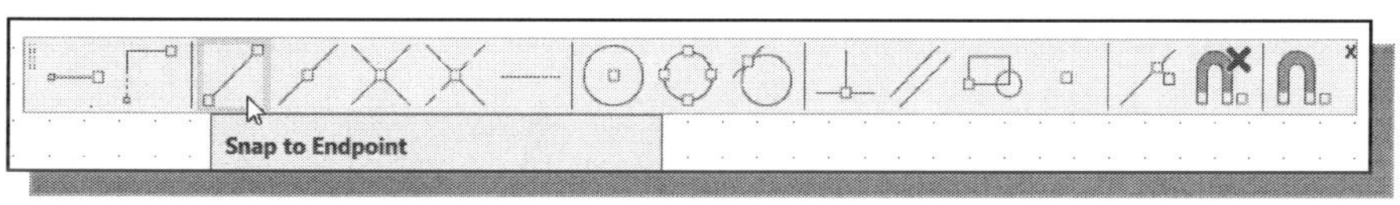

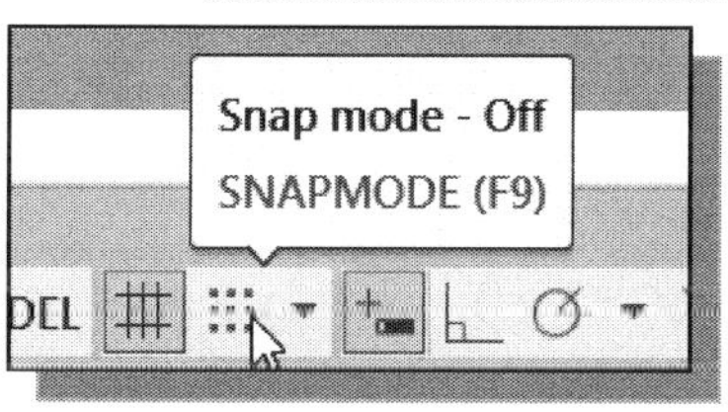

4. We will next turn ***OFF*** the *GRID SNAP* option by toggling off the ***SNAP Mode*** button in the *Status Bar* area.

5. On your own, reset the option buttons in the *Status Bar* area, so that only the *GRID DISPLAY* option is switched ***ON***.

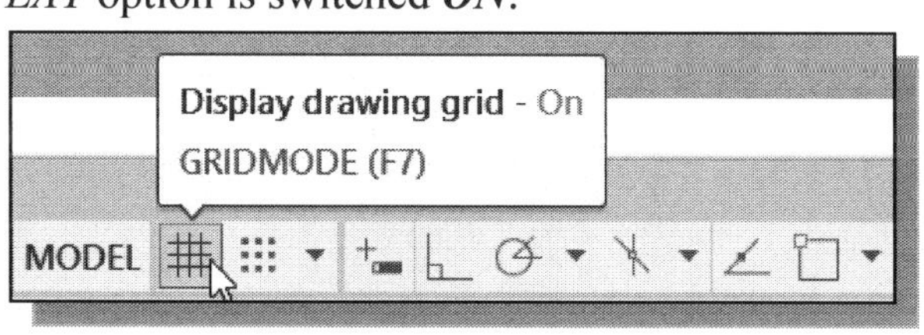

Using the Line Command

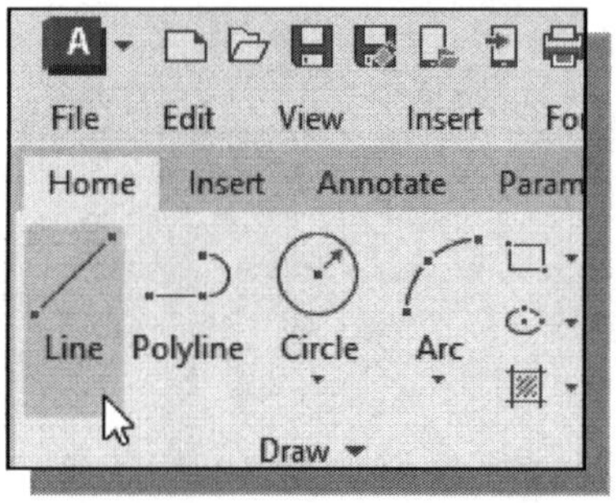

1. Select the **Line** command icon in the *Draw* toolbar. In the command prompt area, near the bottom of the AutoCAD drawing screen, the message "*_line Specify first point:*" is displayed.

2. Pick **Snap to Tangent** in the *Object Snap* toolbar. In the command prompt area, the message "*_tan to*" is displayed. AutoCAD now expects us to select a circle or an arc on the screen.

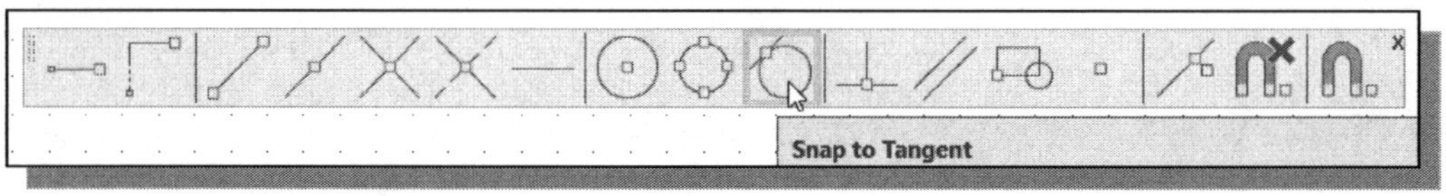

❖ The **Snap to Tangent** option allows us to snap to the point on a circle or arc that, when connected to the last point, forms a line tangent to that object.

3. Pick a location that is near the top left side of the smaller circle on the right; note the tangent symbol is displayed as shown.

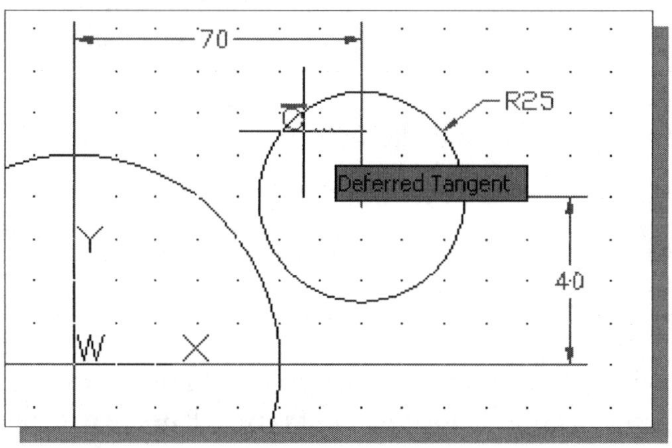

❖ Note that the note "Deferred Tangent" indicates that AutoCAD will calculate the tangent location when the other endpoint of the line is defined.

4. Pick **Snap to Tangent** in the *Object Snap* toolbar. In the command prompt area, the message "*_tan to*" is displayed. AutoCAD now expects us to select a circle or an arc on the screen.

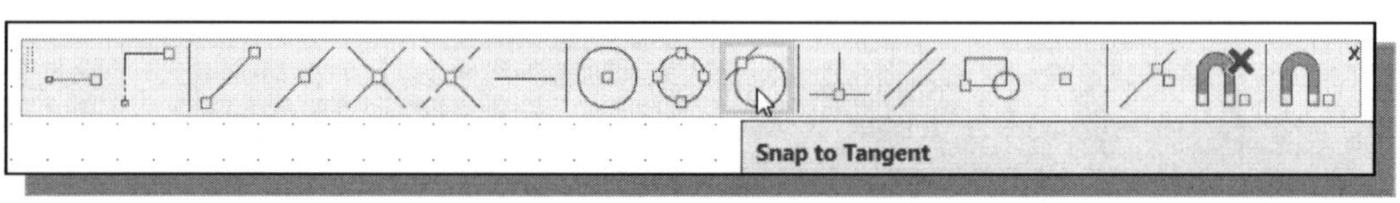

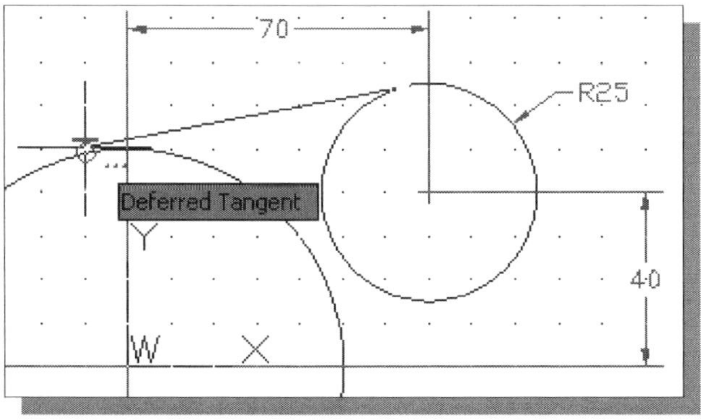

5. Pick a location that is near the top left side of the center circle; note the tangent symbol is displayed as shown.

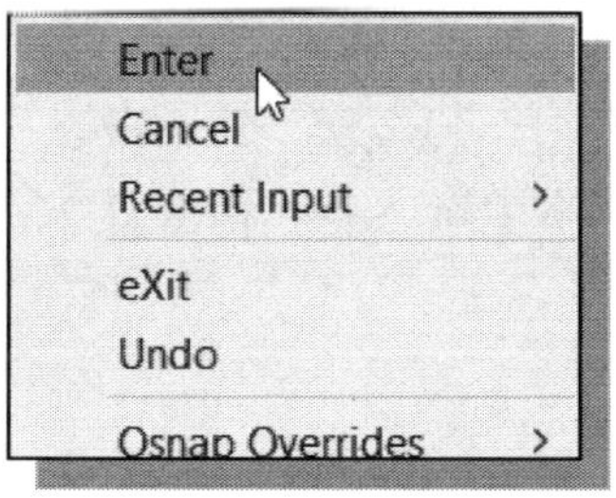

6. Inside the *Drawing Area*, **right-click** to activate the option menu and select **Enter** with the left-mouse-button to end the Line command.

❖ A line tangent to both circles is constructed as shown in the figure.

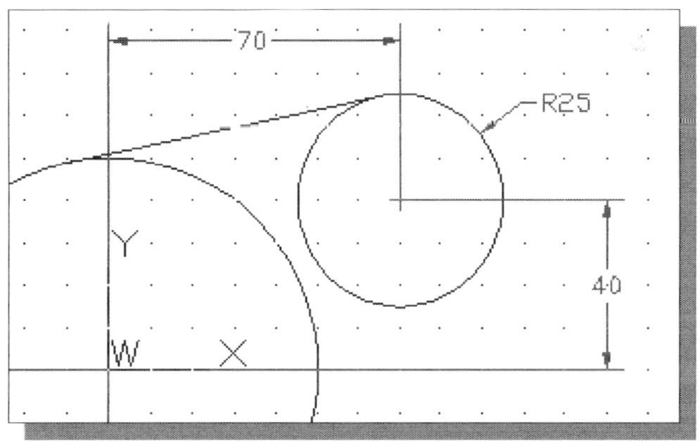

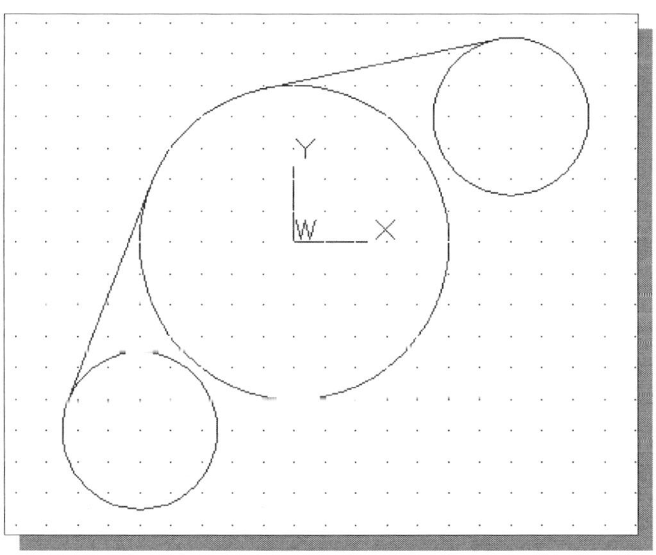

7. On your own, repeat the above steps and create the other tangent line between the center circle and the circle on the left. Your drawing should appear as the figure.

Creating TTR Circles

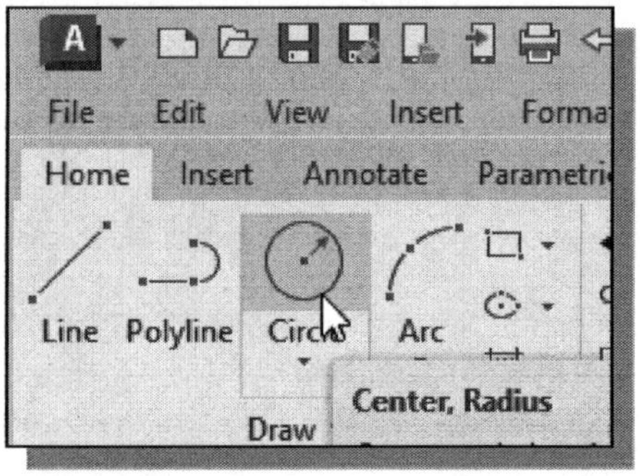

1. Select the **Circle** command icon in the *Draw* toolbar. In the command prompt area, the message "*Specify center point for circle or [3P/2P/Ttr (tan tan radius)]:*" is displayed.

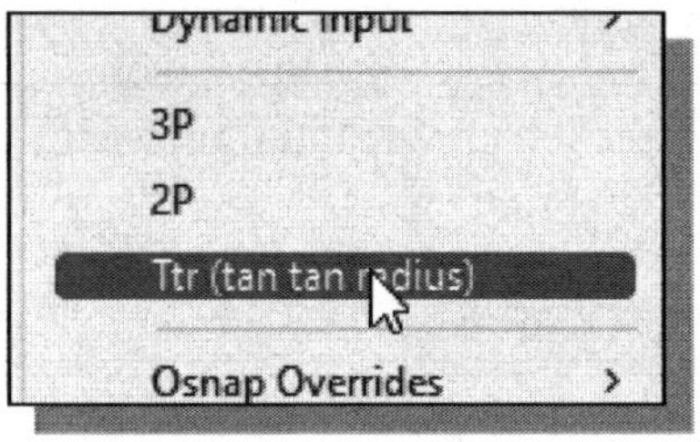

2. Inside the Drawing Area, right-click to activate the option menu and select the **Ttr (tan tan radius)** option. This option allows us to create a circle that is tangent to two objects.

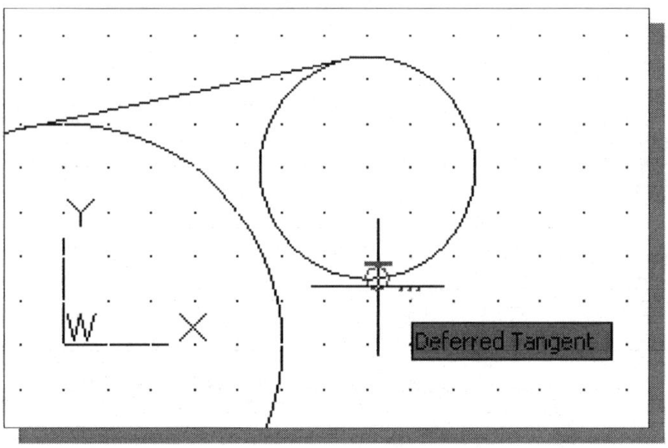

3. Pick a location near the **bottom of the smaller circle** on the right. We will create a circle that is tangent to this circle and the center circle.

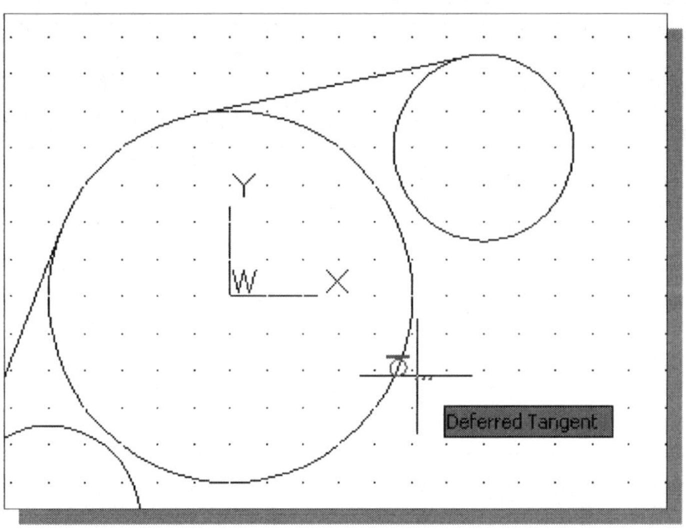

4. Pick the **center circle** by selecting a location that is near the right side of the circle. AutoCAD interprets the locations we selected as being near the tangency.

5. In the command prompt area, the message "*Specify radius of circle*" is displayed. Enter ***50*** as the radius of the circle.

   Specify radius of circle: **50 [ENTER]**

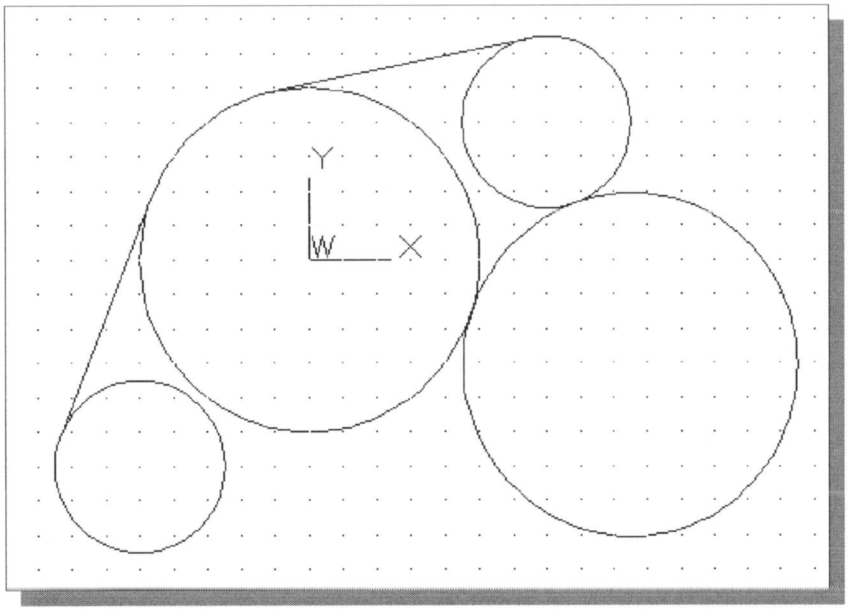

6. On your own, repeat the above steps and create the other TTR circle (radius ***40***). Your drawing should appear as the figure below.

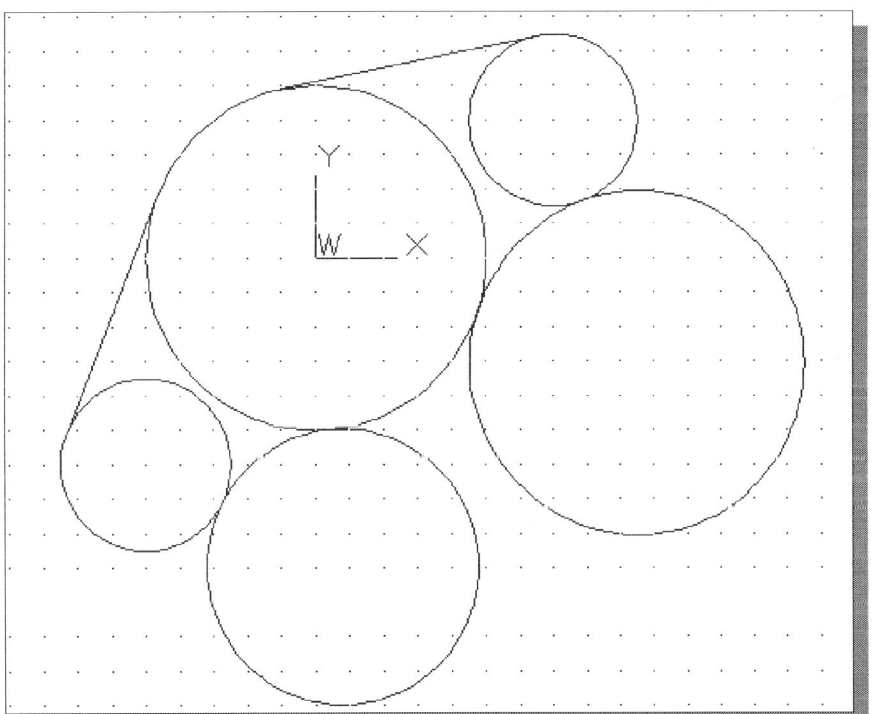

Using the Trim Command

The **Trim** command shortens an object so that it ends precisely at a selected boundary.

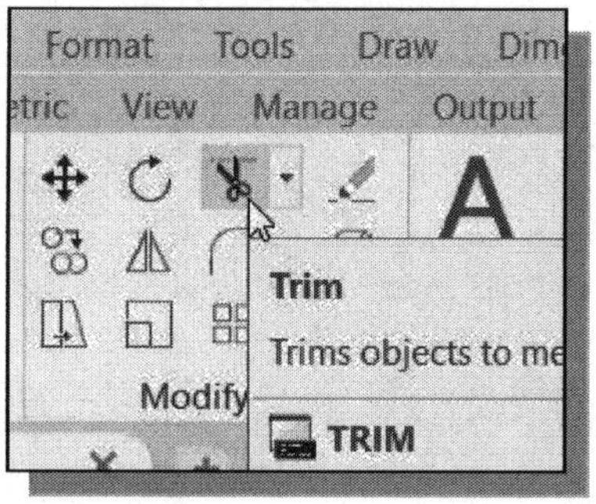

1. Select the **Trim** command icon in the *Modify* toolbar, and click on the down-triangle to display additional icons as shown.

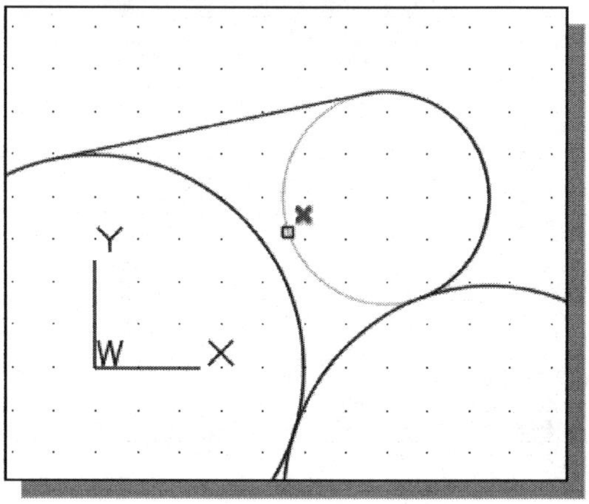

2. The message "*Select object to trim or shift-select object to extend or [Project/Edge/Undo]:*" is displayed in the command prompt area. Move the cursor on the **left** section of the upper right circle and note the selected portion is trimmed as shown.

❖ In AutoCAD, several options are available with the Trim command: (1) We can specify cutting edges at which an object is to stop. Valid cutting edge objects include most 2D geometry such as lines, arcs, circles, ellipses, polylines, splines, and text. For 3D objects, a 2D projection method can also be used, where objects are projected onto the XY plane of the current user coordinate system (UCS). (2) We can select objects to trim by defining a two-point rectangle. (3) We can erase an entire object while in the trim command.

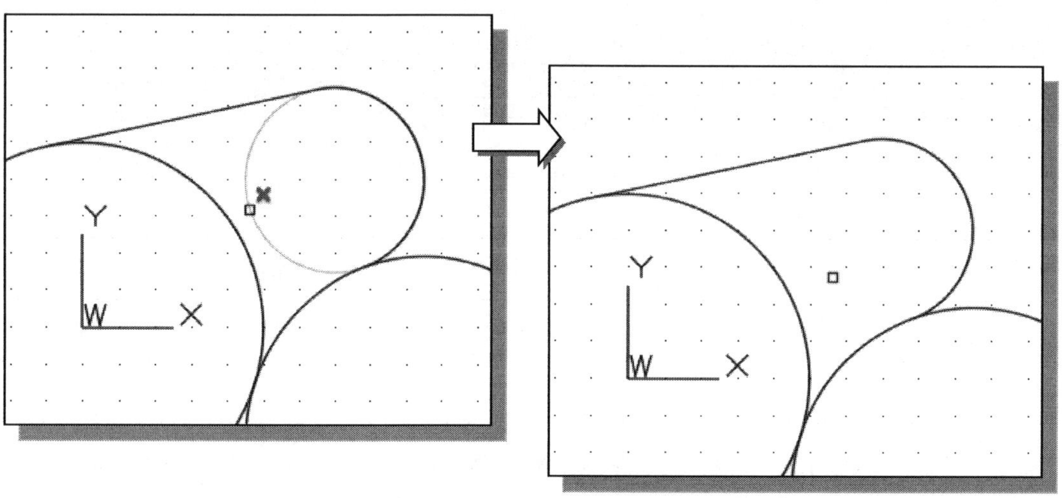

3. Select the upper right side of the center circle to remove the selected portion.

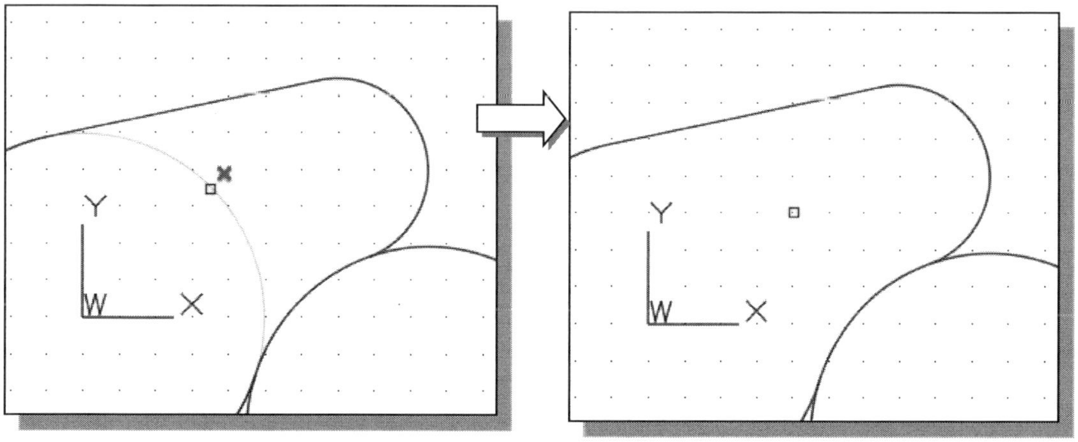

4. Select the upper right side of the circle on the lower right to remove the selected portion.

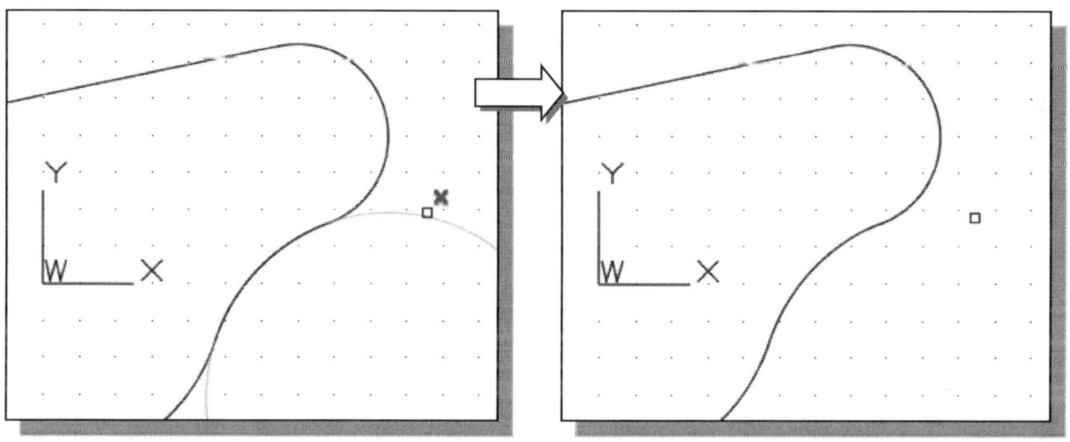

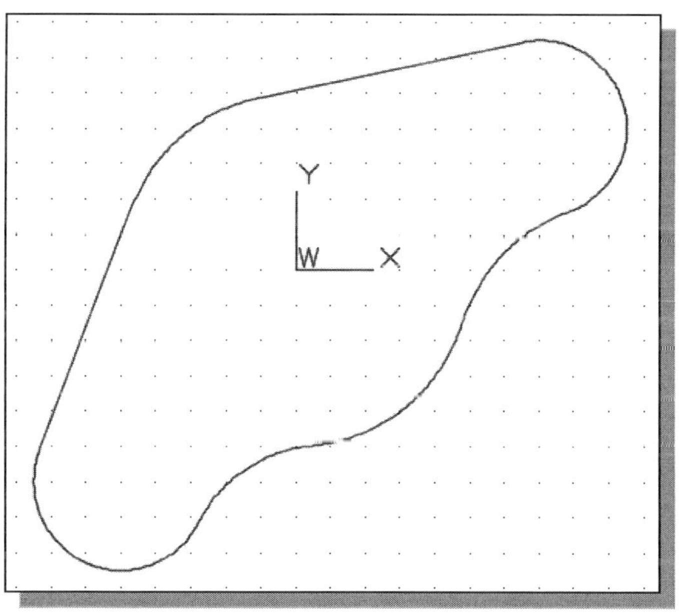

5. On your own, trim the other geometry so that the drawing appears as shown.

6. Inside the *Drawing Area*, **right-click** to activate the option menu and select **Enter** with the left-mouse-button to end the Trim command.

Using the Polygon Command

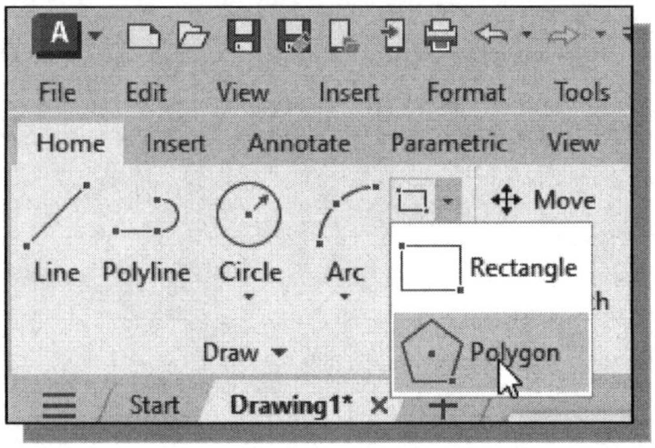

1. Select the **Polygon** command icon in the *Draw* toolbar. Click on the triangle icon next to the rectangle icon to display the additional icon list.

2. Enter ***6*** to create a six-sided hexagon. *polygon Enter number of sides <4>:* **6 [ENTER]**

3. The message "*Specify center of polygon or [Edge]:*" is displayed. Since the center of the large circle is aligned to the origin of the WCS, the center of the polygon can be positioned using several methods. Set the center point to the origin by entering the absolute coordinates. *Specify center of polygon or [Edge]:* **0,0 [ENTER]**

4. In the *command prompt area*, the message "*Enter an option [Inscribed in circle/ Circumscribed about circle] <I>:*" is displayed. Click **Circumscribed about circle** to select the *Circumscribed about circle* option.

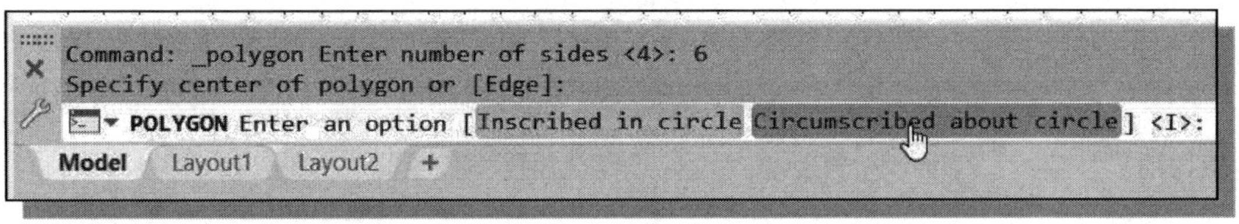

5. In the command prompt area, the message *Specify radius of circle:*" is displayed. Enter ***30*** as the radius.
Specify radius of circle: **30 [ENTER]**

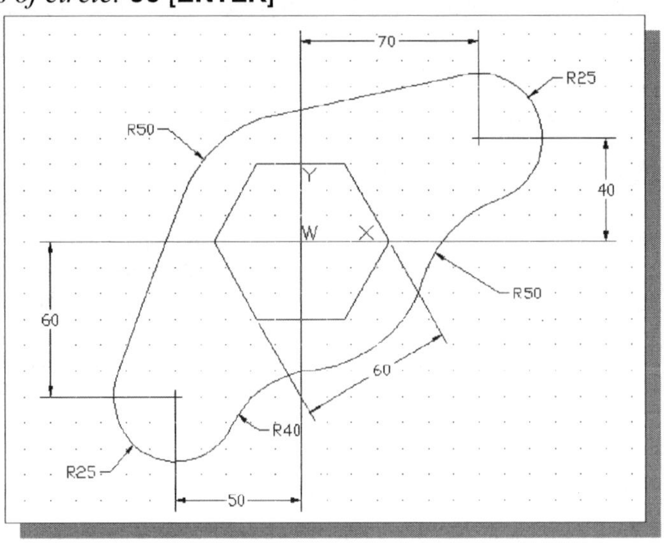

❖ Note that the polygon option [Inscribed in circle/Circumscribed about circle] allows us to create either **flat to flat** or **corner to corner** distance.

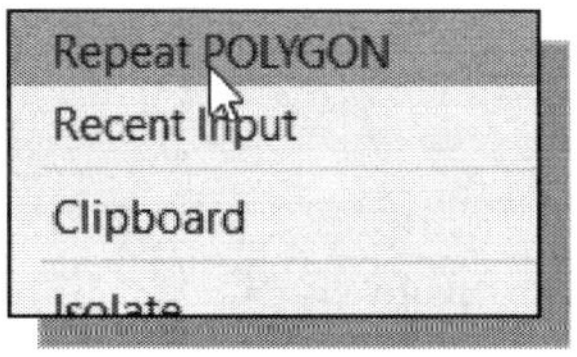

6. Inside the Drawing Area, **right-click** to activate the option menu and select **Repeat Polygon**. In the command prompt area, the message "*_polygon Enter number of sides <6>:*" is displayed.

7. Enter ***4*** to create a four-sided polygon.
   _polygon Enter number of sides <6>: **4 [ENTER]**

8. In the command prompt area, the message "*Specify center of polygon or [Edge]:*" is displayed. Let's use the *Object Snap* options to locate its center location. Pick **Snap to Center** in the *Object Snap* toolbar as shown.

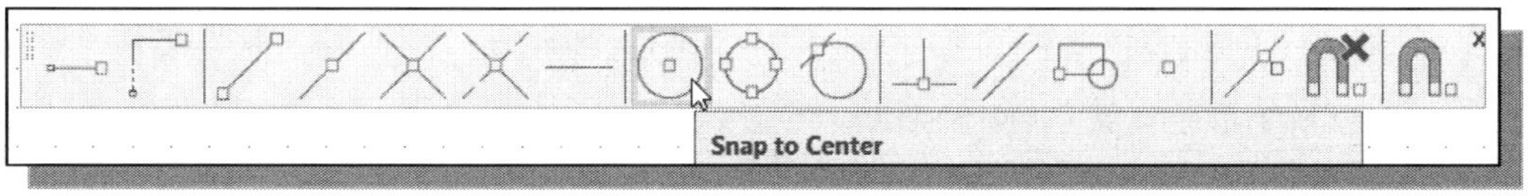

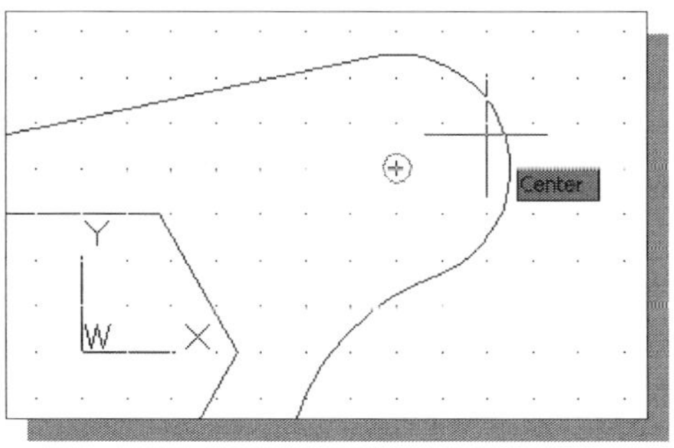

9. Move the cursor on top of the arc on the right and notice the center point is automatically highlighted. Select the arc to accept the highlighted location.

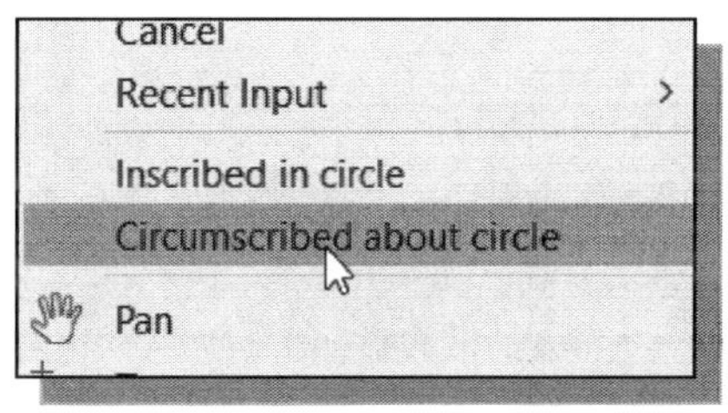

10. Inside the Drawing Area, **right-click** to activate the option menu and select **Circumscribed about circle**.

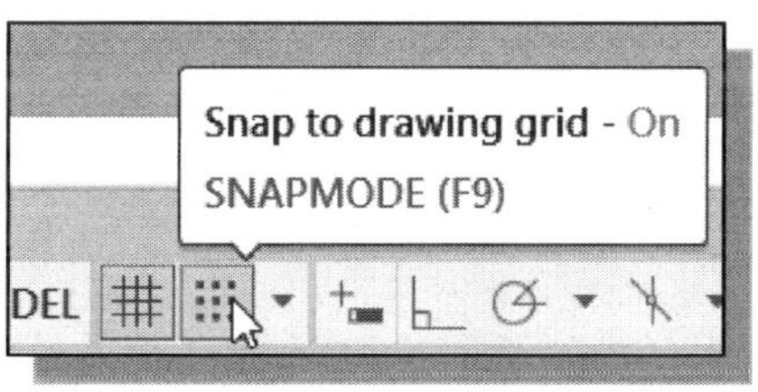

11. Switch ***ON*** the ***GRID SNAP*** option in the *Status Bar* as shown.

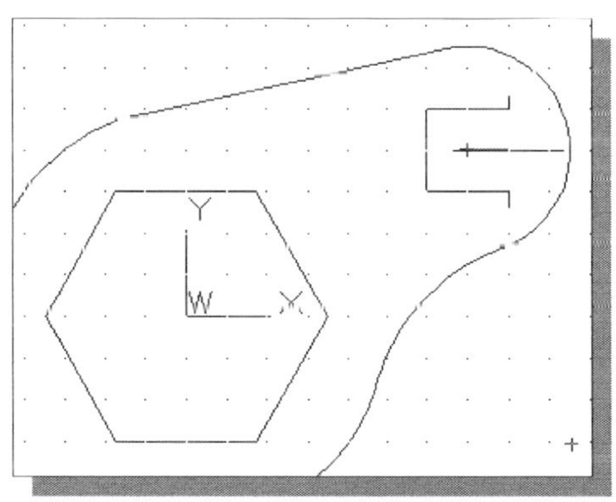

12. Create a square by selecting one of the adjacent grid points next to the center point as shown. Note that the orientation of the polygon can also be adjusted as the cursor is moved to other locations.

Creating a Concentric Circle

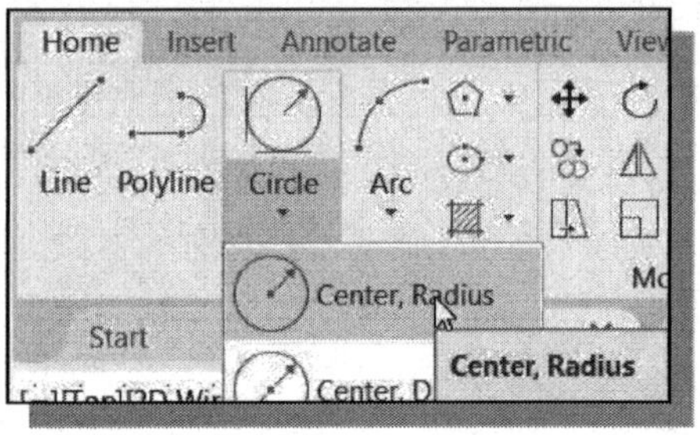

1. Select the **Circle, Radius** command icon in the *Draw* toolbar. In the command prompt area, the message "*Specify center point for circle or [3P/2P/Ttr (tan tan radius)]:*" is displayed.

2. Let's use the *Object Snap* options to assure the center location is aligned properly. Pick **Snap to Center** in the *Object Snap* toolbar as shown.

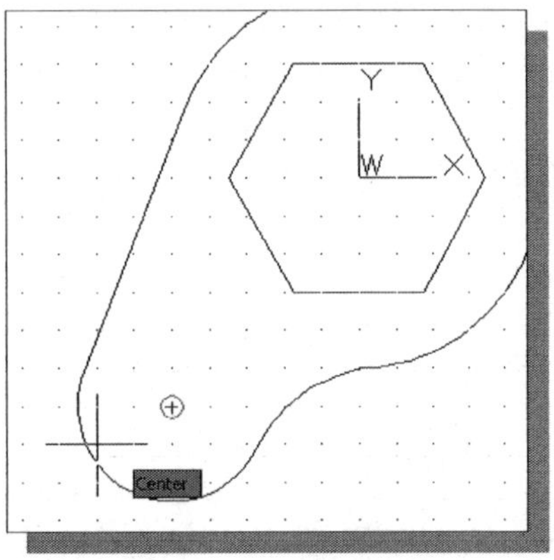

3. Move the cursor on top of the lower arc on the left and notice the center point is automatically highlighted. Select the arc to accept the highlighted location.

4. In the command prompt area, the message "*Specify radius of circle <25>*" is displayed. Enter ***10*** to complete the Circle command.
   Specify radius of circle <25>: **10 [ENTER]**

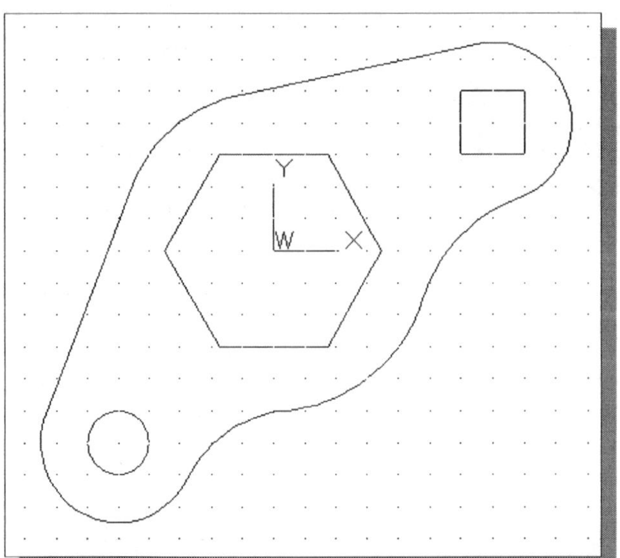

Using the QuickCalc Calculator to Measure Distance and Angle

AutoCAD also provides several tools that will allow us to measure distance, area, perimeter, and even mass properties. With the use of the *Object Snap* options, getting measurements of the completed design can be done very quickly.

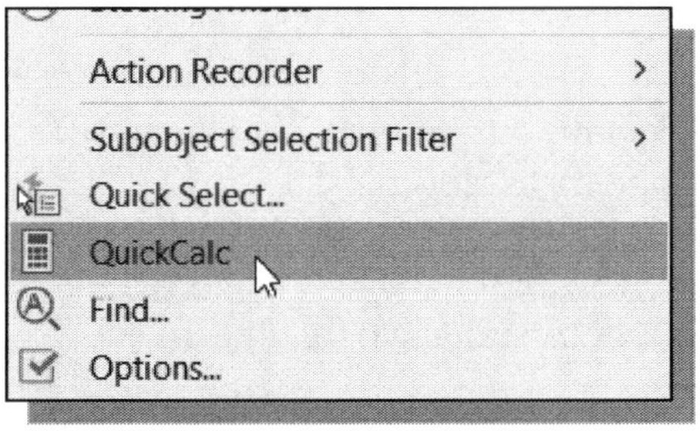

1. Inside the *Drawing Area*, **right-click** once to bring up the option menu.

2. Select **QuickCalc** in the *option menu* as shown.

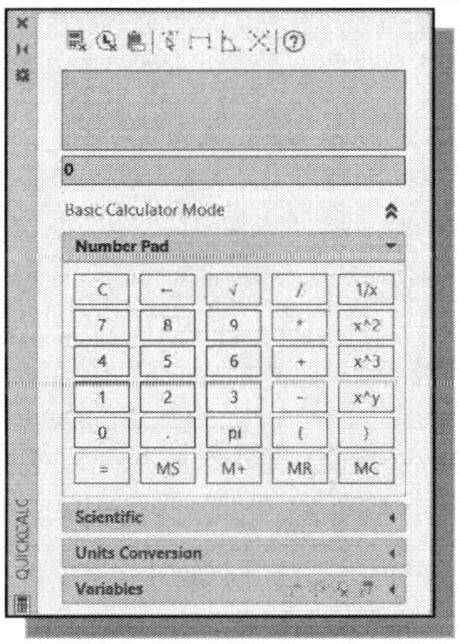

❖ Note that the QuickCalc option brings up the AutoCAD calculator, which can be used to perform a full range of mathematical, scientific, and geometric calculations. We can also use QuickCalc to create and use variables, as well as to convert units of measurement.

3. Click the **Measure Distance** icon, which is located on the top section of the *QuickCalc* calculator pad.

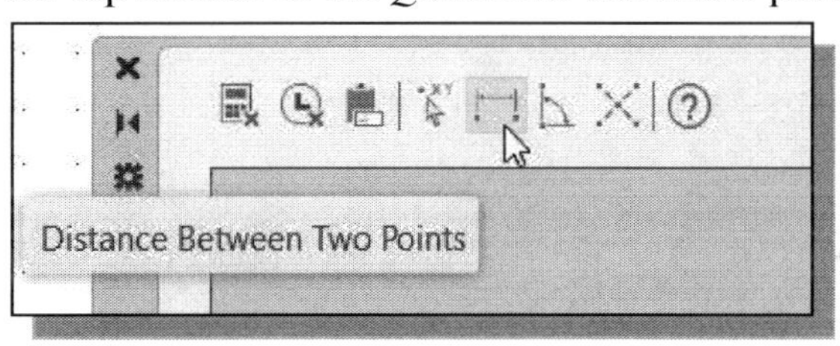

4. Pick **Snap to Endpoint** in the *Object Snap* toolbar.

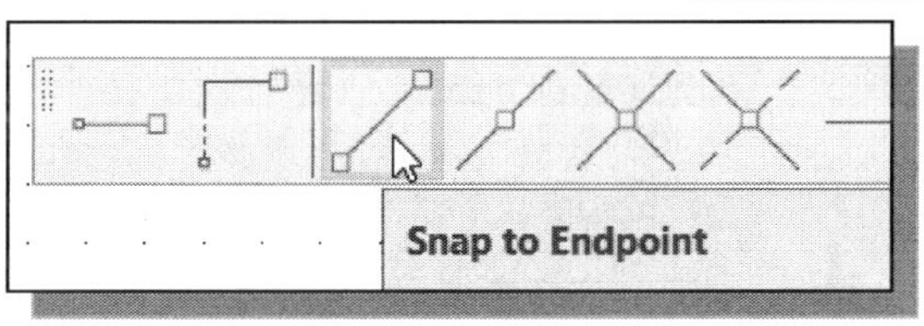

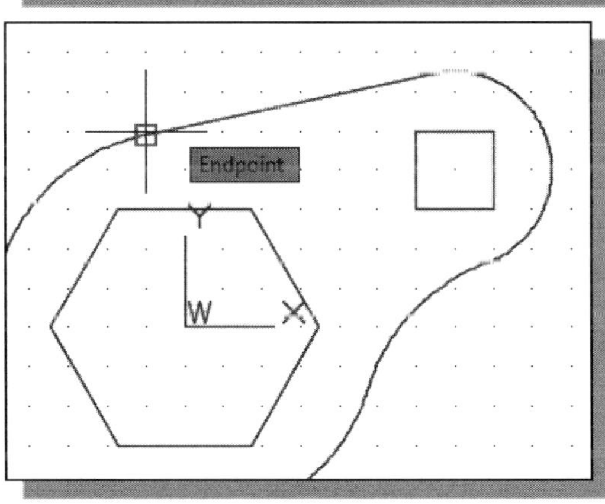

5. Select the **top tangent line**, near the lower endpoint, as shown.

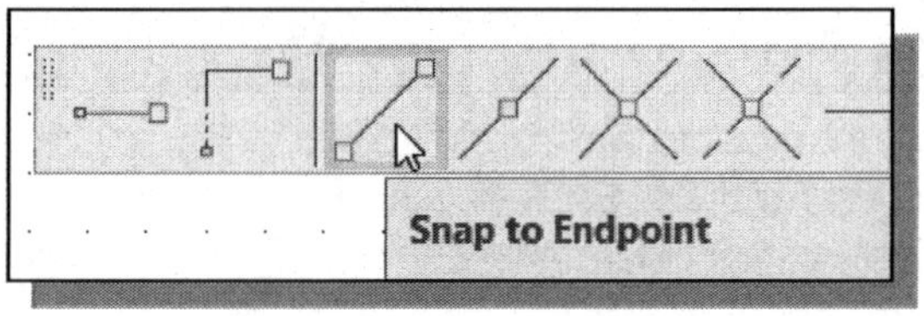

6. Pick **Snap to Endpoint** in the *Object Snap* toolbar.

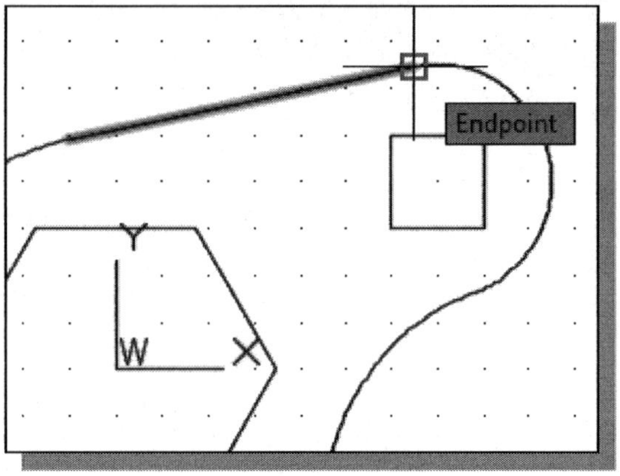

7. Select the tangent line, near the upper endpoint, as shown.

❖ The length of the line is displayed in the *QuickCalc* calculator as shown.

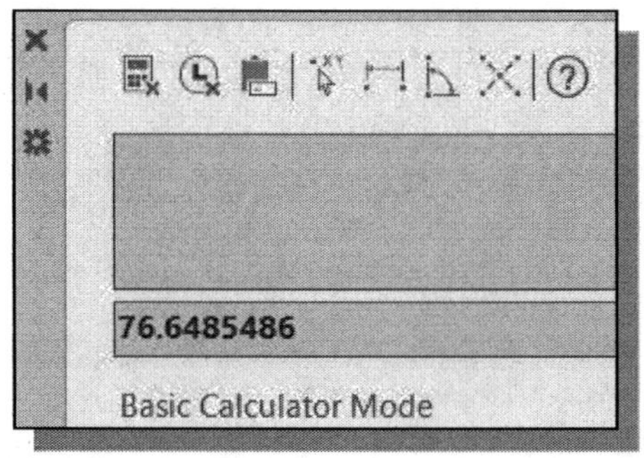

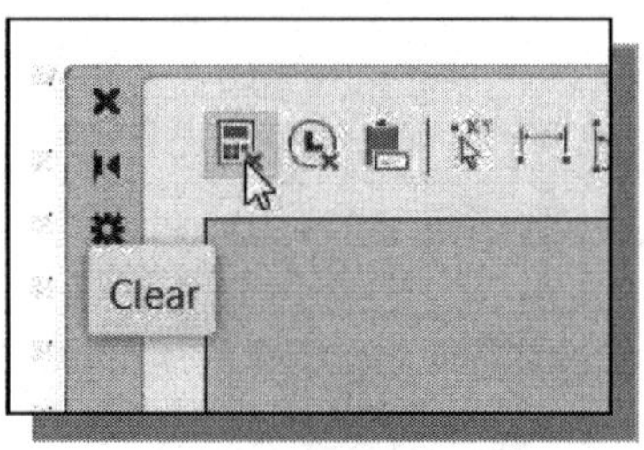

8. Click the **Clear** icon to remove the number displayed.

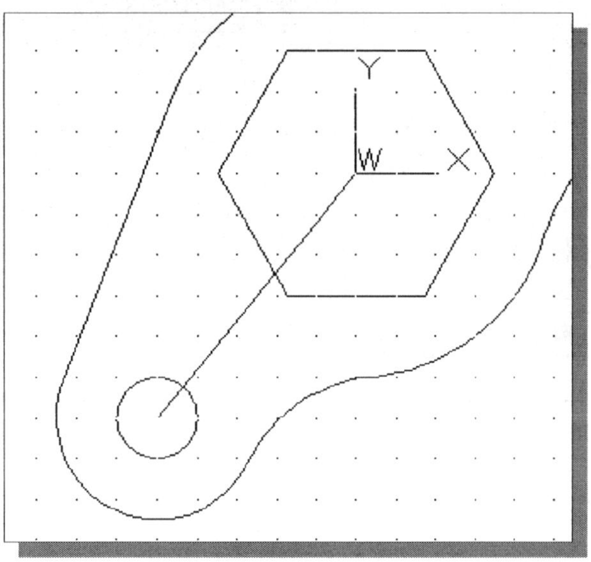

9. On your own, repeat the above steps and measure the center-to-center distance of the lower region of the design as shown. (Hint: use the **Snap to Center** option.)

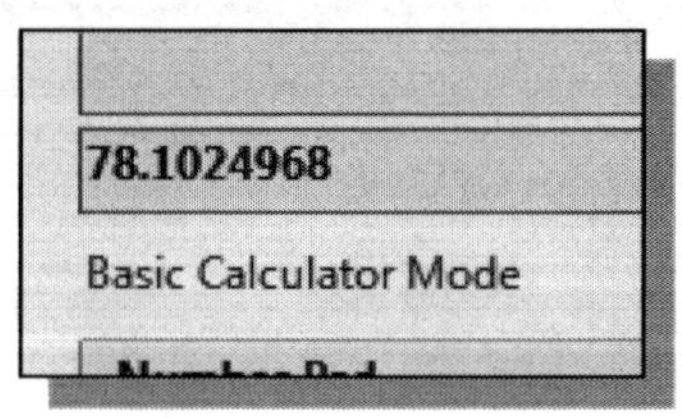

10. Click the **Measure Angle** icon, which is located on the top section of the *QuickCalc* calculator pad.

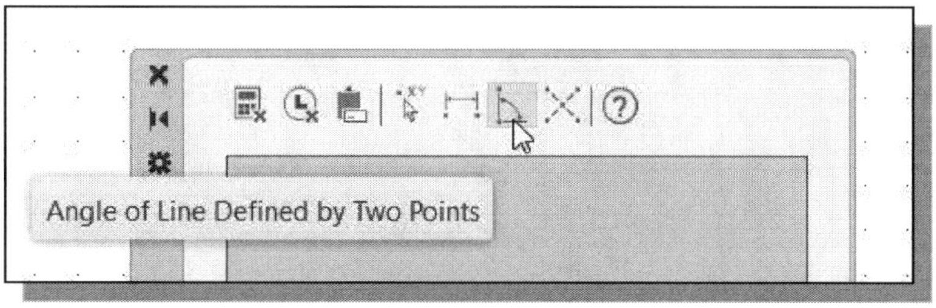

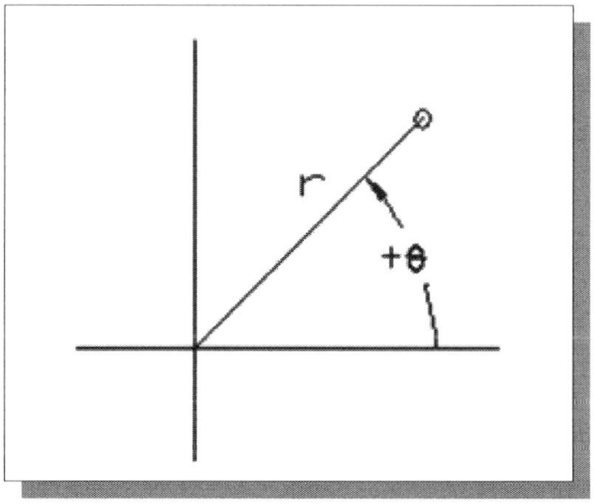

❖ Note that this option allows us to measure the angle between the horizontal axis and the line formed by the two selected points. A positive angle indicates a counterclockwise direction.

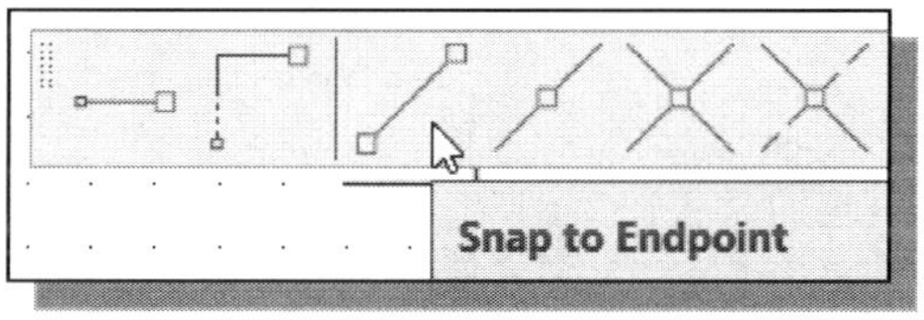

11. Pick **Snap to Endpoint** in the *Object Snap* toolbar.

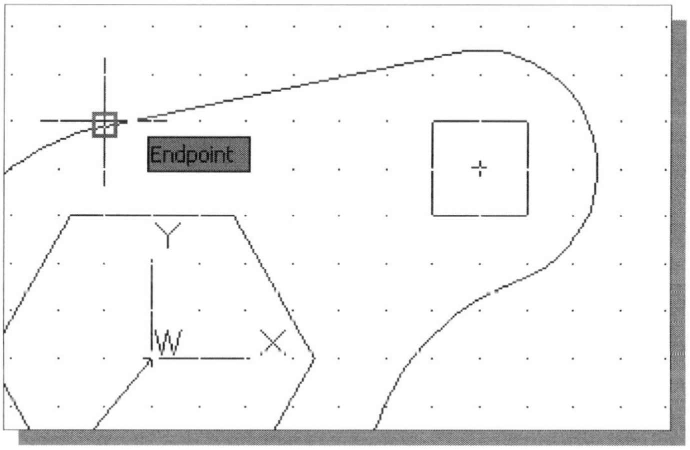

12. Select the tangent line, near the lower endpoint, as shown.

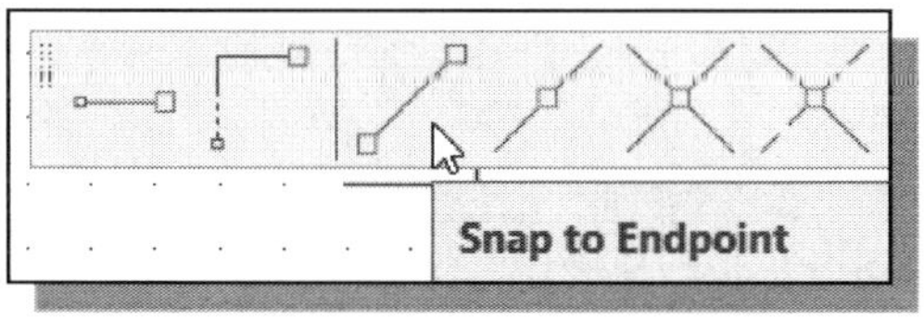

13. Pick **Snap to Endpoint** in the *Object Snap* toolbar.

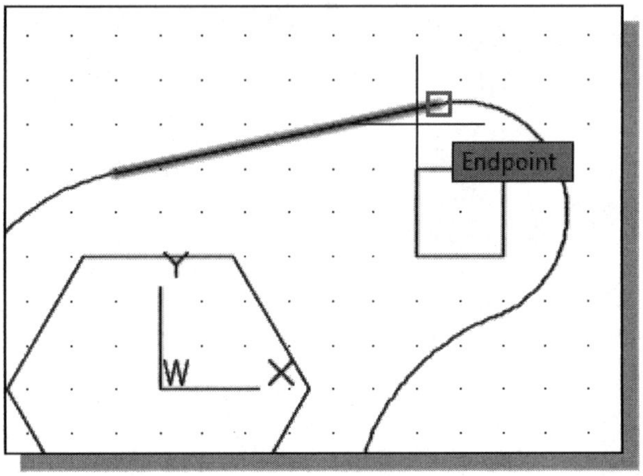

14. Select the tangent line, near the upper endpoint, as shown.

➢ The measured angle is displayed in the calculator pad as shown.

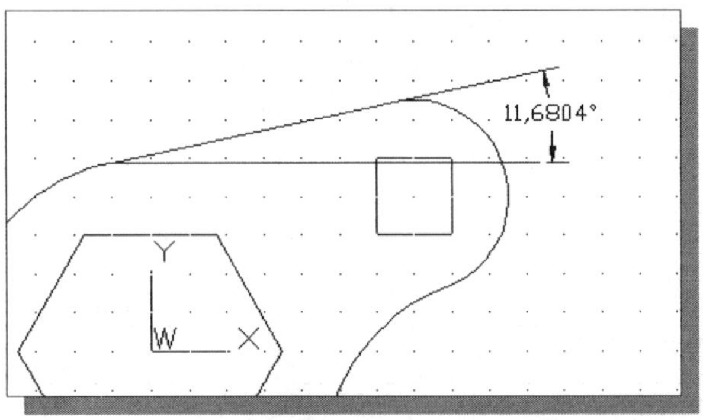

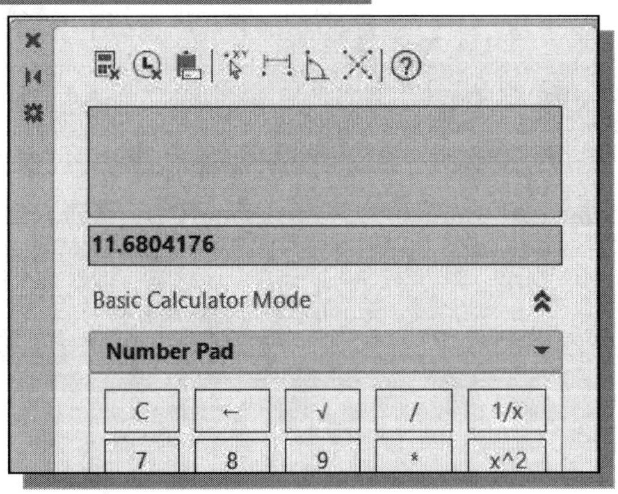

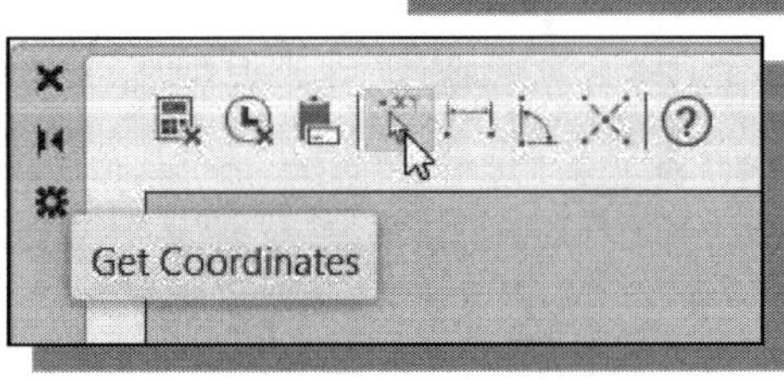

15. On your own, experiment with the available **Get Coordinates** options.

➢ Note also that the QuickCalc calculator can remain active while you are using other AutoCAD commands.

Saving the CAD File

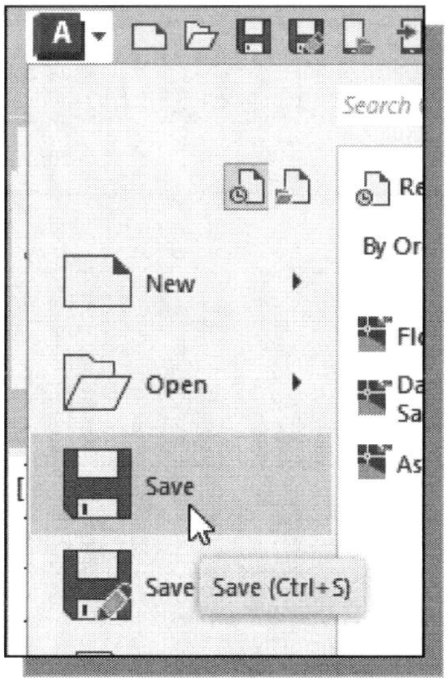

1. In the *Application Menu*, select:

   [Application] → [Save]

   ❖ Note the command can also be activated with quick-key combination of **[Ctrl]+[S]**.

2. In the *Save Drawing As* dialog box, select the folder in which you want to store the CAD file and enter ***RockerArm*** in the *File name* box.

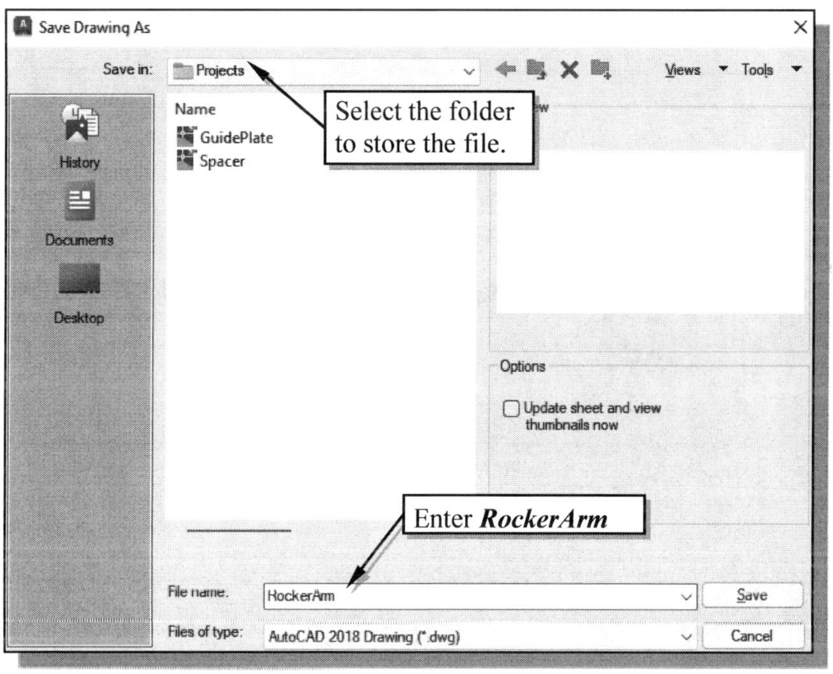

3. Pick **Save** in the *Save Drawing As* dialog box to accept the selections and save the file.

Exit AutoCAD

To exit **AutoCAD 2027**, select **Exit AutoCAD** from the *Application Menu* or type ***QUIT*** at the command prompt.

AutoCAD Quick Keys

Besides using the mouse and/or AutoCAD menu systems, AutoCAD also provides quick keys to access the more commonly used commands, with many of them being a single key stroke.

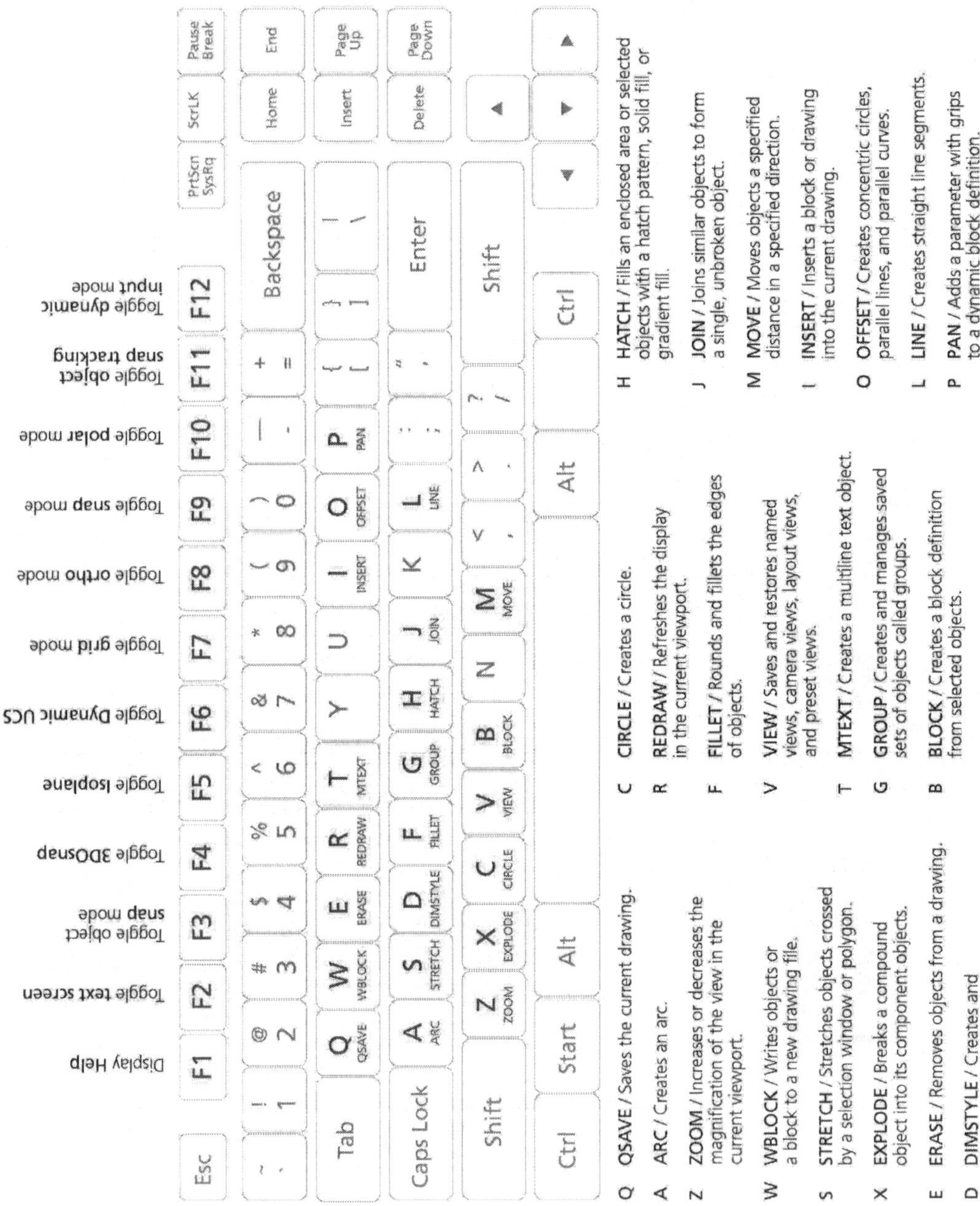

For a more detailed description o the quick keys, refer to the following Autodesk website:
http://www.autodesk.com/store/autocad-shortcuts

Review Questions: (Time: 20 minutes)

1. Describe the procedure to activate the AutoCAD Startup option.

2. List and describe three options in the AutoCAD *Object Snap* toolbar.

3. Which AutoCAD command can we use to remove a portion of an existing entity?

4. Describe the difference between the *circumscribed* and *inscribed* options when using the AutoCAD Polygon command.

5. Create the following triangle and fill in the blanks: Length = ____, Angle = ____. (Dimensions are in inches.)

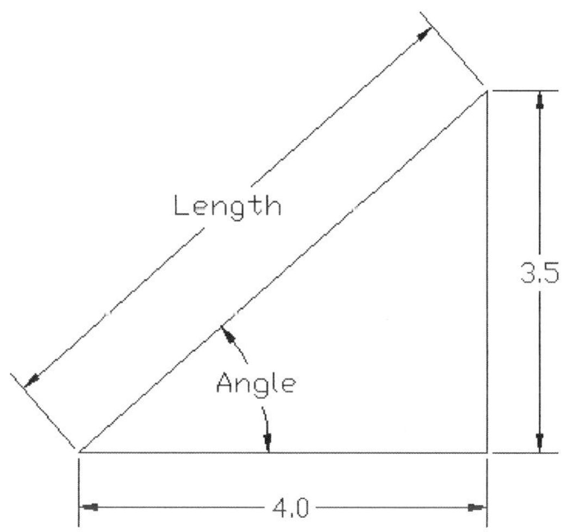

6. Create the following drawing; line *AB* is tangent to both circles. Fill in the blanks: Length = _____, Angle = _____. (Dimensions are in inches.)

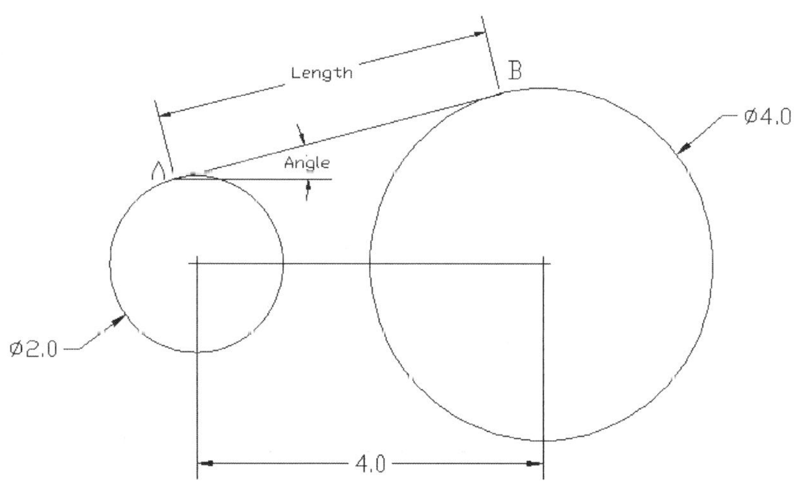

Exercises:

(Unless otherwise specified, dimensions are in inches.) (Time: 120 minutes.)

1. **Adjustable Support**

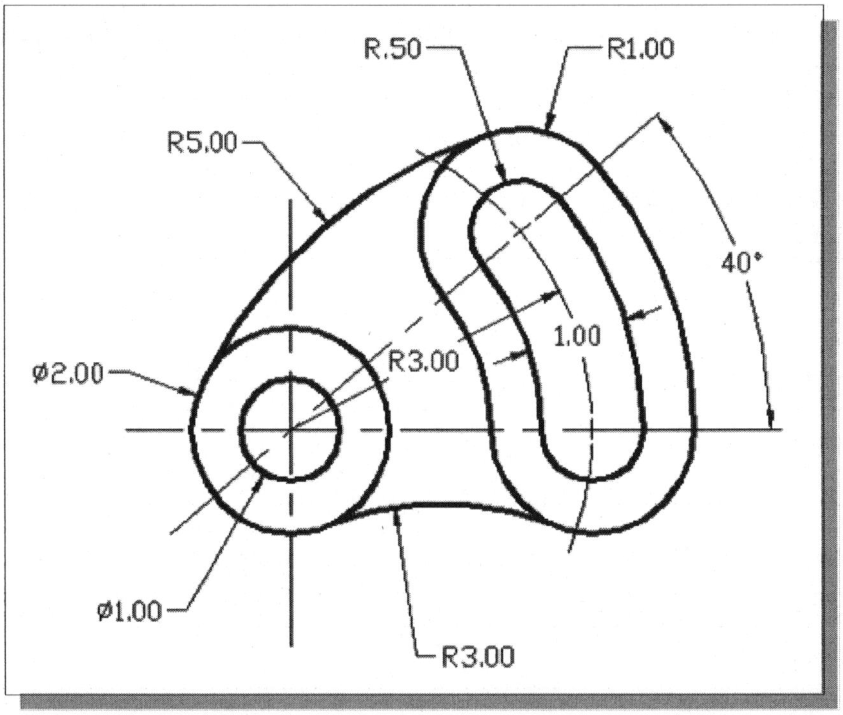

2. **V-Slide Plate** (The design has two sets of parallel lines with implied tangency.)

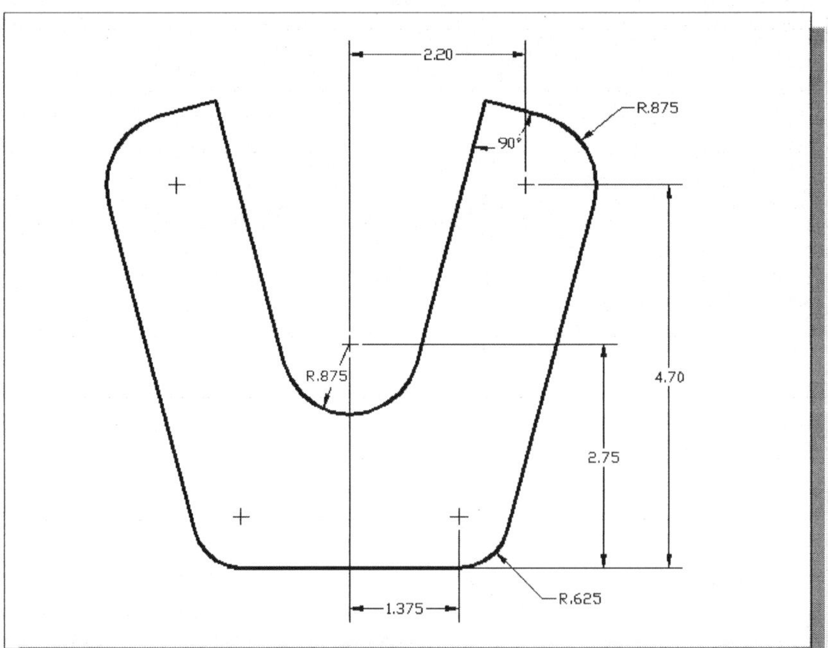

3. **Swivel Base** (Dimensions are in Millimeters.)

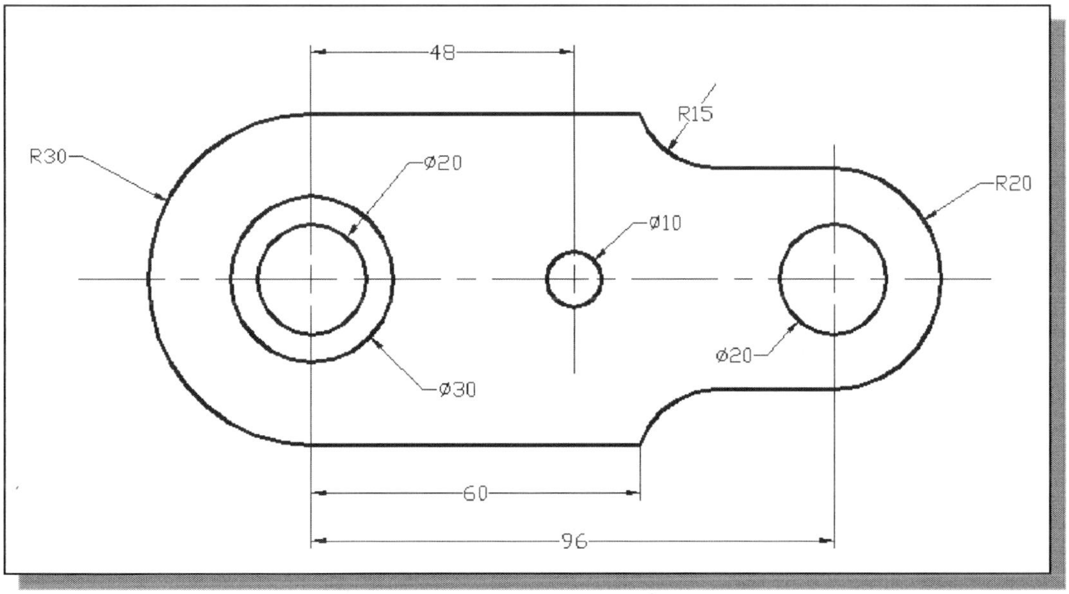

4. **Sensor Mount**

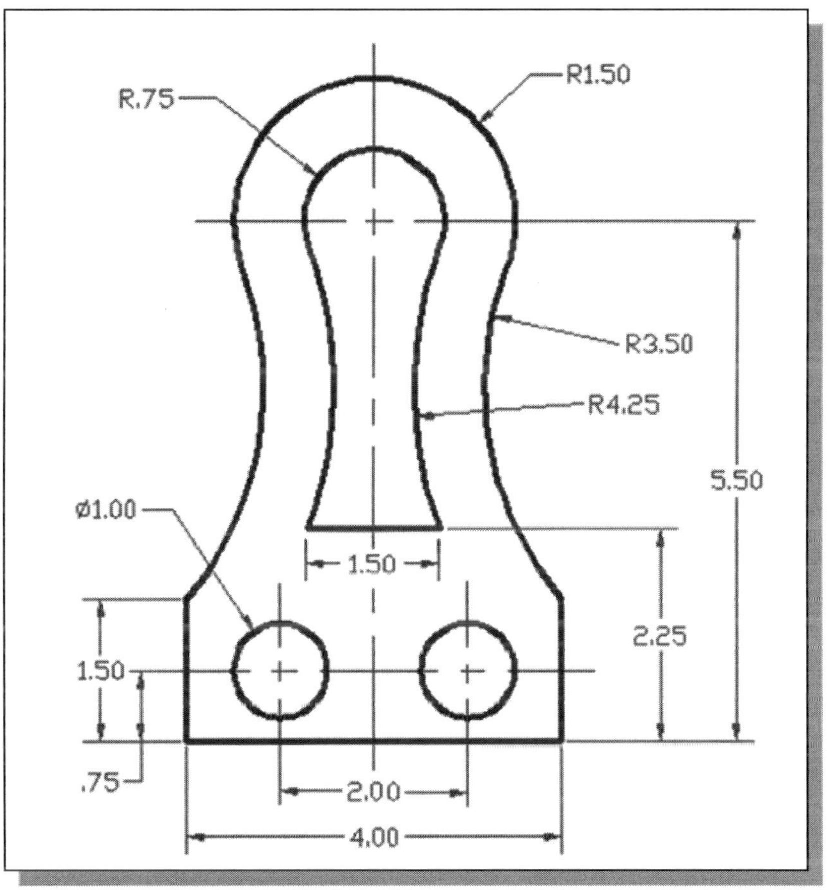

5. **Flat Hook** (Dimensions are in Millimeters. Thickness: 25 mm.)

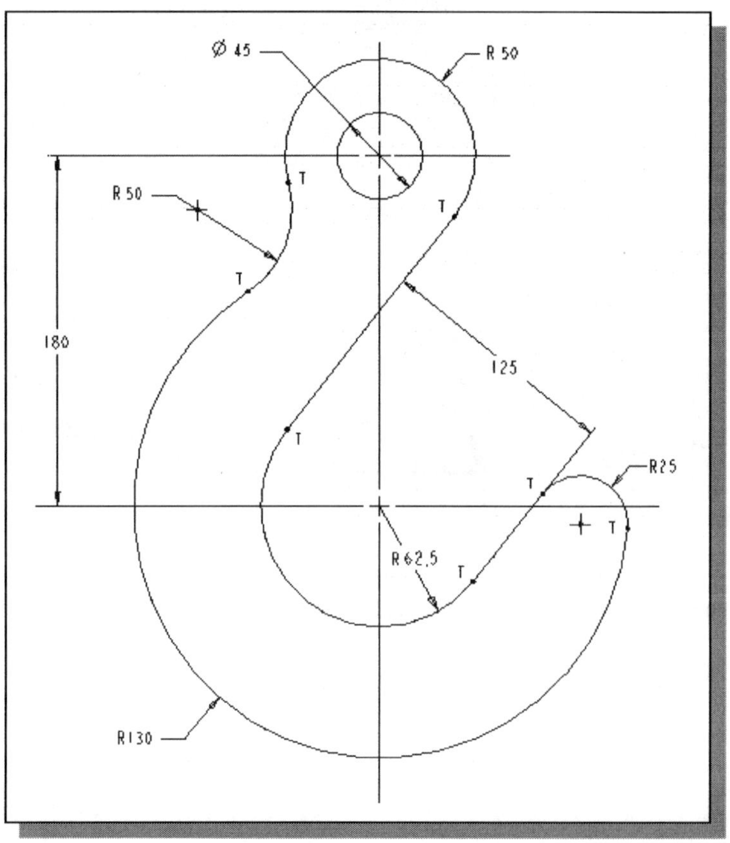

6. **Journal Bracket**

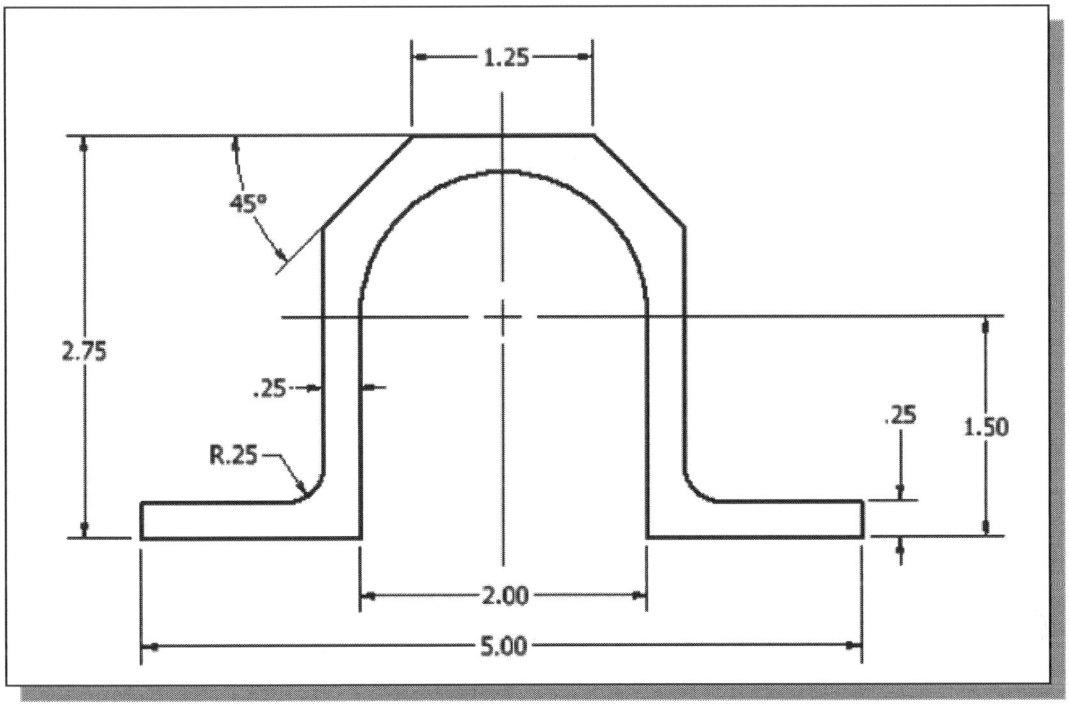

7. **Support Base**

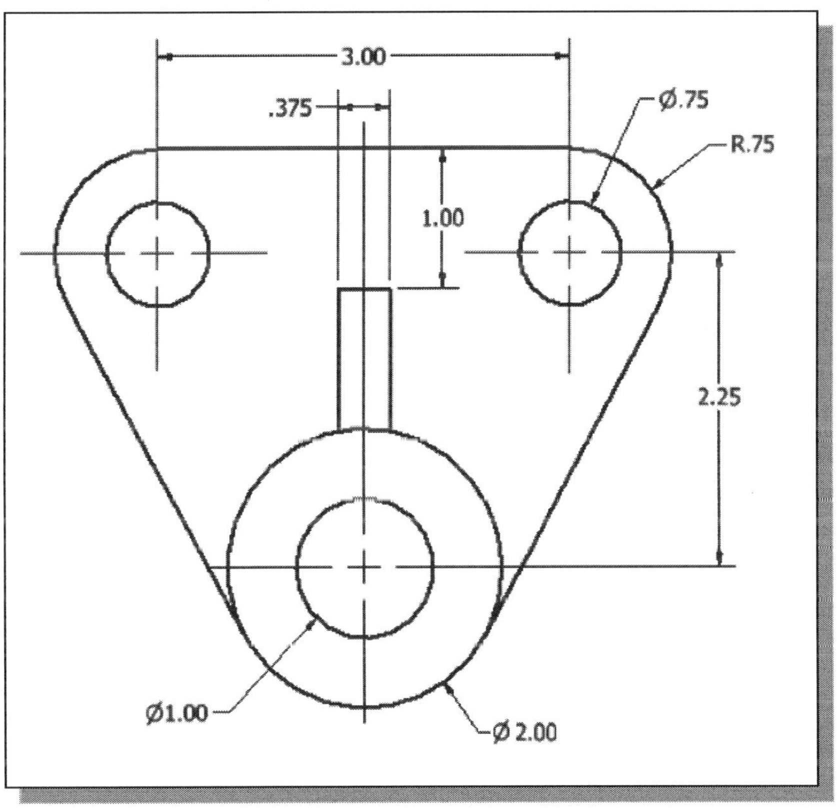

8. **Pivot Arm**

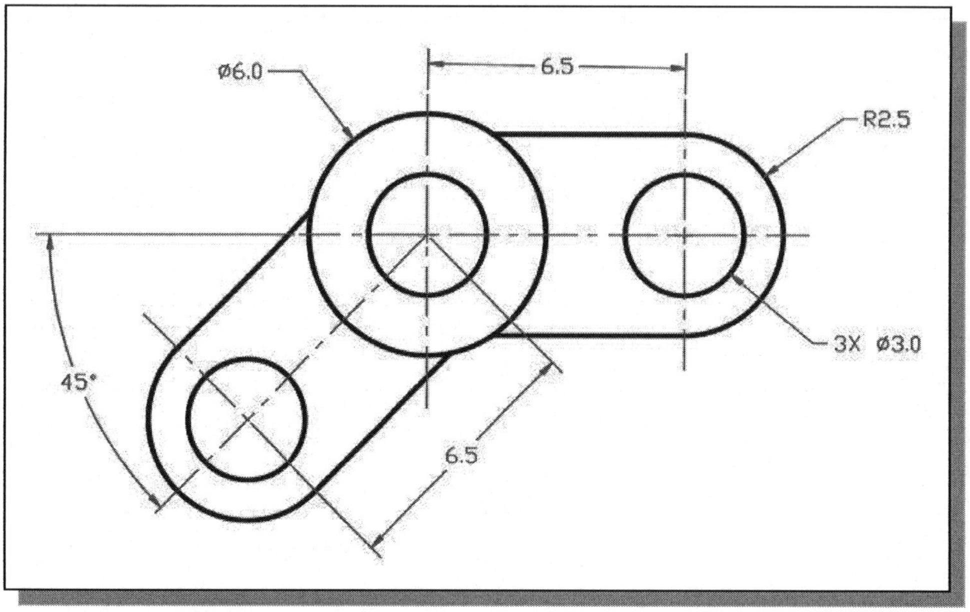

9. **Extruder Cover** (Dimensions are in Millimeters.)

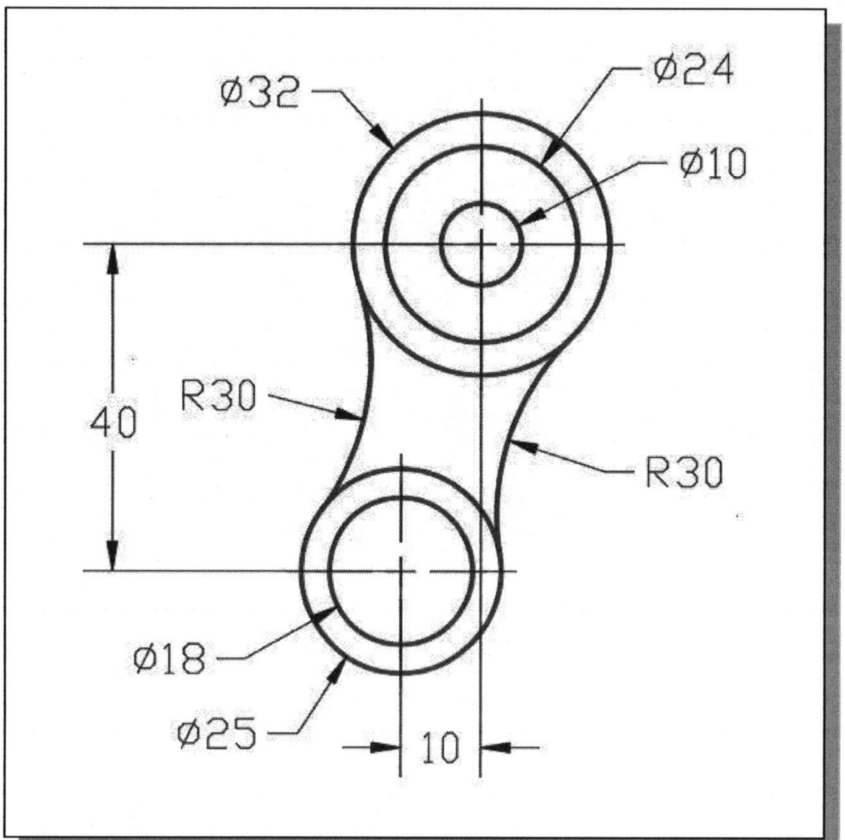

Chapter 3
Geometric Construction and Editing Tools – AutoCAD

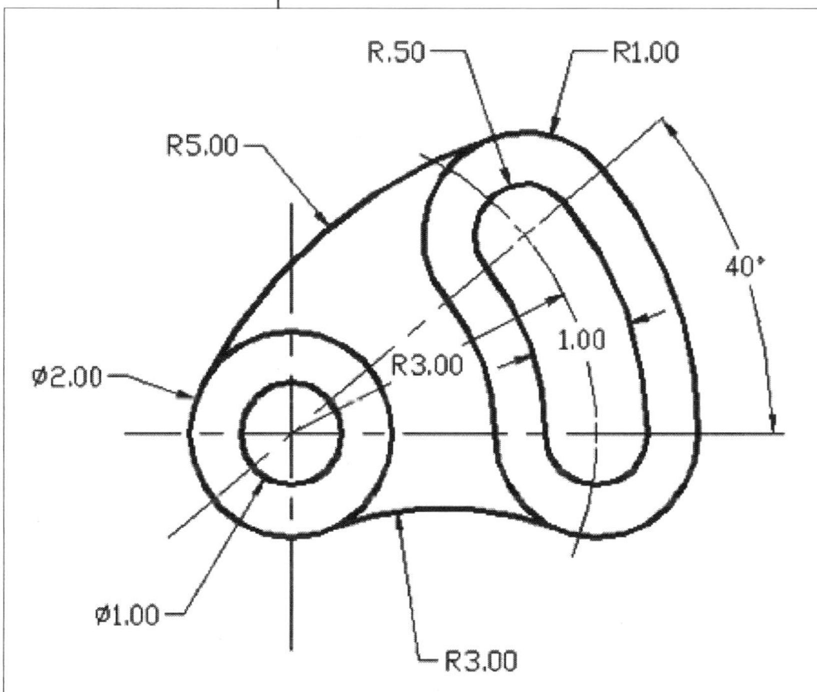

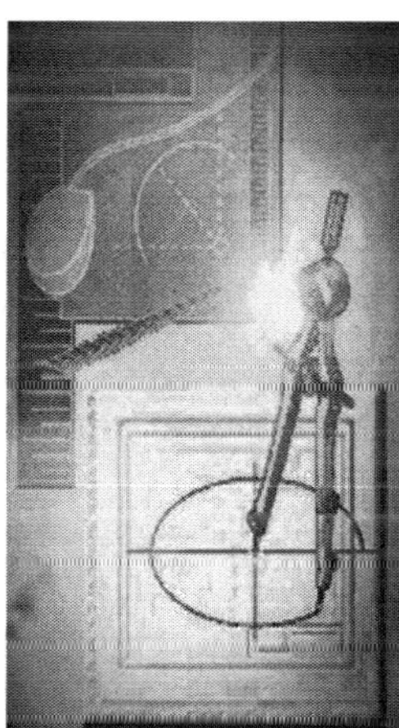

Learning Objectives

- Set up the display of Drawing Units
- Display AutoCAD's toolbars
- Set up and use Object Snaps
- Edit using Extend and Trim
- Use the Fillet command
- Create parallel geometric entities
- Using the Pedit command
- Use the Explode command

Geometric Constructions

The creation of designs usually involves the manipulation of geometric shapes. Traditionally, manual graphical construction used simple hand tools like a T-square, straightedge, scales, triangles, compass, dividers, pencils, and paper. The manual drafting tools are designed specifically to assist in the construction of geometric shapes. For example, the T-square and drafting machine can be used to construct parallel and perpendicular lines very easily and quickly. Today, modern CAD systems provide designers much better control and accuracy in the construction of geometric shapes.

In technical drawings, many of the geometric shapes are constructed with specific geometric properties, such as perpendicularity, parallelism and tangency. For example, in the drawing below, quite a few implied geometric properties are present.

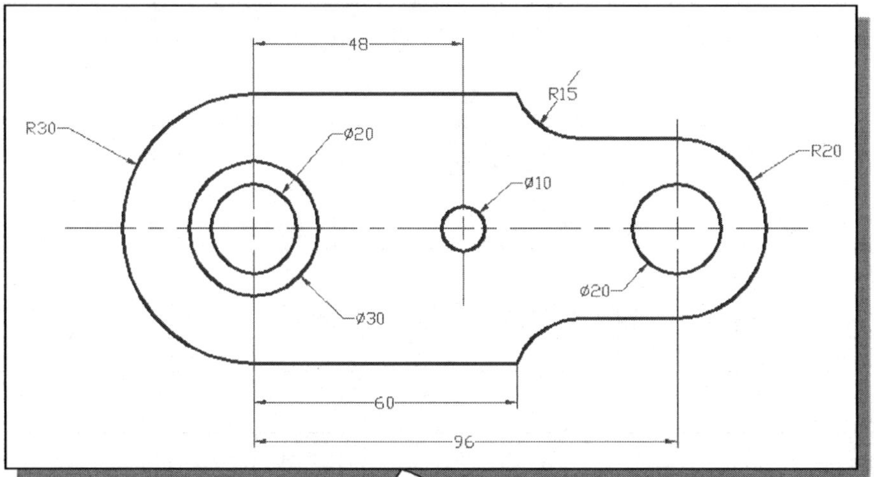

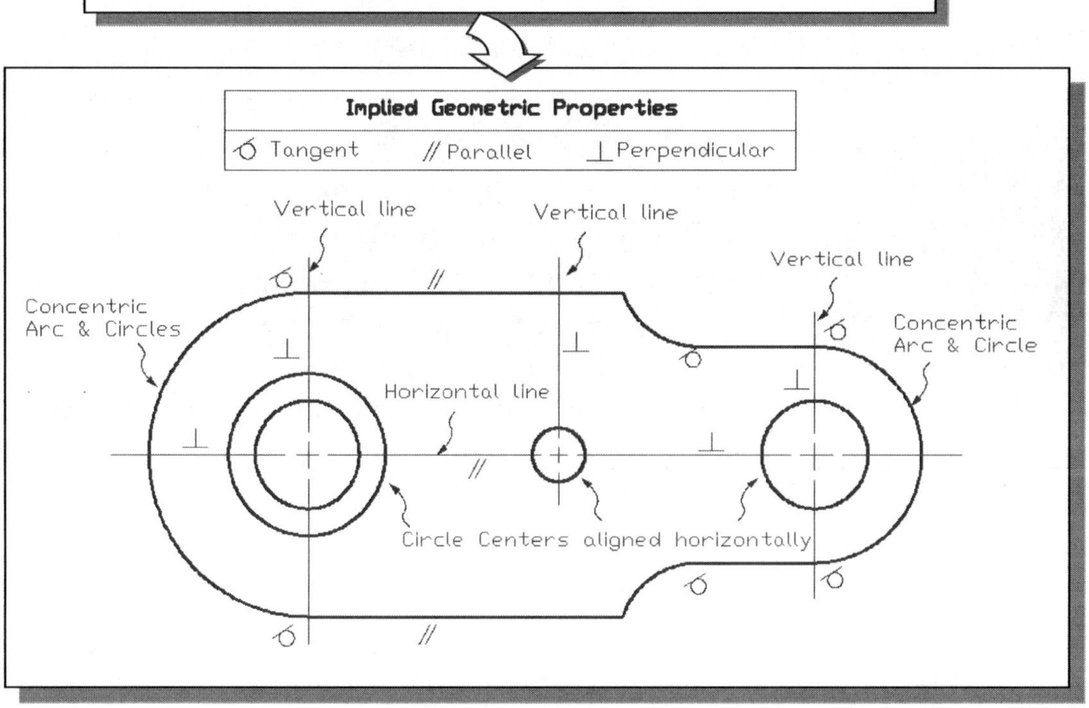

Starting Up AutoCAD 2027

1. Select the AutoCAD 2027 option on the *Program* menu or select the AutoCAD 2027 icon on the *Desktop*. Once the program is loaded into the memory, the **AutoCAD 2027** drawing screen will appear on the screen.

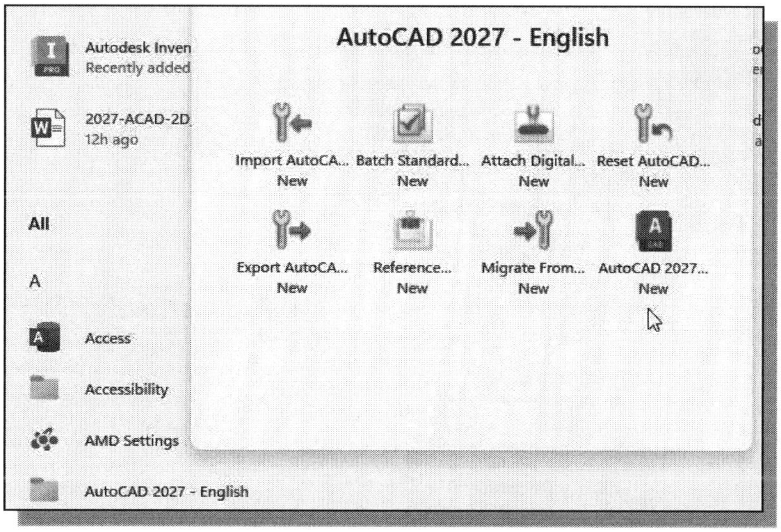

2. In the *Startup* window, select **Start from Scratch**, as shown in the figure below.

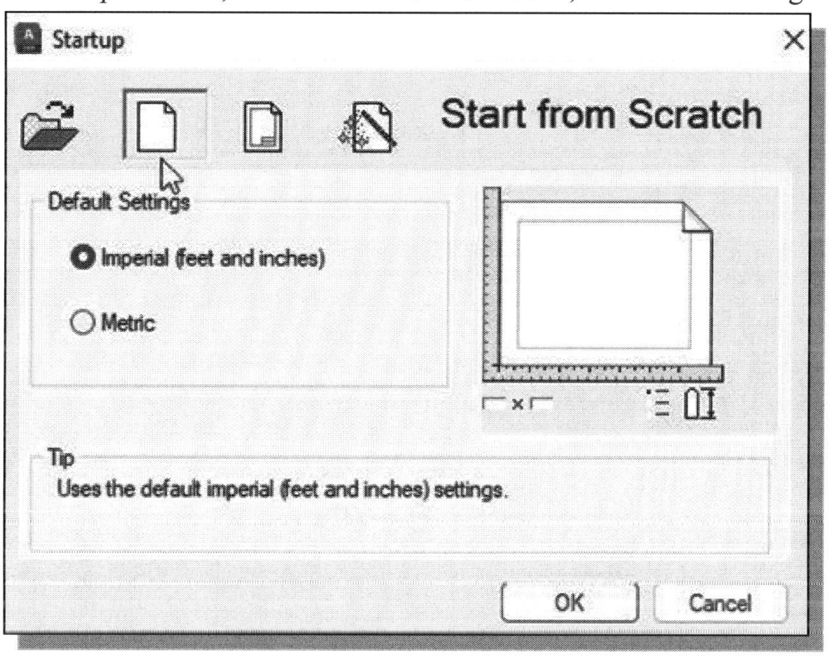

3. In the *Default Settings* section, pick **Imperial (feet and inches)** as the drawing units.

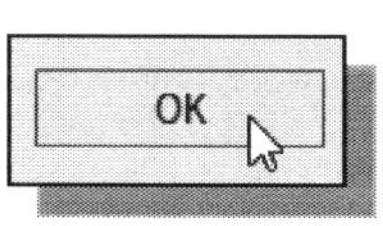

4. Pick **OK** in the *Startup* dialog box to accept the selected settings.

Geometric Construction – CAD Method

The main characteristic of any CAD system is its ability to create and modify 2D/3D geometric entities quickly and accurately. Most CAD systems provide a variety of object construction and editing tools to relieve the designer of the tedious drudgery of this task, so that the designer can concentrate more on design content. A good understanding of the computer geometric construction techniques will enable the CAD users to fully utilize the capability of the CAD systems.

➢ Note that with CAD systems, besides following the classic geometric construction methods, quite a few options are also feasible.

• Bisection of a Line or Arc

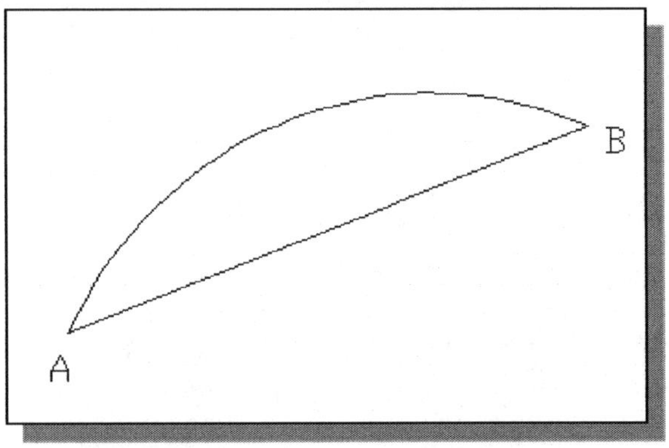

1. Create an arbitrary arc **AB** at any angle, and create line **AB** by connecting the two endpoints of the arc.

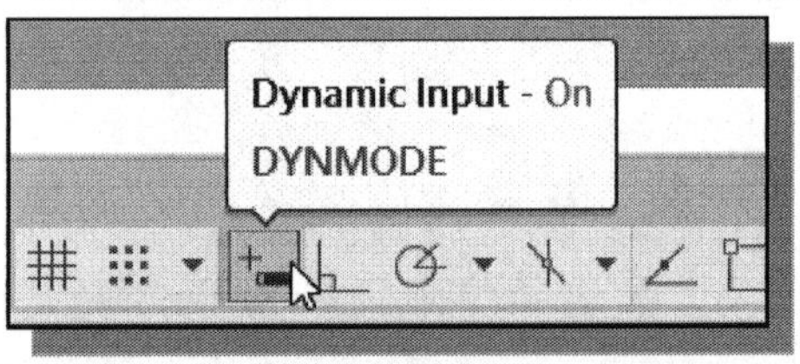

2. Switch ***ON*** only the *Dynamic Input* option by clicking on the buttons in the *Status Bar* area as shown.

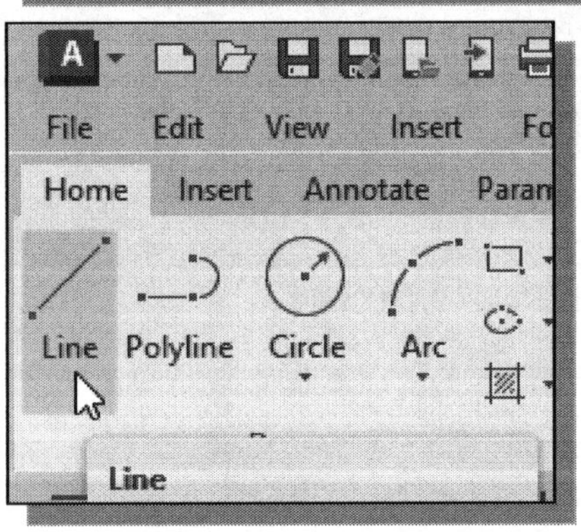

3. Select the **Line** command icon in the *Draw* toolbar. In the command prompt area, near the bottom of the AutoCAD drawing screen, the message "*_line Specify first point:*" is displayed. AutoCAD expects us to identify the starting location of a straight line.

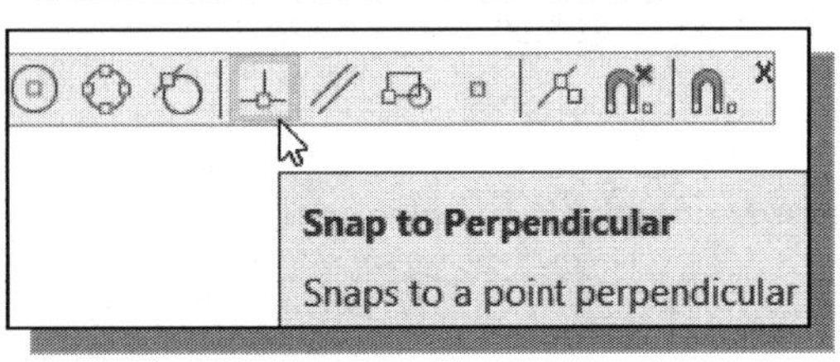

4. Pick **Snap to Perpendicular** in the *Object Snap* toolbar. In the command prompt area, the message "*_per to*" is displayed.

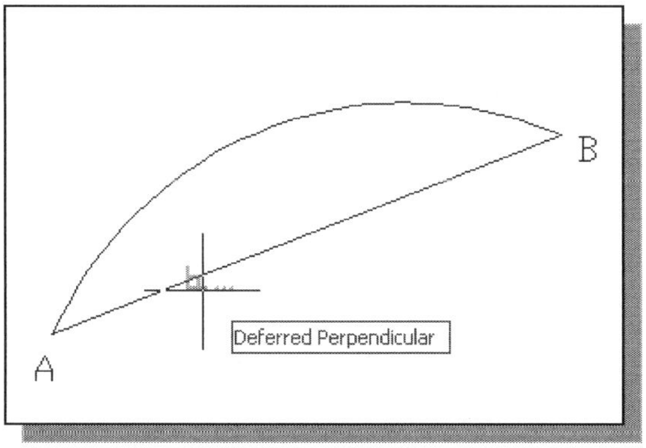

5. Select line **AB** at any position.

❖ Note the displayed tooltip ***Deferred Perpendicular*** indicates the construction is deferred until all inputs are completed.

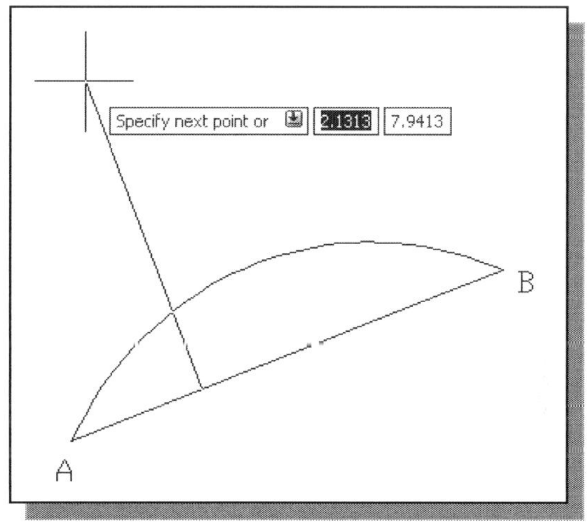

6. Select an arbitrary point above the line as shown.

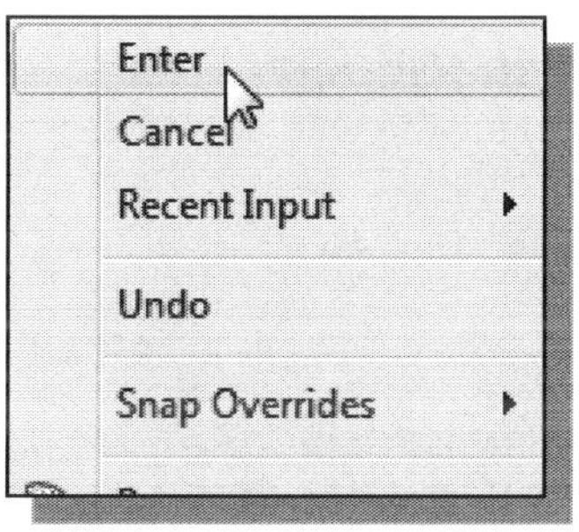

7. Inside the *Drawing Area*, **right-click** to activate the option menu and select **Enter** with the left-mouse-button to end the Line command.

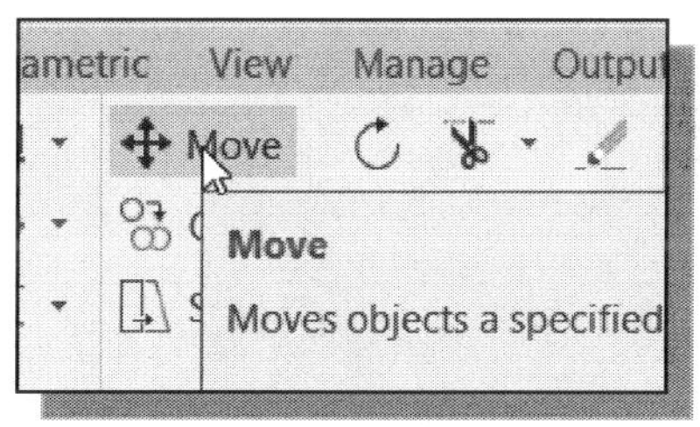

8. Select **Move** in the *Modify* toolbar as shown.

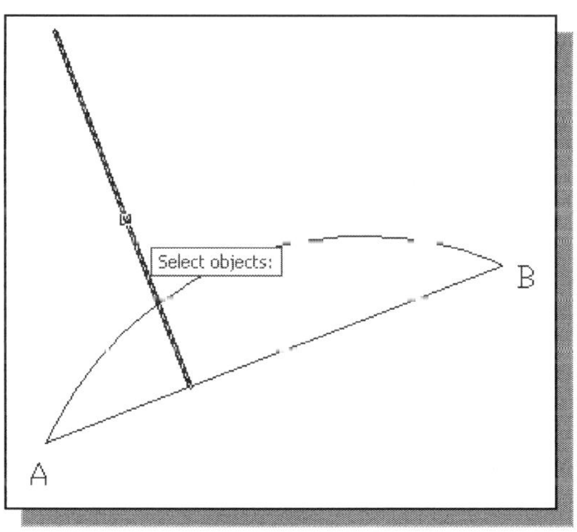

9. Select the **perpendicular line** we just created.

❖ In the *command prompt area*, the message "*Specify the base point or [Displacement]*" is displayed. AutoCAD expects us to select a reference point as the base point for moving the selected object.

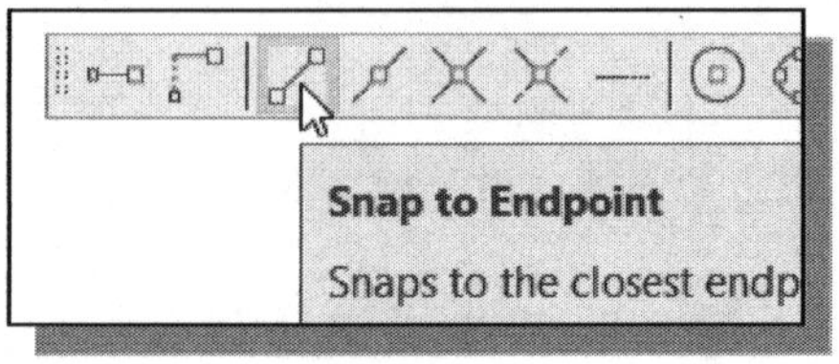

10. Pick **Snap to Endpoint** in the *Object Snap* toolbar.

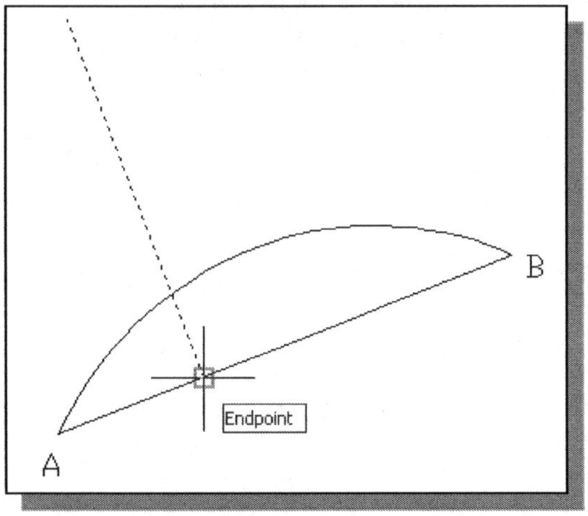

11. Select the lower **Endpoint** of the selected line as shown.

12. Move the cursor inside the Drawing Area, and notice the line is moved to the new cursor location on the screen.

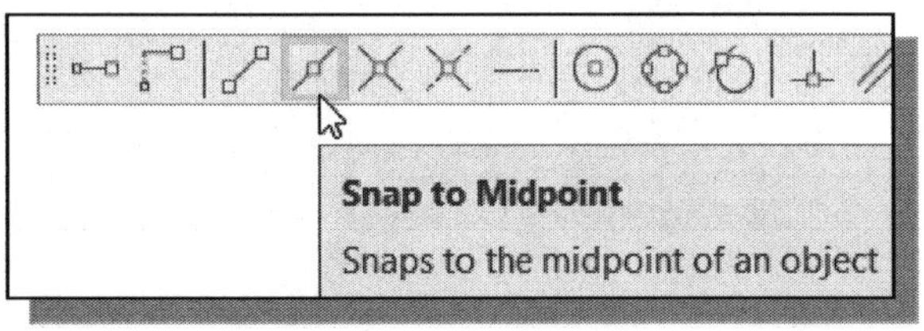

13. Pick **Snap to Midpoint** in the *Object Snap* toolbar.

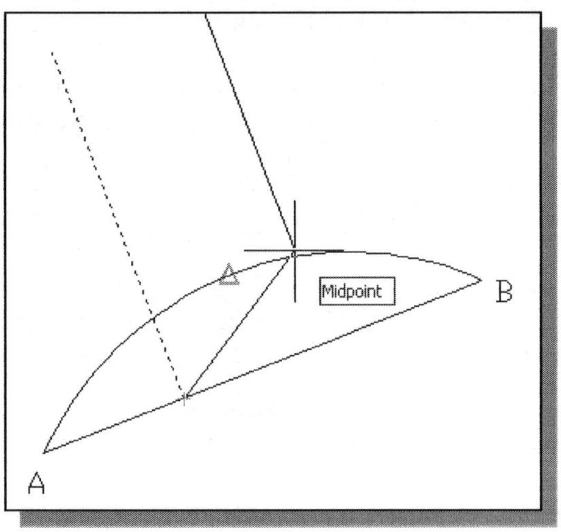

❖ In the command prompt area, the message "*_mid to*" is displayed. AutoCAD now expects us to select an existing arc or line on the screen.

14. Select the arc to move the line to the midpoint of the arc. Note that the midpoint of an arc or a line is displayed when the cursor is on top of the object.

15. On your own, repeat the above process and move the perpendicular line to the midpoint of line **AB**.

➢ The constructed bisecting line is perpendicular to line **AB** and passes through the midpoint of the line or arc **AB**.

• Bisection of an Angle

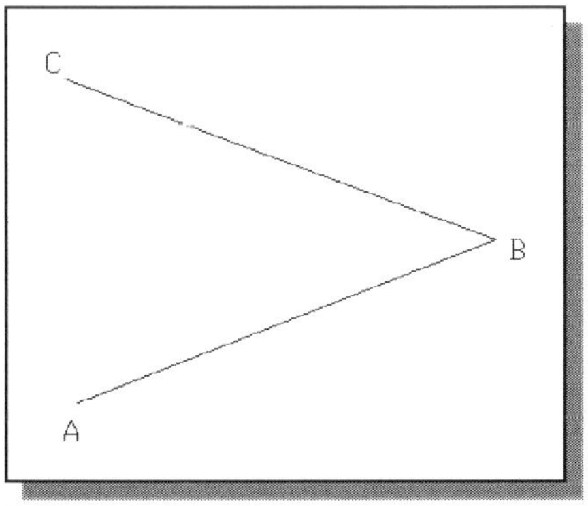

1. Create an arbitrary angle **ABC** as shown in the figure.

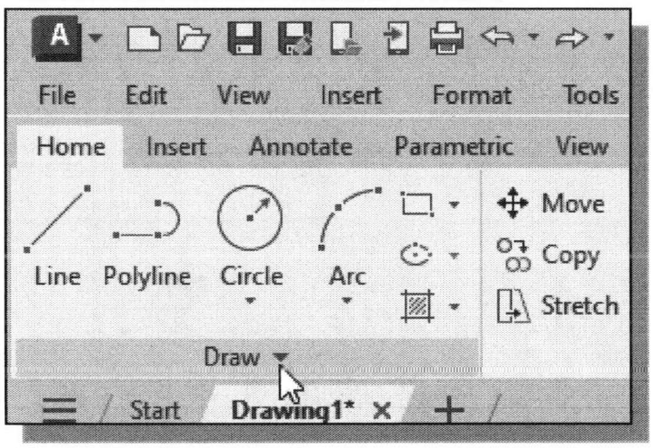

2. Click once with the left-mouse-button on the small triangle in the titlebar of the *Draw* toolbar as shown.

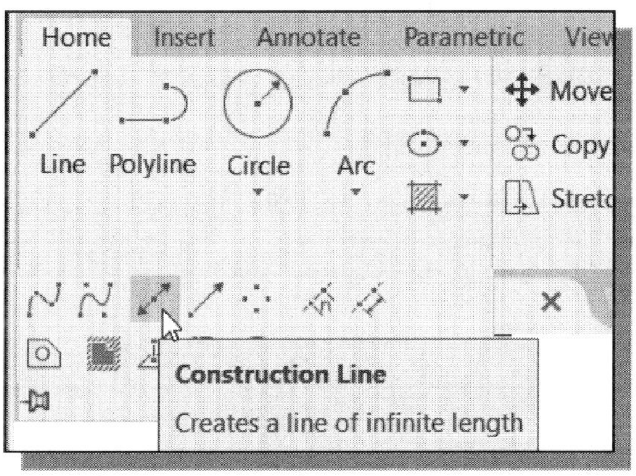

3. Select the **Construction Line** icon in the *Draw* toolbar. In the *command prompt area*, the message "*_xline Specify a point or [Hor/Ver/Ang/Bisect/ Offset]:*" is displayed.

➢ *Construction lines* are lines that extend to infinity. Construction lines are usually used as references for creating other objects.

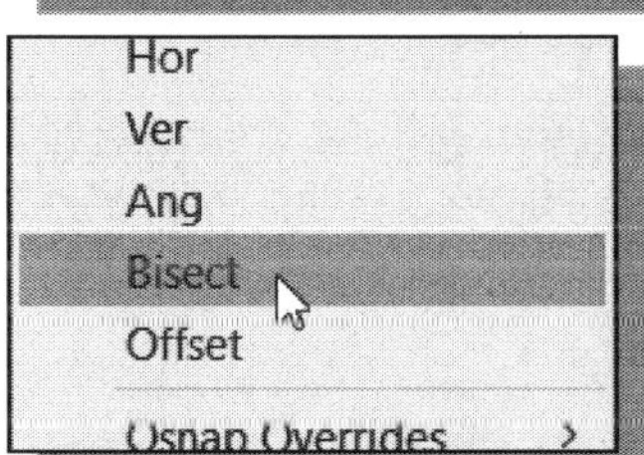

4. Inside the *Drawing Area*, **right-click** once to bring up the option menu.

5. Select **Bisect** from the option list as shown. In the command prompt area, the message "*Specify angle vertex point.*" is displayed.

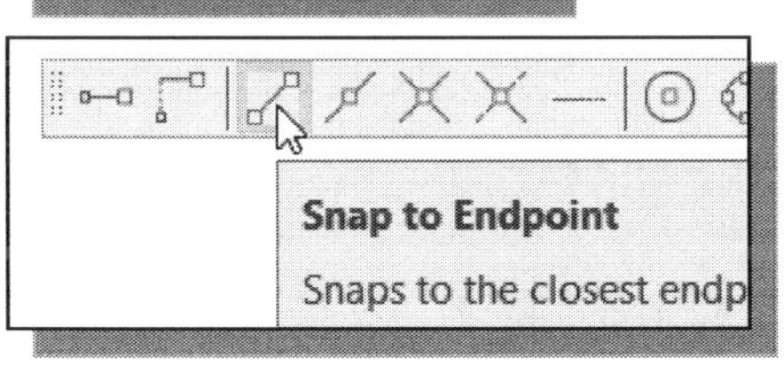

6. Pick **Snap to Endpoint** in the *Object Snap* toolbar.

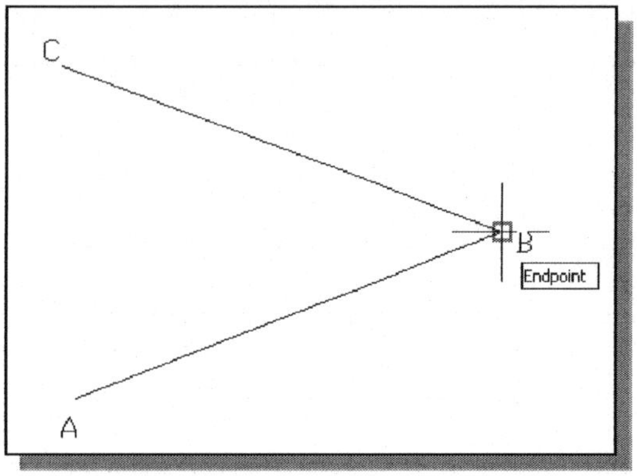

7. Select the vertex point of the angle as shown. In the command prompt area, the message "*Specify angle start point:*" is displayed.

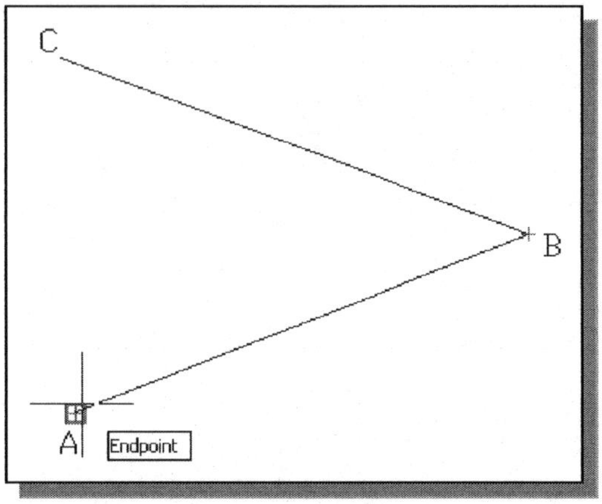

8. Pick **Snap to Endpoint** in the *Object Snap* toolbar.

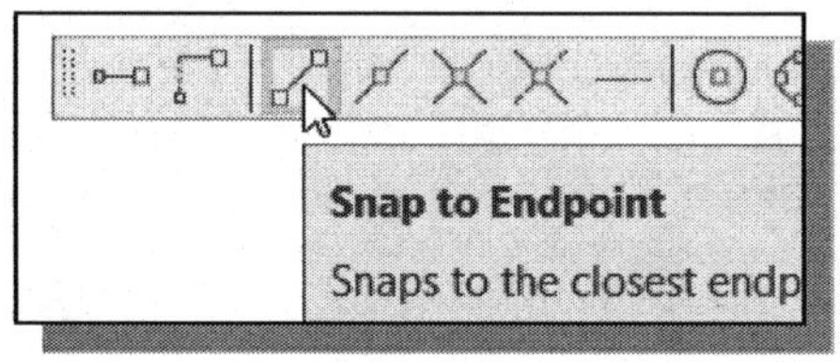

9. Select one of the endpoints, point A or C, of the angle.

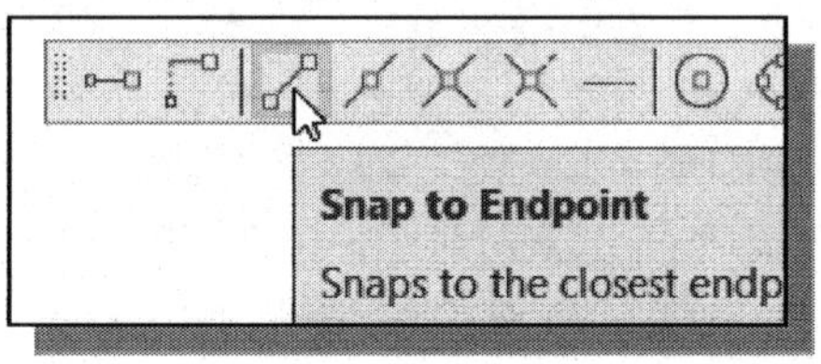

10. Pick **Snap to Endpoint** in the *Object Snap* toolbar.

11. Select the other endpoint of the angle.

➢ Note that the constructed bisection line divides the angle into two equal parts.

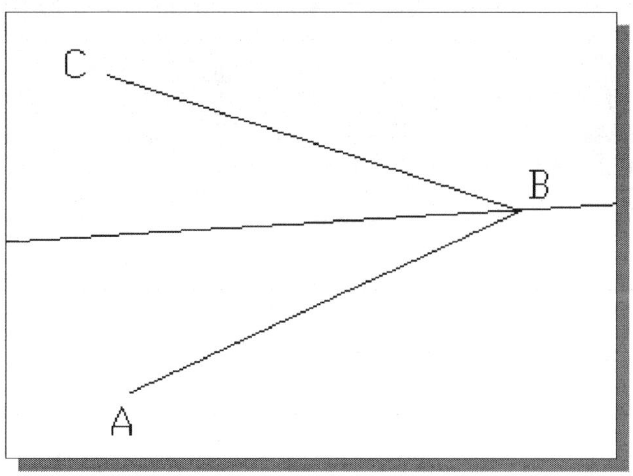

- ## Transfer of an Angle

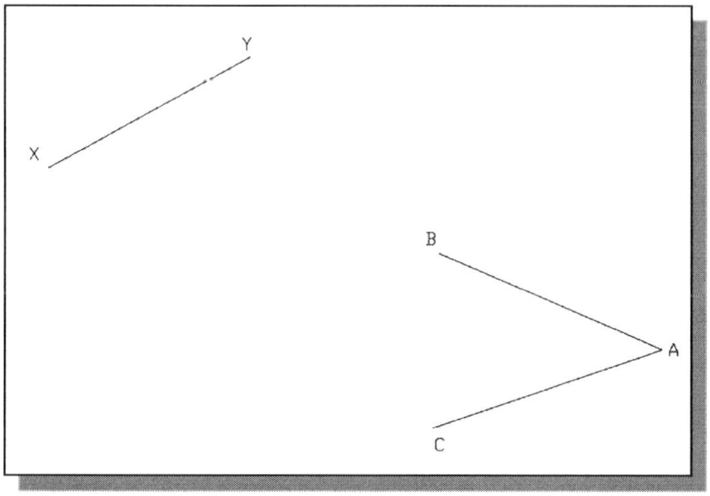

1. Create an arbitrary angle **ABC** and a separate line **XY** as shown in the figure.

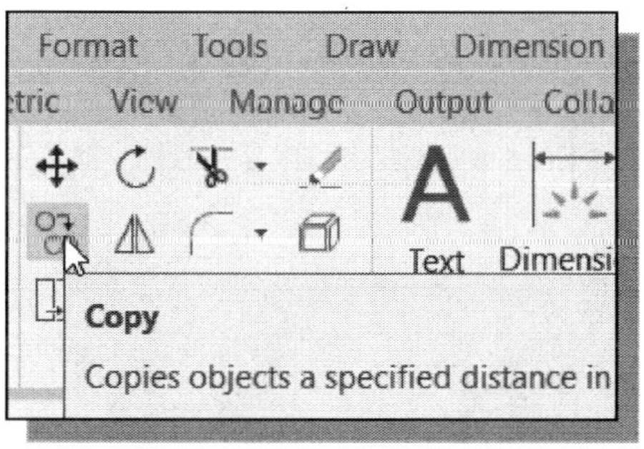

2. Select **Copy** in the *Modify* toolbar as shown.

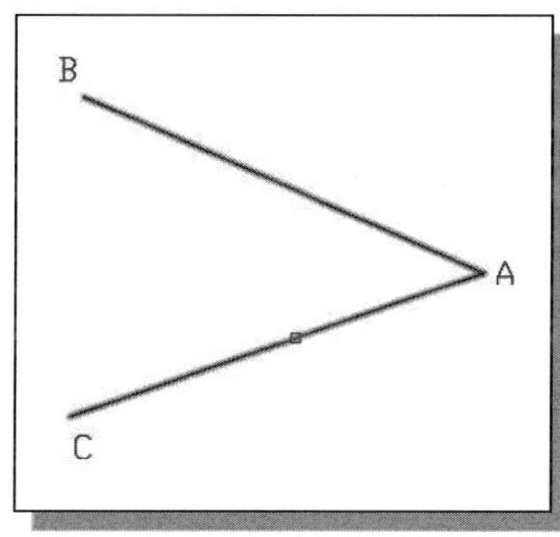

3. Select line AB and AC as the objects to be copied.

4. **Right-click** once to proceed with the Copy command.

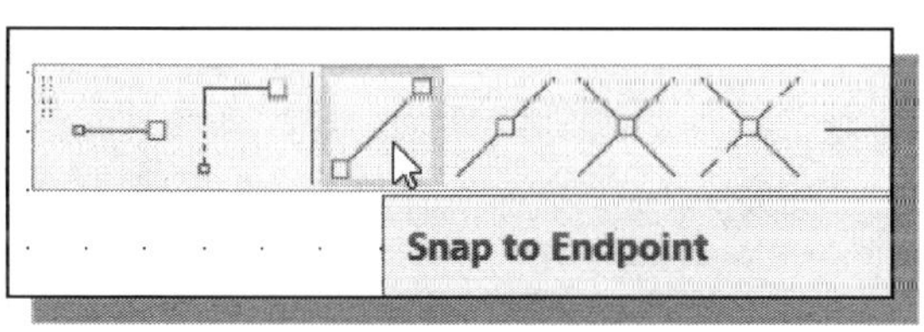

5. Pick **Snap to Endpoint** in the *Object Snap* toolbar.

6. Select point **A** as the base point.

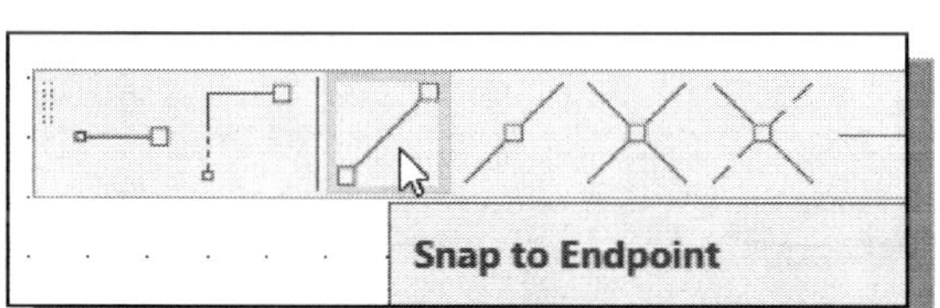

7. Pick **Snap to Endpoint** in the *Object Snap* toolbar.

8. Select point **X** to place the copied lines.

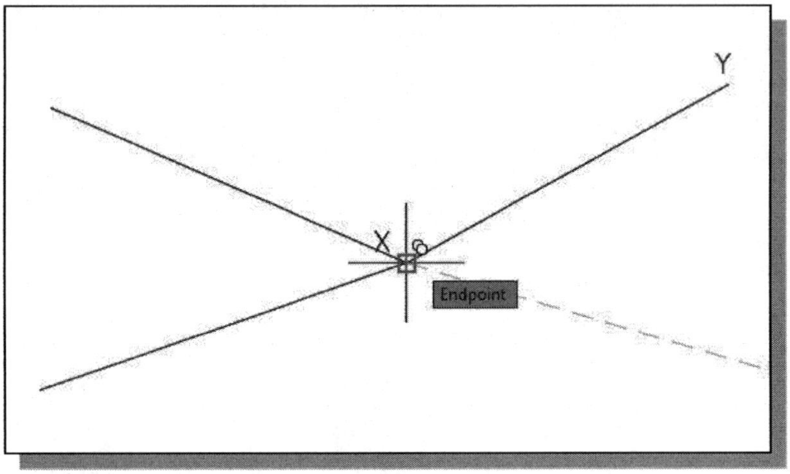

9. Hit the **ENTER** key once to end the **Copy** command.

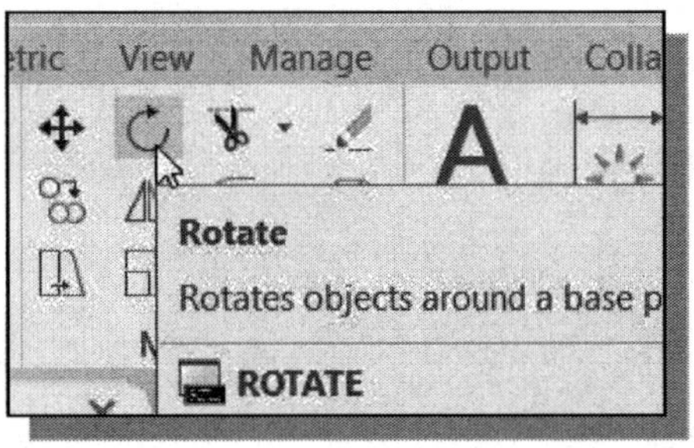

10. Select **Rotate** in the *Modify* toolbar as shown.

11. Select the two lines to the left of **X**.

12. **Right-click** once to proceed with the **Rotate** command.

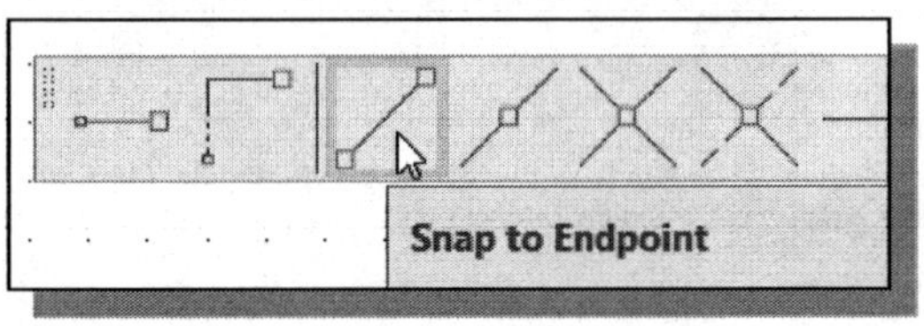

13. Pick **Snap to Endpoint** in the *Object Snap* toolbar.

14. Select point **X** as the base point for the rotation.

15. Inside the *Drawing Area*, **right-click** once to bring up the option menu.

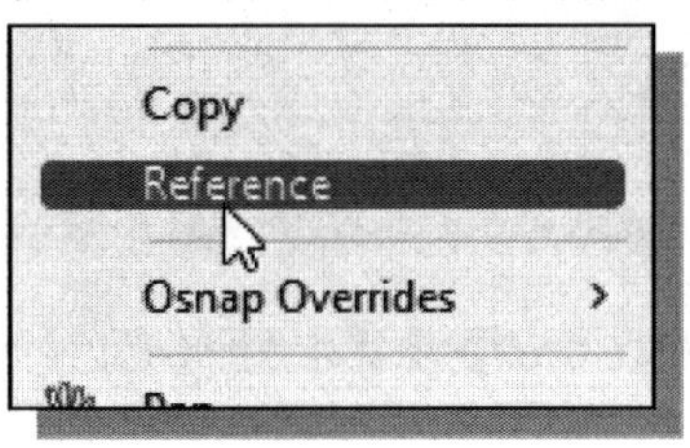

16. Select **Reference** in the option menu as shown.

17. Select point **X** as the first point.

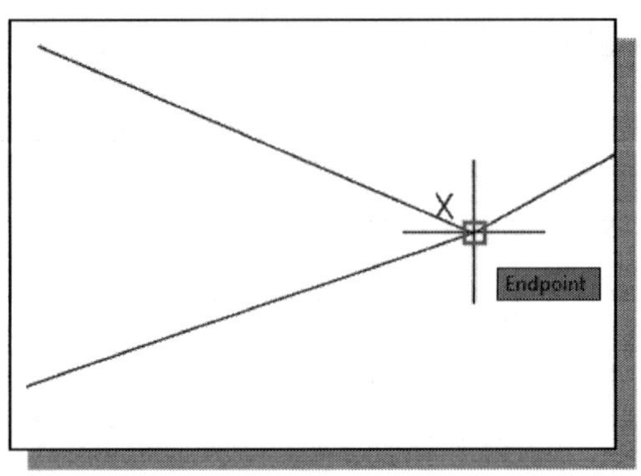

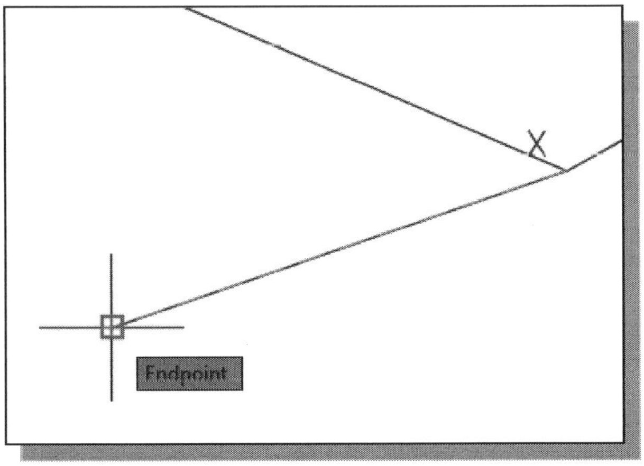

18. Select the left end point of the bottom line as shown.

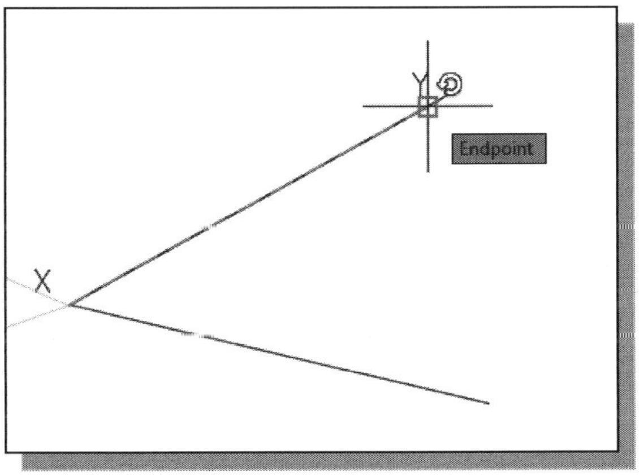

19. Select **Point Y** to align the lines as shown.

➢ Note the **angle** has been transferred to align to the XY line.

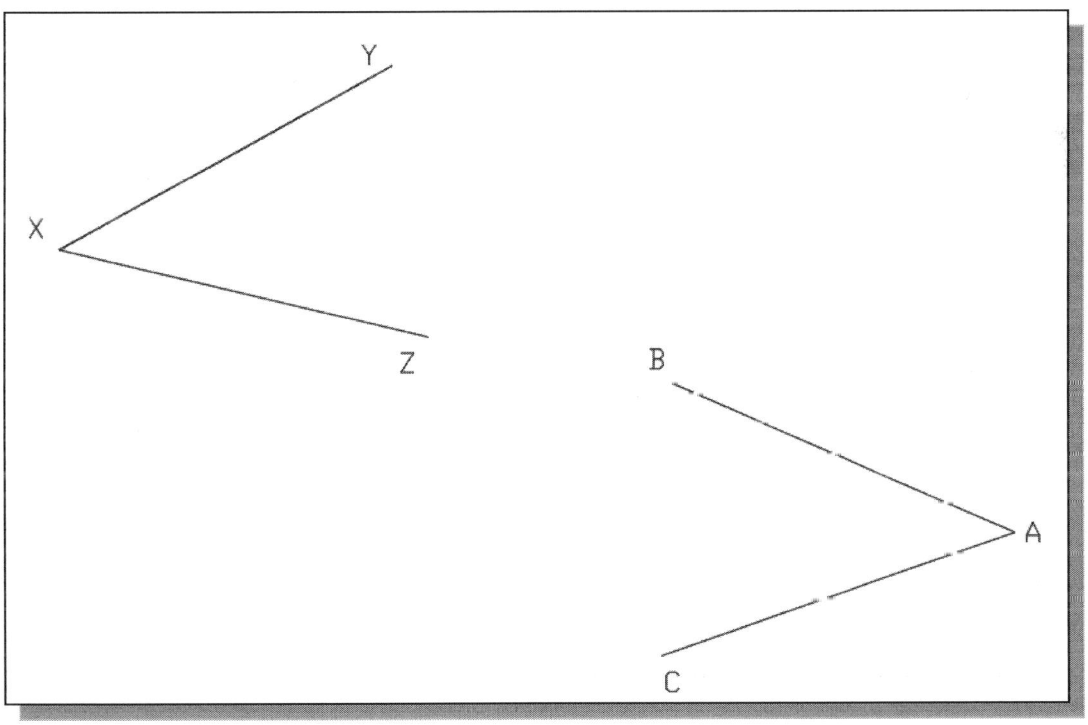

• Dividing a Given Line into a Number of Equal Parts

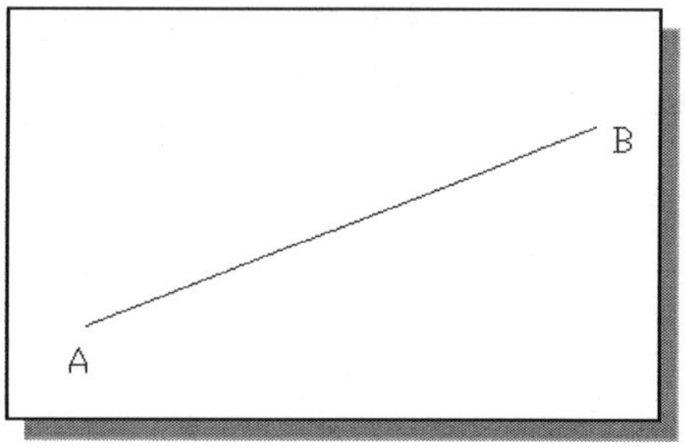

1. Create a line **AB** at an arbitrary angle; the line is to be divided into five equal parts.

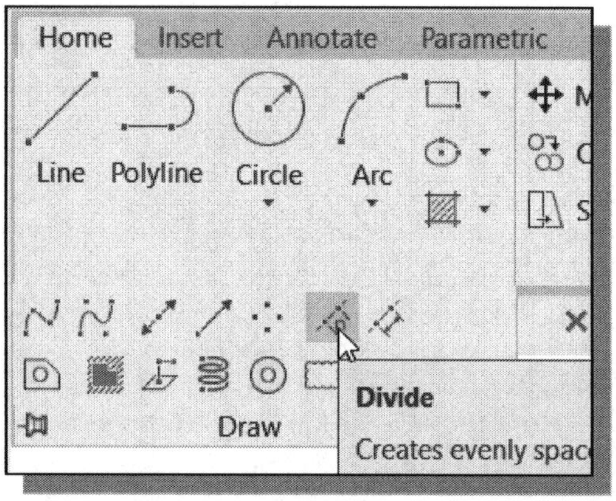

2. In the *Ribbon* toolbar, under *Draw*, select:

   [Divide]

3. Select line **AB**. In the message area, the message “*Enter the number of segments or [Block]:*” is displayed.

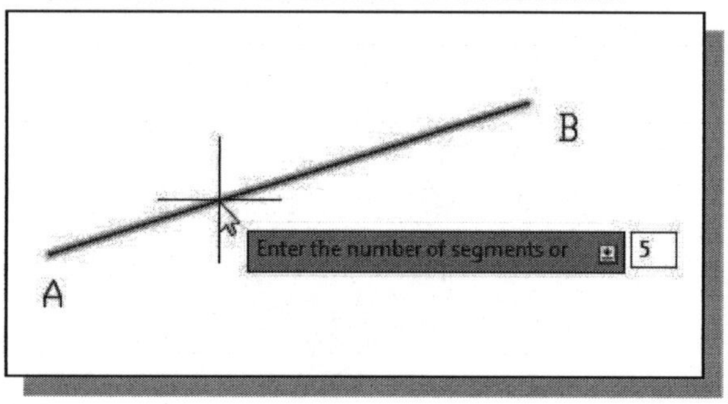

4. Enter **5** as the number of segments needed.

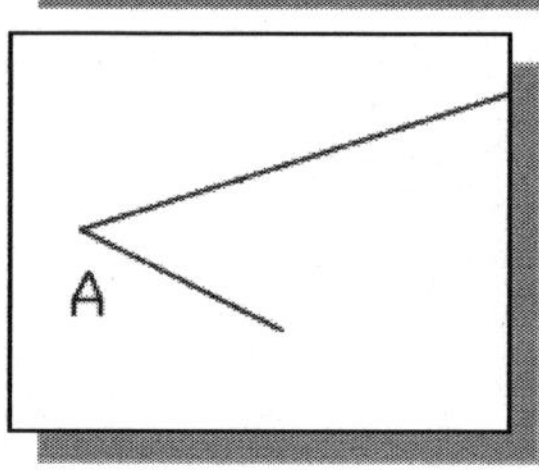

5. On your own, create an arbitrary short line segment at point **A**.

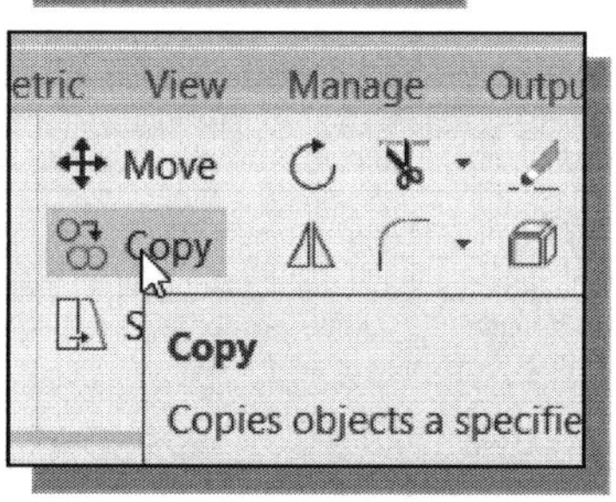

6. Select **Copy** in the *Modify* toolbar as shown.

7. Select the **short line** as the object to be copied.

8. **Right-click** once to proceed with the Copy command.

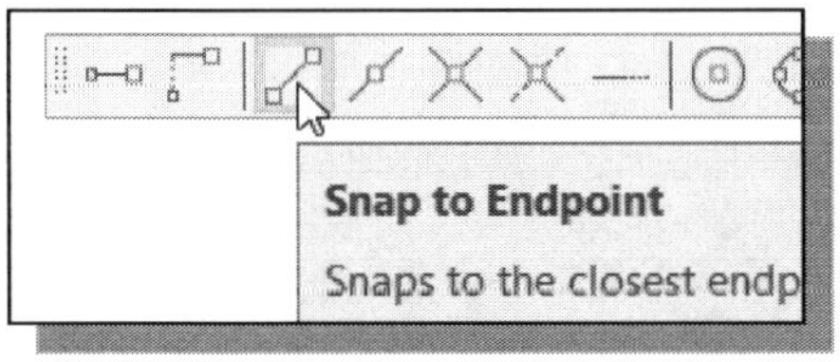

9. Pick **Snap to Endpoint** in the *Object Snap* toolbar.

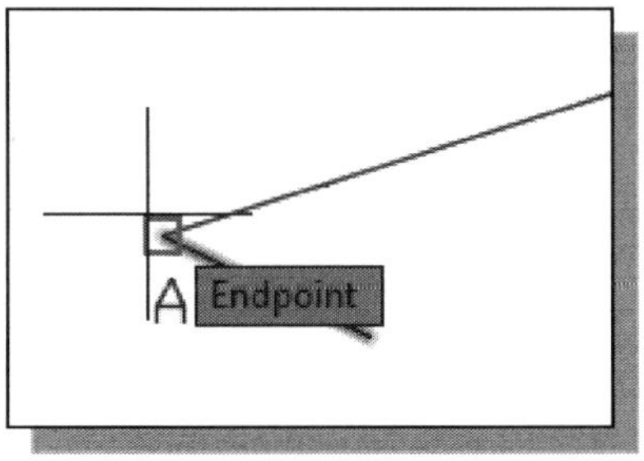

10. **Select** point **A** as the base reference point.

11. Pick **Snap to Node** in the *Object Snap* toolbar.

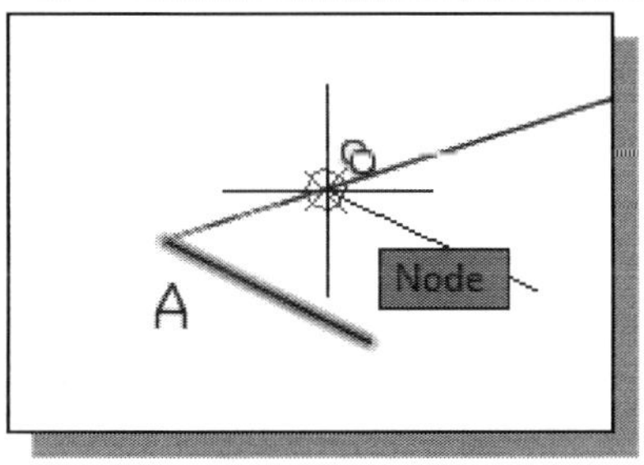

12. Move the cursor along line **AB** and select the next node point as shown.

13. Repeat the above steps and create 3 additional lines at the nodes indicating the division of the line into five equal parts.

➢ We can also change the display of the created Points.

14. In the *Menu Bar*, select:

[Format] → [Point Style]

15. In the *Point Style* window, choose the 4th icon in the second row, as shown.

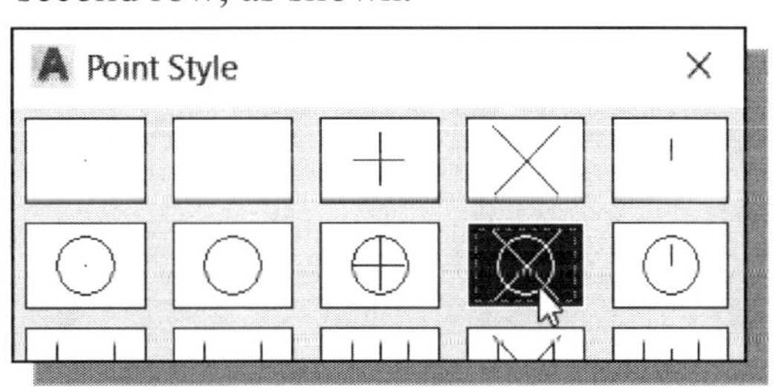

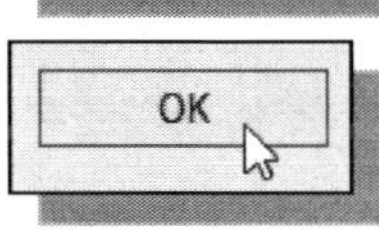

16. Click **OK** to accept the selection and adjust the point style.

• Circle through Three Points

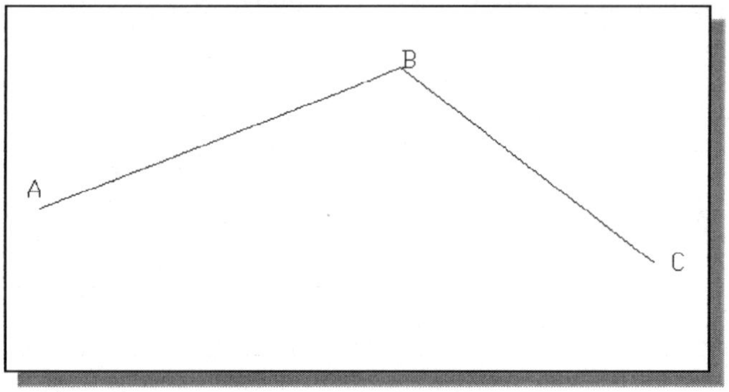

1. Create two arbitrary line segments, **AB** and **BC**, as shown.

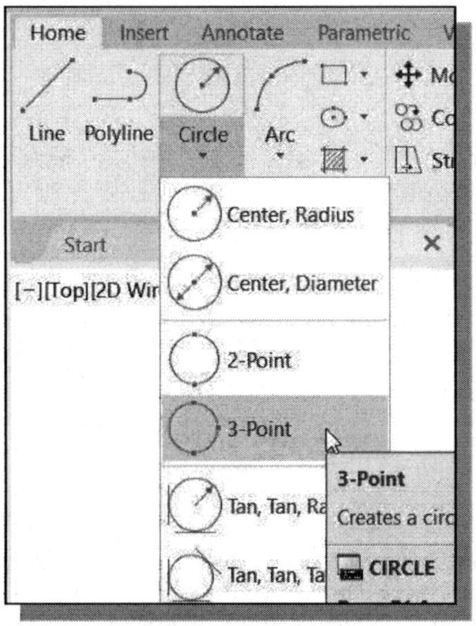

2. Select the **3-Point Circle** command in the *Draw* toolbar as shown.

3. Pick **Snap to Endpoint** in the *Object Snap* toolbar.

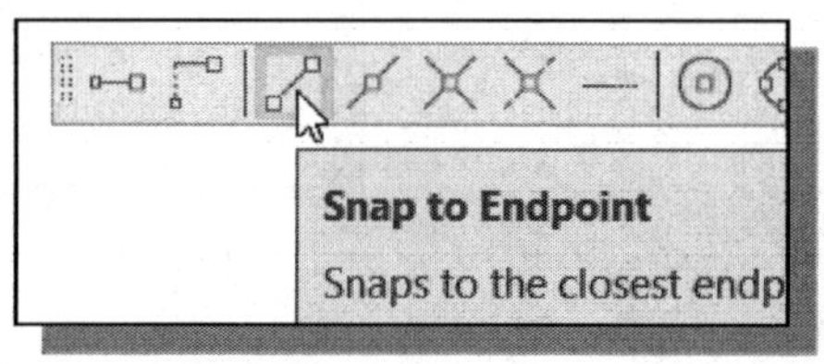

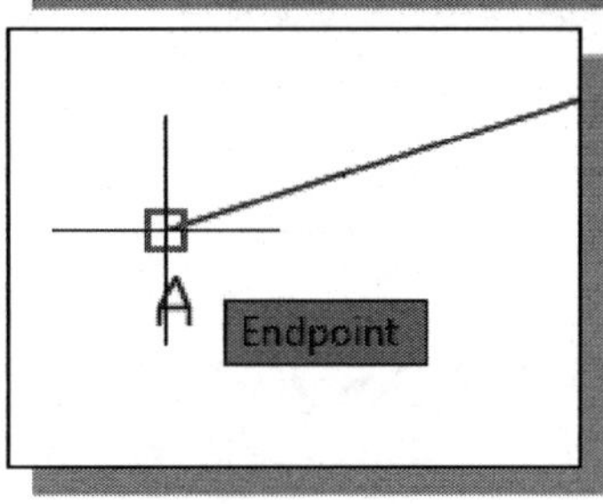

4. Select the first point, point **A**.

5. Repeat the above steps and select points **B** and **C** to create the circle that passes through all three points.

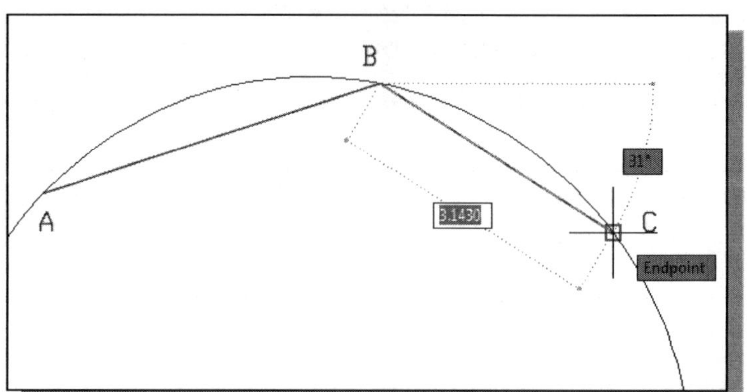

- ## Line Tangent to a Circle from a Given Point

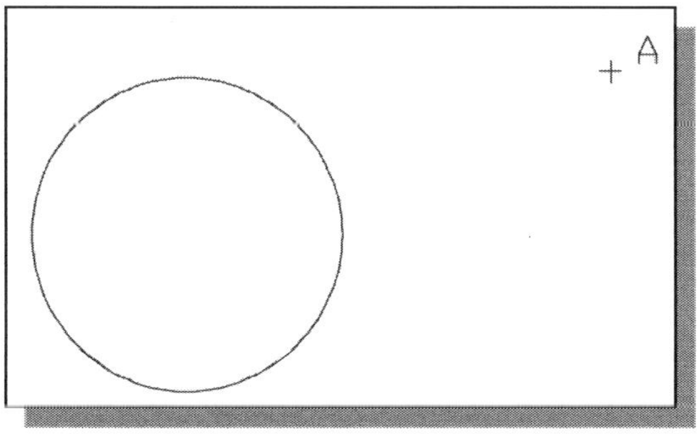

1. Create a circle and a point **A**. (Use the **Point** command to create point **A**.)

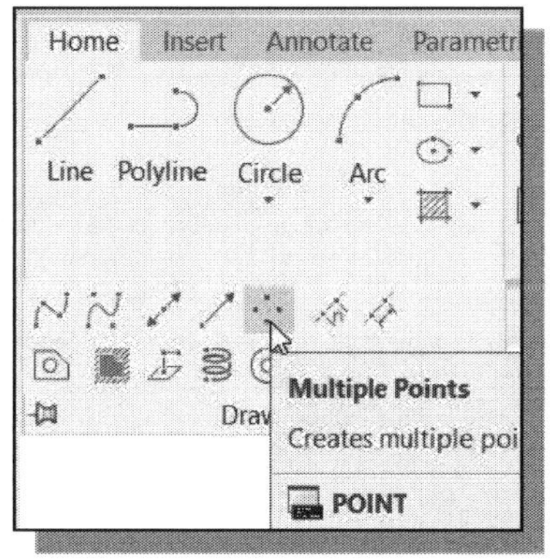

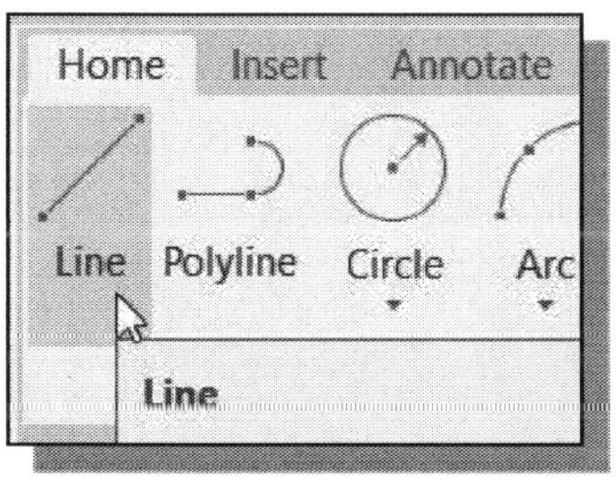

2. Select the **Line** command icon in the *Draw* toolbar. In the command prompt area, near the bottom of the AutoCAD drawing screen, the message "*_line Specify first point:*" is displayed. AutoCAD expects us to identify the starting location of a straight line.

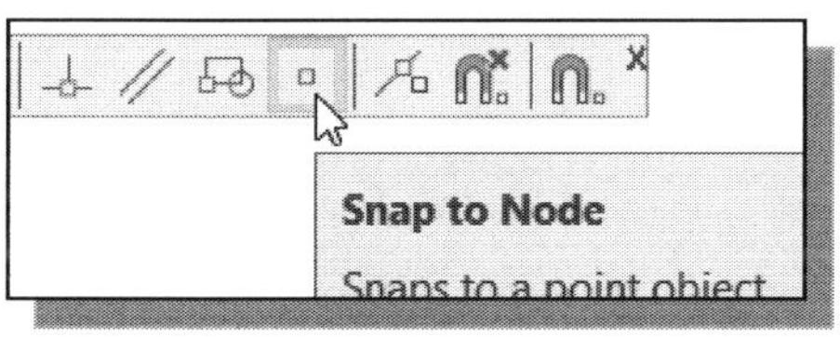

3. Pick **Snap to Node** in the *Object Snap* toolbar.

4. Select point **A** as the starting point of the new line.

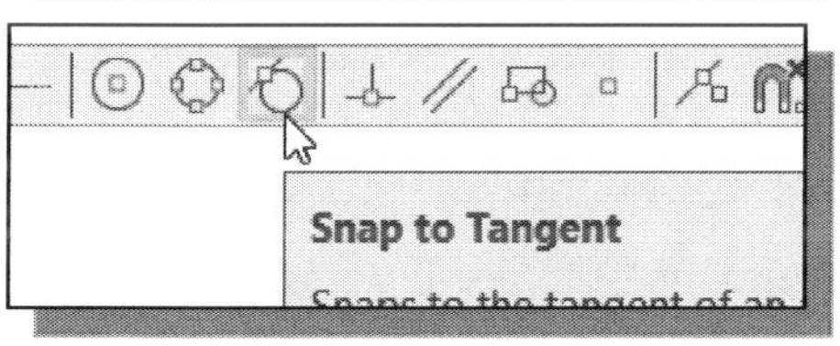

5. Pick **Snap to Tangent** in the *Object Snap* toolbar.

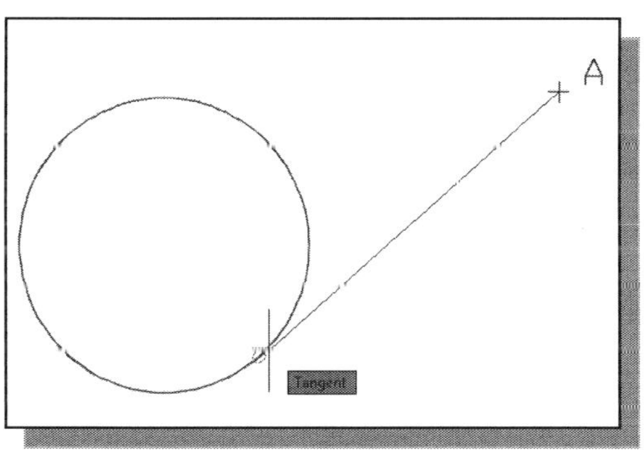

6. Move the cursor on top of the circle and notice the **Tangent** symbol is displayed.

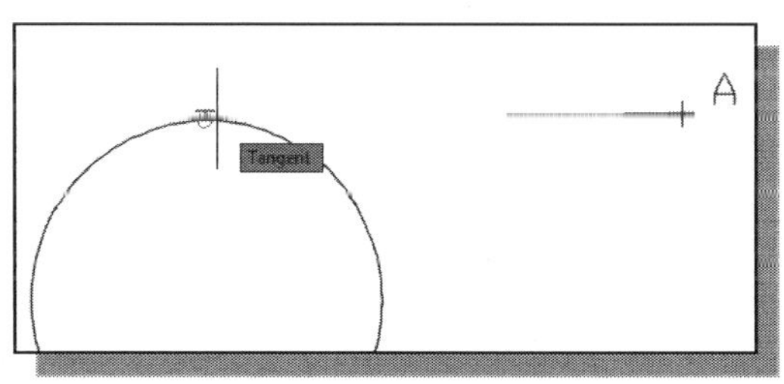

➢ Note that we can create two tangent lines, one to the top and one to the bottom of the circle, from point **A**.

• Circle of a Given Radius Tangent to Two Given Lines

Option I: TTR circle

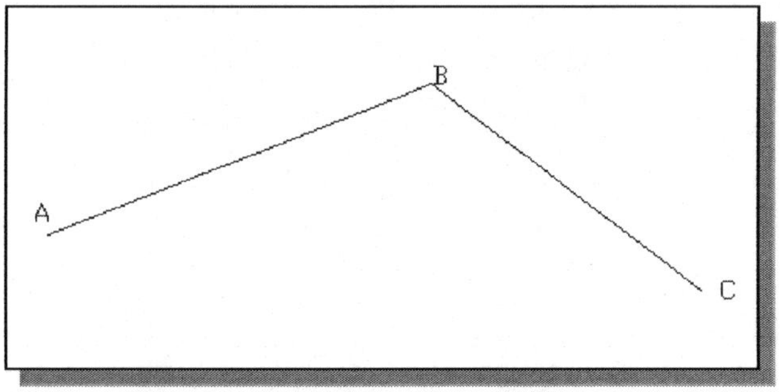

1. Create two arbitrary line segments as shown.

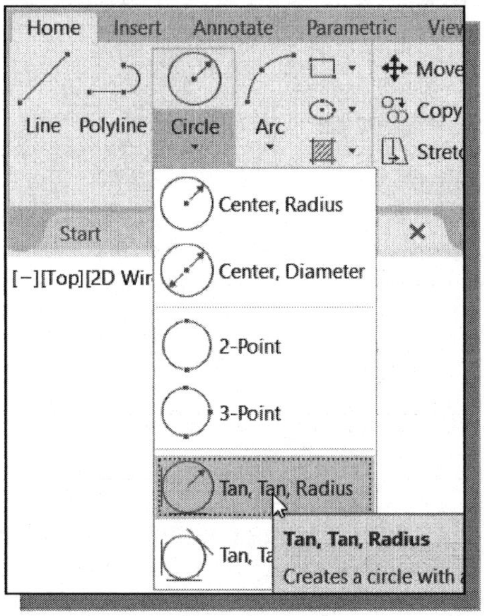

2. Select **TTR Circle** in the *Draw* toolbar as shown.

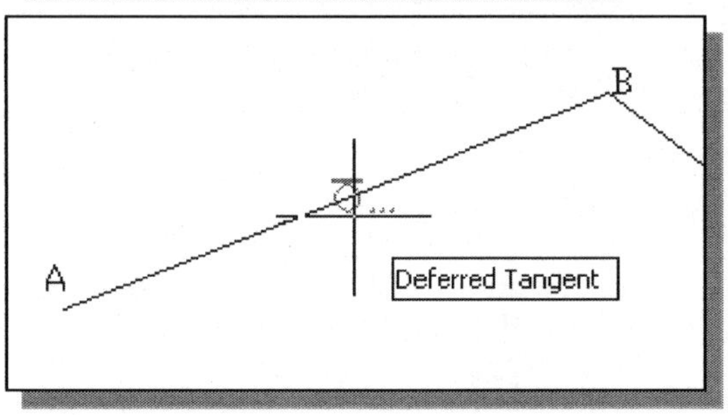

3. Select one of the line segments; note the tangency is deferred until all inputs are completed.

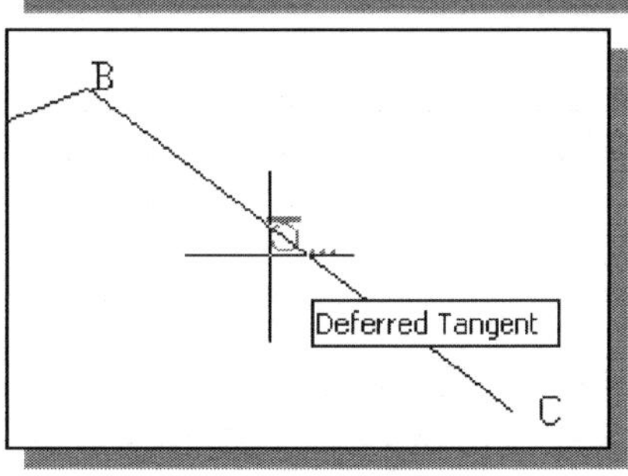

4. Select the other line segment; note the tangency is also deferred until all inputs are completed.

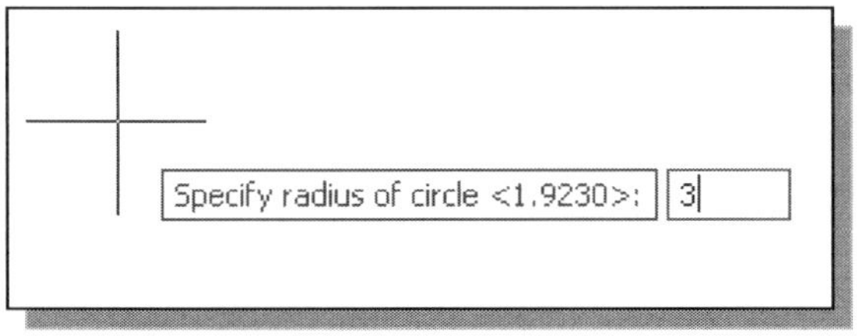

5. Enter ***3*** as the radius of the circle.

➢ The circle is constructed exactly tangent to both lines.

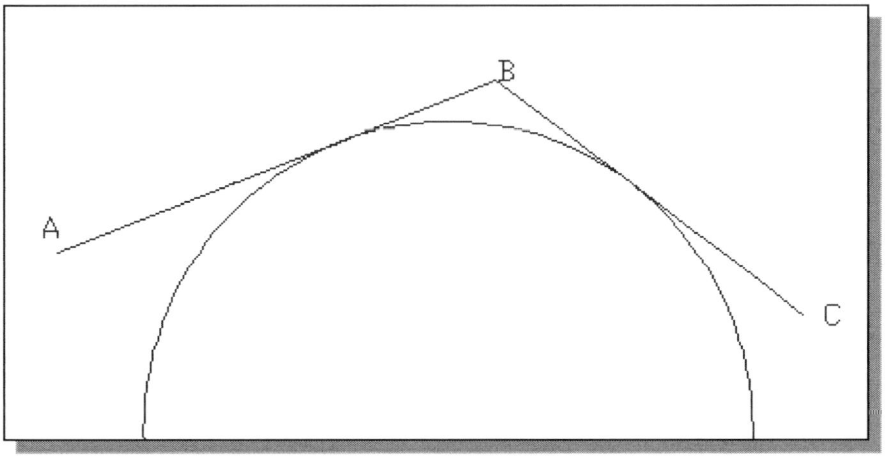

Option II: Fillet Command

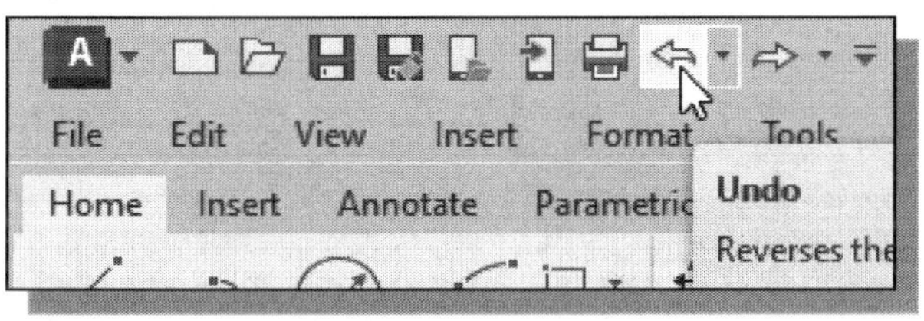

1. Select the **Undo** icon in the *Standard* toolbar as shown. This will undo the last step, the circle.

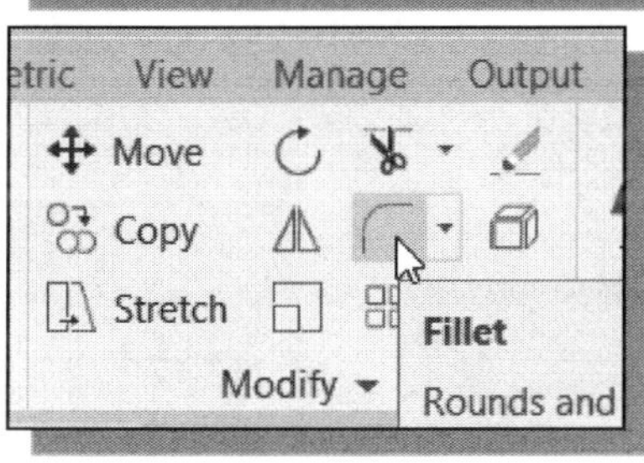

2. Select **Fillet** in the *Modify* toolbar as shown.

3. In the command prompt area, the message "*Select first object or [Undo/Polyline/Radius/Trim/Multiple]*" is displayed. By default, *Mode* is set to **Trim** and the current arc *Radius* is set to **0**.

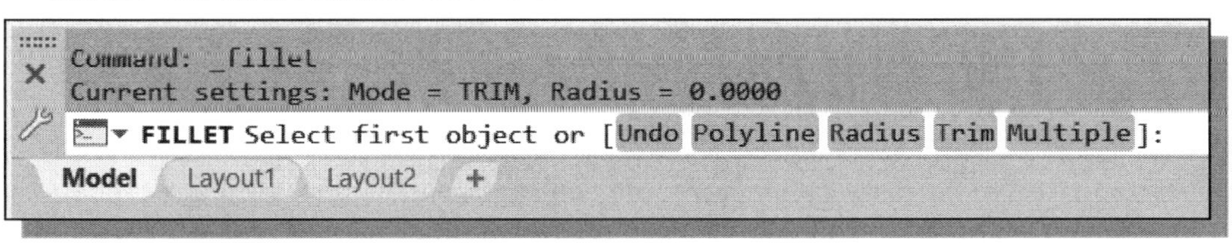

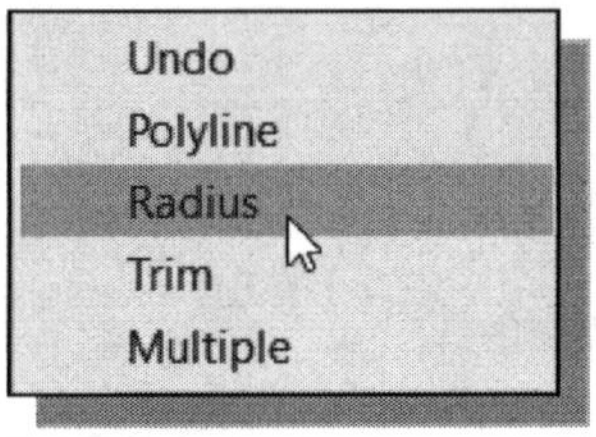

4. Inside the Drawing Area, **right-click** once to bring up the option menu.

5. Select **Radius** to adjust the radius of the fillet.

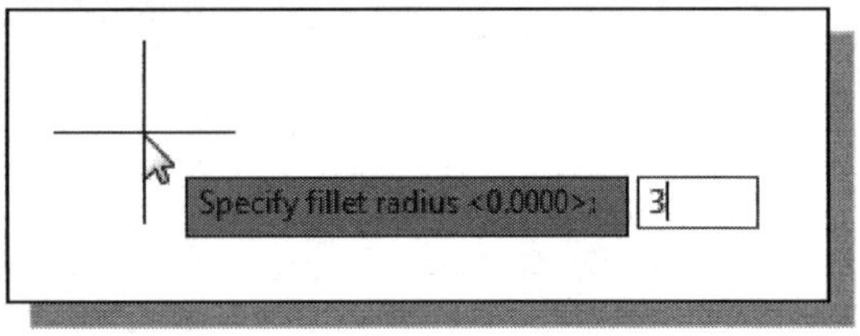

6. Enter ***3*** as the new radius of the Fillet command.

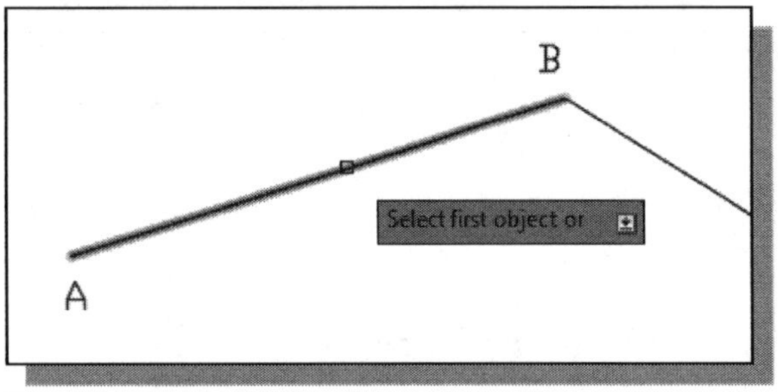

7. Select one of the lines as the first object.

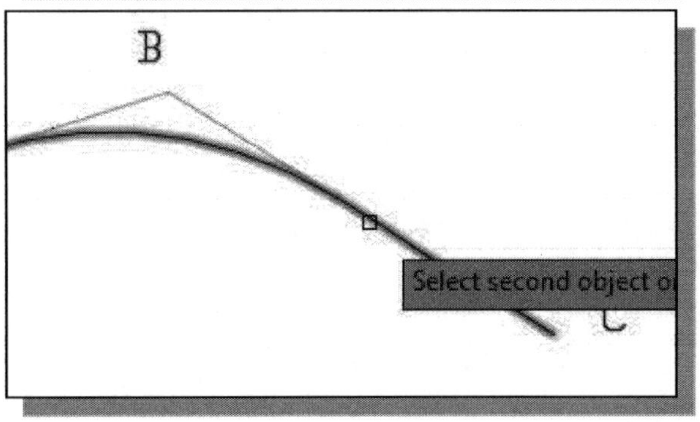

8. Select the other line as the second object.

➤ Note that the default setting of the Fillet command is to trim the edges as shown in the figure below.

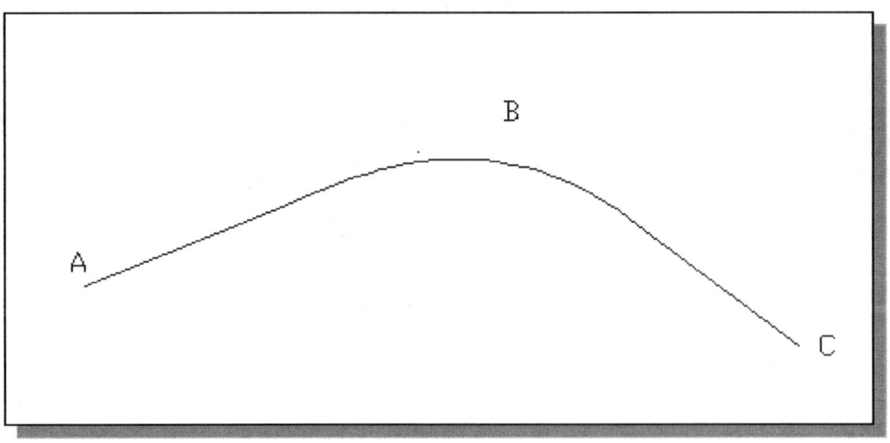

- Note that all of the classical methods for geometric construction, such as the one shown on page 3-14, are also applicable in CAD systems.

The Gasket Design

Exploring the possibilities of a CAD system can be very exciting. For persons who have board drafting experience, the transition from the drafting board to the computer does require some adjustment. However, the essential skills required to work in front of a computer are not that much different from those needed for board drafting. In fact, many of the basic skills acquired in board drafting can also be applied to a computer system. For example, the geometric construction techniques that are typically used in board drafting can be used in AutoCAD. The main difference between using a CAD system over the traditional board drafting is the ability to create and modify geometric entities very quickly and accurately. As was illustrated in the previous sections, a variety of object construction and editing tools, which are available in AutoCAD, are fairly easy to use. It is important to emphasize that a good understanding of the geometric construction fundamentals remains the most important part of using a CAD system. The application of the basic geometric construction techniques is one of the main tasks in using a CAD system.

In the following sections, we will continue to examine more of the geometric construction and editing tools provided by **AutoCAD 2027**. We will be looking at the geometric construction tools, such as Trim, Extend, Edit Polyline and Offset, which are available in **AutoCAD 2027**.

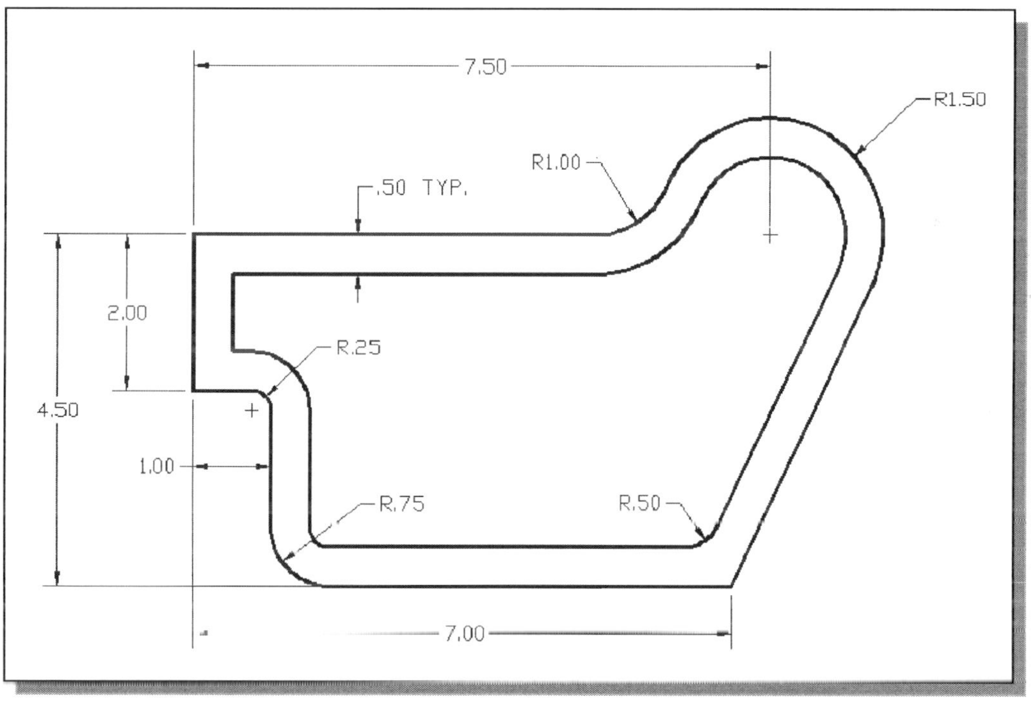

❖ Before continuing to the next page, on your own make a rough sketch showing the steps that can be used to create the design. Be aware that there are many different approaches to accomplishing the same task.

Drawing Units Display Setup

Before creating the first geometric entity, the value of the units within the CAD system should be determined. For example, in one drawing, a unit might equal one millimeter of the real-world object. In another drawing, a unit might equal an inch. The unit type and number of decimal places for object lengths and angles can be set through the **UNITS** command. These *drawing unit settings* control how AutoCAD interprets the coordinate and angle entries and how it displays coordinates and units in the *Status Bar* and in the dialog boxes.

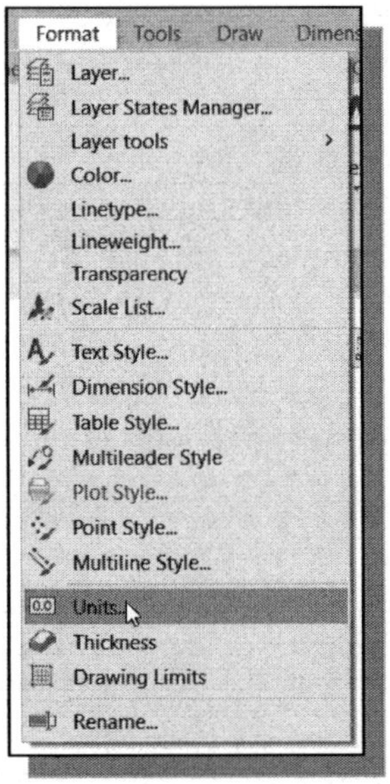

1. In the *Menu Bar* select:

   [Format] → [Units]

2. In the *Drawing Units* dialog box, confirm the *Length Type* to **Decimal**. This is the default measurement to English units, inches.

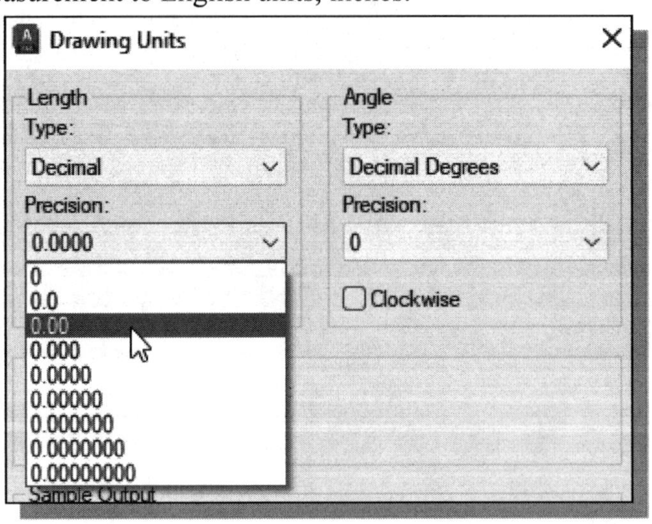

3. Set the *Precision* to **two digits** after the decimal point.

4. Pick **OK** to exit the *Drawing Units* dialog box.

GRID and *SNAP* Intervals Setup

1. In the *Menu Bar*, select:

   [Tools] → [Drafting Settings]

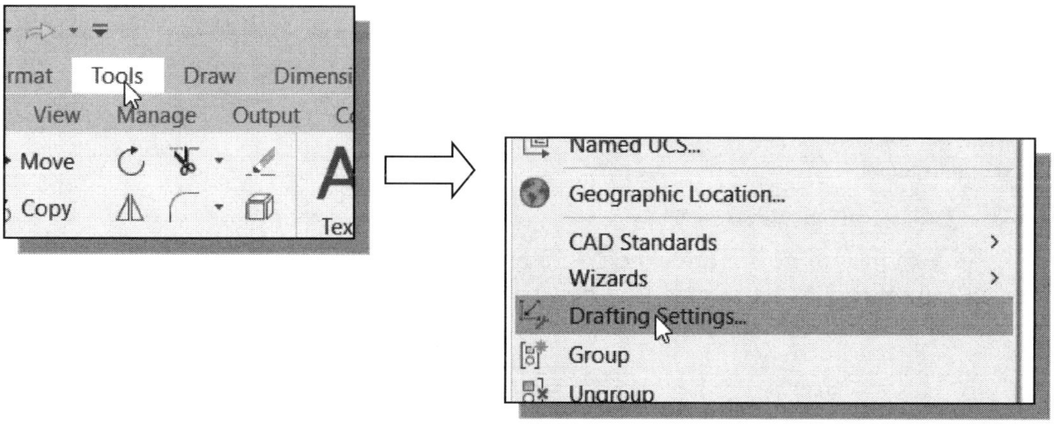

2. In the *Drafting Settings* dialog box, select the **Snap and Grid** tab if it is not the page on top.

3. Change *Grid Spacing* to ***1.00*** for both X and Y directions.

4. Switch **ON** the *Grid On* and *Snap On* options as shown.

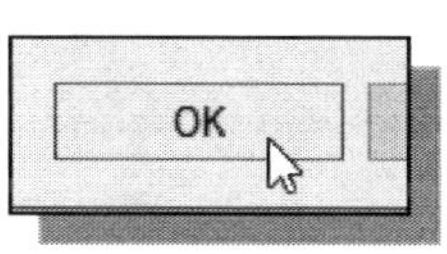

5. Pick **OK** to exit the *Drawing Units* dialog box.

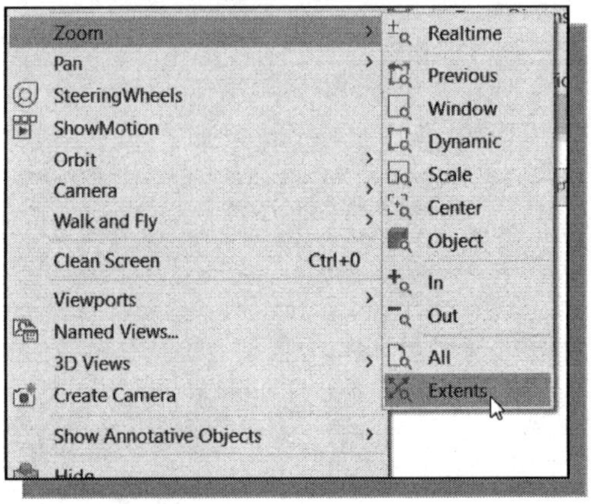

6. On your own, use the **Zoom Extents** command, under the **View** pull-down menu, to reset the display.

❖ Notice in the *Status Bar* area, the *GRID* and *SNAP* options are pressed down indicating they are switched *ON*. Currently, the grid spacing is set to 1 inch and the snap interval is set to 0.5 inch.

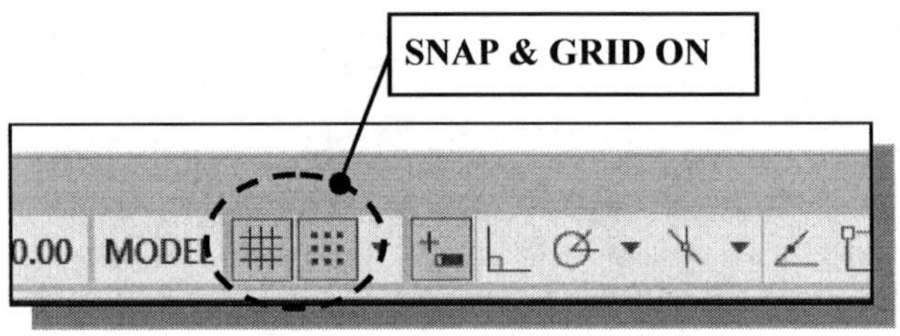

Using the Line Command with ORTHO option

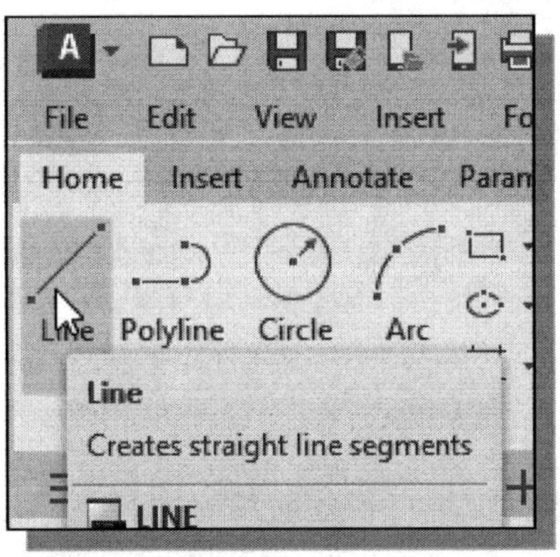

1. Select the **Line** command icon in the *Draw* toolbar. In the command prompt area, near the bottom of the AutoCAD drawing screen, the message "*_line Specify first point:*" is displayed. AutoCAD expects us to identify the starting location of a straight line.

2. In the Drawing Area, move the cursor to **world coordinates (*4,6*)**. **Left-click** to position the starting point of the line at that location.

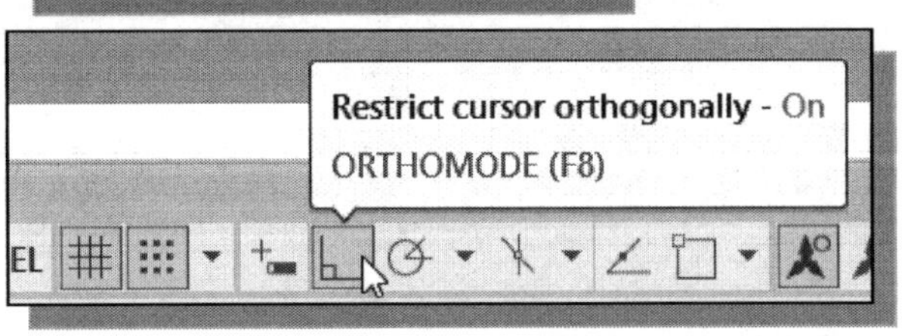

3. We will next turn *off* the *dynamic input* option and switch *ON* the *ORTHO* option by toggling on the ***ORTHO*** button in the *Status Bar* area.

❖ The *ORTHO* option constrains cursor movement to the horizontal or vertical directions, relative to the current coordinate system. With the Line command, we are now restricted to creating only horizontal or vertical lines with the *ORTHO* option.

4. Move the graphics cursor below the last point we selected on the screen and create a vertical line that is **two units** long (*Y coordinate: 4.00*).

5. Move the graphics cursor to the right of the last point and create a horizontal line that is **one unit** long (*X coordinate: 5.00*).

6. Move the graphics cursor below the last point and create a vertical line that is **2.5 units** long (*Y coordinate: 1.50*).

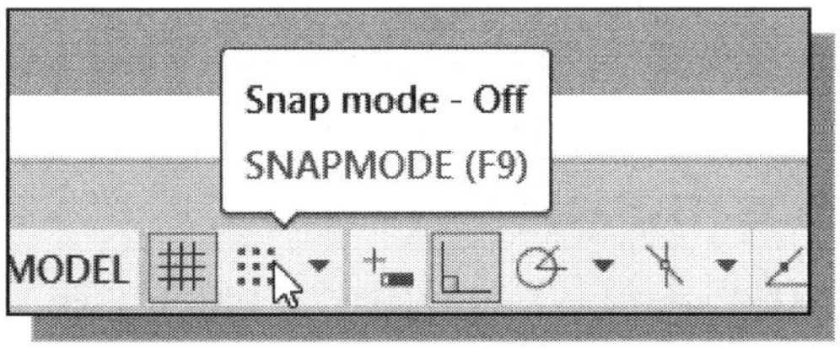

7. Turn ***OFF*** the *SNAP* option in the *Status Bar* area.

8. Move the graphics cursor to the right of the last point and create a horizontal line that is about seven units long (near *X coordinate: 12.00*). As is quite common during the initial design stage, we might not always know all of the dimensions at the beginning.

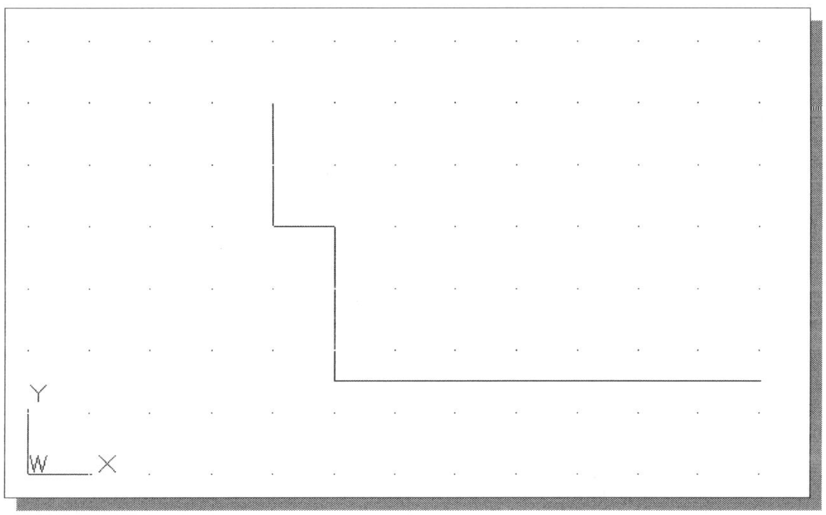

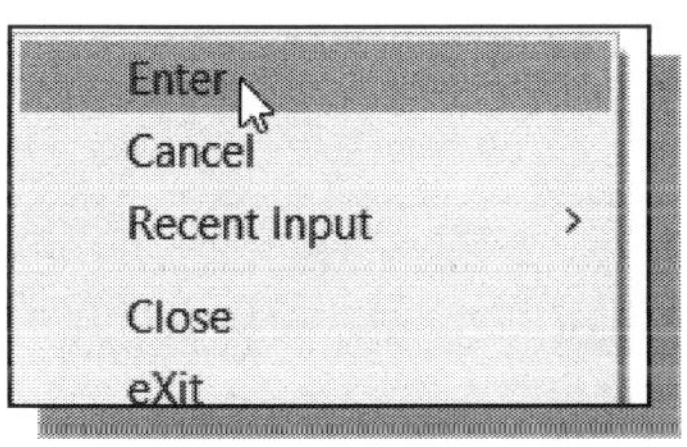

9. Inside the *Drawing Area*, **right-click** to activate the option menu and select **Enter** with the left-mouse-button to end the **Line** command.

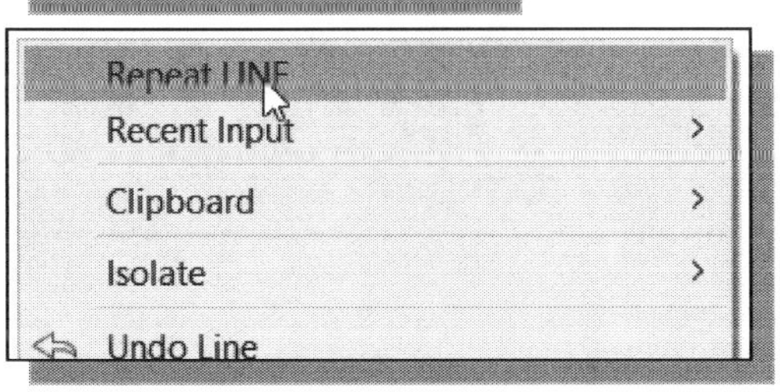

10. Activate the **Line** command by picking the icon in the *Draw* toolbar or **right click** to activate the option menu and select **Repeat Line**.

Object Snap Toolbar

Object Snap is an extremely powerful construction tool available on most CAD systems. During an entity's creation operations, we can snap the cursor to points on objects such as endpoints, midpoints, centers, and intersections. For example, we can quickly draw a line to the center of a circle, the midpoint of a line segment, or the intersection of two lines.

1. Bring up the *Object Snap* toolbar through the **[Tools] → [Toolbars]** menu.

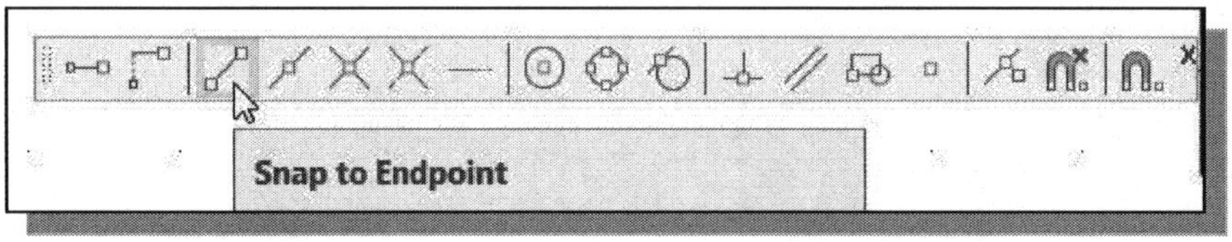

2. In the *Object Snap* toolbar, pick **Snap to Endpoint**. In the command prompt area, the message "*_endp of*" is displayed. AutoCAD now expects us to select a geometric entity on the screen.

❖ The Snap to Endpoint option allows us to snap to the closest endpoint of objects such as lines or arcs. AutoCAD uses the midpoint of the entity to determine which end to snap to.

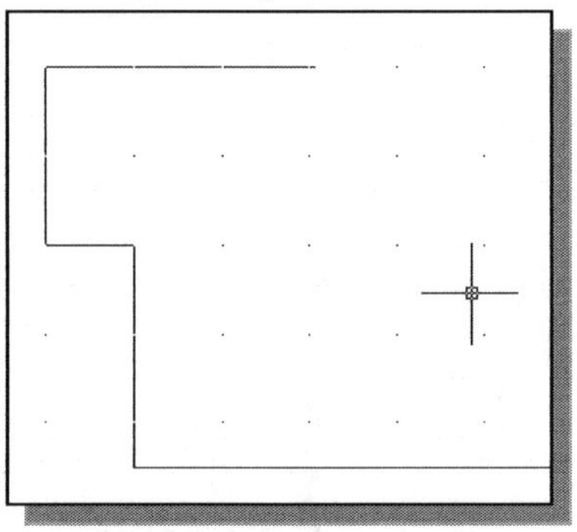

3. Pick the **top left vertical line** by selecting a location above the midpoint of the line. Notice AutoCAD automatically snaps to the top endpoint of the line.

4. Move the graphics cursor to the right of the last point and create a **horizontal line** that is about **three units** long (near *X coordinate: 7.00*).

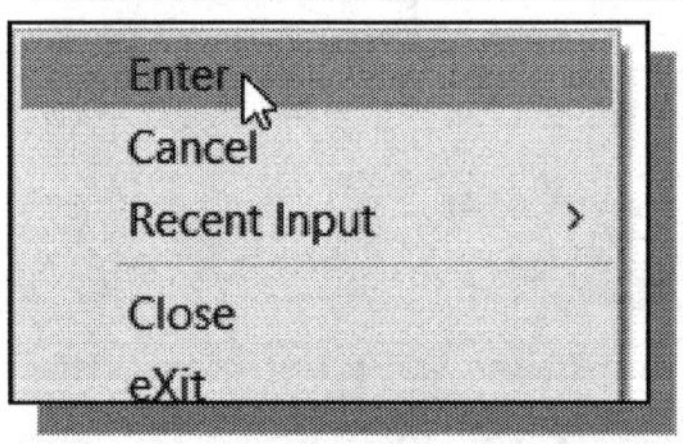

5. Inside the Drawing Area, **right-click** to activate the option menu and select **Enter** with the left-mouse-button to end the **Line** command.

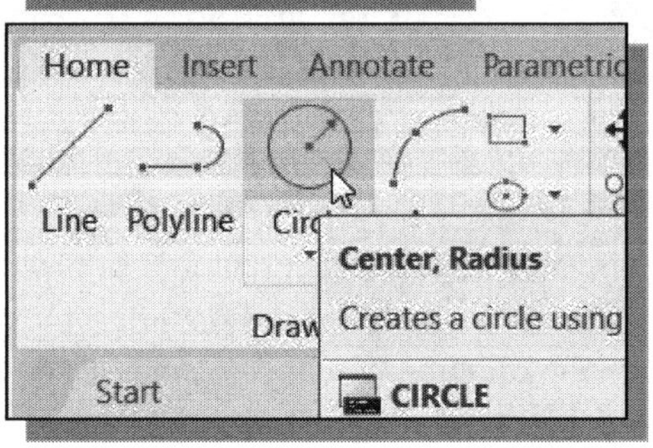

6. Select the **Circle-Radius** command icon in the *Draw* toolbar. In the command prompt area, the message "*Specify center point for circle or [3P/2P/Ttr (tan tan radius)]:*" is displayed.

7. In the *Status Bar* area, switch ***ON*** the *SNAP* option.

8. In the *Drawing Area*, move the cursor to world coordinates (***11.5,6***). **Left-click** to position the center point of the circle at this location.

9. Move the graphics cursor to world coordinates (***13,6***). **Left-click** at this location to create a circle (radius ***1.5*** inches).

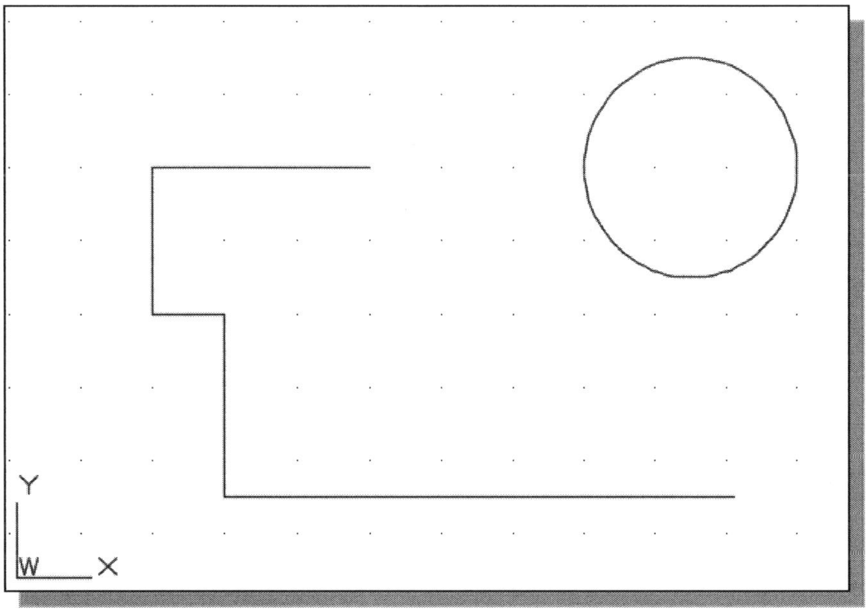

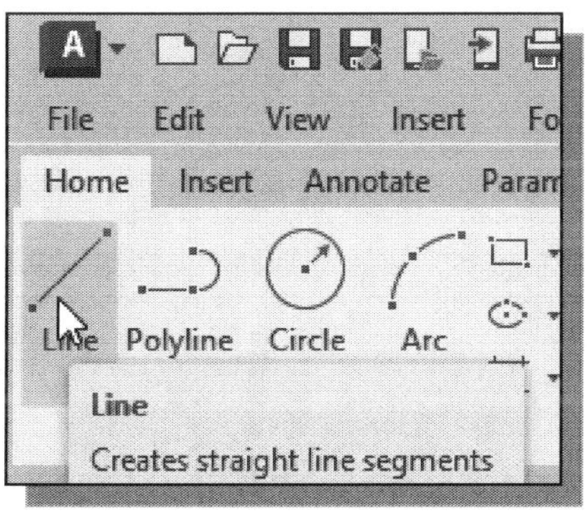

10. Select the **Line** command icon in the *Draw* toolbar. In the command prompt area, the message "*_line Specify first point:*" is displayed.

11. In the *Drawing Area*, move the cursor to world coordinates (***11,1.5***). **Left-click** to position the first point of a line at this location.

12. Pick **Snap to Tangent** in the *Object Snap* toolbar. In the command prompt area, the message "*_tan to*" is displayed. AutoCAD now expects us to select a circle or an arc on the screen.

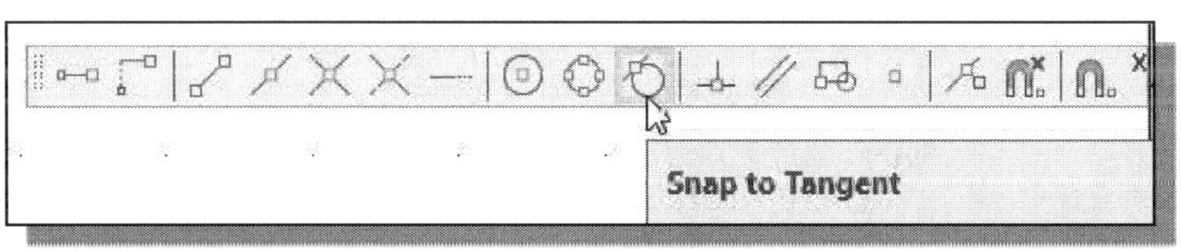

❖ The **Snap to Tangent** option allows us to snap to the point on a circle or arc that, when connected to the last point, forms a line tangent to that object.

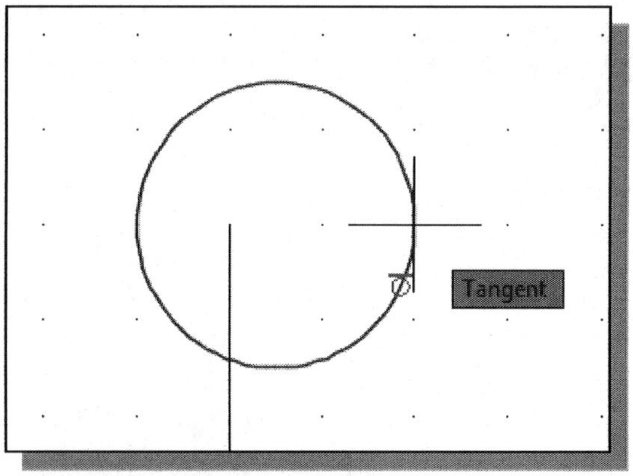

13. Pick a location on the right side of the **circle** and create the line tangent to the circle. Note that the *Object Snap* options take precedence over the *ORTHO* option.

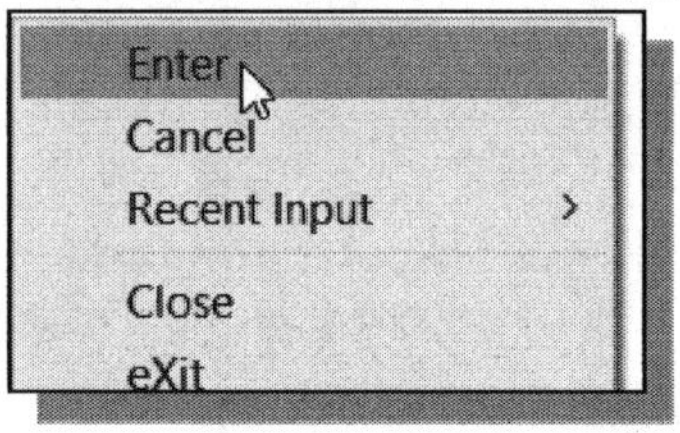

14. Inside the Drawing Area, **right-click** to activate the option menu and select **Enter** with the left-mouse-button to end the **Line** command.

15. In the *Status Bar* area, reset the option buttons so that all of the option buttons are switched ***OFF***.

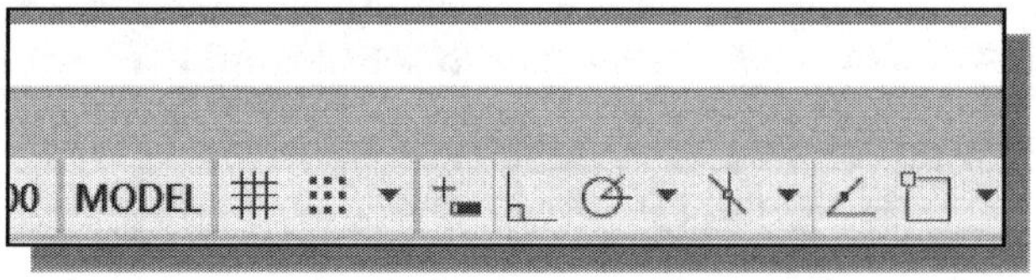

16. Close the *Object Snap* toolbar by **left-clicking** the upper right corner **X** icon.

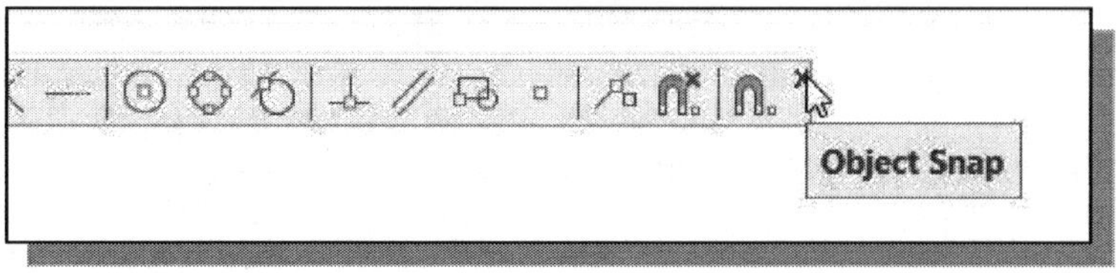

Using the Extend Command

The **Extend** command lengthens an object so that it ends precisely at a selected boundary.

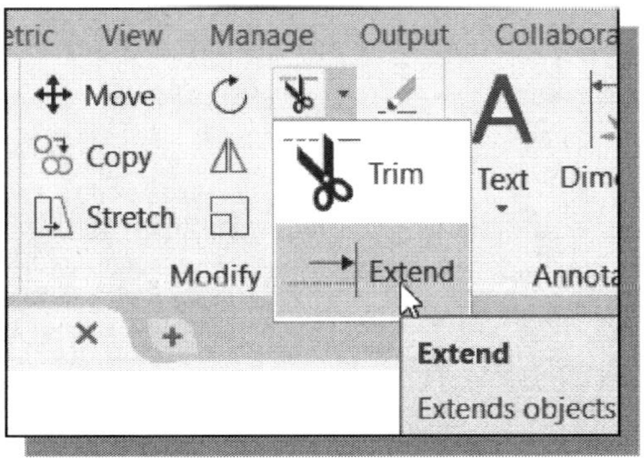

1. Select the **Extend** command icon in the *Modify* toolbar. In the command prompt area, the message "*Select boundary edges... Select objects:*" is displayed.

❖ First, we will use the **Boundary edges option** to select the objects to which we want to extend the object.

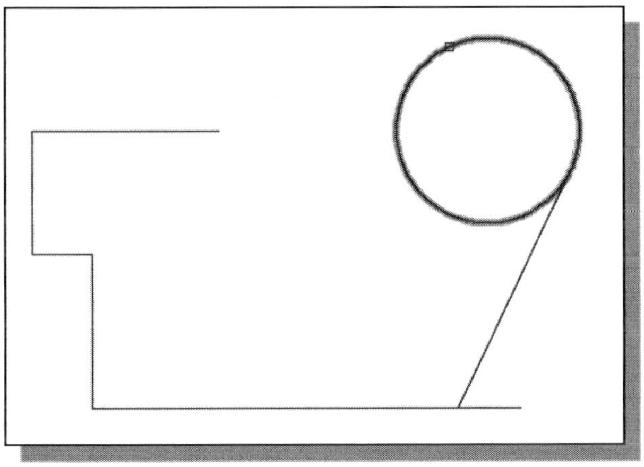

2. In the command prompt area, click **Boundary edges** as shown.

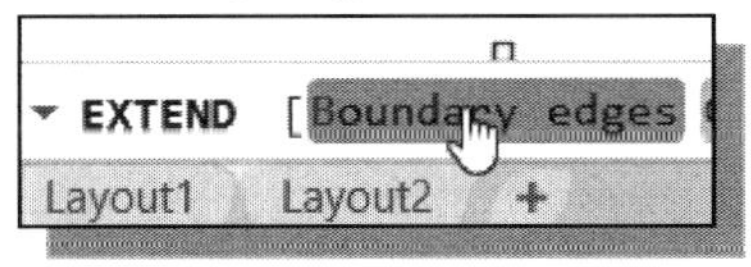

3. Pick the **circle** as the *boundary edge.*

4. Inside the *Drawing Area*, **right-click** to proceed with the **Extend** command.

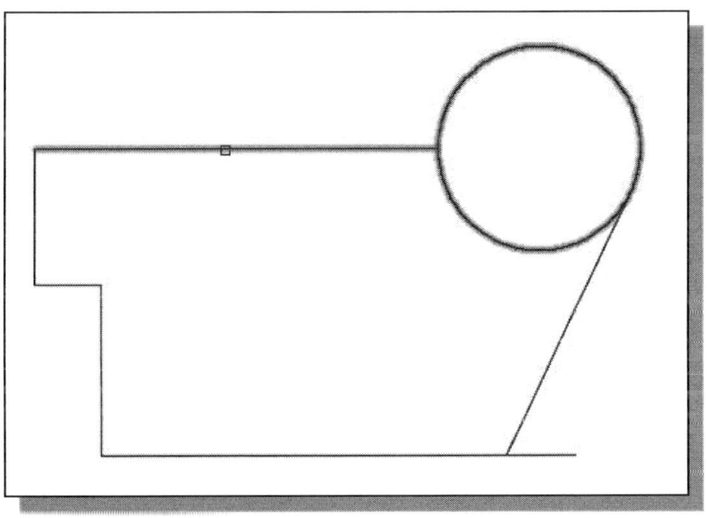

5. The message "*Select object to extend or shift-select object to trim or [Project/Edge/Undo]:*" is displayed in the command prompt area. Extend the **horizontal line** that is to the left side of the circle by clicking near the right endpoint of the line.

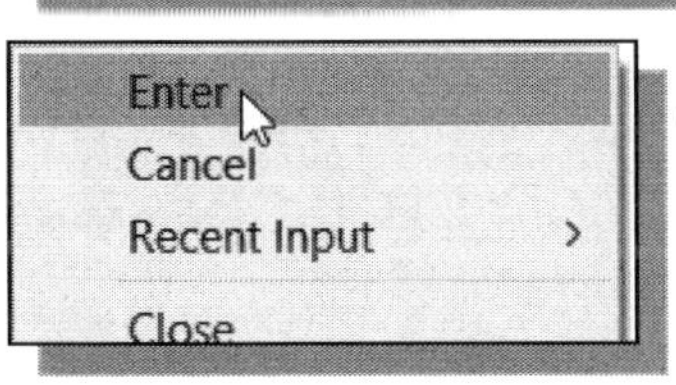

6. Inside the Drawing Area, **right-click** to activate the option menu and select **Enter** with the left-mouse-button to end the **Extend** command.

Using the Trim Command

The Trim command shortens an object so that it ends precisely at a selected boundary.

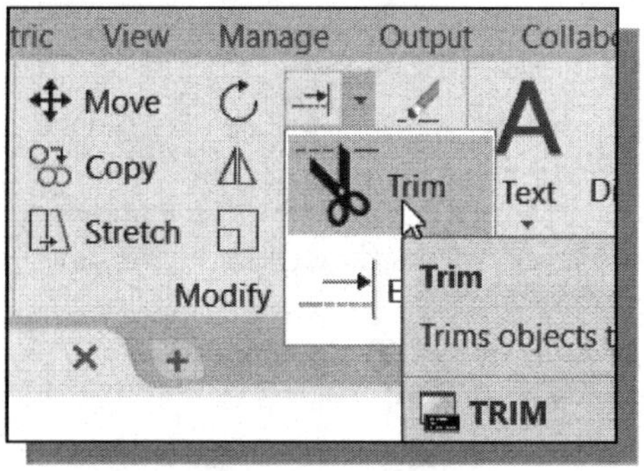

1. Select the **Trim** command icon in the *Modify* toolbar. In the command prompt area, the message "*Select boundary edges... Select objects:*" is displayed.

❖ First, we will select the objects that define the boundary edges to which we want to trim the object.

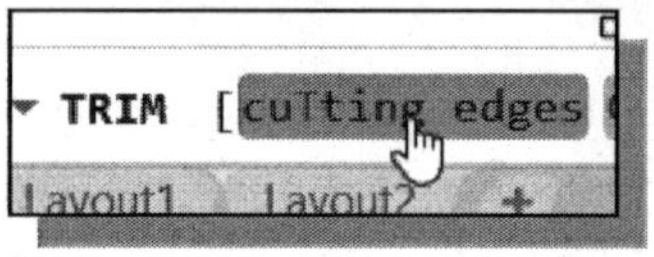

2. In the command prompt area, click **cuTting edges** as shown.

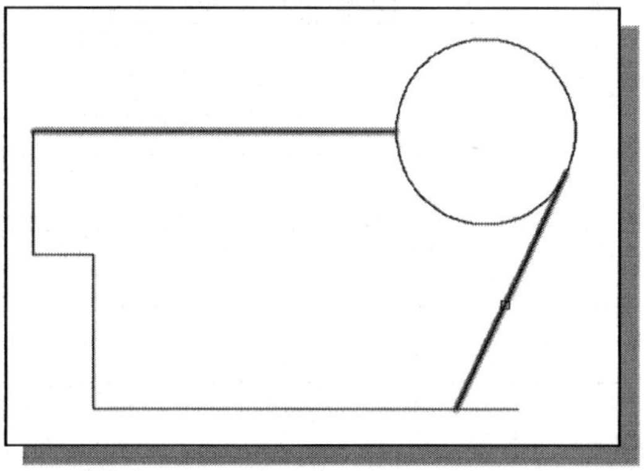

3. Pick the **inclined line** and the **top horizontal line** as the *boundary edges.*

4. Inside the *Drawing Area*, **right-click** to proceed with the Trim command.

5. The message "*Select object to trim or shift-select object to extend or [Fence/Crossing/Project/Edge/eRase/Undo]:*" is displayed in the command prompt area. Pick near the **right endpoint** of the bottom horizontal line.

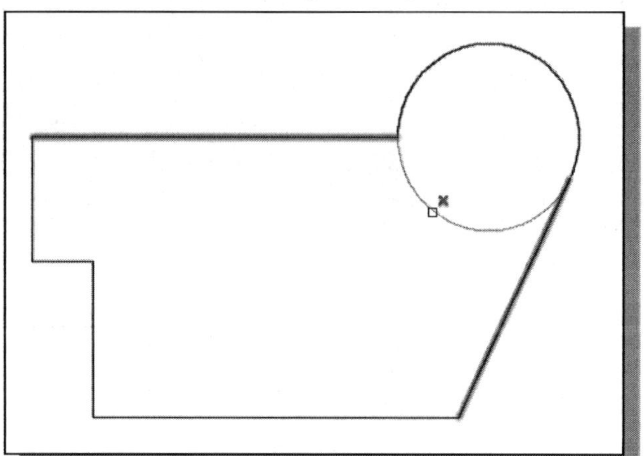

6. Pick the **bottom of the circle** by clicking on the lower portion of the circle.

7. Inside the *Drawing Area*, **right-click** to activate the option menu and select **Enter** with the left-mouse-button to end the Trim command.

- Note that in **AutoCAD 2027**, we can use the Extend command or the Trim command for trimming or extending an object. For example, when using the **Extend** command, we can select an object to *extend* or hold down **SHIFT** and select an object to *trim*.

Creating a TTR Circle

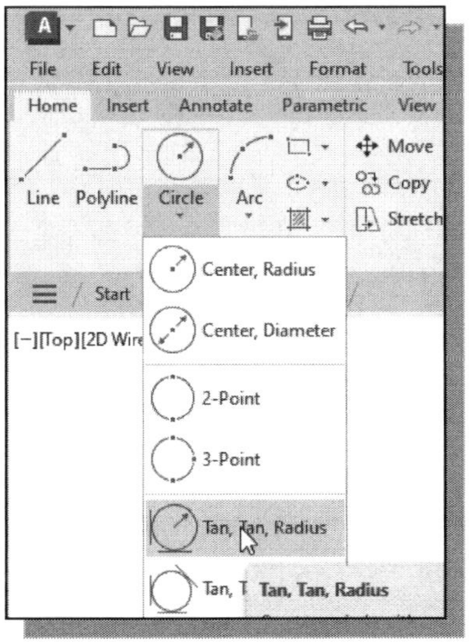

1. In the *Draw* toolbar, click the triangle next to the **Circle** icon to show the additional options.

2. In the displayed list, select the **Tan, Tan, Radius** option. This option allows us to create a circle that is tangent to two objects.

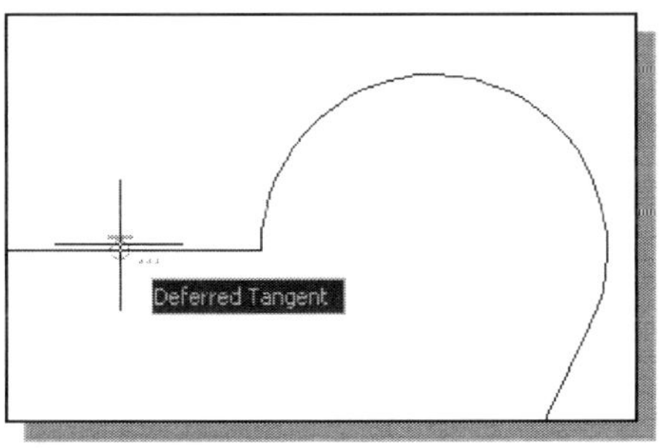

3. Pick the **top horizontal line** that is to the left side of the arc. We will create a circle that is tangent to this line and the circle.

4. Pick the **arc** by selecting a location that is above the right endpoint of the horizontal line. AutoCAD interprets the location we selected as being near the tangency.

5. In the command prompt area, the message "*Specify radius of circle <1.50>*" is displayed.
   Specify radius of circle <1.50>: **1.0 [ENTER]**

➢ On your own, use the **Trim** command and trim the circle, the horizontal line, and the arc as shown.

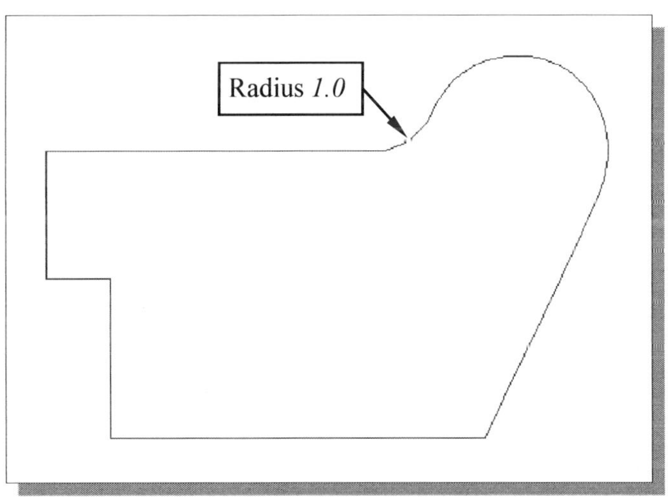

Using the Fillet Command

The **Fillet** command can be used to round or fillet the edges of two arcs, circles, elliptical arcs, or lines with an arc of a specified radius.

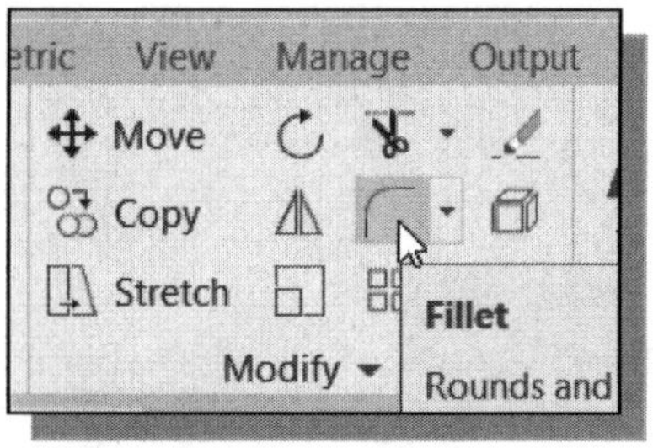

1. Select the **Fillet** command icon in the *Modify* toolbar. In the command prompt area, the message "*Select first object or [Polyline/Radius/Trim]:*" is displayed.

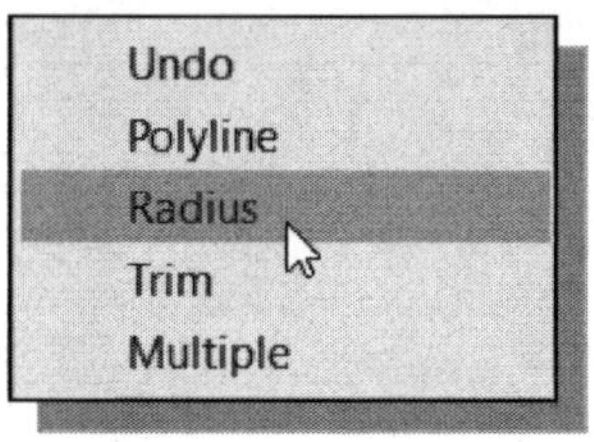

2. Inside the Drawing Area, right-click to activate the option menu and select the **Radius** option with the left-mouse-button to specify the radius of the fillet.

3. In the command prompt area, the message "*Specify fillet radius:*" is displayed.

   Specify fillet radius: **0.75 [ENTER]**

4. Pick the **bottom horizontal line** and the **adjacent vertical line** to create a rounded corner as shown.

➢ On your own, use the **Fillet** command and create a radius ***0.25*** fillet at the corner as shown.

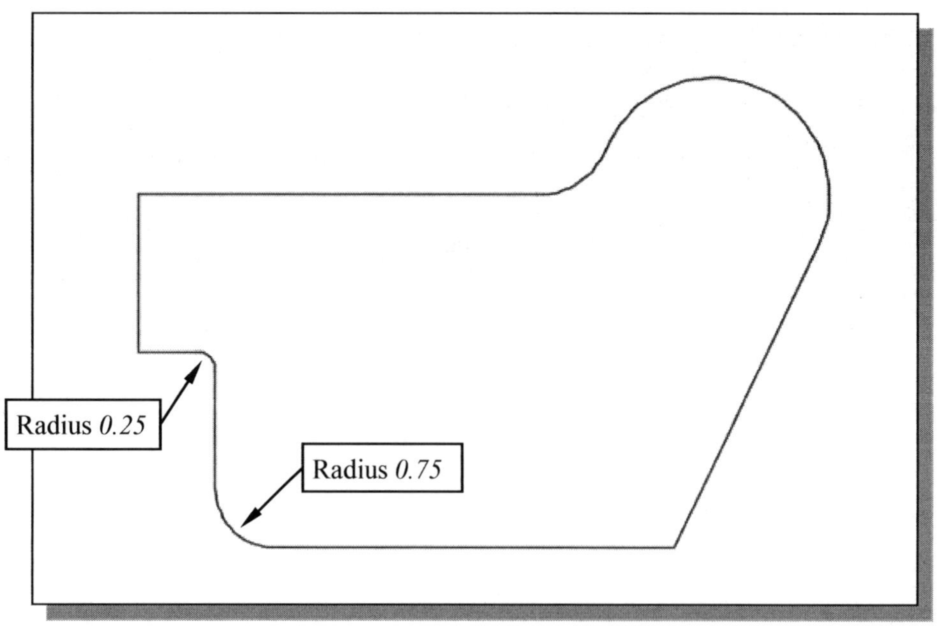

Converting Objects into a Polyline

The next task in our project is to use the **Offset** command and create a scaled copy of the constructed geometry. Prior to using the **Offset** command, we will simplify the procedure by converting all objects into a **compound object – a *polyline*.**

A *polyline* in AutoCAD is a 2D line of adjustable width composed of line and arc segments. A polyline is treated as a single object with definable options.

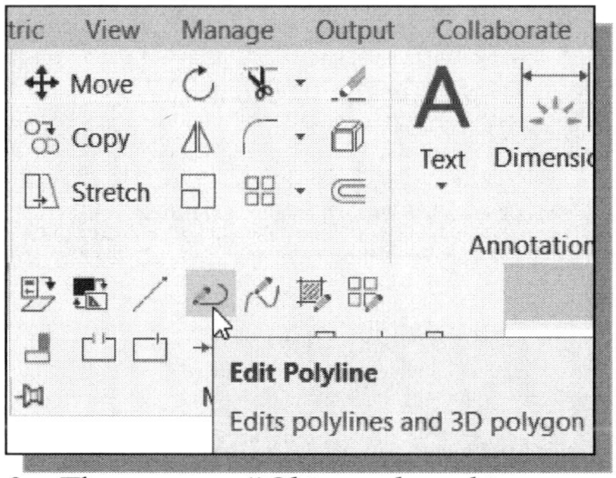

1. In the *Ribbon Toolbars*, select:

   [Modify] → [Edit Polyline]

2. The message "*Select polyline:*" is displayed in the command prompt area. Select **any** of the objects on the screen.

3. The message "*Object selected is not a polyline, Do you want to turn it into one? <Y>*" is displayed in the command prompt area. **Right-click** to accept the *Yes* default.

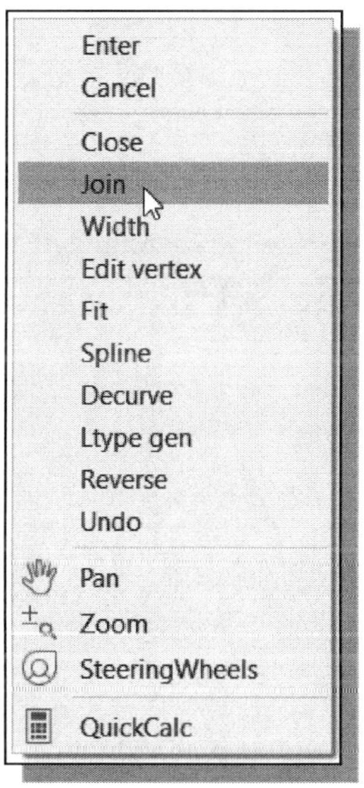

4. Inside the *Drawing Area*, **right-click** once to activate the option menu and select the **Join** option with the left-mouse-button to add objects to the polyline.

5. **Pick all objects** by enclosing them inside a *selection window* (selecting the top left corner first).

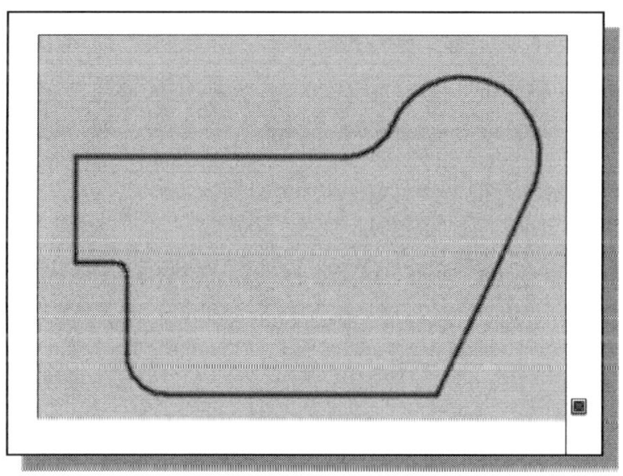

6. Inside the *Drawing Area*, **right-click** once to accept the selected objects.

7. Inside the *Drawing Area*, **right-click** once to activate the option menu and select **Enter** to end the **Edit Polyline** command.

Using the Offset Command

The **Offset** command creates a new object at a specified distance from an existing object or through a specified point.

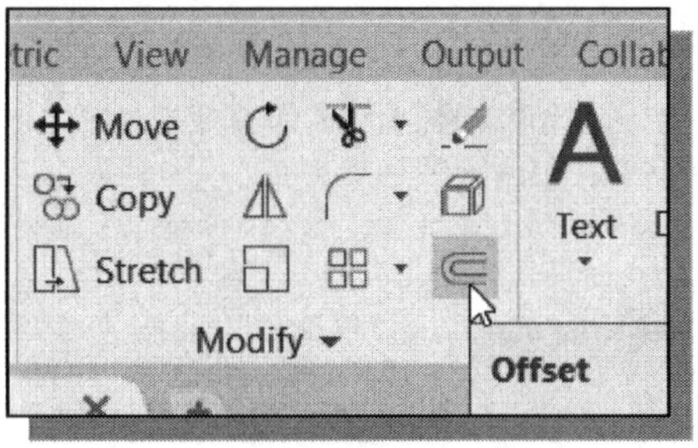

1. Select the **Offset** command icon in the *Modify* toolbar. In the *command prompt area*, the message "*Specify offset distance or [Through]:*" is displayed.

   Specify offset distance or [Through]:
   0.5 [ENTER]

2. In the *command prompt area*, the message "*Select object to offset or <exit>:*" is displayed. Select **any segment** of the polyline on the screen.

➢ Since all the lines and arcs have been converted into a single object, all segments are now selected.

3. AutoCAD next asks us to identify the direction of the offset. Pick a location that is ***inside*** the polyline.

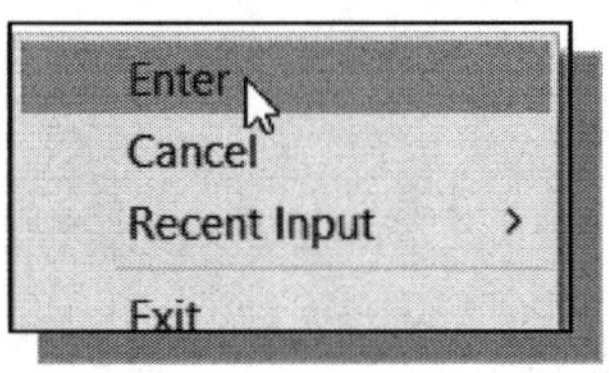

4. Inside the *Drawing Area*, **right-click** and select **Enter** to end the **Offset** command.

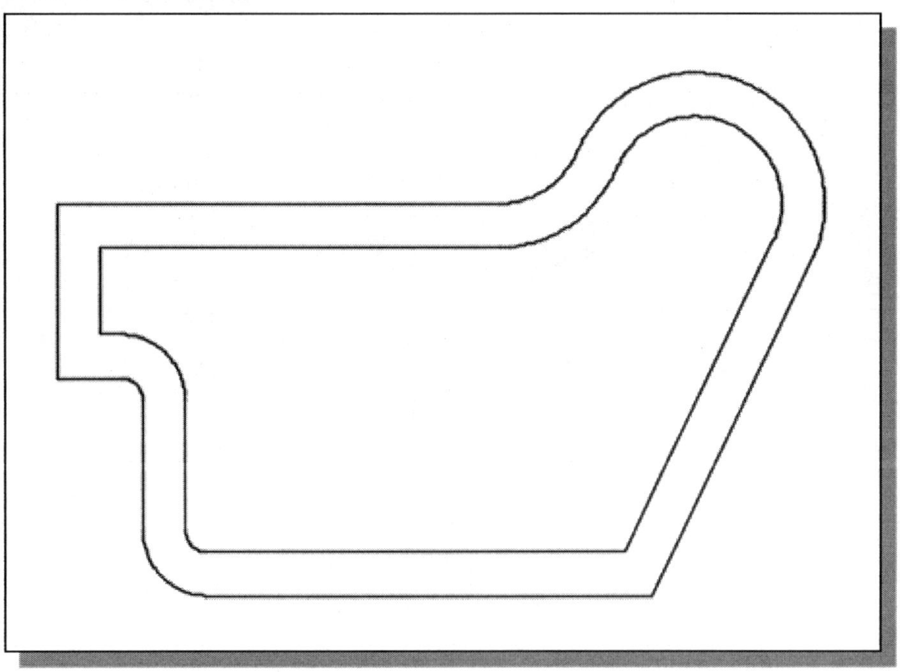

Using the Area Inquiry Tool to Measure Area and Perimeter

AutoCAD also provides several tools that will allow us to measure distance, area, perimeter, and even mass properties. With the use of polylines, measurements of areas and perimeters can be done very quickly.

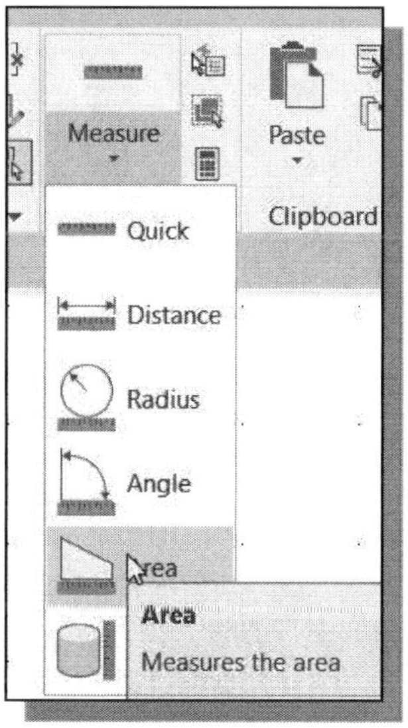

1. In the *Ribbon* tabs area, left-click once on the **Measure** title in the *Utilities* toolbar as shown.

2. In the *Inquiry* toolbar, click on the **Area** icon to activate the Calculates the area and perimeter of selected objects command.

- Note the different **Measure** options that are available in the list.

3. In the command prompt area, the message "*Specify first corner point or [Object/Add/Subtract]:*" is displayed. By default, AutoCAD expects us to select points that will form a polygon. The area and perimeter of the polygon will then be calculated.

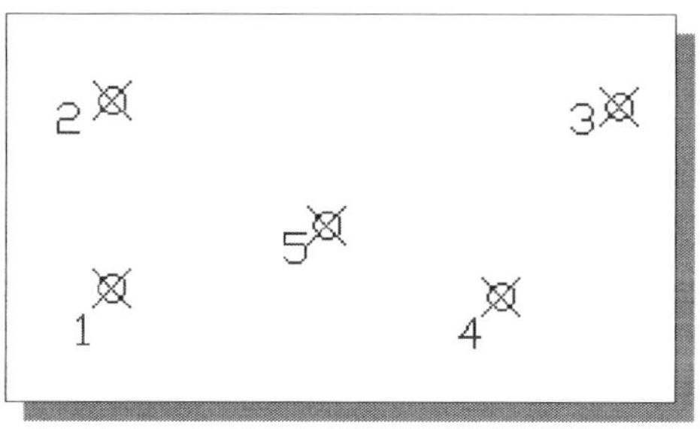

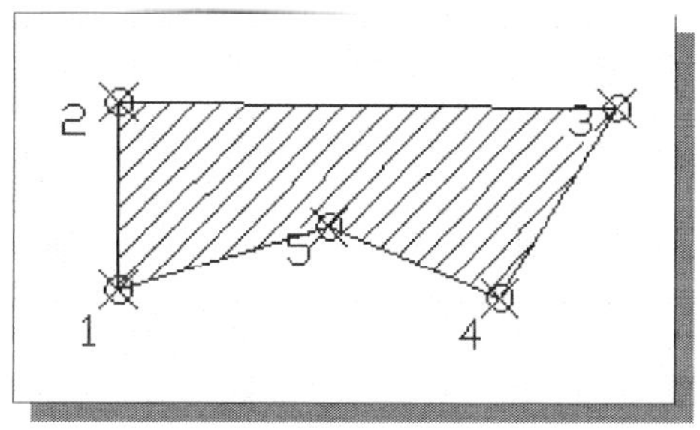

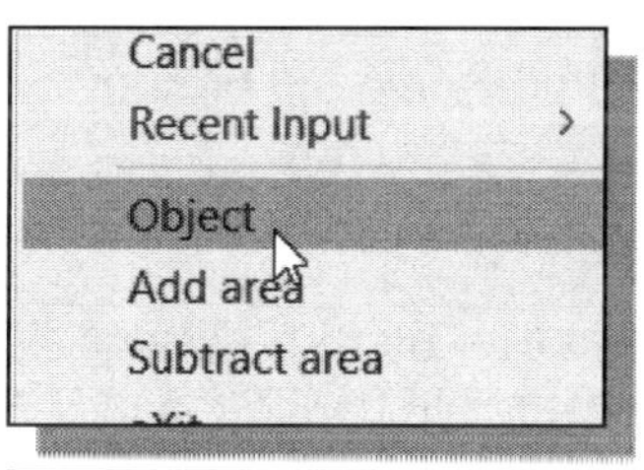

4. AutoCAD can also calculate the area and perimeter of objects that define closed regions. For example, a circle or a rectangle can be selected as both of these objects define closed regions. We can also select a region defined by a *polyline*. To activate this option, **right-click** once inside the Drawing Area and select **Object** as shown.

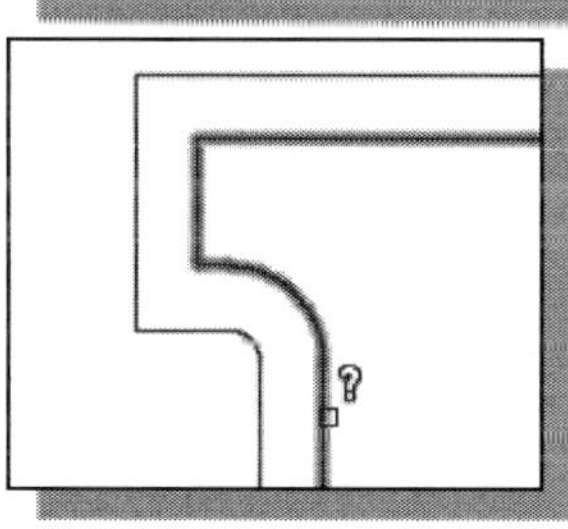

5. In the command prompt area, the message "*Select objects:*" is displayed. Pick the **inside polyline** and the associated area and perimeter information are shown in the prompt area.

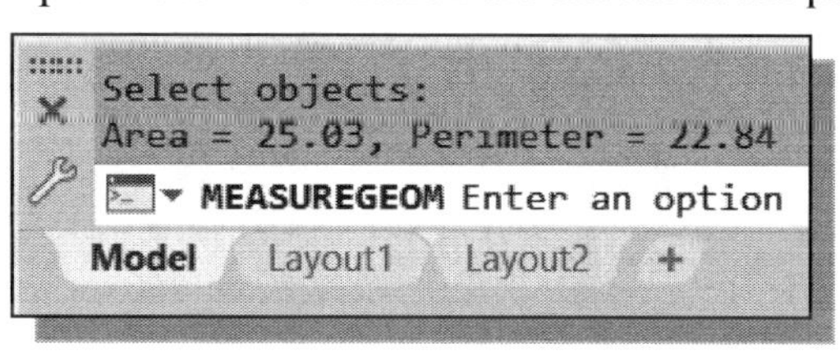

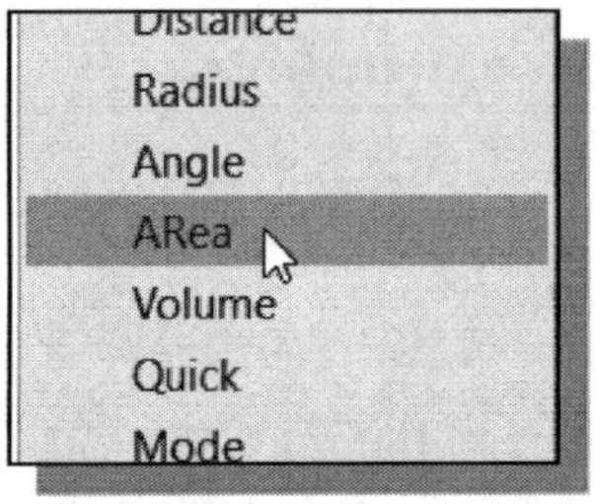

6. Inside the *Drawing Area*, right-click once to bring up the option menu and select **Area** as shown.

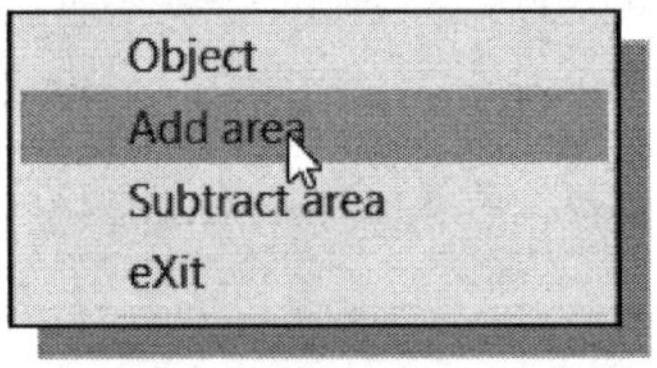

7. We can also select a region defined by multiple *polylines*. To activate this option, **right-click** once inside the Drawing Area and select **Add area** as shown.

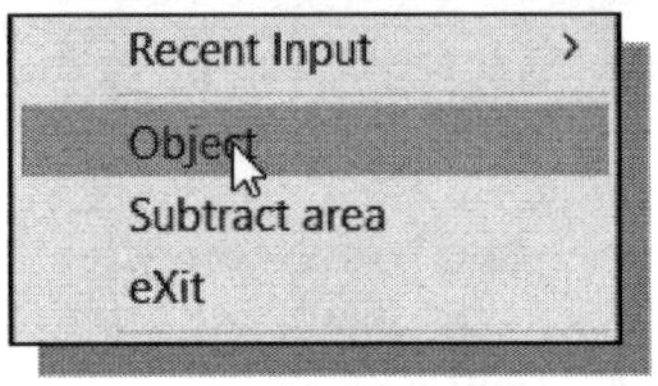

8. To also activate selection of regions *defined* by polylines, **right-click** once inside the *Drawing Area* and select **Object** as shown.

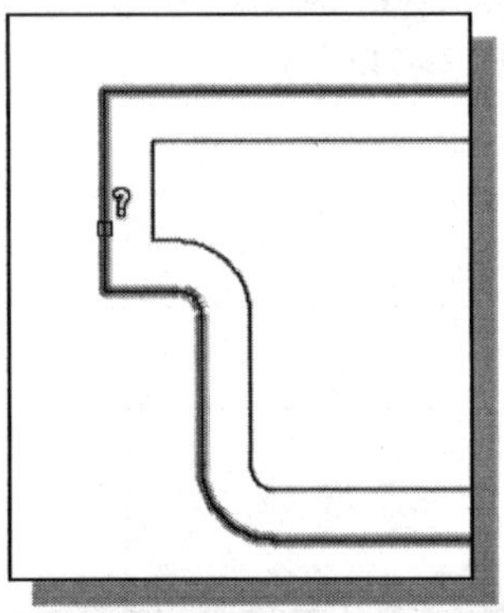

9. In the command prompt area, the message "*[Add Mode] Select objects:*" is displayed. Pick the **outside polyline**. The associated area and perimeter information are shown in the prompt area. **Right-click** once to end the selection.

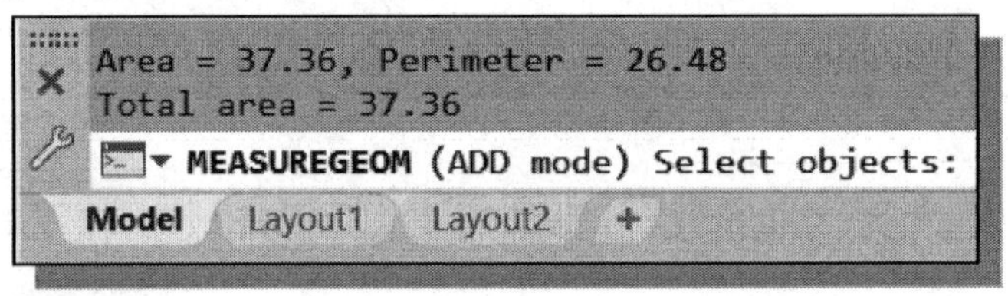

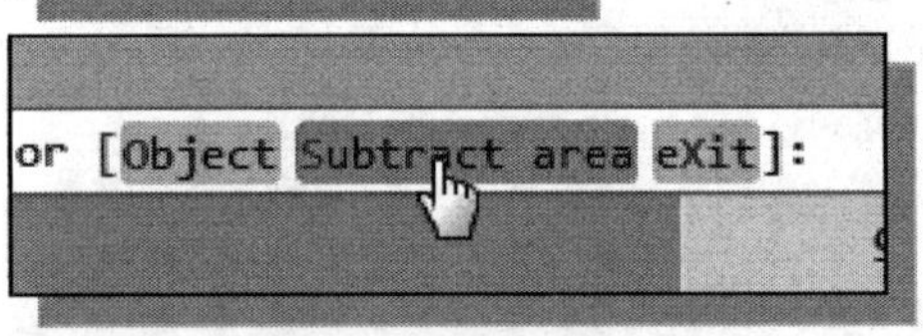

10. Next, we will subtract the region defined by the inside polyline. In the command prompt area, select **Subtract area** as shown.

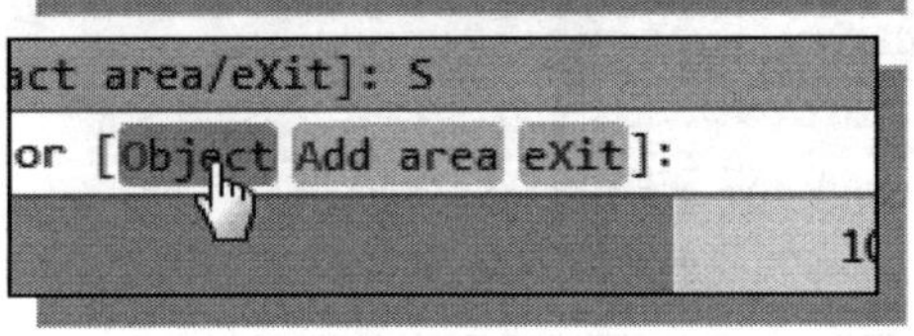

11. To also activate selection of regions defined by polylines, select **Object** in the command prompt area as shown.

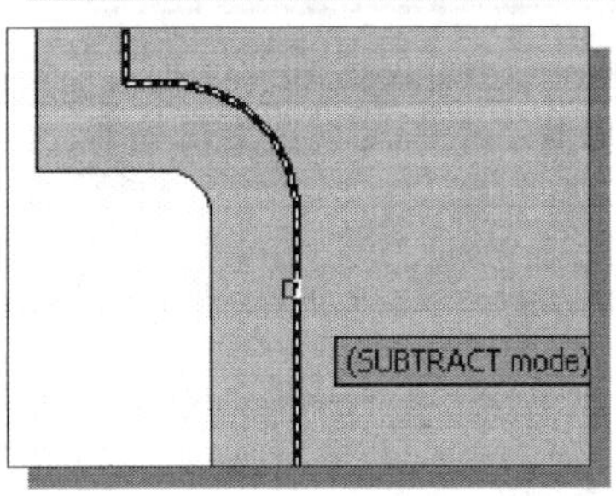

12. In the *command prompt area*, the message "*Select objects:*" is displayed. Pick the **inside polyline** and the area between the two polylines is shown in the *command prompt area.*

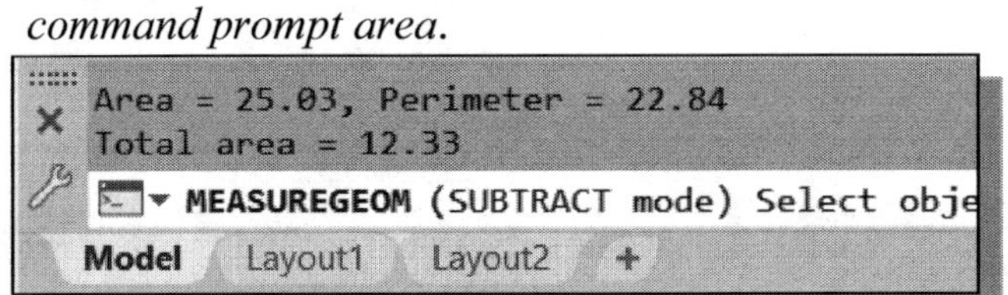

Using the Explode Command

The Explode command breaks a compound object into its component objects.

1. Select the **Explode** command icon in the *Modify* toolbar. In the command prompt area, the message "*Select objects:*" is displayed.

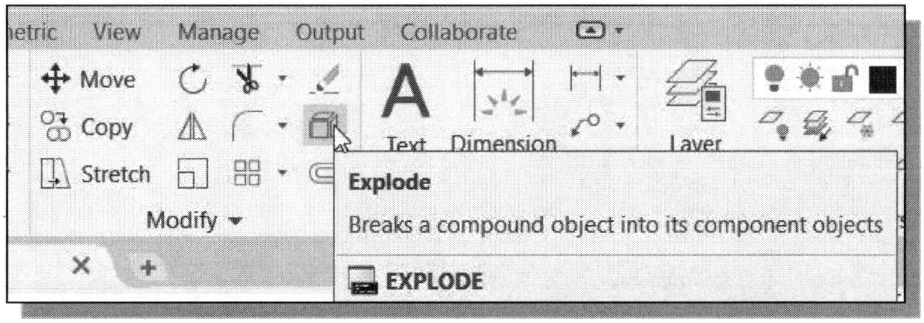

2. Pick the ***inside polyline*** that we created using the Offset command.

3. Inside the Drawing Area, **right-click** to end the Explode command.

Create another Fillet

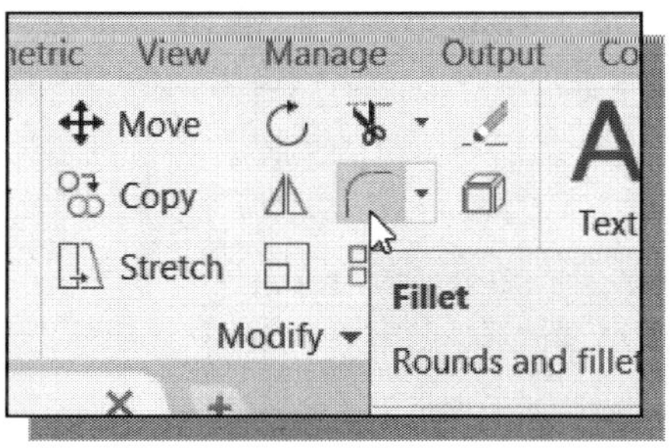

1. Select the **Fillet** command icon in the *Modify* toolbar. In the command prompt area, the message "*Select first object or [Polyline/Radius/Trim]:*" is displayed.

2. On your own, set the *Fillet Radius* to ***0.5.***
   Specify fillet radius: **0.5 [ENTER]**

3. Pick the **horizontal line** and the **adjacent inclined line** to create a rounded corner as shown.

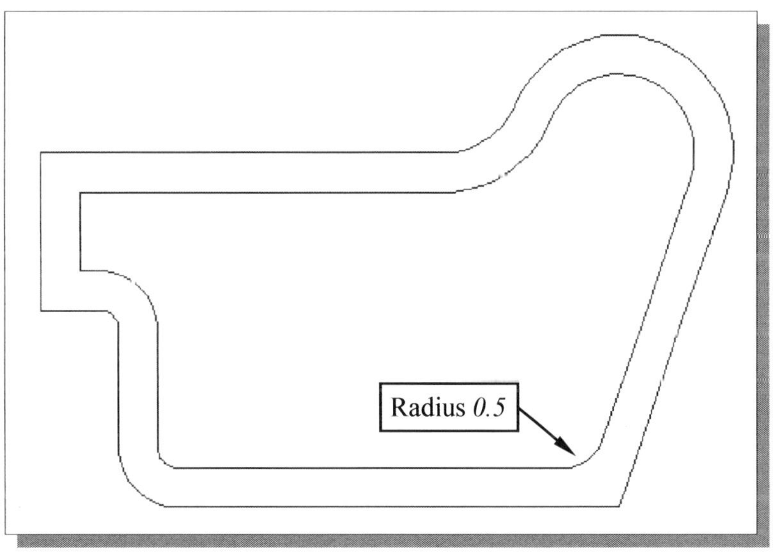

Saving the CAD File

1. In the pull-down menus, select:

   [File] → [Save As]

2. In the *Save Drawing As* dialog box, select the folder in which you want to store the CAD file and enter ***Gasket*** in the *File name* box.

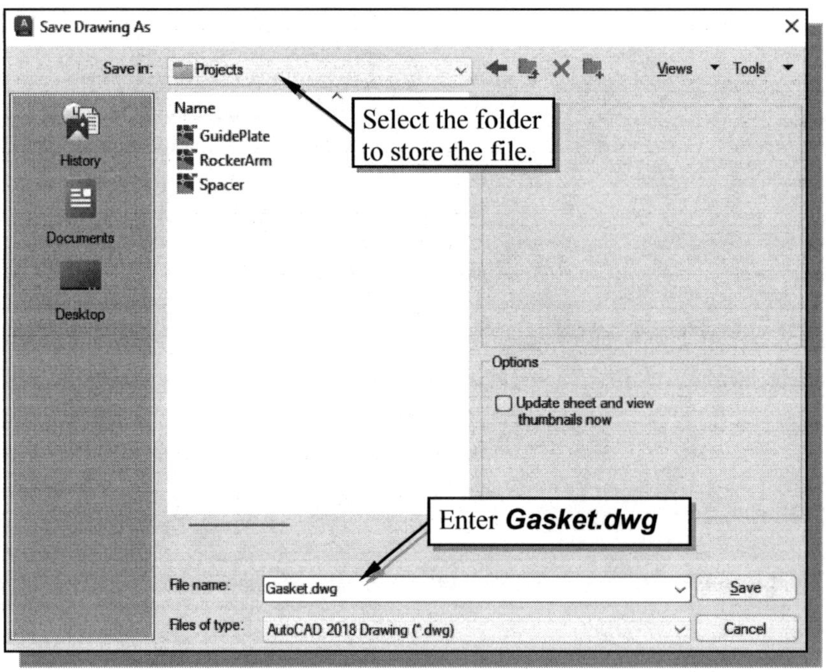

3. Pick **Save** in the *Save Drawing As* dialog box to accept the selections and save the file.

Exit AutoCAD

To exit **AutoCAD 2027**, select **Exit AutoCAD** from the *Application Menu* or type ***QUIT*** at the command prompt.

Review Questions: (Time: 20 minutes)

1. Describe when and why you would use the AutoCAD ***ORTHO*** option.
2. What is the difference between a *line* and a *polyline* in AutoCAD?
3. Which AutoCAD command can we use to break a compound object, such as a polyline, into its component objects?
4. Which AutoCAD command can we use to quickly calculate the area and perimeter of a closed region defined by a polyline?
5. Describe the procedure to calculate the area and perimeter of a closed region defined by a polyline?
6. What does the **Offset** command allow us to do?
7. Create the following triangle and measure the area and perimeter of the triangle.

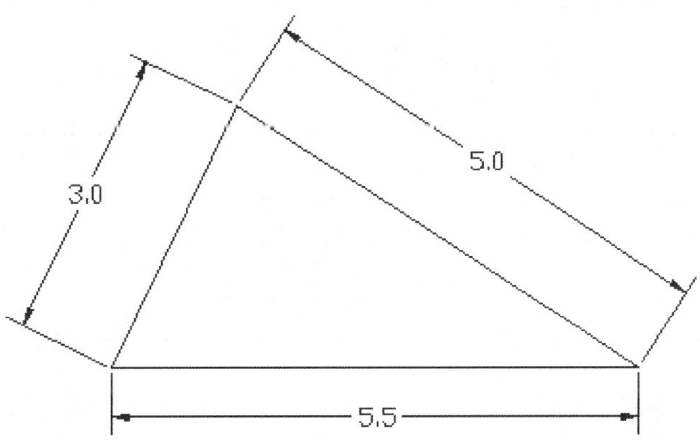

8. Create the following triangle and measure the area and perimeter of the triangle. Also find the angle Θ.

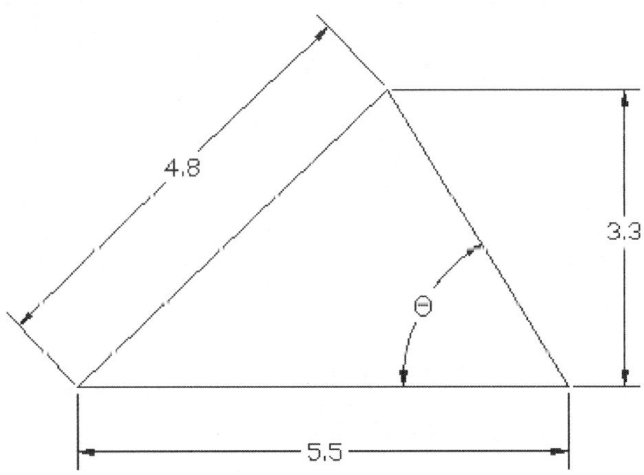

Exercises:

(Unless otherwise specified, dimensions are in inches.) (Time: 90 minutes)

1. **Lines & Squares Pattern**

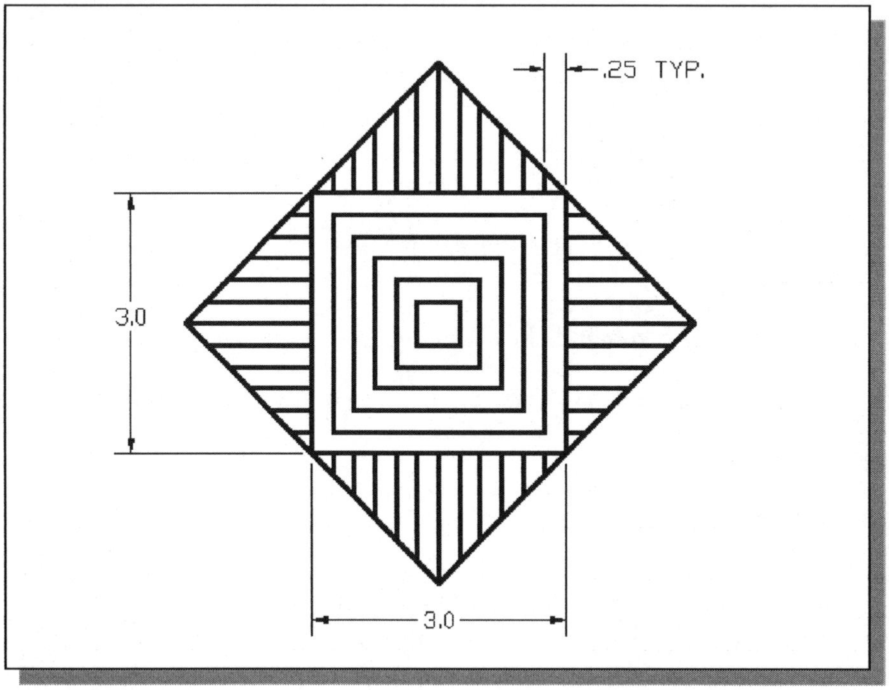

2. **Interlacement Design**

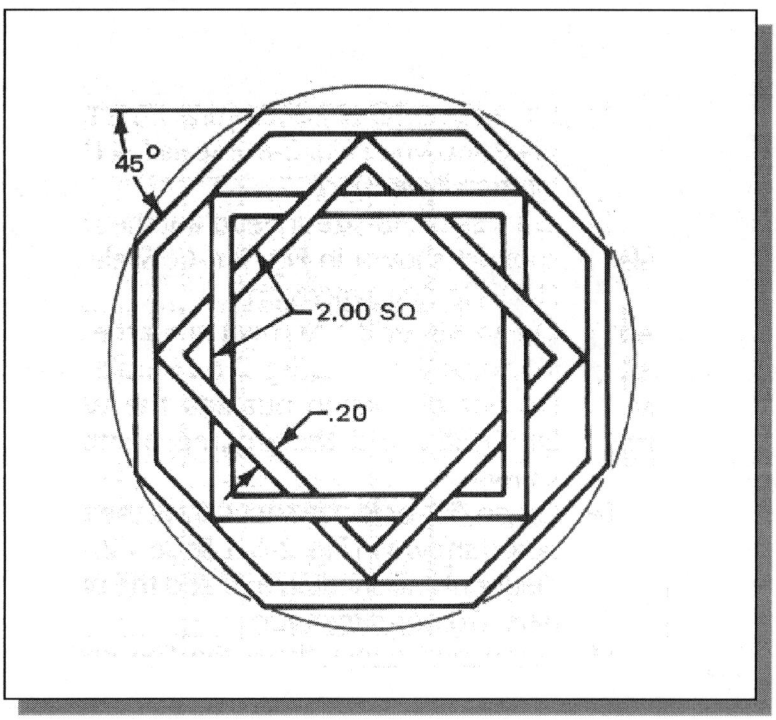

3. **Polygons & Circles Pattern** (Dimensions are in inches.)

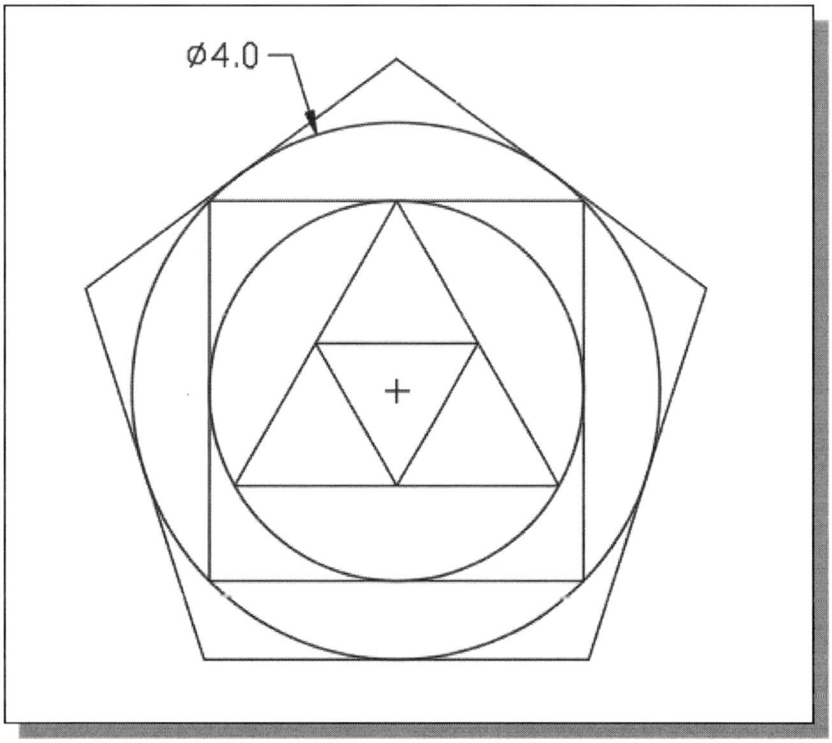

4. **Squares & Circles Pattern** (Dimensions are in inches.)

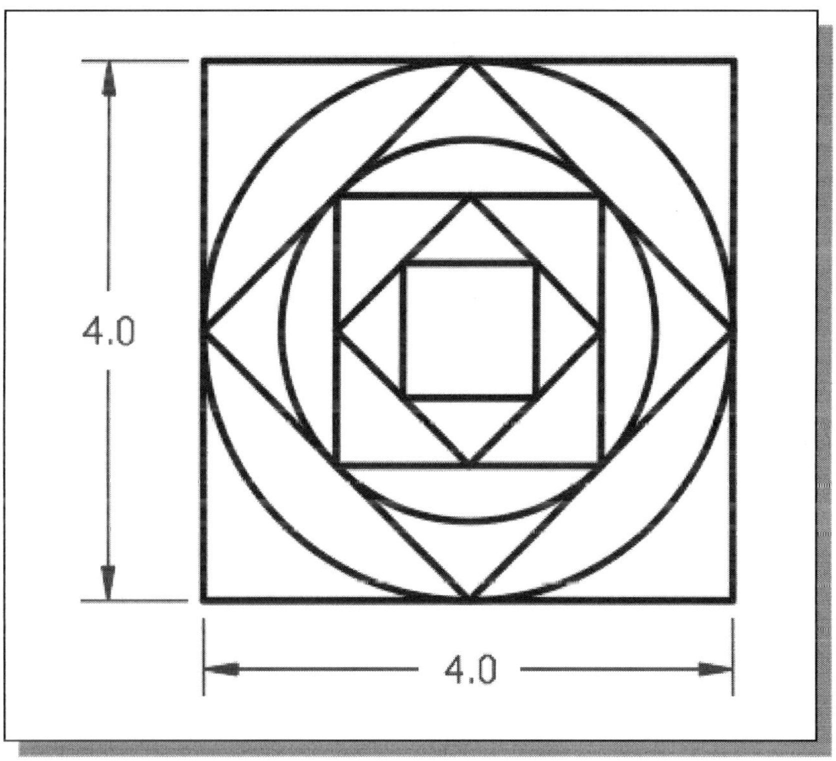

5. **Positioning Spacer** (Dimensions are in inches.)

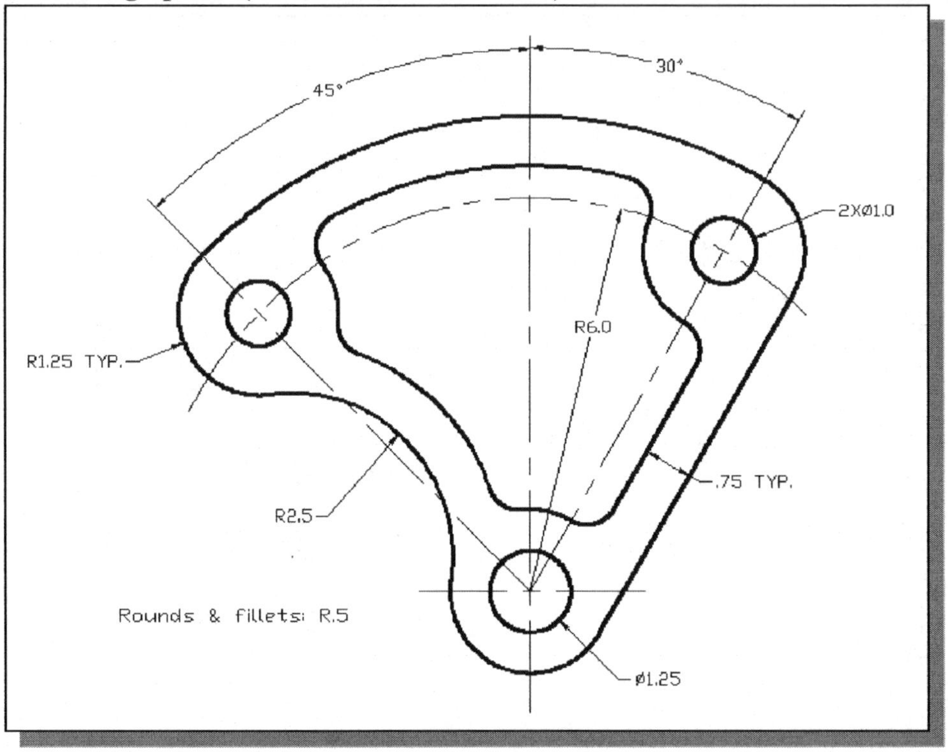

6. **Indexing Base** (Dimensions are in inches.)

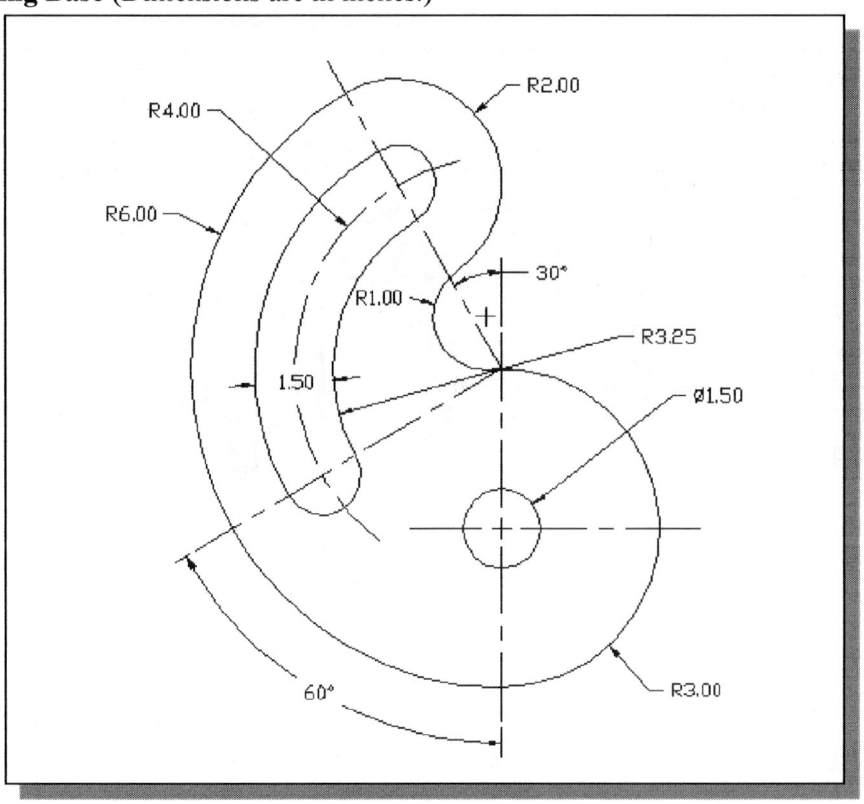

7. **Guide Block** (Dimensions are in inches.)

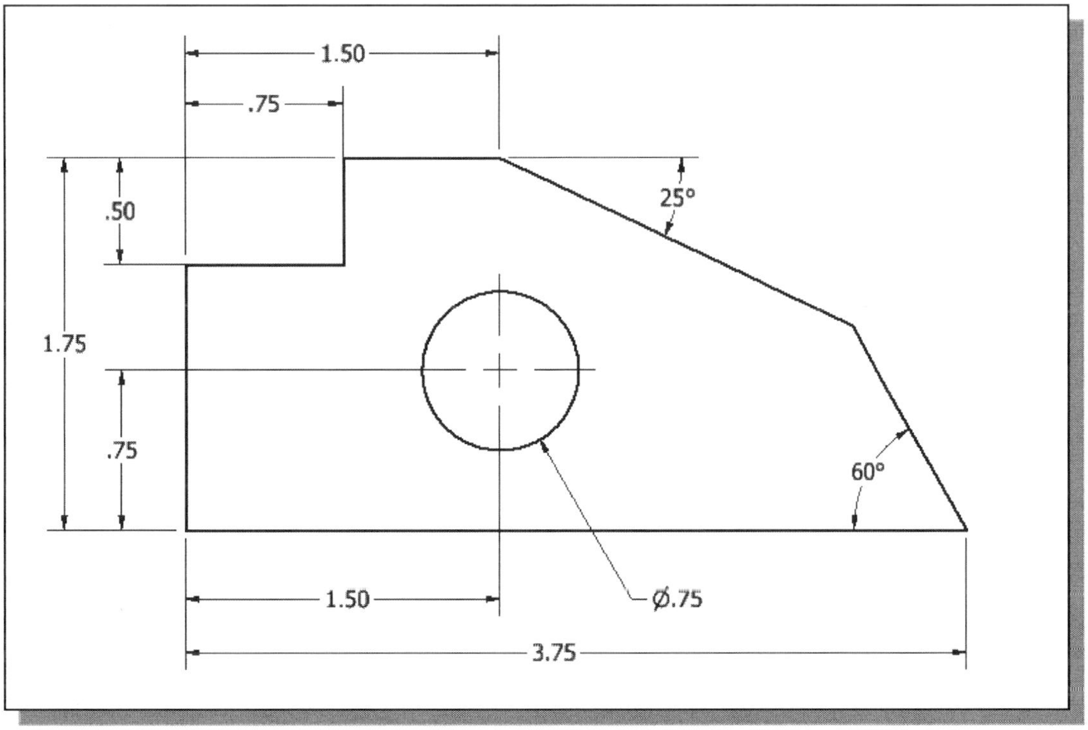

8. **Slider Guide** (Dimensions are in inches.)

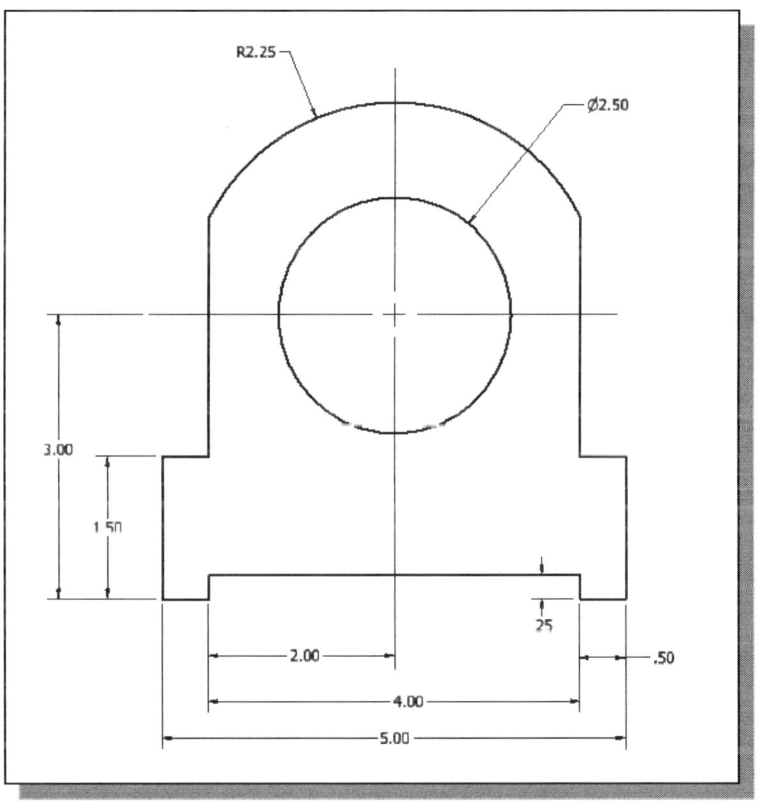

9. **Vent Cover** (Dimensions are in inches.)

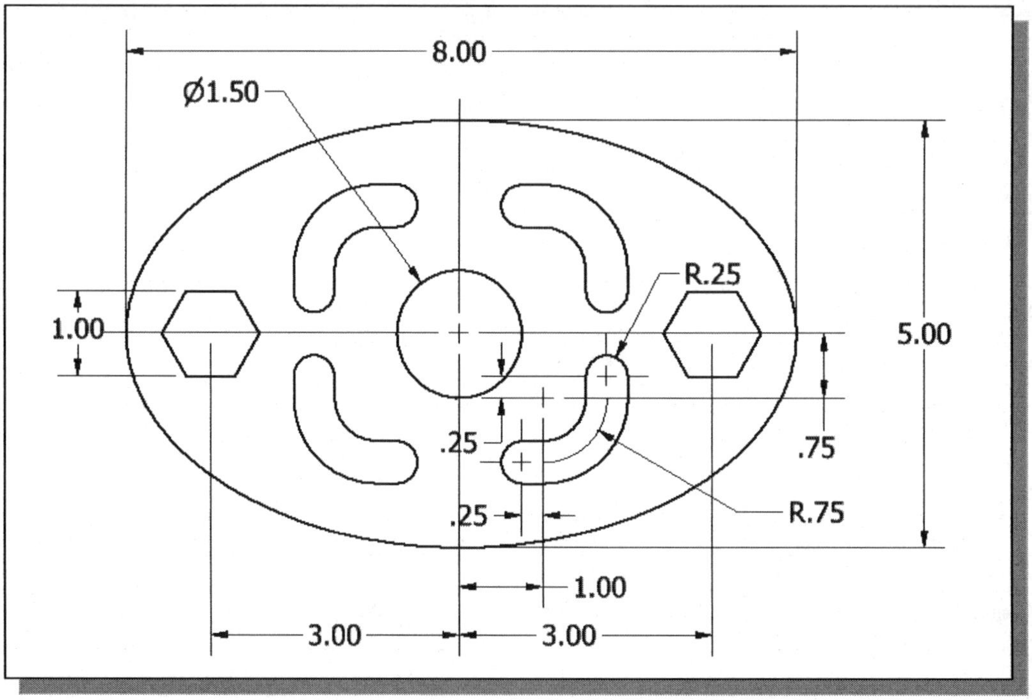

10. **Filter Cap**

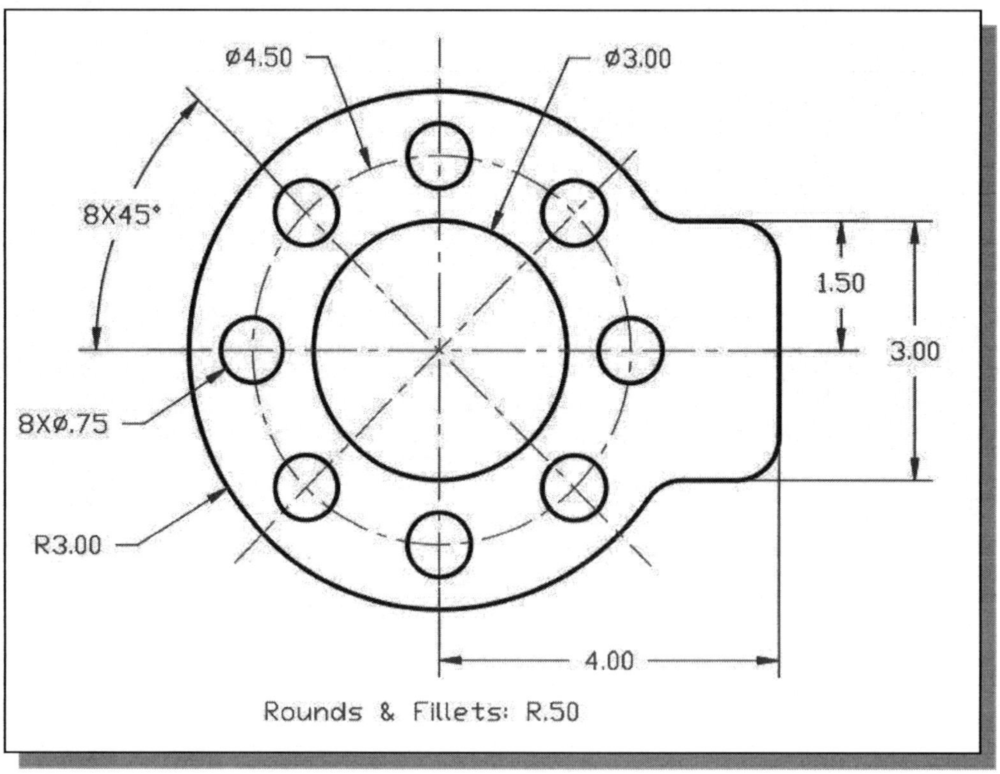

Chapter 4
Orthographic Views in Multiview Drawings – AutoCAD

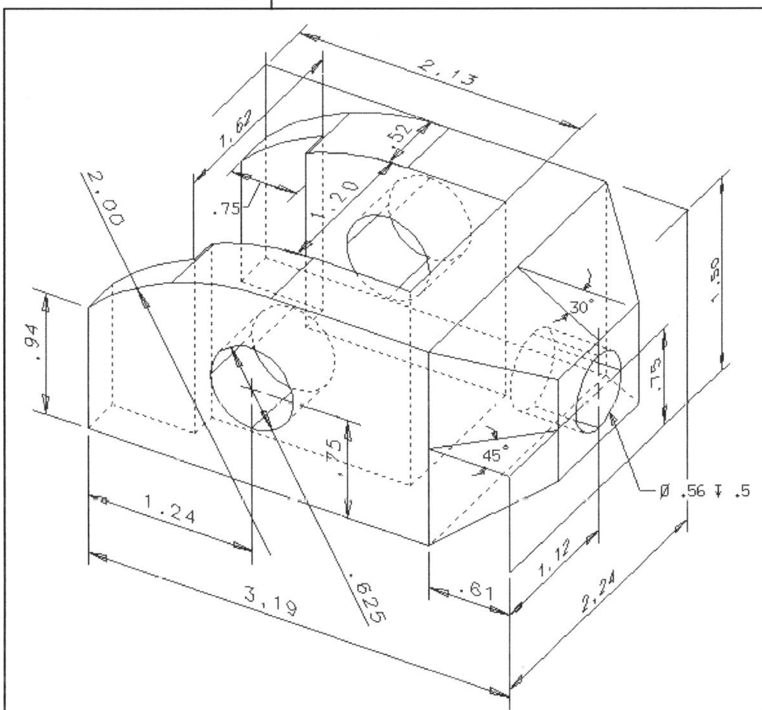

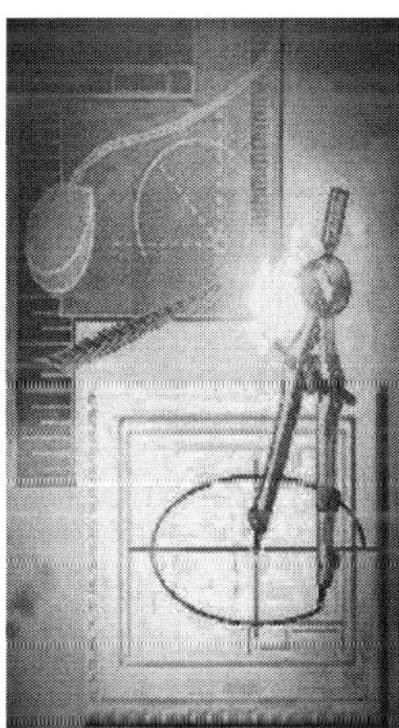

Learning Objectives

- Create 2D orthographic views using AutoCAD
- Use the Construction Line command to draw
- Use Running Object Snaps
- Use AutoCAD's AutoSnap and AutoTrack features
- Create a Miter line to transfer dimensions
- Use Projection lines between orthographic views
- Use the Polar Tracking option

Introduction

Most drawings produced and used in industry are ***multiview drawings***. Multiview drawings are used to provide accurate three-dimensional object information on two-dimensional media, a means of communicating all of the information necessary to transform an idea or concept into reality. The standards and conventions of multiview drawings have been developed over many years, which equip us with a universally understood method of communication. The age of computers has greatly altered the design process, and several CAD methods are now available to help generate multiview drawings using CAD systems.

Multiview drawings usually require several orthographic views to define the shape of a three-dimensional object. Each orthographic view is a two-dimensional drawing showing only two of the three dimensions of the three-dimensional object. Consequently, no individual view contains sufficient information to completely define the shape of the three-dimensional object. All orthographic views must be looked at together to comprehend the shape of the three-dimensional object. The arrangement and relationship between the views are therefore very important in multiview drawings. In this chapter, the common methods of creating two-dimensional orthographic views with AutoCAD are examined.

The Locator Design

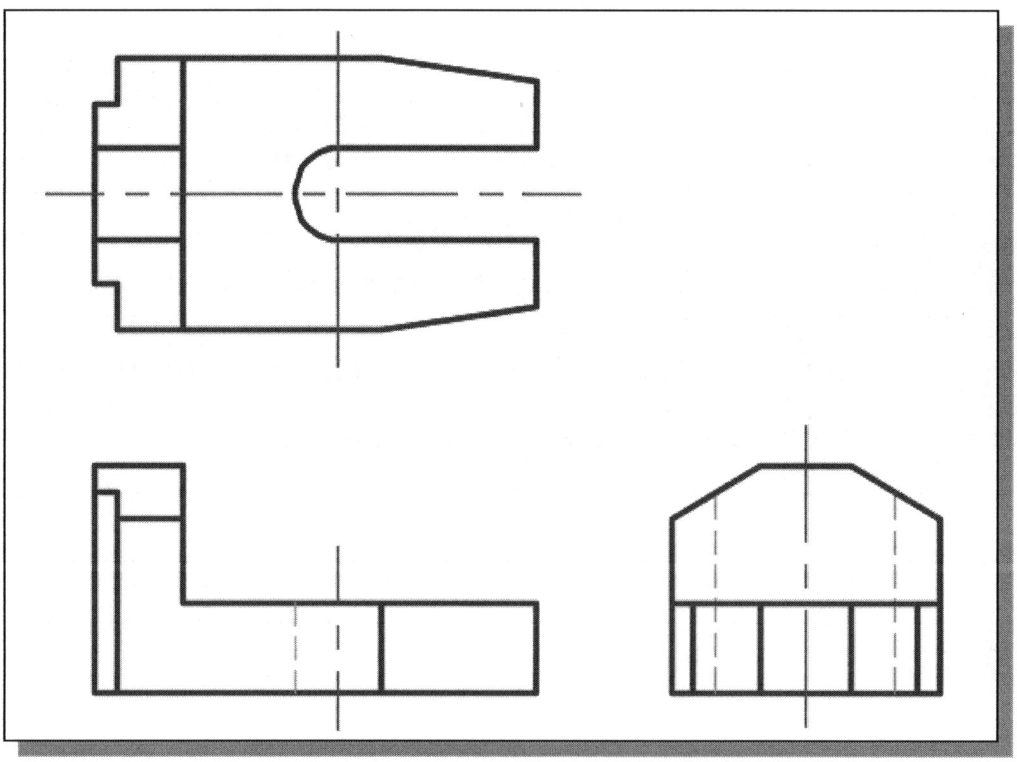

The Locator Part

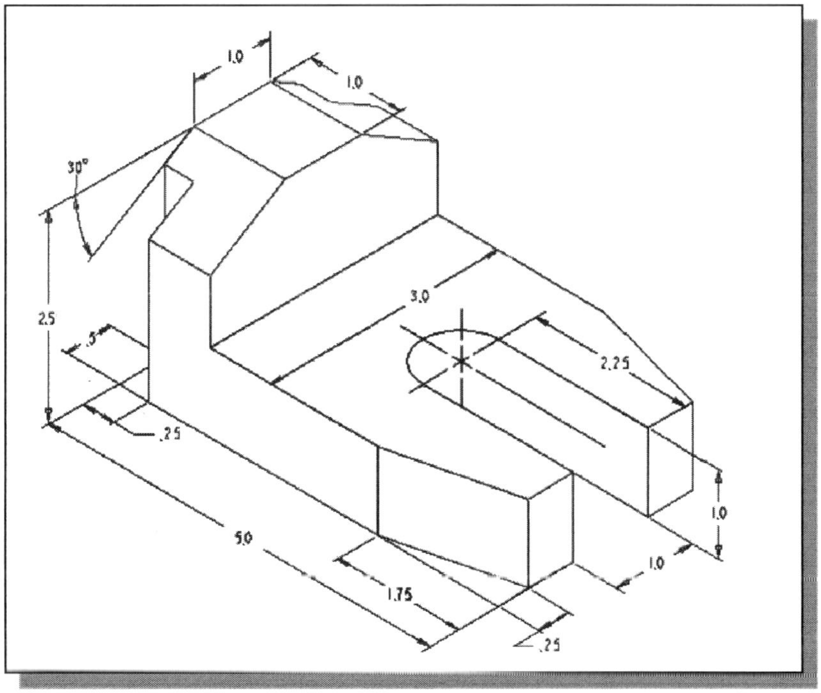

➢ Before going through the tutorial, make a rough sketch of a multiview drawing of the part. How many 2D views will be necessary to fully describe the part? Based on your knowledge of **AutoCAD 2027** so far, how would you arrange and construct these 2D views? Take a few minutes to consider these questions and do preliminary planning by sketching on a piece of paper. You are also encouraged to construct the orthographic views on your own prior to following through the tutorial.

Starting Up AutoCAD 2027

1. Select the **AutoCAD 2027** option on the *Program* menu or select the **AutoCAD 2027** icon on the *Desktop*.

2. In the *Startup* dialog box, select the **Start from Scratch** option with a single click of the left-mouse-button.

3. In the ***Default Settings*** section, pick **Imperial** as the drawing units.

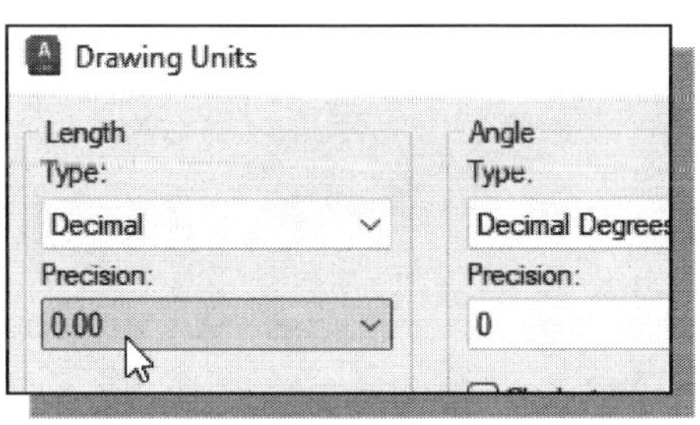

4. On your own, open up the *Units* dialog box, and set the precision to **two decimal places** as shown.

5. On your own, set the ***Grid Spacing*** and ***Snap Spacing*** to ***0.5*** for both X and Y directions.

Layers Setup

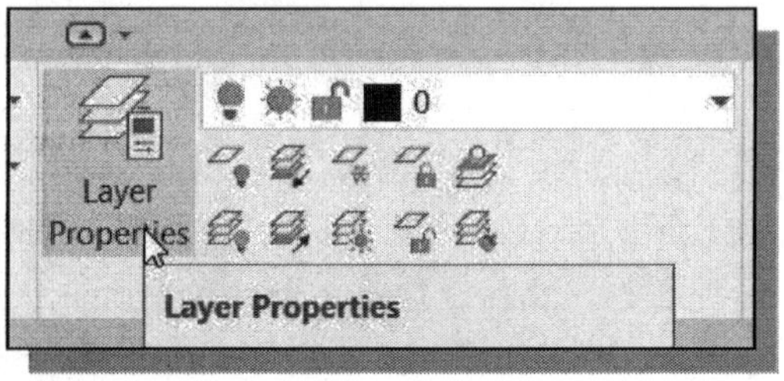

1. Pick **Layer Properties Manager** in the *Layers* toolbar.

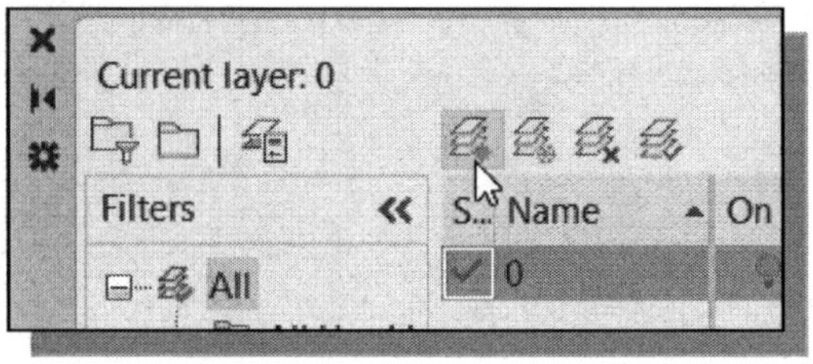

2. Click on the **New Layer** icon to create new layers.

3. Create two **new** layers with the following settings:

Layer	***Color***	***Linetype***
Construction	**White**	**Continuous**
Object	**Blue**	**Continuous**

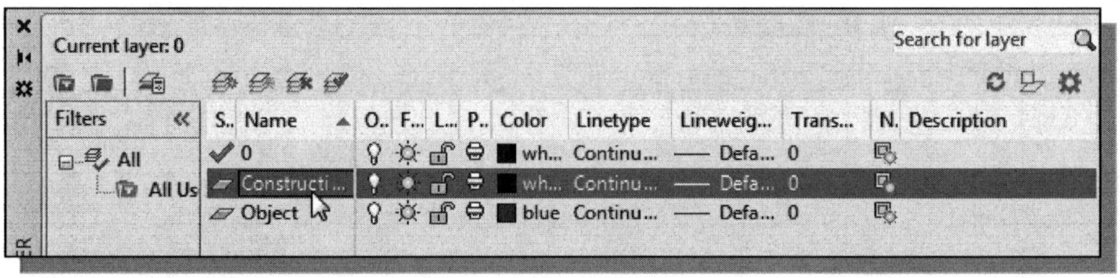

4. Highlight the layer ***Construction*** in the list of layers.

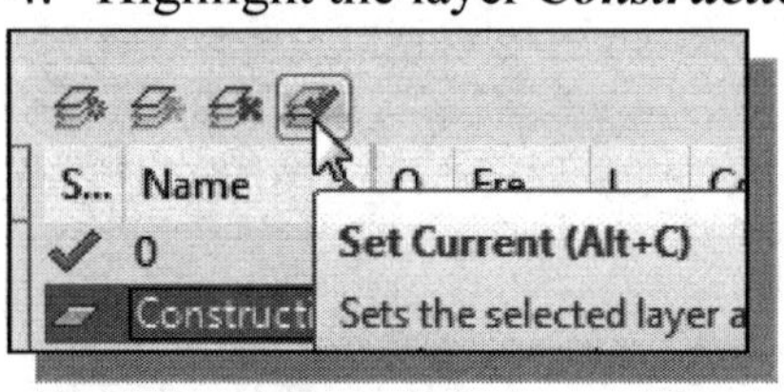

5. Click on the **Current** button to set layer ***Construction*** as the *Current Layer*.

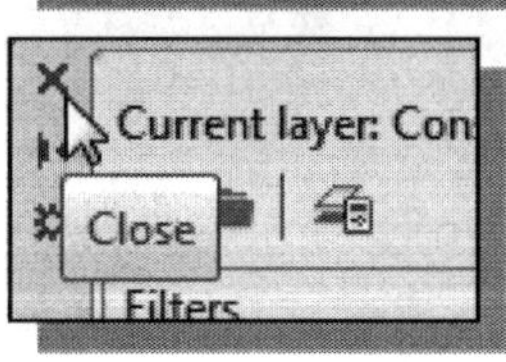

6. Click on the **Close** button to accept the settings and exit the *Layer Properties Manager* dialog box.

7. In the *Status Bar* area, reset the option buttons so that only *SNAP Mode* and *GRID Display* are switched ***ON***.

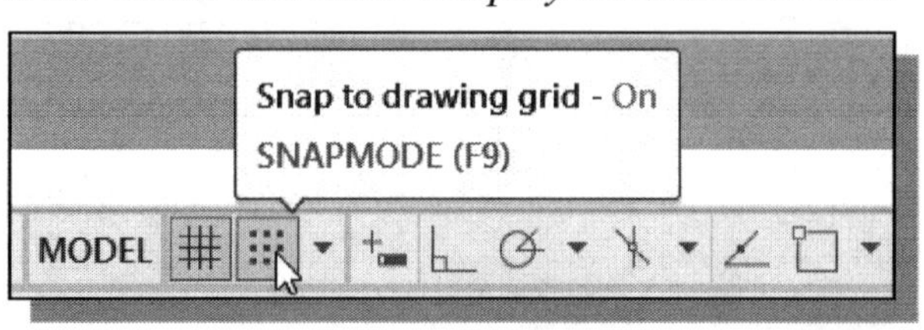

Drawing Construction Lines

Construction lines are lines that extend to infinity. Construction lines are usually used as references for creating other objects. We will also place the construction lines on the *Construction* layer so that the layer can later be frozen or turned off.

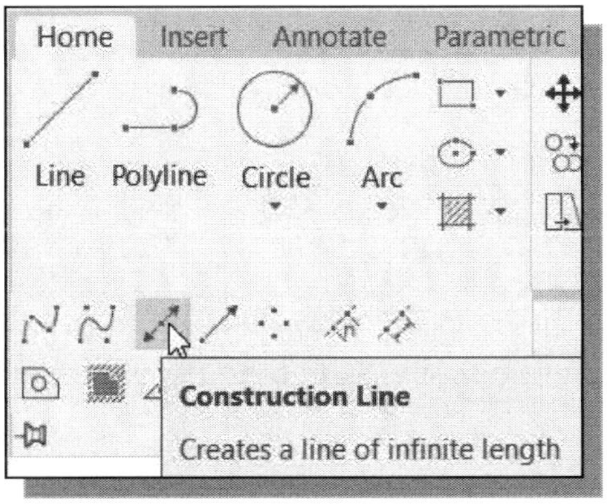

1. Select the **Construction Line** icon in the *Draw* toolbar. In the command prompt area, the message "*_xline Specify a point or [Hor/Ver/Ang/Bisect/ Offset]:*" is displayed.

- To orient construction lines, we generally specify two points. Note that other orientation options are also available.

2. Select a location near the **lower left corner** of the *Drawing Area*. It is not necessary to align objects to the origin of the world coordinate system. CAD systems provide us with many powerful tools to manipulate geometry. Our main goal is to use the CAD system as a flexible and powerful tool and to be very efficient and effective with the systems.

3. Pick a location above the last point to create a **vertical construction line**.

4. Move the cursor toward the right of the first point and pick a location to create a **horizontal construction line**.

5. Inside the *Drawing Area*, **right-click** to end the Construction Line command.

6. In the *Status Bar* area, turn ***OFF*** the *SNAP* option.

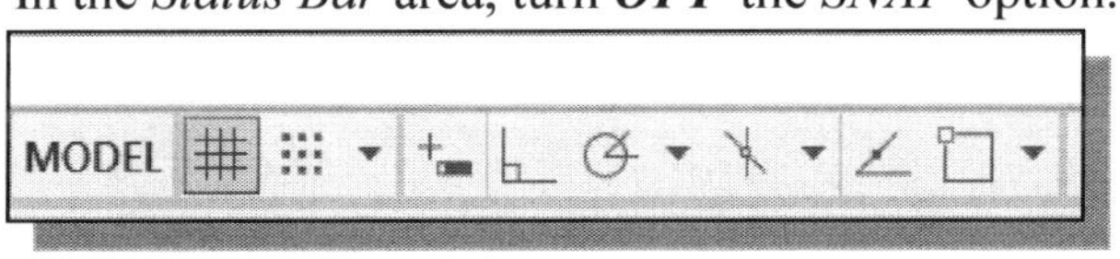

Using the Offset Command

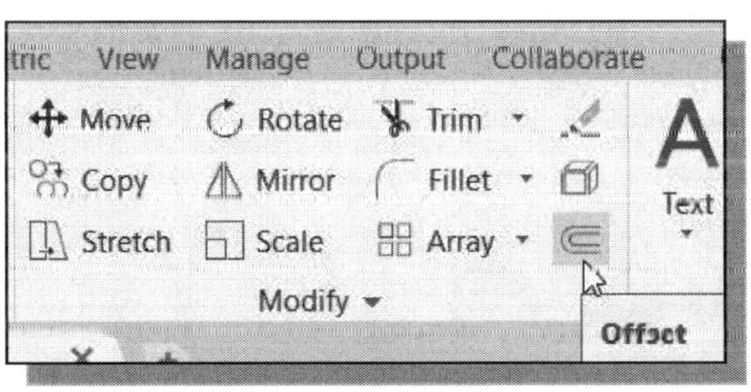

1. Select the **Offset** icon in the *Modify* toolbar. In the *command prompt area*, the message "*Specify offset distance or [Through/Erase/Layer]:*" is displayed.

2. In the *command prompt area*, enter ***5.0*** **[ENTER]**.

3. In the *command prompt area*, the message "*Select object to offset or <exit>:*" is displayed. Pick the **vertical line** on the screen.

4. AutoCAD next asks us to identify the direction of the offset. Pick a location that is to the **right** of the vertical line.

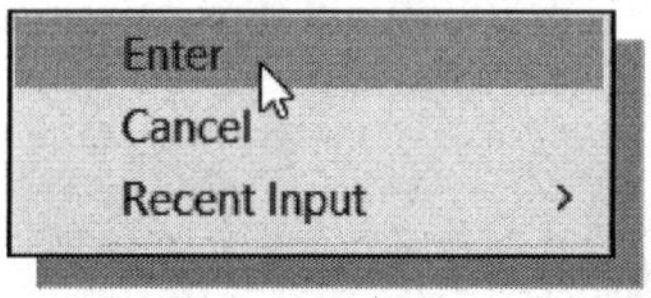

5. Inside the *Drawing Area*, **right-click** and choose **Enter** to end the Offset command.

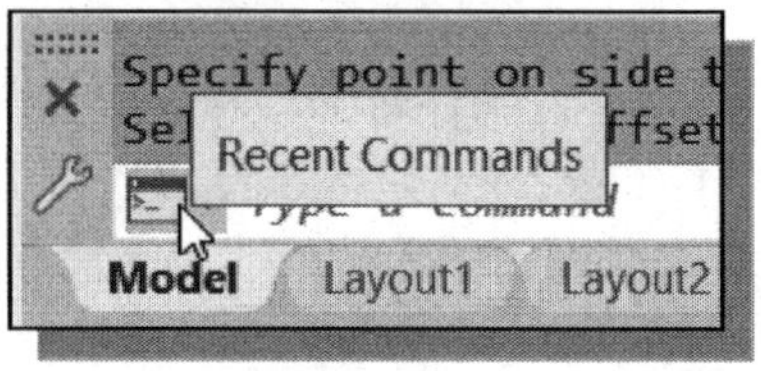

6. In the *command prompt area*, click on the small **triangle icon** to access the list of recent commands.

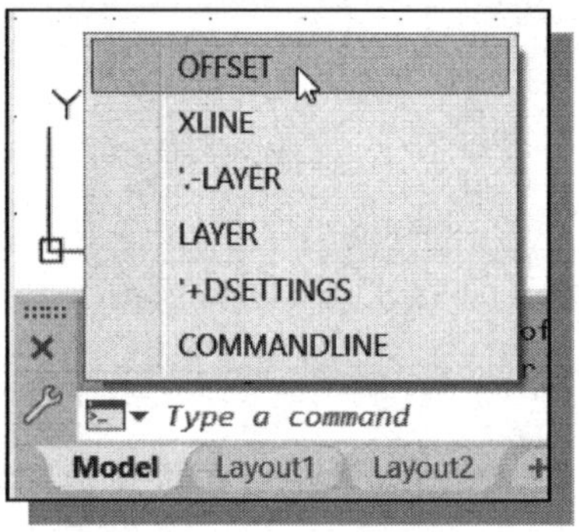

7. Select **Offset** in the pop-up list, to repeat the Offset command.

8. In the *command prompt area*, enter **2.5 [ENTER]**.

9. In the command prompt area, the message "*Select object to offset or <exit>:*" is displayed. Pick the **horizontal line** on the screen.

10. AutoCAD next asks us to identify the direction of the offset. Pick a location that is **above** the horizontal line.

11. Inside the Drawing Area, **right-click** to end the Offset command.

12. Repeat the **Offset** command and create the offset lines as shown.

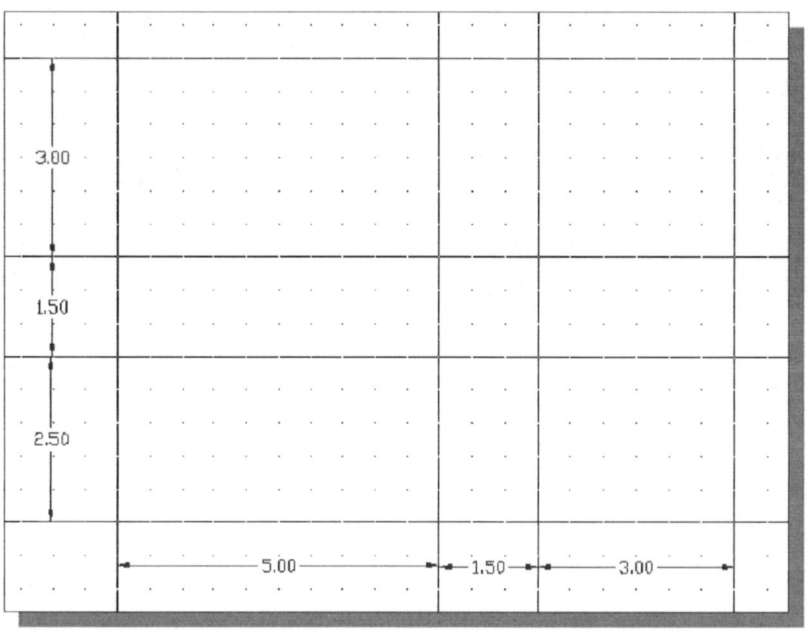

Set Layer Object as the Current Layer

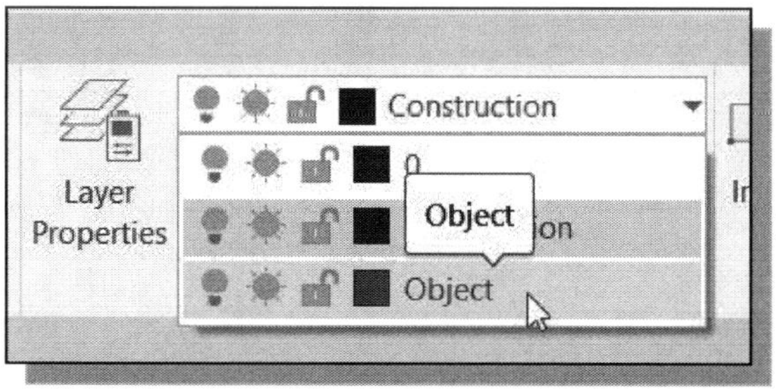

1. On the *Layers* toolbar panel, choose the ***Layer Control*** box with the left-mouse-button.

2. Move the cursor over the name of the layer ***Object***. The tool tip "*Object*" appears.

3. **Left-click once** on the layer *Object* to set it as the *Current Layer*.

Using the Running Object Snaps

In **AutoCAD 2027**, while using geometry construction commands, the cursor can be placed to points on objects such as endpoints, midpoints, centers, and intersections. In AutoCAD, this tool is called the ***Object Snap***.

Object snaps can be turned on in one of two ways:

- **Single Point (or override) Object Snaps**: Sets an object snap for one use.
- **Running Object Snaps**: Sets object snaps *active* until we turn them off.

The procedure we have used so far is the *Single Point Object Snaps* option, where we select the specific object snap from the *Object Snap* toolbar for one use only. The use of the *Running Object Snaps* option to assist the construction is illustrated next.

1. In the *Menu Bar*, select:

   [Tools] → [Drafting Settings]

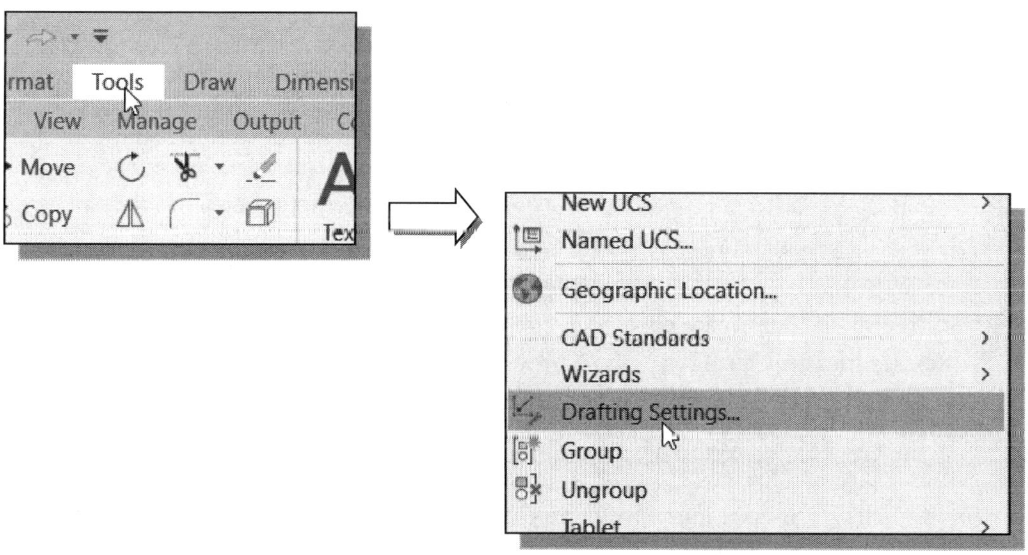

2. In the *Drafting Settings* dialog box select the **Object Snap** tab.

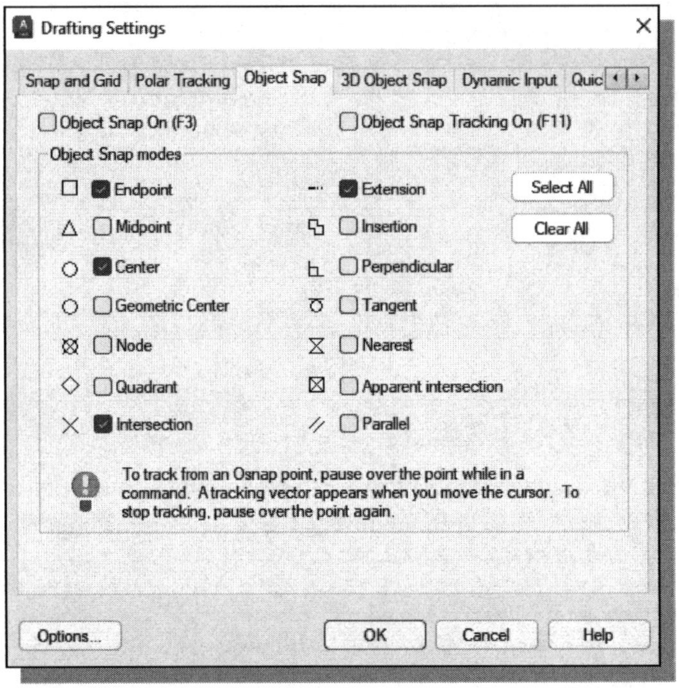

- The *Running Object Snap* options can be turned on or off by clicking the different options listed. Notice the different symbols associated with the different *Object Snap* options.

3. Turn ***ON*** the *Running Object Snap* by clicking the **Object Snap On** box, or hit the **[F3]** key once.

4. Confirm the ***Intersection***, ***Endpoint*** and ***Extension*** options are switched ***ON*** and click on the **OK** button to accept the settings and exit from the *Drafting Settings* dialog box.

❖ Notice in the *Status Bar* area the ***OSNAP*** button is switched ***ON***. We can toggle the *Running Object Snap* option on or off by clicking the *OSNAP* button.

5. Press the **[F3]** key once and notice the *OSNAP* button is switched ***OFF*** in the *Status Bar* area.

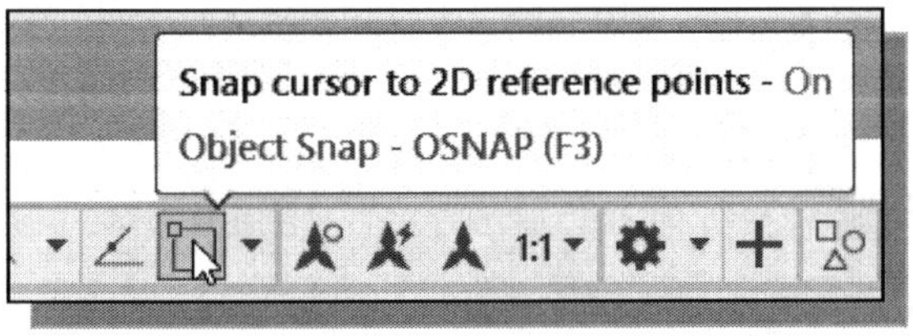

6. Press the **[F3]** key again and notice the *OSNAP* button is now switched ***ON*** in the *Status Bar* area.

➢ **AutoCAD 2027** provides many input methods and shortcuts; you are encouraged to examine the different options and choose the option that best fits your own style.

Creating Object Lines

We will define the areas for the front view, top view and side view by adding object lines using the *Running Object Snap* option.

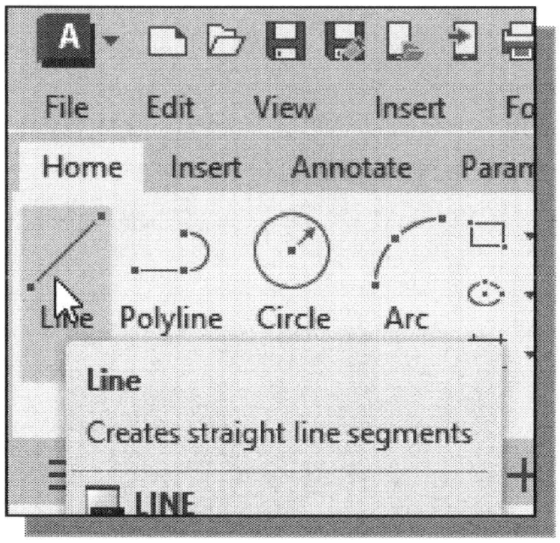

1. Select the **Line** command icon in the *Draw* toolbar. In the command prompt area, the message "*Line Specify first point:*" is displayed.

2. Move the cursor to the **intersection** of any two lines and notice the visual aid automatically displayed at the intersection.

3. Pick the four intersection points closest to the lower left corner to create the four sides of the area of the front view.

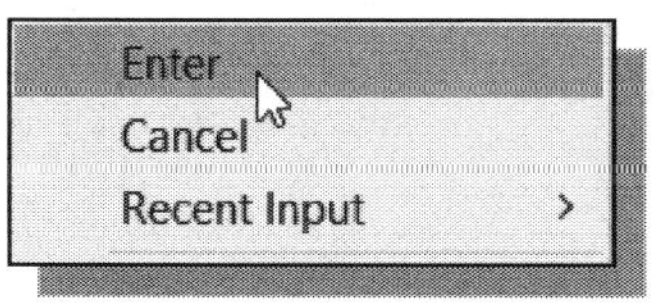

4. Inside the *Drawing Area*, **right-click** once to activate the option menu and select **Enter** with the left-mouse-button to end the **Line** command.

5. Repeat the **Line** command to define the top view and side view as shown.

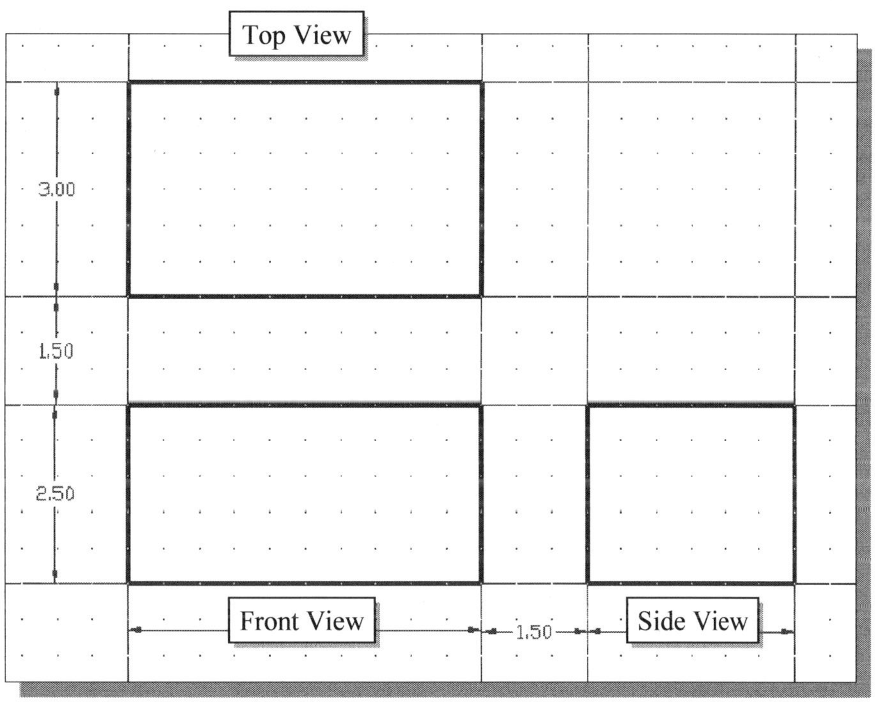

Turn Off the Construction Lines Layer

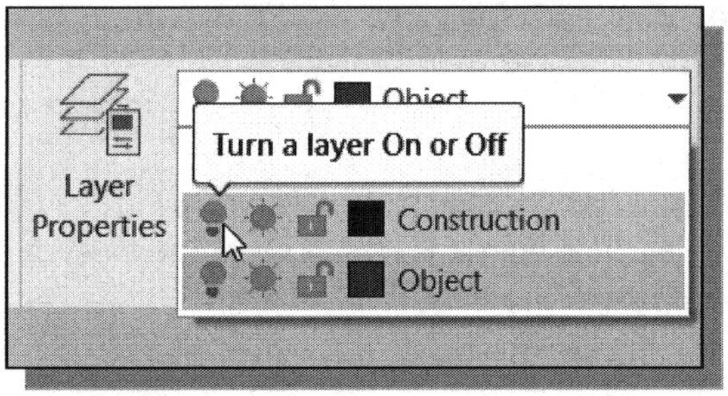

1. On the *Object Properties* toolbar, choose the ***Layer Control*** box with the left-mouse-button.

2. Move the cursor over the lightbulb icon for layer ***Construction***. The tool tip "*Turn a layer On or Off*" appears.

3. **Left-click once** on the *lightbulb* icon and notice the icon color is changed to gray color, representing the layer (layer *Construction*) is turned ***OFF***.

Adding More Objects in the Front View

1. Use the **Offset** command and create the two parallel lines in the front view as shown.

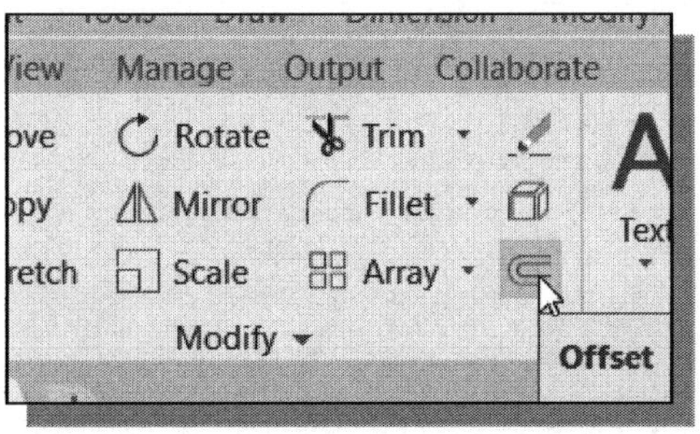

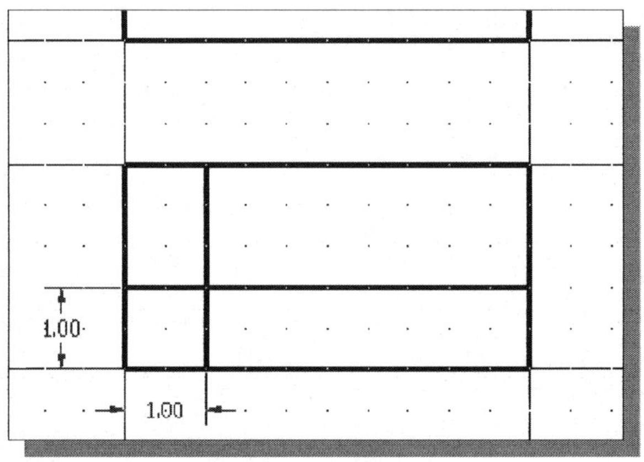

2. Use the **Trim** command and modify the front view as shown.

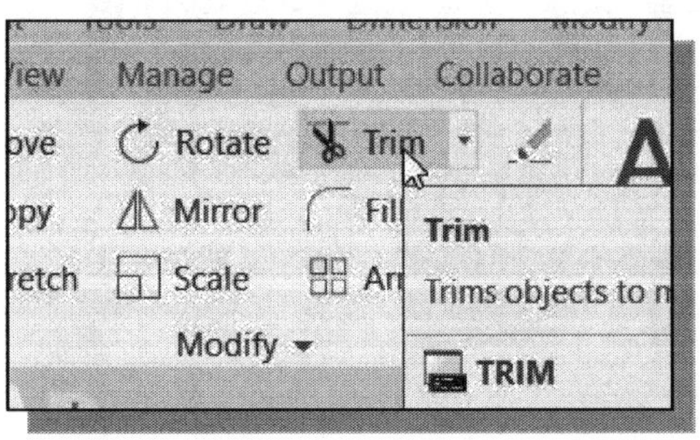

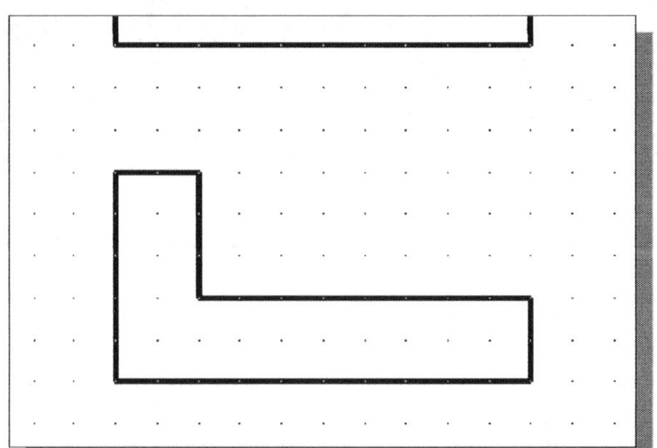

AutoCAD's AutoSnap™ and AutoTrack™ Features

AutoCAD's *AutoSnap* and *AutoTrack* provide visual aids when the *Object Snap* options are switched *on*. The main advantages of *AutoSnap* and *AutoTrack* are as follows:

- **Symbols**: Automatically displays the *Object Snap* type at the object snap location.
- **Tooltips**: Automatically displays the *Object Snap* type below the cursor.
- **Magnet**: Locks the cursor onto a snap point when the cursor is near the point.

With ***Object Snap Tracking***, the cursor can track along alignment paths based on other object snap points when specifying points in a command. To use *Object Snap Tracking*, one or more object snaps must be switched on. The basic rules of using the ***Object Snap Tracking*** option are as follows:

- To track from a *Running Object Snap* point, pause over the point while in a command.
- A tracking vector appears when we move the cursor.
- To stop tracking, pause over the point again.
- When multiple *Running Object Snaps* are on, press the **[TAB]** key to cycle through available snap points when the object snap aperture box is on an object.

1. In the *Status Bar* area, turn **ON** the *OTRACK/AUTOSNAP* option.

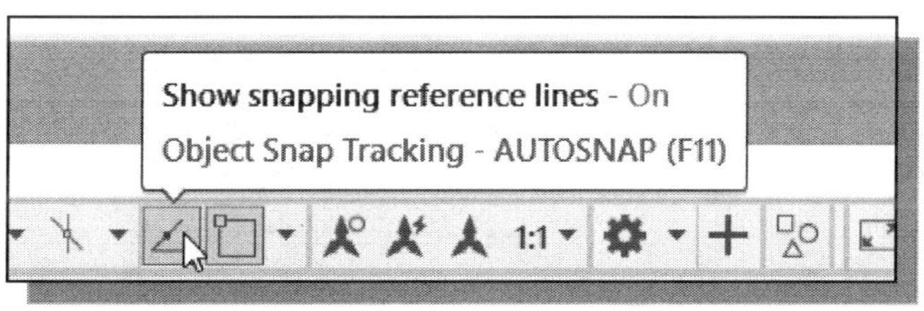

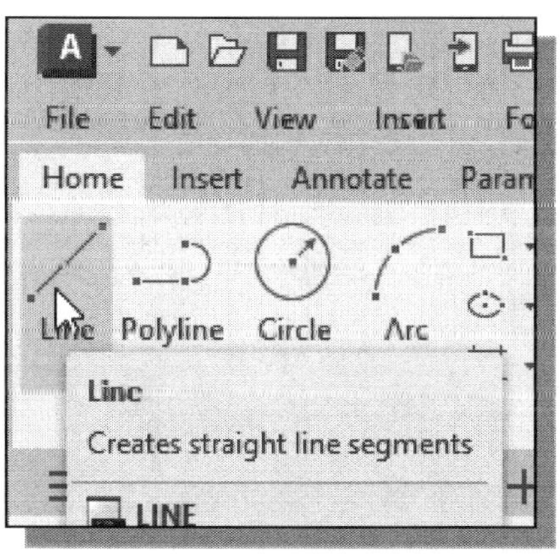

2. Select the **Line** command icon in the *Draw* toolbar. In the command prompt area, the message "*Line Specify first point:*" is displayed.

3. Move the cursor near the top right corner of the vertical protrusion in the front view. Notice that *AUTOSNAP* automatically locks the cursor to the corner and displays the ***Endpoint*** symbol.

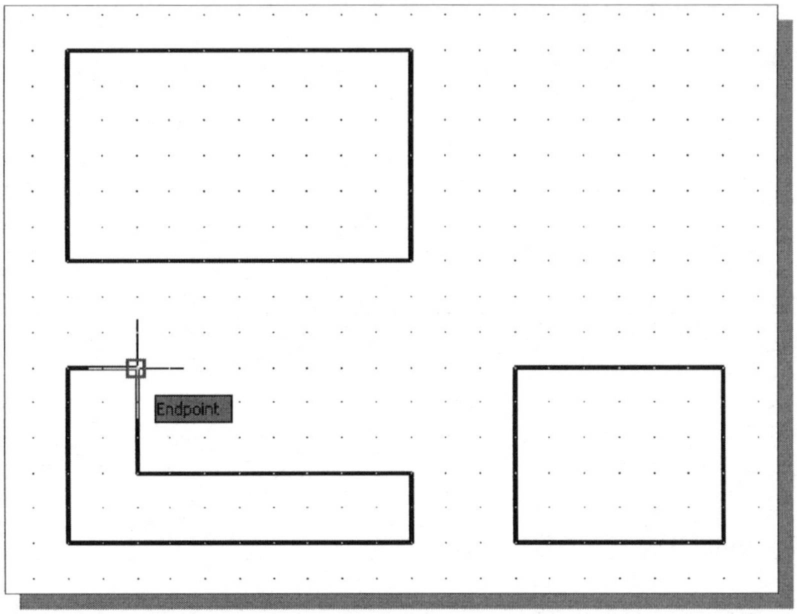

4. Move the cursor upward and notice that *Object Tracking* displays a dashed line, showing the alignment to the top right corner of the vertical protrusion in the front view. Move the cursor near the top horizontal line of the top view and notice that *AUTOSNAP* displays the intersection point.

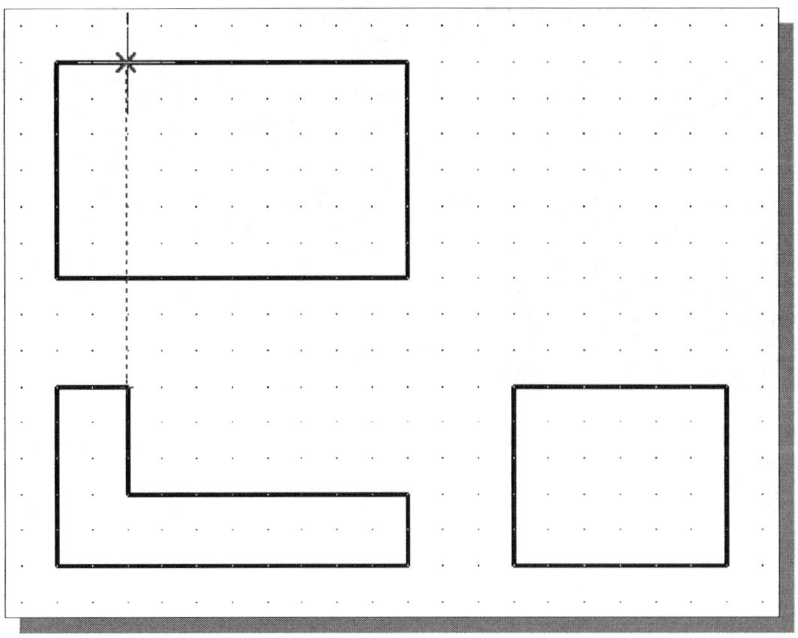

5. Left-click to place the starting point of a line at the intersection.

6. Move the cursor to the top left corner of the front view to activate the tracking feature.

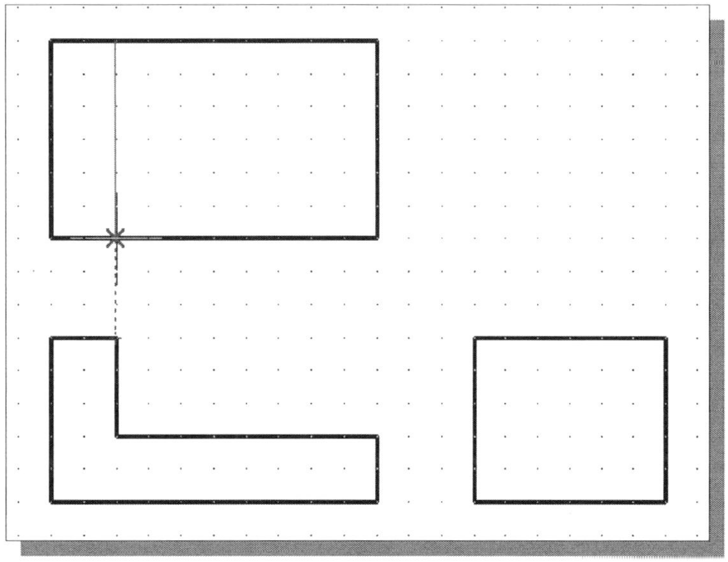

7. Create the line as shown in the above figure.

Adding More Objects in the Top View

1. Use the **Offset** command and create the two parallel lines in the top view as shown.

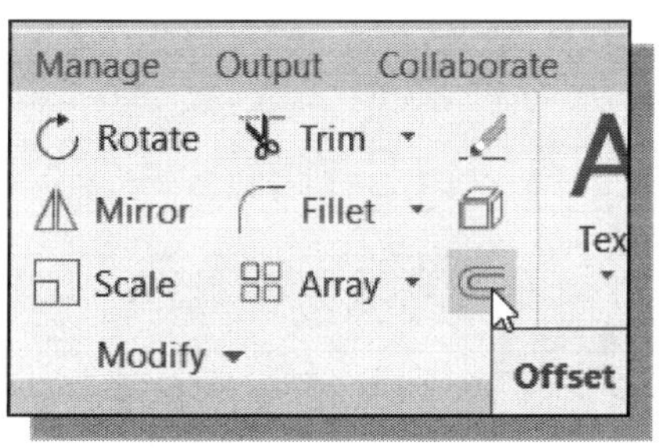

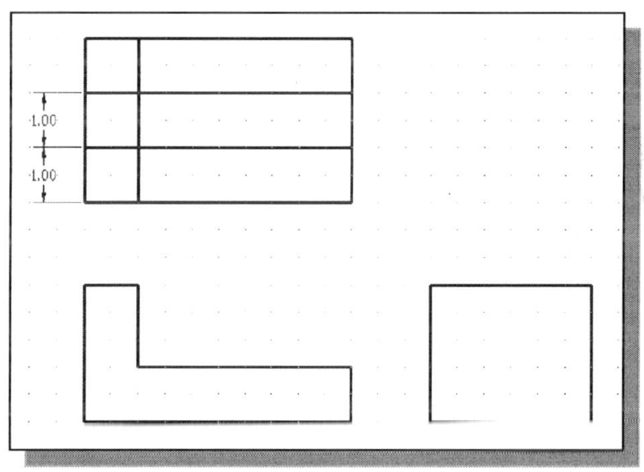

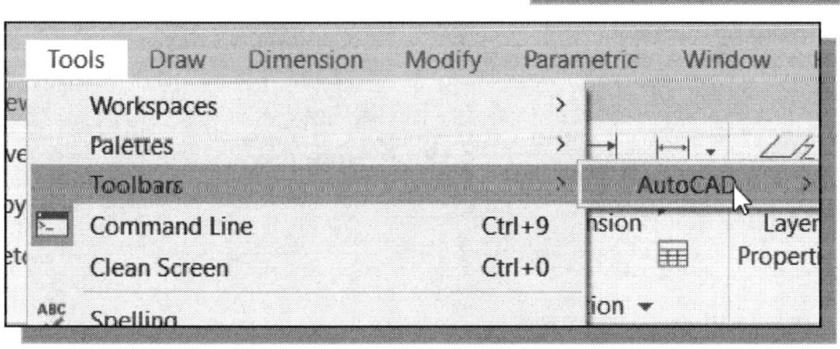

2. On your own, select **[Tools] → [Toolbars] → [Object Snap]** to display the *Object Snap* toolbar on the screen.

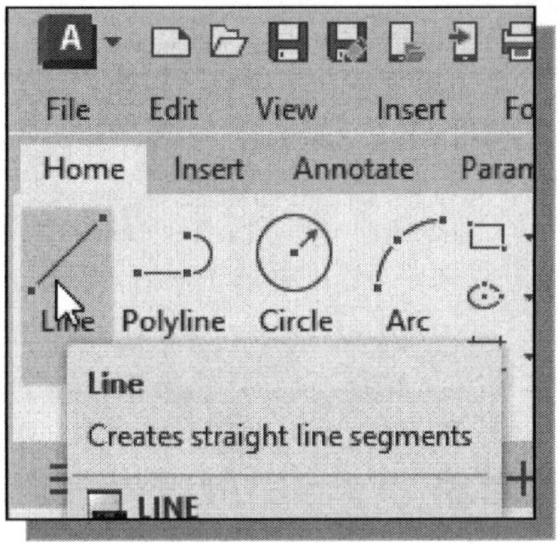

3. Select the **Line** command icon in the *Draw* toolbar. In the command prompt area, the message "*Line Specify first point:*" is displayed.

4. In the *Object Snap* toolbar, pick **Snap From**. In the command prompt area, the message "*_from Base point*" is displayed. AutoCAD now expects us to select a geometric entity on the screen.

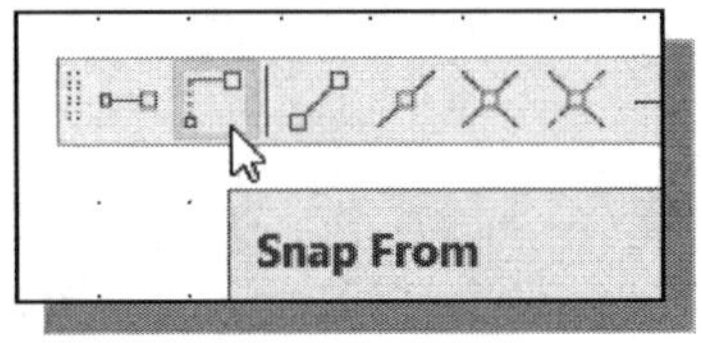

➢ The ***Single Point Object Snap*** overrides the ***Running Object Snap*** option.

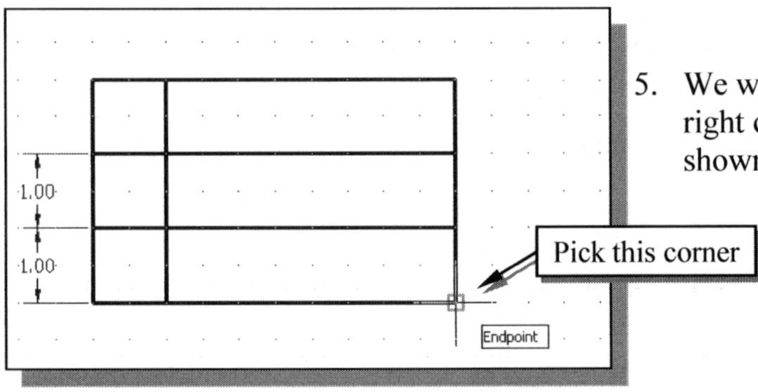

5. We will measure relative to the lower right corner. Pick the corner as shown.

6. In the command prompt area, enter ***@0,0.25*** **[ENTER]**.

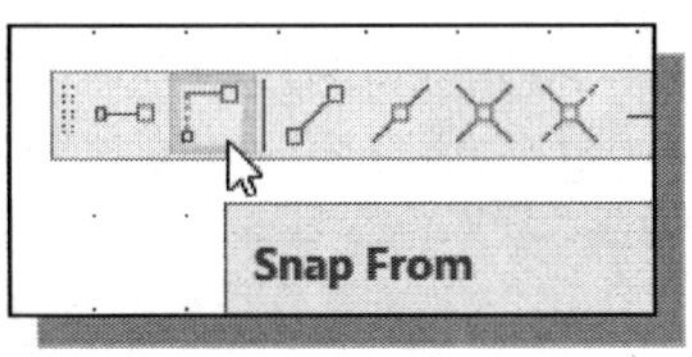

7. In the *Object Snap* toolbar, pick **Snap From**. Pick the lower right corner of the top view again.

8. In the command prompt area, enter ***@-1.75,0*** **[ENTER]**.

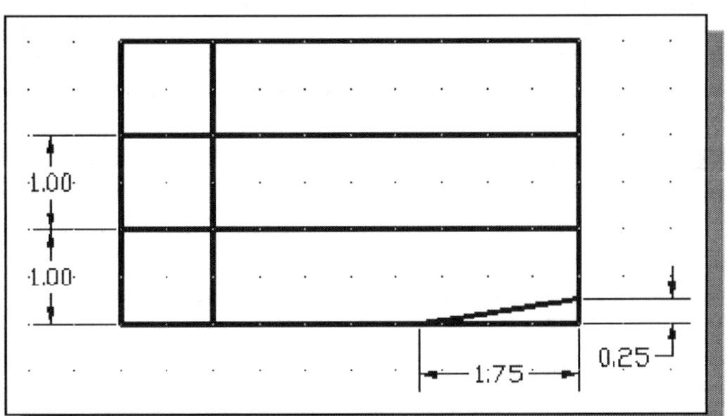

9. Inside the Drawing Area, right-click to activate the option menu and select **Enter** with the left-mouse-button to end the **Line** command.

10. Repeat the procedure and create the line on the top right corner as shown.

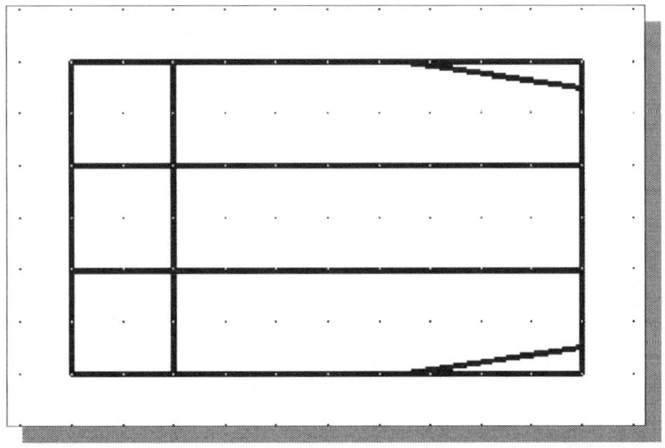

11. Using the *Snap From* option, create the circle (diameter ***1.0***) as shown.

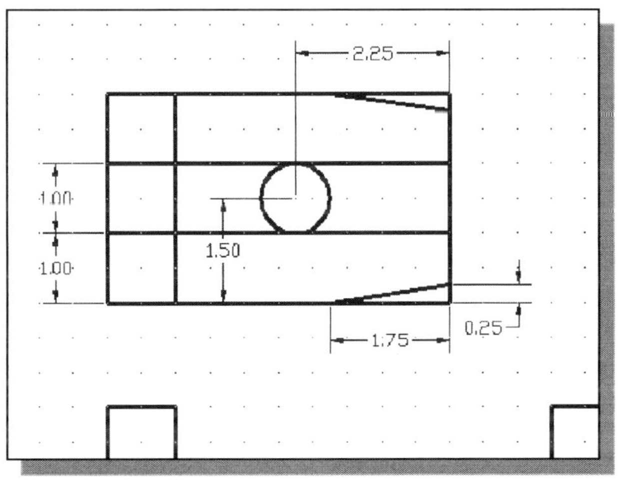

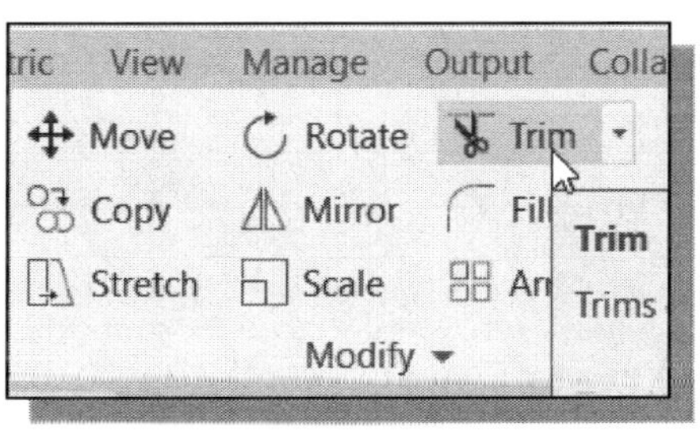

12. Select the **Trim** icon in the *Modify* toolbar.

13. In the command prompt area, click **cuTting edges** as shown.

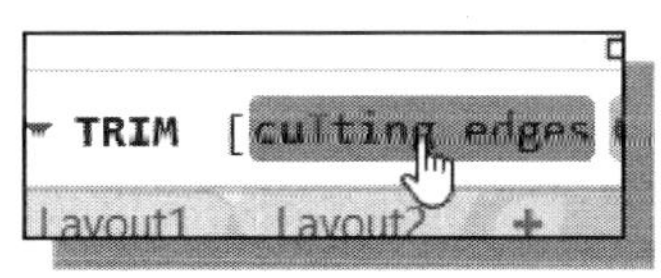

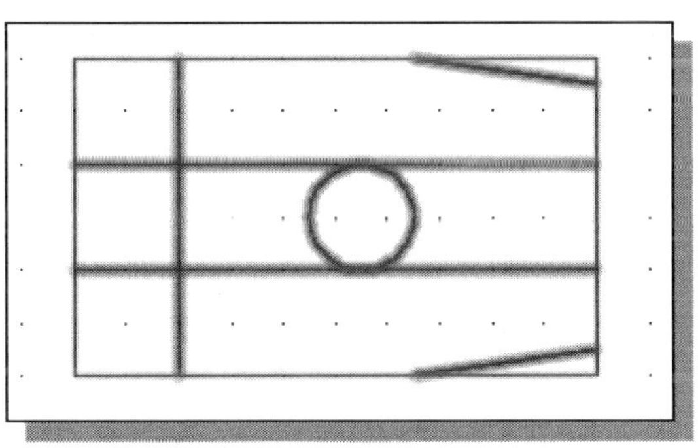

14. Pick the following objects as boundary edges: the circle and the lines that are near the circle.

15. Inside the *Drawing Area*, **right-click** to accept the selected objects.

16. Select the unwanted portions and modify the objects as shown.

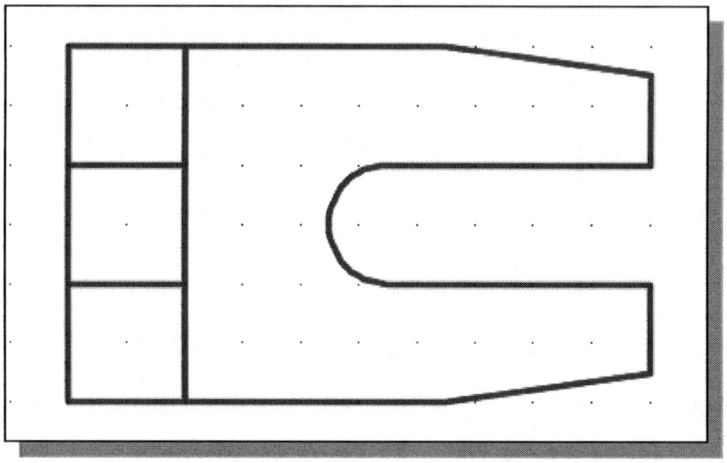

17. On your own, use the **Offset** and **Trim** commands and modify the top view as shown.

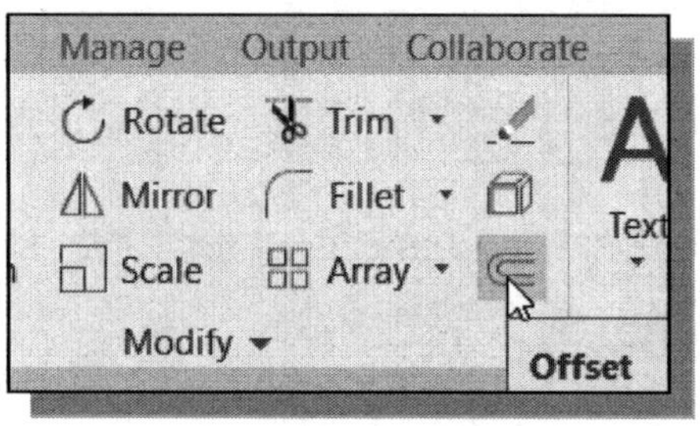

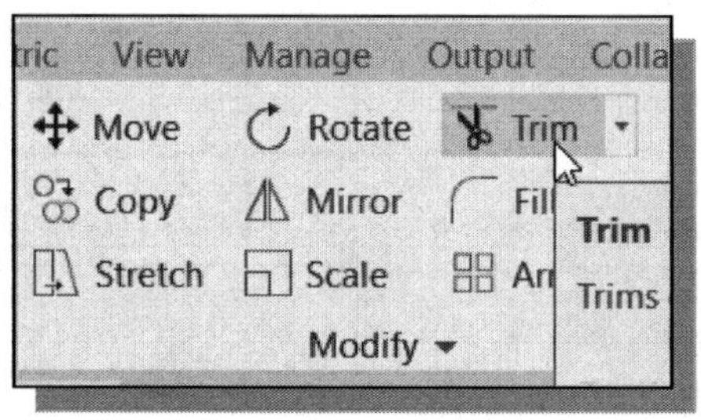

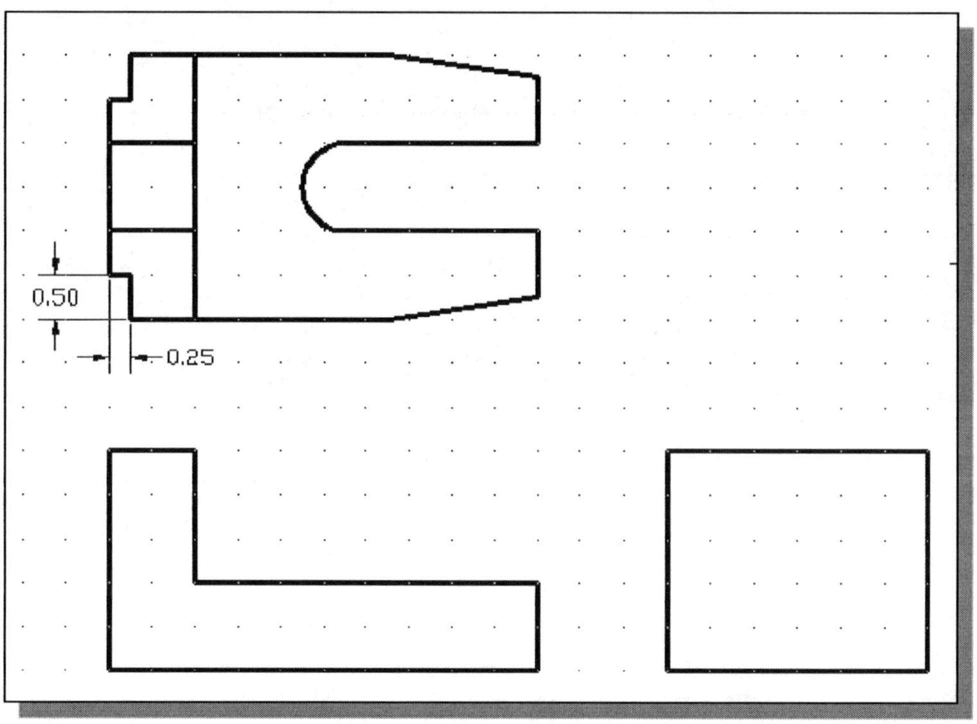

Drawing Using the Miter Line Method

The *45° miter line* method is a simple and straightforward procedure to transfer measurements in between the top view and the side view.

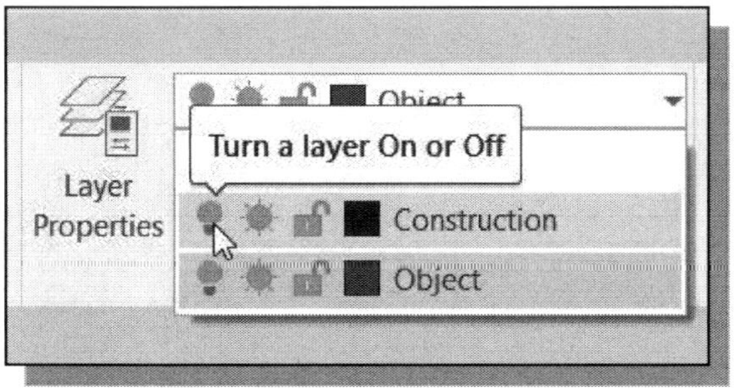

1. On the *Layers* toolbar panel, choose the ***Layer Control*** box by clicking once with the left-mouse-button.

2. Move the cursor over the **light-bulb** icon for layer ***Construction***. The tool tip "*Turn a layer On or Off*" appears.

3. **Left-click once** and notice the icon color is changed to a light color, representing the layer (layer *Construction*) is turned *ON*.

4. **Left-click once** over the name of the layer ***Construction*** to set it as the *Current Layer*.

5. Use the **Line** command and create the *miter line* by connecting the two intersections of the construction lines as shown.

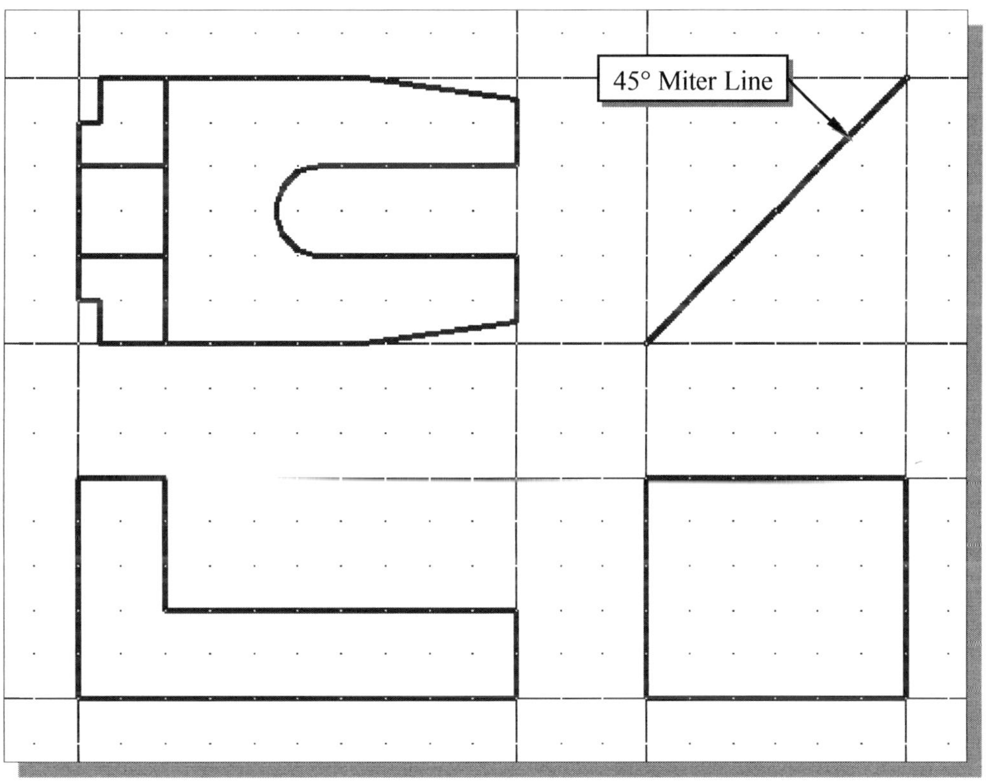

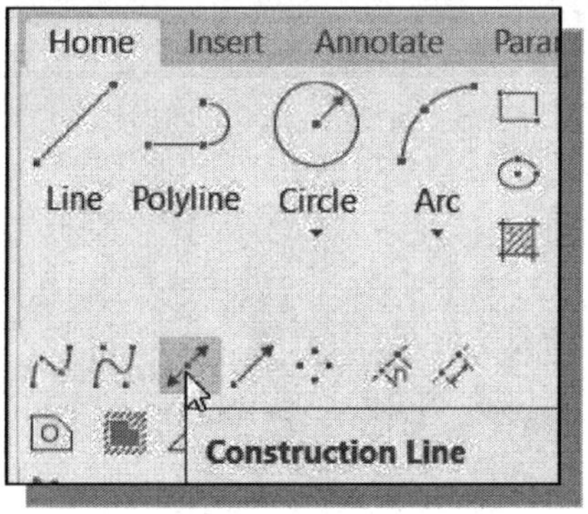

6. Select the **Construction Line** command in the *Draw* toolbar as shown.

7. In the *command prompt area*, select the **Horizontal** option as shown.

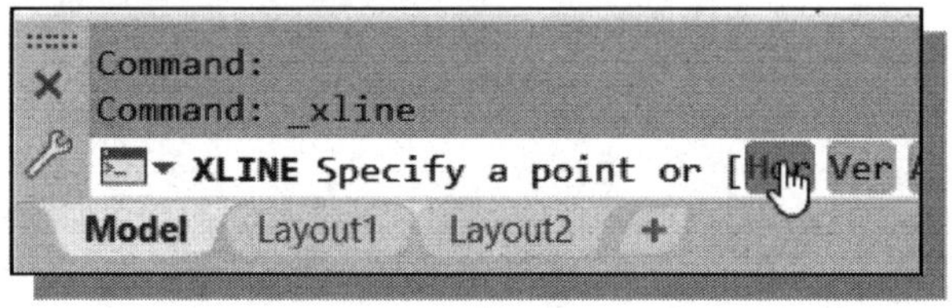

8. On your own, create horizontal projection lines through all the corners in the top view as shown.

9. Use the **Trim** command and trim the projection lines as shown in the figure below.

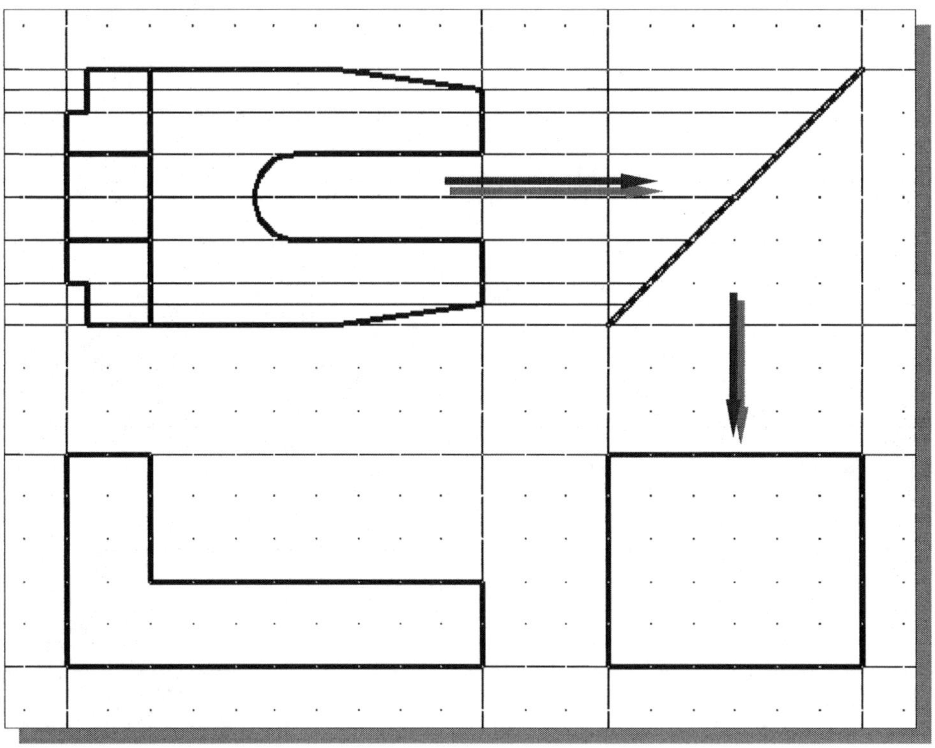

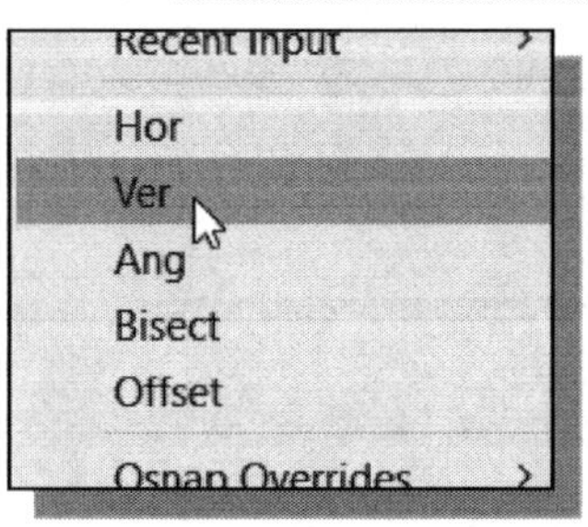

10. On your own, create additional Construction Lines (use the *vertical* option) through all the intersection points that are on the *miter line*.

More Layers Setup

1. Pick ***Layer Properties Manager*** in the *Layers* toolbar panel as shown in the figure below.

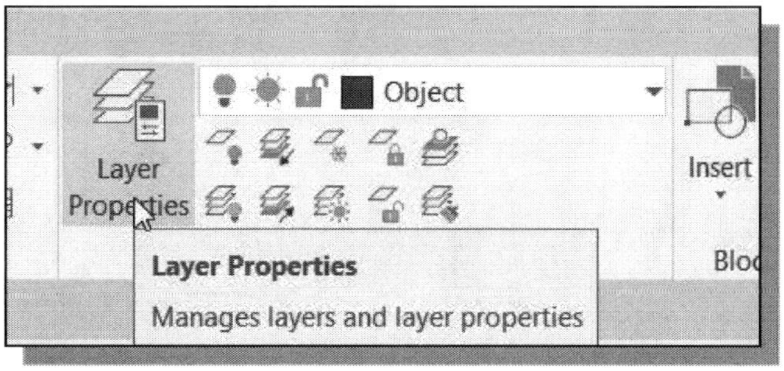

2. Click on the **New** icon to create new layers.

3. Create two **new layers** with the following settings:

Layer	***Color***	***Linetype***
Center	**Red**	**CENTER**
Hidden	**Cyan**	**HIDDEN**

- The default linetype is *Continuous.* To use other linetypes, click on the **Load** button in the *Select Linetype* dialog box and select the desired linetypes.

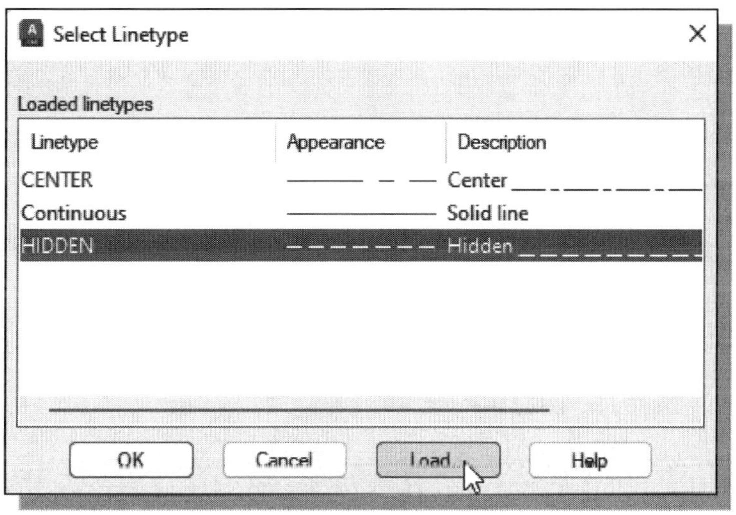

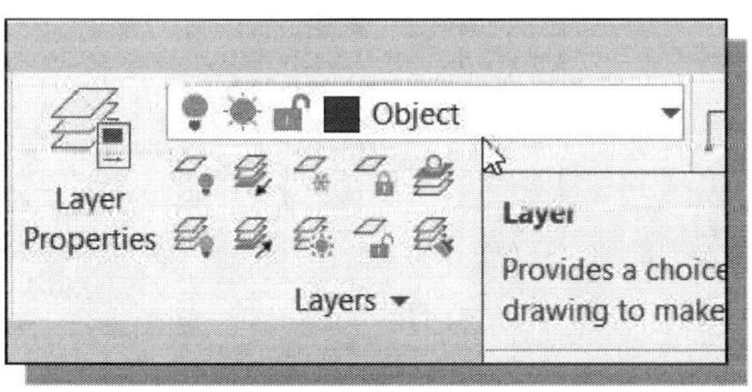

4. On your own, set the layer ***Object*** as the *Current Layer.*

Top View to Side View Projection

1. Using the *Running Object Snaps*, create the necessary **object-lines** in the side view.

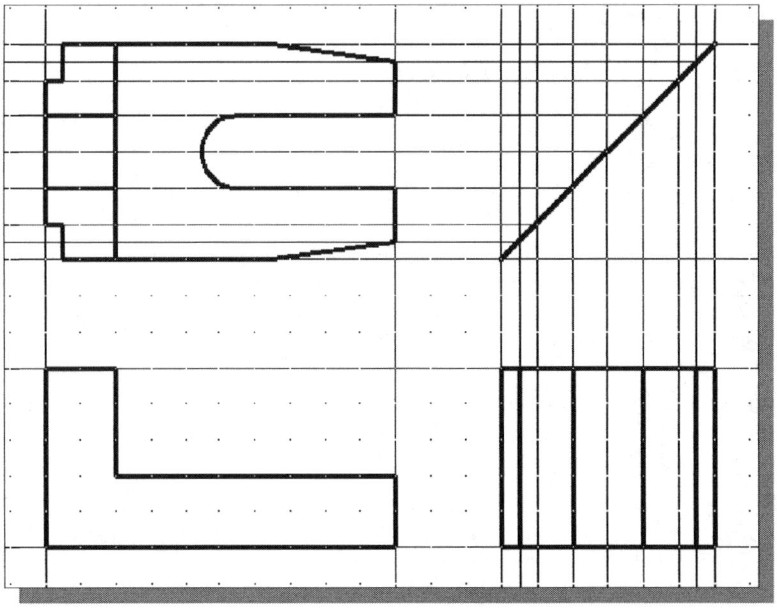

2. Set layer ***Hidden*** as the *Current Layer* and create the two necessary hidden lines in the side view.

3. Set layer ***Center*** as the *Current Layer* and create the necessary centerlines in the side view.

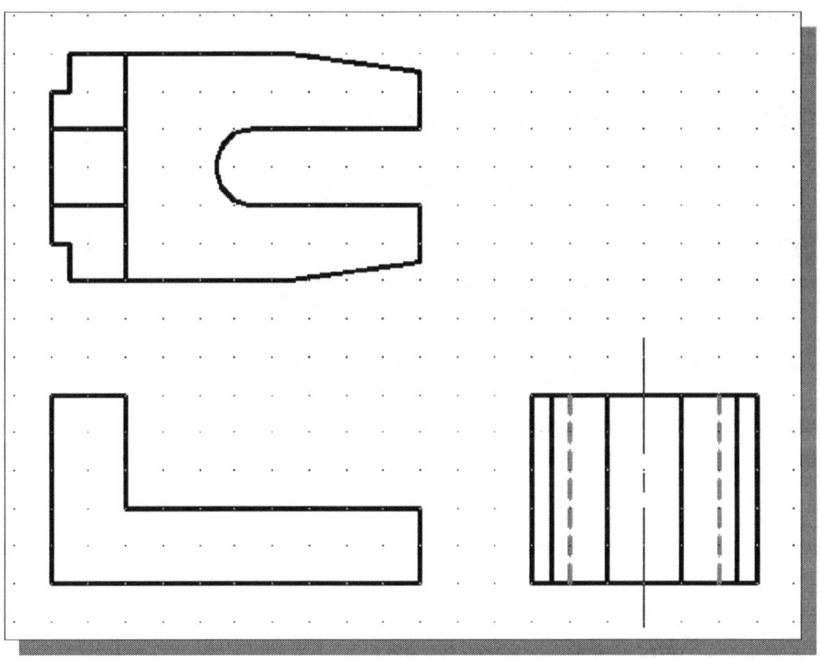

4. In the *Layer Control* box, turn ***OFF*** the ***construction lines***.

5. Set layer ***Object*** as the *Current Layer*.

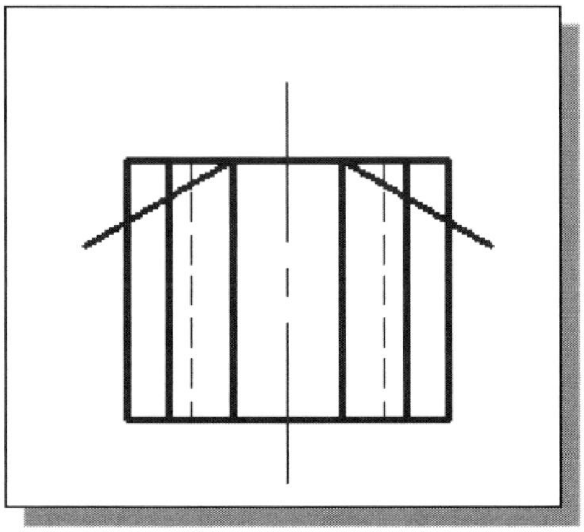

6. Use the **Line** command and create the two 30° inclined lines as shown.

   (Hint: Relative coordinate entries of ***@2.0<-30*** and ***@2.0<210***.)

7. Use the Line command and create a horizontal line in the side view as shown.

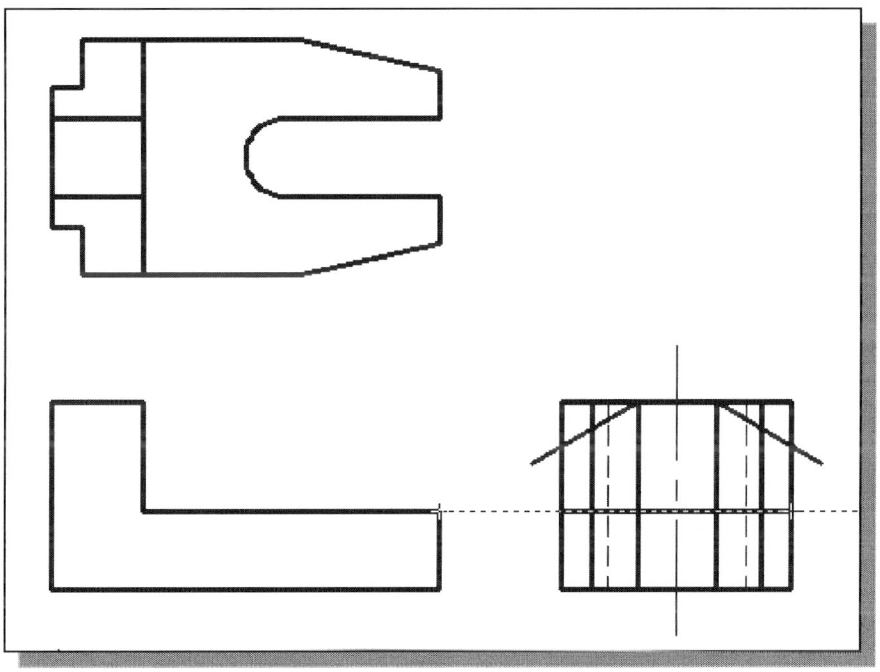

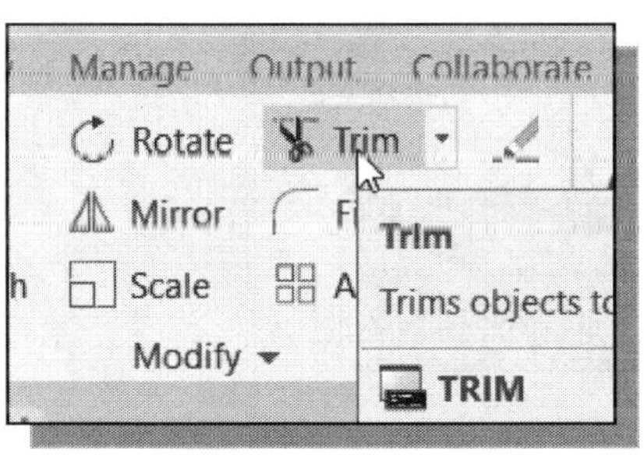

8. On your own, use the **Trim** command and remove the unwanted portions in the side view. Refer to the image shown on the next page if necessary.

Completing the Front View

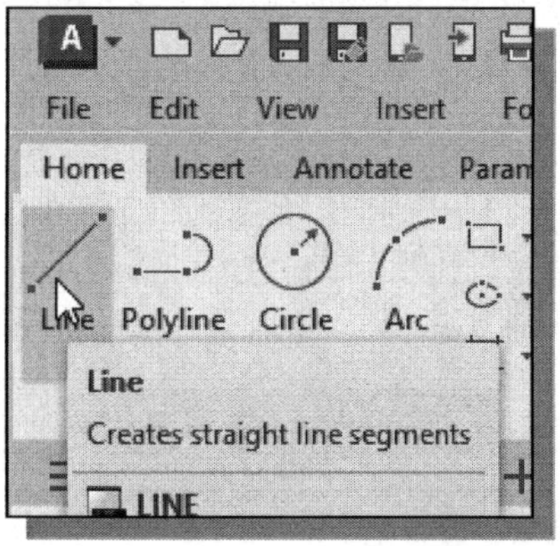

1. Select the **Line** command icon in the *Draw* toolbar. In the command prompt area, the message "*Line Specify first point:*" is displayed.

2. Move the cursor to the top left corner in the side view and the bottom left corner in the top view to activate the *Object Tracking* option to both corners.

3. Left-click once when the cursor is aligned to both corners as shown.

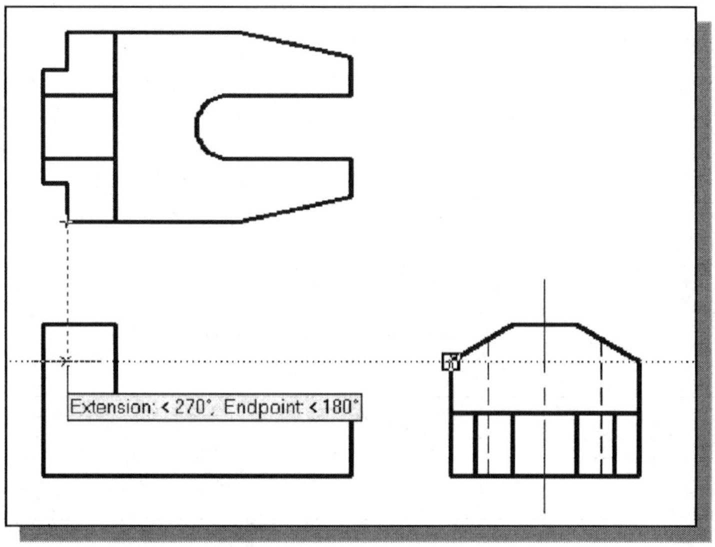

4. Create the **horizontal line** as shown.

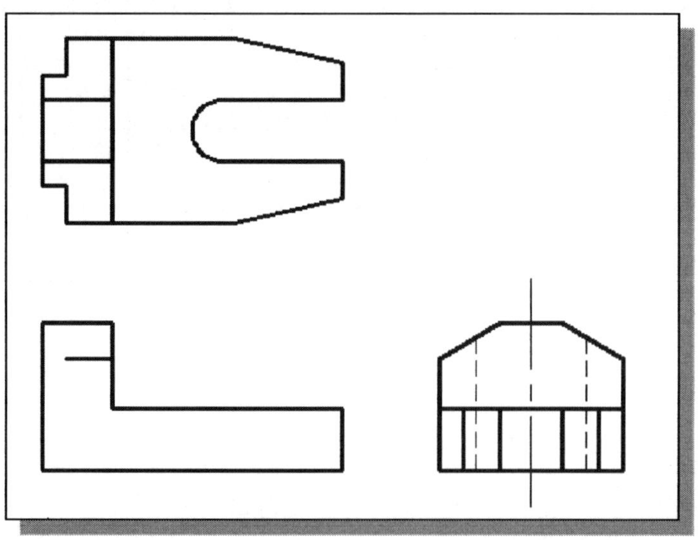

5. Repeat the procedure and create the lines in the front view as shown.

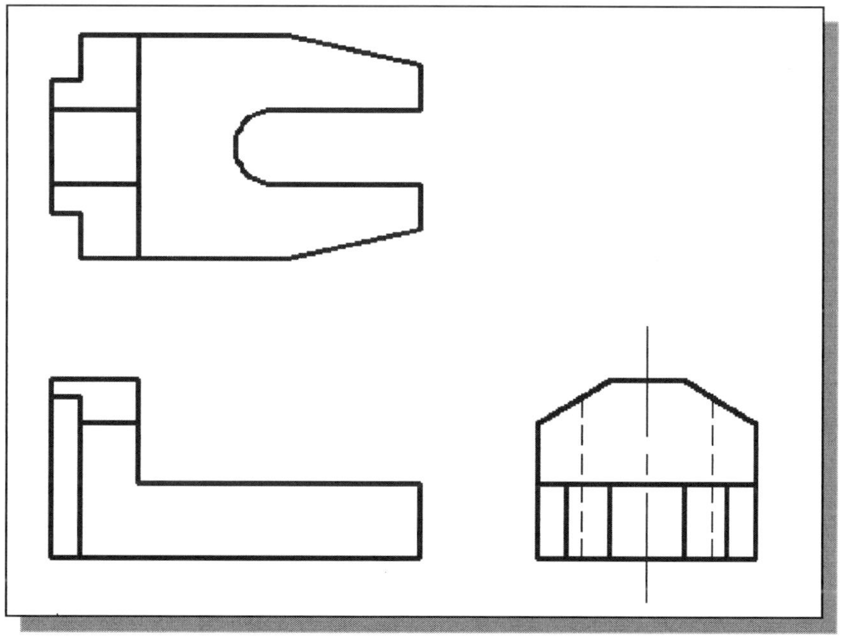

6. Add in any additional object lines that are necessary.

7. Set layer ***Hidden*** as the *Current Layer* and create the necessary hidden lines in the front view.

8. Set layer ***Center*** as the *Current Layer* and create the necessary centerlines in the top view and front view.

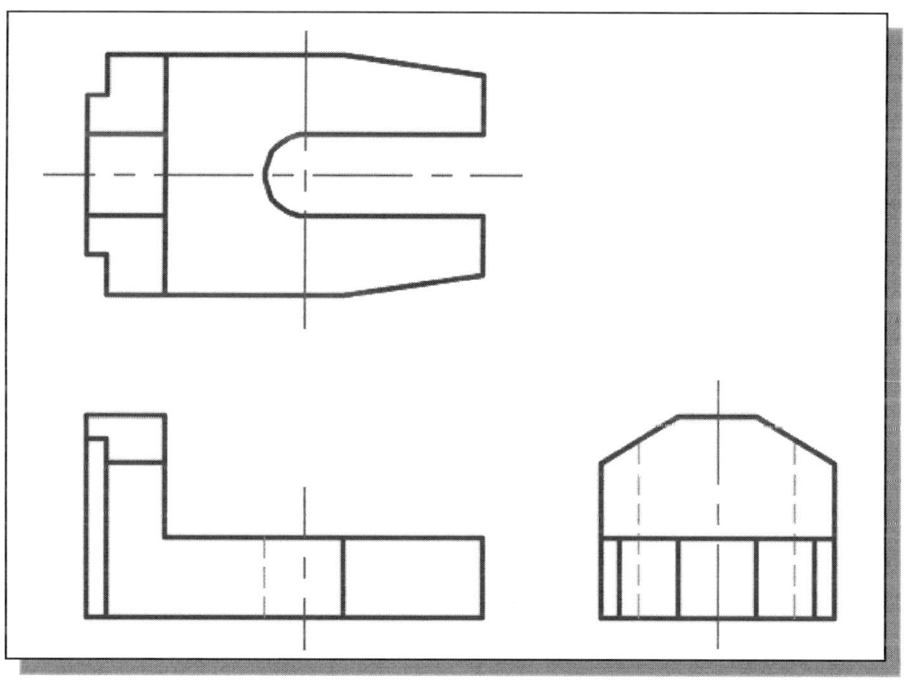

Object Information Using the List Command

AutoCAD provides several tools that will allow us to get information about constructed geometric objects. The **List** command can be used to show detailed information about geometric objects.

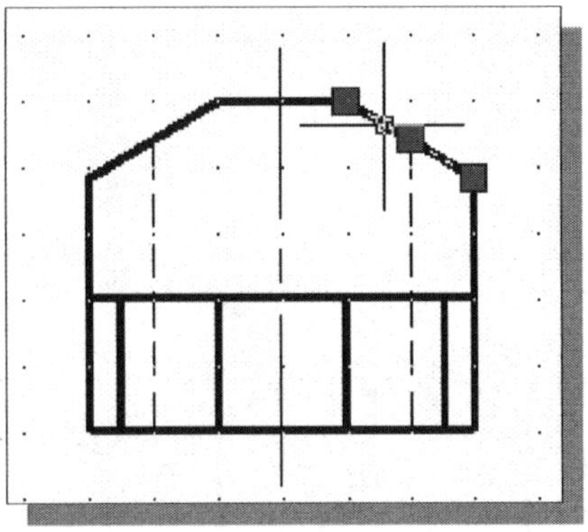

1. Move the cursor to the side view and select the inclined line on the right, as shown in the figure.

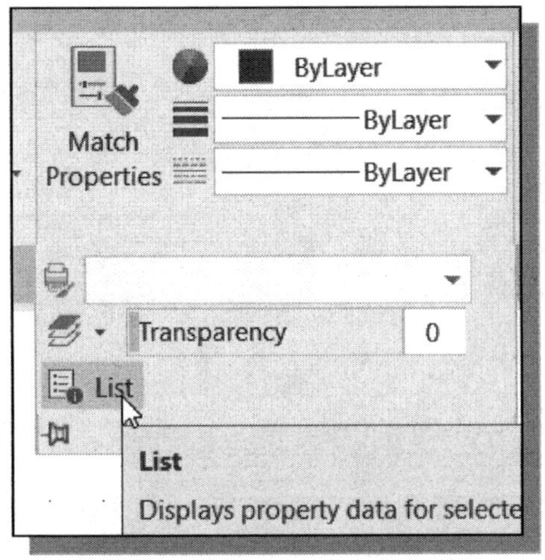

2. In the *Properties* toolbar, click on the **List** icon to activate the command.

- Note the information regarding the selected object is displayed in the *AutoCAD Text Window* as shown.

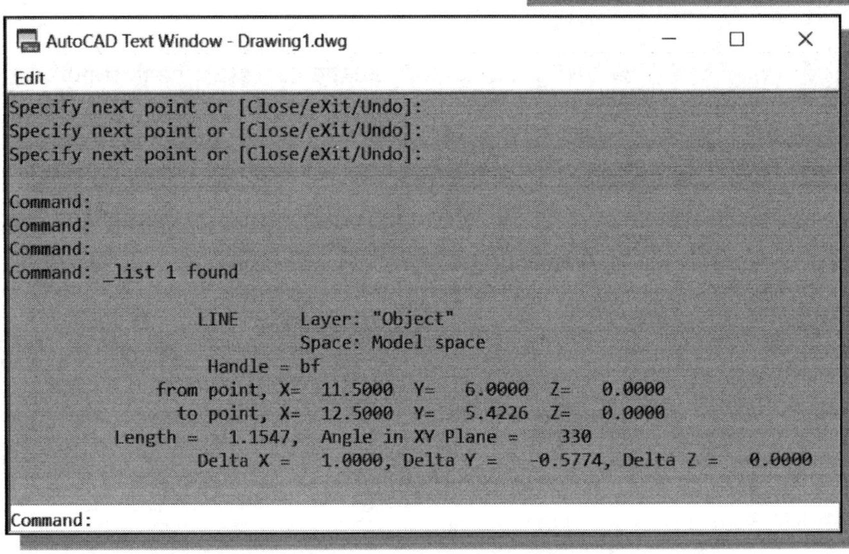

- Note the **List** command can be used to show detailed information about the selected line. The angle and length of the line, as well as the X, Y and Z components between the two endpoints are all listed in a separate window.

3. Press the [**F2**] key once to close the *AutoCAD Text Window*.

4. Press the [**Esc**] key once to deselect the selected line.

Object Information Using the Properties Command

AutoCAD also provides tools that allow us to display and change properties of constructed geometric objects. The **Properties** command not only provides the detailed information about geometric objects—modifications can also be done very quickly.

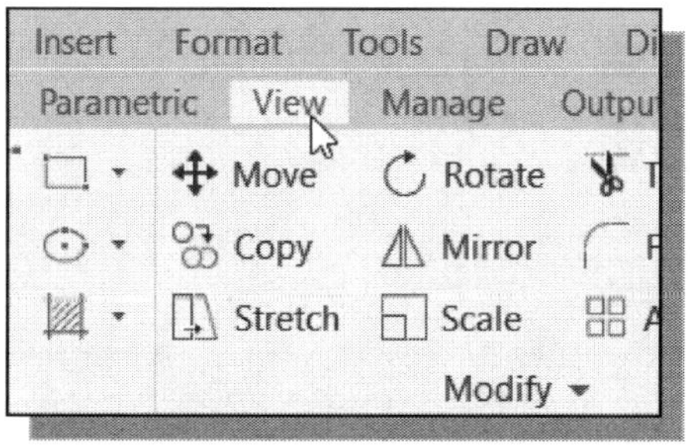

1. In the *Ribbon* tabs area, left-click once on the **View** tab as shown.

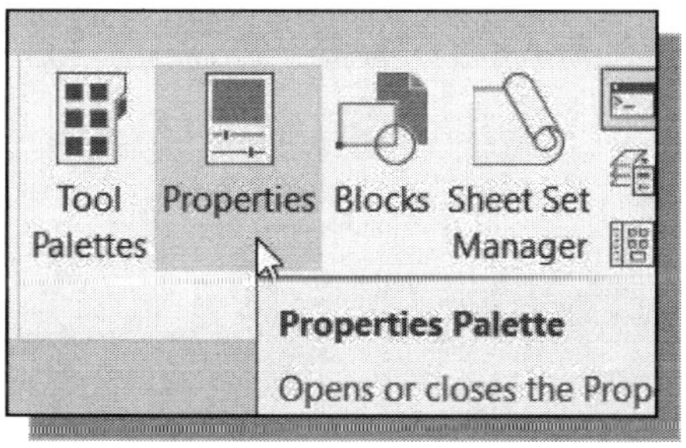

2. In the *Palettes* toolbar, click on the **Properties** icon to activate the command.

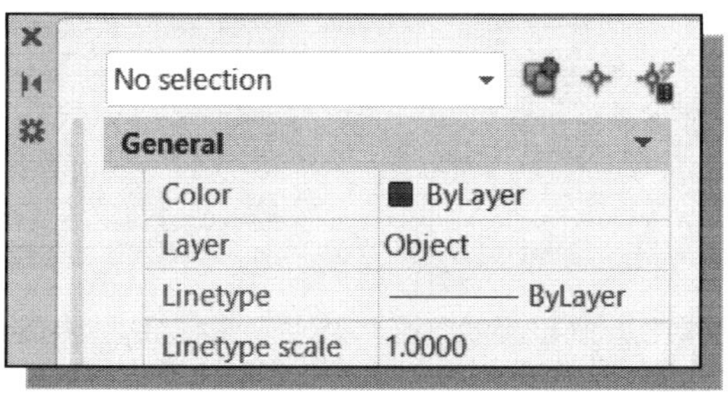

3. Note the *Properties* panel appears on the screen. The "*No selection*" on top of the panel indicates no object has been selected.

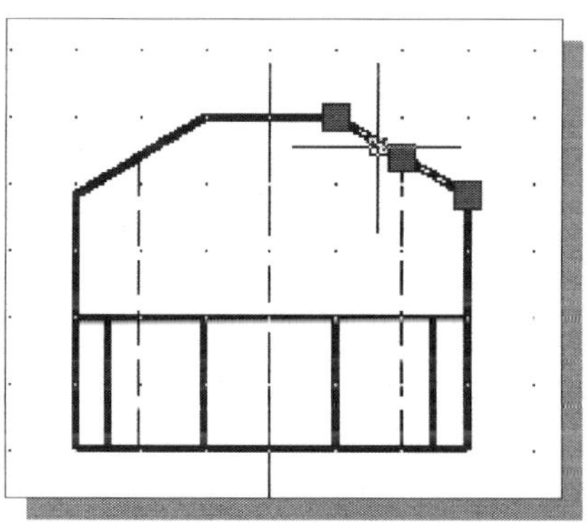

4. Move the cursor to the side view and select the inclined line on the right, as shown in the figure.

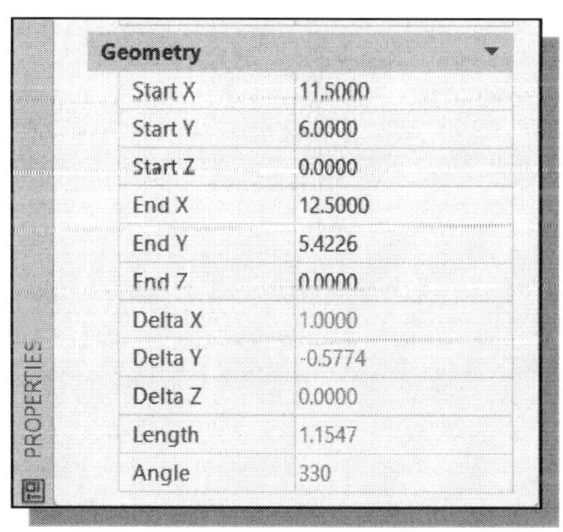

5. The geometry information is listed at the bottom section. Note the line length is *1.1547* and at the angle of *330* degrees.

Review Questions: (Time: 20 minutes)

1. Explain what an orthographic view is and why it is important to engineering graphics.

2. What does the *Running Object Snaps* option allow us to do?

3. Explain how a *miter line* can assist us in creating orthographic views.

4. Describe the AutoCAD *AUTOSNAP* and *AutoTrack* options.

5. List and describe two AutoCAD commands that can be used to get geometric information about constructed objects.

6. List and describe two options you could use to quickly create a 2-inch line attached to a 2-inch circle, as shown in the below figure.

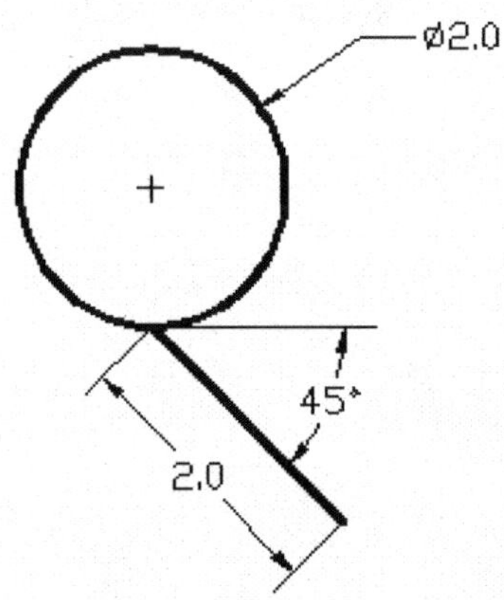

7. What are the length and angle of the inclined line, highlighted in the figure below, in the top view of the *Locator* design?

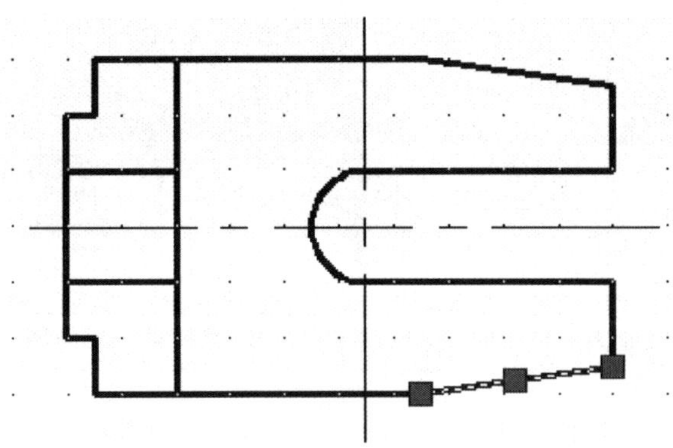

Exercises:

(Unless otherwise specified, dimensions are in inches.) (Time: 175 minutes)

1. **Saddle Bracket**

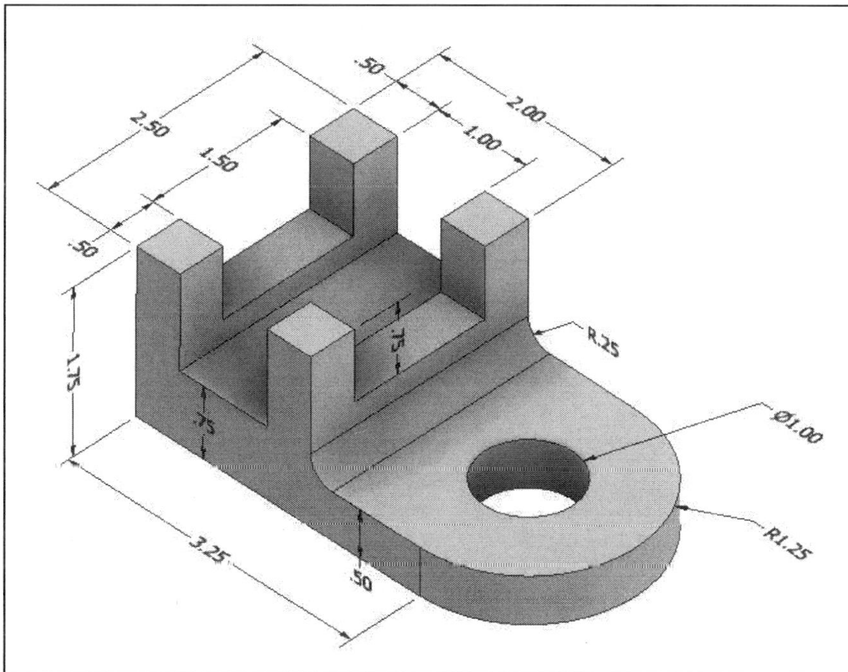

2. **Anchor Base**

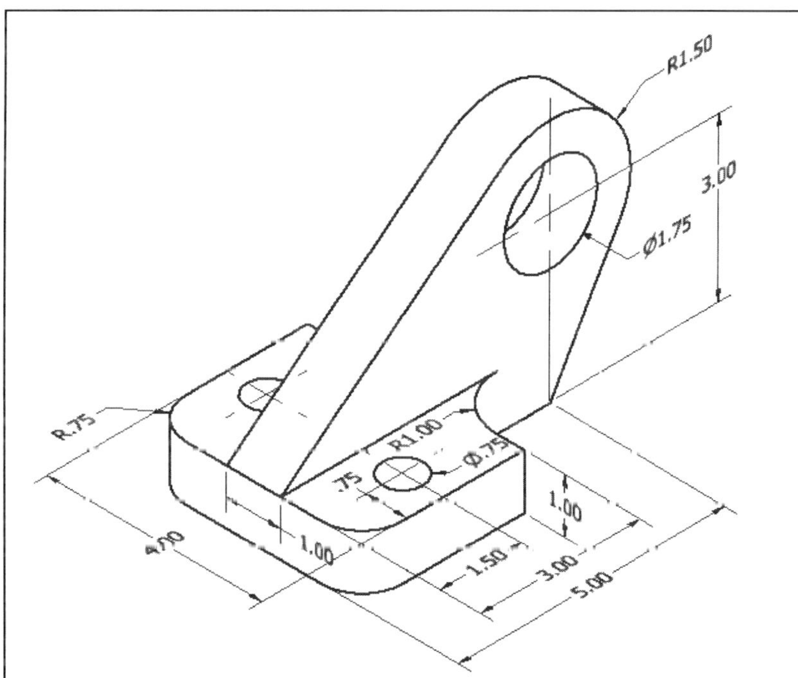

3. **Bearing Base**

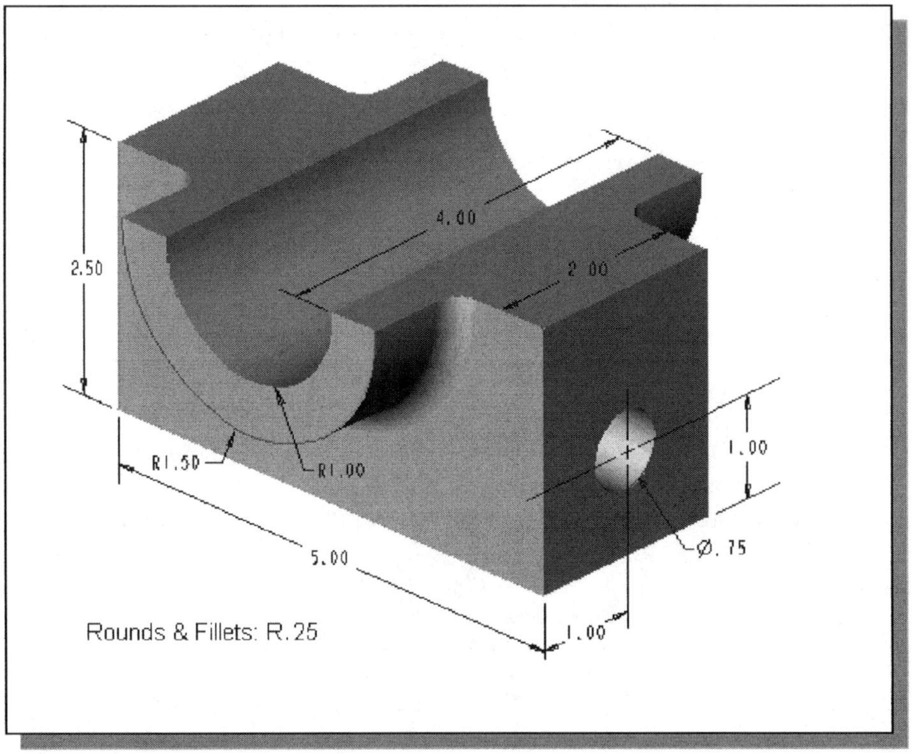

4. **Shaft Support** (Dimensions are in Millimeters. Note the two R40 arcs at the base share the same center.)

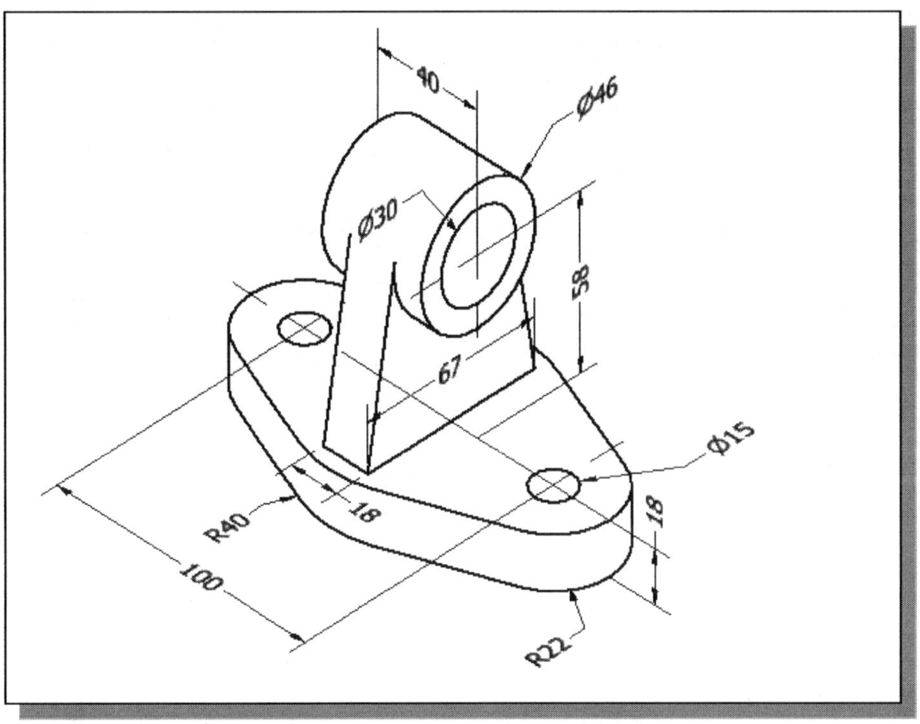

5. **Connecting Rod**

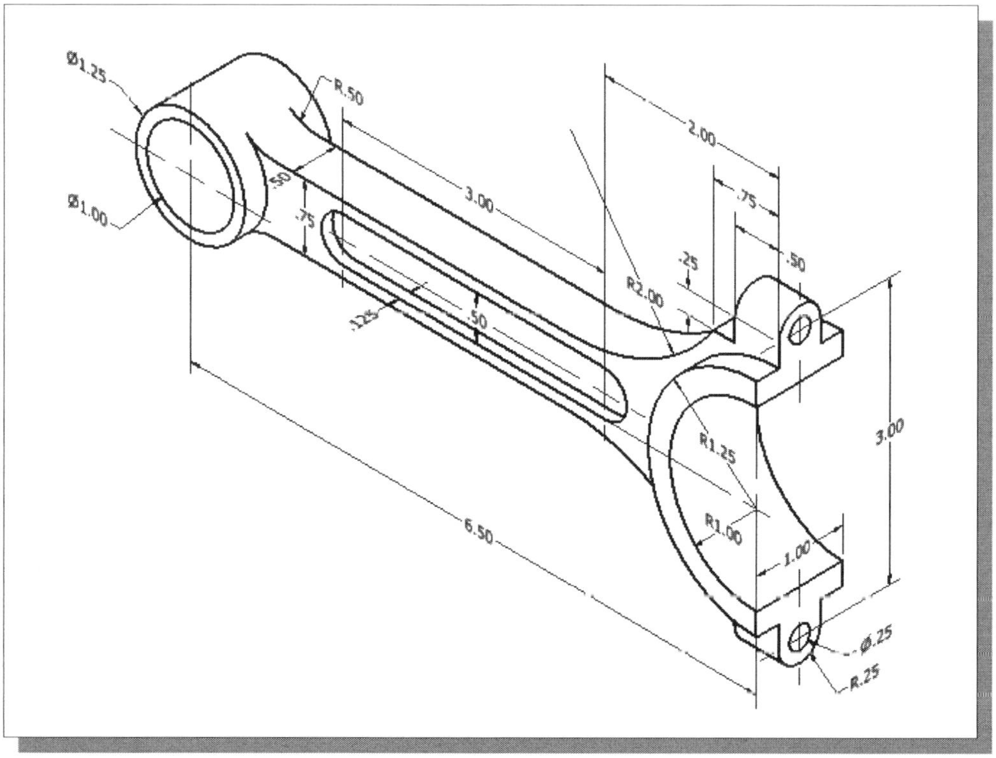

6. **Tube Hanger**

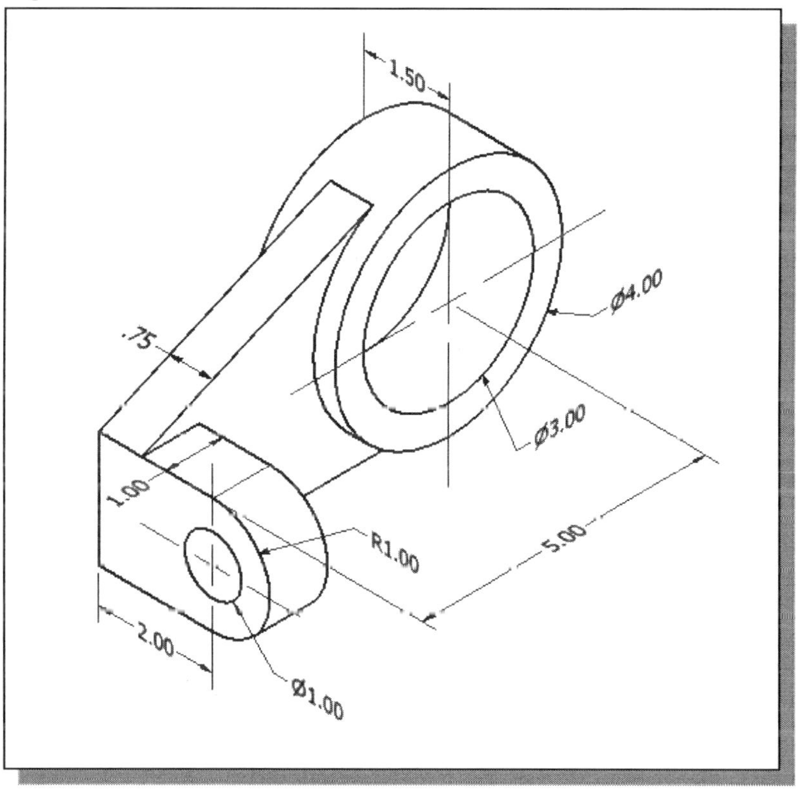

7. **Tube Spacer**

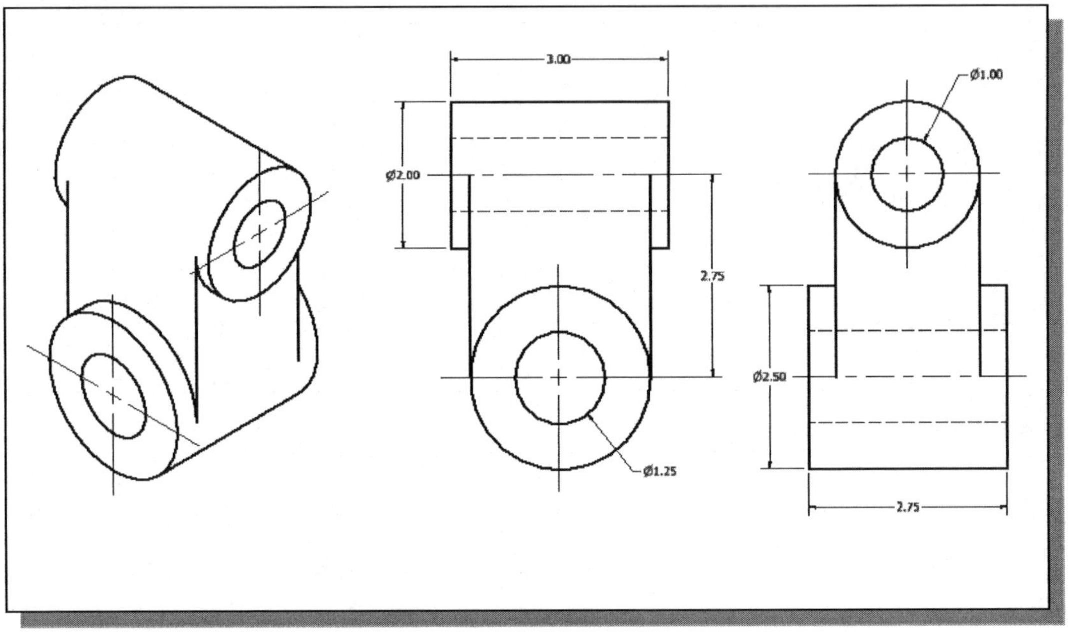

8. **Slider** (Dimensions are in Millimeters.)

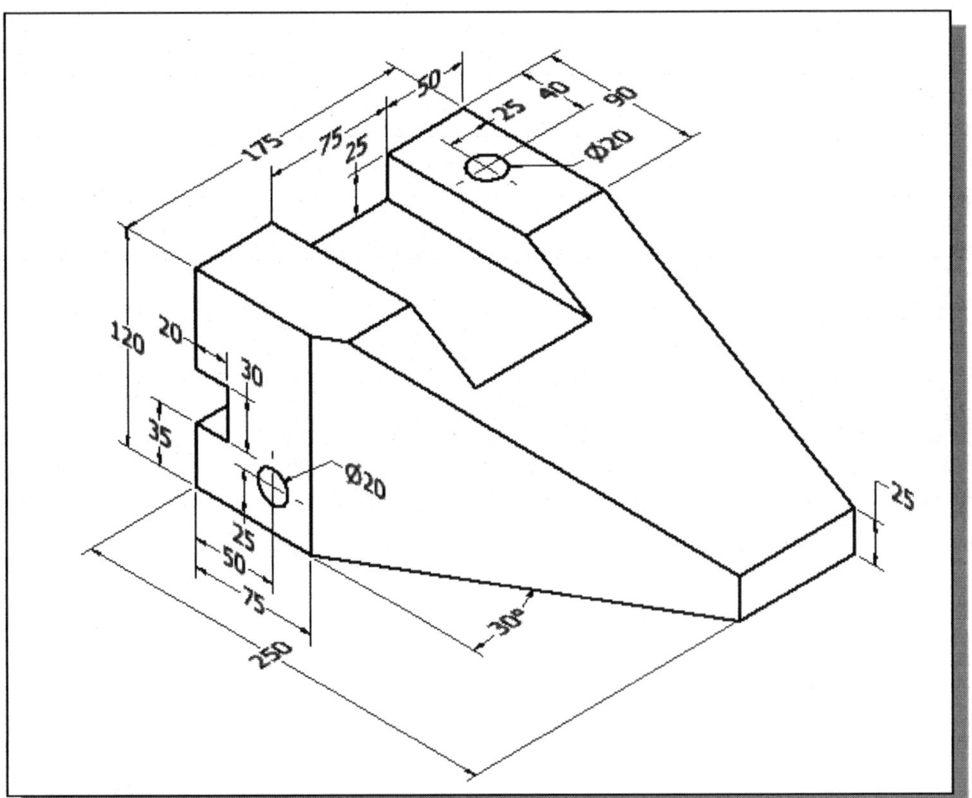

9. **Rod Holder**

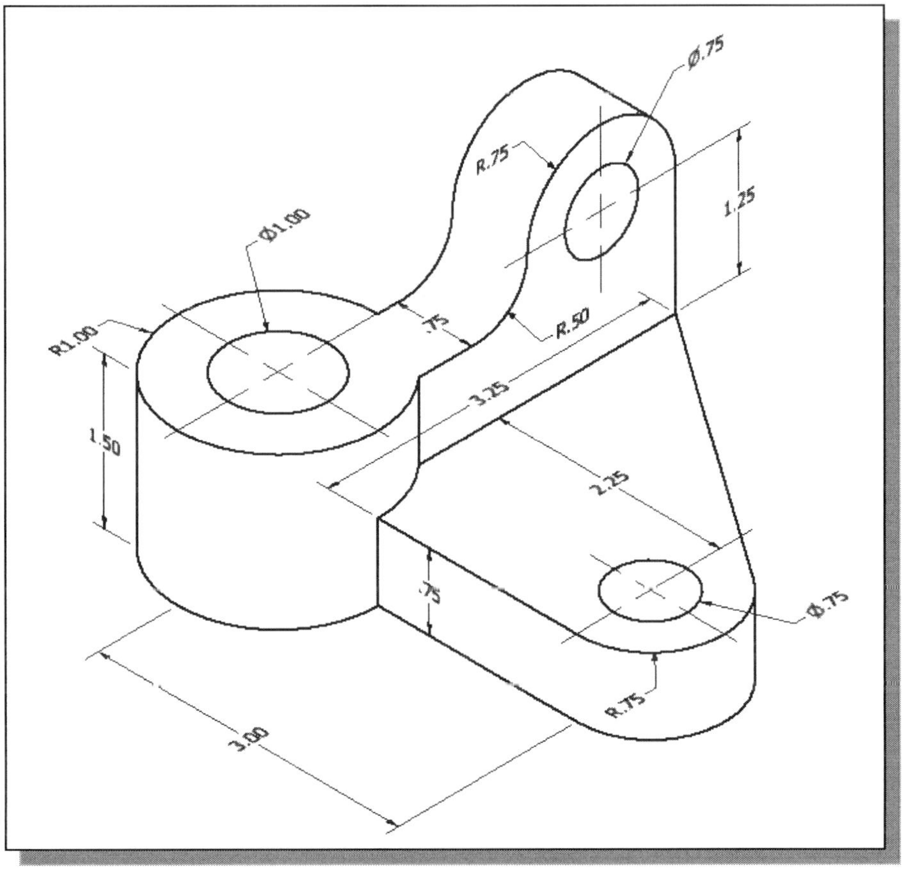

Notes:

Chapter 5

Basic Dimensioning and Notes - AutoCAD

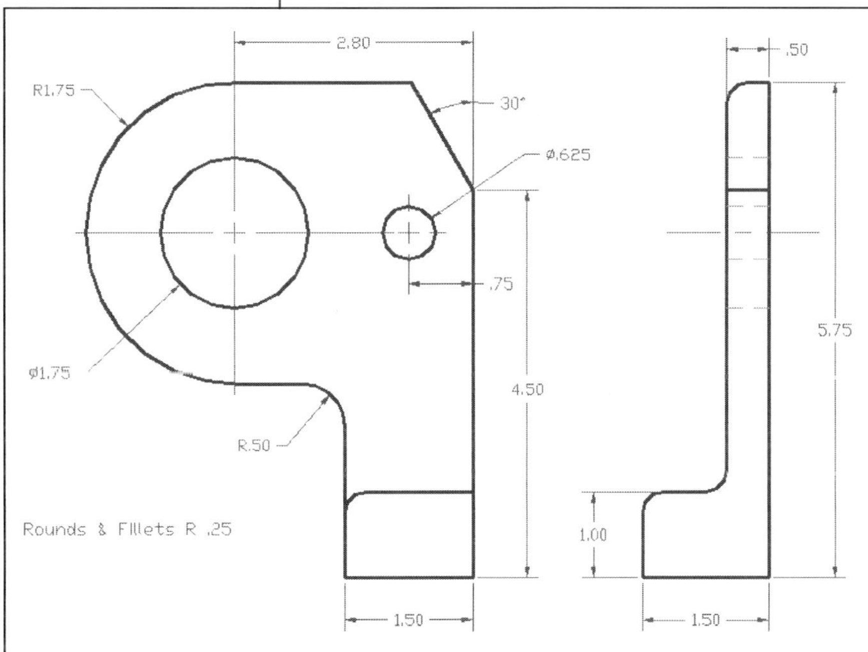

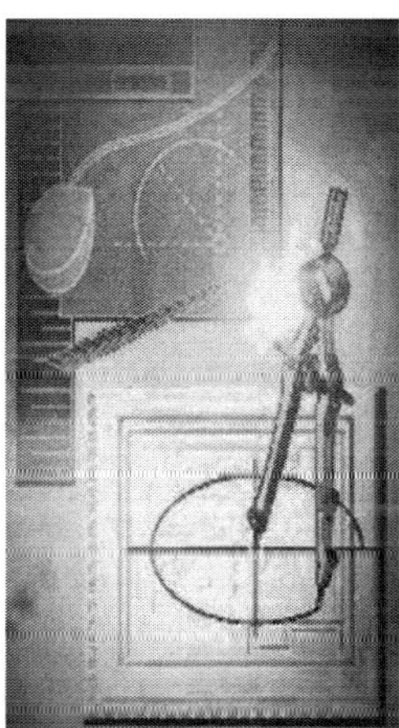

Learning Objectives

- **Understand Dimensioning Nomenclature and Basics**
- **Display and Use the Dimension Toolbar**
- **Use the AutoCAD Dimension Style Manager**
- **Create Center Marks**
- **Add Linear and Angular Dimensions**
- **Use the Multiline Text Command**
- **Create Special Characters in Notes**
- **Use the AutoCAD Classic Workspace**

Introduction

In order to manufacture a finalized design, the complete ***shape*** and ***size*** description must be shown on the drawings of the design. Thus far, the use of AutoCAD 2027 to define the shape of designs has been illustrated. In this chapter, the procedures to convey the ***size*** definitions of designs using **AutoCAD 2027** are discussed. The *tools of size description* are known as *dimensions* and *notes*.

Considerable experience and judgment are required for accurate size description. Detail drawings should contain only those dimensions that are necessary to make the design. Dimensions for the same feature of the design should be given only once in the same drawing. Nothing should be left to chance or guesswork on a drawing. Drawings should be dimensioned to avoid any possibility of questions. Dimensions should be carefully positioned, preferably near the profile of the feature being dimensioned. The designer and the CAD operator should be as familiar as possible with materials, methods of manufacturing, and shop processes.

Traditionally, detailing a drawing is the biggest bottleneck of the design process; and when doing board drafting, dimensioning is one of the most time consuming and tedious tasks. Today, most CAD systems provide what is known as an **auto-dimensioning feature**, where the CAD system automatically creates the extension lines, dimensional lines, arrowheads, and dimension values. Most CAD systems also provide an **associative dimensioning feature** so that the system automatically updates the dimensions when the drawing is modified.

The Bracket Design

Starting Up AutoCAD 2027

1. Select the **AutoCAD 2027** option on the *Program* menu or select the **AutoCAD 2027** icon on the *Desktop*.

2. In the *Startup* window, select **Start from Scratch**, and select the **Imperial (feet and inches)** as the drawing units.

3. In the *Menu Bar*, select:

   [Tools] → [Drafting Settings]

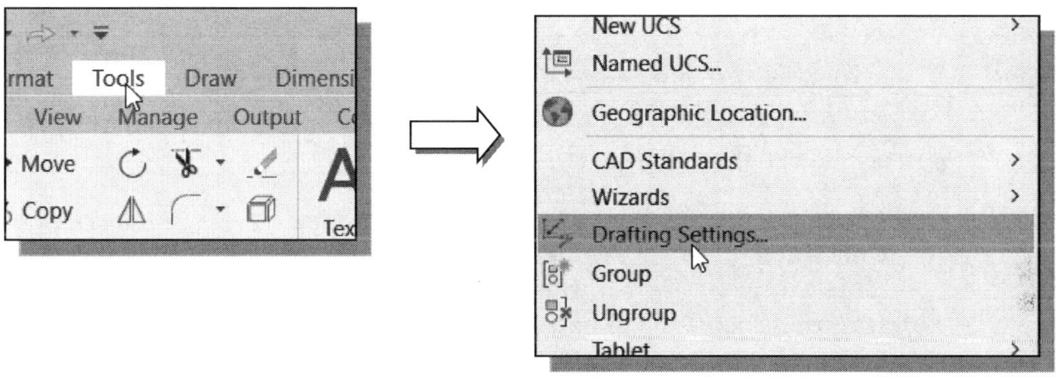

4. In the *Drafting Settings* dialog box, select the **SNAP and GRID** tab if it is not the page on top.

5. Change *Grid Spacing* to ***1.0*** for both X and Y directions.

6. Also adjust the *Snap Spacing* to ***0.5*** for both X and Y directions.

7. Pick **OK** to exit the *Drafting Settings* dialog box.

8. In the *Status Bar* area, reset the option buttons so that only *SNAP Mode* and *GRID Display* are switched ***ON***.

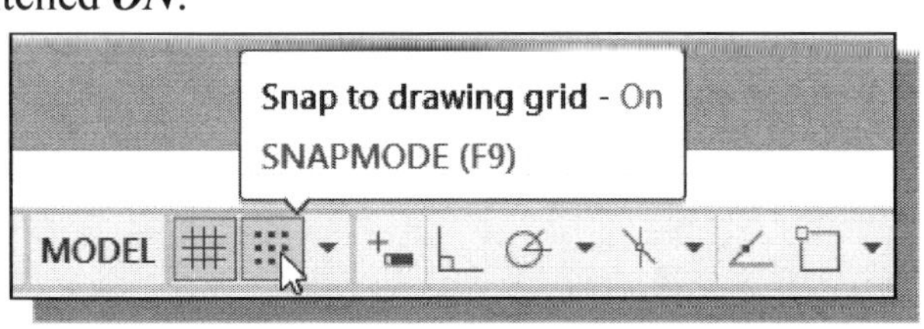

Layers Setup

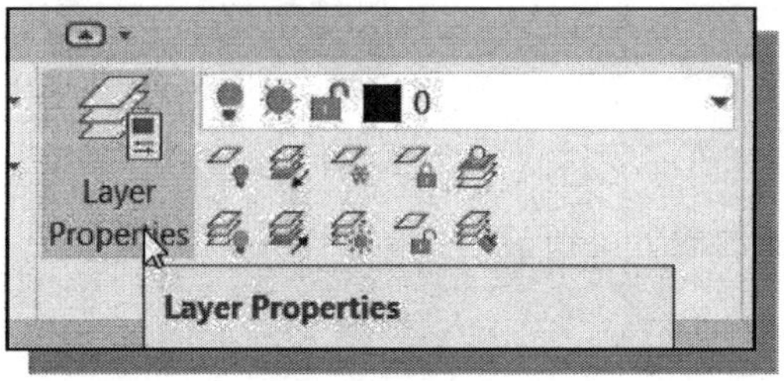

1. Pick ***Layer Properties Manager*** in the *Object Properties* toolbar.

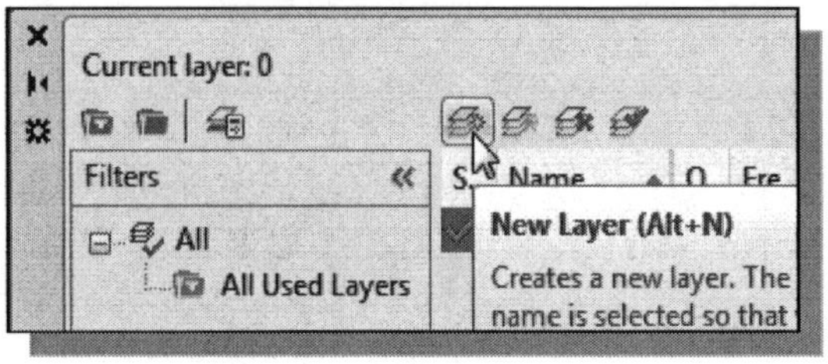

2. In the *Layer Properties Manager* dialog box, click on the **New** button (or the key combination [**Alt+N**]) to create a new layer.

3. Create **layers** with the following settings:

Layer	***Color***	***Linetype***	***Lineweight***
Construction	**Gray(9)**	**Continuous**	**Default**
Object_Lines	**Blue**	**Continuous**	**0.6mm**
Hidden_Lines	**Cyan**	**Hidden**	**0.3mm**
Center_Lines	**Red**	**Center**	**Default**
Dimensions	**Magenta**	**Continuous**	**Default**
Section_Lines	**White**	**Continuous**	**Default**
CuttingPlane_Lines	**Dark Gray(8)**	**Phantom**	**0.6mm**
Title_Block	**Green**	**Continuous**	**1.2mm**
Viewport	**White**	**Continuous**	**Default**

4. Highlight the layer ***Construction*** in the list of layers.

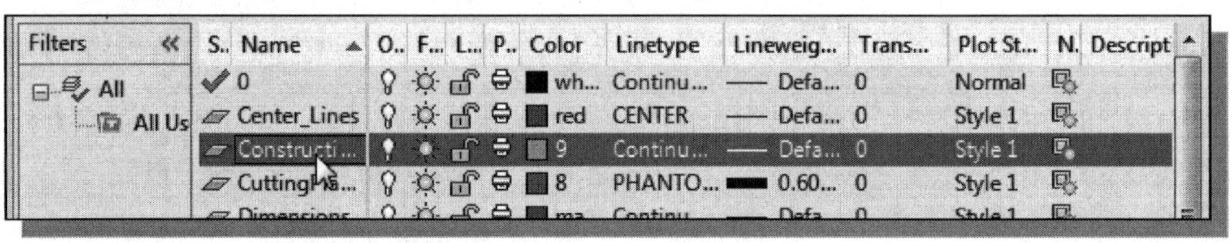

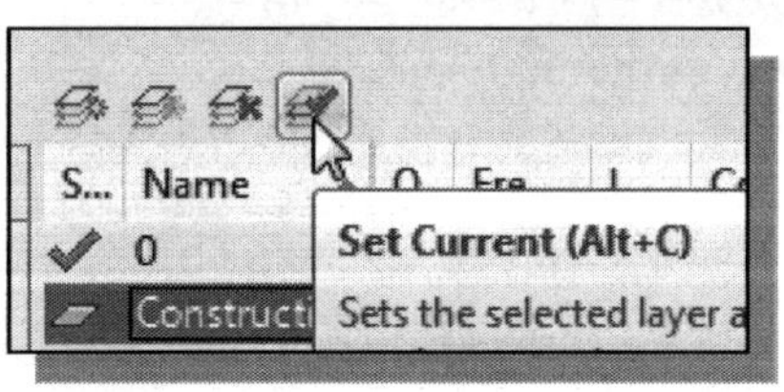

5. Click on the **Current** button to set layer ***Construction*** as the *Current Layer*.

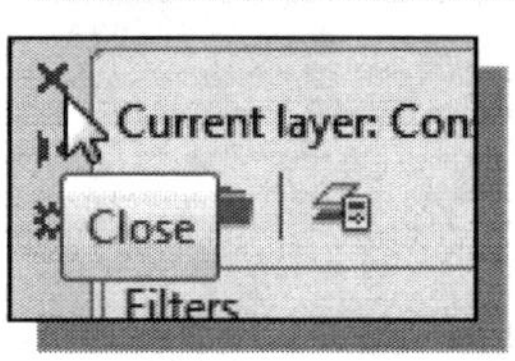

6. Click on the **Close** button to accept the settings and exit the *Layer Properties Manager* dialog box.

The P-Bracket Design

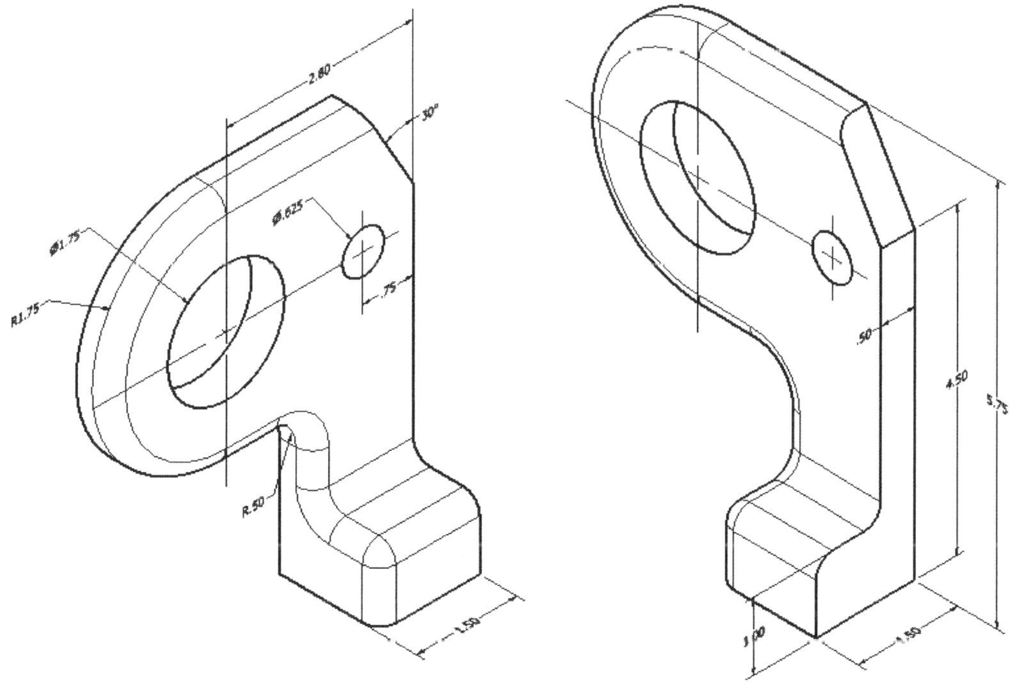

➢ Before going through the tutorial, make a rough sketch of a multiview drawing of the part. How many 2D views will be necessary to fully describe the part? Based on your knowledge of **AutoCAD 2027** so far, how would you arrange and construct these 2D views? Take a few minutes to consider these questions and do preliminary planning by sketching on a piece of paper.

LineWeight Display Control

The *LineWeight Display* control can be accessed through the Status bar area; we will first switch on the icon.

1. To show the icon for the AutoCAD LineWeight Display option, use the *Customization option* at the bottom right corner.

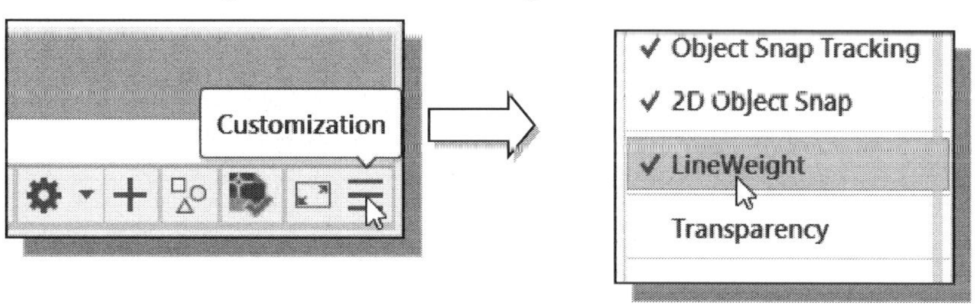

Drawing Construction Lines

We will place the construction lines on the *Construction* layer so that the layer can later be frozen or turned off.

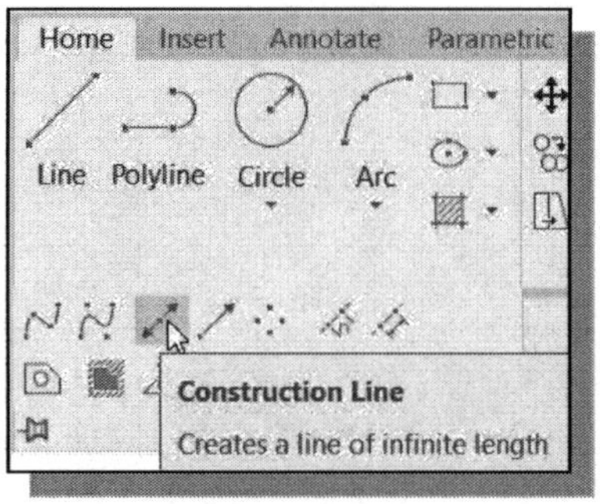

1. Select the **Construction Line** icon in the *Draw* toolbar. In the command prompt area, the message "*_xline Specify a point or [Hor/Ver/Ang/Bisect/ Offset]:*" is displayed.

➢ To orient construction lines, we generally specify two points, although other orientation options are also available.

2. Place the first point at world coordinate (***3,2***) on the screen.

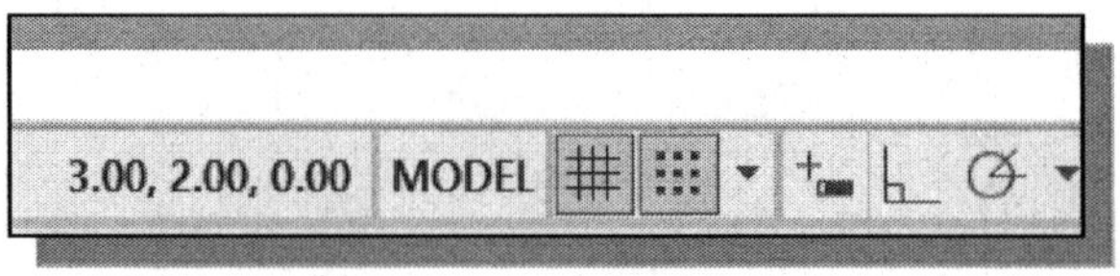

3. Pick a location above the last point to create a **vertical line**.

4. Move the cursor toward the right of the first point and pick a location to create a **horizontal line**.

5. In the *Status Bar* area, turn ***OFF*** the *SNAP* option.

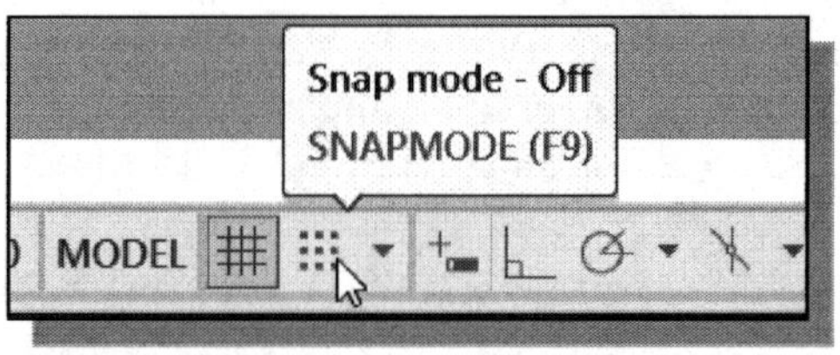

Using the Offset Command

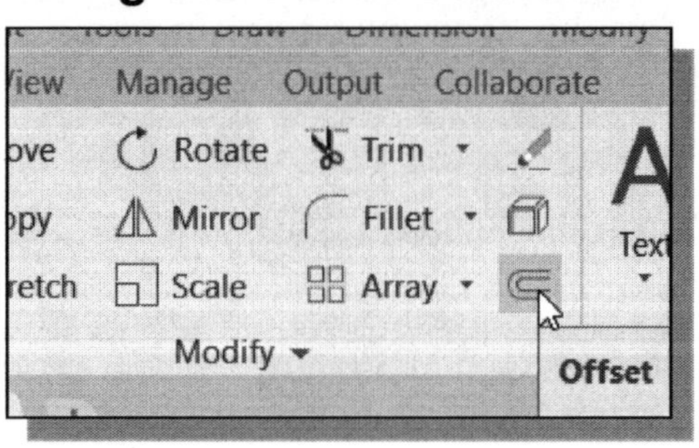

1. Select the **Offset** icon in the *Modify* toolbar. In the command prompt area, the message "*Specify offset distance or [Through]:*" is displayed.

2. In the command prompt area, enter ***2.80*** **[ENTER]**.

3. In the *command prompt area*, the message "*Select object to offset or <exit>:*" is displayed. Pick the **vertical line** on the screen.

4. AutoCAD next asks us to identify the direction of the offset. Pick a location that is to the **right** of the vertical line.

5. Inside the *graphics window*, right-click twice to **end** the **Offset** command.

6. In the *command prompt* area, click on the small icon to access the list of recent commands.

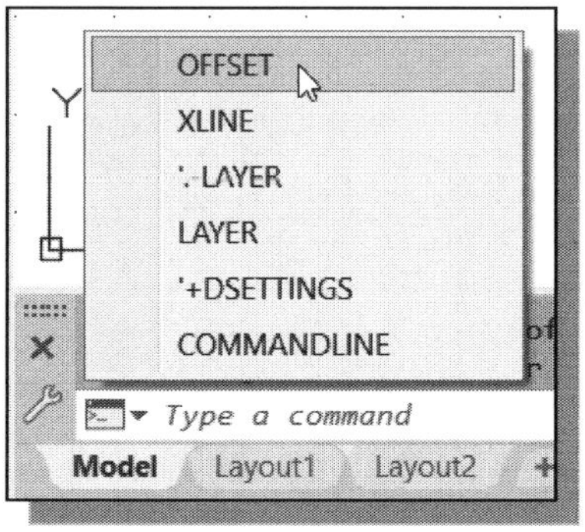

7. Select **Offset** in the pop-up list, to repeat the **Offset** command.

8. In *the command prompt* area, enter ***5.75*** **[ENTER]**.

9. In the *command prompt* area, the message "*Select object to offset or <exit>:*" is displayed. Pick the **horizontal line** on the screen.

10. AutoCAD next asks us to identify the direction of the offset. Pick a location that is **above** the horizontal line.

11. Inside the *graphics window*, **right-click** once to end the **Offset** command.

12. Repeat the **Offset** command and create the lines as shown.

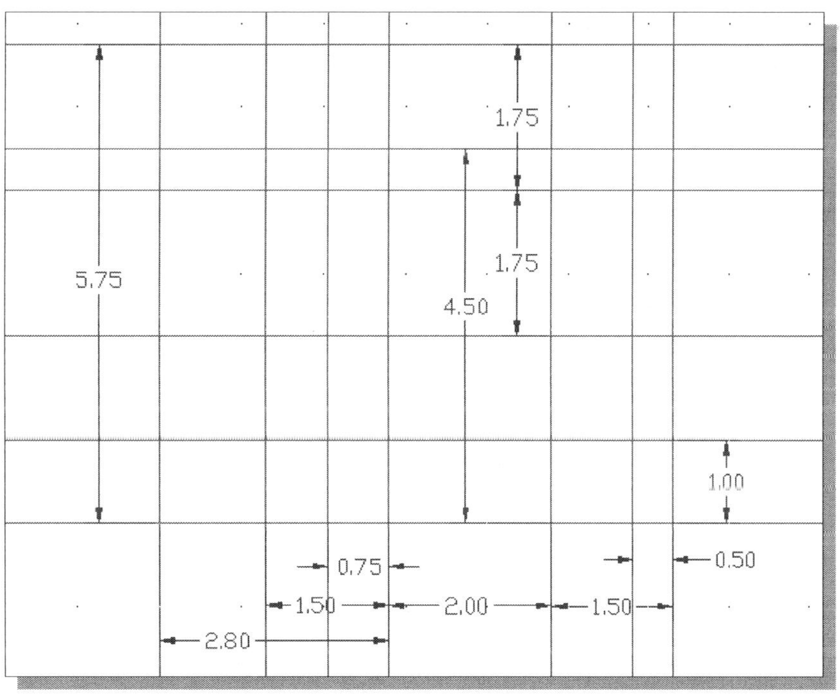

Set Layer Object_Lines as the Current Layer

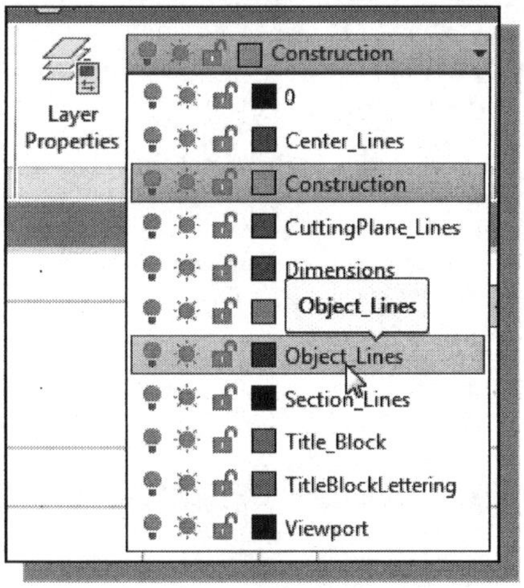

1. On the *Object Properties* toolbar, choose the ***Layer Control*** box with the left-mouse-button.

2. Move the cursor over the name of layer ***Object_Lines*** and the tool tip "*Object_Lines*" appears.

3. **Left-click once** and layer *Object_Lines* is set as the *Current Layer.*

4. In the *Status Bar* area, turn ***ON*** the *Object SNAP, Object TRACKing*, and *Line Weight Display* options.

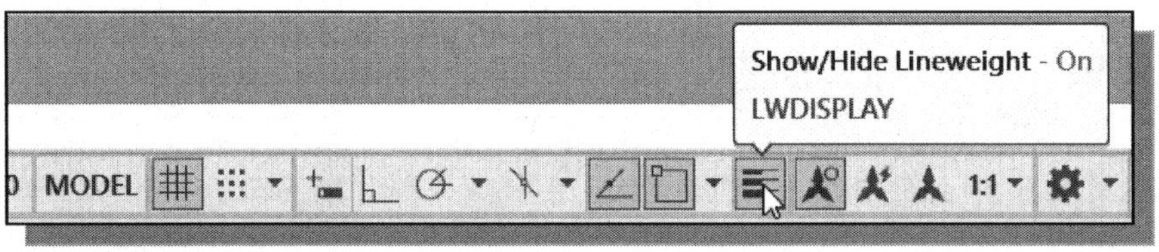

Creating Object Lines

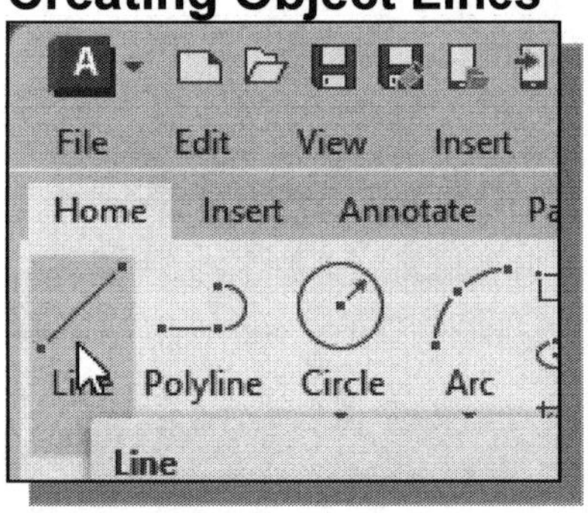

1. Select the **Line** command icon in the *Draw* toolbar. In the command prompt area, the message "*_line Specify first point:*" is displayed.

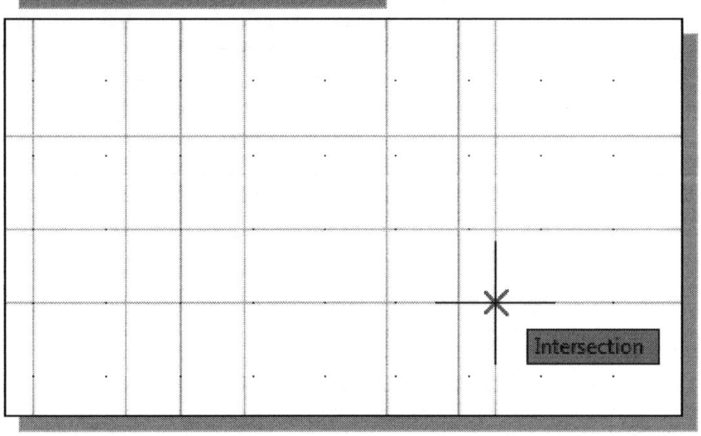

2. Move the cursor to the intersection of the construction lines at the lower right corner of the current sketch, and notice the visual aid automatically displayed at the intersection.

3. Create the object lines as shown below. (Hint: Use the *relative coordinate entry method* and the **Trim** command to construct the **30° line**.)

4. Use the **Arc** and **Circle** commands to complete the object lines as shown.

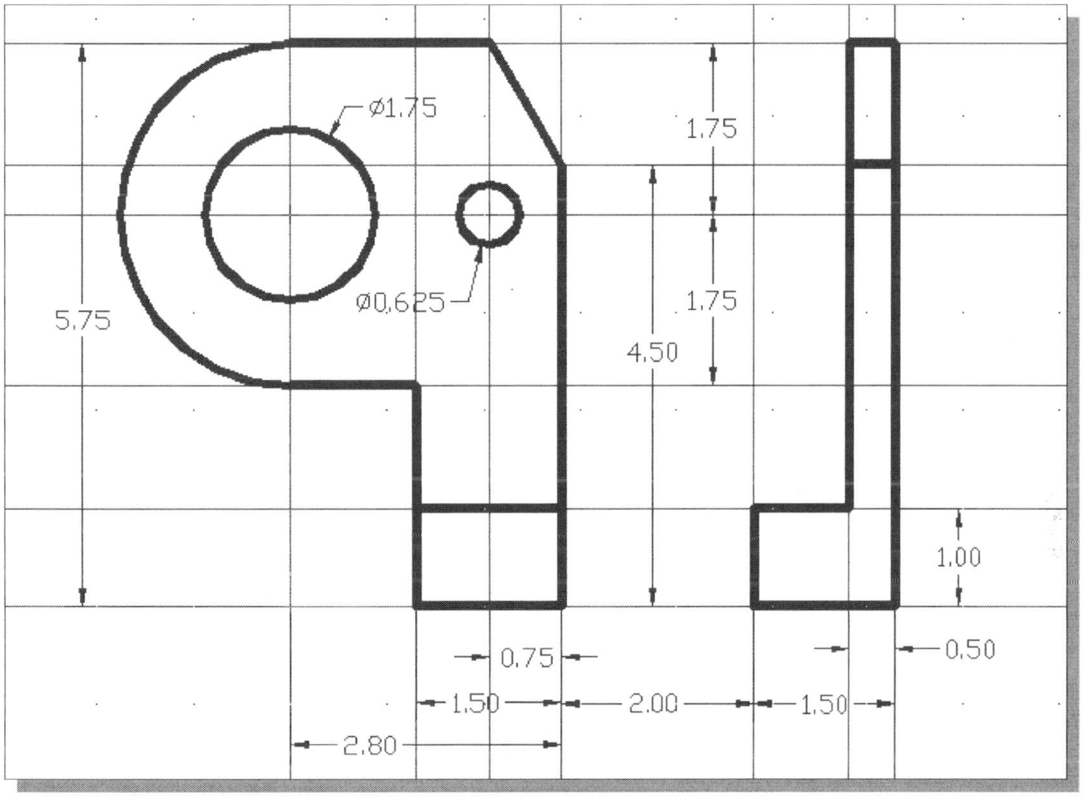

Creating Hidden Lines

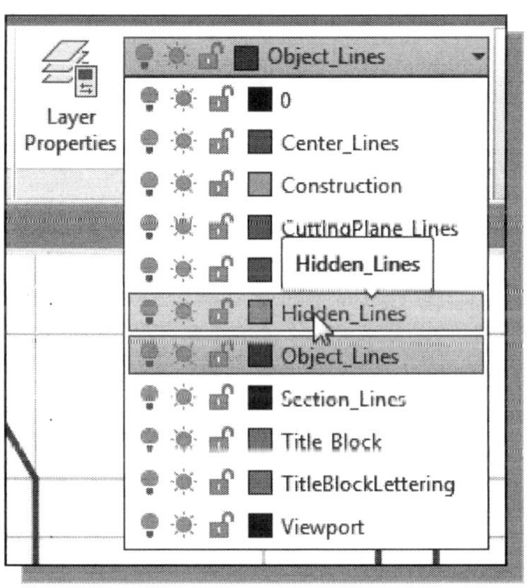

1. On the *Object Properties* toolbar, choose the *Layer Control* box with the left-mouse-button.

2. Move the cursor over the name of layer ***Hidden_Lines***, **left-click once**, and set layer *Hidden_Lines* as the *Current Layer*.

3. On your own, create the five hidden lines in the side view as shown on the next page.

Creating Center Lines

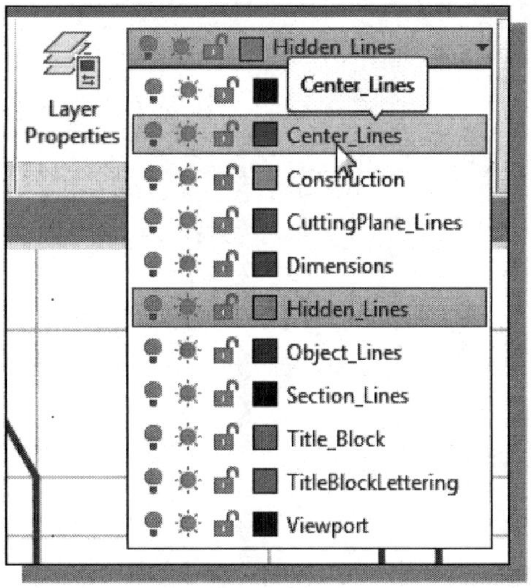

1. On the *Object Properties* toolbar, choose the *Layer Control* box to display the *Layer control list.*

2. Move the cursor over the name of layer ***Center_Lines***, and **left-click once** to set the layer as the *Current Layer.*

3. On your own, create the center line in the side view as shown in the below figure. (The center lines in the front-view will be added using the *Center Mark* option.)

Turn Off the Construction Lines

1. On the *Object Properties* toolbar, choose the *Layer Control* box with the left-mouse-button.

2. Move the cursor over the lightbulb icon for layer *Construction_Lines*, **left-click once**, and notice the icon color is changed to a gray tone color, representing the layer (layer *Construction_Lines*) is turned *OFF.*

3. Move the cursor over the name of layer ***Object_Lines***, **left-click once**, and set layer *Object_Lines* as the *Current Layer.*

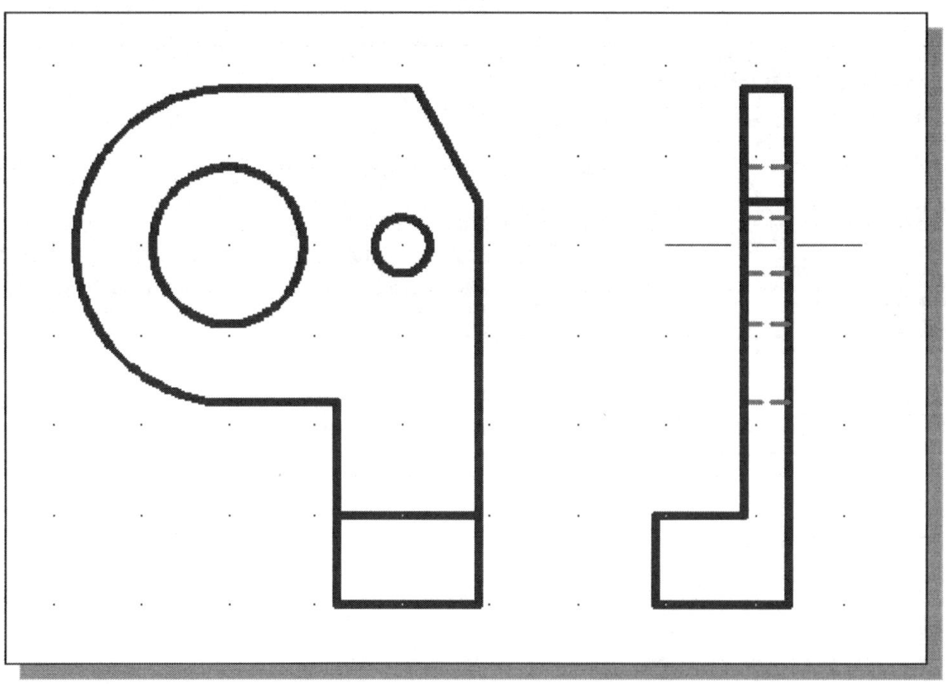

Using the Fillet Command

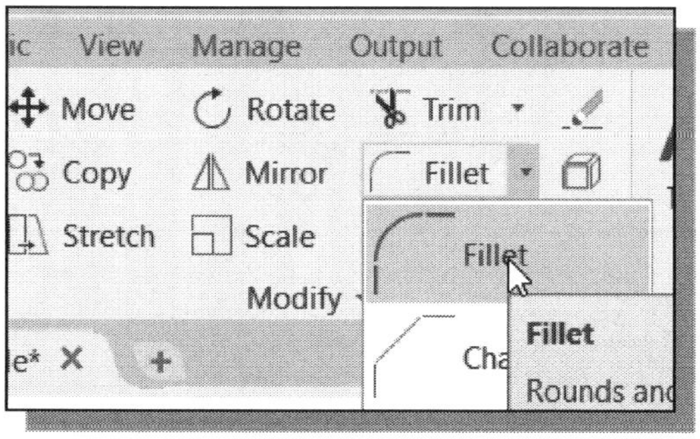

1. Select the **Fillet** command icon in the *Modify* toolbar. In the command prompt area, the message "*Select first object or [Polyline/Radius/Trim]:*" is displayed.

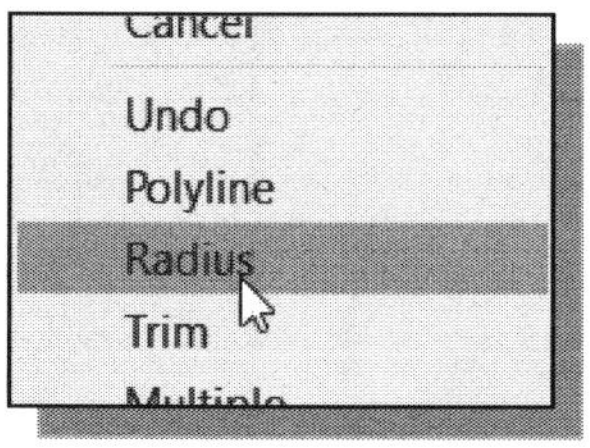

2. Inside the *graphics window*, right-click to activate the *option menu* and select the **Radius** option with the left-mouse-button to specify the radius of the fillet.

3. In the *command prompt* area, the message "*Specify fillet radius:*" is displayed. *Specify fillet radius:* **0.5 [ENTER]**.

4. Pick the **bottom horizontal line** of the front view as the first object to fillet.

5. Pick the **adjacent vertical line** connected to the arc to create a rounded corner as shown.

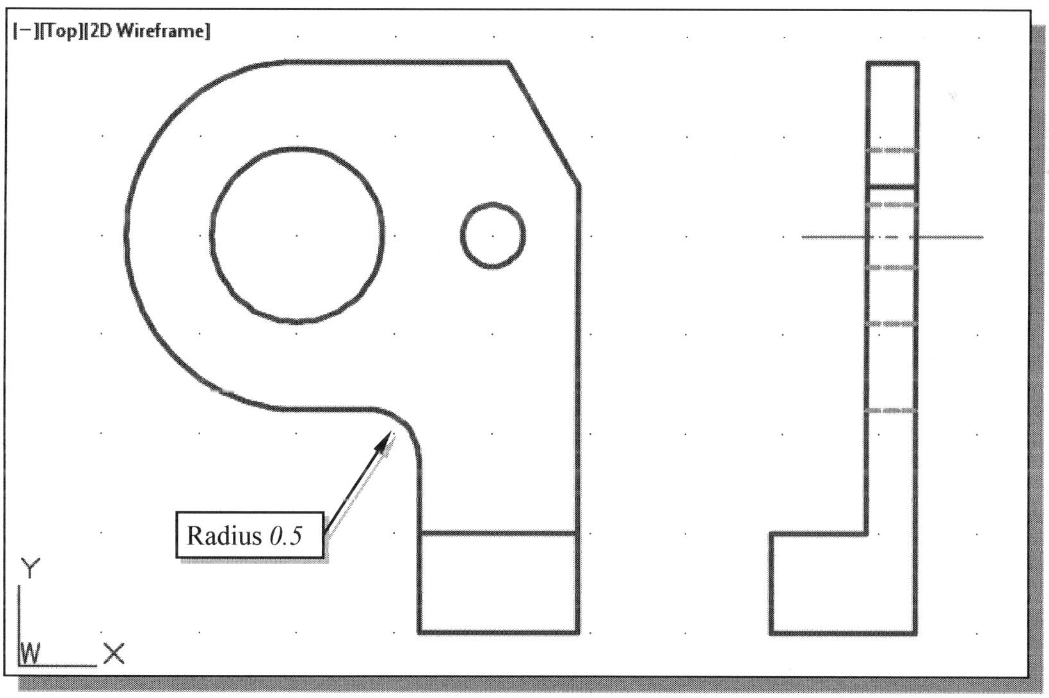

6. Repeat the **Fillet** command and create the four rounded corners (radius ***0.25***) as shown.

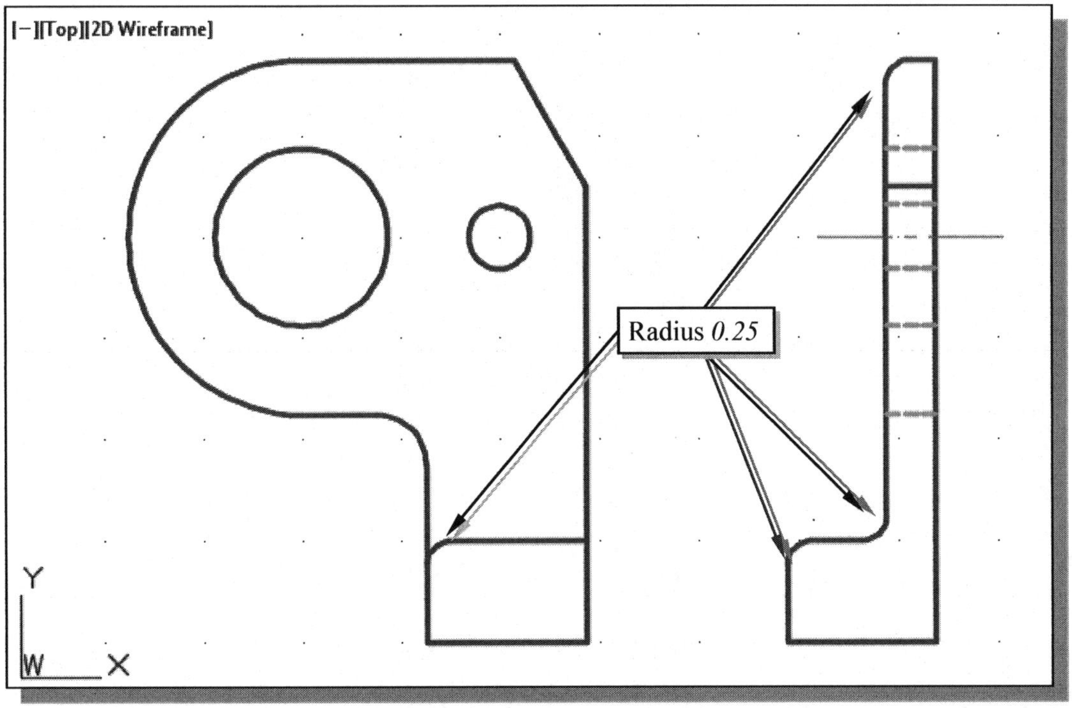

Saving the Completed CAD Design

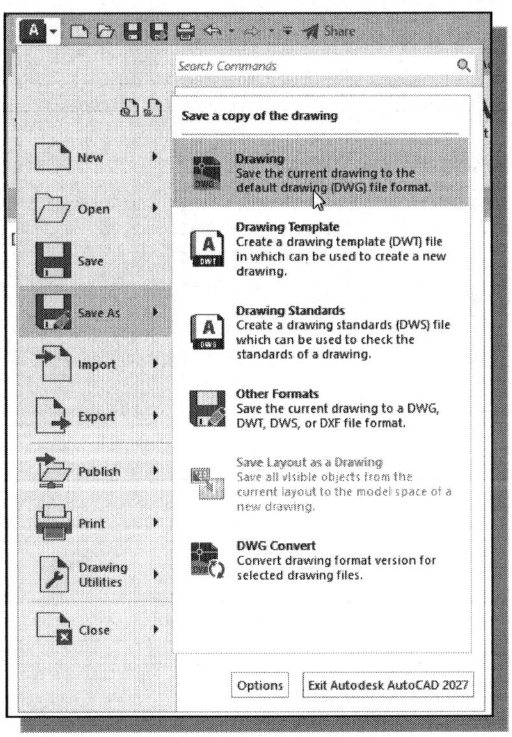

1. In the *Menu Bar*, select:
   [File] → [Save As].

2. In the *Save Drawing As* dialog box, select the folder in which you want to store the CAD file and enter ***Bracket*** in the *File name* box.

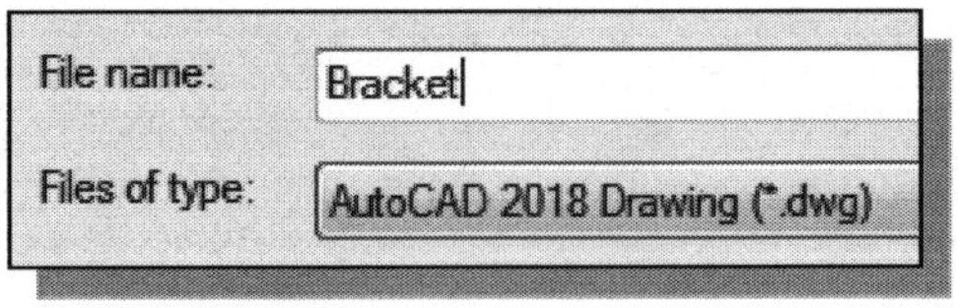

3. Click **Save** in the *Save Drawing As* dialog box to accept the selections and save the file.

Accessing the Dimensioning Commands

The user interface in AutoCAD has gone through several renovations since it was first released back in 1982. The purpose of the renovations is to make commands more accessible. For example, the dimensioning commands can be accessed through several options:

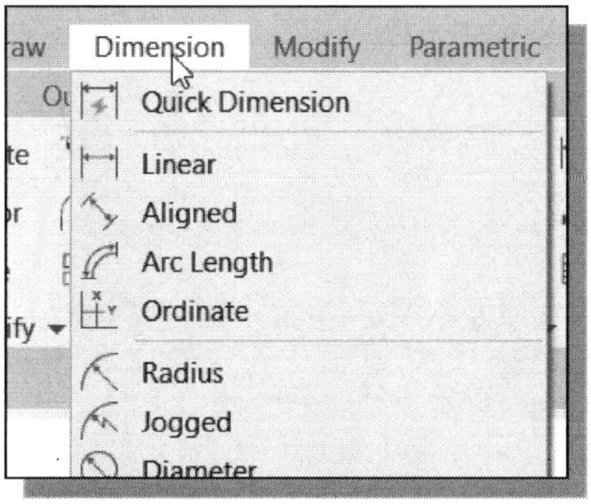

➤ The ***Menu Bar***: The majority of AutoCAD commands can be found in the *Menu Bar*. Specific task related commands are listed under the sub-items of the pull-down list. The commands listed under the *Menu Bar* are more complete, but it might take several clicks to reach the desired command.

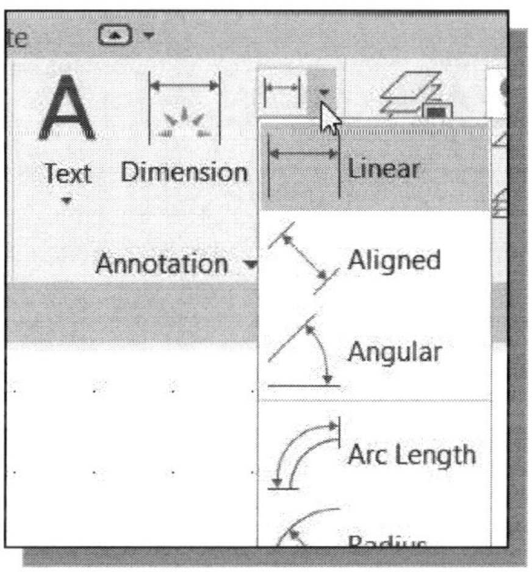

➤ The ***Ribbon* toolbar panels**: The more commonly used dimensioning commands are available in the *Annotation* toolbar as shown.

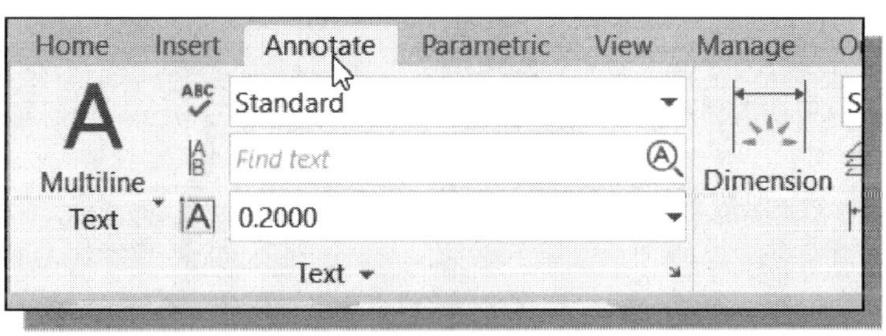

➤ The ***Dimensions* toolbar** under the **Annotate tab**: A more complete set of dimensioning commands.

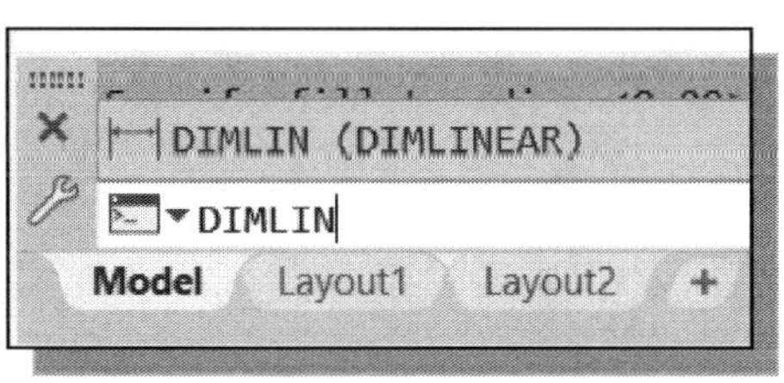

➤ The ***command prompt***: We can also type the command at the command prompt area. This option is always available, with or without displaying the toolbars.

The Dimension Toolbar

The *Dimension* toolbar offers the most flexible option to access the different dimensioning commands. The toolbar contains a more complete list than the *Ribbon* toolbars and this toolbar can be repositioned anywhere on the screen.

1. Move the cursor to the *Menu Bar* area and select:
   [Tools] → [Toolbars] → [AutoCAD] → [Dimension]

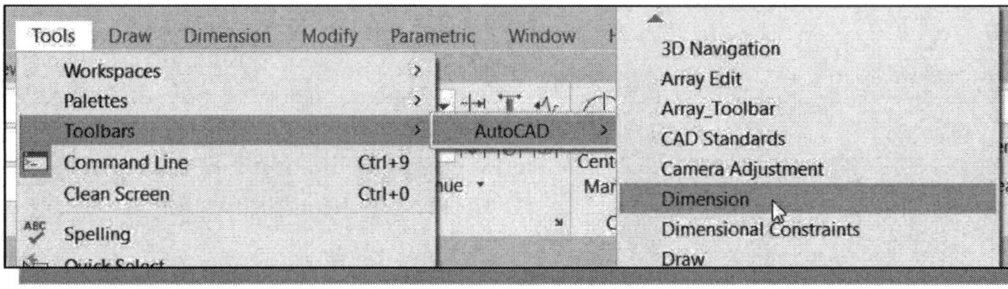

2. Move the cursor over the icons in the *Dimension* toolbar and read the brief description of each icon.

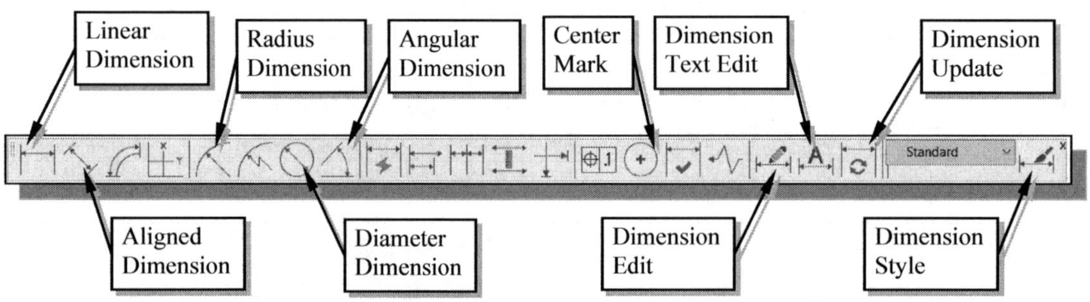

Using Dimension Style Manager

The appearance of the dimensions is controlled by *dimension variables*, which we can set using the *Dimension Style Manager* dialog box.

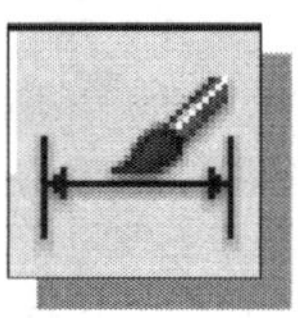

1. In the *Dimension* toolbar, pick **Dimension Style**. The *Dimension Style Manager* dialog box appears on the screen.

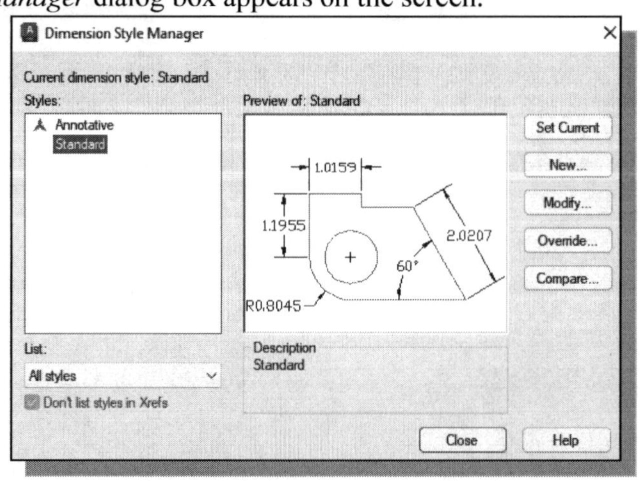

Dimensions Nomenclature and Basics

As it was stated in *Chapter 1*, the rule for creating CAD designs and drawings is that they should be created **full size** using real-world units. The importance of this practice is evident when we begin applying dimensions to the geometry. The features that we specify for dimensioning are measured and displayed automatically.

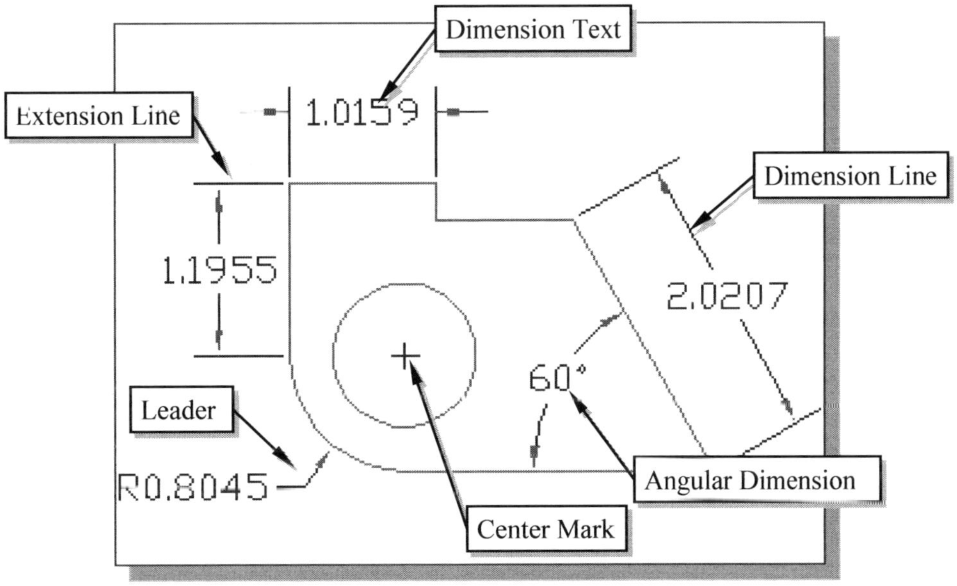

Selecting and placing dimensions can be confusing at times. The two main things to consider are (1) the function of the part and (2) the manufacturing operations. Detail drawings should contain only those dimensions that are necessary to make the design. Dimensions for the same feature of the design should be given only once in the same drawing. Nothing should be left to chance or guesswork on a drawing. Drawings should be dimensioned to avoid any possibility of questions. Dimensions should be carefully positioned, preferably near the profile of the feature being dimensioned.

Notice in the *Dimension Style Manager* dialog box, the AutoCAD default style name is *Standard*. We can create our own dimension style to fit the specific type of design we are working on, such as mechanical or architectual.

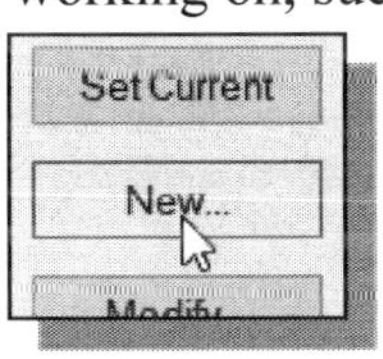

1. Click on the **New** button to create a new dimension style.

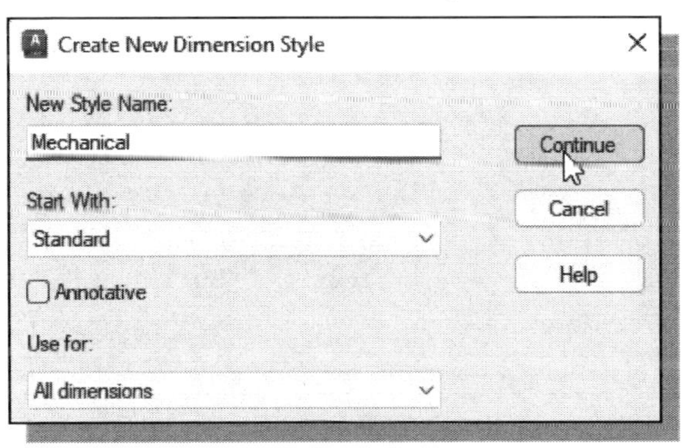

2. In the *Create New Dimension Style* dialog box, enter ***Mechanical*** as the dimension style name.

3. Click on the **Continue** button to proceed.

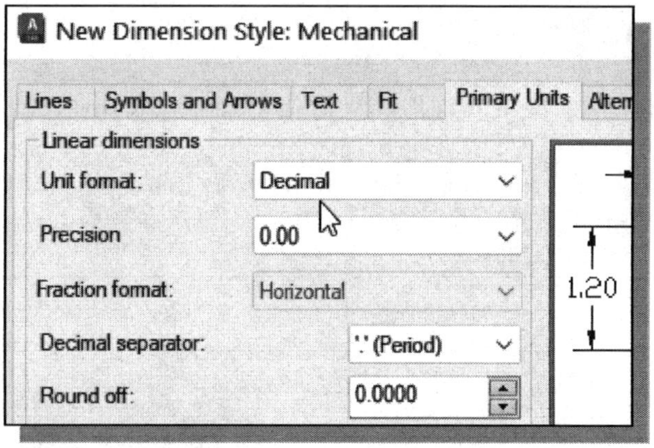

4. Click on the **Primary Units** tab.

5. Select ***Decimal*** as the *Unit format* and precision to **two digits after the decimal point** under the Primary Units tab. Also **suppress** the **leading zeros**.

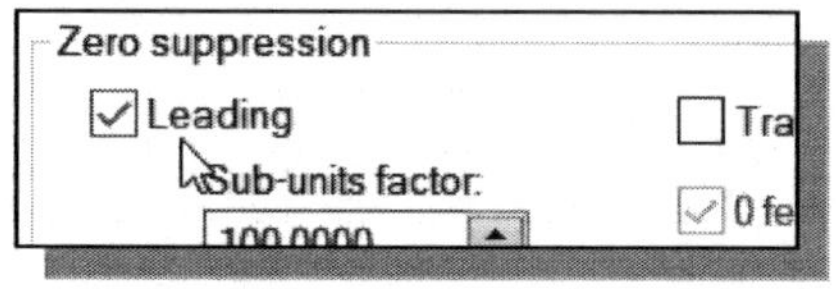

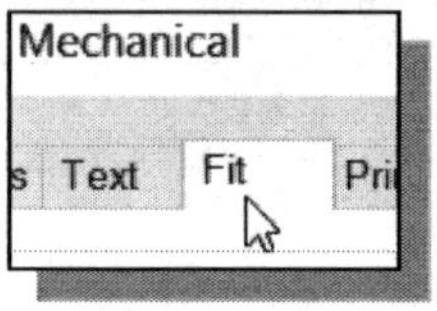

6. Select the **Fit** tab and notice the two options under *Scale for Dimension Features*.

❖ We can manually adjust the dimension scale factor or let AutoCAD automatically adjust the scale factor. For example, our current drawing will fit on A-size paper, and therefore we will use the scale factor of 1; this will assure the height of text size will be 1/8 of an inch on plotted drawing. If we change the Dimension Scale to 2.0 then the plotted text size will be ¼ of an inch on plotted drawing. In chapter 8, we will go over the procedure on using the AutoCAD layout mode, which allows us to plot the same design with different drawing sizes.

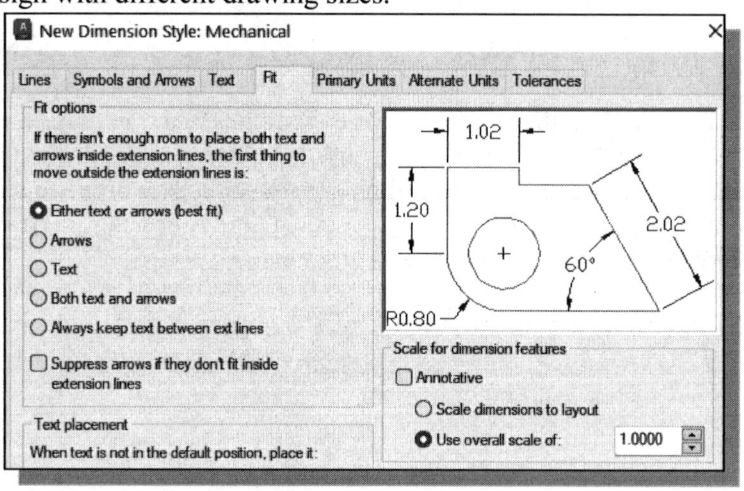

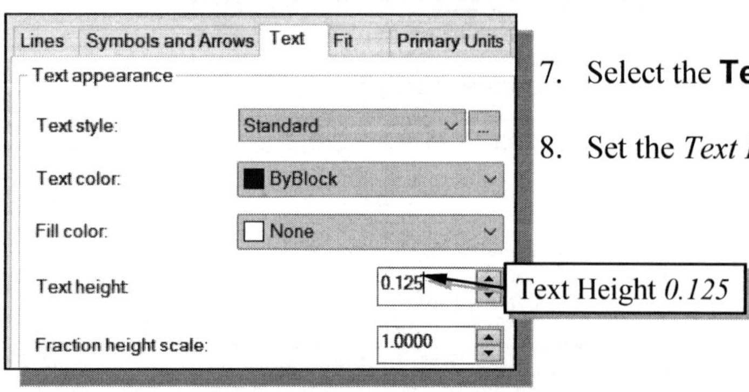

7. Select the **Text** tab.

8. Set the *Text Height* to ***0.125***.

9. Select the **Lines** tab and set *Extend beyond dim lines* to ***0.125***.

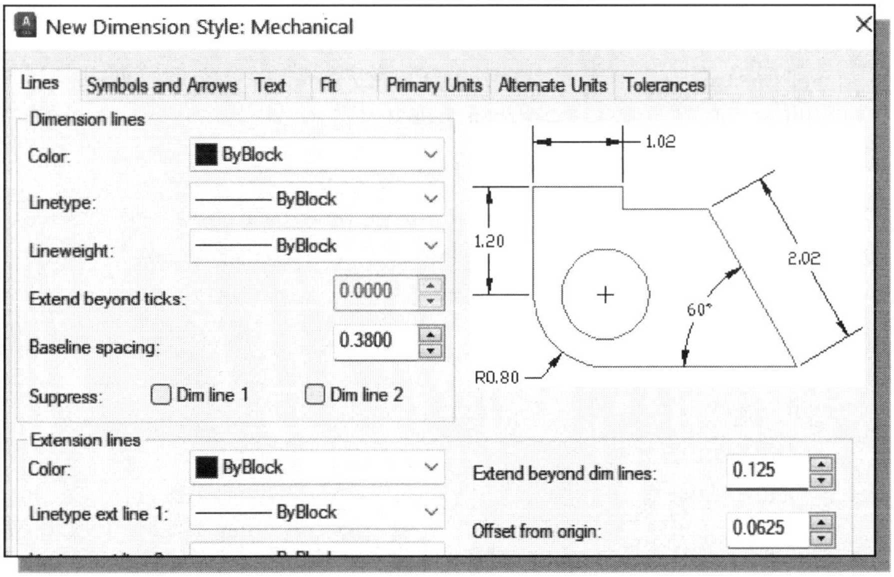

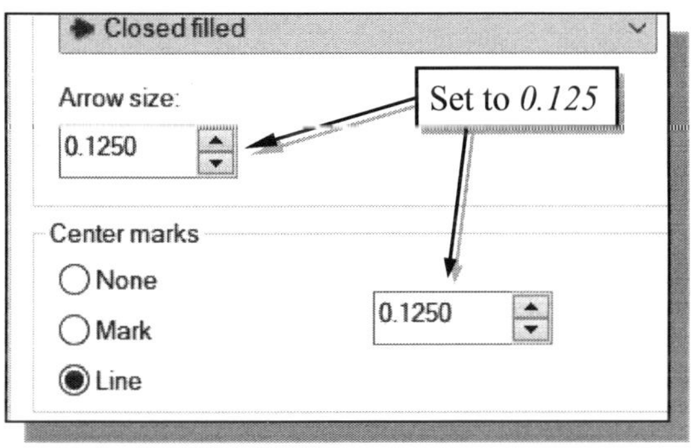

10. Select the **Symbols and Arrows** tab and set *Arrow size* and *Center marks* to ***0.125***. Also set the *Center marks* type to **Line**.

❖ Notice the different options available on this page, options that let us turn off one or both extension lines, dimension lines, and arrowheads.

➢ The **Center Mark** option is used to control the appearance of center marks and centerlines for diameter and radial dimensions.

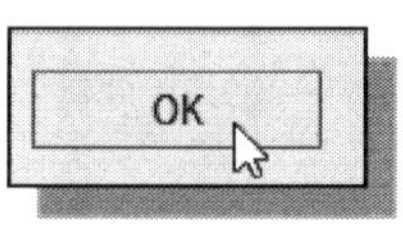

11. Click on the **OK** button to accept the settings and close the dialog box.

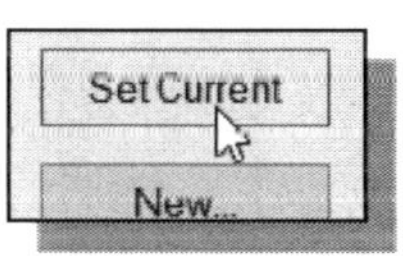

12. Pick the **Set Current** button to make the *Mechanical* dimension style the current dimension style.

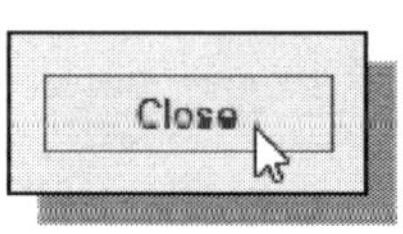

13. Click on the **Close** button to accept the settings and close the *Dimension Style Manager* dialog box.

➢ The **Dimension Style Manager** allows us to easily control the appearance of the dimensions in the drawing.

Using the Center Mark Command

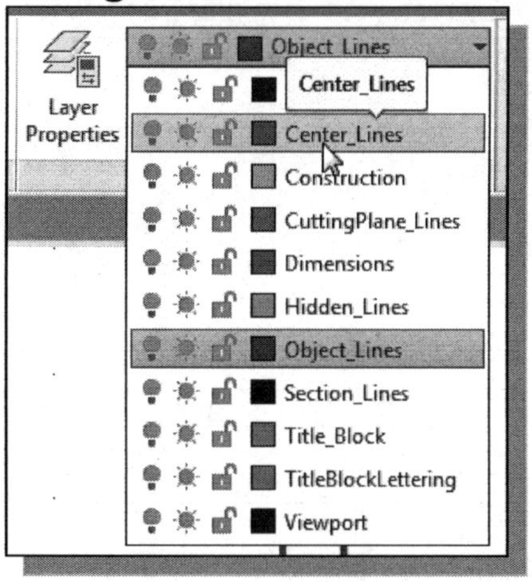

1. On the *Object Properties* toolbar, choose the ***Layer Control*** box with the left-mouse-button.

2. Move the cursor over the name of layer ***Center_Lines***, **left-click once**, and set layer *Center_lines* as the *Current Layer*.

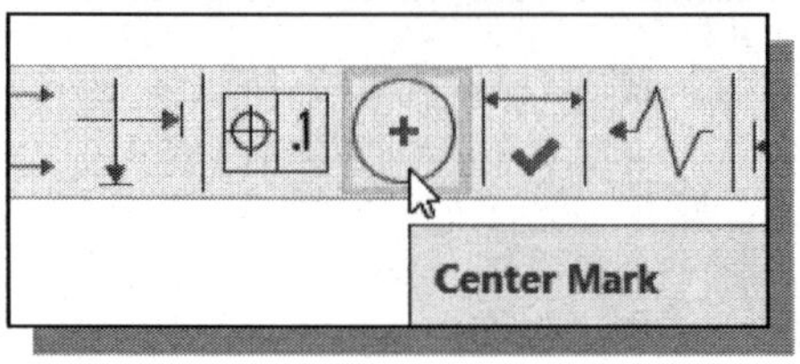

3. In the *Dimension* toolbar, click on the **Center Mark** icon.

4. Pick the **radius 1.75 arc** in the front view and notice AutoCAD automatically places two centerlines through the center of the arc.

5. Repeat the **Center Mark** command and pick the **small circle** to place the centerlines as shown.

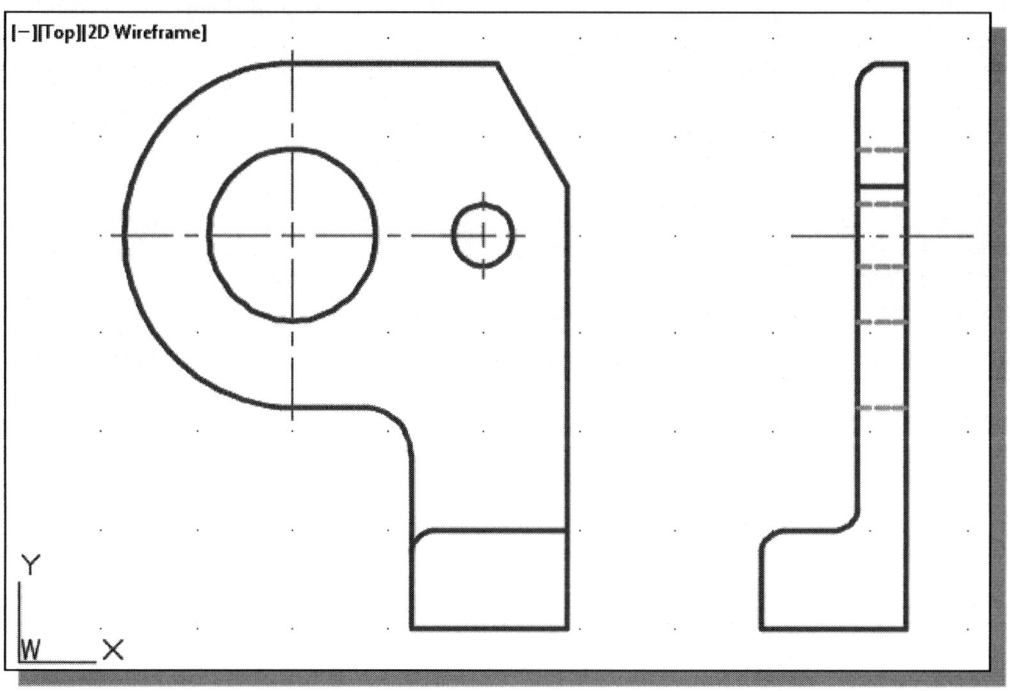

Adding Linear Dimensions

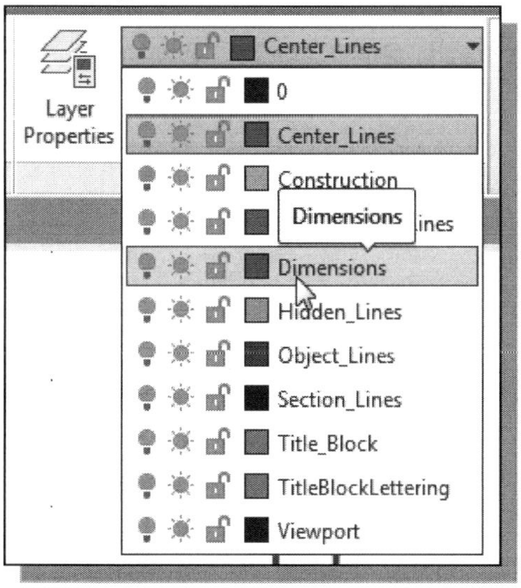

1. On the *Object Properties* toolbar, choose the ***Layer Control*** box with the left-mouse-button.

2. Move the cursor over the name of layer ***Dimensions***, **left-click once**, and set layer *Dimensions* as the *Current Layer*.

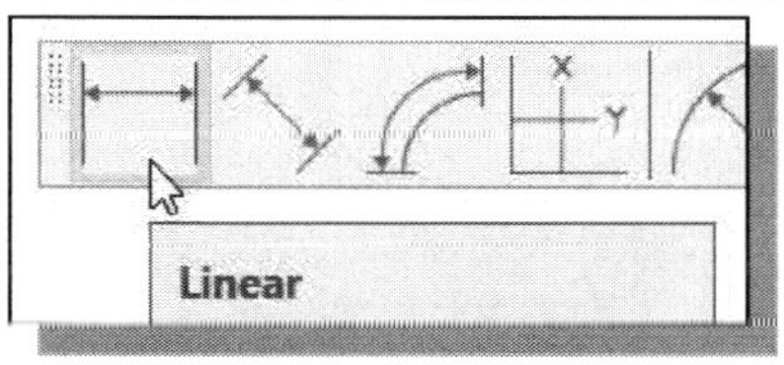

3. In the *Dimension* toolbar, click on the **Linear Dimension** icon.

➢ The Linear Dimension command measures and annotates a feature with a horizontal or vertical dimension.

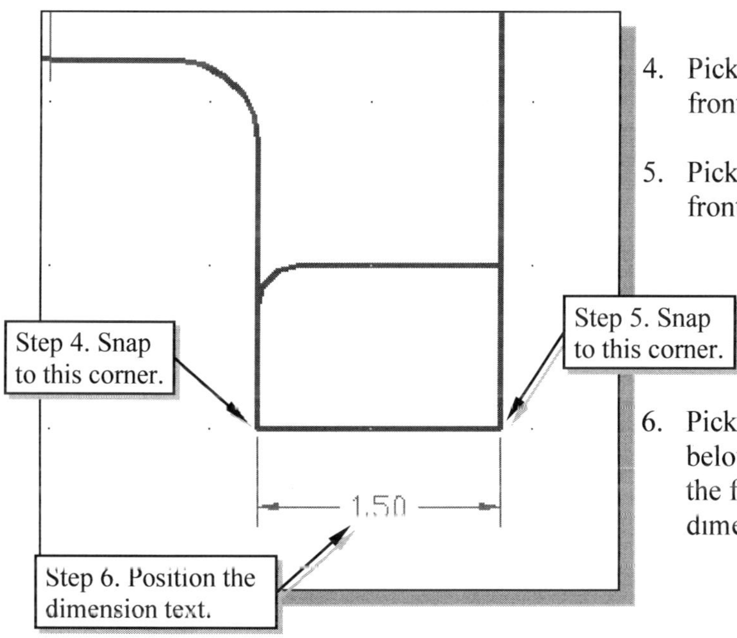

4. Pick the **lower left corner** of the front view of the part.

5. Pick the **lower right corner** of the front view of the part.

6. Pick a point that is about 0.5 inch below the bottom horizontal line of the front view to place the dimension text.

❖ Adding dimensions is very easy with AutoCAD's auto-dimensioning and associative-dimensioning features.

Adding Linear Dimensions Using the Object Option

In AutoCAD 2027, we can create horizontal, vertical, aligned, and radial dimensions with the DIM command. The type of dimension depends on the object that you select and the direction that you drag the dimension line.

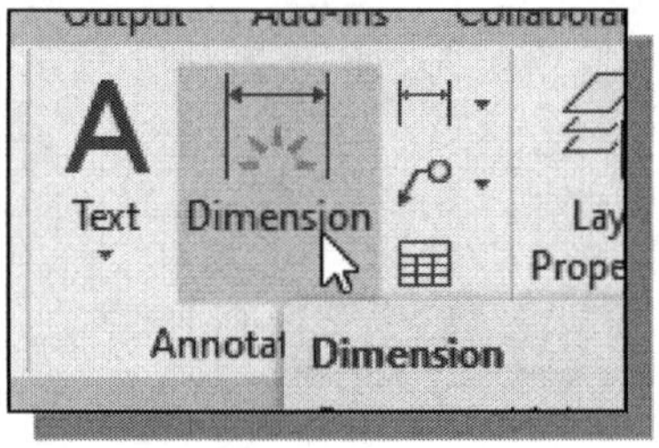

1. In the *Annotation* toolbar, click on the **Dimension** icon.

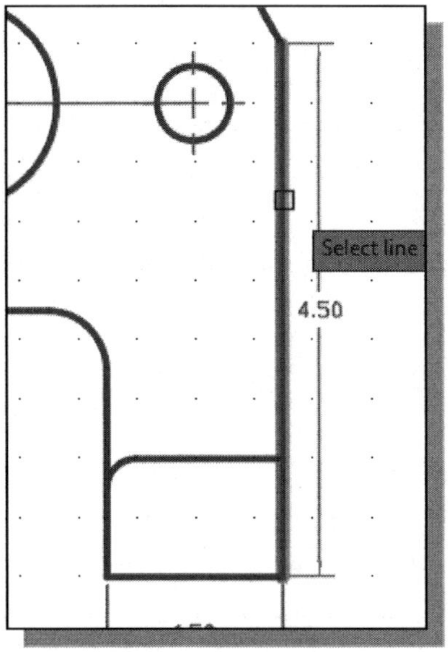

2. Move the cursor on top of the right vertical line in the front view and notice the associated length dimension is displayed next to the line.

3. Left-mouse-click once to accept the displayed dimension.

4. Move the cursor to the right and place the dimension as shown.

5. On your own, repeat the above steps and add the two dimensions in the side view as shown.

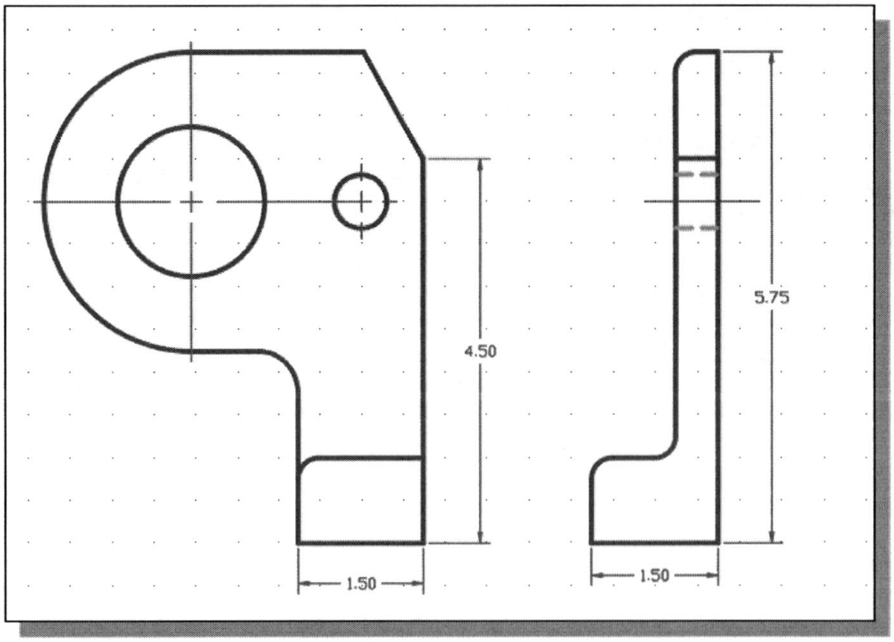

6. Select the right vertical line in the front view, then select the adjacent inclined line to display the related **angular dimension** as shown.

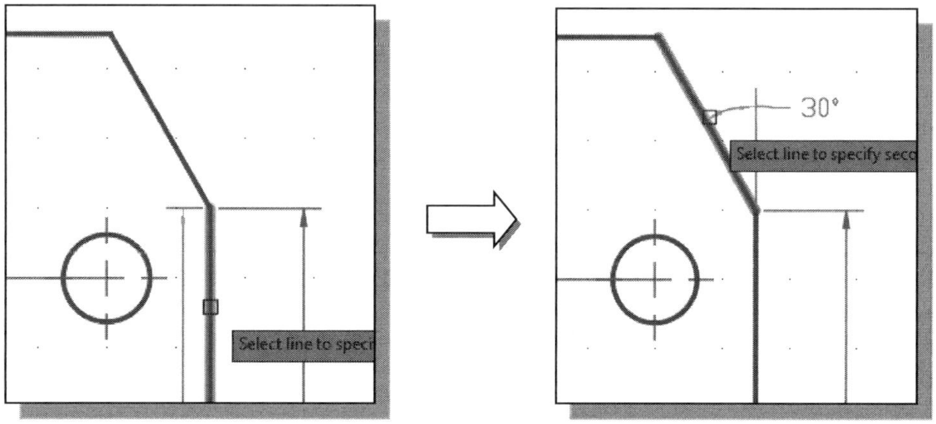

7. Left-mouse-click once to accept the displayed dimension.

8. On your own, move the cursor around and AutoCAD will show the different quadrant angle. Create the angular dimension as shown in the above figure.

9. Repeat the **Linear Dimension** or **Dimension** command and add the necessary linear dimensions as shown.

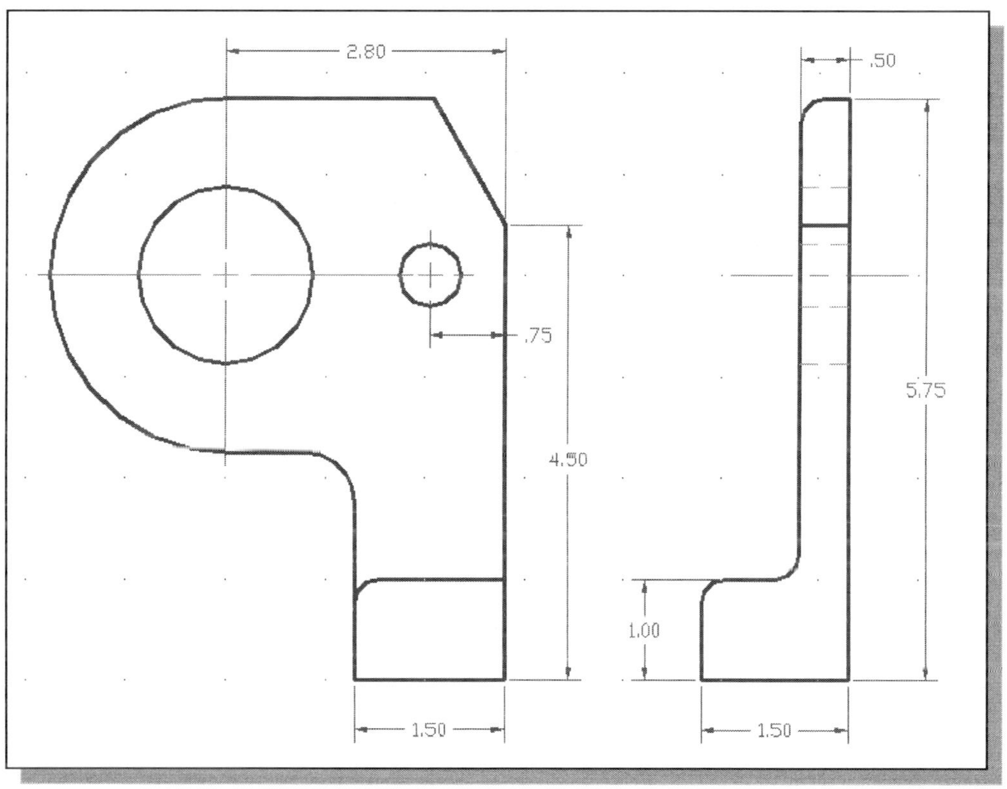

Adding Radius and Diameter Dimensions

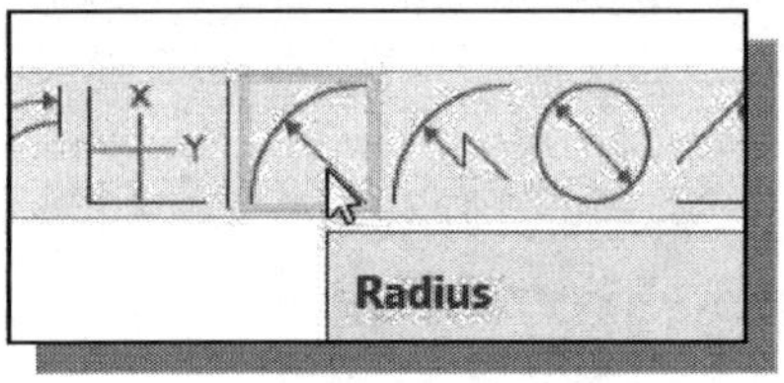

1. In the *Dimension* toolbar, click on the **Radius Dimension** icon.

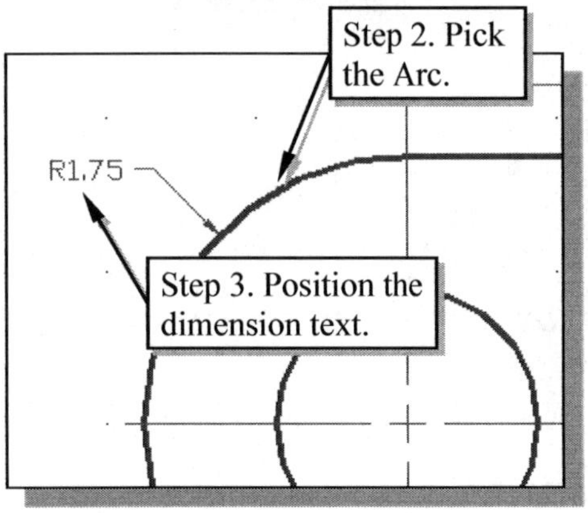

2. Pick the **large arc** in the front view.
3. Pick a point toward the left of the arc to place the dimension text.

4. Use the Radius Dimension and Diameter Dimension commands to add the necessary dimensions as shown.

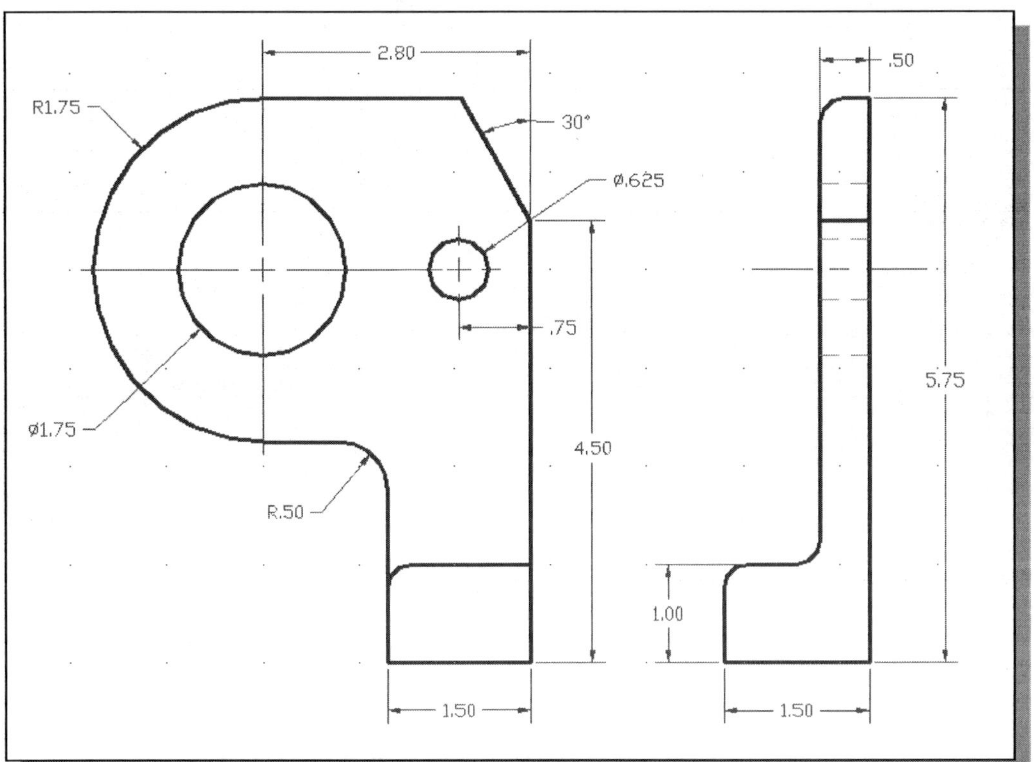

Using the Multiline Text Command

AutoCAD provides two options to create notes. For simple entries, we can use the **Single Line Text** command. For longer entries with internal formatting, we can use the **Multiline Text** command. The procedures for both of these commands are self-explanatory. The **Single Line Text** command, also known as the **Text** command, can be used to enter several lines of text that can be rotated and resized. The text we are typing is displayed on the screen. Each line of text is treated as a separate object in AutoCAD. To end a line and begin another, press the **[ENTER]** key after entering characters. To end the Text command, press the **[ENTER]** key without entering any characters.

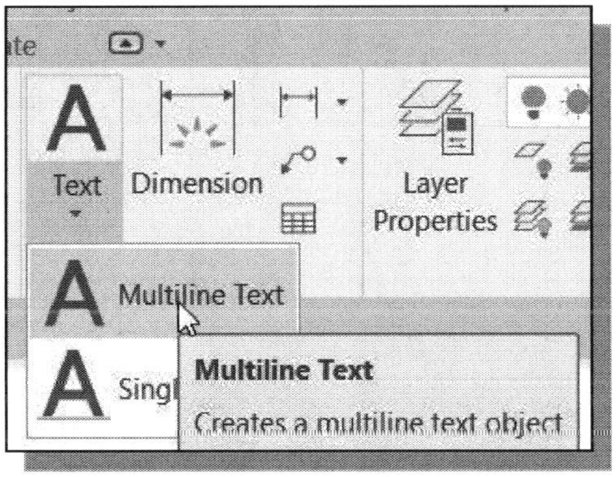

1. In the *Ribbon* toolbar panel, select:

   [Multiline Text]

2. In the *command prompt* area, the message "*Specify start point of text or [Justify/Style]:*" is displayed. Pick a location near the world coordinate ***(1,1.5)***.

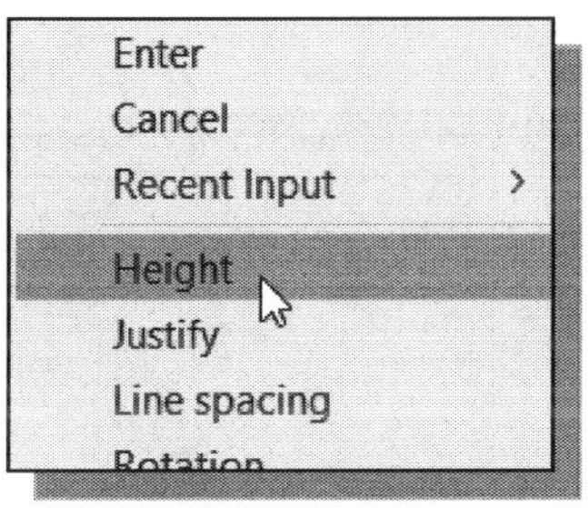

3. Right-click once to bring up the option list and choose **Height**. In the command prompt area, the message "*Specify Height:*" is displayed. Enter ***0.125*** as the text height.

4. Click a position toward the right and create a rectangle representing roughly the area for the notes.

5. In the command prompt area, the message "*Enter Text:*" is displayed. Enter: ***Rounds & Fillets R .25*** **[ENTER]**.

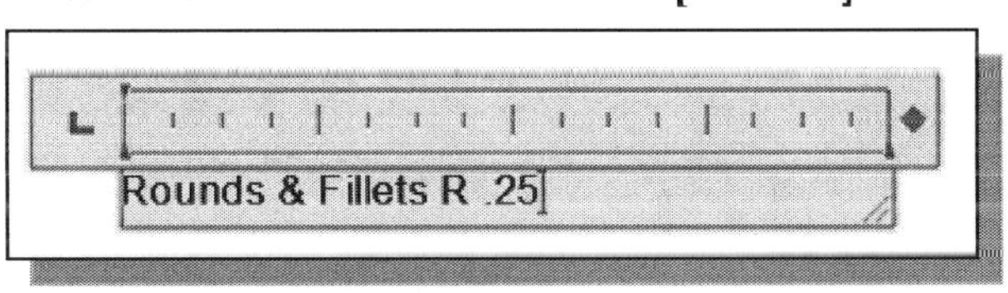

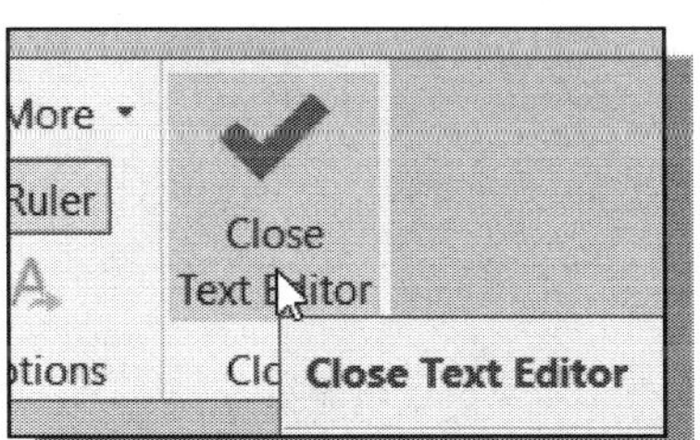

6. Note in the *Ribbon toolbar* area, the different command options are available to adjust the multiline text entered. Click **[Close Text Editor]** once to end the command.

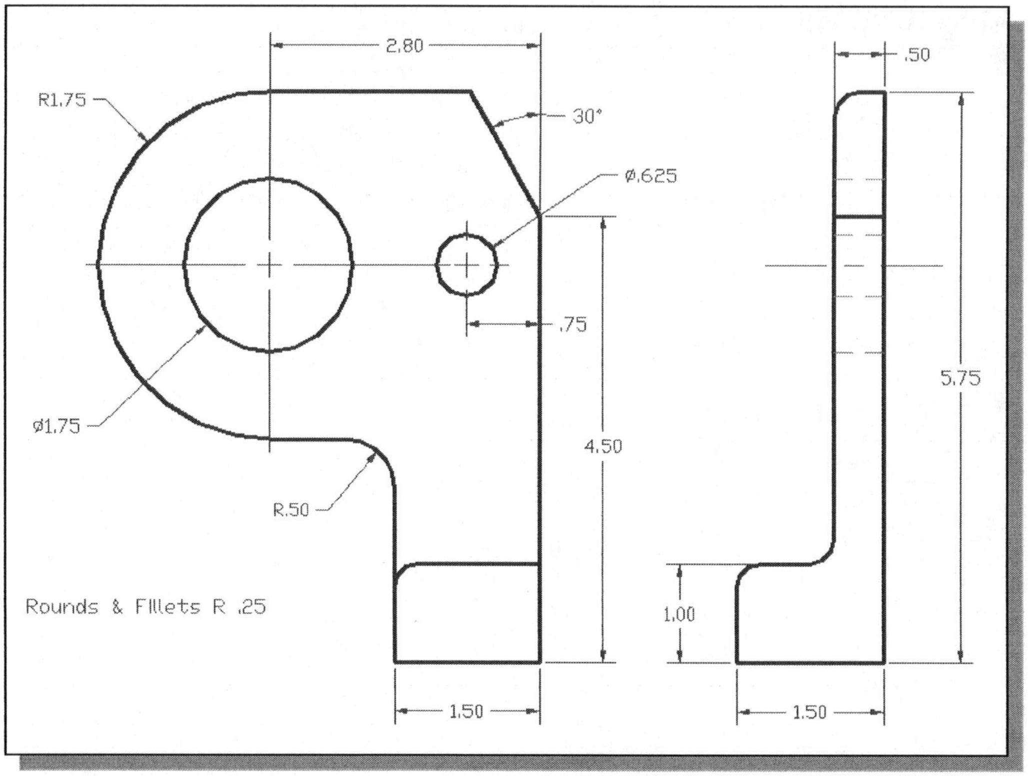

Adding Special Characters

We can add special text characters to the dimensioning text and notes. We can type in special characters during any text command and when entering the dimension text. The most common special characters have been given letters to make them easy to remember.

Code	***Character***	***Symbol***
%%C	Diameter symbol	Ø
%%D	Degree symbol	°
%%P	Plus/Minus sign	±

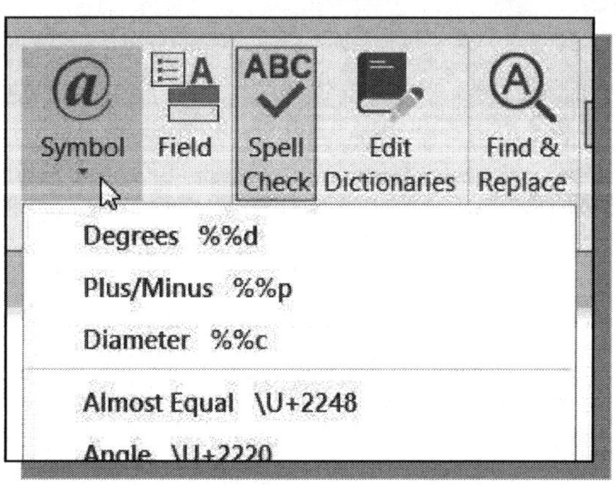

➤ On your own, create notes containing some of the special characters listed.

➤ Note the complete list of special characters can be accessed through the [Multiline Text] → [Symbol] dashboard.

Saving the Design

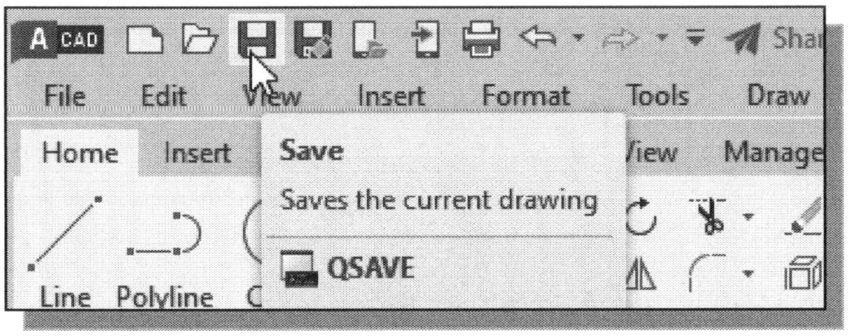

➢ In the *Quick Access Toolbar* area, select the **Save** icon.

A Special Note on Layers Containing Dimensions

AutoCAD creates several hidden **BLOCKS** when we create associative dimensions, and we will take a more in depth look at *blocks* in *Chapter 13*. AutoCAD treats **blocks** as a special type of object called a *named object*. Each kind of *named object* has a *symbol table* or a *dictionary*, and each table or dictionary can store multiple *named objects*. For example, if we create five dimension styles, our drawing's dimension style *symbol table* will have five dimension style records. In general, we do not work with *symbol tables* or *dictionaries* directly.

When we create dimensions in AutoCAD, most of the hidden blocks are placed in the same layer where the dimension was first defined. Some of the definitions are placed in the *DEFPOINTS* layer. When moving dimensions from one layer to another, AutoCAD does not move these definitions. When deleting layers, we cannot delete the current layer, *layer 0*, xref-dependent layers, or a layer that contains visible and/or invisible objects. Layers referenced by block definitions, along with the *DEFPOINTS* layer, cannot be deleted even if they do not contain visible objects.

To delete layers with hidden blocks, first use the **Purge** command **[Application → Drawing Utilities → Purge → Blocks]** to remove the invisible blocks. (We will have to remove all visible objects prior to using this command.) The empty layer can now be *deleted* or *purged*.

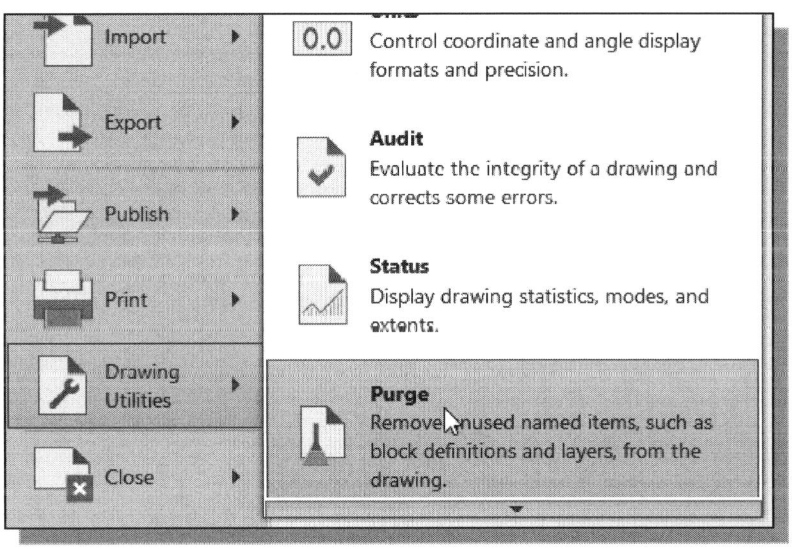

Review Questions: (Time: 25 minutes)

1. Why are dimensions and notes important to a technical drawing?

2. List and describe some of the general-dimensioning practices.

3. What is the effect of *Tolerance Accumulation*? How do we avoid it?

4. Describe the procedure in setting up a new *Dimension Style.*

5. What is the special way to create a diameter symbol when entering a dimension text?

6. What is the text code to create the **Diameter** symbol (Ø) in AutoCAD?

7. Which command can be used to delete layers with hidden blocks? Can we delete *Layer 0*?

8. Which quick-key is used to display and hide the *AutoCAD Text Window*?

9. What are the length and angle of the inclined line, highlighted in the figure below, in the front view of the *P-Bracket* design?

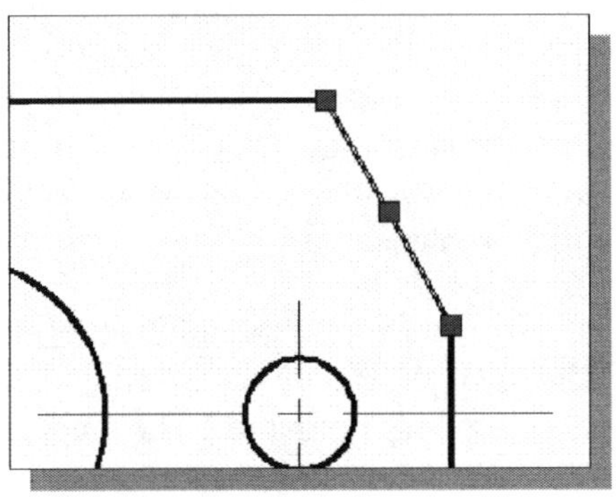

10. Construct the following drawing and measure the angle α.

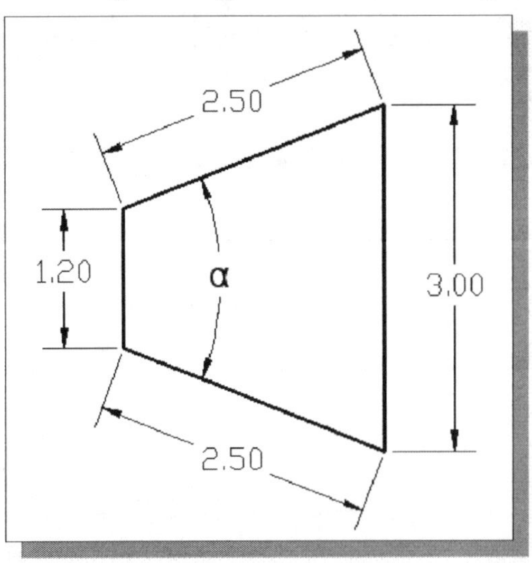

Exercises: (Time: 150 minutes)

1. **Shaft Guide** (Dimensions are in inches.)

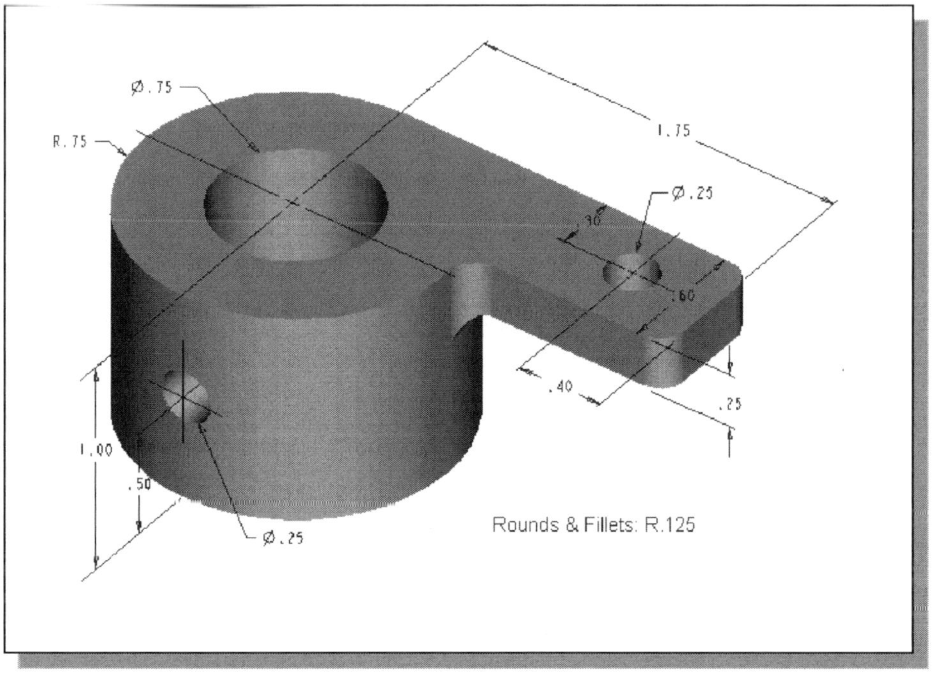

2. **Fixture Cap** (Dimensions are in millimeters.)

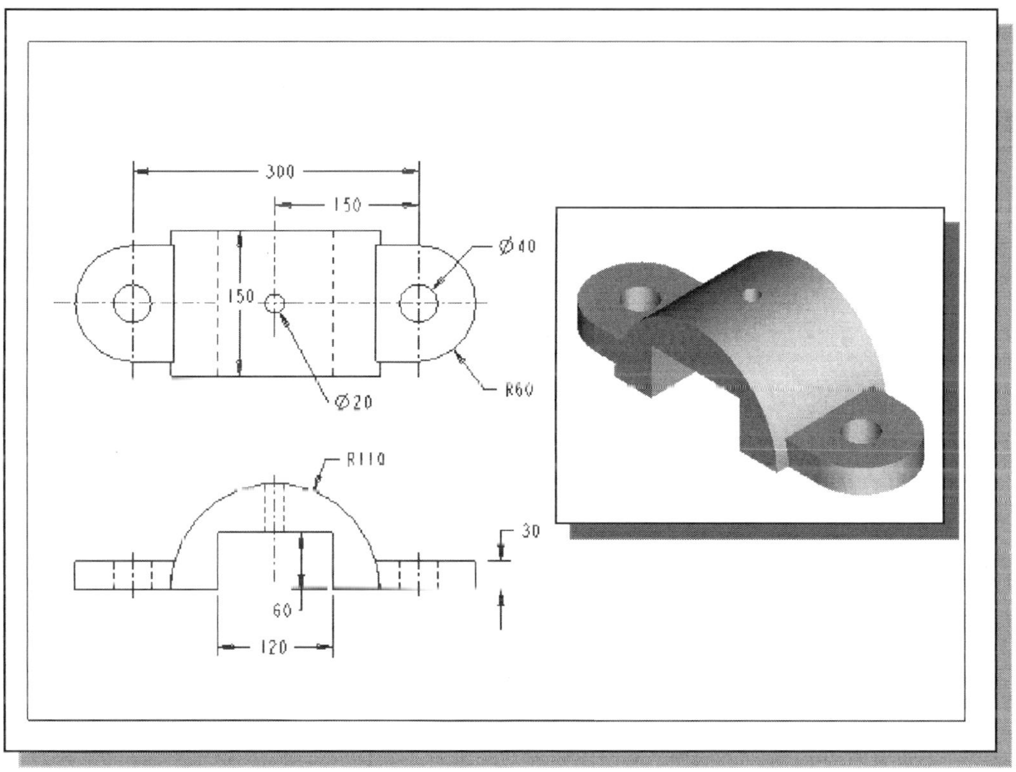

3. **Cylinder Support** (Dimensions are in inches.)

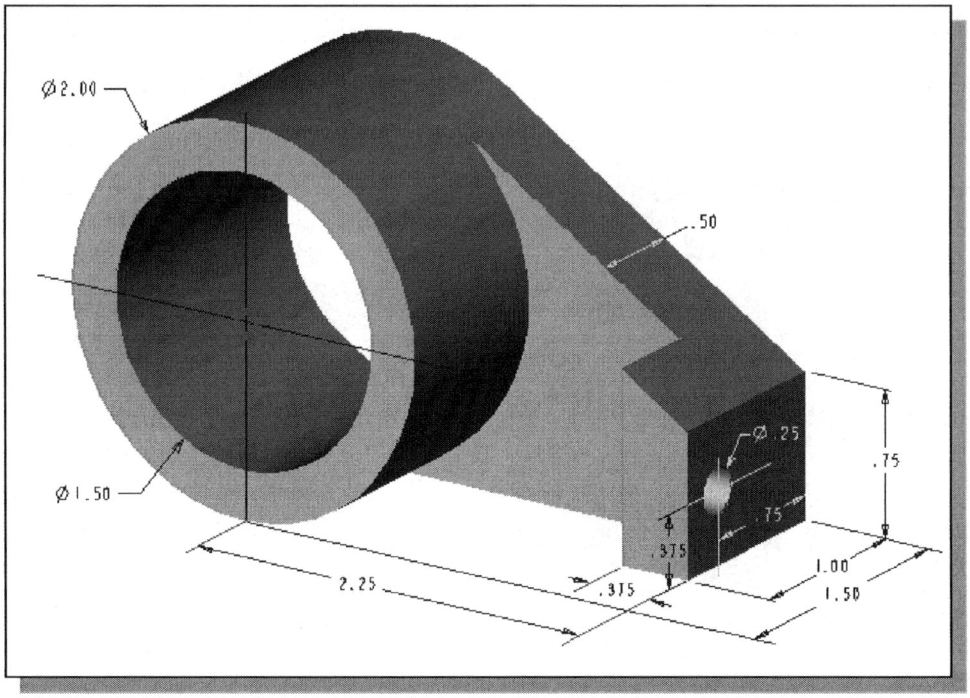

4. **Swivel Base** (Dimensions are in inches. Rounds: R 0.25)

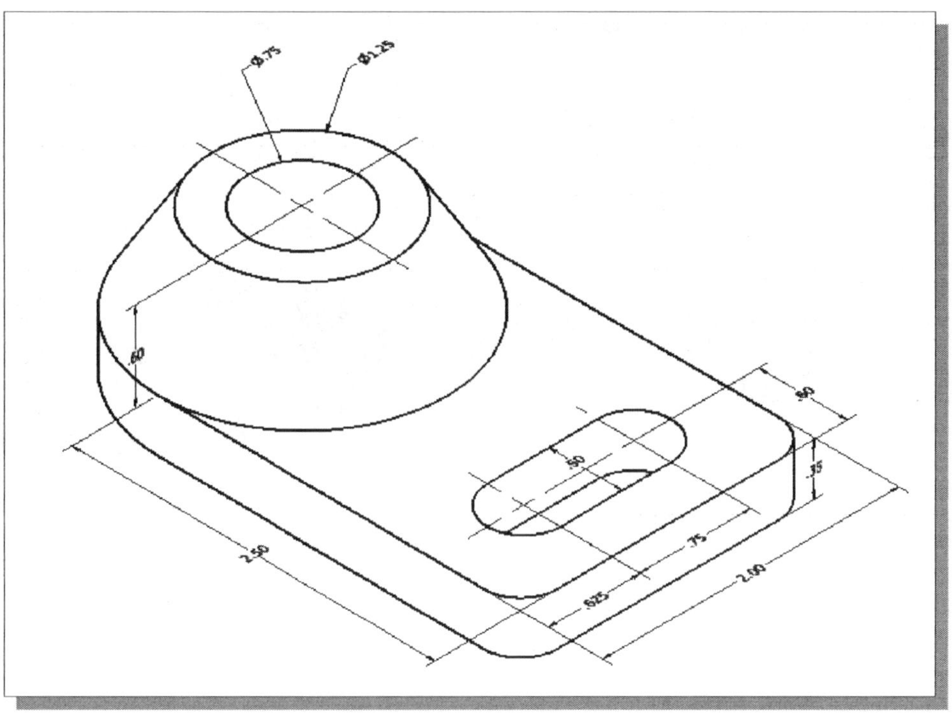

5. **Indexing Stop** (Dimensions are in millimeters.)

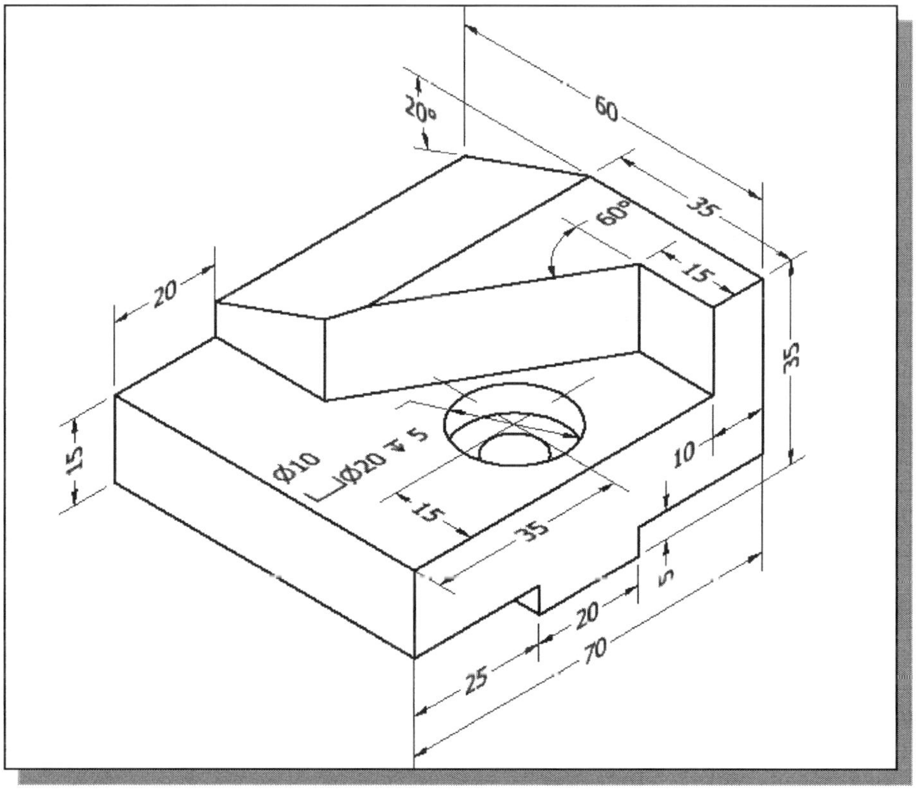

6. **Shaft Guide** (Dimensions are in inches.)

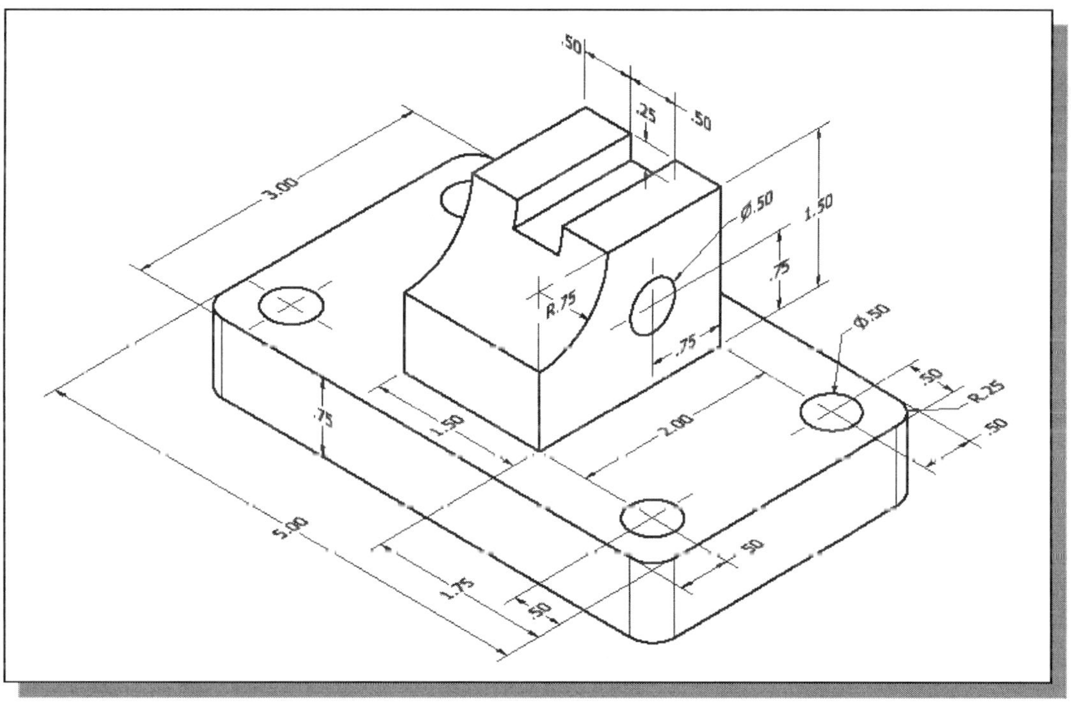

7. **Pivot Holder** (Dimensions are in inches.)

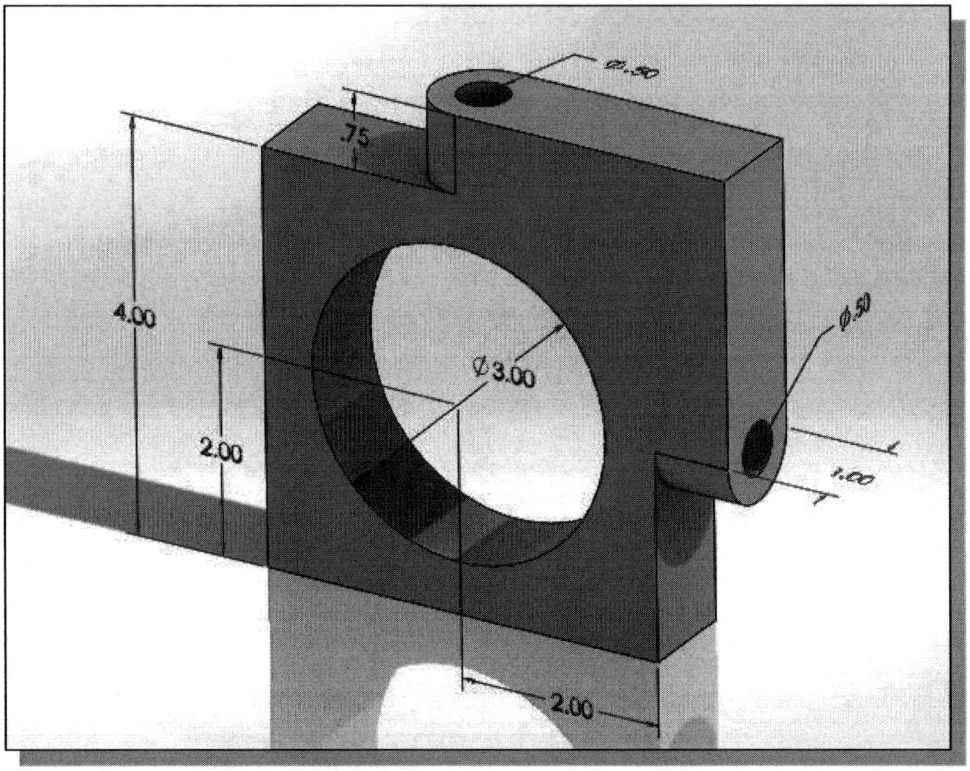

8. **Tube Hanger** (Dimensions are in inches.)

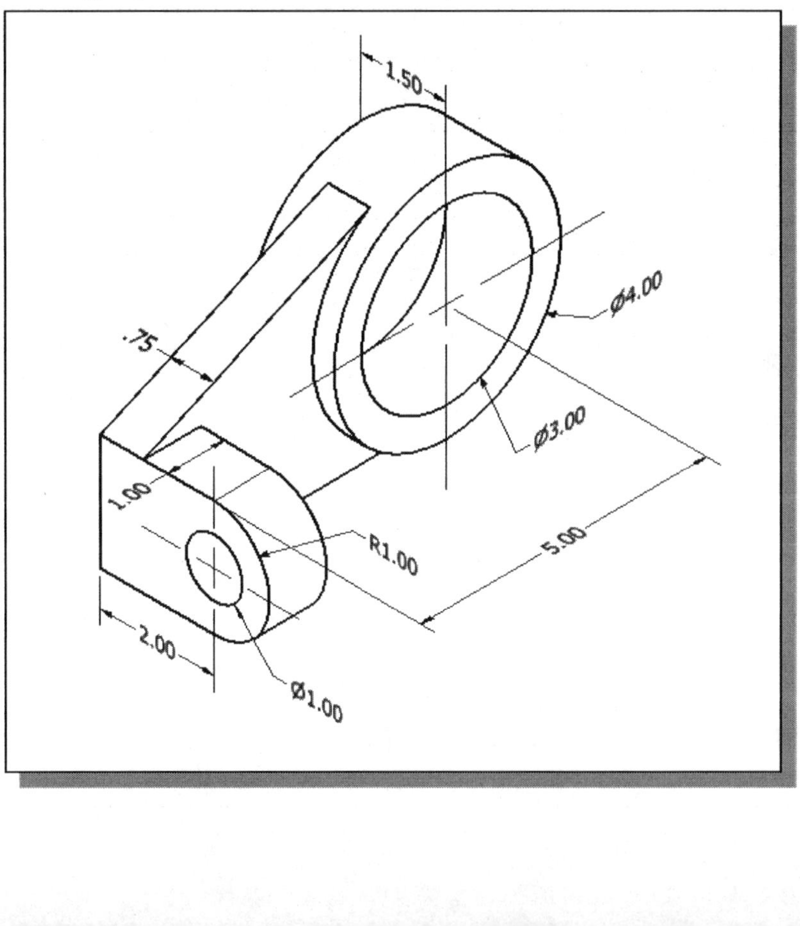

Chapter 6
Pictorials and Sketching

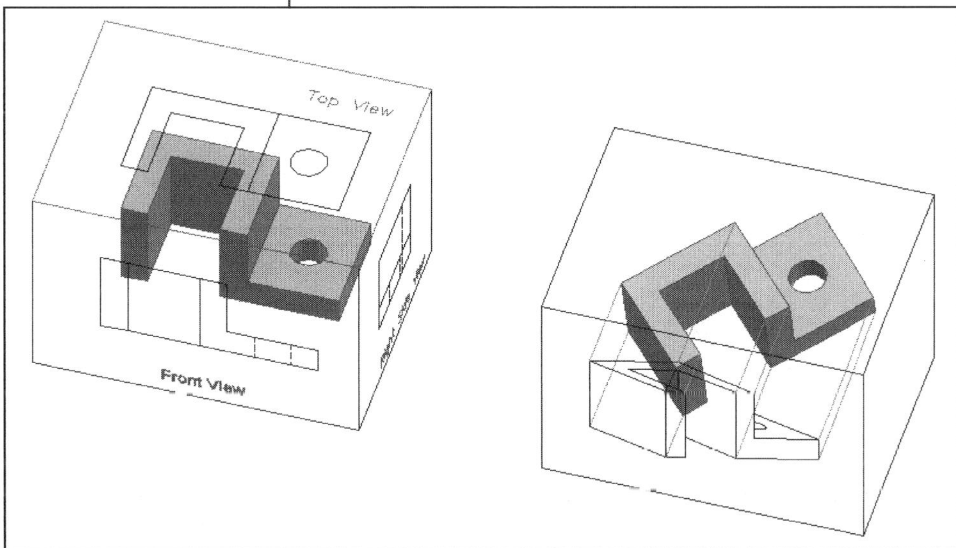

Learning Objectives

- Understand the Importance of Freehand Sketching
- Understand the Terminology Used in Pictorial Drawings
- Understand the Basics of the Following Projection Methods: Axonometric, Oblique and Perspective
- Be Able to Create Freehand 3D Pictorials

Engineering Drawings, Pictorials and Sketching

One of the best ways to communicate one's ideas is through the use of a picture or a drawing. This is especially true for engineers and designers. Without the ability to communicate well, engineers and designers will not be able to function in a team environment and therefore will have only limited value in the profession.

For many centuries, artists and engineers used drawings to express their ideas and inventions. The two figures below are drawings by Leonardo da Vinci (1452-1519) illustrating some of his engineering inventions.

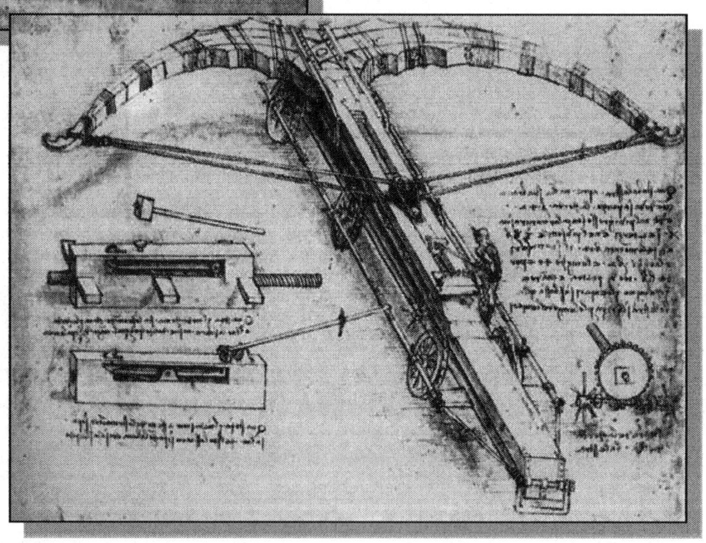

Engineering design is a process to create and transform ideas and concepts into a product definition that meets the desired objective. The engineering design process typically involves three stages: (1) Ideation/conceptual design stage: this is the beginning of an engineering design process, where basic ideas and concepts take shape. (2) Design development stage: the basic ideas are elaborated and further developed. During this stage, prototypes and testing are commonly used to ensure the developed design meets the desired objective. (3) Refine and finalize design stage: This stage of the design process is the last stage of the design process, where the finer details of the design are further refined. Detailed information of the finalized design is documented to assure the design is ready for production.

Two types of drawings are generally associated with the three stages of the engineering process: (1) Freehand Sketches and (2) Detailed Engineering Drawings.

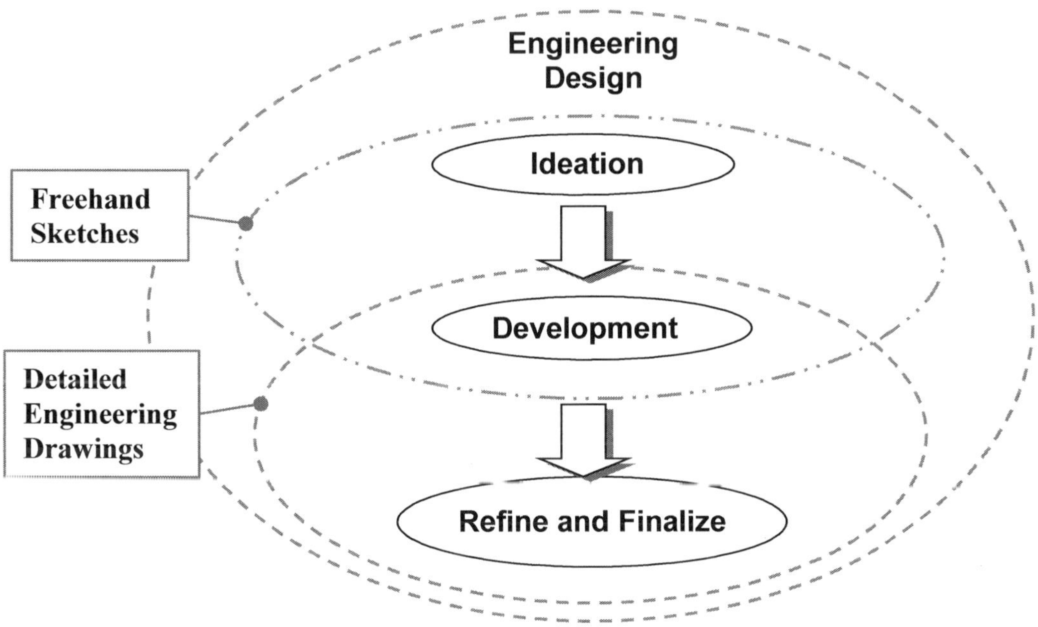

Freehand sketches are generally used in the beginning stages of a design process: (1) to quickly record designer's ideas and help formulate different possibilities, (2) to communicate the designer's basic ideas with others and (3) to develop and elaborate further the designer's ideas/concepts.

During the initial design stage, an engineer will generally picture the ideas in his/her head as three-dimensional images. The ability to think visually, specifically three-dimensional visualization, is one of the most essential skills for an engineer/designer. Freehand sketching is considered as one of the most powerful methods to help develop visualization skills.

Detailed engineering drawings are generally created during the second and third stages of a design process. The detailed engineering drawings are used to help refine and finalize the design and also to document the finalized design for production. Engineering drawings typically require the use of drawing instruments, from compasses to computers, to bring precision to the drawings.

Freehand Sketches and Detailed Engineering Drawings are essential communication tools for engineers. By using the established conventions, such as perspective and isometric drawings, engineers/designers are able to quickly convey their design ideas to others. The ability to sketch ideas is absolutely essential to engineers. The ability to sketch is helpful, not just to communicate with others, but also to work out details in ideas and to identify any potential problems. Freehand sketching requires only simple tools, a pencil and a piece of paper, and can be accomplished almost anywhere and anytime. Creating freehand sketches does not require any artistic ability. Detailed engineering drawing is employed only for those ideas deserving a permanent record.

Freehand sketches and engineering drawings are generally composed of similar information, but there is a tradeoff between time required to generate a sketch/drawing versus the level of design detail and accuracy. In industry, freehand sketching is used to quickly document rough ideas and identify general needs for improvement in a team environment.

Besides the 2D views, described in the previous chapter, there are three main divisions commonly used in freehand engineering sketches and detailed engineering drawings: (1) **Axonometric**, with its divisions into **isometric**, **dimetric** and **trimetric**; (2) **Oblique**; and (3) **Perspective**.

1. **Axonometric projection**: The word *Axonometric* means "to measure along axes." Axonometric projection is a special *orthographic projection* technique used to generate ***pictorials***. **Pictorials** show a 2D image of an object as viewed from a direction that reveals three directions of space. In the figure below, the adjuster model is rotated so that a *pictorial* is generated using *orthographic projection* (projection lines perpendicular to the projection plane) as described in Chapter 4. There are three types of axonometric projections: isometric projection, dimetric projection, and trimetric projection. Typically in an axonometric drawing, one axis is drawn vertically.

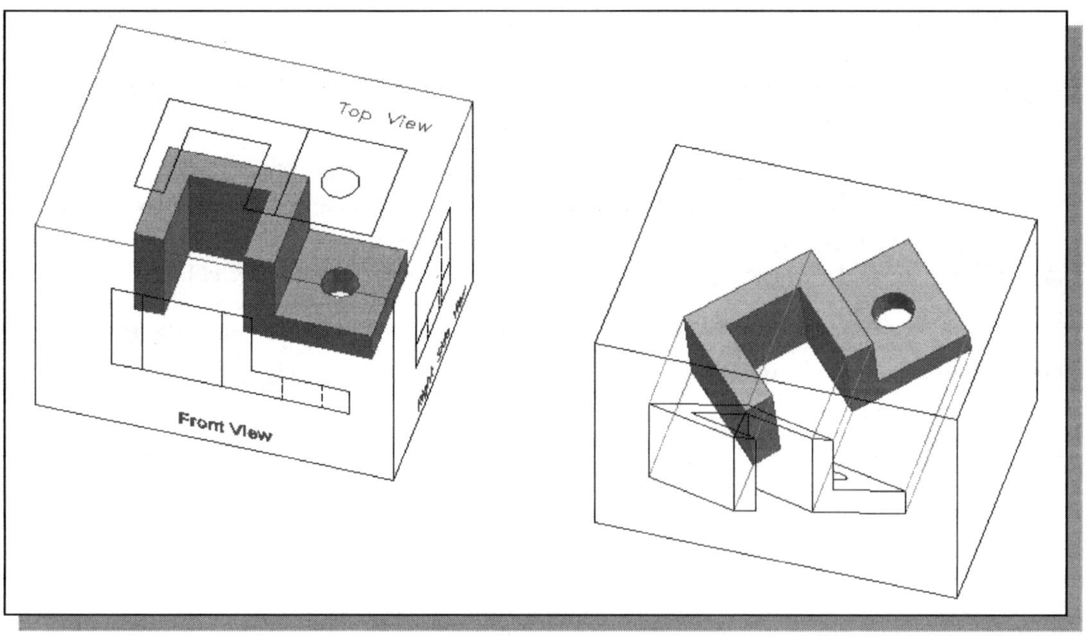

In **isometric projections**, the direction of viewing is such that the three axes of space appear equally foreshortened, and therefore the angles between the axes are equal. In **dimetric projections**, the directions of viewing are such that two of the three axes of space appear equally foreshortened. In **trimetric projections**, the direction of viewing is such that the three axes of space appear unequally foreshortened.

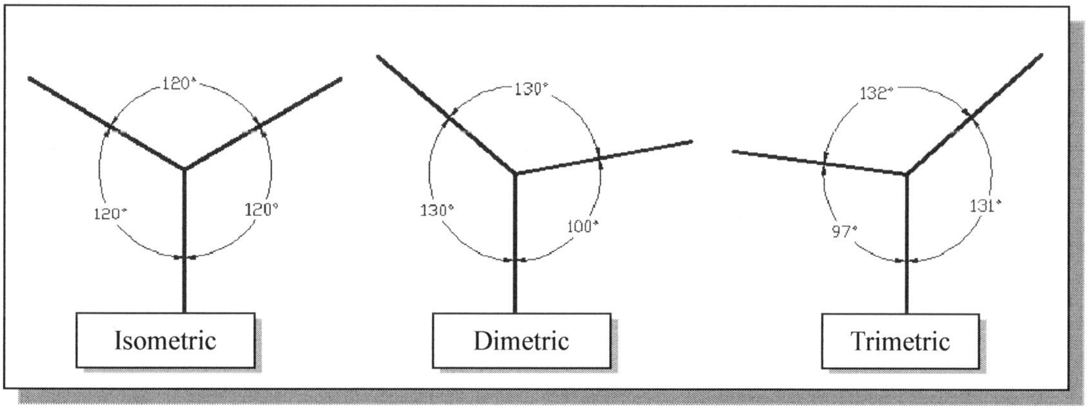

Isometric projection is perhaps the most widely used for pictorials in engineering graphics, mainly because isometric views are the most convenient to draw. Note that the different projection options described here are not particularly critical in freehand sketching as the emphasis is generally placed on the proportions of the design, not the precision measurements. The general procedure to constructing isometric views is illustrated in the following sections.

2. **Oblique Projection** represents a simple technique of keeping the front face of an object parallel to the projection plane and still reveals three directions of space. An **orthographic projection** is a parallel projection in which the projection lines are perpendicular to the plane of projection. An **oblique projection** is one in which the projection lines are other than perpendicular to the plane of projection.

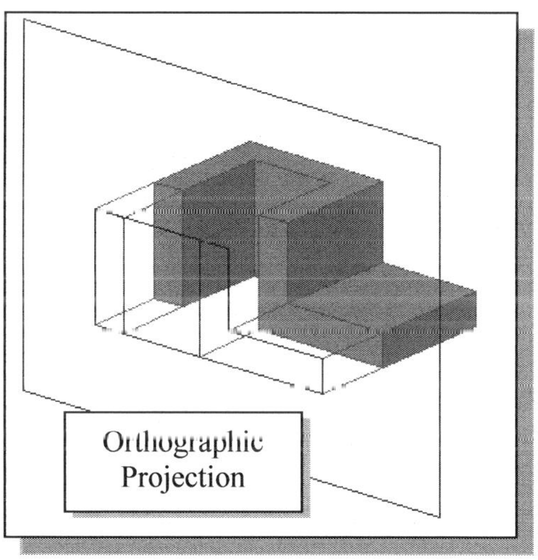

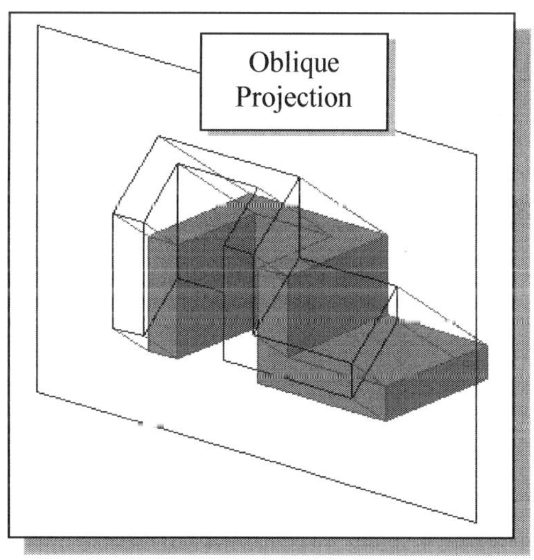

In an oblique drawing, geometry that is parallel to the frontal plane of projection is drawn true size and shape. This is the main advantage of the oblique drawing over the axonometric drawings. The three axes of the oblique sketch are drawn horizontal, vertical, and the third axis can be at any convenient angle (typically between 30 and 60 degrees). The proportional scale along the 3rd axis is typically a scale anywhere between ½ and 1. If the scale is ½, then it is a **Cabinet** oblique. If the scale is 1, then it is a **Cavalier** oblique.

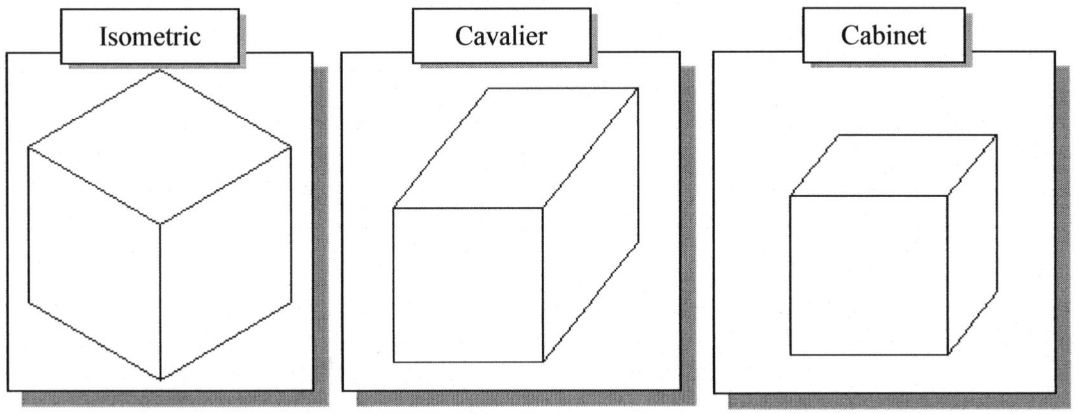

3. **Perspective Projection** adds realism to the three-dimensional pictorial representation; a perspective drawing represents an object as it appears to an observer; objects that are closer to the observer will appear larger to the observer. The key to the perspective projection is that parallel edges converge to a single point, known as the **vanishing point**. If there is just one vanishing point, then it is called a one-point perspective. If two sets of parallel edge lines converge to their respective vanishing points, then it is called a two-point perspective. There is also the case of a three-point perspective in which all three sets of parallel lines converge to their respective vanishing points.

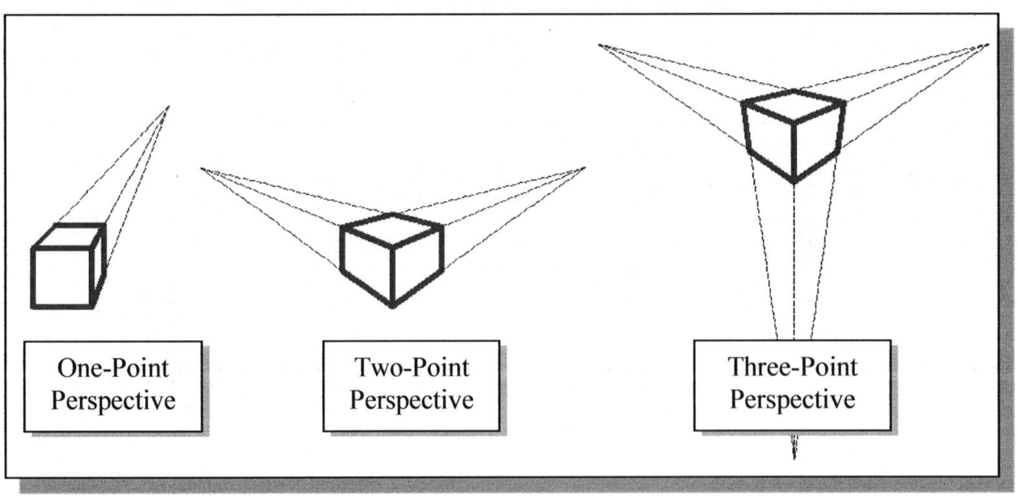

- Although there are specific techniques available to create precise pictorials with known dimensions, in the following sections, the basic concepts and procedures relating to freehand sketching are illustrated.

Isometric Sketching

Isometric drawings are generally done with one axis aligned to the vertical direction. A **regular isometric** is when the viewpoint is looking down on the top of the object, and a **reversed isometric** is when the viewpoint is looking up on the bottom of the object.

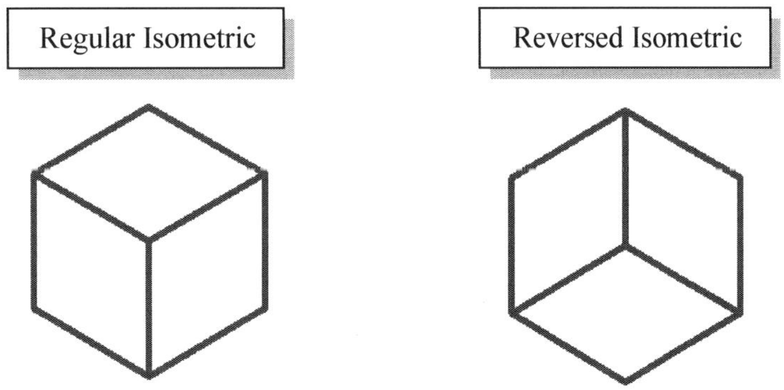

Two commonly used approaches in creating isometric sketches are (1) the **enclosing box** method and (2) the **adjacent surface** method. The enclosing box method begins with the construction of an isometric box showing the overall size of the object. The visible portions of the individual 2D-views are then constructed on the corresponding sides of the box. Adjustments of the locations of surfaces are then made, by moving the edges, to complete the isometric sketch.

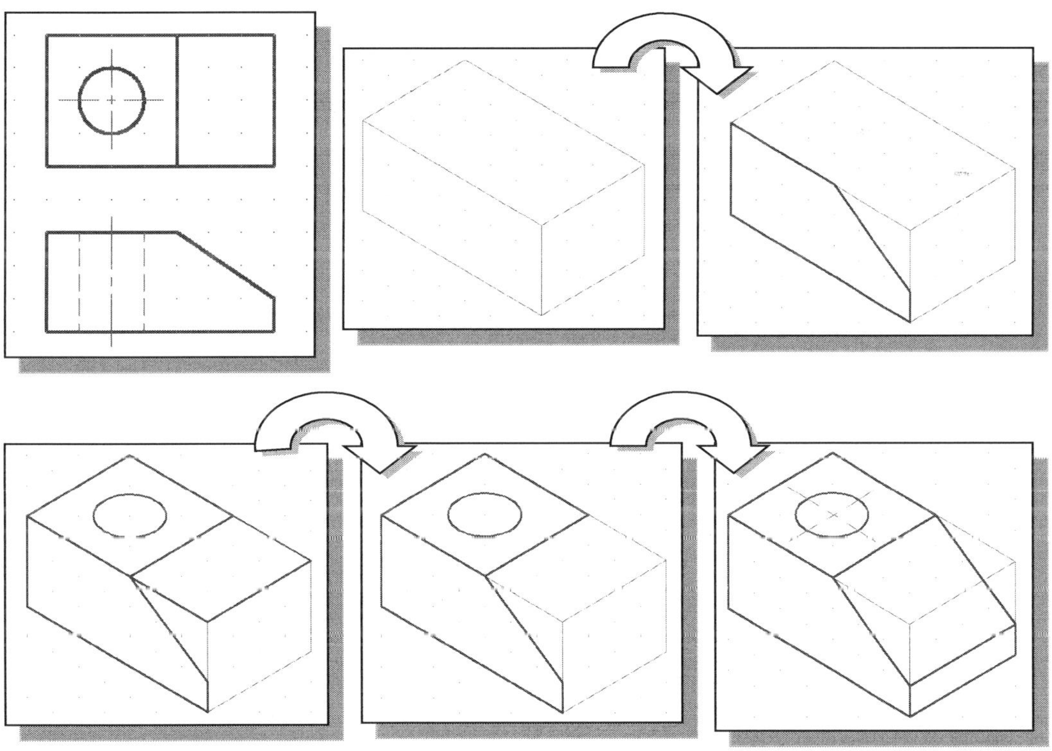

The adjacent surface method begins with one side of the isometric drawing, again with the visible portion of the corresponding 2D-view. The isometric sketch is completed by identifying and adding the adjacent surfaces.

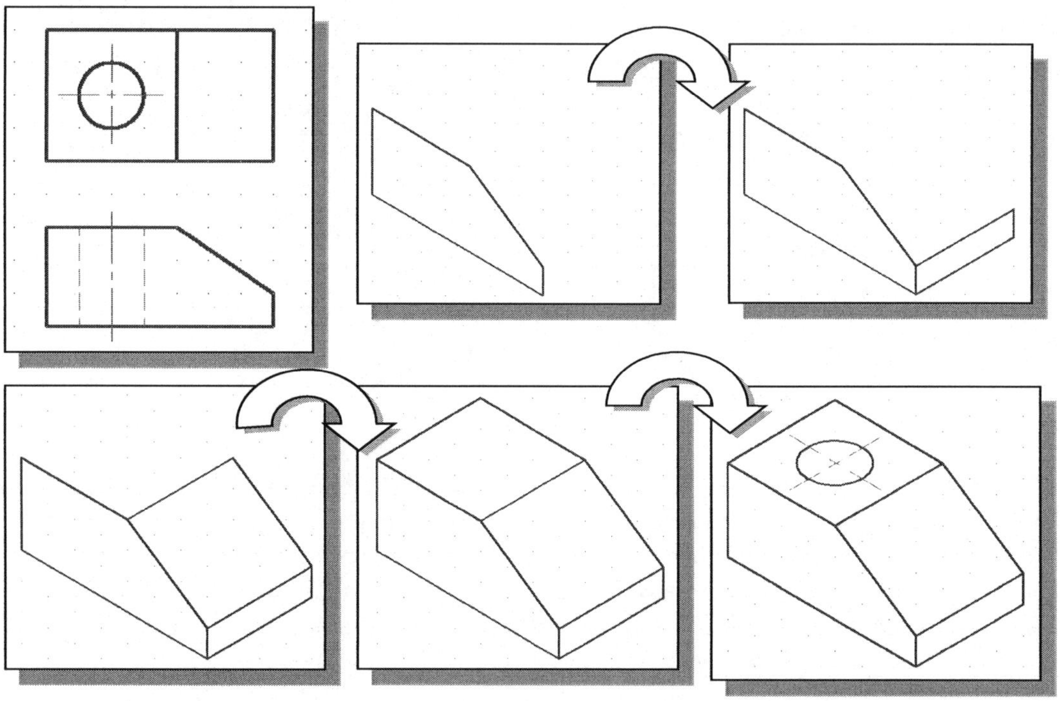

In an isometric drawing, cylindrical or circular shapes appear as ellipses. It can be confusing in drawing the ellipses in an isometric view; one simple rule to remember is the **major axis** of the ellipse is always **perpendicular** to the **center axis** of the cylinder as shown in the figures below.

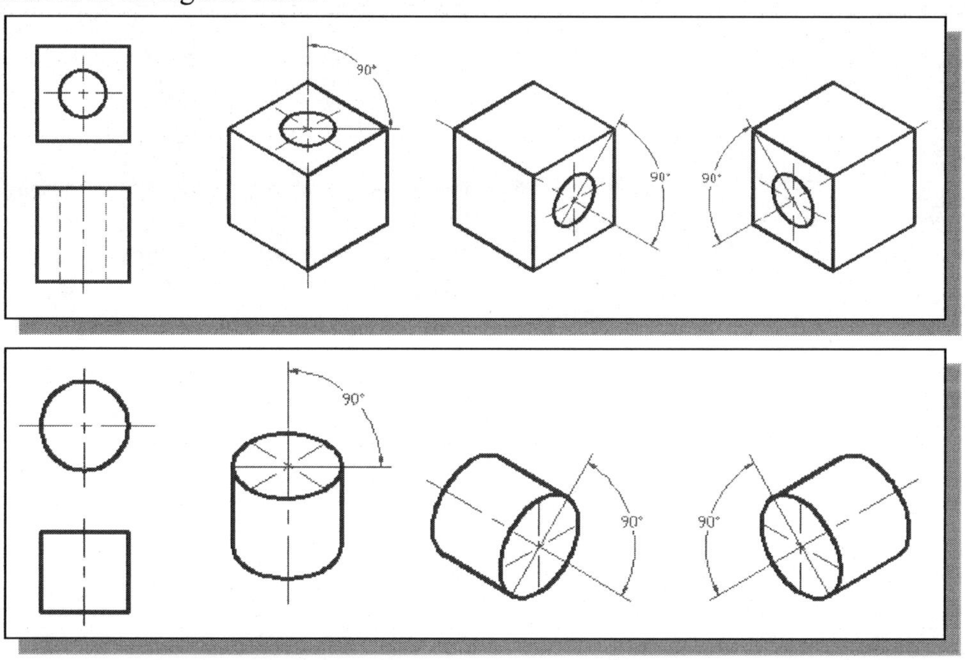

Chapter 6 - Isometric Sketching Exercise 1:

Given the Orthographic Top view and Front view, create the isometric view.

(Note that 3D Models of chapter examples and exercises are available at http://www.sdcpublications.com/downloads/978-1-63057-806-0.)

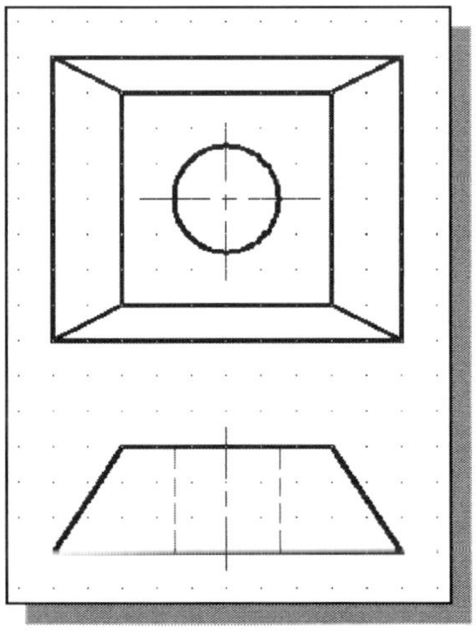

Name: ______________________ Date: ______________

Chapter 6 - Isometric Sketching Exercise 2:

Given the Orthographic Top view and Front view, create the isometric view.

(Note that 3D Models of chapter examples and exercises are available at http://www.sdcpublications.com/downloads/978-1-63057-806-0.)

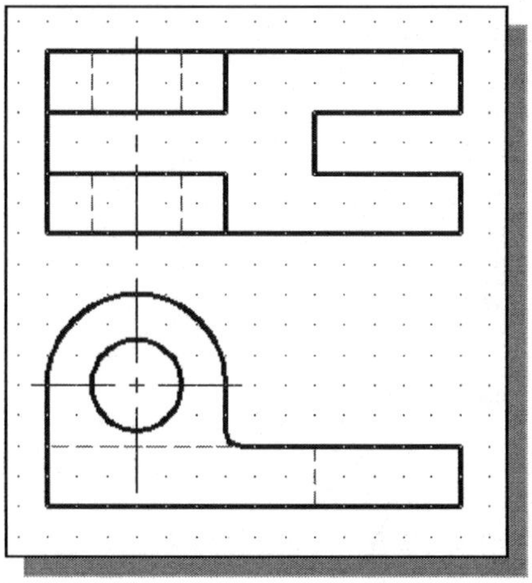

Name: ______________________ Date: ______________

Chapter 6 - Isometric Sketching Exercise 3:

Given the Orthographic Top view and Front view, create the isometric view.

(Note that 3D Models of chapter examples and exercises are available at http://www.sdcpublications.com/downloads/978-1-63057-806-0.)

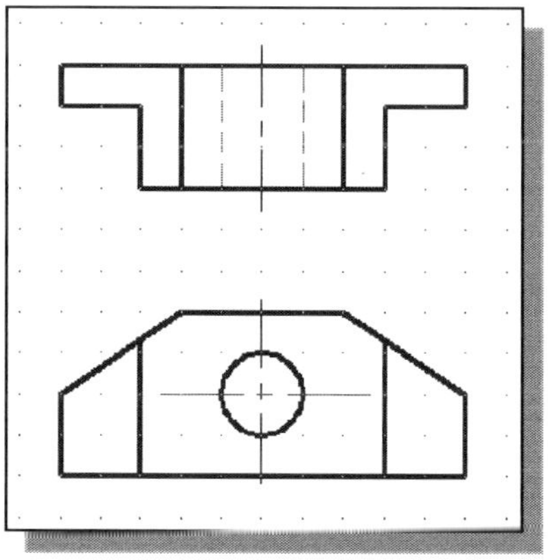

Name: ______________________ Date: ______________

Chapter 6 - Isometric Sketching Exercise 4:

Given the Orthographic Top view and Front view, create the isometric view.

(Note that 3D Models of chapter examples and exercises are available at http://www.sdcpublications.com/downloads/978-1-63057-806-0.)

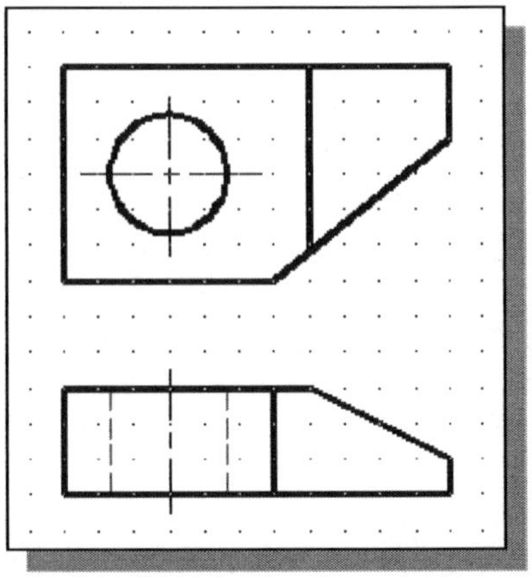

Name: ______________________ Date: ______________

Chapter 6 - Isometric Sketching Exercise 5:

Given the Orthographic Top view, Front view, and Side view create the isometric view.

(Note that 3D Models of chapter examples and exercises are available at http://www.sdcpublications.com/downloads/978-1-63057-806-0.)

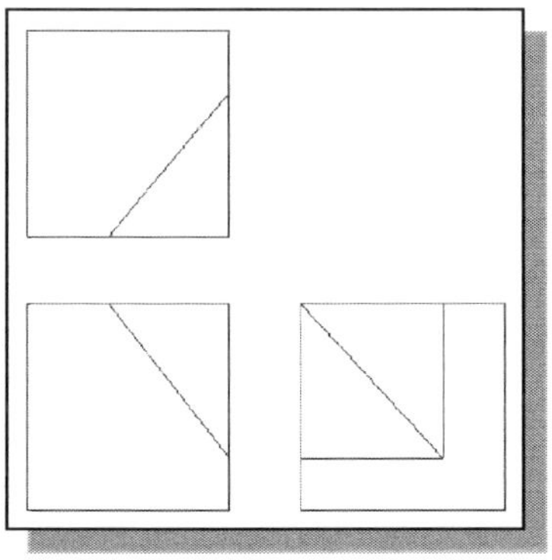

Name: ______________________ Date: ______________

Chapter 6 - Isometric Sketching Exercise 6:

Given the Orthographic Top view, Front view, and Side view create the isometric view.

(Note that 3D Models of chapter examples and exercises are available at http://www.sdcpublications.com/downloads/978-1-63057-806-0.)

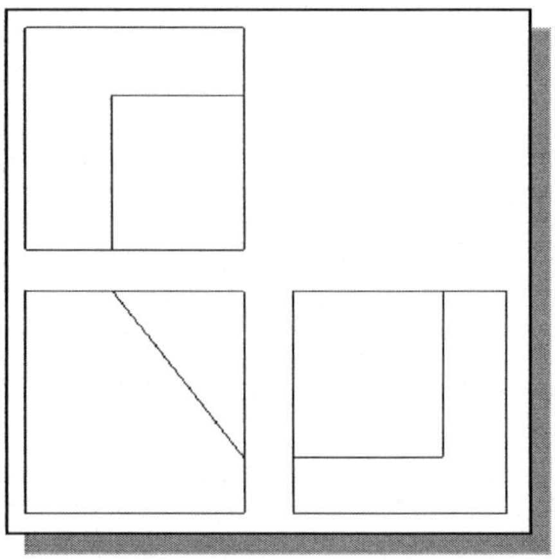

Name: ______________________ Date: ______________

Chapter 6 - Isometric Sketching Exercise 7:

Given the Orthographic Top view, Front view, and Side view create the isometric view.

(Note that 3D Models of chapter examples and exercises are available at http://www.sdcpublications.com/downloads/978-1-63057-806-0.)

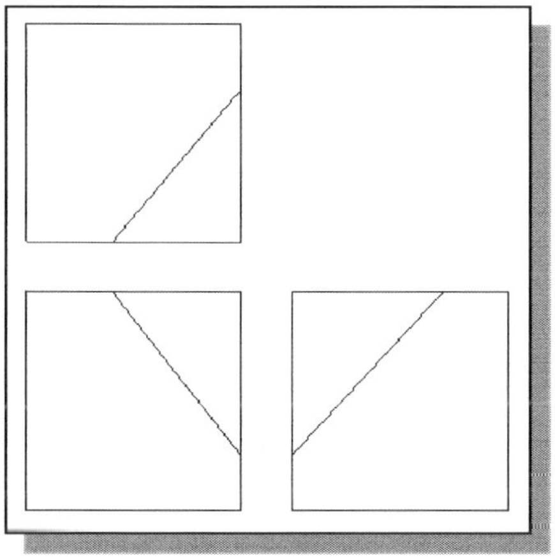

Name: ______________________________ Date: ________________

Chapter 6 - Isometric Sketching Exercise 8:

Given the Orthographic Top view, Front view, and Side view create the isometric view.

(Note that 3D Models of chapter examples and exercises are available at http://www.sdcpublications.com/downloads/978-1-63057-806-0.)

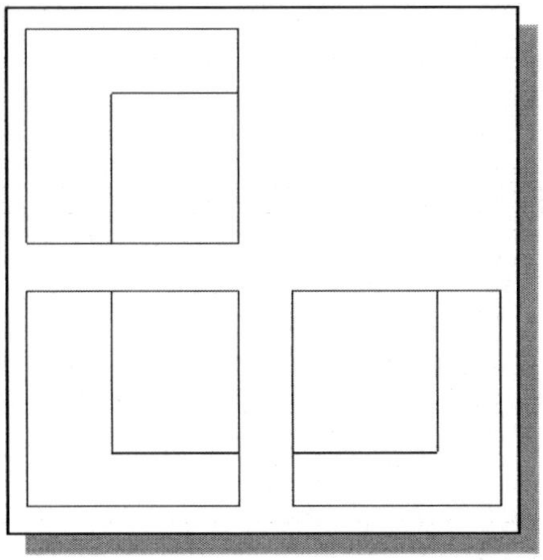

Name: ______________________________ Date: ___________________

Chapter 6 - Isometric Sketching Exercise 9:

Given the Orthographic Top view, Front view, and Side view create the isometric view.

(Note that 3D Models of chapter examples and exercises are available at http://www.sdcpublications.com/downloads/978-1-63057-806-0.)

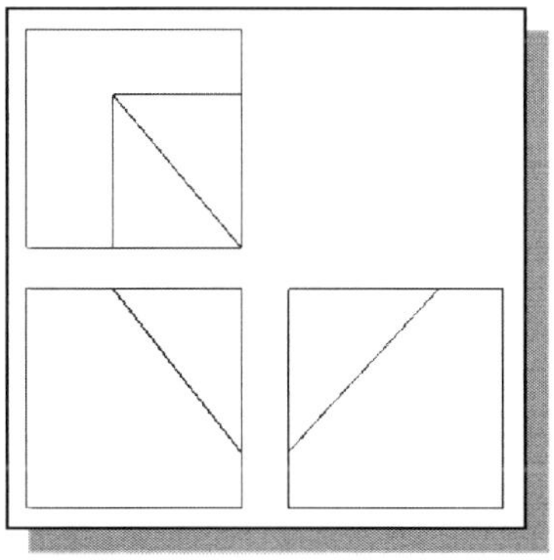

Name: ____________________ Date: ____________

Chapter 6 - Isometric Sketching Exercise 10:

Given the Orthographic Top view, Front view, and Side view create the isometric view.

(Note that 3D Models of chapter examples and exercises are available at http://www.sdcpublications.com/downloads/978-1-63057-806-0.)

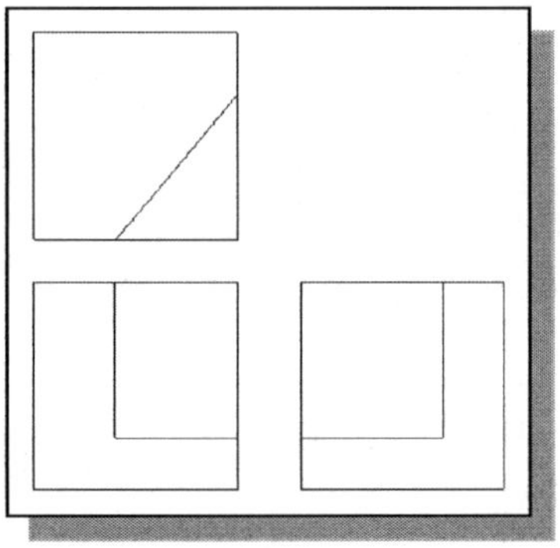

Name: ______________________________ Date: ____________________

Oblique Sketching

Keeping the geometry that is parallel to the frontal plane true size and shape is the main advantage of the oblique drawing over the axonometric drawings. Unlike isometric drawings, circular shapes that are paralleled to the frontal view will remain as circles in oblique drawings. Generally speaking, an oblique drawing can be created very quickly by using a 2D view as the starting point. For designs with most of the circular shapes in one direction, an oblique sketch is the ideal choice over the other pictorial methods.

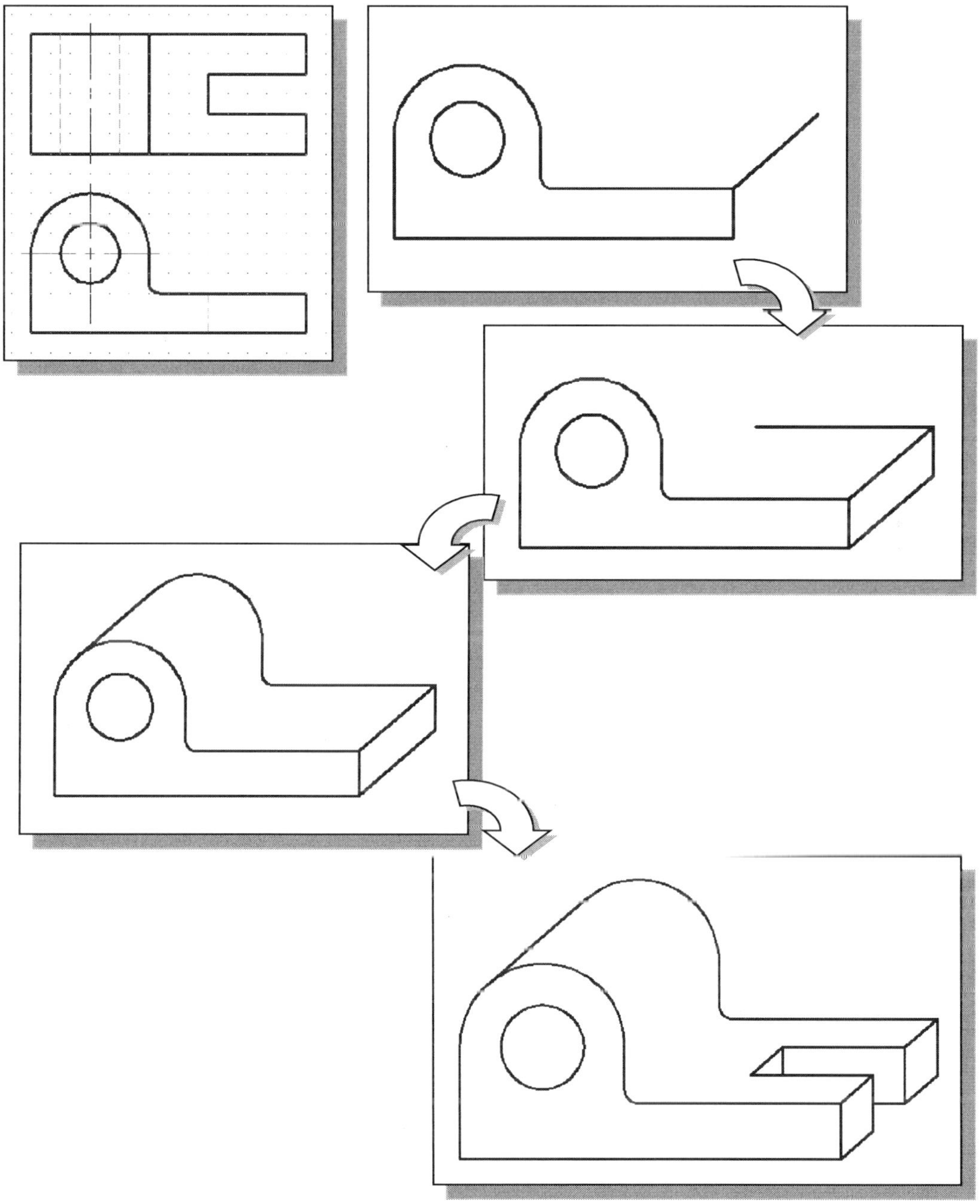

Chapter 6 - Oblique Sketching Exercise 1:

Given the Orthographic Top view and Front view, create the oblique view.

(Note that 3D Models of chapter examples and exercises are available at http://www.sdcpublications.com/downloads/978-1-63057-806-0.)

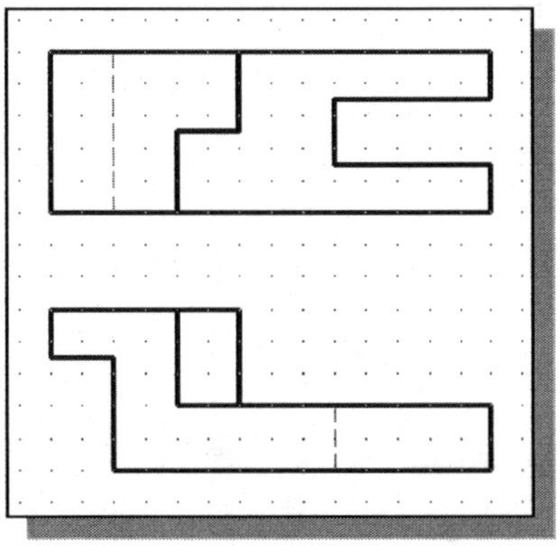

Name: ____________________ Date: ________________

Chapter 6 - Oblique Sketching Exercise 2:

Given the Orthographic Top view and Front view, create the oblique view.

(Note that 3D Models of chapter examples and exercises are available at http://www.sdcpublications.com/downloads/978-1-63057-806-0.)

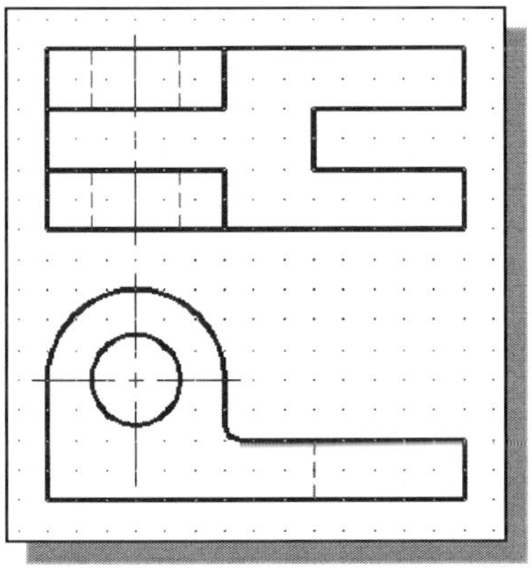

Name: ______________________ Date: ______________

Chapter 6 - Oblique Sketching Exercise 3:

Given the Orthographic Top view and Front view, create the oblique view.

(Note that 3D Models of chapter examples and exercises are available at http://www.sdcpublications.com/downloads/978-1-63057-806-0.)

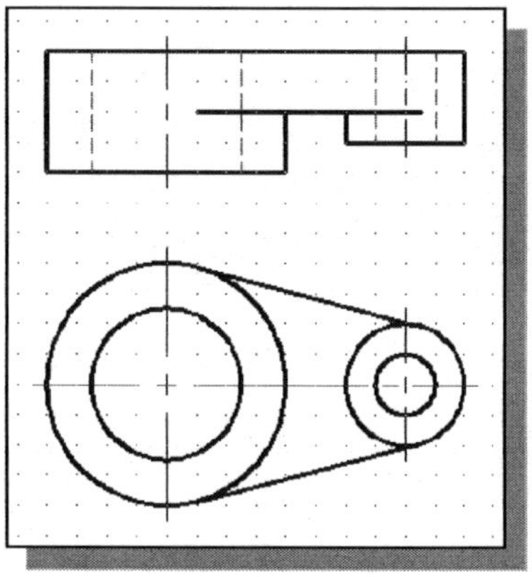

Name: ______________________ Date: ______________

Chapter 6 - Oblique Sketching Exercise 4:

Given the Orthographic Top view and Front view, create the oblique view.

(Note that 3D Models of chapter examples and exercises are available at http://www.sdcpublications.com/downloads/978-1-63057-806-0.)

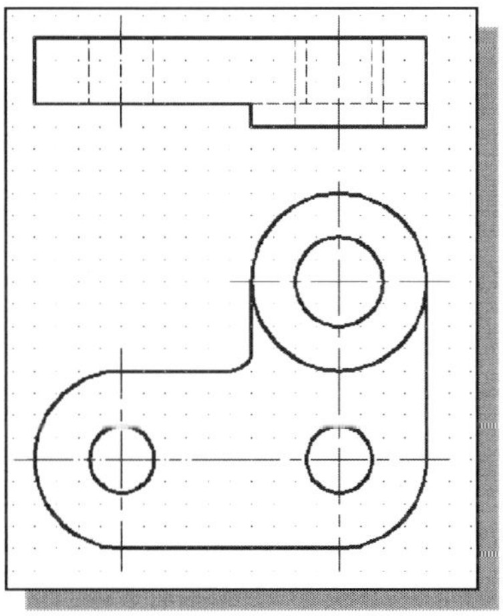

Name: ______________________________ Date: ________________

Chapter 6 - Oblique Sketching Exercise 5:

Given the Orthographic Top view and Front view, create the oblique view.

(Note that 3D Models of chapter examples and exercises are available at http://www.sdcpublications.com/downloads/978-1-63057-806-0.)

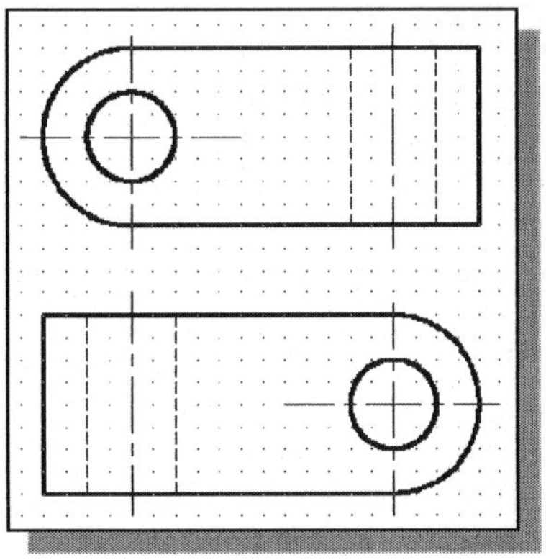

Name: ______________________________ Date: ____________________

Chapter 6 - Oblique Sketching Exercise 6:

Given the Orthographic Top view and Front view, create the oblique view.

(Note that 3D Models of chapter examples and exercises are available at http://www.sdcpublications.com/downloads/978-1-63057-806-0.)

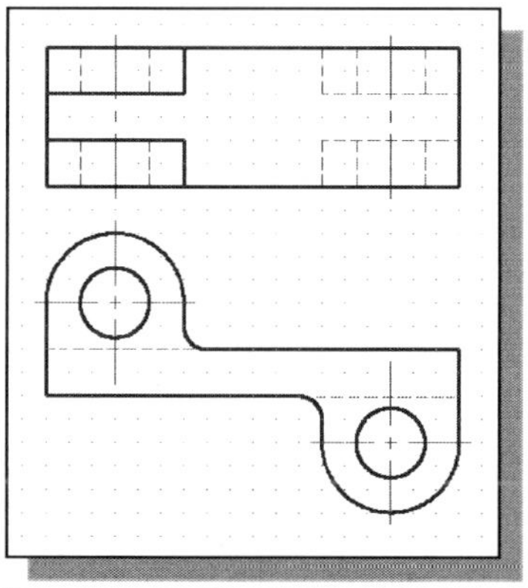

Name: ______________________ Date: ______________

Perspective Sketching

A perspective drawing represents an object as it appears to an observer; objects that are closer to the observer will appear larger to the observer. The key to the perspective projection is that parallel edges converge to a single point, known as the **vanishing point**. The vanishing point represents the position where projection lines converge.

The selection of the locations of the vanishing points, which is the first step in creating a perspective sketch, will affect the looks of the resulting images.

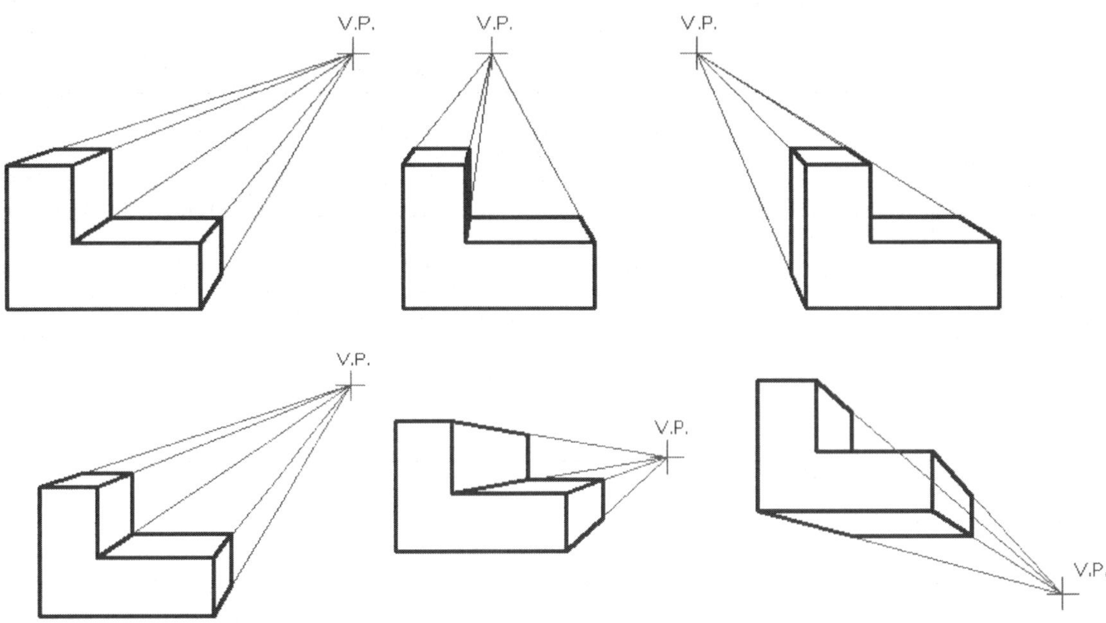

One-point Perspective

One-point perspective is commonly used because of its simplicity. The first step in creating a one-point perspective is to sketch the front face of the object just as in oblique sketching, followed by selecting the position for the vanishing point. For Mechanical designs, the vanishing point is usually placed above and to the right of the picture. The use of construction lines can be helpful in locating the edges of the object and to complete the sketch.

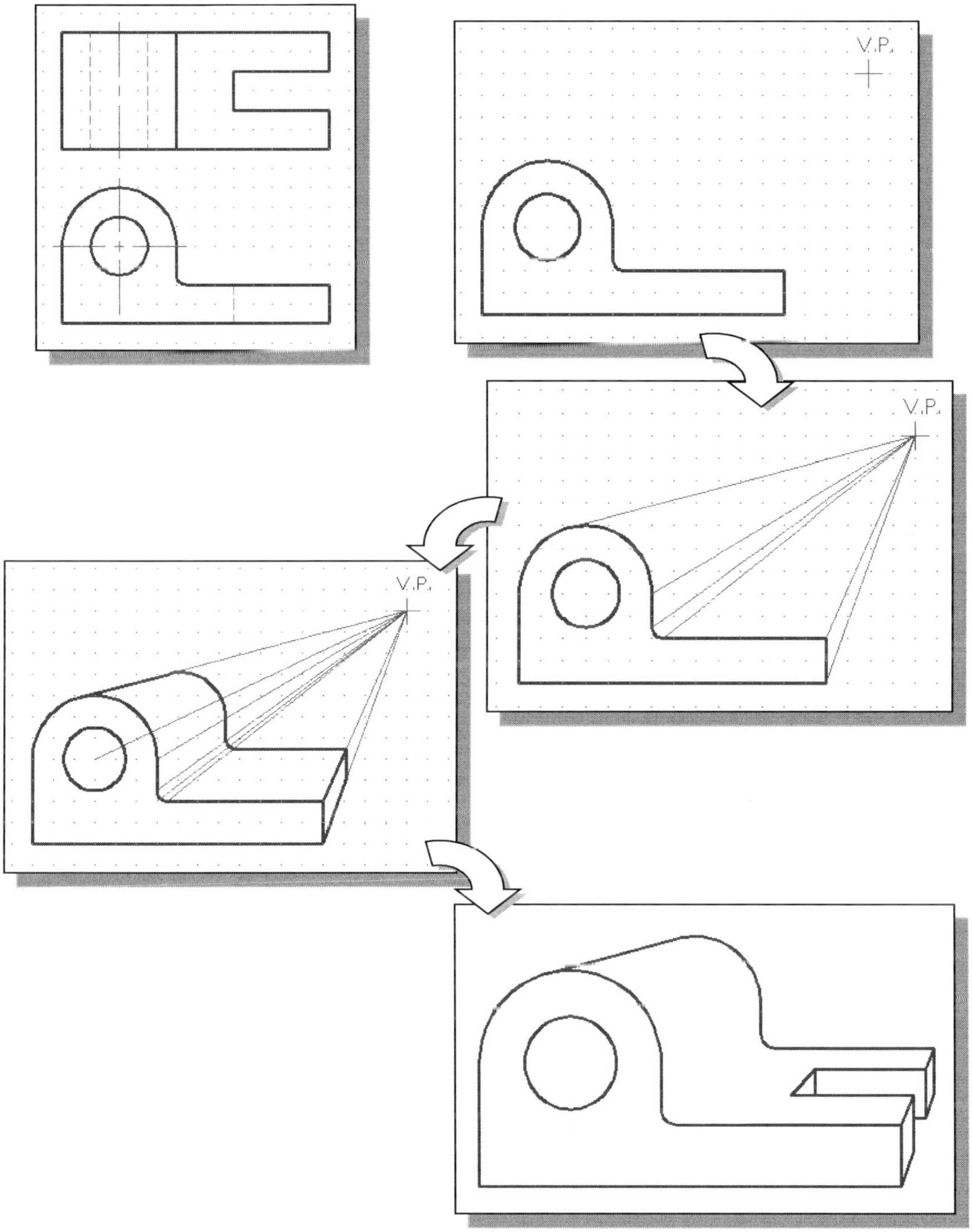

Two-point Perspective

Two-point perspective is perhaps the most popular of all perspective methods. The use of the two vanishing points gives very true to life images. The first step in creating a two-point perspective is to select the locations for the two vanishing points, followed by sketching an enclosing box to show the outline of the object. The use of construction lines can be very helpful in locating the edges of the object and to complete the sketch.

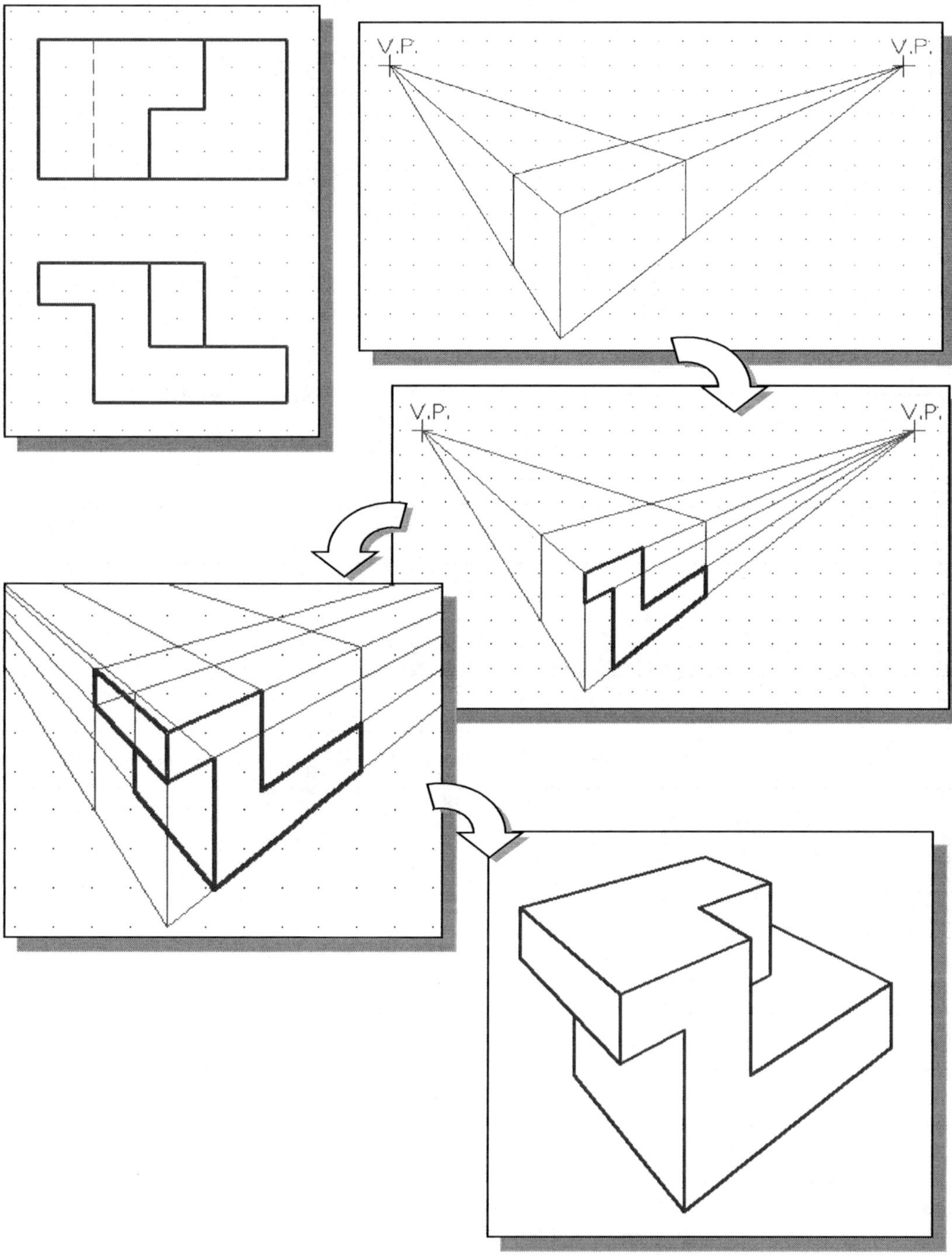

Chapter 6 - Perspective Sketching Exercise 1:

Given the Orthographic Top view and Front view, create one-point or two-point perspective views.

(Note that 3D Models of chapter examples and exercises are available at http://www.sdcpublications.com/downloads/978-1-63057-806-0.)

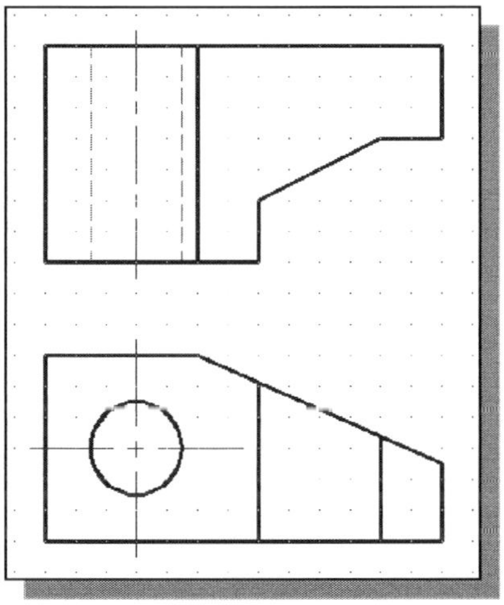

Name: ____________________ Date: ______________

Chapter 6 - Perspective Sketching Exercise 2:

Given the Orthographic Top view and Front view, create one-point or two-point perspective views.

(Note that 3D Models of chapter examples and exercises are available at http://www.sdcpublications.com/downloads/978-1-63057-806-0.)

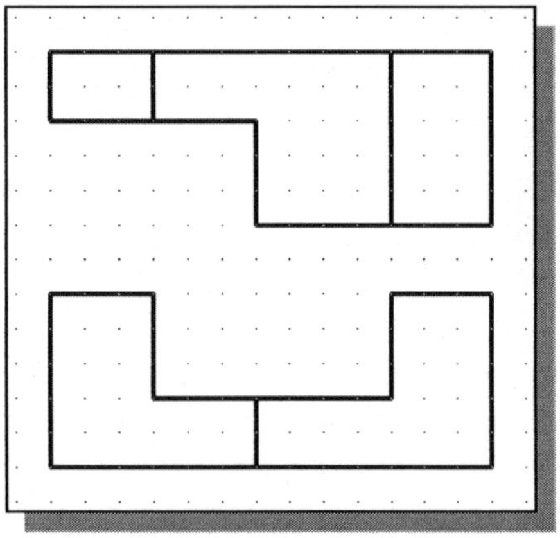

Name: ______________________ Date: ______________

Chapter 6 - Perspective Sketching Exercise 3:

Given the Orthographic Top view and Front view, create one-point or two-point perspective views.

(Note that 3D Models of chapter examples and exercises are available at http://www.sdcpublications.com/downloads/978-1-63057-806-0.)

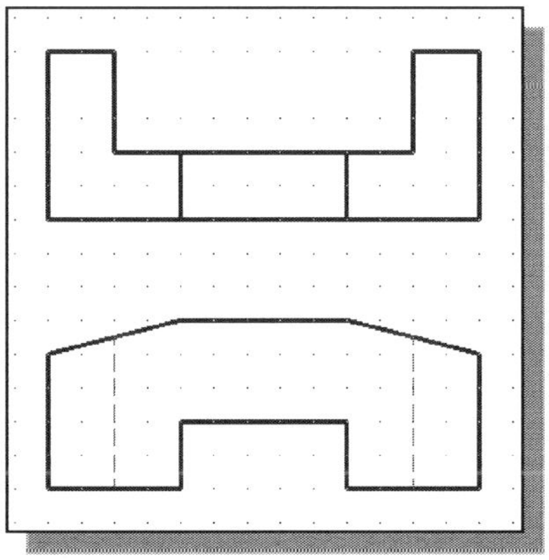

Name: ______________________ Date: ______________

Chapter 6 - Perspective Sketching Exercise 4:

Given the Orthographic Top view and Front view, create one-point or two-point perspective views.

(Note that 3D Models of chapter examples and exercises are available at http://www.sdcpublications.com/downloads/978-1-63057-806-0.)

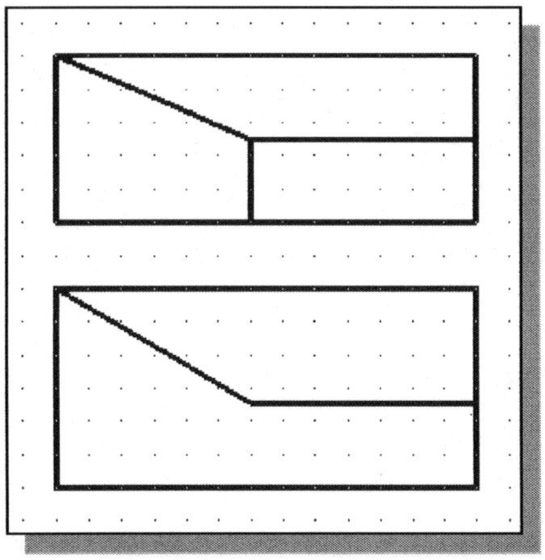

Name: ______________________ Date: ______________

Chapter 6 - Perspective Sketching Exercise 5:

Given the Orthographic Top view and Front view, create one-point or two-point perspective views.

(Note that 3D Models of chapter examples and exercises are available at http://www.sdcpublications.com/downloads/978-1-63057-806-0.)

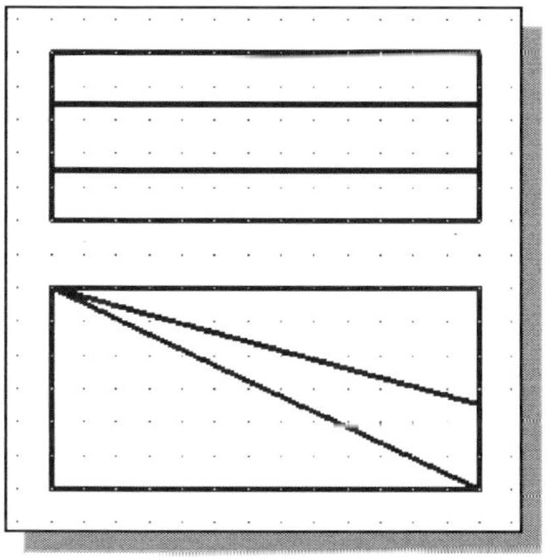

Name: ______________________ Date: ______________

Chapter 6 - Perspective Sketching Exercise 6:

Given the Orthographic Top view and Front view, create one-point or two-point perspective views.

(Note that 3D Models of chapter examples and exercises are available at http://www.sdcpublications.com/downloads/978-1-63057-806-0.)

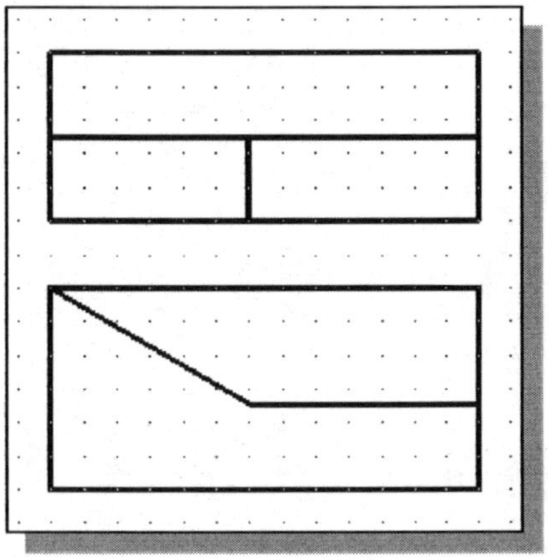

Name: ______________________ Date: ______________

Review Questions:

1. What are the three types of Axonometric projection?

2. Describe the differences between an Isometric drawing and a Trimetric drawing.

3. What is the main advantage of oblique projection over the isometric projection?

4. Describe the differences between a one-point perspective and a two-point perspective.

5. Which pictorial methods maintain true size and shape of geometry on the frontal plane?

6. What is a vanishing point in a perspective drawing?

7. What is a Cabinet Oblique?

8. What is the angle between the three axes in an isometric drawing?

9. In an Axonometric drawing, are the projection lines perpendicular to the projection plane?

10. A cylindrical feature, in a frontal plane, will remain a circle in which pictorial methods?

11. In an Oblique drawing, are the projection lines perpendicular to the projection plane?

12. Create freehand pictorial sketches of:
    - Your desk
    - Your computer
    - One corner of your room
    - The tallest building in your area

Exercises:

Complete the missing views. (Create a pictorial sketch as an aid in reading the views.)

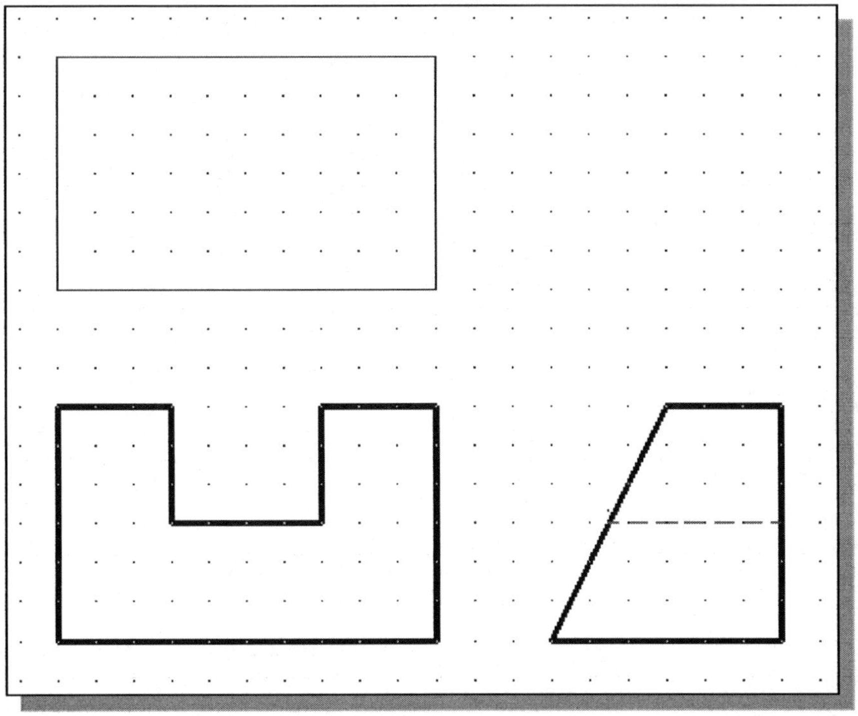

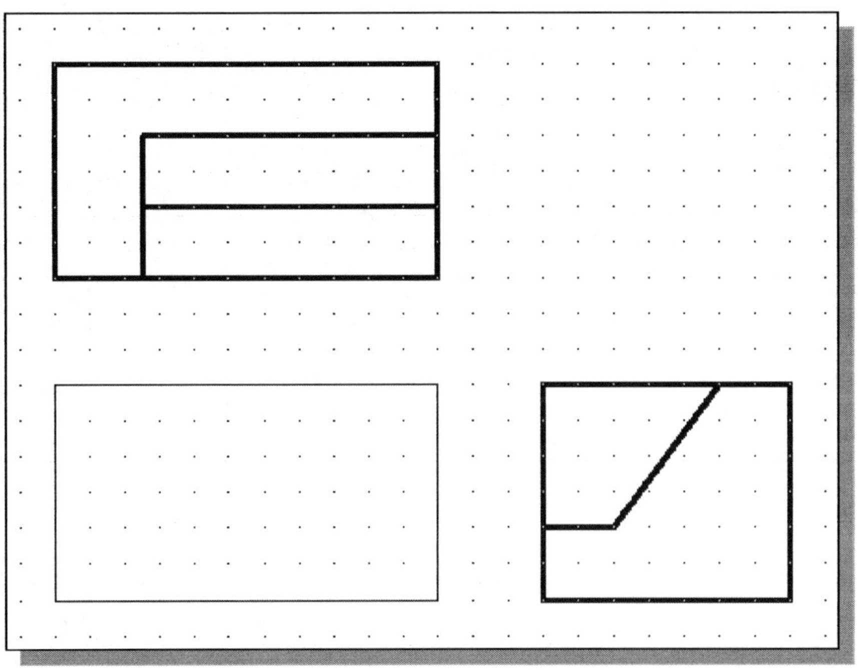

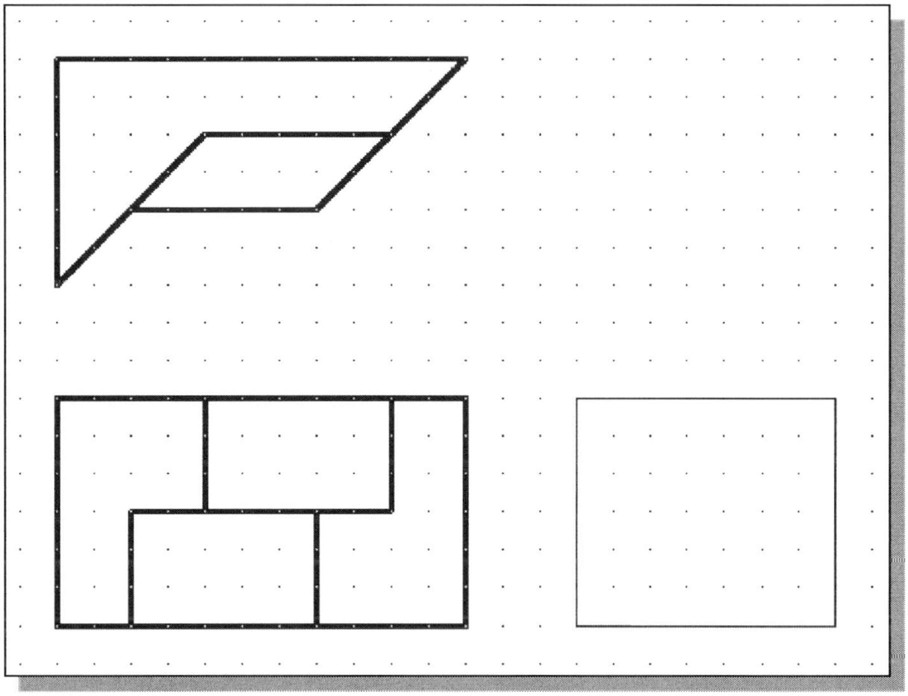

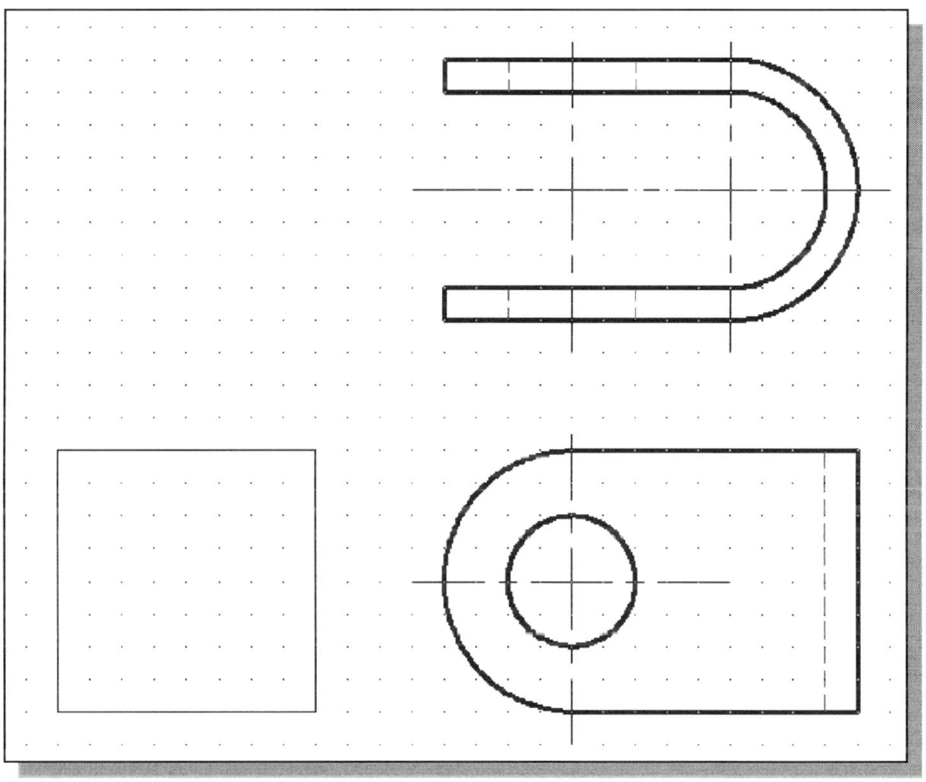

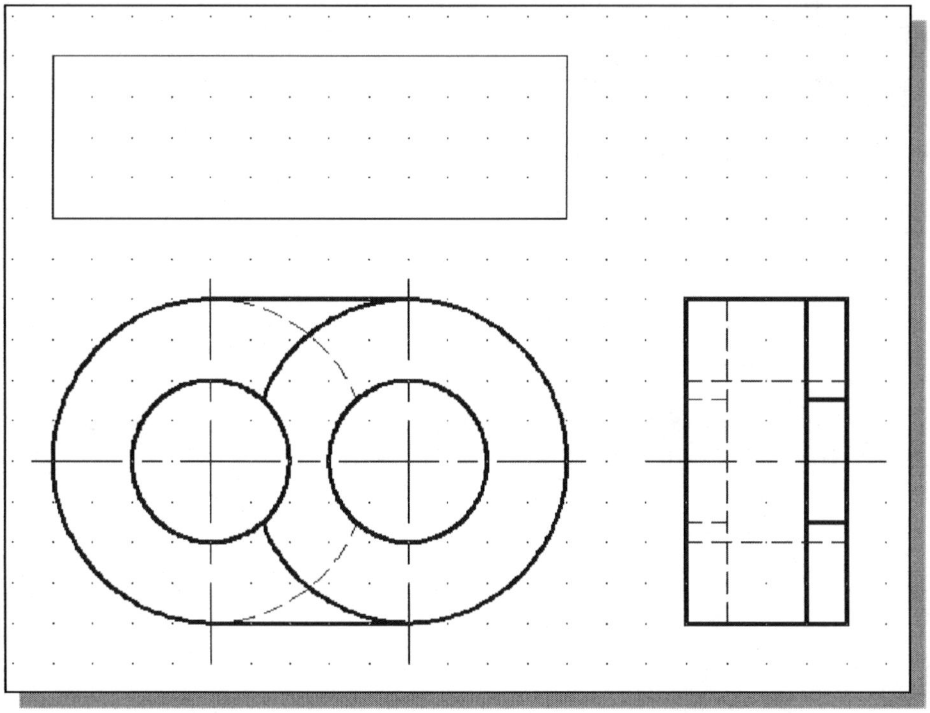

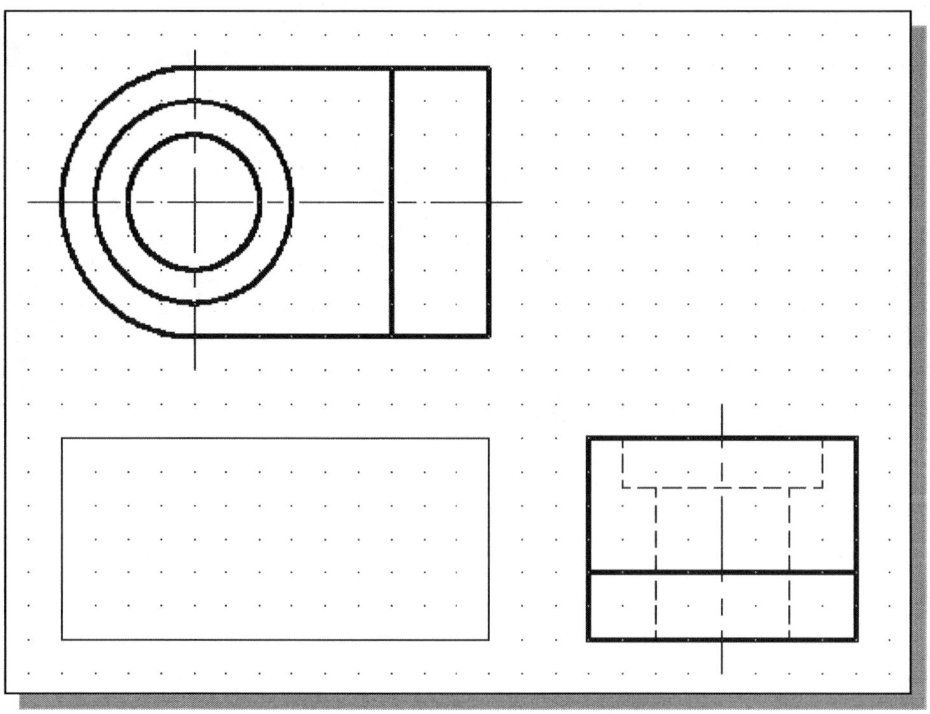

Chapter 7
Parametric Modeling Fundamentals - Autodesk Inventor

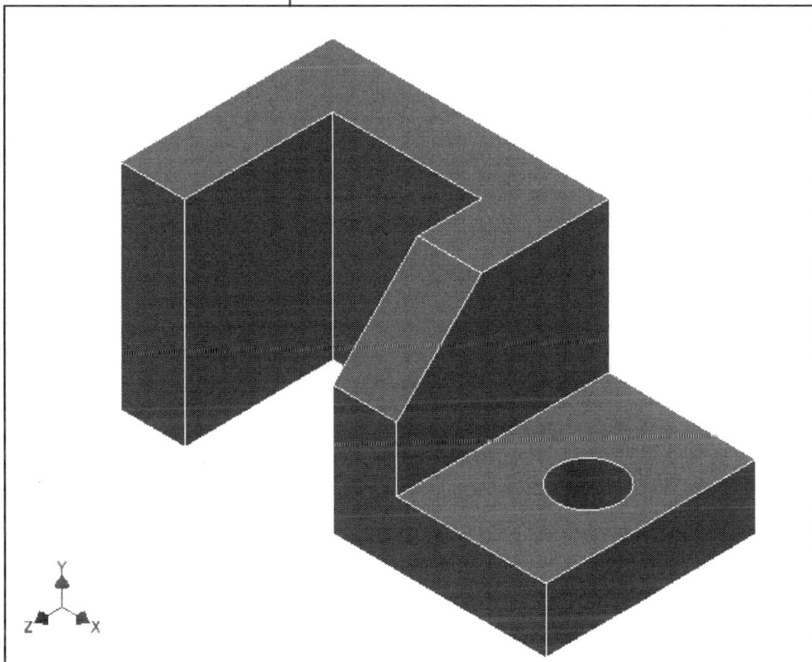

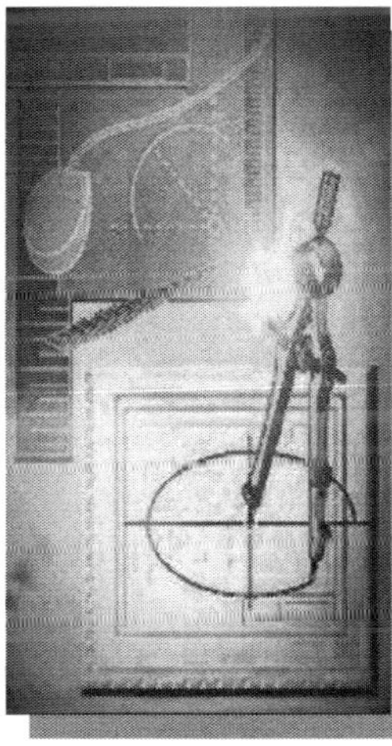

Learning Objectives

- Create Simple Extruded Solid Models
- Understand the Basic Parametric Modeling Procedure
- Create 2D Sketches
- Understand the "Shape before Size" Approach
- Use the Dynamic Viewing Commands
- Create and Edit Parametric Dimensions

Getting Started with Autodesk Inventor

Autodesk Inventor is composed of several application software modules (these modules are called *applications*) all sharing a common database. In this text, the main concentration is placed on the solid modeling modules used for part design. The general procedures required in creating solid models, engineering drawings, and assemblies are illustrated.

How to start Autodesk Inventor depends on the type of workstation and the particular software configuration you are using. With most *Windows* systems, you may select **Autodesk Inventor** on the *Start* menu or select the **Autodesk Inventor** icon on the desktop. Consult your instructor or technical support personnel if you have difficulty starting the software. The program takes a while to load, so be patient.

The tutorials in this text are based on the assumption that you are using Autodesk Inventor's default settings. If your system has been customized for other uses, contact your technical support personnel to restore the default software configuration.

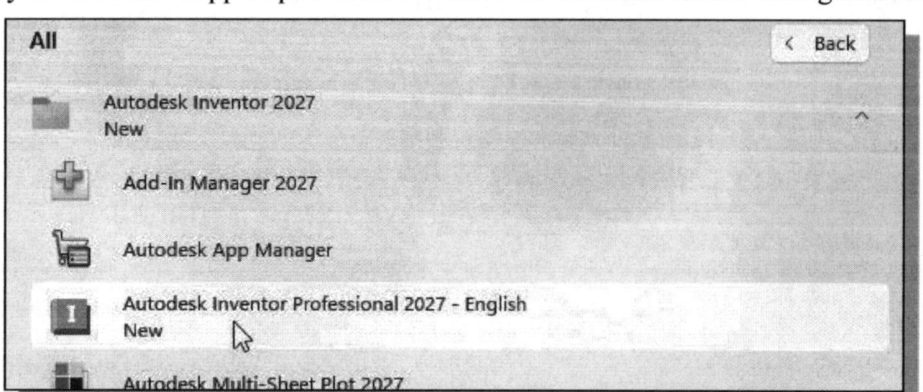

The Screen Layout and Getting Started

Once the program is loaded into the memory, the Inventor window appears on the screen with the *Get Started* options activated.

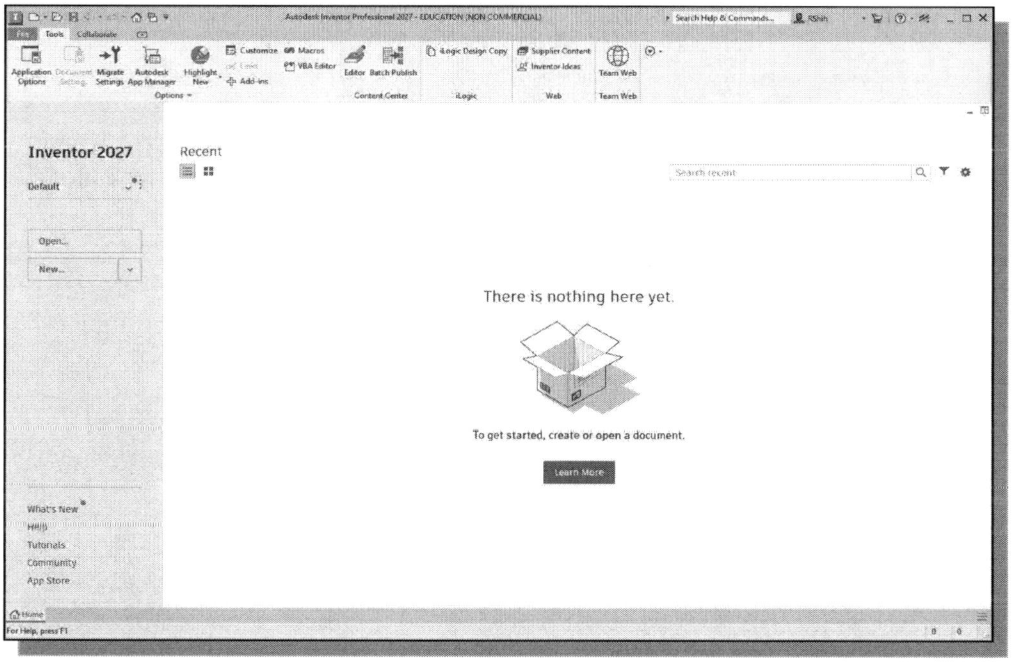

❖ Note that the *Inventor Browser* section contains helpful information in regard to using the Inventor software. For example, clicking the **What's New** option will display the list of new features that are included in this release of Autodesk Inventor.

❖ You are encouraged to browse through the different information available in the *Inventor Browser* section.

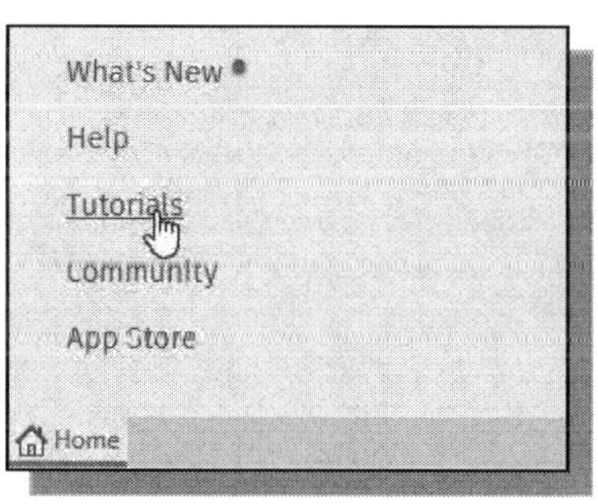

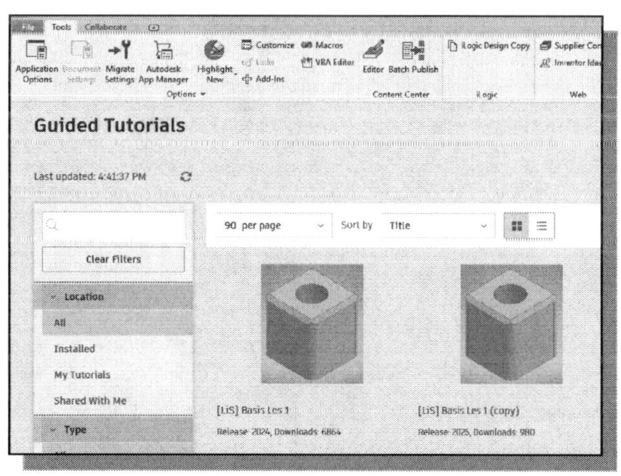

The New File Dialog Box and Units Setup

When starting a new CAD file, the first thing we should do is to choose the units we would like to use. We will use the English (feet and inches) setting for this example.

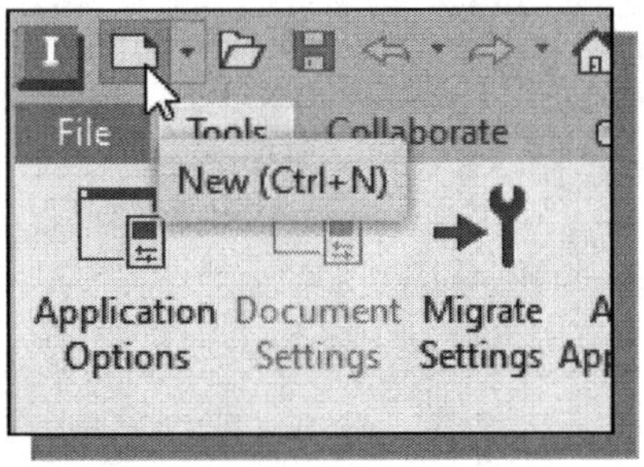

1. Select the **New** icon with a single click of the left-mouse-button in the *Quick Access* toolbar.

❖ Note that the **New** option allows us to start a new modeling task, which can be creating a new model or several other modeling tasks.

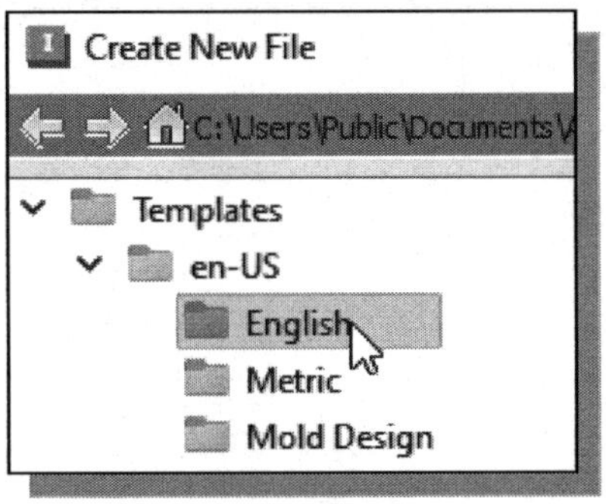

2. Select the **en-US->English** tab in the *New File* dialog box as shown. Note the default tab contains the file options which are based on the default units chosen during installation.

3. Select the **Standard(in).ipt** icon as shown. The different icons are templates for the different modeling tasks. The **idw** file type stands for drawing file, the **iam** file type stands for assembly file, and the **ipt** file type stands for part file. The **ipn** file type stands for assembly presentation.

4. Click **Create** in the *Create New File* dialog box to accept the selected settings.

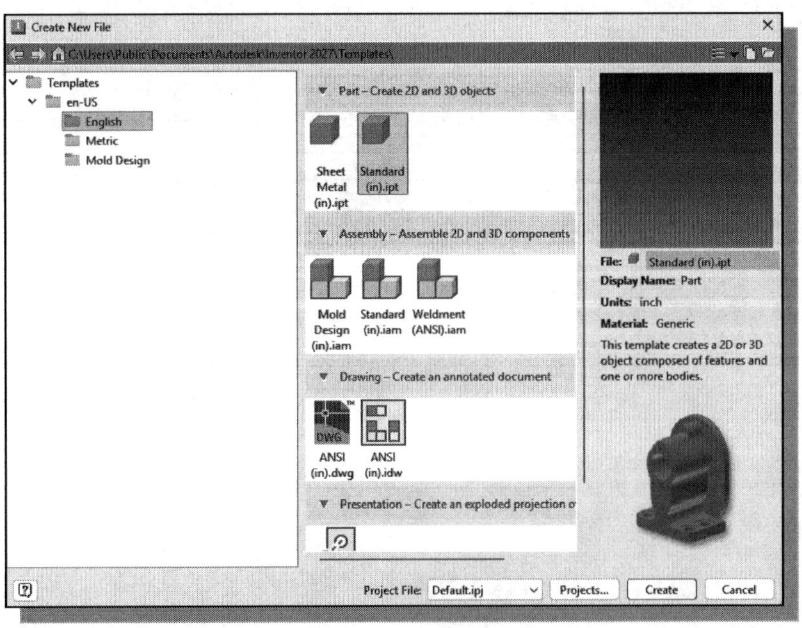

The Default Autodesk Inventor Screen Layout

The default Autodesk Inventor drawing screen contains the *pull-down* menus, the *Standard* toolbar, the *Features* toolbar, the *Sketch* toolbar, the *drawing* area, the *browser* area, and the *Status Bar*. A line of quick text appears next to the icon as you move the *mouse cursor* over different icons. You may resize the Autodesk Inventor drawing window by clicking and dragging the edges of the window, or relocate the window by clicking and dragging the window title area.

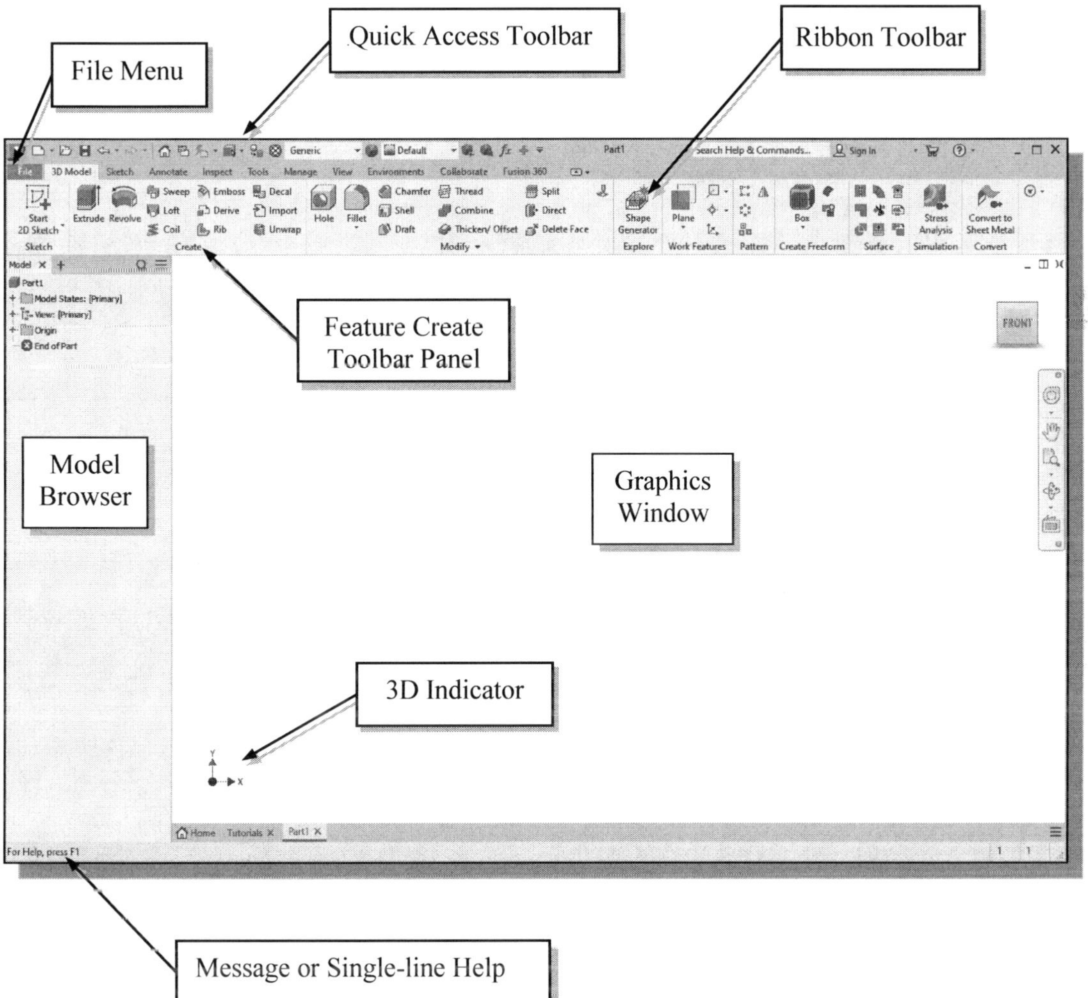

- The ***Ribbon Toolbar*** is a relatively new feature in Autodesk Inventor; the *Ribbon Toolbar* is composed of a series of tool panels, which are organized into tabs labeled by task. The *Ribbon* provides a compact palette of all of the tools necessary to accomplish the different modeling tasks. The drop-down arrow next to any icon indicates additional commands are available on the expanded panel; access the expanded panel by clicking on the drop-down arrow.

- **File Menu**

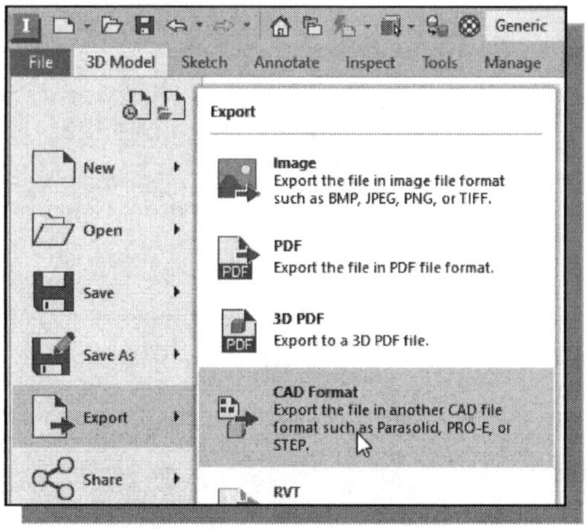

The *File* menu at the upper left corner of the main window contains tools for all file-related operations, such as Open, Save, Export, etc.

- **Quick Access Toolbar**

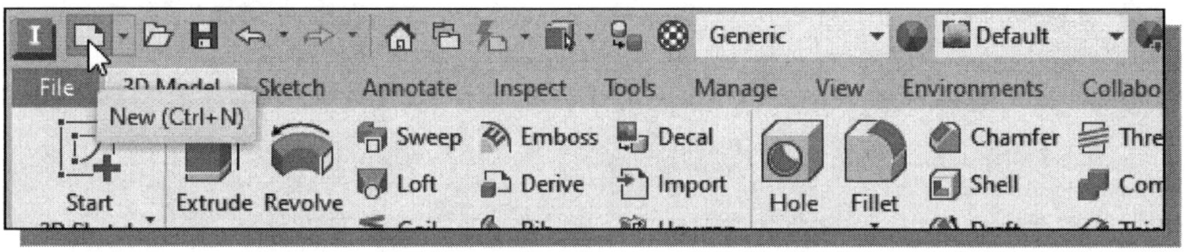

The *Quick Access* toolbar at the top of the *Inventor* window allows us quick access to file-related commands and to Undo/Redo the last operations.

- **Ribbon Tabs and Tool panels**

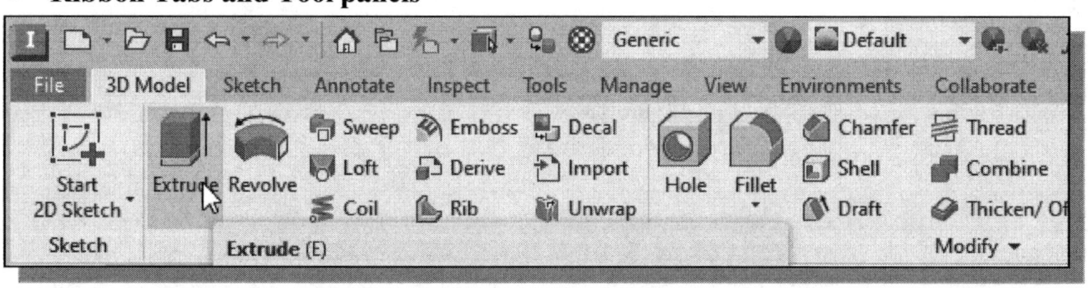

The *Ribbon* is composed of a series of tool panels, which are organized into tabs labeled by task. The assortments of tool panels can be accessed by clicking on the tabs.

- **Online Help Panel**

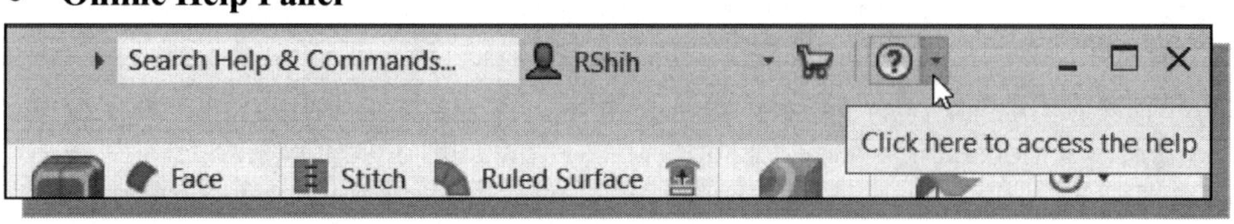

The *Help* options panel provides us with multiple options to access online help for Autodesk Inventor. The ***Online Help system*** provides general help information, such as command options and command references.

- **3D Model Toolbar**

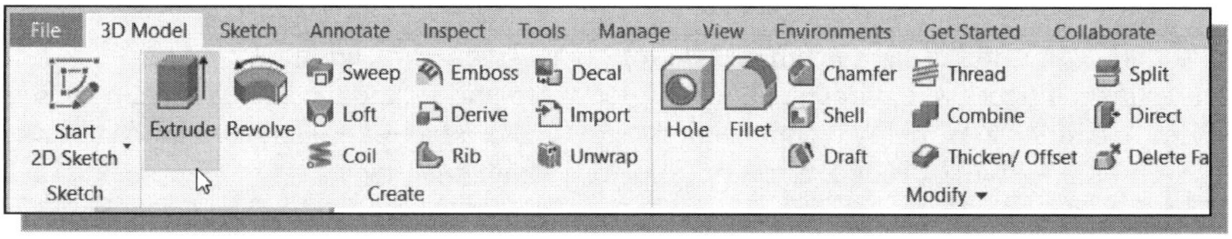

The *3D Model* toolbar provides tools for creating the different types of 3D features, such as **Extrude**, **Revolve**, **Sweep**, etc.

- **Graphics Window**

The *graphics window* is the area where models and drawings are displayed.

- **Message and Status Bar**

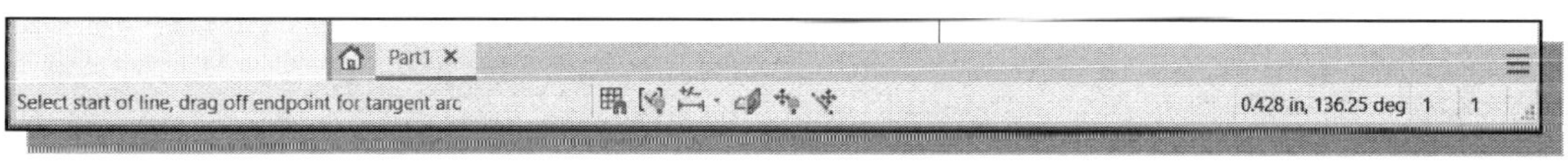

The *Message and Status Bar* area shows a single-line help when the cursor is on top of an icon. This area also displays information pertinent to the active operation. For example, in the figure above, the coordinates and length information of a line are displayed while the *Line* command is activated.

Mouse Buttons

Autodesk Inventor utilizes the mouse buttons extensively. In learning Autodesk Inventor's interactive environment, it is important to understand the basic functions of the mouse buttons. It is highly recommended that you use a mouse or a tablet with Autodesk Inventor since the package uses the buttons for various functions.

- **Left mouse button**
  The **left mouse button** is used for most operations, such as selecting menus and icons, or picking graphic entities. One click of the button is used to select icons, menus and form entries, and to pick graphic items.

- **Right mouse button**
  The **right mouse button** is used to bring up additional available options. The software also utilizes the **right mouse button** the same as the **ENTER** key and is often used to accept the default setting to a prompt or to end a process.

- **Middle mouse button/wheel**
  The middle mouse button/wheel can be used to **Pan** (hold down the wheel button and drag the mouse) or **Zoom** (turn the wheel) realtime.

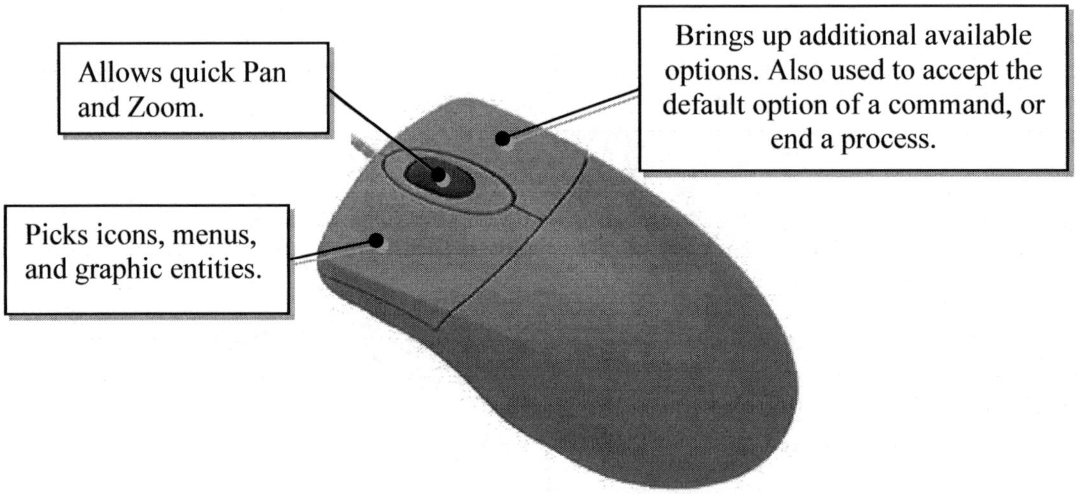

[Esc] – Canceling Commands

The [**Esc**] key is used to cancel a command in Autodesk Inventor. The [**Esc**] key is located near the top-left corner of the keyboard. Sometimes, it may be necessary to press the [**Esc**] key twice to cancel a command; it depends on where we are in the command sequence. For some commands, the [**Esc**] key is used to exit the command.

Autodesk Inventor Help System

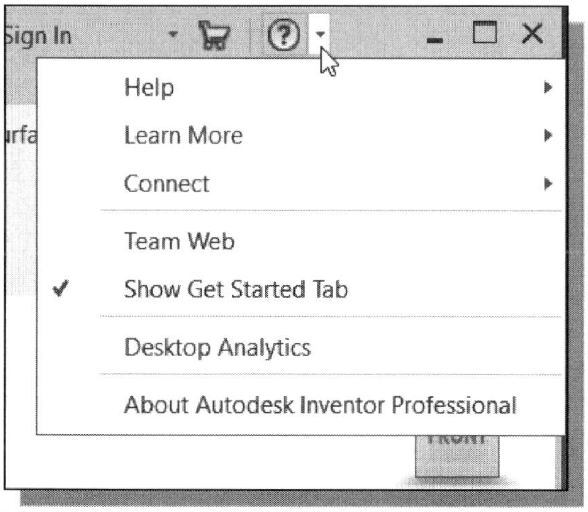

❖ Several types of help are available at any time during an Autodesk Inventor session. Autodesk Inventor provides many help functions, such as:

- Use the ***Help*** button near the upper right corner of the *Inventor* window.

- Help quick-key: Press the [**F1**] key to access the ***Inventor Help* system**.

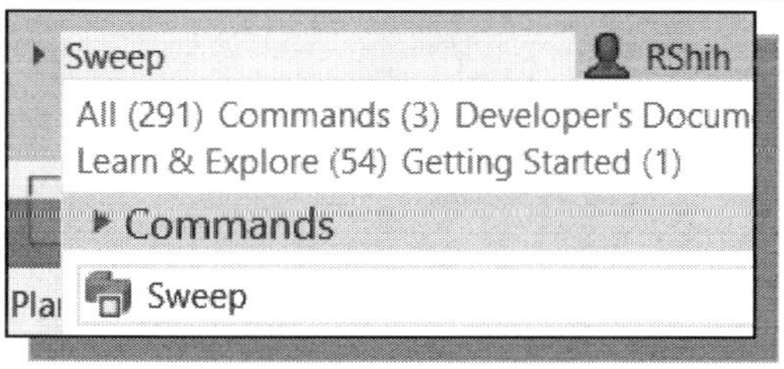

- Use the ***Info Center*** to get information on a specific topic.

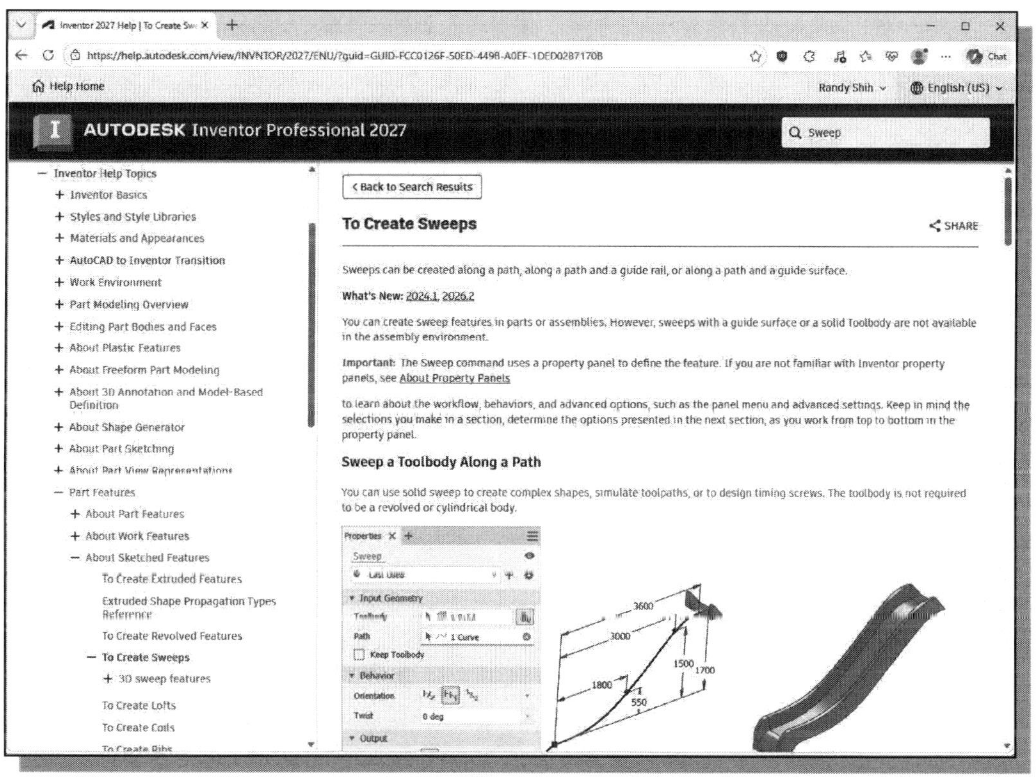

- Use the Internet to access information on the Autodesk community website.

Data Management Using Inventor Project files

With Autodesk Inventor, it is quite feasible to create designs without any regard to using the Autodesk Inventor data management system. Data management becomes critical for projects involving complex designs, especially when multiple team members are involved, or when we are working on integrating multiple design projects, or when it is necessary to share files among the design projects. Autodesk Inventor provides a fairly flexible data management system. It allows one person to use the basic option to help manage the locations of the different design files, or a team of designers can use the data management system to manage their projects stored on a networked computer system.

The Autodesk Inventor data management system organizes files based on **projects**. Each project is identified with a main folder that can contain files and folders associated to the design. In Autodesk Inventor, a *project* file (.ipj) defines the locations of all files associated with the project, including templates and library files.

The Autodesk Inventor data management system uses two types of projects:

- **Single-user Project**
- **Autodesk Vault Project** (installation of ***Autodesk Vault*** software is required)

The ***single-user project*** is for simpler projects where all project files are located on the same computer. The ***Autodesk Vault project*** is more suitable for projects requiring multiple users using a networked computer system.

1. Click on the **Projects** icon with a single click of the left-mouse-button in the *[File]* → *[Manage]* pull-down menu.

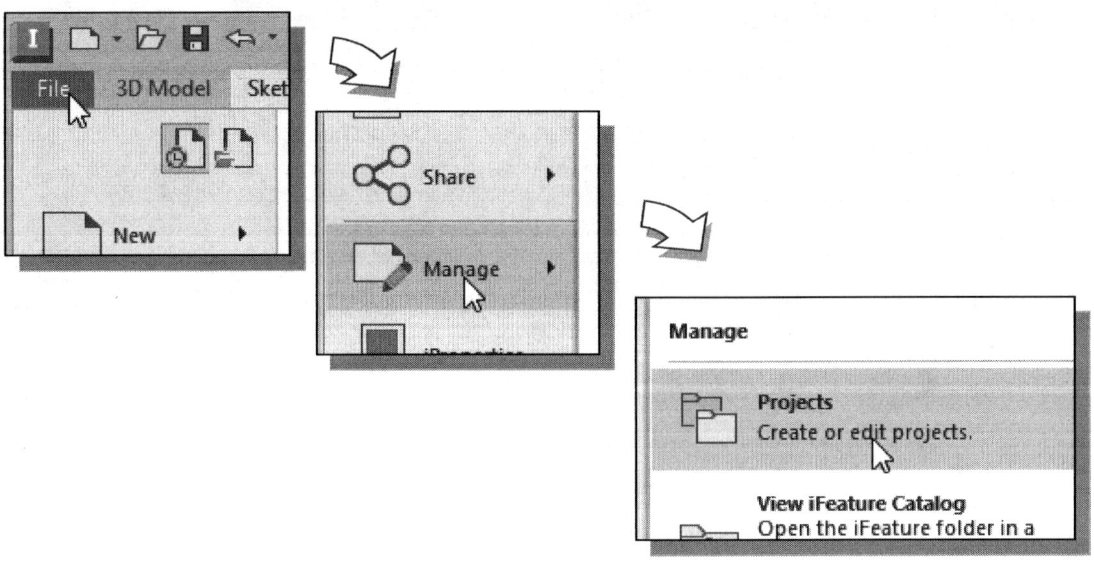

❖ The **Projects Editor** appears on the screen, which allows us to access the settings of new or existing Inventor Single User Project or Autodesk Vault Project.

❖ In the *Projects Editor*: the **Default** project is available.

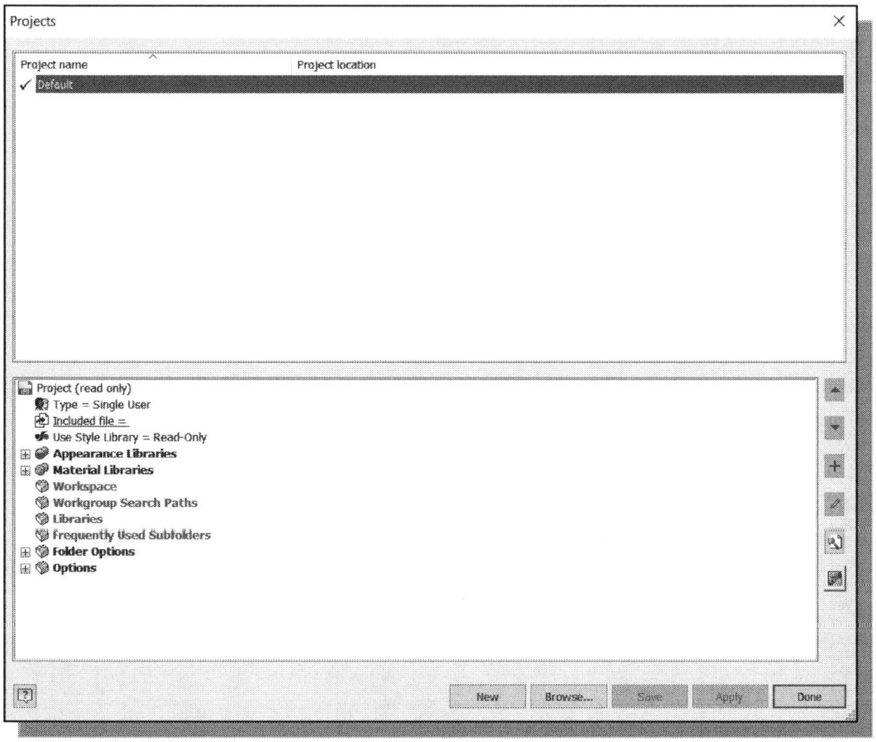

The **Default** project is automatically active by default, and the *default project* does not define any location for files. In other words, the data management system is not used. Using the *default project*, designs can still be created and modified, and any model file can be opened and saved anywhere without regard to project and file management.

Setting up a New Inventor Project

In this section, we will create a new *Inventor* project for the chapters of this book using the *Inventor* built-in **Single User Project** option. Note that it is also feasible to create a separate project for each chapter.

1. Click **New** to begin the setup of a new *project file*.

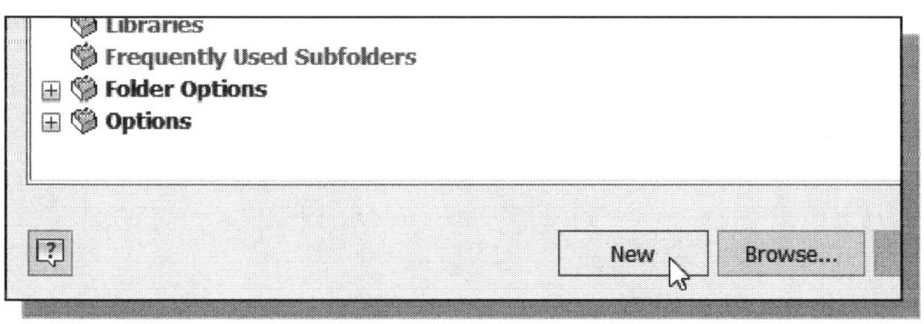

2. The *Inventor project wizard* appears on the screen; select the **New Single User Project** option as shown.

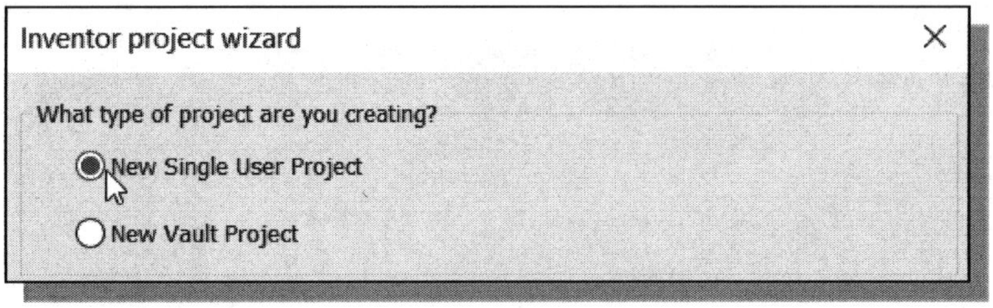

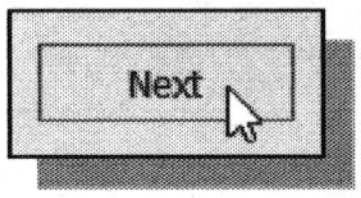

3. Click **Next** to proceed with the next setup option.

4. In the *Project File Name* input box, enter **Parametric-Modeling** as the name of the new project.

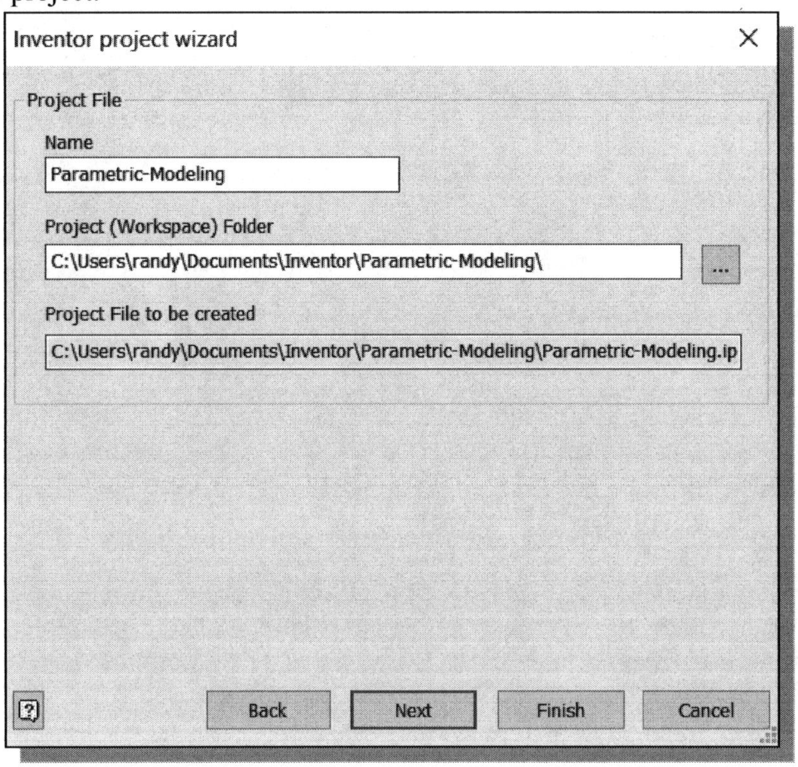

5. In the *Project Folder* input box, note the default folder location, such as **C:\Users\Documents\Inventor \Parametric Modeling\,** and choose a preferred folder name as the folder name of the new project.

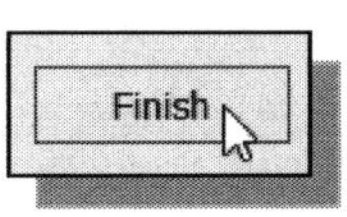

6. Click **Finish** to proceed with the creation of the new project.

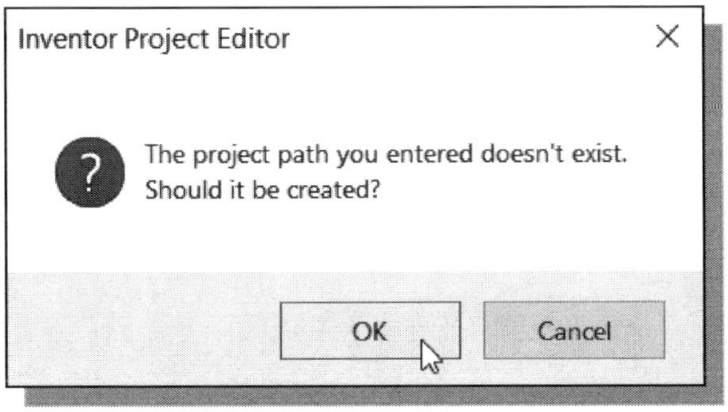

7. A *warning message* appears on the screen, indicating the specified folder does not exist. Click **OK** to create the folder.

8. A second *warning message* appears on the screen, indicating that the newly created project cannot be made active since an *Inventor* file is open. Click **OK** to close the message dialog box.

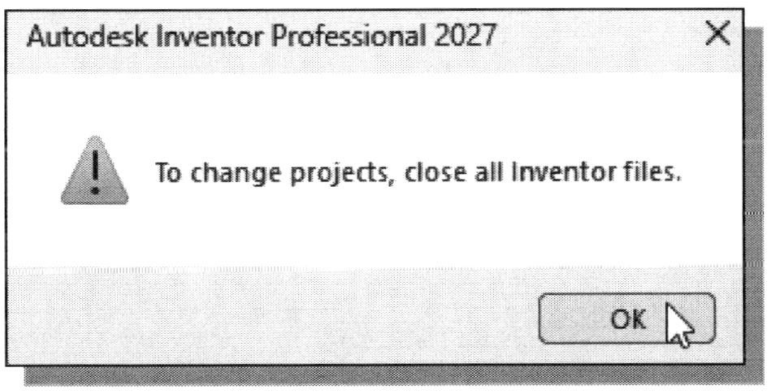

- The new project has been created and its name appears in the project list area as shown in the figure.

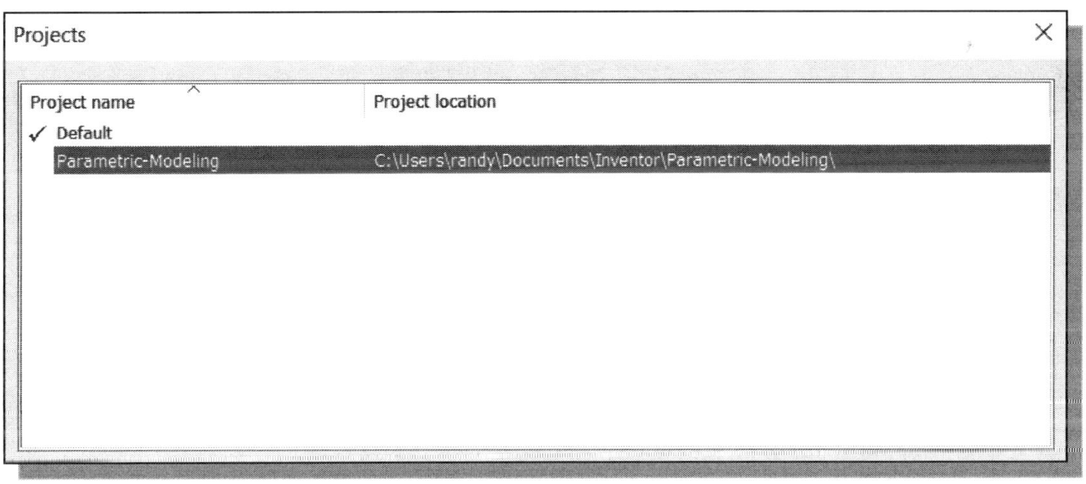

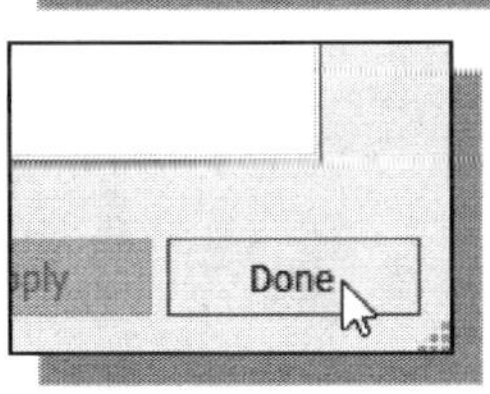

9. Click **Done** to exit the *Inventor Projects Editor* option.

The Content of the Inventor Project File

An *Inventor* project file is actually a text file in .xml format with an .ipj extension. The file specifies the paths to the folder containing the files in the project. To assure that links between files work properly, it is advised to add the locations for folders to the project file before working on model files.

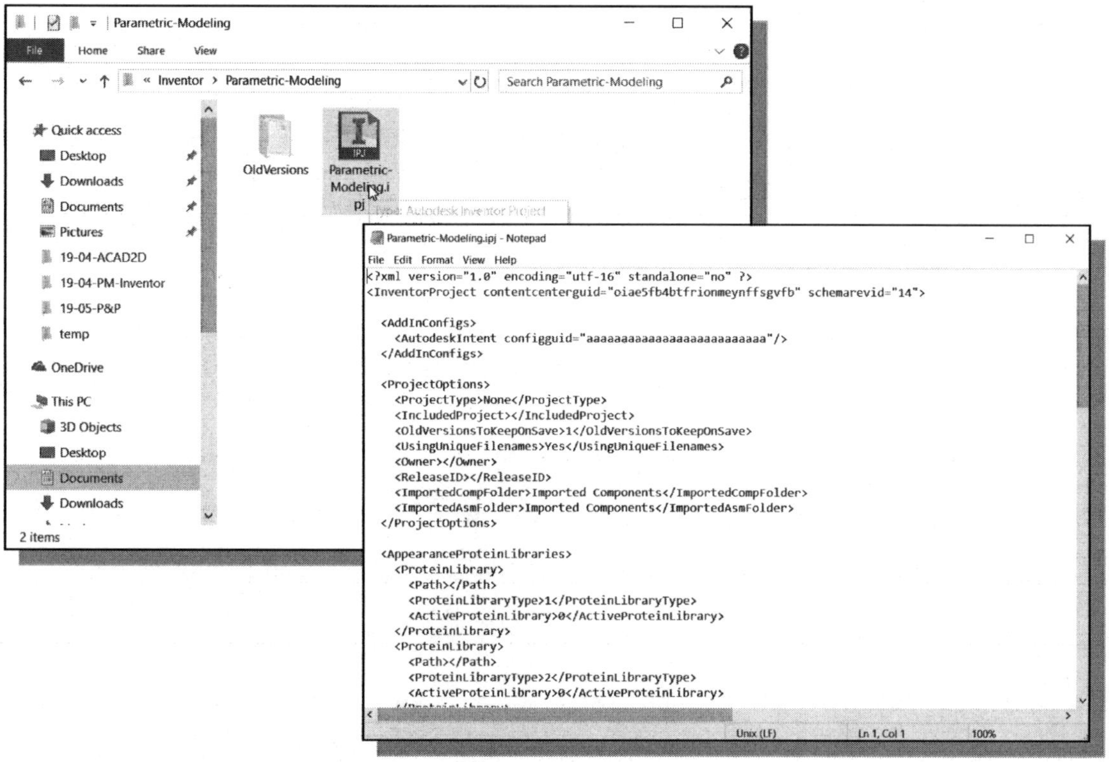

Leaving Autodesk Inventor

To leave the *Application* menu, use the left-mouse-button and click on **Exit Autodesk Inventor** from the pull-down menu.

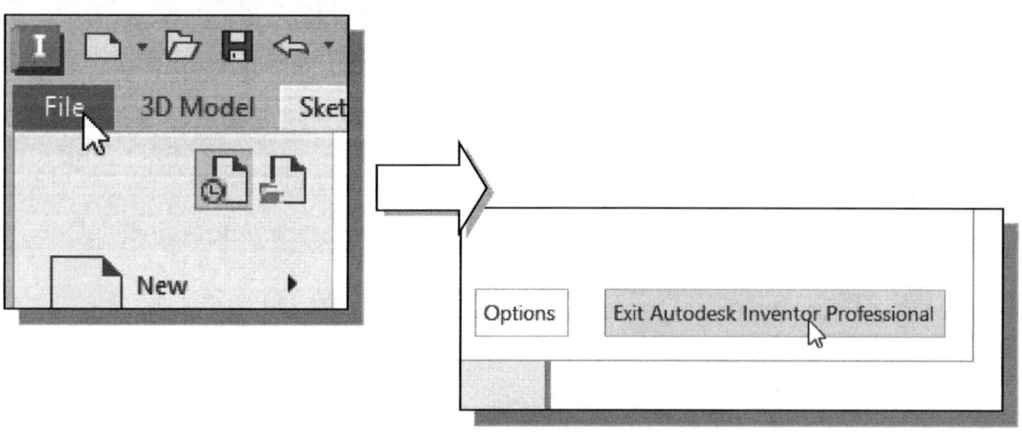

Feature-Based Parametric Modeling

The **feature-based parametric modeling** technique enables the designer to incorporate the original **design intent** into the construction of the model. The word ***parametric*** means the geometric definitions of the design, such as dimensions, can be varied at any time in the design process. Parametric modeling is accomplished by identifying and creating the key features of the design with the aid of computer software. The design variables, described in the sketches as parametric relations, can then be used to quickly modify/update the design.

In Autodesk Inventor, the parametric part modeling process involves the following steps:

1. **Create a rough two-dimensional sketch of the basic shape of the base feature of the design.**

2. **Apply/modify constraints and dimensions to the two-dimensional sketch.**

3. **Extrude, revolve, or sweep the parametric two-dimensional sketch to create the base solid feature of the design.**

4. **Add additional parametric features by identifying feature relations and complete the design.**

5. **Perform analyses on the computer model and refine the design as needed.**

6. **Create the desired drawing views to document the design.**

The approach of creating two-dimensional sketches of the three-dimensional features is an effective way to construct solid models. Many designs are in fact the same shape in one direction. Computer input and output devices we use today are largely two-dimensional in nature, which makes this modeling technique quite practical. This method also conforms to the design process that helps the designer with conceptual design along with the capability to capture the ***design intent***. Most engineers and designers can relate to the experience of making rough sketches on restaurant napkins to convey conceptual design ideas. Autodesk Inventor provides many powerful modeling and design tools, and there are many different approaches to accomplishing modeling tasks. The basic principle of **feature-based modeling** is to build models by adding simple features one at a time. In this chapter, the general parametric part modeling procedure is illustrated; a very simple solid model with extruded features is used to introduce the Autodesk Inventor user interface. The display viewing functions and the basic two-dimensional sketching tools are also demonstrated.

The Adjuster Design

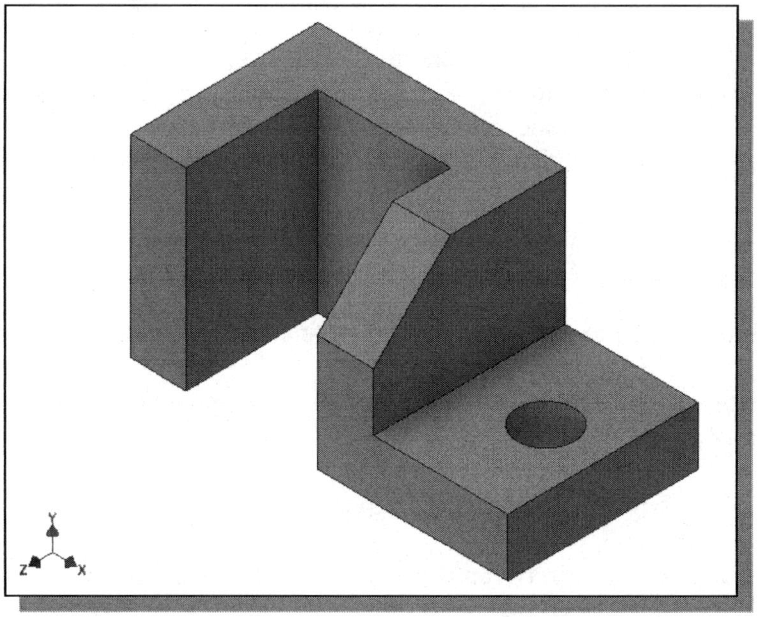

Starting Autodesk Inventor

1. Select the **Autodesk Inventor** option on the *Start* menu or select the **Autodesk Inventor** icon on the desktop to start Autodesk Inventor. The Autodesk Inventor main window will appear on the screen.

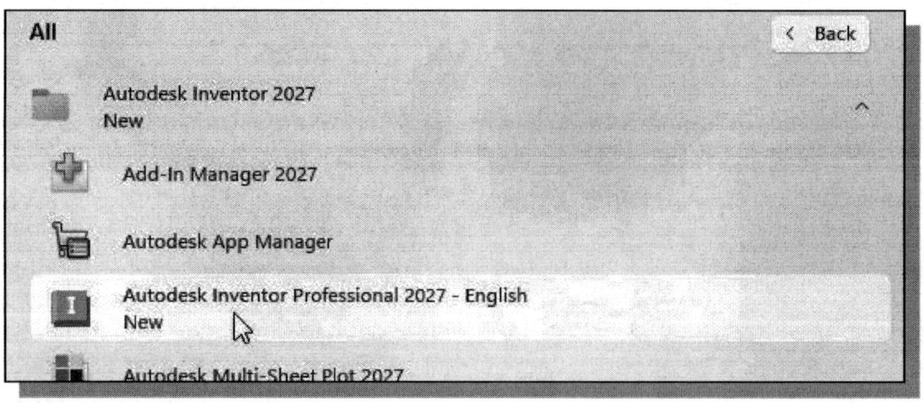

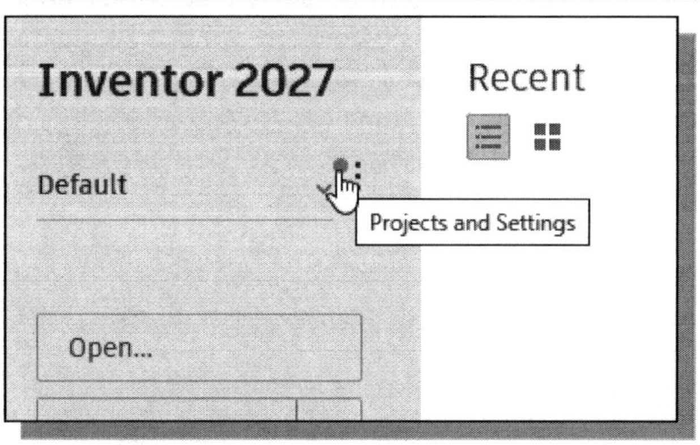

2. Select the **Settings** option next to the *Projects* icon with a single click of the left-mouse-button.

3. In the *Projects List*, confirm the ***Parametric-Modeling*** project is activated as the activate project as shown.

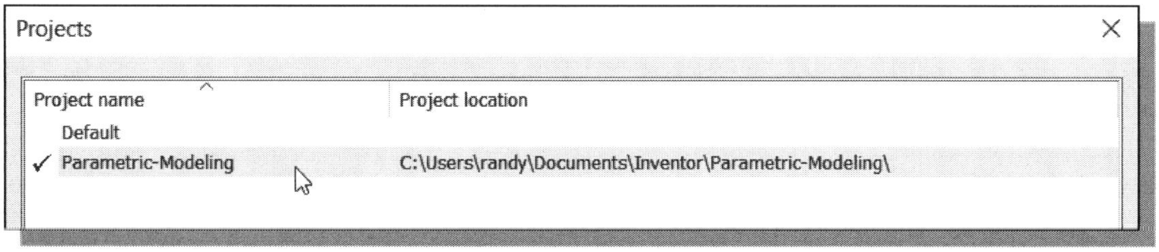

- Note that Autodesk Inventor will keep this activated project as the default project until another project is activated.

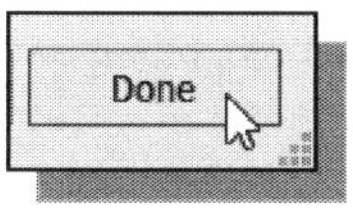

4. Click **Done** to accept the setting and end the *Projects Editor*.

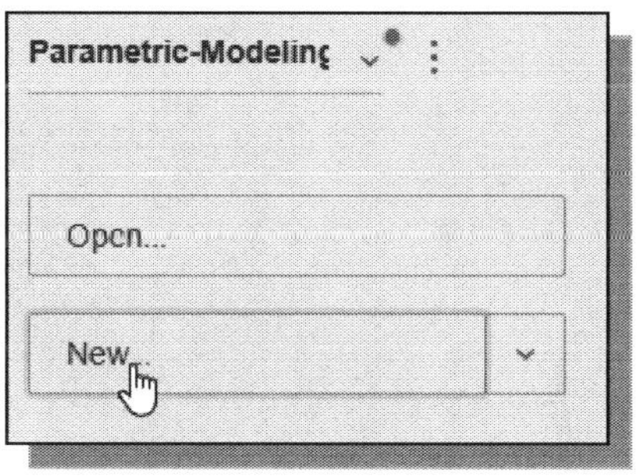

5. Select the **New File** icon with a single click of the left-mouse-button as shown in the figure.

- Notice the ***Parametric-Modeling*** project name is displayed above as the active project.

6. Select the **en-US → English** tab as shown below. When starting a new CAD file, the first thing we should do is choose the units we would like to use. We will use the English setting (inches) for this example.

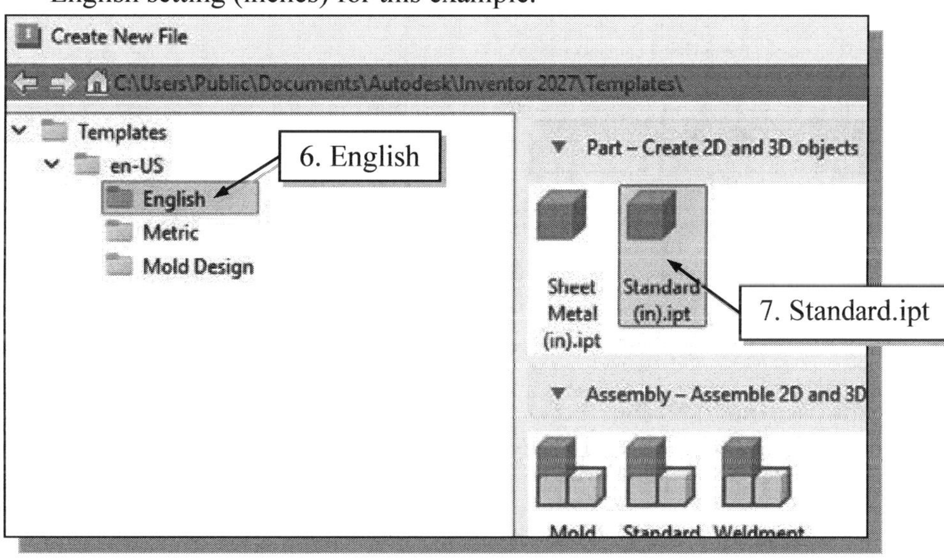

7. Select the **Standard(in).ipt** icon as shown.

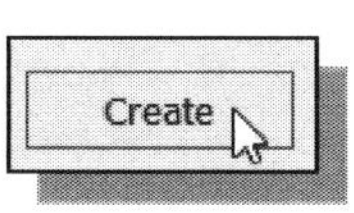

8. Pick **Create** in the *New File* dialog box to accept the selected settings.

The Default Autodesk Inventor Screen Layout

The default Autodesk Inventor drawing screen contains the *pull-down* menus, the *Standard* toolbar, the *3D Model* toolbar, the *Sketch* toolbar, the *drawing* area, the *browser* area, and the *Status Bar*. A line of quick text appears next to the icon as you move the *mouse cursor* over different icons. You may resize the *Autodesk Inventor* drawing window by clicking and dragging the edges of the window, or relocate the window by clicking and dragging the window title area.

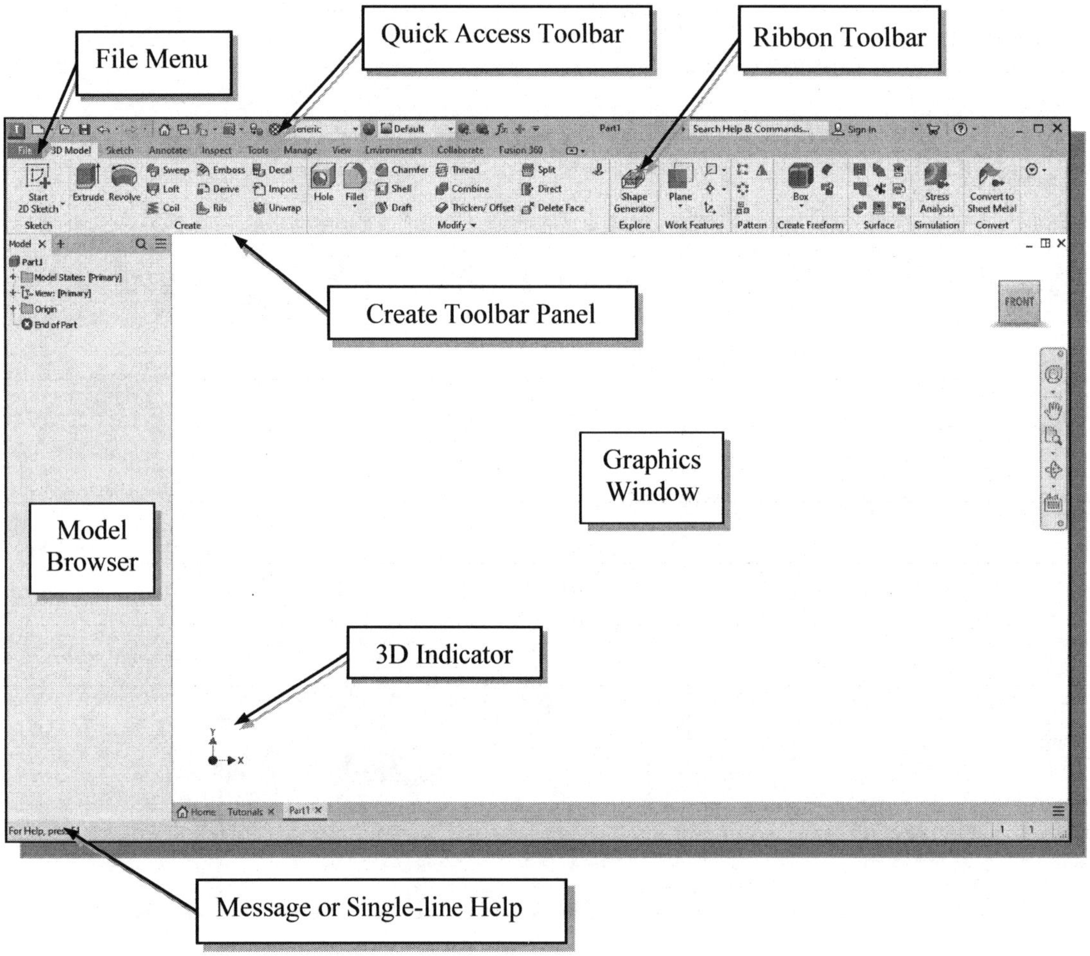

The ***Ribbon Toolbar*** is a relatively new feature in Autodesk Inventor; the *Ribbon Toolbar* is composed of a series of tool panels, which are organized into tabs labeled by task. The *Ribbon* provides a compact palette of all of the tools necessary to accomplish the different modeling tasks. The drop-down arrow next to any icon indicates additional commands are available on the expanded panel; access the expanded panel by clicking on the drop-down arrow.

Sketch Plane – It is an XY monitor, but an XYZ World

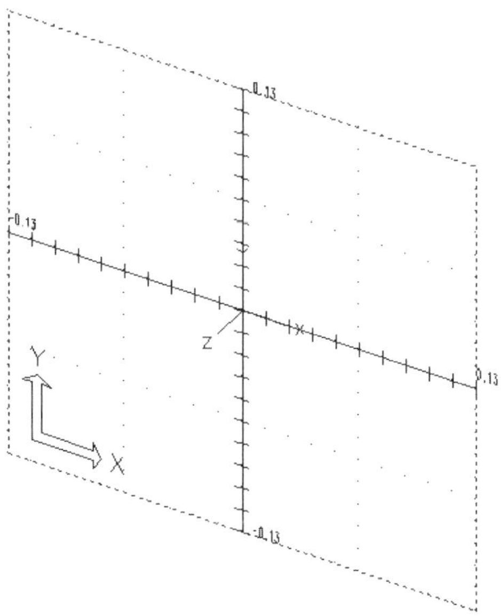

Design modeling software is becoming more powerful and user friendly, yet the system still does only what the user tells it to do. When using a geometric modeler, we therefore need to have a good understanding of what its inherent limitations are.

In most 3D geometric modelers, 3D objects are located and defined in what is usually called **world space** or **global space**. Although a number of different coordinate systems can be used to create and manipulate objects in a 3D modeling system, the objects are typically defined and stored using the world space. The world space is usually a **3D Cartesian coordinate system** that the user cannot change or manipulate.

In engineering designs, models can be very complex, and it would be tedious and confusing if only the world coordinate system were available. Practical 3D modeling systems allow the user to define **Local Coordinate Systems (LCS)** or **User Coordinate Systems (UCS)** relative to the world coordinate system. Once a local coordinate system is defined, we can then create geometry in terms of this more convenient system.

Although objects are created and stored in 3D space coordinates, most of the geometric entities can be referenced using 2D Cartesian coordinate systems. Typical input devices such as a mouse or digitizer are two-dimensional by nature; the movement of the input device is interpreted by the system in a planar sense. The same limitation is true of common output devices, such as displays and plotters. The modeling software performs a series of three-dimensional to two-dimensional transformations to correctly project 3D objects onto the 2D display plane.

The Autodesk Inventor ***sketching plane*** is a special construction approach that enables the planar nature of the 2D input devices to be directly mapped into the 3D coordinate system. The *sketching plane* is a local coordinate system that can be aligned to an existing face of a part, or a reference plane.

Think of the sketching plane as the surface on which we can sketch the 2D sections of the parts. It is similar to a piece of paper, a whiteboard, or a chalkboard that can be attached to any planar surface. The first sketch we create is usually drawn on one of the established datum planes. Subsequent sketches/features can then be created on sketching planes that are aligned to existing **planar faces of the solid part** or **datum planes.**

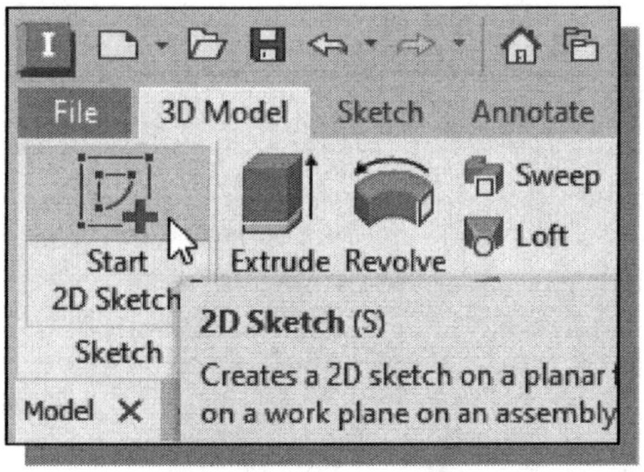

1. Activate the **Start 2D Sketch** icon with a single click of the left-mouse-button.

2. Move the cursor over the edge of the *XY Plane* in the graphics area. When the *XY Plane* is highlighted, click once with the **left-mouse-button** to select the *Plane* as the sketch plane for the new sketch.

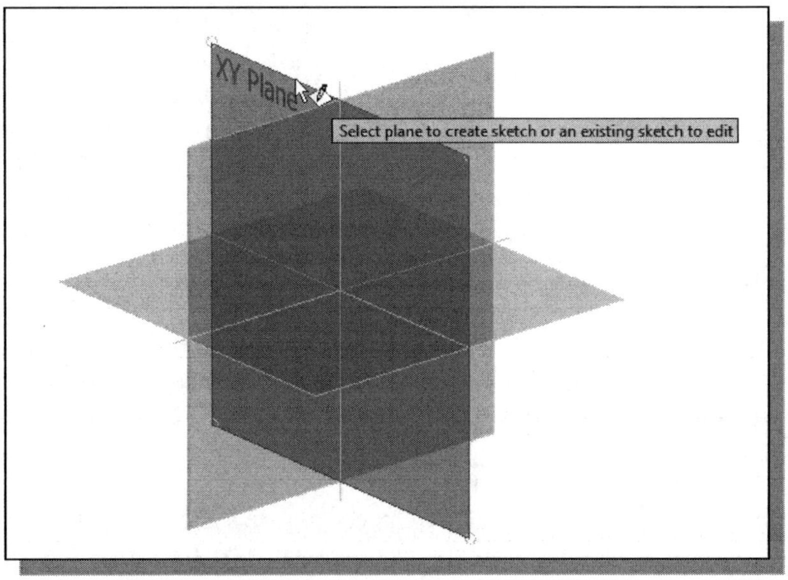

- The *sketching plane* is a reference location where two-dimensional sketches are created. Note that the *sketching plane* can be any planar part surface or datum plane.

3. Confirm the main *Ribbon* area is switched to the **Sketch** toolbars; this indicates we have entered the 2D Sketching mode.

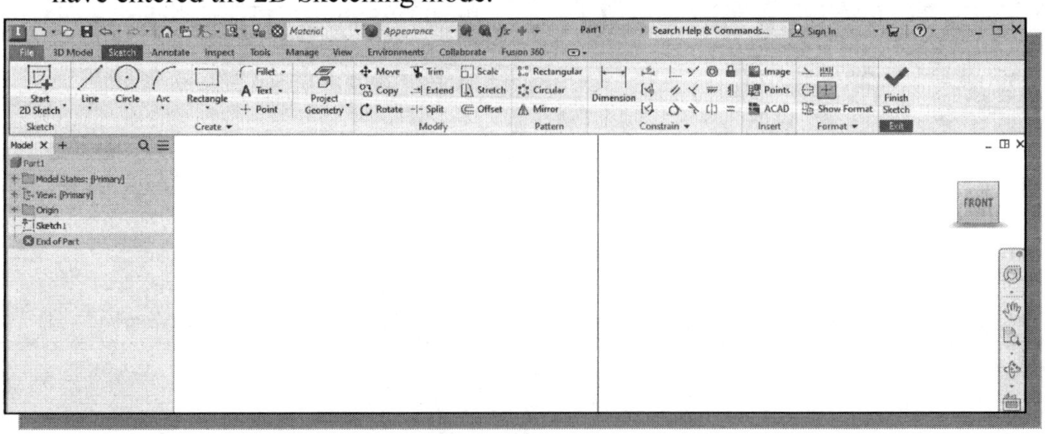

Create A Rough Sketch

Quite often during the early design stage, the shape of a design may not have any precise dimensions. Most conventional CAD systems require the user to input the precise lengths and locations of all geometric entities defining the design, which are not available during the early design stage. With *parametric modeling*, we can use the computer to elaborate and formulate the design idea further during the initial design stage. With Autodesk Inventor, we can use the computer as an electronic sketchpad to help us concentrate on the formulation of forms and shapes for the design. This approach is the main advantage of *parametric modeling* over conventional solid-modeling techniques.

As the name implies, a ***rough sketch*** is not precise at all. When sketching, we simply sketch the geometry so that it closely resembles the desired shape. Precise scale or lengths are not needed. Autodesk Inventor provides many tools to assist us in finalizing sketches. For example, geometric entities such as horizontal and vertical lines are set automatically. However, if the rough sketches are poor, it will require much more work to generate the desired parametric sketches. Here are some general guidelines for creating sketches in Autodesk Inventor:

- **Create a sketch that is proportional to the desired shape.** Concentrate on the shapes and forms of the design.

- **Keep the sketches simple.** Leave out small geometry features such as fillets, rounds and chamfers. They can easily be placed using the Fillet and Chamfer commands after the parametric sketches have been established.

- **Exaggerate the geometric features of the desired shape.** For example, if the desired angle is 85 degrees, create an angle that is 50 or 60 degrees. Otherwise, Autodesk Inventor might assume the intended angle to be a 90-degree angle.

- **Draw the geometry so that it does not overlap.** The geometry should eventually form a closed region. *Self-intersecting* geometry shapes are not allowed.

- **The sketched geometric entities should form a closed region.** To create a solid feature, such as an extruded solid, a closed region is required so that the extruded solid forms a 3D volume.

➢ **Note:** The concepts and principles involved in *parametric modeling* are very different, and sometimes they are totally opposite, to those of conventional computer aided drafting. In order to understand and fully utilize Autodesk Inventor's functionality, it will be helpful to take a *Zen* approach to learning the topics presented in this text: **Have an open mind and temporarily forget your experiences using conventional Computer Aided Drafting systems.**

Step 1: Creating a Rough Sketch

The *Sketch* toolbar provides tools for creating the basic geometry that can be used to create features and parts.

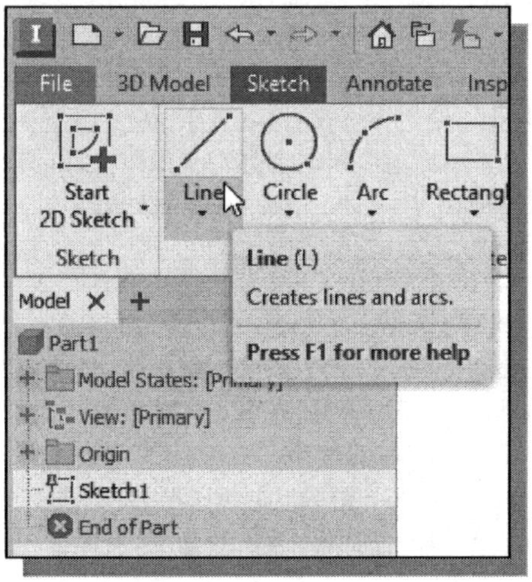

1. Move the graphics cursor to the **Line** icon in the *Sketch* toolbar. A *Help-tip box* appears next to the cursor and a brief description of the command is displayed at the bottom of the drawing screen: "*Creates Straight lines and arcs.*"

2. Select the icon by clicking once with the **left-mouse-button**; this will activate the Line command. Autodesk Inventor expects us to identify the starting location of a straight line.

Graphics Cursors

Notice the cursor changes from an arrow to a crosshair when graphical input is expected.

1. Left-click a starting point for the shape, roughly just below and to the right of the center of the graphics window.

2. As you move the graphics cursor, you will see a digital readout next to the cursor and also in the *Status Bar* area at the bottom of the window. The readout gives you the cursor location, the line length, and the angle of the line measured from horizontal. Move the cursor around and you will notice different symbols appear at different locations.

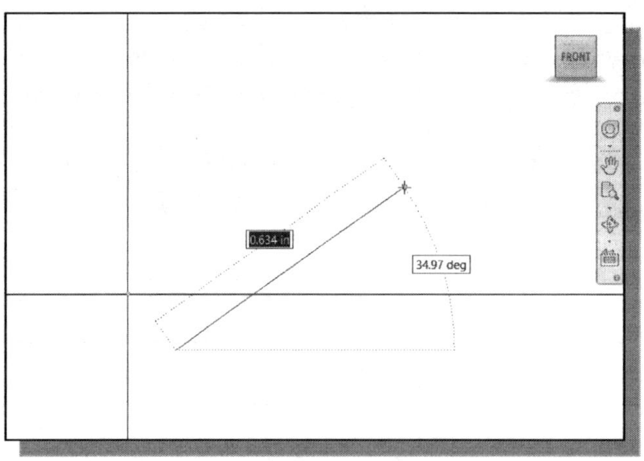

➢ The readout displayed next to the cursor is called the ***Dynamic Input***. This option is part of the **Heads-Up Display** option that is now available in Inventor. Note that *Dynamic Input* can be used for entering precise values, but its usage is somewhat limited in *parametric modeling*.

3. Move the graphics cursor toward the right side of the graphics window and create a horizontal line as shown below (**Point 2**). Notice the geometric constraint symbol, a short horizontal line indicating the geometric property, is displayed.

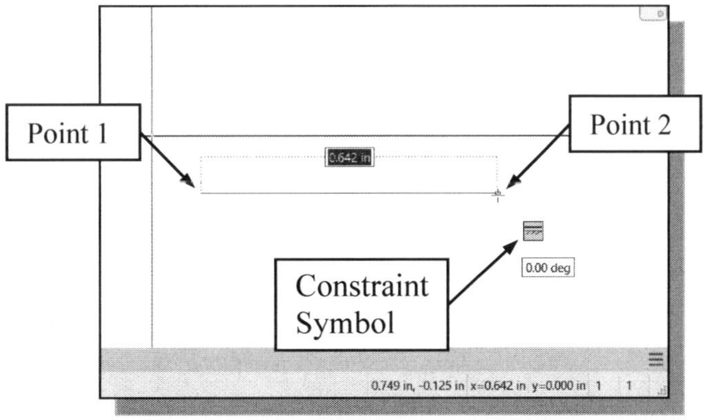

Geometric Constraint Symbols

Autodesk Inventor displays different visual clues, or symbols, to show you alignments, perpendicularities, tangencies, etc. These constraints are used to capture the *design intent* by creating constraints where they are recognized. Autodesk Inventor displays the governing geometric rules as models are built. To prevent constraints from forming, hold down the [**Ctrl**] key while creating an individual sketch curve. For example, while sketching line segments with the **Line** command, endpoints are joined with a **Coincident** *constraint*, but when the [**Ctrl**] key is pressed and held, the inferred constraint will not be created.

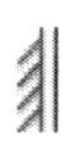	**Vertical**	indicates a line is vertical
	**Horizontal**	indicates a line is horizontal
- - - -	**Dashed line**	indicates the alignment is to the center point or endpoint of an entity
	**Parallel**	indicates a line is parallel to other entities
	**Perpendicular**	indicates a line is perpendicular to other entities
	Coincident	indicates the cursor is at the endpoint of an entity
	**Concentric**	indicates the cursor is at the center of an entity
	**Tangent**	indicates the cursor is at tangency points to curves

1. Complete the sketch as shown below, creating a closed region ending at the starting point (**Point 1**). Do not be overly concerned with the actual size of the sketch. Note that all line segments are sketched horizontally or vertically.

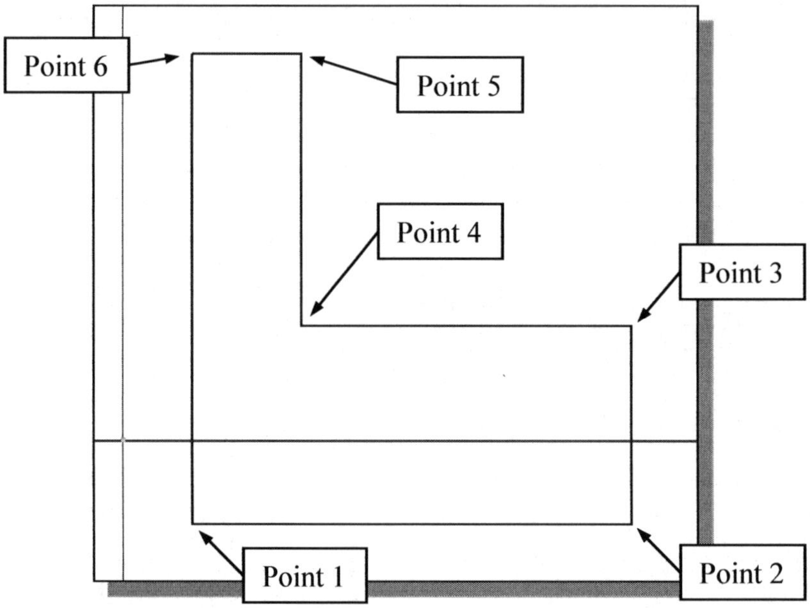

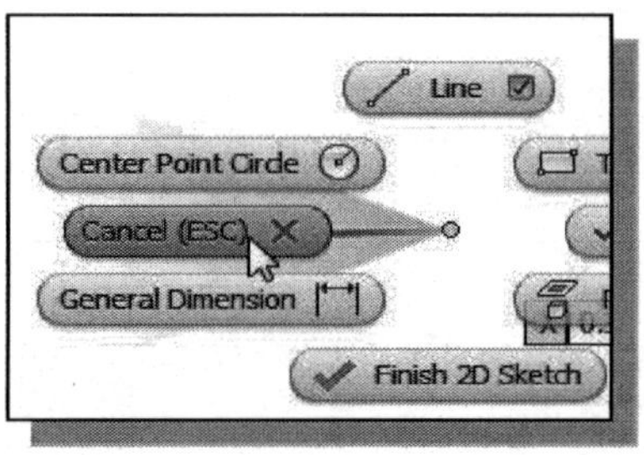

2. Inside the graphics window, click once with the **right-mouse-button** to display the option menu. Select Cancel [Esc] in the pop-up menu, or hit the [**Esc**] key once to end the Sketch Line command.

Step 2: Apply/Modify Constraints and Dimensions

As the sketch is made, Autodesk Inventor automatically applies some of the geometric constraints (such as horizontal, parallel, and perpendicular) to the sketched geometry. We can continue to modify the geometry, apply additional constraints, and/or define the size of the existing geometry. In this example, we will illustrate adding dimensions to describe the sketched entities.

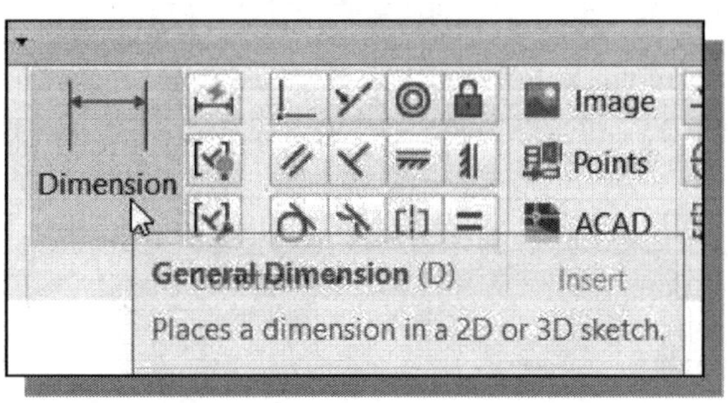

1. Move the cursor to the *Constrain* toolbar area; it is the toolbar next to the *2D Draw* toolbar. Note the first icon in this toolbar is the General Dimension icon. The Dimension command is generally known as **Smart Dimensioning** in parametric modeling.

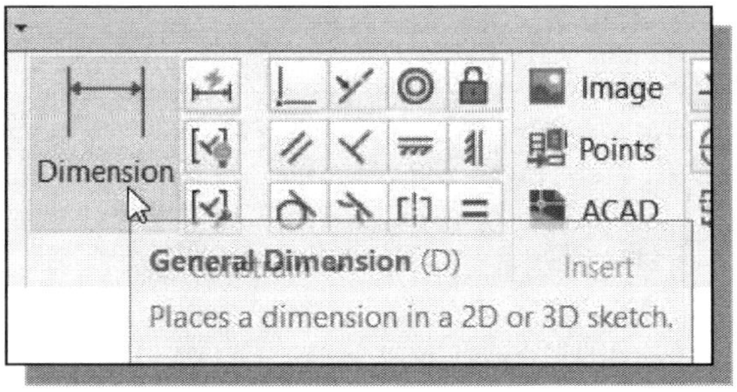

2. Move the cursor on top of the Dimension icon. The Smart Dimensioning command allows us to quickly create and modify dimensions. **Left-click** once on the icon to activate the Dimension command.

3. The message "*Select Geometry to Dimension*" is displayed in the *Status Bar* area at the bottom of the *Inventor* window. Select the bottom horizontal line by left-clicking once on the line.

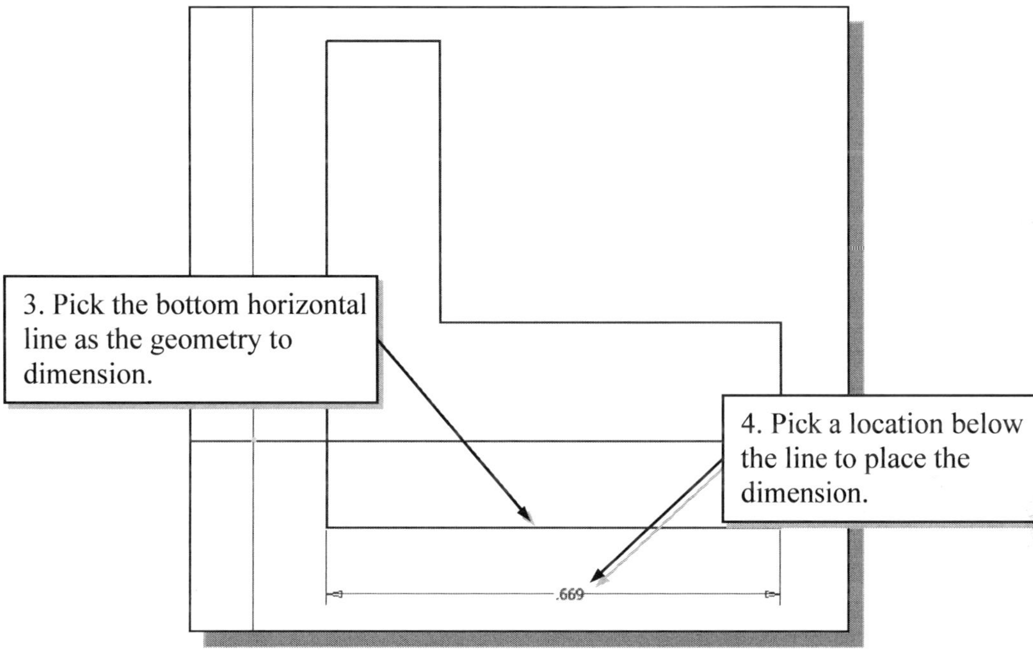

4. Move the graphics cursor below the selected line and **left-click** to place the dimension. (Note that the value displayed on your screen might be different than what is shown in the figure above.)

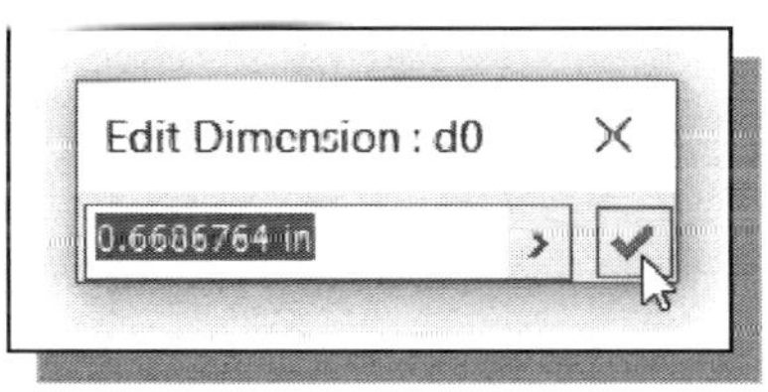

5. Accept the *default value* by clicking on the **Accept** button as shown.

❖ The General Dimension command will create a length dimension if a single line is selected.

6. The message "*Select Geometry to Dimension*" is displayed in the *Status Bar* area, located at the bottom of the *Inventor* window. Select the top-horizontal line as shown below.

7. Select the bottom-horizontal line as shown below.

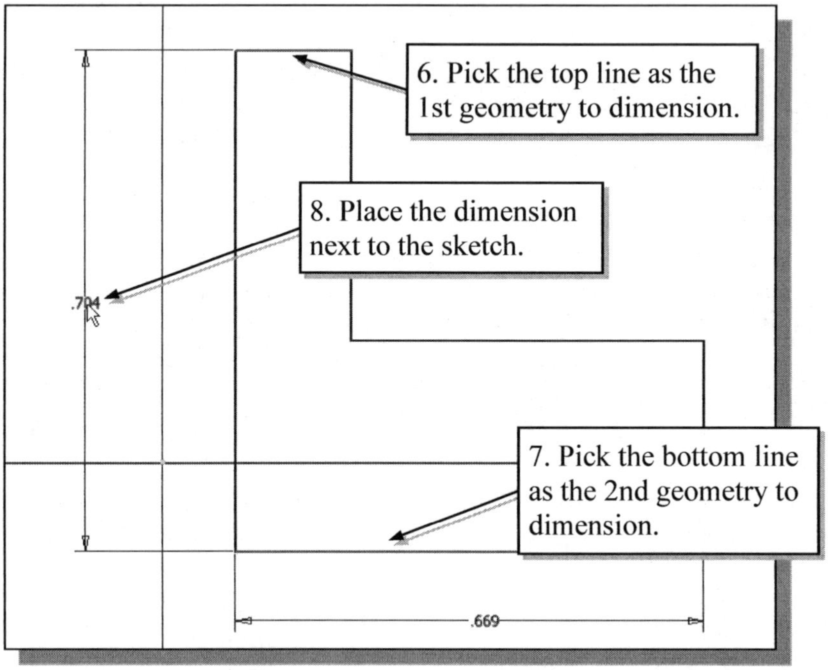

8. Pick a location to the left of the sketch to place the dimension.

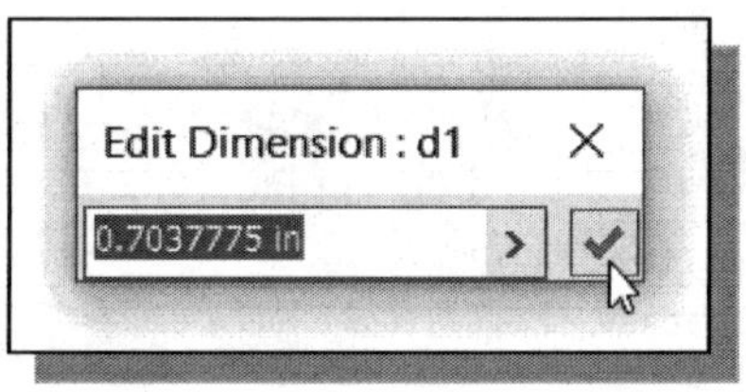

9. Accept the default value by clicking on the **Accept** button.

❖ When two parallel lines are selected, the **General Dimension** command will create a dimension measuring the distance between them.

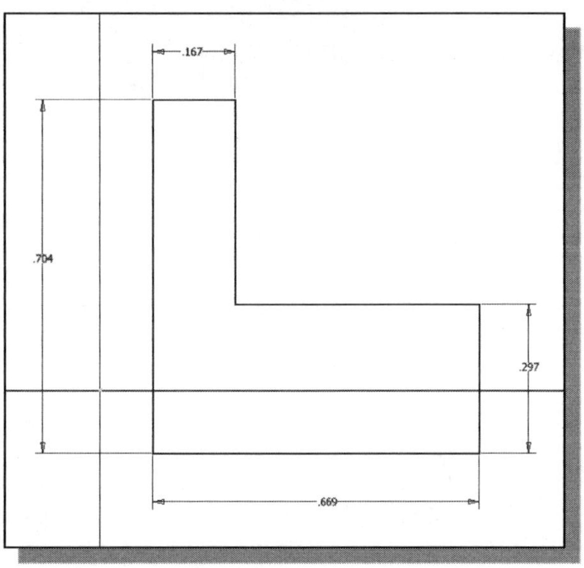

10. On your own, repeat the above steps and create additional dimensions (accepting the default values created by Inventor) so that the sketch appears as shown.

Dynamic Viewing Functions – Zoom and Pan

Autodesk Inventor provides a special user interface called *Dynamic Viewing* that enables convenient viewing of the entities in the graphics window.

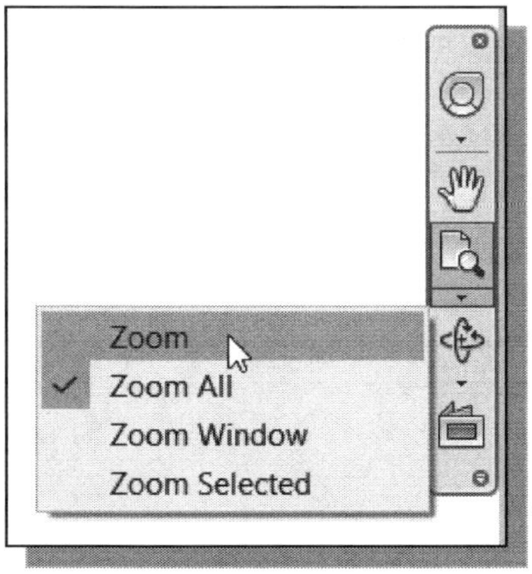

1. Click on the **Zoom** icon located in the *Navigation* bar as shown.
2. Move the cursor near the center of the graphics window.
3. Inside the graphics window, **press and hold down the left-mouse-button**, then move downward to enlarge the current display scale factor.
4. Press the [**Esc**] key once to exit the Zoom command.

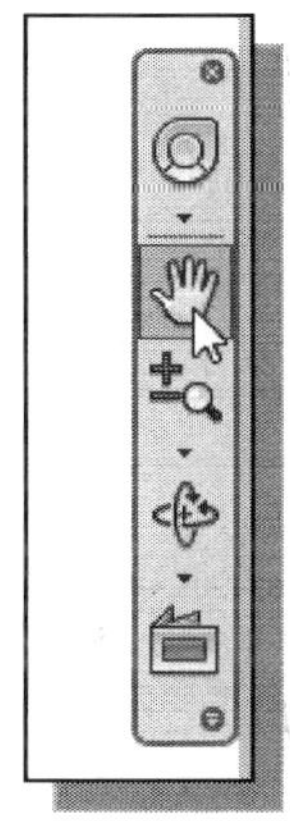

5. Click on the **Pan** icon located above the Zoom command in the *Navigation* bar. The icon is the picture of a hand.

➢ The Pan command enables us to move the view to a different position. This function acts as if you are using a video camera.

6. On your own, use the Zoom and Pan options to reposition the sketch near the center of the screen.

Modifying the Dimensions of the Sketch

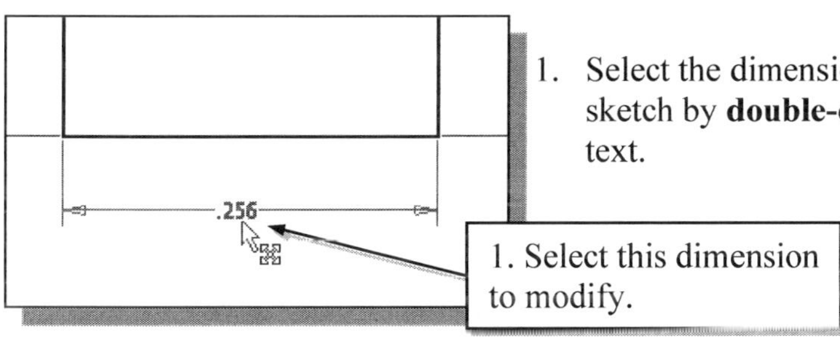

1. Select the dimension that is at the bottom of the sketch by **double-clicking** on the dimension text.

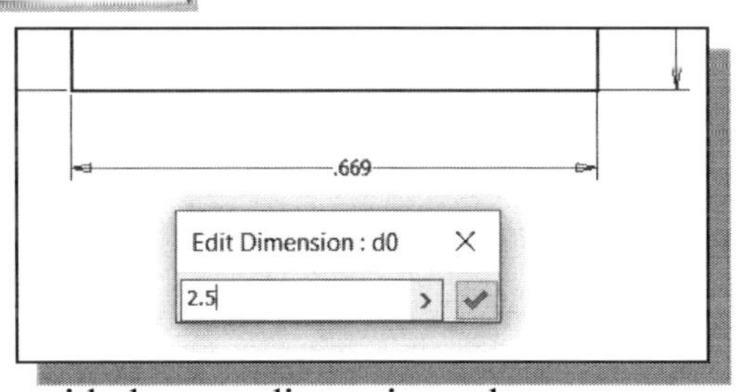

2. In the *Edit Dimension* window, the current length of the line is displayed. Enter **2.5** to set the length of the line.
3. Click on the **Accept** icon to accept the entered value.

➢ Autodesk Inventor will now update the profile with the new dimension value.

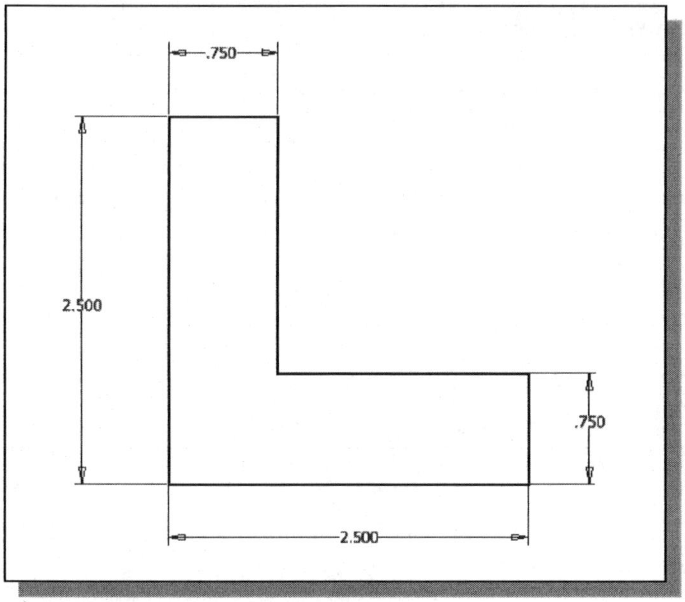

4. On your own, repeat the above steps and adjust the dimensions so that the sketch appears as shown.

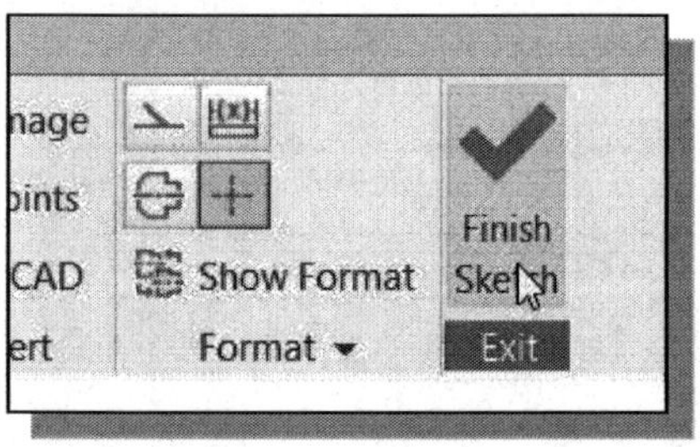

5. In the *Ribbon* toolbar, click once with the **left-mouse-button** to select **Finish Sketch** in the *Ribbon* area to end the **Sketch** option.

Step 3: Completing the Base Solid Feature

Now that the 2D sketch is completed, we will proceed to the next step: create a 3D part from the 2D profile. Extruding a 2D profile is one of the common methods that can be used to create 3D parts. We can extrude planar faces along a path. We can also specify a height value and a tapered angle. In Autodesk Inventor, each face has a positive side and a negative side; the current face we are working on is set as the default positive side. This positive side identifies the positive extrusion direction and it is referred to as the face's ***normal***.

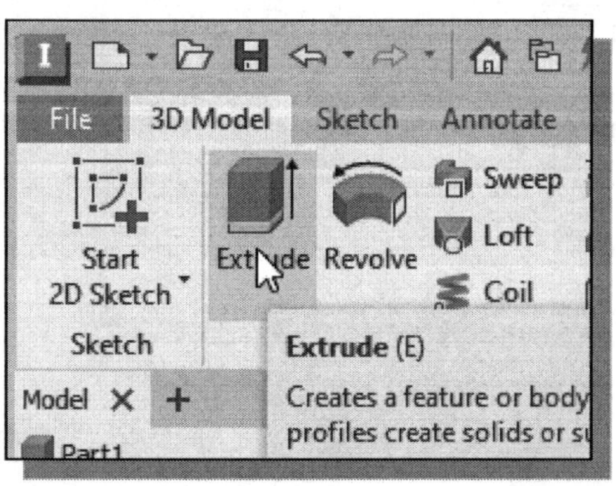

1. In the 3D Model tab, select the **Extrude** command by clicking the left-mouse-button on the icon as shown.

2. In the *Extrude* edit box, enter **2.5** as the extrusion distance. Notice that the sketch region is automatically selected as the extrusion profile.

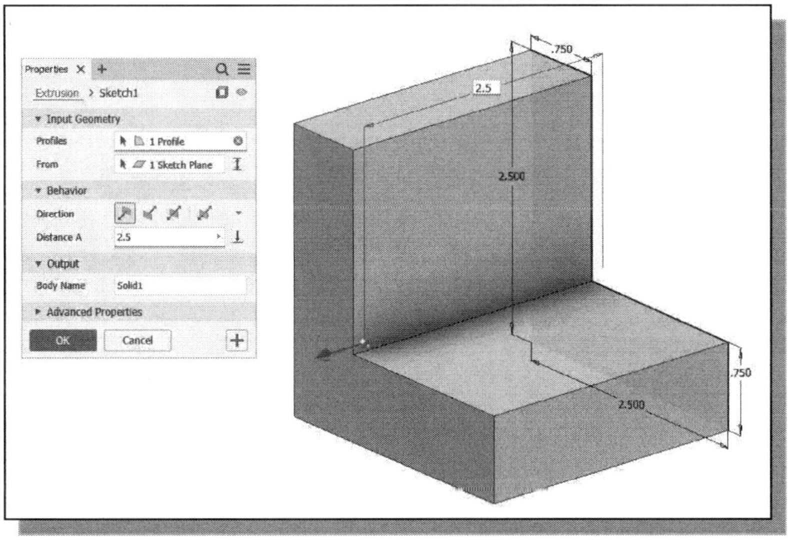

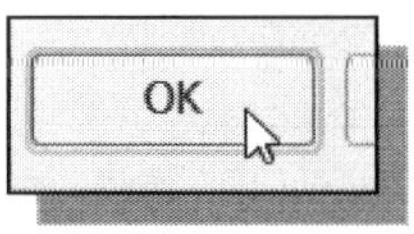

3. Click on the **OK** button to proceed with creating the 3D part.

➢ Note that all dimensions disappeared from the screen. All parametric definitions are stored in the **Autodesk Inventor database** and any of the parametric definitions can be re-displayed and edited at any time.

Isometric View

Autodesk Inventor provides many ways to display views of the three-dimensional design. Several options are available that allow us to quickly view the design to track the overall effect of any changes being made to the model. We will first orient the model to display in the *isometric view* by using the pull-down menu.

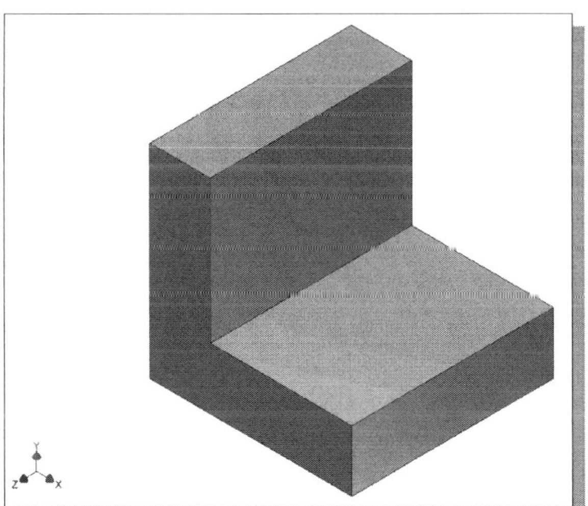

1. Hit the function key **[F6]** once to automatically adjust the display and also reset the display to the *isometric* view.

❖ Note that most of the view-related commands can be accessed in the **ViewCube** and/or the *Navigation* bar located to the right side of the graphics window.

❖ Dynamic Rotation of the 3D Block – Free Orbit

The **Free Orbit** command allows us to:

- Orbit a part or assembly in the graphics window. Rotation can be around the center mark, free in all directions, or around the X/Y-axes in the *3D-Orbit* display.
- Reposition the part or assembly in the graphics window.
- Display isometric or standard orthographic views of a part or assembly.

The **Free Orbit** tool is accessible while other tools are active. Autodesk Inventor remembers the last used mode when you exit the **Orbit** command.

1. Click on the **Orbit** icon in the *Navigation* bar.

➢ The *3D Orbit* display is a circular rim with four handles and a center mark. *3D Orbit* enables us to manipulate the view of 3D objects by clicking and dragging with the left-mouse-button:

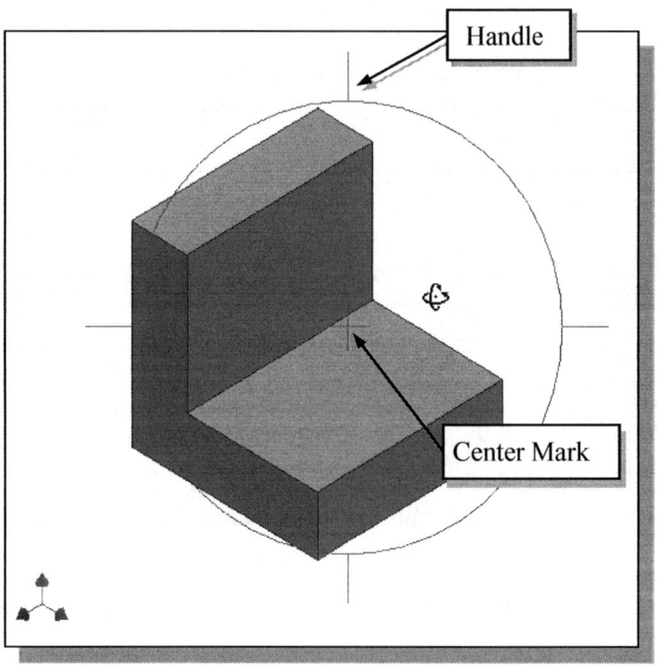

- Drag with the left-mouse-button near the center for free rotation.
- Drag on the handles to orbit around the horizontal or vertical axes.
- Drag on the rim to orbit about an axis that is perpendicular to the displayed view.
- Single left-click to align the center mark of the view.

2. Inside the *circular rim*, press down the left-mouse-button and drag in an arbitrary direction; the **3D Orbit** command allows us to freely orbit the solid model.

3. Move the cursor near the circular rim and notice the cursor symbol changes to a single circle. Drag with the left-mouse-button to orbit about an axis that is perpendicular to the displayed view.

4. Single left-click near the top-handle to align the selected location to the center mark in the graphics window.

5. Activate the **Constrained Orbit** option by clicking on the associated icon as shown.

❖ *The Constrained Orbit can be used to rotate the model about axes in Model Space, equivalent to moving the eye position about the model in latitude and longitude.*

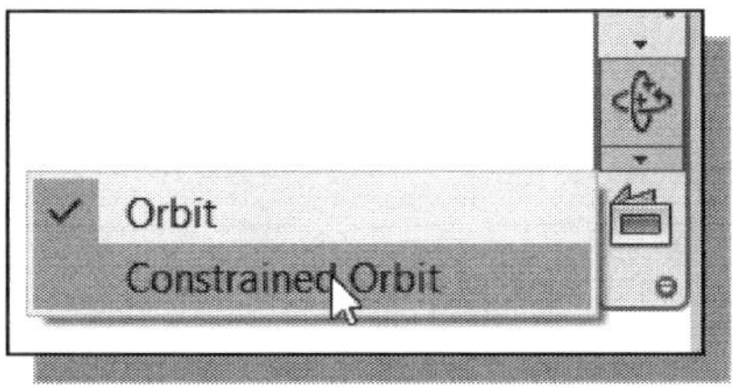

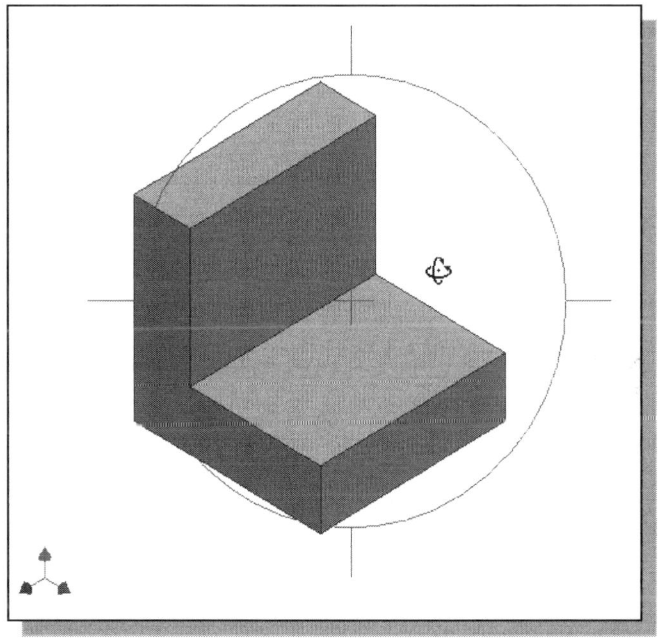

6. On your own, use the different options described in the above steps and familiarize yourself with both of the **3D Orbit** commands. Reset the display to the *Isometric* view as shown in the above figure before continuing to the next section.

❖ Note that while in the **3D Orbit** mode, a horizontal marker will be displayed next to the cursor if the cursor is away from the circular rim. This is the **exit marker**. Left-clicking once will allow you to exit the **3D Orbit** command.

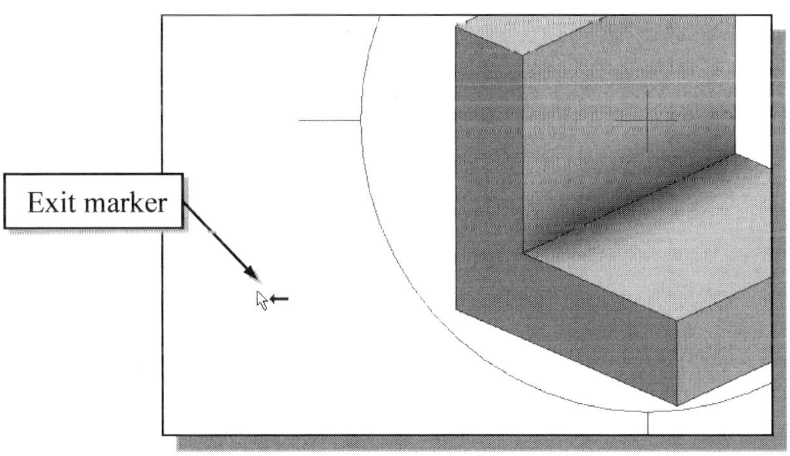

Dynamic Viewing – Quick Keys

We can also use the function keys on the keyboard and the mouse to access the *Dynamic Viewing* functions.

❖ Panning – (1) F2 and drag with the left-mouse-button

Hold the **F2** function key down and drag with the left-mouse-button to pan the display. This allows you to reposition the display while maintaining the same scale factor of the display.

Pan

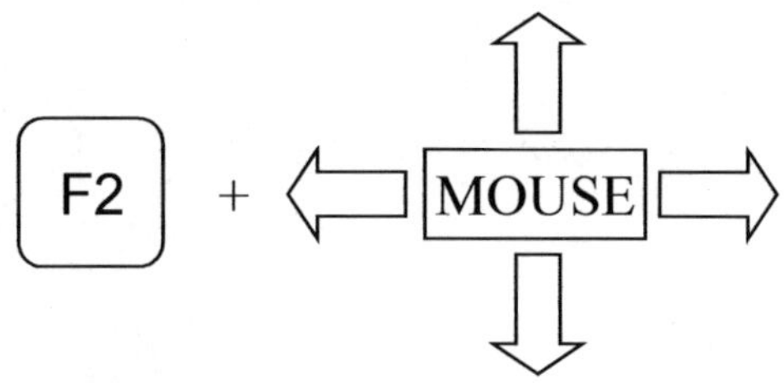

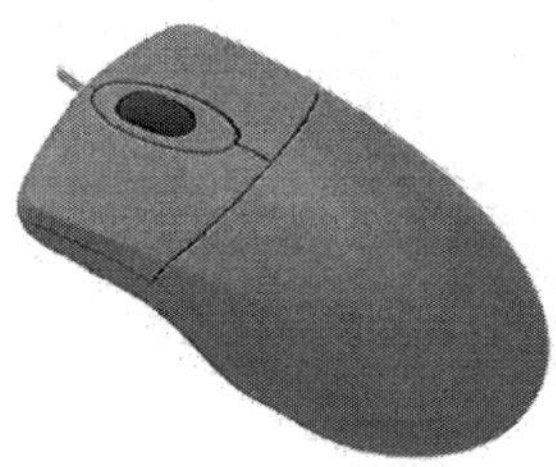

(2) Press and drag with the mouse wheel

Pressing and dragging with the mouse wheel can also reposition the display.

❖ Zooming – (1) F3 and drag with the left-mouse-button

Hold the **F3** function key down and drag with the left-mouse-button vertically on the screen to adjust the scale of the display. Moving upward will reduce the scale of the display, making the entities display smaller on the screen. Moving downward will magnify the scale of the display.

Zoom

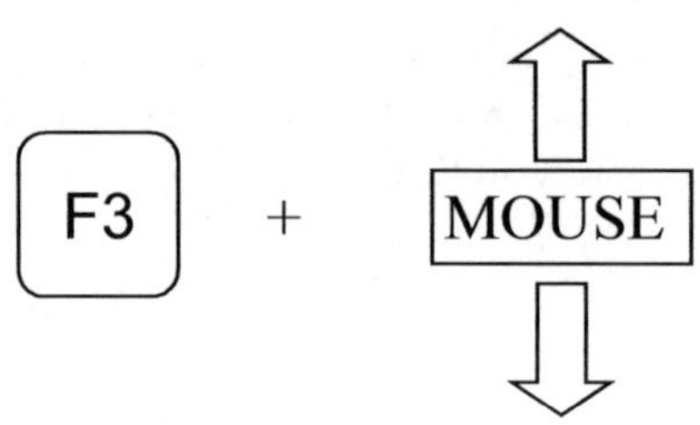

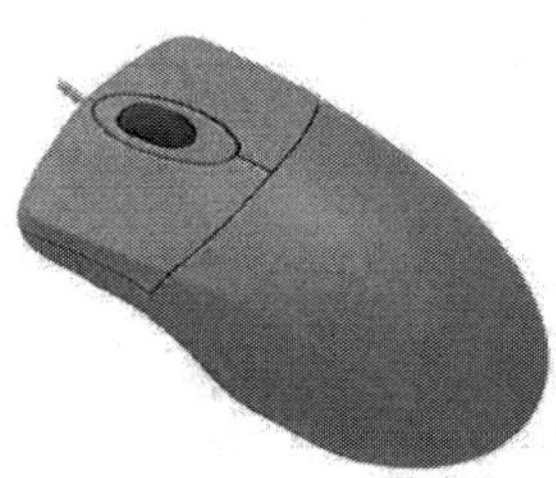

(2) Turning the mouse wheel

Turning the mouse wheel can also adjust the scale of the display. Turning forward will reduce the scale of the display, making the entities display smaller on the screen. Turning backward will magnify the scale of the display.

❖ 3D Dynamic Rotation – Shift and drag with the middle-mouse-button

Hold the **Shift** key down and drag with the middle-mouse-button to orbit the display. Note that the 3D dynamic rotation can also be activated using the **F4** function key and the left-mouse-button.

Dynamic Rotation

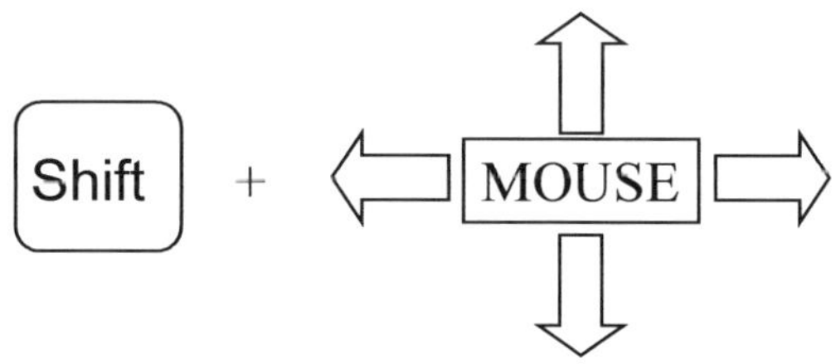

Viewing Tools – Standard Toolbar

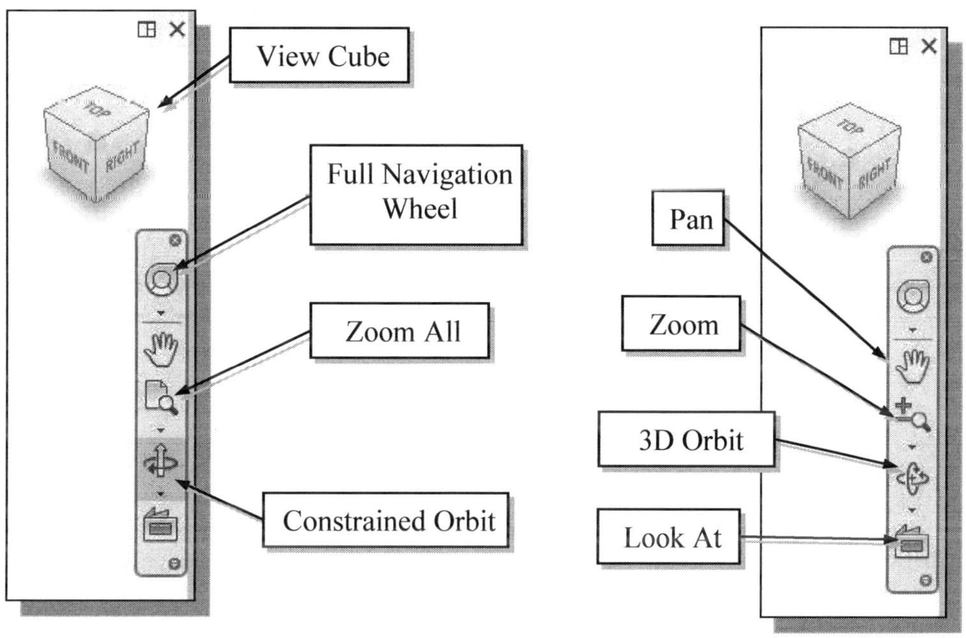

Zoom All – Adjusts the view so that all items on the screen fit inside the graphics window.

Zoom Window – Use the cursor to define a region for the view; the defined region is zoomed to fill the graphics window.

Zoom – Moving upward will reduce the scale of the display, making the entities display smaller on the screen. Moving downward will magnify the scale of the display.

Pan – This allows you to reposition the display while maintaining the same scale factor of the display.

Zoom Selected – In a part or assembly, zooms the selected edge, feature, line, or other element to fill the graphics window. You can select the element either before or after clicking the Zoom button. (Not used in drawings.)

Orbit – In a part or assembly, adds an orbit symbol and cursor to the view. You can orbit the view planar to the screen around the center mark, around a horizontal or vertical axis, or around the X and Y axes. (Not used in drawings.)

Look At – In a part or assembly, zooms and orbits the model to display the selected element planar to the screen or a selected edge or line horizontal to the screen. (Not used in drawings.)

View Cube – The ViewCube is a 3D navigation tool that appears, by default, when you enter Inventor. The ViewCube is a clickable interface which allows you to switch between standard and isometric views.

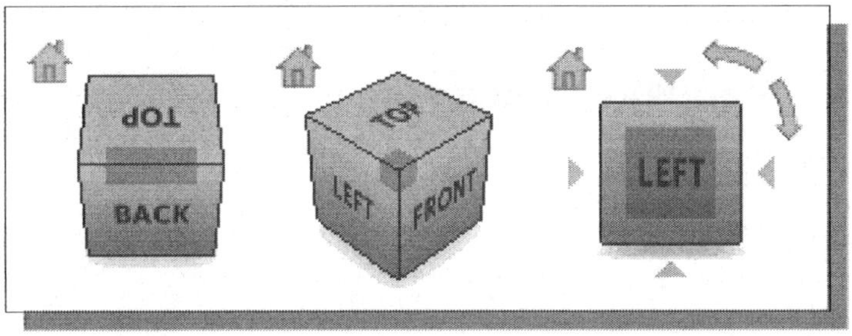

Once the ViewCube is displayed, it is shown in one of the corners of the graphics window over the model in an inactive state. The ViewCube also provides visual feedback about the current viewpoint of the model as view changes occur. When the cursor is positioned over the ViewCube, it becomes active and allows you to switch to one of the available preset views, roll the current view, or change to the Home view of the model.

1. Move the cursor over the ViewCube and notice the different sides of the ViewCube become highlighted and can be activated.

2. Single left-click when the front side is activated as shown. The current view is set to view the front side.

3. Move the cursor over the counterclockwise arrow of the ViewCube and notice the orbit option becomes highlighted.

4. Single left-click to activate the counterclockwise option as shown. The current view is orbited 90 degrees; we are still viewing the front side.

5. Move the cursor over the left arrow of the ViewCube and notice the orbit option becomes highlighted.

6. Single left-click to activate the left arrow option as shown. The current view is now set to view the top side.

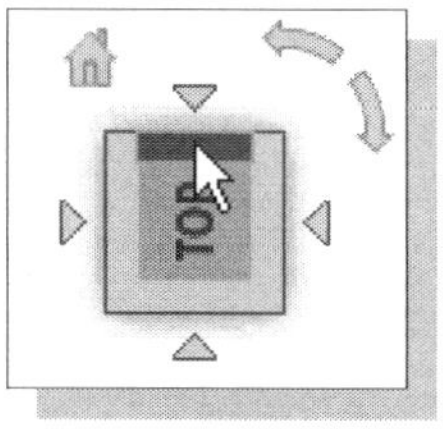

7. Move the cursor over the top edge of the ViewCube and notice the roll option becomes highlighted.

8. Single left-click to activate the roll option as shown. The view will be adjusted to roll 45 degrees.

9. Move the cursor over the ViewCube and drag with the left-mouse-button to activate the **Free Rotation** option.

10. Move the cursor over the home icon of the ViewCube and notice the Home View option becomes highlighted.

11. Single left-click to activate the **Home View** option as shown. The view will be adjusted back to the default ***isometric view***.

Full Navigation Wheel – The Navigation Wheel contains tracking menus that are divided into different sections known as wedges. Each wedge on a wheel represents a single navigation tool. You can pan, zoom, or manipulate the current view of a model in different ways. The 3D Navigation Wheel and 2D Navigation Wheel (mostly used in the 2D drawing mode) have some or all of the following options:

Zoom – Adjusts the magnification of the view.
Center – Centers the view based on the position of the cursor over the wheel.
Rewind – Restores the previous view.
Forward – Increases the magnification of the view.
Orbit – Allows 3D free rotation with the left-mouse-button.
Pan – Allows panning by dragging with the left-mouse-button.
Up/Down – Allows panning with the use of a scroll control.
Walk – Allows *walking*, with linear motion perpendicular to the screen, through the model space.
Look – Allows rotation of the current view vertically and horizontally.

3D Full Navigation Wheel

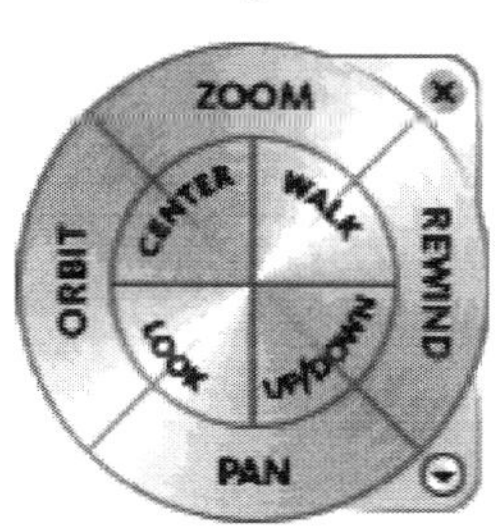

2D Full Navigation Wheel

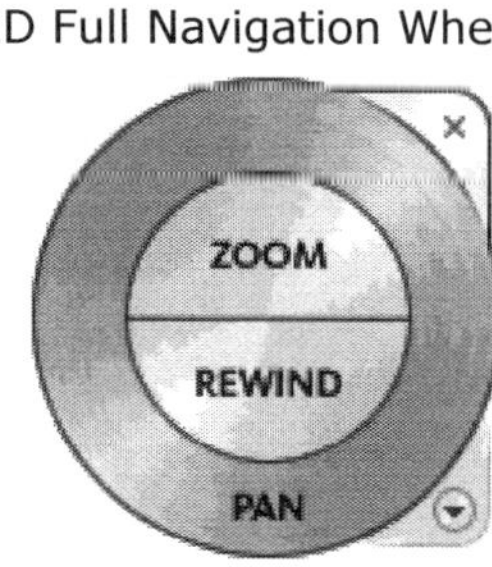

1. Activate the **Full Navigation Wheel** by clicking on the icon as shown.

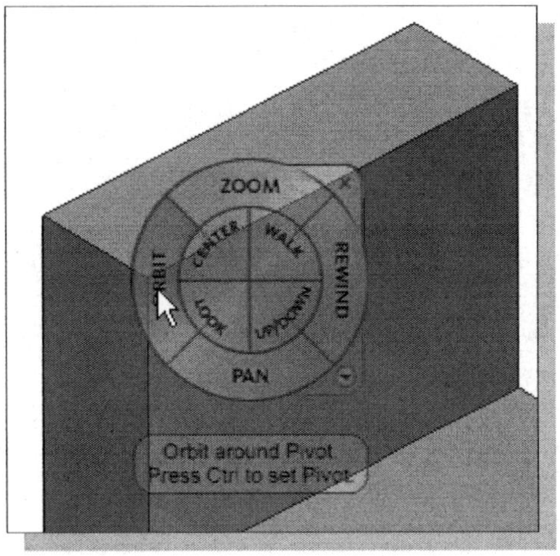

2. Move the cursor in the graphics window and notice the **Full Navigation Wheel** menu follows the cursor on the screen.

3. Move the cursor on the **Orbit** option to highlight the option.

4. Click and drag with the left-mouse-button to activate the **Free Rotation** option.

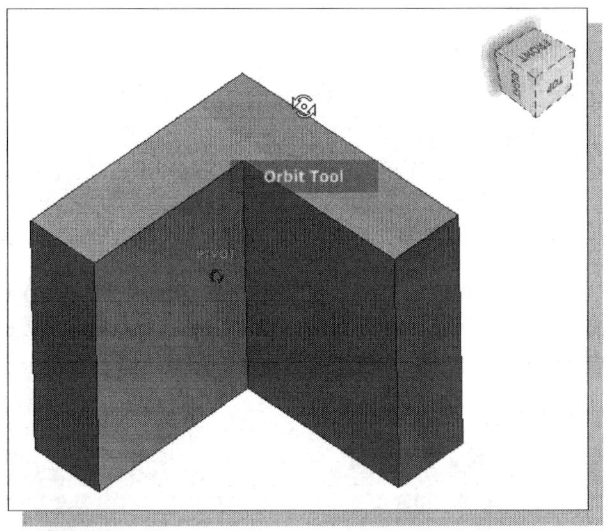

5. Drag with the left-mouse-button and notice the **ViewCube** also reflects the model orientation.

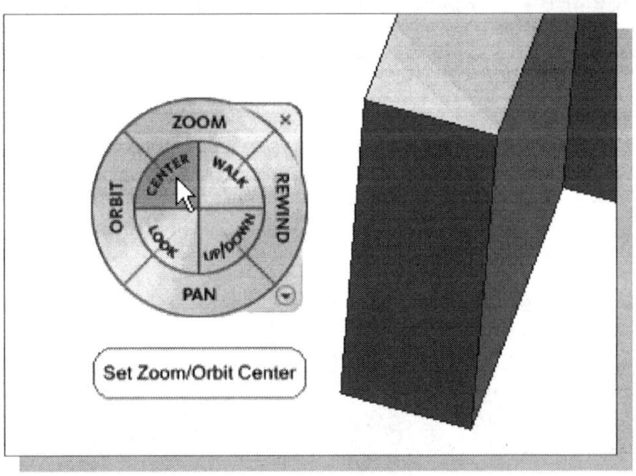

6. Move the cursor to the left side of the model and click the **Center** option as shown. The display is adjusted so the selected point is the new **Zoom/Orbit** center.

7. On your own, experiment with the other available options.

Display Modes

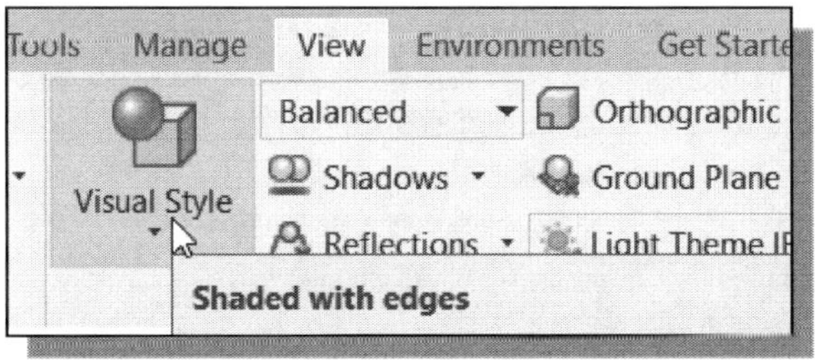

- The **Visual Style** in the *View* tab has eleven display-modes ranging from very realistic renderings of the model to very artistic representations of the model. The more commonly used modes are as follows:

❖ **Realistic Shaded Solid:**

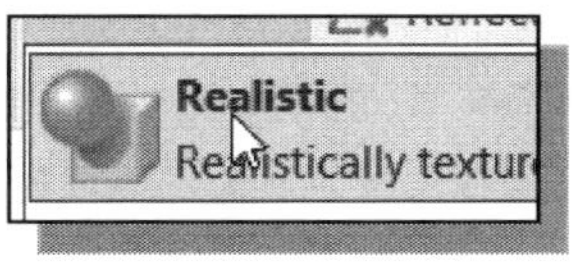

The *Realistic Shaded Solid* display mode generates a high-quality shaded image of the 3D object.

❖ **Standard Shaded Solid:**

The *Standard Shaded Solid* display option generates a shaded image of the 3D object that requires fewer computer resources compared to the realistic rendering.

❖ **Wireframe Image:**

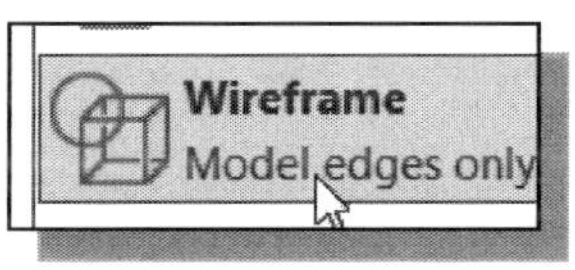

The *Wireframe Image* display option allows the display of the 3D objects using the basic wireframe representation scheme.

❖ **Wireframe with Hidden-Edges:**

The *Wireframe with Hidden-Edges* option can be used to generate an image of the 3D object with all the back lines shown as hidden-lines.

Orthographic vs. Perspective

Besides the above basic display modes, we can also choose orthographic view or perspective view of the display. Click on the triangle icon next to the *display mode button* on the *View* toolbar.

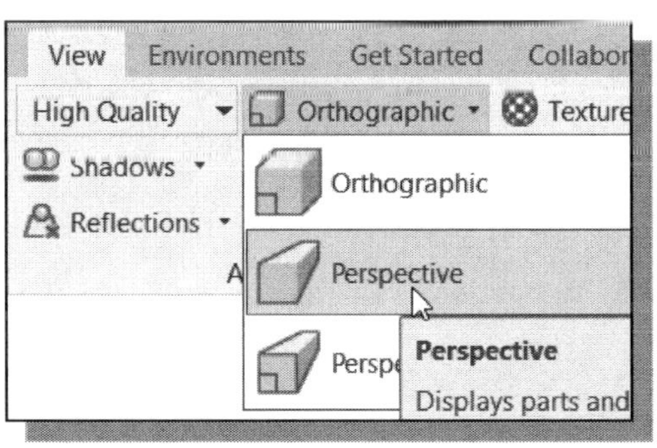

❖ **Orthographic**
The first icon allows the display of the 3D object using the parallel edges representation scheme.

❖ **Perspective**
The second icon allows the display of the 3D object using the perspective, nonparallel edges, and representation scheme.

Disable the Heads-Up Display Option

The **Heads-Up Display** option in Inventor provides mainly the **Dynamic Input** function, which can be quite useful for 2D drafting activities. For example, in the use of a 2D drafting CAD system, most of the dimensions of the design would have been determined by the documentation stage. However, in *parametric modeling*, the usage of the *Dynamic Input* option is quite limited, as this approach does not conform to the "**shape before size**" design philosophy.

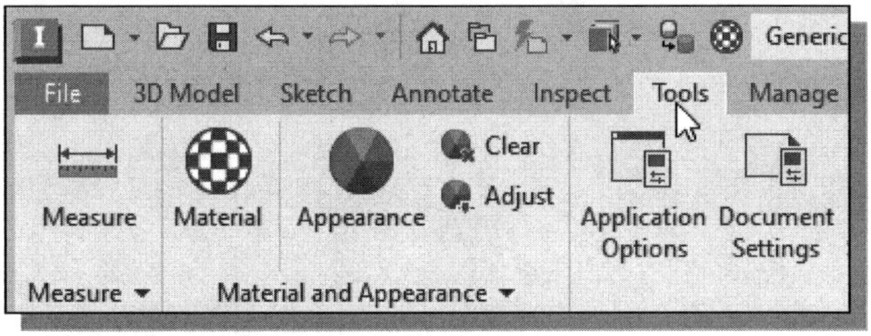

1. Select the **Tools** tab in the *Ribbon* as shown.

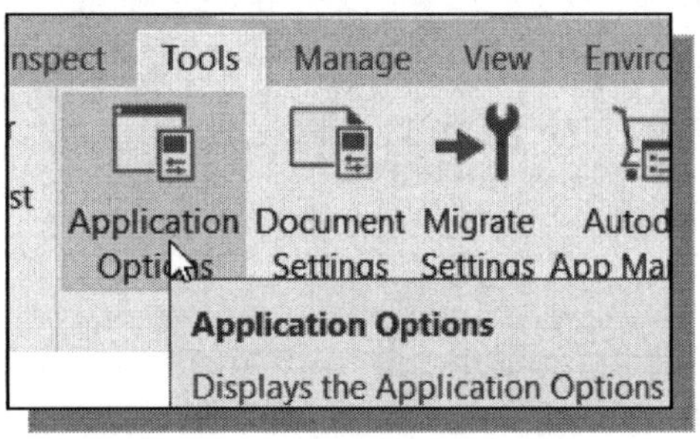

2. Select **Application Options** in the options toolbar as shown.

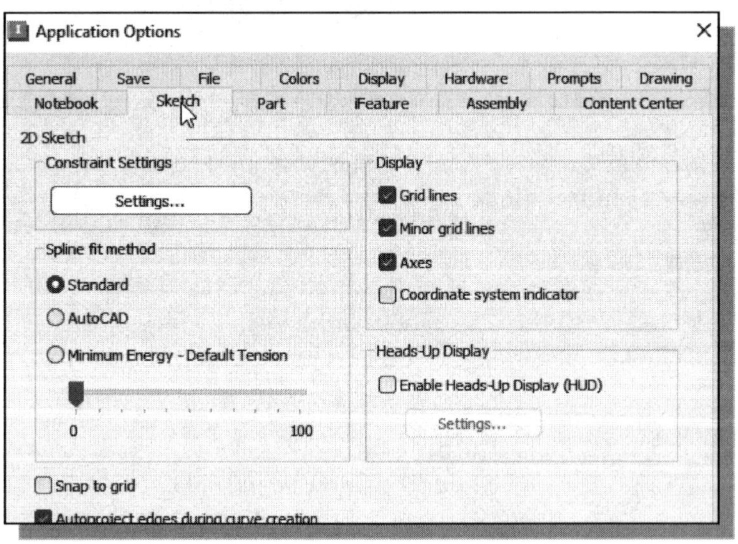

3. Select the **Sketch** tab to display the sketch related settings.

4. In the *Heads-Up Display* section, turn **OFF** the ***Enable Heads-Up Display***, ***Snap to Grid*** options and switch **On** the **Grid lines**, **Minor grid lines** and **Axes** options in the *Display* section as shown.

5. On your own, examine the other sketch settings that are available.

6. Click **OK** to accept the settings.

Step 4-1: Adding an Extruded Feature

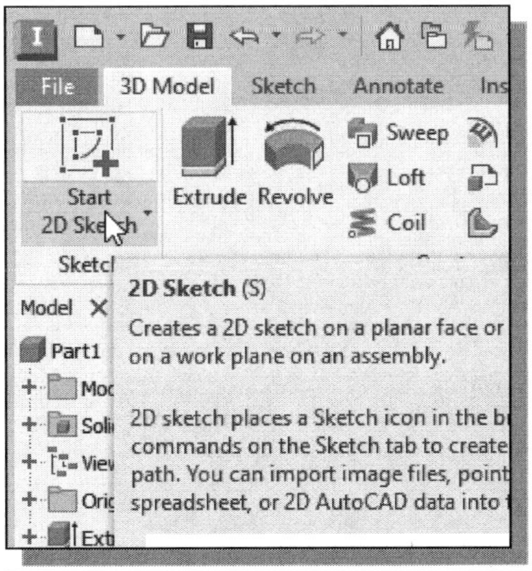

1. Activate the *3D Model* tab and select the **Start 2D Sketch** command by left-clicking once on the icon.

2. In the *Status Bar* area, the message "*Select plane to create sketch or an existing sketch to edit*" is displayed. Autodesk Inventor expects us to identify a planar surface where the 2D sketch of the next feature is to be created. Notice that Autodesk Inventor will automatically highlight feasible planes and surfaces as the cursor is on top of the different surfaces. Pick the top horizontal face of the 3D solid object.

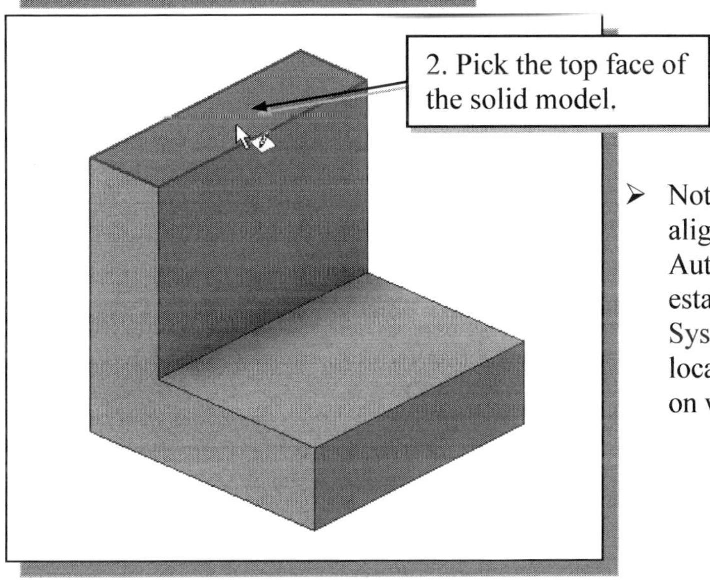

➢ Note that the sketch plane is aligned to the selected face. Autodesk Inventor automatically establishes a User-Coordinate-System (UCS) and records its location with respect to the part on which it was created.

- Next, we will create and profile another sketch, a rectangle, which will be used to create another extrusion feature that will be added to the existing solid object.

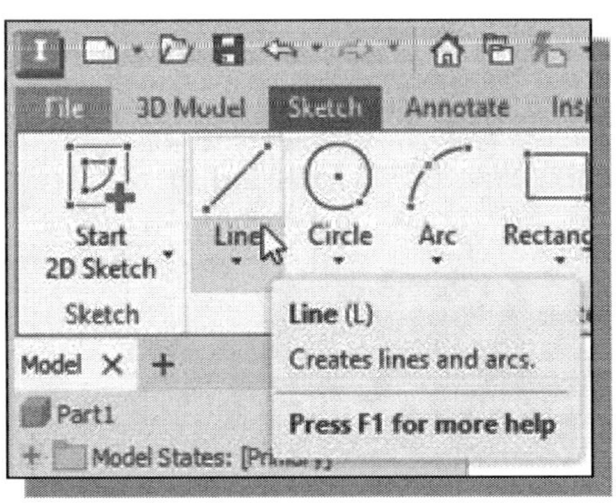

3. Select the **Line** command by clicking once with the **left-mouse-button** on the icon in the *Sketch* tab on the Ribbon.

4. Create a sketch with segments perpendicular/parallel to the existing edges of the solid model as shown below.

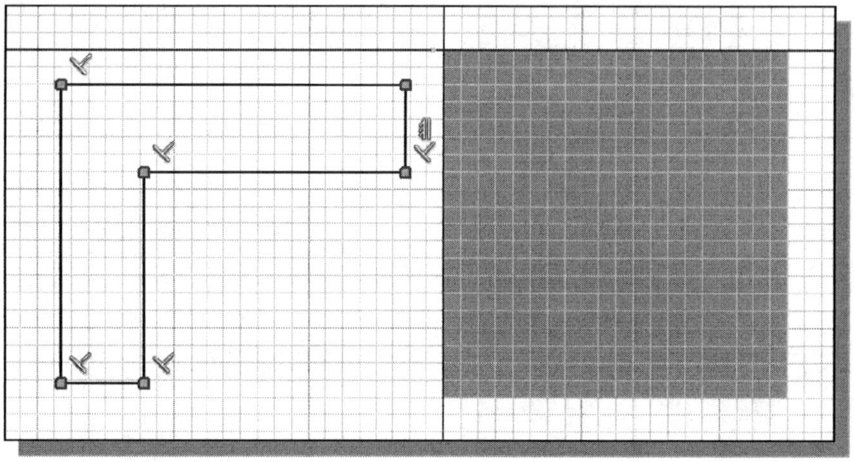

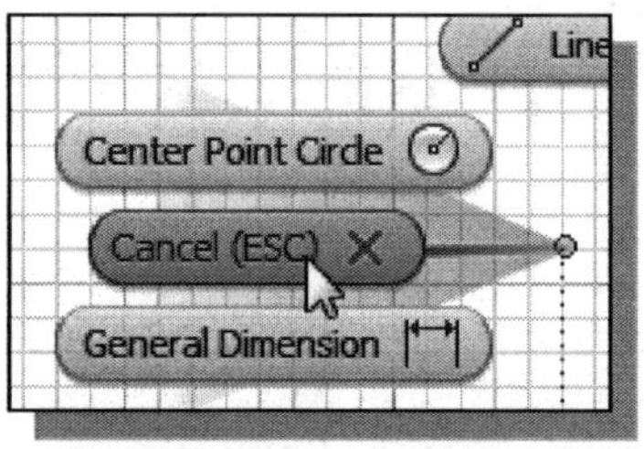

5. Inside the graphics window, click once with the **right-mouse-button** to display the option menu. Select **Cancel (ESC)** in the pop-up menu to end the Line command.

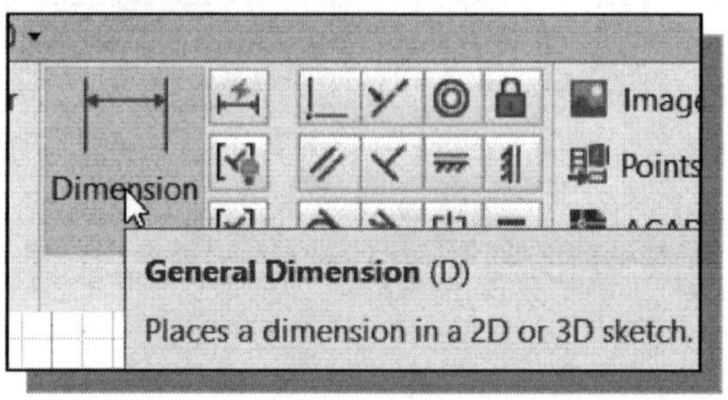

6. Select the **General Dimension** command in the *Sketch* toolbar. The General Dimension command allows us to quickly create and modify dimensions. Left-click once on the icon to activate the General Dimension command.

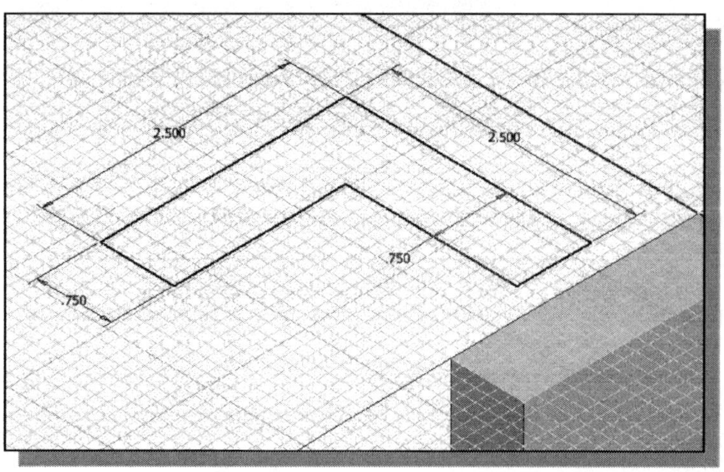

7. Hit the function key **[F6]** once to switch the display to the isometric display as shown.

8. Create the **four dimensions** to describe the size of the sketch as shown in the figure.

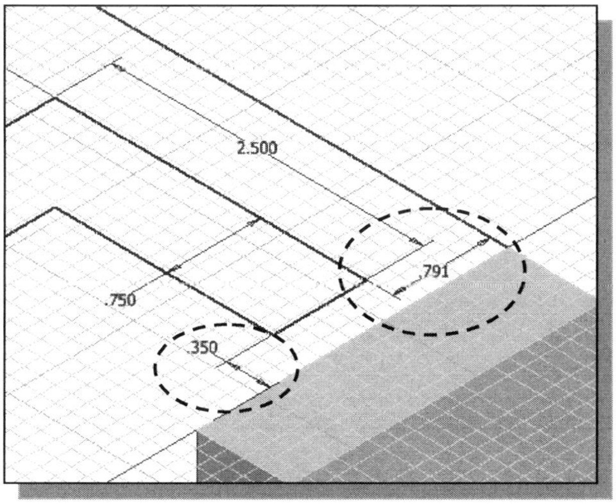

9. Create the two location dimensions to describe the position of the sketch relative to the top corner of the solid model as shown.

10. On your own, modify the two location dimensions to **0.0** and adjust the size dimensions as shown in the figure below.

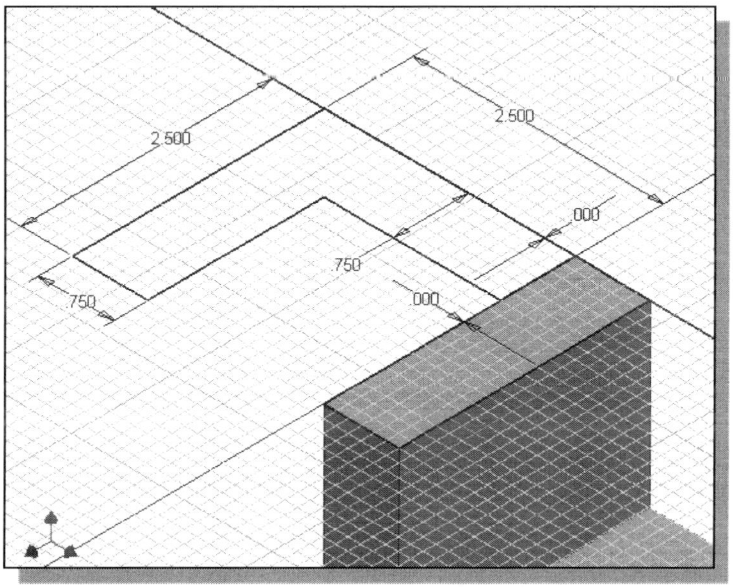

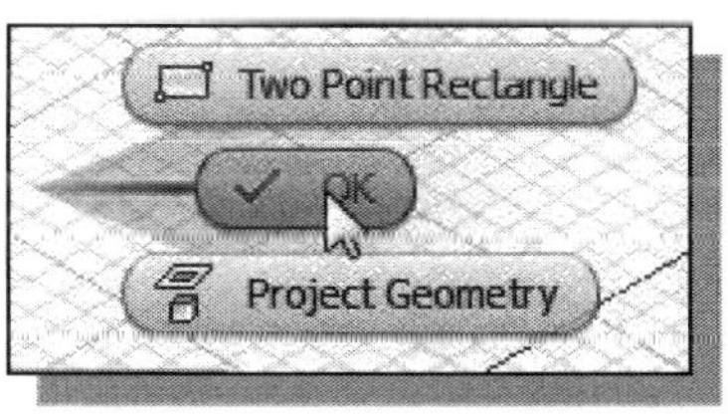

11. Inside the graphics window, click once with the **right-mouse-button** to display the option menu. Select **OK** in the pop-up menu to end the General Dimension command.

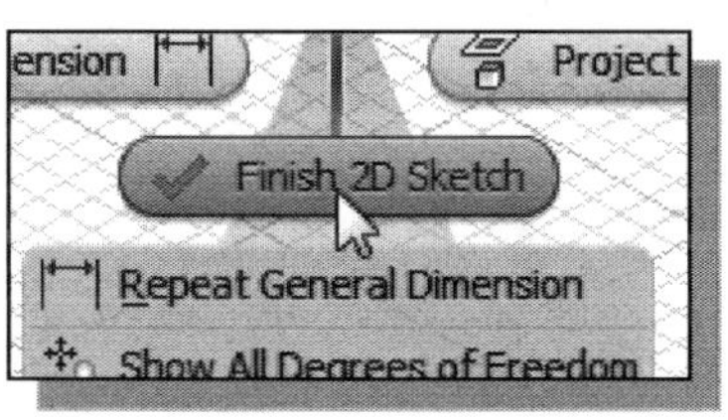

12. Inside the graphics window, click once with the **right-mouse-button** to display the option menu. Select **Finish 2D Sketch** in the pop-up menu to end the Sketch option.

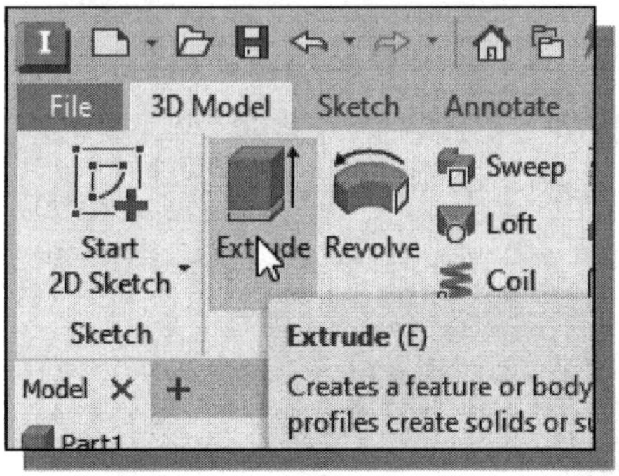

13. In the *3D Model* tab select the **Extrude** command by left-clicking on the icon.

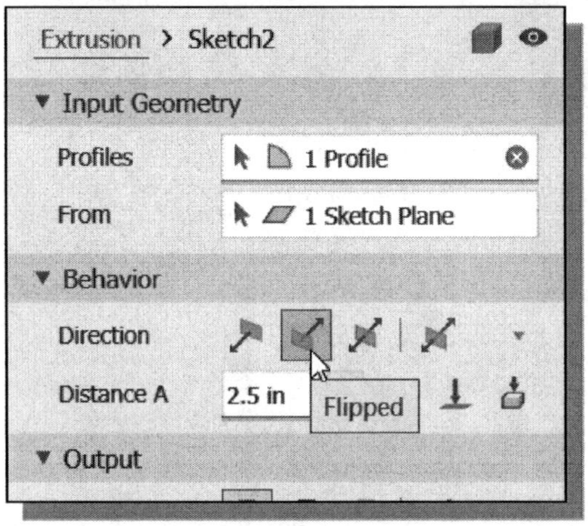

14. In the *Extrude* dialog box, enter **2.5** as the extrude distance as shown.

15. Click on the **Flipped icon** to reverse the *Extrusion Direction* as shown.

16. Confirm the *Boolean* option is set to **Join** and click on the **OK** button to proceed with creating the extruded feature.

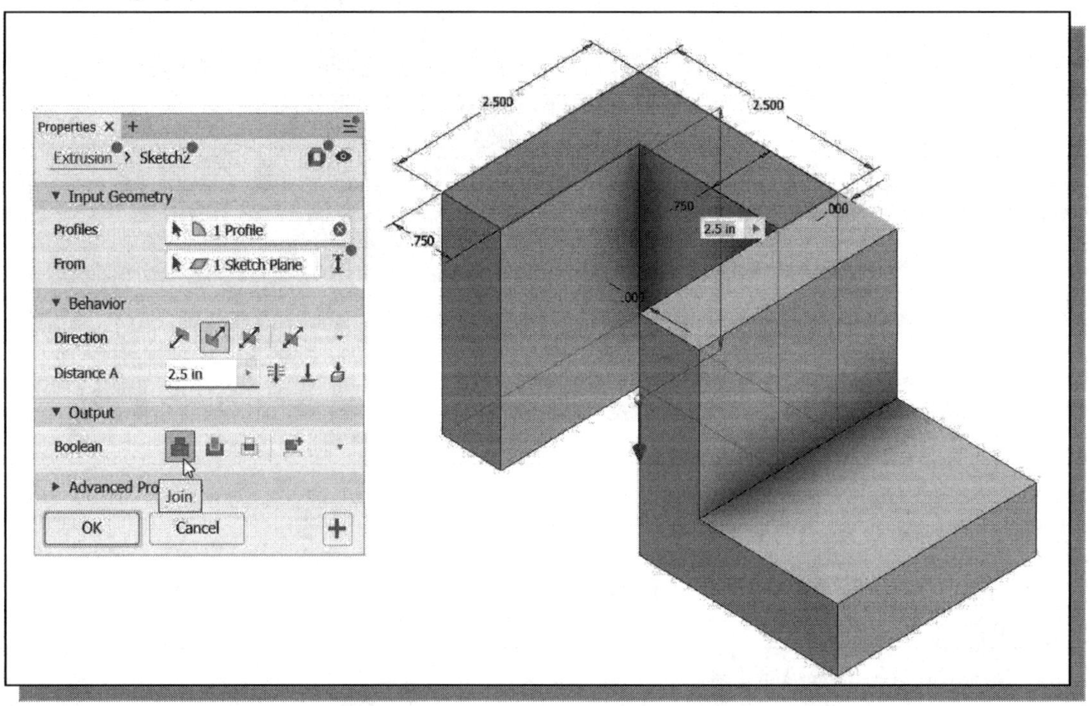

Step 4-2: Adding a Cut Feature

Next, we will create and profile a circle, which will be used to create a cut feature that will be added to the existing solid object.

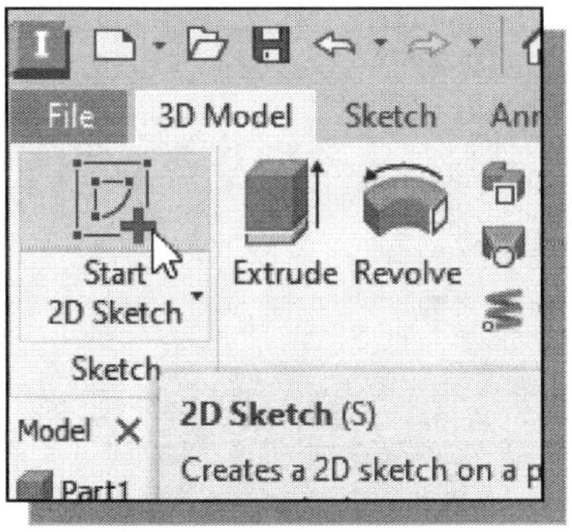

1. In the *3D Model* tab select the **Start 2D Sketch** command by left-clicking once on the icon.

2. In the *Status Bar* area, the message "*Select plane to create sketch or an existing sketch to edit.*" is displayed. Autodesk Inventor expects us to identify a planar surface where the 2D sketch of the next feature is to be created. Pick the top horizontal face of the 3D solid model as shown.

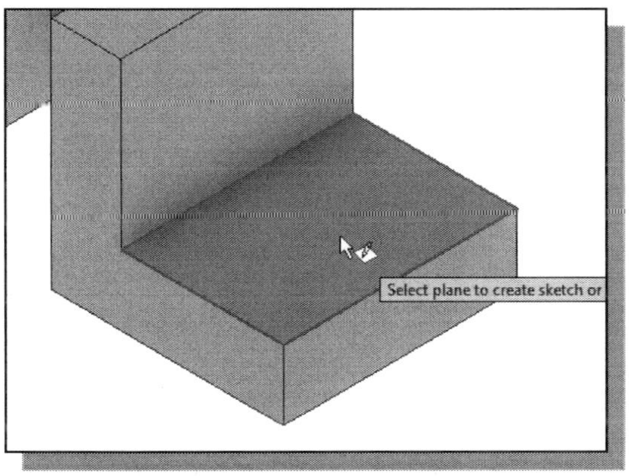

➢ Note that the sketch plane is aligned to the selected face. Autodesk Inventor automatically establishes a User-Coordinate-System (UCS) and records its location with respect to the part on which it was created.

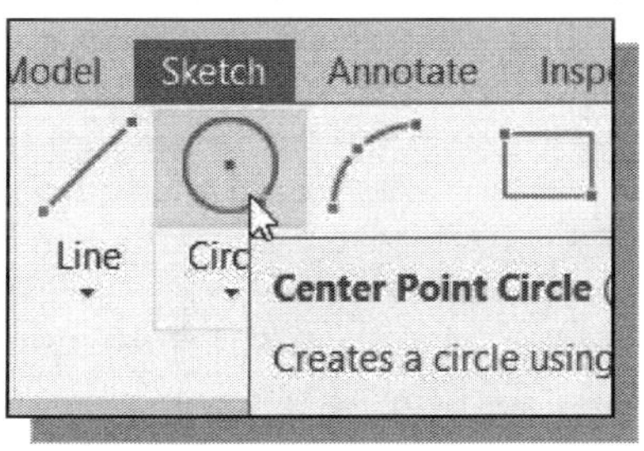

3. Select the **Center point circle** command by clicking once with the **left-mouse-button** on the icon in the *Sketch* tab on the Ribbon.

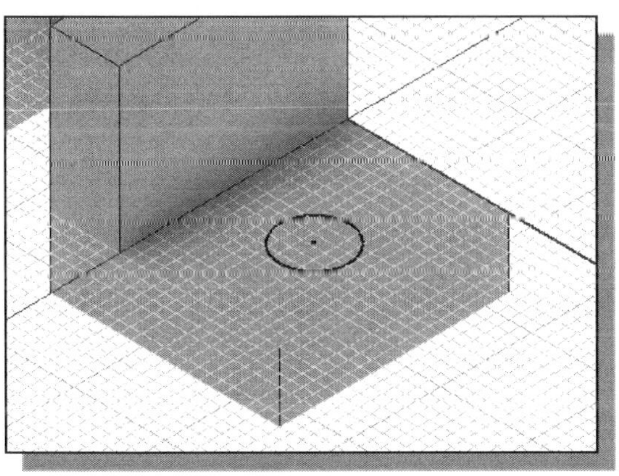

4. Create a circle of arbitrary size on the top face of the solid model as shown.

5. On your own, create and modify the dimensions of the sketch as shown in the figure.

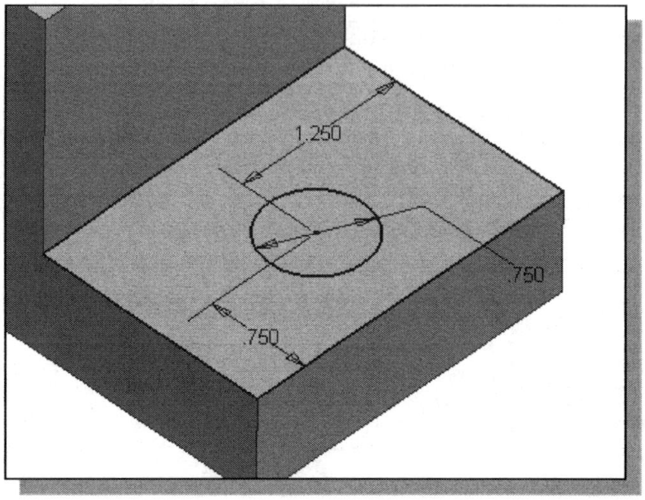

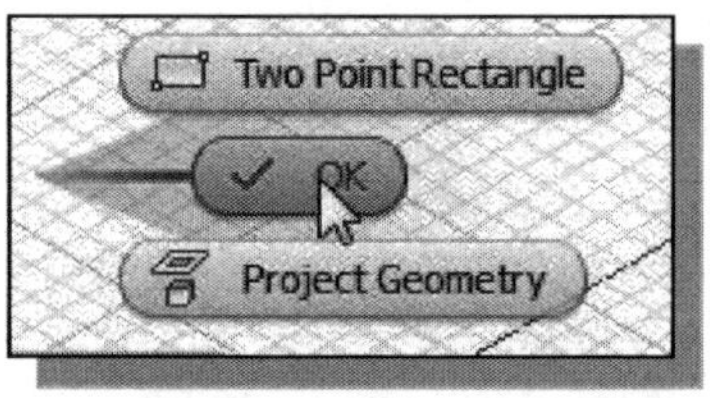

6. Inside the graphics window, click once with the **right-mouse-button** to display the option menu. Select **OK** in the pop-up menu to end the General Dimension command.

7. Inside the graphics window, click once with the **right-mouse-button** to display the option menu. Select **Finish 2D Sketch** in the pop-up menu to end the Sketch option.

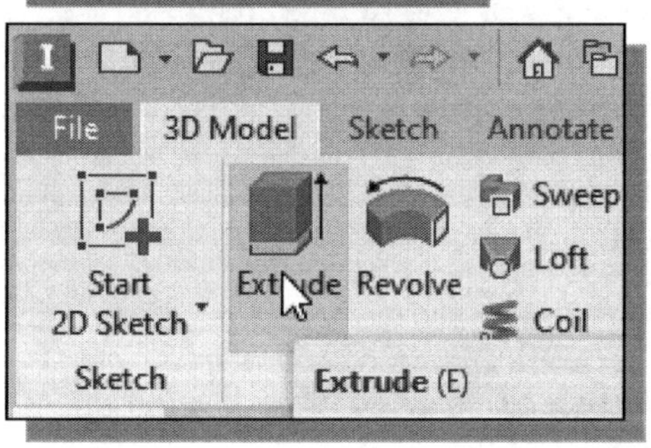

8. In the *3D Model* tab select the **Extrude** command by clicking the left-mouse-button on the icon.

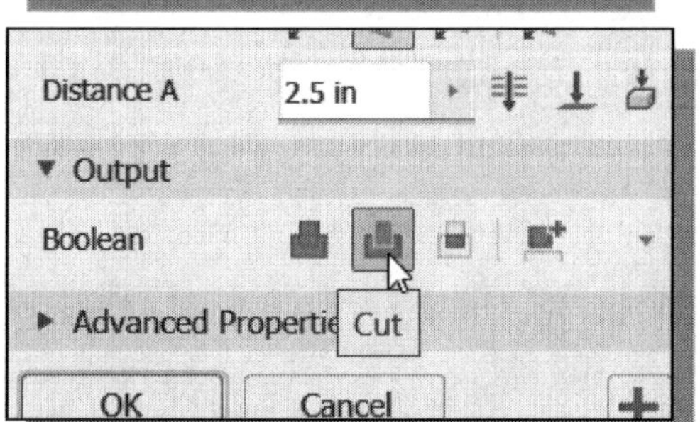

9. Select the **CUT** option in the *Output - Boolean option* list to set the extrusion operation to ***Cut***.

10. Set the *Extents* option to **Through All** as shown. The *All* option instructs the software to calculate the extrusion distance and assures the created feature will always cut through the full length of the model.

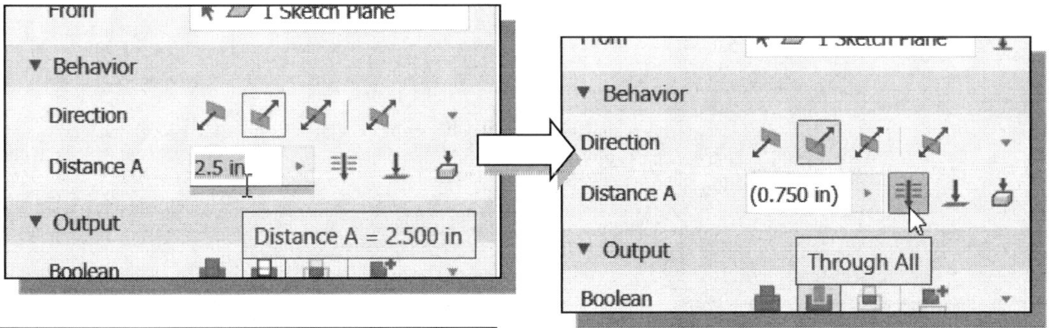

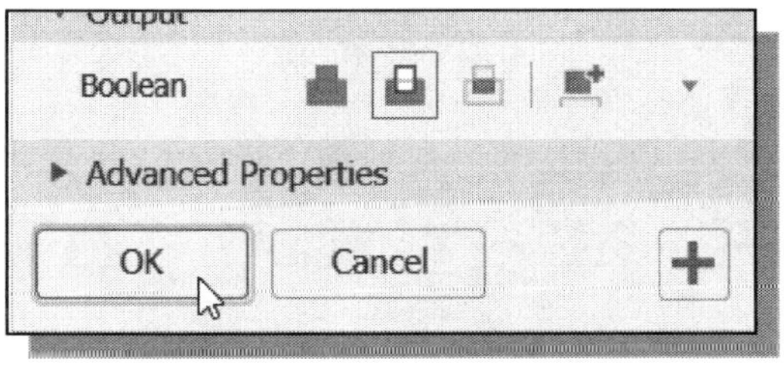

11. Click on the **OK** button to proceed with creating the extruded feature.

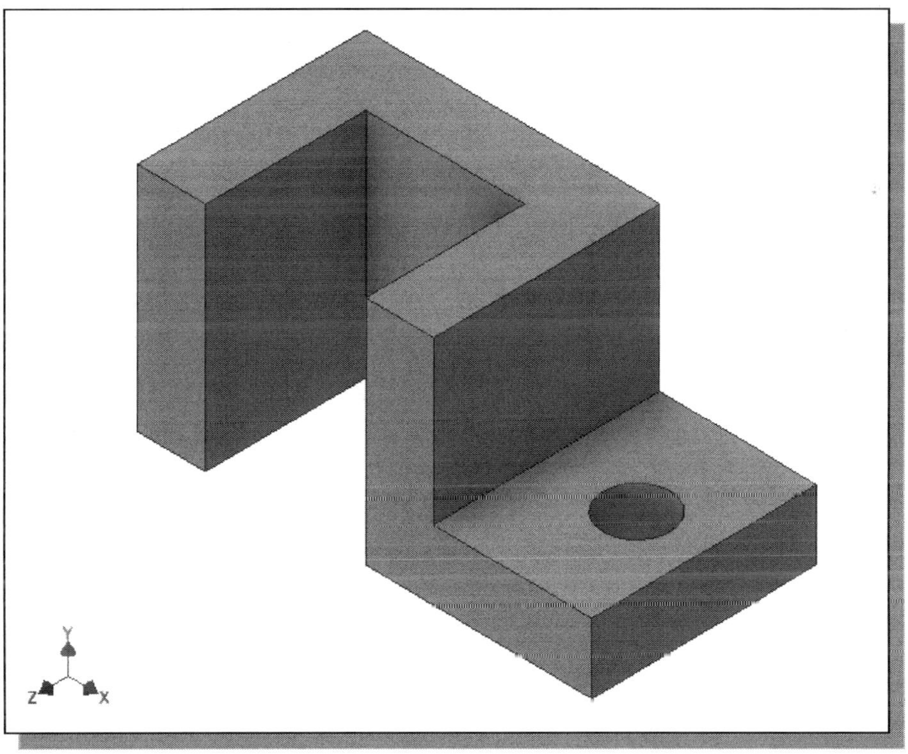

- In *Autodesk Inventor*, the **Extrude** command can be used to create solid features by either adding or subtracting extruded features.

Step 4-3: Adding another Cut Feature

Next, we will create and profile a triangle, which will be used to create a cut feature that will be added to the existing solid object.

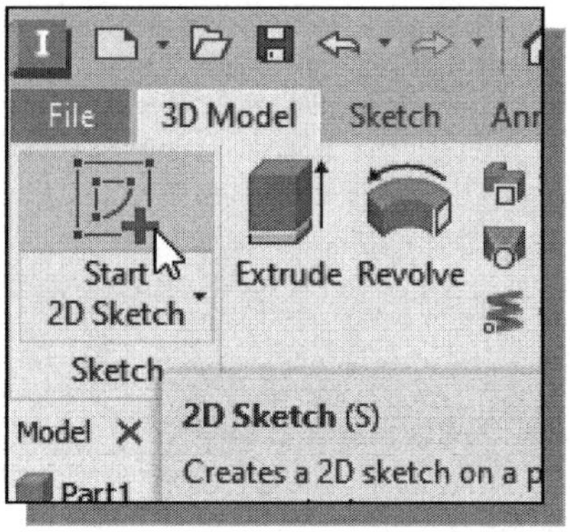

1. In the *3D Model* tab select the **Start 2D Sketch** command by left-clicking once on the icon.

2. In the *Status Bar* area, the message "*Select plane to create sketch or an existing sketch to edit.*" is displayed. Autodesk Inventor expects us to identify a planar surface where the 2D sketch of the next feature is to be created. Pick the vertical face of the 3D solid model next to the horizontal section as shown.

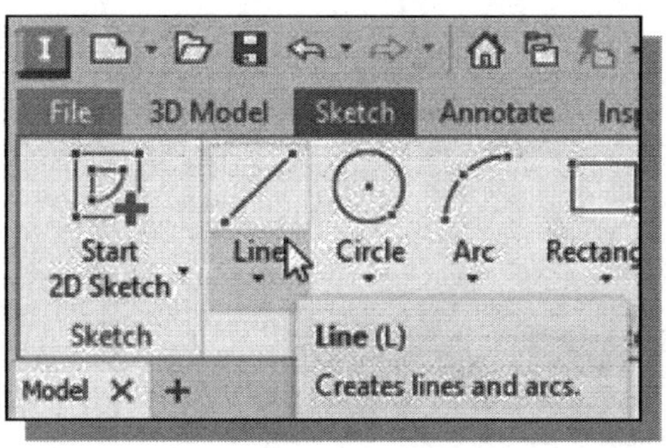

3. Select the **Line** command by clicking once with the **left-mouse-button** on the icon in the *Sketch* ribbon.

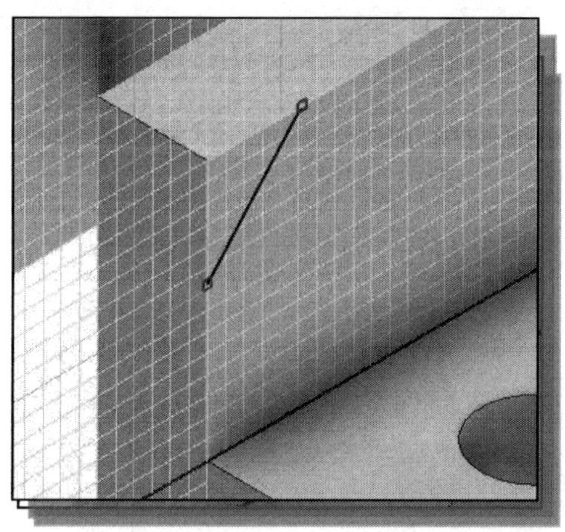

4. Create an **inclined line segment** near the upper left corner of the model as shown. (Do not align the endpoints to the midpoint of the existing edges.)

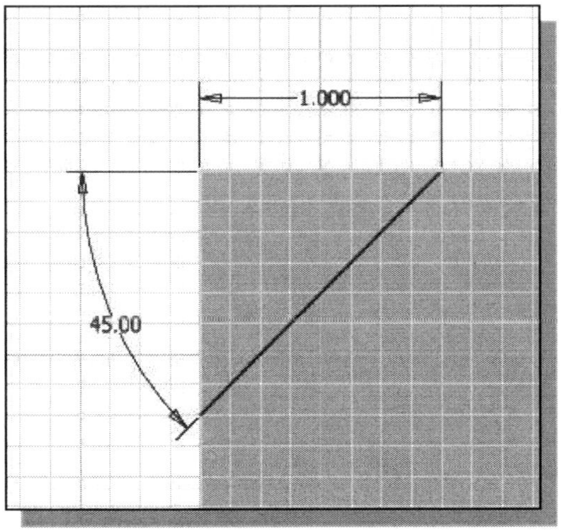

5. On your own, create and modify the two dimensions of the sketch as shown in the figure. (Hint: create the angle dimension by selecting the two adjacent lines and place the angular dimension inside the desired quadrant.)

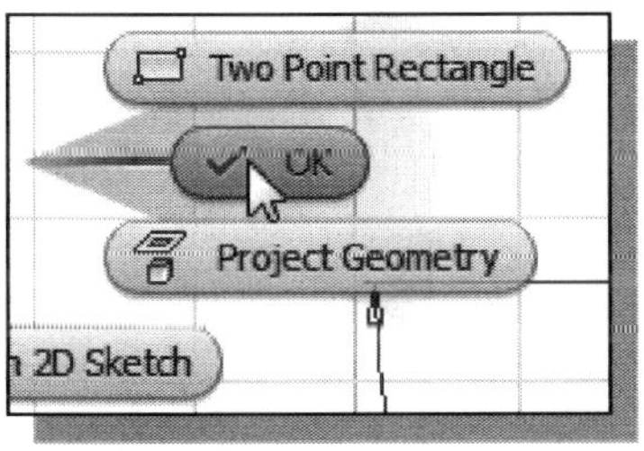

6. Inside the graphics window, click once with the **right-mouse-button** to display the option menu. Select **OK** in the pop-up menu to end the General Dimension command.

7. Select **Finish 2D Sketch** in the *Ribbon toolbar* to end the Sketch option.

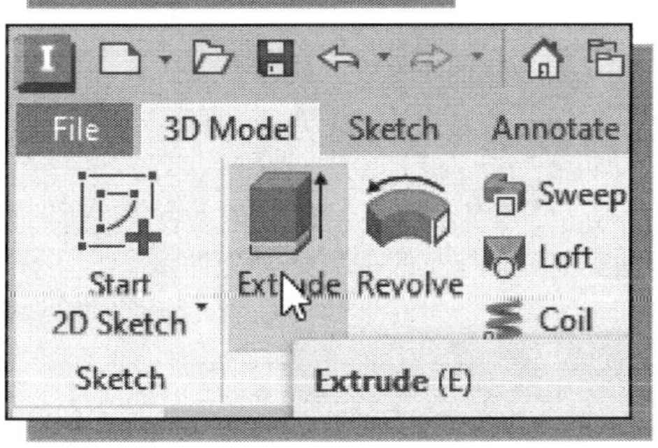

8. In the *3D Model* tab, select the **Extrude** command by left-clicking the icon.

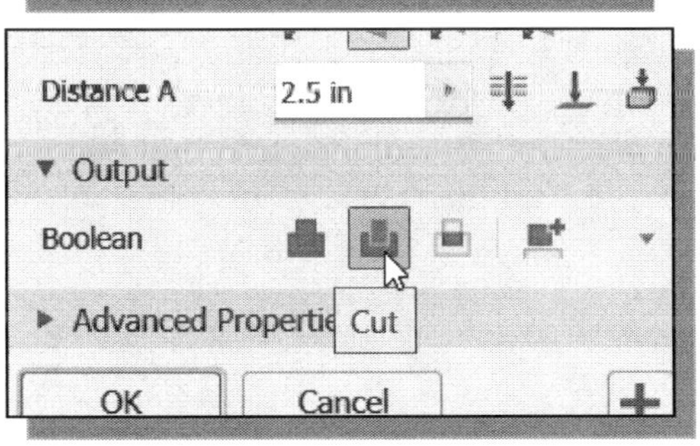

9. Select the **CUT** option in the *Boolean option* list to set the extrusion operation to ***Cut***.

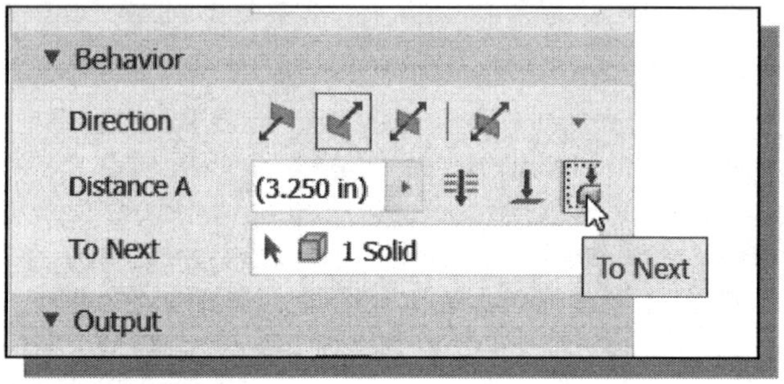

10. Set the *Extents* option to **To Next** as shown. The *To Next* option instructs the software to calculate the extrusion distance and assures the created feature will always cut through the proper length of the model.

11. Click on the **OK** button to proceed with creating the extruded feature.

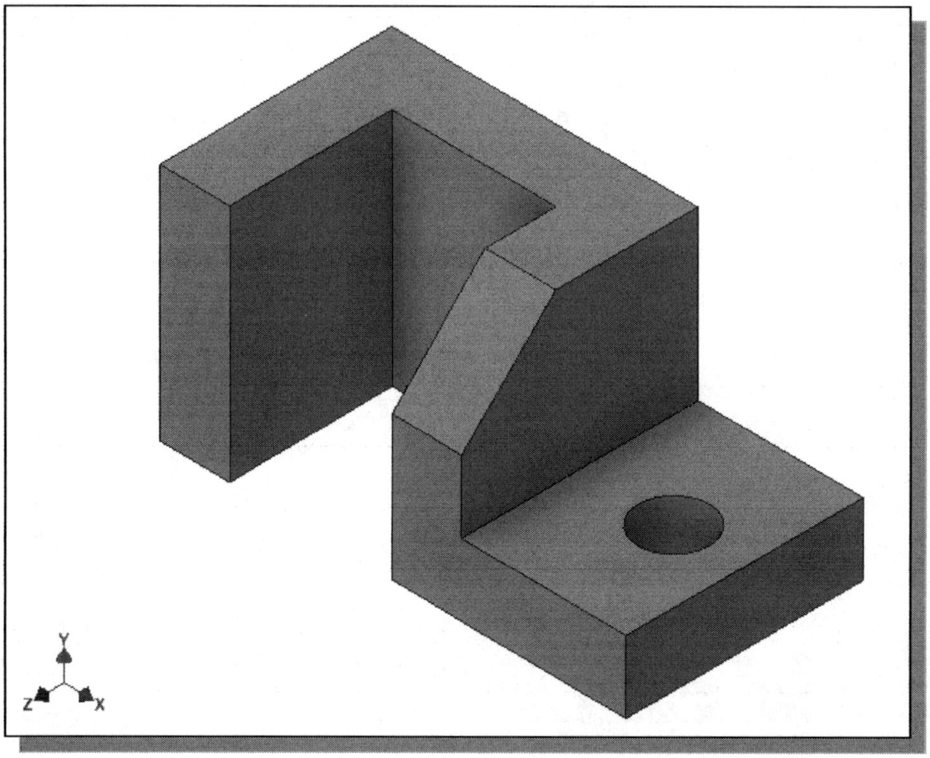

Save the Model

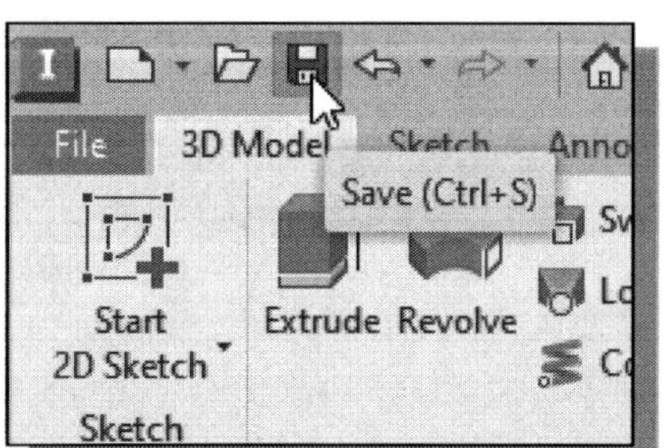

1. Select **Save** in the *Quick Access* toolbar, or you can also use the "**Ctrl-S**" combination (hold down the "Ctrl" key and hit the "S" key once) to save the part.

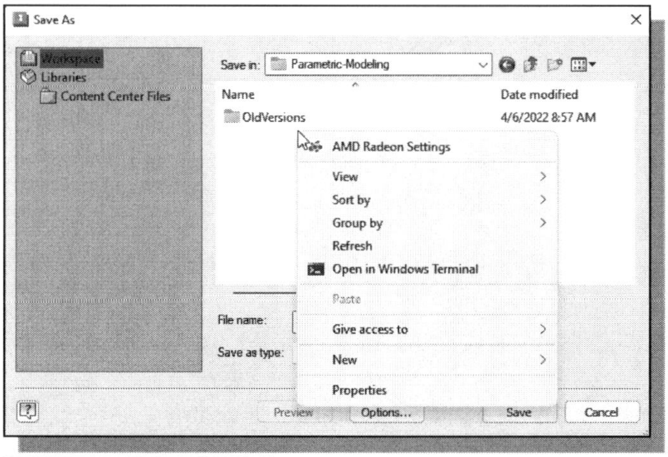

2. In the *Save As* dialog box, **right-click** once in the *list area* to bring up the *option menu.*

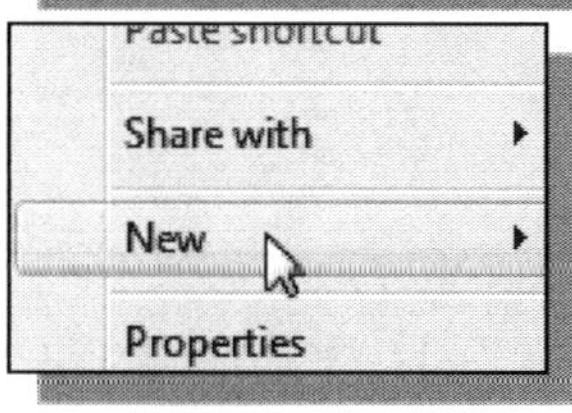

3. In the *option list*, select **New** as shown.

4. In the second *option list*, select **Folder** to create a subfolder.

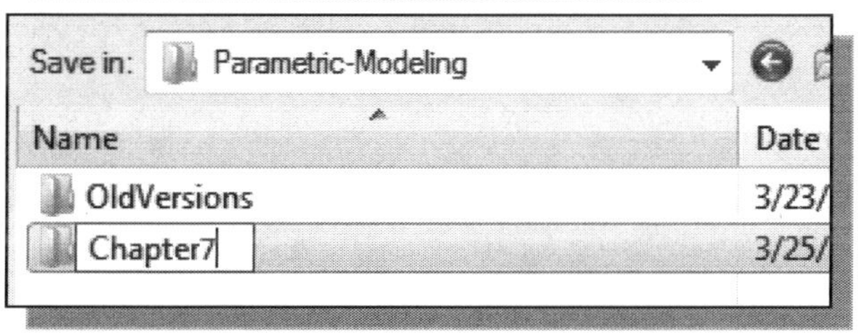

5. Enter **Chapter7** as the new folder name as shown.

6. **Double-click** on the Chapter7 folder to open it.

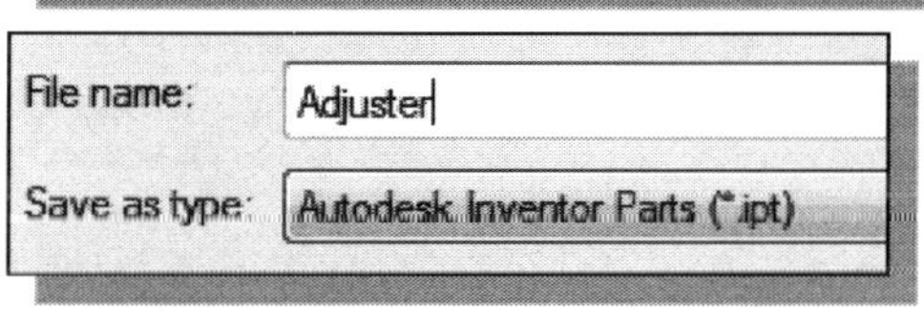

7. In the *file name* editor box, enter **Adjuster** as the file name.

8. Click on the **Save** button to save the file.

❖ You should form a habit of saving your work periodically, just in case something goes wrong while you are working on it. In general, you should save your work at an interval of every 15 to 20 minutes. You should also save before making any major modifications to the model.

Review Questions: (Time: 20 minutes)

1. What is the first thing we should set up in Autodesk Inventor when creating a new model?

2. Describe the general *parametric modeling* procedure.

3. Describe the general guidelines in creating *Rough Sketches*.

4. What is the main difference between a rough sketch and a *profile*?

5. List two of the geometric constraint symbols used by Autodesk Inventor.

6. What was the first feature we created in this lesson?

7. How many solid features were created in the tutorial?

8. How do we control the size of a feature in parametric modeling?

9. Which command was used to create the last cut feature in the tutorial? How many dimensions do we need to fully describe the cut feature?

10. List and describe three differences between parametric modeling and traditional 2D Computer Aided Drafting techniques.

Exercises: (Time: 150 minutes. All dimensions are in inches.)

1. **Inclined Support** (Thickness: **.5**)

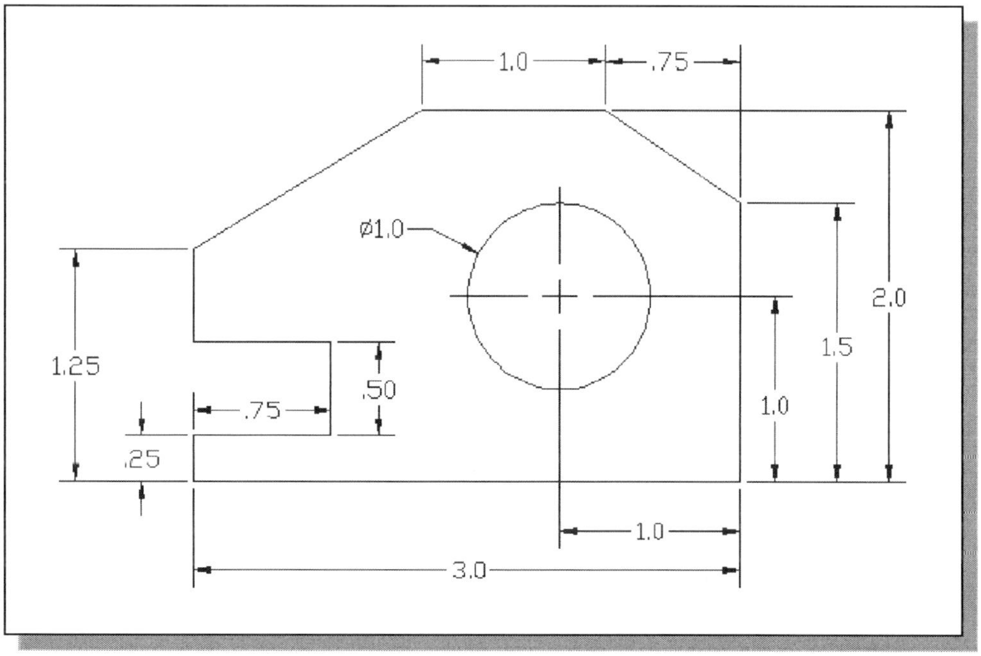

2. **Spacer Plate** (Thickness: **.125**)

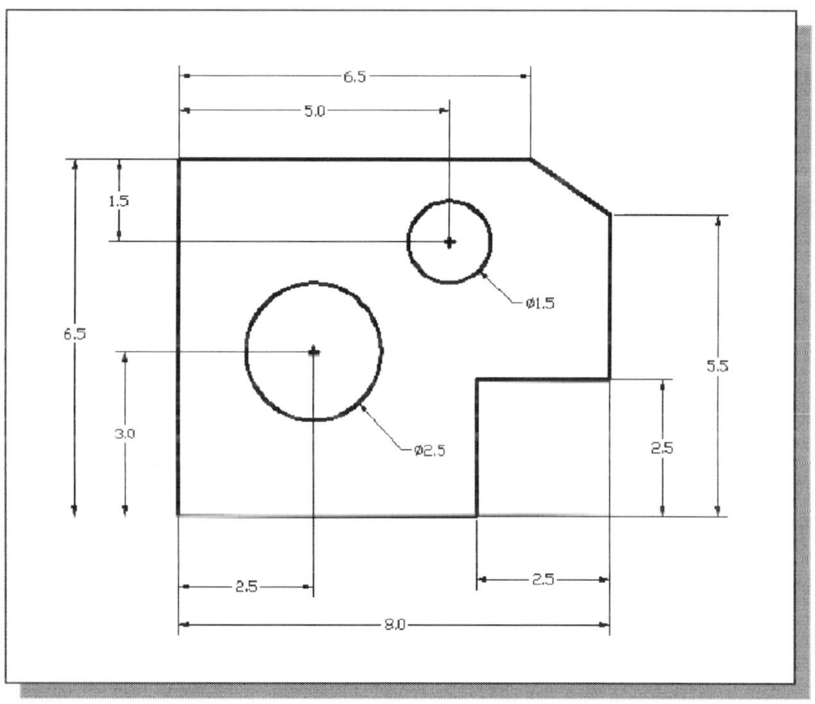

3. **Positioning Stop**

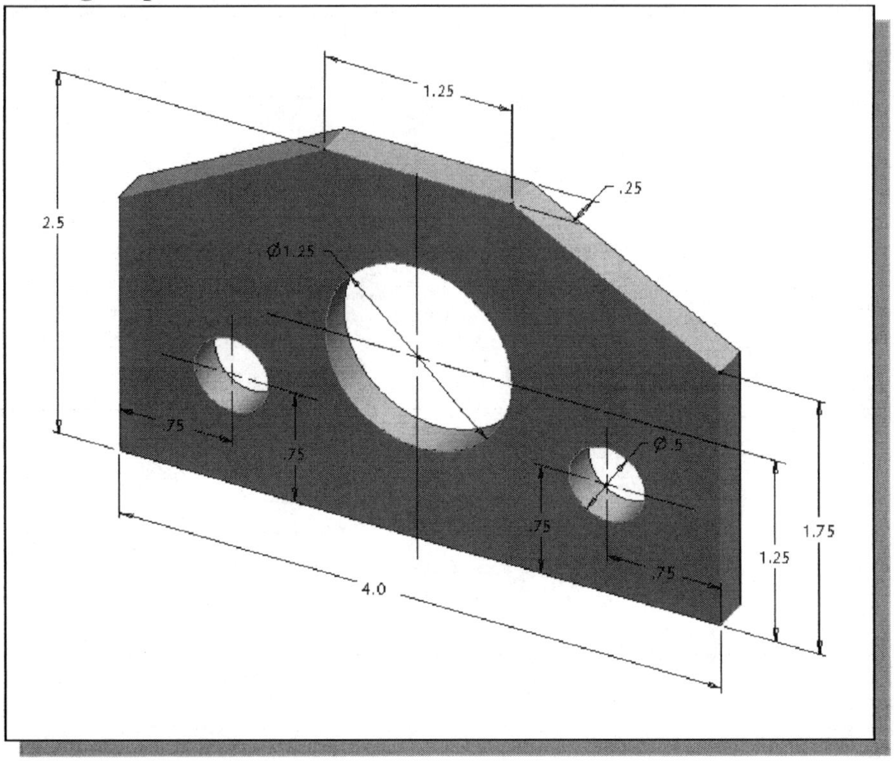

4. **Guide Block**

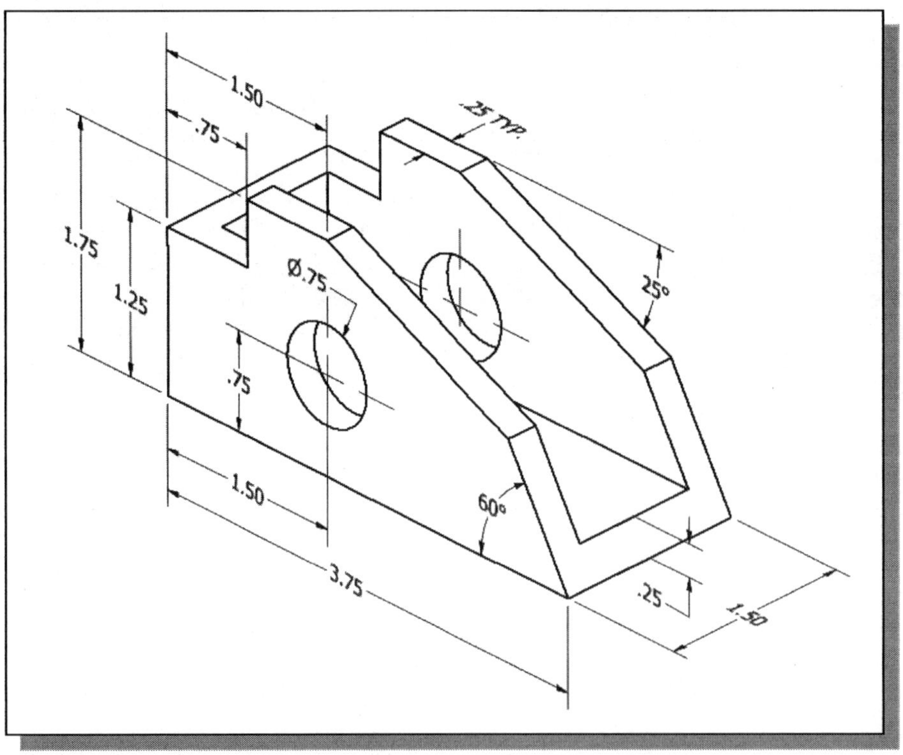

5. **Slider Block**

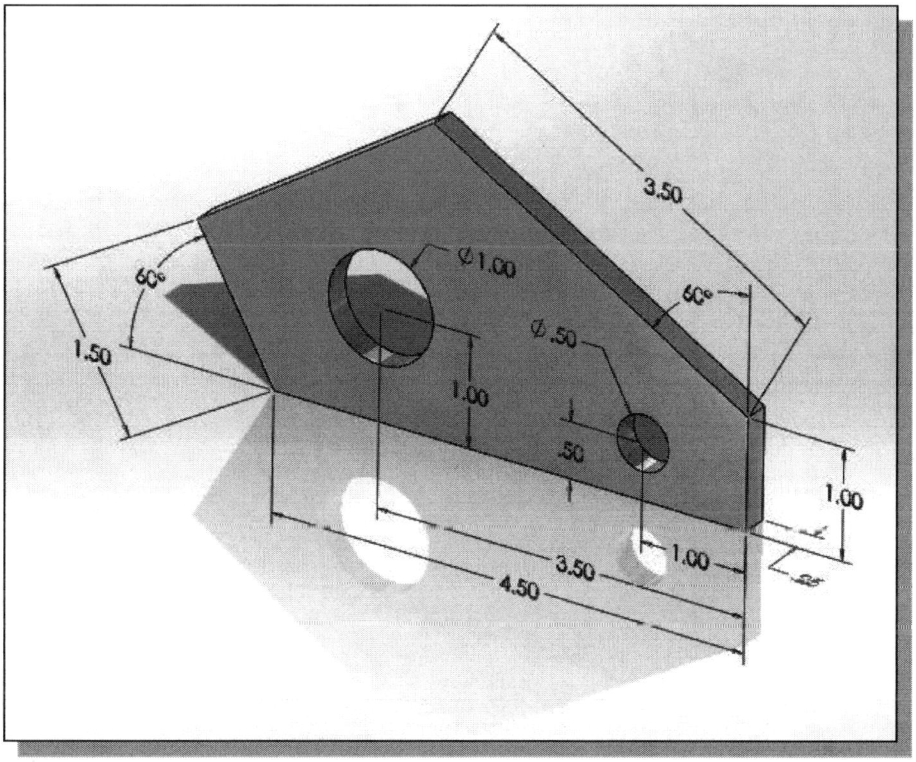

6. **Angle Lock**

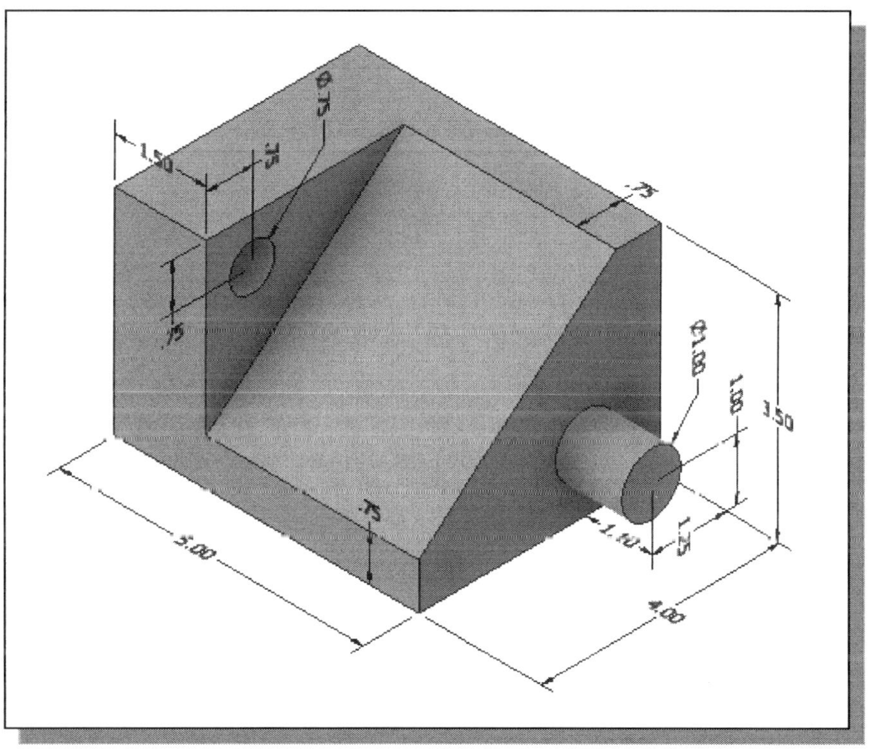

7. Coupler

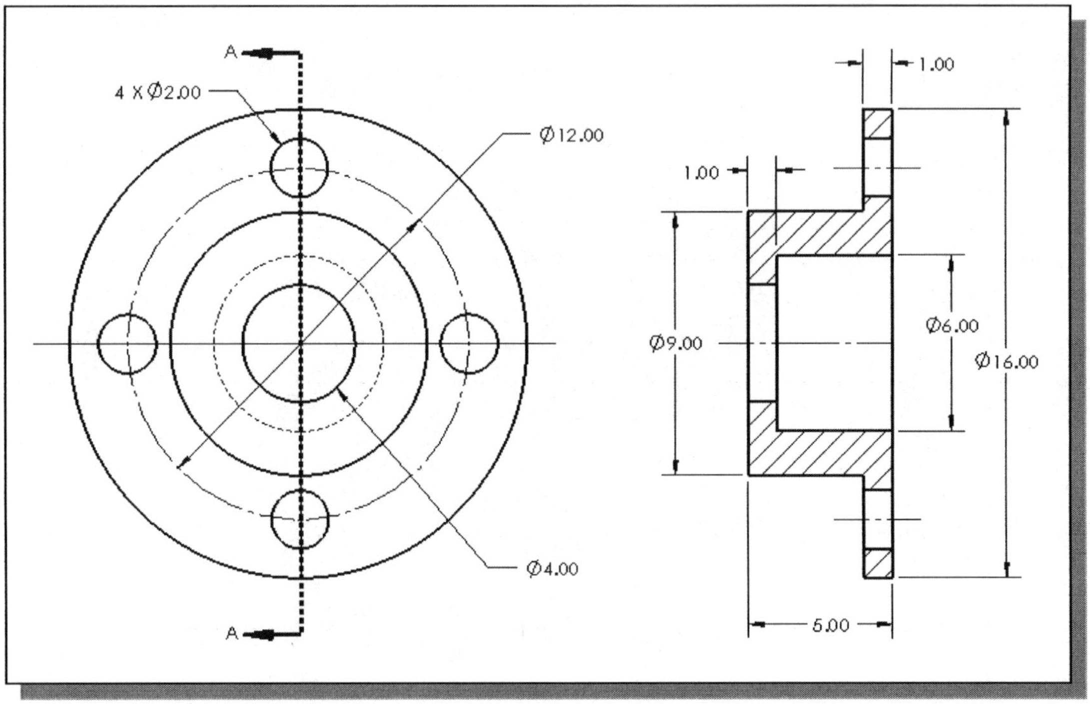

Chapter 8
Constructive Solid Geometry Concepts - Autodesk Inventor

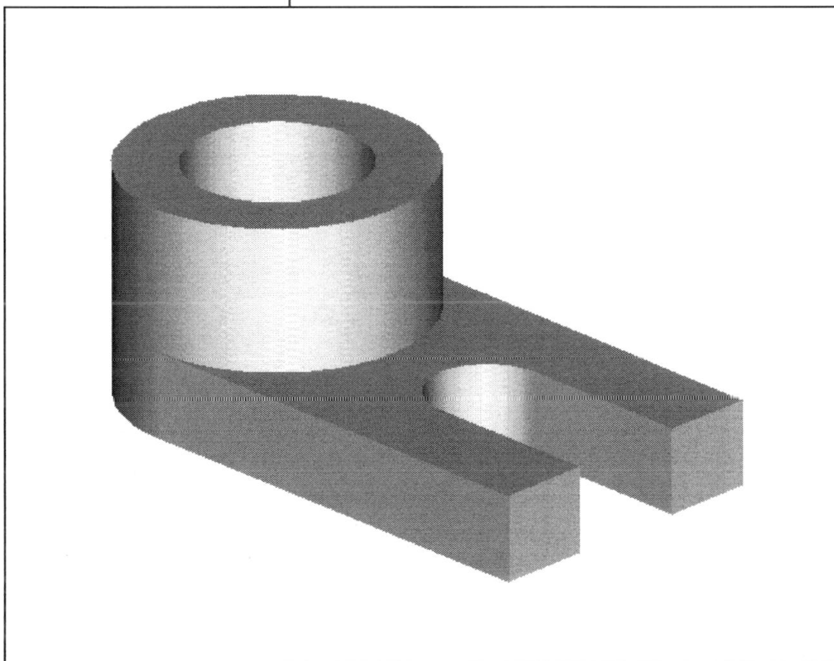

Learning Objectives

- Understand Constructive Solid Geometry Concepts
- Create a Binary Tree
- Understand the Basic Boolean Operations
- Set up Grid and Snap Intervals
- Understand the Importance of Order of Features
- Create Placed Features
- Use the Different Extrusion Options

Introduction

In the 1980s, one of the main advancements in **solid modeling** was the development of the **Constructive Solid Geometry** (CSG) method. CSG describes the solid model as combinations of basic three-dimensional shapes (**primitive solids**). The basic primitive solid set typically includes Rectangular-prism (Block), Cylinder, Cone, Sphere, and Torus (Tube). Two solid objects can be combined into one object in various ways using operations known as **Boolean operations**. There are three basic Boolean operations: **JOIN (Union)**, **CUT (Difference)**, and **INTERSECT**. The *JOIN* operation combines the two volumes included in the different solids into a single solid. The *CUT* operation subtracts the volume of one solid object from the other solid object. The *INTERSECT* operation keeps only the volume common to both solid objects. The CSG method is also known as the **Machinist's Approach**, as the method is parallel to machine shop practices.

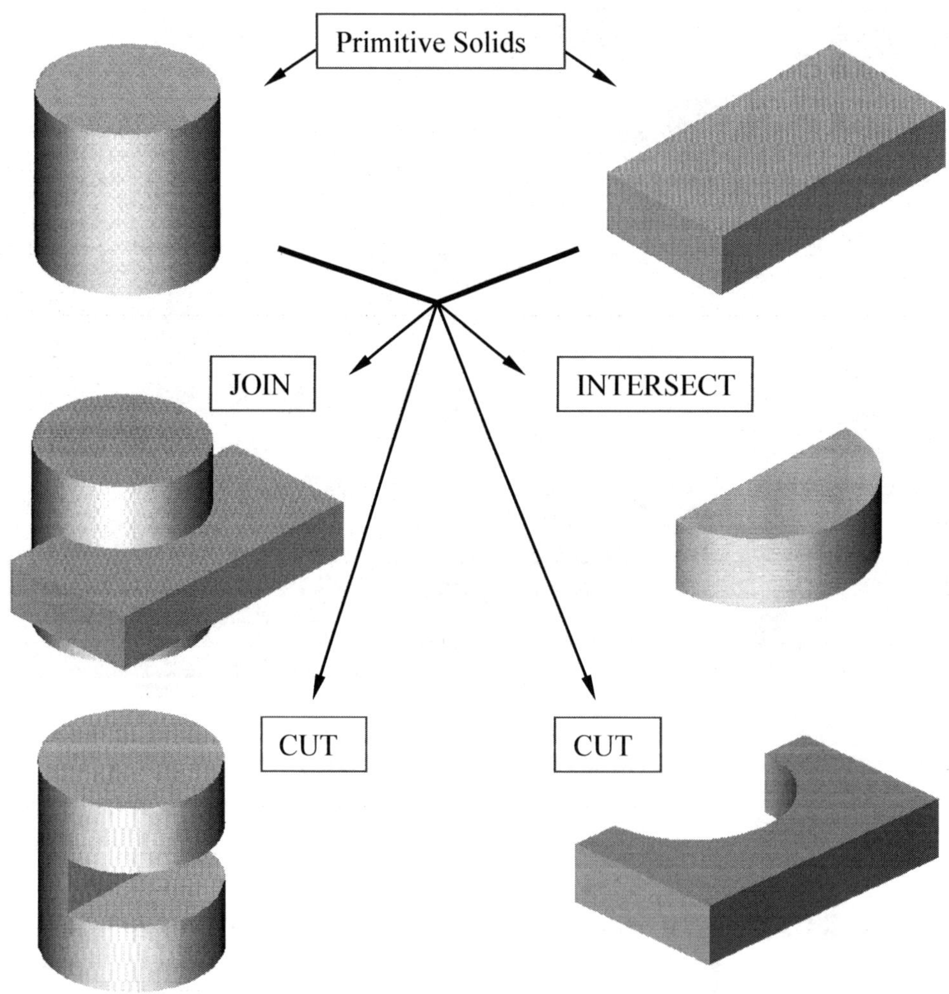

Binary Tree

The CSG is also referred to as the method used to store a solid model in the database. The resulting solid can be easily represented by what is called a **binary tree**. In a binary tree, the terminal branches (leaves) are the various primitives that are linked together to make the final solid object (the root). The binary tree is an effective way to keep track of the *history* of the resulting solid. By keeping track of the history, the solid model can be re-built by re-linking through the binary tree. This provides a convenient way to modify the model. We can make modifications at the appropriate links in the binary tree and re-link the rest of the history tree without building a new model.

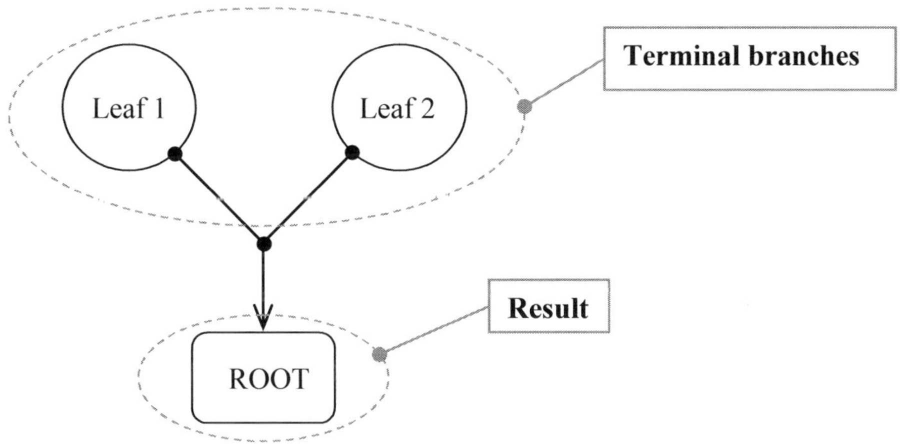

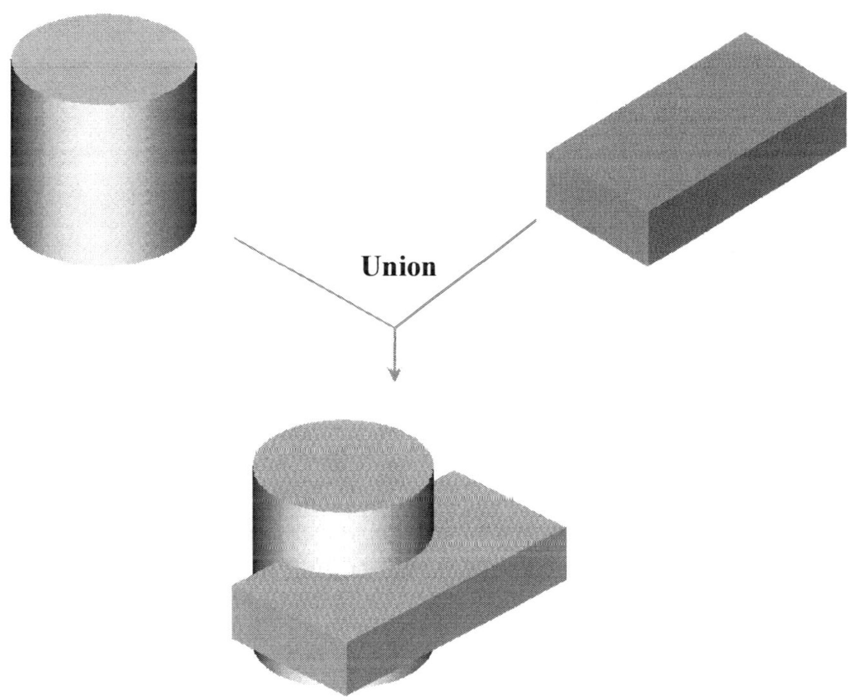

The Locator Design

The CSG concept is one of the important building blocks for feature-based modeling. In Autodesk Inventor, the CSG concept can be used as a planning tool to determine the number of features that are needed to construct the model. It is also good practice to create features that are parallel to the manufacturing process required for the design. With parametric modeling, we are no longer limited to using only the predefined basic solid shapes. In fact, any solid features we create in Autodesk Inventor are used as primitive solids; parametric modeling allows us to maintain full control of the design variables that are used to describe the features. In this lesson, a more in-depth look at the parametric modeling procedure is presented. The equivalent CSG operation for each feature is also illustrated.

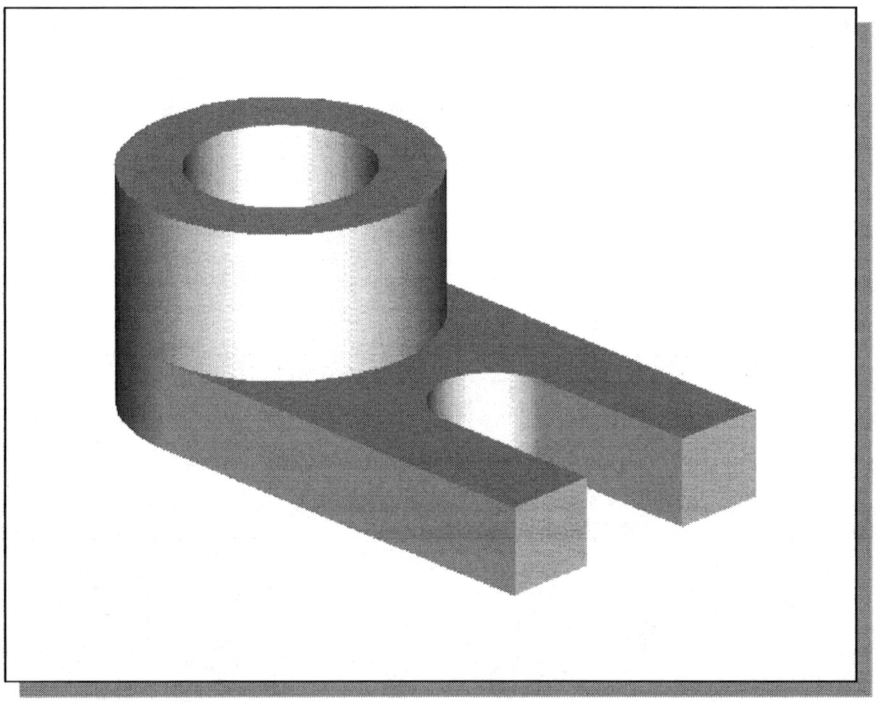

- Before going through the tutorial, on your own make a sketch of a CSG binary tree of the ***Locator*** design using only two basic types of primitive solids: cylinder and rectangular prism. In your sketch, how many *Boolean operations* will be required to create the model? What is your choice of the first primitive solid to use, and why? Take a few minutes to consider these questions and do the preliminary planning by sketching on a piece of paper. Compare the sketch you make to the CSG binary tree steps shown on the next page. Note that there are many different possibilities in combining the basic primitive solids to form the solid model. Even for the simplest design, it is possible to take several different approaches to creating the same solid model.

Modeling Strategy – CSG Binary Tree

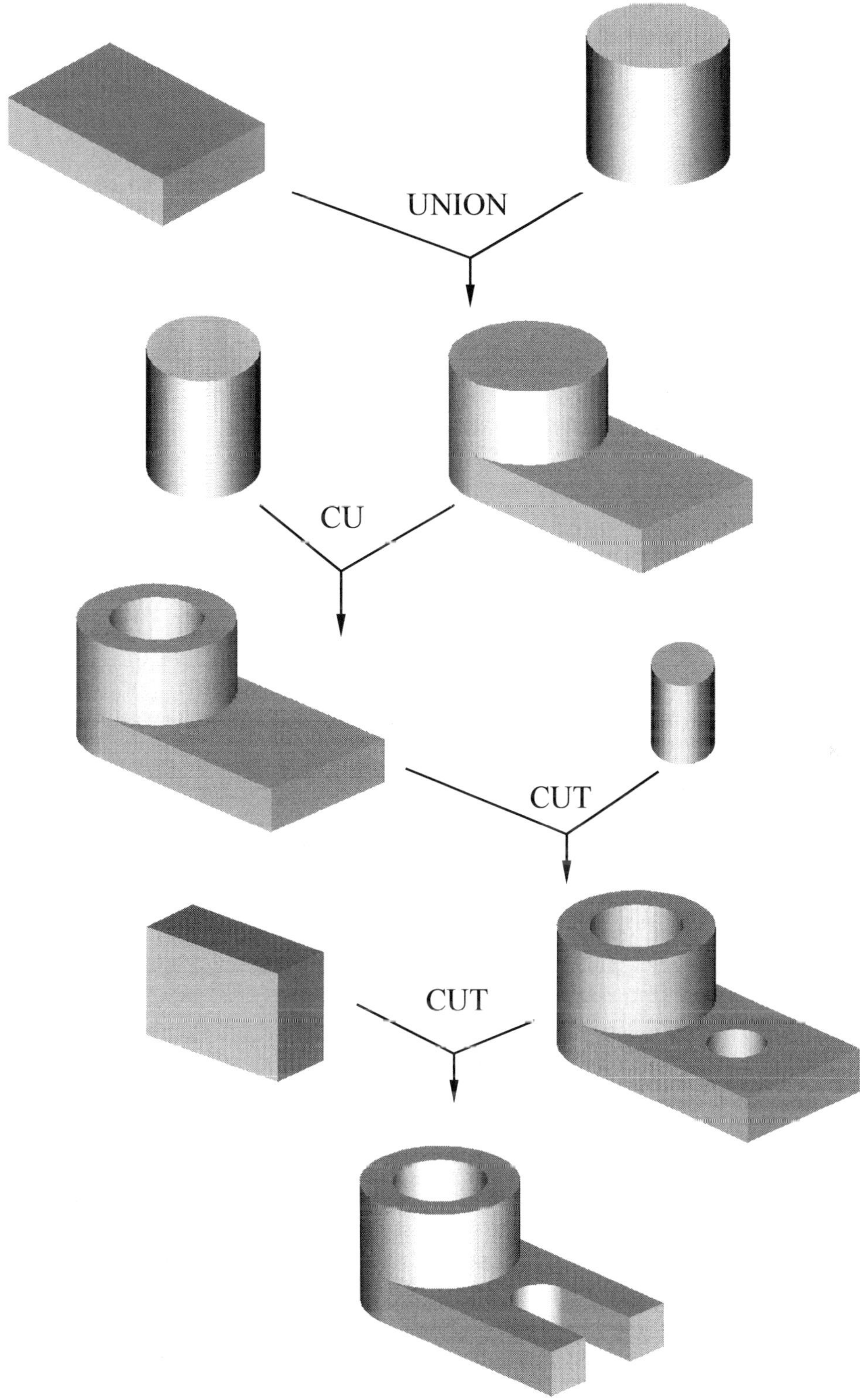

Starting Autodesk Inventor

1. Select the **Autodesk Inventor** option on the *Start* menu or select the **Autodesk Inventor** icon on the desktop to start Autodesk Inventor. The Autodesk Inventor main window will appear on the screen.

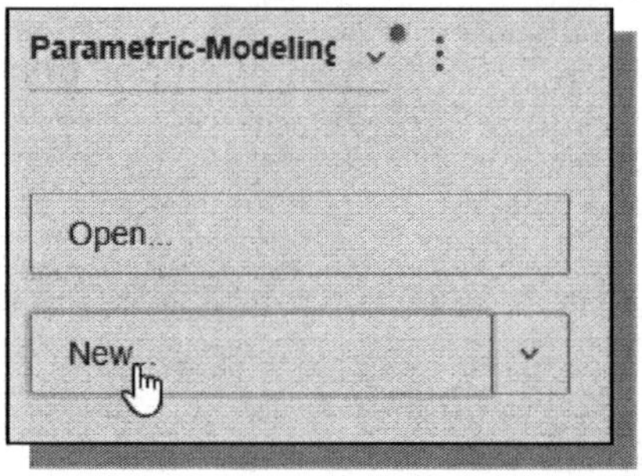

2. Select the **New File** icon with a single click of the left-mouse-button as shown.

❖ Every object we construct in a CAD system is measured in units. We should determine the value of the units within the CAD system before creating the first geometric entities. For example, in one model, a unit might equal one millimeter of the real-world object; in another model, a unit might equal an inch. In Autodesk Inventor, the ***Choose Template*** option is used to control how Autodesk Inventor interprets the coordinate and angle entries.

3. Select the **Metric** tab as shown below. We will use the millimeter (mm) setting for this example.

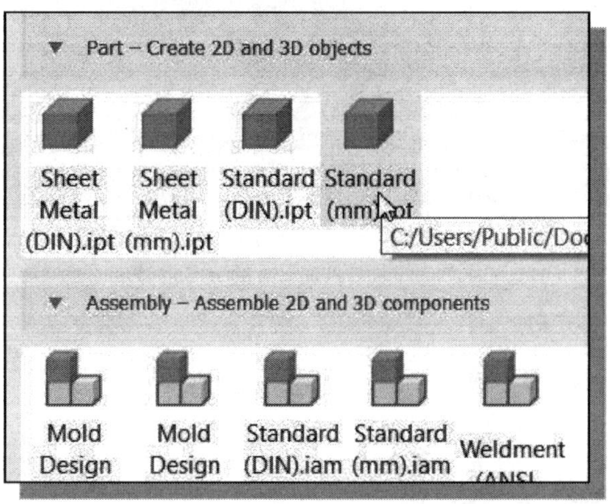

4. In the *New File – Part Template* area, select the **Standard(mm).ipt** icon as shown.

5. Confirm the ***Parametric-Modeling*** project is activated; note the **Projects** button is available to view/modify the active project.

6. Pick **Create** in the *Startup* dialog box to accept the selected settings.

Base Feature

In *parametric modeling*, the first solid feature is called the **base feature**, which usually is the primary shape of the model. Depending upon the design intent, additional features are added to the base feature.

Some of the considerations involved in selecting the base feature are:

- **Design intent** – Determine the functionality of the design; identify the feature that is central to the design.

- **Order of features** – Choose the feature that is the logical base in terms of the order of features in the design. Consider creating the design using as few features as possible.

- **Ease of making modifications** – Select a base feature that is more stable and is less likely to be changed.

1. Activate the **Start 2D Sketch** icon with a single click of the left-mouse-button.

2. Move the cursor over the edge of the *XZ Plane* in the graphics area. When the *XZ Plane* is highlighted, click once with the **left-mouse-button** to select the *Plane* as the sketch plane for the new sketch.

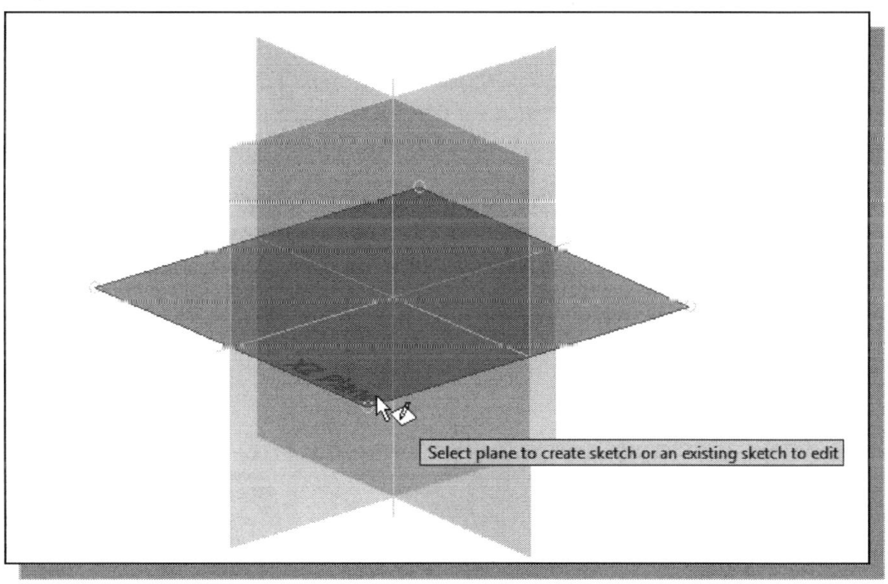

GRID Display Setup

1. In the *Ribbon* toolbar panel, select **[Tools] → [Document Settings]**.

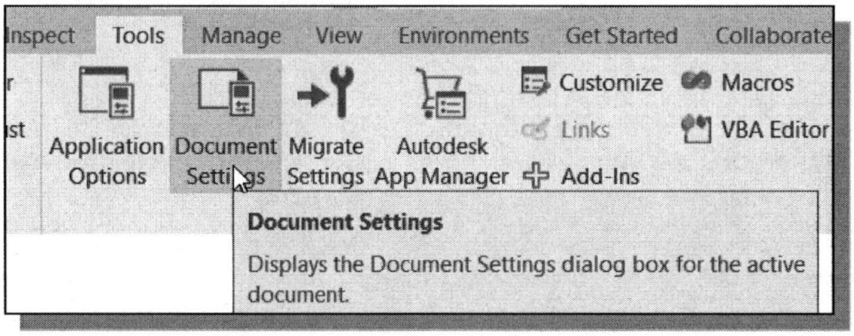

2. In the *Document Settings* dialog box, click on the **Sketch** tab as shown in the below figure.

3. Set the *X* and *Y Snap Spacing* to **5 mm**.

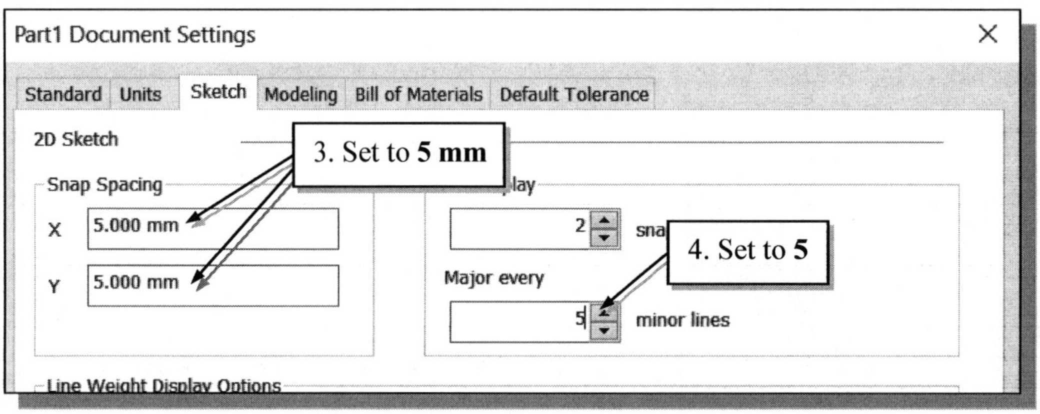

4. Change *Grid Display* to display one *major line* every **5** *minor lines.*

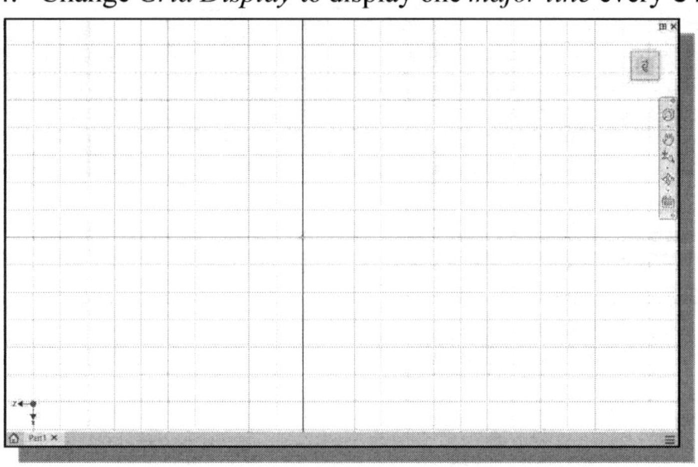

5. Pick **OK** to exit the *Sketch Settings* dialog box.

➢ Note that although the **Snap to grid** option is also available, its usage in parametric modeling is not recommended.

➢ On your own, use the dynamic **Zoom** function to view the grid setup. Refer to Page 7-38 on how to switch on the *grid lines display* options if necessary.

➢ A rectangular block will be first created as the base feature of the ***Locator*** design.

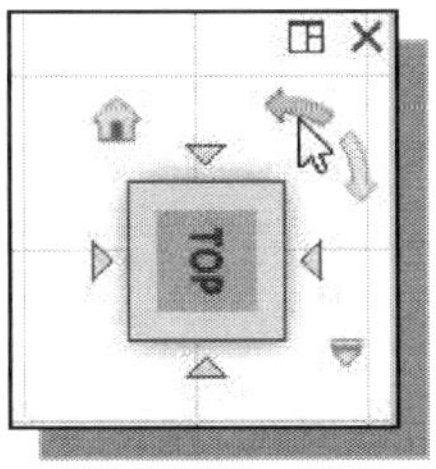

6. Click on the **rotate-left arrow** on the view cube to rotate the display.

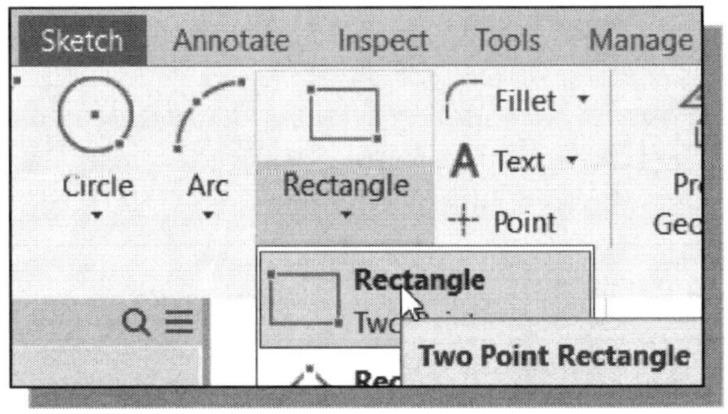

7. Switch back to the *Sketch* tab and select the **Two point rectangle** command by clicking once with the **left-mouse-button**.

8. Create a rectangle of arbitrary size by selecting two locations on the screen as shown below.

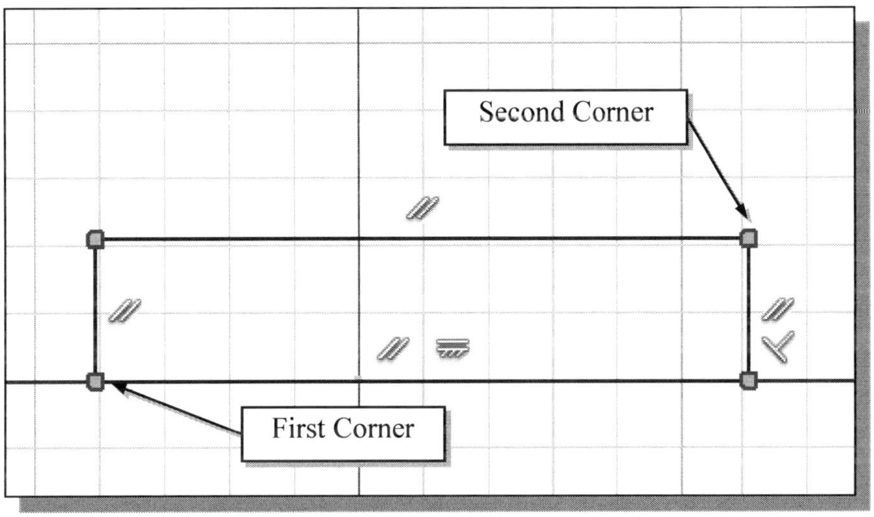

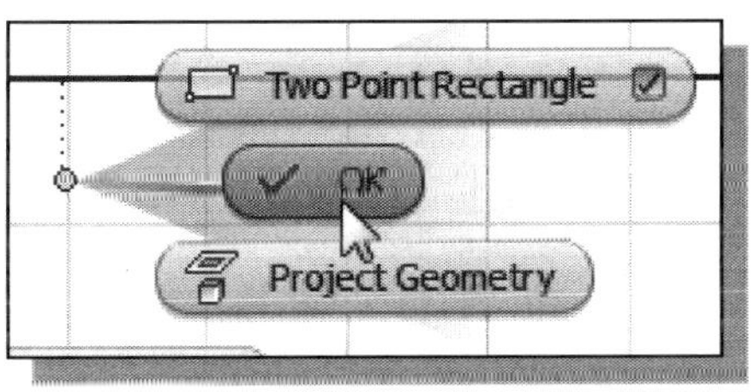

9. Inside the graphics window, click once with the **right-mouse-button** to bring up the option menu.

10. Select **OK** to end the Rectangle command.

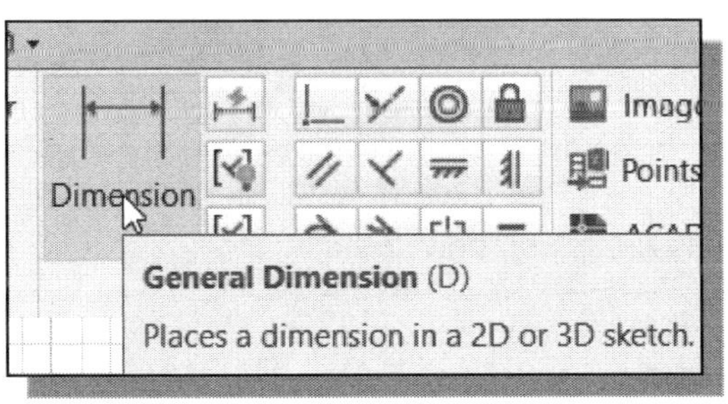

11. Activate the **General Dimension** command by clicking once with the left-mouse-button. The General Dimension command allows us to quickly create and modify dimensions.

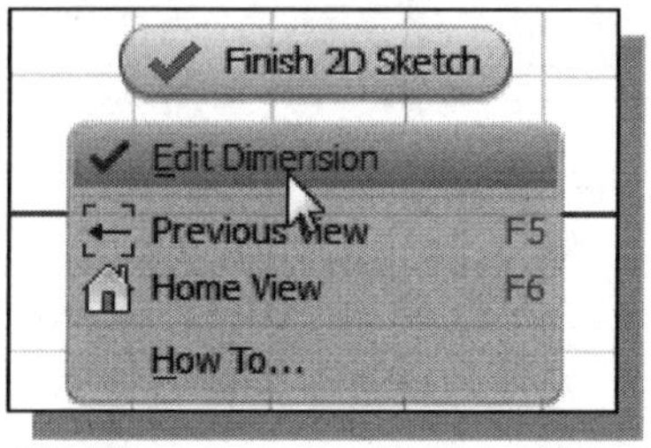

12. Inside the graphics window, click once with the right-mouse-button to bring up the option menu and click **Edit Dimension** to turn **OFF** the editing option while creating dimensions.

13. The message "*Select Geometry to Dimension*" is displayed in the *Status Bar* area at the bottom of the Autodesk Inventor window. Select the bottom horizontal line by left-clicking once on the line.

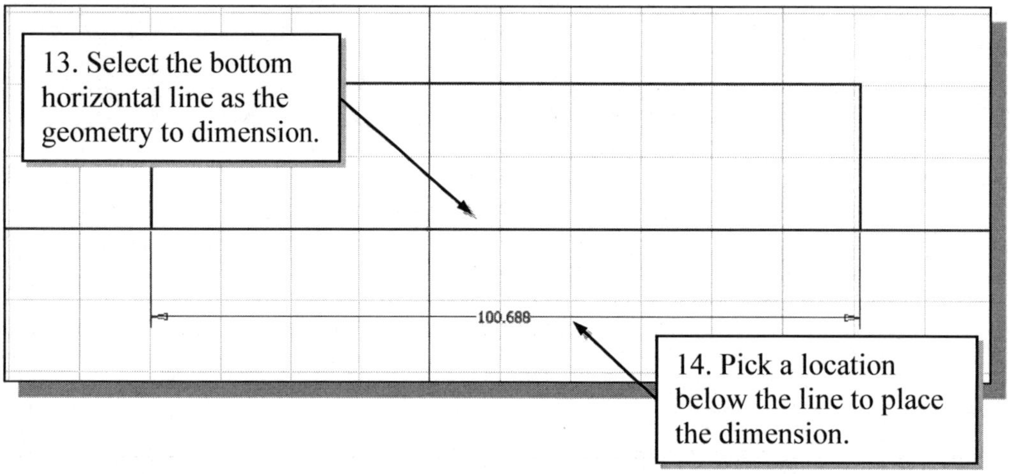

14. Move the graphics cursor below the selected line and left-click to place the dimension. (Note that the value displayed on your screen might be different than what is shown in the above figure.)

15. On your own, create a vertical size dimension of the sketched rectangle as shown.

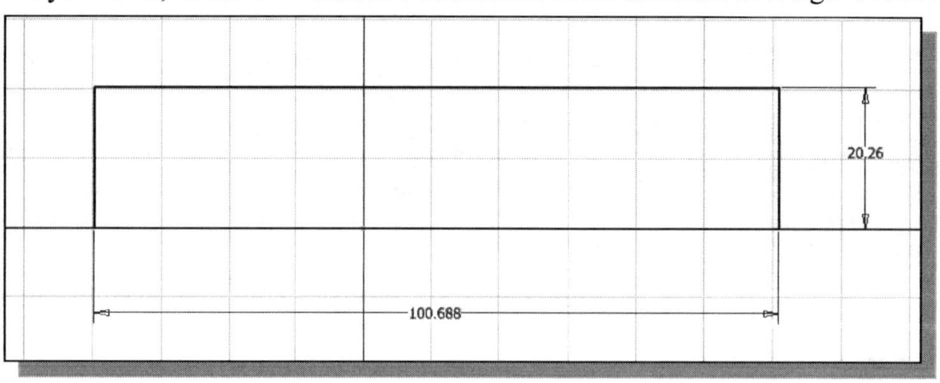

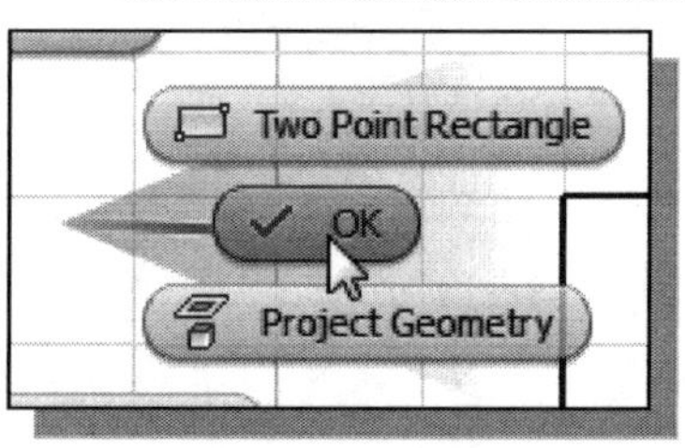

16. Inside the graphics window, click once with the right-mouse-button to bring up the option menu and click **OK** to end the *Dimension* command.

Model Dimensions Format

1. In the *Ribbon* tabs, select
   [Tools] → [Document Settings].

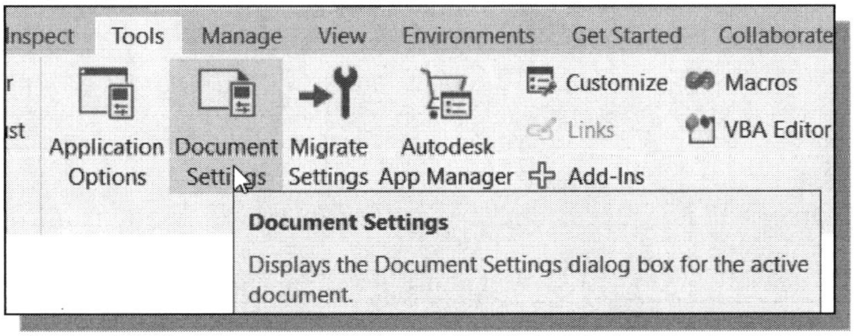

2. In the *Document Settings* dialog box, set the *Modeling Dimension Display* to **Display as value** as shown in the figure.

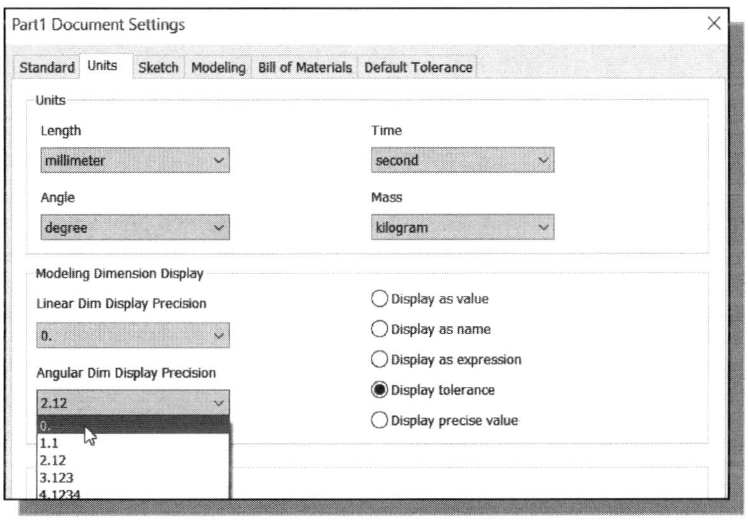

3. Also set the precision to ***no digits*** after the decimal point for both the *linear dimension* and *angular dimension* displays as shown in the above figure.

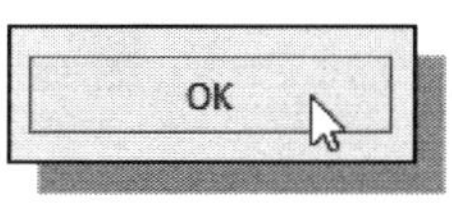

4. Pick **OK** to exit the *Document Settings* dialog box.

Modifying the Dimensions of the Sketch

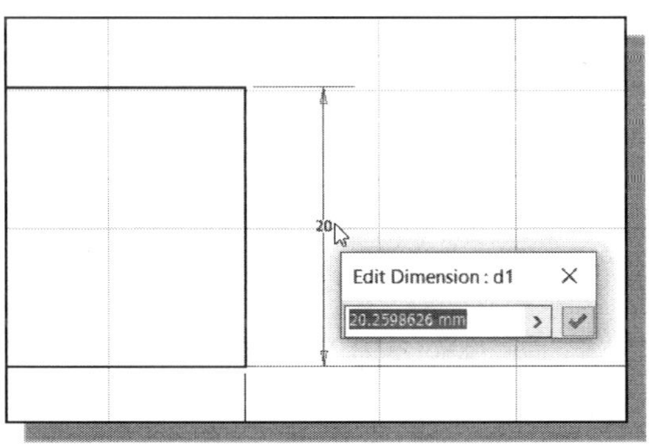

1. Select the height dimension that is to the right side of the sketch by ***double-clicking*** with the left-mouse-button on the dimension text.

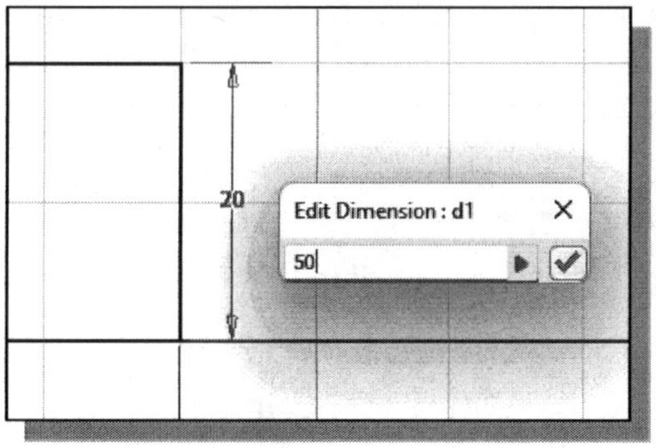

2. In the *Edit Dimension* window, the current length of the line is displayed. Enter **50** to set the selected length of the sketch to 50 millimeters.

3. Click on the **Accept** icon to accept the entered value.

➢ Autodesk Inventor will now update the profile with the new dimension value.

4. On your own, repeat the above steps and adjust the dimensions so that the sketch appears as shown below. Also **exit** the Dimension command.

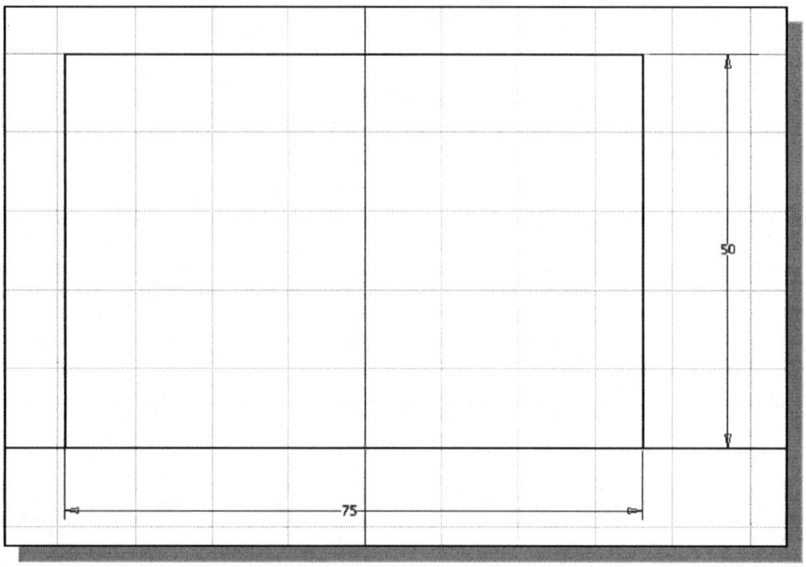

Repositioning Dimensions

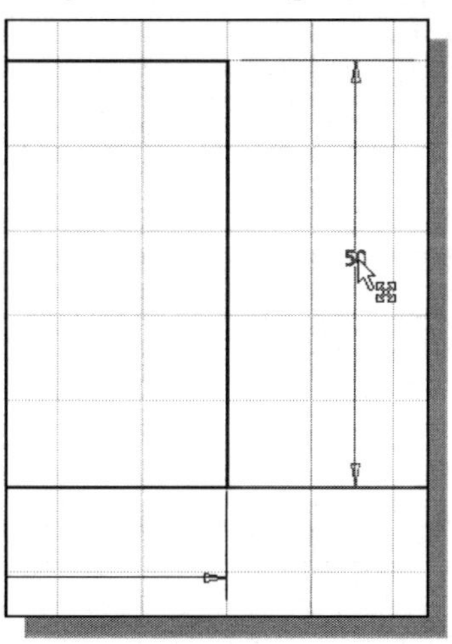

1. Move the cursor near the vertical dimension; note that the dimension is highlighted. Move the cursor slowly until a small arrows marker appears next to the cursor, as shown in the figure.

2. Drag with the **left-mouse-button** to reposition the selected dimension.

3. Repeat the above steps to reposition the horizontal dimension.

Using the Measure Tools

Autodesk Inventor also provides several measuring tools that allow us to measure area, perimeter and additional information of the constructed 2D sketches.

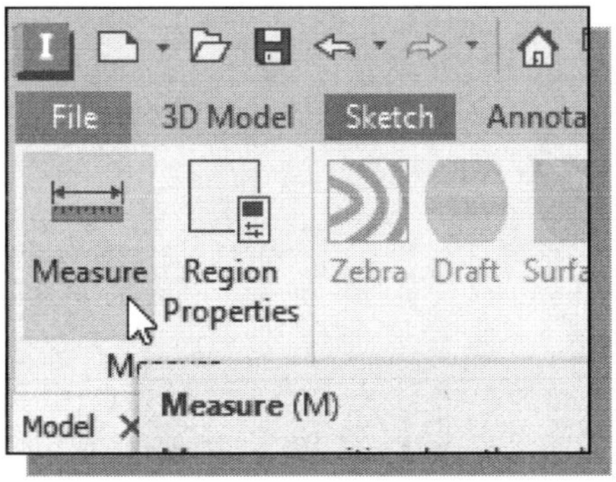

1. In the ***Inspect*** *Ribbon tab*, left-click once on the **Measure** option as shown.

- Note that **other** measurement options are also available in the toolbar.

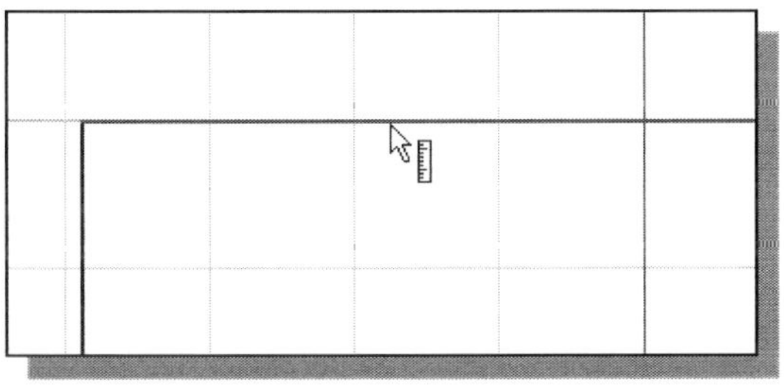

2. Click on the top edge of the rectangle as shown.

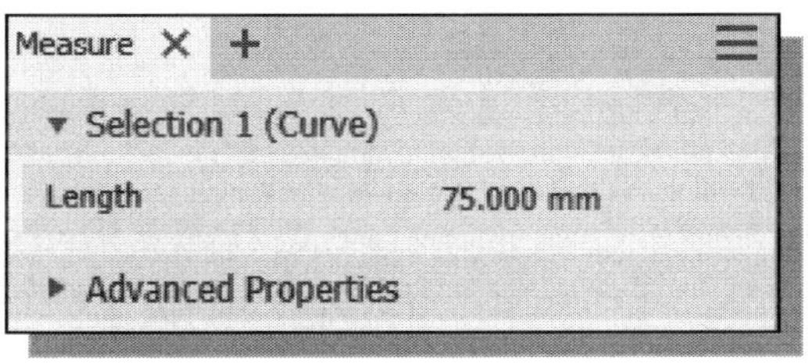

3. The associated length measurement of the selected geometry is displayed in the *Length* dialog box as shown.

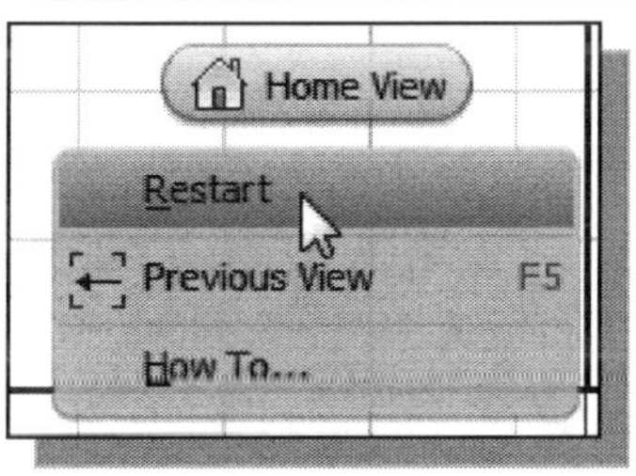

4. Inside the *graphics window*, right-click once to bring up the **Option menu** and select **Restart** as shown.

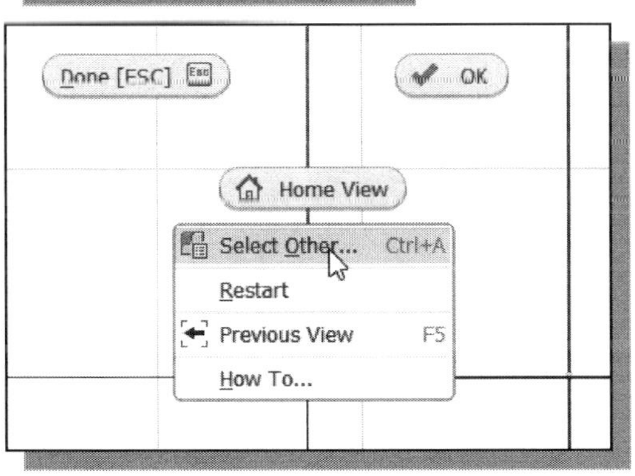

5. Move the cursor on top of any of the edges and click once with the right-mouse-button to bring up the **Option menu** and choose **Select Other...** as shown.

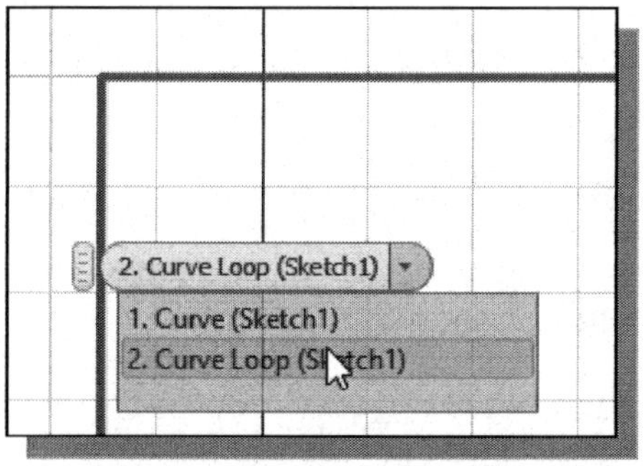

6. In the *Selection list*, left-click once to pick the **Curve Loop** option as shown.

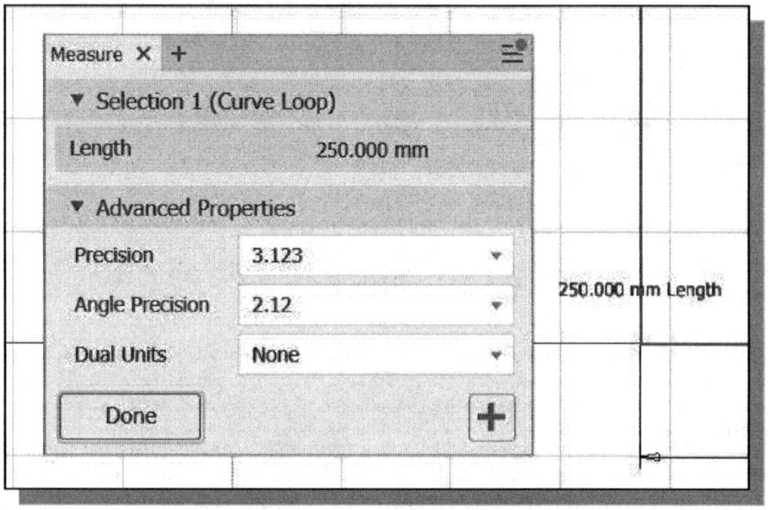

- The *perimeter* of the rectangle is displayed as shown.

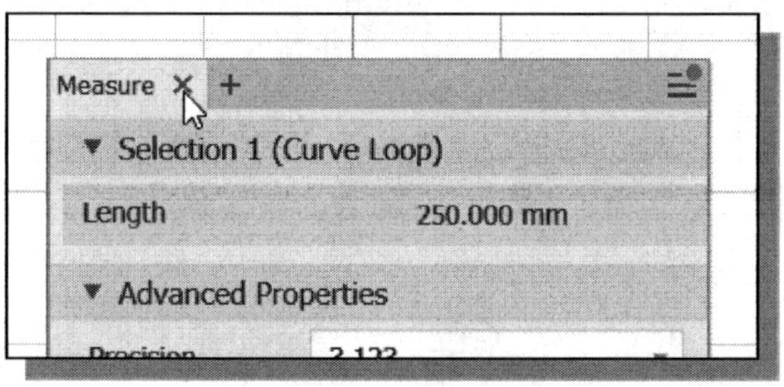

7. Click on the [**X**] icon to end the Measure command as shown.

8. In the *Inspect Ribbon tab*, left-click once on the **Region Properties** option as shown.

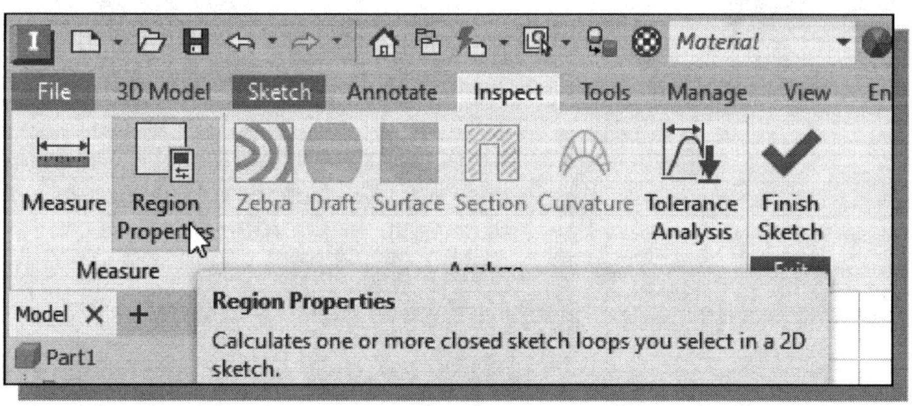

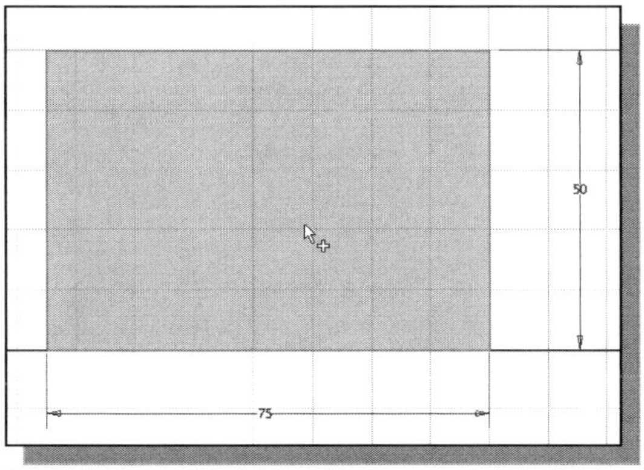

9. Click on the inside of the rectangle; notice the region is highlighted as the cursor is moved inside the rectangle, as shown.

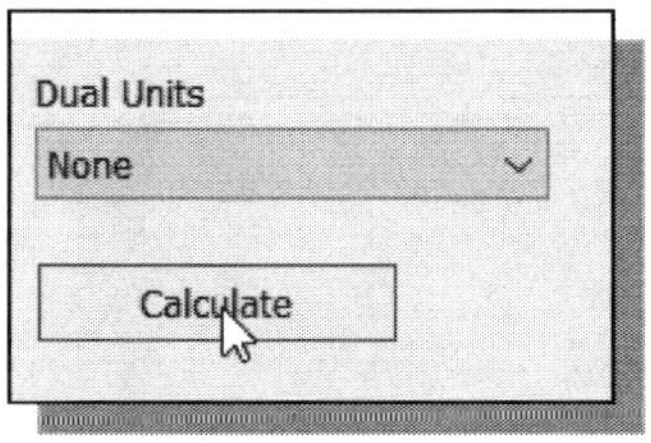

10. In the ***Region Properties*** dialog box, click on the **Calculate** button to perform the calculations of the associated geometry information.

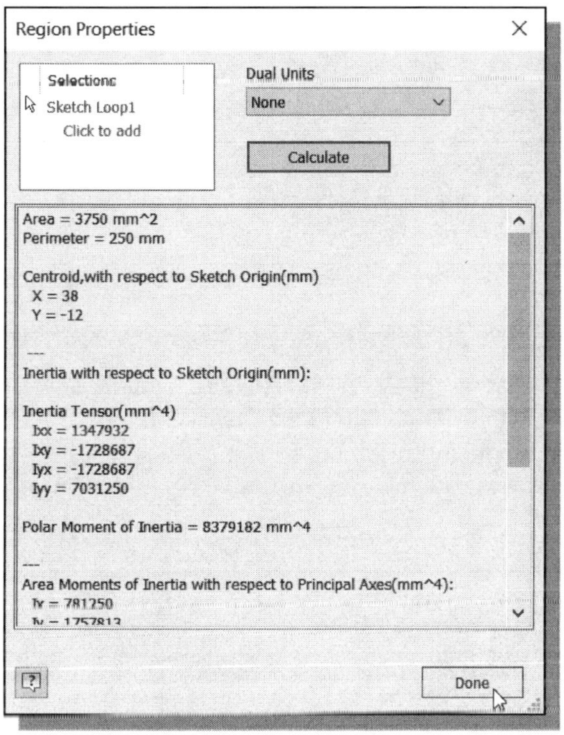

❖ In the ***Region Properties*** dialog box, the detailed region properties are calculated and displayed, including the *Area Moments of Inertia*, *Area* and *Perimeter*.

11. Click **Done** to exit the **Region Properties** command.

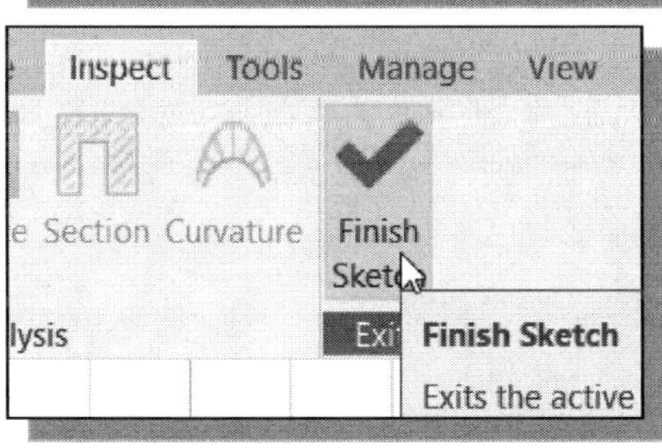

12. Select **Finish Sketch** in the *Ribbon* to end the **Sketch** option.

Completing the Base Solid Feature

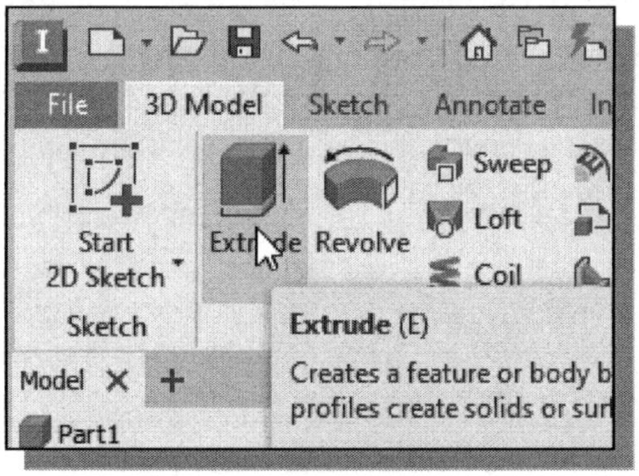

1. In the *3D Model tab* select the **Extrude** command by clicking the left-mouse-button on the icon.

2. In the *Extrude* pop-up window, enter **15** as the extrusion distance. Notice that the sketch region is automatically selected as the extrusion profile.

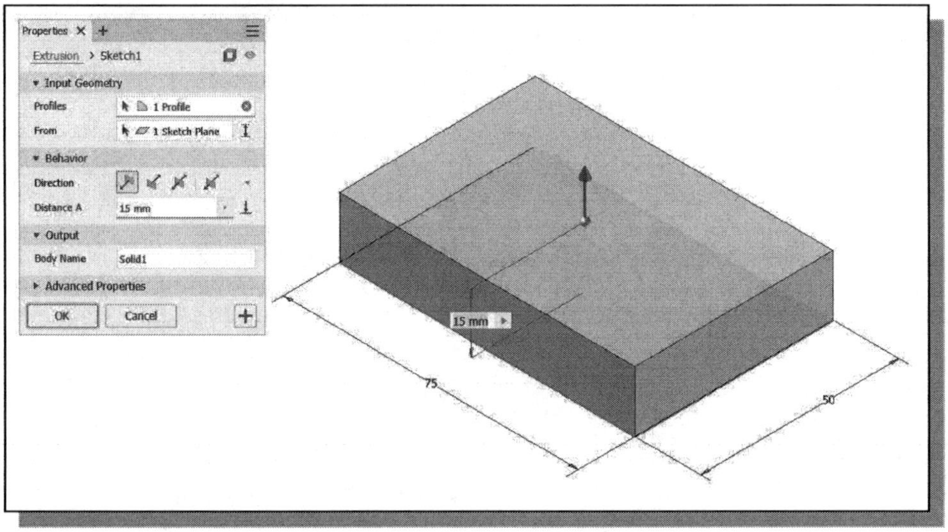

3. Click on the **OK** button to proceed with creating the 3D part. Use the *Dynamic Viewing* options to view the created part. Press **F6** to change the display to the isometric view as shown before going to the next section.

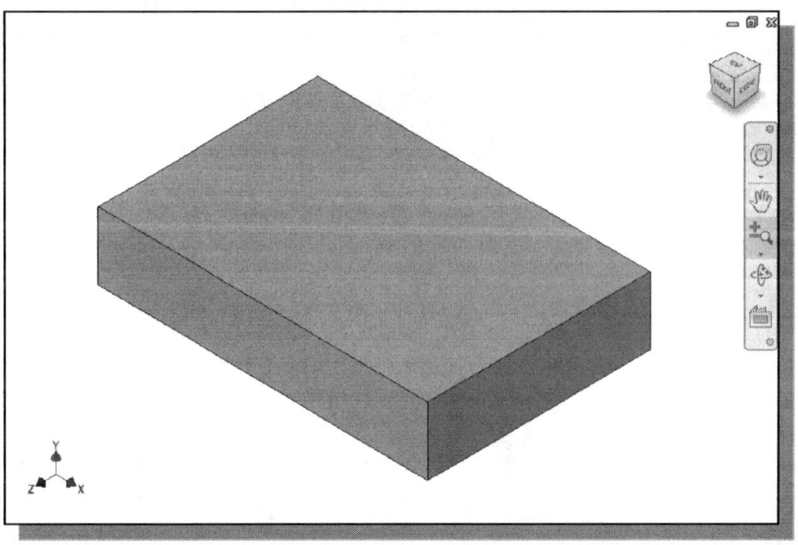

Creating the Next Solid Feature

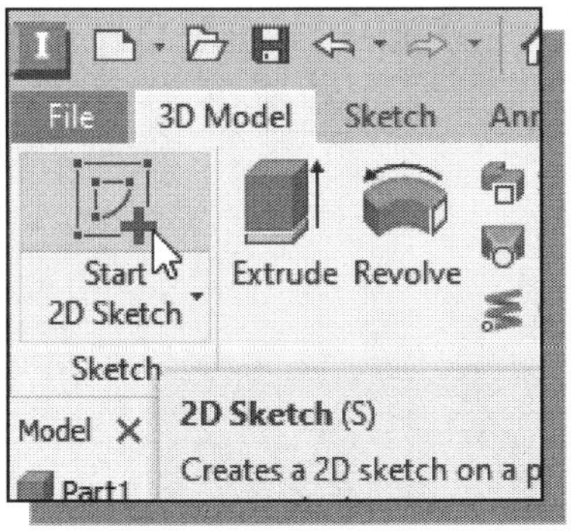

1. In the *3D Model tab* select the **Start 2D Sketch** command by left-clicking once on the icon.

2. In the *Status Bar* area, the message "*Select plane to create sketch or an existing sketch to edit*" is displayed. Autodesk Inventor expects us to identify a planar surface where the 2D sketch of the next feature is to be created. Move the graphics cursor on the 3D part and notice that Autodesk Inventor will automatically highlight feasible planes and surfaces as the cursor is on top of the different surfaces.

3. Use the **ViewCube** to adjust the display viewing the bottom face of the solid model as shown below.

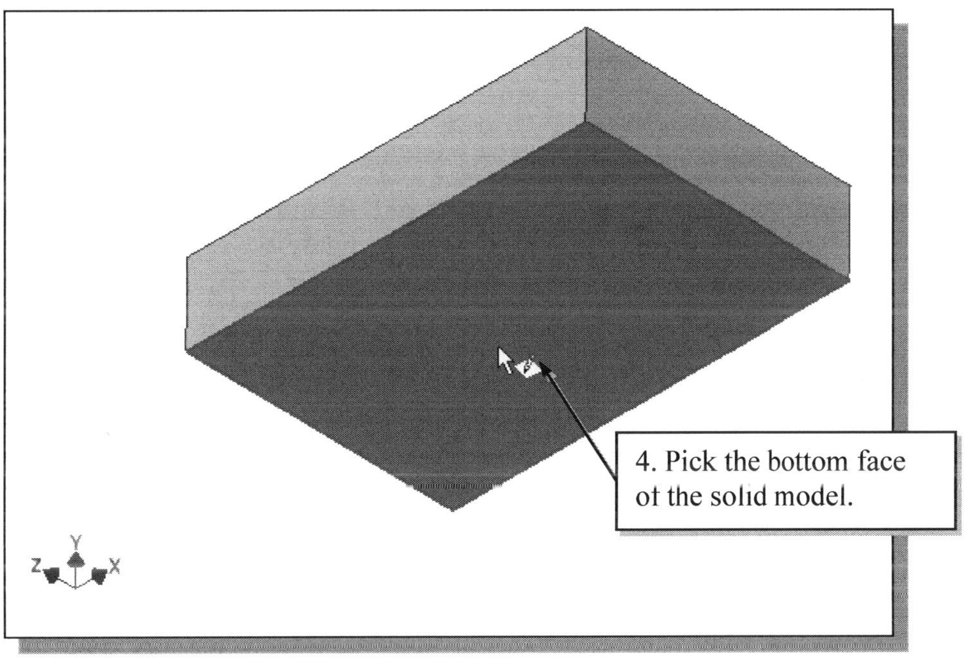

4. Pick the bottom face of the 3D model as the sketching plane.

➢ Note that the sketching plane is aligned to the selected face. Autodesk Inventor automatically establishes a User-Coordinate-System (UCS) and records its location with respect to the part on which it was created.

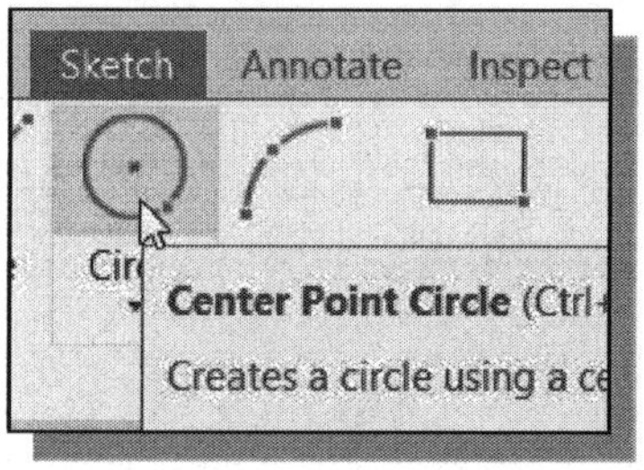

5. Select the **Center Point Circle** command by clicking once with the left-mouse-button on the icon in the *Sketch* tab.

➢ We will align the center of the circle to the midpoint of the base feature.

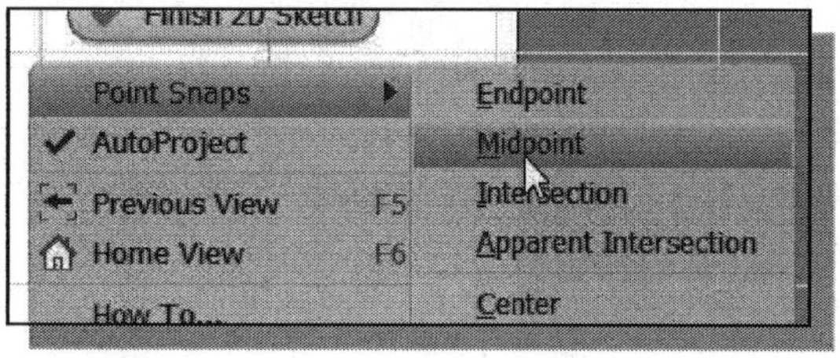

6. Inside the graphics window, click once with the **right-mouse-button** to bring up the option menu and choose the snap to **Midpoint** option.

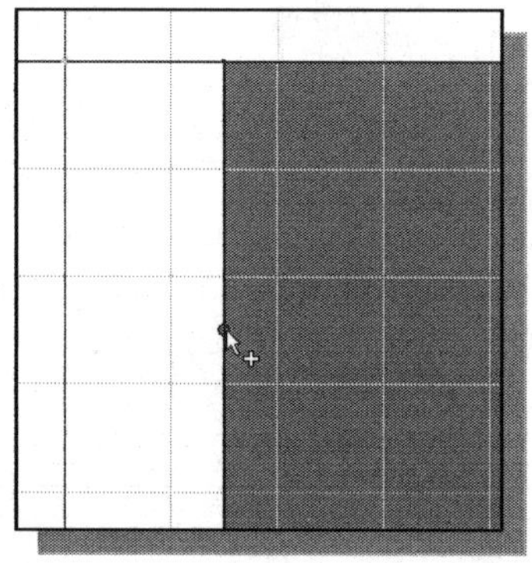

7. Select the bottom edge of the base feature to align the center point of the new circle.

8. Select the green dot to align the midpoint of the line.

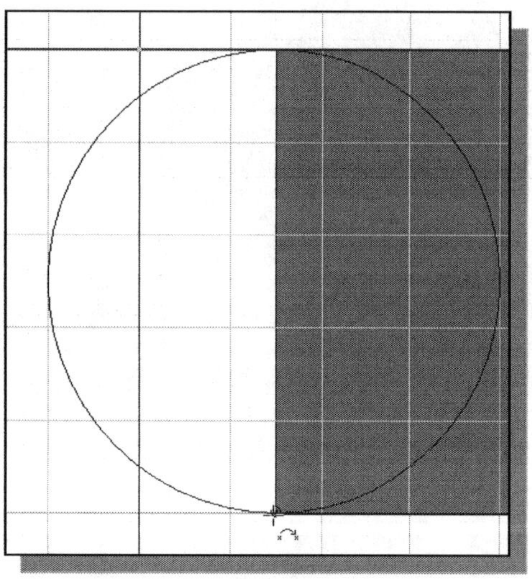

9. Select the bottom corner of the base feature to create a circle as shown in the figure.

10. Inside the *graphics window*, click once with the right-mouse-button to display the option menu. Select **OK** to end the Circle command.

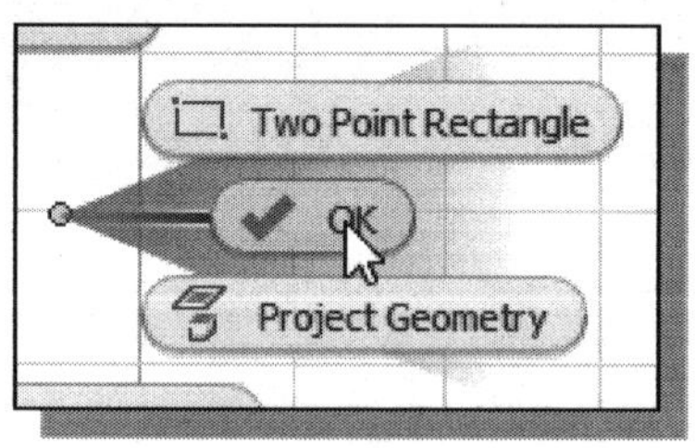

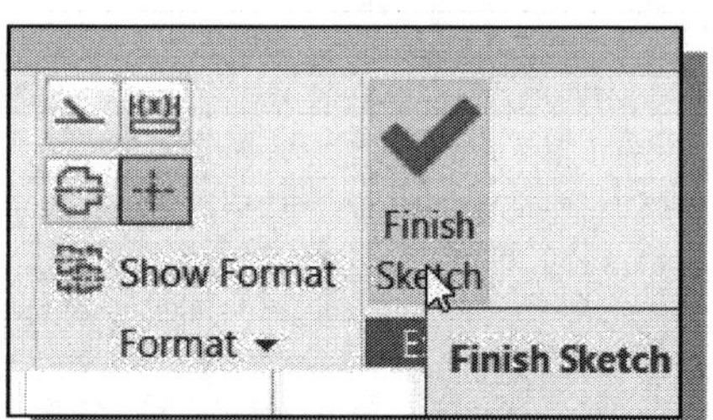

11. In the *Ribbon* toolbar, select **Finish Sketch** to exit the Sketch mode.

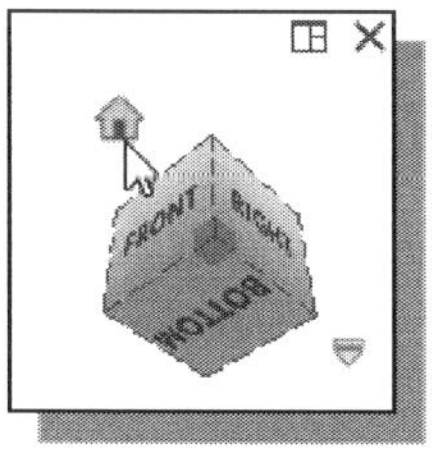

12. Press the function key **F6** once or select **Home View** in the **ViewCube** to change the display to the isometric view as shown.

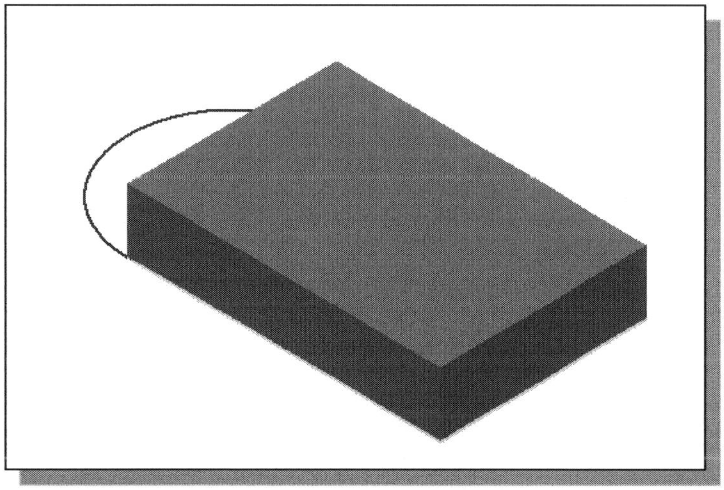

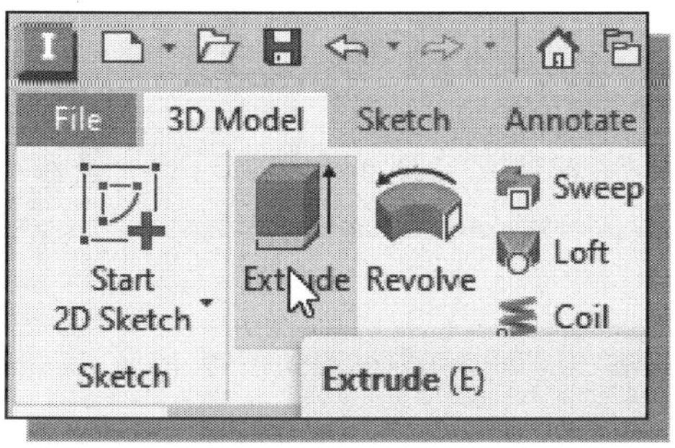

13. In the *3D Model tab*, select the **Extrude** command by left-clicking the icon.

14. Autodesk Inventor next expects us to select the region to be used to create the feature. First select inside the semi-circle region under the solid feature as shown.

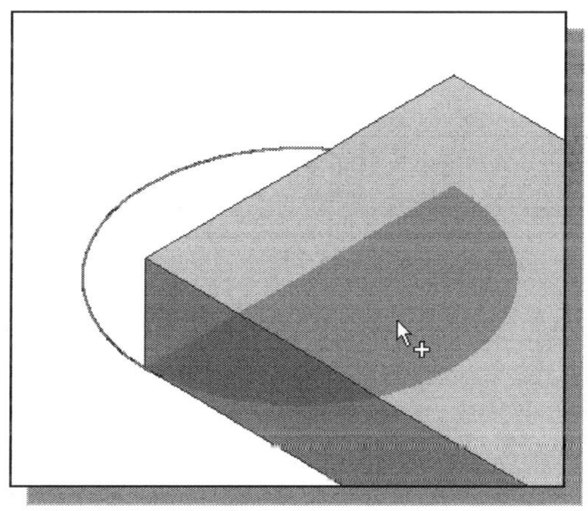

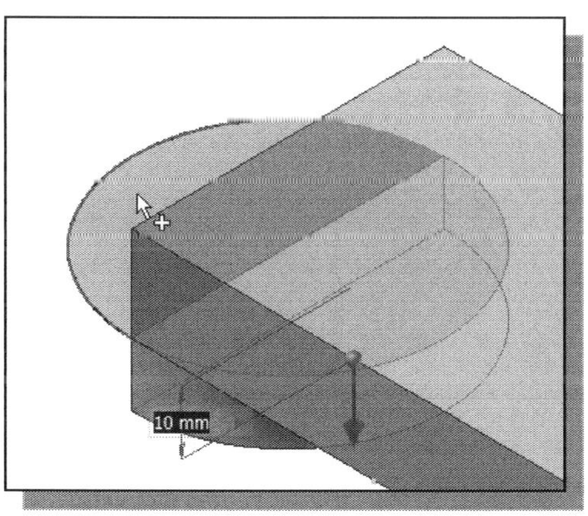

15. Select inside the other semi-circle region outside the solid feature as shown.

- Note that Autodesk Inventor creates the extruded feature downward as shown.

16. In the *Extrude* pop-up control, enter **40** as the blind extrusion distance as shown below. Set the solid operation to **Join** and click on the **Flip direction** button to reverse the direction of extrusion (upward) as shown below.

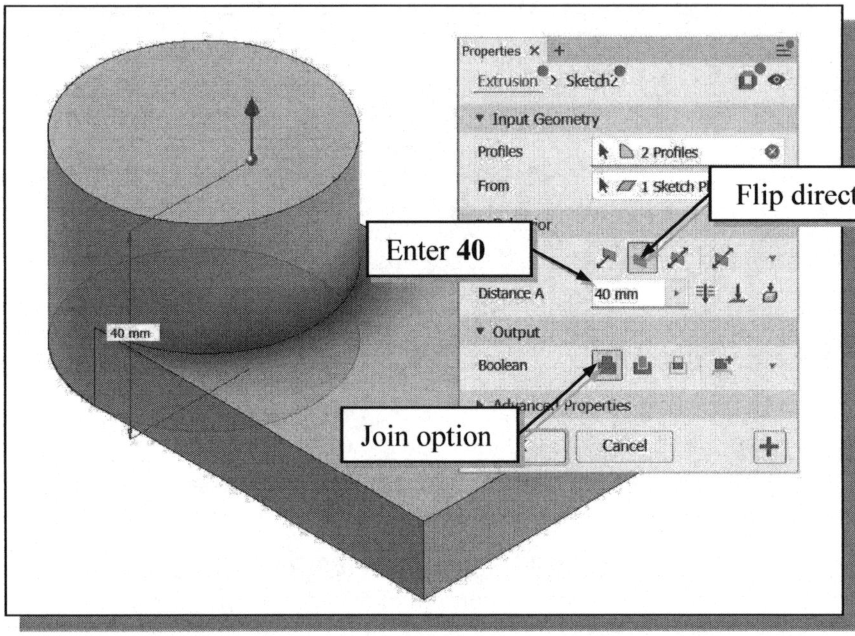

➤ Note that most of the settings can also be set through the icons displayed on the screen.

17. Click on the **OK** button to proceed with the *Join* operation.

- The two features are joined together into one solid part; the *CSG-Union* operation was performed.

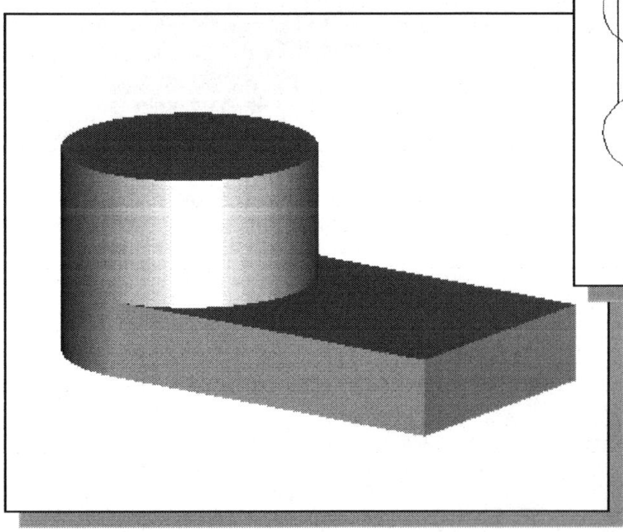

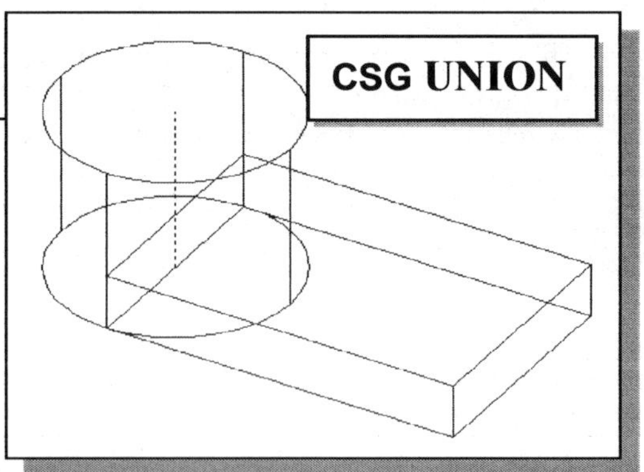

Creating a Cut Feature

We will create a circular cut as the next solid feature of the design. We will align the sketch plane to the top of the last cylinder feature.

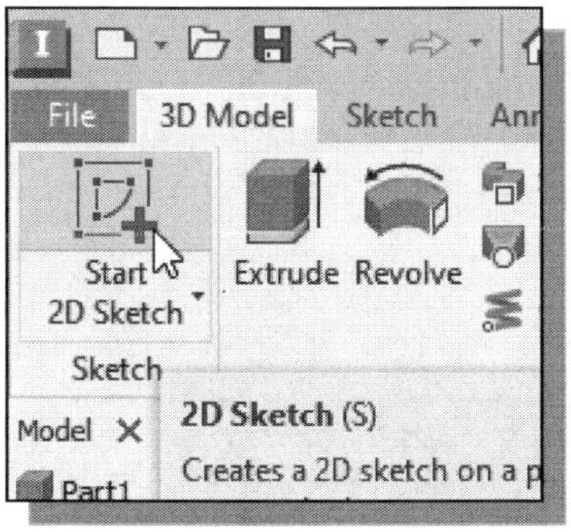

1. In the *3D Model tab* select the **Start 2D Sketch** command by left-clicking once on the icon.

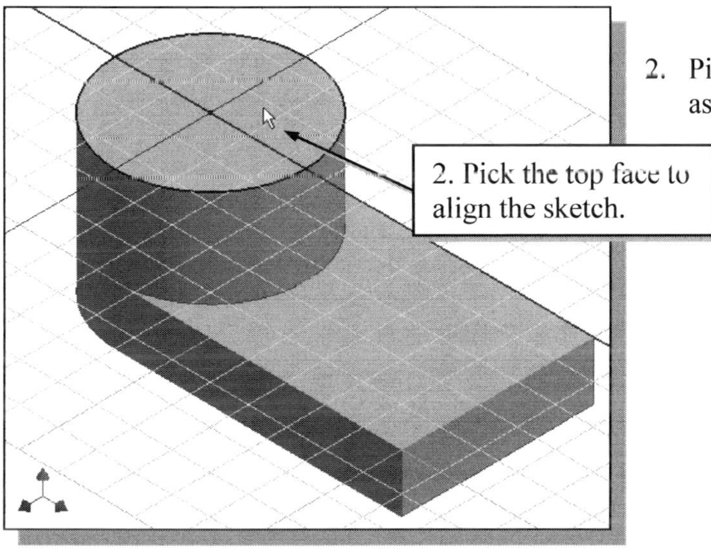

2. Pick the top face of the cylinder as shown.

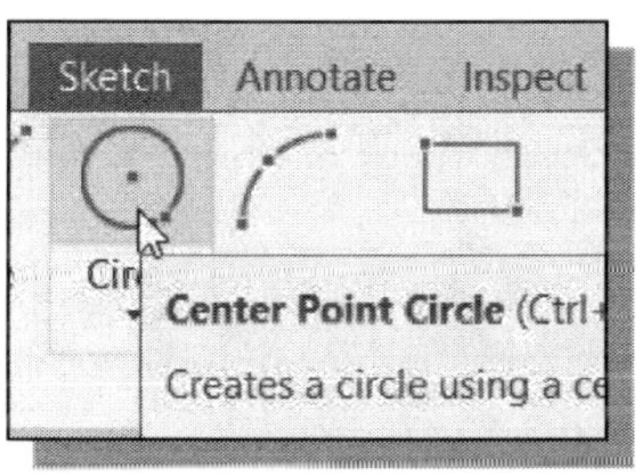

3. Select the **Center Point Circle** command by clicking once with the **left-mouse button** on the icon in the *Sketch tab* of the Ribbon toolbar.

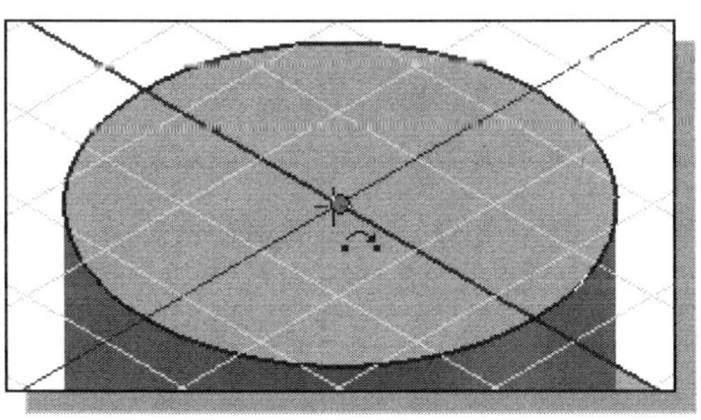

4. Select the **Center** point of the top face of the 3D model as shown.

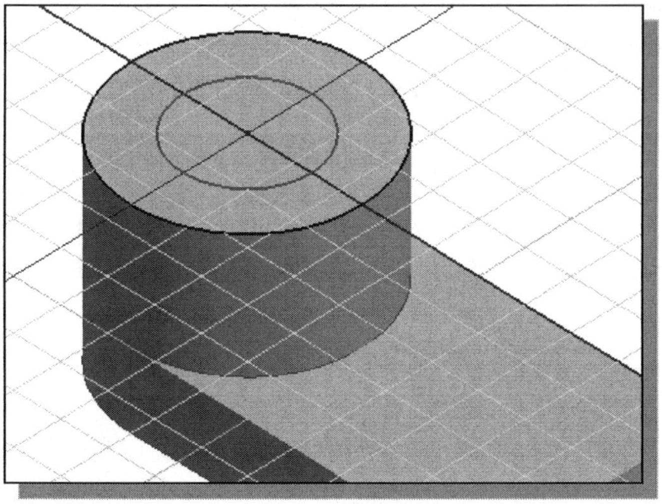

5. Sketch a circle of arbitrary size inside the top face of the cylinder as shown to the left.

6. Use the right-mouse-button to display the option menu and select **OK** in the pop-up menu to end the **Circle** command.

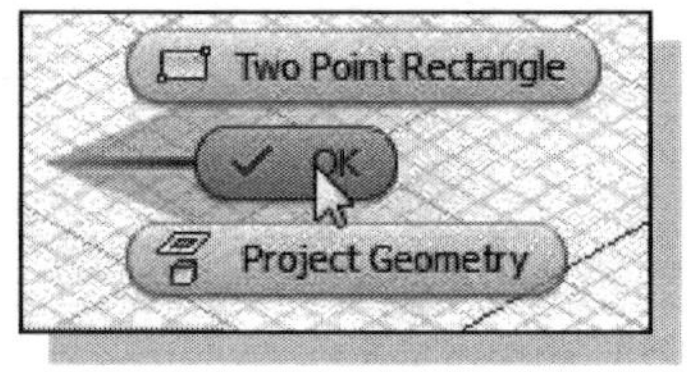

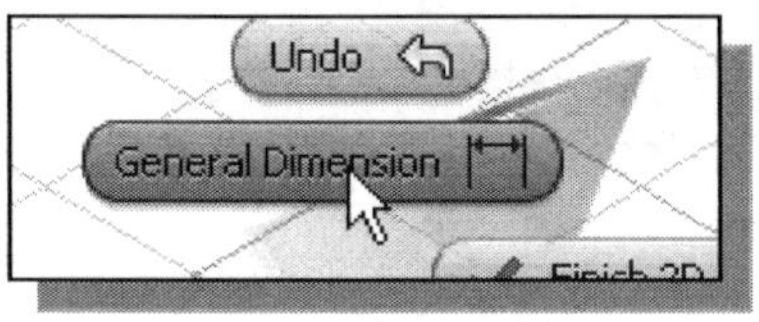

7. Inside the graphics window, click once with the **right-mouse-button** to display the option menu. Select the **General Dimension** option in the pop-up menu.

8. Create a dimension to describe the size of the circle and set it to **30mm**.

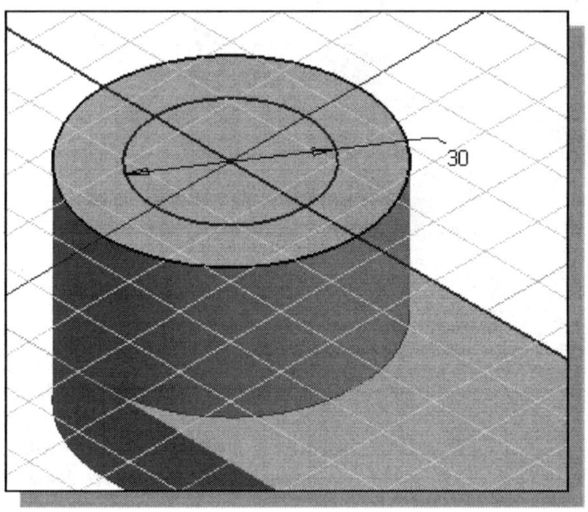

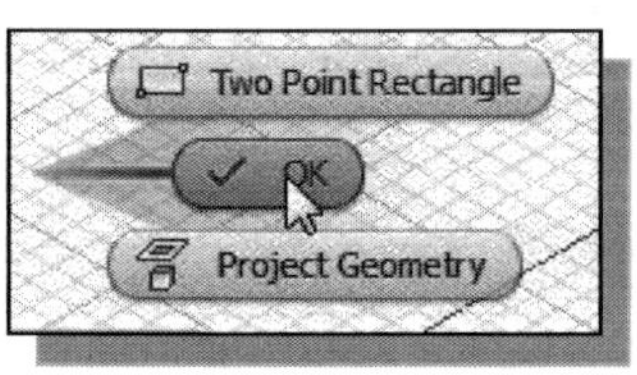

9. Inside the graphics window, click once with the right-mouse-button to display the option menu. Select **OK** in the pop-up menu to end the **Dimension** command.

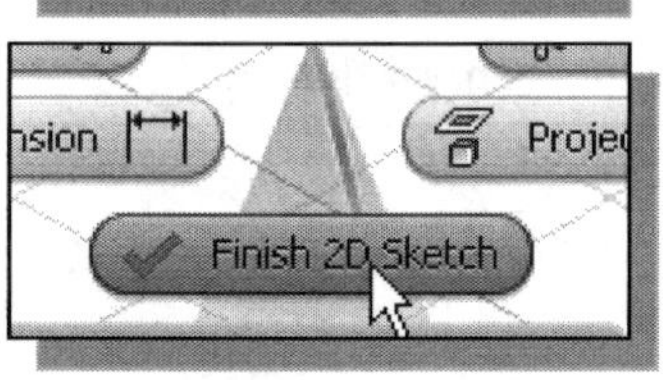

10. Inside the graphics window, click once with the right-mouse-button to display the option menu. Select **Finish 2D Sketch** in the pop-up menu to end the **Sketch** option.

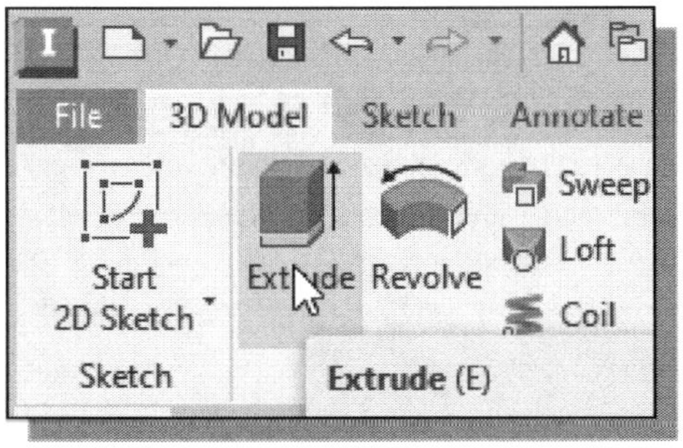

11. In the *3D Model tab*, select the **Extrude** command by left-clicking on the icon.

12. Click on the inside of the sketched circle as the profile to be extruded.

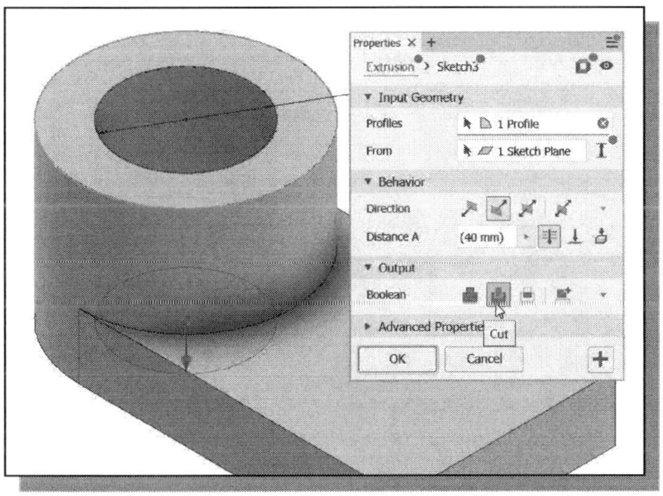

13. In the *Extrusion* pop-up window, set the operation option to **Cut**. Select **Through All** as the *Extents* option, as shown below. Confirm the arrowhead points downward.

14. Click on the **OK** button to proceed with the *Cut* operation.

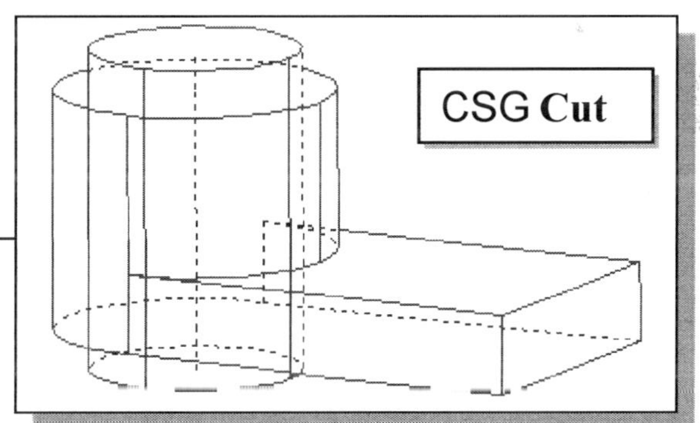

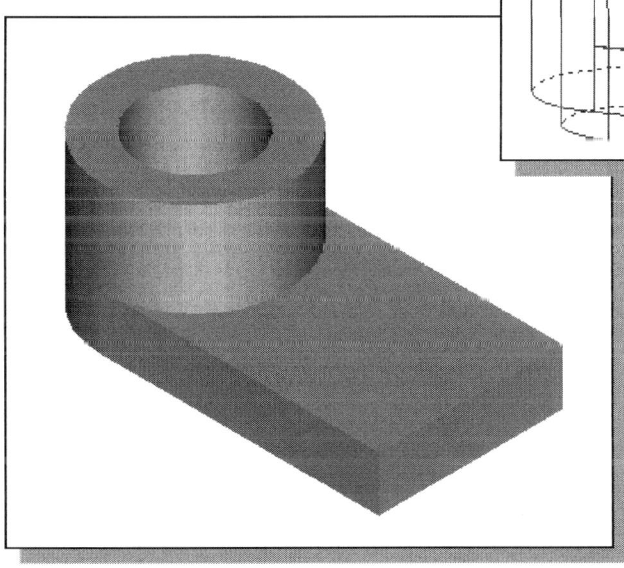

- The circular volume is removed from the solid model; the *CSG-Cut* operation resulted in a single solid.

Sketched Features vs. Placed Features

In Autodesk Inventor, there are two types of geometric features: **placed features** and **sketched features**. The last cut feature we created is a *sketched feature*, where we created a rough sketch and performed an extrusion operation. We can also create a hole feature, which is a placed feature. A *placed feature* is a feature that does not need a sketch and can be created automatically. Holes, slots, fillets, chamfers, and shells are all placed features.

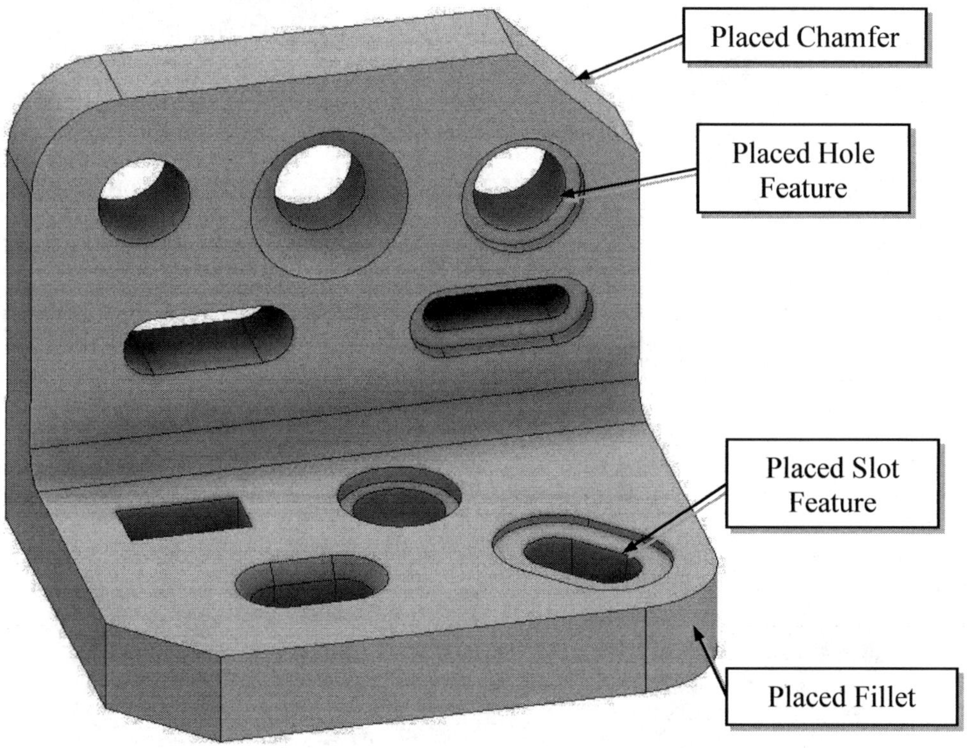

Hole tool: Quickly place holes using presets, or specify the hole dimensions, drill point, termination, and thread type options using the property panel.

Slot tool: Quickly place slots using presets, or specify the slot dimensions. Other options, such as sharp corner, fillets, counter bore, counter sink options.

Fillet tool: Quickly place rounded corners, both curving inward and outward. Basic option is done by selecting edges; more complicated options such as varying radii can also be created.

Creating a Placed Hole Feature

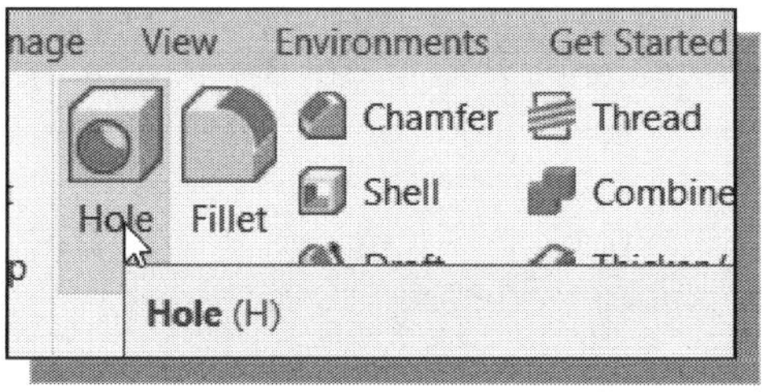

1. In the *Create* toolbar, select the **Hole** command by left-clicking on the icon.

2. Pick a location inside the top horizontal surface of the base feature as shown.

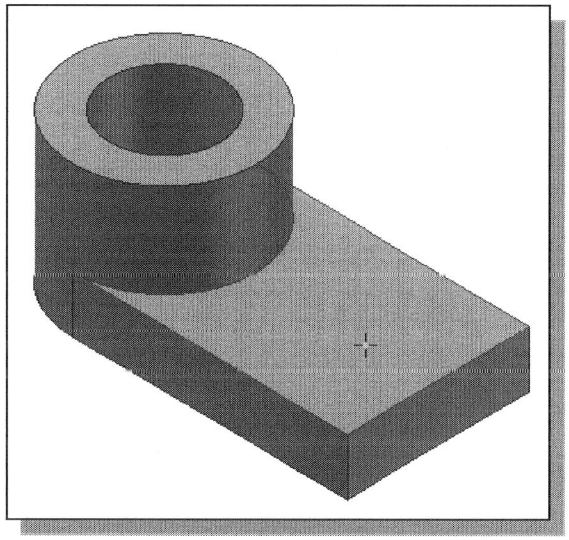

3. Enter **20 mm** as the diameter of the hole as shown. **Do Not** click the OK button yet.

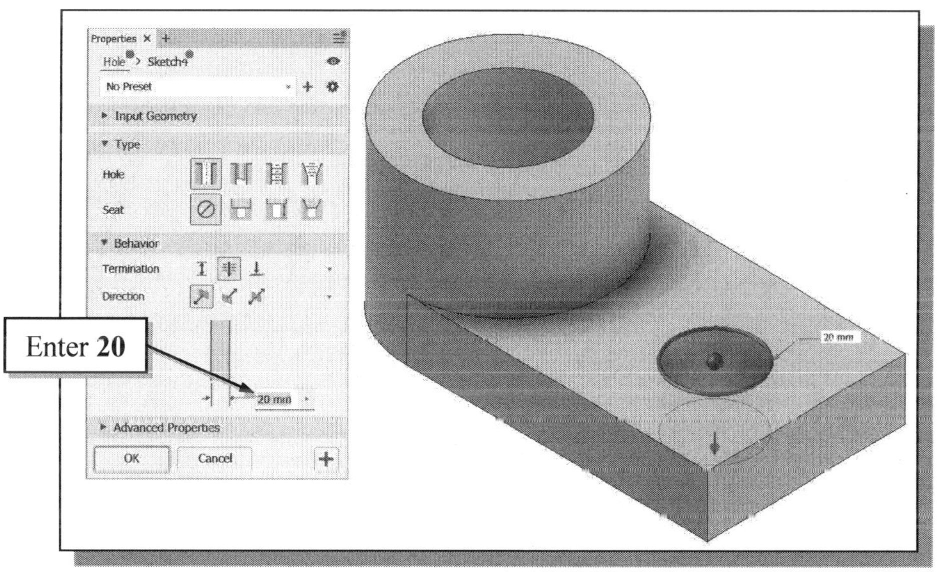

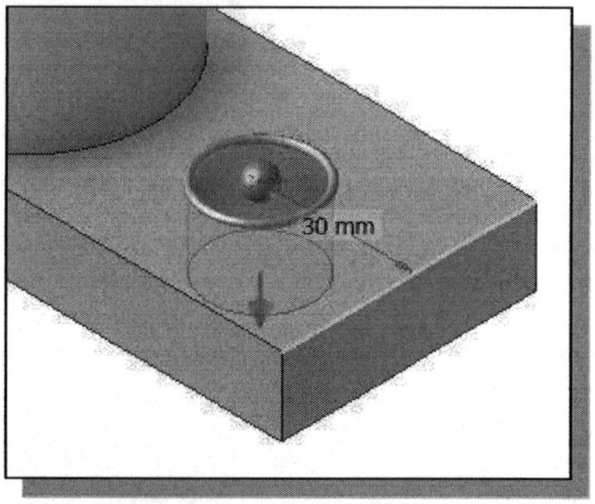

4. Pick the **right-edge** of the top face of the base feature as shown. This will be used as the first reference for placing the hole on the plane.

5. Enter **30** mm as the distance as shown. **Do Not** click the OK button yet.

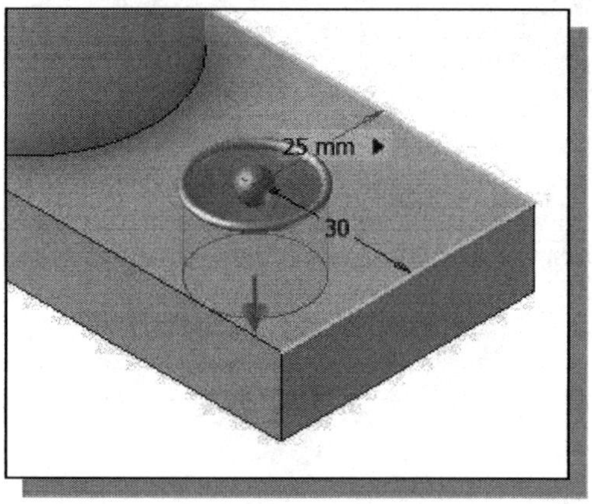

6. Pick the **adjacent edge** of the top face as shown. This will be used as the second reference for placing the hole on the plane.

7. Enter **25** mm as the distance as shown.

8. In *Holes* dialog box, set the *Termination* option to **Through All**.

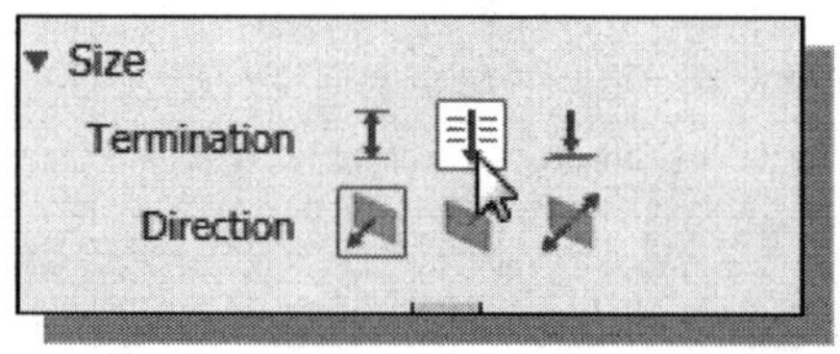

9. Click on the **OK** button to proceed with the *Hole* feature.

- The circular volume is removed from the solid model; the *CSG-Cut* operation resulted in a single solid.

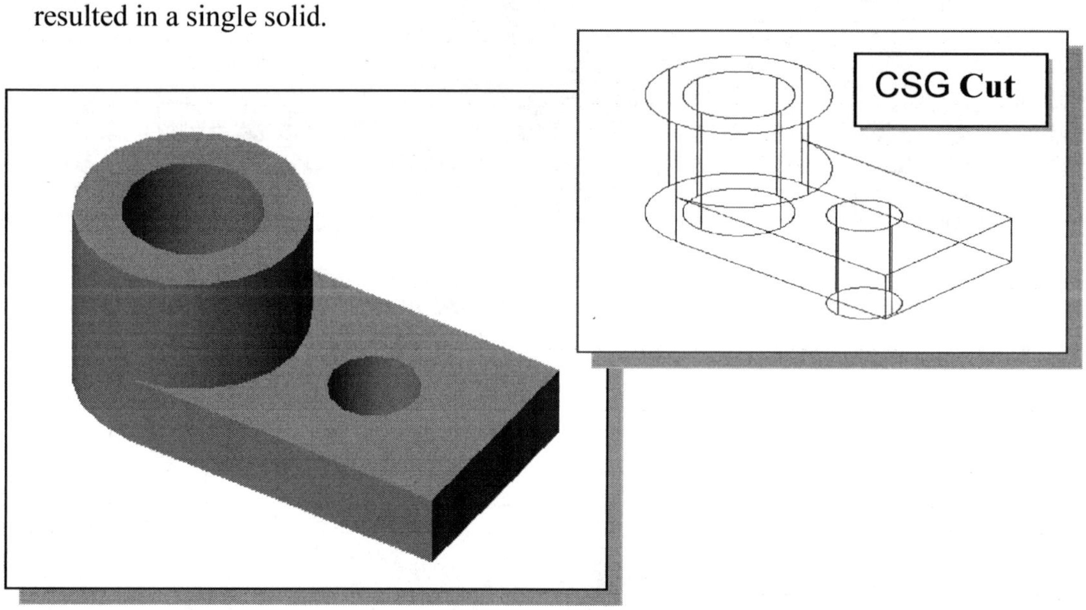

Creating a Rectangular Cut Feature

Next create a rectangular cut as the last solid feature of the ***Locator***.

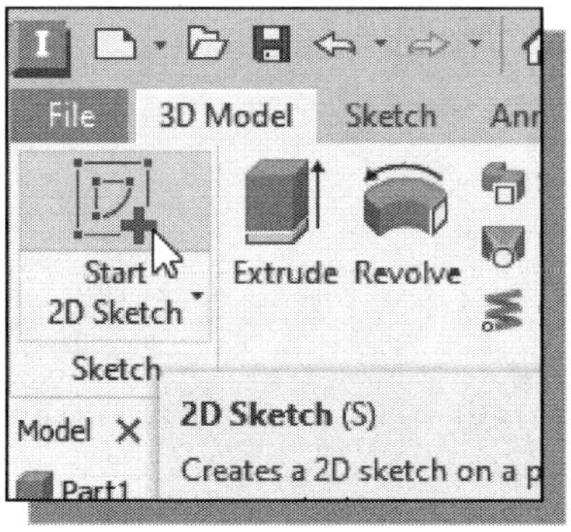

1. In the *3D Model* tab select the **Start 2D Sketch** command by left-clicking once on the icon.

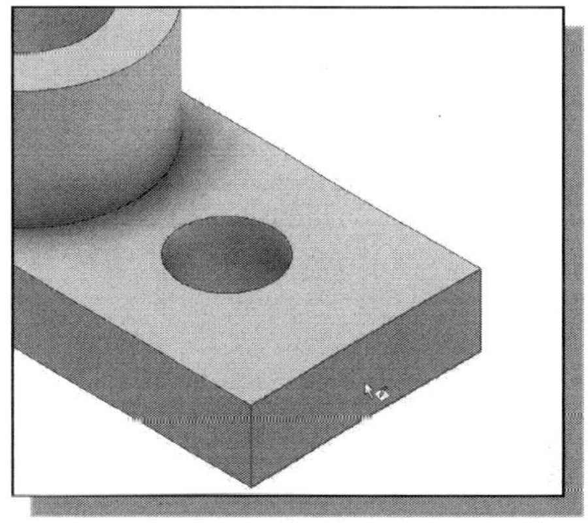

2. Pick the right face of the base feature as shown.

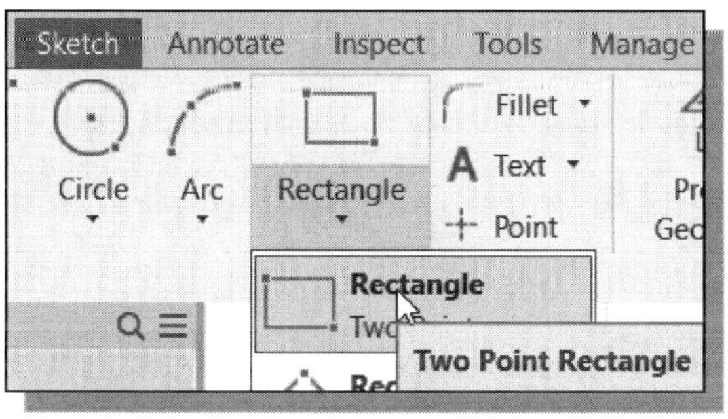

3. Select the **Two point rectangle** command by clicking once with the left-mouse-button on the icon in the *Sketch tab* of the Ribbon toolbar.

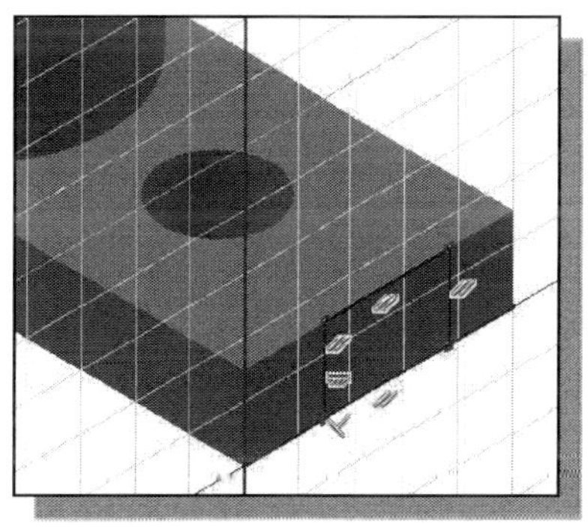

4. Create a rectangle that is aligned to the top and bottom edges of the base feature as shown. (Hit [**F6**] to set the display orientation if necessary.)

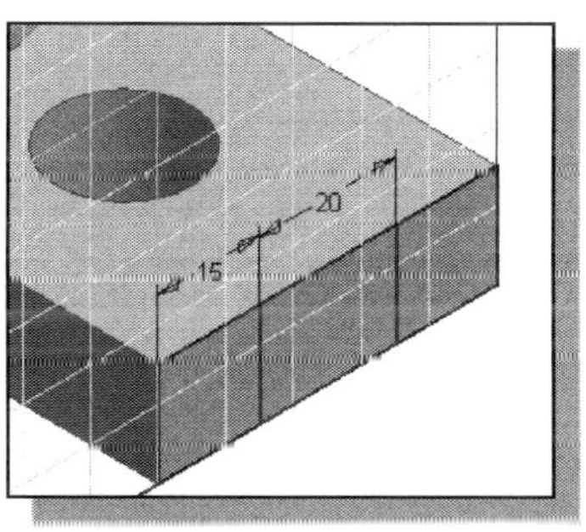

5. On your own, create and modify the two dimensions as shown.

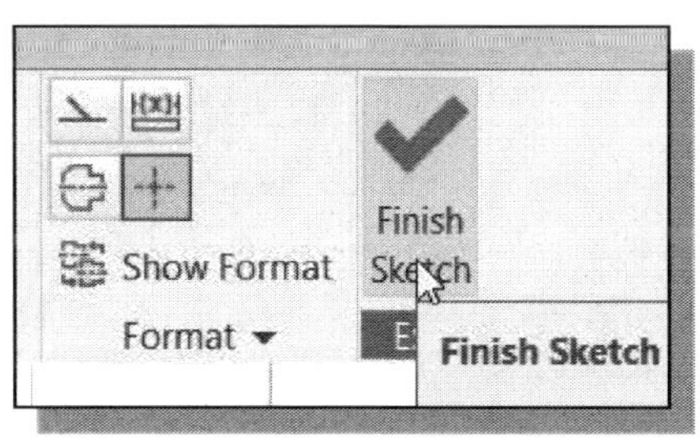

6. Select **Finish Sketch** in the *Ribbon* toolbar to end the **Sketch** option.

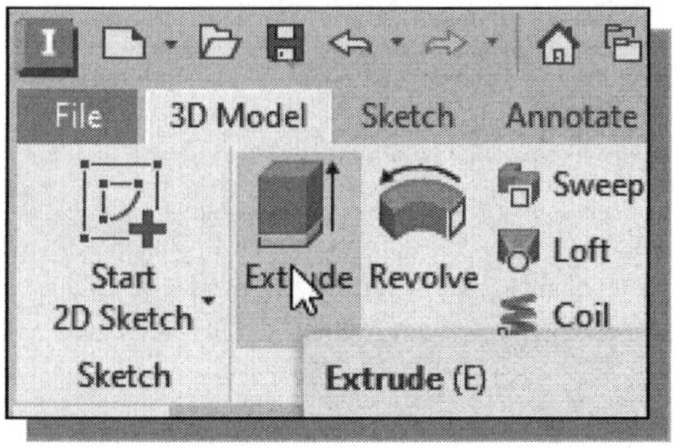

7. In the *3D Model* tab, select the **Extrude** command by left-clicking on the icon.

8. In the *Extrude* pop-up window, the **Profile** button is pressed down; Autodesk Inventor expects us to identify the profile to be extruded. Move the cursor inside the rectangle we just created and left-click once to select the region as the profile to be extruded.

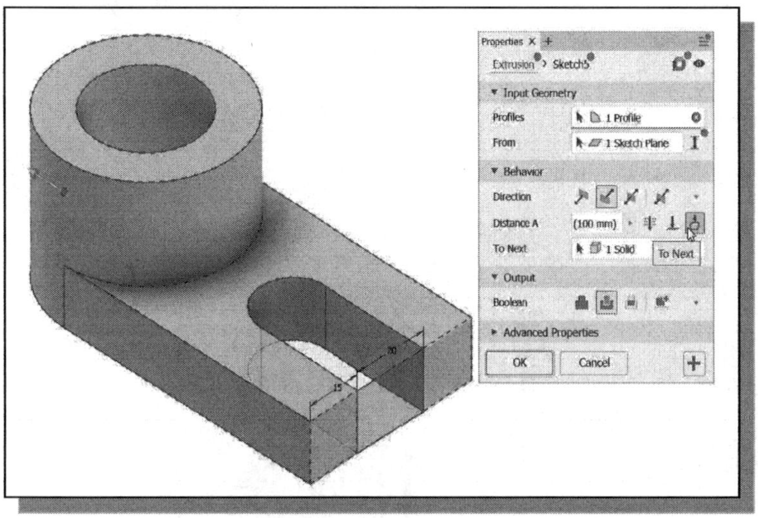

9. In the *Extrude* pop-up window, set the operation option to **Cut**. Select **To Next** as the *Distance* option as shown. Set the arrowhead points toward the center of the solid model.

10. Click on the **OK** button to create the *Cut* feature and complete the design.

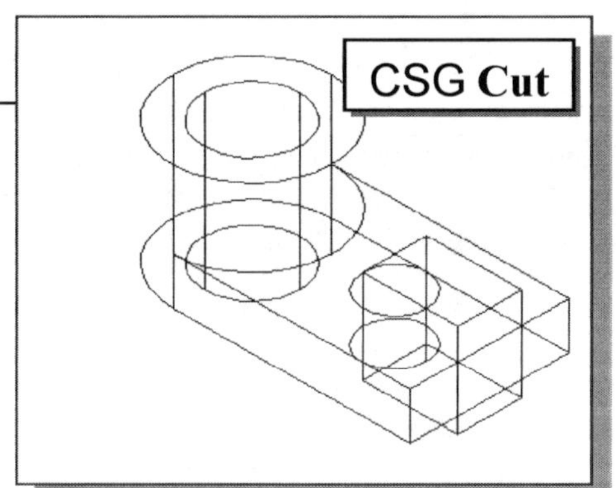

Save the Model

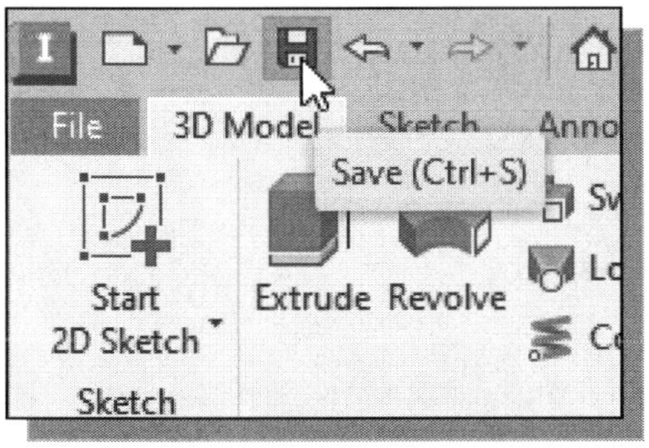

1. Select **Save** in the *Quick Access Toolbar*, or you can also use the "**Ctrl-S**" combination (hold down the "Ctrl" key and hit the "S" key once) to save the part.

2. Switch to the **Parametric Modeling** *folder* if it is not the current folder.

3. In the *Save As* dialog box, **right-click** once in the *list area* to bring up the *option menu*.

4. In the *option list*, select **New** as shown.

5. In the second *option list*, select **Folder** to create a subfolder.

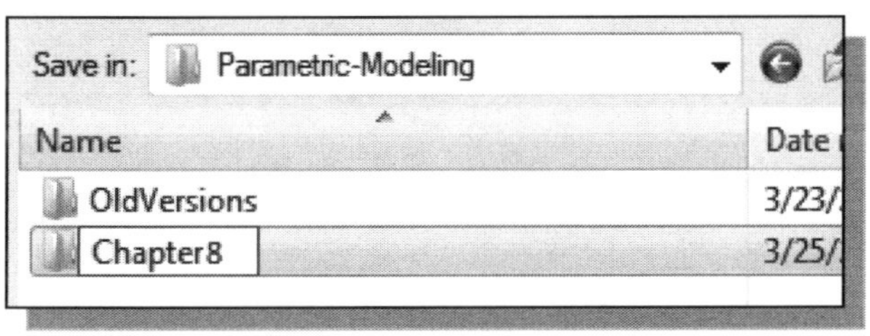

6. Enter **Chapter8** as the new folder name as shown.

7. **Double-click** on the Chapter8 folder to open it.

8. In the *file name* editor box, enter **Locator** as the file name.

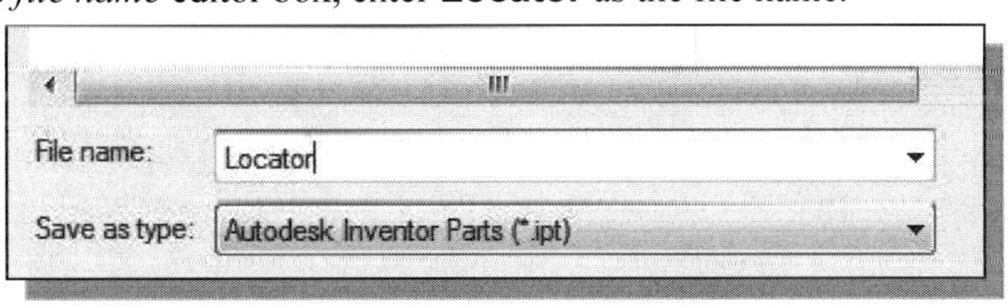

9. Click on the **Save** button to save the file.

Review Questions:

1. List and describe three basic *Boolean operations* commonly used in computer geometric modeling software.

2. What is a *primitive solid*?

3. What does *CSG* stand for?

4. Which *Boolean operation* keeps only the volume common to the two solid objects?

5. What is the main difference between a *CUT feature* and a *HOLE feature* in *Autodesk Inventor*?

6. Create the following 2D Sketch and measure the associated area and perimeter.

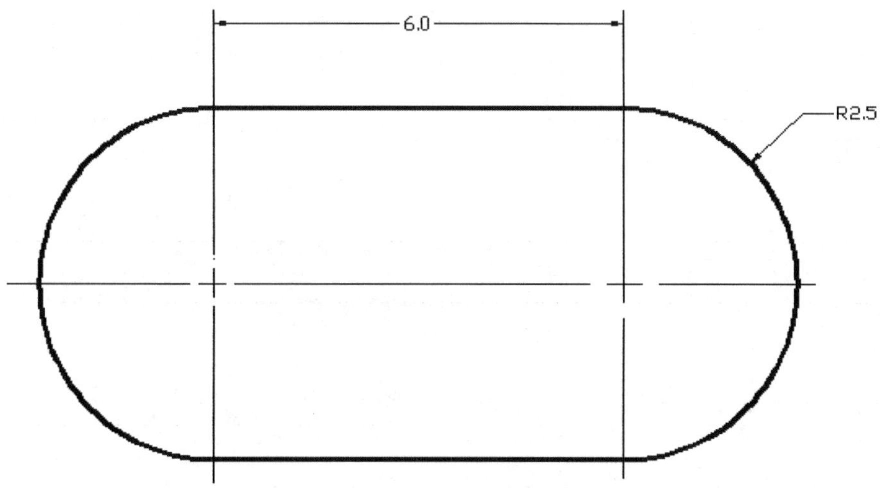

7. Using the CSG concepts, create *Binary Tree* sketches showing the steps you plan to use to create the two models shown on page 8-31.

Exercises:

1. **Latch Clip** (Dimensions are in inches. Thickness: 0.25 inches.)

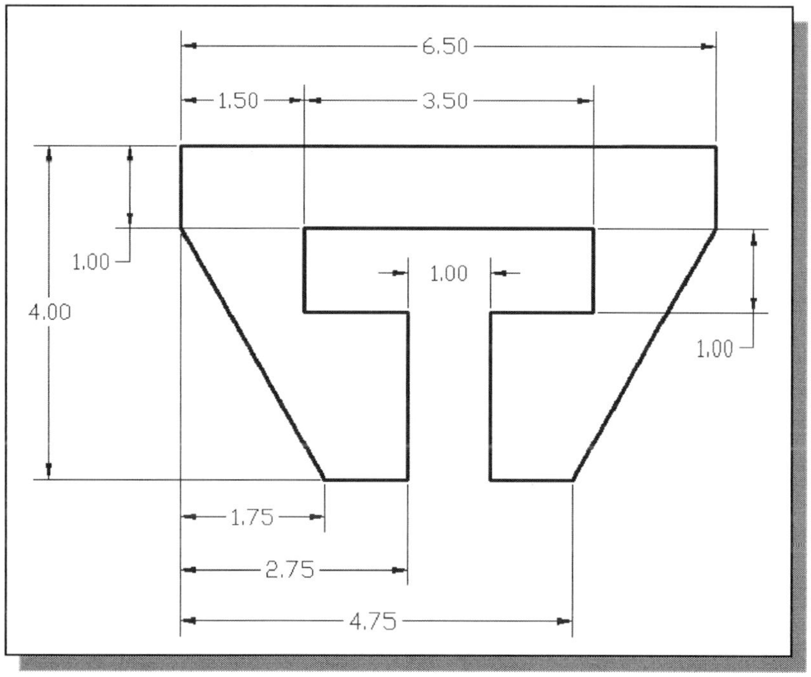

2. **Guide Plate** (Dimensions are in inches. Thickness: 0.25 inches. Boss height 0.125 inches. The two diameter 1.00 holes are through holes.)

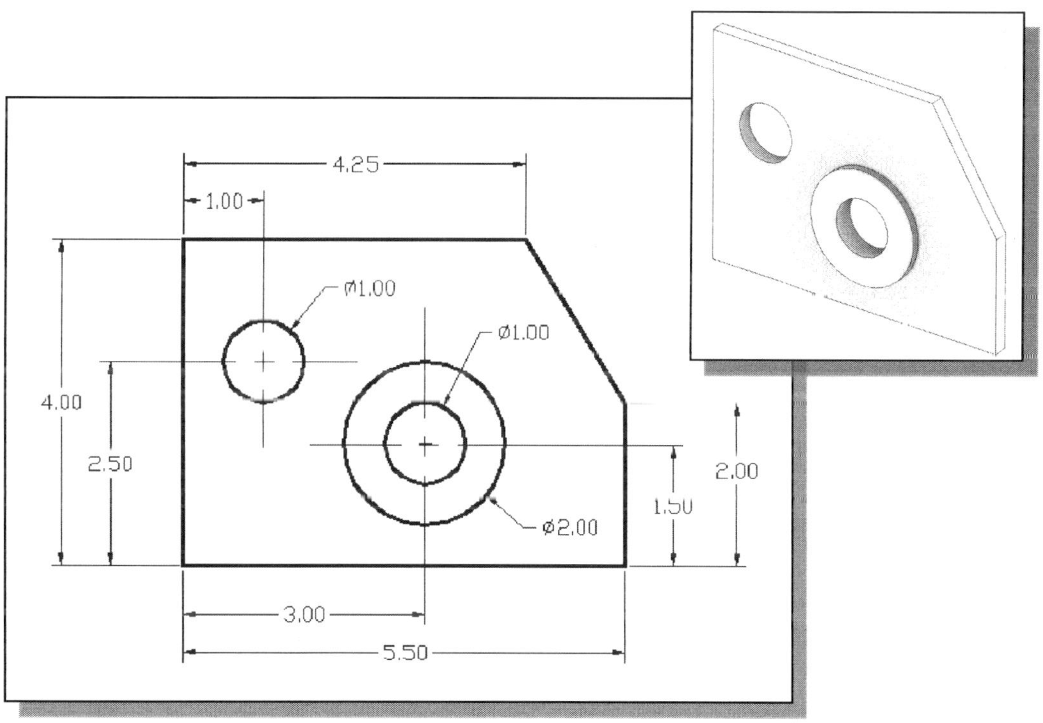

3. **Angle Slider** (Dimensions are in millimeters.)

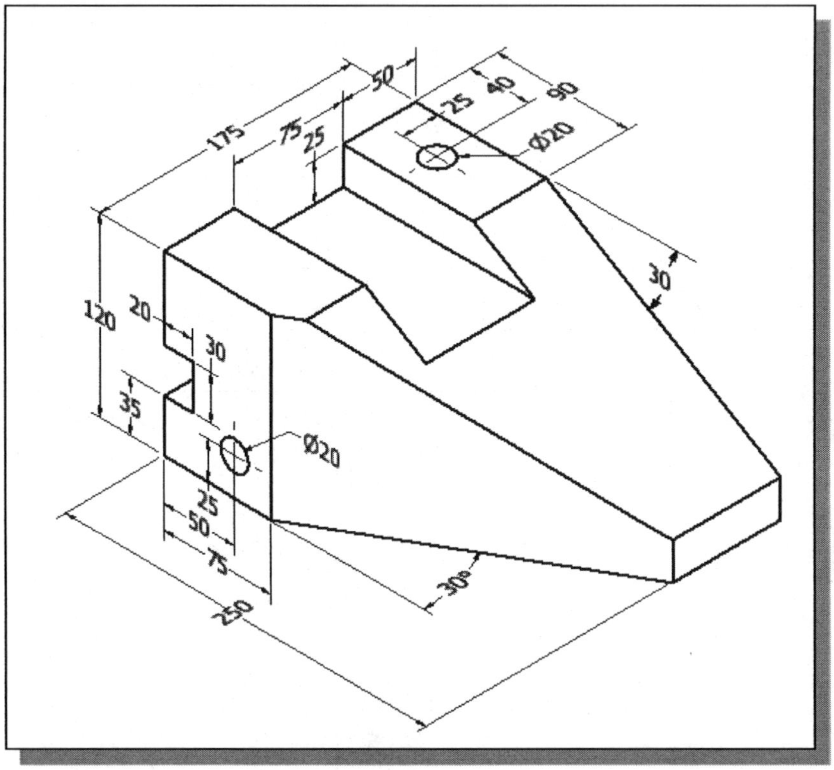

4. **Coupling Base** (Dimensions are in inches.)

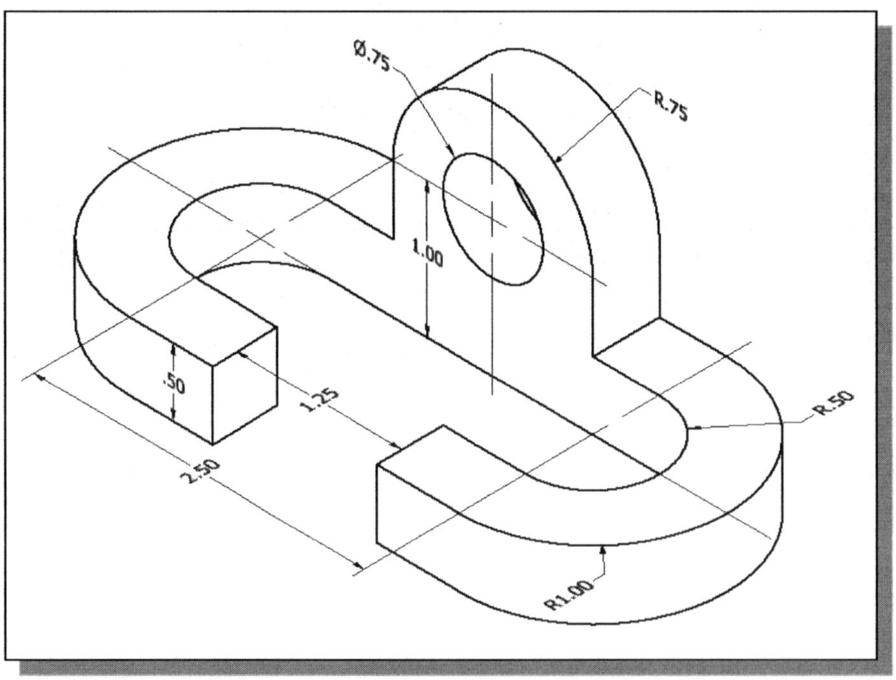

5. **Indexing Guide** (Dimensions are in inches.)

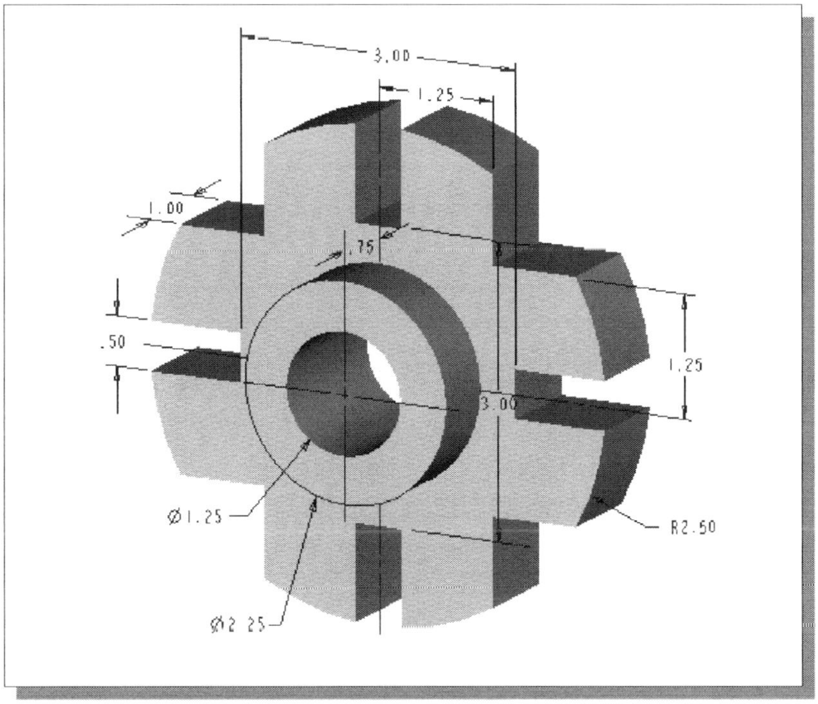

6. **L-Bracket** (Dimensions are in inches.)

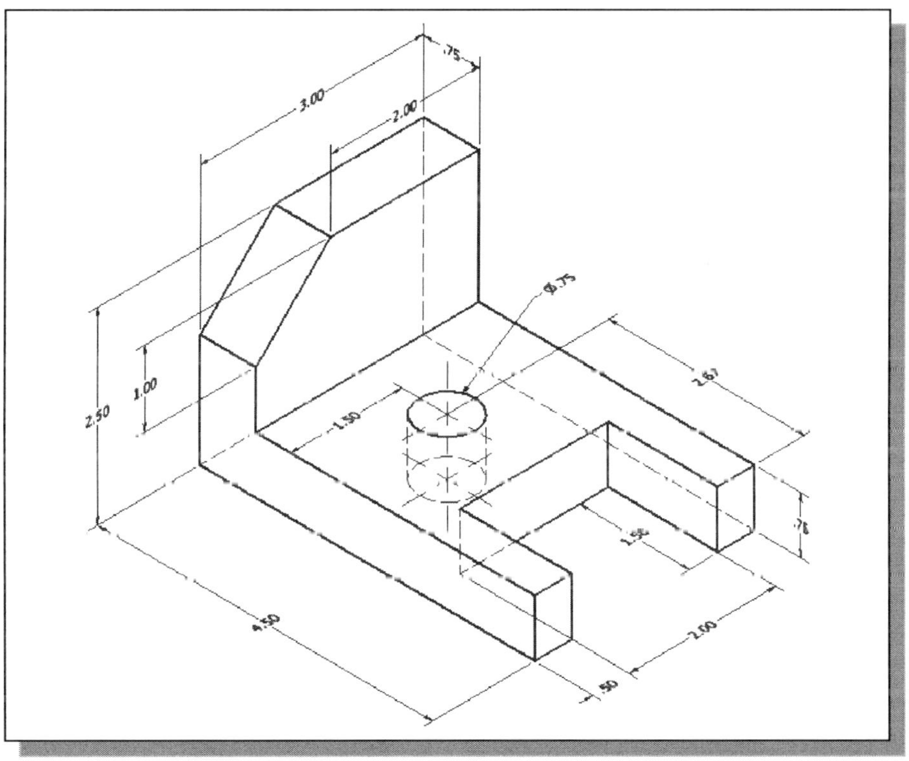

7. **Slide Base** (Dimensions are in inches.)

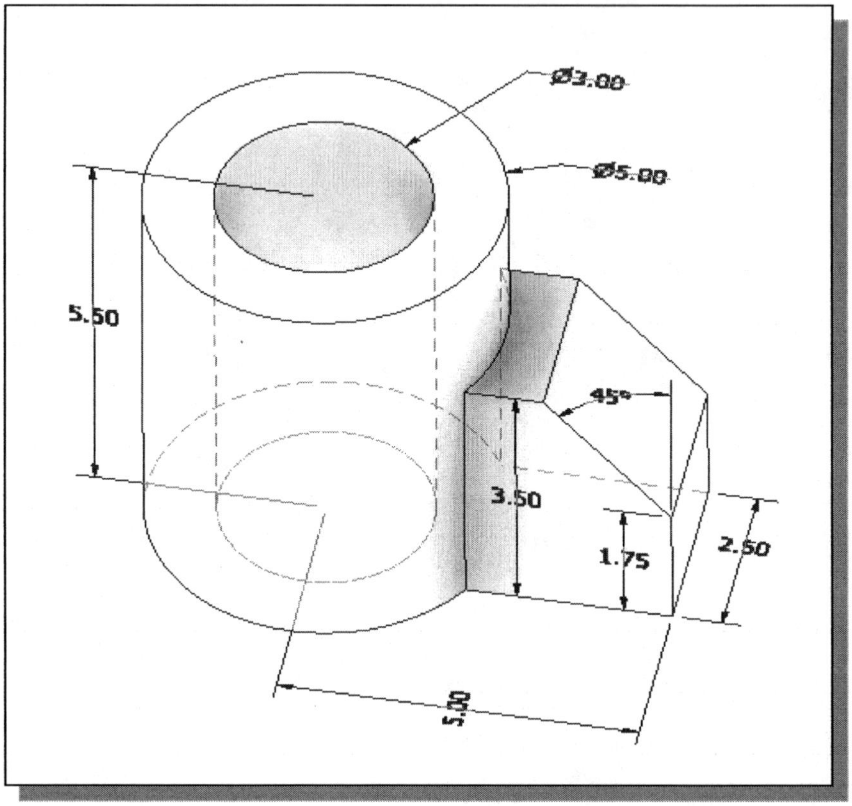

Chapter 9
Model History Tree - Autodesk Inventor

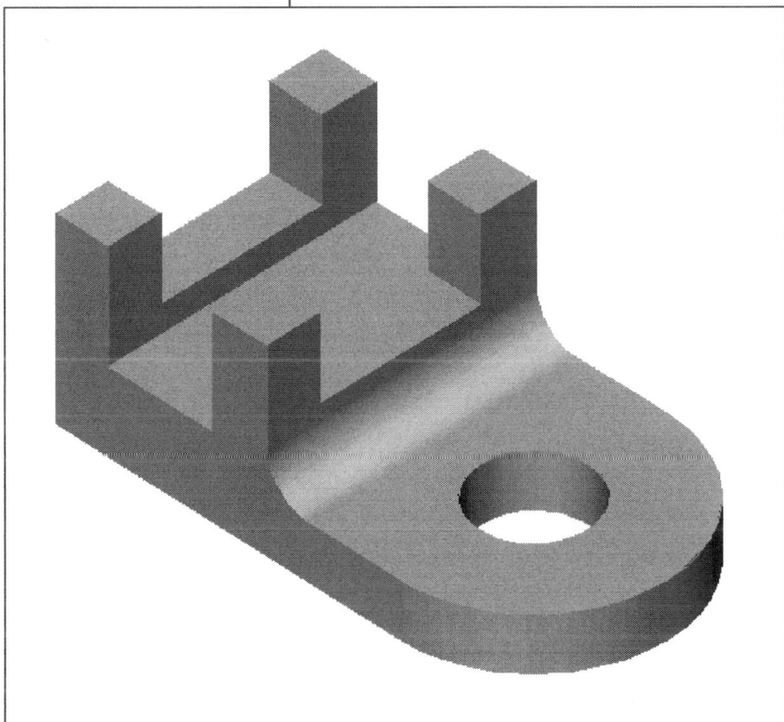

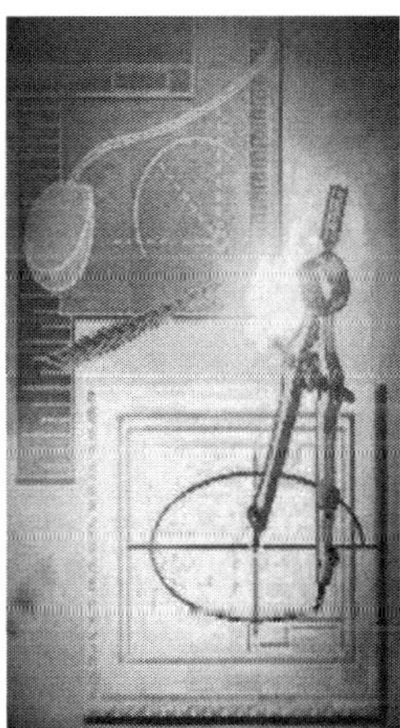

Learning Objectives

- Understand Feature Interactions
- Use the Part Browser
- Modify and Update Feature Dimensions
- Perform History-Based Part Modifications
- Change the Names of Created Features
- Implement Basic Design Changes

Introduction

In Autodesk Inventor, the **design intents** are embedded into features in the **history tree**. The structure of the model history tree resembles that of a **CSG binary tree**. A CSG binary tree contains only *Boolean relations*, while the **Autodesk Inventor history tree** contains all features, including *Boolean relations*. A history tree is a sequential record of the features used to create the part. This history tree contains the construction steps, plus the rules defining the design intent of each construction operation. In a history tree, each time a new modeling event is created previously defined features can be used to define information such as size, location, and orientation. It is therefore important to think about your modeling strategy before you start creating anything. It is important, but also difficult, to plan ahead for all possible design changes that might occur. This approach in modeling is a major difference in **FEATURE-BASED CAD SOFTWARE**, such as Autodesk Inventor, from previous generation CAD systems.

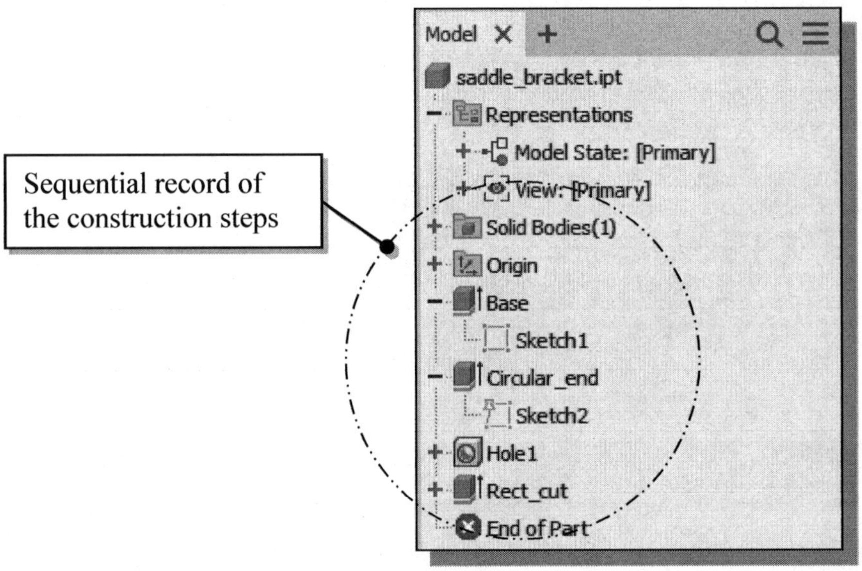

Feature-based parametric modeling is a cumulative process. Every time a new feature is added, a new result is created, and the feature is also added to the history tree. The database also includes parameters of features that were used to define them. All of this happens automatically as features are created and manipulated. At this point, it is important to understand that all of this information is retained, and modifications are done based on the same input information.

In Autodesk Inventor, the history tree gives information about modeling order and other information about the feature. Part modifications can be accomplished by accessing the features in the history tree. It is therefore important to understand and utilize the feature history tree to modify designs. Autodesk Inventor remembers the history of a part, including all the rules that were used to create it, so that changes can be made to any operation that was performed to create the part. In Autodesk Inventor, to modify a feature we access the feature by selecting the feature in the ***browser*** window.

The Saddle Bracket Design

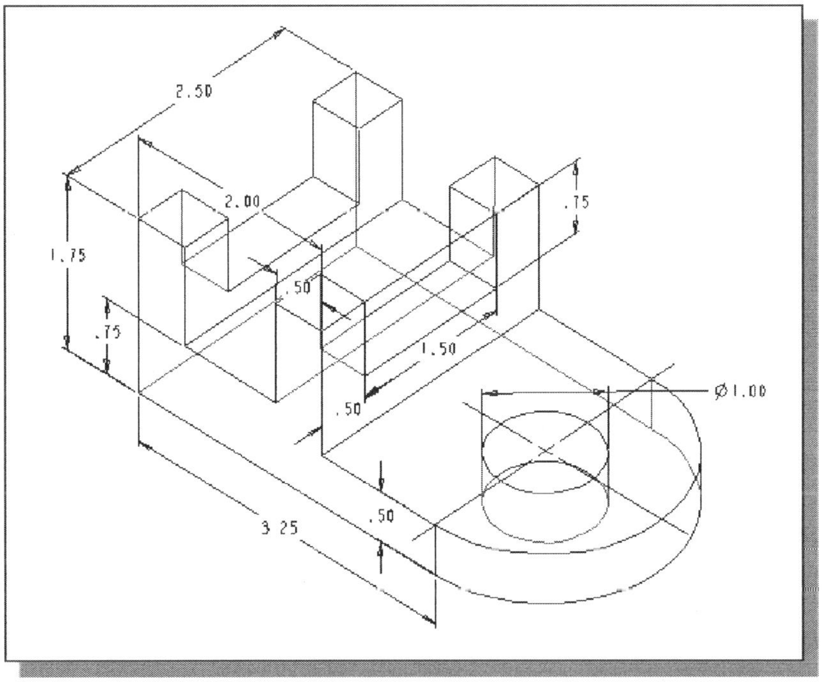

❖ Based on your knowledge of Autodesk Inventor so far, how many features would you use to create the design? Which feature would you choose as the **BASE FEATURE**, the first solid feature, of the model? What is your choice in arranging the order of the features? Would you organize the features differently if additional fillets were to be added in the design? Take a few minutes to consider these questions and do preliminary planning by sketching on a piece of paper. You are also encouraged to create the model on your own prior to following through the tutorial.

Starting Autodesk Inventor

1. Select the **Autodesk Inventor** option on the *Start* menu or select the **Autodesk Inventor** icon on the desktop to start Autodesk Inventor. The Autodesk Inventor main window will appear on the screen.

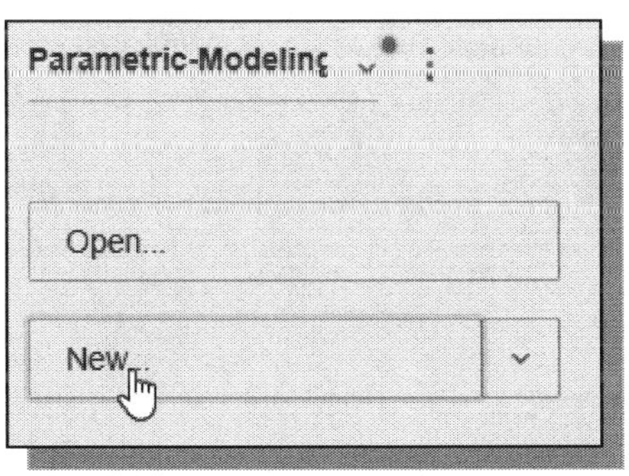

2. Once the program is loaded into memory, select the **New File** icon with a single click of the left-mouse-button in the *Launch* toolbar.

3. Select the **en-US->English** tab, and in the *Part template* area select **Standard(in).ipt**.

4. Click **Create** in the *New File* dialog box to accept the selected settings to start a new model.

Modeling Strategy

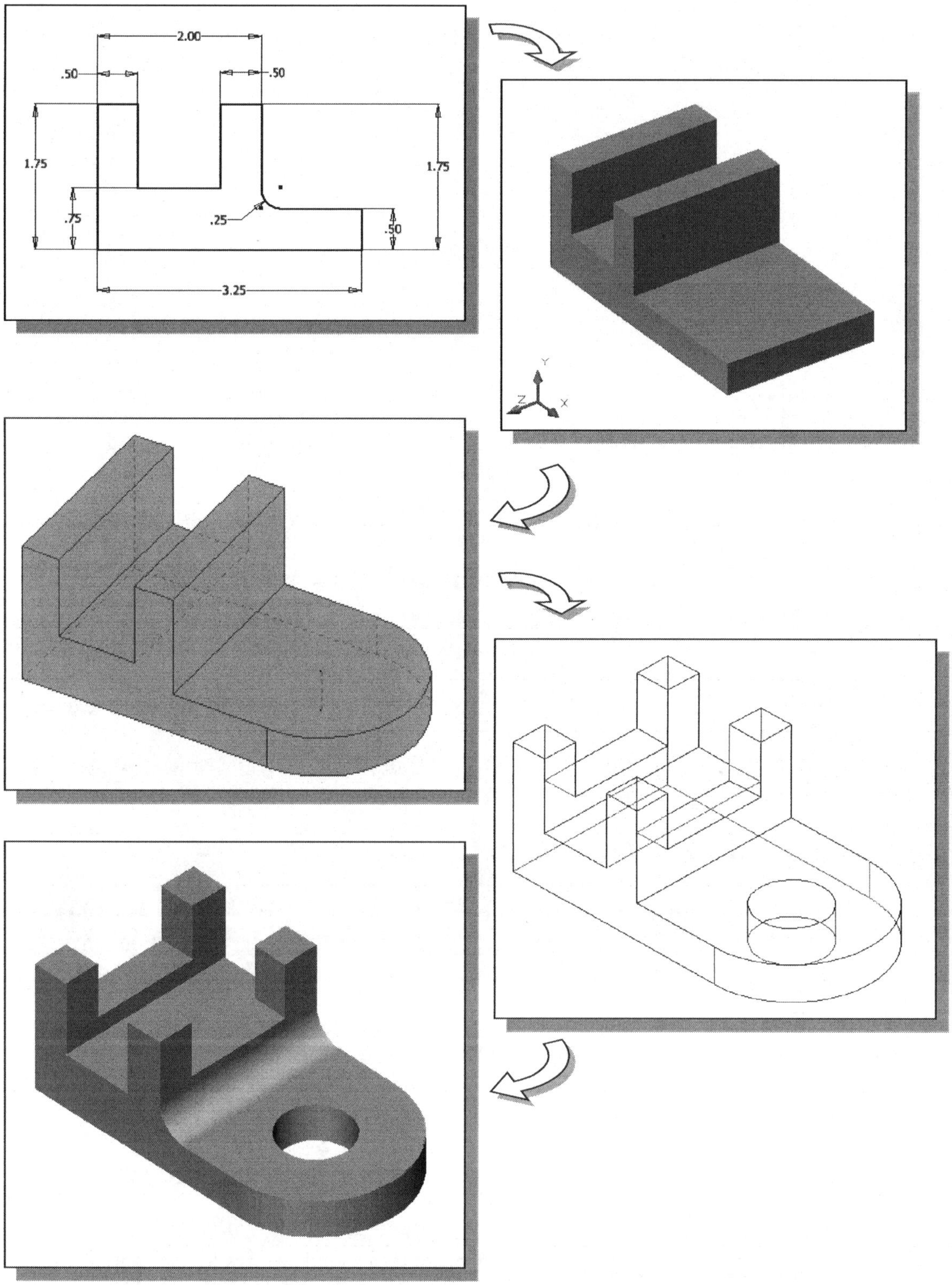

The Autodesk Inventor Browser

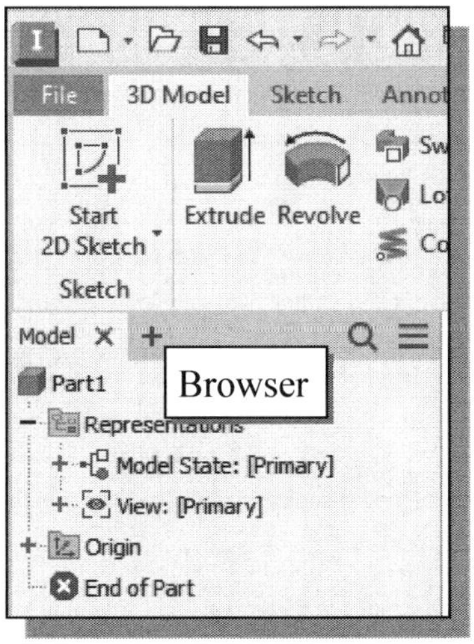

- In the Autodesk Inventor screen layout, the ***browser*** is located to the left of the graphics window. Autodesk Inventor can be used for part modeling, assembly modeling, part drawings, and assembly presentation. The *browser* window provides a visual structure of the features, constraints, and attributes that are used to create the part, assembly, or scene. The *browser* also provides right-click menu access for tasks associated specifically with the part or feature, and it is the primary focus for executing many of the Autodesk Inventor commands.

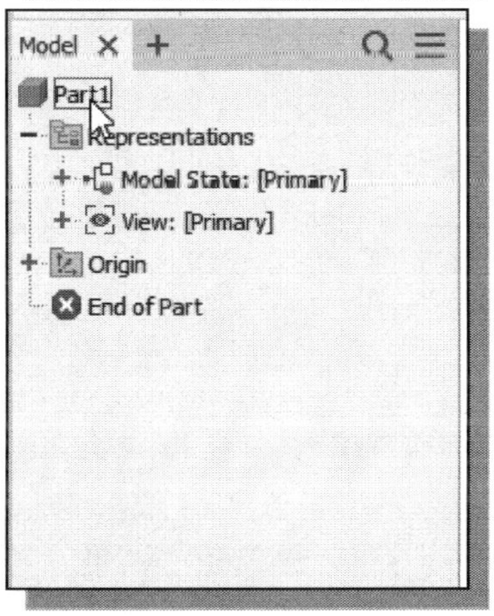

- The first item displayed in the *browser* is the name of the part, which is also the file name. By default, the name "**Part1**" is used when we first started Autodesk Inventor. The *browser* can also be used to modify parts and assemblies by moving, deleting, or renaming items within the hierarchy. Any changes made in the *browser* directly affect the part or assembly and the results of the modifications are displayed on the screen instantly. The *browser* also reports any problems and conflicts during the modification and updating procedure.

Creating the Base Feature

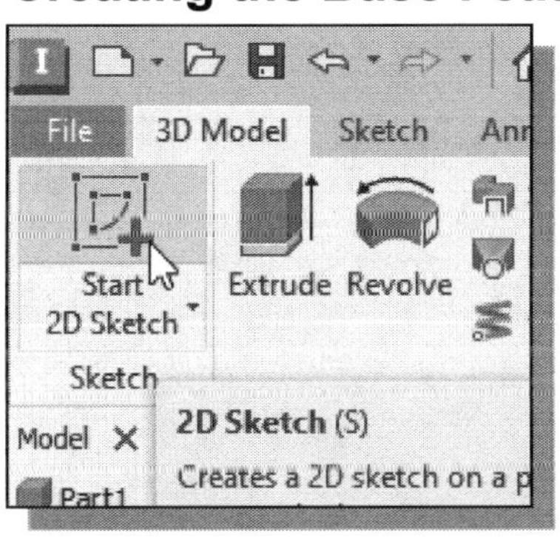

1. Move the graphics cursor to the **Start 2D Sketch** icon in the *Sketch toolbar* under the *3D Model tab*. A *Help-tip box* appears next to the cursor and a brief description of the command is displayed at the bottom of the drawing screen.

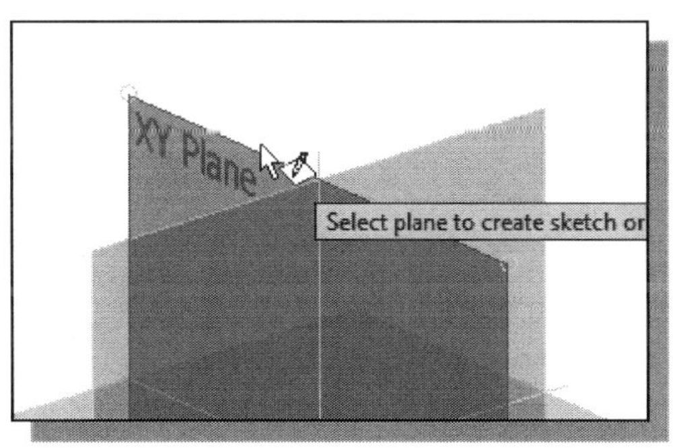

2. Move the cursor over the edge of the *XY Plane* in the graphics area. When the *XY Plane* is highlighted, click once with the **left-mouse-button** to select the *Plane* as the sketch plane for the new sketch.

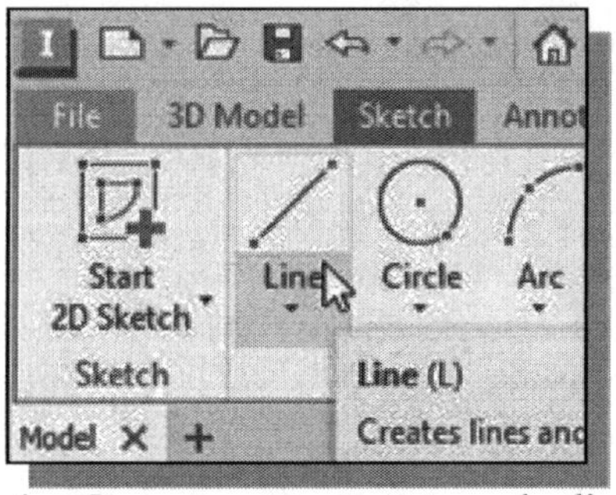

3. Select the **Line** icon by clicking once with the left-mouse-button; this will activate the **Line** command.

4. On your own, create and adjust the geometry by adding and modifying dimensions as shown below.

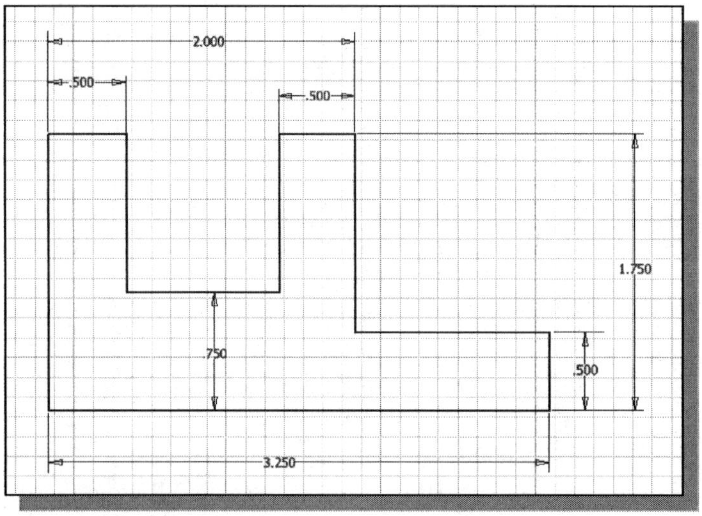

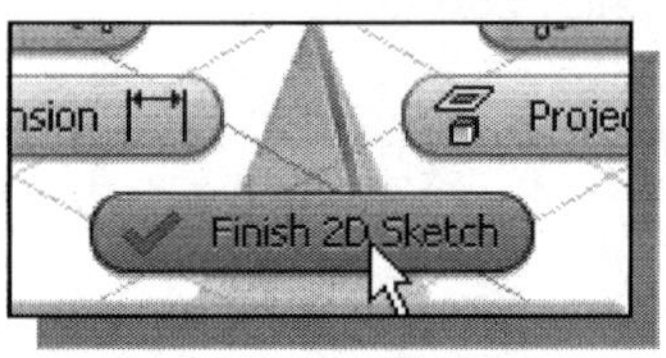

5. Inside the graphics window, click once with the right-mouse-button to display the option menu. Select **Finish 2D Sketch** in the pop-up menu to end the **Sketch** option.

6. On your own, use the dynamic viewing functions to view the sketch. Click the home view icon to change the display to the *isometric* view before proceeding to the next step.

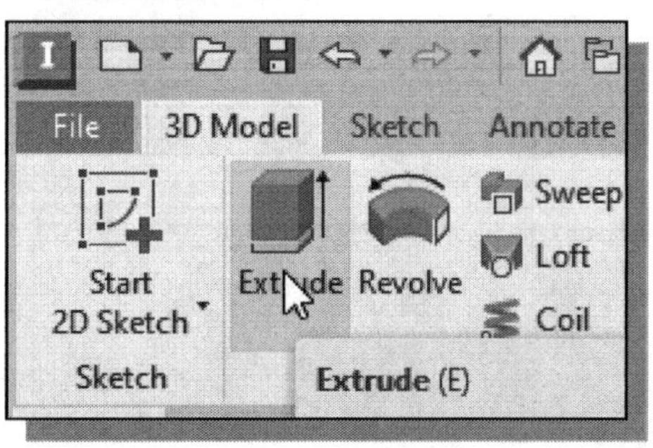

7. In the *Sketch toolbar* under the *3D Model tab*, select the **Extrude** command by left-clicking on the icon.

8. In the *Distance* option box, enter **2.5** as the total extrusion distance.

9. In the *Extrude* pop-up window, left-click once on the **Symmetric** icon. The **Symmetric** option allows us to extrude in both directions of the sketched profile.

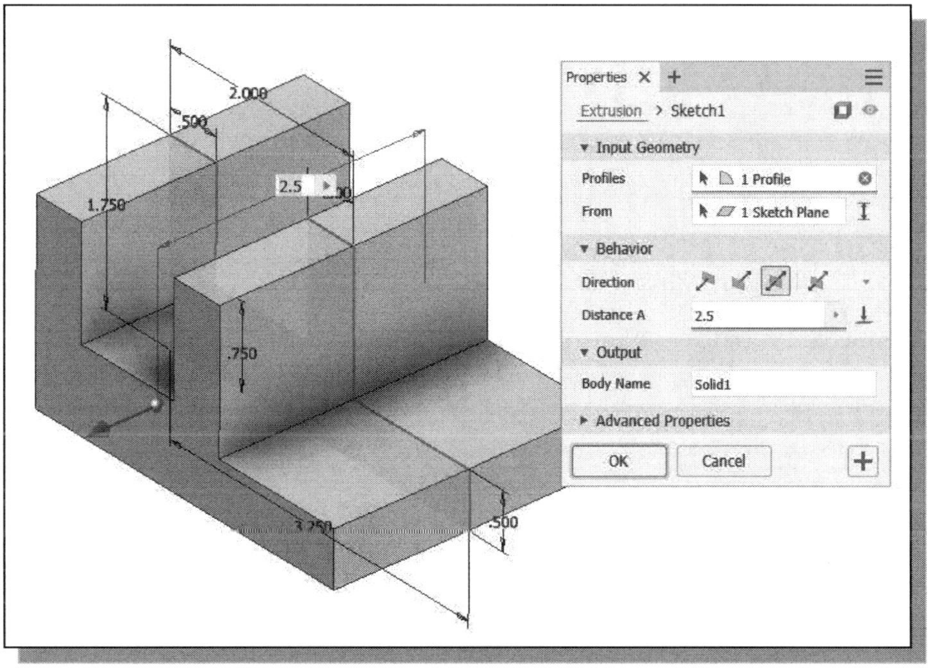

10. Click on the **OK** button to accept the settings and create the base feature.

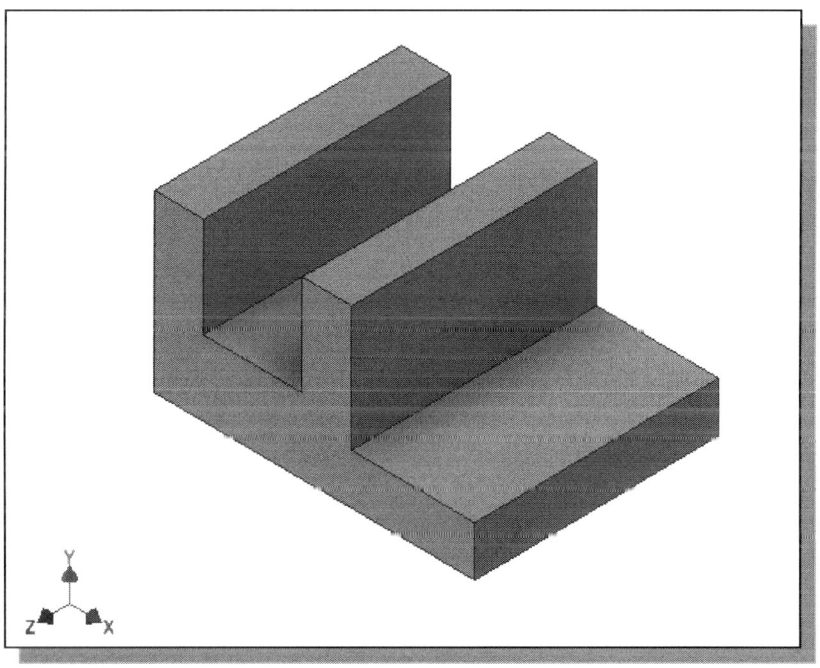

➢ On your own, use the *Dynamic Viewing* functions to view the 3D model. Also notice the extrusion feature is added to the *Model Tree* in the *browser* area.

Adding the Second Solid Feature

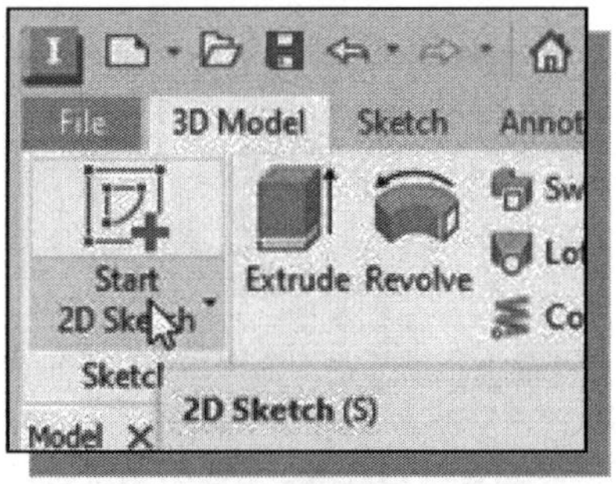

1. In the *Sketch toolbar* under the *3D Model tab* select the **Start 2D Sketch** command by left-clicking once on the icon.

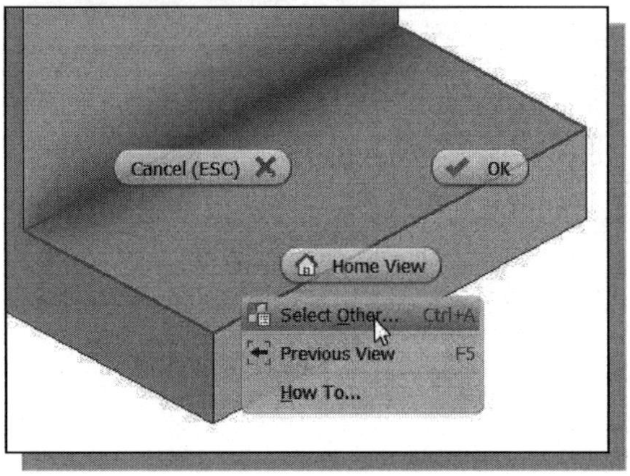

2. In the *Status Bar* area, the message "*Select plane to create sketch or an existing sketch to edit.*" is displayed. Move the cursor inside the upper horizontal face of the 3D object as shown below.

3. Click once with the **right-mouse-button** to bring up the option menu and choose **Select Other** to switch to the next feasible choice.

4. On your own, click on the down arrow to examine all possible surface selections.

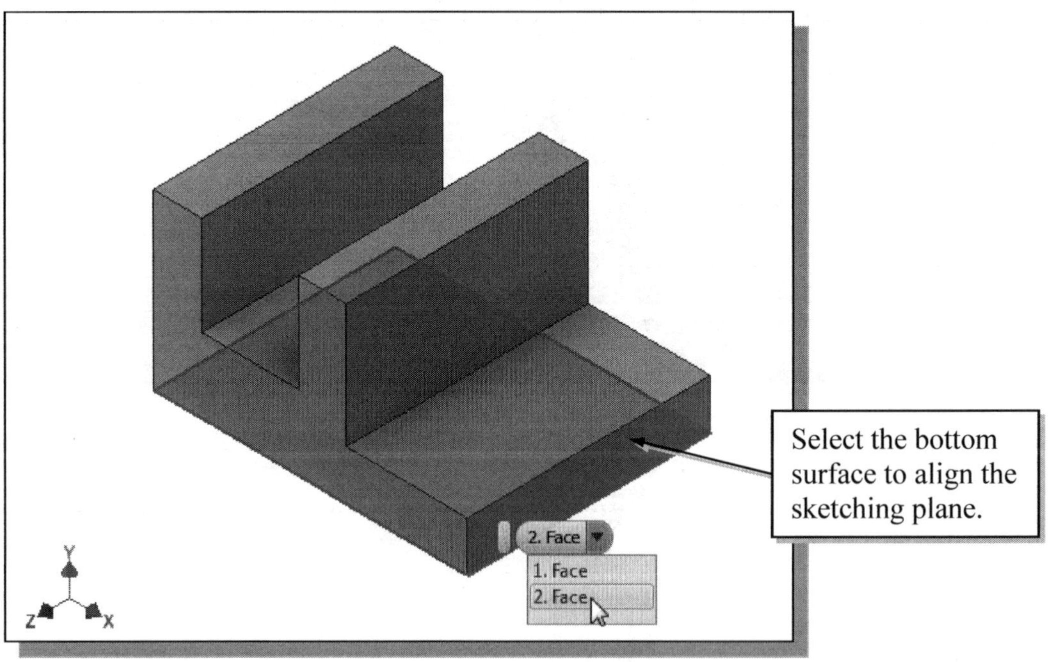

5. Select the **bottom horizontal face** of the solid model when it is highlighted as shown in the above figure.

Creating a 2D Sketch

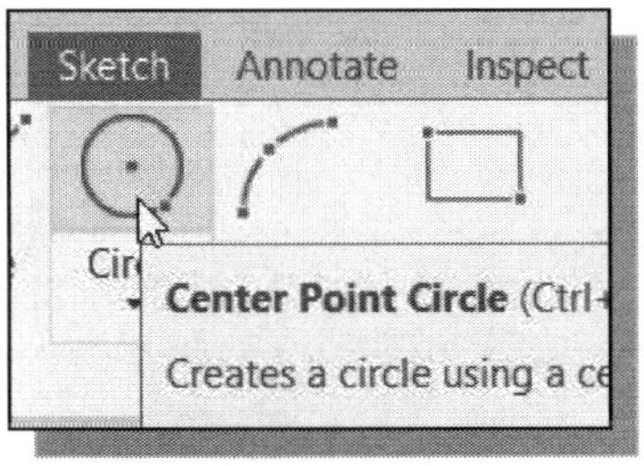

1. Select the **Center Point Circle** command by clicking once with the left-mouse-button on the icon in the *Sketch* tab.

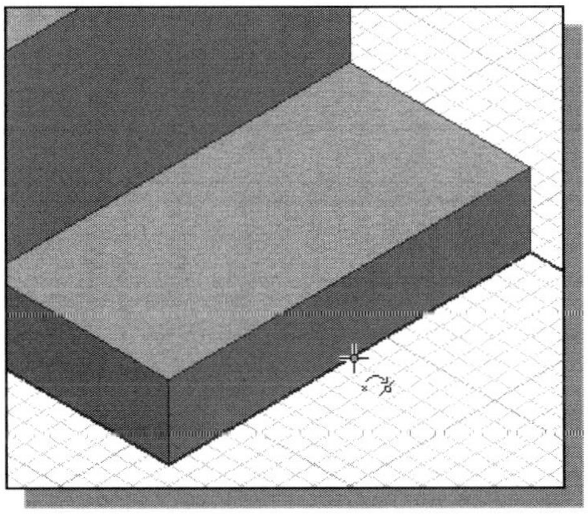

➢ We will align the center of the circle to the midpoint of the base feature.

2. On your own, use the snap to midpoint option to pick the midpoint of the edge when the midpoint is displayed with GREEN color as shown in the figure. (Hit [F6] to set the display orientation if necessary.)

3. Select the front corner of the base feature to create a circle as shown below.

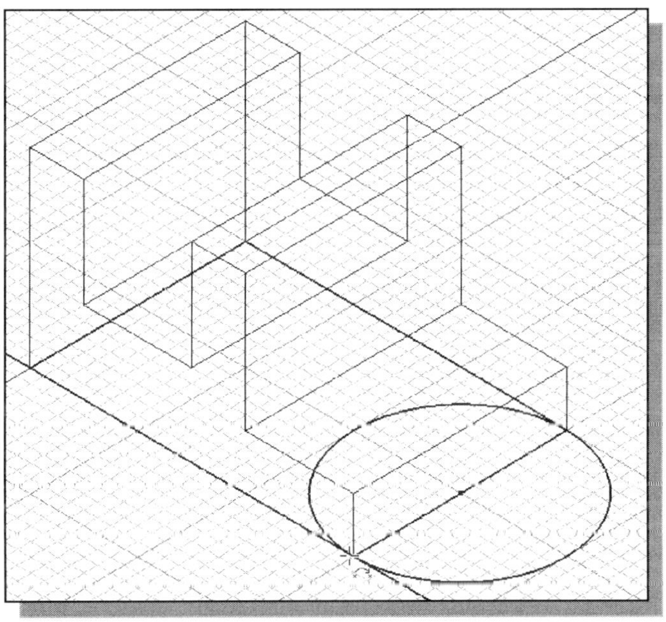

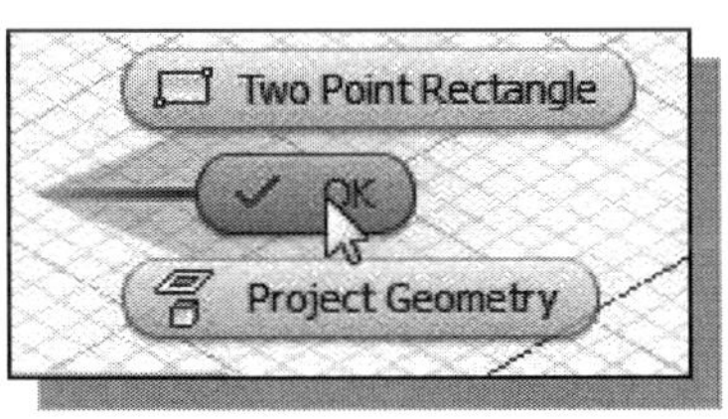

4. Inside the graphics window, click once with the right-mouse-button to display the option menu. Select **OK** in the pop-up menu to end the Circle command.

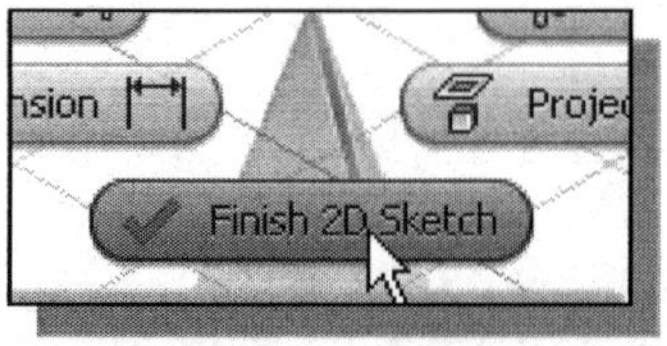

5. Inside the graphics window, click once with the right-mouse-button to display the option menu. Select **Finish 2D Sketch** in the pop-up menu to end the Sketch option.

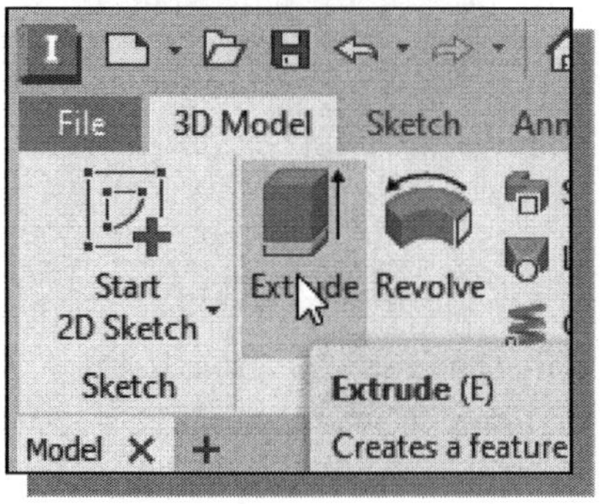

6. In the *Features* toolbar (the toolbar that is located to the left side of the graphics window), select the **Extrude** command by clicking the left-mouse-button on the icon.

7. Move the cursor to the outside **semi-circle** we just created and left-click once to select the region as the **profile** to be extruded.

8. In the *Extrude* pop-up control, set the operation option to **Join.**

9. Also set the *Distance* option to **To Selected Face** as shown below.

10. Select the top face of the base feature as the termination surface for the extrusion.

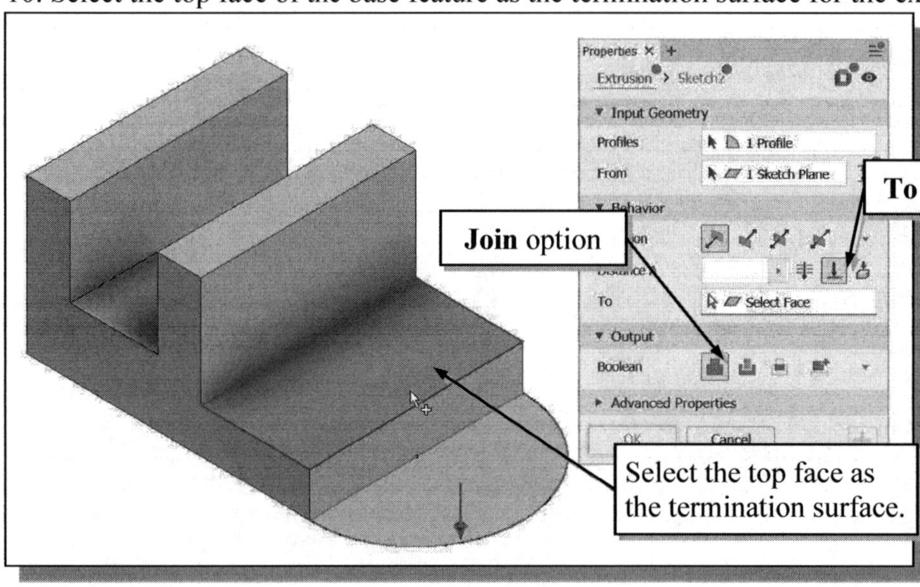

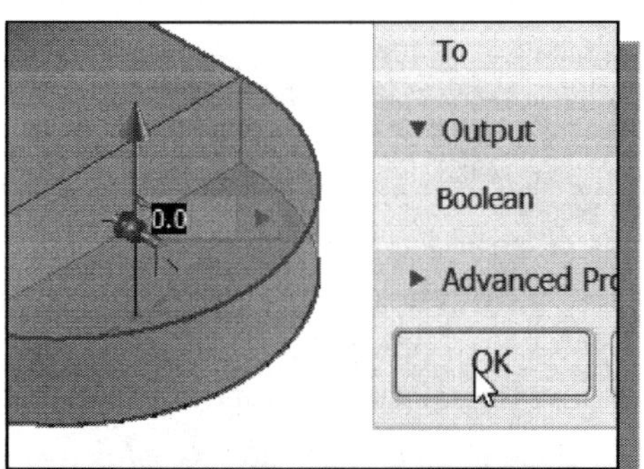

11. Click on the **OK** button to proceed with the *Join* operation.

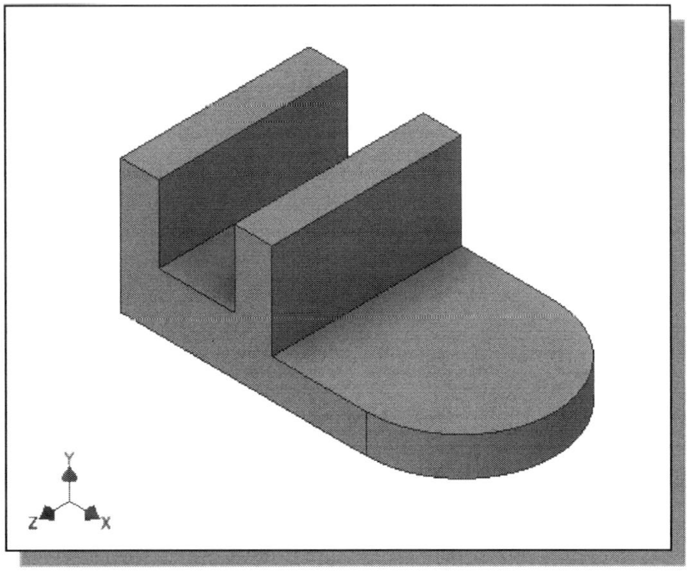

Renaming the Part Features

Currently, our model contains two extruded features. The feature is highlighted in the display area when we select the feature in the *browser* window. Each time a new feature is created, the feature is also displayed in the *Model Tree* window. By default, Autodesk Inventor will use generic names for part features. However, when we begin to deal with parts with a large number of features, it will be much easier to identify the features using more meaningful names. Two methods can be used to rename the features: 1. **Clicking** twice on the name of the feature and 2. Using the **Properties** option. In this example, the use of the first method is illustrated.

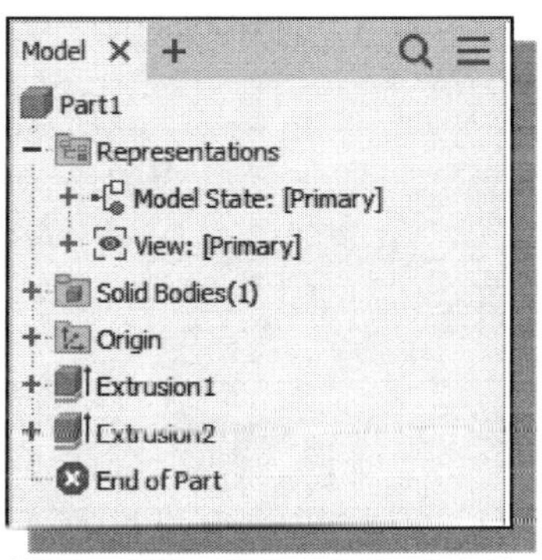

1. Select the first extruded feature in the *model browser* area by left-clicking once on the name of the feature, **Extrusion1**. Notice the selected feature is highlighted in the graphics window.

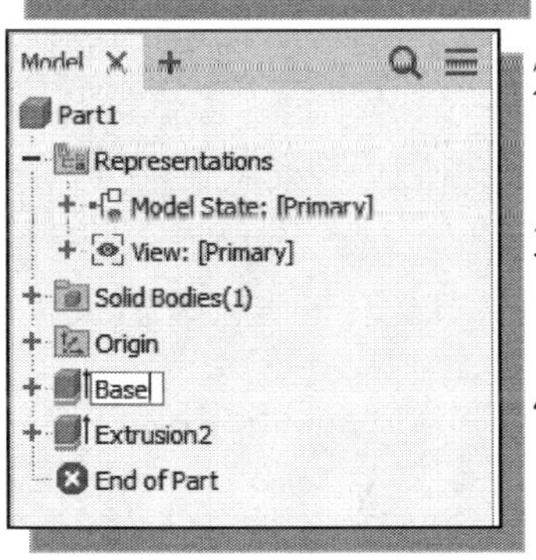

2. Left-click again on the feature name to enter the *Edit* mode as shown.

3. Enter **Base** as the new name for the first extruded feature.

4. On your own, rename the second extruded feature to **Circular_End**.

Adjusting the Width of the Base Feature

One of the main advantages of parametric modeling is the ease of performing part modifications at any time in the design process. Part modifications can be done through accessing the features in the history tree. Autodesk Inventor remembers the history of a part, including all the rules that were used to create it, so that changes can be made to any operation that was performed to create the part. For our ***Saddle Bracket*** design, we will reduce the size of the base feature from 3.25 inches to 3.0 inches, and the extrusion distance to 2.0 inches.

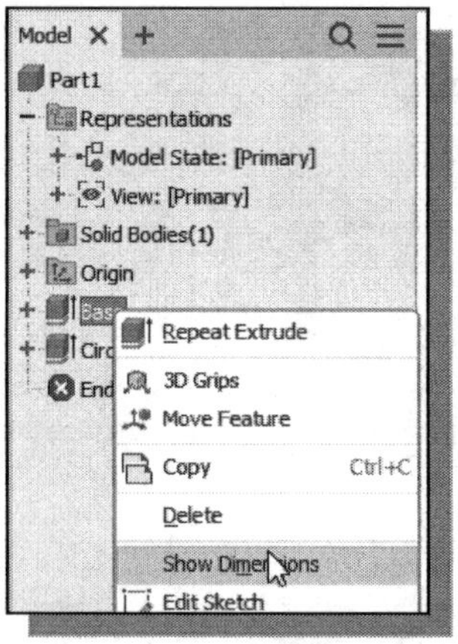

1. Select the first extruded feature, **Base**, in the *browser* area. Notice the selected feature is highlighted in the graphics window.

2. Inside the *browser* area, **right-mouse-click** on the first extruded feature to bring up the option menu and select the **Show Dimensions** option in the pop-up menu.

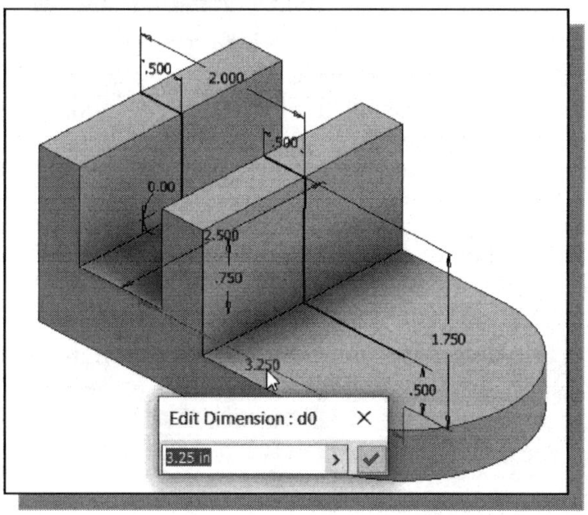

3. All dimensions used to create the **Base** feature are displayed on the screen. Select the overall width of the **Base** feature, the **3.25** dimension value, by double-clicking on the dimension text as shown.

4. Enter **3.0** in the *Edit Dimension* window.

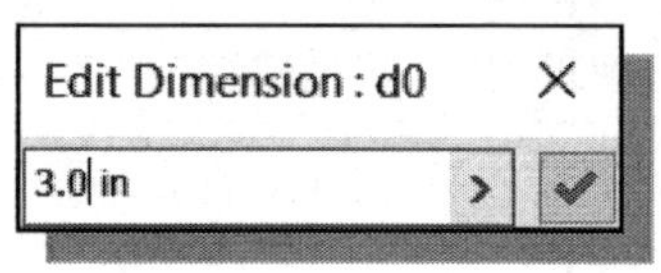

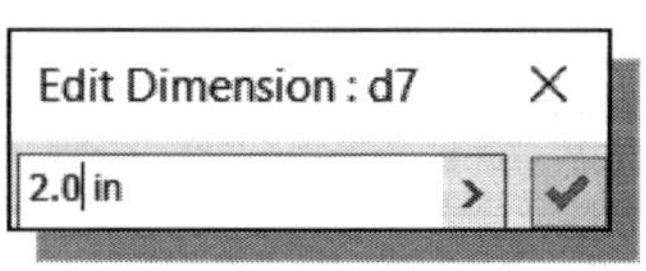

5. On your own, repeat the above steps and modify the extruded distance from **2.5** to **2.0**.

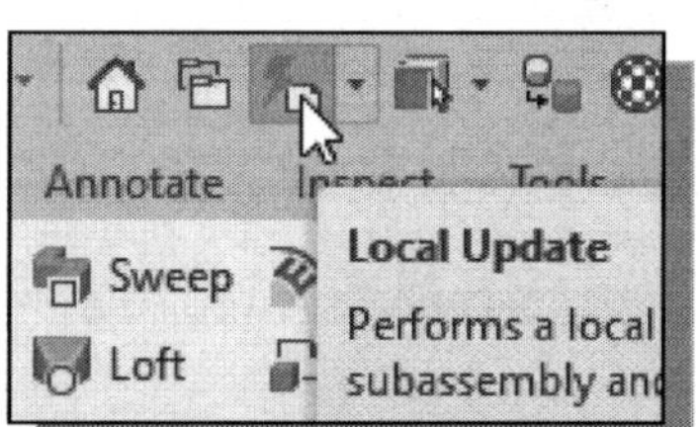

6. Click **Local Update** in the *Quick Access Toolbar*.

➢ Note that Autodesk Inventor updates the model by re-linking all elements used to create the model. Any problems or conflicts that occur will also be displayed during the updating process.

Adding a Placed Feature

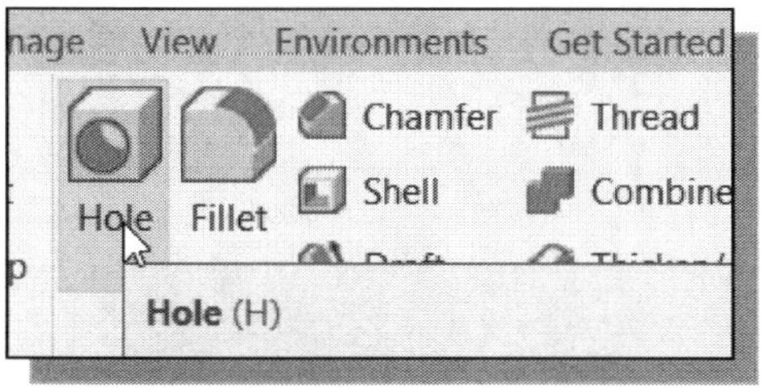

1. In the *Sketch tab*, select the **Hole** command by left-clicking on the icon.

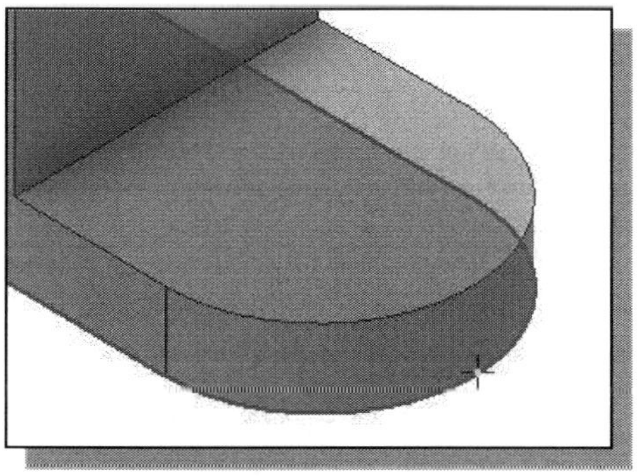

2. Pick the **bottom plane** of the solid model as the placement plane as shown.

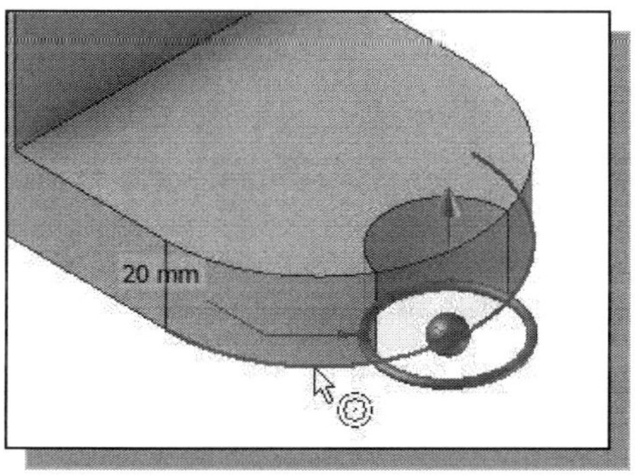

3. Pick the **bottom arc** and notice the *concentric reference symbol* appears indicating the center of the hole will be aligned to the center of the selected arc.

4. Set the hole diameter to **0.75 in** as shown.

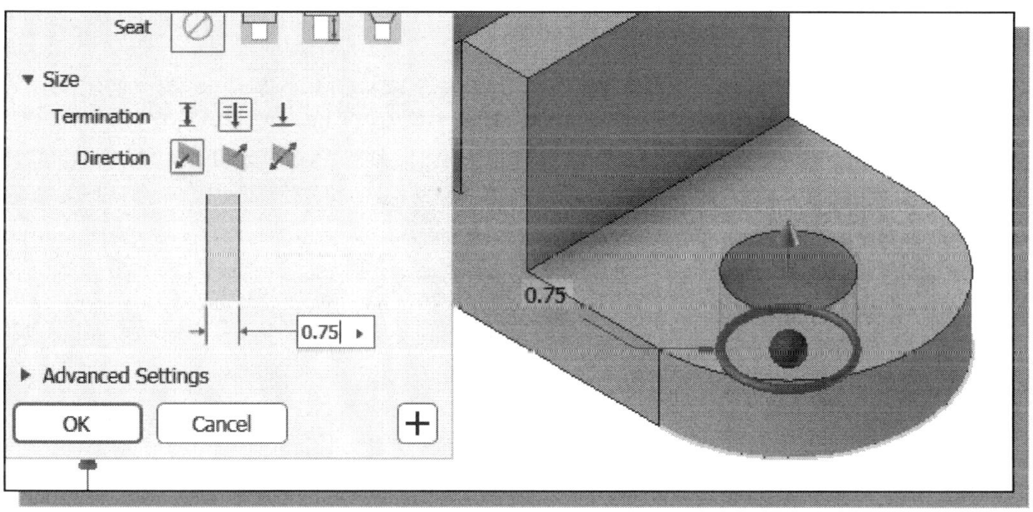

5. Set the termination option to **Through All** as shown.

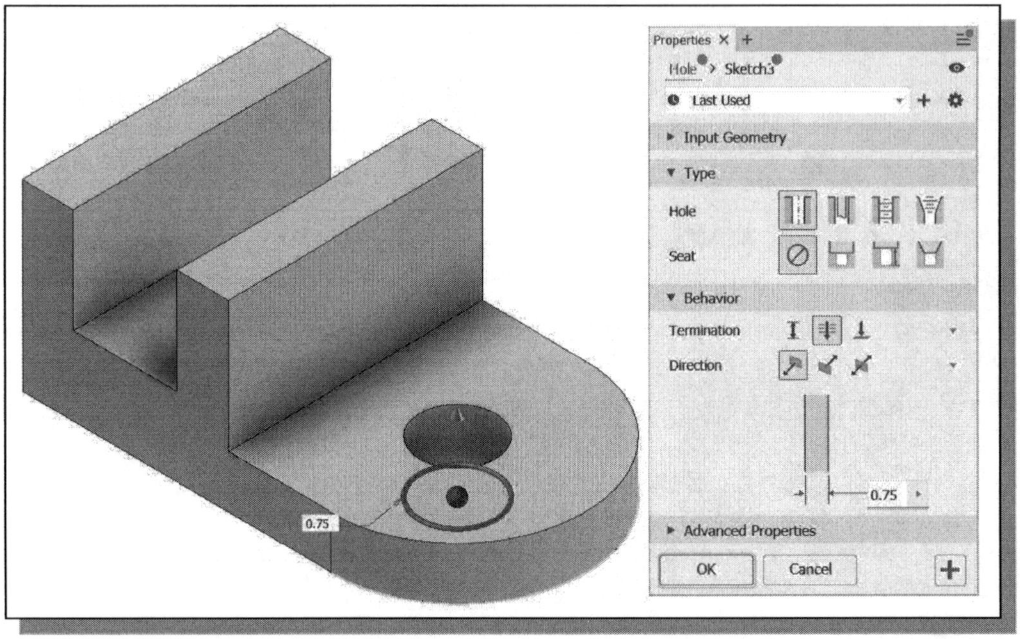

6. Click **OK** to accept the settings and create the *Hole* feature.

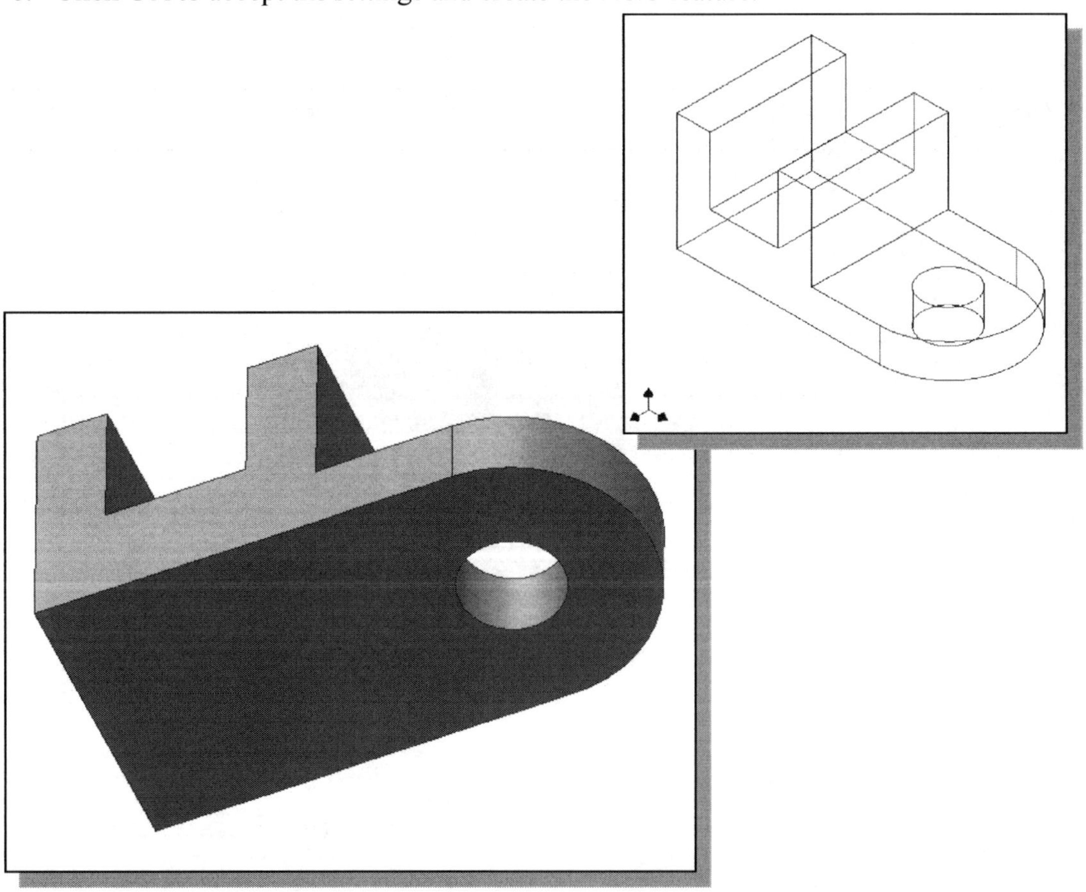

Creating a Rectangular Cut Feature

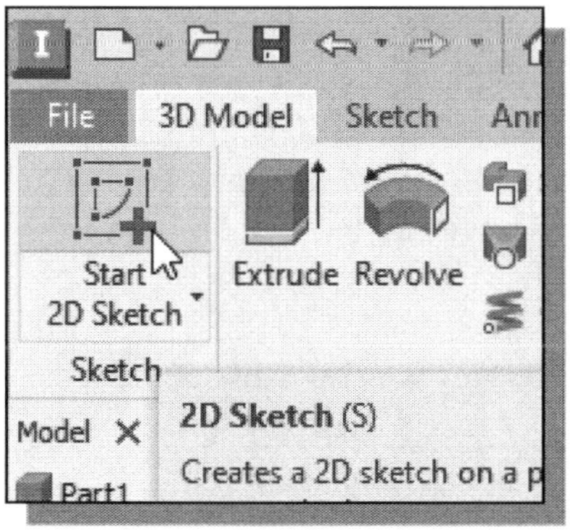

1. In the *Sketch toolbar* under the *3D Model tab* select the **Start 2D Sketch** command by left-clicking once on the icon.

2. Pick the **vertical face** of the solid as shown. (Note the alignment of the origin of the sketch plane.)

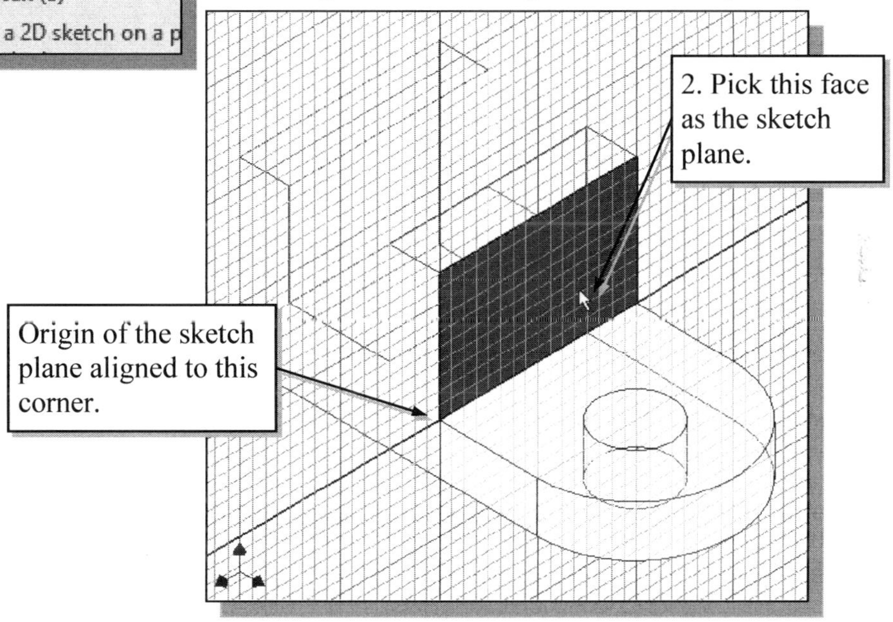

➢ On your own, create a rectangular cut (**1.0 x 0.75**) feature (**To Next** option) as shown and rename the feature to **Rect_Cut**.

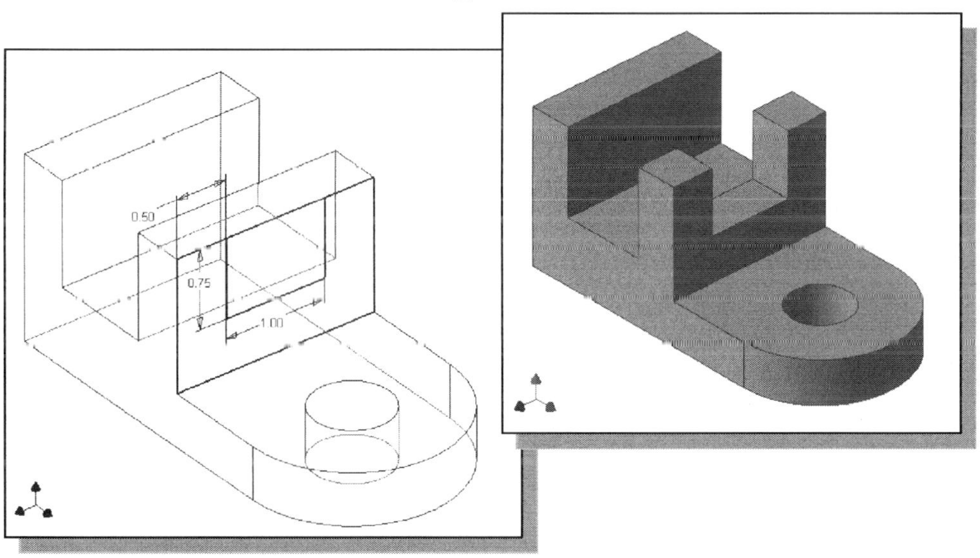

History-Based Part Modifications

Autodesk Inventor uses the *history-based part modification* approach, which enables us to make modifications to the appropriate features and re-link the rest of the history tree without having to reconstruct the model from scratch. We can think of it as going back in time and modifying some aspects of the modeling steps used to create the part. We can modify any feature that we have created. As an example, we will adjust the depth of the rectangular cutout.

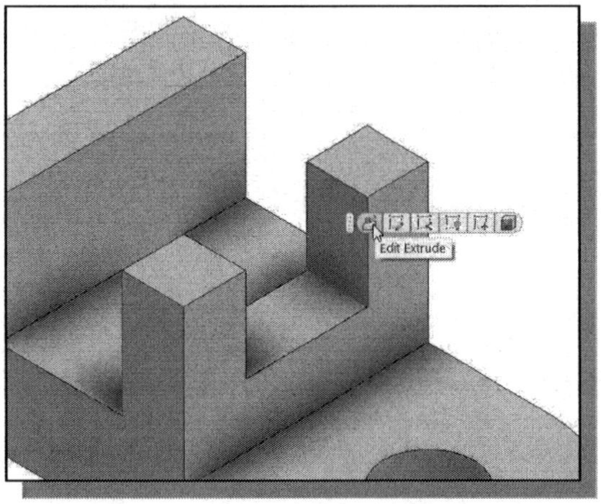

1. In the *graphics* window, select the last cut feature, **Rect_Cut**, by left-clicking on one surface of the feature.

2. Select **Edit Feature** in the pop-up menu. Notice the *Extrude* dialog box appears on the screen.

- Note that the feature pop-up options are also available through the Model History Tree, as shown on the next page.

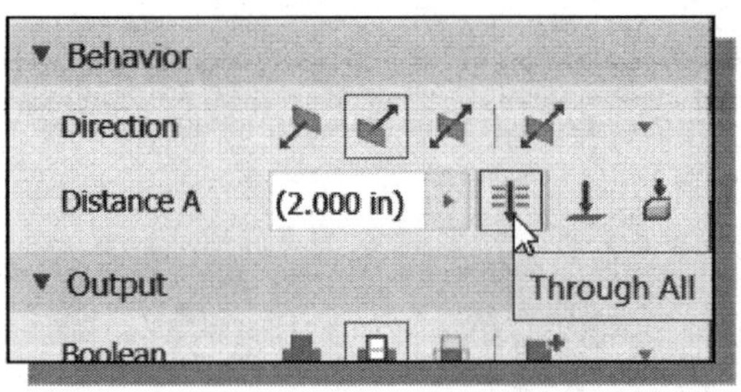

3. In the *Extrude* dialog box, set the termination *Extents* to the **Through All** option.

4. Click on the **OK** button to accept the settings.

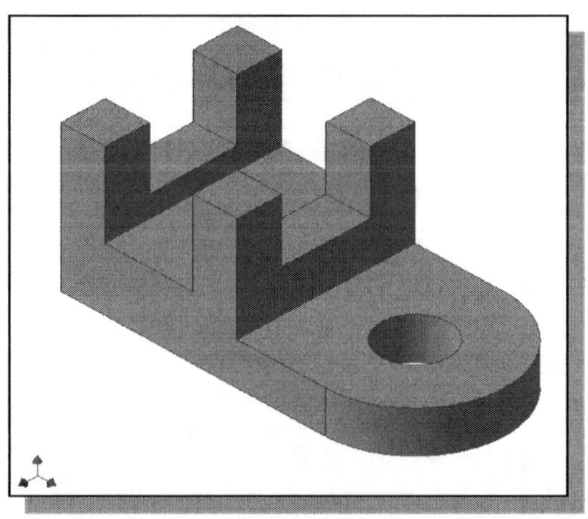

- As can be seen, the history-based modification approach is very straight forward, and it only took a few seconds to adjust the cut feature to the **Through All** option.

A Design Change

Engineering designs usually go through many revisions and changes. Autodesk Inventor provides an assortment of tools to handle design changes quickly and effectively. We will demonstrate some of the tools available by changing the **Base** feature of the design.

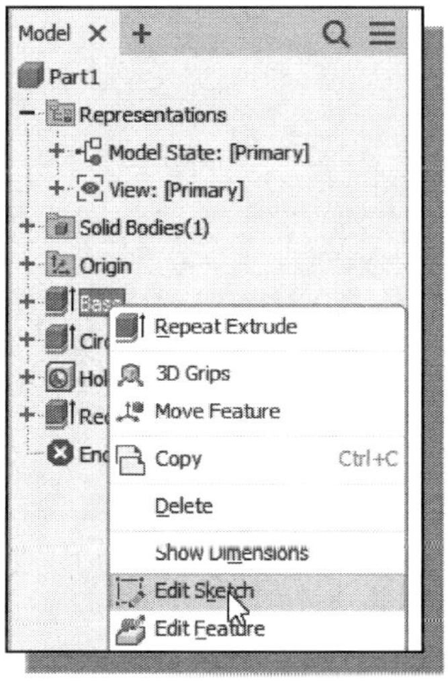

1. In the *browser* window, select the **Base** feature by left-clicking once on the name of the feature.

2. In the *browser*, right-click once on the **Base** feature to bring up the option menu; then pick **Edit Sketch** in the pop-up menu.

3. Click **Home** to reset the display to ***Isometric***.

❖ Autodesk Inventor will now display the original 2D sketch of the selected feature in the graphics window. We have literally gone back to the point where we first created the 2D sketch. Notice the feature being modified is also highlighted in the desktop *browser*.

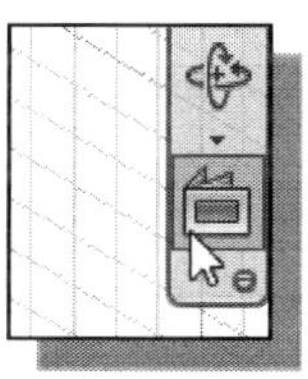

4. Click on the **Look At** icon in the *Standard* toolbar area.

- The **Look At** command automatically aligns the *sketch plane* of a selected entity to the screen.

5. Select any line segment of the 2D sketch to reset the display to align to the 2D sketch.

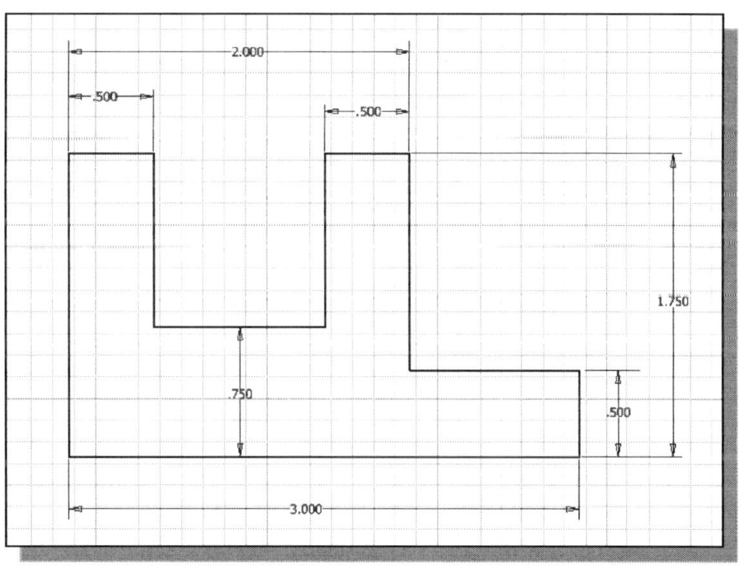

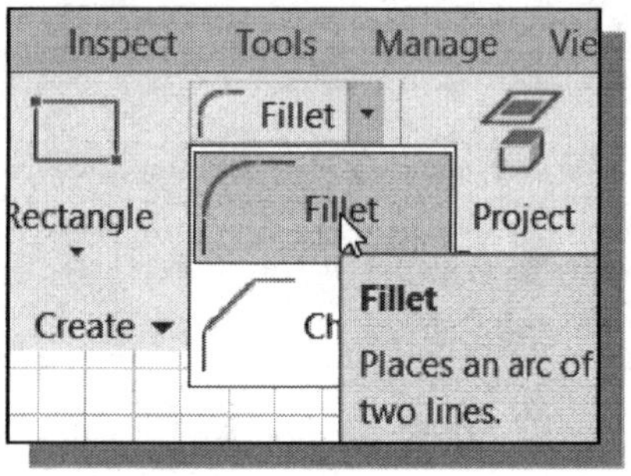

6. Select the **Fillet** command in the *2D Sketch* toolbar.

7. In the graphics window, enter **0.25** as the new radius of the fillet.

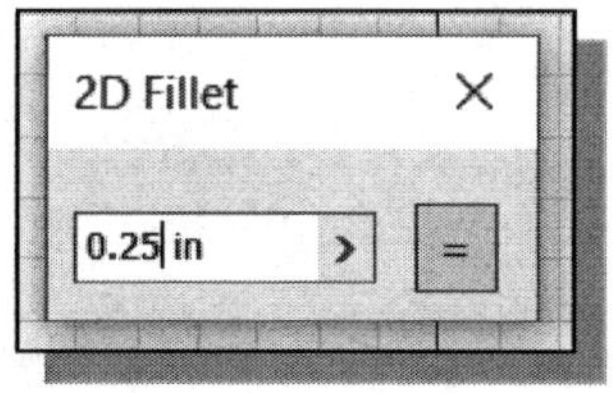

8. Select the two edges as shown to create the fillet.

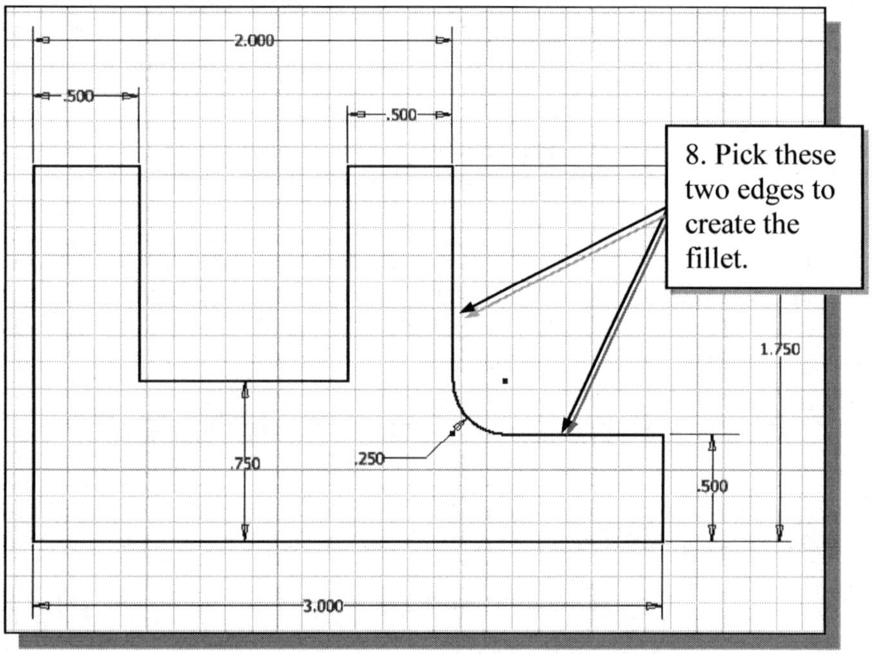

- Note that the fillet is created automatically with the dimension attached. The attached dimension can also be modified through the history tree.

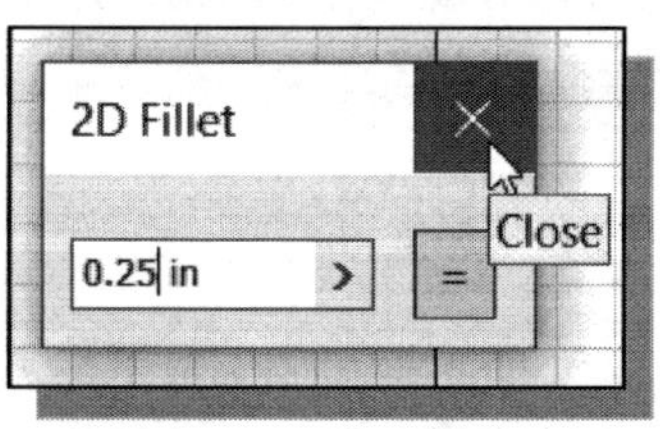

9. Click on the [**X**] icon in the *2D Fillet* window to end the **Fillet** command.

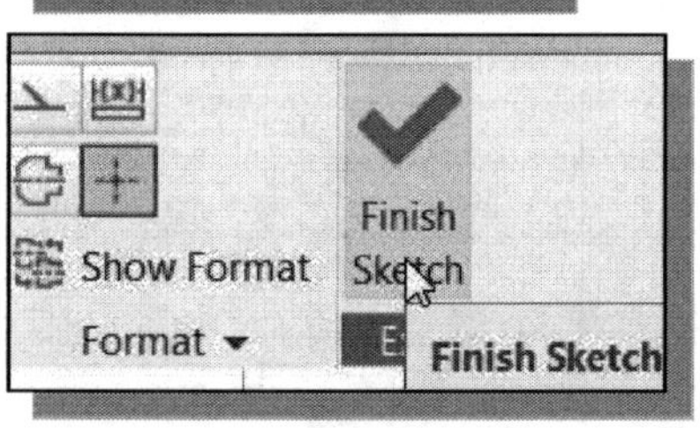

10. Select **Finish Sketch** in the *Ribbon* toolbar to end the **Sketch** option.

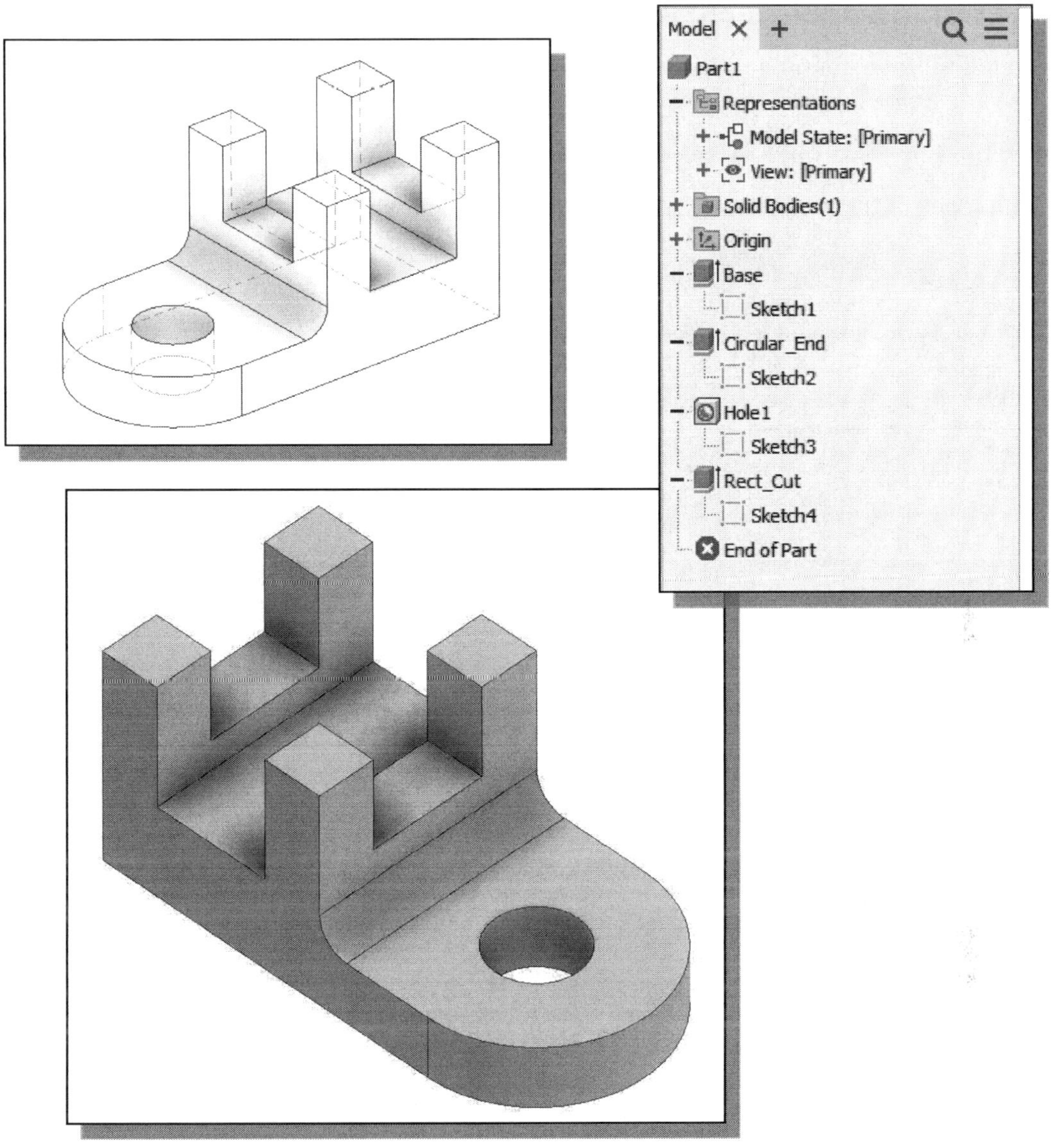

❖ In a typical design process, the initial design will undergo many analyses, testing, and reviews. The *history-based part modification* approach is an extremely powerful tool that enables us to quickly update the design. At the same time, it is quite clear that PLANNING AHEAD is also important in doing feature-based modeling.

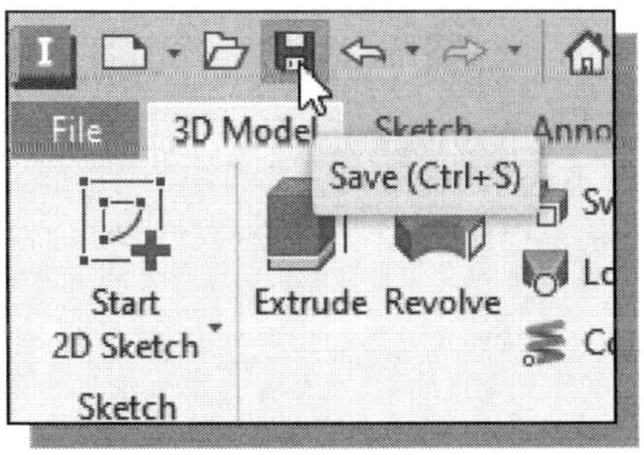

11. On your own, create the **Chapter9** folder and save the model as *Saddle_Bracket.ipt.*

Assigning and Calculating the Associated Physical Properties

Autodesk Inventor models have properties called **iProperties**. The *iProperties* can be used to create reports and update assembly bills of materials, drawing parts lists, and other information. With *iProperties*, we can also set and calculate physical properties for a part or assembly using the material library. This allows us to examine the physical properties of the model, such as weight or center of gravity.

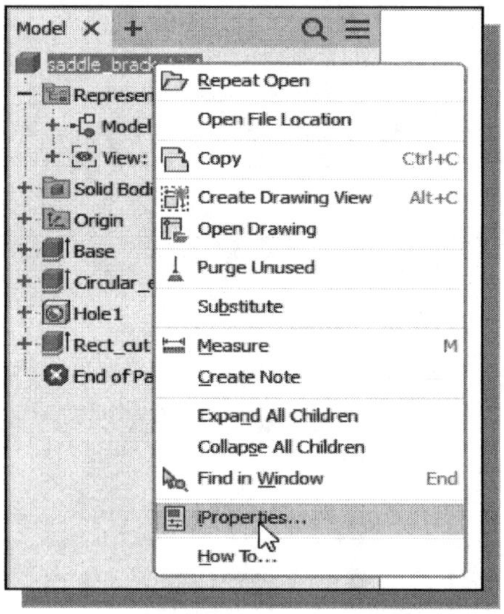

1. In the *browser*, **right-click** once on the ***part name*** to bring up the option menu; then pick **iProperties** in the *pop-up* menu.

2. On your own, look at the different information listed in the *iProperties* dialog box.

3. Click on the **Physical** tab; this is the page that contains the physical properties of the selected model.

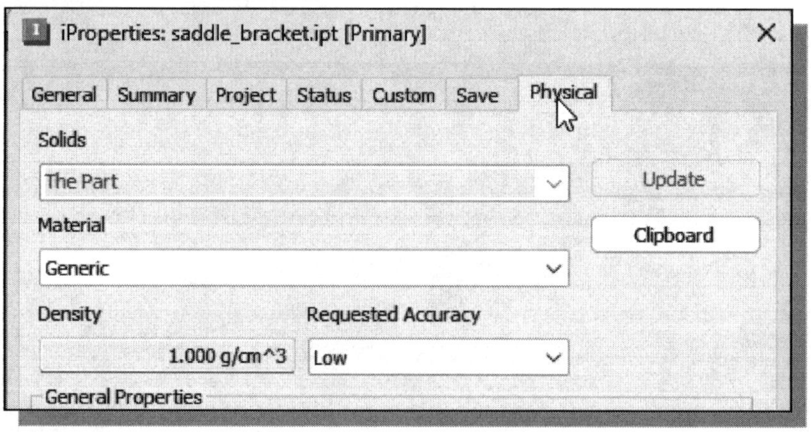

- Note that the *Material* option is not assigned, and none of the physical properties are shown.

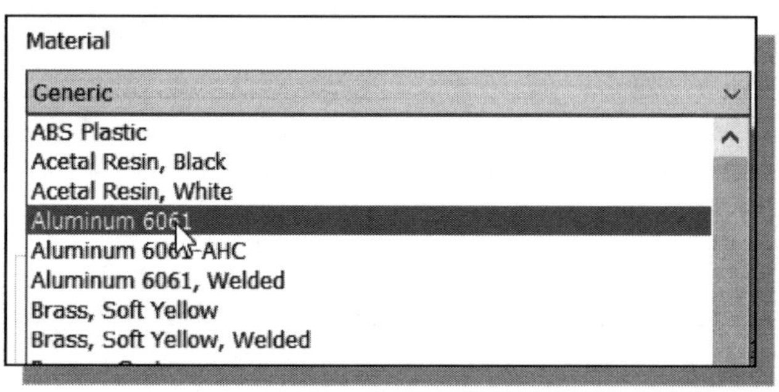

4. Click the down-arrow in the *Material* option to display the material list, and select **Aluminum-6061** as shown.

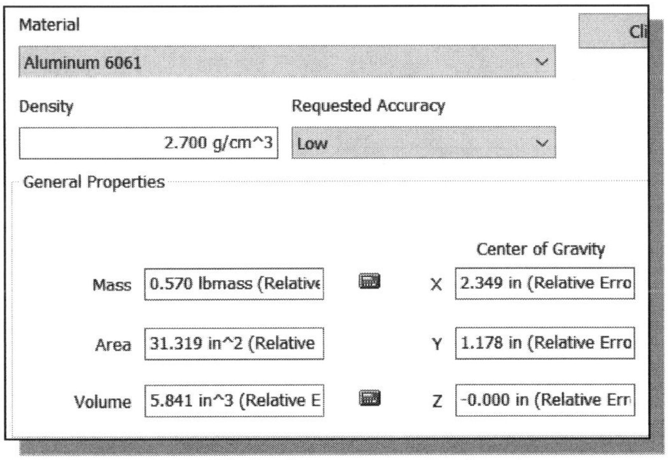

❖ Note the *General Properties* area now has the *Mass*, *Area*, *Volume* and the *Center of Gravity* information of the model based on the density of the selected material.

5. Click on the **Global** button to display the *Mass Moments Inertial* of the design.

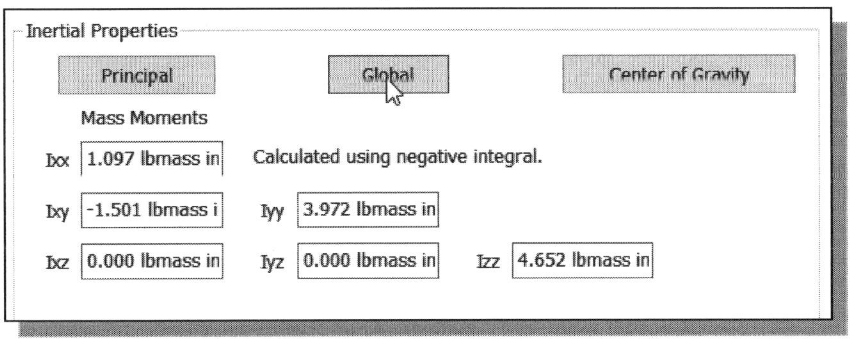

6. On your own, select **Cast Iron** as the *Material* type and compare the differences in using the different materials.

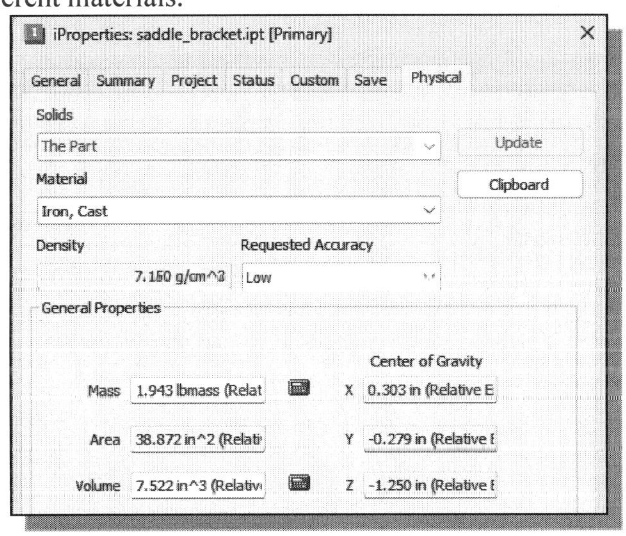

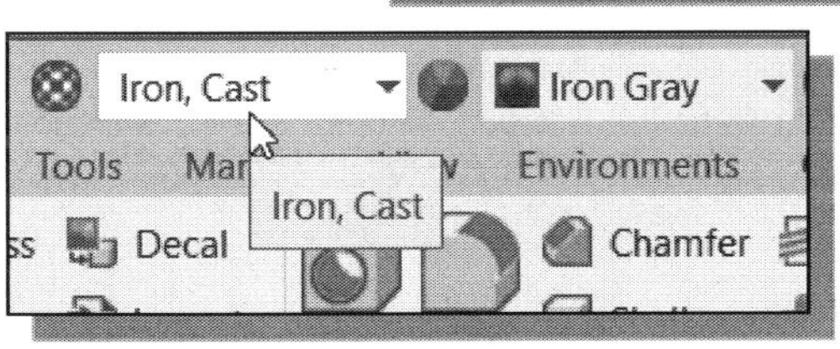

❖ Also note the *Material* can be assigned through the quick access menu as shown.

Review Questions:

1. What are stored in the Autodesk Inventor *History Tree*?

2. When extruding, what is the difference between *Distance* and *Through All*?

3. Describe the *history-based part modification* approach.

4. What determines how a model reacts when other features in the model change?

5. Describe the steps to rename existing features.

6. Describe two methods available in Autodesk Inventor to *modify the dimension values* of parametric sketches.

7. Create *History Tree sketches* showing the steps you plan to use to create the two models shown on page 9-24.

Exercises:

1. **C-Clip** (Dimensions are in inches. Plate thickness: **0.25 inches**.)

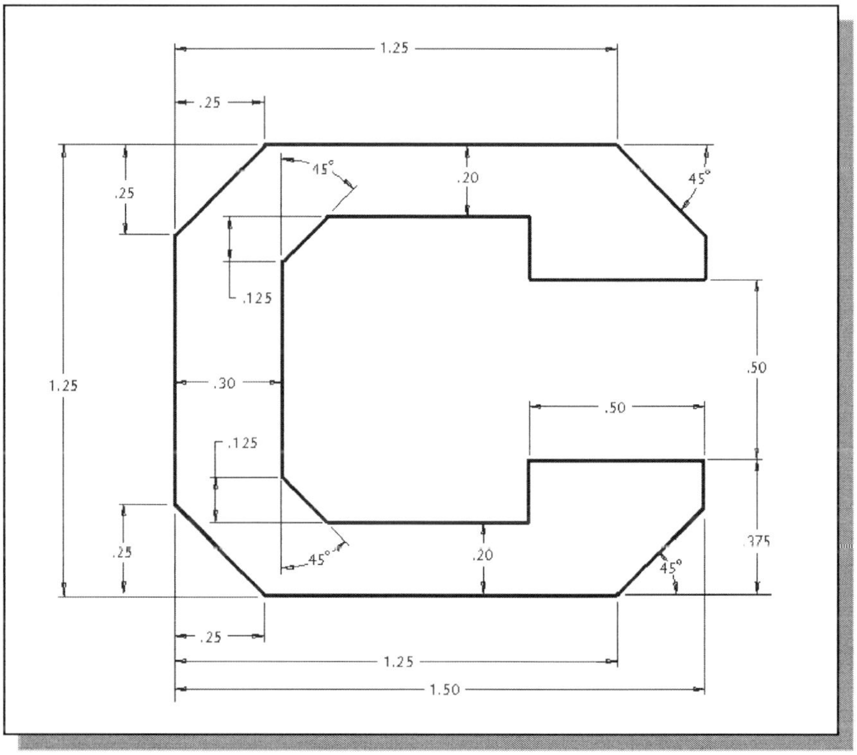

2. **Tube Mount** (Dimensions are in inches.)

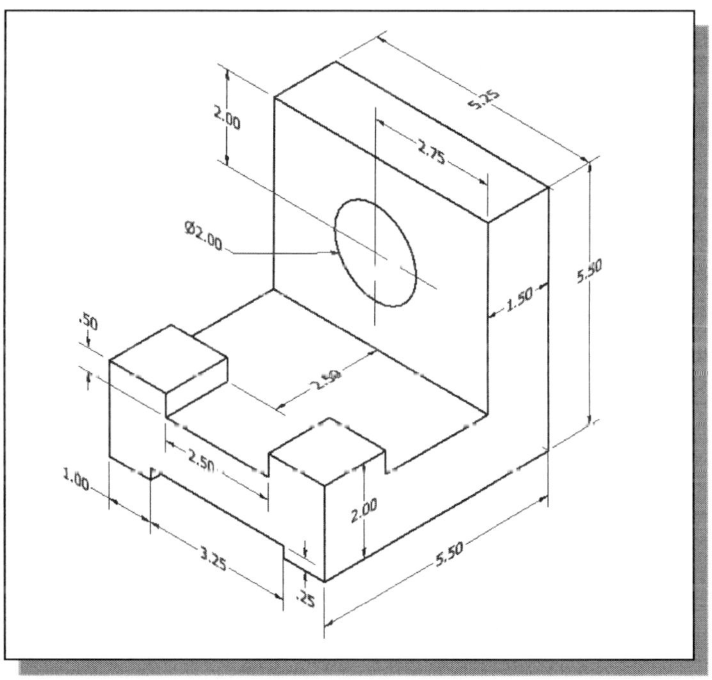

3. **Hanger Jaw** (Dimensions are in inches. Volume =?)

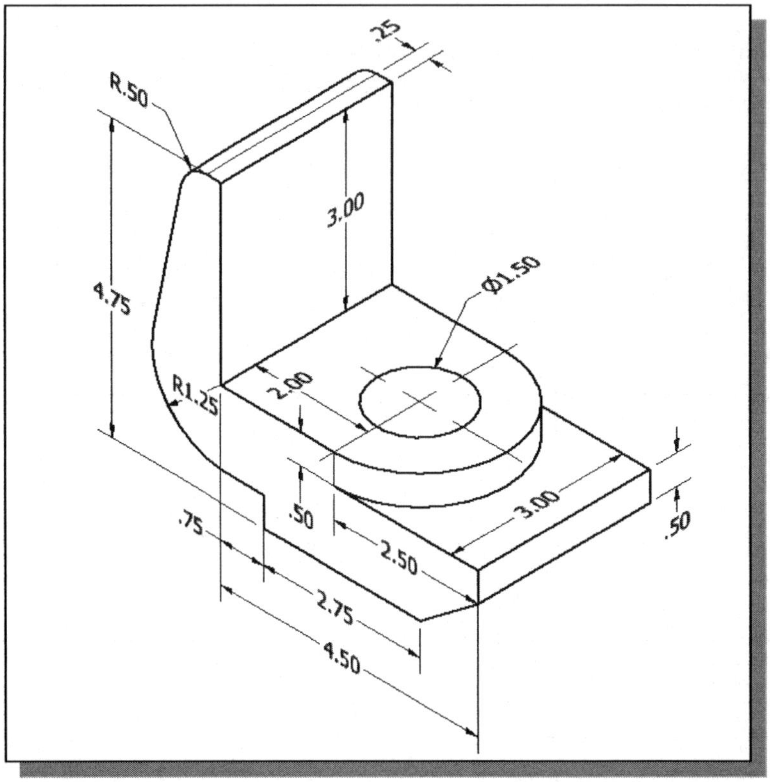

4. **Transfer Fork** (Dimensions are in inches. Material: **Cast Iron.** Volume =?)

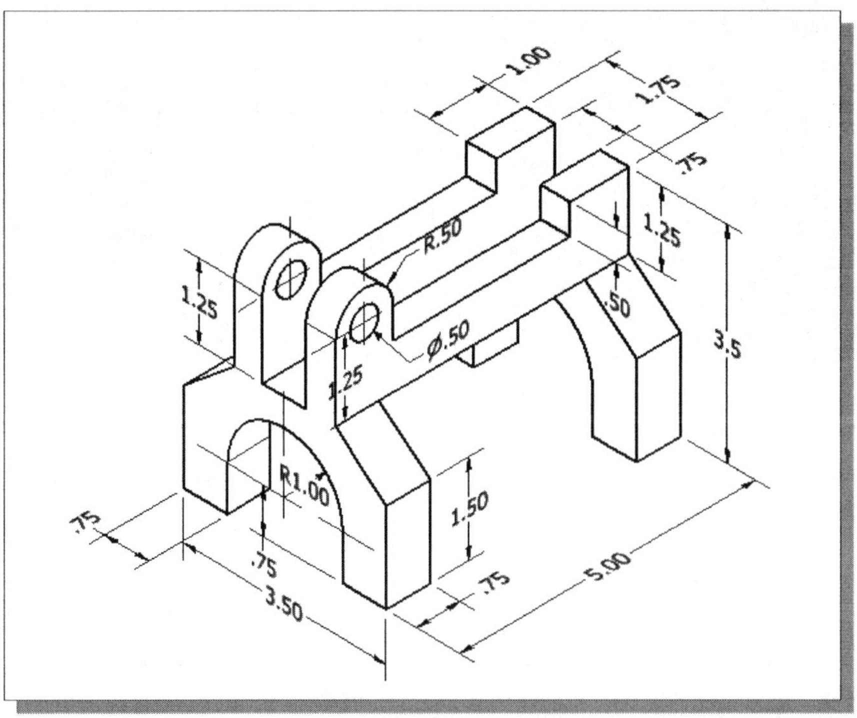

5. **Guide Slider** (Material: **Cast Iron**. Weight and Volume =?)

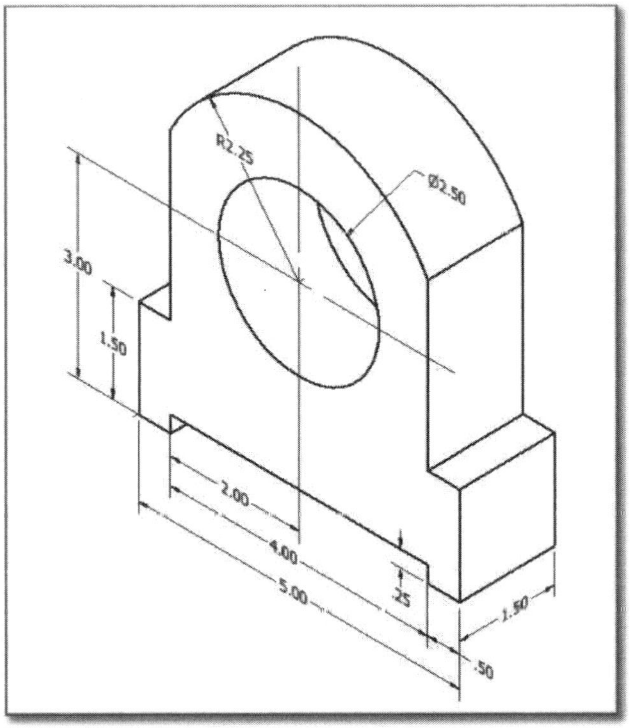

6. **Shaft Guide** (Material: **Aluminum-6061**. Mass and Volume =?)

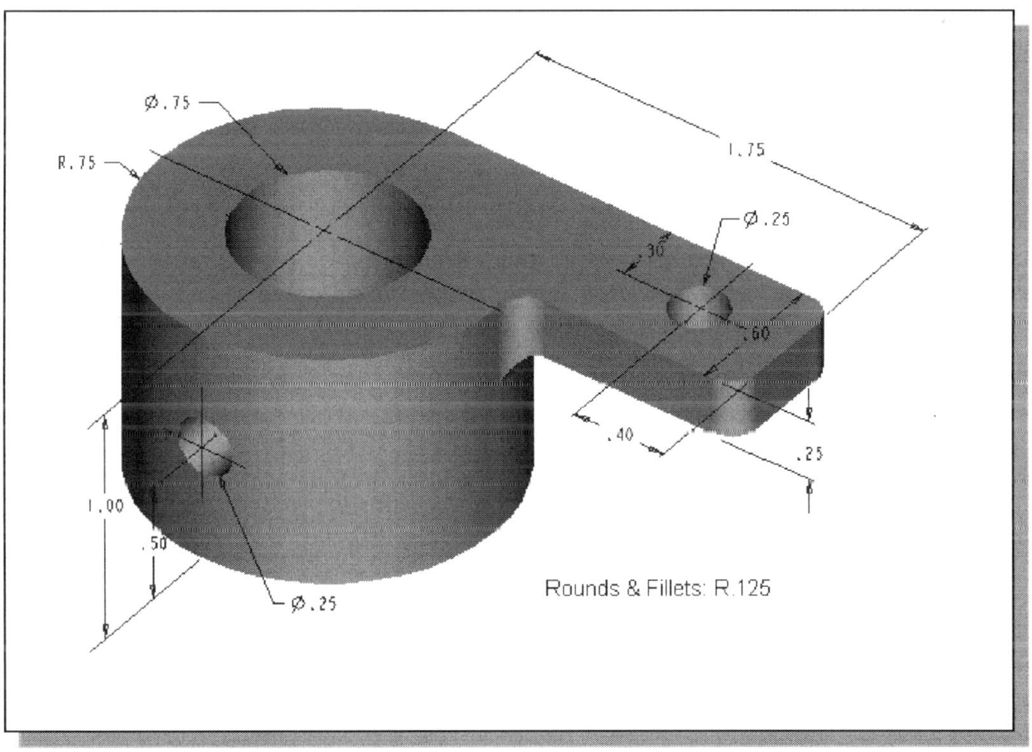

7. **Idler Mount** (Dimensions are in inches. Center to center distance: 6.0)

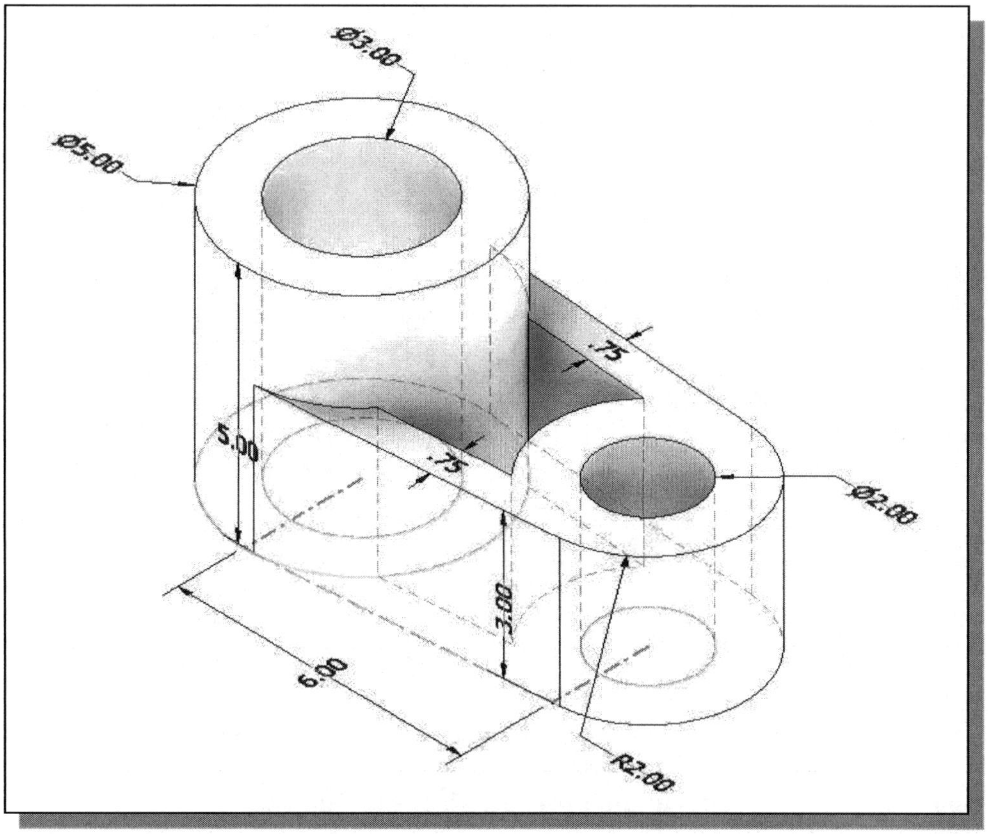

Chapter 10
Parametric Constraints Fundamentals - Autodesk Inventor

Learning Objectives

- Create Parametric Relations
- Use Dimensional Variables
- Display, Add, and Delete Geometric Constraints
- Understand and Apply Different Geometric Constraints
- Display and Modify Paramotric Relations
- Create Fully Constrained Sketches

Constraints and Relations

A primary and essential difference between parametric modeling and previous generation computer modeling is that parametric modeling captures the *design intent*. In the previous lessons, we have seen that the design philosophy of "*shape before size*" is implemented through the use of Autodesk Inventor's Profile and Dimension commands. In performing geometric constructions, dimensional values are necessary to describe the **SIZE** and **LOCATION** of constructed geometric entities. Besides using dimensions to define the geometry, we can also apply geometric rules to control geometric entities. More importantly, Autodesk Inventor can capture design intent through the use of **geometric constraints**, **dimensional constraints**, and **parametric relations**. In Autodesk Inventor, there are two types of constraints: **geometric constraints** and **dimensional constraints**. For part modeling in Autodesk Inventor, constraints are applied to *2D sketches*. **Geometric constraints** are **geometric restrictions** that can be applied to geometric entities; for example, *horizontal*, *parallel*, *perpendicular*, and *tangent* are commonly used *geometric constraints* in parametric modeling. **Dimensional constraints** are used to describe the SIZE and LOCATION of individual geometric shapes. One should also realize that depending upon the way the constraints are applied, the same results can be accomplished by applying different constraints to the geometric entities. In Autodesk Inventor, **parametric relations** are user-defined mathematical equations composed of dimensional variables and/or *design variables*. In parametric modeling, features are made of geometric entities with both relations and constraints describing individual design intent. In this lesson, we will discuss the fundamentals of parametric relations and geometric constraints.

Create a Simple Triangular Plate Design

In parametric modeling, **geometric properties** such as *horizontal*, *parallel*, *perpendicular*, and *tangent* can be applied to geometric entities automatically or manually. By carefully applying proper **geometric constraints**, very intelligent models can be created. This concept is illustrated by the following example.

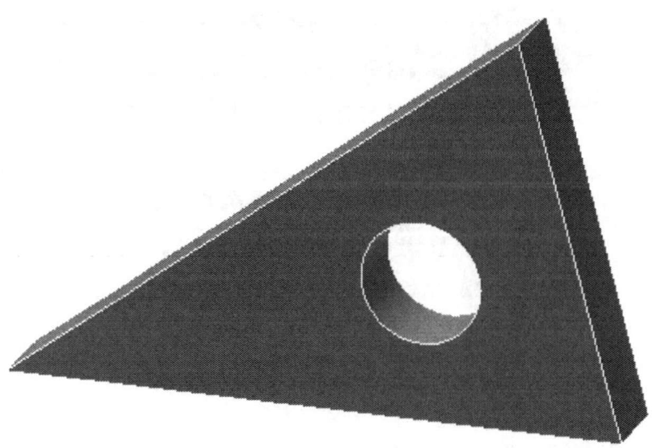

Fully Constrained Geometry

In Autodesk Inventor, as we create 2D sketches, geometric constraints such as *horizontal* and *parallel* are automatically added to the sketched geometry. In most cases, additional constraints and dimensions are needed to fully describe the sketched geometry beyond the geometric constraints added by the system. Although we can use Autodesk Inventor to build partially constrained or totally unconstrained solid models, the models may behave unpredictably as changes are made. In most cases, it is important to consider the design intent and to add proper constraints to geometric entities. In the following sections, a simple triangle is used to illustrate the different tools that are available in Autodesk Inventor to create/modify geometric and dimensional constraints.

Starting Autodesk Inventor

1. Select the **Autodesk Inventor** option on the *Start* menu or select the **Autodesk Inventor** icon on the desktop to start Autodesk Inventor. The Autodesk Inventor main window will appear on the screen. Once the program is loaded into memory, the *Startup* dialog box appears at the center of the screen.

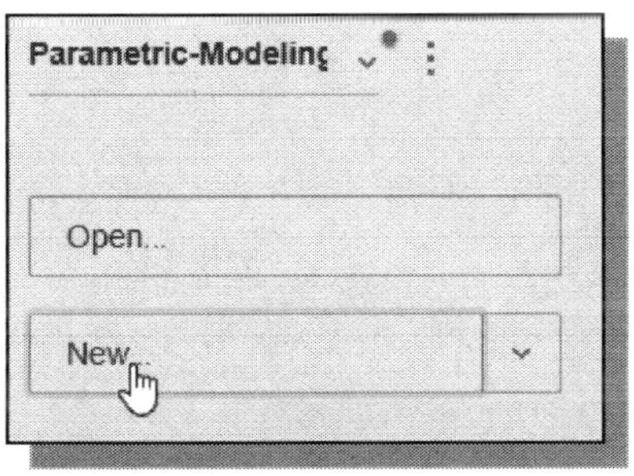

2. Select the **New** icon with a single click of the left-mouse-button in the left panel as shown.

3. Select the **en-US→English** tab and in the *Part template* area, select **Standard(in).ipt**.

4. Click **Create** in the *New File* dialog box to accept the selected settings to start a new model.

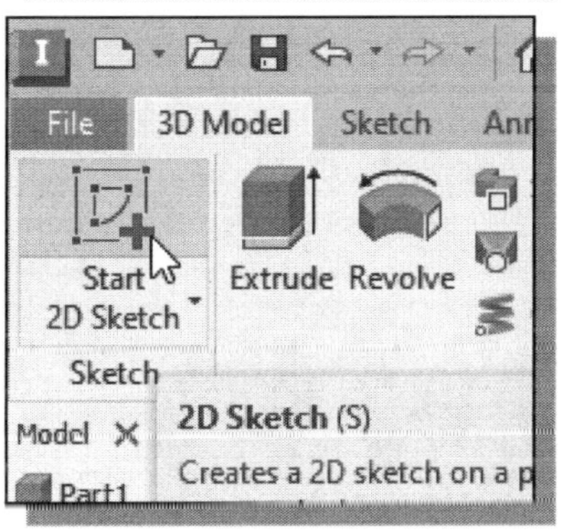

5. Click once with the left-mouse-button to select the **Start 2D Sketch** command.

6. Click once with the **left-mouse-button** to select the *XY Plane* as the sketch plane for the new sketch.

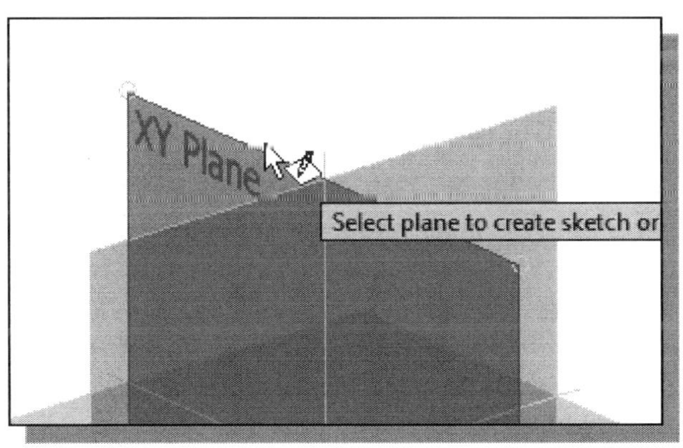

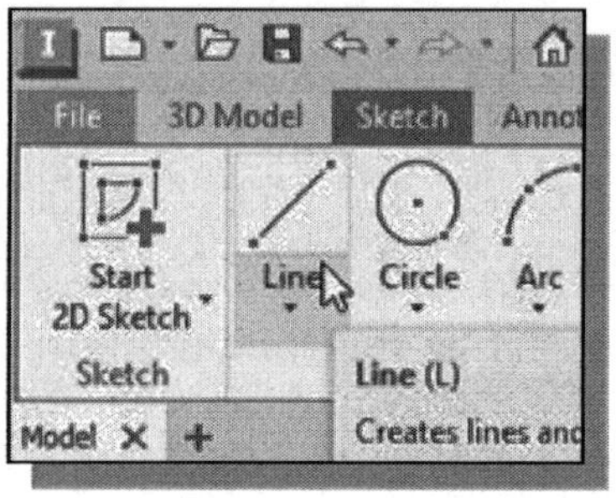

7. Click the **Line** icon in the *Sketch* tab to activate the command. A Help-tip box appears next to the cursor, and a brief description of the command is displayed at the bottom of the drawing screen: "Creates Straight line and arcs."

8. Create a triangle of arbitrary size positioned near the center of the screen as shown below. (Note that the base of the triangle is **horizontal.**) Hit the **[Esc]** key once to end the line command.

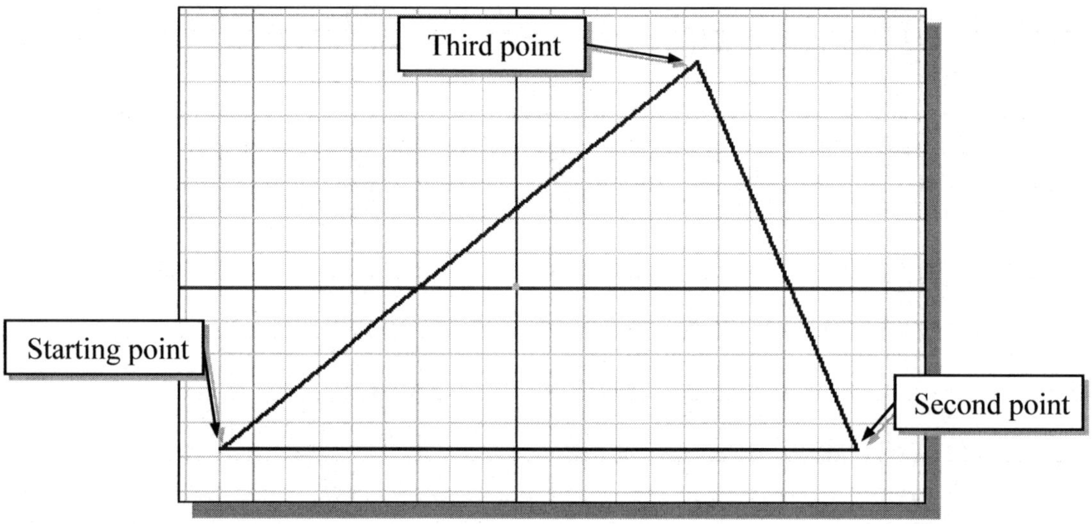

Displaying Existing Constraints

1. Select the **Show Constraints** command in the *Constrain* toolbar. This icon allows us to display constraints that are already applied to the 2D profiles. Left-click once on the icon to activate **Show Constraints.**

➢ In *parametric modeling*, constraints are typically applied as geometric entities are created. Autodesk Inventor will attempt to add proper constraints to the geometric entities based on the way the entities were created. Constraints are displayed as symbols next to the entities as they are created. The current profile consists of three line entities, three straight lines. The horizontal line has a **Horizontal constraint** applied to it.

2. Select the horizontal line and notice the number of constraints applied is displayed in the message area.

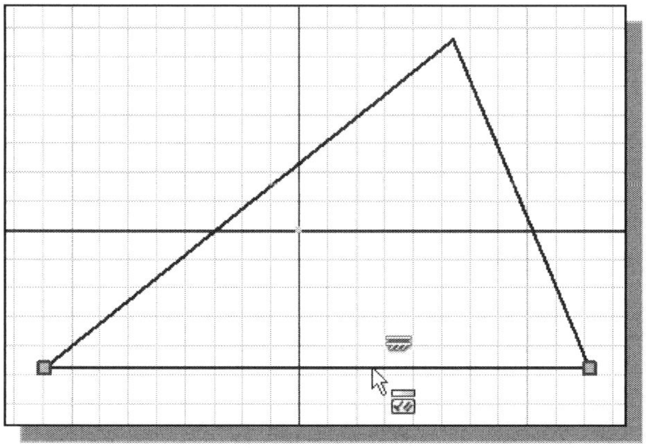

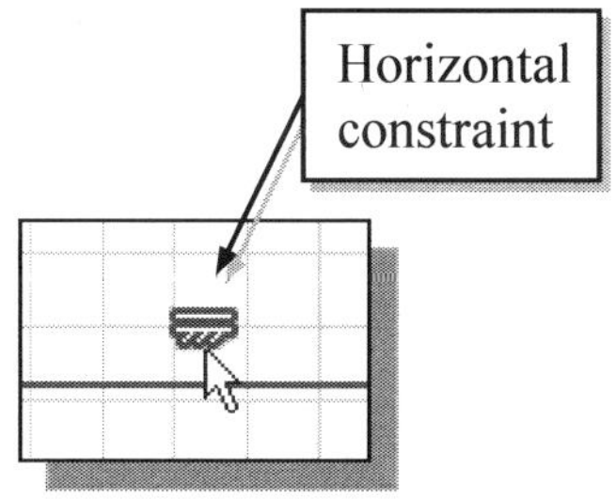

3. On your own, move the cursor on top of the other two lines and notice no additional constraints exist on the other two entities.

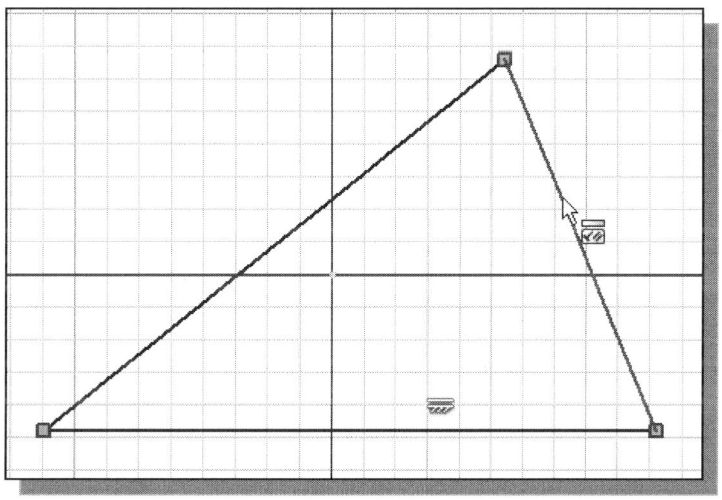

4. Move the cursor on top of the displayed constraint and notice the highlighted endpoint/line indicating the location/entities where the constraints are applied.

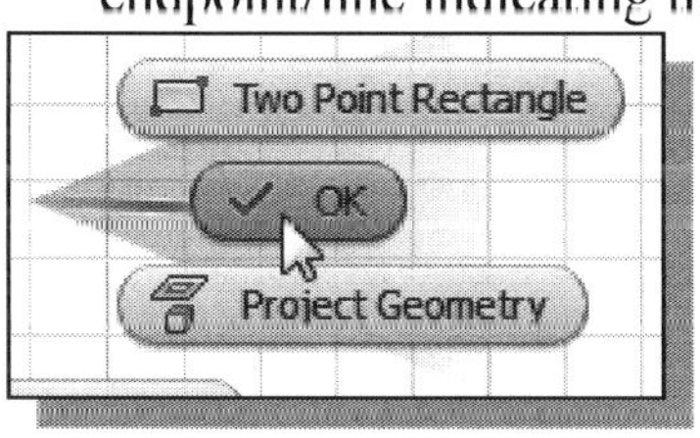

5. Inside the graphics window, right-click to bring up the option menu and select **OK** to end the Show Constraints command.

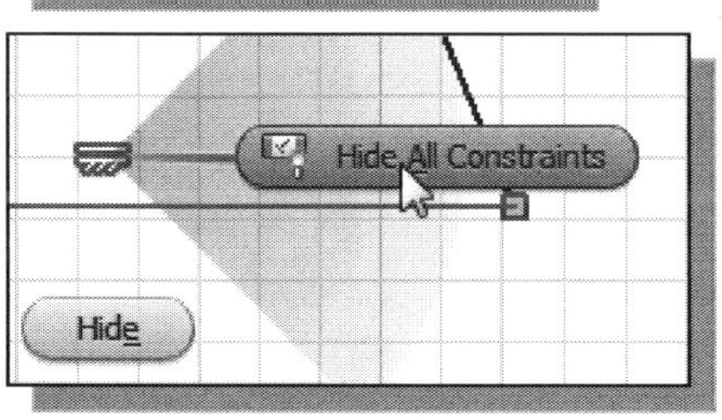

6. Right-click on the **horizontal** constraint icon to bring up the option list and select the **Hide All Constraints** option as shown.

Applying Geometric/Dimensional Constraints

In Autodesk Inventor, twelve types of constraints are available for 2D sketches.

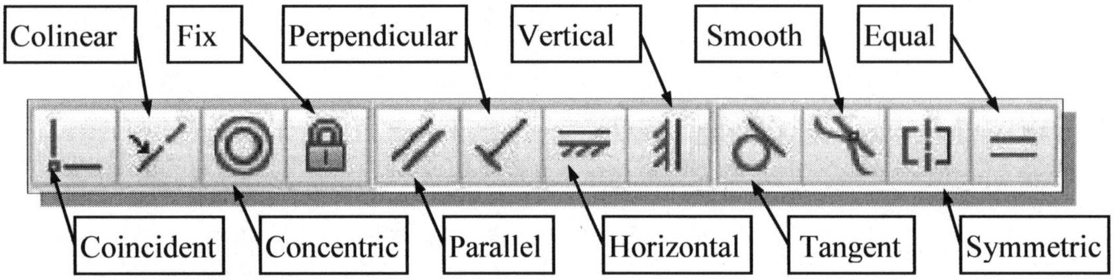

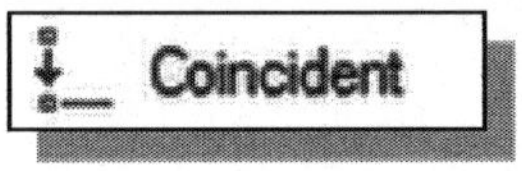

Coincident constraint: Constrains two points together or one point to a curve.

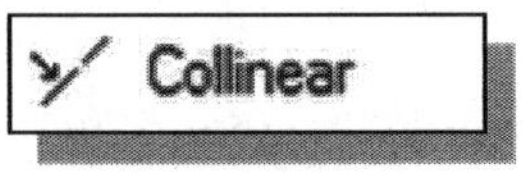

Collinear constraint: Causes two lines or ellipse axes to lie along the same line.

Concentric constraint: Constrains two arcs, circles, or ellipses to the same center point.

Fixed location constraint: Constrains points or curves to a fixed location relative to the sketch coordinate system.

Parallel constraint: Causes selected lines or ellipse axes to lie parallel to one another.

Perpendicular constraint: Causes selected curves or ellipse axes to lie at right angles to one another.

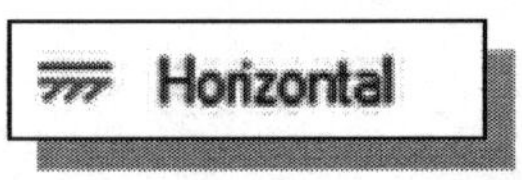

Horizontal constraint: Causes lines, ellipse axes, or pairs of points to lie parallel to the X-axis of the sketch coordinate system.

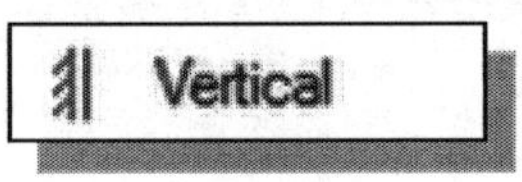

Vertical constraint: Causes lines, ellipse axes, or pairs of points to lie parallel to the Y-axis of the sketch coordinate system.

Tangent constraint: Constrains two curves to be tangent to one another.

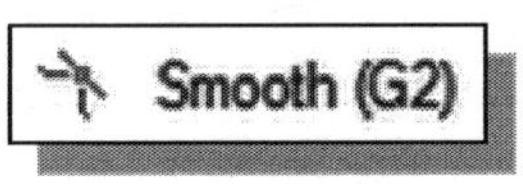

Smooth (G2) constraint: Creates a curvature continuous (G2) condition between a spline and a line, arc, or spline.

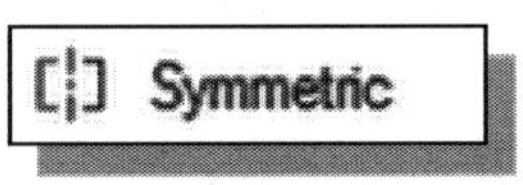

Symmetric constraint: Constrains lines or curves to become symmetrically constrained about a selected line.

Equal constraint: Selected arcs/circles constrained to the same radius or selected lines to the same length.

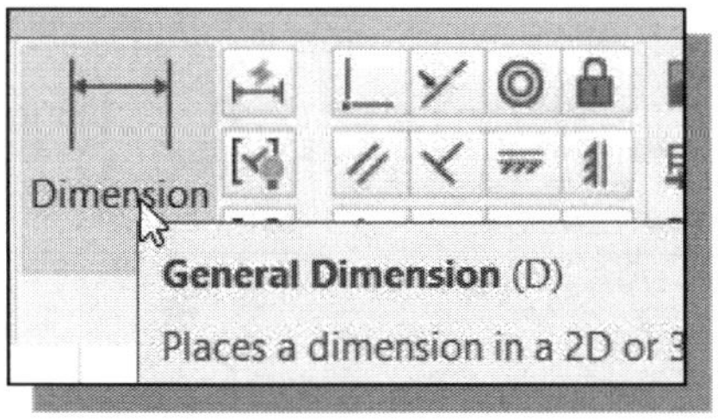

1. Select the **General Dimension** command in the *Sketch* toolbar. The General Dimension command allows us to quickly create and modify dimensions. Left-click once on the icon to activate the General Dimension command.

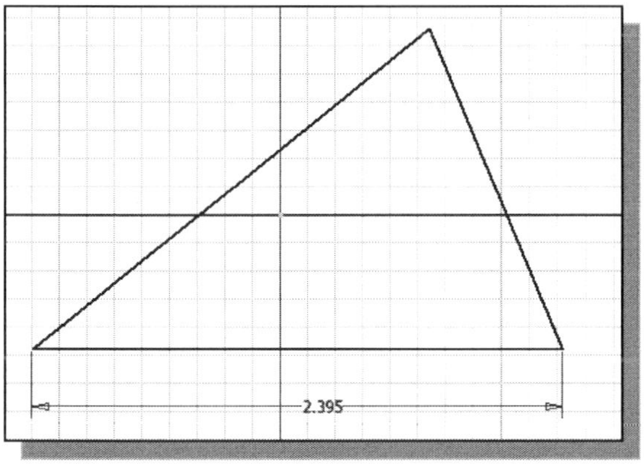

2. On your own, create the dimension as shown in the figure below. (Note that the displayed value might be different on your screen.)

❖ Note, *Inventor* identifies the need for additional dimensions at the bottom of the screen.

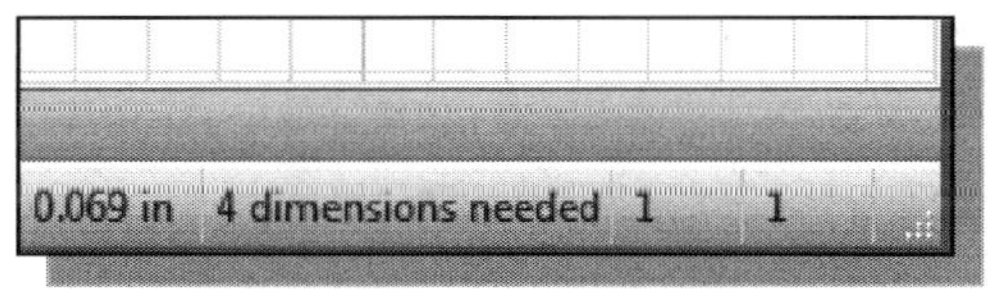

3. Move the cursor on top of the different **Constraint** icons. A *Help-tip box* appears next to the cursor and a brief description of the command is displayed at the bottom of the drawing screen as the cursor is moved over the different icons.

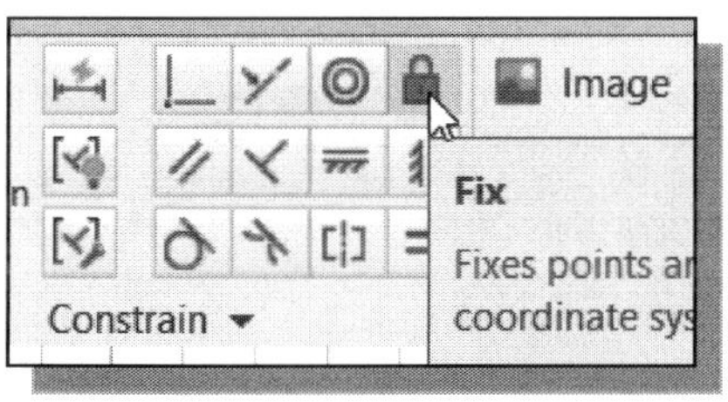

4. Click on the **Fix** constraint icon to activate the command.

5. Pick the **lower right corner** of the triangle to make the corner a fixed point.

6. Inside the graphics window, right-click to bring up the option menu and select **OK** to end the Fix Constraints command.

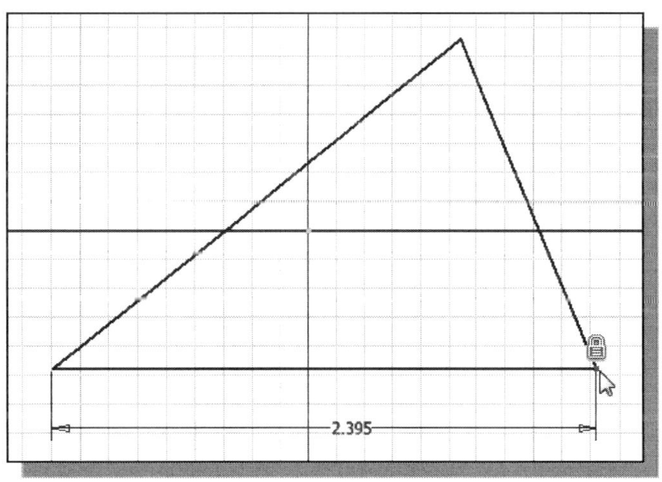

➢ Geometric constraints can be used to control the direction in which changes can occur. For example, in the current design we are adding a horizontal dimension to control the length of the horizontal line. If the length of the line is modified to a greater value, Autodesk Inventor will lengthen the line toward the left side. This is due to the fact that the **Fix** constraint will restrict any horizontal movement of the horizontal line toward the right side.

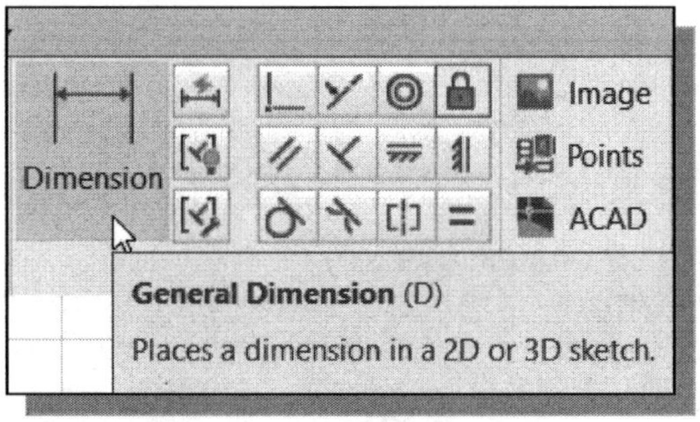

7. Select the **General Dimension** command in the *2D Sketch* toolbar.

8. Click on the dimension text to open the *Edit Dimension* window.

9. Enter a value that is greater than the displayed value to observe the effects of the modification.

10. On your own, use the **Undo** command to reset the dimension value to the previous value.

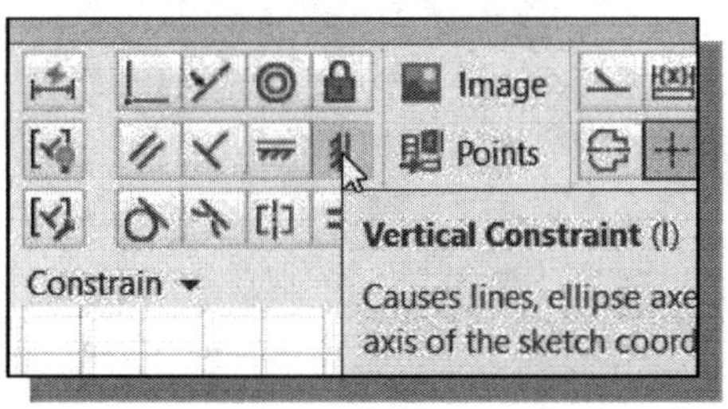

11. Select the **Vertical** constraint icon in the *2D Constraints* toolbar.

12. Pick the inclined line on the right to make the line vertical as shown in the figure below.

13. Hit the [**Esc**] key once to end the **Vertical Constraint** command.

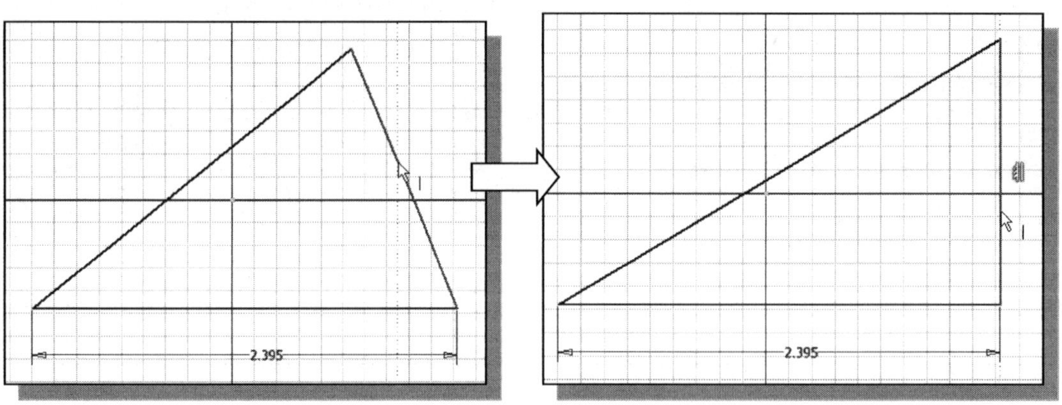

➢ You should think of the constraints and dimensions as defining elements of the geometric entities. How many more constraints or dimensions will be necessary to fully constrain the sketched geometry? Which constraints or dimensions would you use to fully describe the sketched geometry?

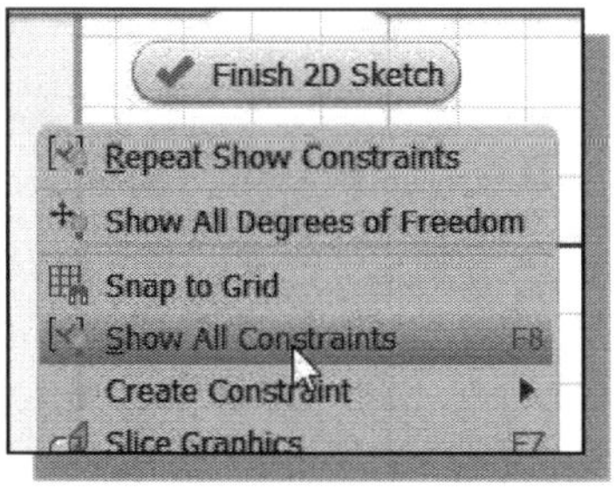

14. Inside the graphics window, click once with the **right-mouse-button** to display the option menu. Select **Show All Constraints** in the pop-up menu to show all the applied constraints. (Note that function key **F8** can also be used to activate this command.)

15. Move the cursor on top of the top corner of the triangle. (Note the display of the two Coincident constraints at the top corner.)

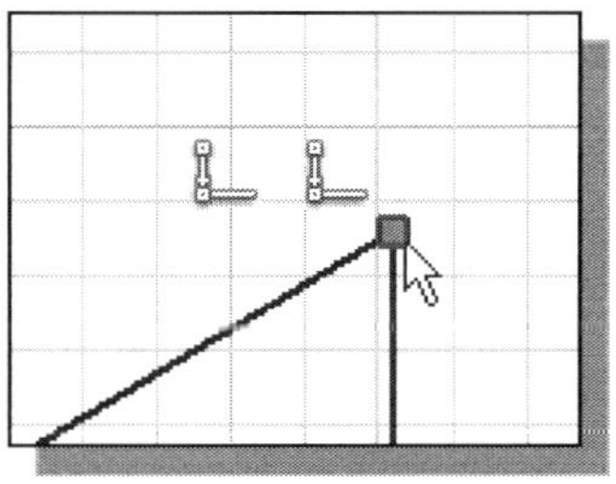

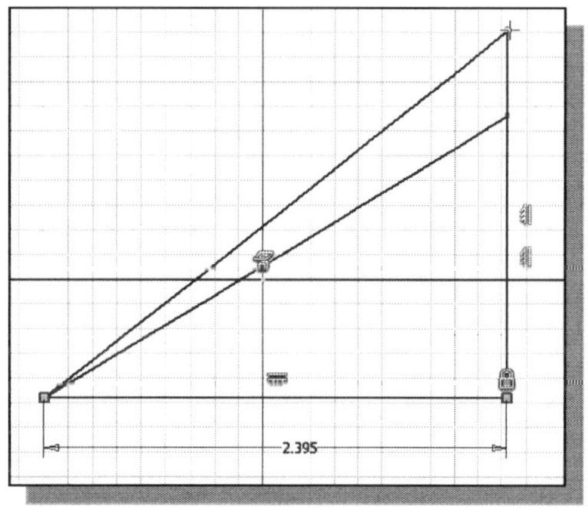

16. Drag the top corner of the triangle and note that the corner can be moved to a new location. Release the mouse button at a new location and notice the corner is adjusted only in an upward or downward direction. Note that the two adjacent lines are automatically adjusted to the new location.

17. On your own, experiment with dragging the other corners to new locations.

- The three constraints that are applied to the geometry provide a full description for the location of the two lower corners of the triangle. The Vertical constraint, along with the Fix constraint at the lower right corner, does not fully describe the location of the top corner of the triangle. We will need to add additional information, such as the length of the vertical line or an angle dimension.

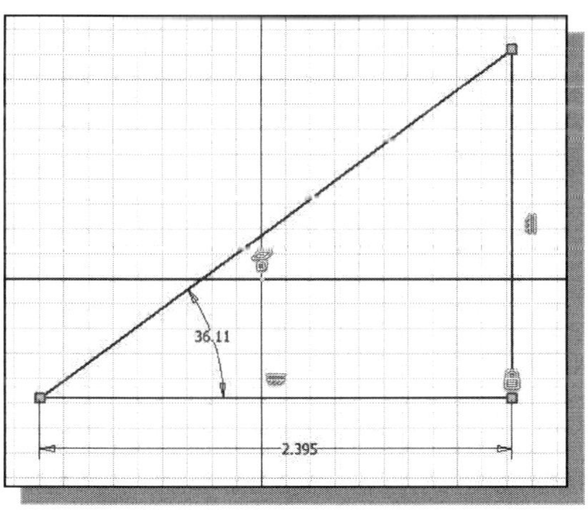

18. On your own, add an angle dimension to the left corner of the triangle.

19. Press the [**Esc**] key once to exit the General Dimension command.

20. On your own, try changing the angle to **45°** and observe the adjustment of the triangle with the adjustment.

- Note the sketched geometry is now fully constrained with the added dimension.

Over-Constraining and Driven Dimensions

We can use Autodesk Inventor to build partially constrained or totally unconstrained solid models. In most cases, these types of models may behave unpredictably as changes are made. However, Autodesk Inventor will not let us over-constrain a sketch; additional dimensions can still be added to the sketch, but they are used as references only. These additional dimensions are called ***driven dimensions***. *Driven dimensions* do not constrain the sketch; they only reflect the values of the dimensioned geometry. They are enclosed in parentheses to distinguish them from normal (parametric) dimensions. A *driven dimension* can be converted to a normal dimension only if another dimension or geometric constraint is removed.

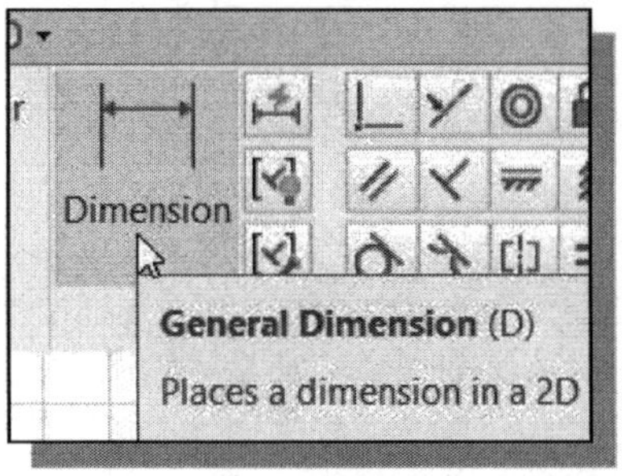

1. Select the **General Dimension** command in the *Sketch* toolbar.

2. Select the **vertical line.**

3. Pick a location that is to the right side of the triangle to place the dimension text.

4. A warning dialog box appears on the screen stating that the dimension we are trying to create will over-constrain the sketch. Click on the **Accept** button to proceed with the creation of a driven dimension.

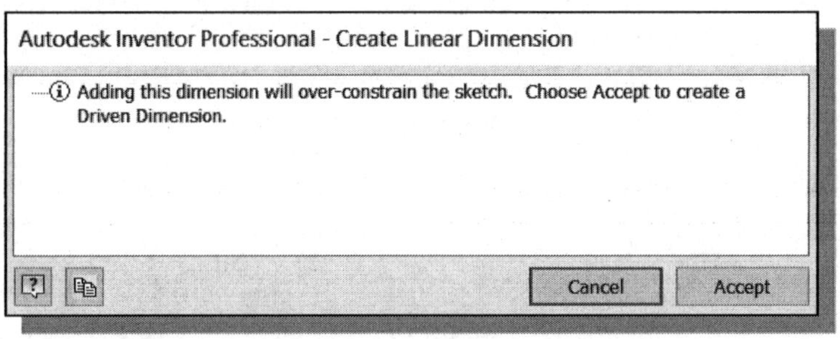

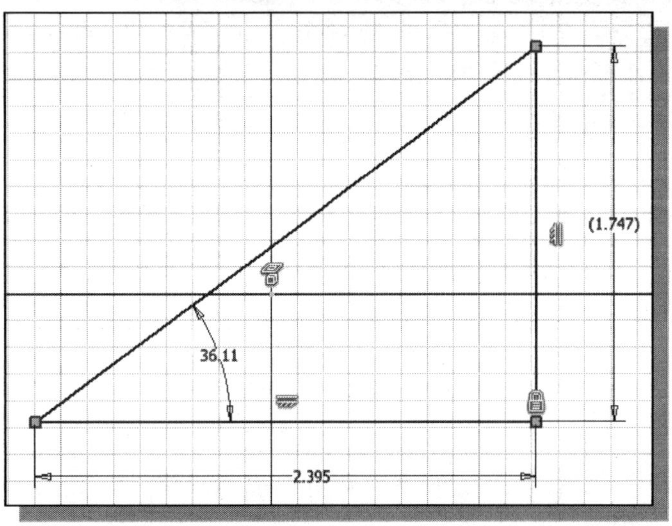

5. On your own, modify the angle dimension to **35°** and observe the changes of the 2D sketch and the driven dimension.

❖ Note that Inventor has indicated the sketch is **Fully Constrained.**

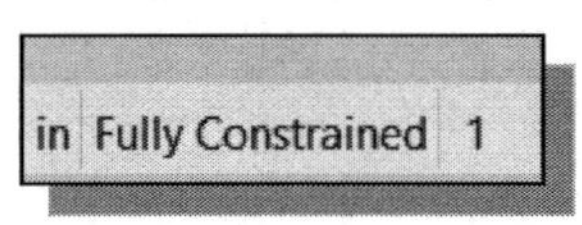

Deleting Existing Constraints

1. On your own, display all the active constraints if they are not already displayed. (Hint: Use the **Show Constraints** command in the *Sketch* toolbar or **Show All Constraints** in the option menu.)

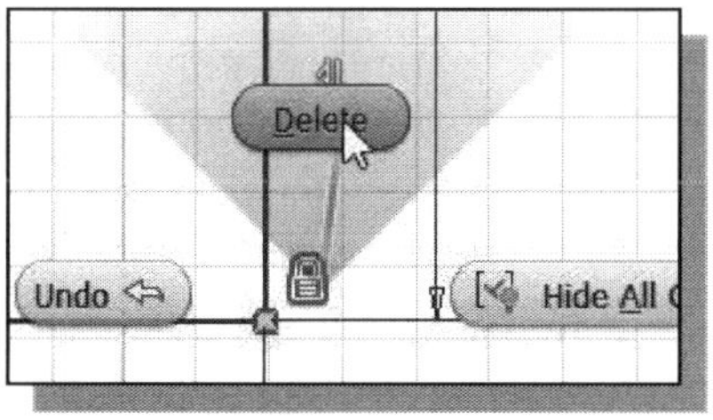

2. Move the cursor on top of the **Fix** constraint icon and **right-click** once to bring up the option menu.

3. Select **Delete** to remove the Fix constraint that is applied to the lower right corner of the triangle.

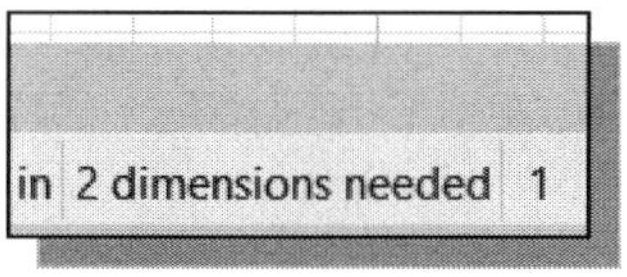

❖ Note the removal of the **Fix** constraint has caused the need for **two additional dimensions**.

4. On your own, hide all the constraints with the [**F9**] key and drag the top corner of the triangle upward and note that the entire triangle is free to move in all directions. Release the mouse button to move the triangle to the new location.

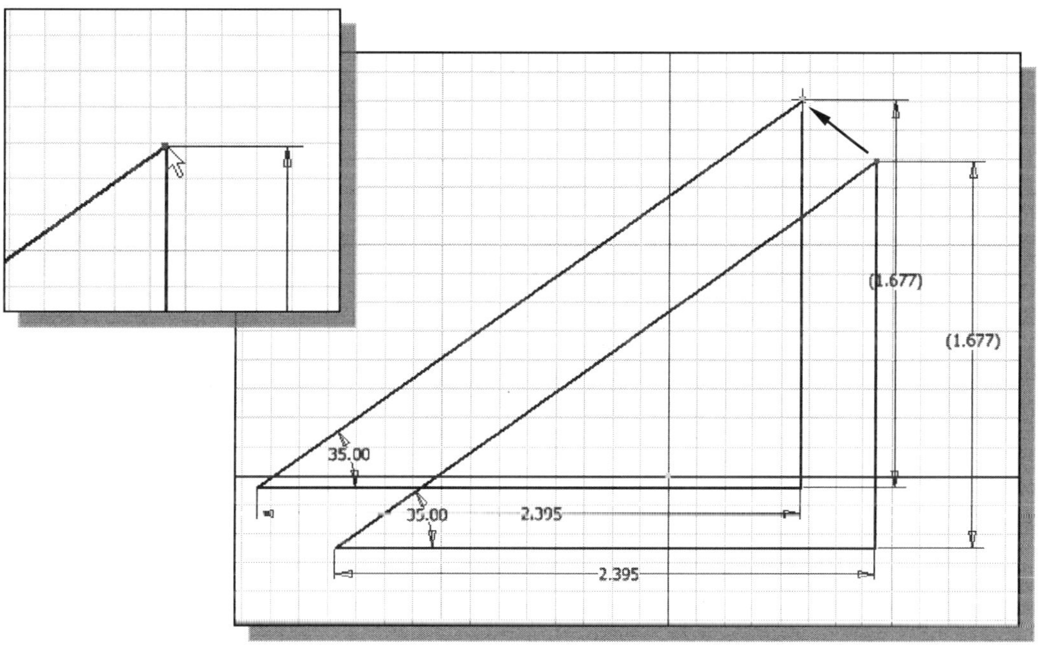

5. On your own, delete the reference dimension on the right and experiment with dragging the corners and the line segments to move the triangle to new locations.

❖ **Dimensional constraints** are used to describe the SIZE and LOCATION of individual geometric shapes. **Geometric constraints** are **geometric restrictions** that can be applied to geometric entities. The constraints applied to the triangle are sufficient to maintain its size and shape, but the geometry can be moved around; its location definition isn't complete.

Using the Auto Dimension Command

In Autodesk Inventor, the Auto Dimension command can be used to assist in creating a fully constrained sketch. **Fully constrained** sketches can be updated more predictably as design changes are implemented. The general procedure for applying dimensions to sketches is to use the General Dimension command to add the more critical dimensions, and then use the Auto Dimension command to add the additional dimensions/constraints to fully constrain the sketch. The Auto Dimension command can also be used to apply the missing dimensions that are needed. It is also important to realize that different sets of dimensions and geometric constraints can be applied to the same sketch to accomplish a fully constrained geometry.

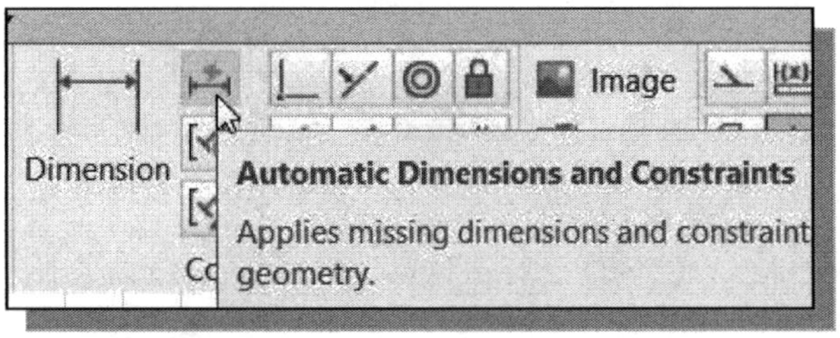

1. Click on the **Auto Dimension** icon in the *Constrain* toolbar.

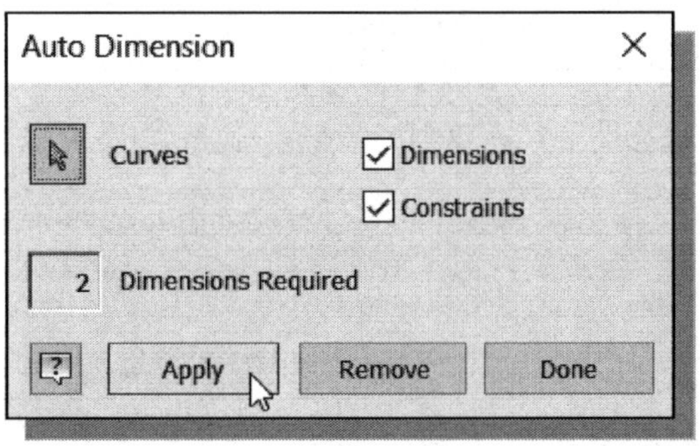

❖ Note that Autodesk Inventor indicates the sketch is missing two locational dimensions.

2. Click **Apply** to the Auto Dimension command.

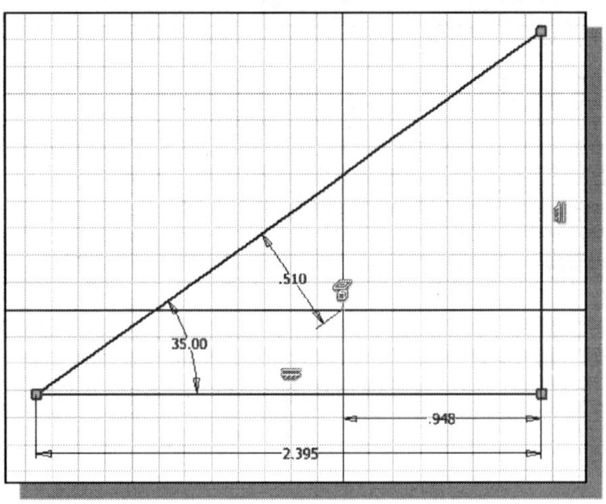

- Note that the Auto Dimension command added two dimensions measuring from the **Origin**, the intersection of the horizontal and vertical axes.

➢ The two newly added dimensions do not change the size of the triangle; they are used to position the triangle.

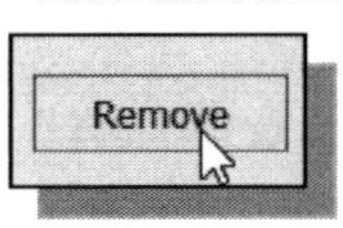

3. Click **Remove** to undo the Auto Dimension command. Note that only the dimensions created by the Auto Dimension command are affected.

4. Click **Done** to close the dialog box and exit the Auto Dimension command.

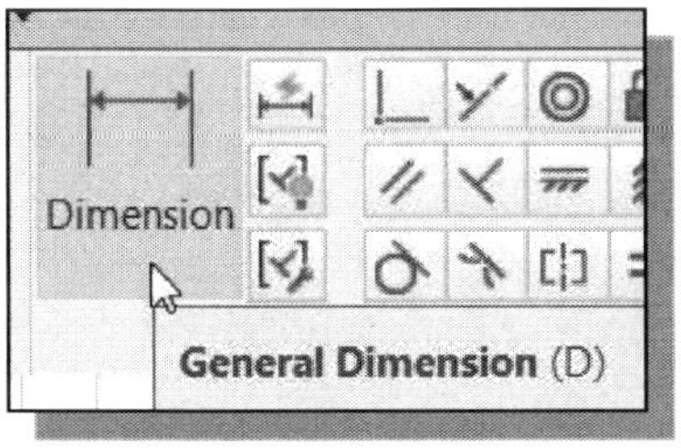

5. Activate the **General Dimension** command in the *Constrain* toolbar.

6. On your own, create the two locational dimensions, measuring the lower right corner to the origin as shown.

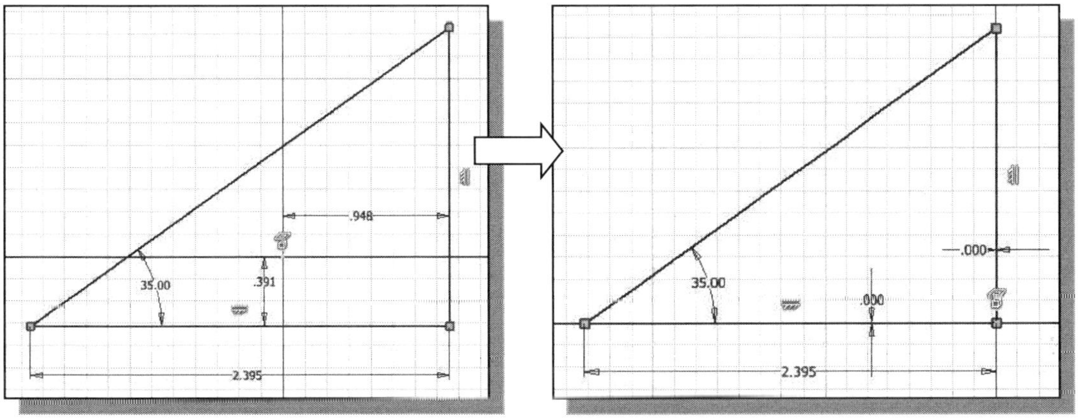

7. On your own, set the two dimensions to **0.0** and observe the alignment of the lower right corner of the triangle to the *Origin*.

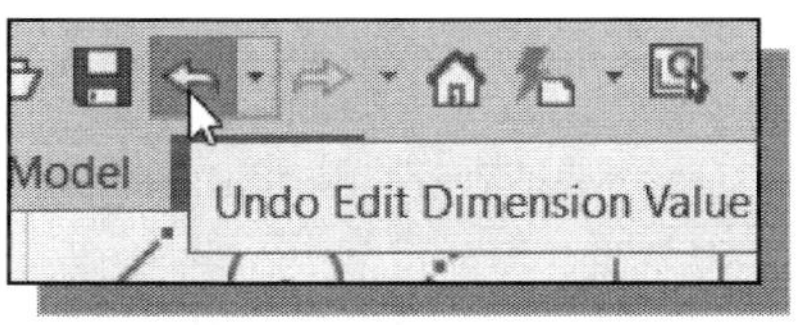

8. On your own, click the **Undo** button several times to return to the point before the two location dimensions were added.

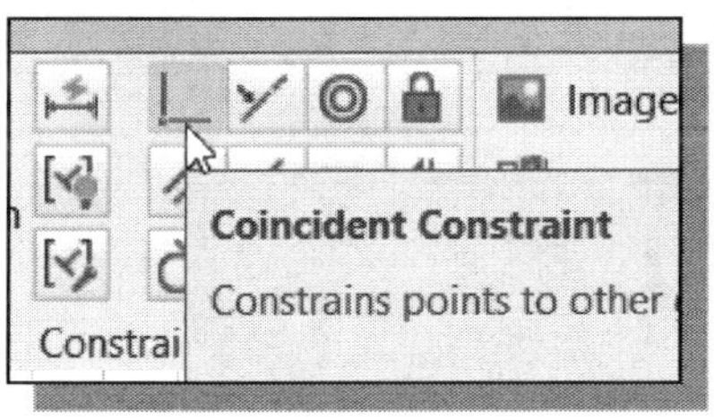

9. Activate the **Coincident Constraint** command in the *Constrain* toolbar.

10. Select the **lower right corner** of the triangle and the **Origin** to fully constrain the sketch as shown.

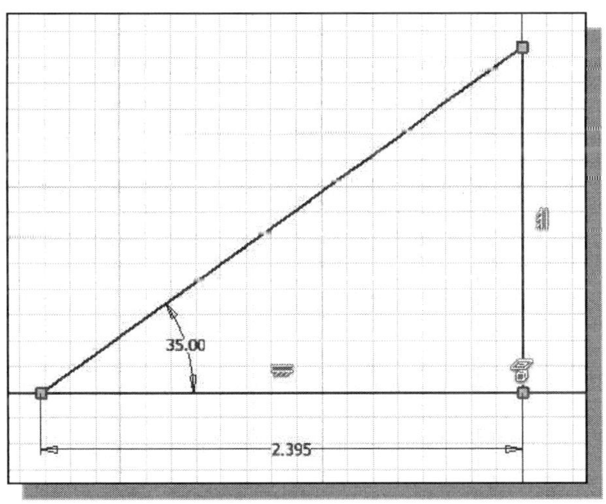

➢ In parametric modeling, it is desired to create fully constrained sketches.

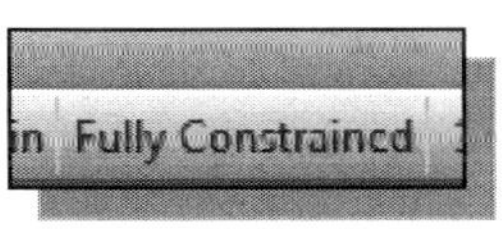

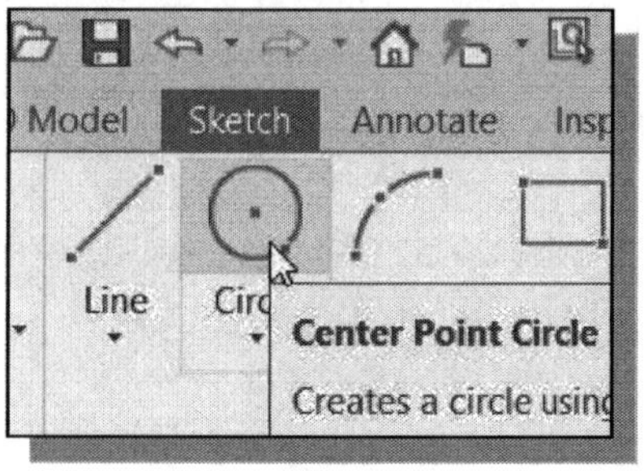

11. Select the **Center Point Circle** command by clicking once with the left-mouse-button on the icon in the *Sketch* toolbar.

12. On your own, create a circle of arbitrary size inside the triangle as shown below.

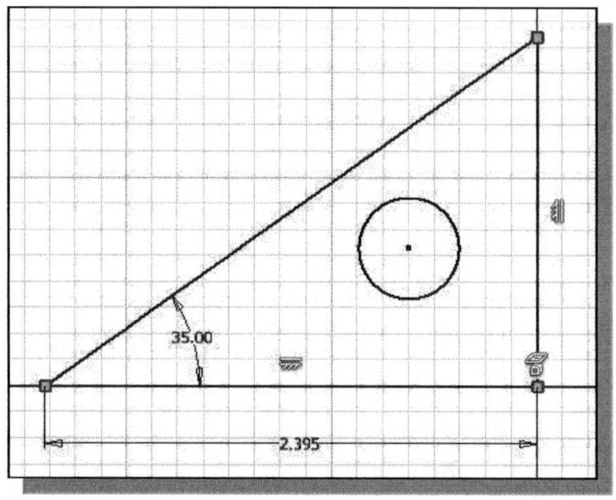

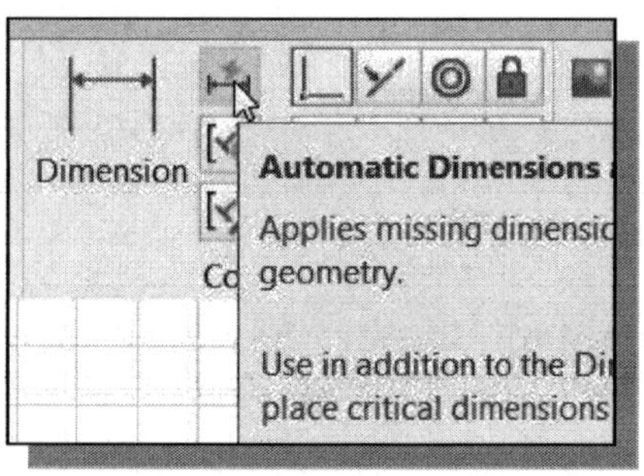

13. Click on the **Auto Dimension** icon in the *Sketch* panel.

❖ Note that *Autodesk Inventor* confirms that the sketch is not fully constrained and "*3 Dimensions Required*" to fully constrain the circle. What are the dimensions and/or constraints that can be applied to fully constrain the circle?

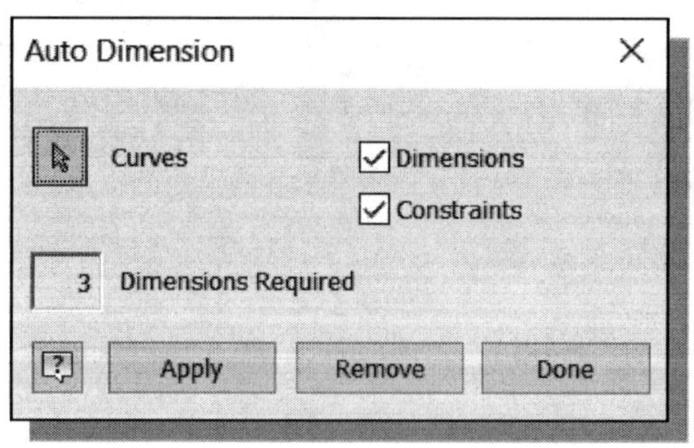

14. Click **Done** to exit the Auto Dimension command.

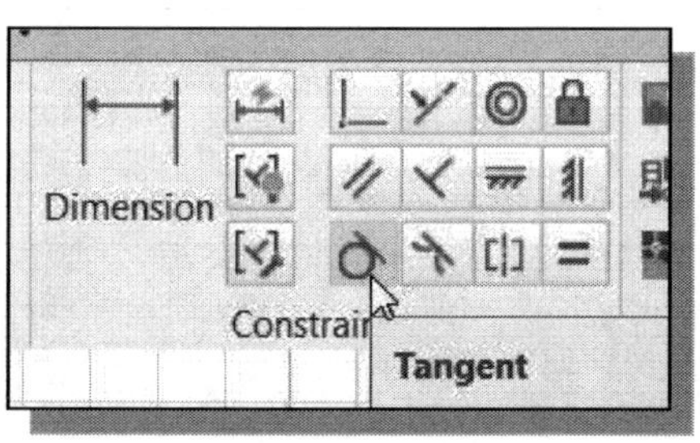

15. Click on the **Tangent** constraint icon in the *Sketch* toolbar.

16. Pick the circle by left-clicking once on the geometry.

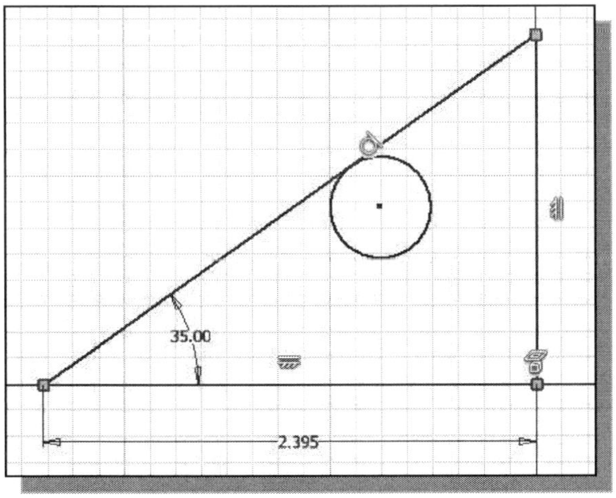

17. Pick the inclined line. The sketched geometry is adjusted as shown.

18. Inside the graphics window, click once with the right-mouse-button to display the option menu. Select **OK** in the pop-up menu to end the **Tangent** command.

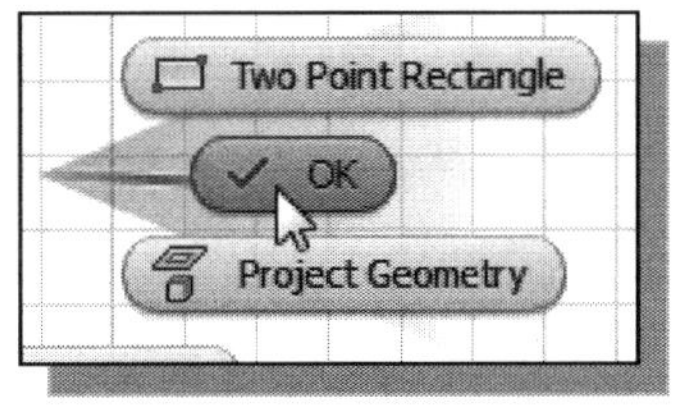

- How many more constraints or dimensions do you think will be necessary to fully constrain the circle? Which constraints or dimensions would you use to fully constrain the geometry?

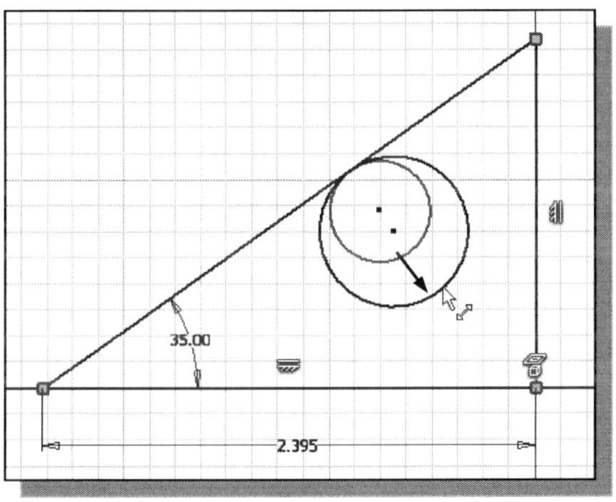

19. Move the cursor on top of the right side of the circle, and then drag the circle toward the right edge of the graphics window. Notice the size of the circle is adjusted while the system maintains the **Tangent** constraint.

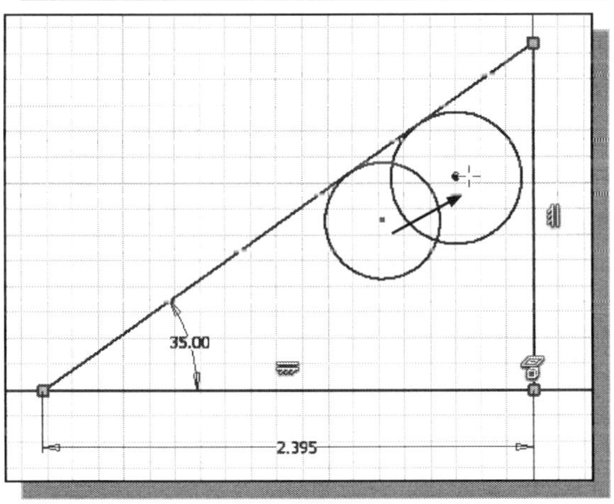

20. Drag the center of the circle toward the upper right direction. Notice the **Tangent** constraint is always maintained by the system.

➢ On your own, experiment with adding additional constraints and/or dimensions to fully constrain the sketched geometry. Use the **Undo** command to undo any changes before proceeding to the next section.

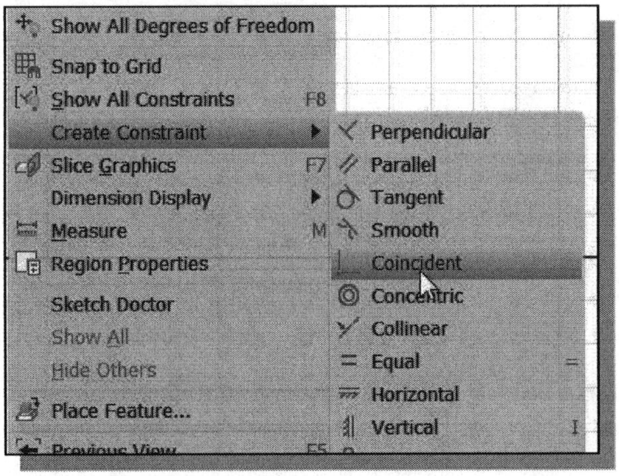

21. Inside the *graphics window*, click once with the **right-mouse-button** to display the option menu. Select **Create Constraint → Coincident** in the pop-up menus.

- The option menu is a quick way to access many of the commonly used commands in Autodesk Inventor.

22. Pick the **vertical line**.

23. Pick the center of the circle to align the **center** of the circle and the vertical line.

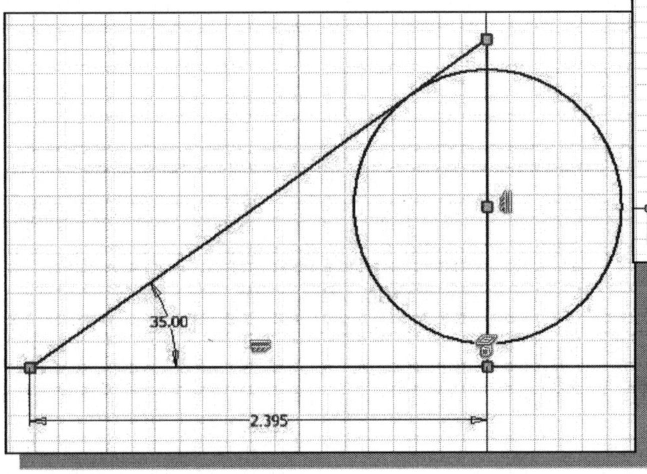

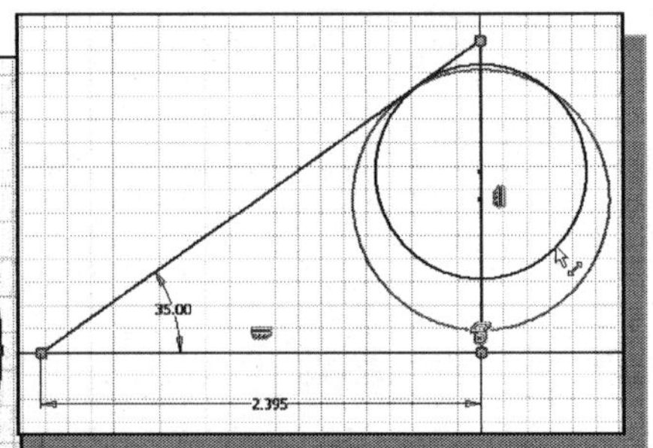

- Is the circle fully constrained?

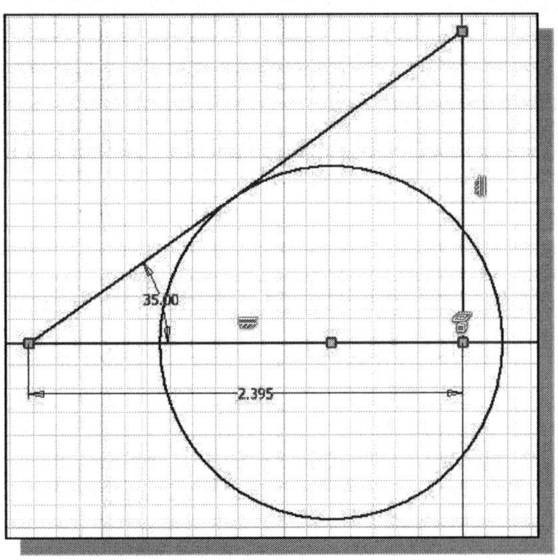

24. On your own, **delete** the **Coincident** constraint we just applied and add a **Coincident** constraint between the center of the circle and the horizontal line.

- How many more constraints or dimensions do you think will be necessary to fully constrain the circle? Which constraints or dimensions would you use to fully constrain the geometry?

❖ The application of different constraints affects the geometry differently. The design intent is maintained in the CAD model's database and thus allows us to create very intelligent CAD models that can be modified and revised fairly easily. On your own, experiment and observe the results of applying different constraints to the triangle. For example: (1) adding another **Fix** constraint to the top corner of the triangle; (2) deleting the horizontal dimension and adding another **Fix** constraint to the left corner of the triangle; and (3) adding another **Tangent** constraint and adding the size dimension to the circle.

25. On your own, modify the 2D sketch as shown below.

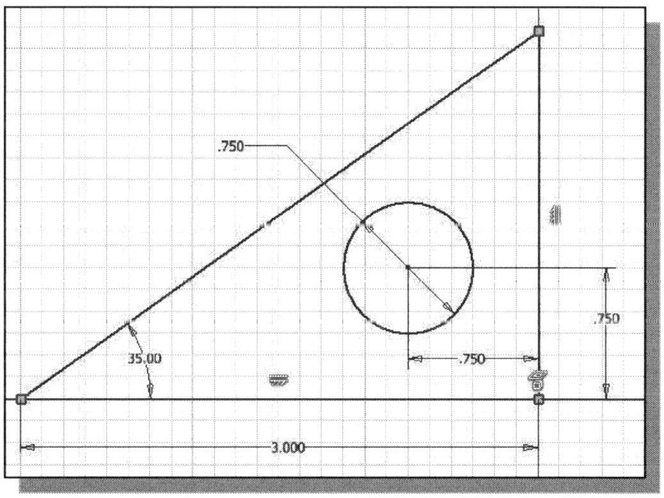

➢ On your own, use the **Extrude** command and create a 3D solid model with a plate thickness of **0.25**. Also experiment with modifying the parametric relations and dimensions through the *part browser*.

Constraint and Sketch Settings

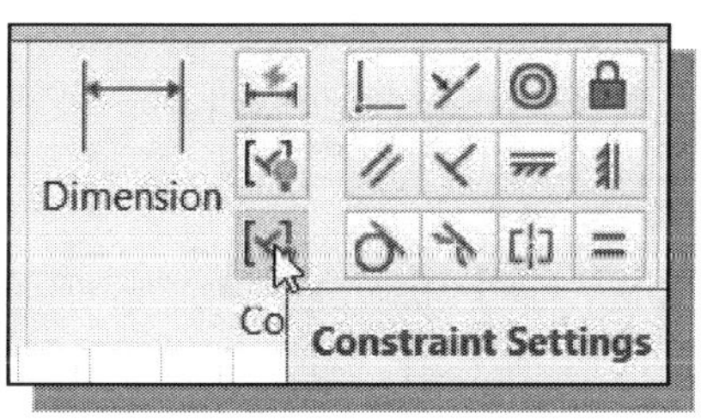

- Click on the **Constraint Settings** icon to access the constraint settings dialog box.

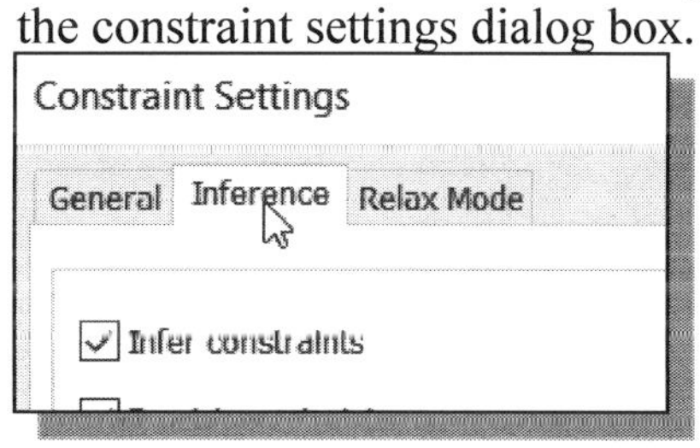

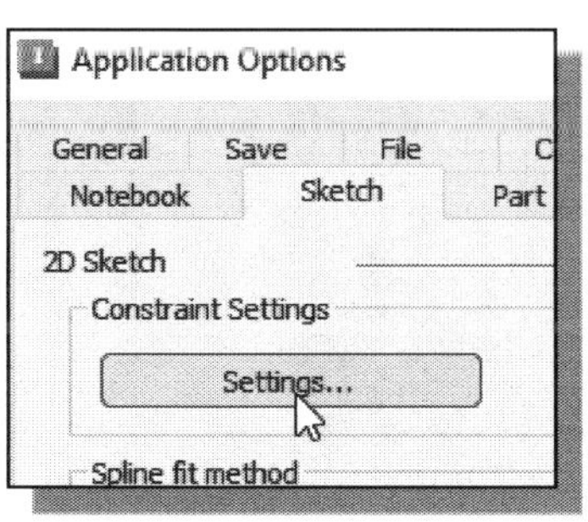

- Note the settings can also be accessed through **Application Options** in the **Tools** pull-down menu. Switch to the **Sketch** tab then click on **Constraint Settings** to display and/or modify the constraint settings.

Parametric Relations

In parametric modeling, dimensions are design parameters that are used to control the sizes and locations of geometric features. Dimensions are more than just values; they can also be used as feature control variables. This concept is illustrated by the following example.

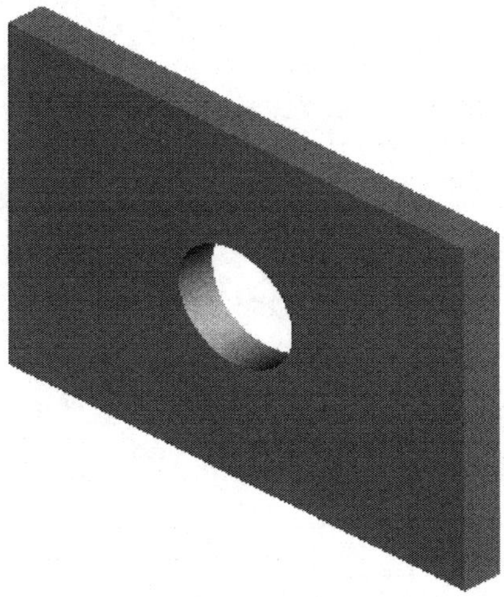

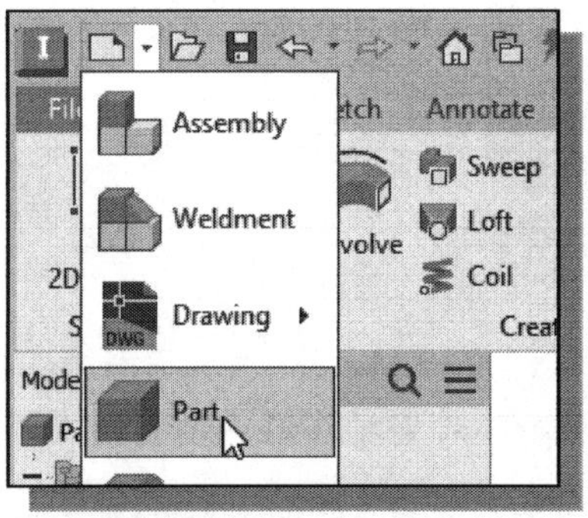

1. Start a new drawing by left-clicking once on the **New → Part** icon in the *Standard* toolbar.

- Another graphics window appears on the screen. We can switch between the two models by clicking on the different graphics windows.

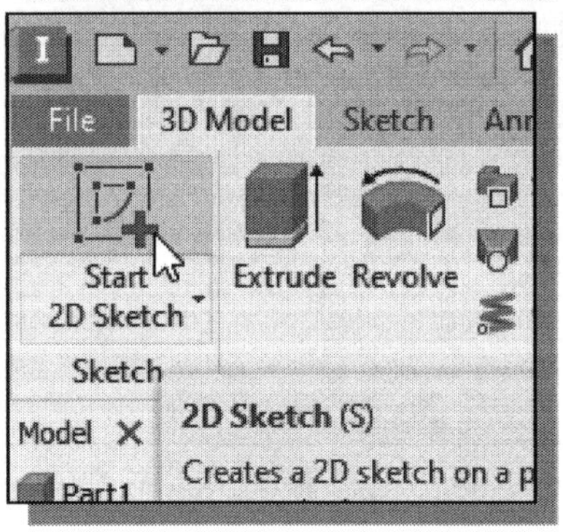

2. Select the **Start 2D Sketch** command with the left-mouse-button.

3. Select the *XY Plane* as the sketch plane for the new sketch with the **left-mouse-button**.

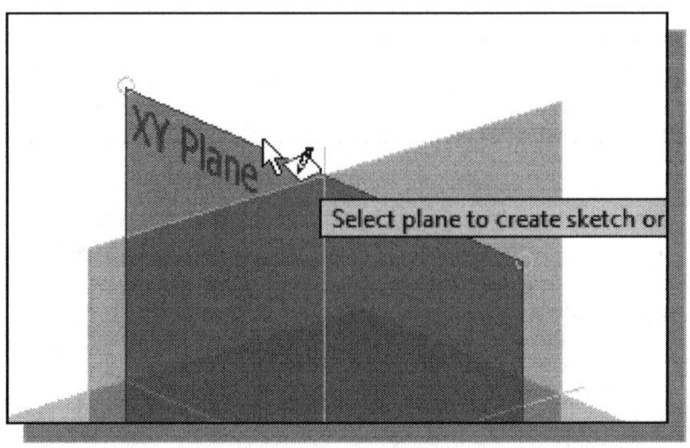

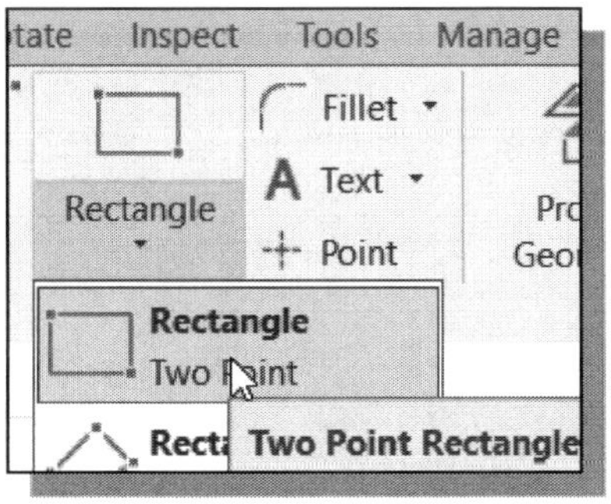

4. Select the **Two point rectangle** command by clicking once with the left-mouse-button on the icon in the *Sketch* toolbar.

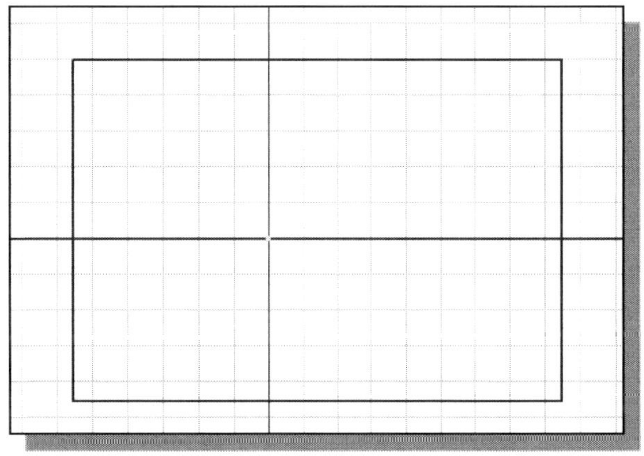

5. Create a rectangle of arbitrary size positioned near the center of the screen.

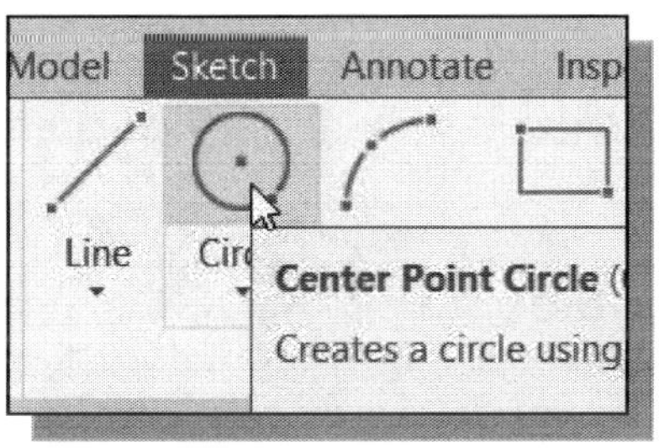

6. Select the **Center Point Circle** command by clicking once with the left-mouse-button on the icon in the *Sketch* toolbar.

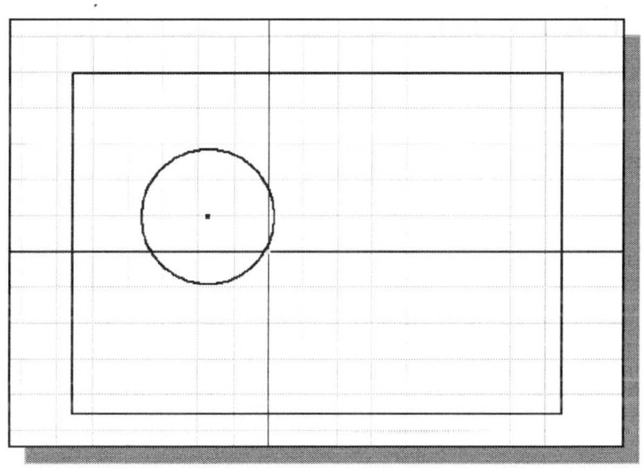

7. Create a **circle** of arbitrary size inside the rectangle as shown.

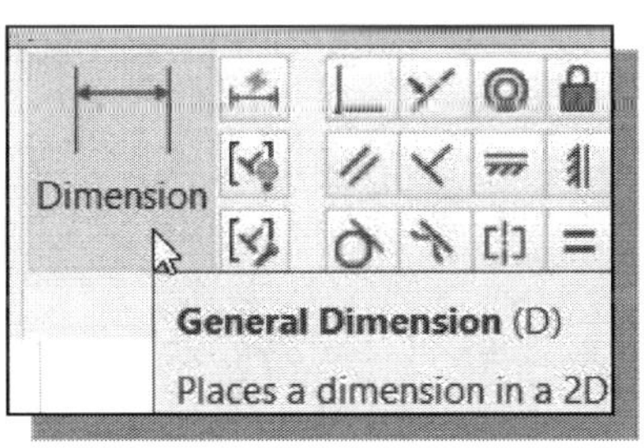

8. Select the **General Dimension** command in the *Sketch* toolbar.

9. On your own, create and adjust the geometry by modifying the dimensions as shown below. (Note: Align the center of the circle to the origin to fully constrain the sketch.)

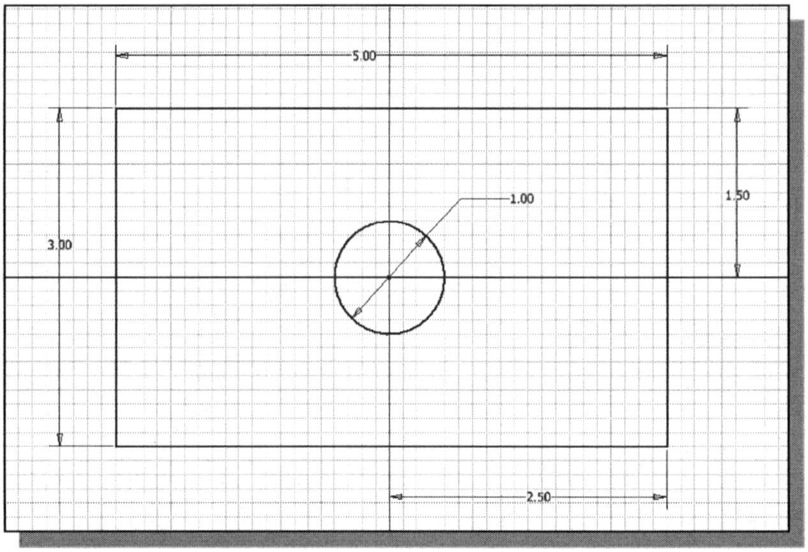

- On your own, change the overall width of the rectangle to **6.0** and the overall height of the rectangle to **3.6** and observe the location of the circle in relation to the edges of the rectangle. Adjust the dimensions back to **5.0** and **3.0** as shown in the above figure before continuing.

Dimensional Values and Dimensional Variables

Initially in Autodesk Inventor, values are used to create different geometric entities. The text created by the Dimension command also reflects the actual location or size of the entity. Each dimension is also assigned a name that allows the dimension to be used as a control variable. The default format is "dxx," where the "xx" is a number that Autodesk Inventor increments automatically each time a new dimension is added.

Let us look at our current design, which represents a plate with a hole at the center. The dimensional values describe the size and/or location of the plate and the hole. If a modification is required to change the width of the plate, the location of the hole will remain the same as described by the two location dimensional values. This is okay if that is the design intent. On the other hand, the *design intent* may require (1) keeping the hole at the center of the plate and (2) maintaining the size of the hole to be one-third of the height of the plate. We will establish a set of parametric relations using the dimensional variables to capture the design intent described in statements (1) and (2) above.

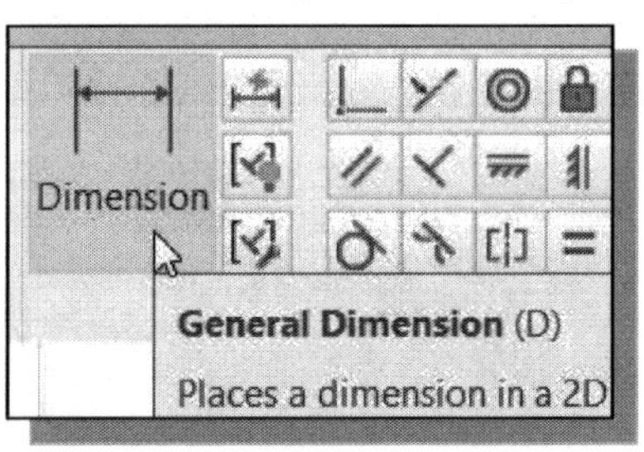

1. Left-click once on the **General Dimension** icon to activate the General Dimension command.

2. Click on the **width dimension** of the rectangle to display the *Edit Dimension* window.

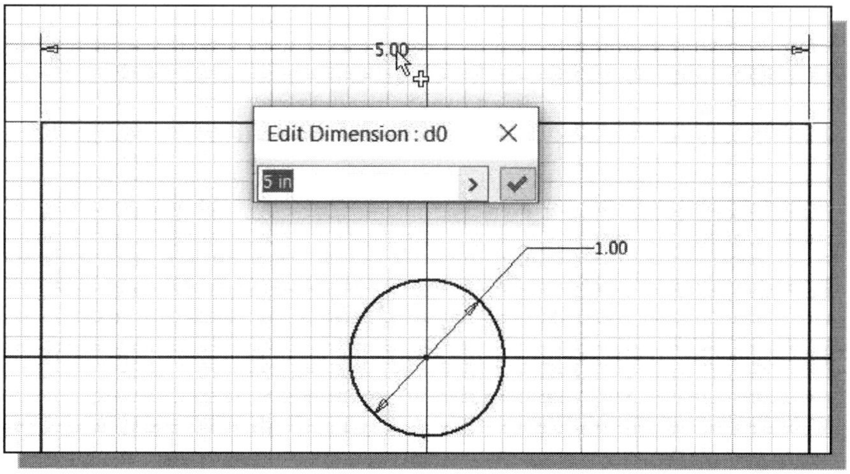

- Notice the ***variable name* d0** is displayed in the title area of the *Edit Dimension* window and also in the cursor box when the cursor is moved near the text box.

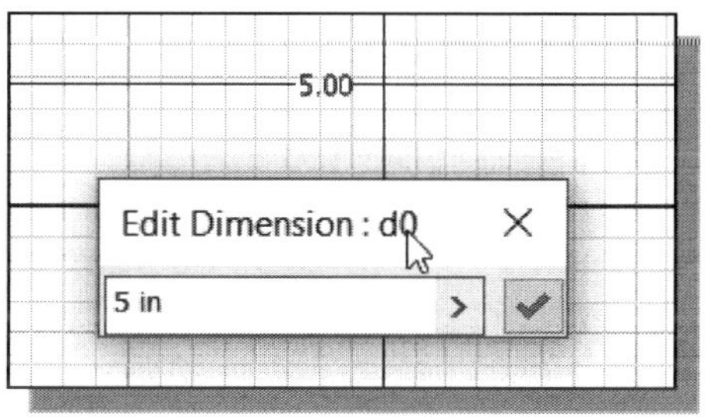

3. Click on the ***check mark*** button to close the *Edit Dimension* window.

Parametric Equations

Each time we add a dimension to a model, that value is established as a parameter for the model. We can use parameters in equations to set the values of other parameters.

1. Click on the **horizontal location dimension** of the circle to display the *Edit Dimension* window.

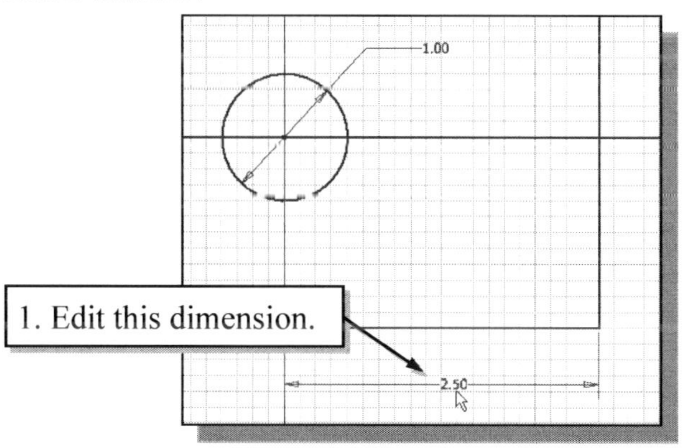

2. Click on the width dimension of the rectangle **d0** (value of **5.0**). Notice the selected variable name is automatically entered in the *Edit Dimension* window.

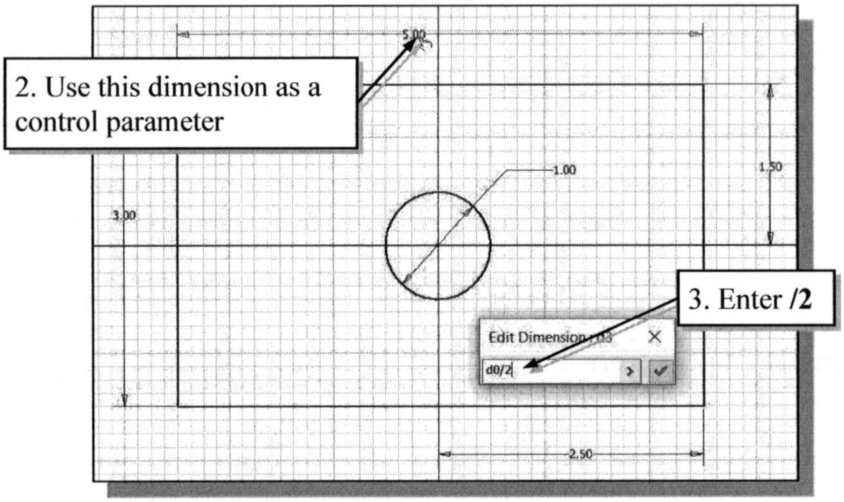

3. In the *Edit Dimension* window, enter **/2** to set the horizontal location dimension of the circle to be one-half of the width of the rectangle.

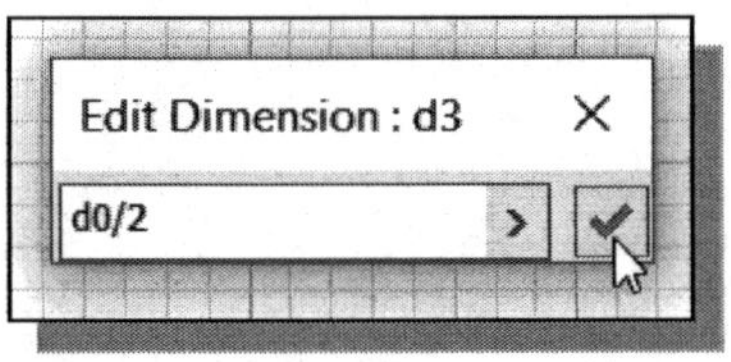

4. Click on the ***check mark*** button to close the *Edit Dimension* window.

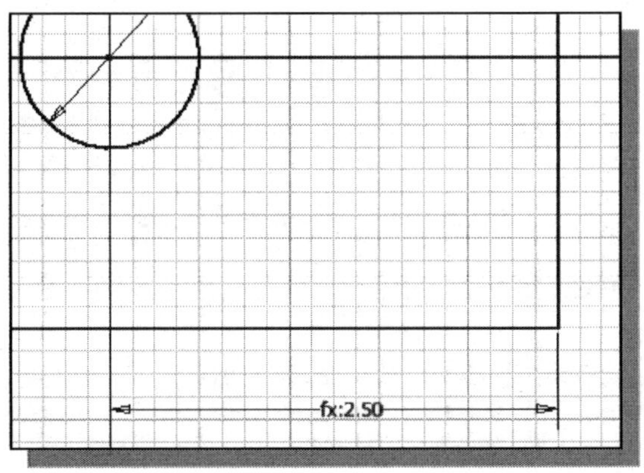

❖ Notice the derived dimension values are displayed with **fx** in front of the numbers. The parametric relations we entered are used to control the location of the circle; the location is based on the height and width of the rectangle.

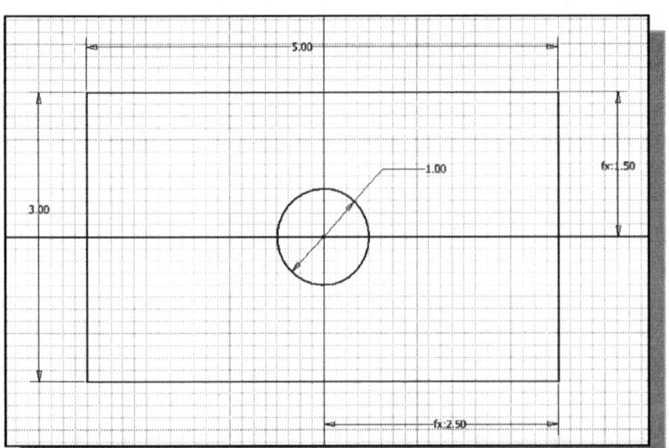

5. On your own, repeat the above steps and set the vertical location dimension to one-half of the height of the rectangle.

Viewing the Established Parameters and Relations

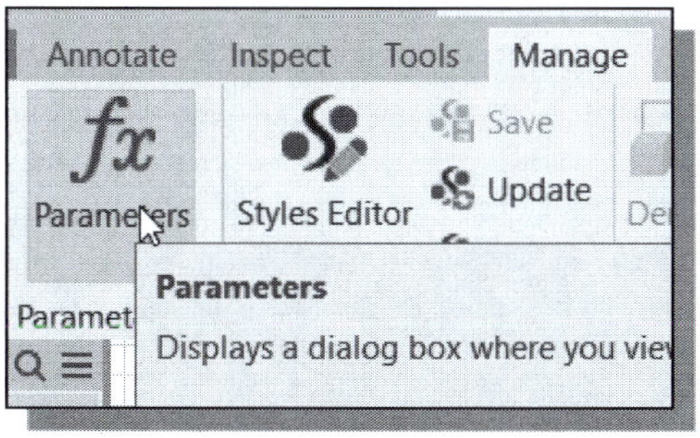

1. In the *Manage* toolbar select the **Parameters** command by left-clicking once on the icon.

- The **Parameters** command can be used to display all dimensions used to define the model. We can also create additional parameters as design variables, which are called ***user parameters***.

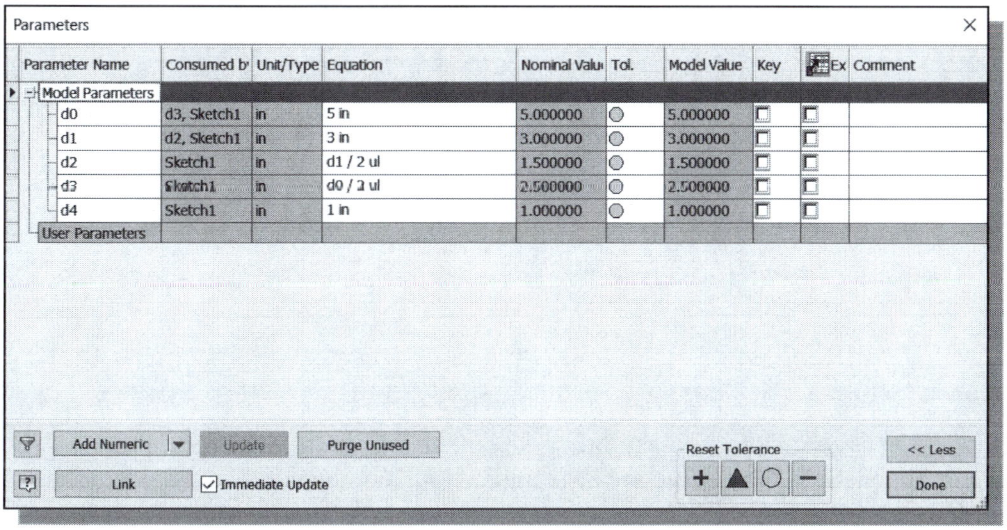

2. Click on the **1.0** value in the equation section of the *Parameters* window. Enter **d1/3** as the parametric relation to set the size of the circle to be one-third of the height of the rectangle as shown below.

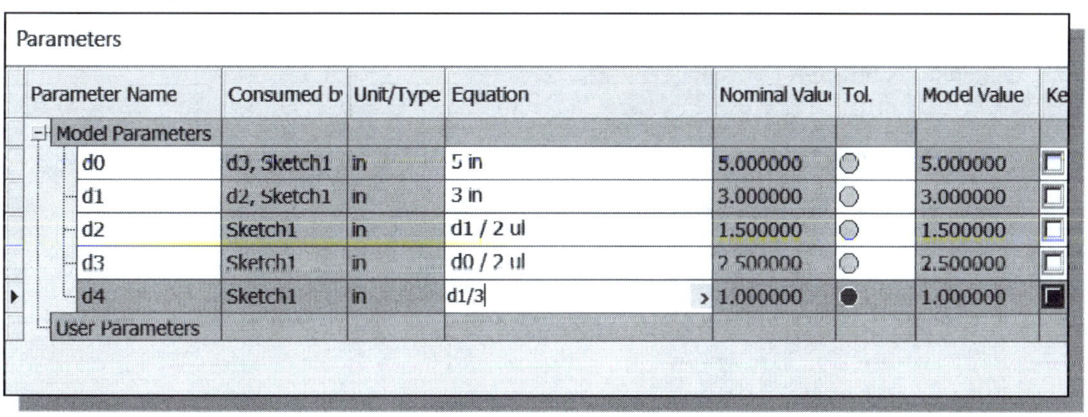

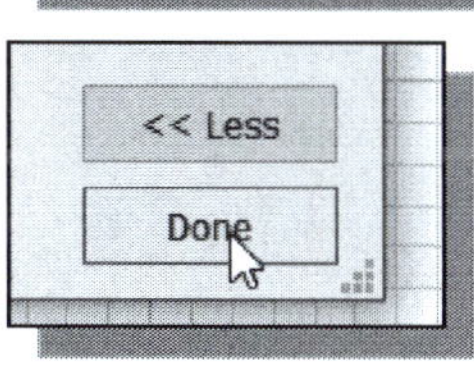

3. Click on the **Done** button to accept the settings.

4. On your own, change the dimensions of the rectangle to **6.0 x 3.6** and observe the changes to the location and size of the circle. (Hint: Double-click the dimension text to bring up the *Edit Dimension* window.)

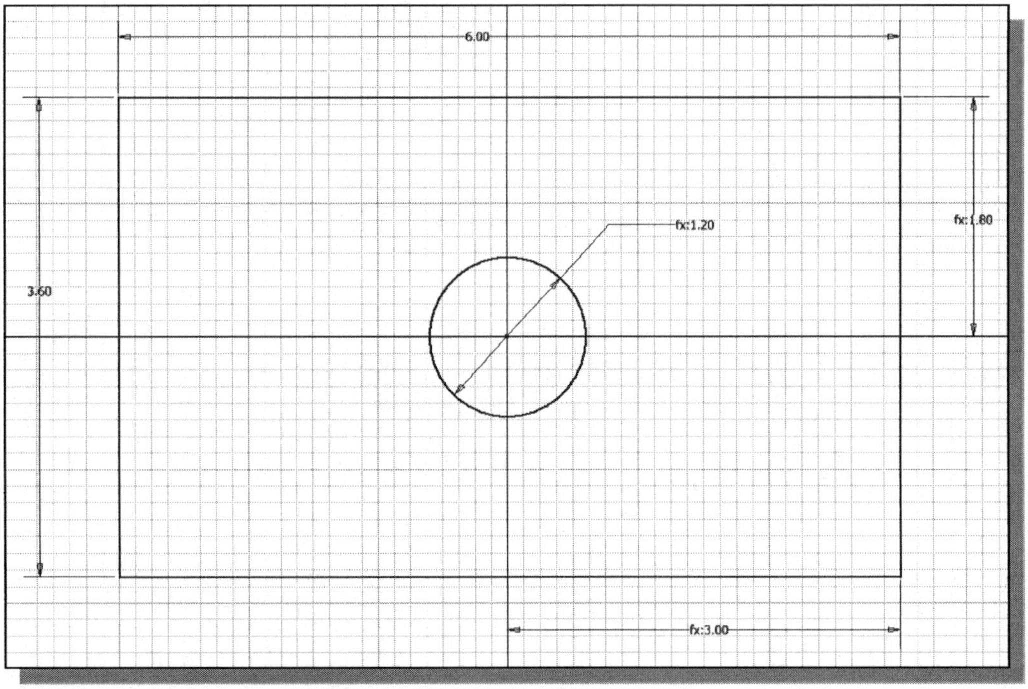

❖ *Autodesk Inventor* automatically adjusts the dimensions of the design, and the parametric relations we entered are also applied and maintained. The dimensional constraints are used to control the size and location of the hole. The design intent, previously expressed by statements (1) and (2) at the beginning of this section, is now embedded into the model.

➢ On your own, use the **Extrude** command and create a 3D solid model with a plate thickness of **0.25**. Also, experiment with modifying the parametric relations and dimensions through the *part browser*.

Saving the Model File

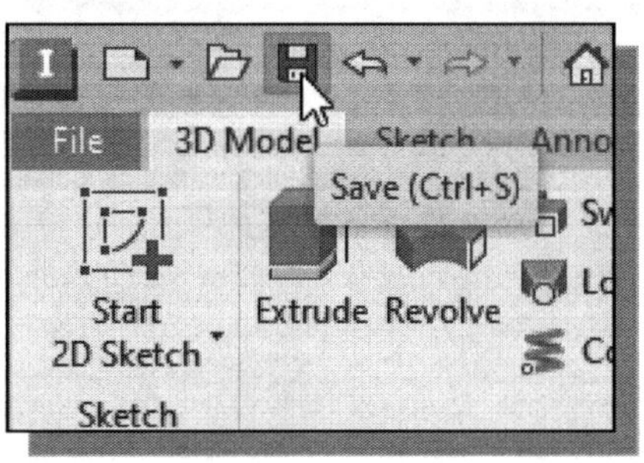

1. Select **Save** in the *Standard* toolbar. We can also use the "**Ctrl-S**" combination (press down the "Ctrl" key and hit the "S" key once) to save the part.

2. In the pop-up window, enter **Plate** as the name of the file.

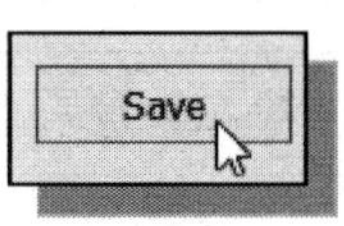

3. Click on the **SAVE** button to save the file.

Using the Measure Tools

Besides using the measure tools to get geometric information at the 2D level, the measure tools can also be used on 3D models.

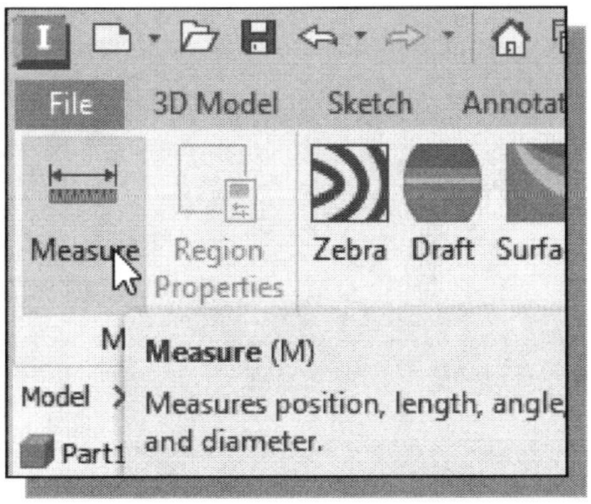

1. In the *Inspect Ribbon tab*, left-click once on the **Measure** option as shown.

2. Click on the top edge of the rectangular plate as shown.

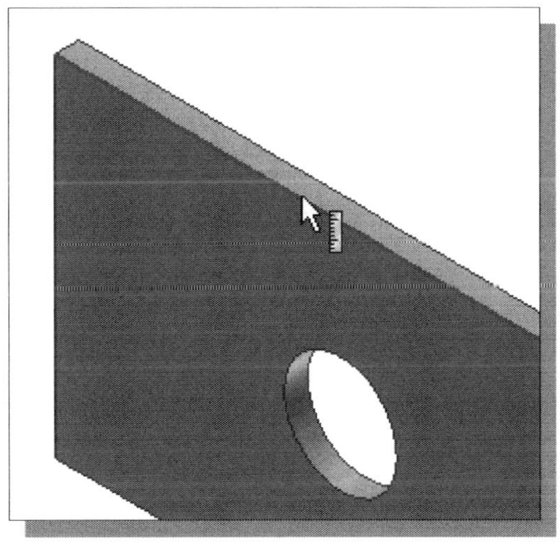

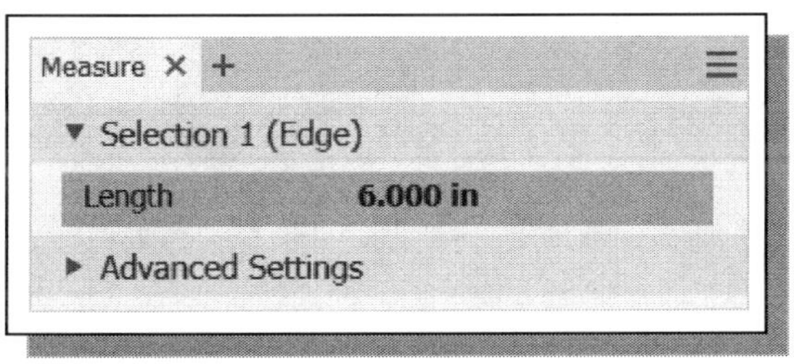

3. The associated length measurement of the selected geometry is displayed in the *Length* dialog box as shown.

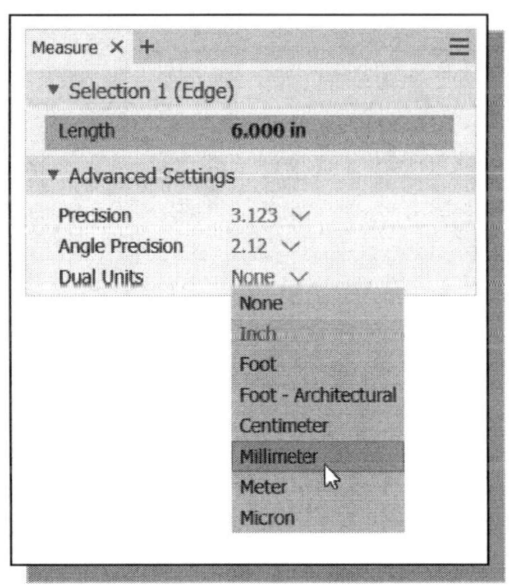

4. Click on the **triangular icon** of the **Advanced Settings** option list to display the available options.

5. Choose [**Dual Units**] → [**Millimeter**] to also display the measurement in mm.

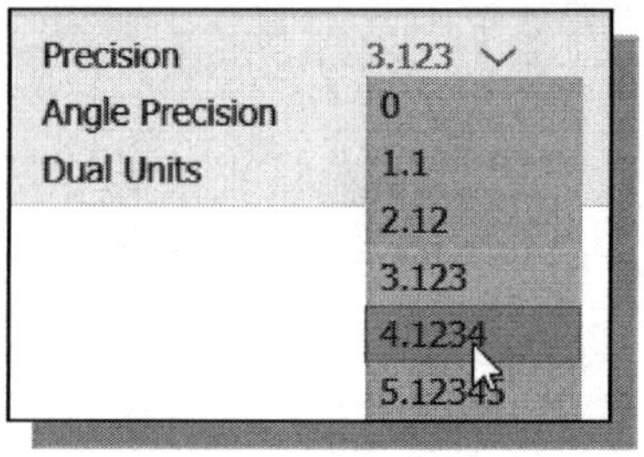

6. On your own, set the precision to show 4 decimal places as shown.

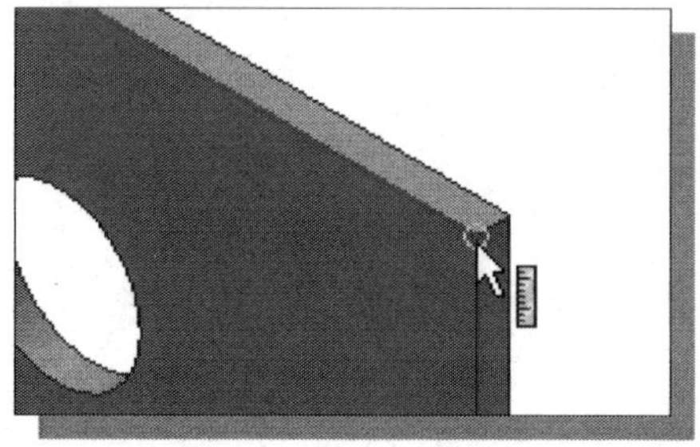

7. Click the **top-right corner** of the 3D model as shown.

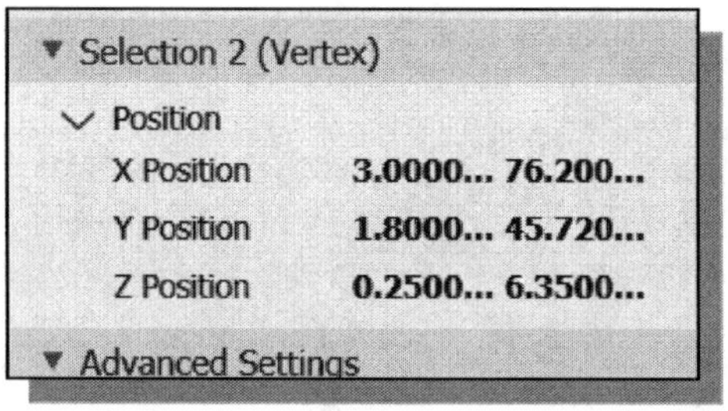

❖ Notice the information regarding the selected point is displayed in the *Measure* dialog box. The absolute position of the point is displayed. (Note the displayed numbers may be different on your screen.)

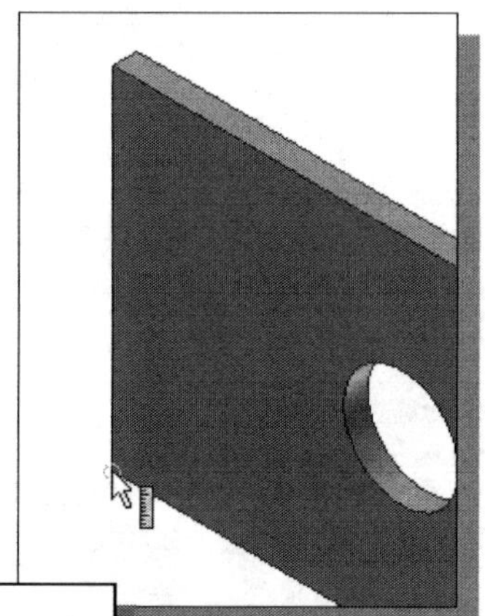

8. Select the front left bottom corner as the second location for the Measure Length command. The distance in between the two selected objects is calculated and displayed as shown.

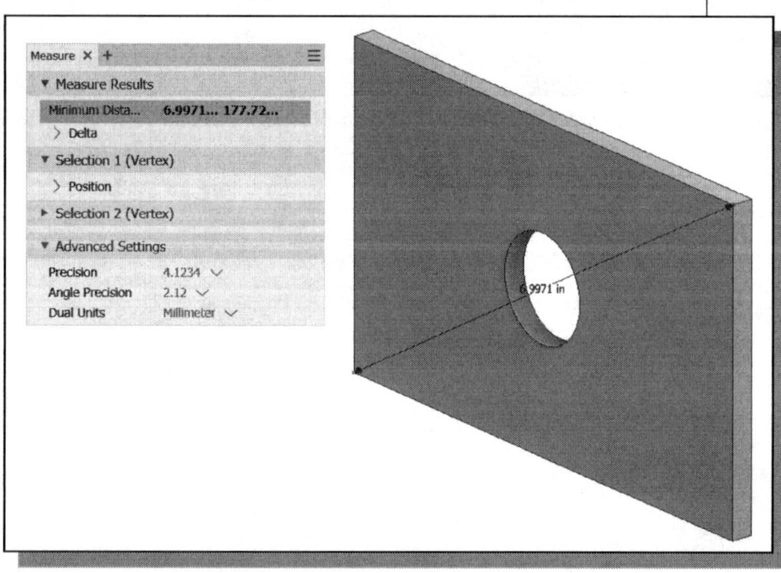

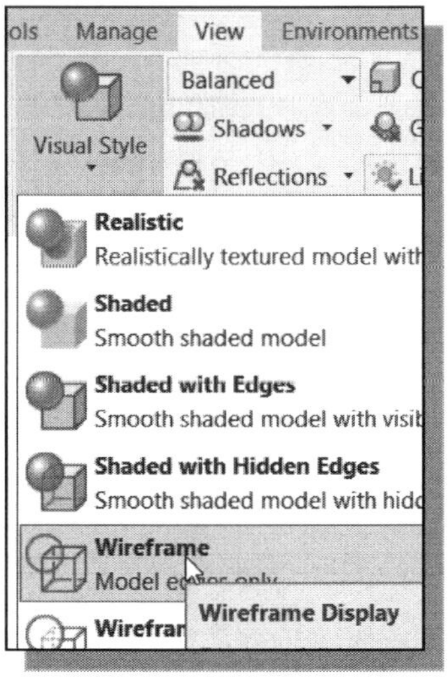

9. Set the display option to **Wireframe Display** by clicking the associated icon in the *Display* toolbar as shown.

10. Select the left vertical plane by clicking on the selection arrows. (Hint: Use the **Select Other** option if you are having difficulty selecting it.)

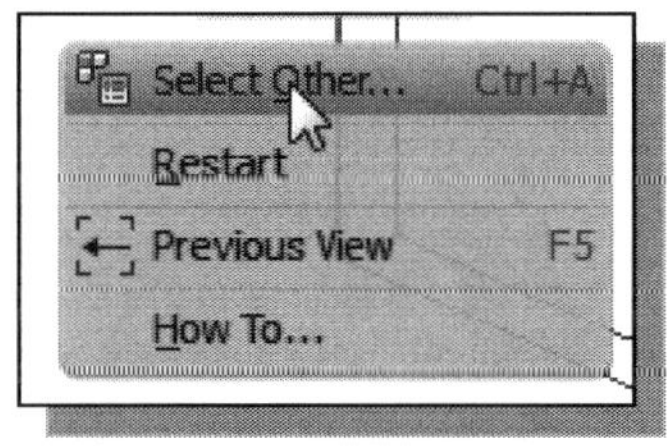

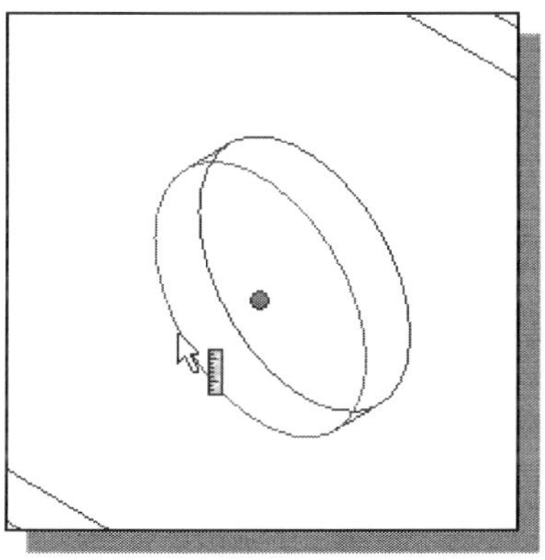

11. Select the circular hole in the front face; notice the center point is highlighted (the actual point used for the calculation) as shown.

❖ Different types of entities can be selected, and the measurements are calculated accordingly.

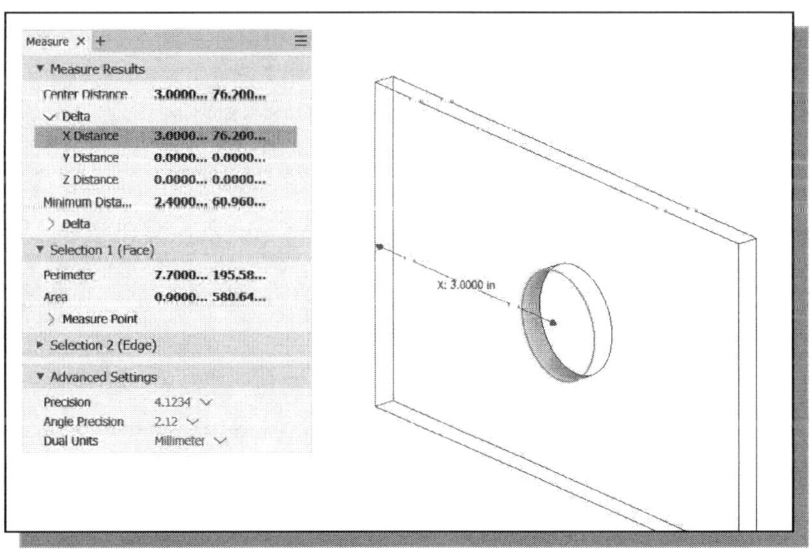

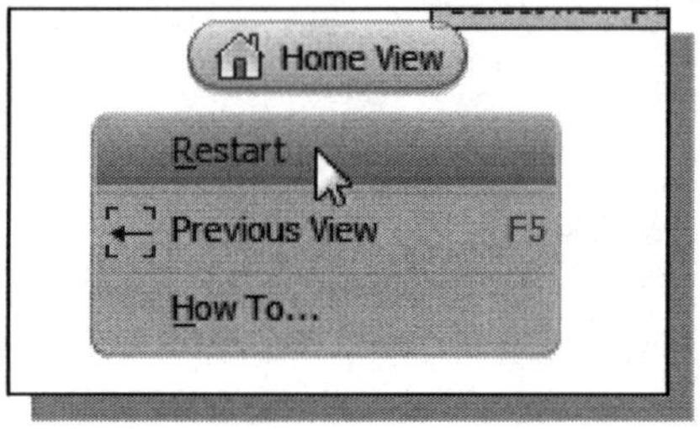

12. On your own, reset the **Measure** option by selecting **Restart** in the option list as shown.

13. Click on the front face of the plate model to display the area of the selected surface.

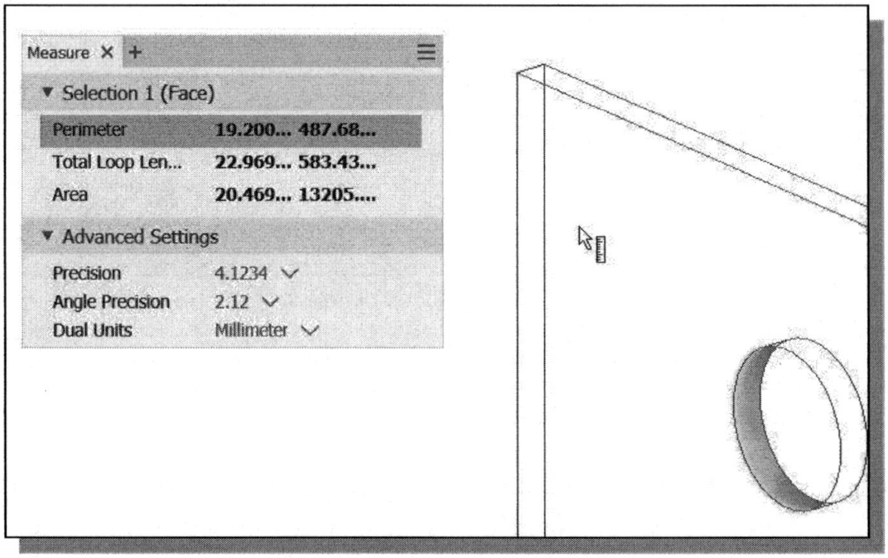

14. Note that we can also measure cylindrical surfaces by selecting the cylindrical surface as shown.

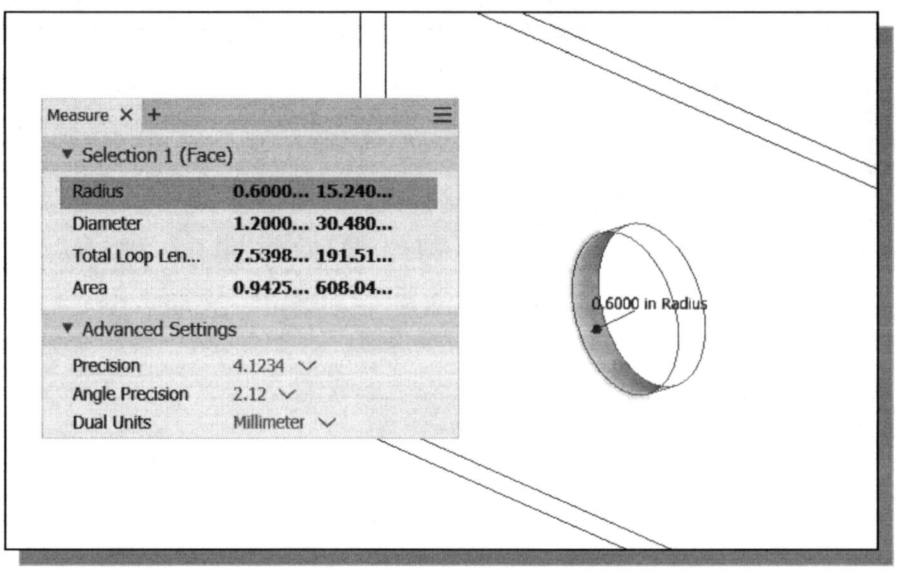

15. On your own, experiment with the different **measure tools** available.

Review Questions:

1. What is the difference between *dimensional* constraints and *geometric* constraints?

2. How can we confirm that a sketch is fully constrained?

3. How do we distinguish between derived dimensions and regular dimensions on the screen?

4. Describe the procedure to Display/Edit user-defined equations.

5. List and describe three different geometric constraints available in Autodesk Inventor.

6. Does Autodesk Inventor allow us to build partially constrained or totally unconstrained solid models? What are the advantages and disadvantages of building these types of models?

7. How do we display and examine the existing constraints that are applied to the sketched entities?

8. Describe the advantages of using parametric equations.

9. Can we delete an applied constraint? How?

10. Create the following 2D Sketch and measure the associated area and perimeter.

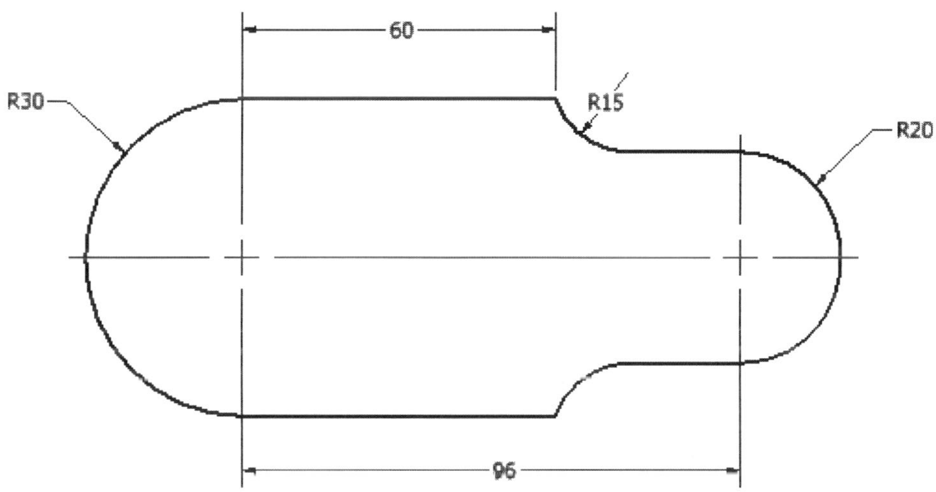

11. Describe the purpose and usage of the Auto Dimension command.

Exercises:

(Create and establish three parametric relations for each of the following designs.)

1. **Swivel Base** (Dimensions are in millimeters. Base thickness: **10 mm.** Boss: **5 mm.**)

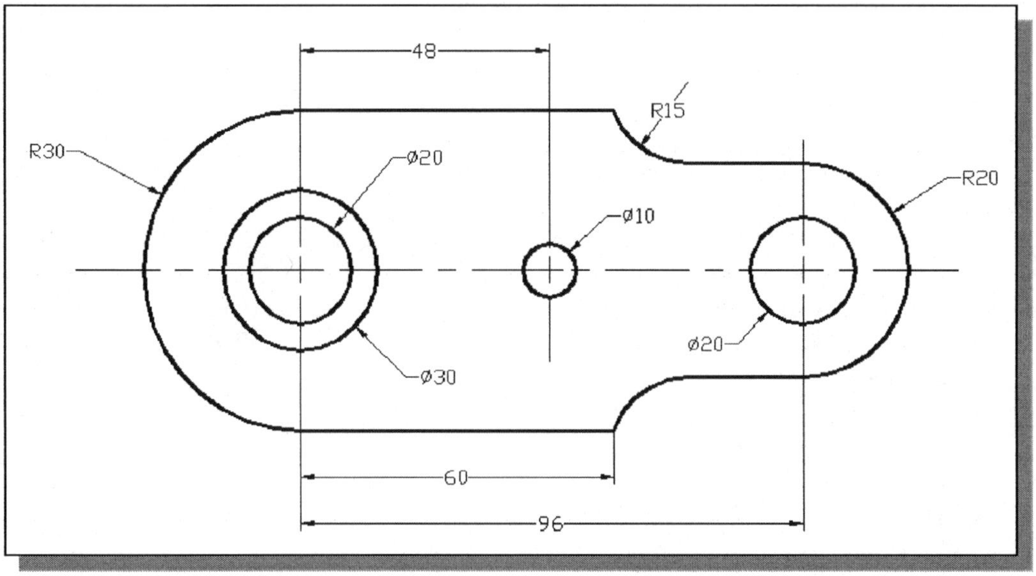

2. **Anchor Base** (Dimensions are in inches.)

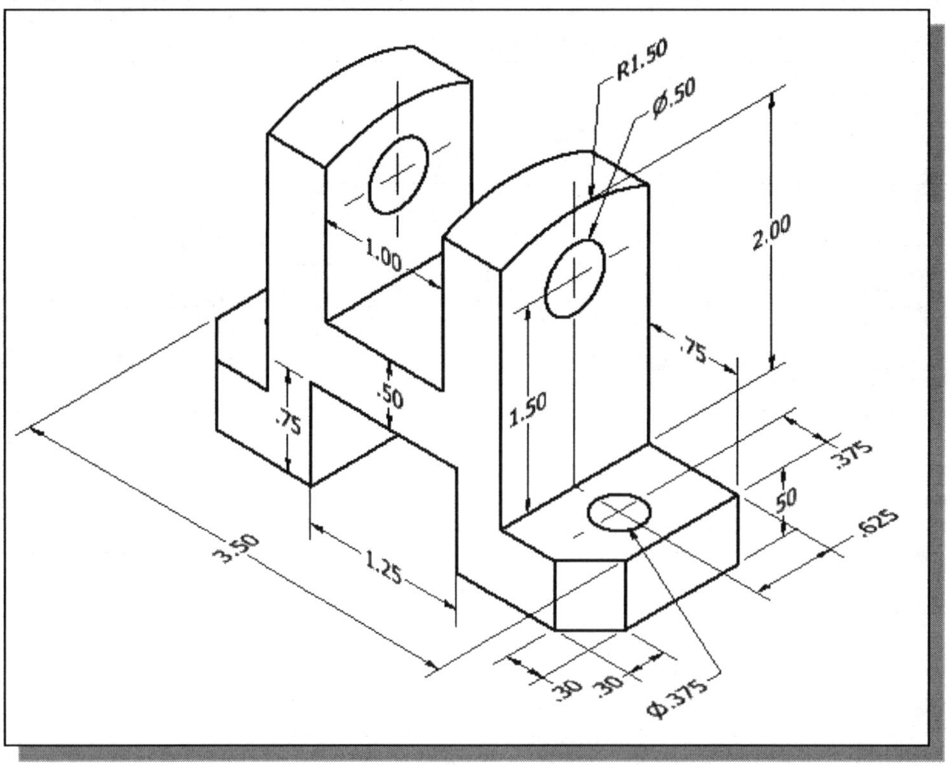

3. **Wedge Block** (Dimensions are in inches.)

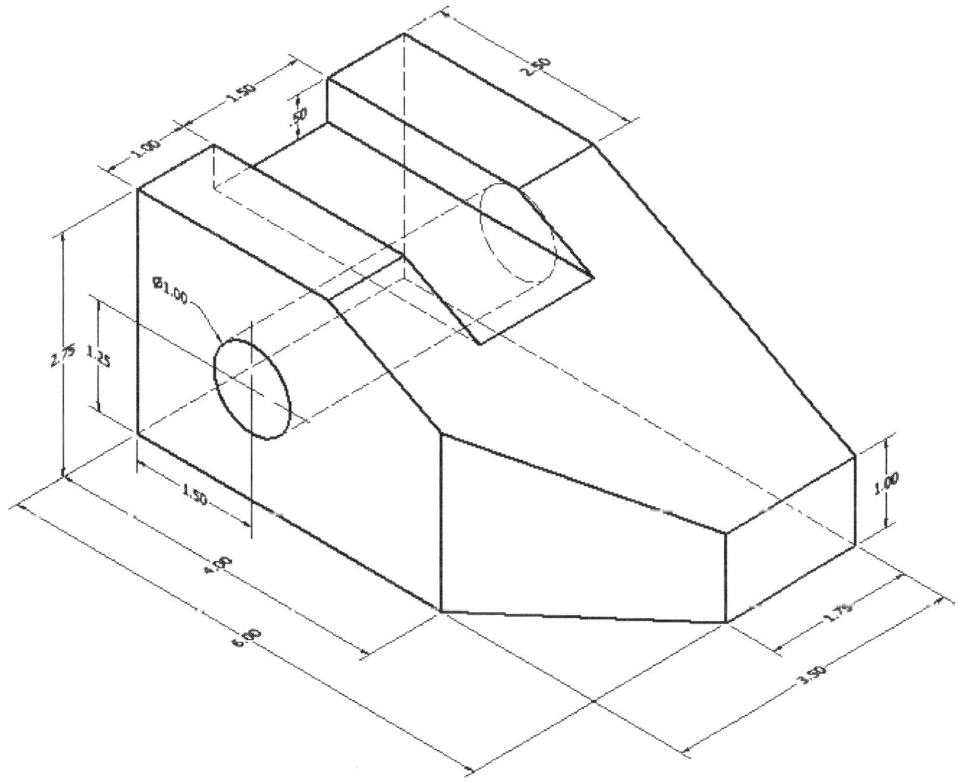

4. **Hinge Guide** (Dimensions are in inches.)

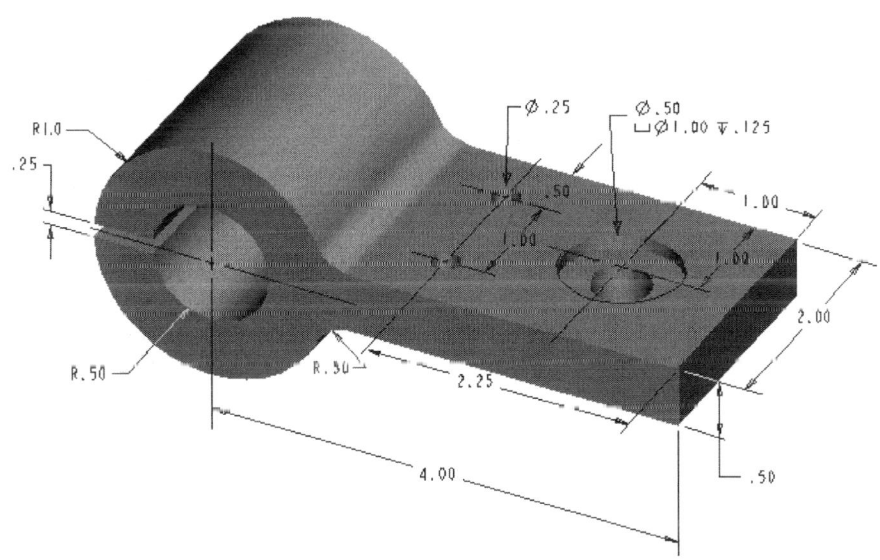

5. **Rod Slide** (Dimensions are in inches.)

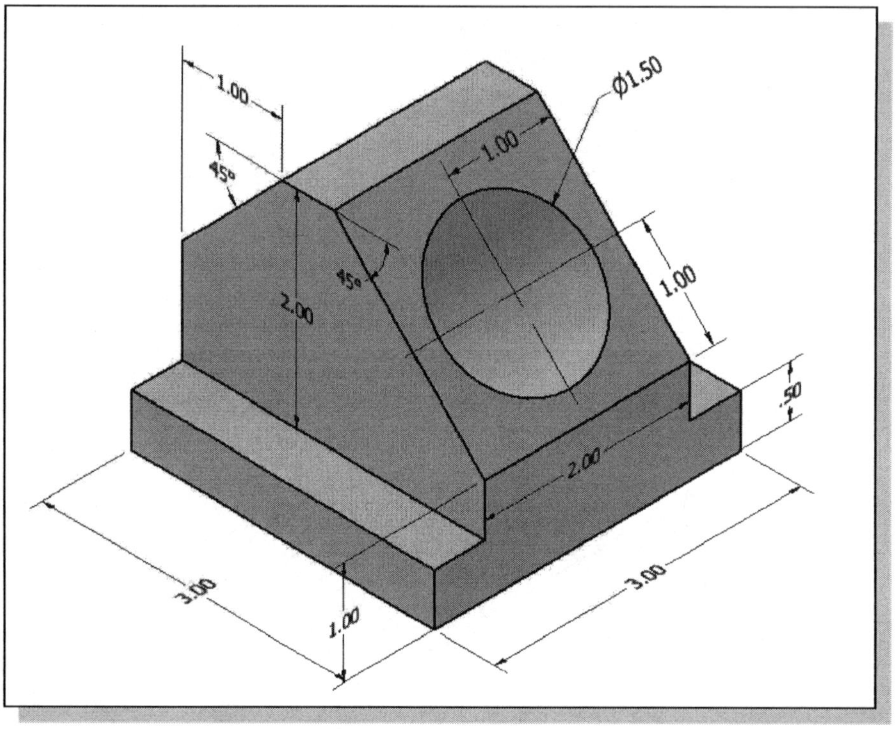

6. **Support Fixture** (Dimensions are in inches.)

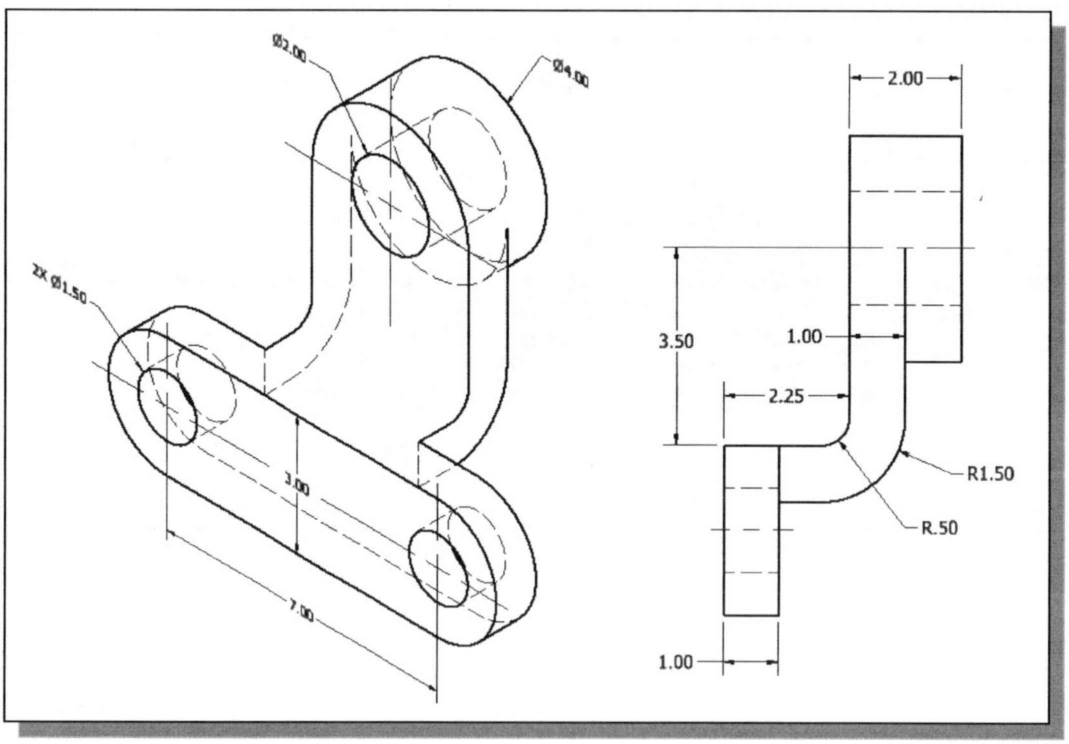

7. **Extruder Base** (Dimensions are in mm.)

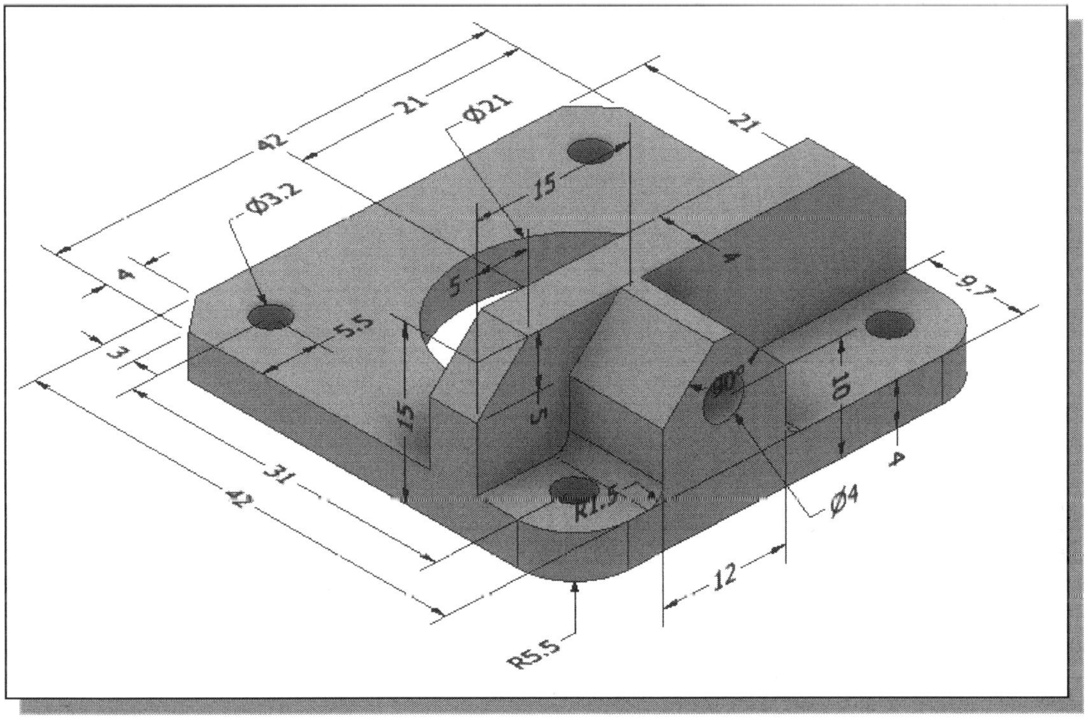

Notes:

Chapter 11
Geometric Construction Tools - Autodesk Inventor

Learning Objectives

- Apply Geometry Constraints
- Use the Trim/Extend Command
- Use the Offset Command
- Understand the Profile Sketch Approach
- Create Projected Geometry
- Understand and Use Reference Geometry
- Edit with Click and Drag
- Use the Auto Dimension Command

Introduction

The main characteristics of solid modeling are the accuracy and completeness of the geometric database of the three-dimensional objects. However, working in three-dimensional space using input and output devices that are largely two-dimensional in nature is potentially tedious and confusing. Autodesk Inventor provides an assortment of two-dimensional construction tools to make the creation of wireframe geometry easier and more efficient. Autodesk Inventor includes two types of wireframe geometry: ***curves*** and ***profiles***. Curves are basic geometric entities such as lines, arcs, etc. Profiles are a group of curves used to define a boundary. A *profile* is a closed region and can contain other closed regions. Profiles are commonly used to create extruded and revolved features. An *invalid profile* consists of self-intersecting curves or open regions. In this lesson, the basic geometric construction tools, such as Trim and Extend, are used to create profiles. The Autodesk Inventor's ***profile sketch*** approach to creating profiles is also introduced. Mastering the geometric construction tools along with the application of proper constraints and parametric relations is the true essence of *parametric modeling*.

The Gasket Design

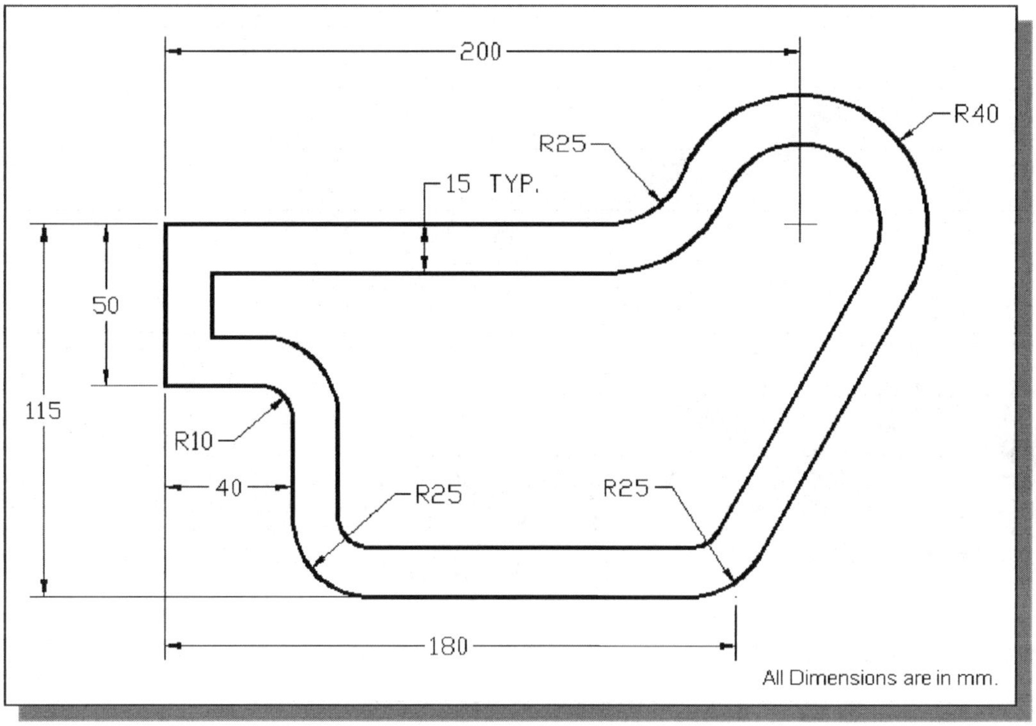

❖ Based on your knowledge of Autodesk Inventor so far, how would you create this design? What is the most difficult geometry involved in the design? Take a few minutes to consider a modeling strategy and do preliminary planning by sketching on a piece of paper. You are also encouraged to create the design on your own prior to following through the tutorial.

Modeling Strategy

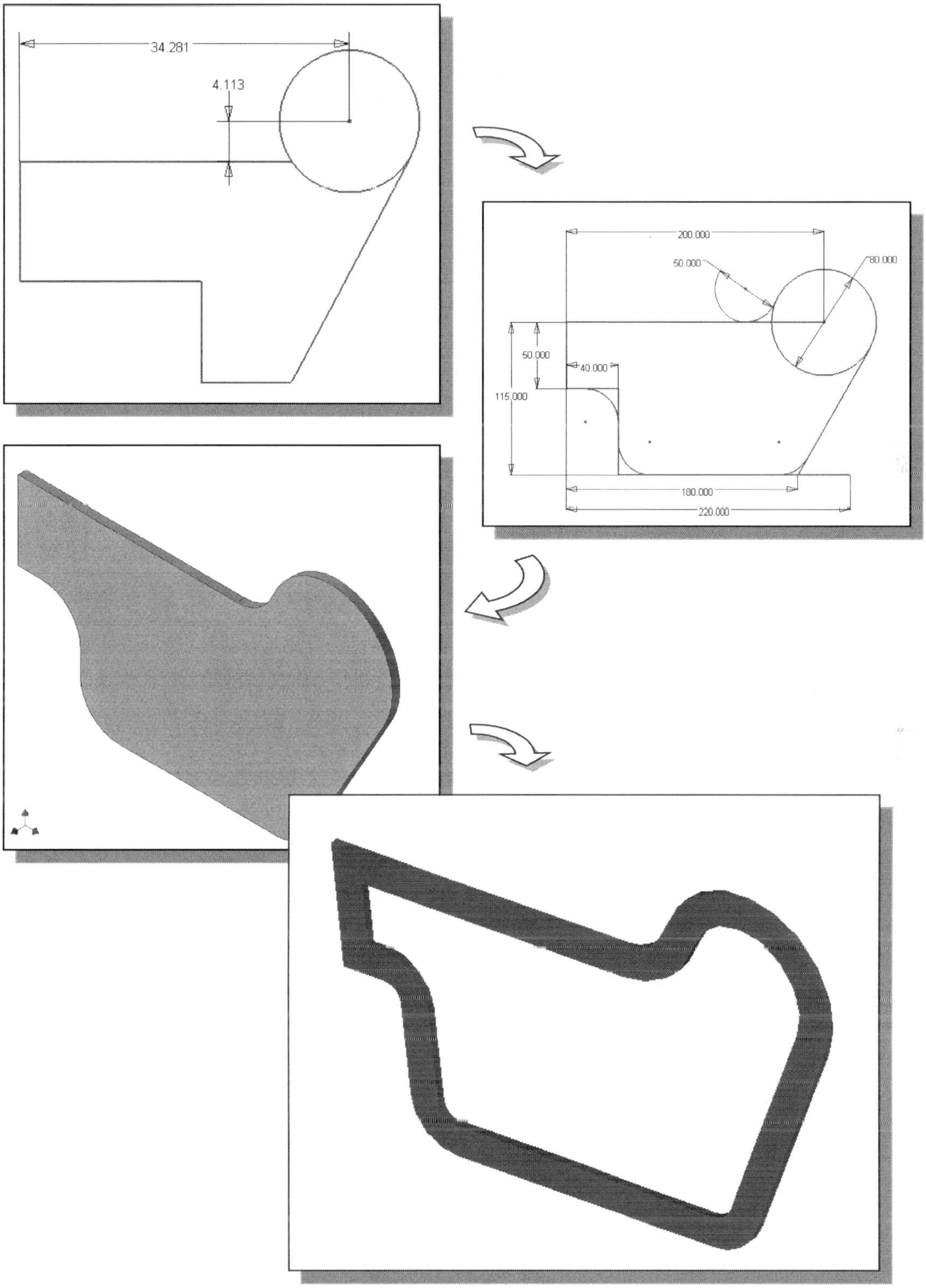

Starting Autodesk Inventor

1. Select the **Autodesk Inventor** option on the *Start* menu or select the **Autodesk Inventor** icon on the desktop to start Autodesk Inventor. The Autodesk Inventor main window will appear on the screen.

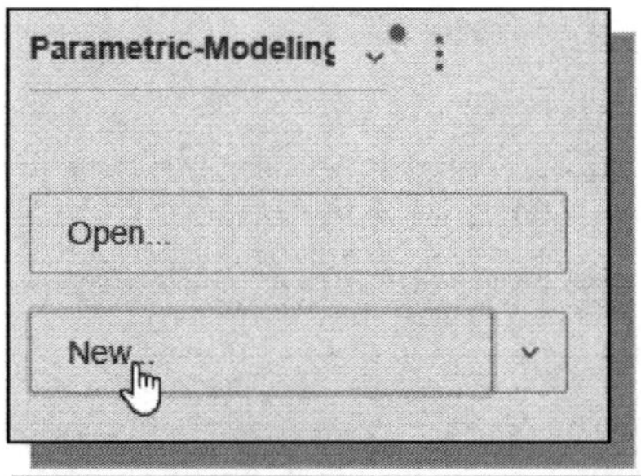

2. Select the **New File** icon with a single click of the left-mouse-button as shown.

3. Select the **Metric** tab as shown. We will use the millimeter (mm) setting for this design.

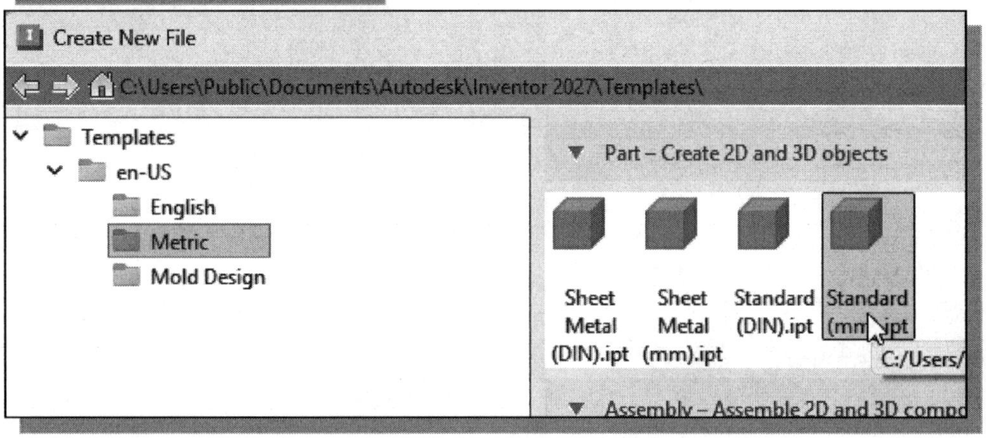

4. In the *New File* dialog box, use the scroll bar on the right and select the **Standard(mm).ipt** icon as shown.

5. Click **Create** in the *New File* dialog box to accept the selected settings to start a new model.

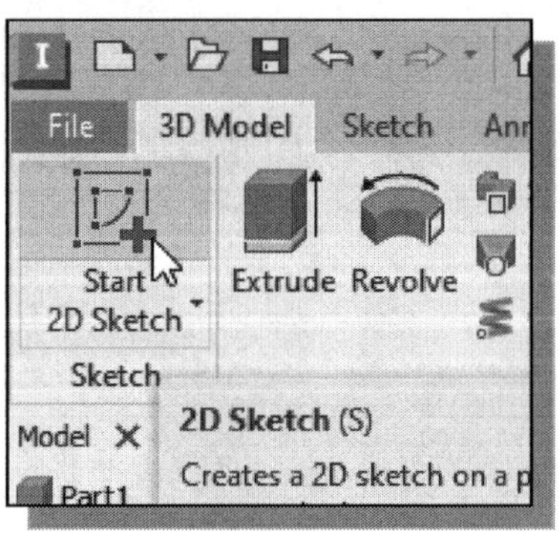

6. Click once with the left-mouse-button to select the **Start 2D Sketch** command. Click once with the **left-mouse-button** to select the *XY Plane* as the sketch plane for the new sketch.

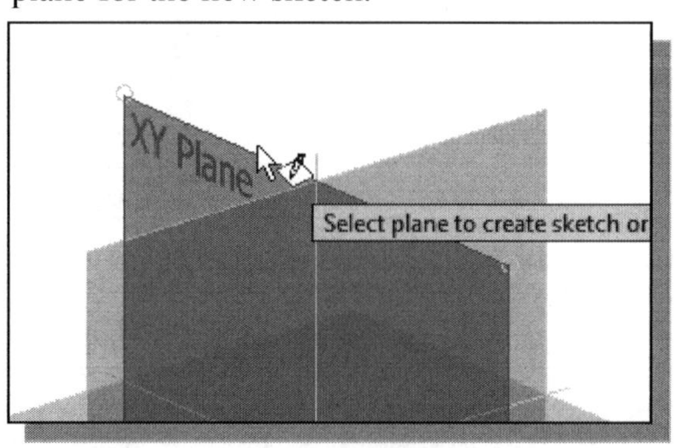

Create a 2D Sketch

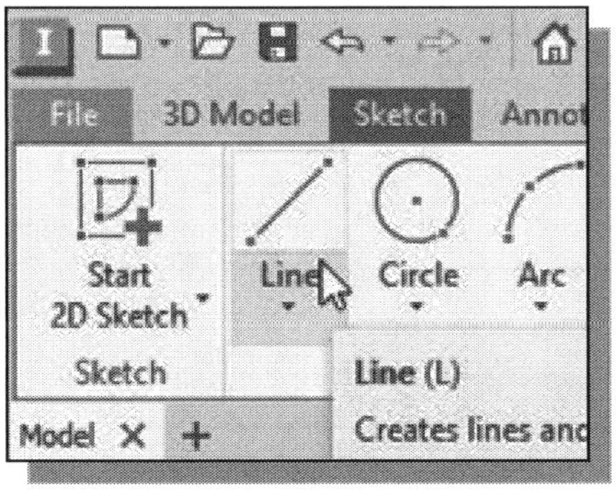

1. Click on the **Line** icon in the *Sketch* tab on the Ribbon.

2. Create a sketch as shown in the figure below. Start the sketch from the top right corner. The line segments are all parallel and/or perpendicular to each other. We will intentionally create arbitrary line segments, as it is quite common during the initial design stage that most of the shapes and forms are undetermined.

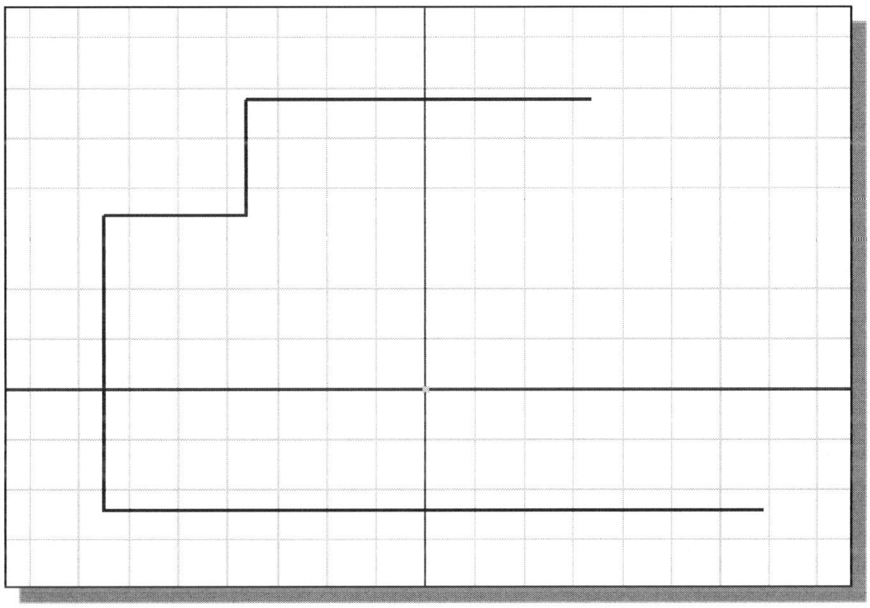

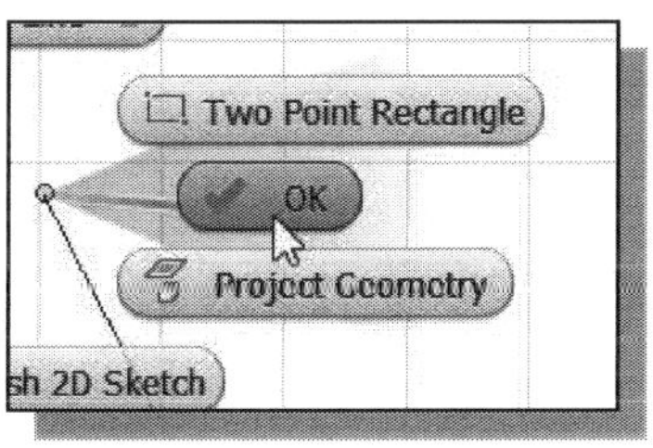

3. Inside the graphics window, right-click to bring up the option menu, and select **OK** to end the **Line** command.

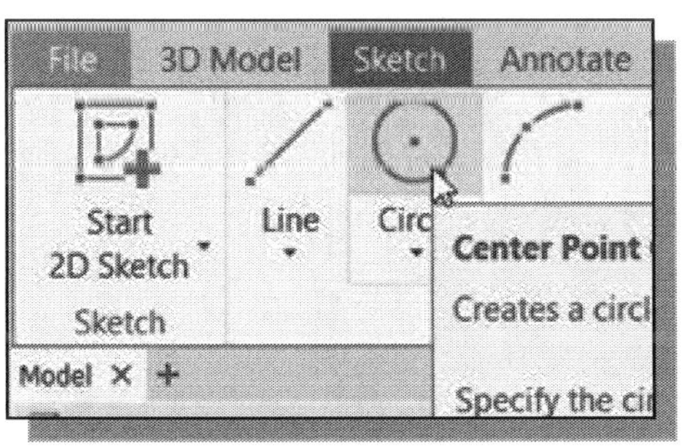

4. Select the **Center Point Circle** command by clicking once with the left-mouse-button on the icon in the *Sketch* tab on the Ribbon.

5. Pick a location that is above the bottom horizontal line as the center location of the circle.

6. Move the cursor toward the right and create a circle of arbitrary size by clicking once with the left-mouse-button.

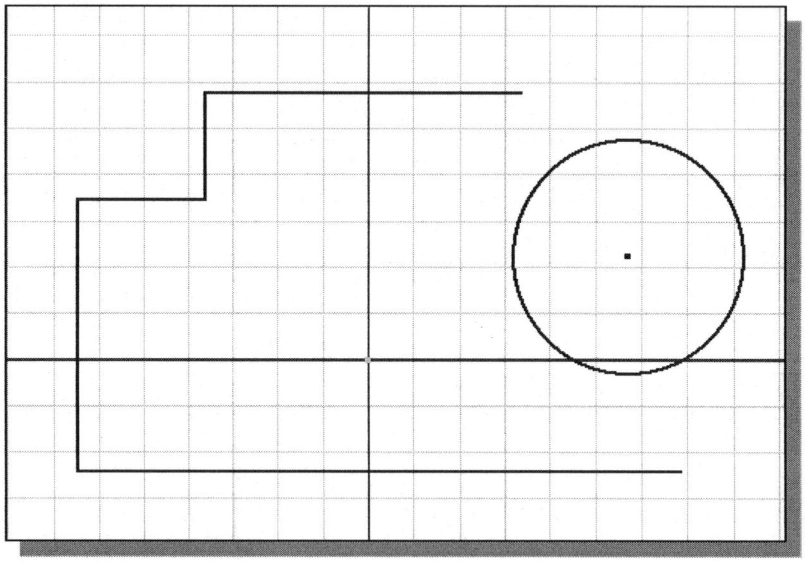

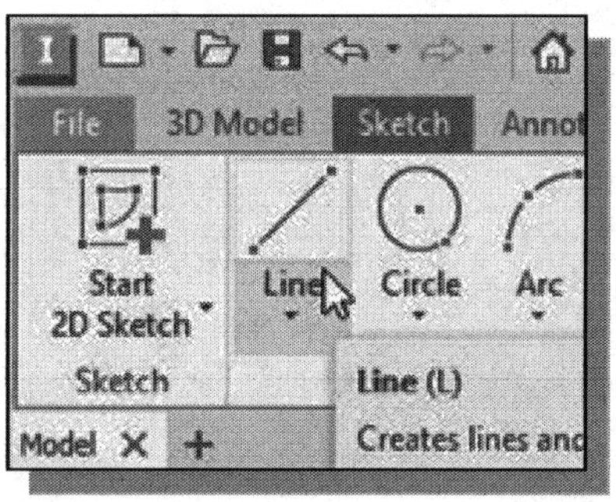

7. Click on the **Line** icon in the *Sketch* tab on the Ribbon.

8. Move the cursor near the upper portion of the circle and pick a location on the circle when the **Coincident** constraint symbol is displayed.

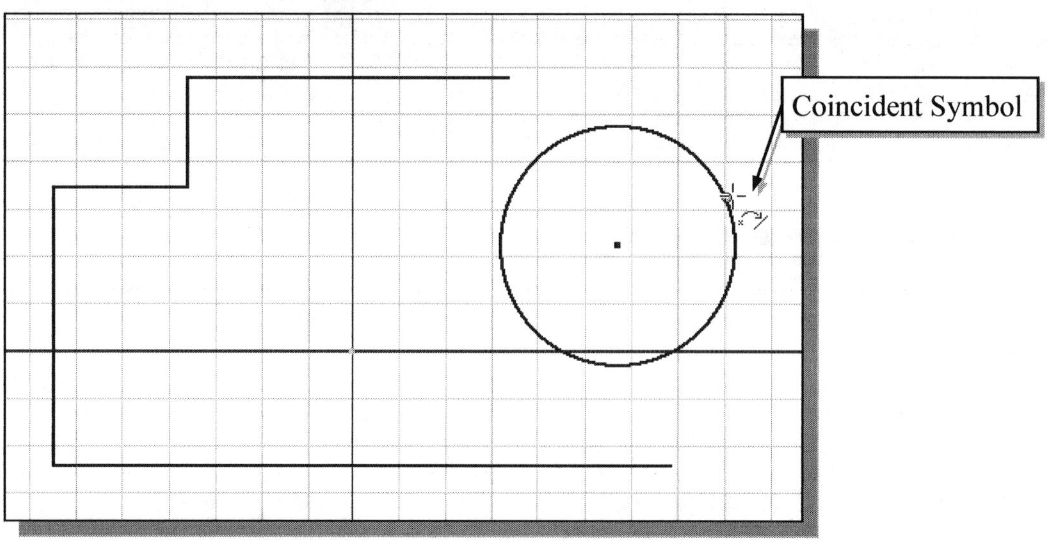

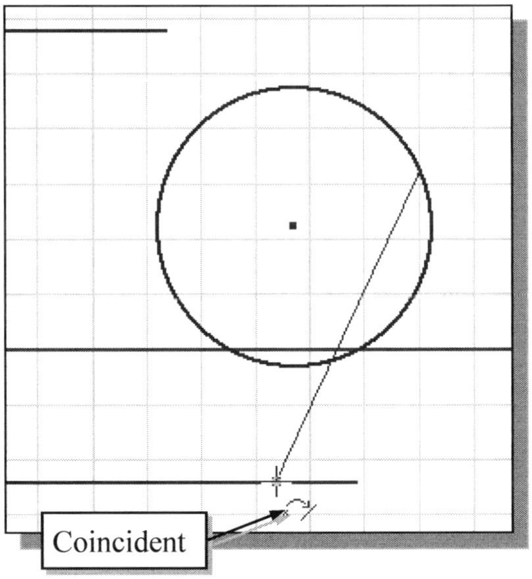

9. For the other end of the line, select a location that is on the lower horizontal line and about one-third from the right endpoint. Notice the Coincident constraint symbol is displayed when the cursor is on the horizontal line.

10. Inside the graphics window, right-click to bring up the option menu and select **OK** to end the Line command.

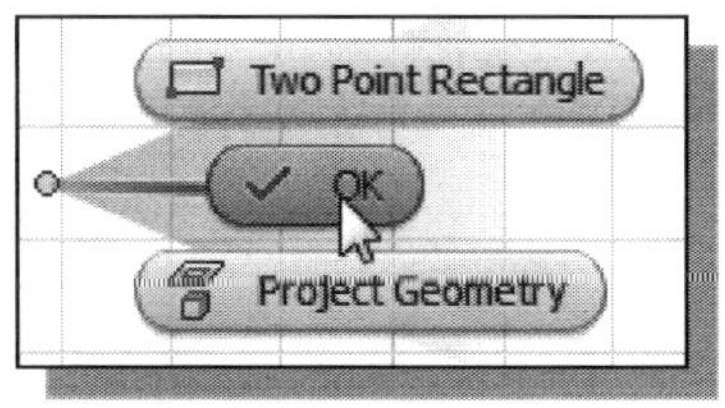

Edit the Sketch by Dragging the Sketched Entities

In Autodesk Inventor, we can click and drag any under-constrained curve or point in the sketch to change the size or shape of the sketched profile. As illustrated in the previous chapter, this option can be used to identify under-constrained entities. This *Editing by dragging* method is also an effective visual approach that allows designers to quickly make changes.

1. Move the cursor on the lower left vertical edge of the sketch. Click and drag the edge to a new location that is toward the right side of the sketch.

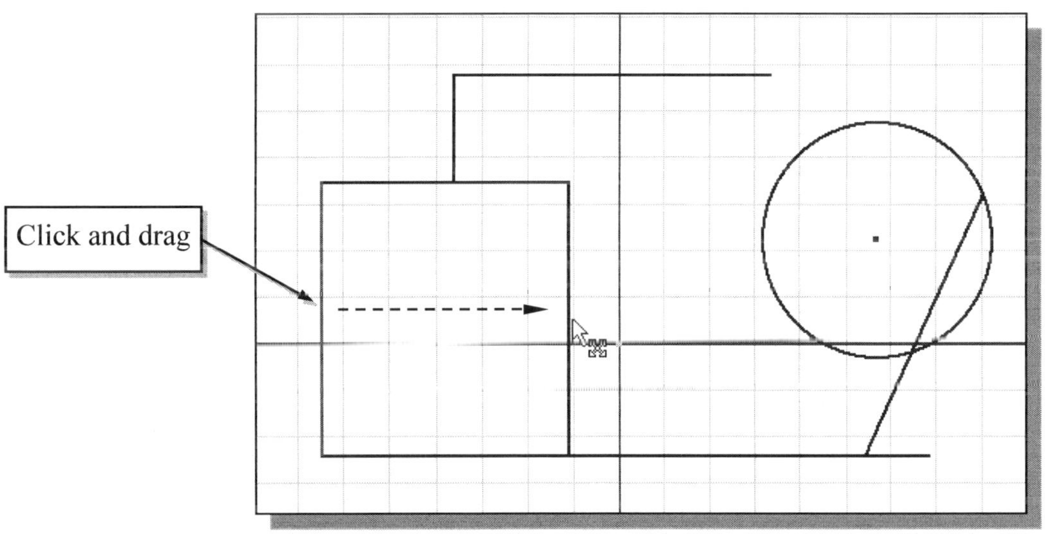

❖ Note that we can only drag the vertical edge horizontally; the connections to the two horizontal lines are maintained while we are moving the geometry.

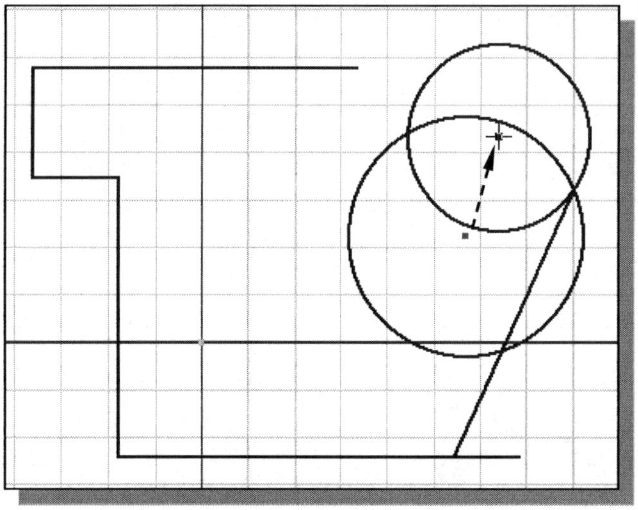

2. Click and drag the center point of the circle to a new location.

❖ Note that as we adjust the size and the location of the circle, the connection to the inclined line is maintained.

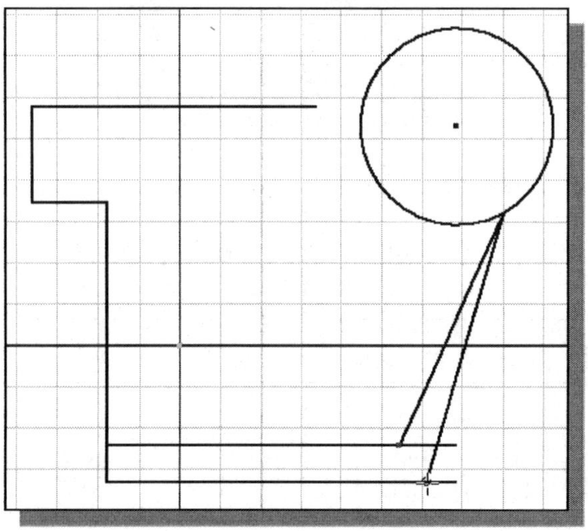

3. Click and drag the lower endpoint of the inclined line to a new location.

❖ Note that as we adjust the size and the location of the inclined line the location of the bottom horizontal edge is also adjusted.

❖ Note that several changes occur as we adjust the size and the location of the inclined line. The location of the bottom horizontal line and the length of the vertical line are adjusted accordingly.

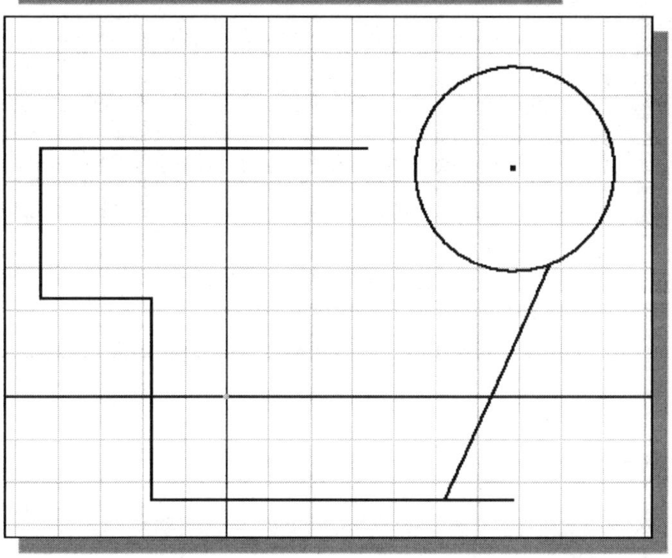

4. On your own, adjust the sketch so that the shape of the sketch appears roughly as shown.

❖ The *Editing by dragging* method is an effective approach that allows designers to explore and experiment with different design concepts.

Add Additional Constraints

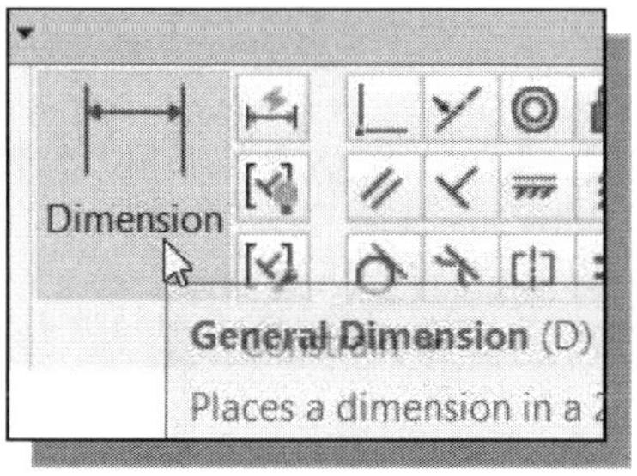

1. Choose **General Dimension** in the *Sketch* panel.

2. Add the horizontal location dimension, from the top left vertical edge to the center of the circle as shown. (Do not be overly concerned with the dimensional value; we are still working on creating a *rough sketch*.)

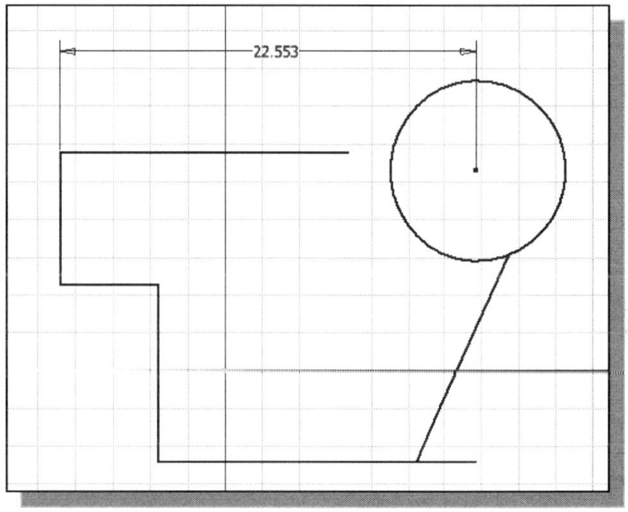

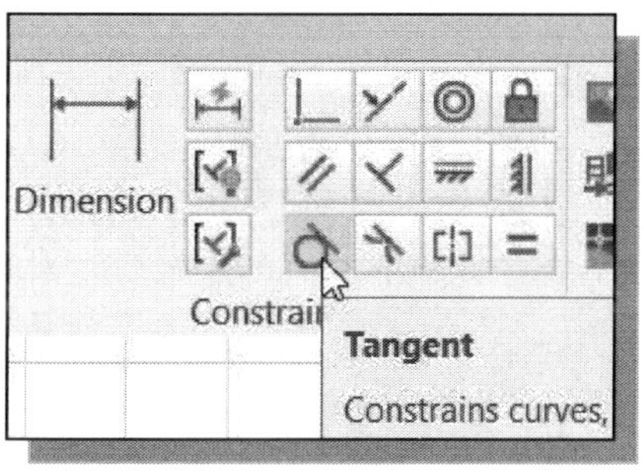

3. Click on the **Tangent** constraint icon in the *Sketch* panel.

4. Pick the inclined line by left-clicking once on the geometry.

5. Pick the circle. The sketched geometry is adjusted as shown below.

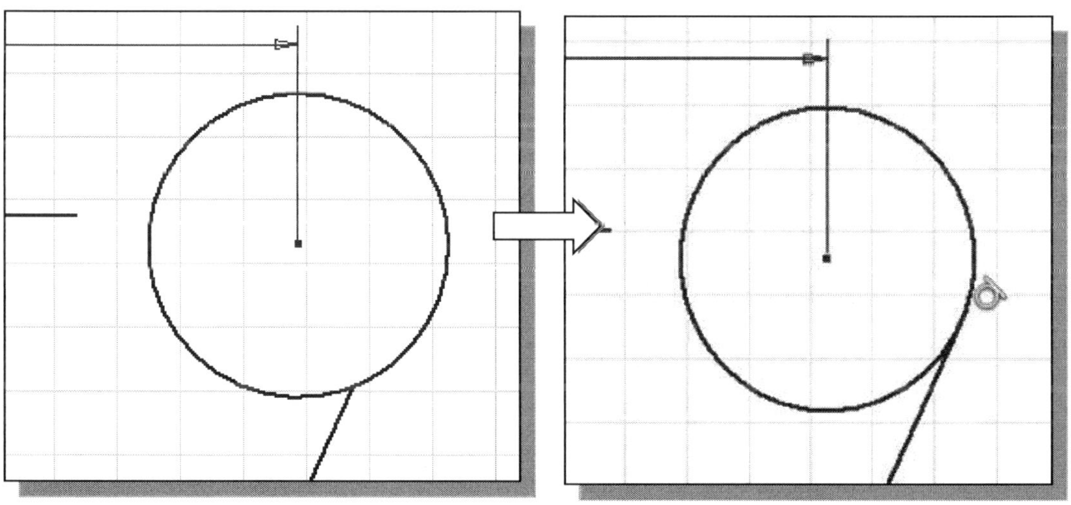

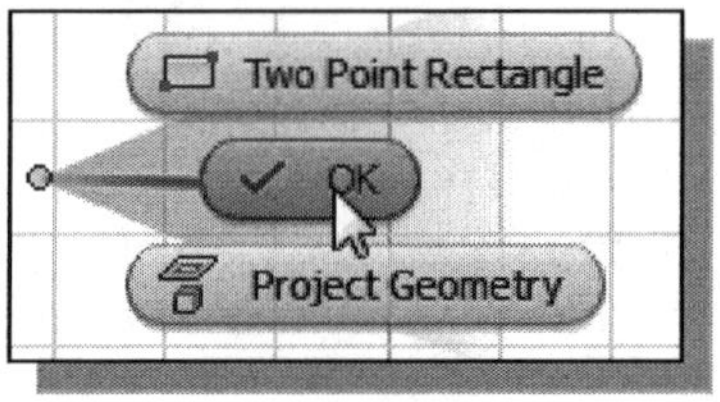

6. Inside the graphics window, right-click to bring up the option menu.

7. In the option menu, select **OK** to end the Tangent command.

8. Use the drag and drop approach, of the circle center, to observe the relations of the sketched geometry.

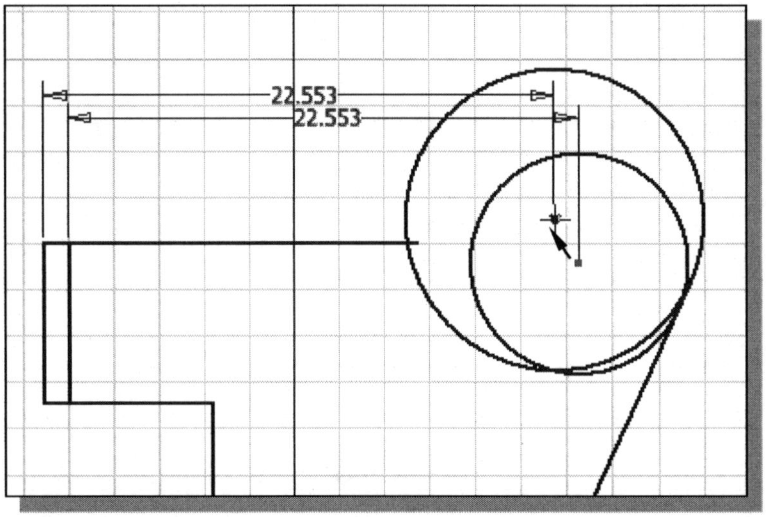

❖ Note that the dimension we added now restricts the horizontal movement of the center of the circle. The tangent relation to the inclined line is maintained.

Use the Trim and Extend Commands

In the following sections, we will illustrate using the Trim and Extend commands to complete the desired 2D profile.

The **Trim** and **Extend** commands can be used to shorten/lengthen an object so that it ends precisely at a boundary. As a general rule, Autodesk Inventor will try to clean up sketches by forming a closed region sketch. Also note that while we are in either **Trim** or **Extend**, we can press the [**Shift**] key to switch to the opposite operation.

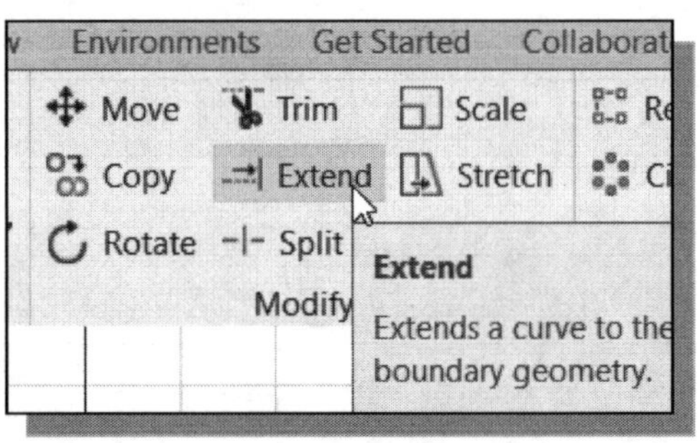

1. Choose **Extend** in the *Modify toolbar* panel. The message "*Extend curves*" is displayed in the prompt area.

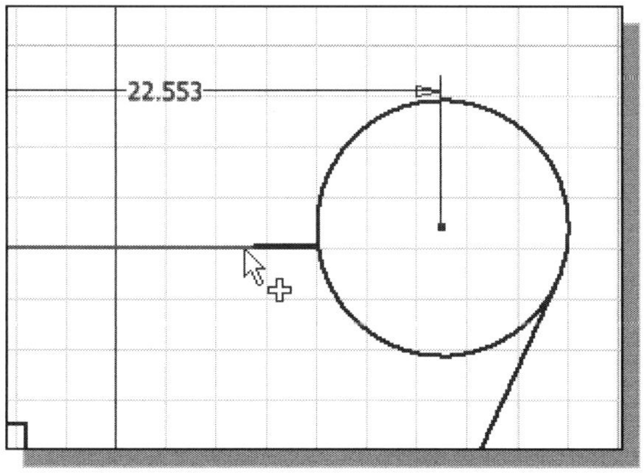

2. We will first extend the top horizontal line to the circle. Move the cursor near the right-hand endpoint of the top horizontal line. Autodesk Inventor will automatically display the possible result of the selection.

3. Next, we will trim the bottom horizontal line to the inclined line. The Trim operation can be activated by selecting the Trim icon in the *Sketch* panel or by pressing down the [**Shift**] key while we are in the Extend command. Move the cursor near the right-hand endpoint of the bottom horizontal line and select the line and press down the [**Shift**] key. Autodesk Inventor will display a dashed line indicating the portion of the line that will be trimmed.

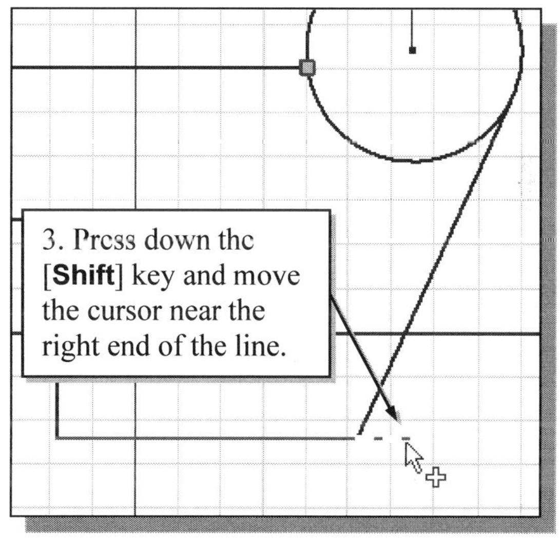

4. Left-click once on the line to perform the **Trim** operation.

5. On your own, create the vertical location dimension as shown below.

6. Adjust the dimension to **0.0** so that the horizontal line and the center of the circle are aligned horizontally.

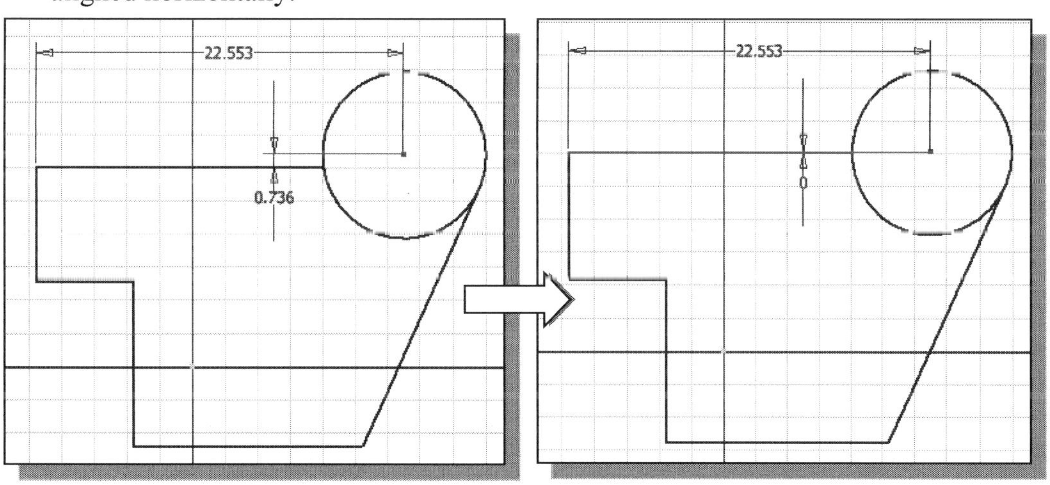

7. On your own, create the **height dimension** to the left and use the **Show Constraints** command to examine the applied constraints. Confirm that a **Perpendicular constraint** is applied to the horizontal and vertical lines as shown.

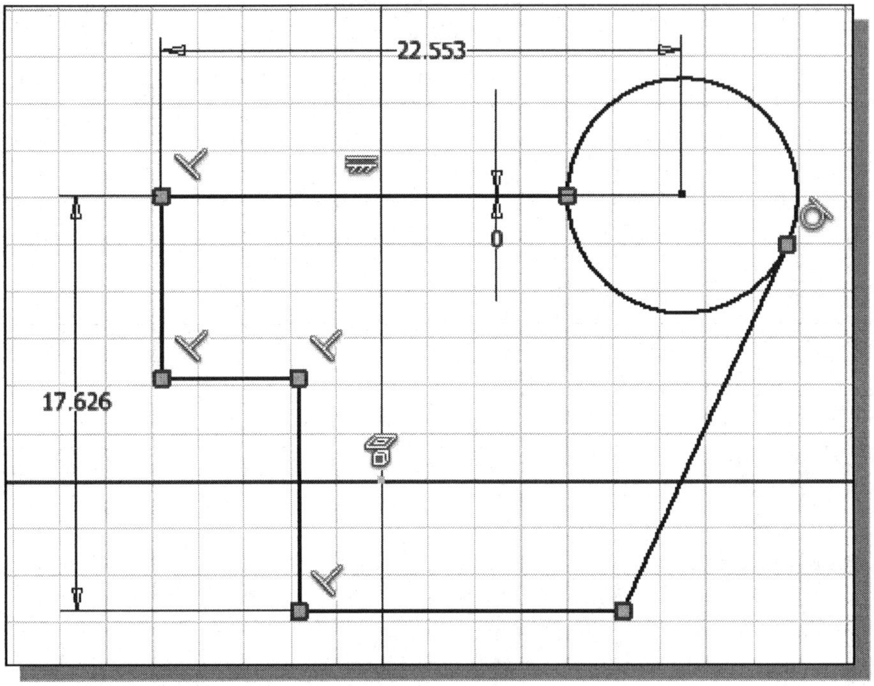

The Auto Dimension Command

In Autodesk Inventor, we can use the **Auto Dimension** command to assist in creating a fully constrained sketch. Fully constrained sketches can be updated more predictably as design changes are implemented. The general procedure for applying dimensions to sketches is to use the **General Dimension** command to add the desired key dimensions, and then use the **Auto Dimension** command as a quick way to calculate all other sketch dimensions necessary. Autodesk Inventor remembers which dimensions were added by the user and which were calculated by the system, so that automatic dimensions do not replace the desired dimensions.

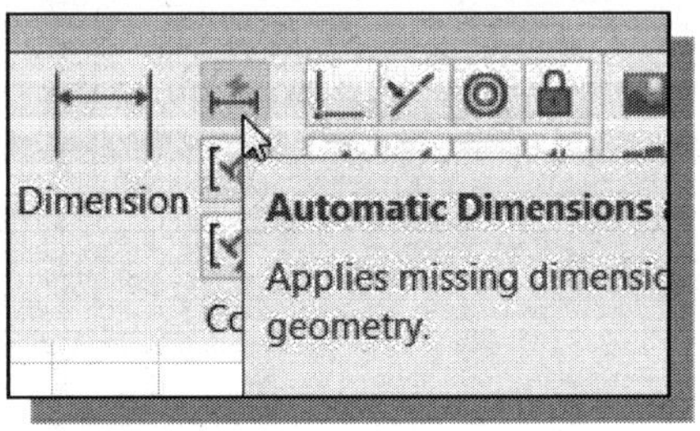

1. Click on the **Auto Dimension** icon in the *Sketch* panel.

- Note that 6 dimensions are needed to fully constrain the sketch, as indicated in the *Status Bar*.

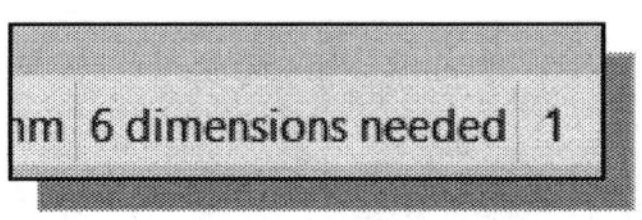

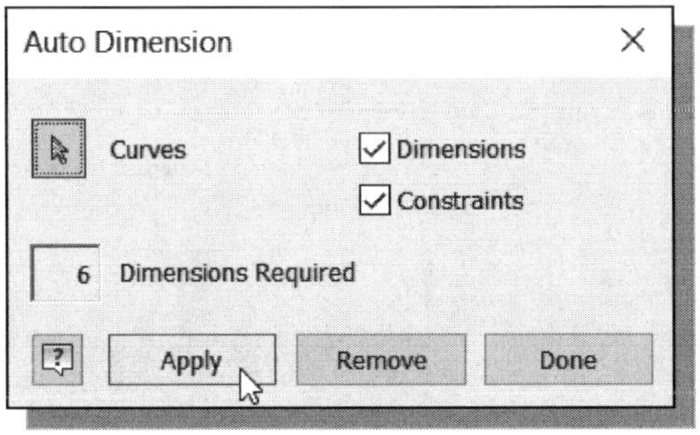

2. The *Auto Dimension* dialog box appears on the screen. Confirm that the **Dimensions** and **Constraints** options are switched *ON* as shown.

3. Click on the **Apply** button to proceed with the Auto Dimension command.

➢ Note that the system automatically calculates additional dimensions for all created geometric entities. Note that at times, the system applied dimensions might not be adequate for the designs. It is best to apply all the key dimensions prior to using the **Auto Dimension** command.

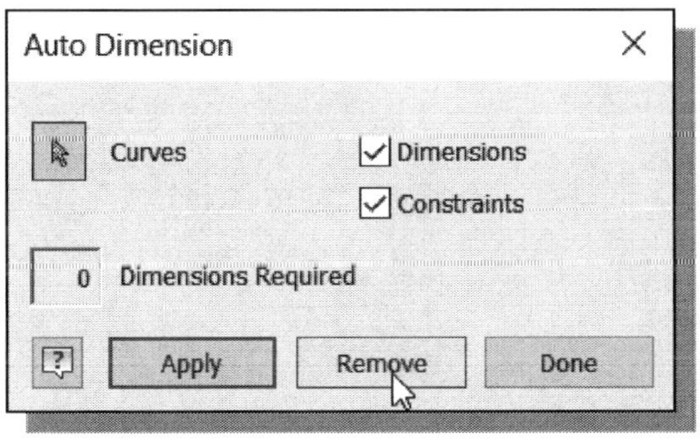

➢ The dimensions created by the **Auto Dimension** command can also be **Removed**.

4. Click on the **Remove** button to undo the dimensions created by the *Auto Dimension* command.

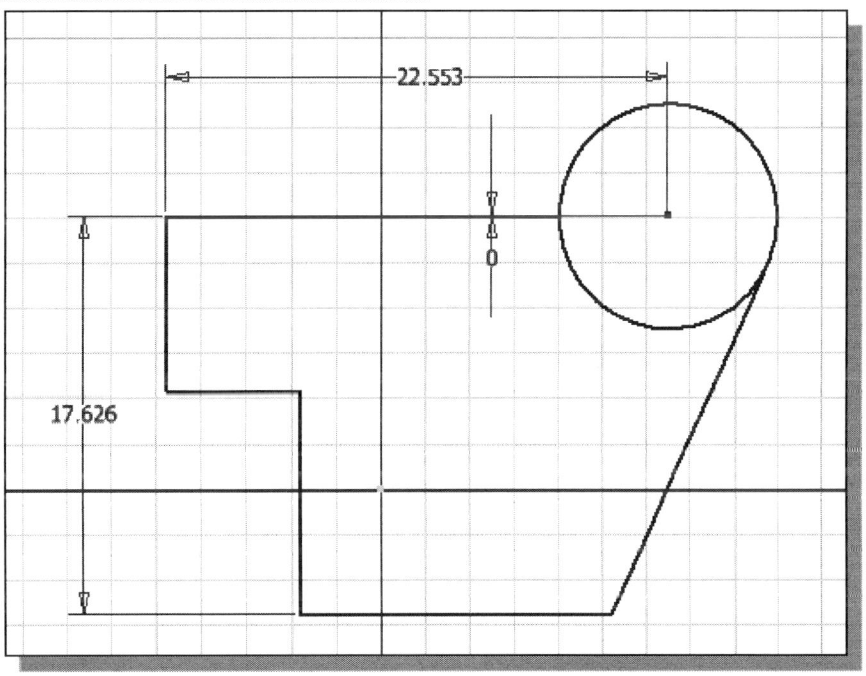

➢ Note the **Remove** option only removes the dimensions created by the **Auto Dimension** command but maintains the dimensions created by the user.

5. On your own, **trim** the circle and add the additional dimensions as shown.

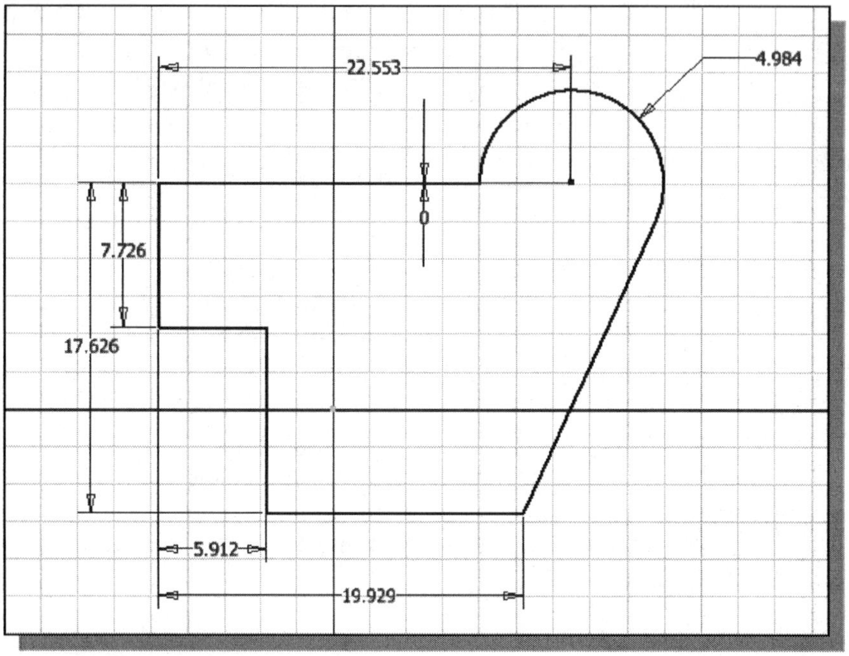

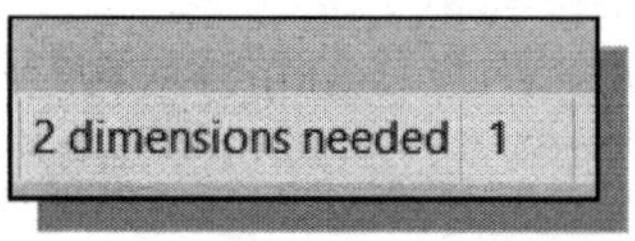

6. Note the display in the *Status Bar* indicates two additional dimensions are still needed to fully constrain the sketch.

Create Fillets and Completing the Sketch

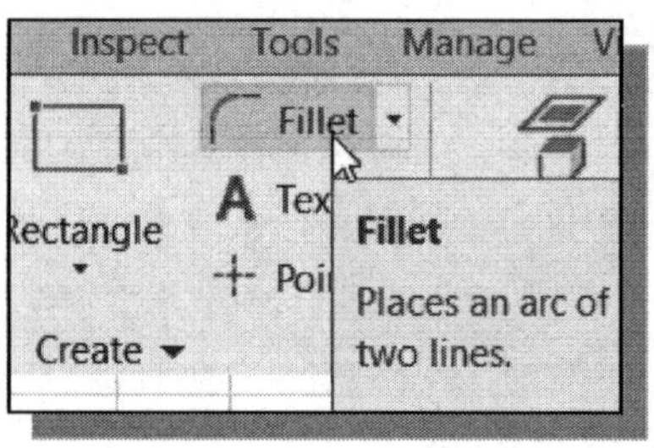

1. Click on the **Fillet** icon in the *Sketch* panel.

2. The *2D Fillet* radius dialog box appears on the screen. Use the **default** radius value and click on the top horizontal line and the arc to create a fillet as shown.

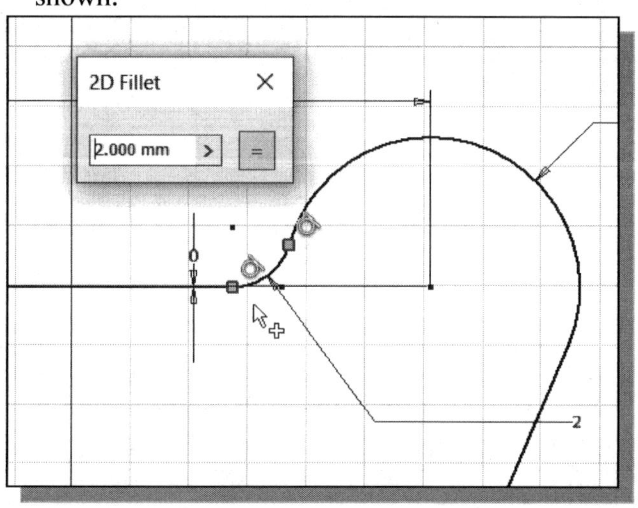

3. On your own, create the three additional fillets as shown in the below figure. Note that the **Equal** constraint is activated, and all rounds and fillets are created with the constraint.

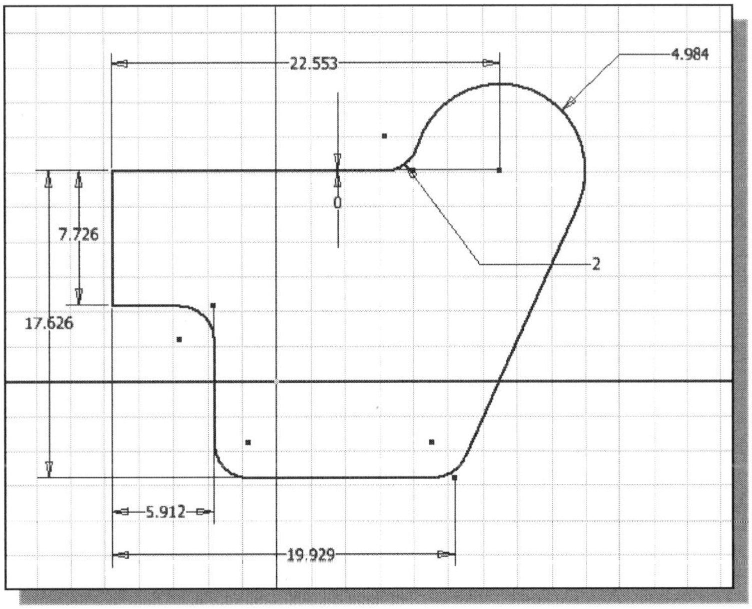

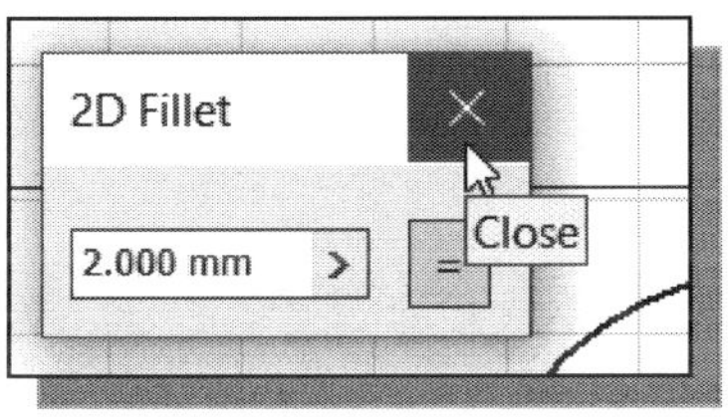

4. Click on the [**X**] icon to close the *2D Fillet* dialog box and end the **Fillet** command.

Fully Constrained Geometry

1. Click on the **Fix** constraint icon in the *Sketch Panel.*

2. Apply the **Fix** constraint to the center of the large arc as shown below.

➢ Note that the sketch is now fully constrained.

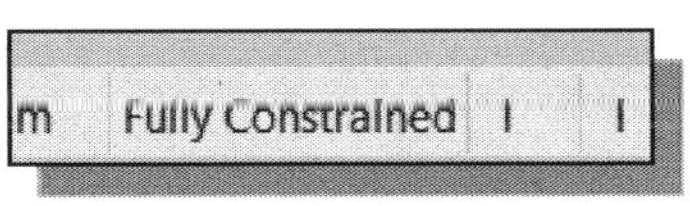

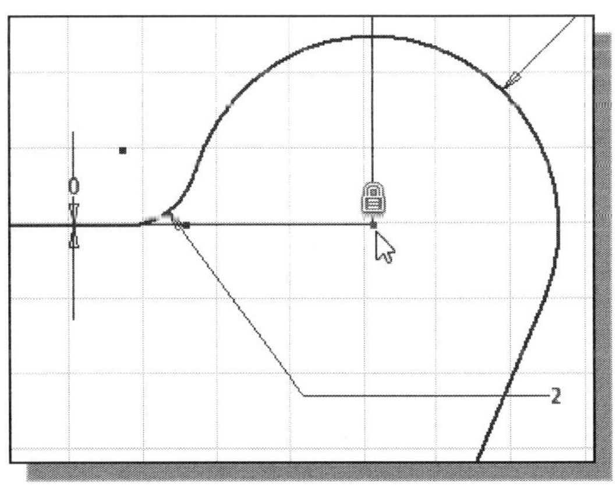

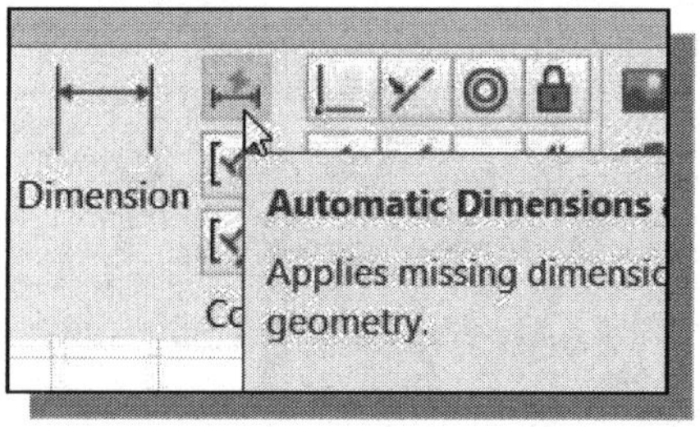

3. Click on the **Auto Dimension** icon in the *Sketch* panel.

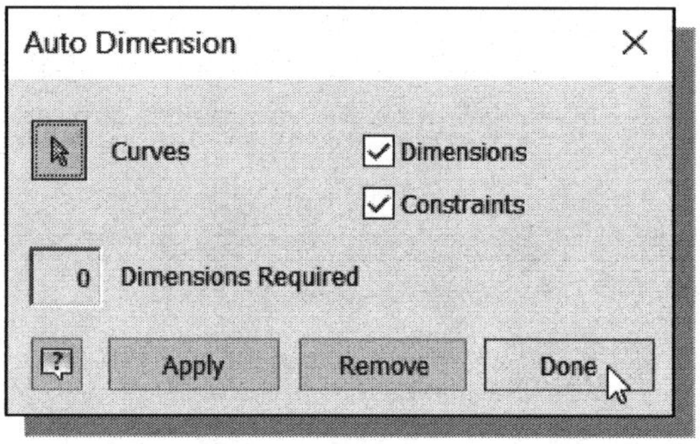

➢ Note that the system automatically recalculates if any additional dimension is needed for all created geometric entities. The applied Fix constraint provided the previously missing location dimensions for the created sketches.

4. Click **Done** to exit the Auto Dimension command.

5. On your own, complete the sketch by adjusting the dimensions to the desired values as shown below. (Hint: Change the larger values first.)

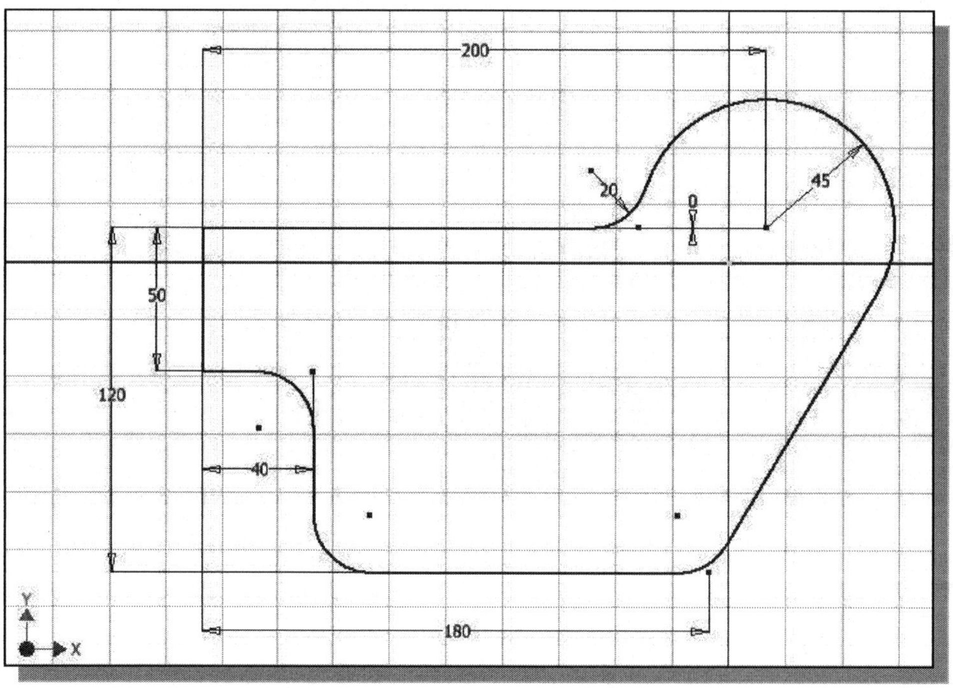

❖ Note that by applying proper geometric and dimensional constraints to the sketched geometry a *constraint network* is created that assures the geometry shape behaves predictably as changes are made.

Profile Sketch

In Autodesk Inventor, ***profiles*** are closed regions that are defined from sketches. Profiles are used as cross sections to create solid features. For example, **Extrude**, **Revolve**, **Sweep**, **Loft**, and **Coil** operations all require the definition of at least a single profile. The sketches used to define a profile can contain additional geometry since the additional geometry entities are consumed when the feature is created. To create a profile we can create single or multiple closed regions, or we can select existing solid edges to form closed regions. A profile cannot contain self-intersecting geometry; regions selected in a single operation form a single profile. As a general rule, we should dimension and constrain profiles to prevent them from unpredictable size and shape changes. Autodesk Inventor does allow us to create under-constrained or non-constrained profiles; the dimensions and/or constraints can be added/edited later.

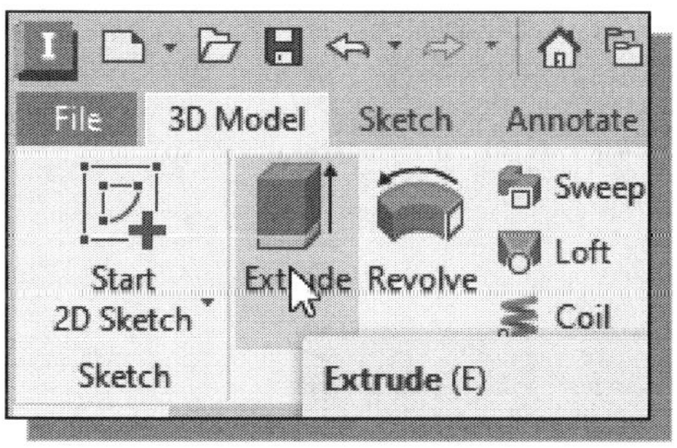

1. In the *3D Model* tab, select the **Extrude** command by left-clicking once on the icon.

❖ Note that Autodesk Inventor automatically highlights the closed region of the sketch. The defining geometry now forms the **profile** required for the *Extrude* operation.

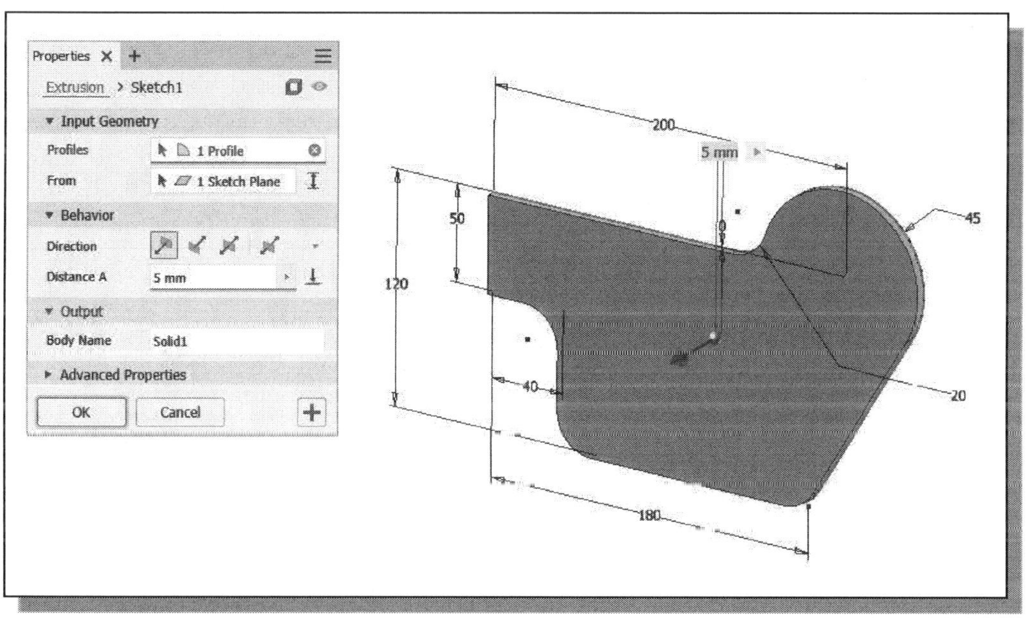

2. In the *Extrude* dialog box, enter **5 mm** as the extrusion distance as shown.

3. Click on the **OK** button to accept the settings and create the solid feature.

❖ Note that all the sketched geometry entities and dimensions are consumed and have disappeared from the screen when the feature is created.

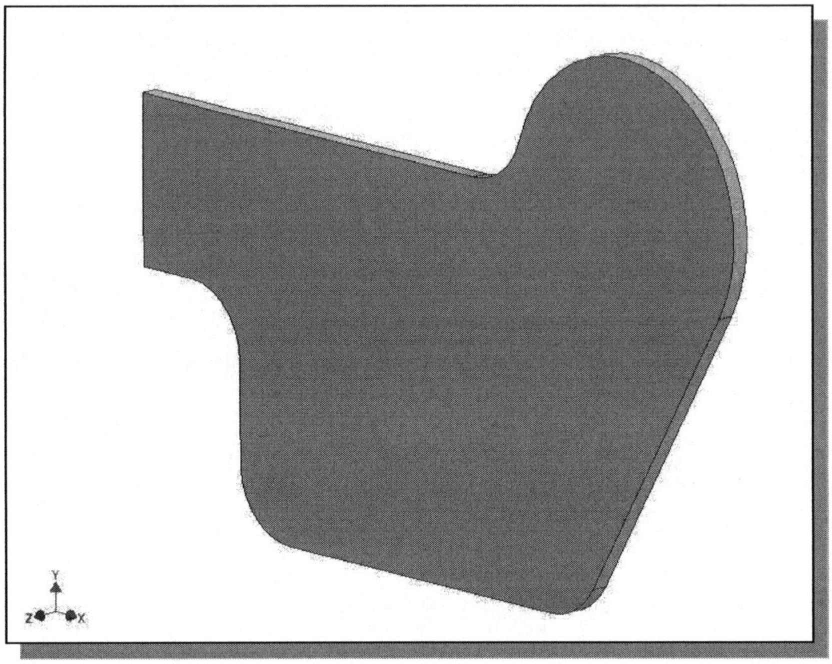

Redefine the Sketch and Profile

Engineering designs usually go through many revisions and changes. Autodesk Inventor provides an assortment of tools to handle design changes quickly and effectively. We will demonstrate some of the tools available by changing the base feature of the design. The profile used to create the extrusion is selected from the sketched geometry entities. In Autodesk Inventor, any profile can be edited and/or redefined at any time. It is this type of functionality in parametric solid modeling software that provides designers with greater flexibility and the ease to experiment with different design considerations.

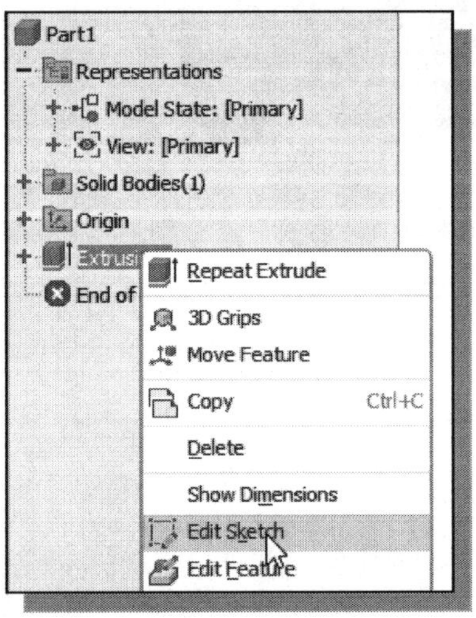

1. In the *browser*, **right-click** once on the **Extrusion1** feature to bring up the option menu, and then pick **Edit Sketch** in the pop-up menu.

2. On your own, create a circle and a rectangle of arbitrary sizes, positioned as shown in the figure below. We will intentionally under-constrain the new sketch to illustrate the flexibility of the system.

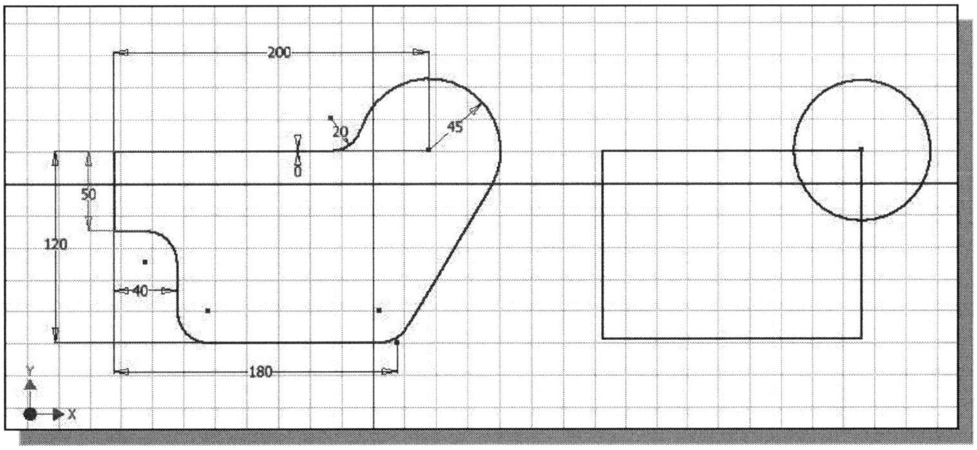

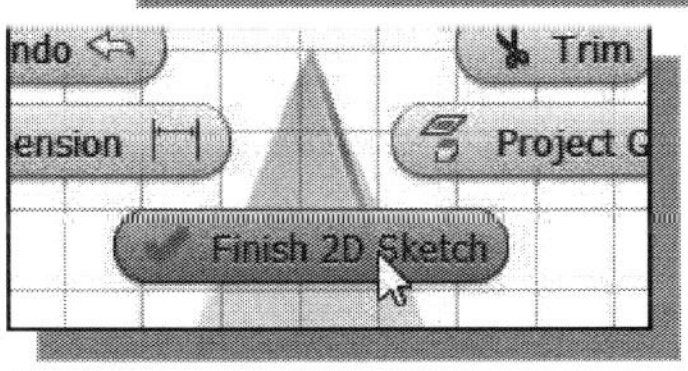

3. Inside the *graphics window*, click once with the right-mouse-button to display the option menu. Select **Finish 2D Sketch** in the pop-up menu to end the Sketch option.

➤ Note that, at this point, the solid model remains the same as before. We will next redefine the profile used for the base feature.

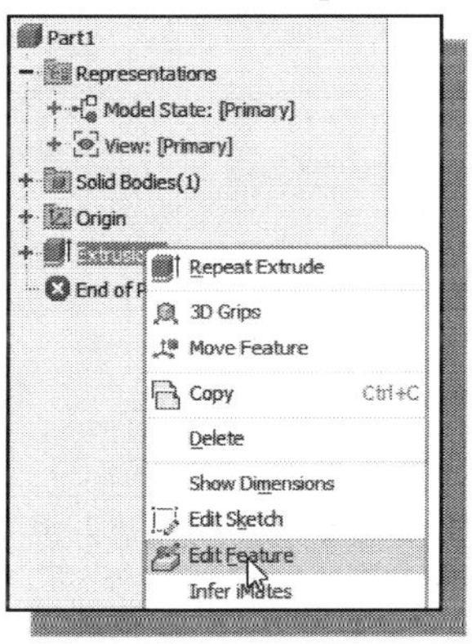

4. In the *browser*, right-click once on the Extrusion1 feature to bring up the option menu, and then pick **Edit Feature** in the pop-up menu.

❖ Autodesk Inventor will now display the 2D sketch of the selected feature in the graphics window. We have literally gone back in time to the point where we defined the extrusion feature.

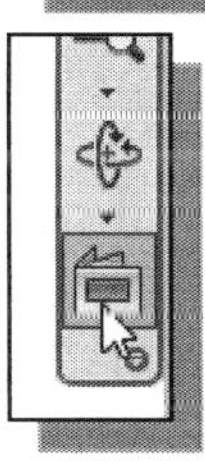

5. Click on the **Look At** icon in the *Standard* toolbar area.

6. Click on the front face of the gasket design.

- The **Look At** command automatically aligns the *sketch plane* of a selected entity to the screen.

7. Select any line segment of the 2D sketch.

8. Click on the **Zoom All** icon in the *Standard* toolbar.

➢ We have literally gone back to the point where we first defined the 2D profile. The original sketch and the new sketch we just created are wireframe entities recorded by the system as belonging to the same **SKETCH**, but only the **PROFILED** entities are used to create the feature.

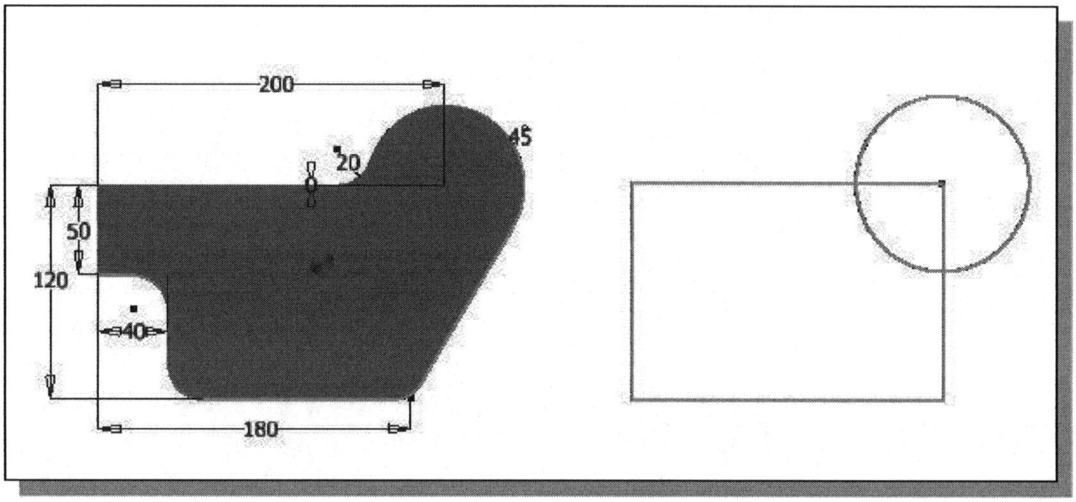

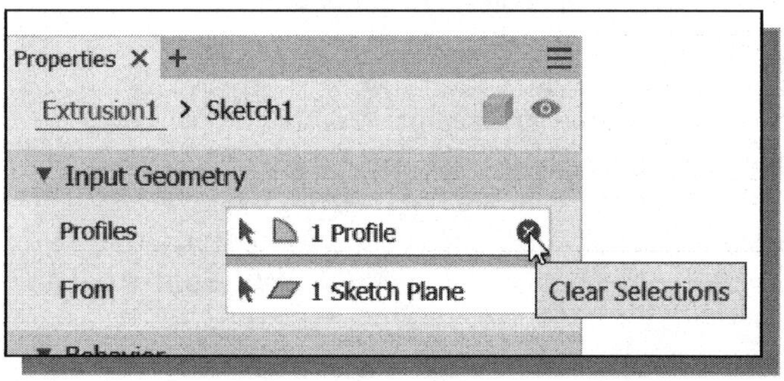

9. In the *Extrude* control panel, click on the **[x]** button to clear the current selected 2D profile.

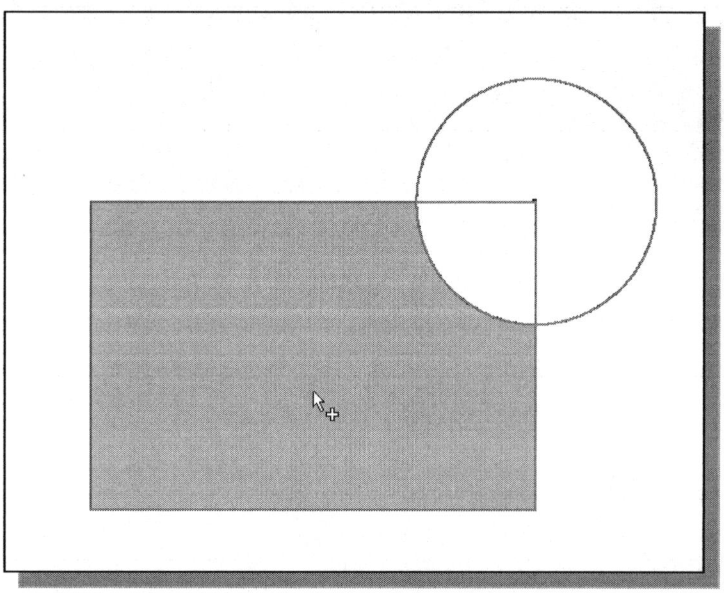

10. Click inside the lower region of the rectangle of the sketch on the right side of the graphics window.

➢ Autodesk Inventor automatically selects the geometry entities that form a closed region to define the profile.

11. Click the inside regions of the circle and complete the profile definition as shown in the figure below.

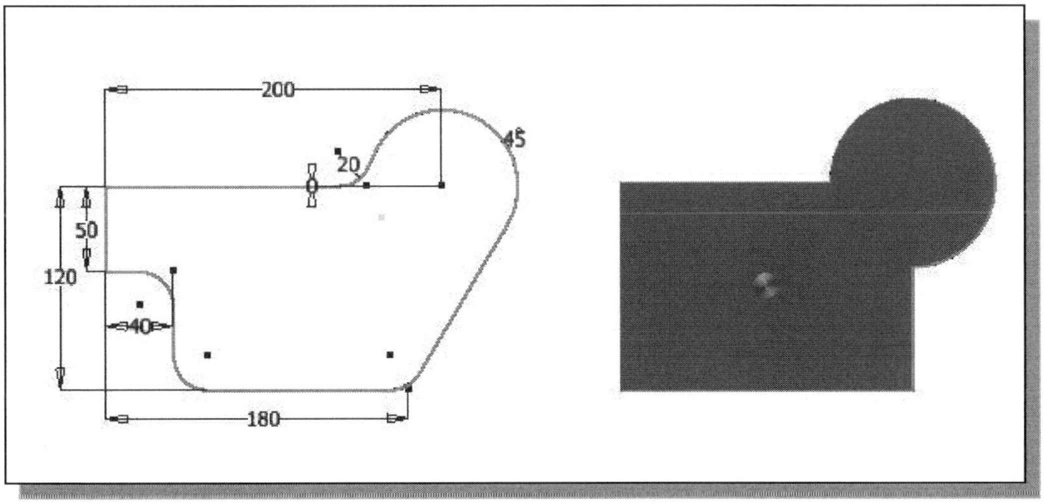

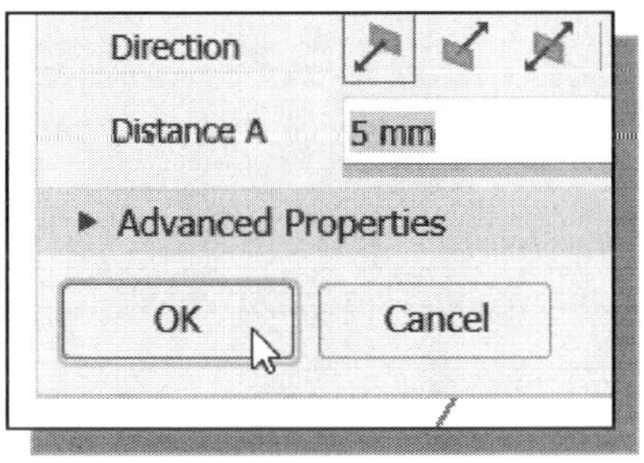

12. In the *Extrude* control panel, click on the **OK** button to accept the settings and update the solid feature.

- The feature is recreated using the newly sketched geometric entities, which are under-constrained and with no dimensions. The profile is created with extra wireframe entities by selecting multiple regions. The extra geometry entities can be used as construction geometry to help in defining the profile. This approach encourages engineering content over drafting technique, which is one of the key features of Autodesk Inventor over other solid modeling software.

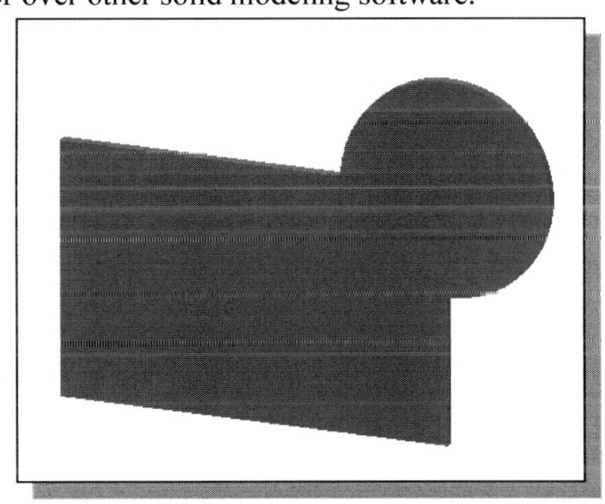

13. On your own, repeat the above steps and reset the profile back to the original gasket sketch.

Create an Offset Cut Feature

To complete the design, we will create a cutout feature by using the **Offset** command. First, we will set up the sketching plane to align with the front face of the 3D model.

1. In the *3D Model* tab select the **Start 2D Sketch** command by left-clicking once on the icon.

2. In the *Status Bar* area, the message "*Select plane to create sketch or an existing sketch to edit.*" is displayed. Select the **front face** of the 3D model in the graphics window.

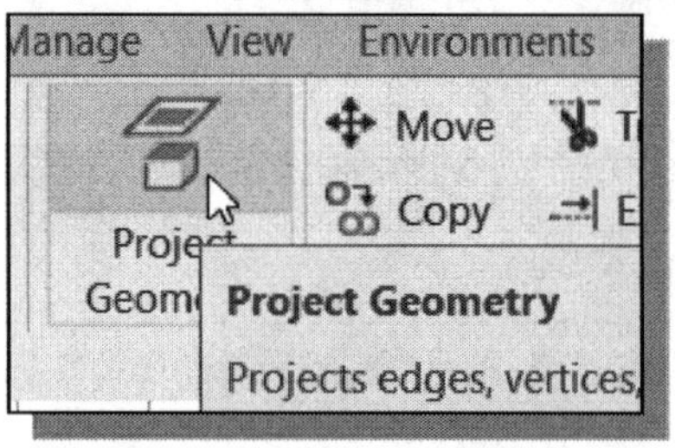

3. Click on the **Project Geometry** icon in the *2D Create* panel.

4. Select the front face of the gasket model, and notice the outline of the design has been projected onto the sketching plane.

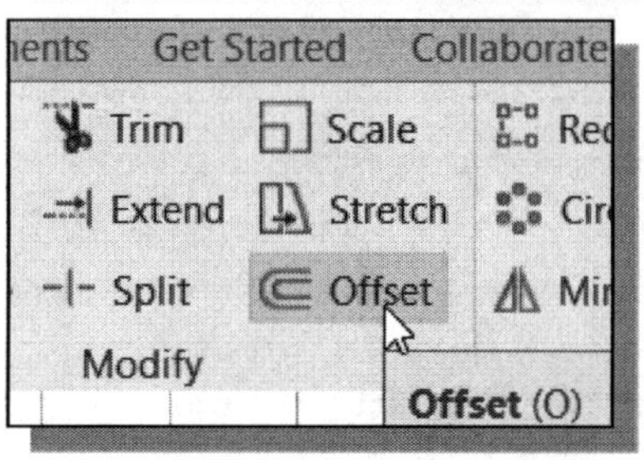

5. Click on the **Offset** icon in the *Sketch* tab on the Ribbon.

6. *Right-click* once to bring up the option menu and activate "**Loop select**" if necessary, as shown.

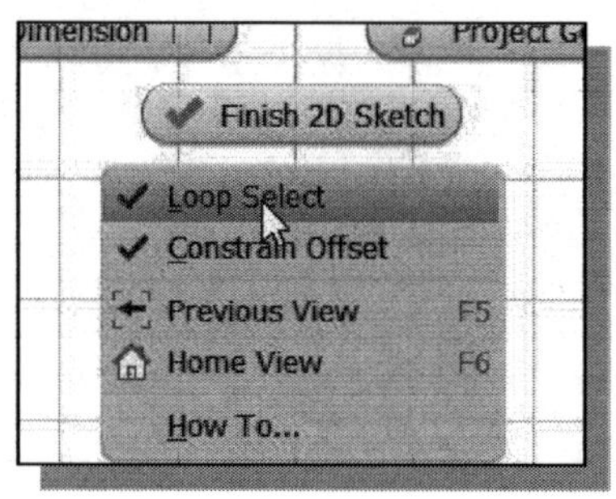

7. Select any edge of the **front face** of the 3D model. Autodesk Inventor will automatically select all of the connecting geometry to form a closed region.

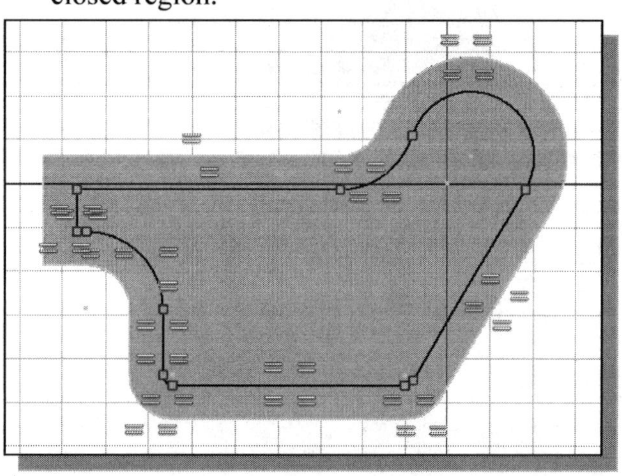

8. Move the cursor toward the center of the selected region and notice an offset copy of the outline is displayed.

9. Left-click once to create the offset profile as shown.

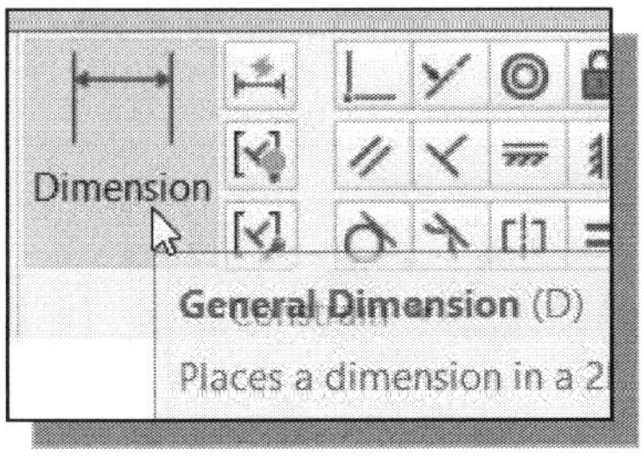

10. On your own, use the **General Dimension** command to create the offset dimension as shown in the figure below.

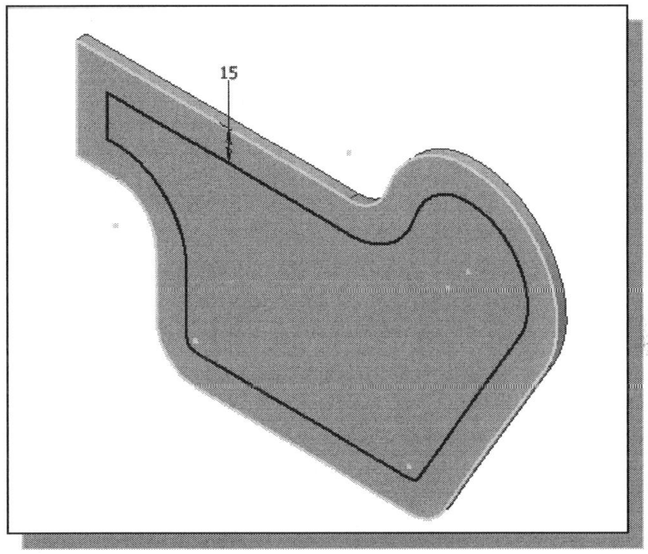

11. Modify the offset dimension to **15 mm** as shown in the figure to the right.

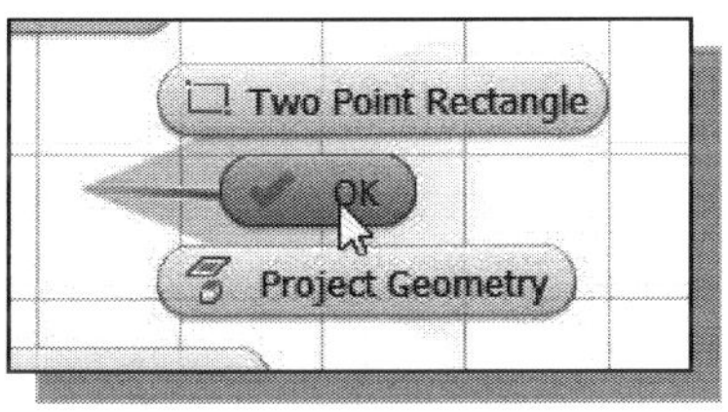

12. Inside the graphics window, click once with the right-mouse-button to display the option menu. Select **OK** in the pop-up menu to end the General Dimension command.

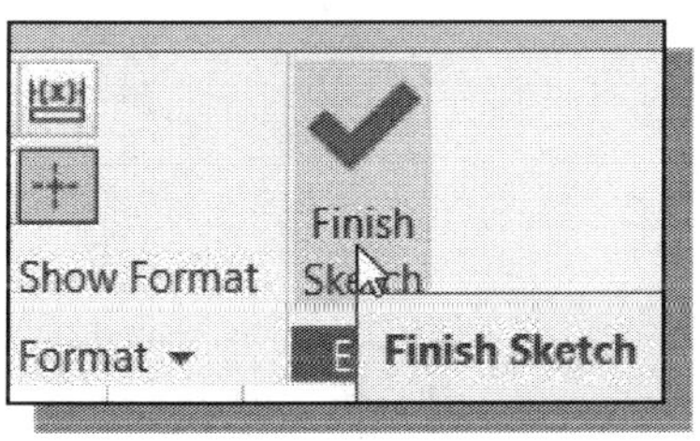

13. Inside the graphics window, click once with the right-mouse-button to display the option menu. Select **Finish Sketch** in the pop-up menu to end the Sketch option.

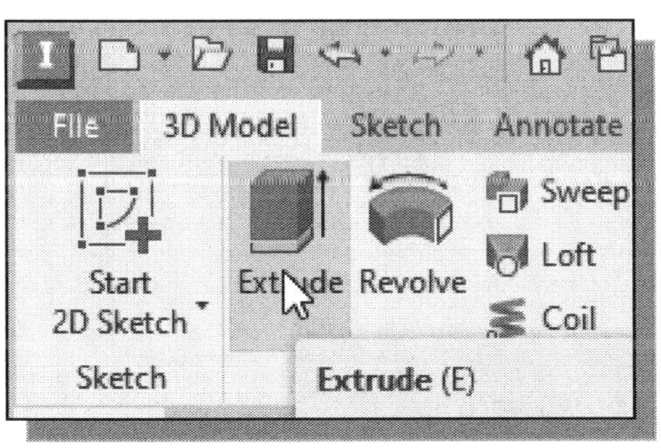

14. In the *3D Model* toolbar (the toolbar that is located to the left side of the graphics window), select the **Extrude** command by left-clicking on the icon.

15. Select the **inside region** of the offset geometry as the profile for the extrusion.

16. Inside the *Extrude* dialog box, select the **Cut** operation, set the *Extents* to **All** and set the direction of the cutout as shown in the figure below.

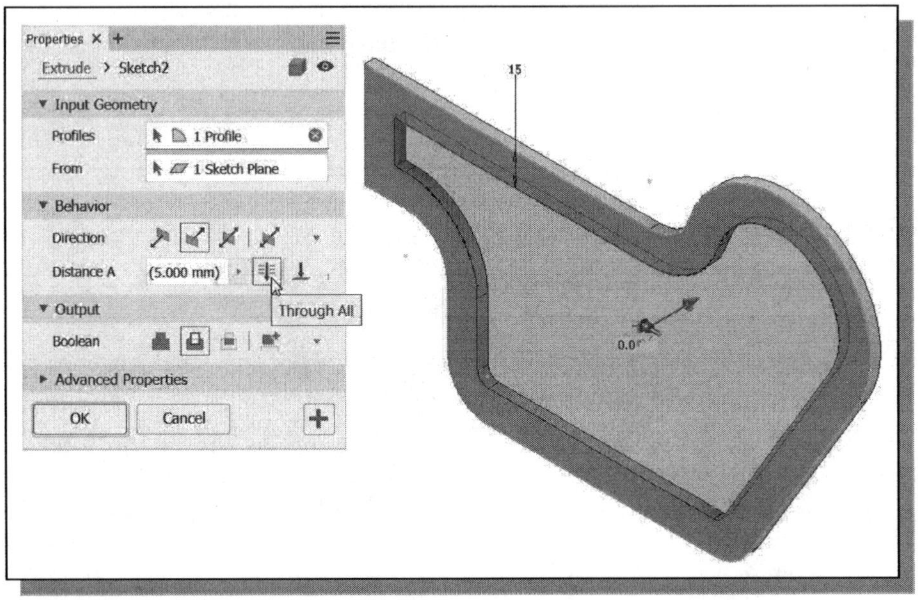

17. In the *Extrude* dialog box, click on the **OK** button to accept the settings and create the solid feature.

➤ The offset geometry is associated with the original geometry. On your own, adjust the overall height of the design to **150 millimeters** and confirm that the offset geometry is adjusted accordingly.

Review Questions:

1. What are the two types of wireframe geometry available in Autodesk Inventor?
2. Can we create a profile with extra 2D geometry entities?
3. How do we access the Autodesk Inventor's **Edit Sketch** option?
4. How do we create a *profile* in Autodesk Inventor?
5. Can we build a profile that consists of self-intersecting curves?
6. Describe the procedure to create a copy of a sketched 2D wireframe geometry.
7. Can we create additional entities in a 2D sketch, without using them at all?
8. How do we align the *sketch plane* of a selected entity to the screen?
9. Describe the steps we used to switch existing profiles in the tutorial.
10. Describe the advantages of using the Offset command vs. creating a separate sketch.

Exercises:

1. **V-slide Plate** (Dimensions are in inches. Plate Thickness: **0.25**)

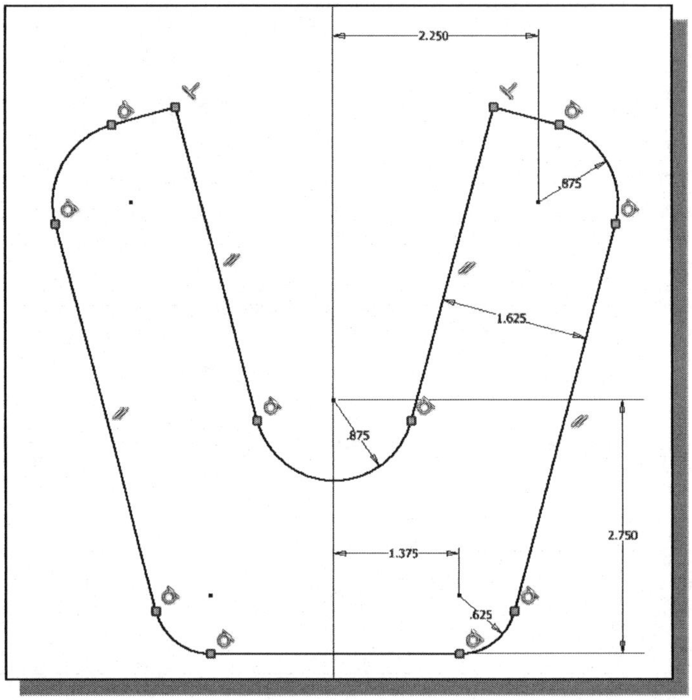

2. **Shaft Support** (Dimensions are in millimeters. Note the two R40 arcs at the base share the same center.)

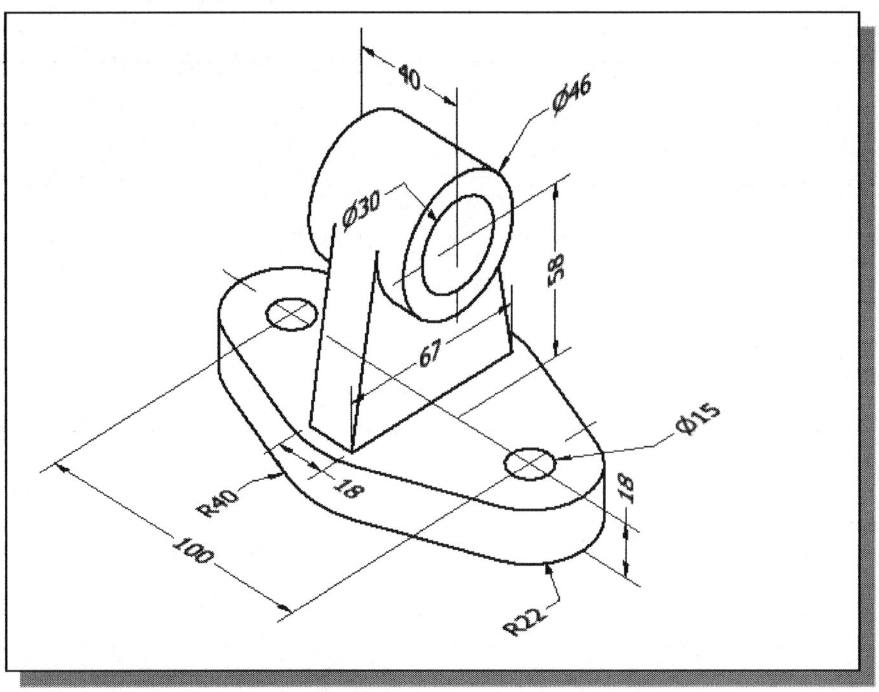

3. **Vent Cover** (Thickness: **0.125** inches. Hint: Use the Ellipse command.)

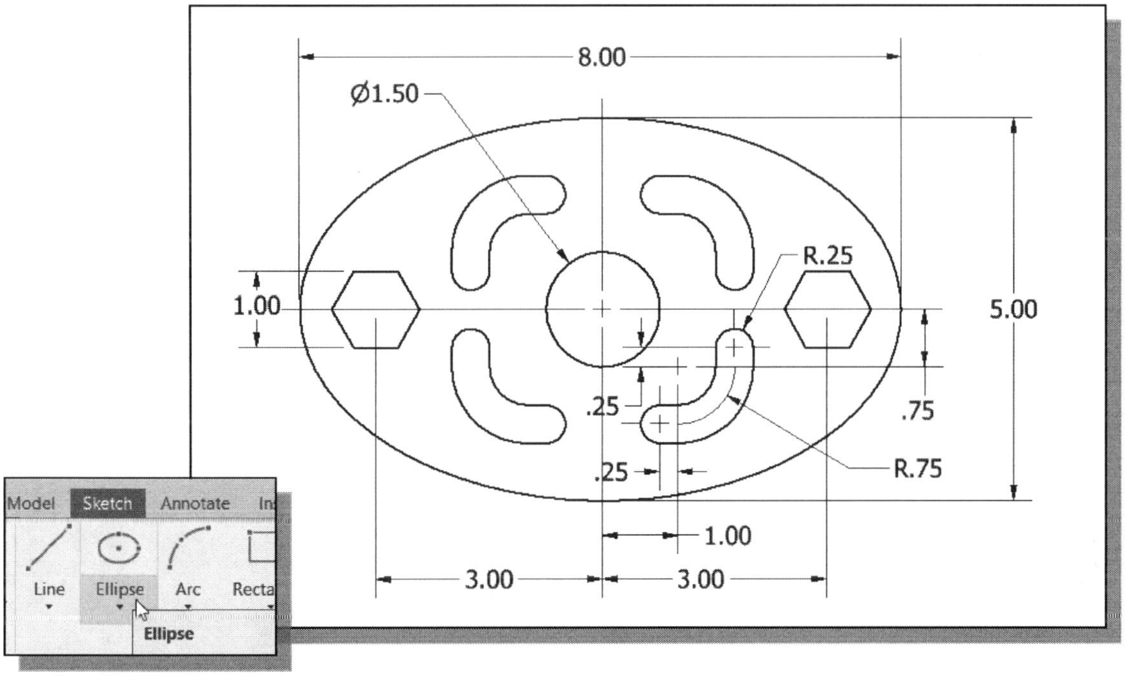

4. **Anchor Base** (Dimensions are in inches.)

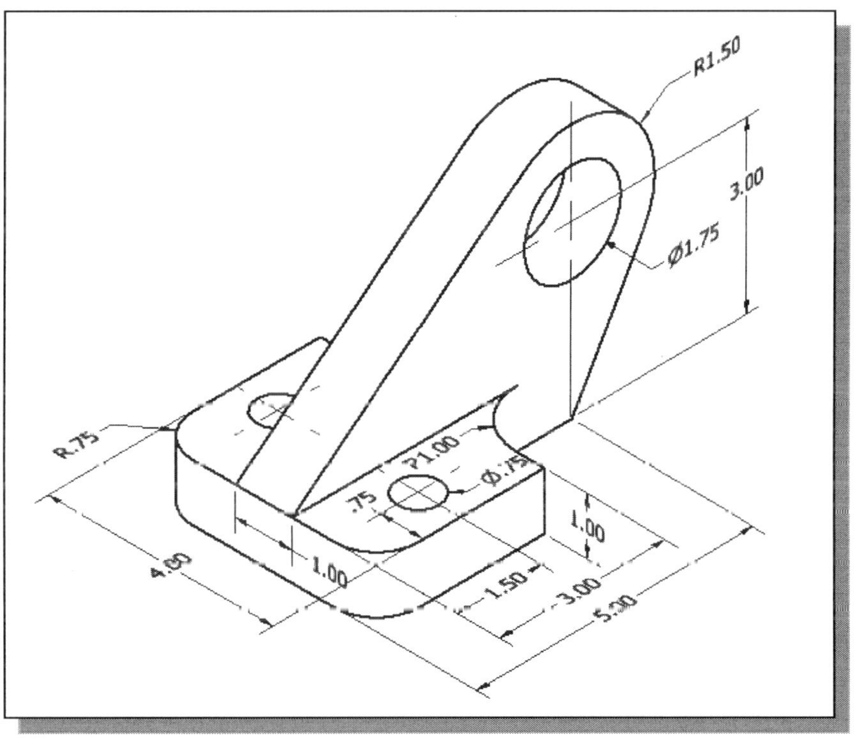

5. **Tube Spacer** (Dimensions are in inches.)

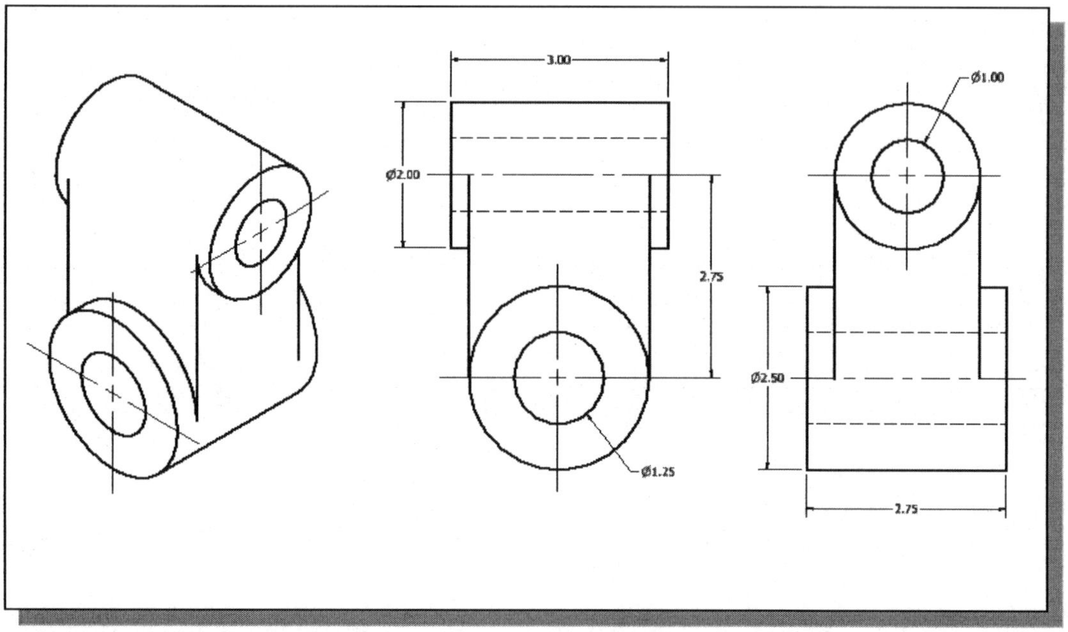

6. **Pivot Lock** (Dimensions are in inches. The circular features in the design are all aligned to the two centers at the base.)

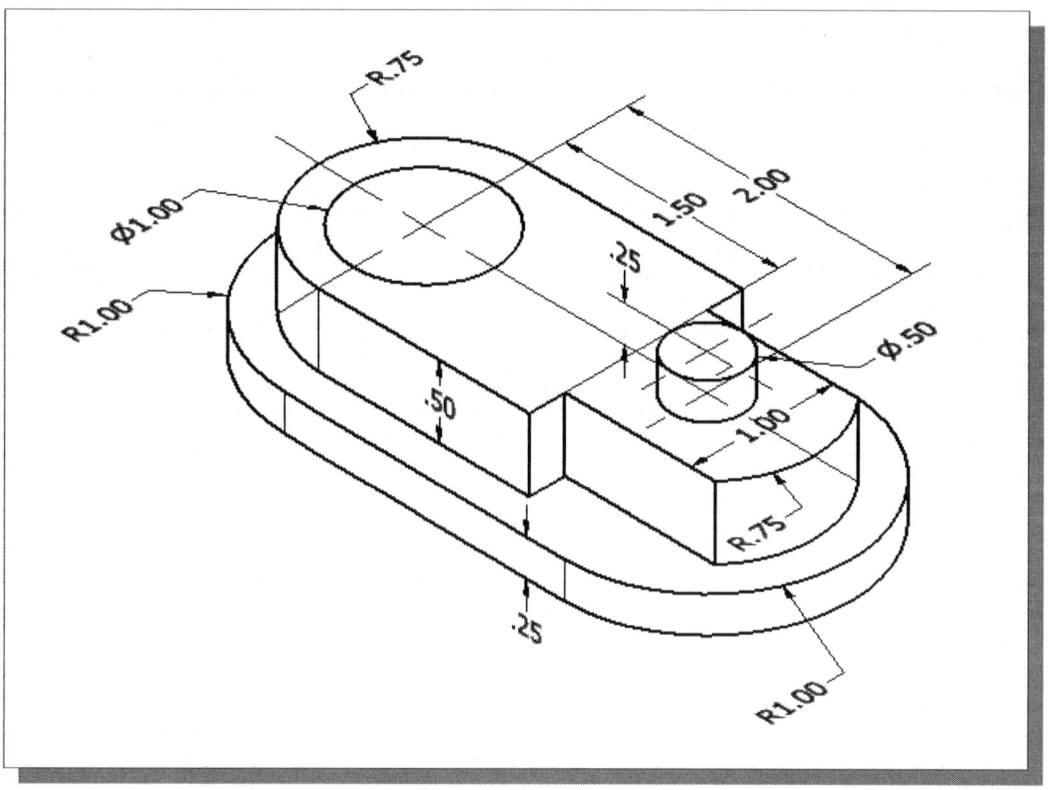

7. **Lock-ring** (Dimensions are in inches.)

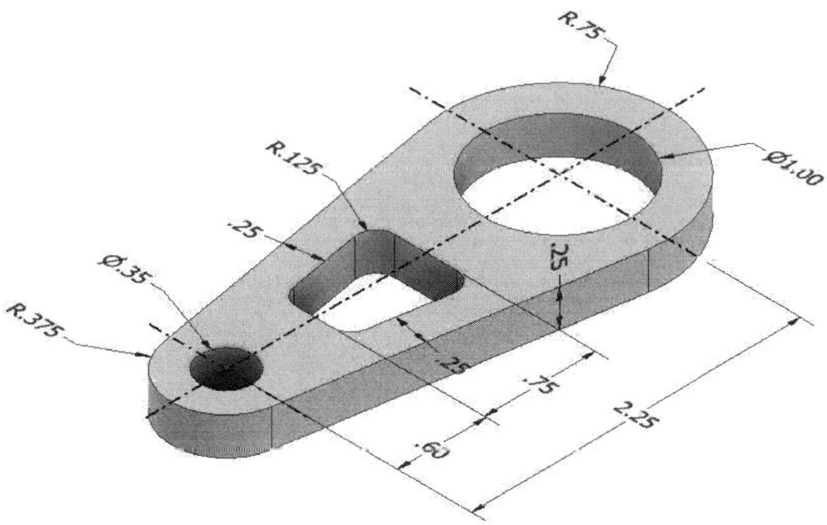

Notes:

Chapter 12
Parent/Child Relationships and the BORN Technique - Autodesk Inventor

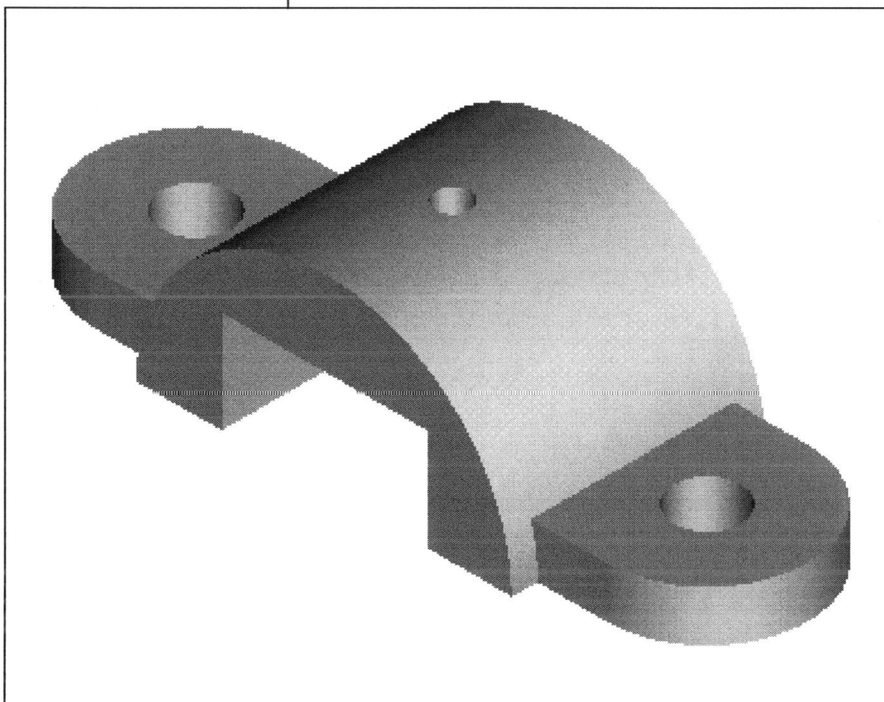

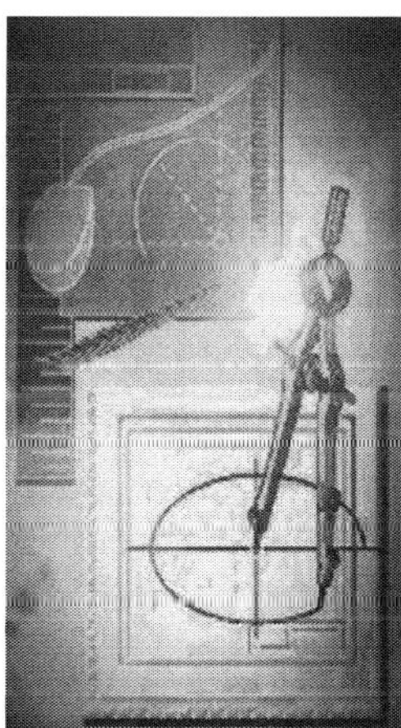

Learning Objectives

- ♦ Understand the Concept and Usage of the BORN Technique
- ♦ Understand the Importance of Parent/Child Relations in Features
- ♦ Use the Suppress Feature Option
- ♦ Resolve Undesired Feature Interactions

Introduction

The parent/child relationship is one of the most powerful aspects of ***parametric modeling***. In Autodesk Inventor, each time a new modeling event is created, previously defined features can be used to define information such as size, location, and orientation. The referenced features become **Parent** features to the new feature, and the new feature is called the **Child** feature. The parent/child relationships determine how a model reacts when other features in the model change, thus capturing design intent. It is crucial to keep track of these parent/child relations. Any modification to a parent feature can change one or more of its children.

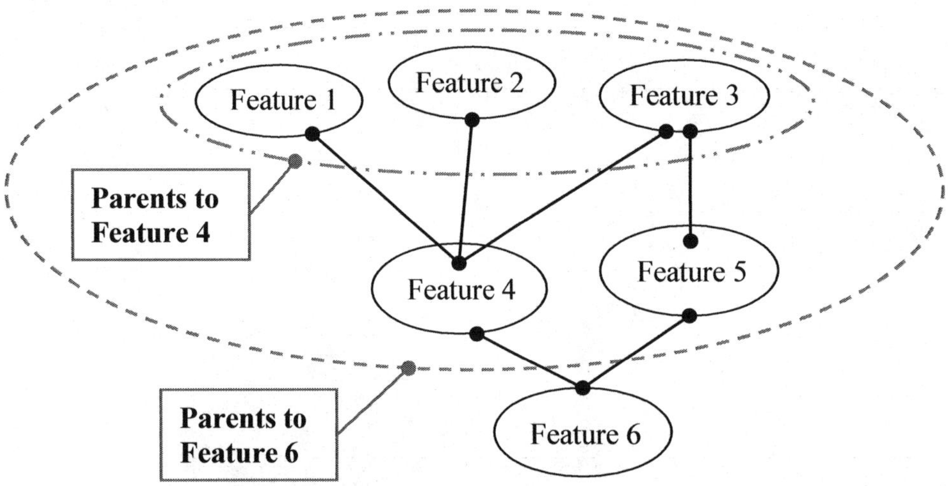

Parent/child relationships can be created *implicitly* or *explicitly*; implicit relationships are implied by the feature creation method, and explicit relationships are entered manually by the user. In the previous chapters, we first select a sketching plane before creating a 2D profile. The selected surface becomes a parent of the new feature. If the sketching plane is moved, the child feature will move with it. As one might expect, parent/child relationships can become quite complicated when the features begin to accumulate. It is therefore important to think about modeling strategy before we start to create anything. The main consideration is to try to plan ahead for possible design changes that might occur which would be affected by the existing parent/child relationships. Parametric modeling software, such as Autodesk Inventor, also allows us to adjust feature properties so that any feature conflicts can be quickly resolved.

The BORN Technique

In *parametric modeling*, the ***base feature*** (the *first solid feature* of the solid model) is the center of all features and is considered the key feature of the design. All subsequent features are built by referencing the first feature. Much emphasis is placed on the selection of the *base feature.*

A more advanced technique of creating solid models is what is known as the "**Base Orphan Reference Node**" (**BORN**) technique. The basic concept of the BORN technique is to use a *Cartesian coordinate system* as the first feature prior to creating any solid features. With the *Cartesian coordinate system* established, we then have three mutually perpendicular datum planes (namely the *XY*, *YZ*, and *ZX planes*), three datum axes and a datum point available to use as sketching planes. The three datum planes can also be used as references for dimensions and geometric constructions. Using this technique, the first node in the history tree is called an "orphan," meaning that it has no history to be replayed. The technique of using the reference geometry in this "base node" is therefore called the "Base Orphan Reference Node" (BORN) technique.

Autodesk Inventor automatically establishes a set of reference geometry when we start a new part, namely a *Cartesian coordinate system* with three work planes, three work axes, and a work point. All subsequent solid features can then use the coordinate system and/or reference geometry as sketching planes. The *base feature* is still important, but the *base feature* is no longer the ONLY choice for creating subsequent solid features. This approach provides us with more options while we are creating parametric solid models. More importantly, this approach provides greater flexibility for part modifications and design changes. This approach is also very useful in creating assembly models, which will be illustrated in the later chapters of this text.

The U-Bracket Design

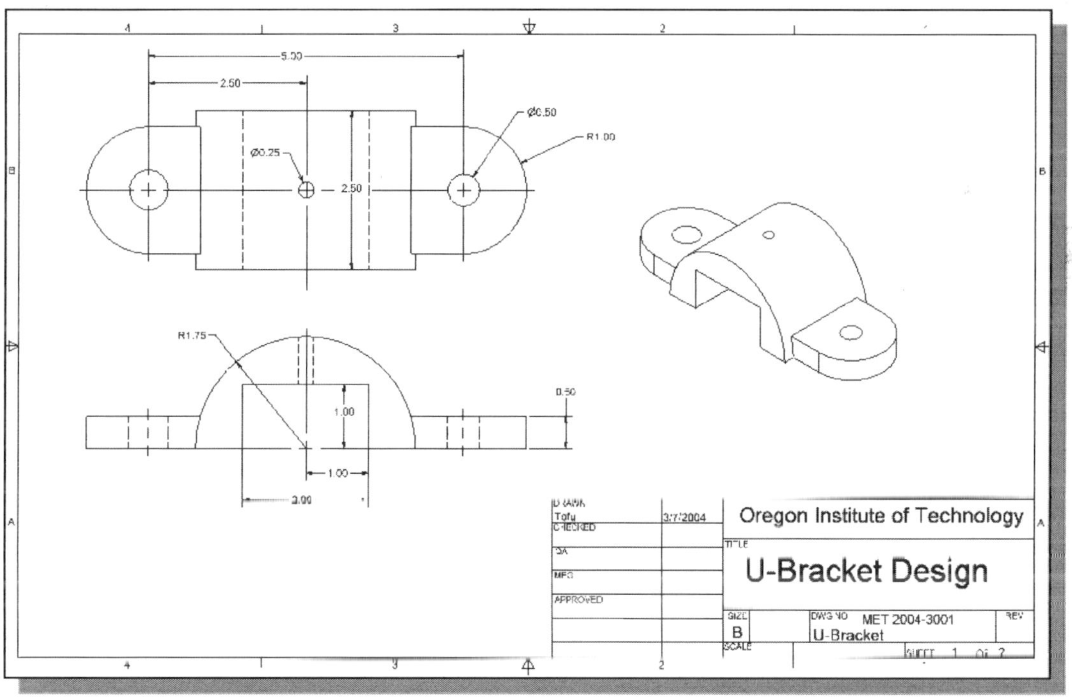

➢ Based on your knowledge of *Inventor* so far, how many features would you use to create the model? Which feature would you choose as the **base feature**? What is your choice for arranging the order of the features? Would you organize the features differently if the rectangular cut at the center is changed to a circular shape (Radius: 1.25 inch)?

Sketch Plane Settings

1. Select the Autodesk Inventor option on the *Start* menu or select the Autodesk Inventor icon on the desktop to start Autodesk Inventor. The Autodesk Inventor main window will appear on the screen.

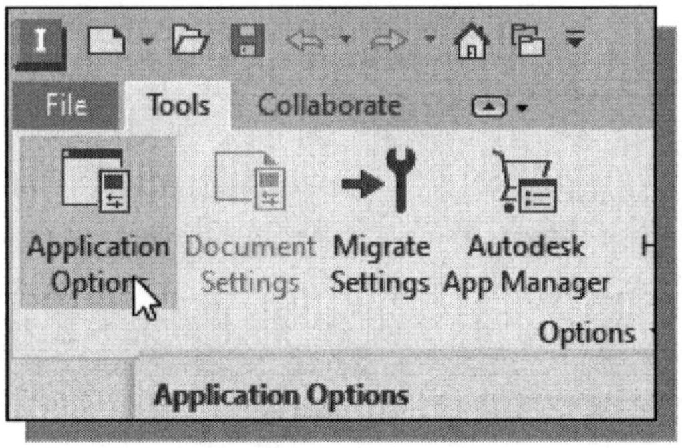

2. Select **Application Options** in the **Tools** pull-down menu.

- The **Application Options** menu allows us to set behavioral options, such as *color*, *file locations*, etc.

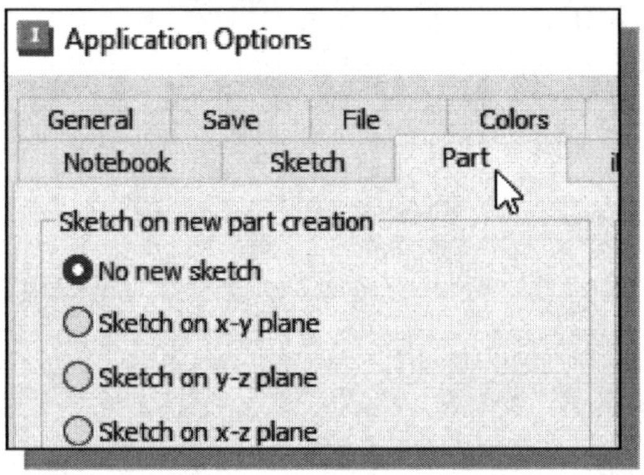

3. Click on the **Part** tab to display and/or modify the default sketch plane settings.

- Note that a sketch plane can be aligned to one of the work planes during new part creation. Confirm the **No new sketch** option is set as shown.

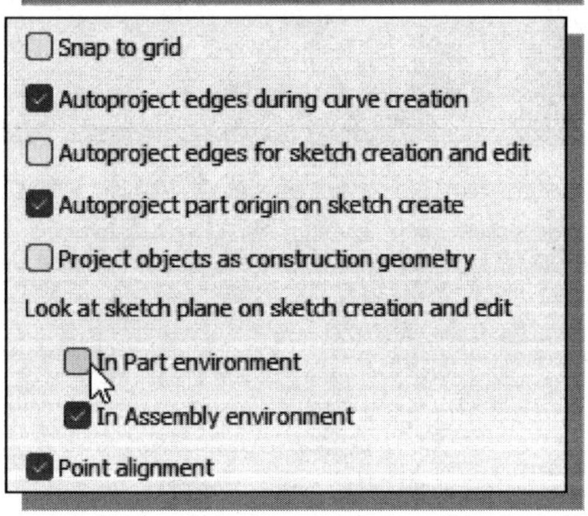

4. Click on the **Sketch** tab to examine/modify the default sketching settings.

5. Turn ***OFF*** the ***Look at sketch plane on sketch creation - In Part environment*** option as shown.

6. Click on the **OK** button to accept the setting.

- Note that the new settings will take effect when a new part file is created.

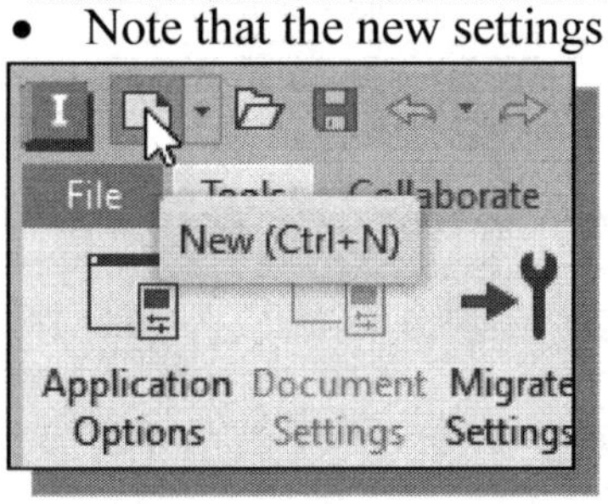

7. Click on the **New** icon in the *Standard* toolbar.

8. On your own, open a new ***English*** units **standard (in) part** file.

Apply the BORN Technique

1. In the *Part Browser* window, click on the [**+**] symbol in front of the ***Origin*** feature to display more information on the feature.

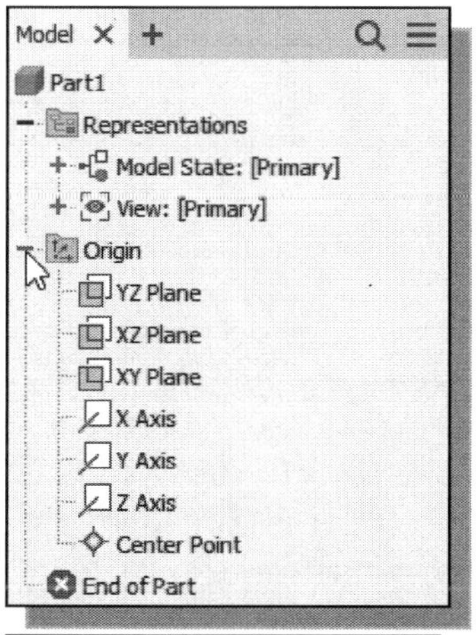

❖ In the *Part Browser* window, notice a new part name appeared with seven work features established. The seven work features include three *work planes*, three *work axes*, and a *work point*. By default, the three work planes and work axes are aligned to the **world coordinate system** and the work point is aligned to the *origin* of the **world coordinate system**.

2. Inside the *browser* window, move the cursor on top of the third work plane, the **XY Plane**. Notice a rectangle, representing the work plane, appears in the graphics window.

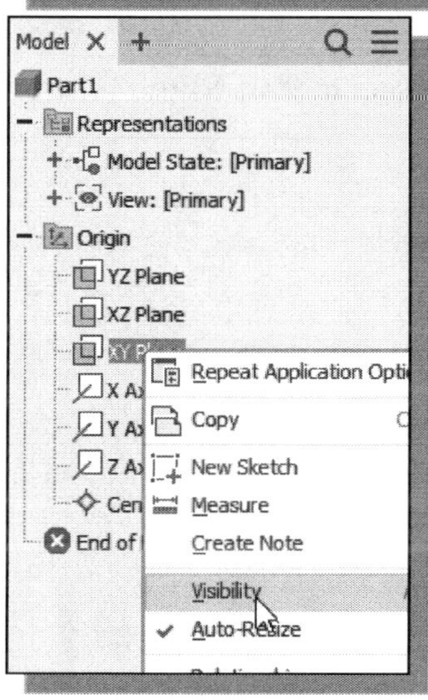

3. Inside the *browser* window, click once with the right-mouse-button on XY Plane to display the option menu. Click on **Visibility** to toggle on the display of the plane.

4. On your own, repeat the above steps and toggle ***ON*** the display of all of the *work planes* and the *center point* on the screen.

5. On your own, use the *Dynamic Viewing* options (ViewCube, 3D Orbit, Zoom and Pan) to view the default work features.

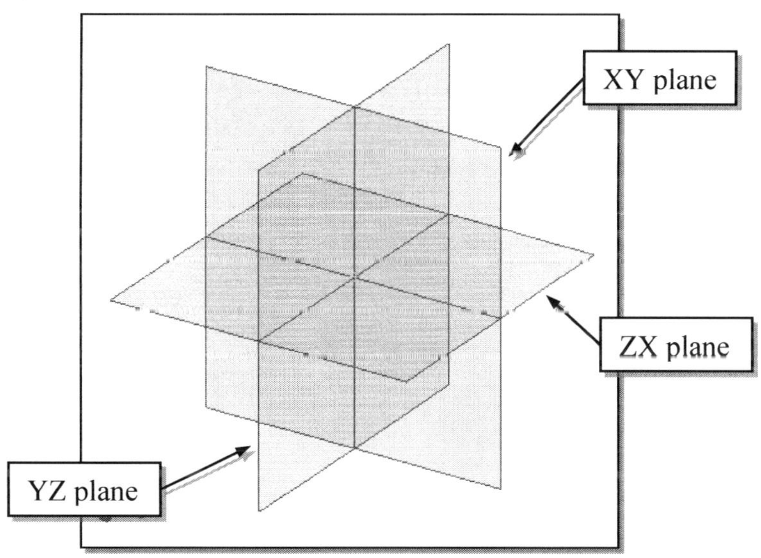

❖ By default, the basic set of work planes is aligned to the world coordinate system; the work planes are the first features of the part. We can now proceed to create solid features referencing the three mutually perpendicular datum planes.

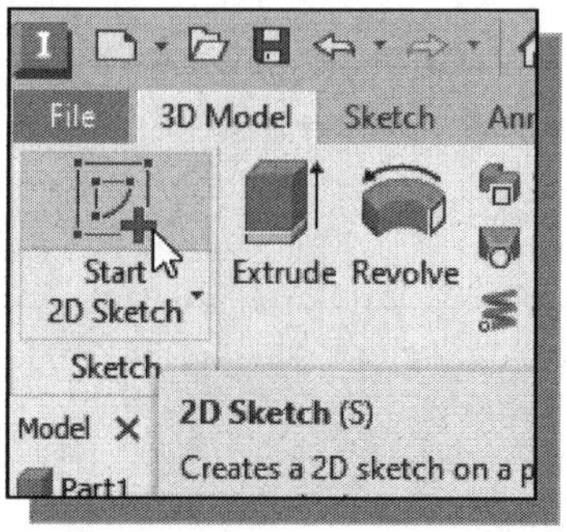

6. In the *Sketch* toolbar select the **Start 2D Sketch** command by left-clicking once on the icon.

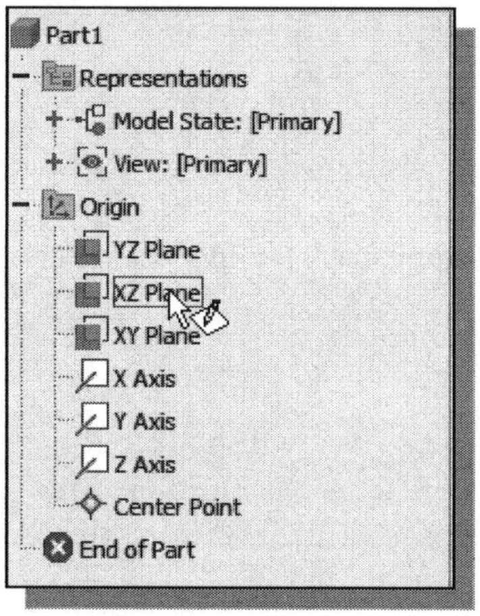

7. In the *Status Bar* area, the message "*Select plane to create sketch or an existing sketch to edit.*" is displayed. Autodesk Inventor expects us to identify a planar surface where the 2D sketch of the next feature is to be created. Move the graphics cursor on top of the **XZ Plane**, inside the *browser* window as shown, and notice that Autodesk Inventor will automatically highlight the corresponding plane in the graphics window. Left-click once to select the XZ Plane as the sketching plane.

❖ Autodesk Inventor allows us to identify and select features in the graphics window as well as in the *browser* window.

- Note that since both of the ***Look at sketch plane on sketch creation*** options are turned ***OFF***, the view will be adjusted back to the default ***isometric view***.

➢ Note the alignment of the sketch plane is set to the XZ plane as shown.

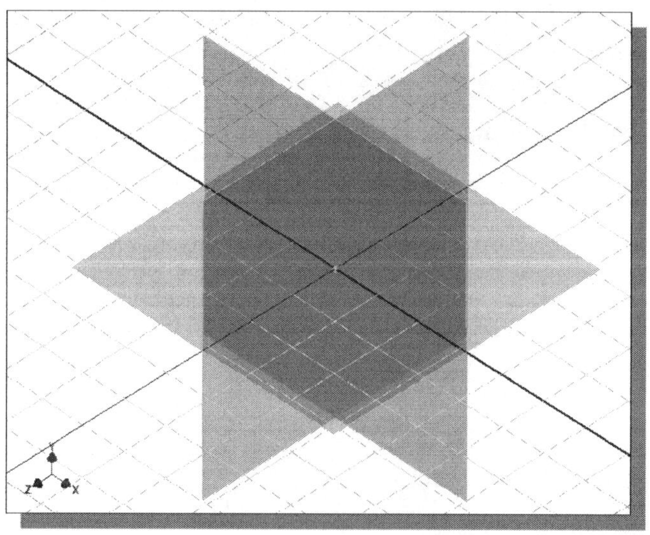

Create a 2D Sketch for the Base Feature

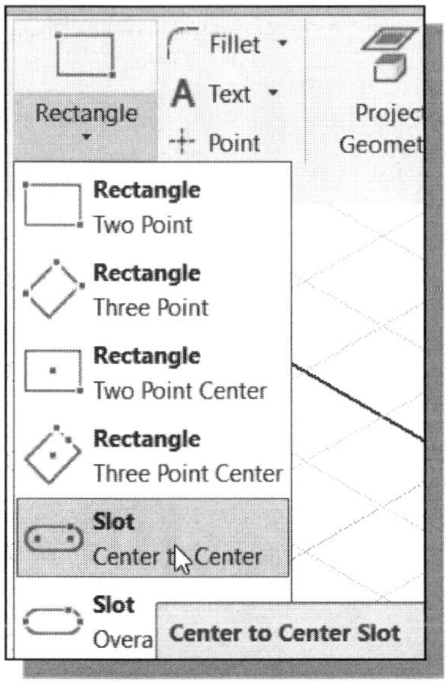

1. Select the **Center to Center Slot** command by clicking once with the **left-mouse-button** on the icon in the *Draw* toolbar.

2. Create a horizontal line, representing center to center distance of the slot, in front of the work planes as shown below. (Note the **Horizontal** symbol indicates the alignment of the sketched line.)

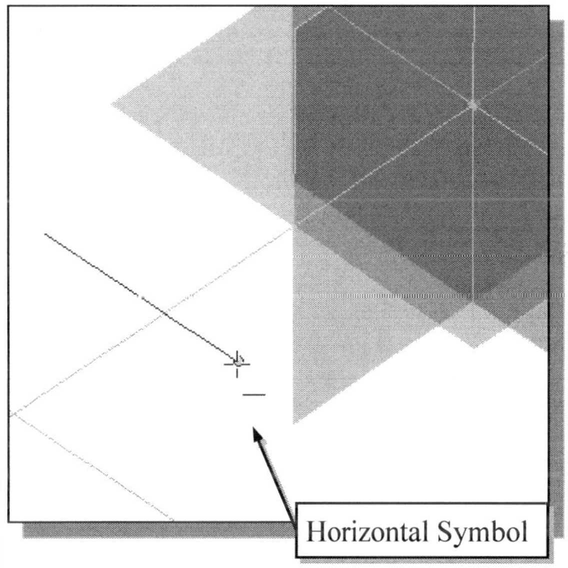

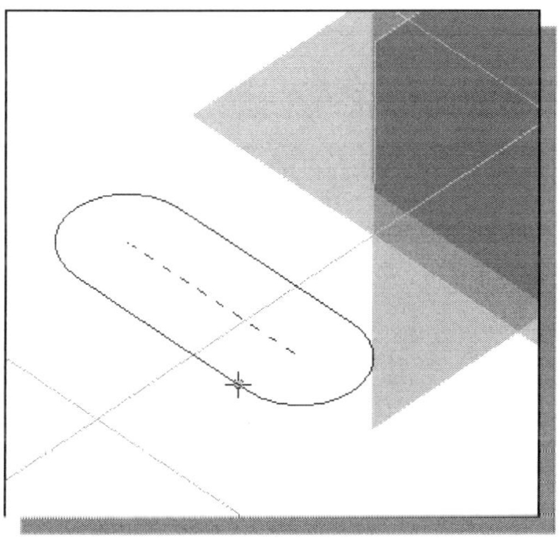

3. Move the cursor outward to define the size of the center to center slot; click once with the left-mouse-button to create the shape.

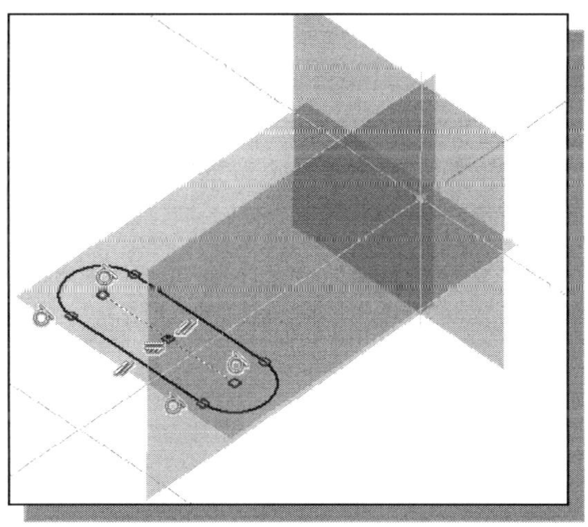

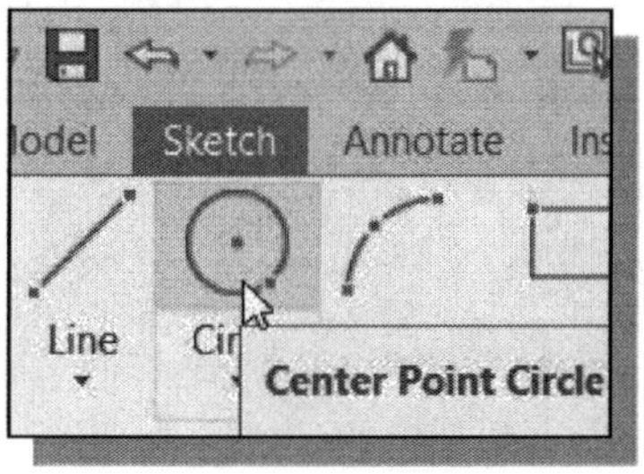

4. Choose **Center Point Circle** in the *Draw* toolbar.

5. On your own, create the two inner circles; the center points of the circles are coincident to the centers of the overall slot.

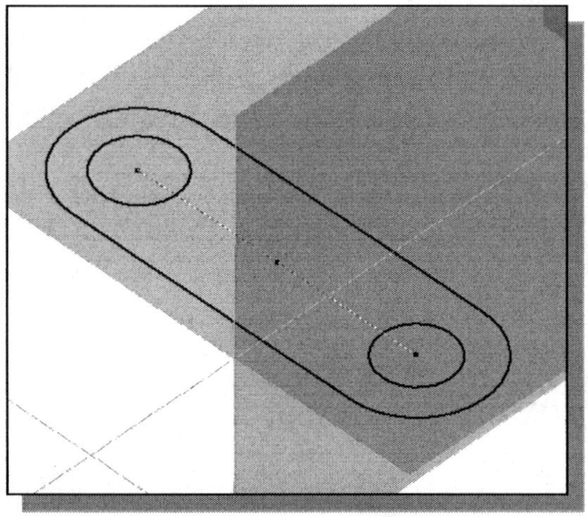

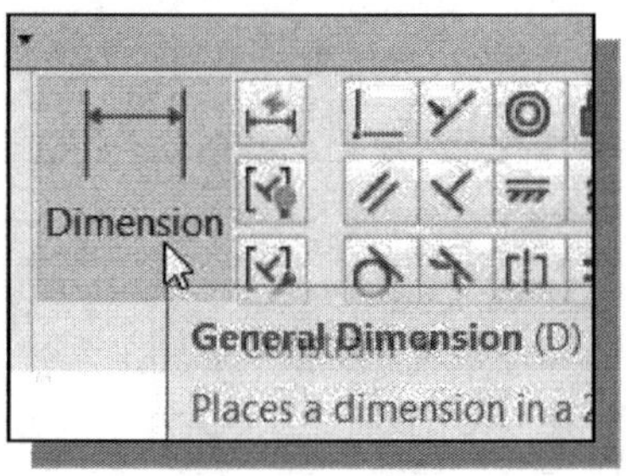

6. Left-click once on the **General Dimension** icon to activate the General Dimension command.

7. On your own, set the display orientation to the Top view position as shown in the below figure.

8. On your own, create the dimensions, referencing the origin point, to fully constrain the sketch as shown. (Do not be overly concerned with the actual numbers displayed; the dimensions will be adjusted in the next steps.)

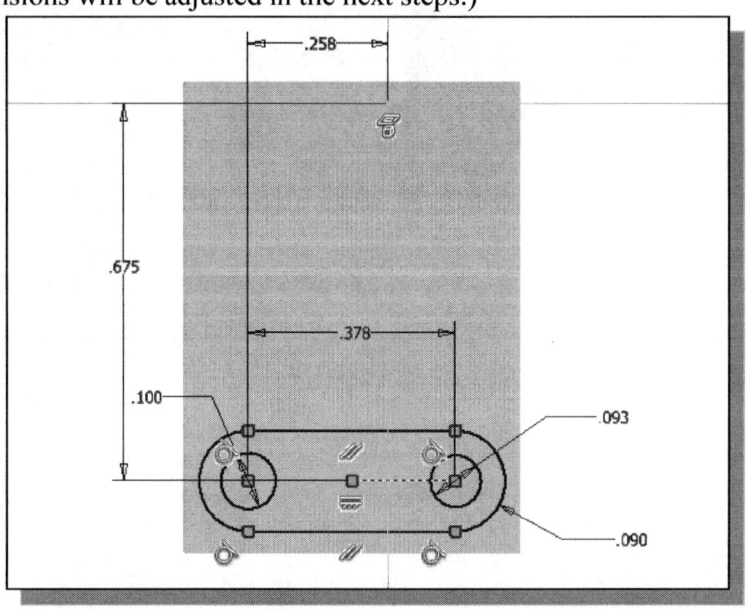

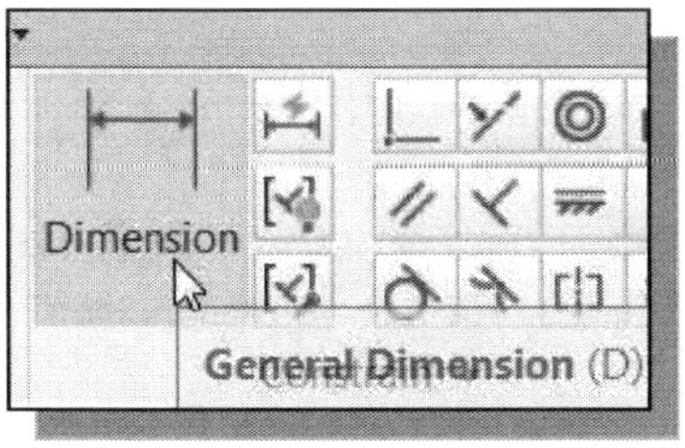

9. Choose **General Dimension** in the *Constrain* panel.

10. On your own, adjust the dimensions as shown in the figure.

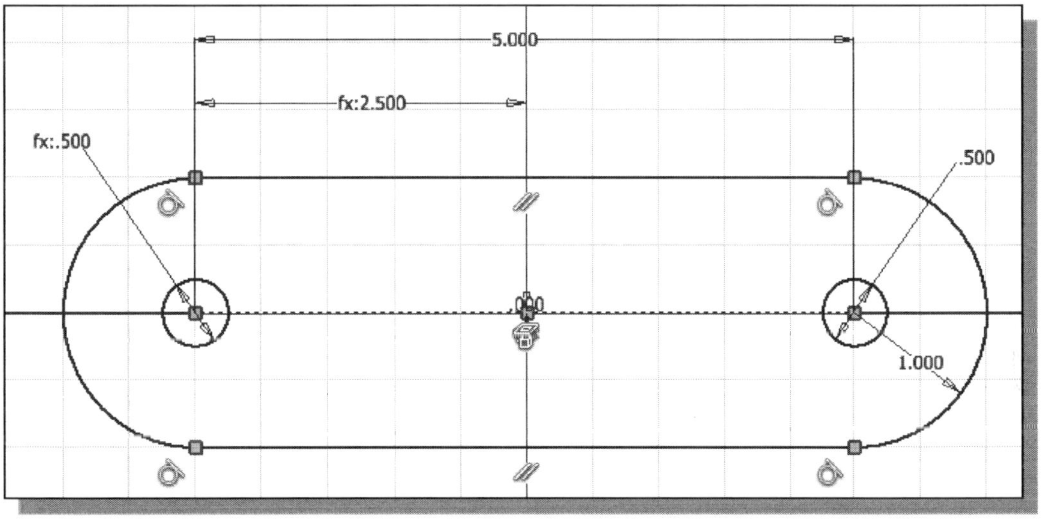

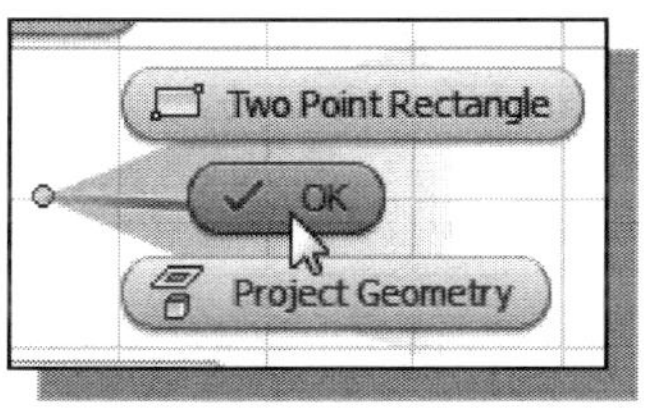

11. Inside the graphics window, click once with the right-mouse-button to display the option menu. Select **OK** in the pop-up menu to end the General Dimension command.

12. On your own, use the **Parameters** command to examine the two parametric equations used.

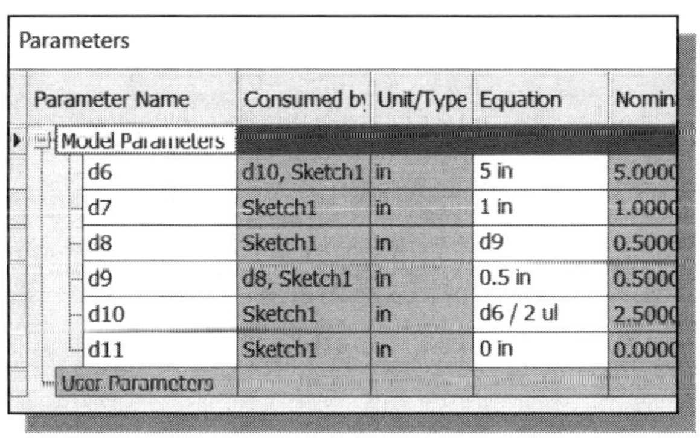
Parameters

Parameter Name	Consumed by	Unit/Type	Equation	Nomin
Model Parameters				
d6	d10, Sketch1	in	5 in	5.000
d7	Sketch1	in	1 in	1.000
d8	Sketch1	in	d9	0.500
d9	d8, Sketch1	in	0.5 in	0.500
d10	Sketch1	in	d6 / 2 ul	2.500
d11	Sketch1	in	0 in	0.000
User Parameters				

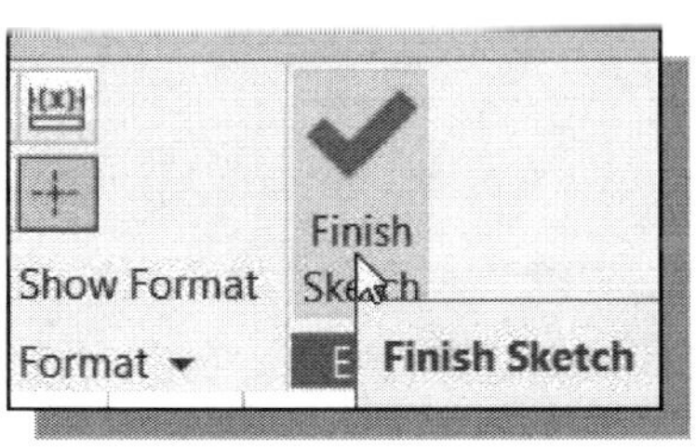

13. In the *Ribbon toolbar* area, select **Finish Sketch** in the pop-up menu to end the Sketch option.

Create the First Extrude Feature

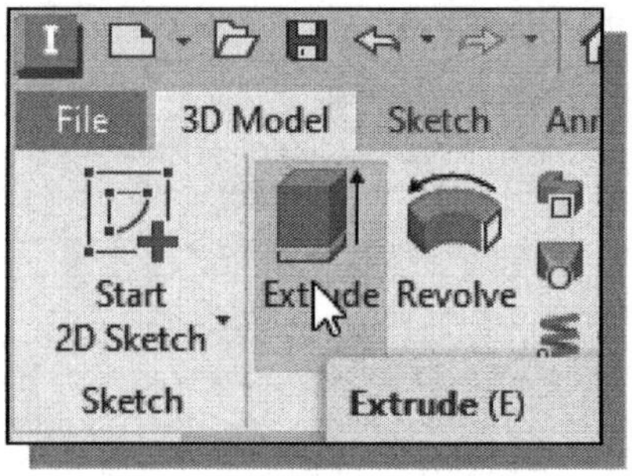

1. In the *Create* toolbar, select the **Extrude** command by clicking once with the left-mouse-button on the icon.

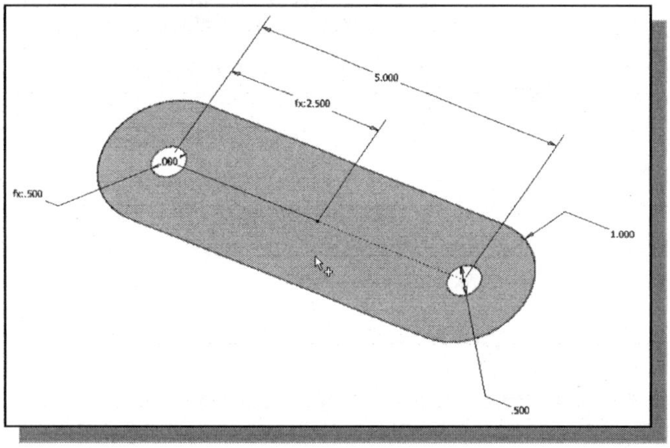

2. Select the inside regions of the sketch to define the profile of the extrusion as shown.

3. In the *Distance* option box, enter **0.5** as the extrusion distance.

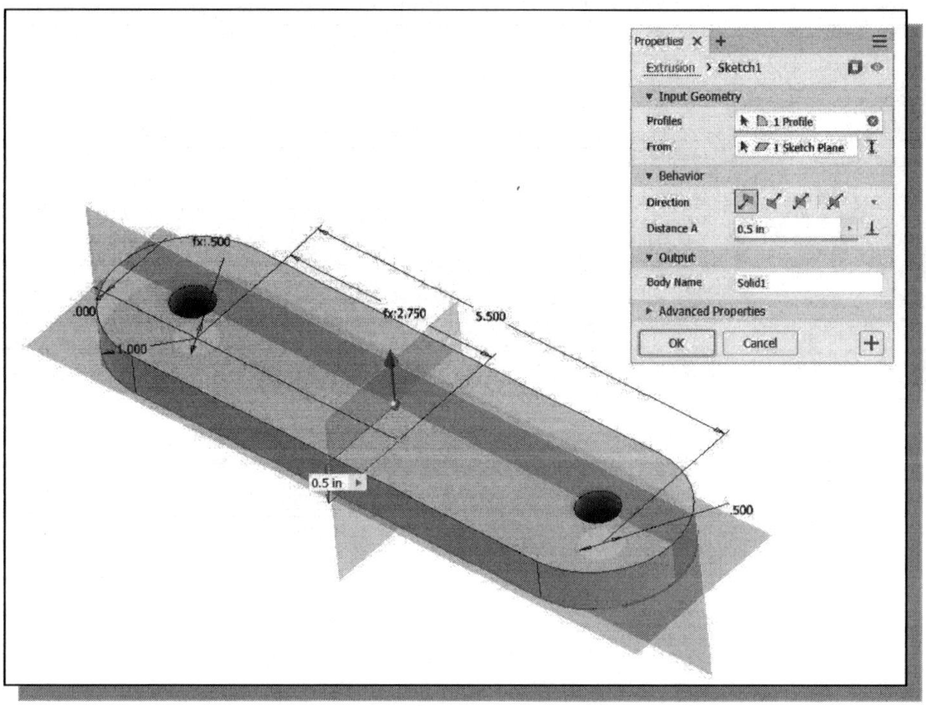

4. In the *Extrude* pop-up control, click on the **OK** button to create the base feature.

The Implied Parent/Child Relationships

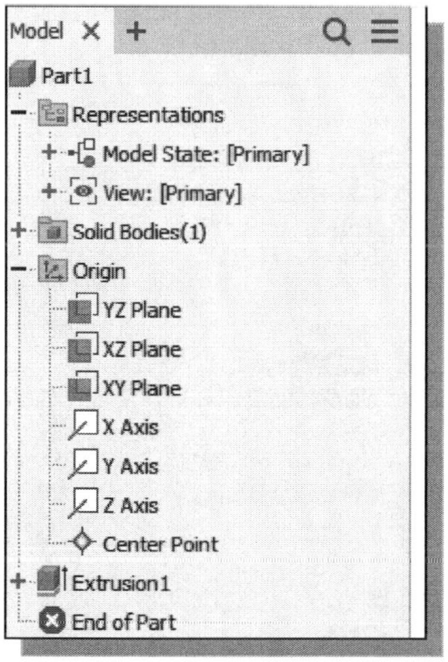

- The *Model Tree* shows two main features: the ***Origin*** (default work features) and the base feature (**Extrusion1** shown in the figure) we just created. The parent/child relationships were established implicitly when we created the base feature: (1) XZ workplane was selected as the sketch plane; (2) Center Point was used as the reference point to align the 2D sketch of the base feature.

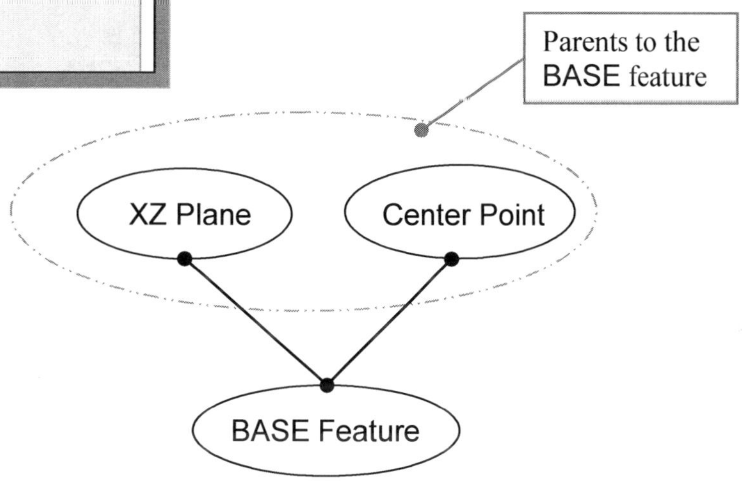

Create the Second Solid Feature

For the next solid feature, we will create the top section of the design. Note that the center of the base feature is aligned to the Center Point of the default work features. This was done intentionally so that additional solid features can be created referencing the default work features. For the second solid feature, the XY workplane will be used as the sketch plane.

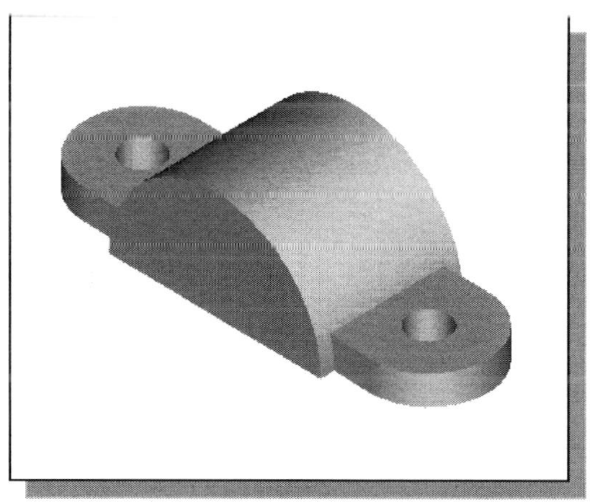

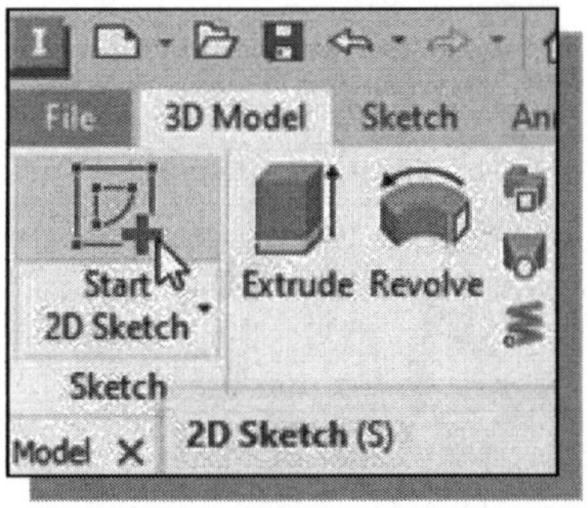

1. In the *Sketch* toolbar select the **Start 2D Sketch** command by left-clicking once on the icon.

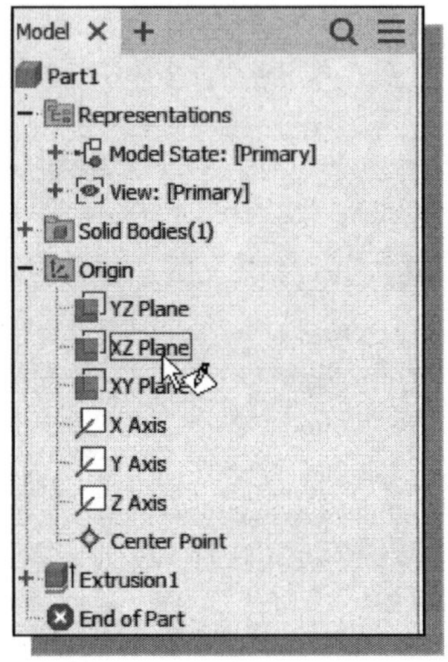

2. In the *Status Bar* area, the message "*Select face, work plane, sketch or sketch geometry.*" is displayed. Pick the **XY Plane** by clicking the work plane name inside the *browser* as shown.

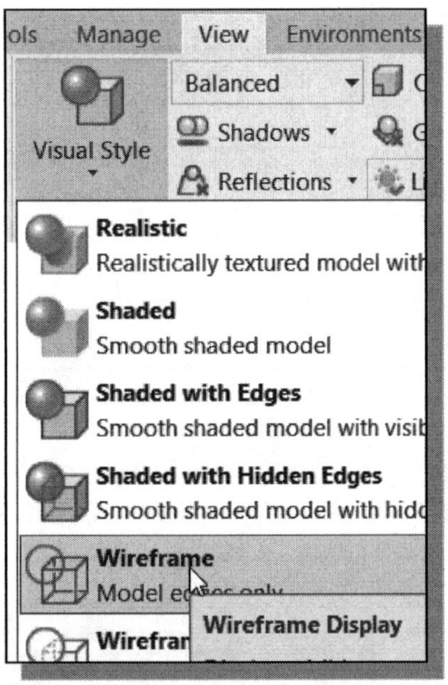

3. Select the **View** tab in the *Ribbon* panel as shown.
4. Select **Wireframe** display mode under the *Visual Style* icon as shown.

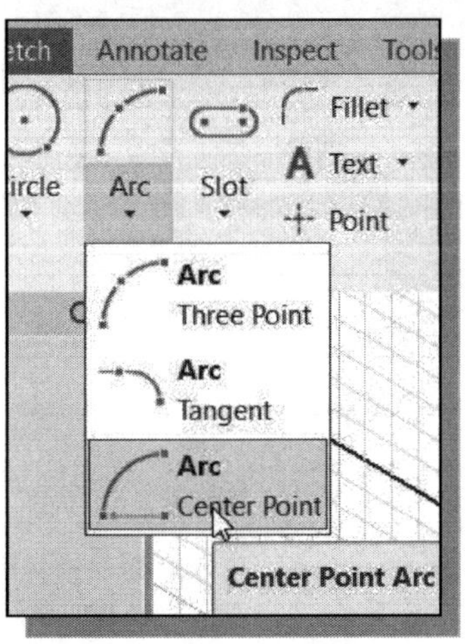

5. Select the **Sketch** tab in the *Ribbon.*
6. Select the **Center point arc** command by clicking once with the left-mouse-button on the icon in the *icon stack* as shown.
7. Pick the **center point** and watch for the Green dot for alignment as the center location of the new arc.

8. On your own, create a semi-circle of arbitrary size, with the center point aligned to the origin and both endpoints aligned to the X-axis, as shown below.

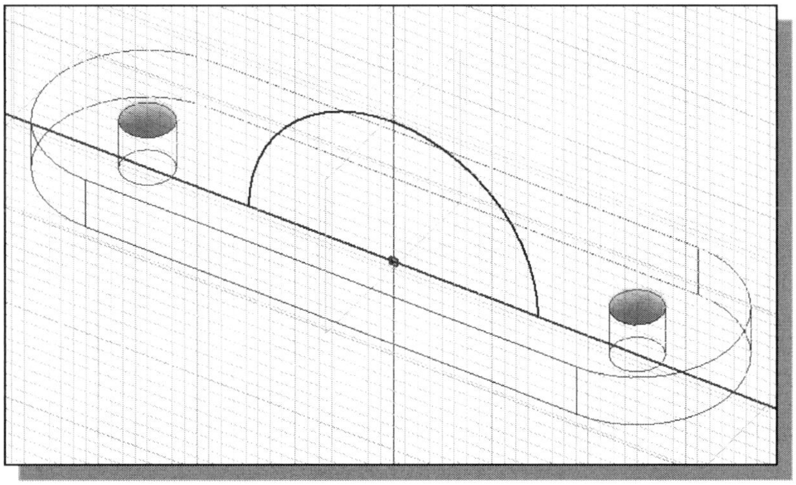

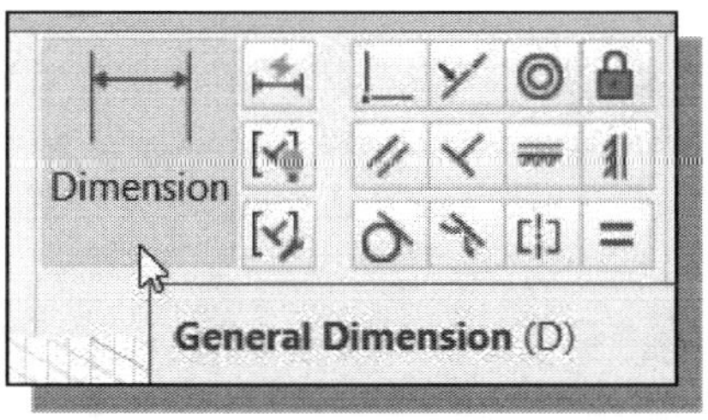

9. Move the cursor on top of the **General Dimension** icon. Left-click once on the icon to activate the General Dimension command.

10. On your own, create and adjust the radius of the arc to **1.75**.

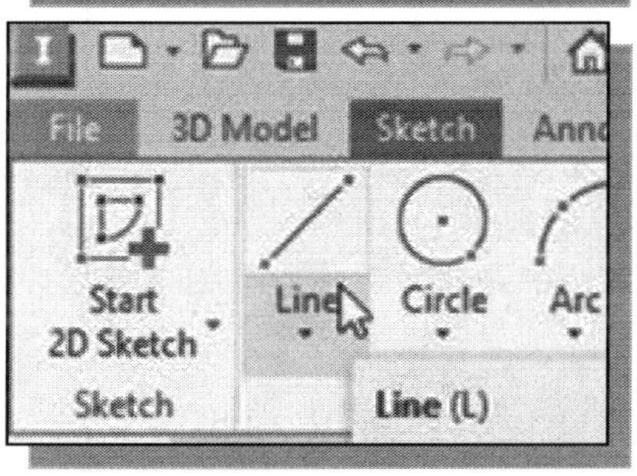

11. Select the **Line** command in the *Draw* toolbar.

12. Create a line connecting the two endpoints of the arc as shown in the figure below. (Hint: Use the **Coincident** constraint to help align the line to the origin if necessary.)

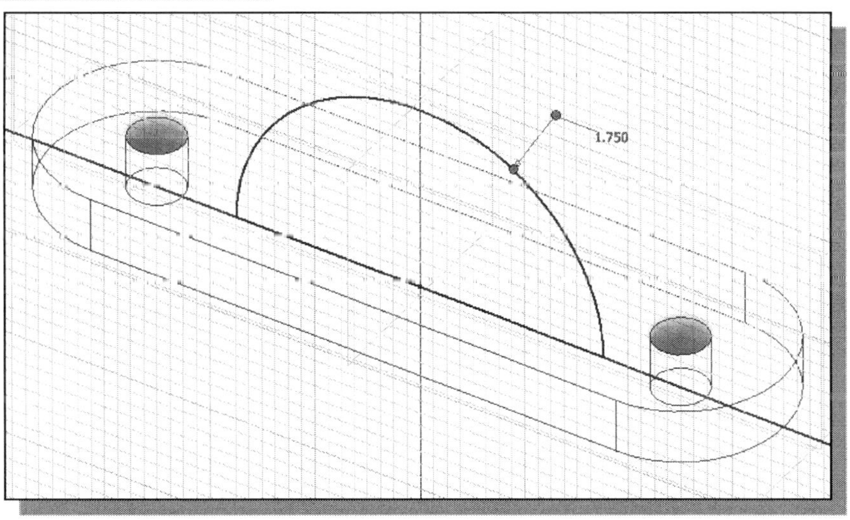

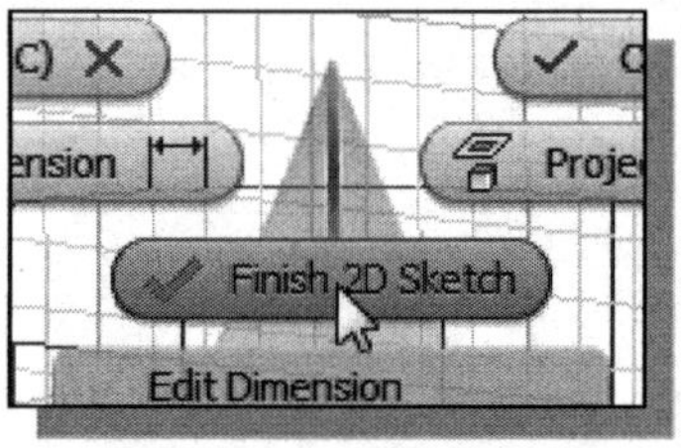

13. Inside the graphics window, click once with the right-mouse-button to display the option menu. Select **Finish 2D Sketch** in the pop-up menu to end the Sketch option.

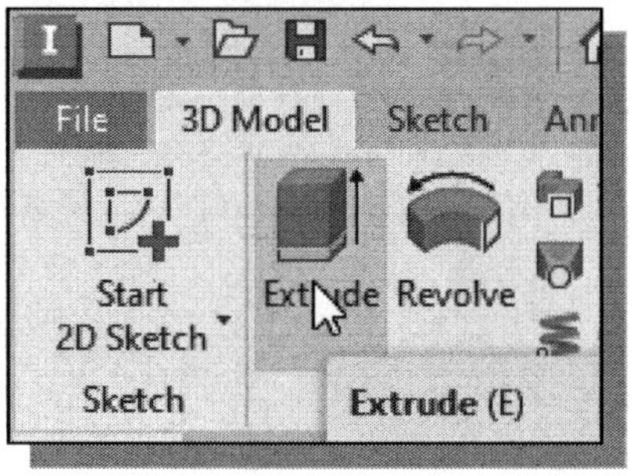

14. In the *Create* toolbar, select the **Extrude** command by clicking once with the left-mouse-button on the icon.

15. Select the inside region of the sketched arc-line curves as the profile to be extruded.

16. In the *Extrude* dialog box, set to the **Symmetric** option.

17. In the *Distance* value box, set the extrusion distance to **2.5**.

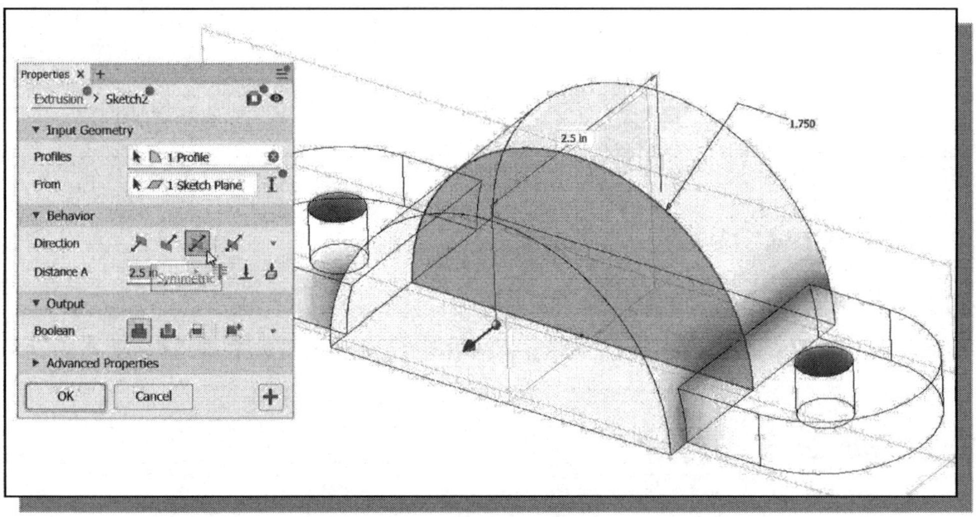

18. Click on the **OK** button to proceed with the Extrude operation.

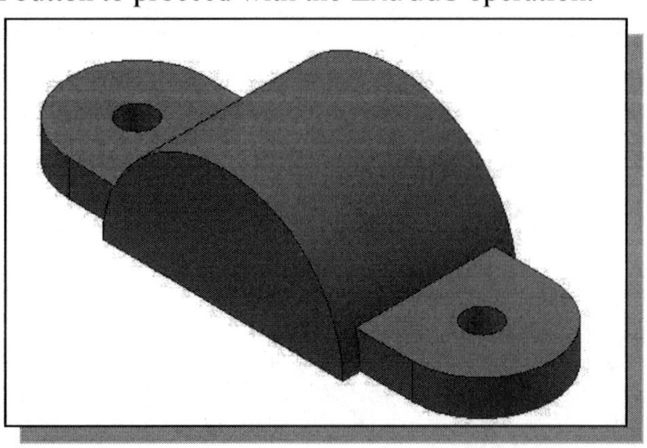

Create a Cut Feature

A rectangular cut will be created as the next solid feature.

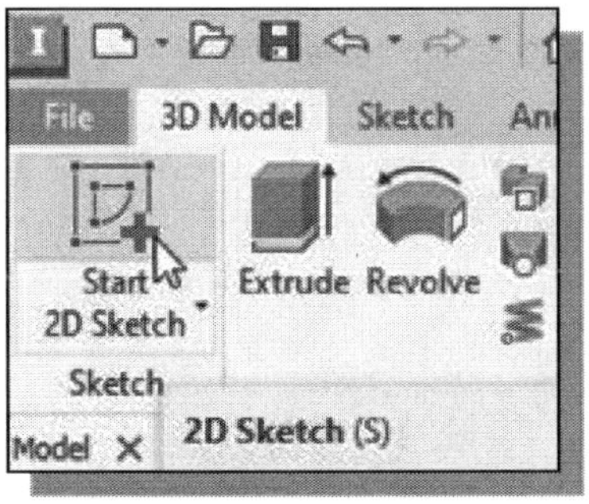

1. In the *Sketch* toolbar select the **Start 2D Sketch** command by left-clicking once on the icon.

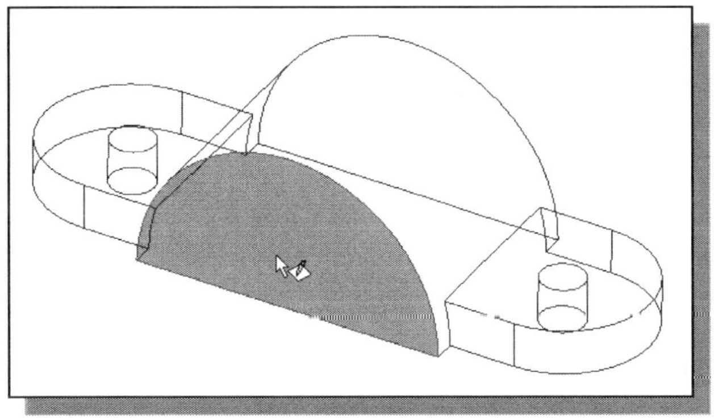

2. In the *Status Bar* area, the message "*Select plane to create sketch or an existing sketch to edit*" is displayed. Pick the front vertical face of the solid model shown.

3. On your own, create a rectangle and apply the dimensions as shown below. (Hint: Use the **YZ Plane** to assure the proper alignment of the 2D sketch.)

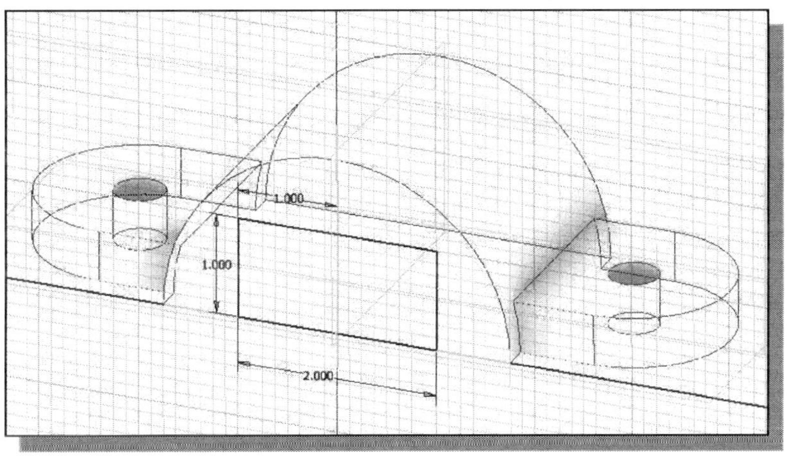

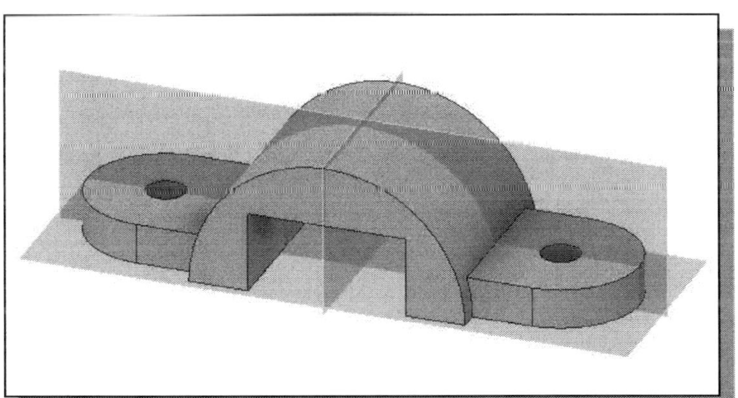

4. On your own, use the **Extrude** command and create a cutout that cuts through the entire 3D solid model as shown.

The Second Cut Feature

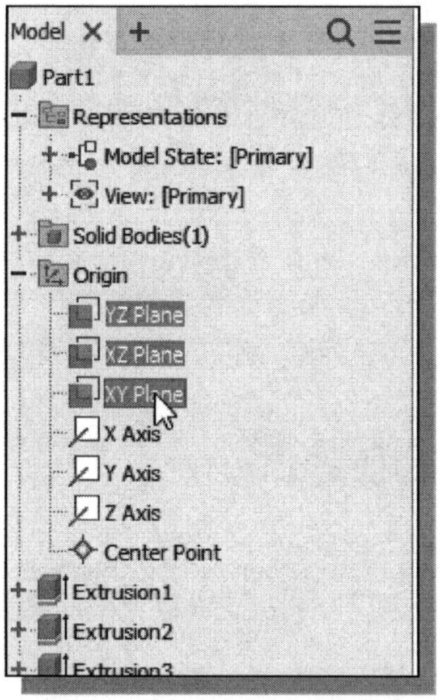

1. In the *Model Tree area*, select all of the **Datum Planes** while holding down the [**SHIFT**] key.

2. *Right-click* on any of the selected items to display the option menu and turn **OFF** the visibility of the selected items as shown.

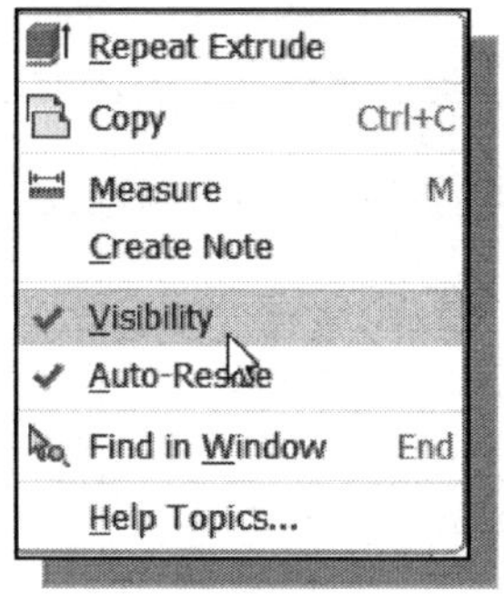

3. In the *Sketch* toolbar select the **Start 2D Sketch** command by left-clicking once on the icon.

4. In the *Status Bar* area, the message "*Select face, work plane, sketch or sketch geometry*" is displayed. Select the horizontal face of the last cut feature as the *sketching plane.*

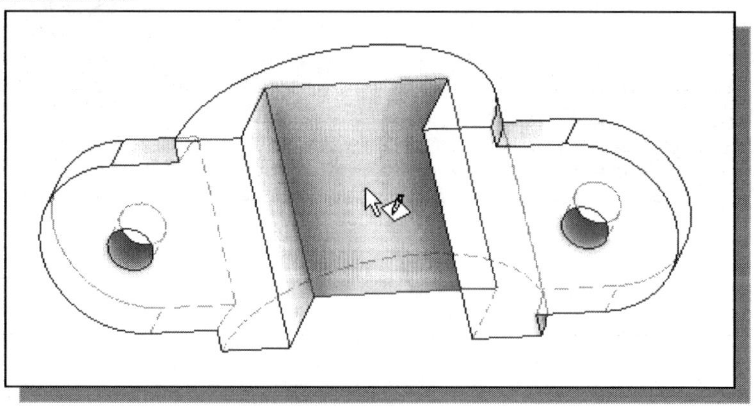

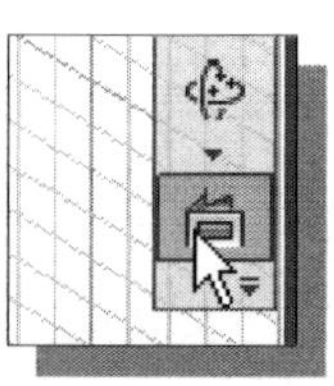

5. In the *Standard* toolbar area, click on the **Look At** button.

6. Select one of the edges of the highlighted sketching plane.

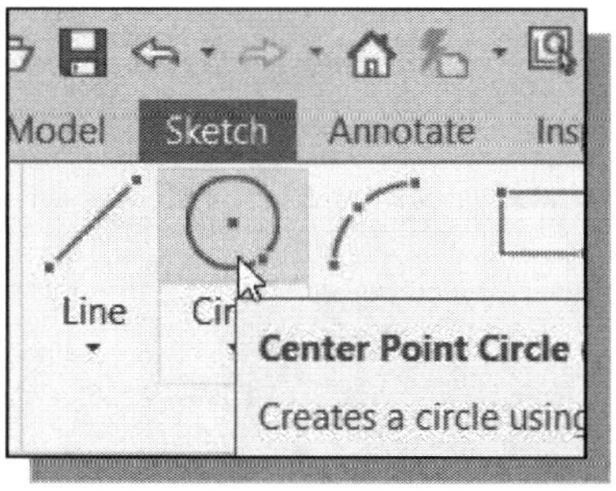

7. Select the **Center Point Circle** command by clicking once with the left-mouse-button on the icon in the *Draw* panel.

8. Pick the **center point**, located at the center of the part, to align the center of the new circle.

9. On your own, create a circle of arbitrary size.

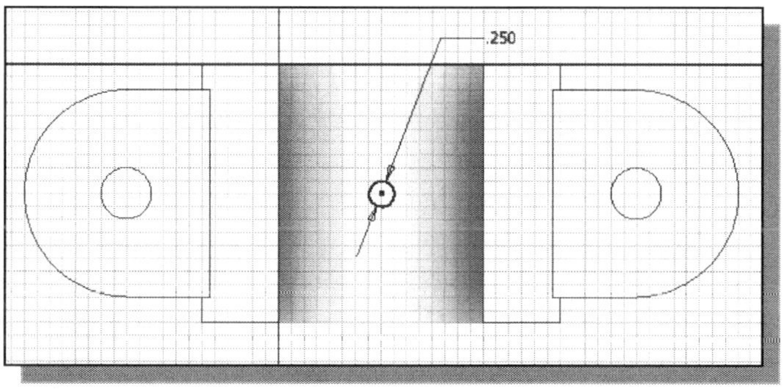

10. On your own, add the size dimension of the circle and set the dimension to **0.25**.

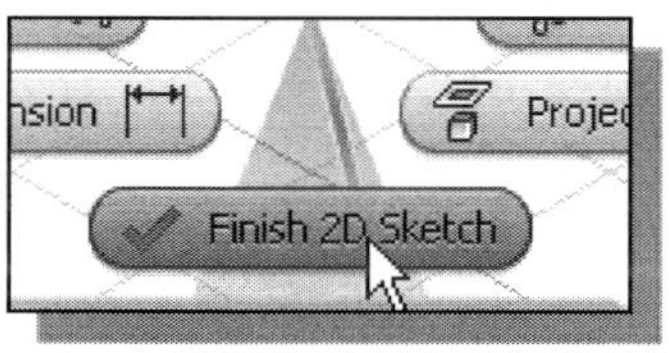

11. Inside the graphics window, click once with the right-mouse-button to display the option menu. Select **Finish 2D Sketch** in the pop-up menu to end the Sketch option.

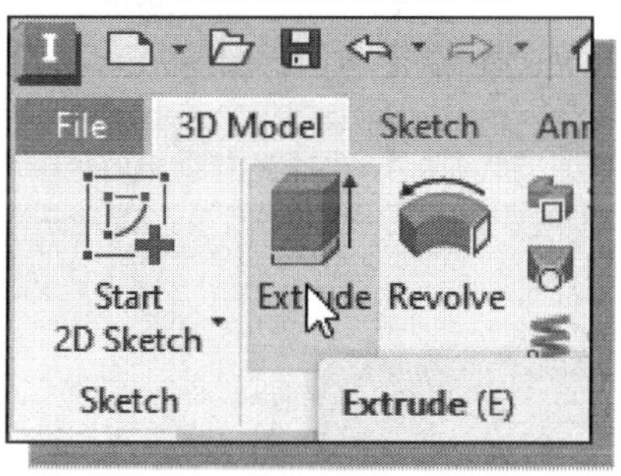

12. In the *Create toolbar*, select the **Extrude** command by clicking once with the left-mouse-button on the icon.

13. Select the inside region of the sketched circle as the profile to be extruded.

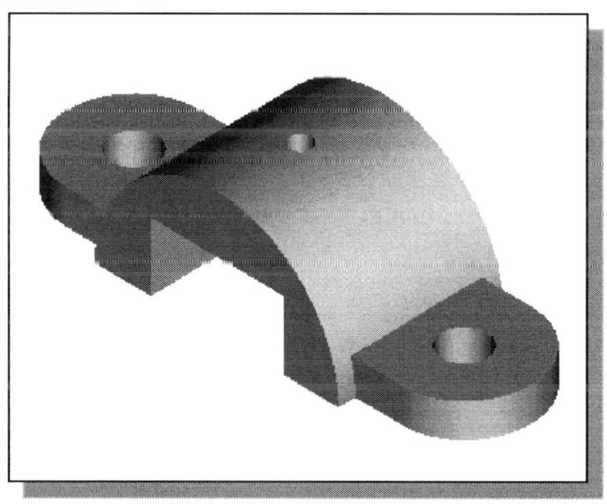

14. In the *Extrude* control panel, set to the **Cut – Through All** option.

15. Click on the **OK** button to proceed with creating the cut feature.

Examine the Parent/Child Relationships

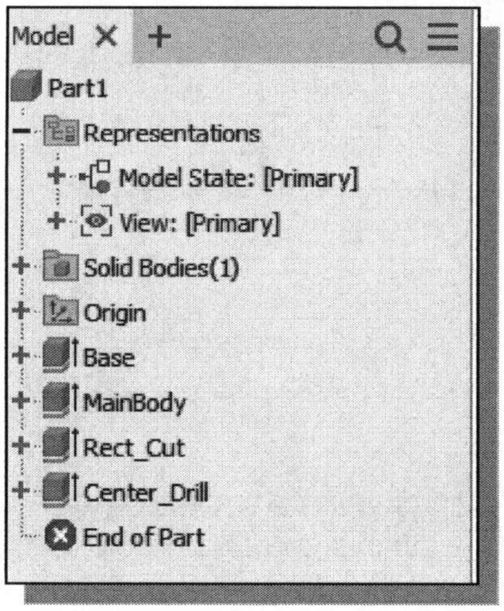

1. On your own, rename the feature names to **Base**, **MainBody**, **Rect_Cut** and **Center_Drill** as shown in the figure.

The *Model Tree* window now contains seven items: the ***Origin*** (default work features) and four solid features. All of the parent/child relationships were established implicitly as we created the solid features. As more features are created, it becomes much more difficult to make a sketch showing all the parent/child relationships involved in the model. On the other hand, it is not really necessary to have a detailed picture showing all the relationships among the features. In using a feature-based modeler, the main emphasis is to consider the interactions that exist between the **immediate features**. Treat each feature as a unit by itself and be clear on the parent/child relationships for each feature. Thinking in terms of *features* is what distinguishes *feature-based modeling* and the previous generation solid modeling techniques. Let us take a look at the last feature we created, the **Center_Drill** feature. What are the parent/child relationships associated with this feature? (1) Since this is the last feature we created, it is not a parent feature to any other features. (2) Since we used one of the surfaces of the rectangular cutout as the sketching plane, the **Rect_Cut** feature is a parent feature to the **Center_Drill** feature. (3) We also used the Origin as a reference point to align the center; therefore, the ***Origin*** is also a parent to the **Center_Drill** feature.

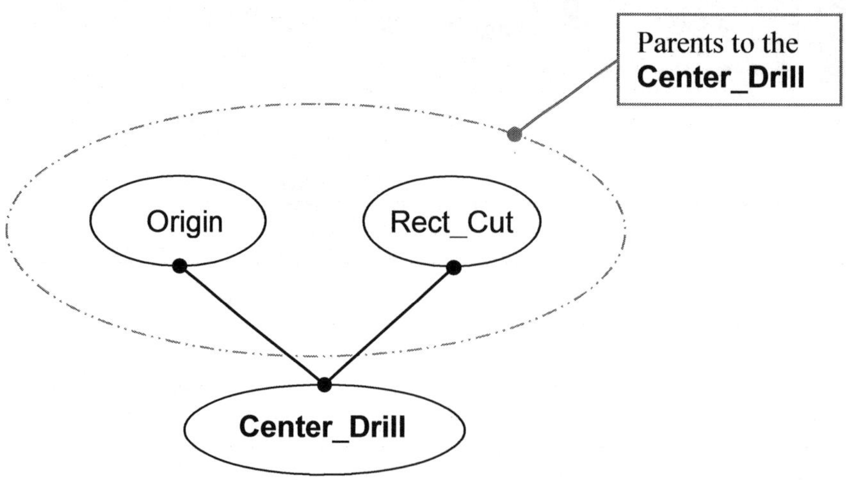

Modify a Parent Dimension

Any changes to the parent features will affect the child feature. For example, if we modify the height of the **Rect_Cut** feature from 1.0 to 0.75, the depth of the child feature (**Center_Drill** feature) will be affected.

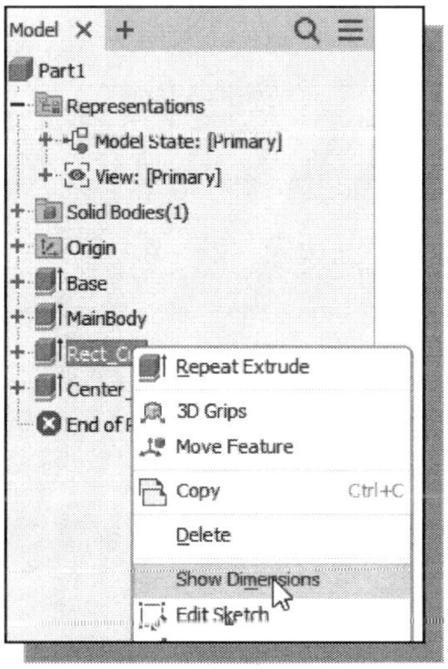

1. In the *Model Tree* window, right-click on **Rect_Cut** to bring up the option menu.

2. In the option menu, select **Show Dimensions**.

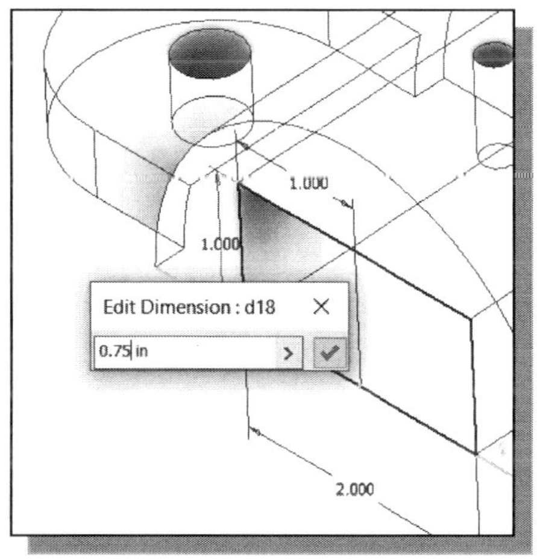

3. Select the height dimension (1.0) by double-clicking on the dimension.

4. Enter **0.75** as the new height dimension as shown.

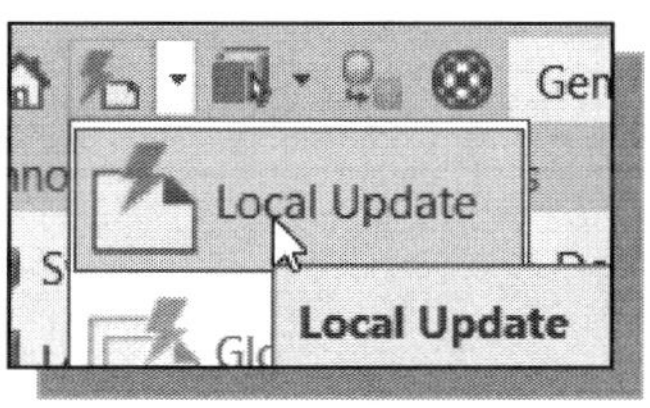

5. Click on the **Update** button in the *Quick Access Toolbar* area to proceed with updating the solid model.

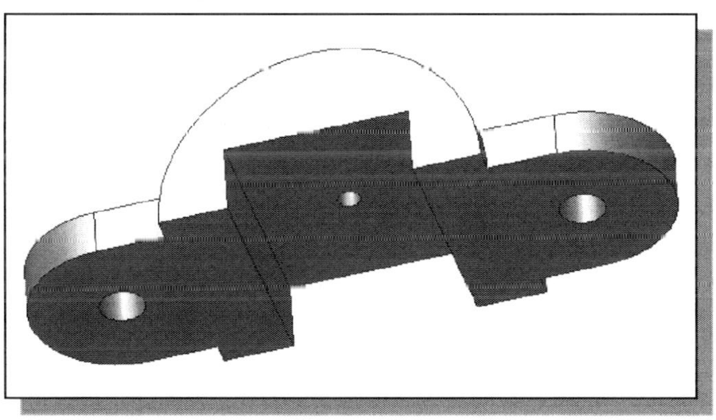

➢ Note that the position of the **Center_Drill** feature is also adjusted as the placement plane is lowered. The drill-hole still goes through the main body of the *U-Bracket* design. The parent/child relationship assures the intent of the design is maintained.

6. On your own, adjust the height of the **Rect_Cut** feature back to **1.0** inch before proceeding to the next section.

A Design Change

Engineering designs usually go through many revisions and changes. For example, a design change may call for a circular cutout instead of the current rectangular cutout feature in our model. Autodesk Inventor provides an assortment of tools to handle design changes quickly and effectively. In the following sections, we will demonstrate some of the more advanced tools available in Autodesk Inventor, which allow us to perform the modification of changing the rectangular cutout (2.0 × 1.0 inch) to a circular cutout (radius: 1.25 inch).

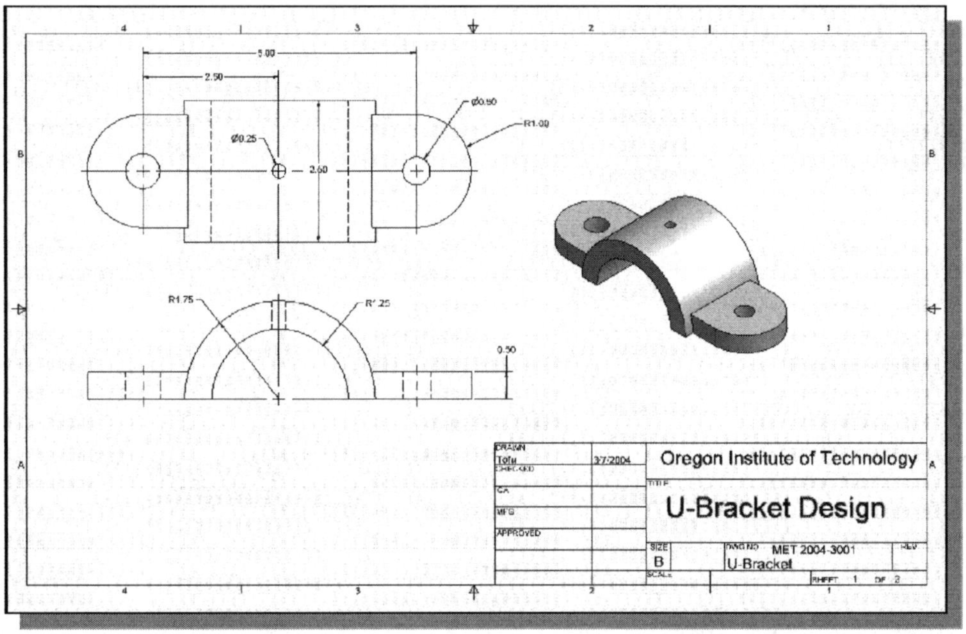

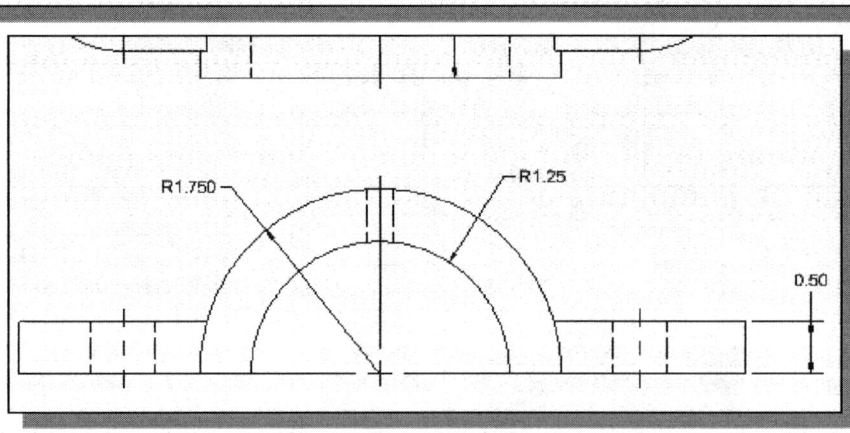

❖ Based on your knowledge of Autodesk Inventor so far, how would you accomplish this modification? What other approaches can you think of that are also feasible? Of the approaches you came up with, which one is the easiest to do and which is the most flexible? If this design change was anticipated right at the beginning of the design process, what would be your choice in arranging the order of the features? You are encouraged to perform the modifications prior to following through the rest of the tutorial.

Feature Suppression

With Autodesk Inventor, we can take several different approaches to accomplish this modification. We could (1) create a new model, or (2) change the shape of the existing cut feature using the **Redefine** command, or (3) perform **feature suppression** on the rectangular cut feature and add a circular cut feature. The third approach offers the most flexibility and requires the least amount of editing to the existing geometry. **Feature suppression** is a method that enables us to disable a feature while retaining the complete feature information; the feature can be reactivated at any time. Prior to adding the new cut feature, we will first suppress the rectangular cut feature.

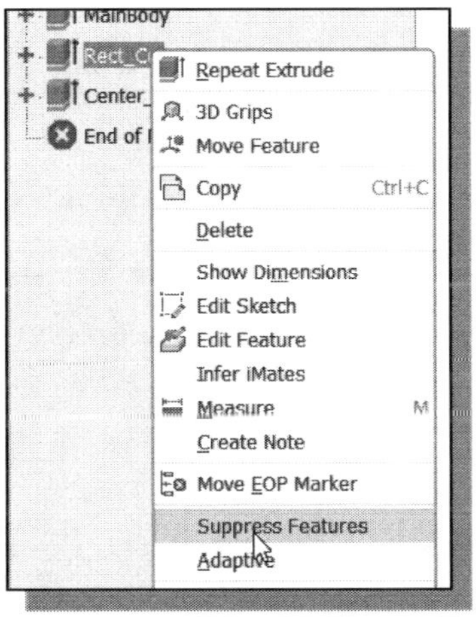

1. Move the cursor inside the *Model Tree* window. Click once with the right-mouse-button on **Rect_Cut** to bring up the option menu.

2. Pick **Suppress** in the pop-up menu.

❖ With the *Suppress* command, the Rect_Cut and Center_Drill features have disappeared in the display area. The child feature cannot exist without its parent(s), and any modification to the parent (Rect_Cut) influences the child (Center_Drill).

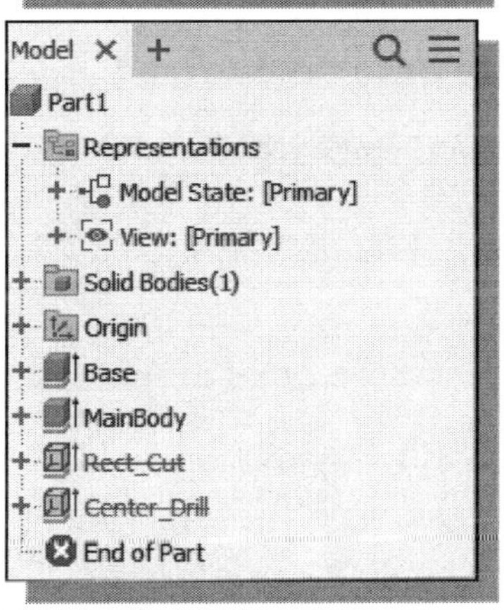

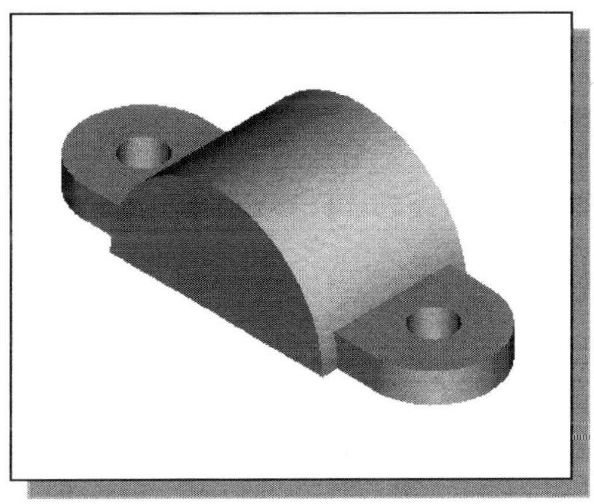

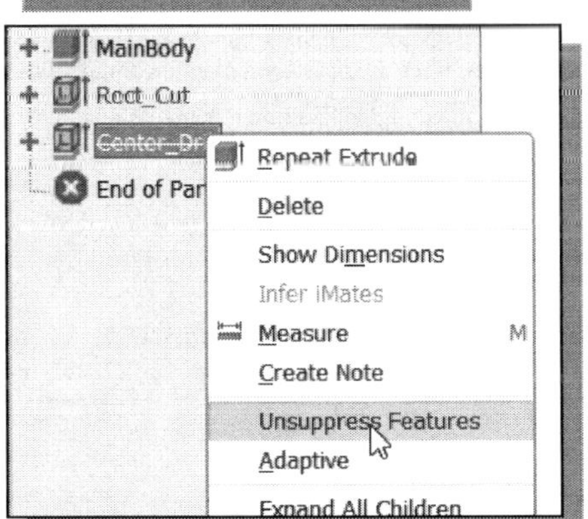

3. Move the cursor inside the *Model Tree* window. Click once with the right-mouse-button on top of **Center_Drill** to bring up the option menu.

4. Pick **Unsuppress Features** in the pop-up menu.

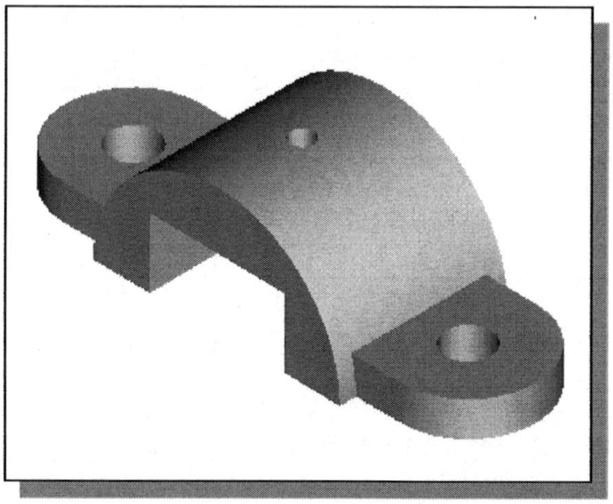

➢ In the display area and the *Model Tree* window, both the **Rect_Cut** feature and the **Center_Drill** feature are re-activated. The child feature cannot exist without its parent(s); the parent (Rect_Cut) must be activated to enable the child (Center_Drill).

A Different Approach to the Center_Drill Feature

The main advantage of using the BORN technique is to provide greater flexibility for part modifications and design changes. In this case, the Center_Drill feature can be placed on the XZ workplane and therefore not be linked to the Rect_Cut feature.

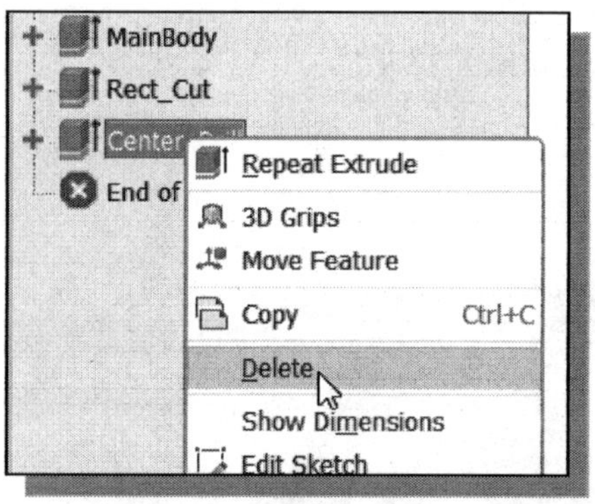

1. Move the cursor inside the *Model Tree* window. Click once with the **right-mouse-button** on top of **Center_Drill** to bring up the option menu.

2. Pick **Delete** in the pop-up menu.

3. In the *Delete Features* window, confirm the **consumed sketches and features** option is switched ***ON***.

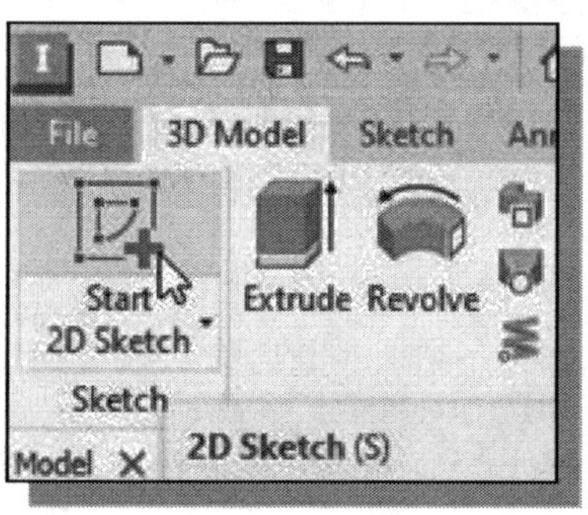

4. Click **OK** to proceed with the Delete command.

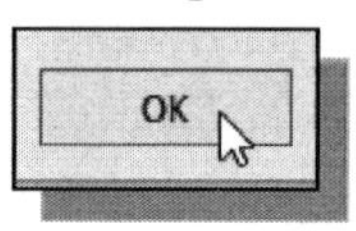

5. In the *Sketch* toolbar select the **Start 2D Sketch** command by left-clicking once on the icon.

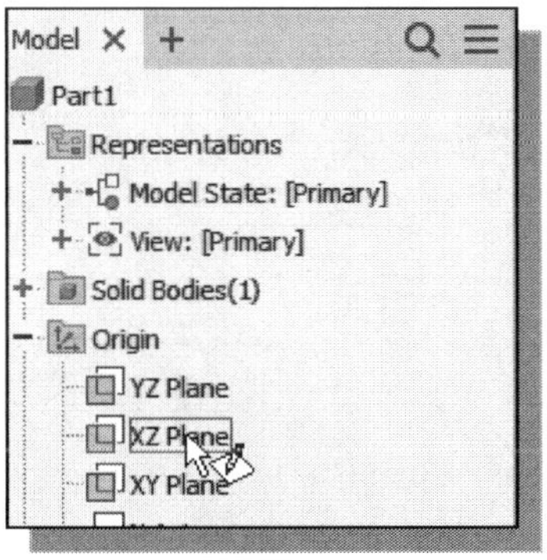

6. In the *Status Bar* area, the message "*Select plane to create sketch or an existing sketch to edit*" is displayed. Pick the **XZ Plane** in the *Model Tree* window as shown.

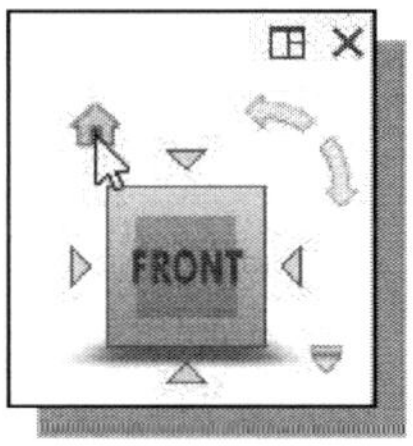

7. Inside the graphics area, single left-click to activate the **Home View** option as shown. The view will be adjusted back to the default ***isometric view***.

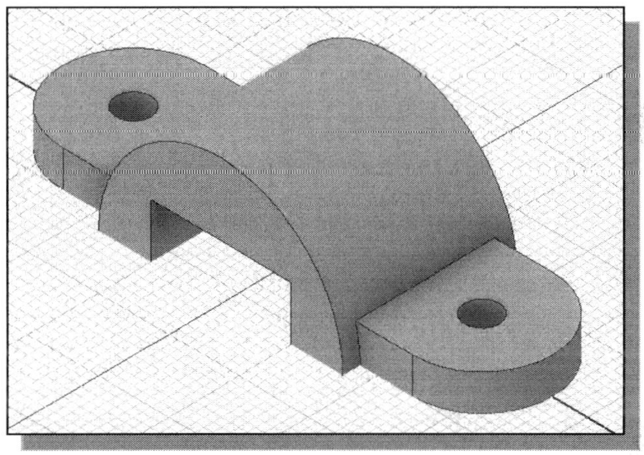

➢ Note the alignment of the sketch plane is set to the XZ plane as shown.

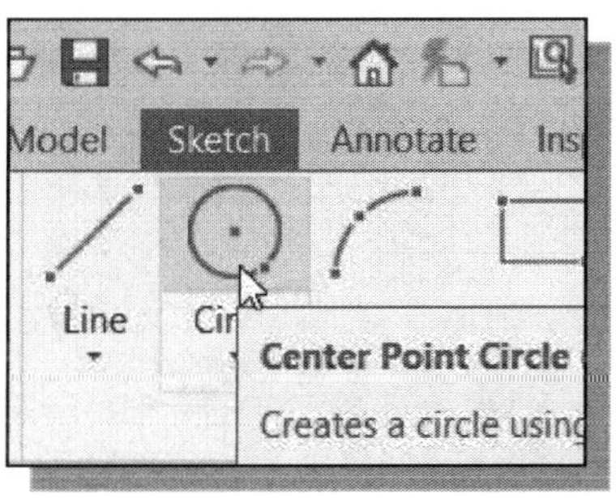

8. Select the **Center Point Circle** command by clicking once with the left-mouse-button on the icon in the *Draw* panel.

9. Pick the center point to align the center of the new circle. Select another location to create a circle of arbitrary size.

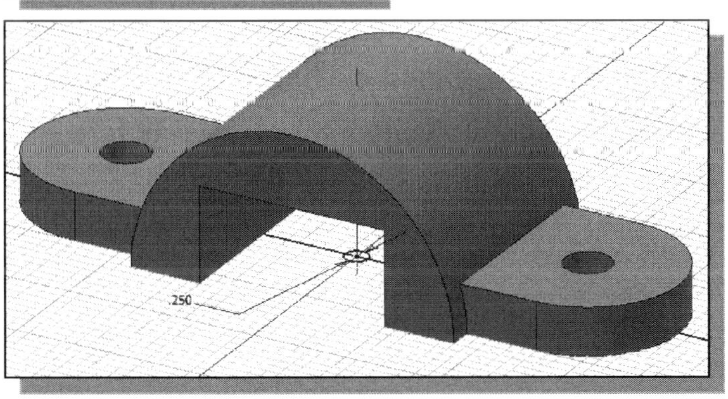

10. On your own, add the size dimension of the circle and set the dimension to **0.25**.

11. On your own, complete the extrude cut feature, cutting upward through the main body of the design.

Suppress the Rect_Cut Feature

Now the new **Center_Drill** feature is no longer a child of the **Rect_Cut** feature, any changes to the **Rect_Cut** feature do not affect the **Center_Drill** feature.

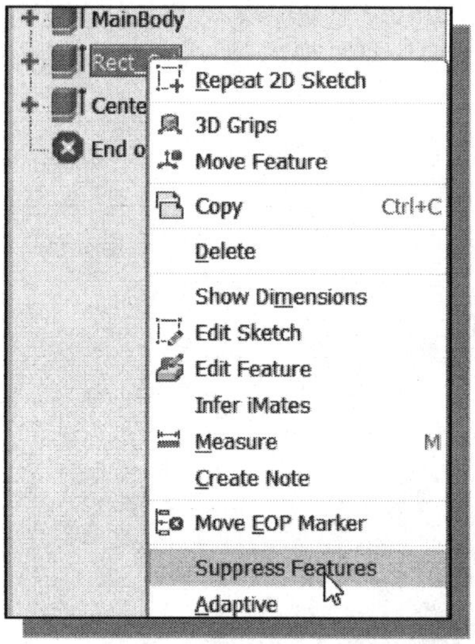

1. Move the cursor inside the *Model Tree* window. Click once with the right-mouse-button on top of **Rect_Cut** to bring up the option menu.

2. Pick **Suppress Features** in the pop-up menu.

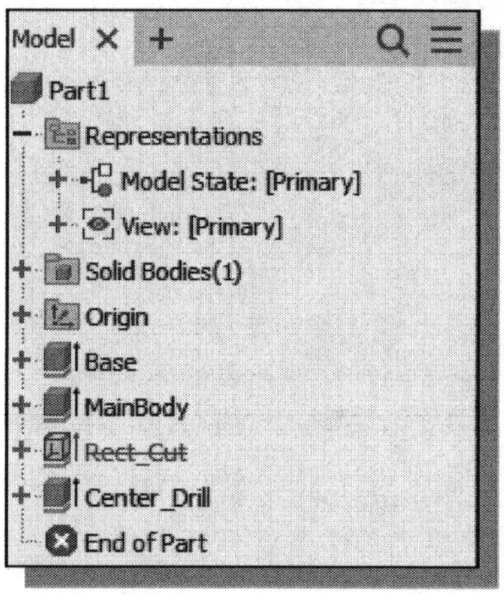

❖ The **Rect_Cut** feature is now disabled without affecting the ***new*** **Center_Drill** feature.

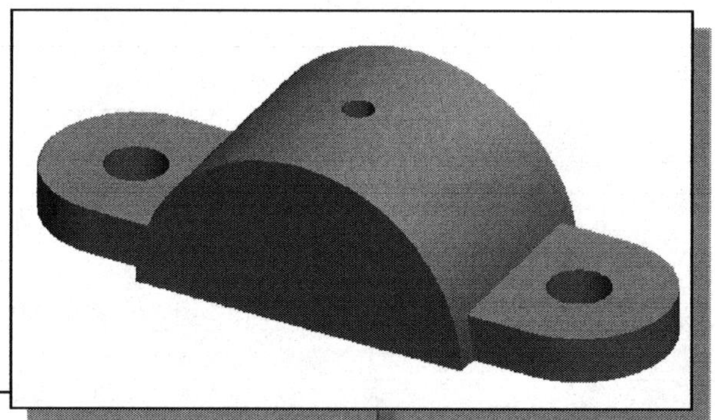

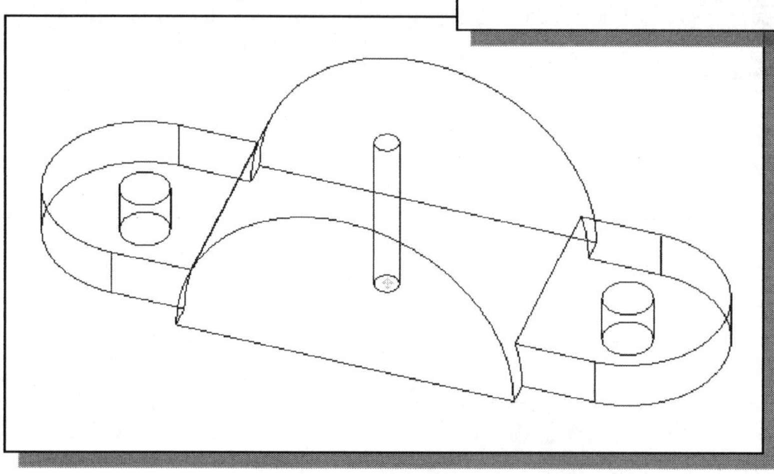

Create a Circular Cut Feature

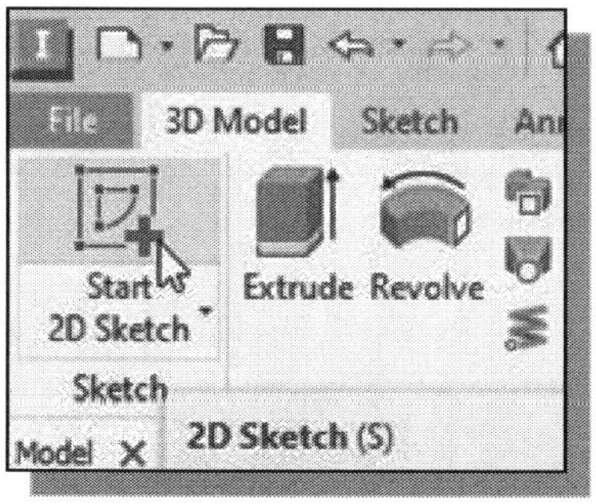

1. In the *Sketch* toolbar select the **Start 2D Sketch** command by left-clicking once on the icon.

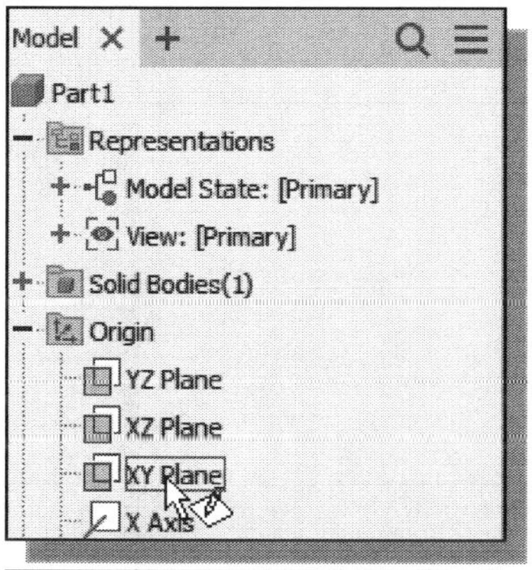

2. In the *Status Bar* area, the message "*Select face, work plane, sketch or sketch geometry*" is displayed. Pick the **XY Plane** in the *Model Tree* window as shown.

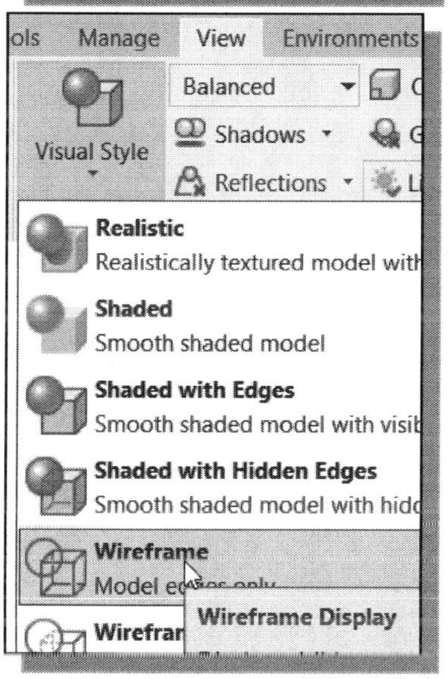

3. Activate the **View** tab in the *Ribbon* panel as shown.

4. Select **Wireframe** display mode under the *Visual Style* icon as shown.

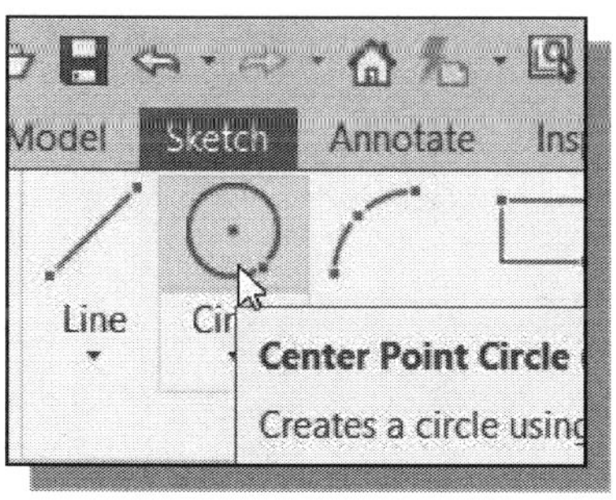

5. Select the **Center Point Circle** command by clicking once with the left-mouse-button on the icon in the *Draw* panel.

6. Pick the **center point** at the origin to align the center of the new circle.

7. On your own, create a circle of arbitrary size.

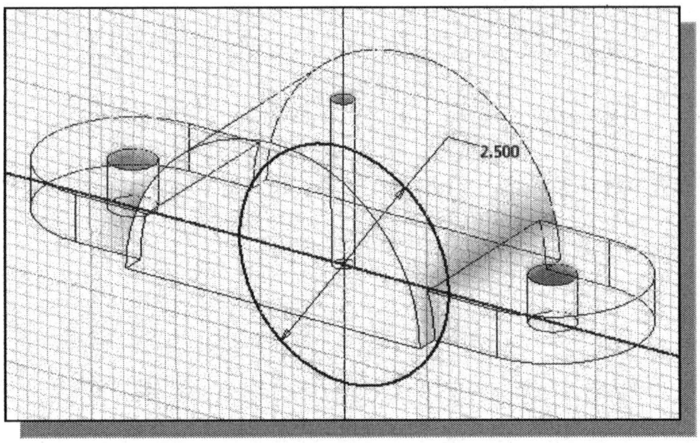

8. On your own, create the size dimension of the circle and set the dimension to **2.5** as shown in the figure.

9. On your own, complete the **cut** feature using the **Symmetric - All** command.

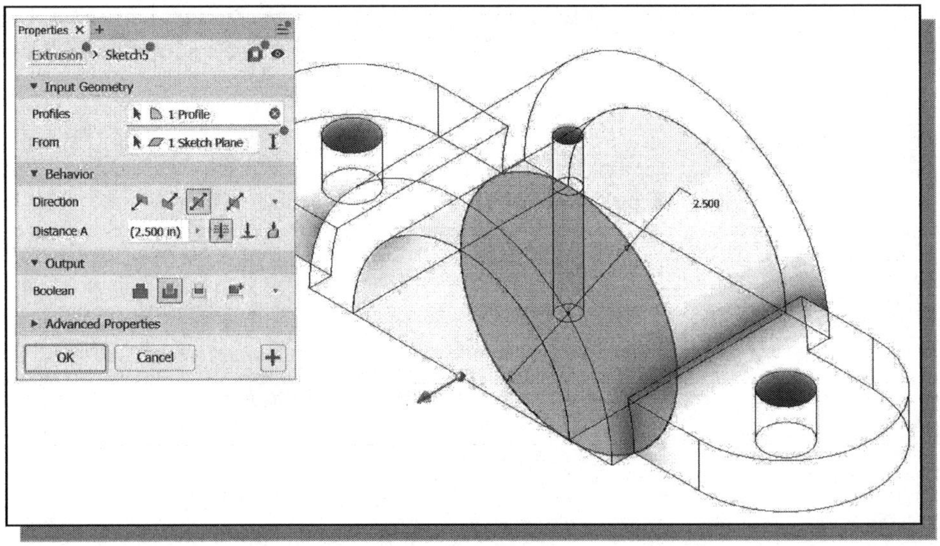

❖ Note that the parents of the Circular_Cut feature are the XY Plane and the Center Point.

➢ On your own, save the model as **U-Bracket**; this model will be used again in the next chapter.

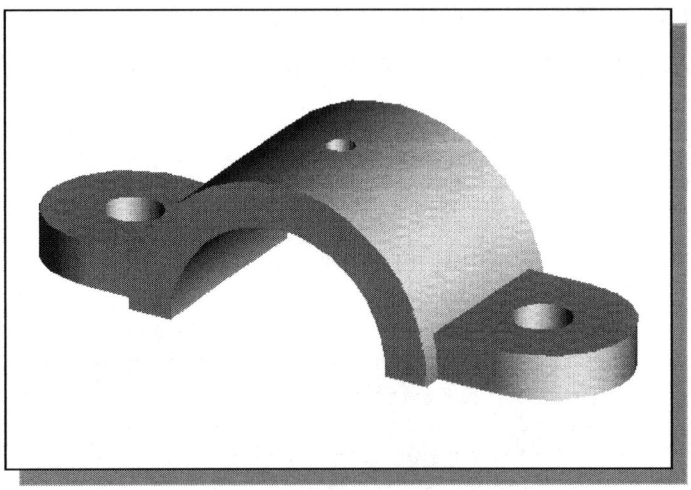

A Flexible Design Approach

In a typical design process, the initial design will undergo many analyses, tests, reviews and revisions. Autodesk Inventor allows the users to quickly make changes and explore different options of the initial design throughout the design process.

The model we constructed in this chapter contains two distinct design options. The *feature-based parametric modeling* approach enables us to quickly explore design alternatives, and we can include different design ideas into the same model. With parametric modeling, designers can concentrate on improving the design, and the design process becomes quicker and requires less effort. The key to successfully using parametric modeling as a design tool lies in understanding and properly controlling the interactions of features, especially the parent/child relations.

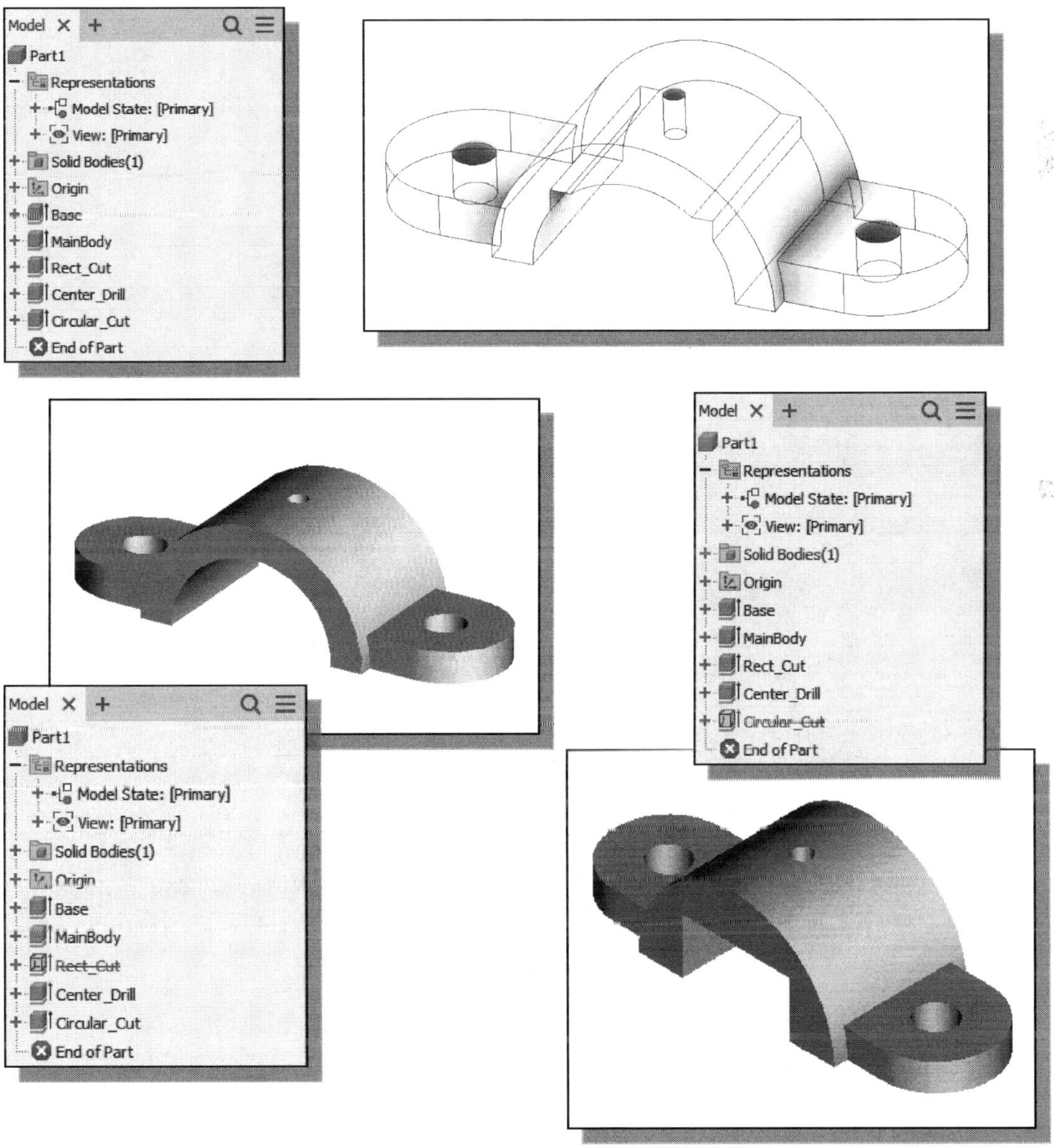

View and Edit Material Properties

The *Inventor Material Library* provides many commonly used materials. The material properties listed in the *Material Library* can be edited and new materials can be added.

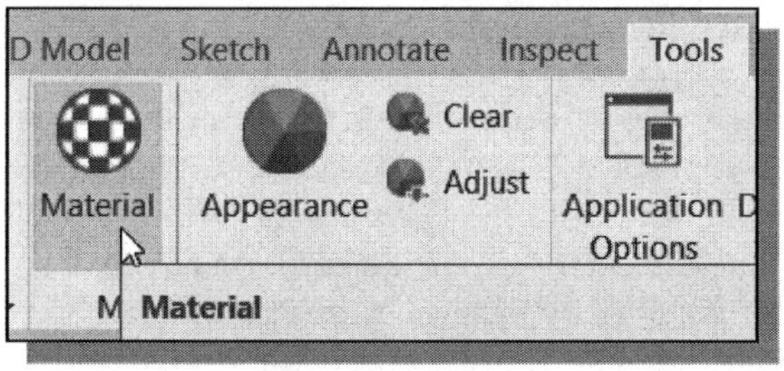

1. In the *Tools* tab, click **Material** as shown.

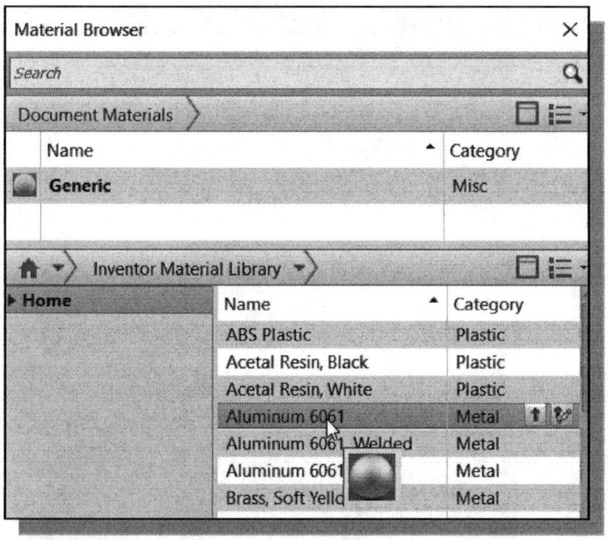

2. In the *Inventor Material* library group, select **Aluminum-6061**.

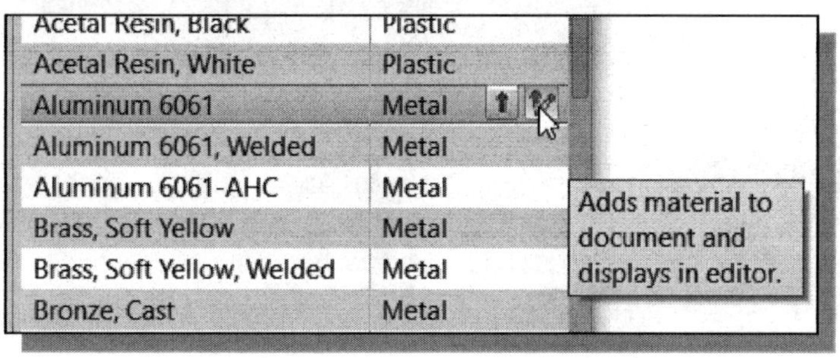

3. Click the **Add Material to document and display in editor** icon as shown.

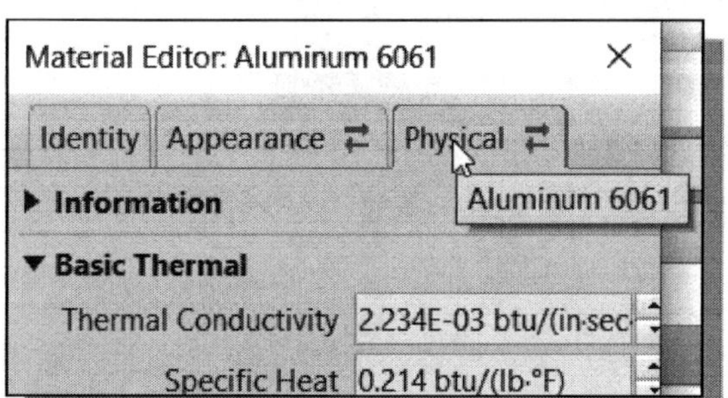

4. Click on the **Physical Aspect** tab to view the associated material properties.

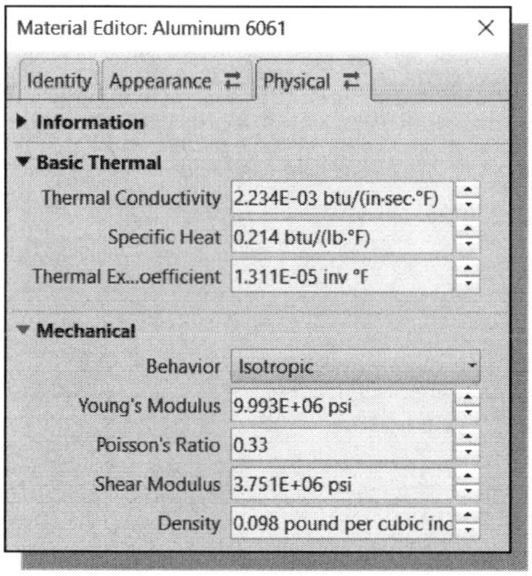

5. Expand the **Mechanical** properties list as shown.

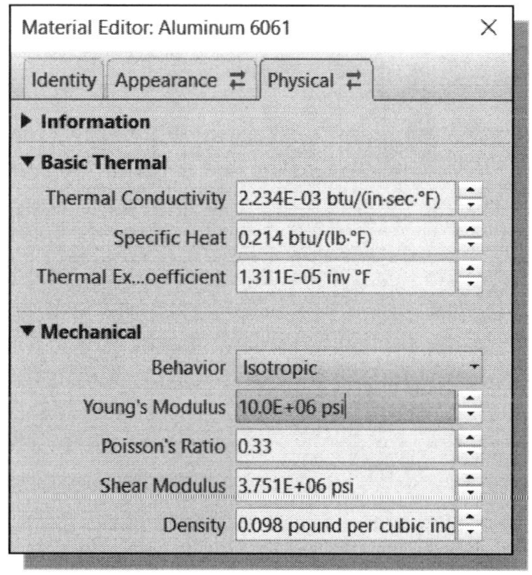

6. Enter **10.0E6 psi** as the new value for ***Young's Modulus***.

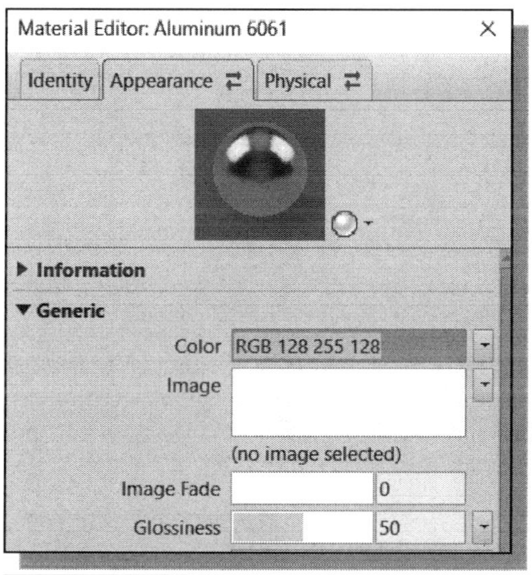

7. On your own, edit the material **Appearance - Glossiness** to **50** and color to **light green** as shown in the figure.

8. Click **OK** to accept the changes and close the editor.

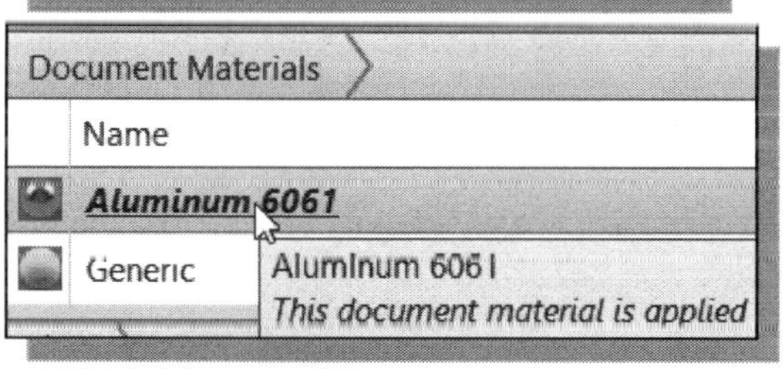

❖ Note the **Aluminum-6061** material in the document material list is highlighted showing the applied material properties.

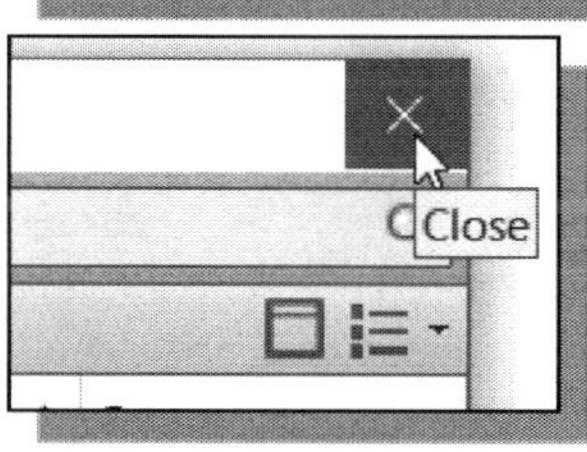

9. Click **Close** to exit the **Material Browser**.

- Note the new material setting is assigned to the model which can be shown under any of the shaded display modes.

Review Questions:

1. Why is it important to consider the parent/child relationships between features?
2. Describe the procedure to suppress a feature.
3. What is the basic concept of the BORN technique?
4. What happens to a feature when it is suppressed?
5. How do you identify a suppressed feature in a model?
6. What is the main advantage of using the BORN technique?
7. Create sketches showing the steps you plan to use to create the models shown on the next page:

Exercises: (Dimensions are in inches unless otherwise specified.)

1. **Swivel Yoke** (Material: Cast Iron)

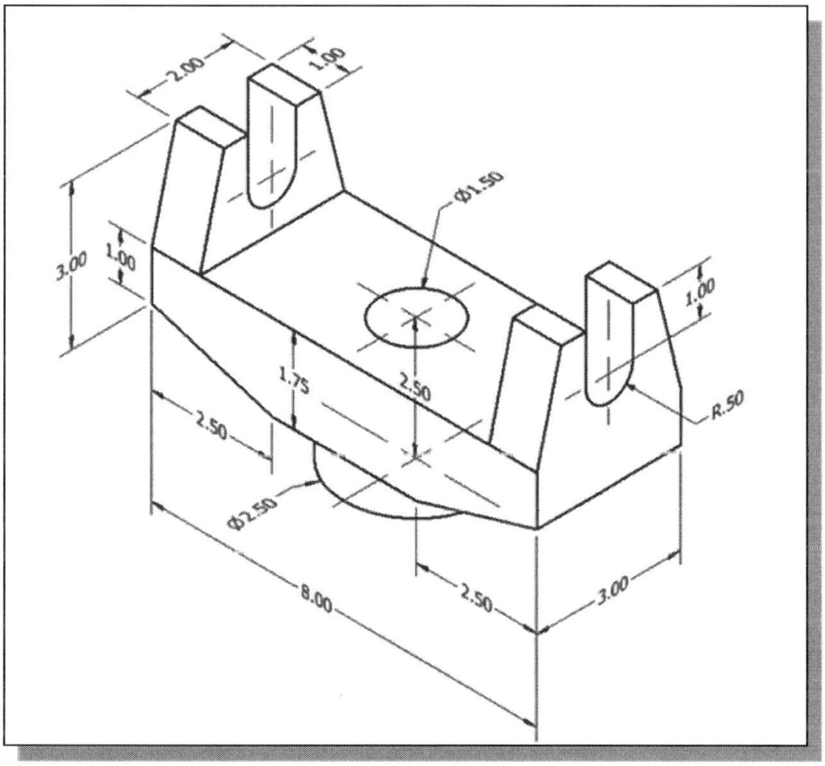

2. **Angle Bracket** (Material: Carbon Steel)

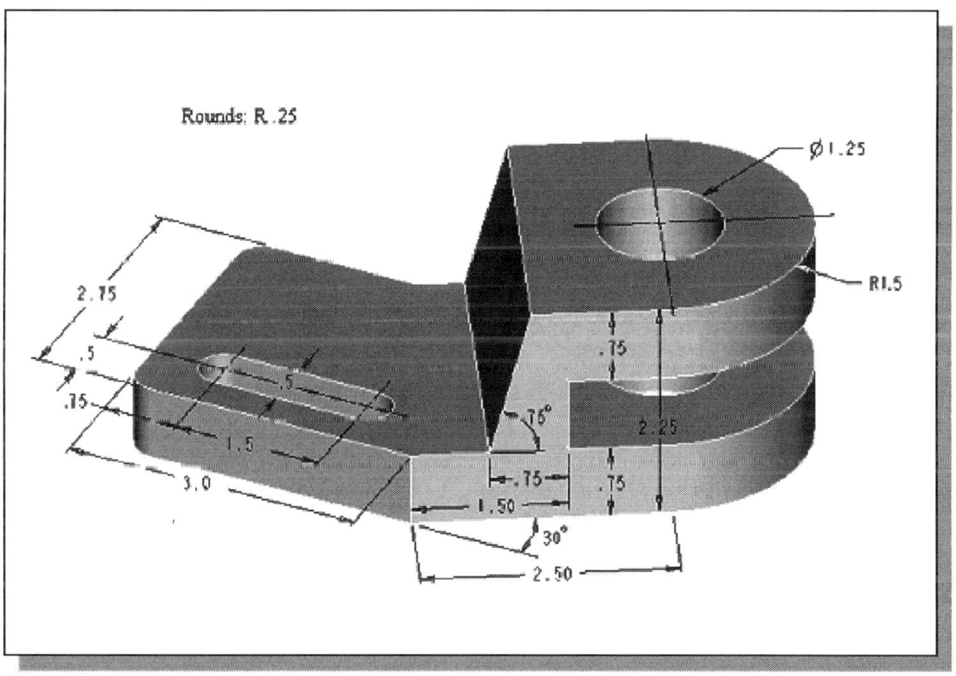

3. **Connecting Rod** (Material: Carbon Steel)

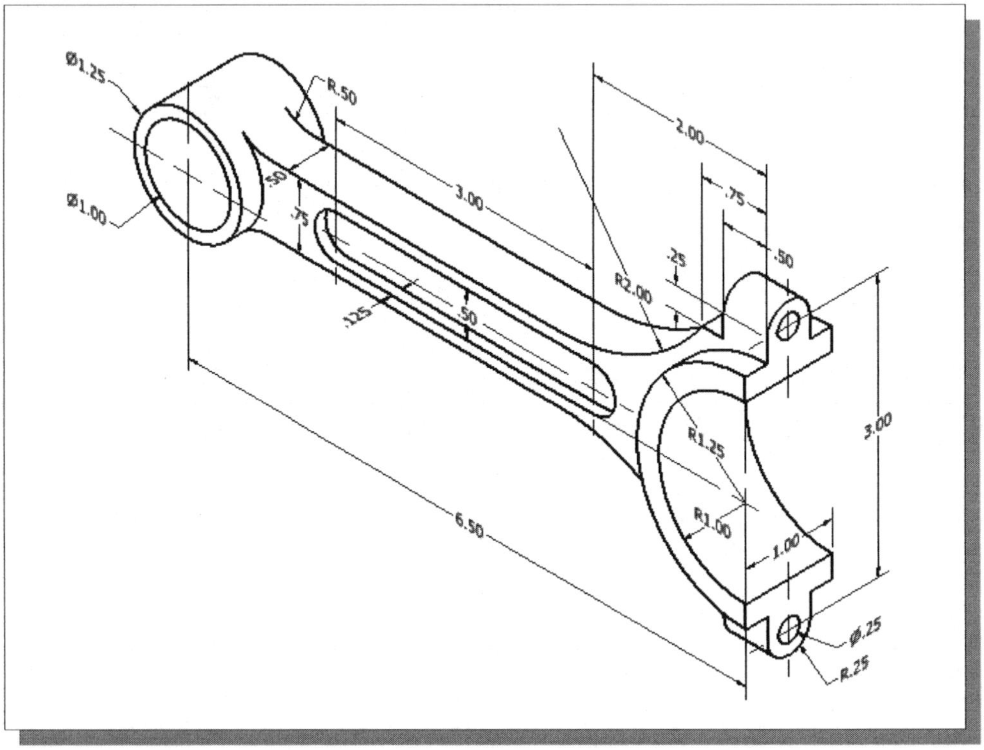

4. **Tube Hanger** (Material: Aluminum 6061)

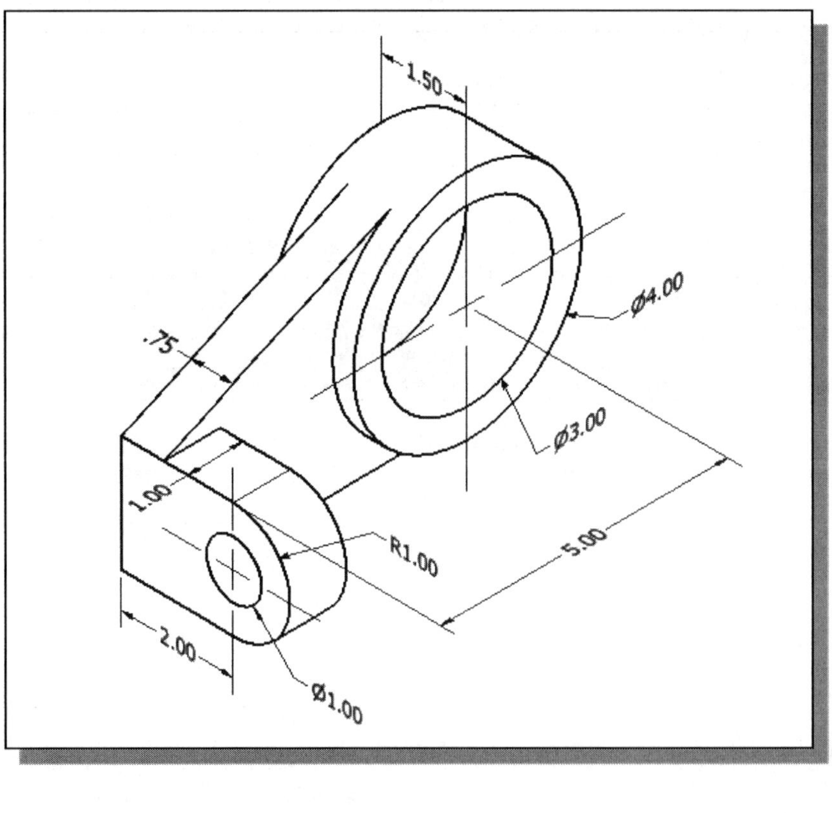

5. **Angle Latch** (Dimensions are in mm, Material: Brass)

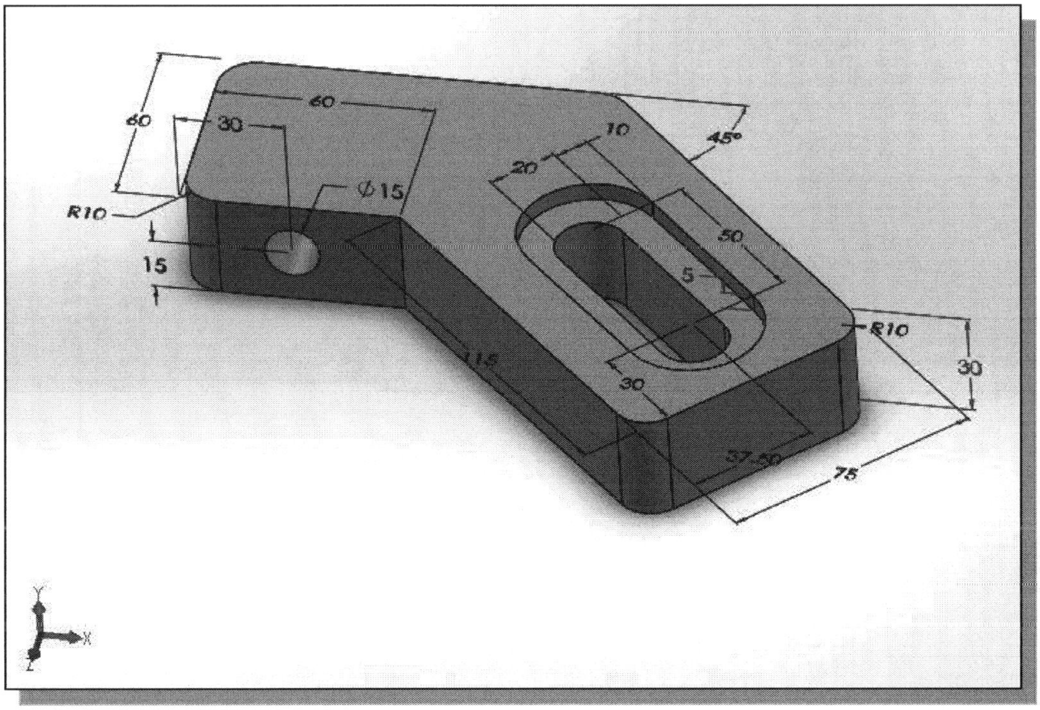

6. **Inclined Lift** (Material: Mild Steel)

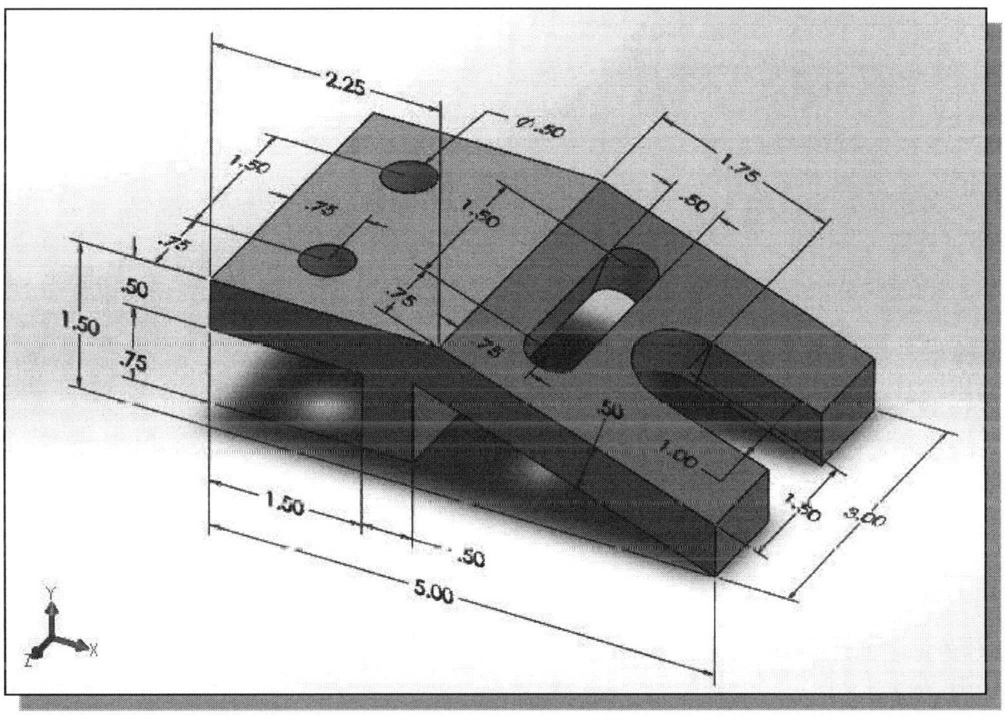

7. **Support Mount** (Material: **Mild Steel)**

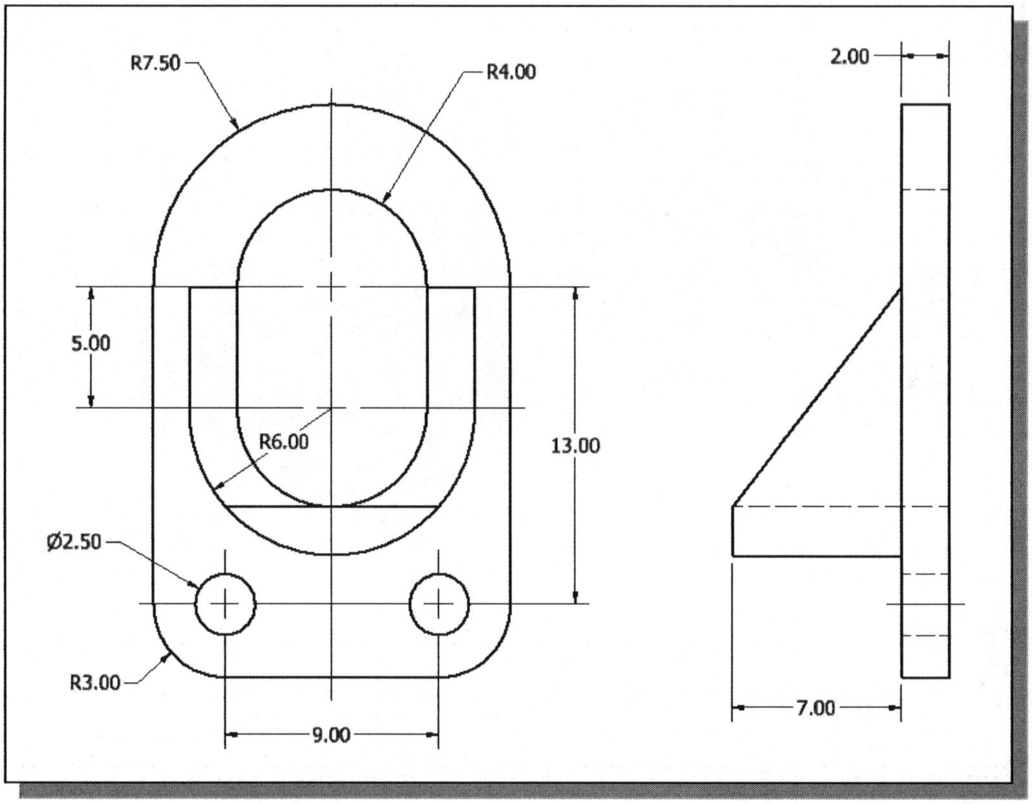

Chapter 13
Part Drawings and 3D Model-Based Definition - Autodesk Inventor

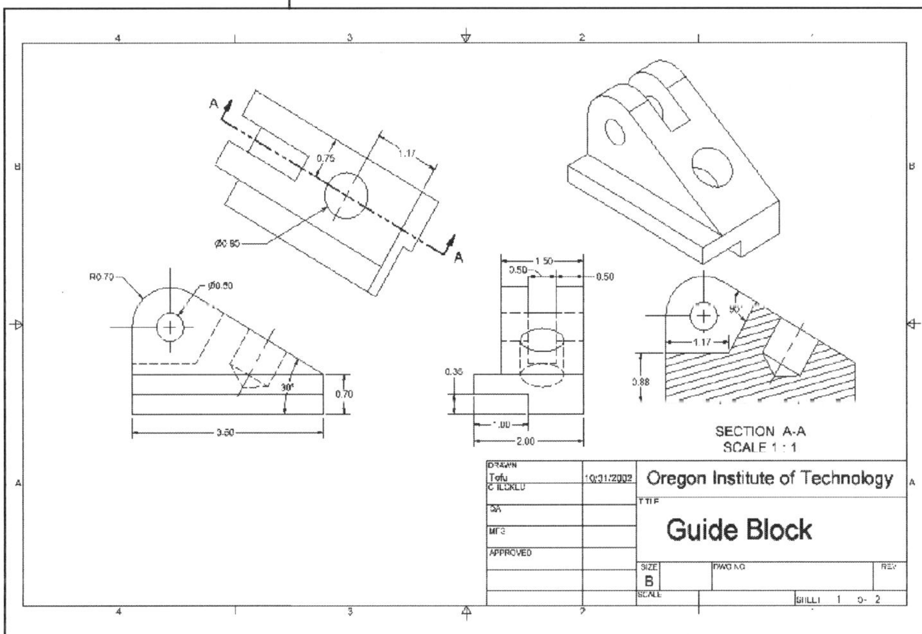

Learning Objectives

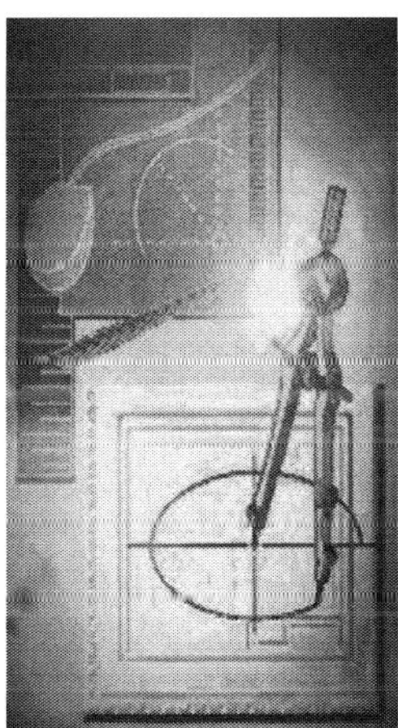

- Create Drawing Layouts from Solid Models
- Understand Associative Functionality
- Use the Default Borders and Title Block in the Layout Mode
- Arrange and Manage 2D Views in Drawing Mode
- Display and Hide Feature Dimensions
- Create Reference Dimensions
- Create 3D Model-Based Definition on Solid Models

Drawings from Parts and Associative Functionality

With the software/hardware improvements in solid modeling, the importance of two-dimensional drawings is decreasing. Drafting is considered one of the downstream applications of using solid models. In many production facilities, solid models are used to generate machine tool paths for *computer numerical control* (CNC) machines. Solid models are also used in *rapid prototyping* to create 3D physical models out of plastic resins, powdered metal, etc. Ideally, the solid model database should be used directly to generate the final product. However, the majority of applications in most production facilities still require the use of two-dimensional drawings. Using the solid model as the starting point for a design, solid modeling tools can easily create all the necessary two-dimensional views. In this sense, solid modeling tools are making the process of creating two-dimensional drawings more efficient and effective.

Autodesk Inventor provides associative functionality in the different Autodesk Inventor modes. This functionality allows us to change the design at any level, and the system reflects it at all levels automatically. For example, a solid model can be modified in the *Part Modeling Mode* and the system automatically reflects that change in the *Drawing Mode*. We can also modify a feature dimension in the *Drawing Mode*, and the system automatically updates the solid model in all modes.

In this lesson, the general procedure of creating multi-view drawings is illustrated. The *U_Bracket* design from the last chapter is used to demonstrate the associative functionality between the model and drawing views.

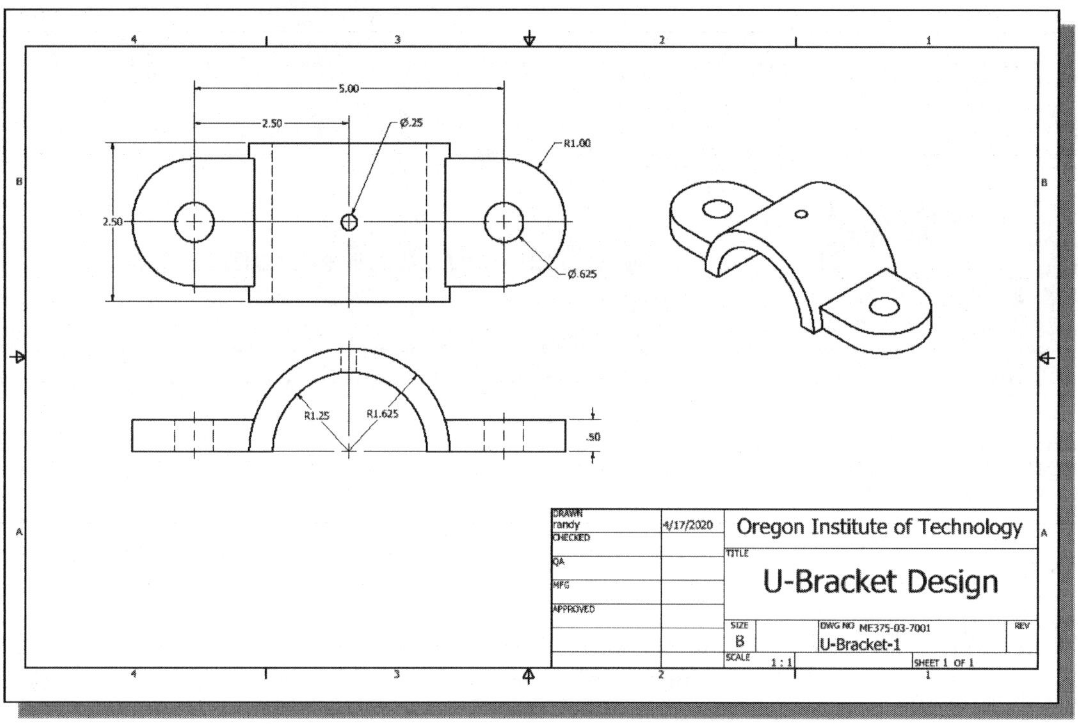

3D Model-Based Definition

Model-based definition (MBD) is the practice of using 3D models within 3D CAD software to provide specifications for individual components and assemblies. The types of information included are geometric dimensioning and tolerancing (GD&T), component level materials, assembly level bills of materials, engineering configurations, design intent, etc. With this new set of tools, the mental translation of 3D models to two-dimensional (2D) drawings for communicating information and then back to 3D models for manufacturing is replaced with a representative 3D prototype that provides all necessary information to communicate and manufacture the product. This approach means faster and more precise product communication, which can greatly improve the product development process.

Autodesk Inventor provides users with the ability to access powerful digital product information for communication and in support of operations such as inspection, manufacturing, or marketing. With software/hardware improvements, it is now feasible to use the solid modeling software to document and communicate all production and manufacturing information in a three-dimensional (3D) environment. In *Autodesk Inventor 2027*, exciting tools are now available for documenting and communicating product designs. We can apply 3D-based annotation, in conjunction with engineering drawing conventions, directly to the solid model or assembly. This new solids-based documentation approach provides the ability to create, manage, and deliver process-specific information without the need for paper-based documentation. In this lesson, the general procedure of creating 3D model-based definition is also illustrated.

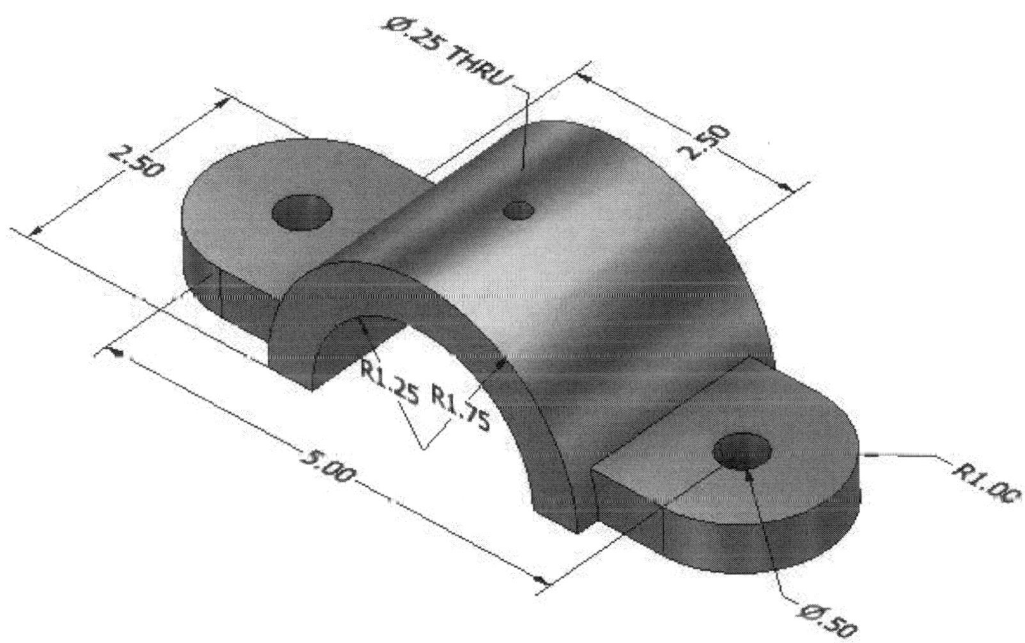

Starting Autodesk Inventor

1. Select the **Autodesk Inventor** option on the *Start* menu or select the **Autodesk Inventor** icon on the desktop to start Autodesk Inventor. The Autodesk Inventor main window will appear on the screen.

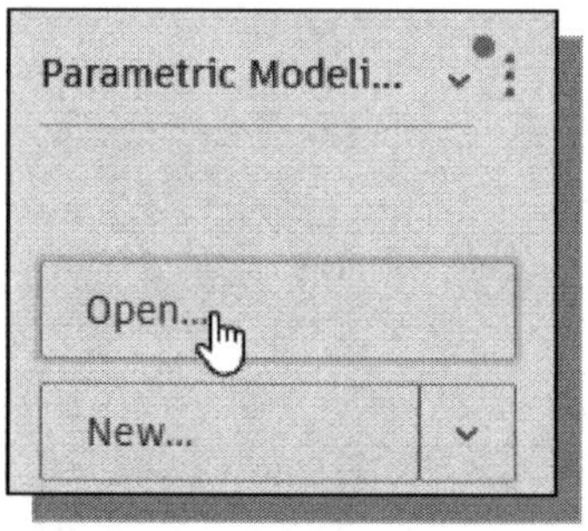

2. Once the program is loaded into memory, select the **Open** option as shown.

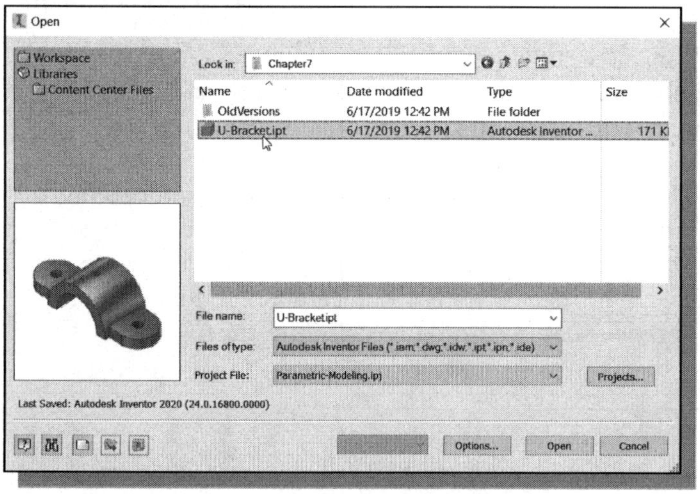

3. In the *File name* list box, select the **U-Bracket.ipt** file. (Use the **Projects** option to locate the file if the wrong project is displayed in the *Project File* box.)

4. Click on the **Open** button to accept the selected settings.

Drawing Mode – 2D Paper Space

Autodesk Inventor allows us to generate 2D engineering drawings from solid models so that we can plot the drawings to any exact scale on paper. An engineering drawing is a tool that can be used to communicate engineering ideas/designs to manufacturing, purchasing, service, and other departments. Until now we have been working in ***model space*** to create our design in ***full size***. We can arrange our design on a two-dimensional sheet of paper so that the plotted hardcopy is exactly what we want. This two-dimensional sheet of paper is known as ***paper space*** in *AutoCAD* and *Autodesk Inventor*. We can place borders and title blocks, objects that are less critical to our design, on *paper space*. In general, each company uses a set of standards for drawing content, based on the type of product and also on established internal processes. The appearance of an engineering drawing varies depending on when, where, and for what purpose it is produced. However, the general procedure for creating an engineering drawing from a solid model is fairly well defined. *In Autodesk Inventor*, creation of 2D engineering drawings from solid models consists of four basic steps: drawing sheet formatting, creating/positioning views, annotations, and printing/plotting.

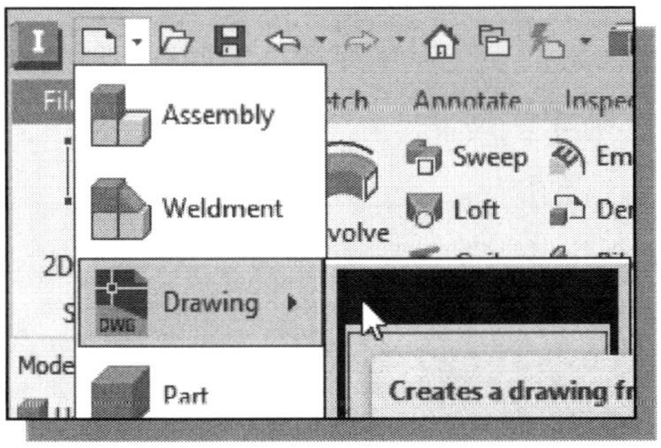

1. Click on the **drop-down arrow** next to the **New File** icon in the *Quick Access* toolbar area to display the available **New File** options.

2. Select **Drawing**, without choosing any drawing option, from the option list.

➢ Note that a new graphics window appears on the screen. We can switch between the solid model and the drawing by clicking the corresponding tabs or graphics windows.

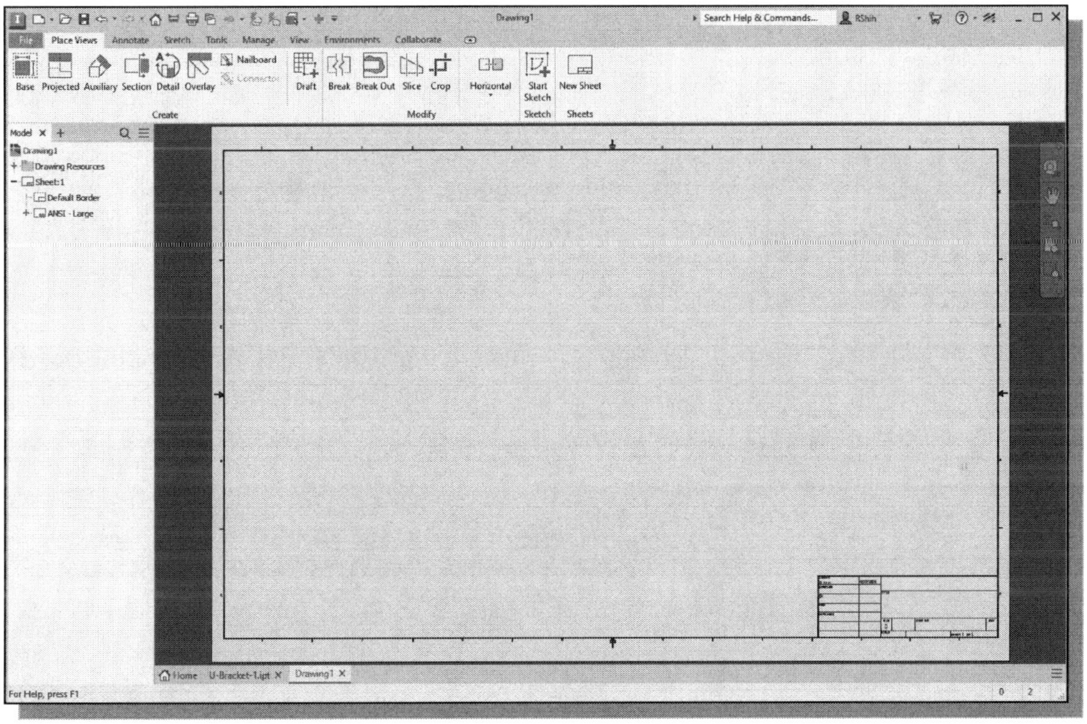

❖ In the graphics window, *Autodesk Inventor* displays a default drawing sheet that includes a title block. The drawing sheet is placed on the 2D paper space, and the title block also indicates the paper size being used.

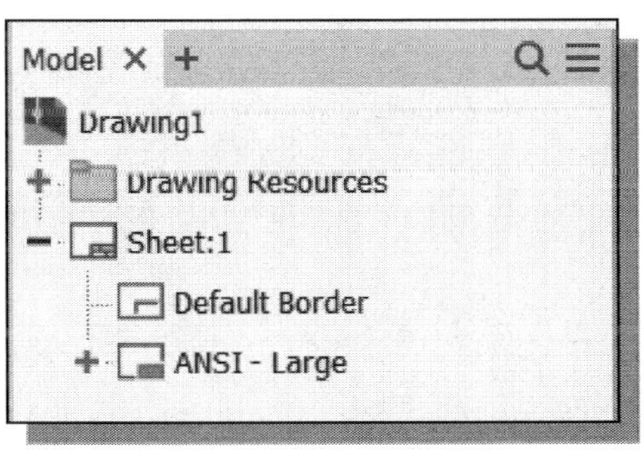

➢ In the *browser* area, the **Drawing1** icon is displayed at the top, which indicates that we have switched to ***Drawing Mode***. **Sheet1** is the current drawing sheet that is displayed in the graphics window.

Drawing Sheet Format

1. Choose the **Manage** tab in the *Ribbon* toolbar.

2. Click **Styles Editor** in the *Styles and Standards* toolbar as shown.

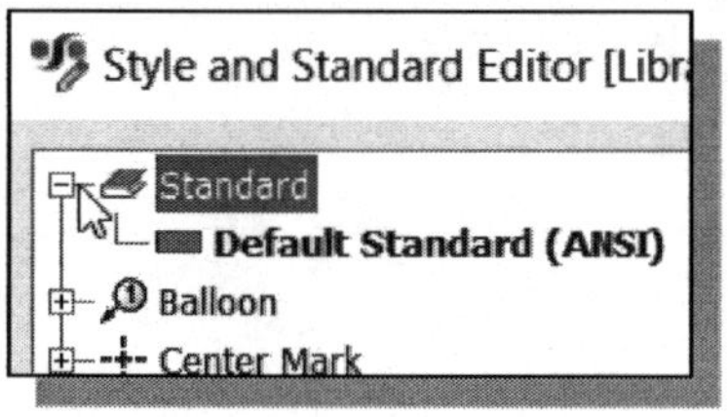

3. Click on the [+] sign in front of **Standard** to display the current active standard. Note that there can only be **one active standard** for each drawing.

4. Set the *Filter Styles Setting* to display **All Styles**. Note that besides the default ANSI drafting standard, other standards, such as ISO, GB, BSI, DIN, and JIS, are also available.

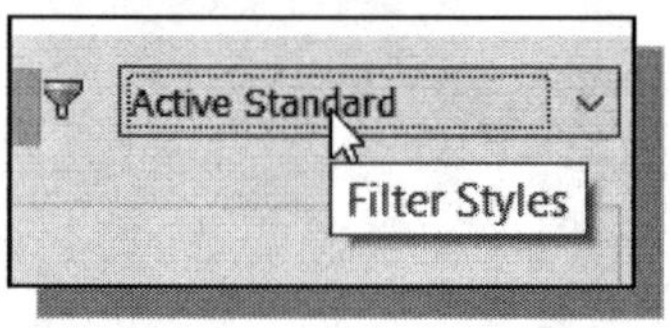

5. Set the *Filter Styles Setting* to display **Active Standard** and note only the active standard is displayed.

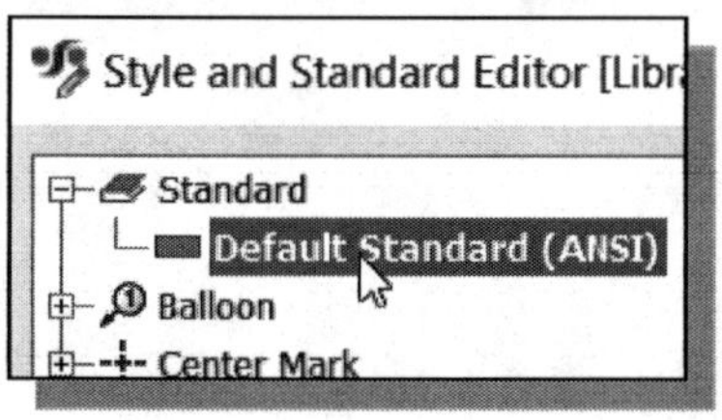

6. Click **Default Standard (ANSI)** to toggle the display of detailed settings for the current standard.

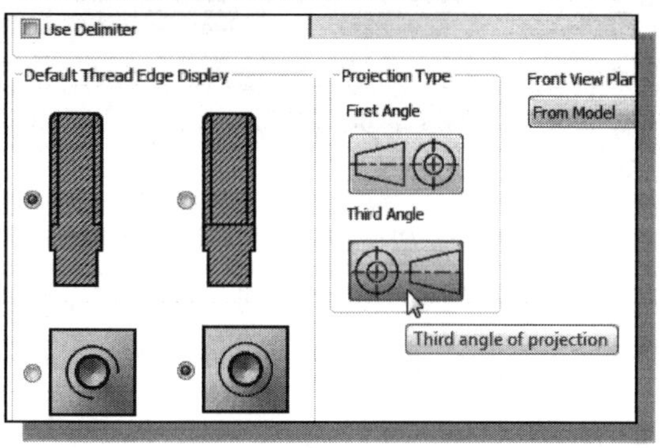

7. In the *View Preferences* page, confirm that the *Projection Type* is set to **Third Angle of projection**.

❖ Notice the different settings available in the *General* option window, such as the *Units* setting and the *Line Weight* setting.

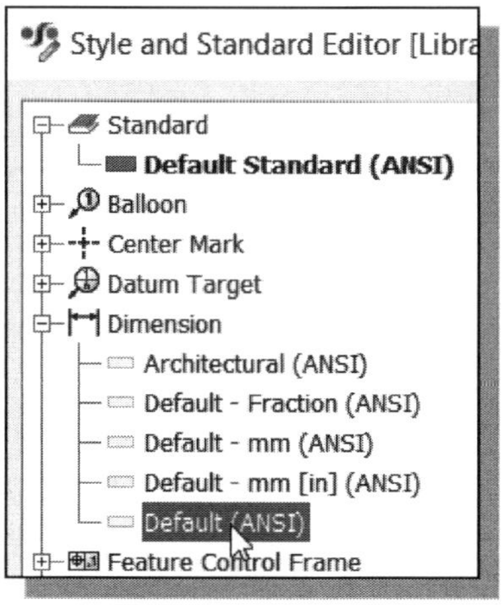

8. Choose **Default (ANSI)** in the **Dimension** list as shown.

➢ Note that the default *Dimension Style* in Inventor is based on the ANSI Y14.5-1994 standard.

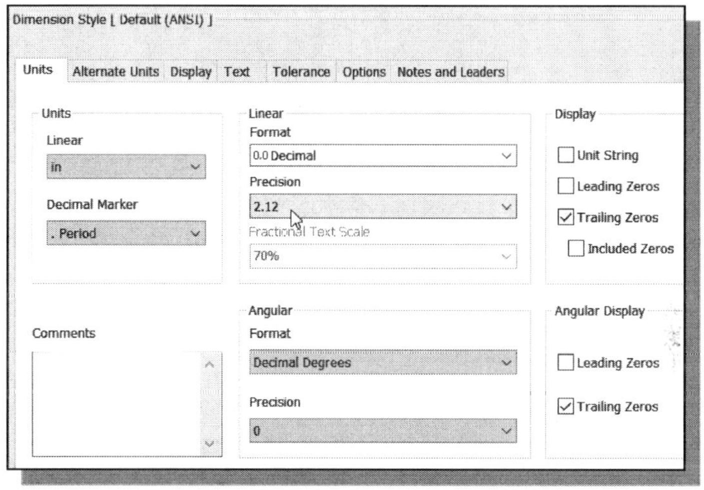

9. The **Units** tab contains the settings for linear/angular units. Note that the *Linear* units are set to **Decimal** and the *Precision* for linear dimensions is set to two digits after the decimal point.

10. Click on the **Text** tab to display and examine the settings for dimension text. Note that the default *Dimension Style*, DEFAULT-ANSI, cannot be modified. However, new *Dimension Styles* can be created and modified.

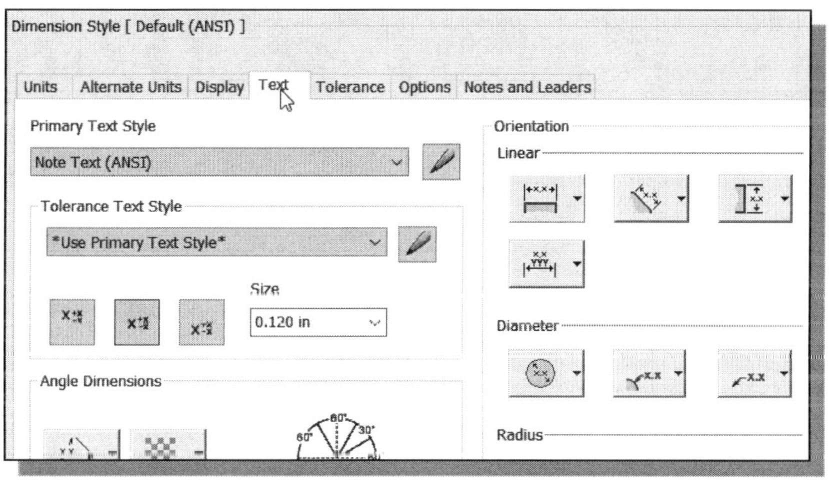

➢ On your own, click on the other tabs and examine the other *Settings* available.

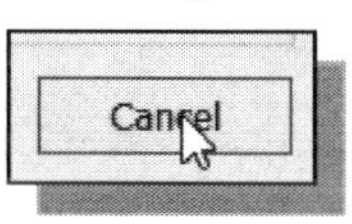

11. Click on the **Cancel** button to exit the *Style and Standard Editor* dialog box.

Using the Pre-defined Drawing Sheet Formats

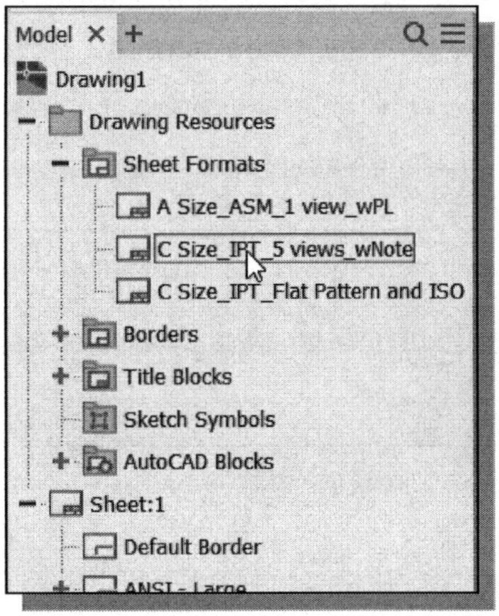

1. Inside the *Drawing Browser* window, click on the **[>]** symbol in front of **Drawing Resources** to display the available options.

2. Click on the **[>]** symbol in front of **Sheet Formats** to display the available pre-defined sheet formats.

❖ Notice several pre-defined *sheet formats*, each with a different view configuration, are available in the *browser* window.

3. Inside the *browser* window, **double-click** on the **C size IPT 5 view** sheet format.

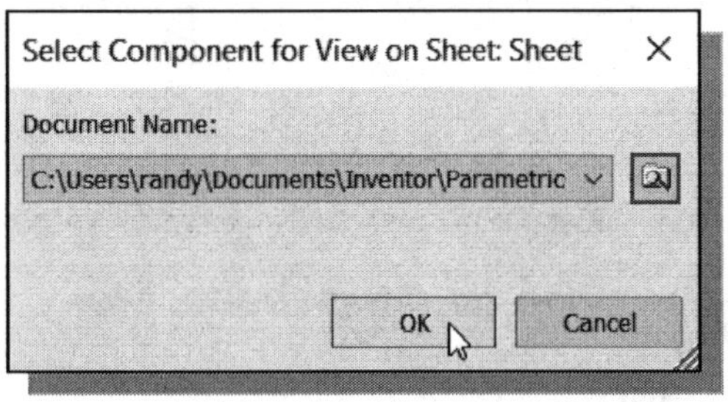

4. Click on the **OK** button to accept the default part file and generate the 2D views.

➢ The ***U-Bracket*** model is the only model opened. By default, all of the 2D drawings will be generated from this model file.

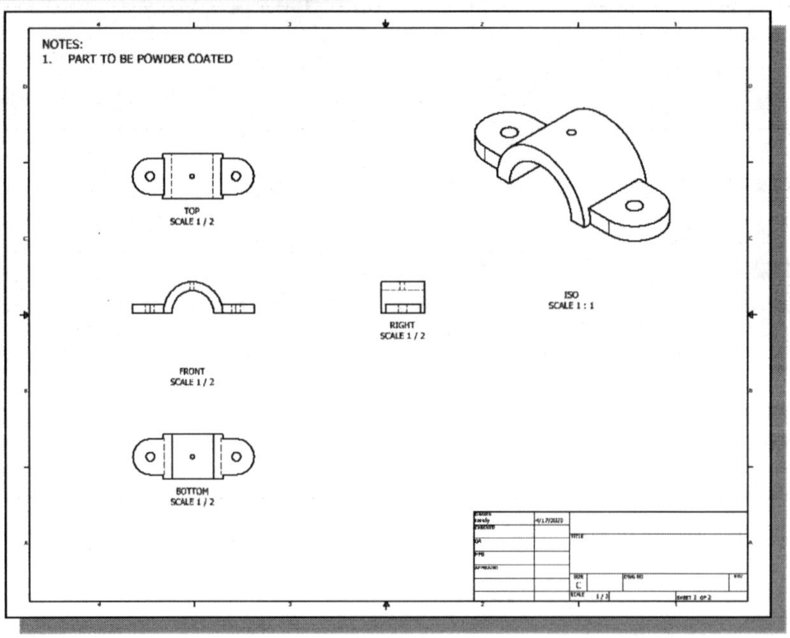

❖ We have created a C-size drawing of the *U-Bracket* model. Autodesk Inventor automatically generates and positions five of the pre-defined views of the model inside the title block.

Activate, Delete and Edit Drawing Sheets

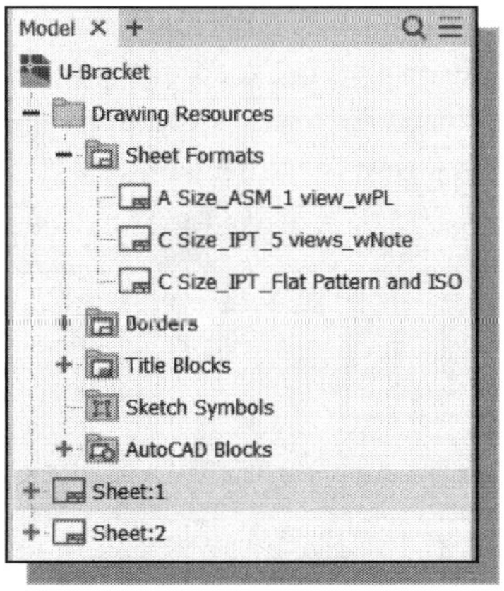

❖ Note that we have created two drawing sheets, displayed in the *Drawing Browser* window as Sheet1, and Sheet2. Autodesk Inventor allows us to create multiple 2D drawings from the same model file, which can be used for different purposes.

➢ In most cases, the pre-defined *sheet formats* can be used to quickly set up the views needed. However, it is also important to understand the concepts and principles involved in setting up the views. In the next sections, the procedures to set up drawing sheets and different types of views are illustrated.

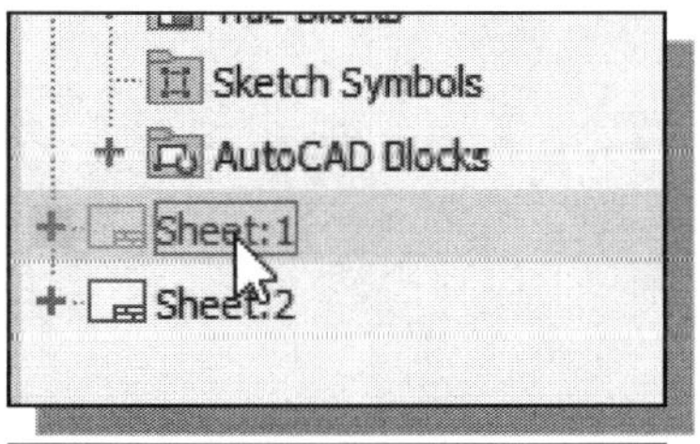

1. Inside the *Drawing Browser* window, double-click on **Sheet1** to activate this drawing sheet.

   • Alternatively, use the right-mouse-click and select **Activate** in the option menu.

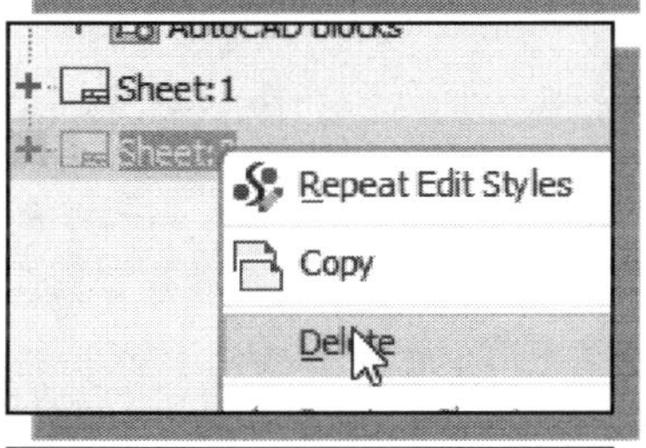

2. Inside the *Drawing Browser* window, right-click on **Sheet2** to display the option menu.

3. Select **Delete Sheet** in the option menu to remove the Sheet2 drawing.

4. In the *warning window*, click on the **OK** button to proceed with deleting the drawing.

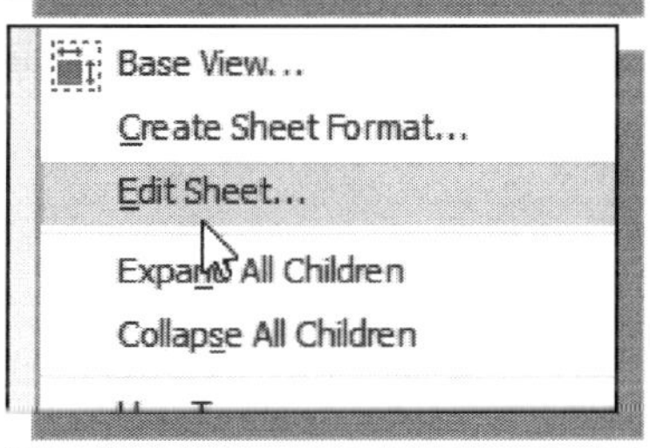

5. Inside the *Drawing Browser* window, **right-click** on **Sheet1** to display the *option menu.*

6. Select **Edit Sheet** in the option menu to display the settings for the *Sheet1* drawing.

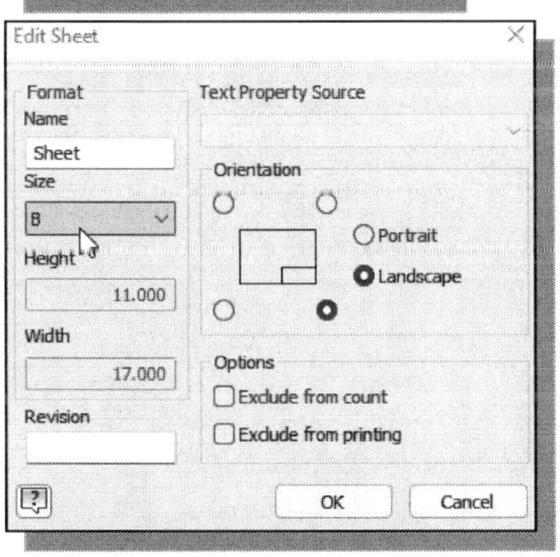

7. Set the sheet size to **B-size** and click on the **OK** button to exit the *Edit Sheet* dialog box.

Add a Base View

In *Autodesk Inventor Drawing Mode*, the first drawing view we create is called a **base view**. A *base view* is the primary view in the drawing; other views can be derived from this view. When creating a *base view*, Autodesk Inventor allows us to specify the view to be shown. By default, Autodesk Inventor will treat the *world XY plane* as the front view of the solid model. Note that there can be more than one *base view* in a drawing.

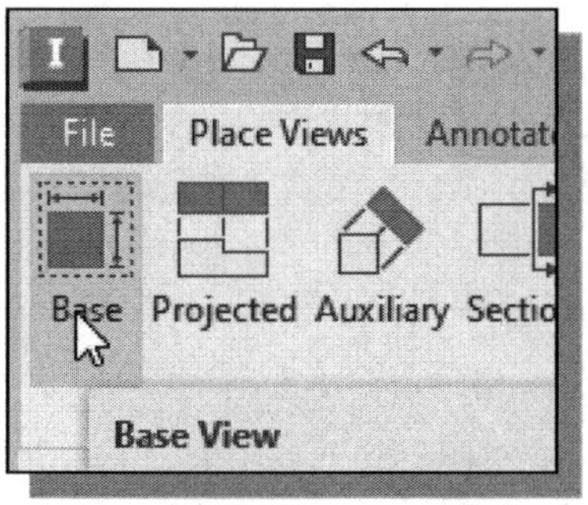

1. Click on the **Base View** in the *Place Views* panel to create a base view.

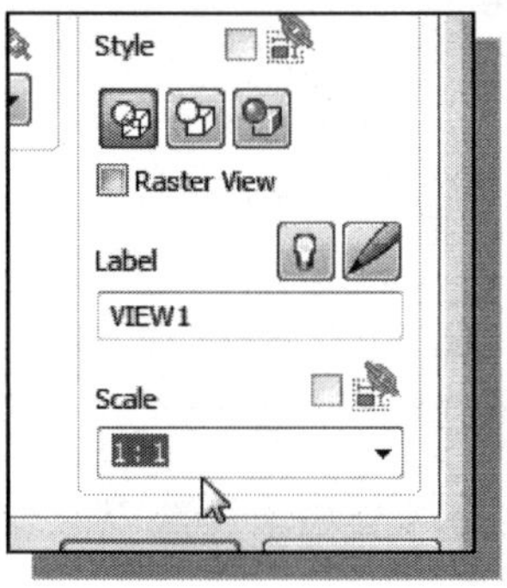

2. In the *Drawing View* dialog box, set the **Scale** to **1 : 1** and Style to **Hidden Line** as shown in the figure below.

3. In the *graphics area*, click on the arrows to switch to different views; set it to the **Front View** as shown in the below figure.

4. Inside the *graphics window,* drag and place the ***base*** view near the lower left corner of the graphics window as shown below. Click **OK** to place the *base view* and close the *Drawing View* dialog box.

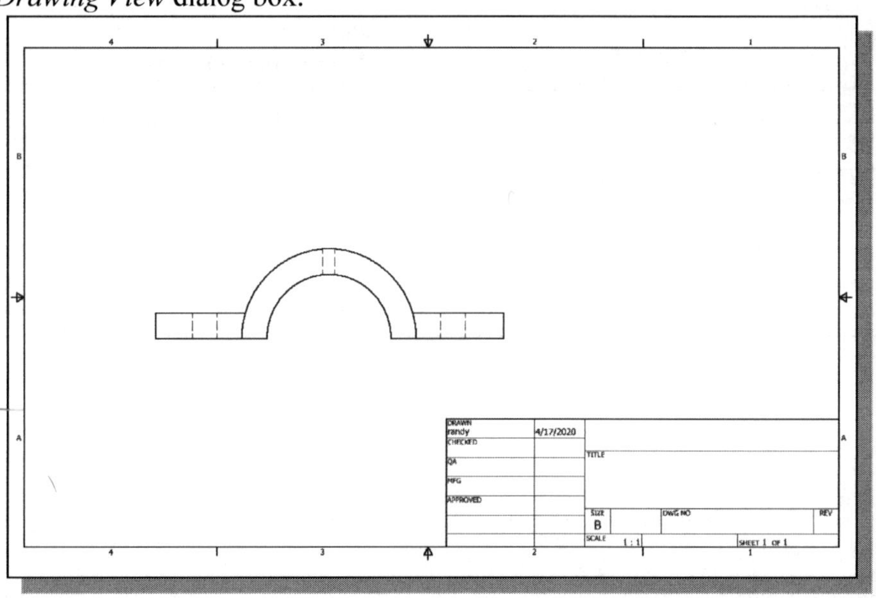

Create Projected Views

In *Autodesk Inventor Drawing Mode*, **projected views** can be created with a first-angle or third-angle projection, depending on the drafting standard used for the drawing. We must have a base view before a projected view can be created. Projected views can be orthographic projections or isometric projections. Orthographic projections are aligned to the base view and inherit the base view's scale and display settings. Isometric projections are not aligned to the base view.

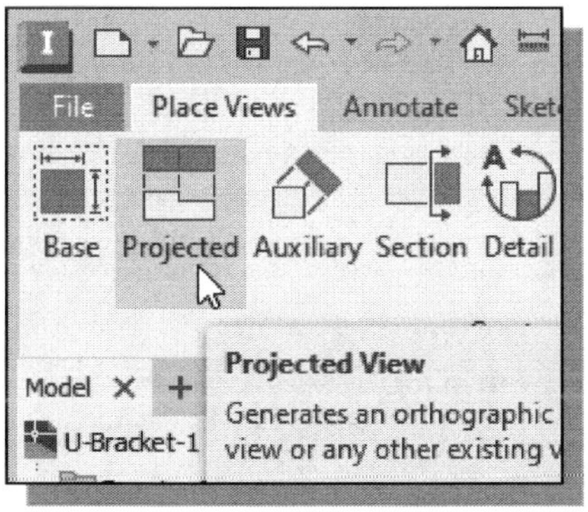

1. Click the **Projected View** button in the *Place Views* panel; this command allows us to create projected views.

2. Select the **base view** as the main view for the projected views.

3. Move the cursor **above** the *base view* and select a location to position the projected side view of the model.

4. Move the cursor toward the upper right corner of the title block and select a location to position the isometric view of the model as shown below.

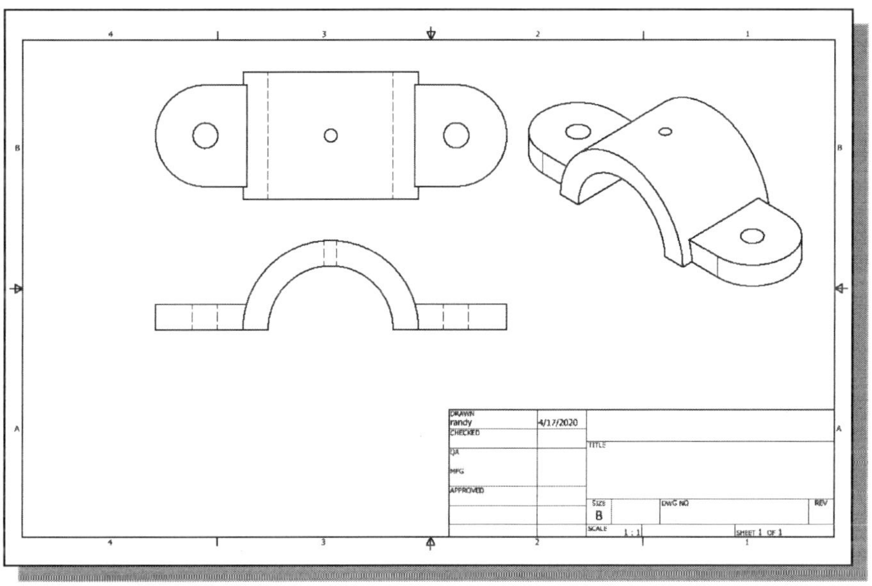

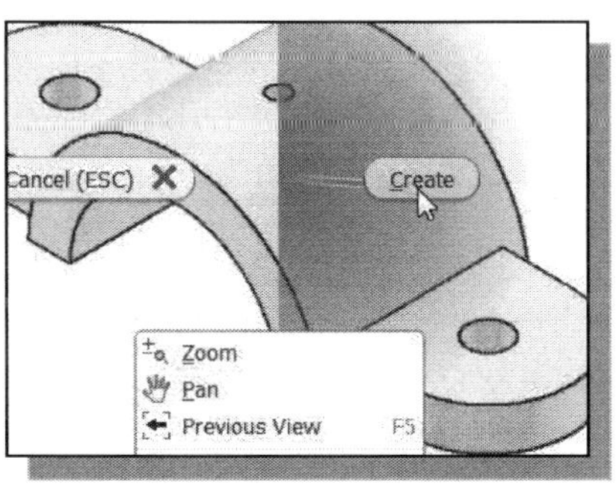

5. Inside the *graphics window*, right-click once to bring up the **option menu**.

6. Select **Create** to proceed with creating the two projected views.

Adjust the View Scale

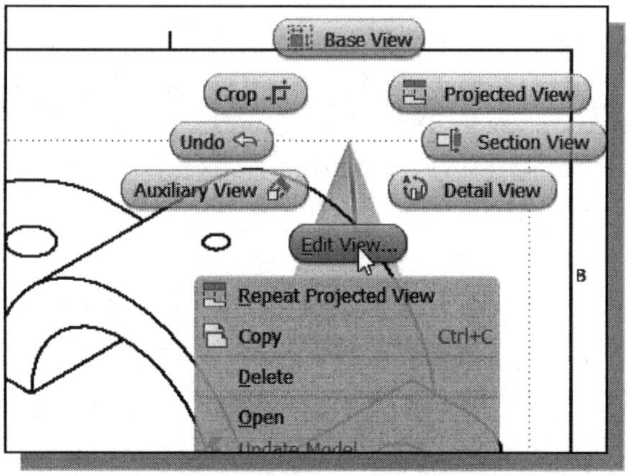

1. Move the cursor on top of the *isometric view* and watch for the box around the entire view indicating the view is selectable as shown in the figure. **Right-click** once to bring up the *option menu.*

2. Select **Edit View** in the option menu.

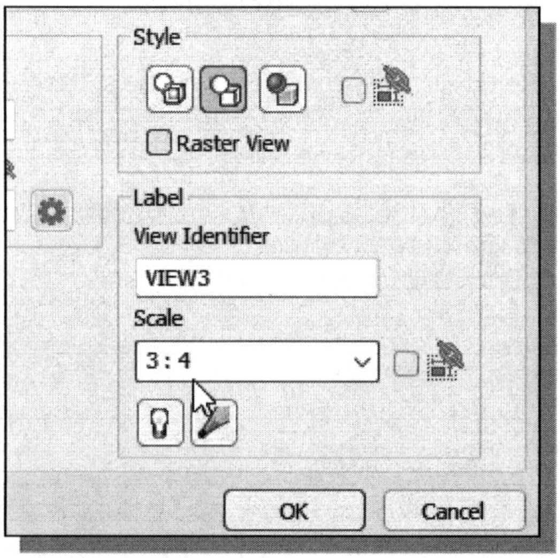

3. Inside the *Drawing View* dialog box set the *Scale* to **3:4** as shown in the figure.

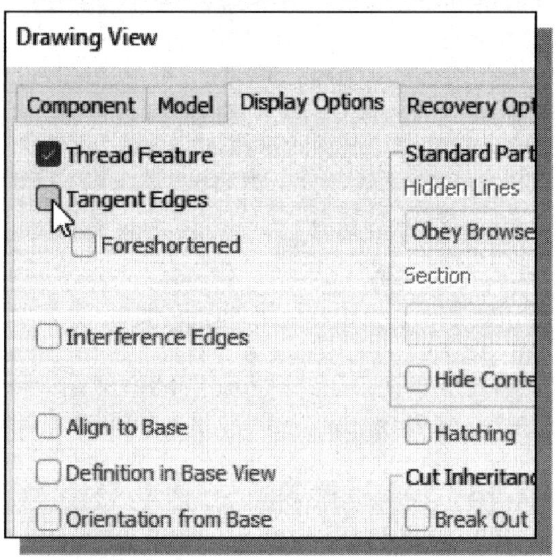

4. Click on the **Display Options** tab and turn ***OFF*** the **Tangent Edges** option as shown.

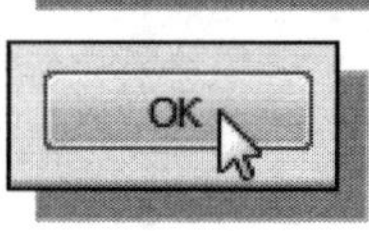

5. Click on the **OK** button to accept the settings and proceed with updating the drawing views.

Repositioning Views

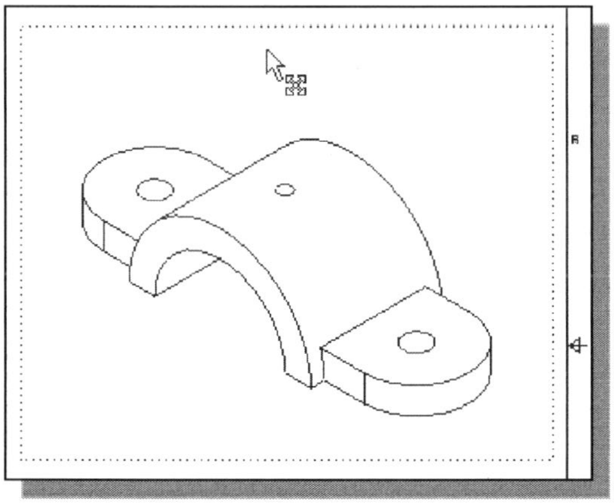

1. Move the cursor on top of the isometric view and watch for the **four-arrow Move symbol** as the cursor is near the border indicating the view can be dragged to a new location as shown in the figure.

2. Press and hold down the left-mouse-button and reposition the view to a new location.

3. On your own, reposition the views we have created so far. Note that the top view can be repositioned only in the vertical direction. The top view remains aligned to the base view, the front view.

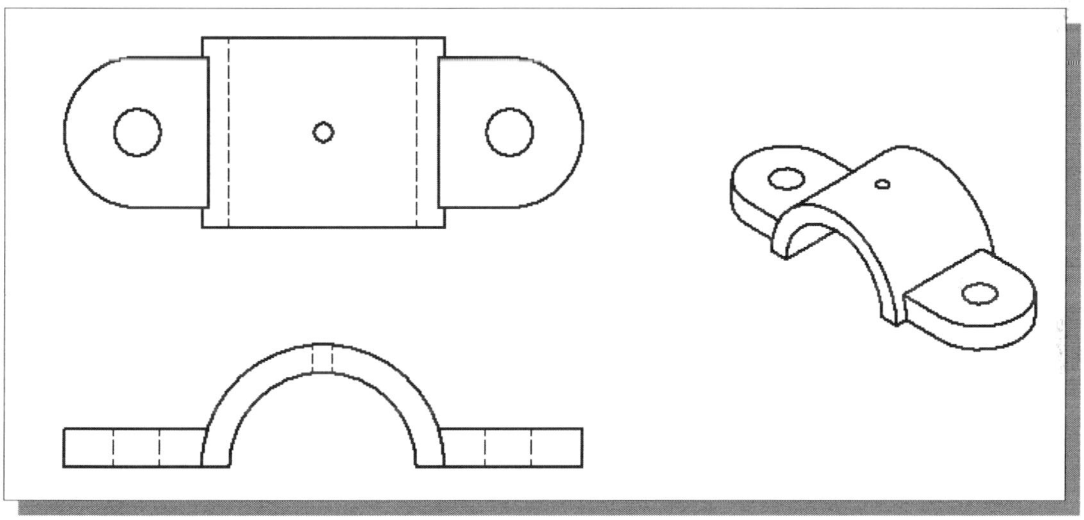

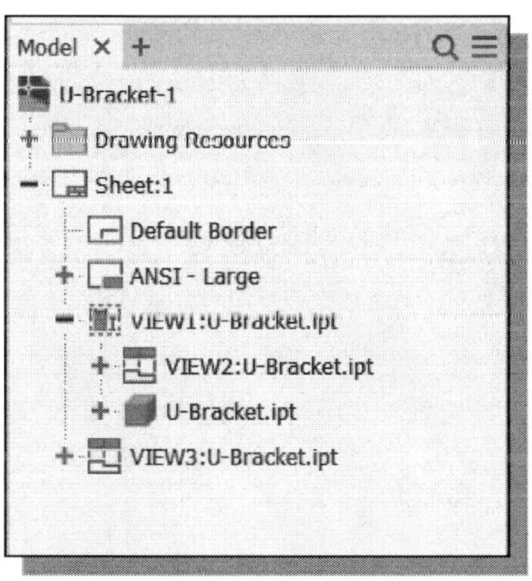

➢ Note that in the *Drawing Browser* area, a hierarchy of the created views is displayed under Sheet1. The base view, View1, is listed as the first view created, with View2 linked to it. The top view, View2, is projected from the base view, View1. The implied parent/child relationship is maintained by the system. Drawing views are associated with the model and the drawing sheets. As we create views from the base view, they are nested beneath the base view in the *browser*.

Display Feature Dimensions

By default, feature dimensions are not displayed in 2D views in Autodesk Inventor. We can change the default settings while creating the views or switch on the display of the parametric dimensions using the option menu.

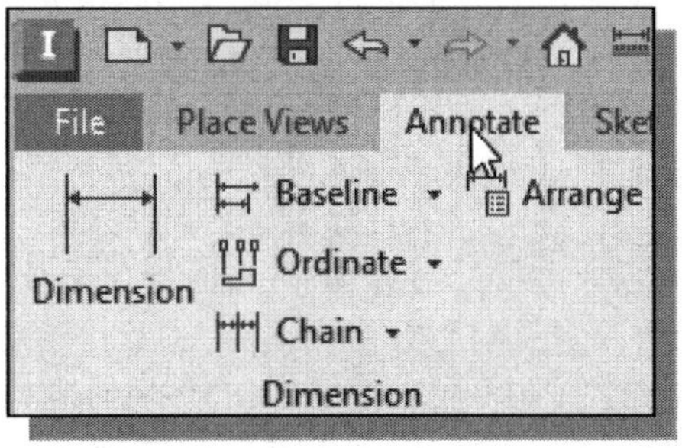

1. Select **Annotate** by left-clicking once in the *Ribbon* toolbar system.

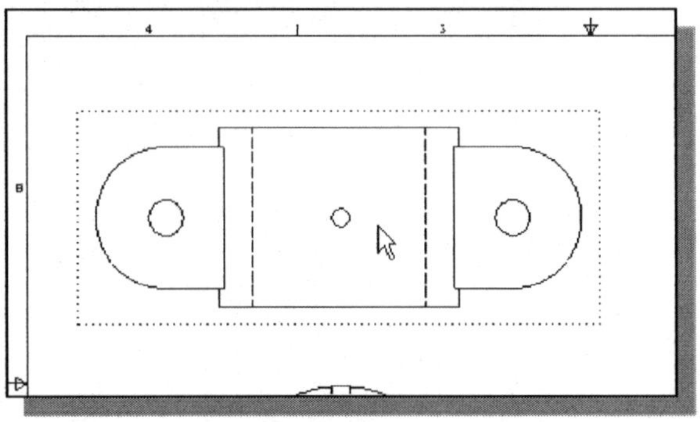

2. Move the cursor on top of the ***top*** view of the model and watch for the box around the entire view indicating the view is selectable as shown in the figure.

3. Inside the graphics window**, right-click** once on the top view to bring up the option menu.

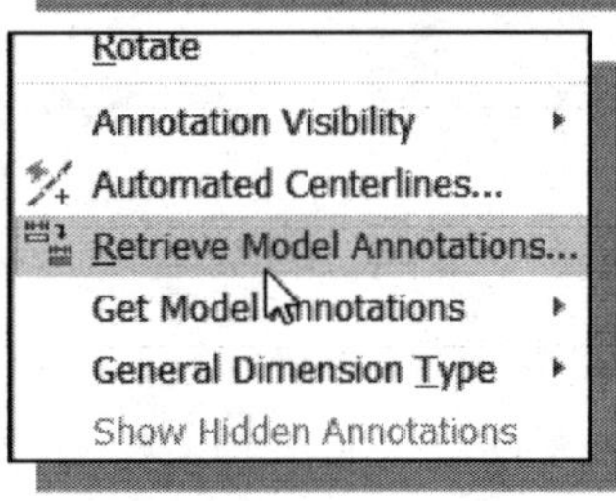

4. Select **Retrieve Model Annotations** to display the parametric dimensions used to create the model. Note the command can also be accessed through the *Ribbon* toolbar.

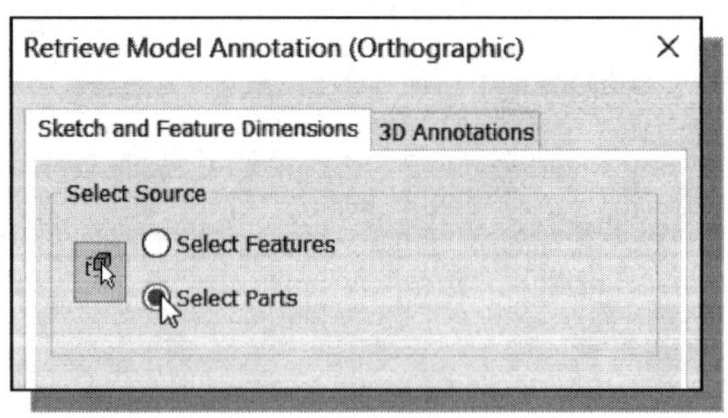

5. In the *Sketch and Features Dimensions* tab, set the *Select Source* option to **Select Parts** as shown.

6. Move the *Retrieve Model annotations* dialog box by pressing the title of the box and dragging with the left-mouse button to the right side of the view.

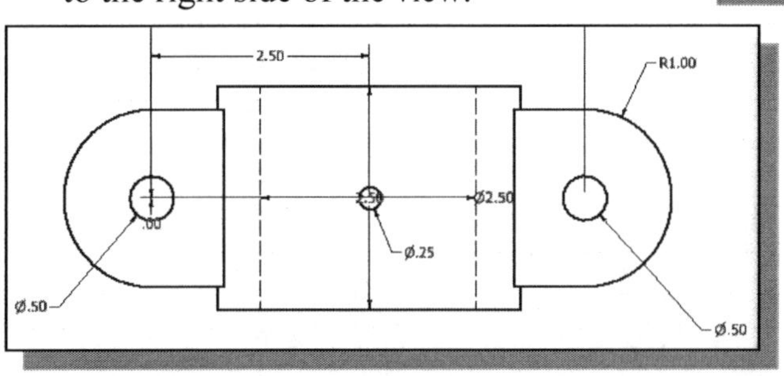

➢ Note that many of the dimensions used to create the part are now displayed in the selected view.

➢ The system now expects us to select the dimensions to retrieve.

7. On your own, select the dimensions to retrieve by left-clicking once on the dimensions as shown. (Note that only selected dimensions are retrieved.)

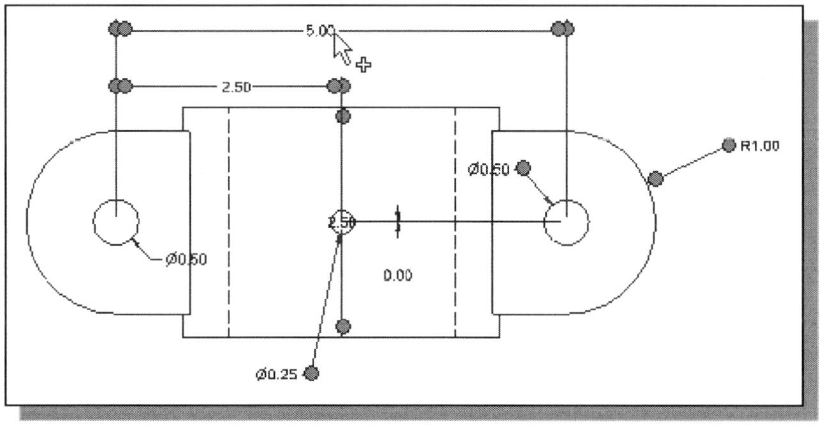

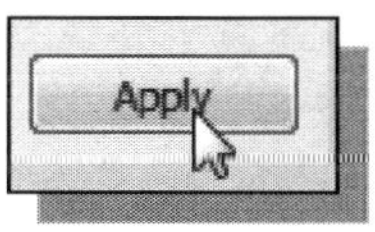

8. Click on the **Apply** button to proceed with retrieving the selected dimensions.

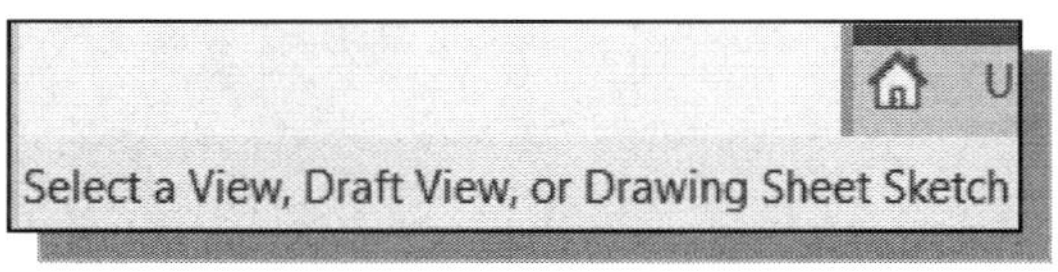

9. In the *message* area, the Inventor system expects us to **Select a View** as shown.

10. Select the ***front*** view.

11. On your own, retrieve the three dimensions as shown.

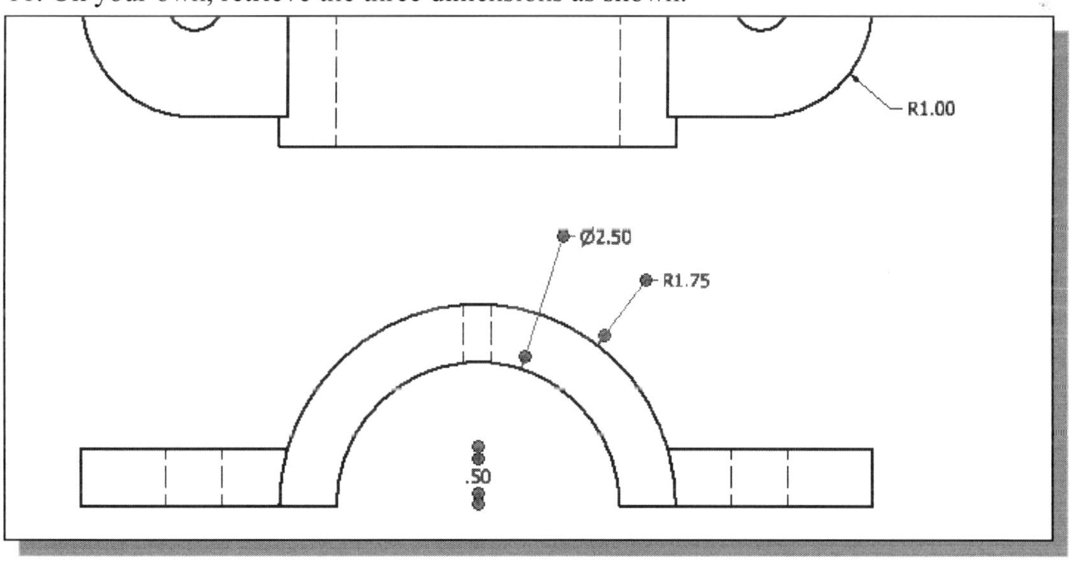

12. Click on the **OK** button to end the Retrieve Model Annotations command.

Repositioning and Hiding Feature Dimensions

1. Move the cursor on top of the width dimension text **5.00**, and watch for when the dimension text becomes highlighted with the four-arrow symbol indicating the dimension is selectable.

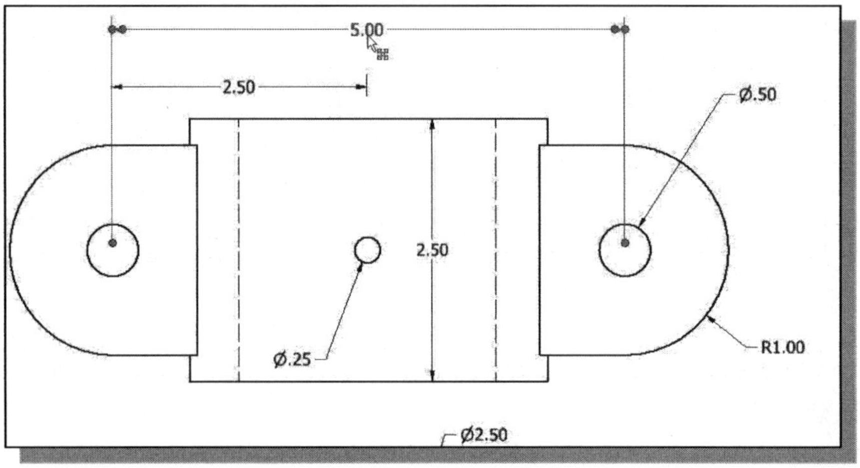

2. Reposition the dimension by using the left-mouse-button and drag the dimension text to a new location.

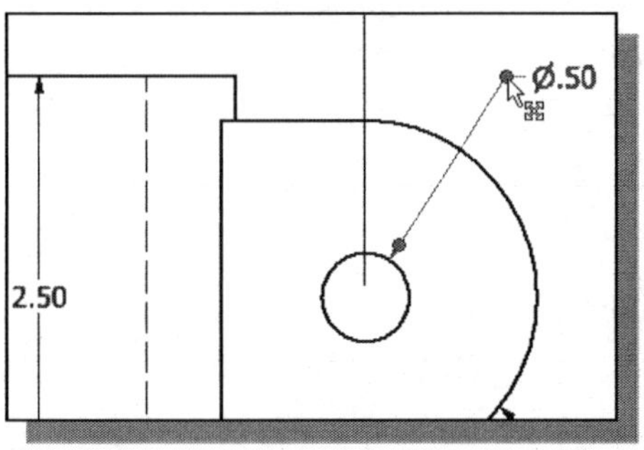

3. Move the cursor on top of the diameter dimension **0.5** and drag the grip point green dot associated with the dimension to reposition the dimension. Note that we can also drag on the dimension text, which only repositions the text.

4. On your own, reposition the dimensions displayed in the *top* view as shown in the figure below.

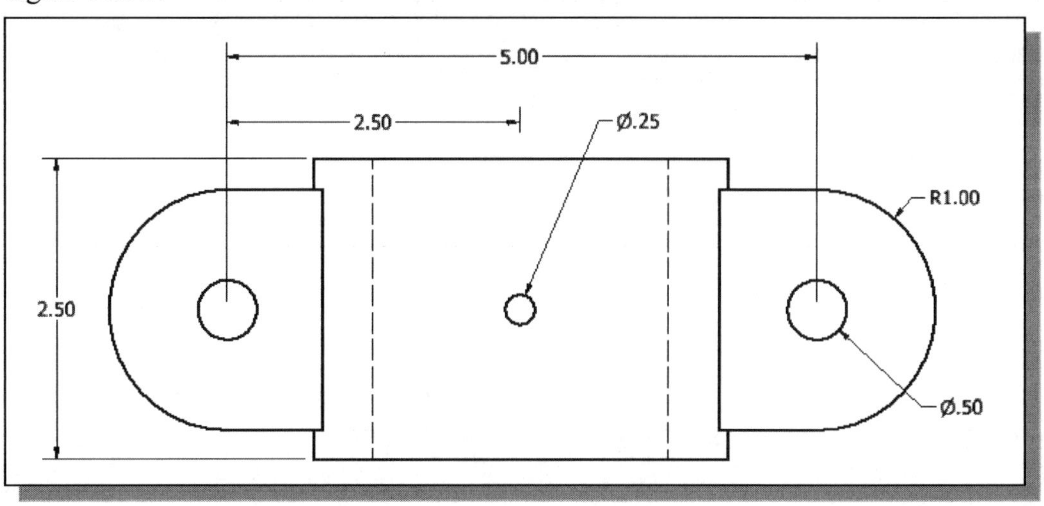

5. Move the cursor on top of the radius dimension **R 1.75** and notice two green grip points appear. The grip points can be used to reposition the dimension.

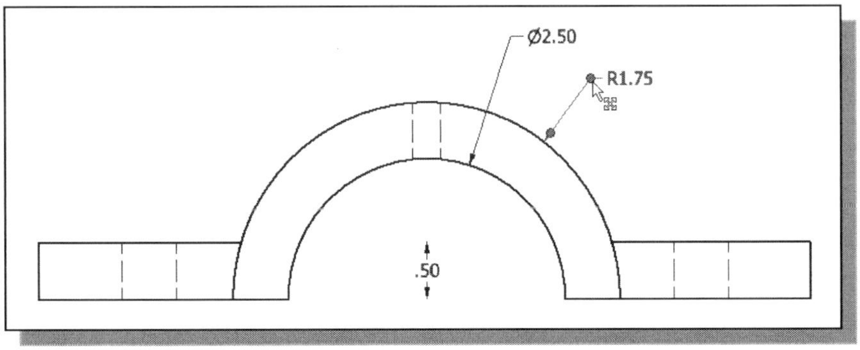

6. Use the left-mouse-button and drag the grip point near the center of the view and notice the arrowhead is automatically adjusted to the inside, as shown in the figures below.

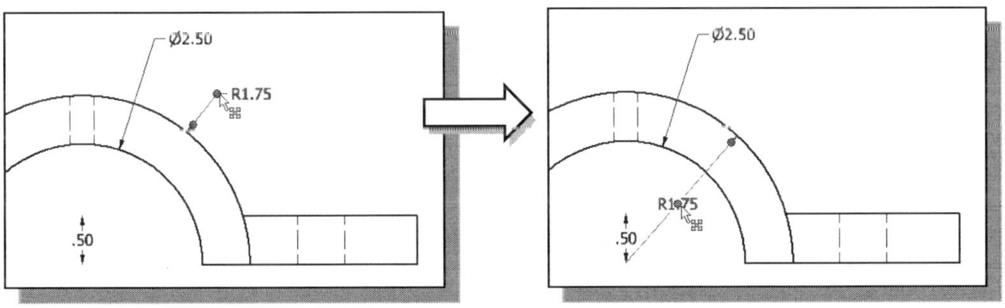

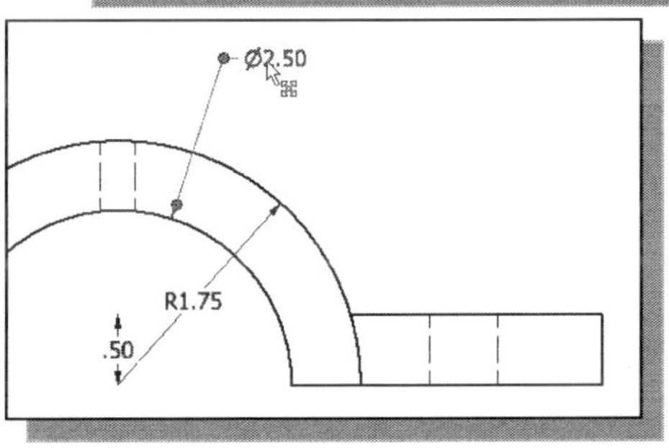

7. Move the cursor on top of the diameter dimension **2.50** and left-mouse-click once to select the dimension.

8. Right-click once on the dimension text to bring up the **option menu**.

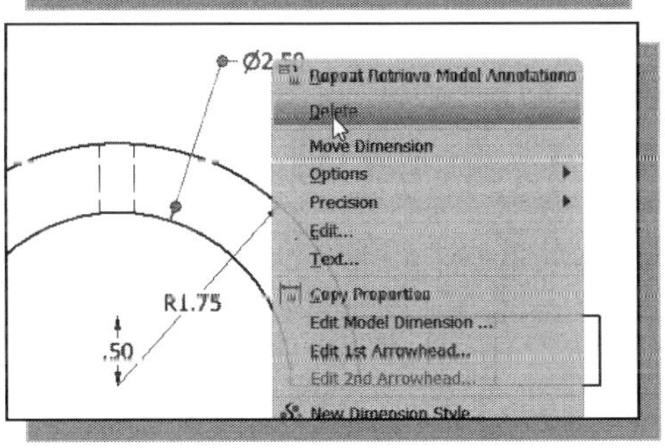

9. Select **Delete** to remove the dimension from the display.

➢ Note that the feature dimension is deleted from the display, but the removed dimension still remains in the database. In other words, the feature dimension is turned off or is hidden. Any feature dimensions can be removed from the display just as they can be displayed.

Add Additional Dimensions – Reference Dimensions

Besides displaying the **feature dimensions**, dimensions used to create the features, we can also add additional **reference dimensions** in the drawing. *Feature dimensions* are used to control the geometry, whereas *reference dimensions* are controlled by the existing geometry. In the drawing layout, therefore, we can ***add*** *or* ***delete*** *reference dimensions*, but we can only *hide* the *feature dimensions.* One should try to use as many *feature dimensions* as possible and add *reference dimensions* only if necessary. It is also more effective to use *feature dimensions* in the drawing layout since they are created when the model was built. Note that additional *Drawing Mode* entities, such as lines and arcs, can be added to drawing views. Before *Drawing Mode* entities can be used in a reference dimension, they must be associated to a *drawing view*.

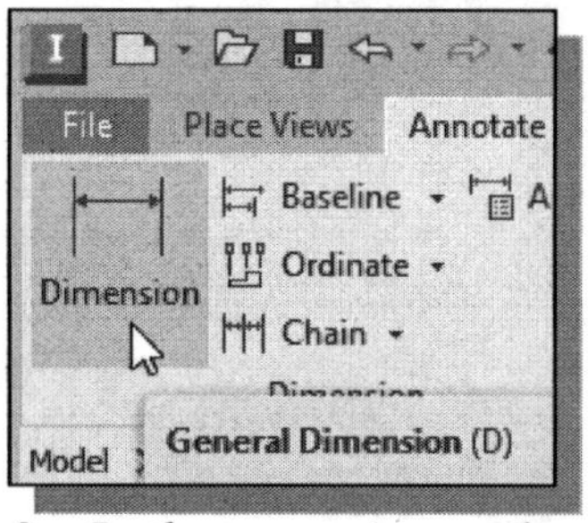

1. Click on the **General Dimension** button.

➢ Note the **General Dimension** command is similar to the **Smart Dimensioning** command in the *3D Modeling Mode.*

2. In the prompt area, the message "*Select first object:*" is displayed. Select the smaller arc of the front view.

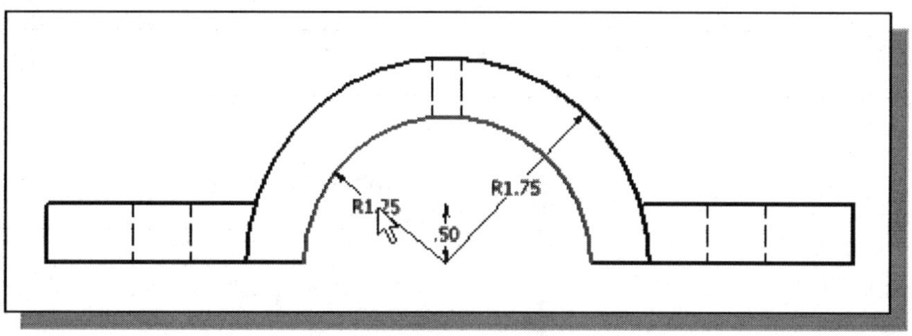

3. Place the dimension text on the inside of the arc as shown in the above figure.

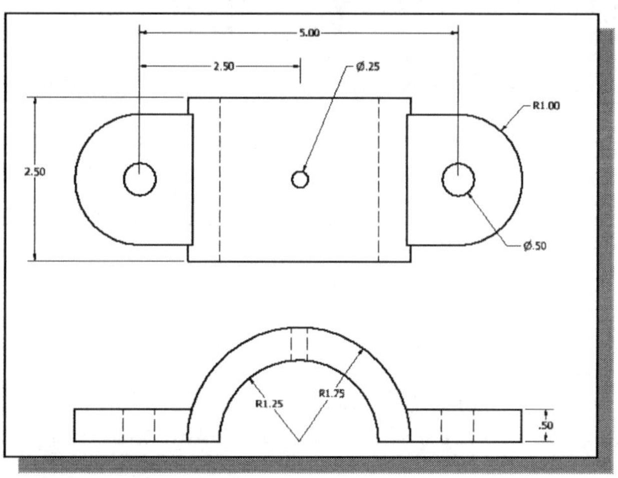

4. On your own, position the necessary dimensions for the design as shown in the figure.

➢ Note the extension lines can also be repositioned by dragging the associated grip points.

Add Center Marks and Center Lines

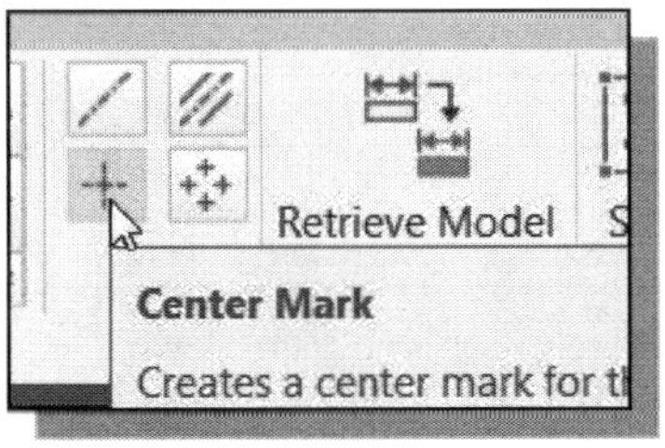

1. Click on the **Center Mark** button in the *Drawing Annotation* window.

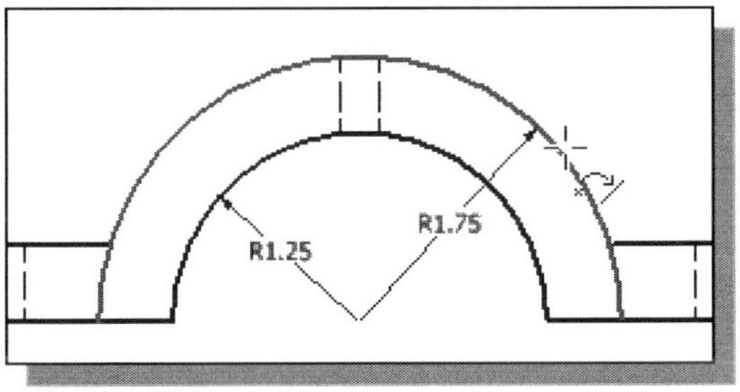

2. Click on the larger arc in the front view to add the center mark.

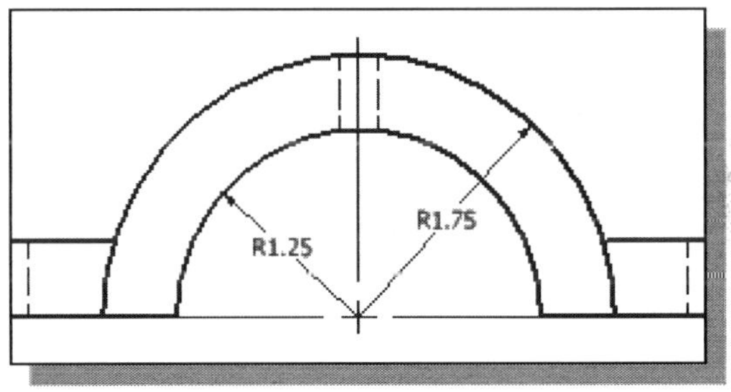

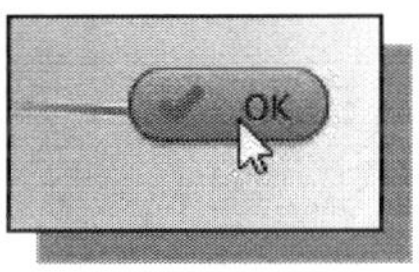

3. Inside the *graphics window*, click once with the **right-mouse-button** to display the option menu. Select **OK** in the pop-up menu to end the Center Mark command.

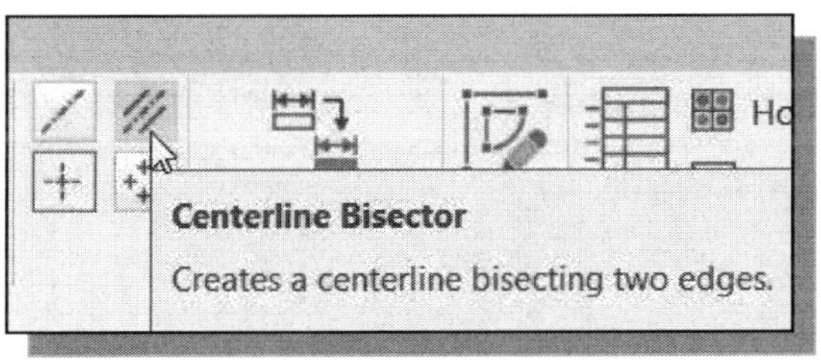

4. Select **Centerline Bisector** from the option list.

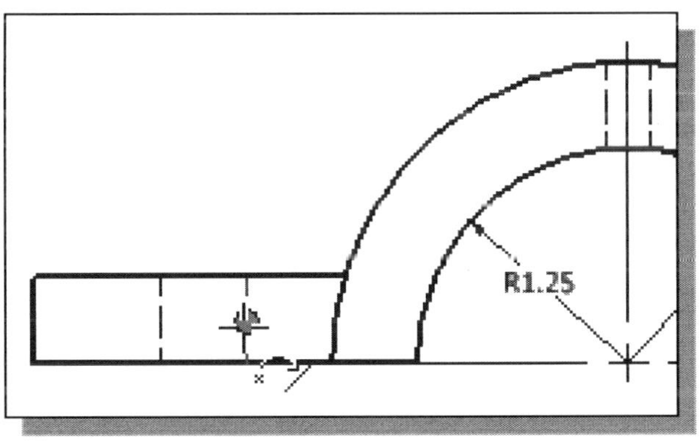

5. Click on the two hidden edges of one of the *drill* features of the front view as shown in the figure.

6. On your own, repeat the above step and create another centerline on the right side of the front view as shown.

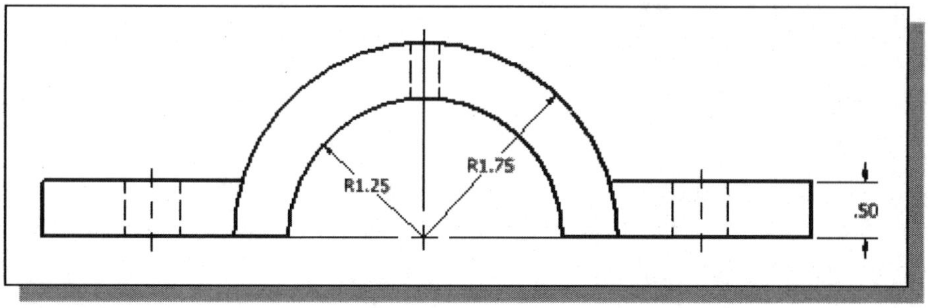

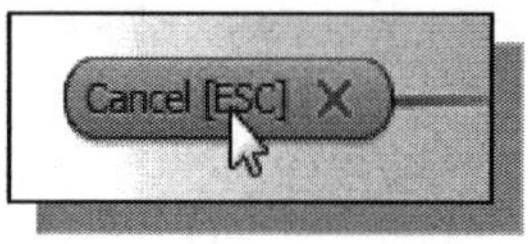

7. Inside the graphics window, click once with the right-mouse-button to display the option menu. Select **Cancel [ESC]** in the pop-up menu to end the Centerline Bisector command.

8. On your own, repeat the above steps and create additional centerlines as shown in the figure below.

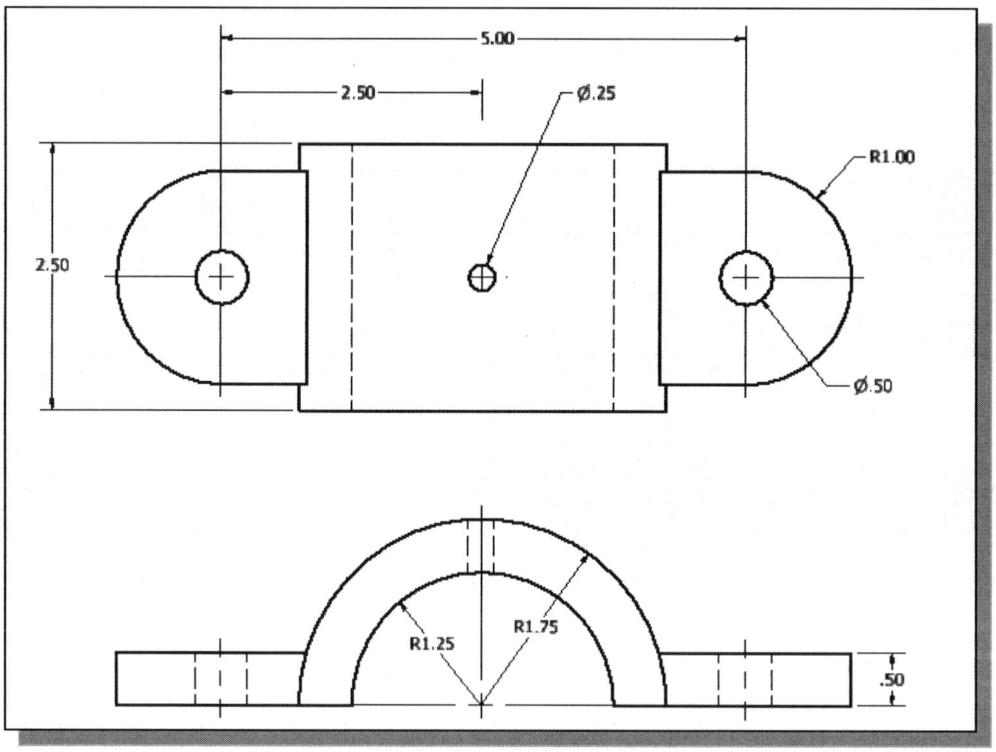

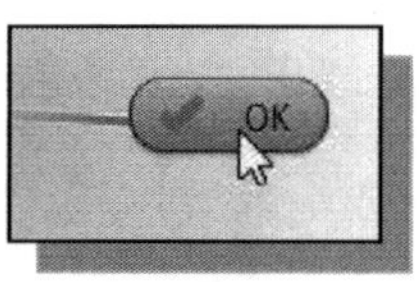

9. Inside the graphics window, click once with the right-mouse-button to display the option menu. Select **OK** in the pop-up menu to end the Centerline command.

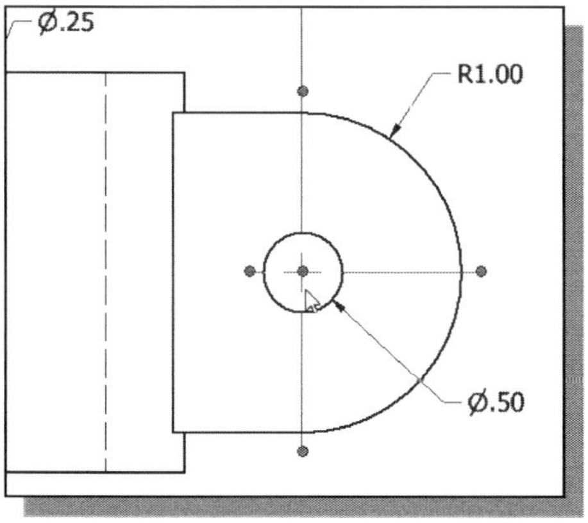

10. Click on the right centerlines in the *top* view as shown.

11. Adjust the length of the horizontal centerline by dragging on one of the grip points as shown.

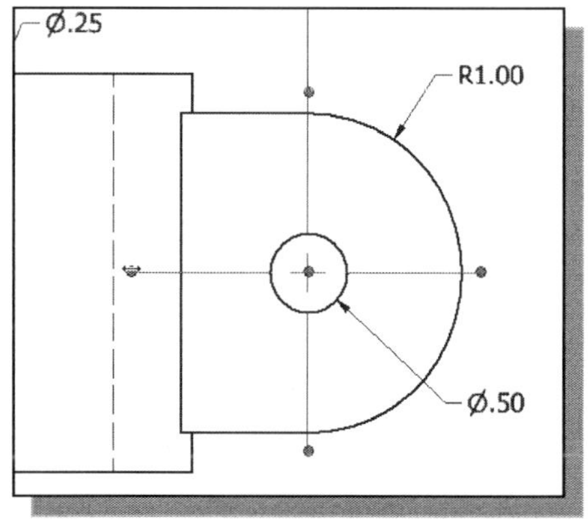

12. On your own, repeat the above steps and adjust the dimensions/centerlines as shown below.

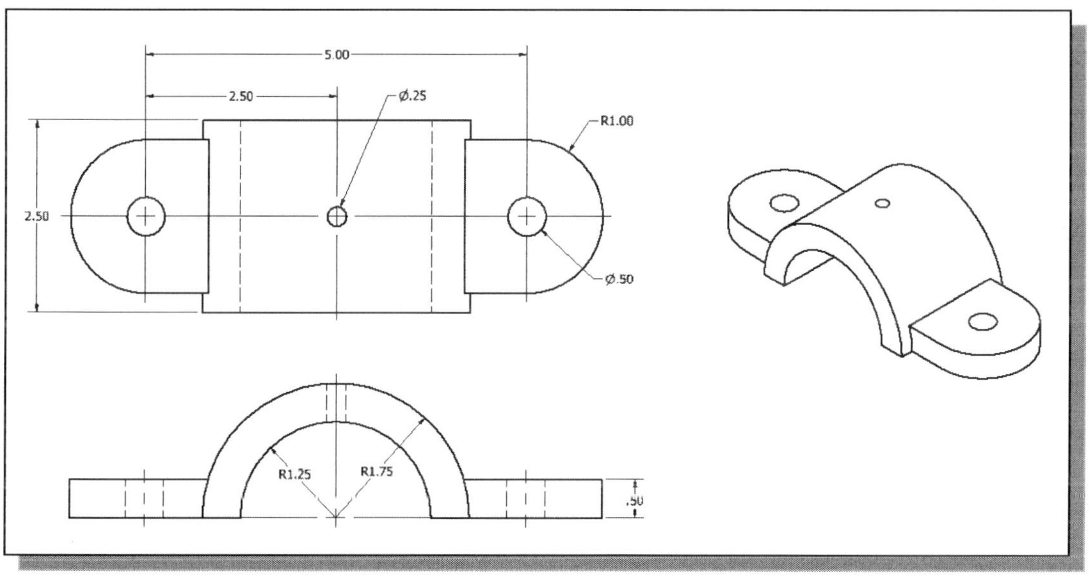

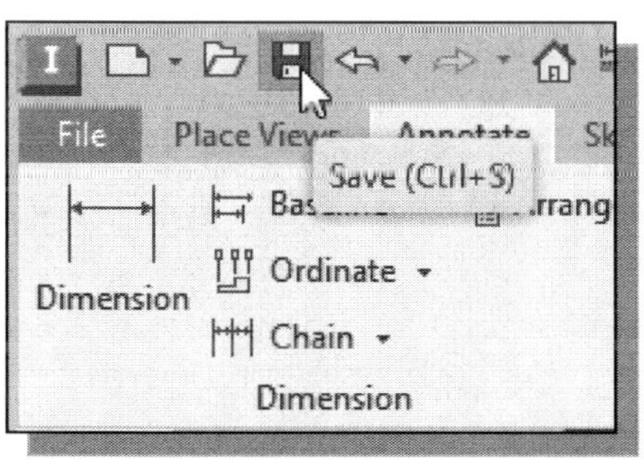

13. Click on the **Save File** icon in the *Standard* toolbar as shown.

14. Click the **Save** button to use the default drawing name.

Complete the Drawing Sheet

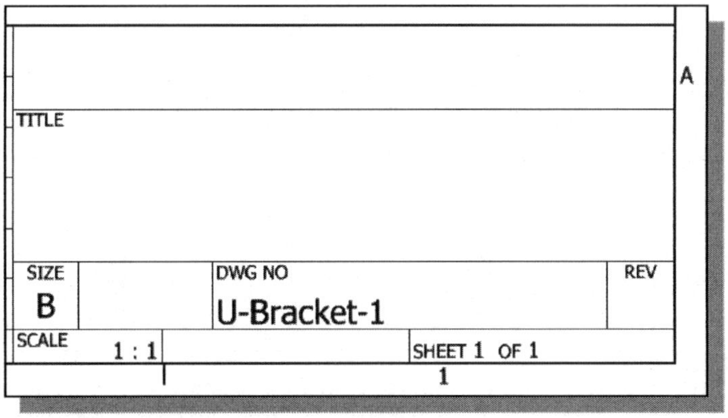

1. On your own, use the **Zoom** and the **Pan** commands to adjust the display as shown; this is so that we can complete the title block.

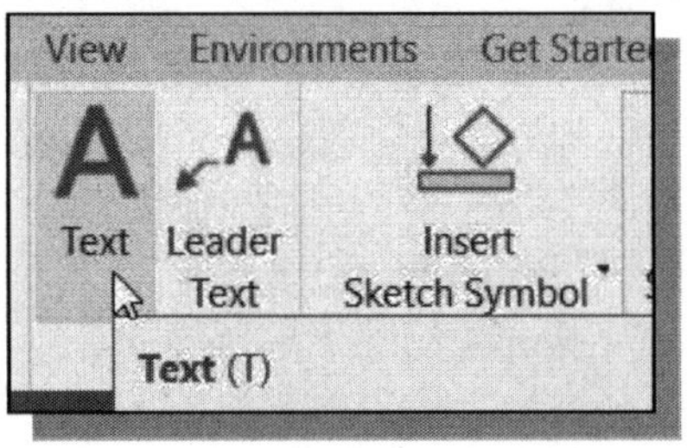

2. In the *Drawing Annotation* window, click on the **Text** button.

3. Pick a location that is inside the top block area as the location for the new text to be entered.

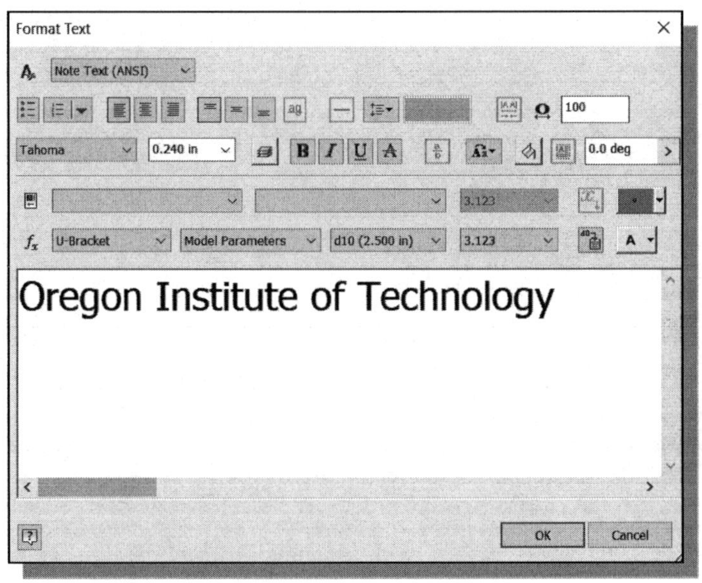

4. In the *Format Text* dialog box, enter the name of your organization. Also note the different settings available.

5. Click **OK** to proceed.

6. On your own, repeat the above steps and complete the title block.

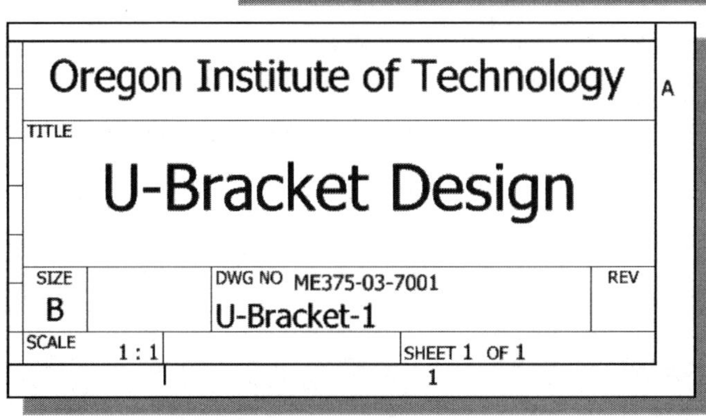

Associative Functionality – Modifying Feature Dimensions

Autodesk Inventor's *associative functionality* allows us to change the design at any level, and the system reflects the changes at all levels automatically.

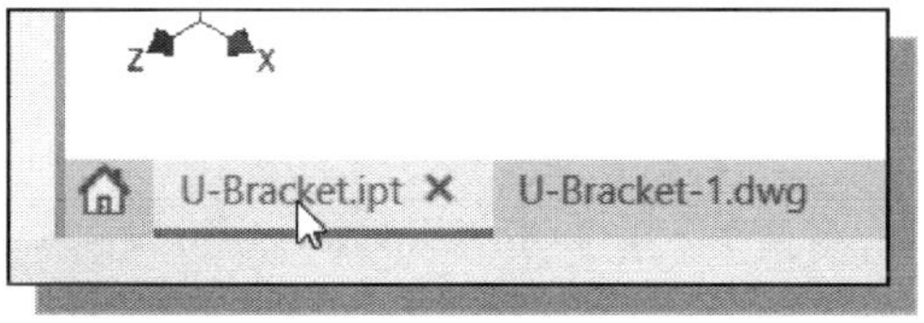

1. Click on the ***U-Bracket*** part window or tab to switch to the *Solid Model.*

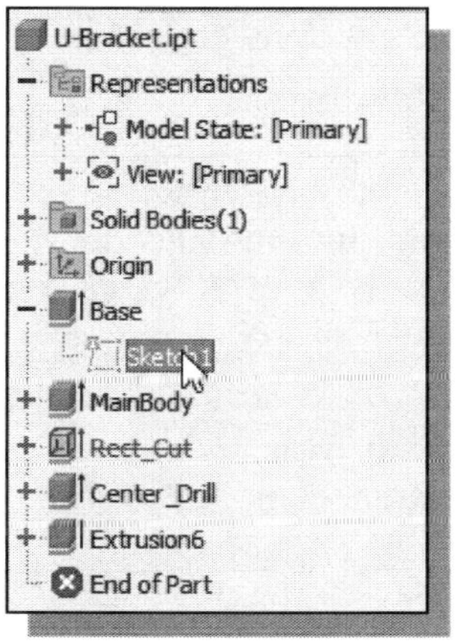

2. In the *browser* window, click once on the [+] sign in front of the **Base** (Extrusion1) to expand the menu list.

3. Select **Sketch1** to display the sketch and dimensions in the graphics area.

4. Choose **Make Sketch visible** as shown.

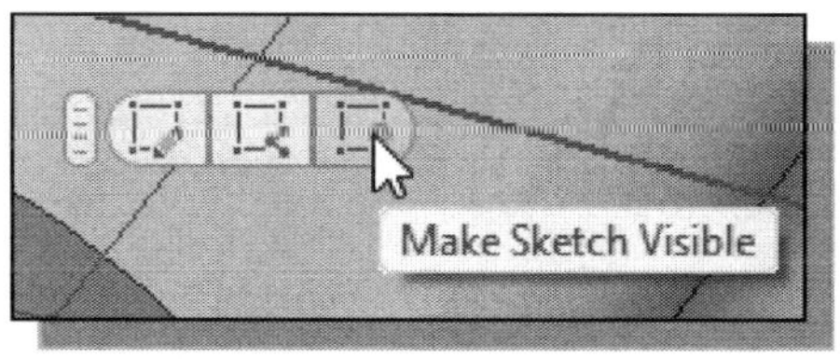

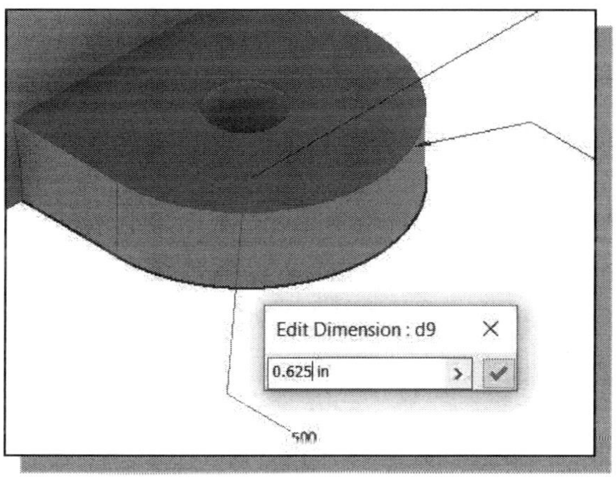

5. Double-click on the diameter dimensions (**0.50**) of the drill feature on the base feature as shown in the figure.

6. In the *Edit Dimension* dialog box, enter **0.625** as the new diameter dimension.

7. Click on the **check mark** button to accept the new setting.

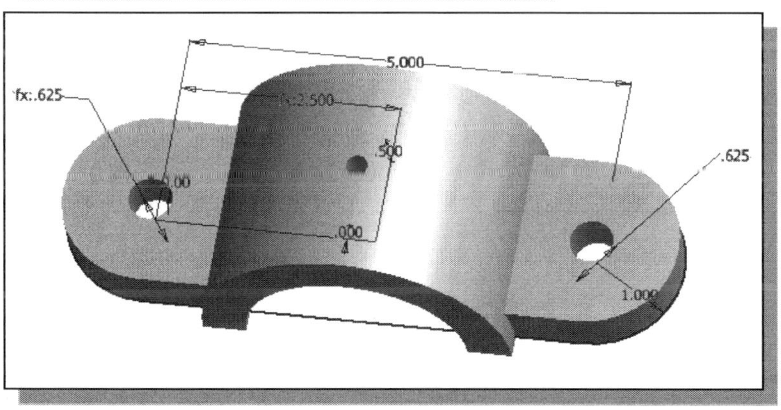

8. On your own, confirm the diameter of the other drill feature is also set to **0.625** as shown.

9. Click on the **Update** button in the *Standard* toolbar area to proceed with updating the solid model.

10. Click on the ***U-Bracket-1*** drawing graphics window or tab to switch to the *Multi-View Drawing*.

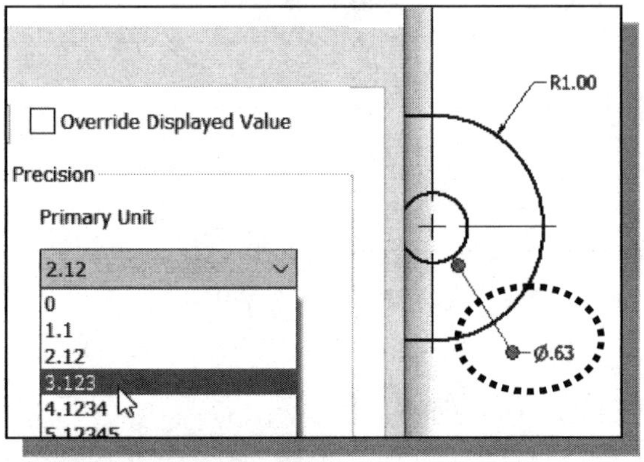

11. Inside the *graphics window*, double-click on the **0.63** dimension in the ***top*** view to bring up the *Precision and Tolerance* dialog box.

12. Set the *Precision* option to **3 digits after the decimal point** as shown.

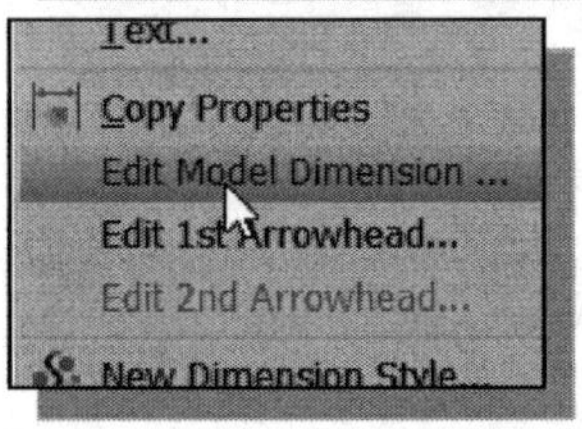

13. Inside the graphics window, right-click once on the **R 1.75** dimension in the *front* view to bring up the option menu.

14. Select **Edit Model Dimension** in the pop-up menu.

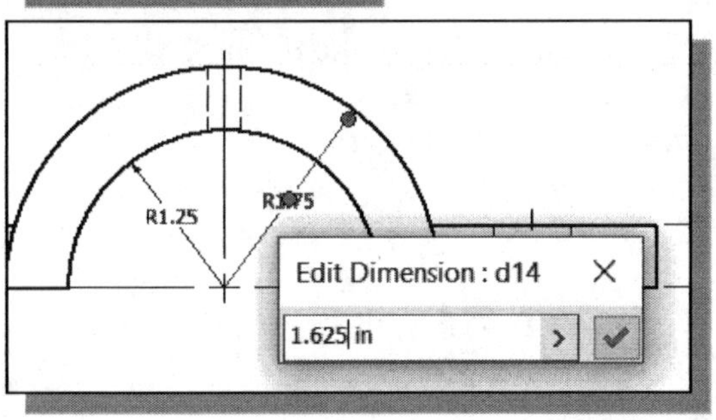

15. Change the dimension to **1.625**.

16. Click on the **check mark** button to accept the setting.

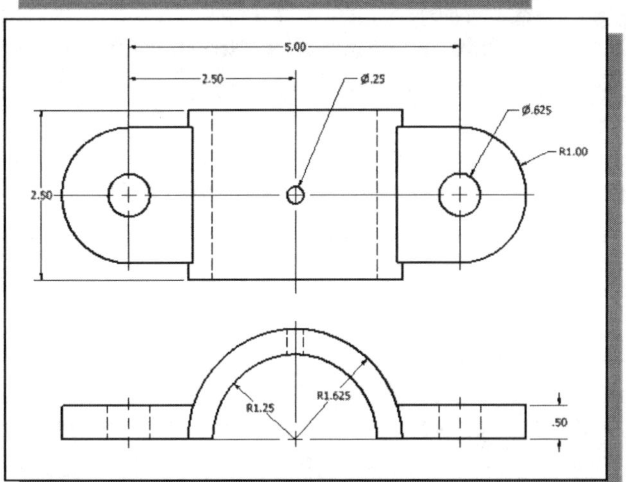

➢ Note the geometry of the cut feature is updated in all views automatically.

❖ On your own, switch to the *Part Modeling Mode* and confirm the design is updated as well.

➢ The completed multi-view drawing should appear as shown on the next page.

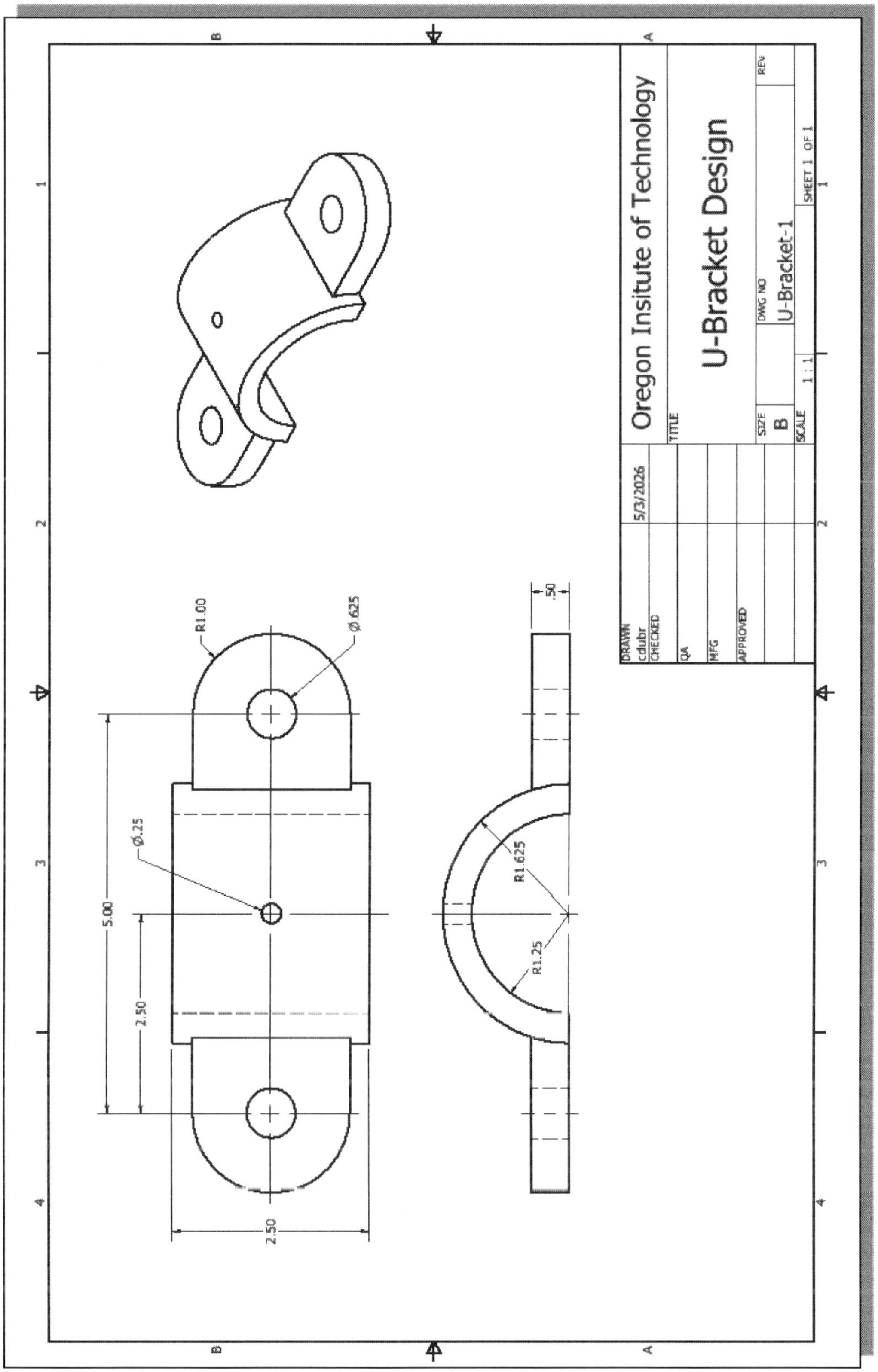
Oregon Insitute of Technology
U-Bracket Design
DRAWN
cdubr
5/3/2026
CHECKED
QA
MFG
APPROVED
TITLE
SIZE
B
DWG NO
U-Bracket-1
REV
SCALE
1 : 1
SHEET 1 OF 1
R1.00
Ø.625
Ø.25
5.00
2.50
2.50
.50
R1.625
R1.25

3D Model-Based Definition

The 3D Model-Based Definition (MBD) functionality is also available in Autodesk Inventor 2026. Modern 3D CAD applications allow for the insertion of engineering information such as dimensions, GD&T, notes and other product details directly within the 3D digital data set for components and assemblies. MBD uses such capabilities to establish the 3D digital data set as the source of these specifications and design authority for the product. The 3D digital data set may contain enough information to manufacture and inspect a product without the need for 2D engineering drawings.

Autodesk has partnered with *Sigmetrix/Advanced Dimensional Management*, leading providers of tolerance analysis and GD&T software and training, to help users apply semantic GD&T properly per the rules of the ASME Y14.5 and applicable ISO GPS standards. Autodesk Inventor 2027 supports both ASME and ISO standards. Inventor 2027 provides API access to all the MBD data, which means that downstream software can directly access the Product Manufacturing Information from the model.

The new Annotate ribbon provides a suite of tools for annotating models and exporting data sets to 3D PDF and other 3D formats. The 3D Annotation tools are divided into three categories: Geometric Annotation, General Annotation, and Notes.

Geometric Annotation tools are related to GD&T and GPS. The **Tolerance Feature** tool is used to apply geometric tolerances to features. The **DRF** tool is used to define Datum Reference Frames and datum systems. The **Tolerance Advisor** tool provides feedback on completeness of the GD&T scheme, error messages and warnings as the GD&T is applied.

General Annotation includes the **Dimension** tool, the **Hole/Thread Note** tool, and the **Surface Texture** tool. The *Dimension* tool is used to apply dimensions and directly-toleranced dimensions. The *Hole/Thread Note* is used to annotate complex holes and threaded holes. The *Surface Texture* tool is used to define surface texture requirements.

Notes are used to apply notes and general profile tolerances. Local notes may be defined using the *Leader Text* tool. General notes may be defined by the *General Note* tool. Default profile tolerances may be defined by the *General Profile Note* tool.

With this set of MBD tools, the mental translation of 3D models to two-dimensional (2D) drawings for communicating information and then back to 3D models for manufacturing is replaced by a simplified approach. The 3D annotation approach means faster and more precise product communication, which can improve the product development process.

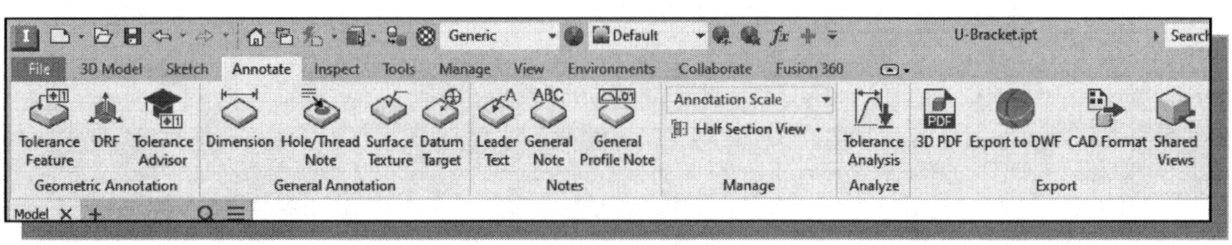

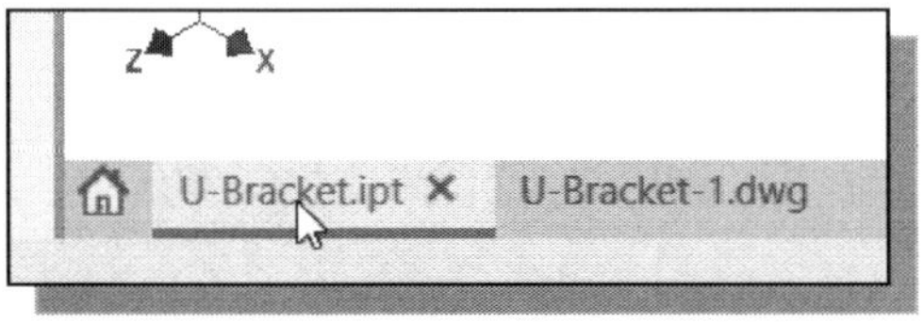

1. Click on the ***U-Bracket*** part window or tab to switch to the *Solid Model*.

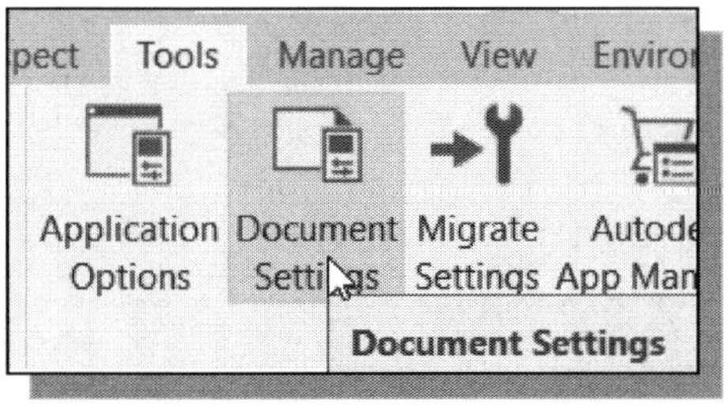

2. Click on the **Tools** tab and pick the *Document Settings* as shown.

3. Confirm the *Annotations Standard* is set to **ASME** as the *annotation* standard as shown.

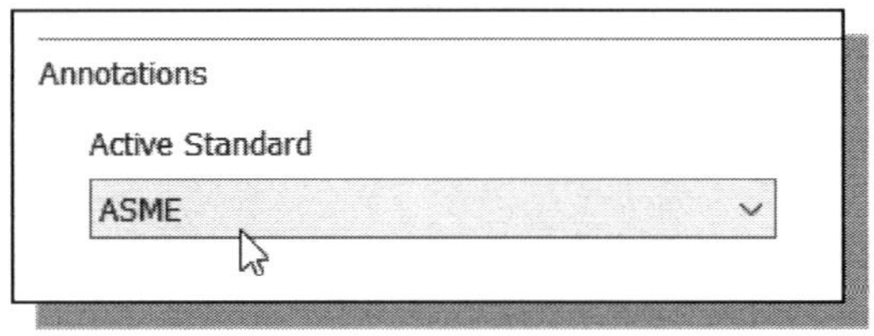

4. Click **Close** to accept the settings.

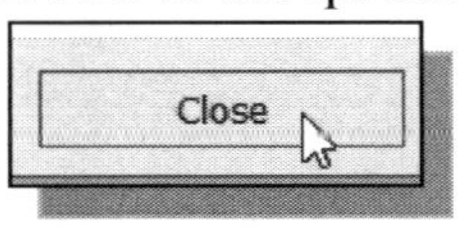

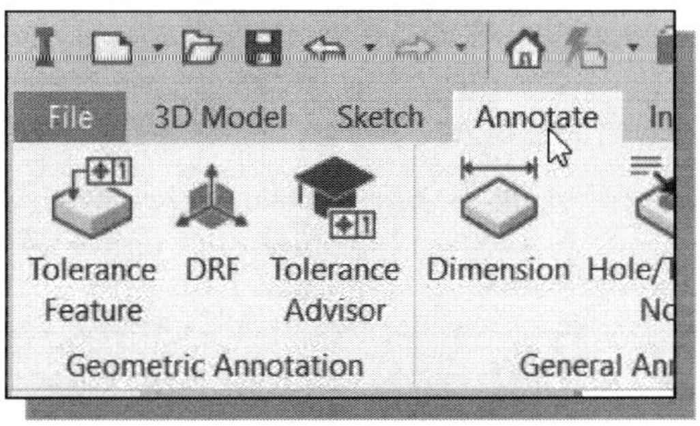

5. Click on the **Annotate** tab to switch to the *MBD toolbar set* as shown.

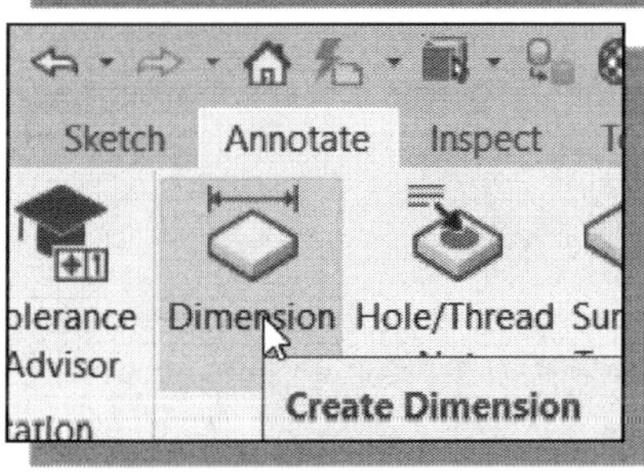

6. Activate the **Create Dimension** command in the *General Annotation* toolbar as shown.

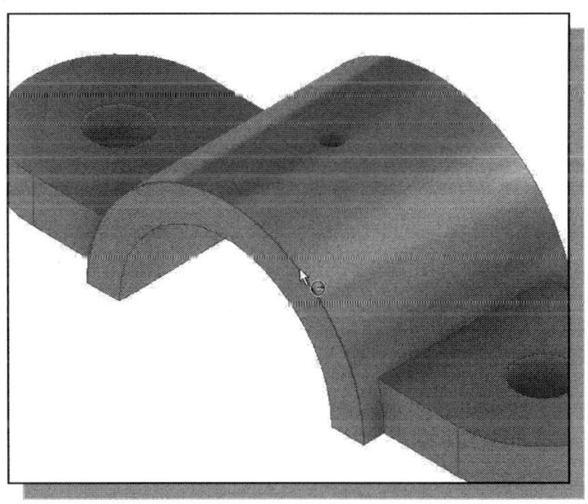

7. Click on the **large arc** on the front section of the solid model as shown.

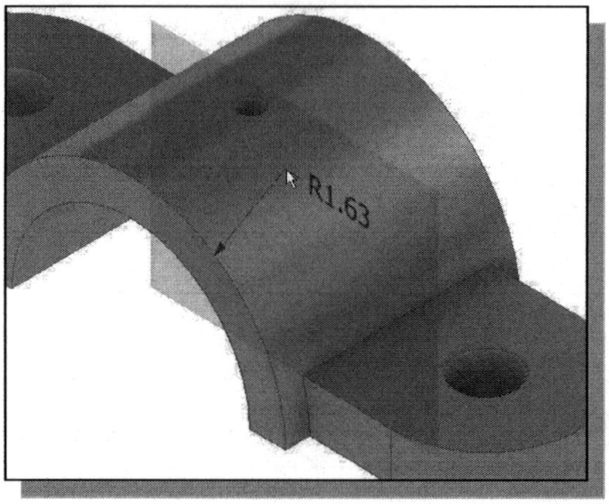

8. On your own, place the dimension above the arc as shown in the figure.

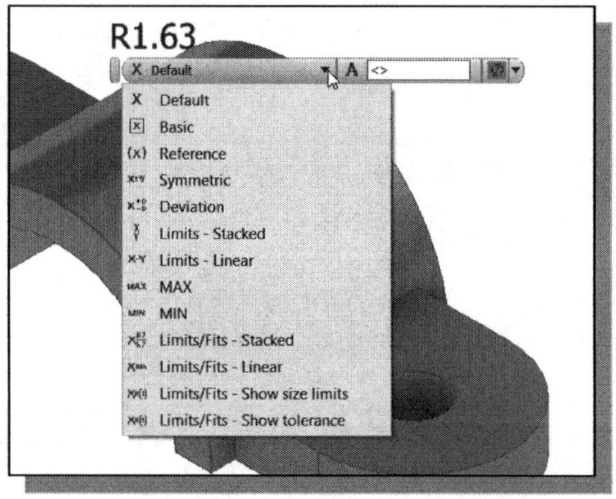

9. Display the first option list and note the different GD&T options available for the associated dimension.

10. On your own, use the **Edit Dimension** icon and change the number of digits displayed.

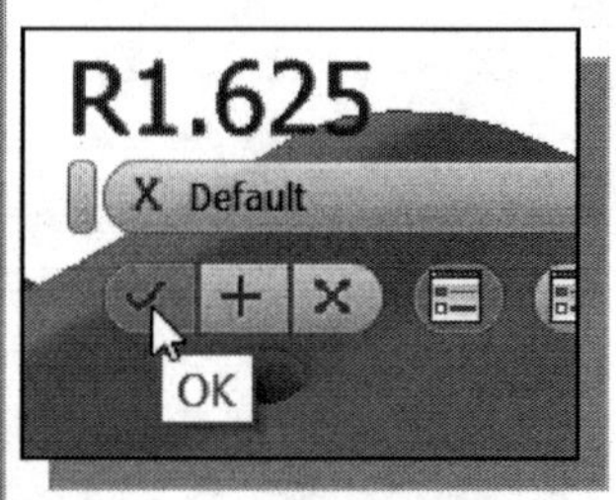

11. Click **OK** to accept the setting and create the dimension as shown.

12. On your own, repeat the above steps and add the other arc dimension as shown.

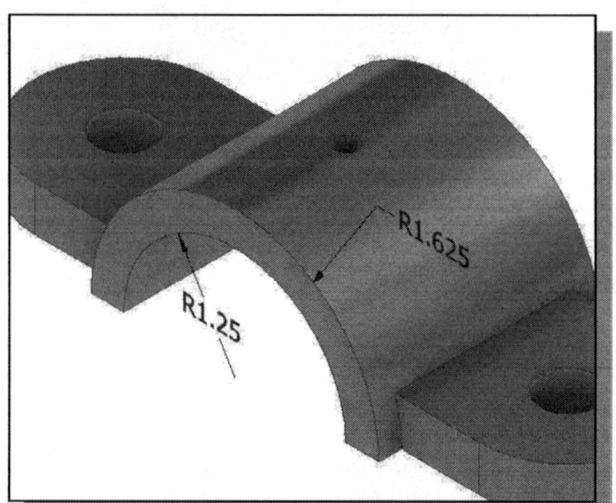

➤ Note that the radius and diameter dimensions are placed on the same plane of the selected arc and circle. The 3D annotation command will automatically select the placement plane if the selected geometry lies on a specific plane.

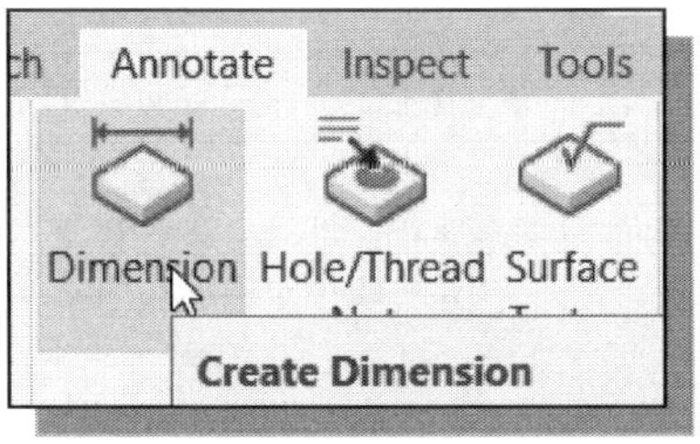

13. Activate the **Create Dimension** command in the *General Annotation* toolbar as shown.

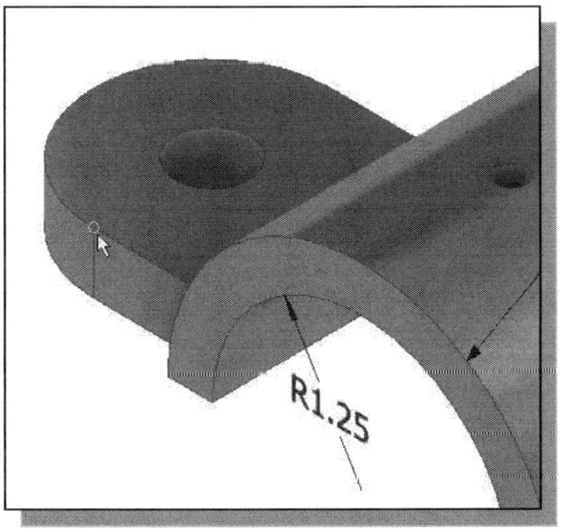

14. Click on the arc endpoint on the left section of the solid model as shown.

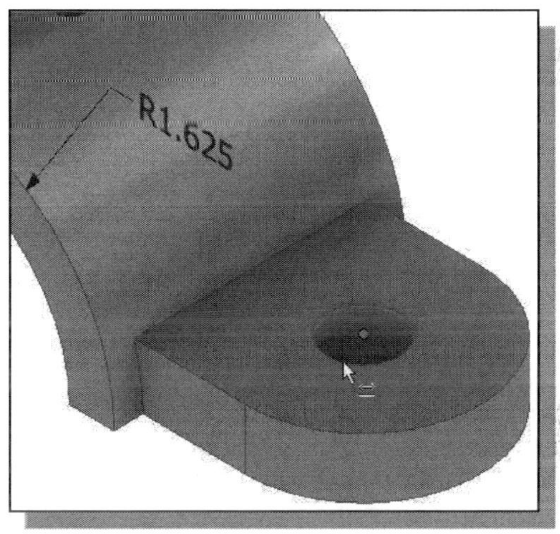

15. Click on the top circle on the right section of the solid model as shown.

➢ Note that by selecting a circle, we also set the placement plane for the dimension.

16. On your own, place the dimension in front of the solid model as shown.

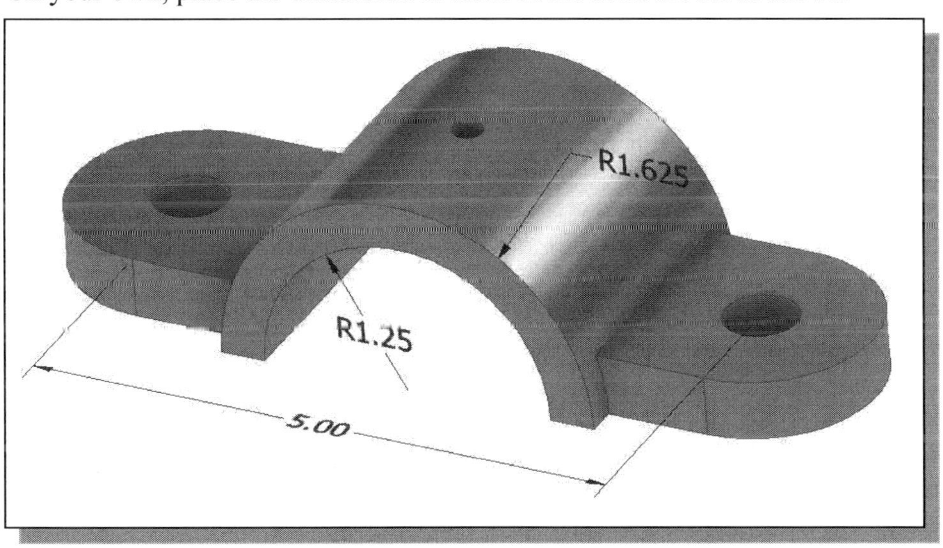

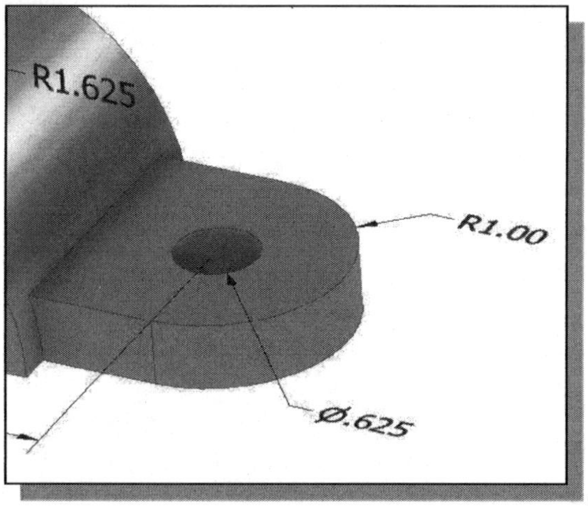

17. On your own, repeat the above steps and create the arc and hole dimensions as shown.

18. On your own, use the dynamic rotation option to view the bottom of the design as shown.

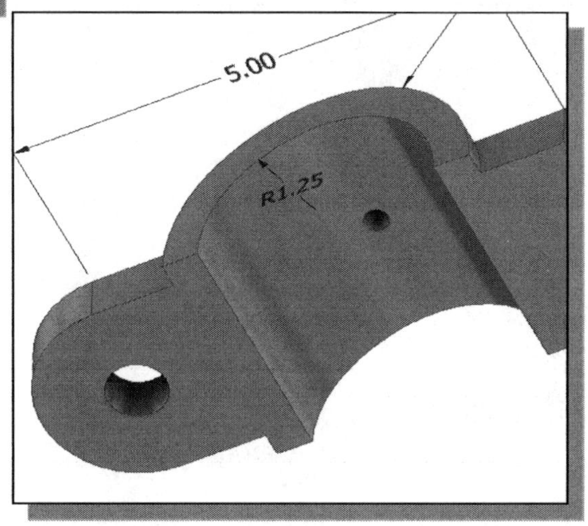

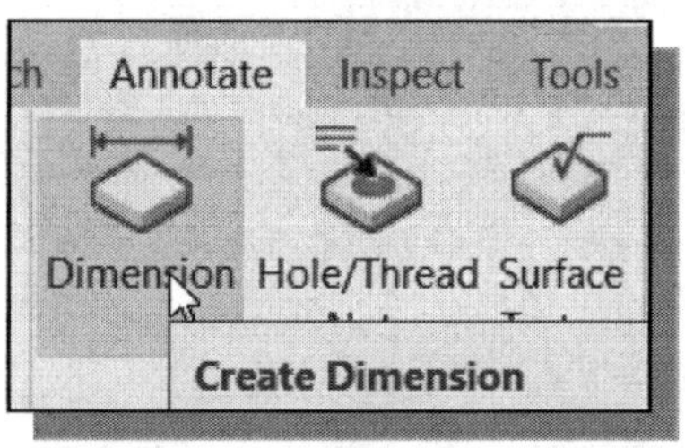

19. Activate the **Create Dimension** command in the *General Annotation* toolbar as shown.

20. On your own, select the straight edge and create the dimension as shown.

➤ Note the **General Dimension** command in *3D Annotation* behaves similarly to the **Smart Dimensioning** command in the *3D Modeling Mode. Inventor* will automatically create the proper dimensions based on the selected geometry.

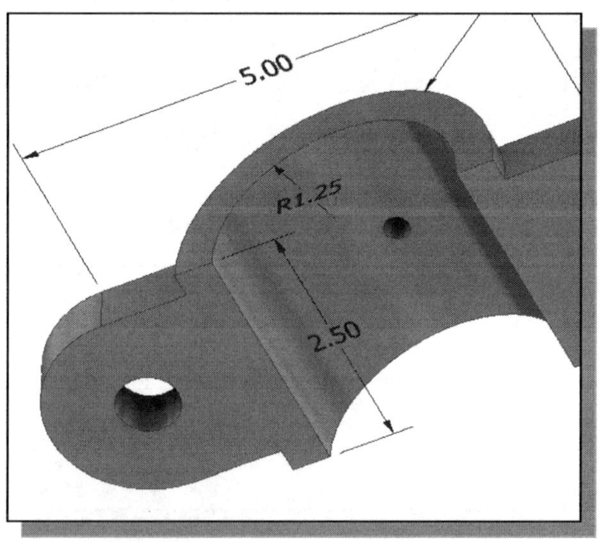

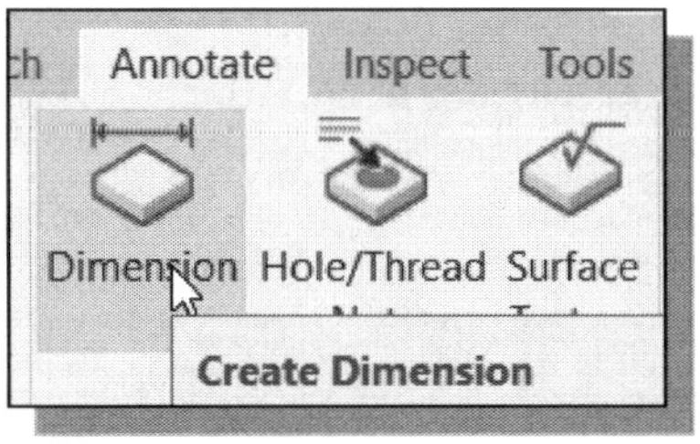

21. Activate the **Create Dimension** command in the General Annotation toolbar as shown.

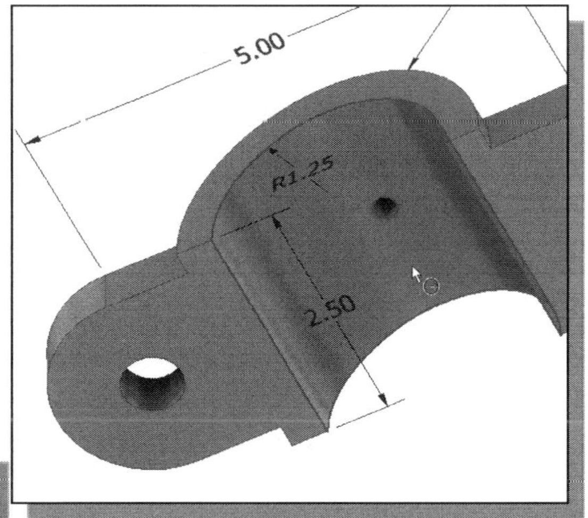

22. Select the inside **cylindrical surface** as shown.

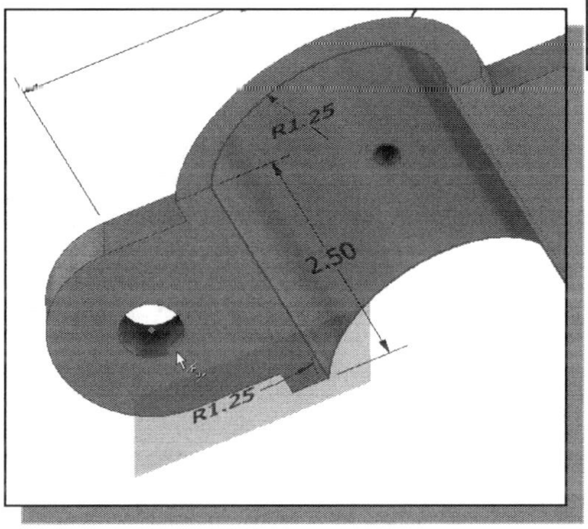

23. Click on the **bottom circle** on the left section of the solid model as shown.

24. On your own, place the dimension as shown.

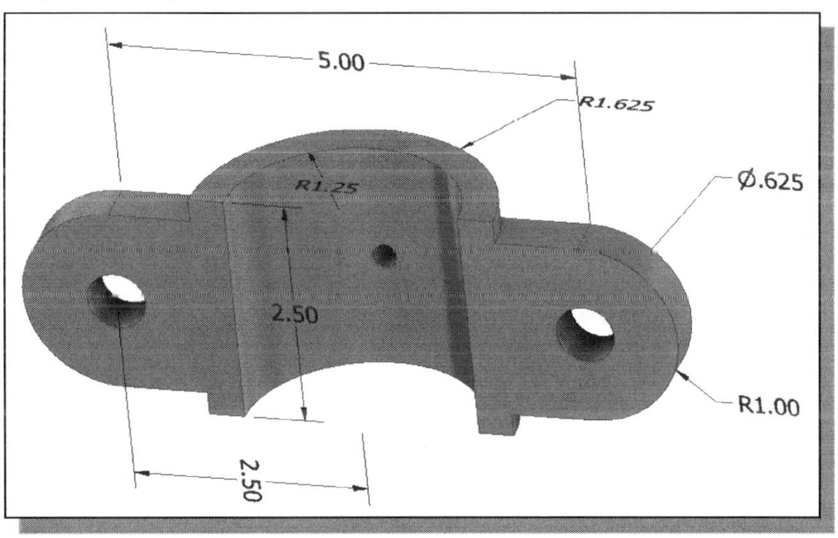

25. Press the function key **F6** once or select **Home View** in the **ViewCube** to change the display back to the default isometric view.

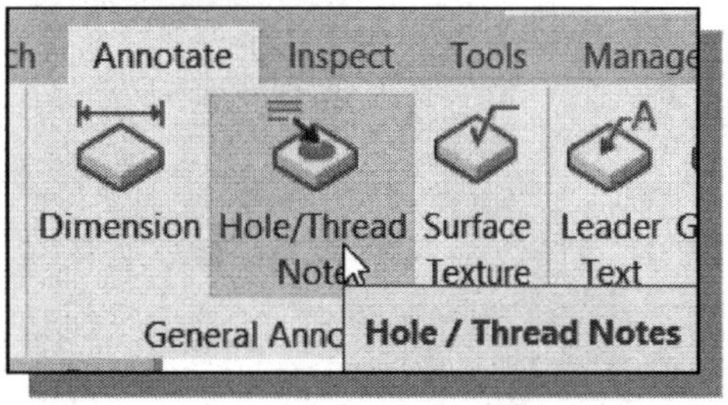

26. Activate the **Hole/Thread Note** command in the *General Annotation* toolbar as shown.

27. Select the **center drill hole** as shown.

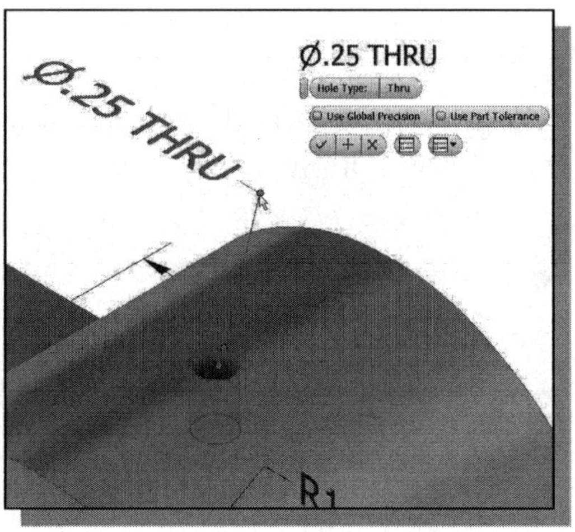

28. Place the dimension toward the left side as shown. Note the different options available of the selected hole feature.

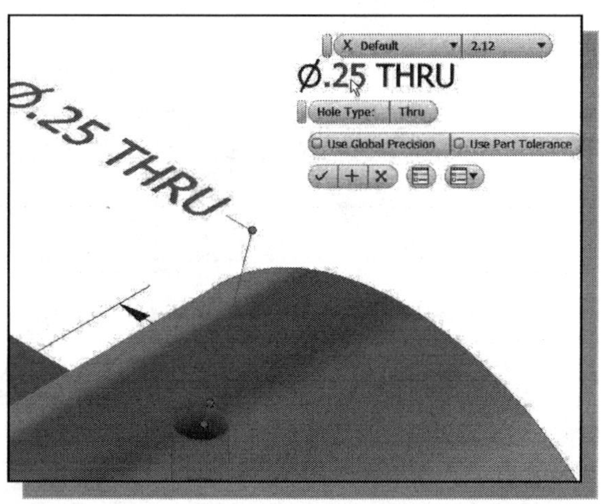

29. Move the cursor on top of the diameter value and **left-click** on the text to display additional dimension options.

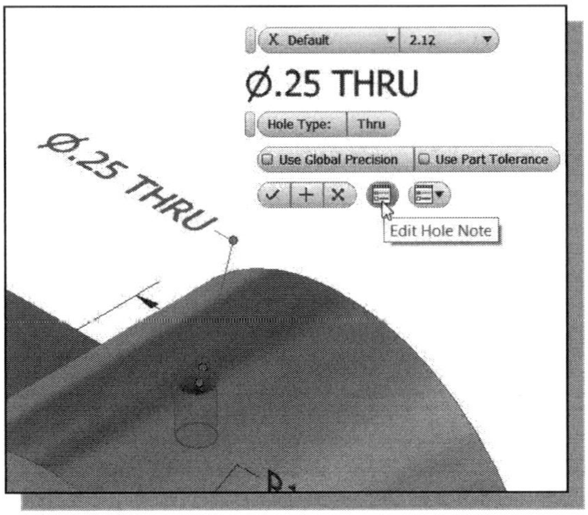

30. Click on the **Edit Hole Note** icon as shown. We will use this option to identify the related features for the small drill hole at the center.

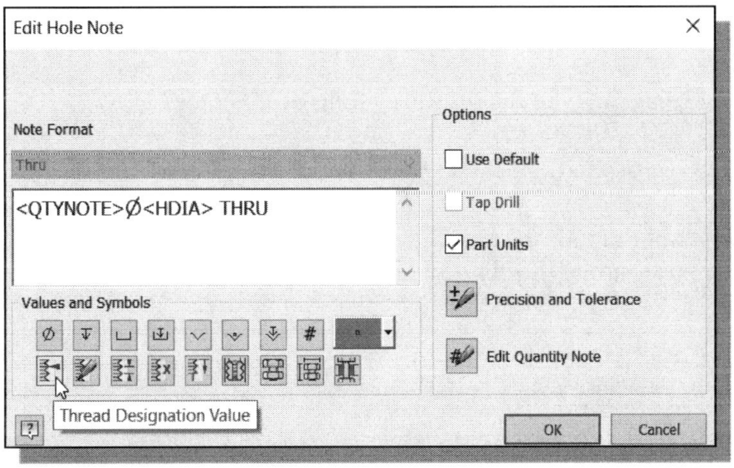

31. Note that we can add additional threads information to the *Hole Note*.

32. Click **OK** to close the *Editor*.

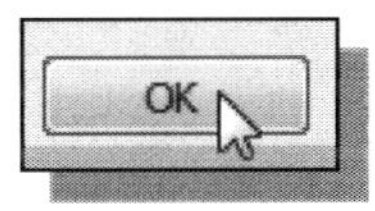

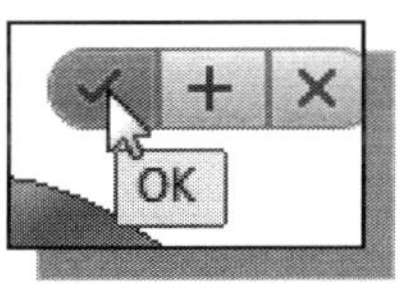

33. Click **OK** to accept the settings and create the dimension and complete the addition of the 3D model-based definition.

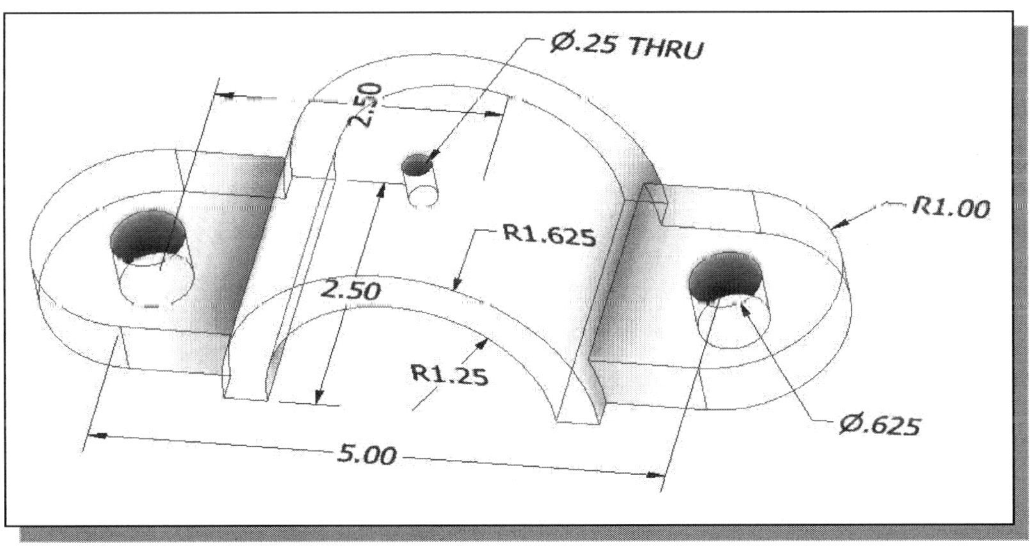

Review Questions: (Time: 25 minutes)

1. What does Autodesk Inventor's *associative functionality* allow us to do?
2. How do we move a view on the *Drawing Sheet*?
3. How do we display feature/model dimensions in the drawing mode?
4. What is the difference between a *feature dimension* and a *reference dimension*?
5. How do we reposition dimensions?
6. What is a *base view*?
7. Can we delete a drawing view? How?
8. Can we adjust the length of centerlines in the drafting mode of Inventor? How?
9. Describe the purpose and usage of the Leader Text command.
10. Describe the advantages of using the **3D Model Based Definition** approach as a documentation tool over the traditional multiview drawing approach.

Exercises: Create the Solid models and the associated 2D drawings and also create the associated MBD of the following exercises.

1. **Slide Mount** (Dimensions are in inches.)

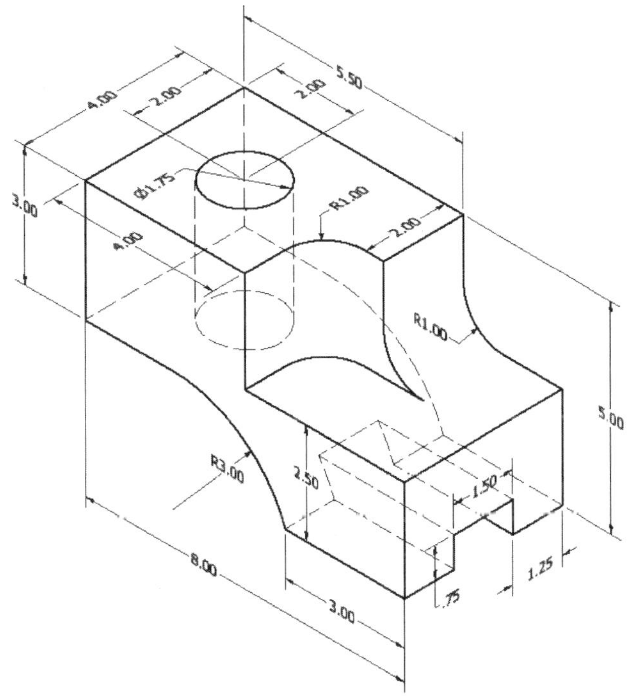

2. **Corner Stop** (Dimensions are in inches.)

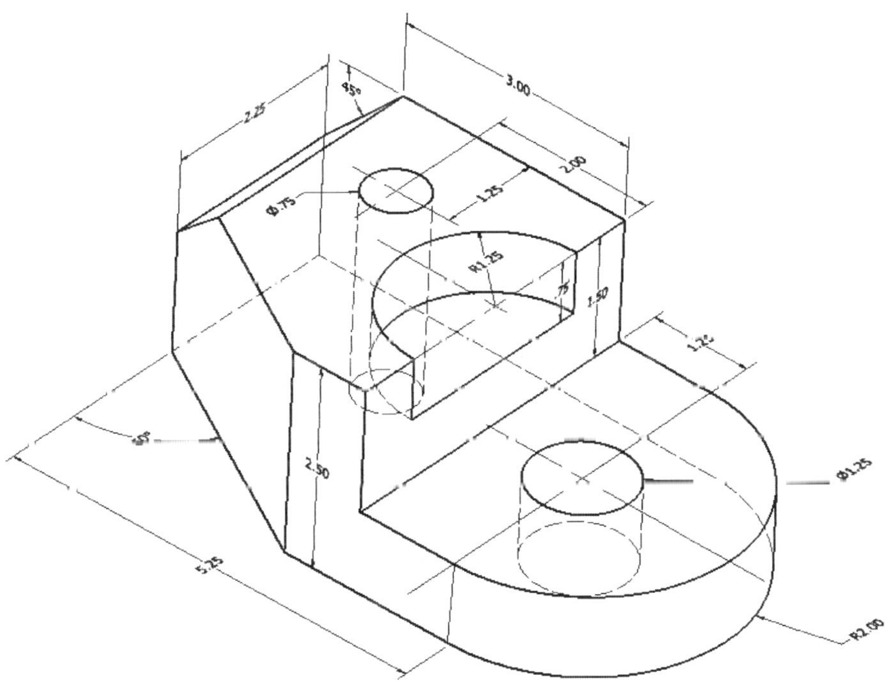

3. **Switch Base** (Dimensions are in inches.)

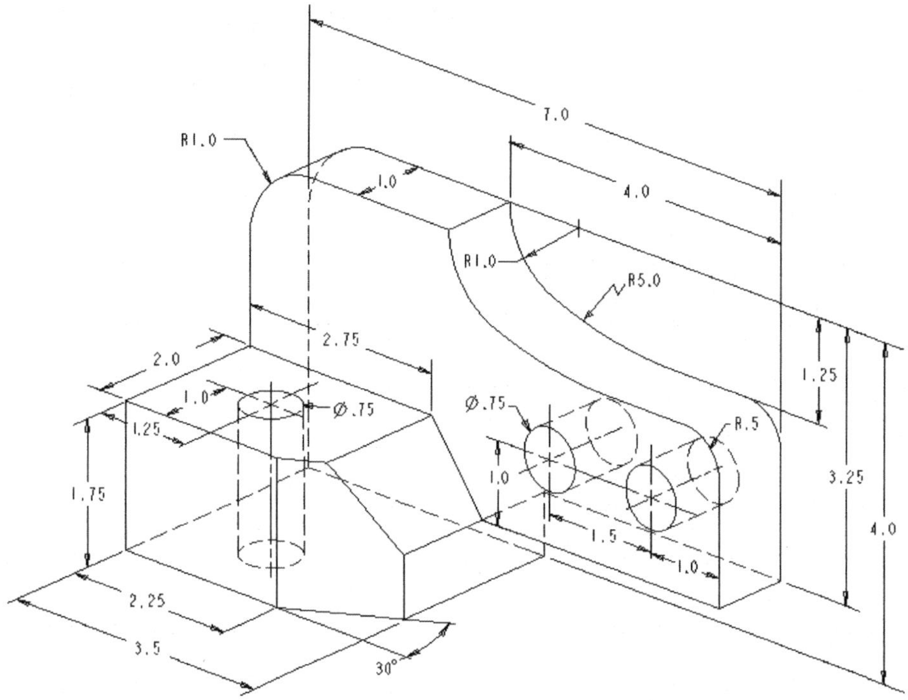

4. **Angle Support** (Dimensions are in inches.)

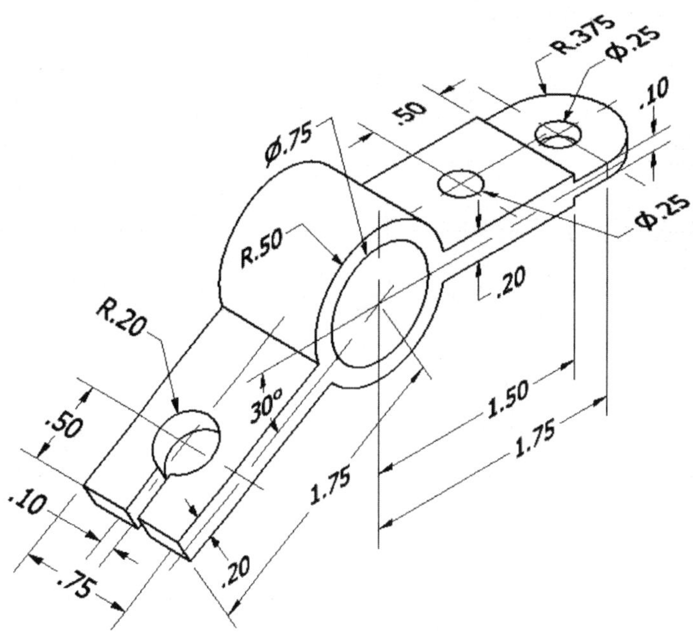

5. **Block Base** (Dimensions are in inches. Plate Thickness: 0.25)

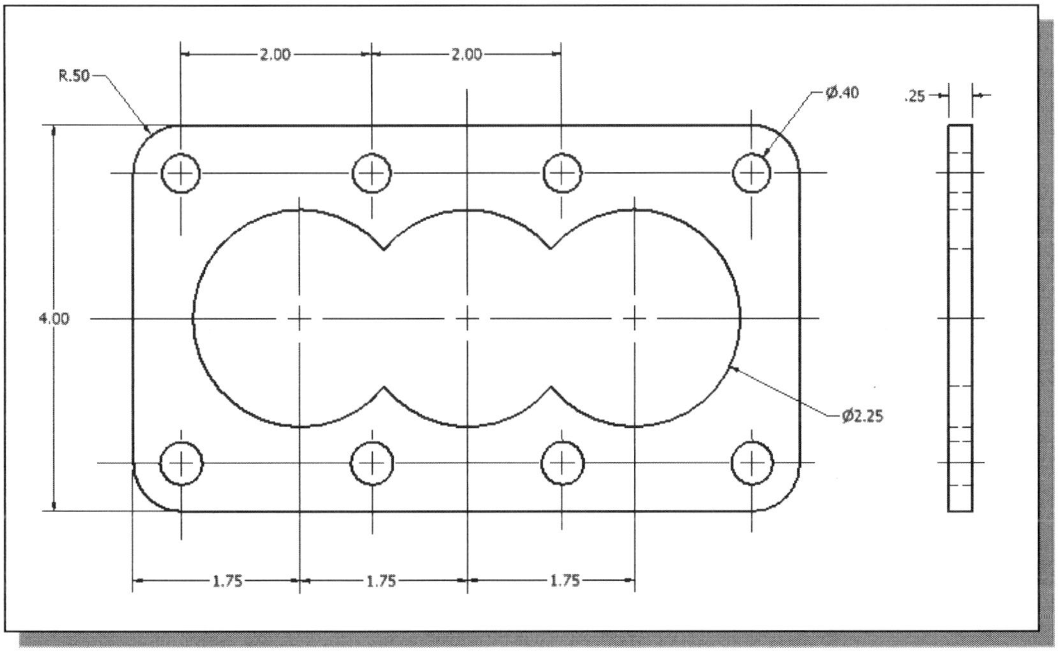

6. **Shaft Guide** (Dimensions are in inches.)

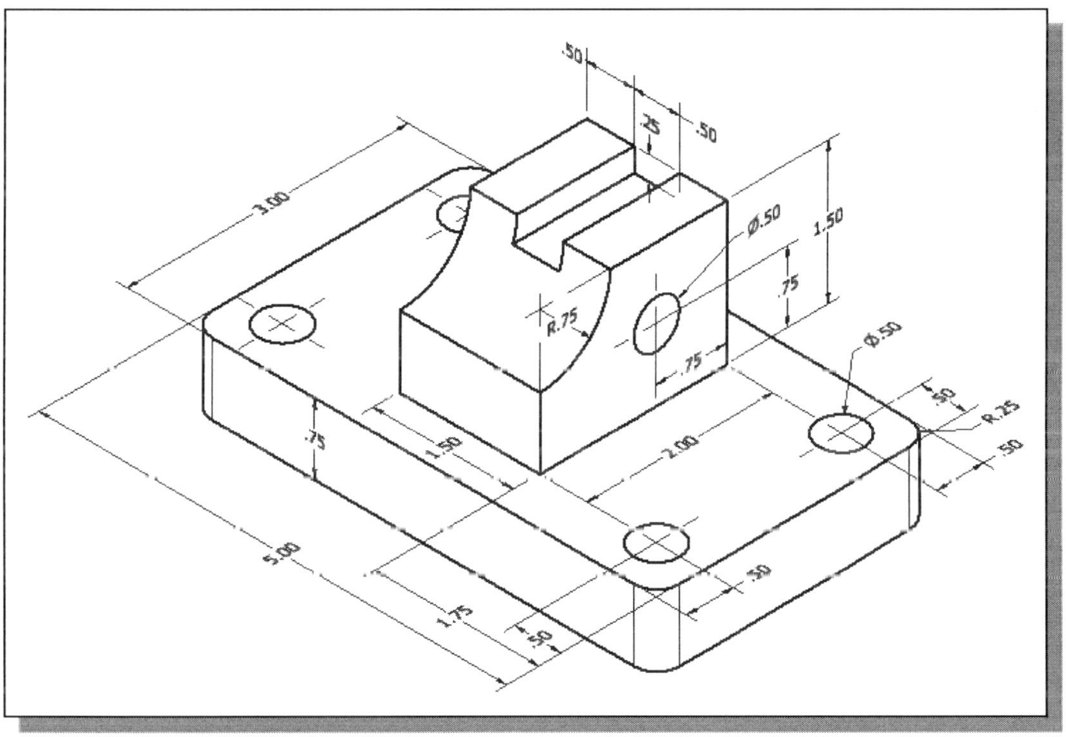

Notes:

Chapter 14
Symmetrical Features in Designs - Autodesk Inventor

Learning Objectives

- ♦ Create Revolved Features
- ♦ Use the Mirror Feature Command
- ♦ Create New Borders and Title Blocks
- ♦ Create Circular Patterns
- ♦ Create and Modify Linear Dimensions
- ♦ Use Autodesk Inventor's Associative Functionality
- ♦ Identify Symmetrical Features in Designs

Introduction

In parametric modeling, it is important to identify and determine the features that exist in the design. *Feature-based parametric modeling* enables us to build complex designs by working on smaller and simpler units. This approach simplifies the modeling process and allows us to concentrate on the characteristics of the design. Symmetry is an important characteristic that is often seen in designs. Symmetrical features can be easily accomplished by the assortment of tools that are available in feature-based modeling systems, such as Autodesk Inventor.

The modeling technique of extruding two-dimensional sketches along a straight line to form three-dimensional features, as illustrated in the previous chapters, is an effective way to construct solid models. For designs that involve cylindrical shapes, shapes that are symmetrical about an axis, revolving two-dimensional sketches about an axis can form the needed three-dimensional features. In solid modeling, this type of feature is called a ***revolved feature***.

In Autodesk Inventor, besides using the **Revolve** command to create revolved features, several options are also available to handle symmetrical features. For example, we can create multiple identical copies of symmetrical features with the **Feature Pattern** command or create mirror images of models using the **Mirror Feature** command. We can also use *construction geometry* to assist the construction of more complex features. In this lesson, the construction and modeling techniques of these more advanced options are illustrated.

A Revolved Design: Pulley

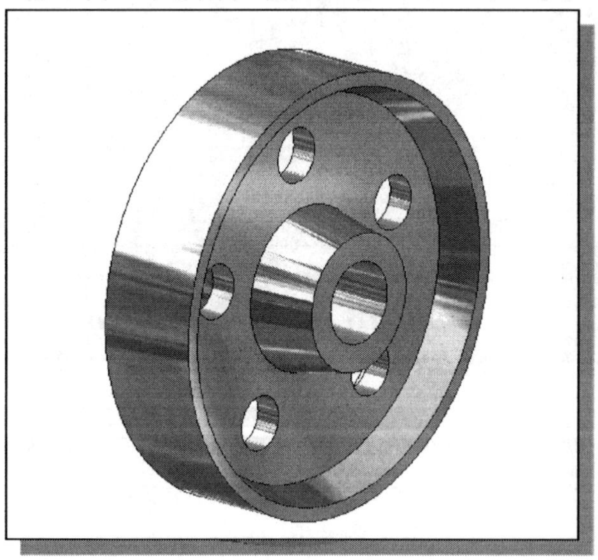

- ❖ Based on your knowledge of Autodesk Inventor, how many features would you use to create the design? Which feature would you choose as the **base feature** of the model? Identify the symmetrical features in the design and consider other possibilities in creating the design. You are encouraged to create the model on your own prior to following through the tutorial.

Modeling Strategy – A Revolved Design

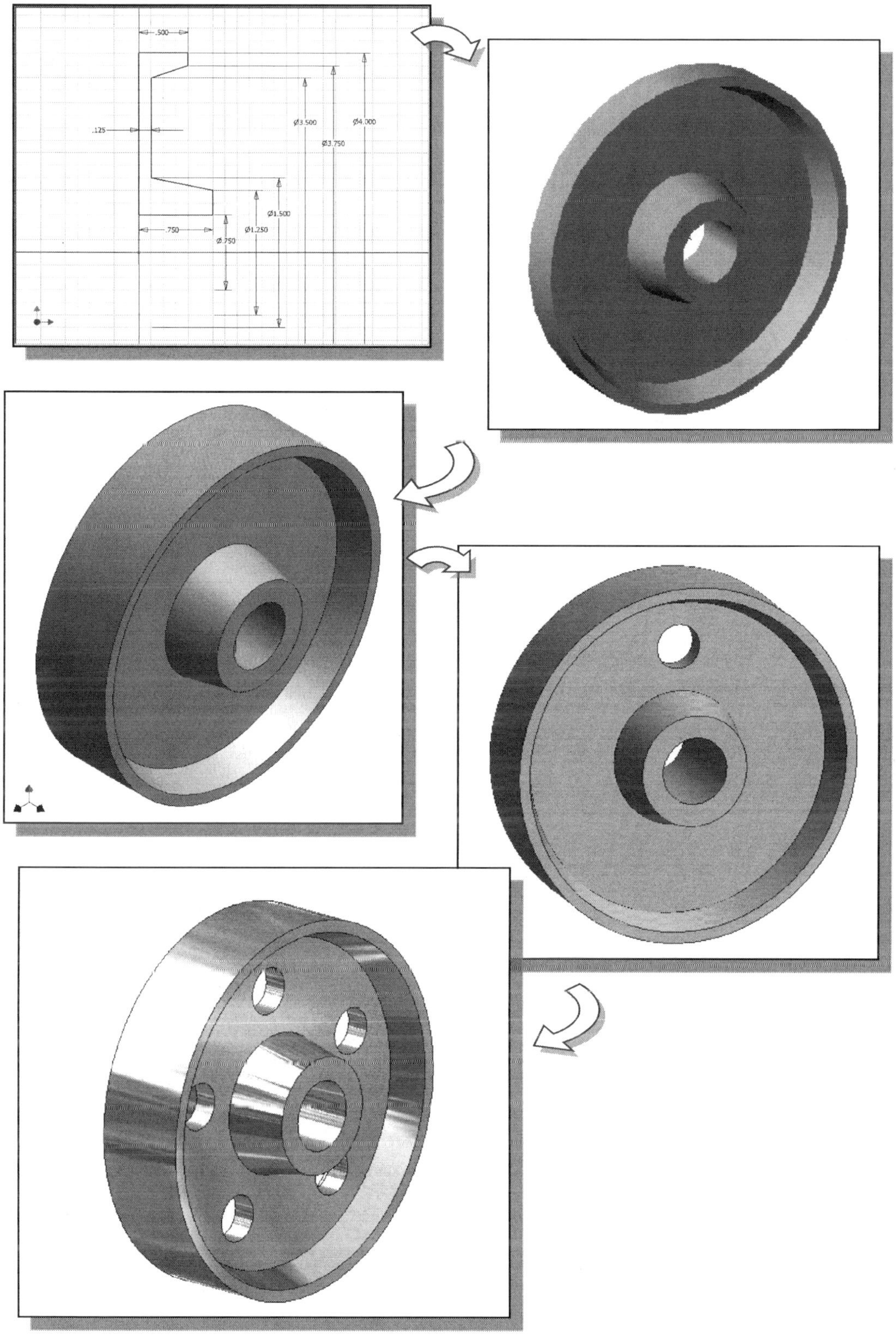

Starting Autodesk Inventor

1. Select the **Autodesk Inventor** option on the *Start* menu or select the **Autodesk Inventor** icon on the desktop to start Autodesk Inventor. The Autodesk Inventor main window will appear on the screen.

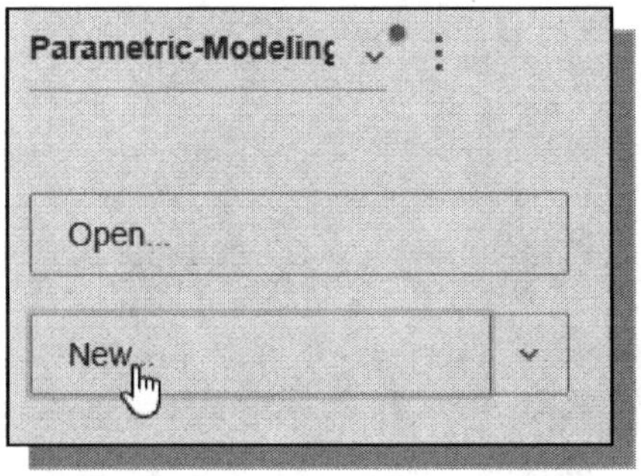

2. Select the **New File** icon with a single click of the left-mouse-button.

3. Select the **English** units set and in the *Part File* area, select **Standard(in).ipt**.

4. Click **Create** in the *New File* dialog box to start a new model.

Set Up the Display of the Sketch Plane

1. In the *Part Browser* window, click on the [+] symbol in front of the **Origin** feature to display more information on the feature.

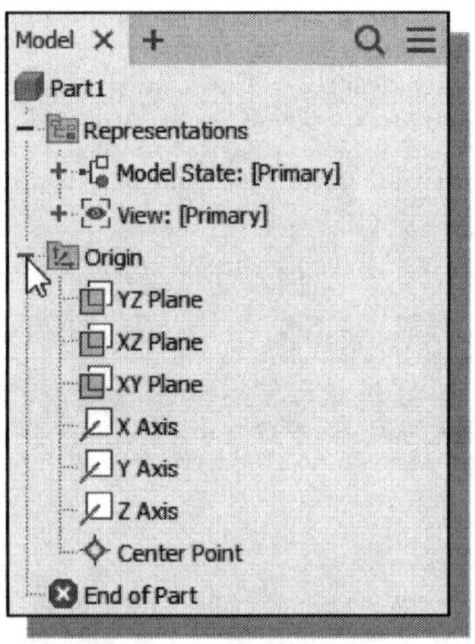

❖ In the *browser* window, notice a new part name appeared with seven work features established. The seven work features include three *work planes*, three *work axes* and a *work point*. By default, the three work planes and work axes are aligned to the **world coordinate system** and the work point is aligned to the *origin* of the **world coordinate system**.

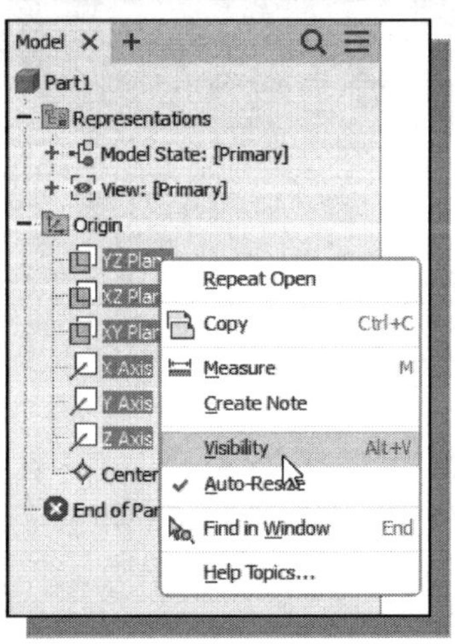

2. Inside the *browser* window, select the three work planes by holding down the **[Ctrl]** key and clicking with the left-mouse-button.

3. Click the right-mouse-button on any of the work features to display the option menu. Click on **Visibility** to toggle ***ON*** the display of the plane.

Creating a 2D Sketch for the Base feature

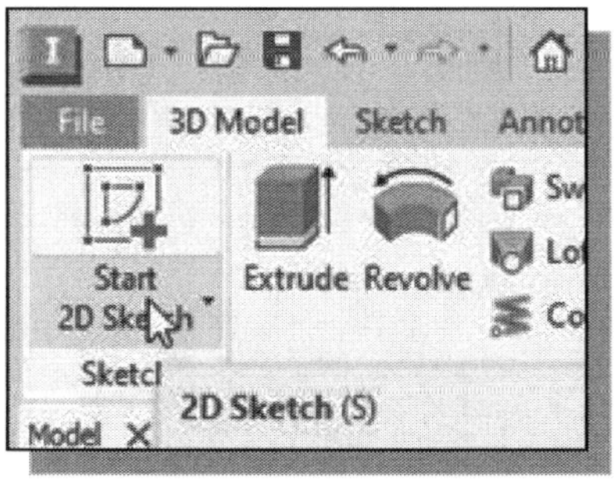

1. In the *Sketch* toolbar select the **Start 2D Sketch** command by left-clicking once on the icon.

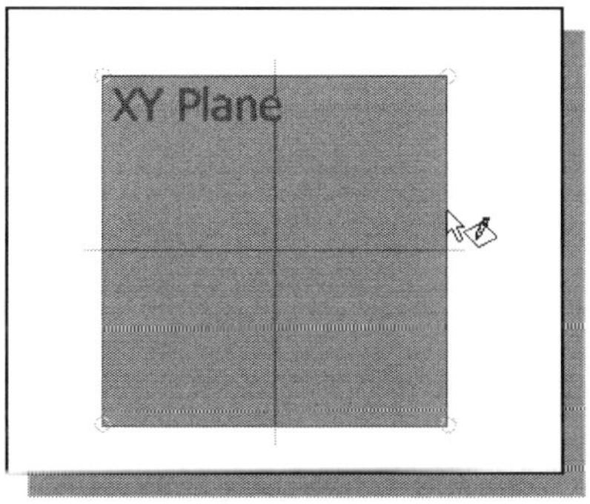

2. In the *Status Bar* area, the message "*Select plane to create sketch or an existing sketch to edit.*" is displayed. Select the **XY Plane** by clicking on the plane inside the graphics window, as shown.

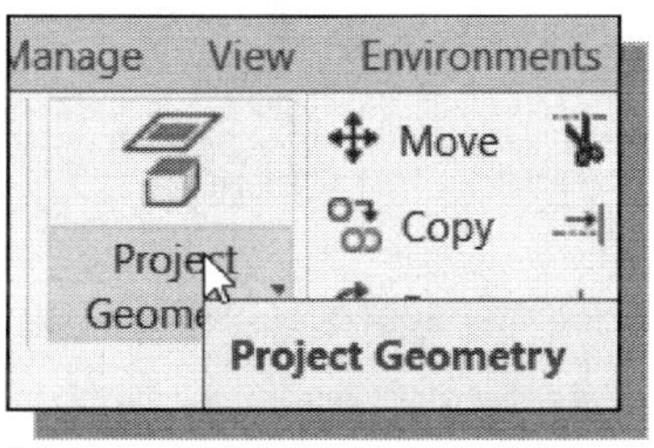

3. Select the **Project Geometry** command in the *2D Sketch* panel. The Project Geometry command allows us to project existing features onto the active sketching plane. Left-click once on the icon to activate the Project Geometry command.

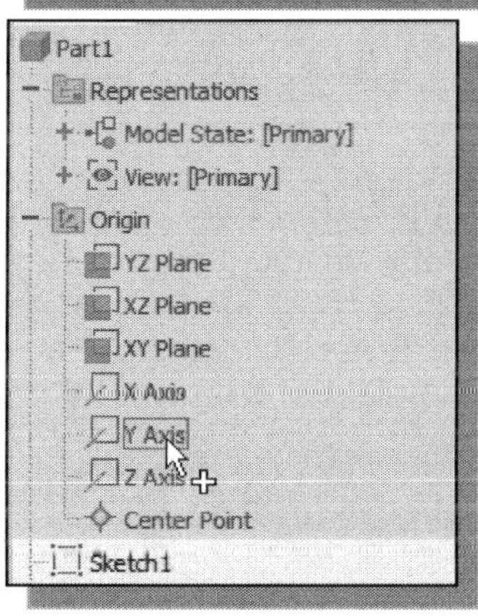

4. In the *Status Bar* area, the message "*Select edge, vertex, work geometry or sketch geometry to project.*" is displayed. Inside the *browser* window, select the **X-axis** and **Y-axis** to project these entities onto the sketching plane.

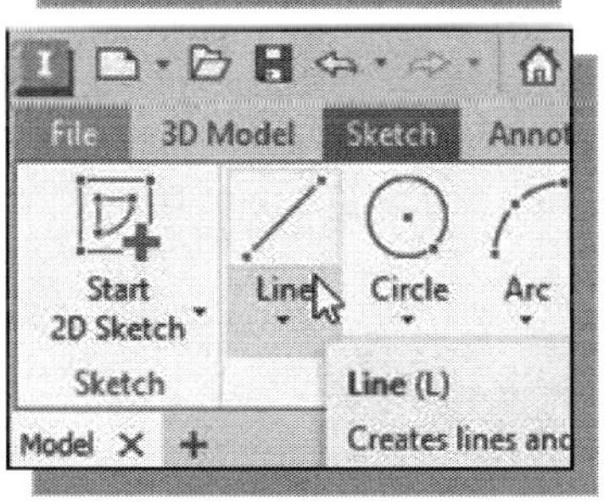

5. Select the **Line** option in the *2D Sketch* panel. A *Help-tip box* appears next to the cursor and a brief description of the command is displayed at the bottom of the drawing screen: "*Creates Straight lines and arcs.*"

6. Create a closed-region sketch with the starting point aligned to the projected **Y-axis** as shown below. (Note that the ***Pulley*** design is symmetrical about a horizontal axis as well as a vertical axis, which allows us to simplify the 2D sketch as shown below.)

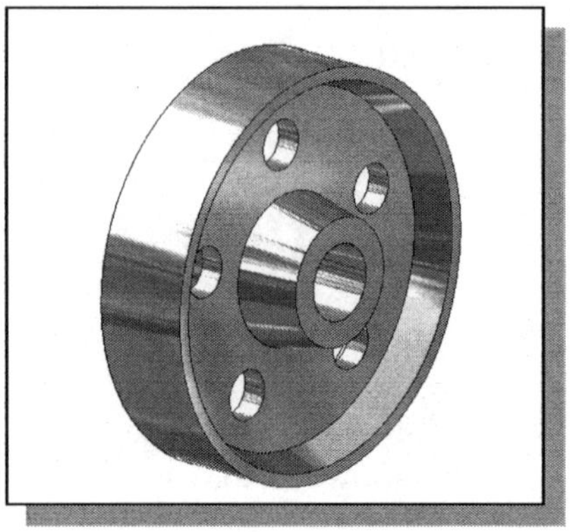

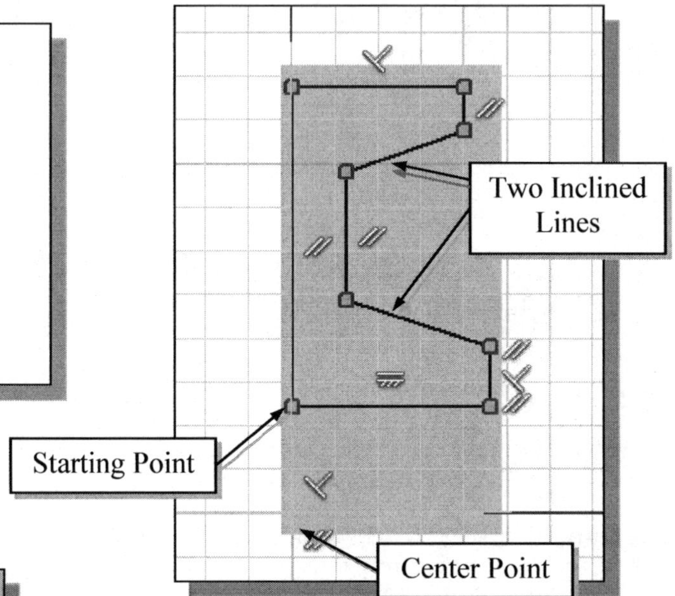

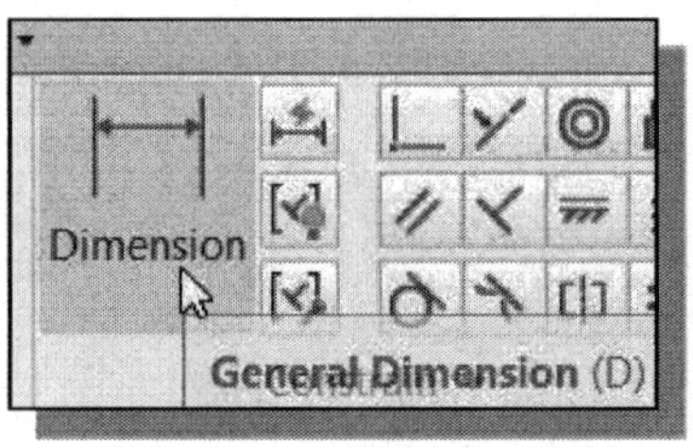

7. Select the **General Dimension** command in the *2D Sketch* panel.

8. Pick the **X-axis** as the first entity to dimension as shown in the figure below.

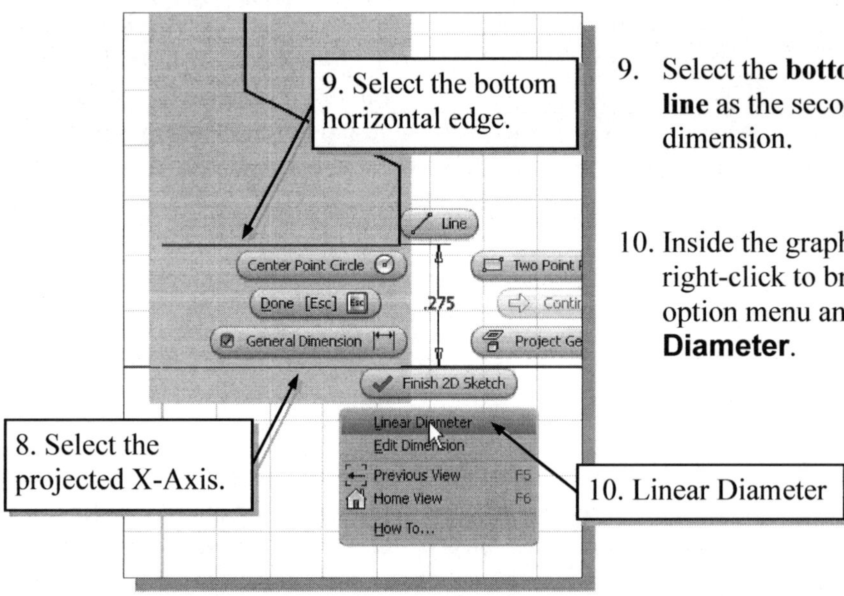

9. Select the **bottom horizontal line** as the second object to dimension.

10. Inside the graphics window, right-click to bring up the option menu and select **Linear Diameter**.

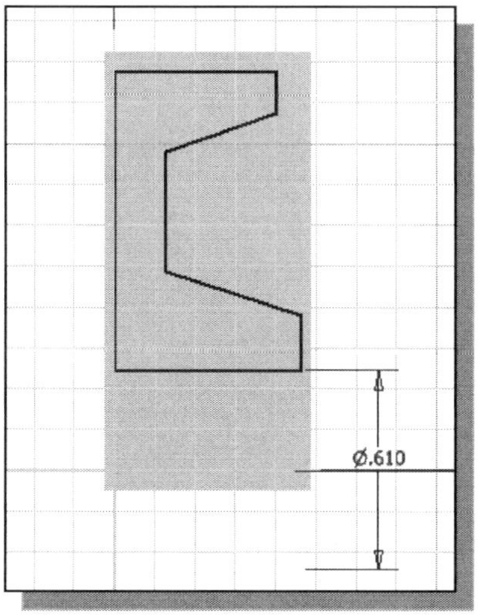

11. Place the dimension text to the right side of the sketch.

- To create a dimension that will account for the symmetrical nature of the design, pick the axis of symmetry, pick the entity, select **Linear Diameter** in the option menu, and then place the dimension.

12. Pick the projected **X-axis** as the first entity to dimension as shown in the figure below.

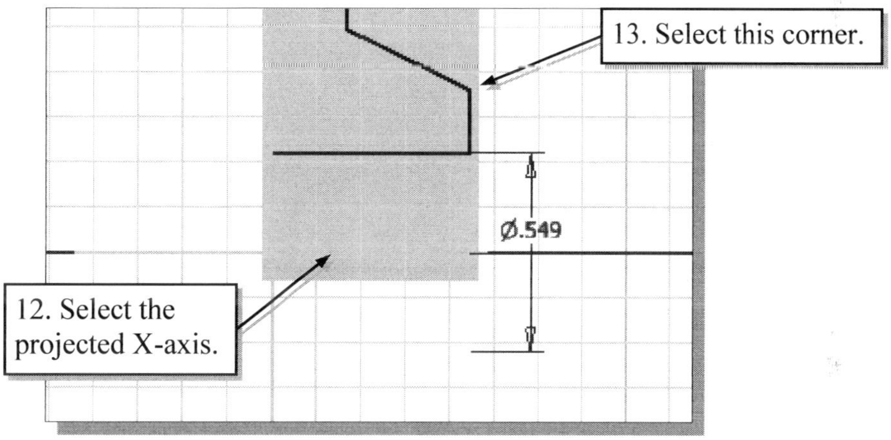

13. Select the **corner point** as the second object to dimension as shown in the above figure.

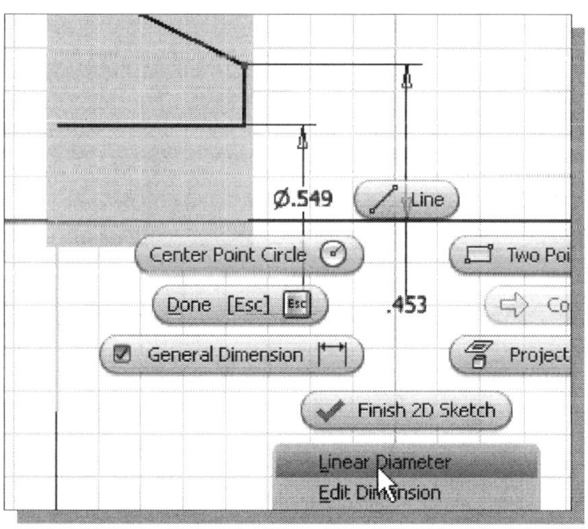

14. Inside the graphics window, right-click to bring up the option menu and select **Linear Diameter**.

15. Place the dimension text toward the right side of the sketch.

16. On your own, create and adjust the vertical size/location dimensions as shown below. (Hint: Modify the larger dimensions first.)

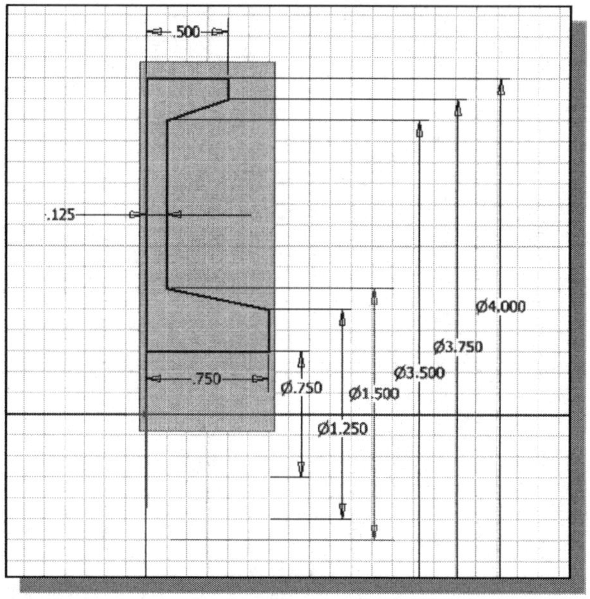

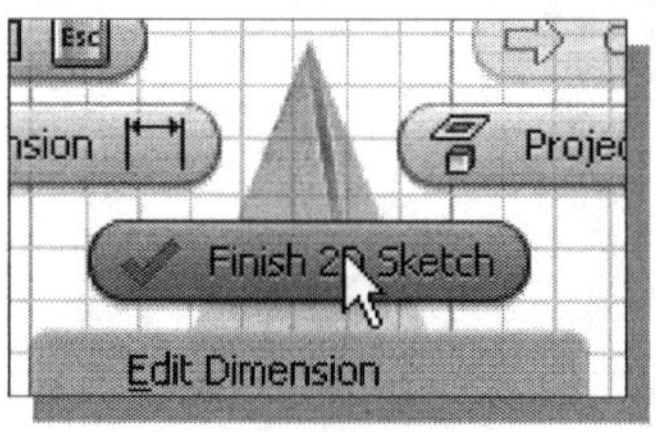

17. Inside the graphics window, click once with the right-mouse-button to display the option menu. Select **Finish 2D Sketch** in the pop-up menu to end the **Sketch** option.

➢ On your own, use the **3D-Rotate** command to confirm the completed sketch and dimensions are on a 2D plane.

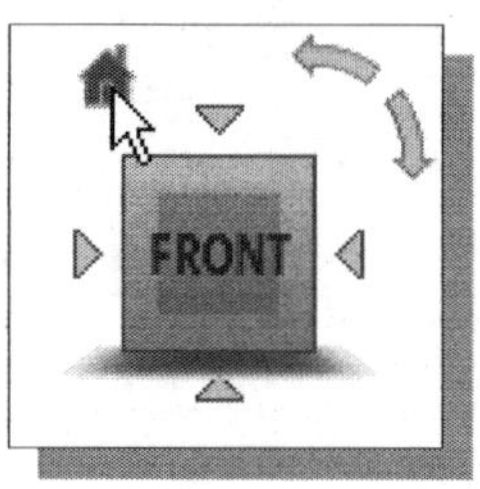

18. Select **Home View** in the **ViewCube** to adjust the display of the 2D sketch to the isometric view.

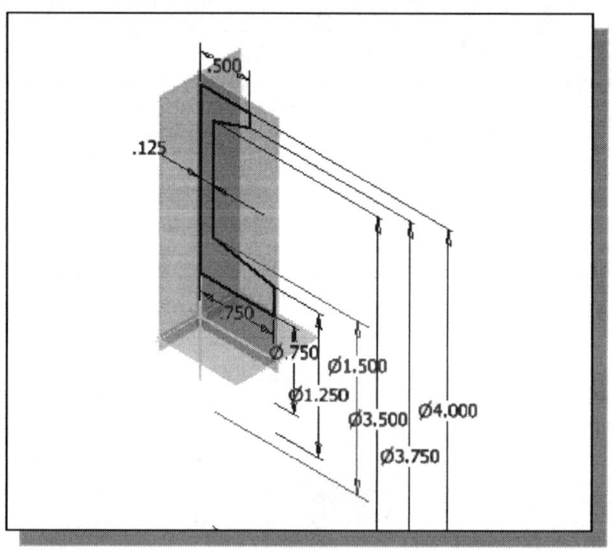

Create the Revolved Feature

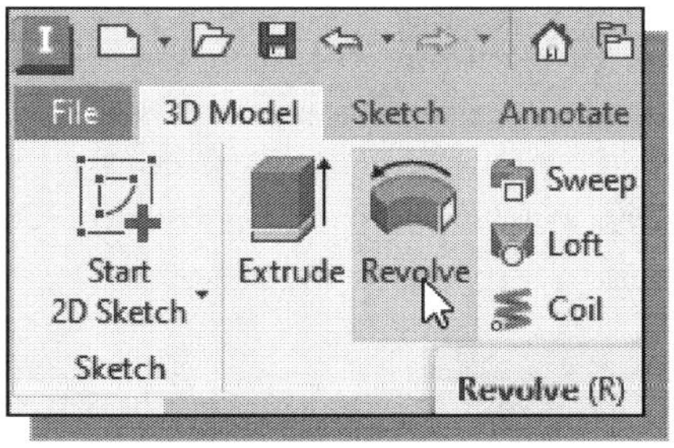

1. In the *Create Feature* panel select the **Revolve** command by clicking the left-mouse-button on the icon.

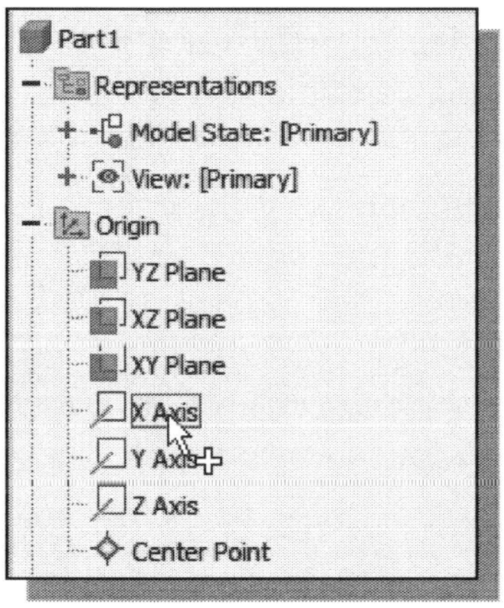

2. In the *Revolve* dialog box, the **Axis** button is activated indicating Autodesk Inventor expects us to select the revolution axis for the revolved feature. Select **X-Axis** as the axis of rotation in the *browser* window as shown.

3. In the *Revolve* dialog box, confirm the termination *Extents* option is set to **Full** as shown.

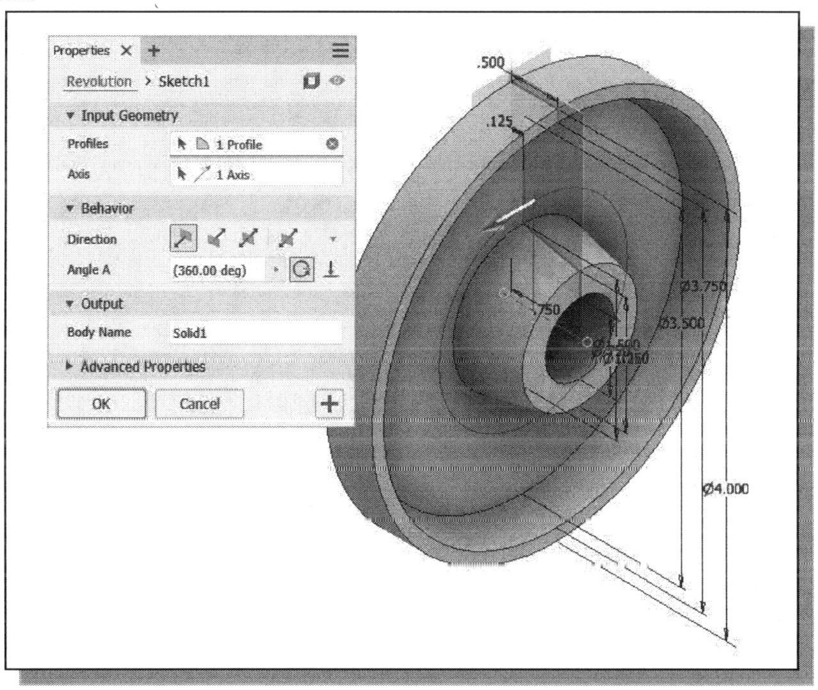

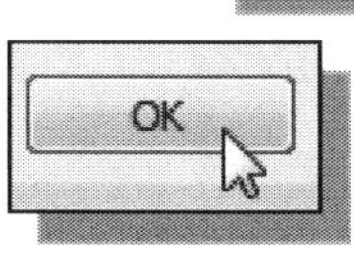

4. Click on the **OK** button to accept the settings and create the revolved feature.

Mirroring Features

In Autodesk Inventor, features can be mirrored to create and maintain complex symmetrical features. We can mirror a feature about a work plane or a specified surface. We can create a mirrored feature while maintaining the original parametric definitions, which can be quite useful in creating symmetrical features. For example, we can create one quadrant of a feature, and then mirror it twice to create a solid with four identical quadrants.

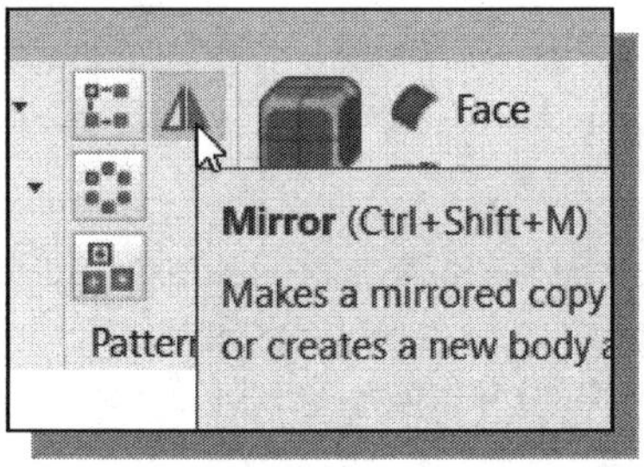

1. In the *Pattern* panel, select the **Mirror Feature** command by left-clicking on the icon.

2. In the *Mirror Pattern* dialog box, the **Features** button is activated. Autodesk Inventor expects us to select features to be mirrored. In the prompt area, the message *"Select feature to pattern"* is displayed. Select **any edge** of the 3D base feature.

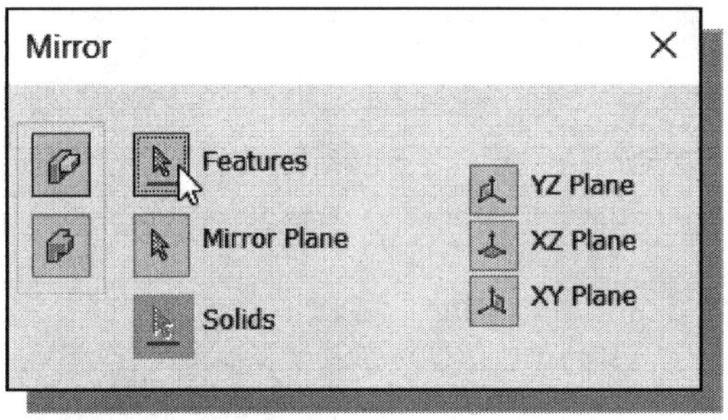

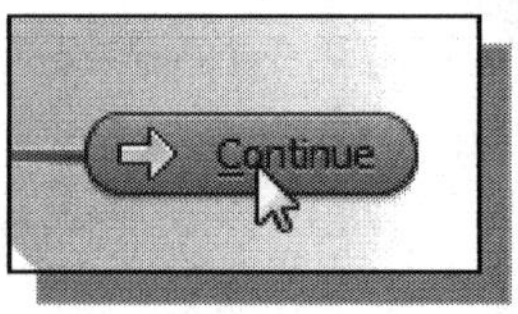

3. Inside the graphics window, **right-click** to bring up the **option menu**.

4. Select **Continue** in the option list to proceed with the Mirror Feature command.

5. In the *Mirror Pattern* dialog box, we can also activate the **Mirror Plane** option by clicking on the icon. Autodesk Inventor expects us to select a planar surface about which to mirror.

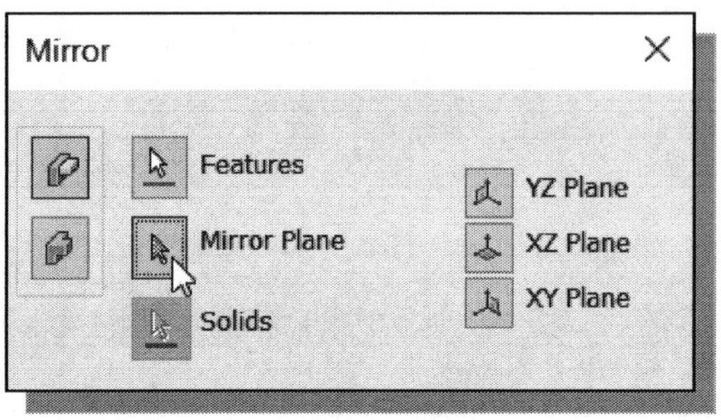

6. On your own, use the **ViewCube** or the **3D-Rotate** function key [**F4**] to dynamically rotate the solid model so that we are viewing the back surface as shown.

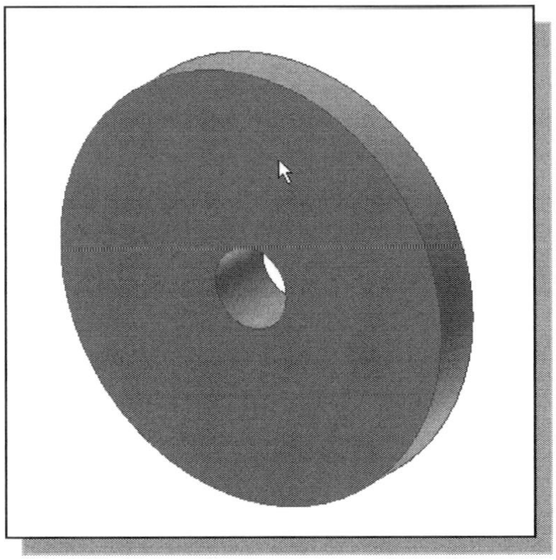

7. Select the surface as shown to the left as the planar surface about which to mirror.

8. Click on the **OK** button to accept the settings and create a mirrored feature.

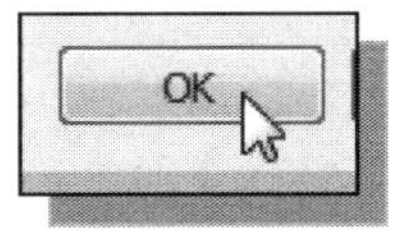

9. On your own, use the **ViewCube** or the **3D-Rotate** function key [**F4**] to dynamically rotate the solid model and view the resulting solid.

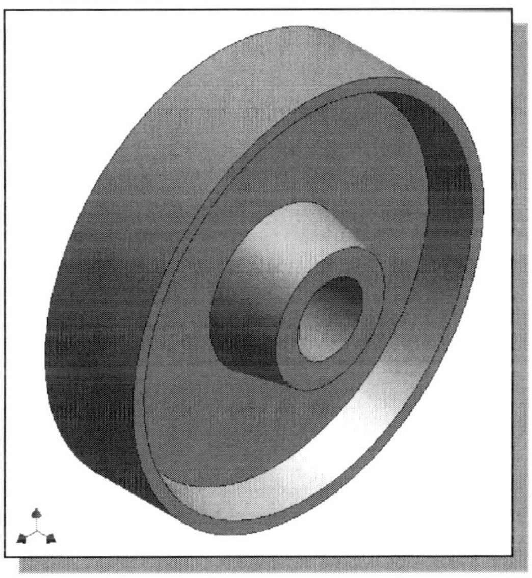

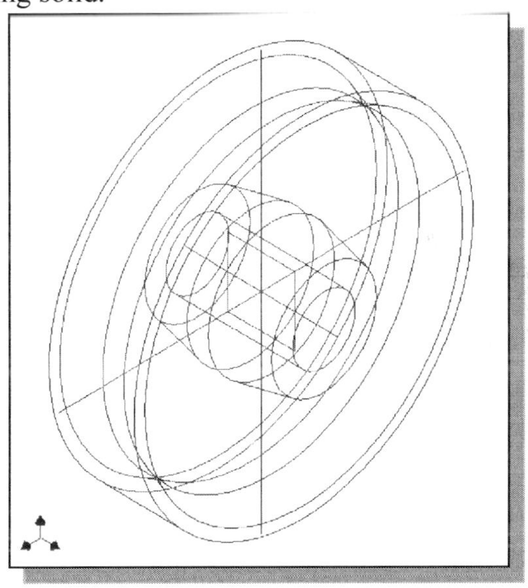

➢ Now is a good time to save the model (quick-key: [**Ctrl**] + [**S**]). It is a good habit to save your model periodically, just in case something might go wrong while you are working on it. You should also save the model after you have completed any major constructions.

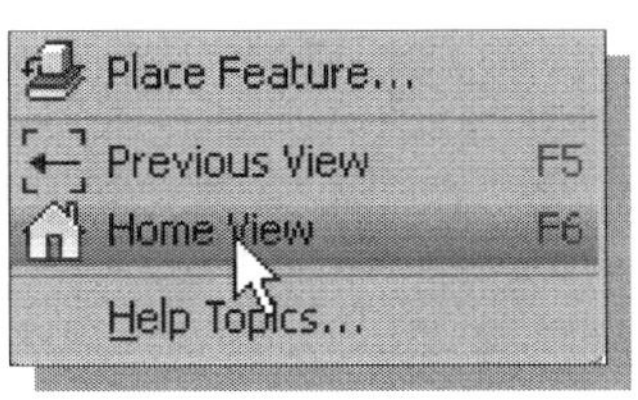

10. Inside the graphics window, right-click to bring up the option menu.

11. Select **Home View** in the option list to adjust the display of the 2D sketch on the screen.

Create a Pattern Leader Using Construction Geometry

In Autodesk Inventor, we can also use **construction geometry** to help define, constrain, and dimension the required geometry. **Construction geometry** can be lines, arcs, and circles that are used to line up or define other geometry but are not themselves used as the shape geometry of the model. When profiling the rough sketch, Autodesk Inventor will separate the construction geometry from the other entities and treat them as construction entities. Construction geometry can be dimensioned and constrained just like any other profile geometry. When the profile is turned into a 3D feature, the construction geometry remains in the sketch definition but does not show in the 3D model. Using construction geometry in profiles may mean fewer constraints and dimensions are needed to control the size and shape of geometric sketches. We will illustrate the use of the construction geometry to create a cut feature.

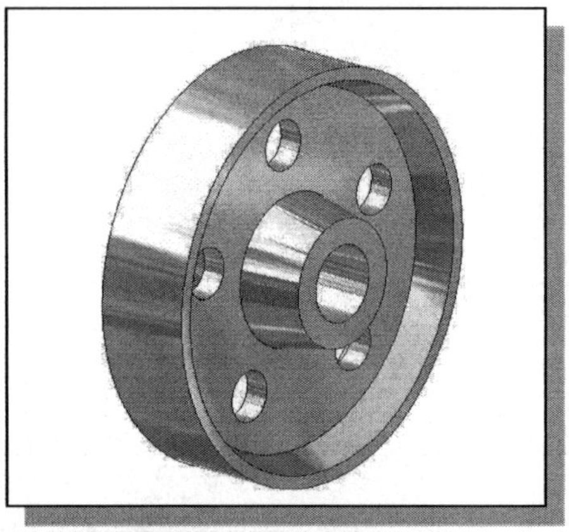

- The *Pulley* design requires the placement of five identical holes on the base solid. Instead of creating the five holes one at a time, we can simplify the creation of these holes by using the Pattern command, which allows us to create duplicate features. Prior to using the Pattern command, we will first create a ***pattern leader***, which is a regular extruded feature.

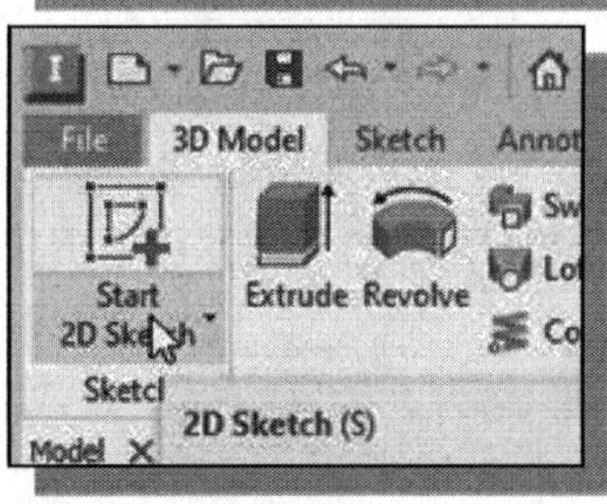

1. In the *Sketch* toolbar select the **Start 2D Sketch** command by left-clicking once on the icon.

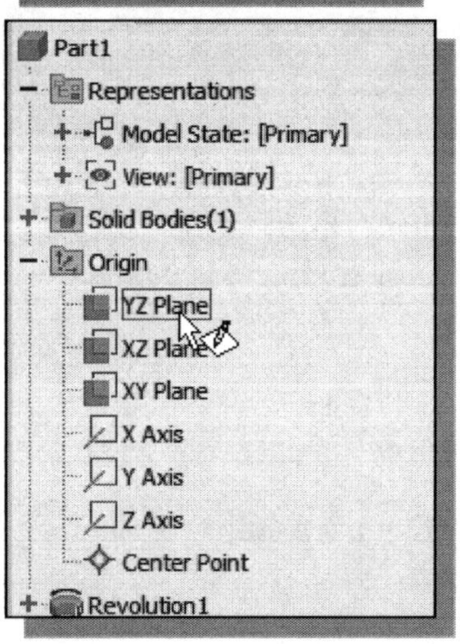

2. In the *Status Bar* area, the message "*Select face, work plane, sketch or sketch geometry.*" is displayed. Pick the YZ Plane, inside the *browser* window, as shown.

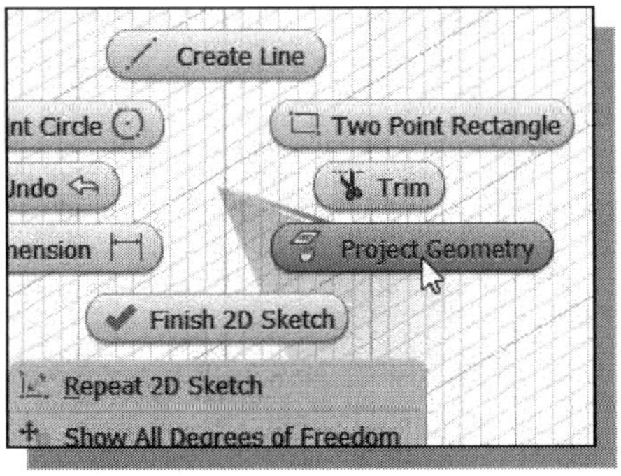

3. Inside the graphics window, **right-click** to bring up the option menu.

4. Select **Project Geometry** in the option menu. The **Project Geometry** command allows us to project existing geometry to the active sketching plane.

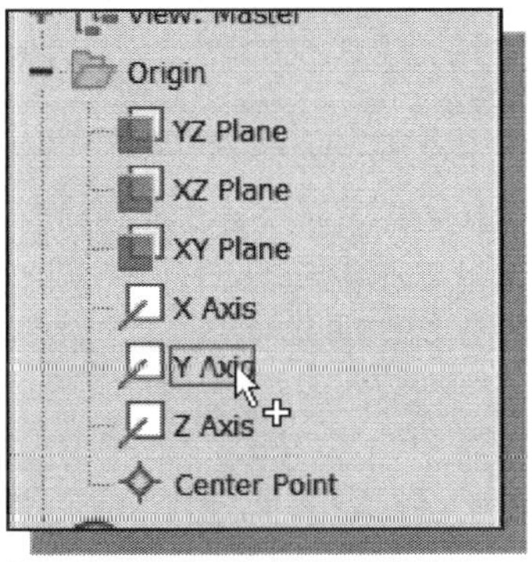

5. In the *Status Bar* area, the message "*Select edge, vertex, work geometry or sketch geometry to project.*" is displayed. Inside the *browser* window, select the **Y-axis** and **Z-axis** to project these entities onto the sketching plane.

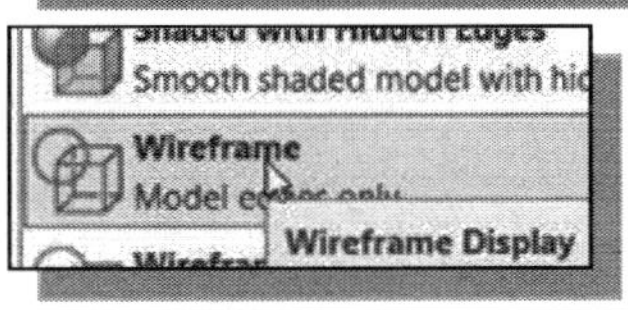

6. On your own, set the display to *wireframe* by clicking on the **Wireframe Display** icon in the *View* panel.

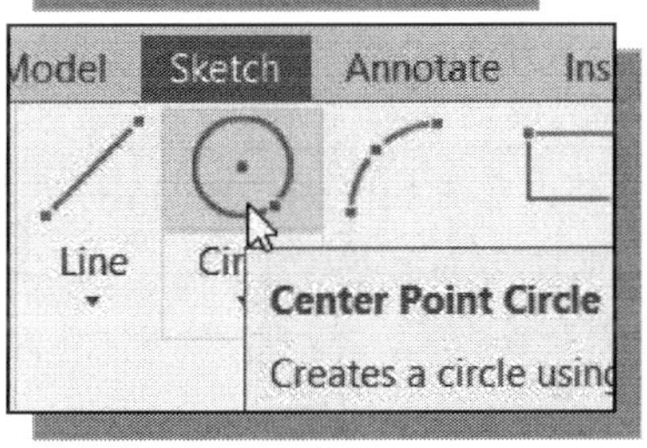

7. Select the **Center Point Circle** command by clicking once with the left-mouse-button on the icon in the *2D Sketch* panel.

8. Create a circle of arbitrary size as shown below.

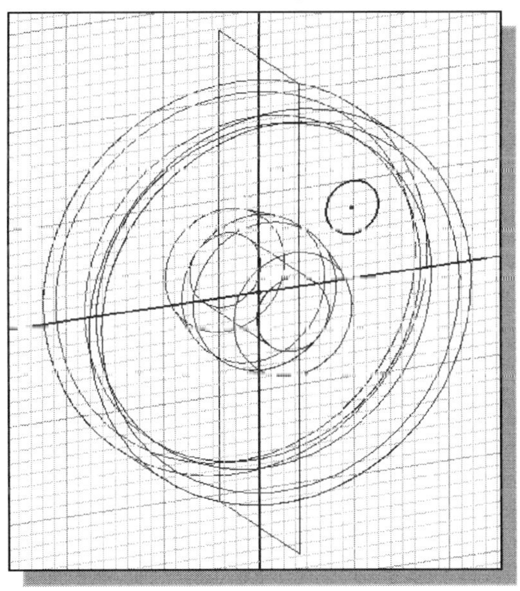

9. In the *Standard* toolbar area, click on the **Look At** button.

10. Select the circle we just created to orient the display of the sketching plane on the screen.

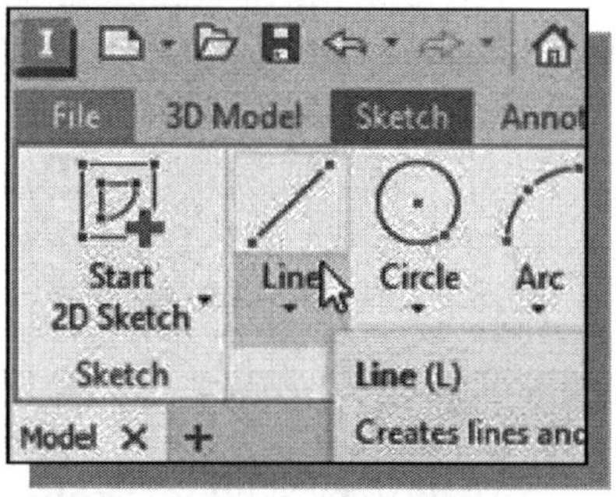

11. Select the **Line** command in the *2D Sketch* panel. A brief description of the command is displayed at the bottom of the drawing screen: "*Creates Straight lines and arcs.*"

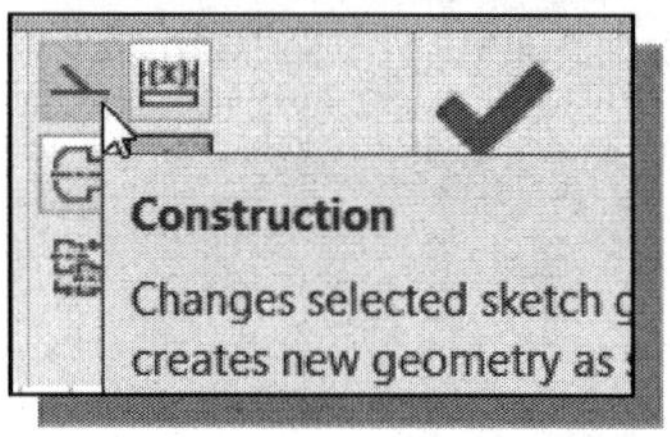

12. Set the *Style* option to **Construction** as shown.

13. Create a *construction line* by connecting from the center of the circle we just created to the projected center point (***origin***) at the center of the 3D model as shown below.

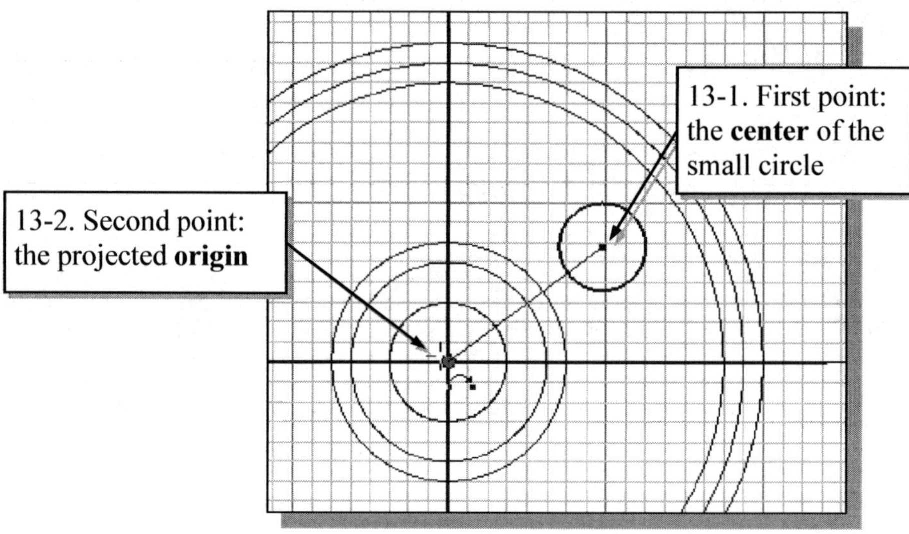

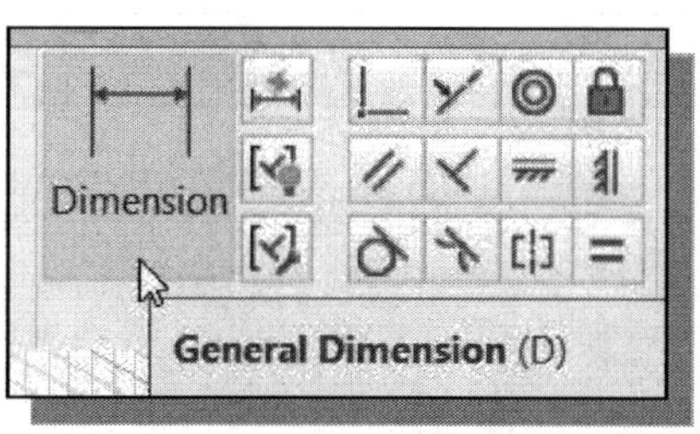

14. Select the **General Dimension** command in the *Constrain* panel.

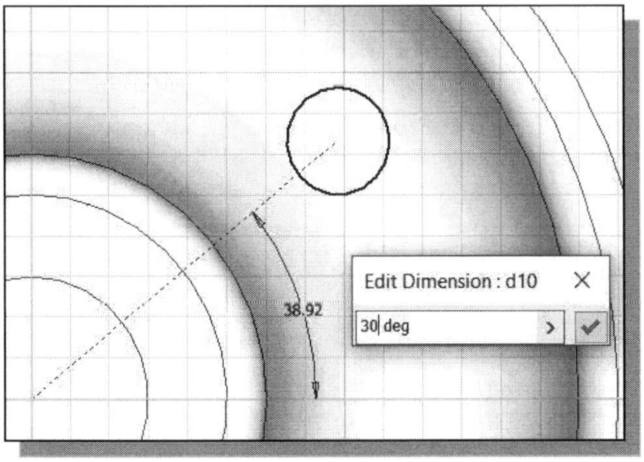

15. Pick the **horizontal axis** as the first entity to dimension as shown in the figure.

16. Select the **construction line** as the second object to dimension.

17. Place the dimension text to the right of the model as shown.

18. On your own, set the angle dimension to **30** as shown in the above figure.

➢ Note that the small circle moves as the location of the construction line is adjusted by the *angle dimension* we created.

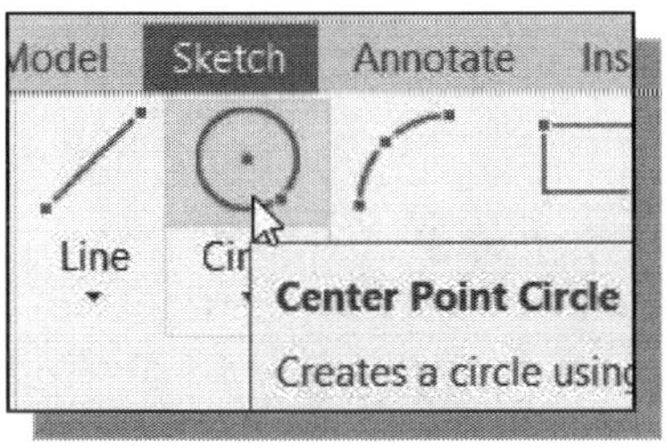

19. Select the **Center Point Circle** command by clicking once with the left-mouse-button on the icon in the *Draw* panel.

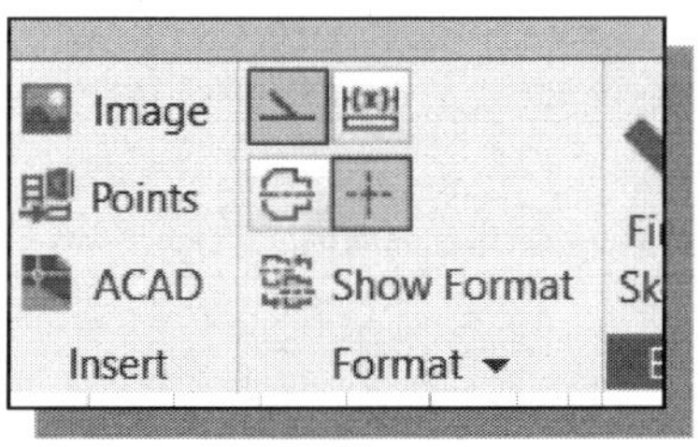

20. Confirm the *Style* option is still set to **Construction**.

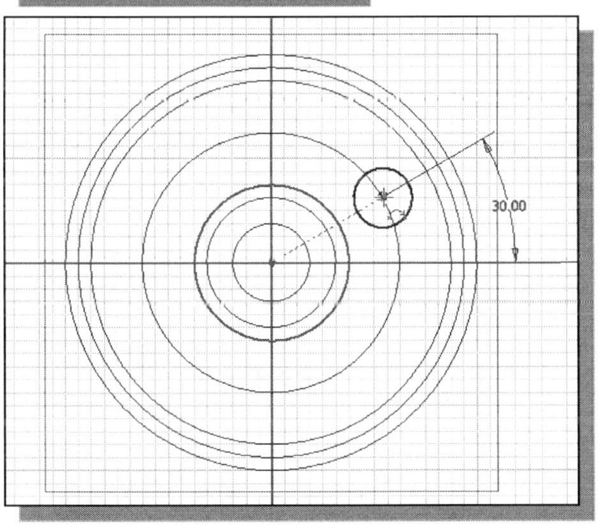

21. Create a *construction circle* by placing the center at the projected center point (***origin***).

22. Pick the **center** of the small circle to set the size of the construction circle as shown.

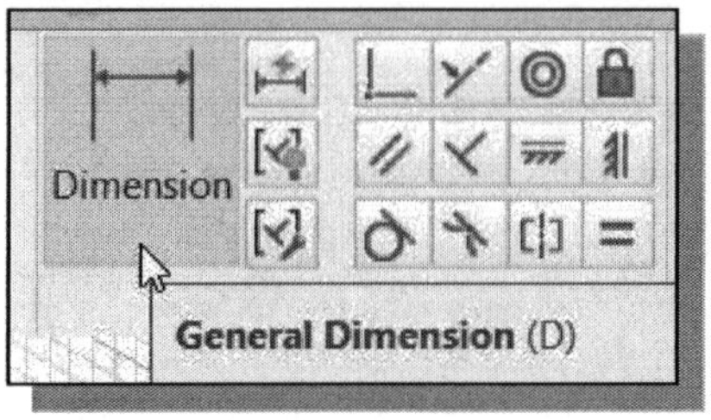

23. Select the **General Dimension** command in the *Constrain* panel.

24. On your own, create the two diameter dimensions, **.5** and **2.5**, as shown below.

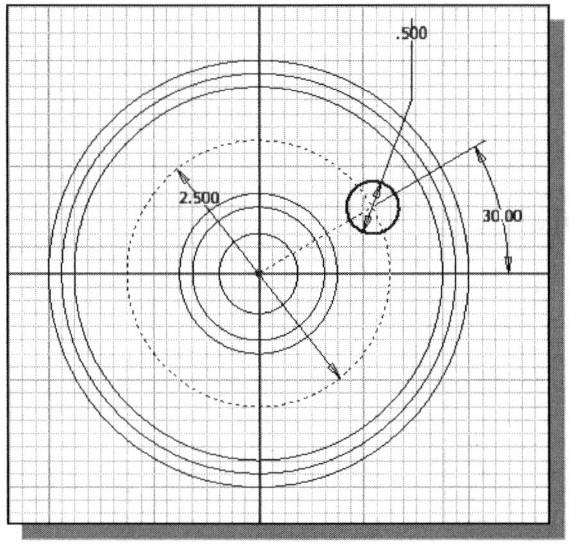

25. Inside the graphics window, click once with the right-mouse-button to display the option menu. Select **Finish Sketch** in the pop-up menu to end the **Sketch** option.

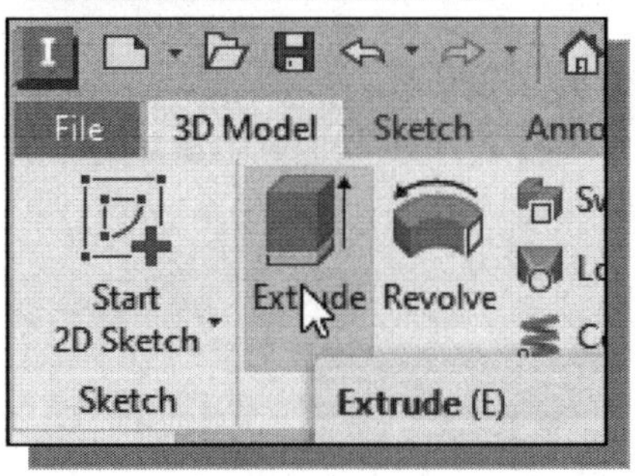

26. In the *Create Features* panel select the **Extrude** command by left-clicking on the icon.

27. Pick the inside region of the circle to set up the profile of the extrusion.

28. Inside the *Extrude* dialog box, select the **Cut** operation for **Symmetric (both directions)**, and set the *Extents* to **All** as shown.

29. Click on the **OK** button to accept the settings and create the cut feature.

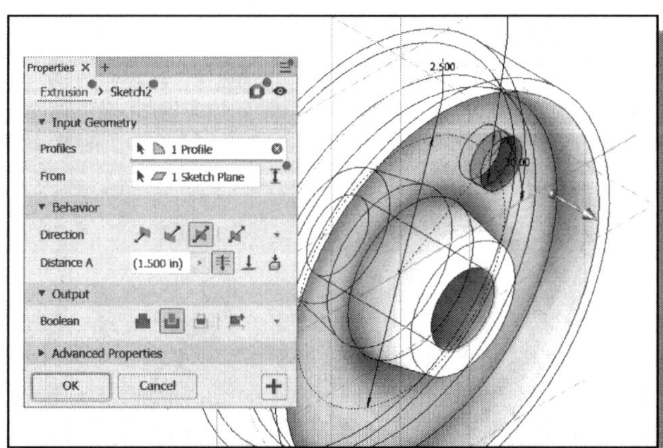

30. On your own, adjust the angle dimension applied to the construction line of the cut feature to **90** and observe the effect of the adjustment.

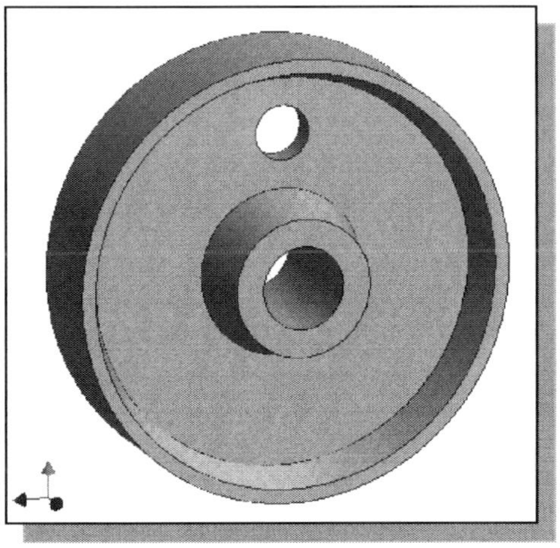

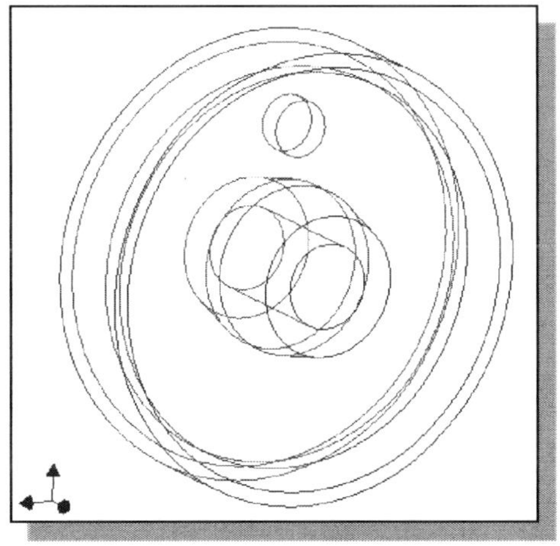

Circular Pattern

In Autodesk Inventor, existing features can be easily duplicated. The **Pattern** command allows us to create both rectangular and polar arrays of features. The patterned features are parametrically linked to the original feature; any modifications to the original feature are also reflected in the arrayed features.

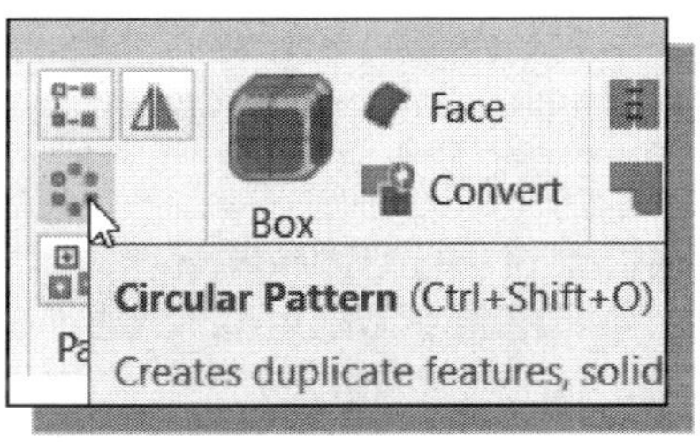

1. In the *Pattern Features* panel, select the **Circular Pattern** command by left-clicking once on the icon.

2. The message "*Select Feature to be arrayed:*" is displayed in the command prompt window. Select the **circular cut feature** when it is highlighted as shown.

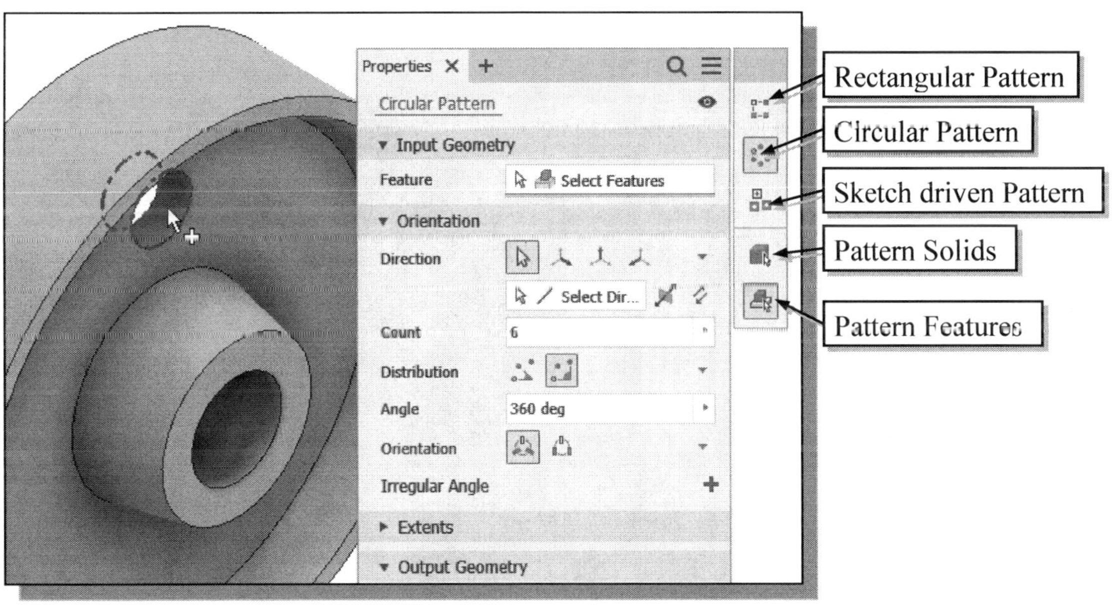

3. Inside the graphics window, **right-click** to bring up the **option menu**.

4. Select **Continue** in the option list to proceed with the Circular Pattern command.

5. Autodesk Inventor expects us to select an axis to pattern about. In the prompt area, the message "*Define the axis of revolution*" is displayed. Select the **X-Axis** in the *browser* window or the inside cylindrical surface in the graphics window.

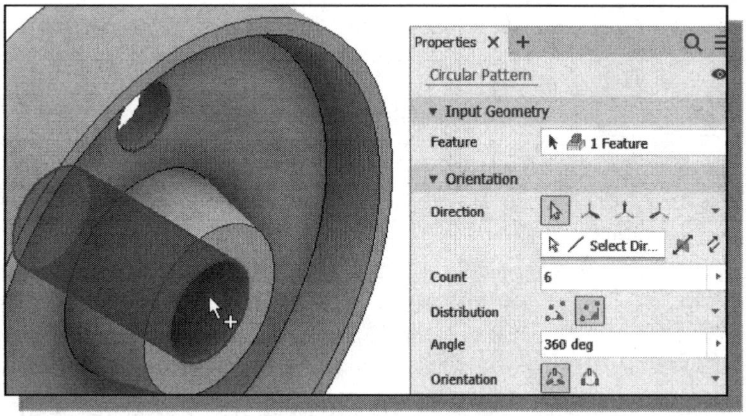

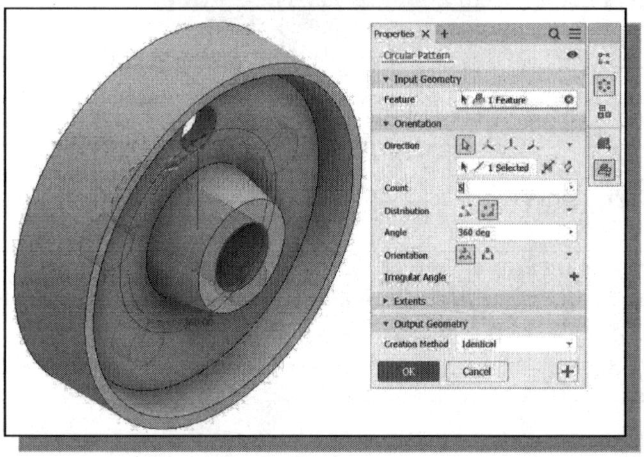

6. In the *Circular Pattern* dialog box, enter **5** in the ***Count*** box and **360** in the ***Angle*** box as shown. (Note the different options available for the Circular Pattern command.)

7. Click on the **OK** button to accept the settings and create the *circular pattern*.

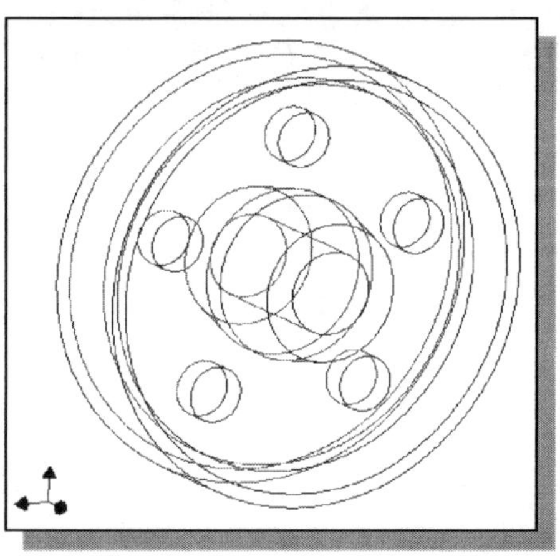

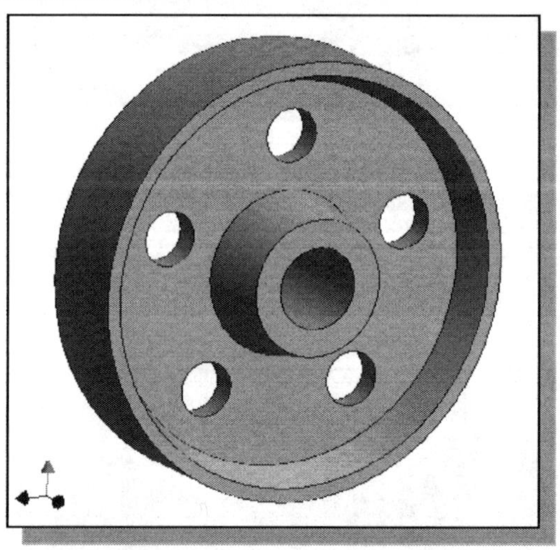

Examine the Design Parameters

1. In the *Manage* tab select the **Parameters** command by left-clicking once on the icon. The *Parameters* pop-up window appears.

2. Scroll down to the bottom of the list and locate the two dimensions used to create the circular pattern (the d15 & d16 dimensions in the below figure).

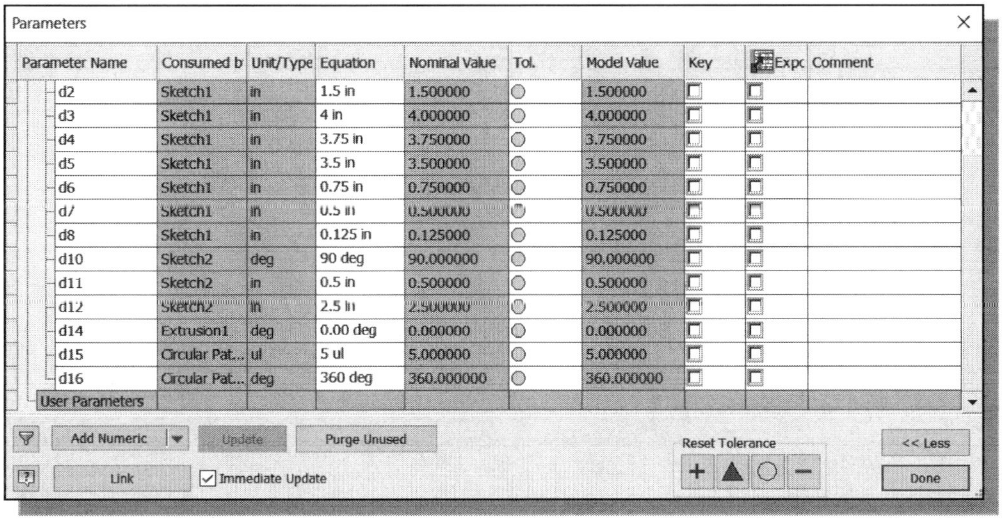

3. Click on the **Done** button to accept the settings.

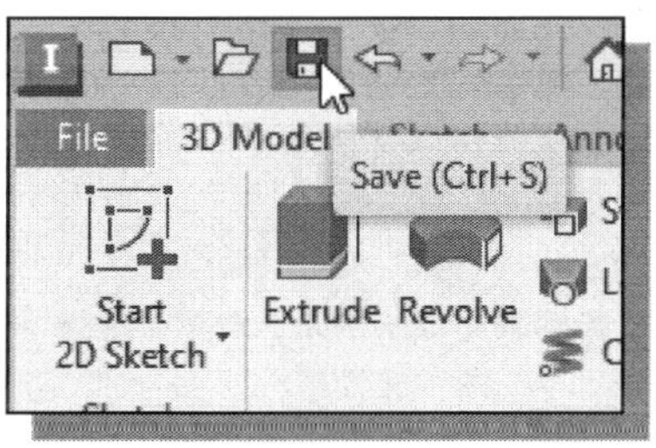

4. Select **Save** in the *Standard* toolbar; we can also use the "**Ctrl-S**" combination (press down the [Ctrl] key and hit the [S] key once) to save the part as ***Pulley*** in the **Chapter14** folder.

Drawing Mode – Defining a New Border and Title Block

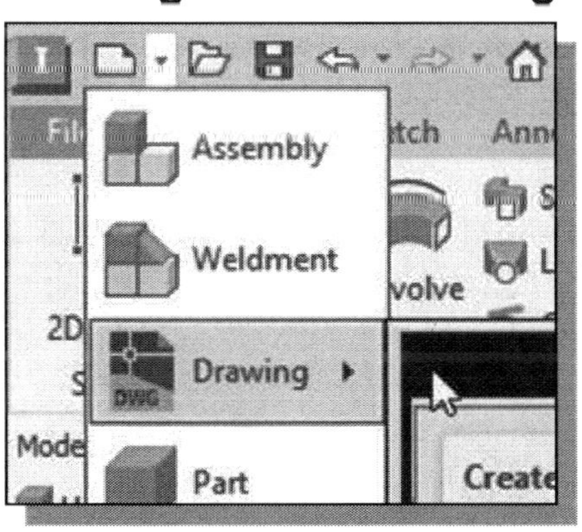

1. Click on the **drop-down arrow** next to the **New File** button in the *Quick Access* toolbar area to display the available new file options.

2. Select **Drawing** from the drop-down list.

➢ Note that a new graphics window appears on the screen. We can switch between the solid model and the drawing by clicking the corresponding graphics window.

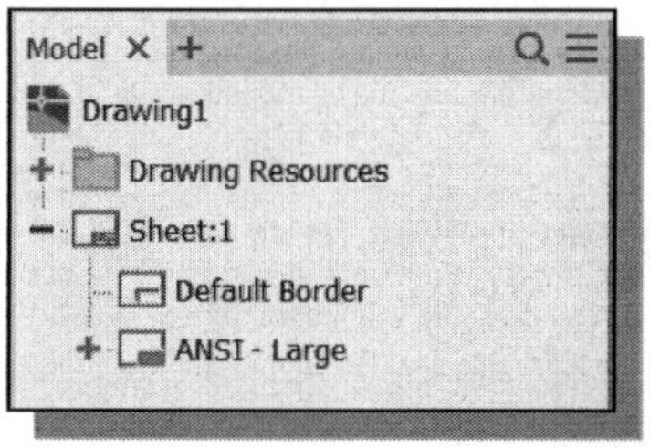

3. Inside the drawing *browser* window, click on the [**+**] symbol in front of **Sheet1** to display the settings.

4. On your own, **delete** the **Default Border** and the **ANSI-Large** ***title block***. (Hint: right-click on the names to bring up the option menu.)

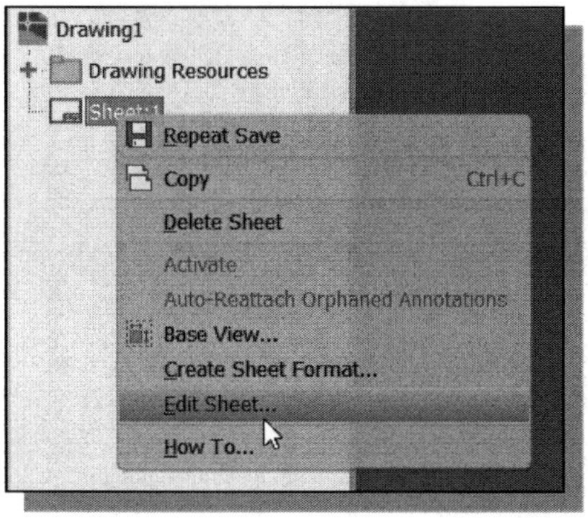

5. Inside the drawing *browser* window, **right-click** on **Sheet1** to bring up the option menu.

6. Select **Edit Sheet** in the option list.

7. In the *Edit Sheet* dialog box, set the sheet size to **A** (8.5 × 11).

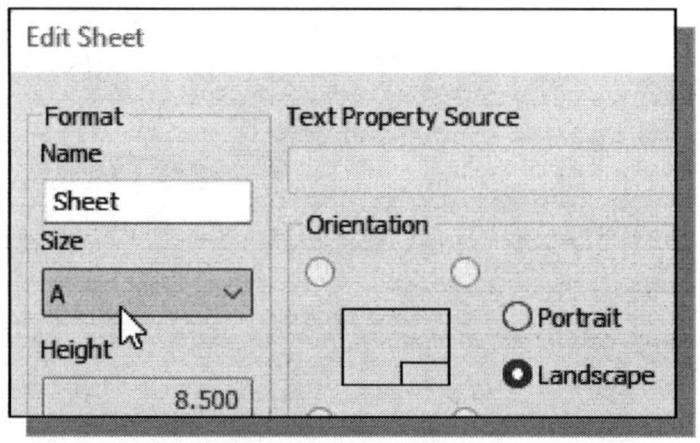

8. Confirm the page *Orientation* is set to **Landscape** and click on the **OK** button to accept the settings.

9. In the *Ribbon* toolbar panel, select **Manage → Define New Border**.

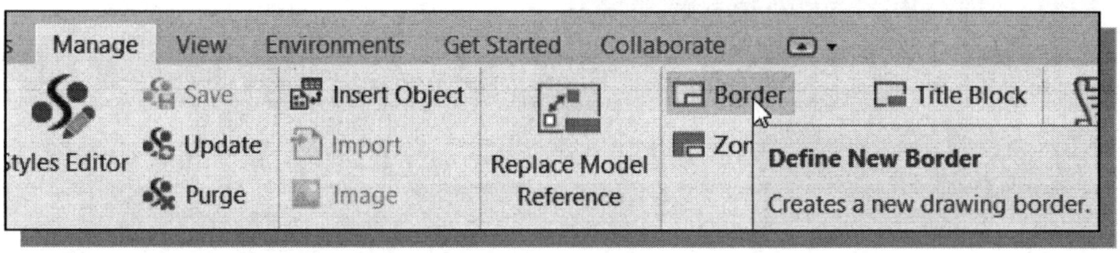

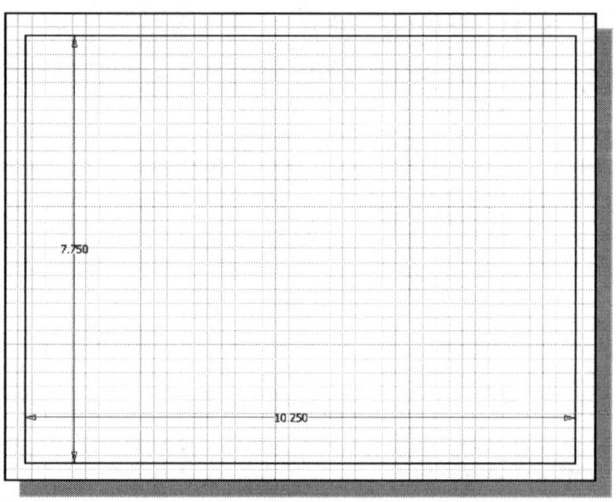

10. On your own, create a rectangle (**7.75** × **10.25**) using the **Two Point Rectangle** command and the **General Dimension** command.

11. Drag and drop the edges of the rectangle and position the rectangle to the center of the sheet.

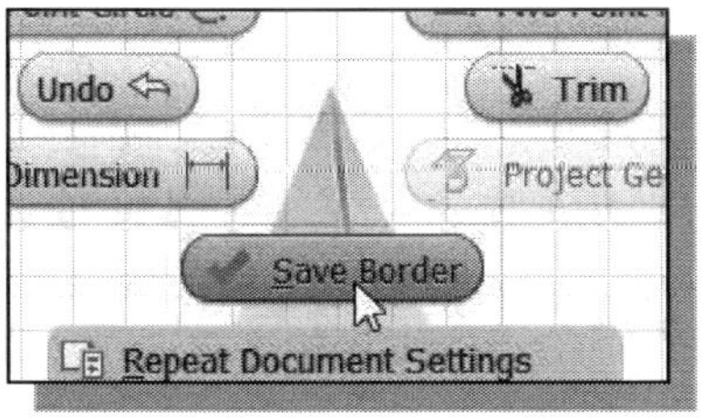

12. Inside the graphics window, **right-click** to bring up the option menu.

13. Select **Save Border** in the option list.

14. In the *Border* dialog box, enter **A-Size** as the new border name.

15. Click on the **Save** button to end the Define New Border command.

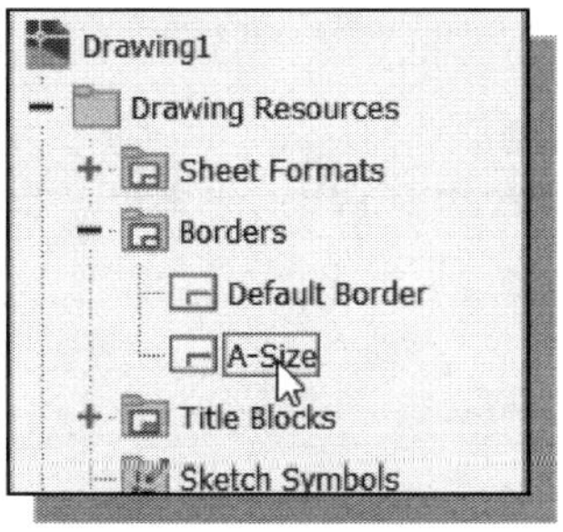

16. Inside the *browser* window, expand the **Drawing Resources** list by clicking on the [**+**] symbol.

17. **Double-click** on the **A-size** border, the border we just created, to place the border in the current drawing. Note that none of the dimensions used to construct the border are displayed.

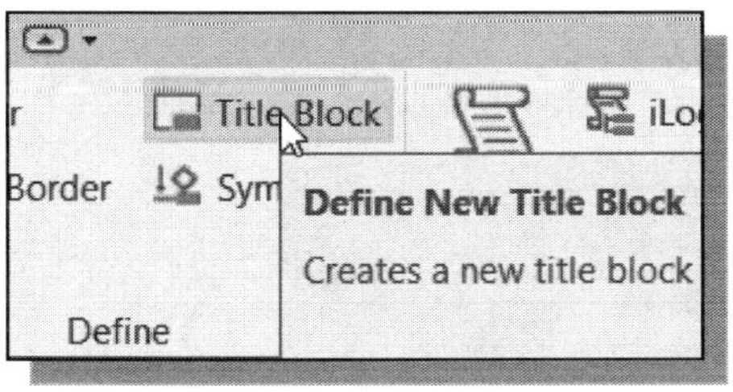

18. In the Define Toolbar, select **[Define] → [Title Block]**.

19. On your own, create a title block using the **Two Point Rectangle**, **Line**, **General Dimension**, and **Text** commands.

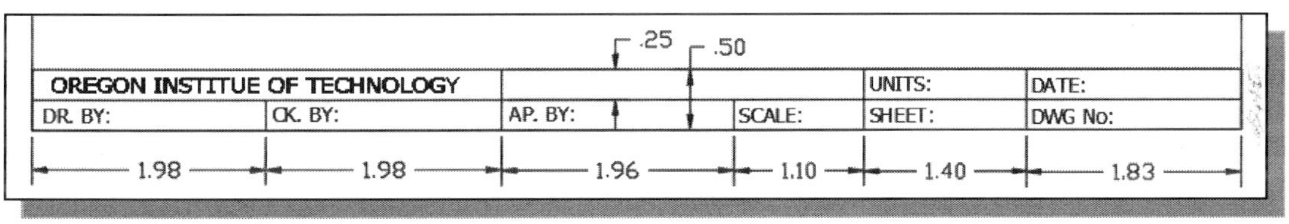

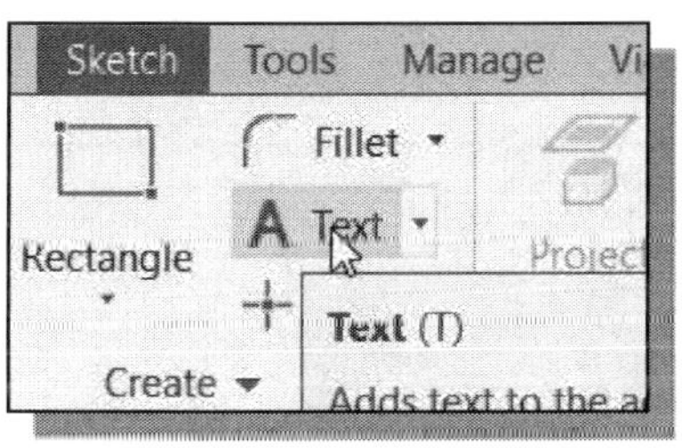

20. In the *Create toolbar*, activate the **Text** command as shown.

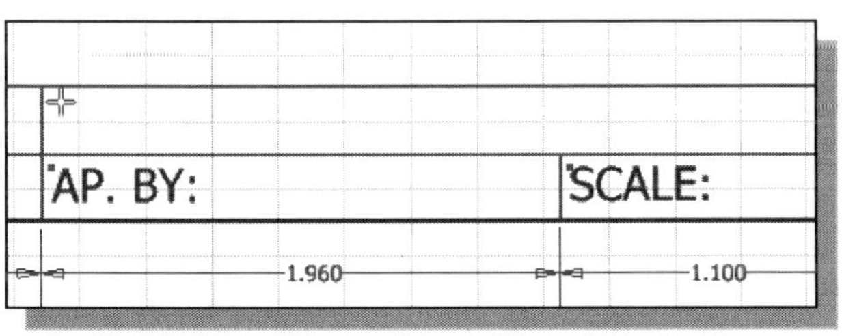

21. Click near the top left corner of the *Title Box*, the second box of the top section in the title block we just created, as shown.

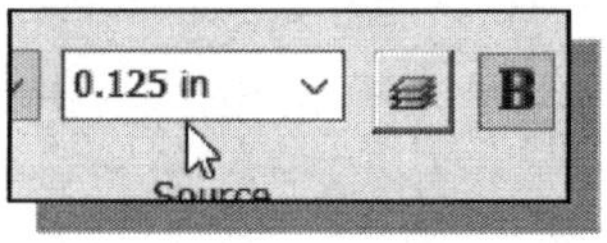

22. In the *Format Text dialog* box, adjust the text size to **0.125** as shown.

23. In the *Format Text dialog* box, select **Standard iProperties** and **Title** as the *Type* and *Property* parameter as shown.

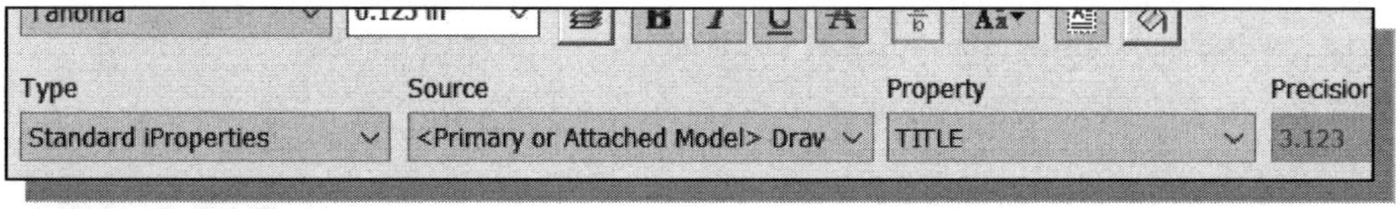

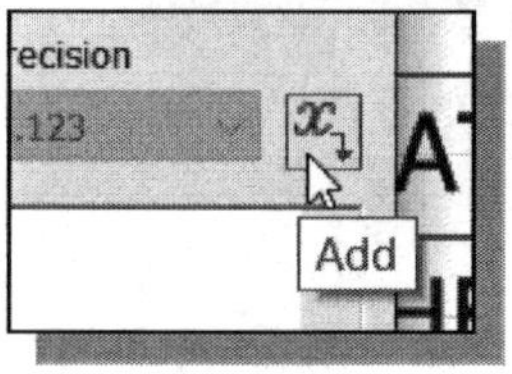

24. Click on the **Add Text Parameter** icon to insert the associated iProperty information to the title block.

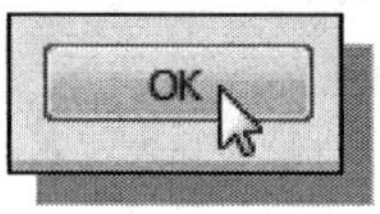

25. Click on the **OK** button to accept the settings.

26. On your own, repeat the above process to add the **Standard iProperty - Creation Date** to the *Date Box* as shown.

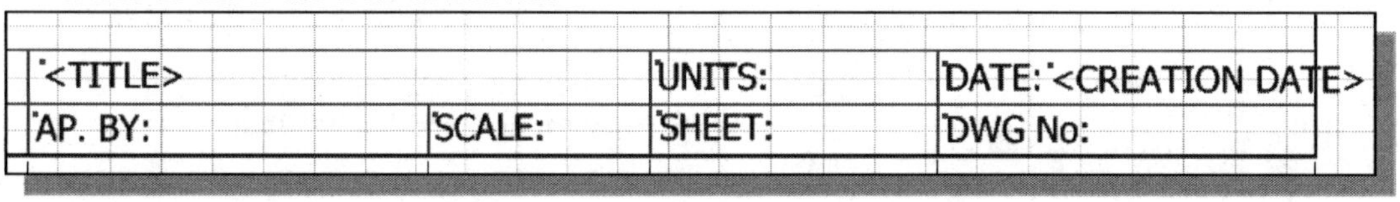

27. On your own, repeat the above steps and add in the associated Standard iProperties for the bottom line of the title block as shown.

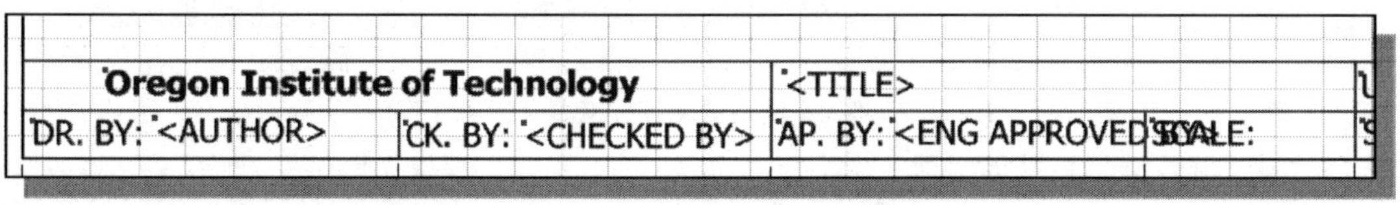

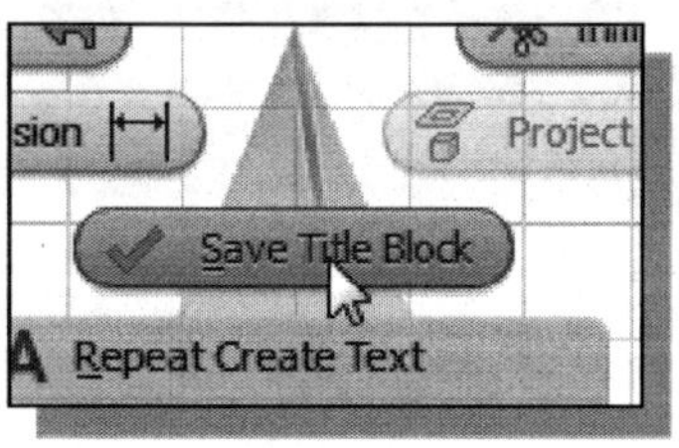

28. Inside the *graphics window*, right-click to bring up the option menu.

29. Select **Save Title Block** in the option list.

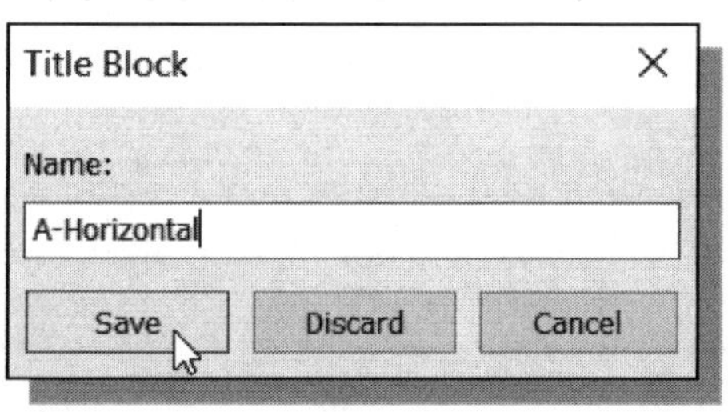

30. In the *Title Block* dialog box, enter **A-Horizontal** as the new title block name.

31. Click on the **Save** button to end the Define New Title Block command.

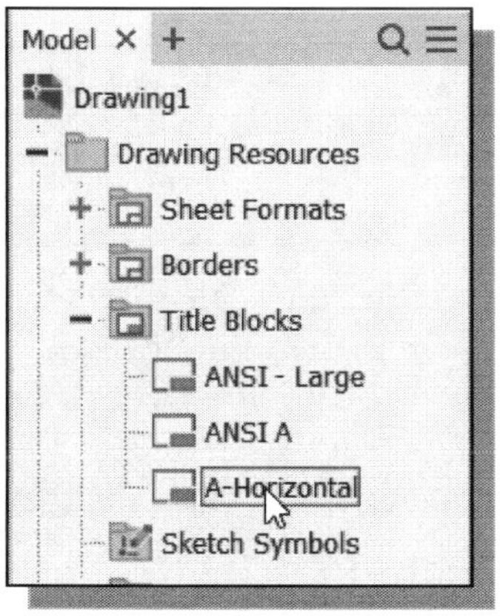

32. Inside the *browser* window, expand the **Title Blocks** list by clicking on the [**+**] symbol.

33. Double-click on the **A-Horizontal** title block, the title block we just created, to place it into the current drawing.

Create a Drawing Template

In Autodesk Inventor, each new drawing is created from a template. During the installation of Autodesk Inventor, a default drafting standard was selected which sets the default template used to create drawings. We can use this template or another predefined template, modify one of the predefined templates, or create our own templates to enforce drafting standards and other conventions. Any drawing file can be used as a template; a drawing file becomes a template when it is saved in the *Templates* folder. Once the template is saved, we can create a new drawing file using the new template.

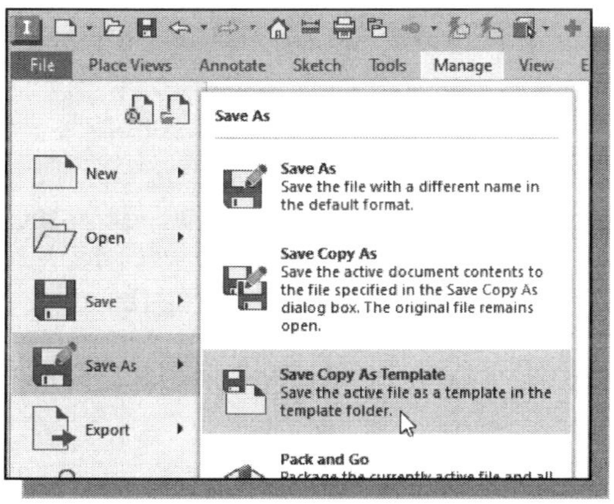

1. Select **Save Copy As Template** in the *File Menu*; we will save the current drawing as a template file.

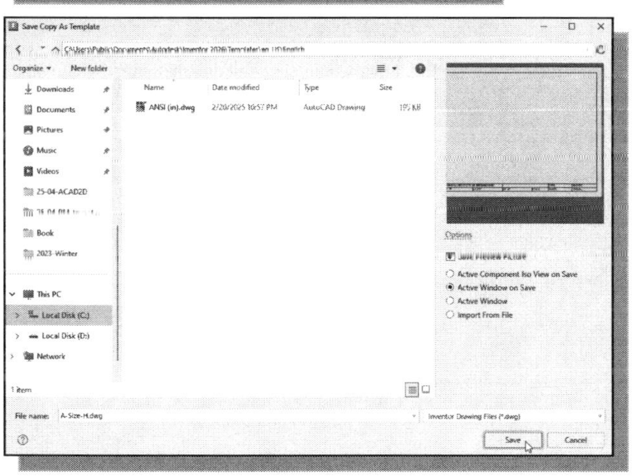

2. In the *Save As* dialog box, switch to the *Public User - Inventor* folder: **Inventor 2027 → Templates → en-US→ English** directory.

3. Enter **A-Size-H.dwg** as the template filename.

4. Click on the **Save** button to create a drawing template file.

Create the Necessary Views

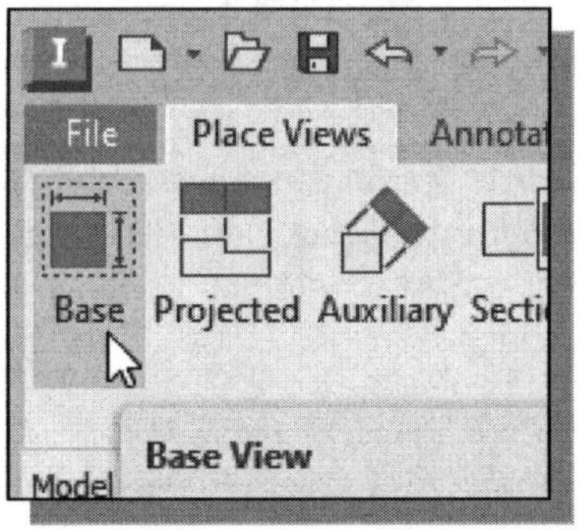

1. Click on **Base View** in the *Place Views* panel to create a base view.

2. In the *Drawing View* dialog box, set the scale to **3 : 4** and select the ***left*** view as shown in the figure below.

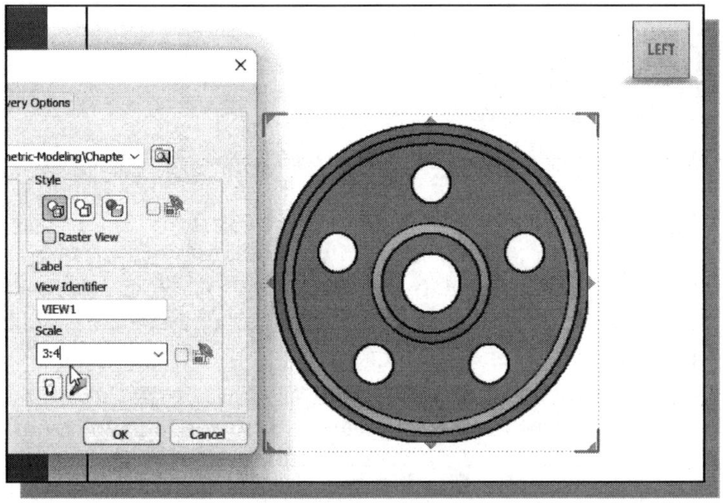

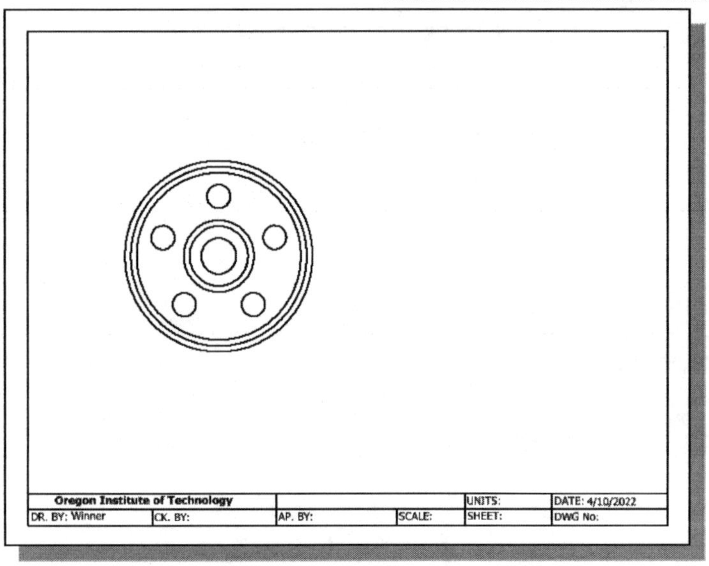

3. Move the cursor inside the graphics window and place the **base view** toward the left side of the border as shown. (If necessary, drag the *Drawing View* dialog box to another location on the screen.)

4. Click on the **OK** button to accept the setting.

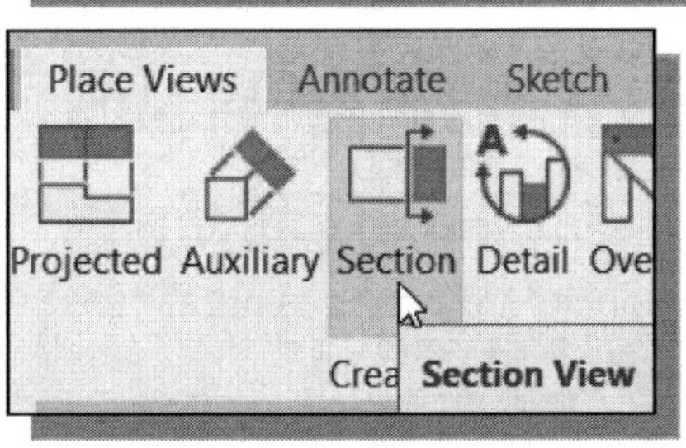

5. Click on the **Section View** button in the *Place Views* panel to create a section view.

6. Click on the **base view** to select the view where the section line is to be created.

7. Inside the graphics window, align the cursor to the center of the base view and create the vertical cutting plane line as shown.

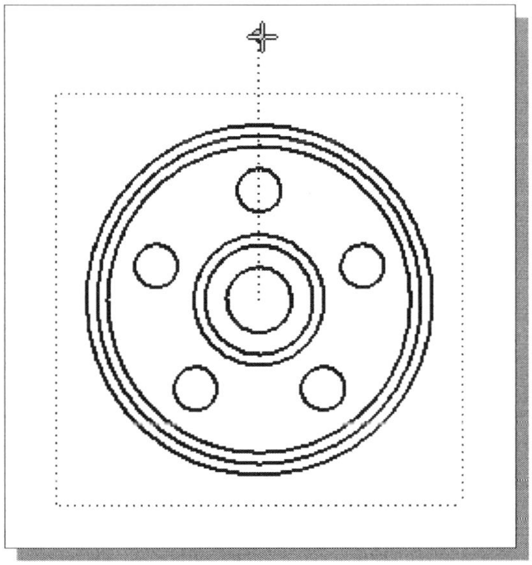

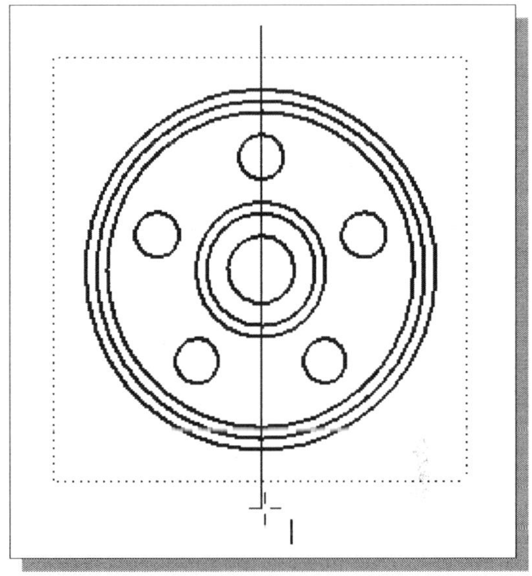

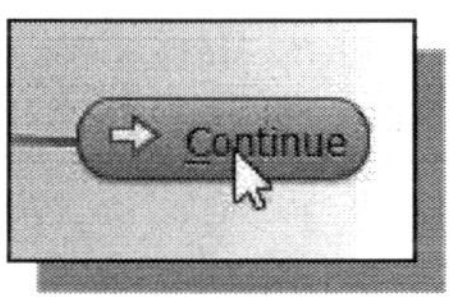

8. Inside the *graphics window*, right-click once to bring up the **option menu**.

9. Select **Continue** to proceed with the Section View command.

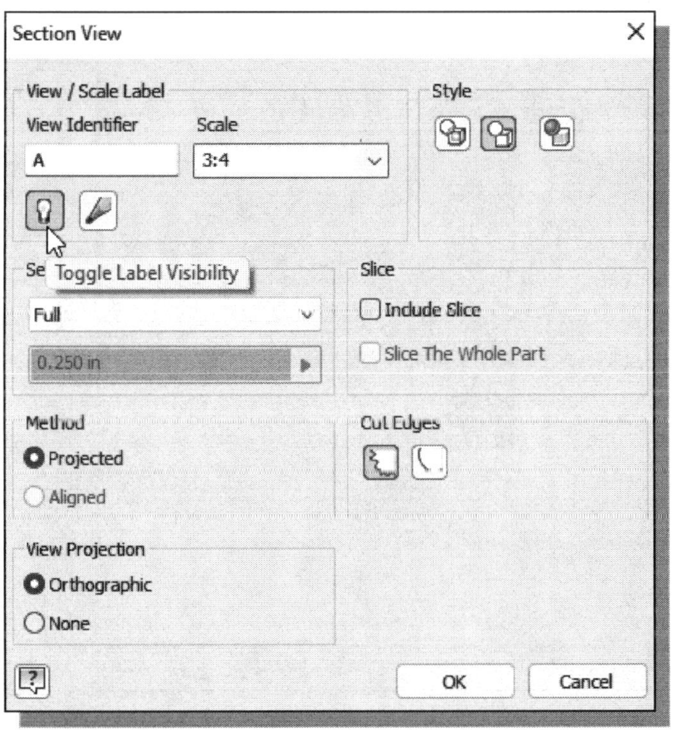

10. Inside the *Section View* dialog box, toggle ***OFF*** the **Label Visibility** option as shown.

11. Set the *Display Style* to **Hidden Line Removed**, as shown. (**DO NOT** click on the **OK** button.)

12. Next, Autodesk Inventor expects us to place the projected section. Select a location that is toward the right side of the base view as shown in the figure.

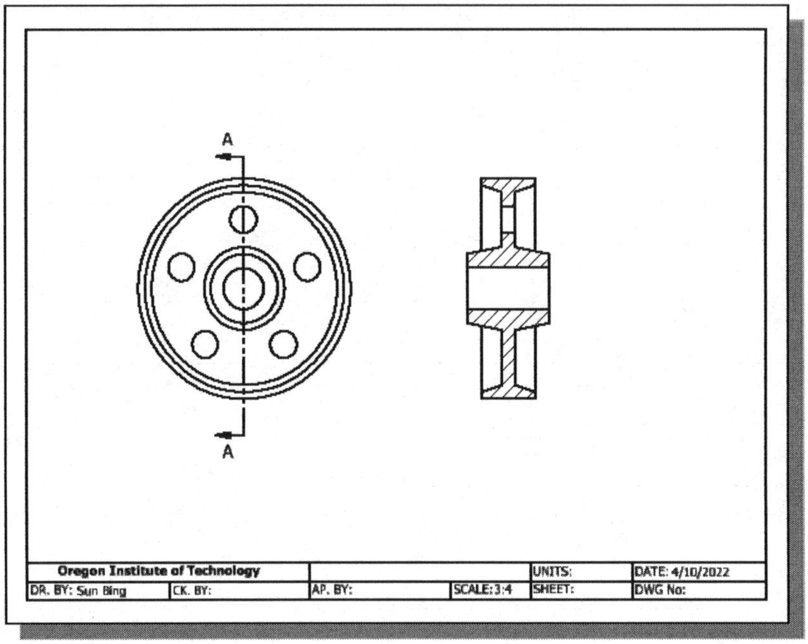

13. On your own, use the Projected View option and create an ***isometric*** **view** (Iso Top Left – ¾ scale) of the design and place the view toward the right side of the section view as shown below.

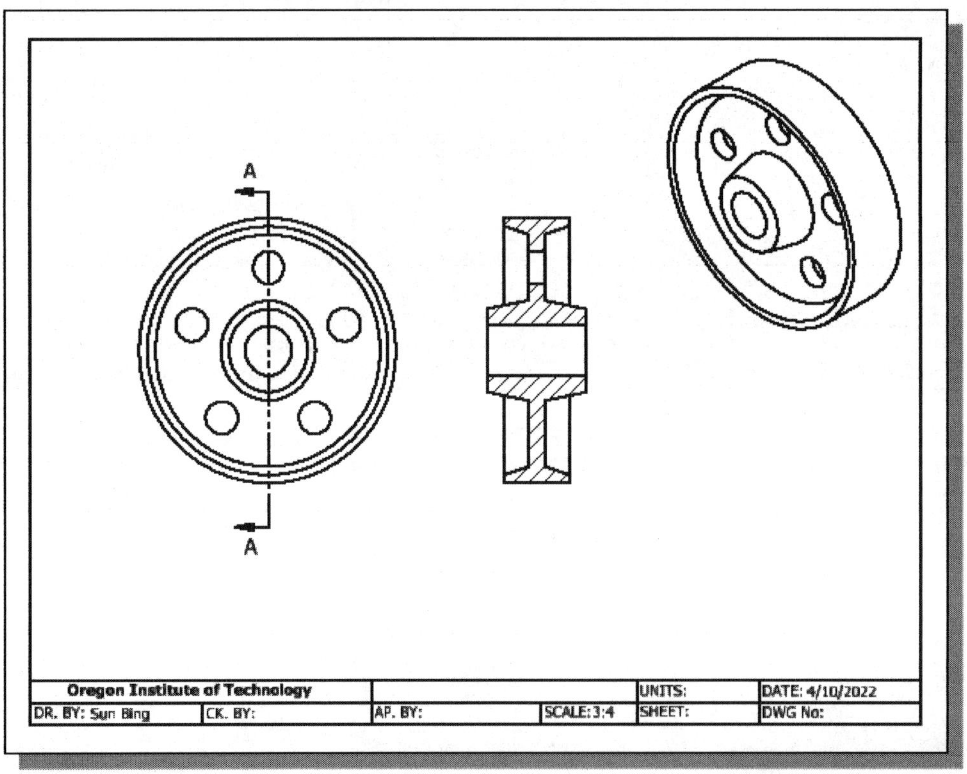

Retrieve Model Annotations – Features Option

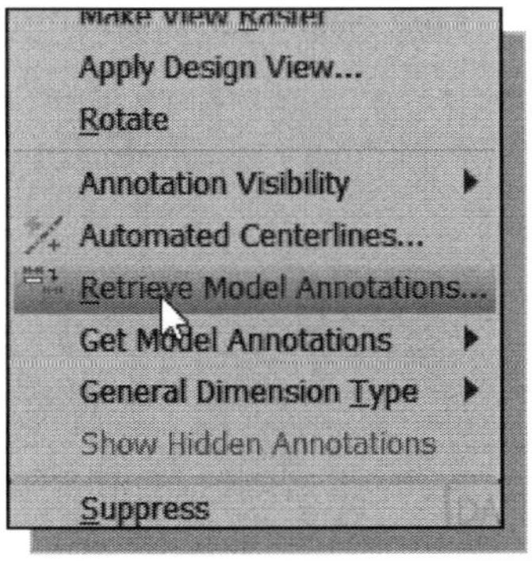

1. Move the cursor on top of the ***section* view** of the model and watch for the box around the entire view indicating the view is selectable as shown in the figure.

2. Inside the *graphics window*, **right-click** once to bring up the option menu.

3. Select **Retrieve Model Annotations** to display the parametric dimensions used to create the model.

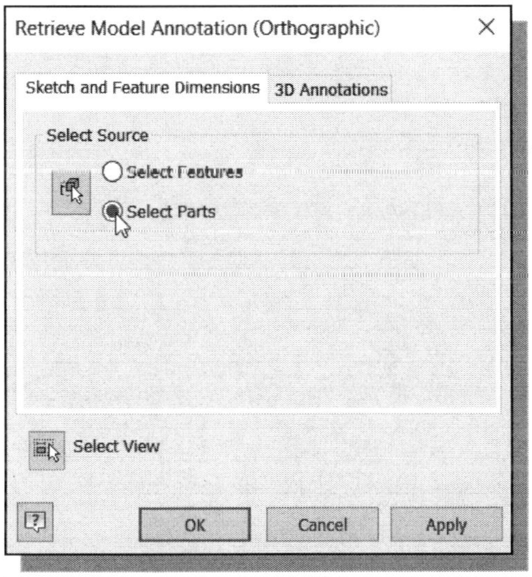

4. In the *Retrieve Model Annotations* dialog box, set the *Select Source* option to **Select Parts** as shown.

➢ The dimensions used to create the revolved feature are now displayed in the section view.

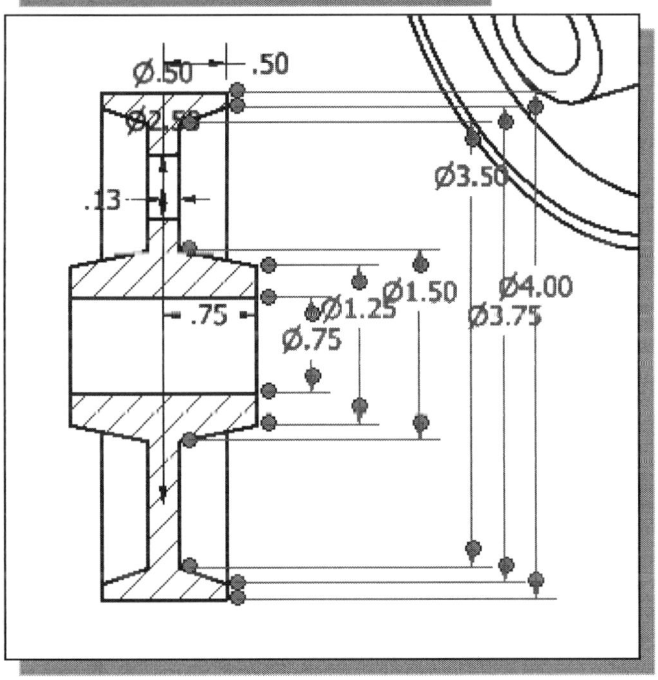

5. On your own, select the desired **model dimensions** to be displayed.

6. Click on the **Apply** button and notice the selected dimensions changed color indicating they have been retrieved.

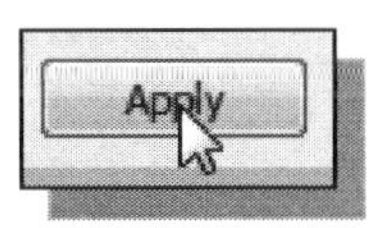

7. Note that the **Select View** button is activated; click on the Base view to continue with the Retrieve Model Annotations command.

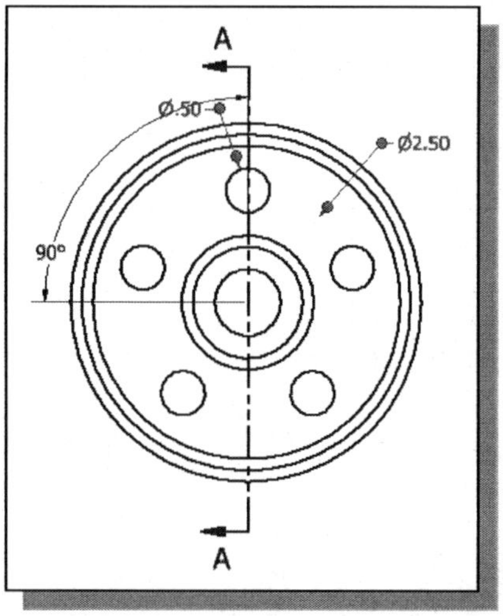

8. On your own, retrieve the model dimensions on the base view as shown.

9. On your own, reposition the views and dimensions as shown in the figure.

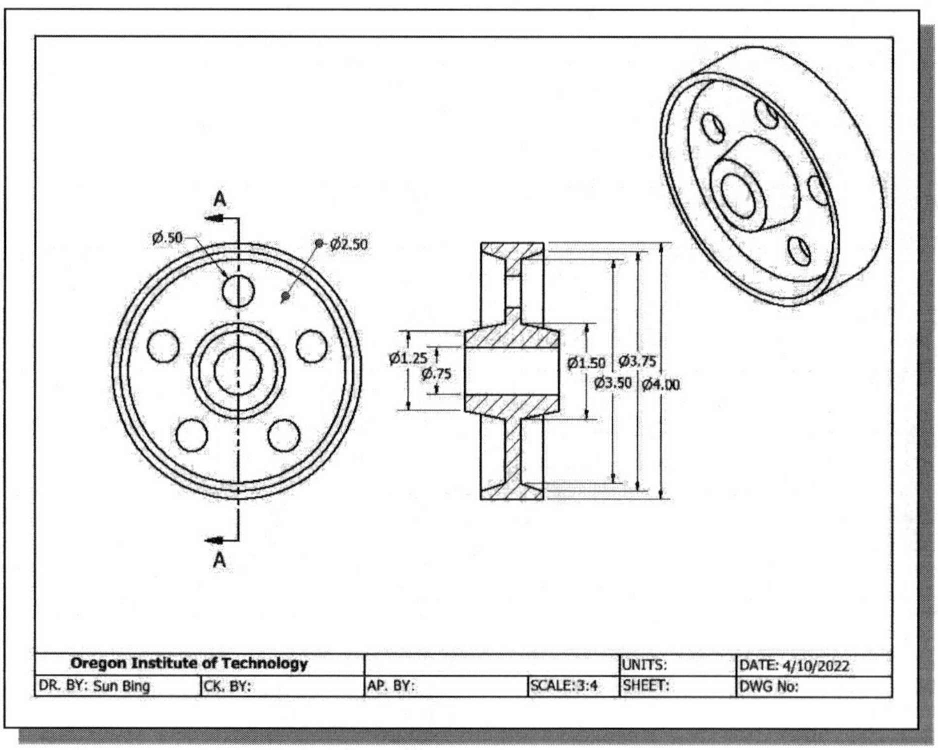

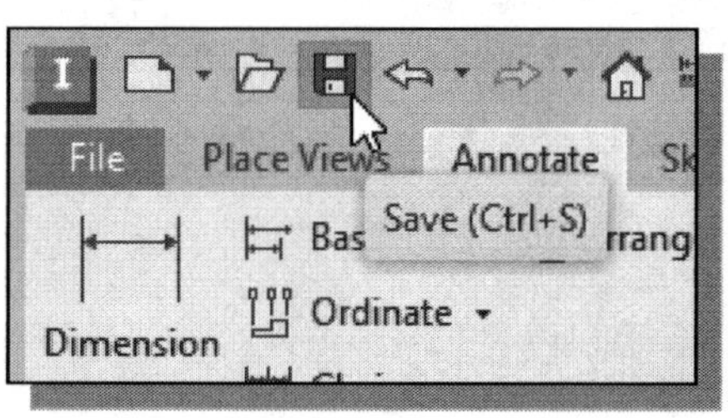

10. On your own, use the **Save** command and save the drawing as ***pulley.dwg***.

Associative Functionality – A Design Change

Autodesk Inventor's *associative functionality* allows us to change the design at any level, and the system reflects the changes at all levels automatically. We will illustrate the associative functionality by changing the circular pattern from five holes to six holes.

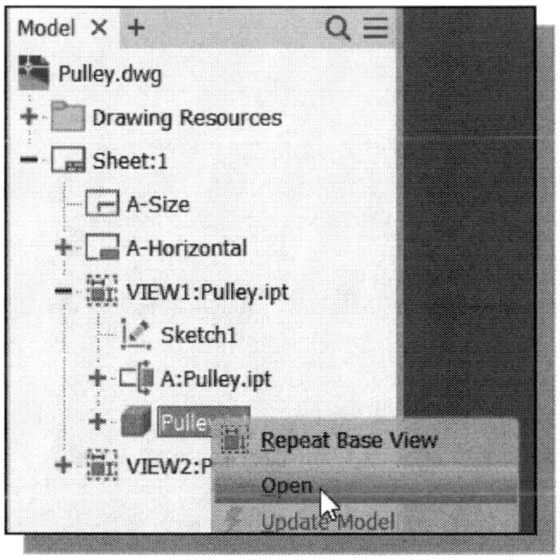

1. Inside the *Model Tree* window, below the VIEW1 list, right-click on the **Pulley.ipt** part name to bring up the option menu.

2. Select **Open** in the pop-up menu to switch to the associated solid model.

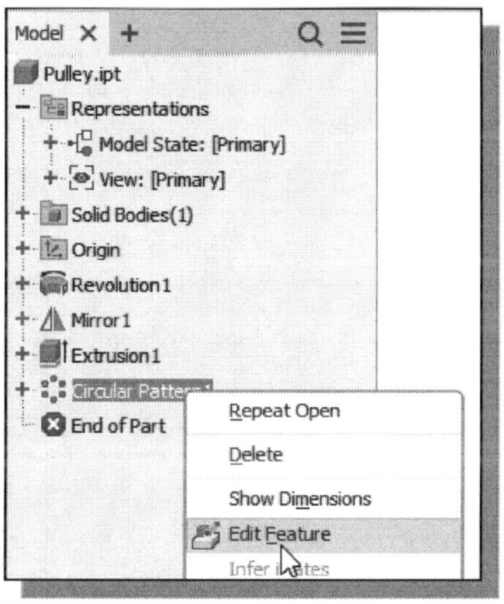

3. Inside the *Model Tree* window, right-click on the CircularPattern1 feature to bring up the option menu.

4. Select **Edit Feature** in the pop-up menu to bring up the associated feature option.

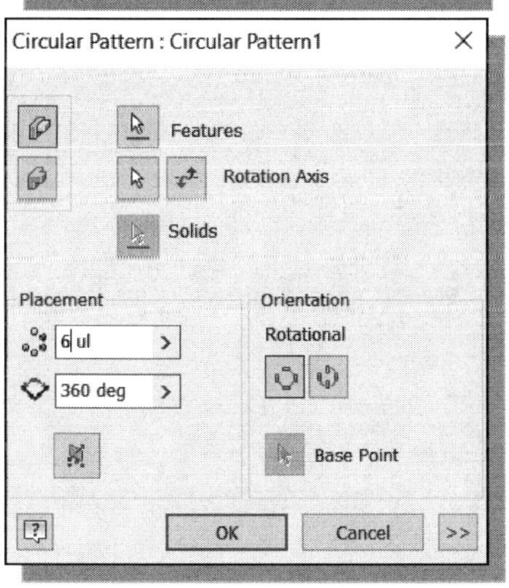

5. In the *Circular Pattern* dialog box, change the number to **6** as shown.

6. Click on the **OK** button to accept the setting.

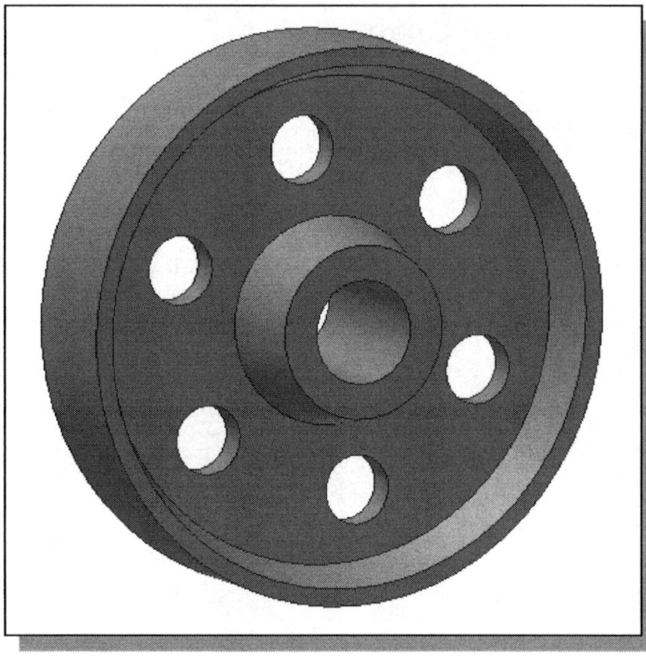

❖ The solid model is updated showing the 6 equally spaced holes as shown.

7. Switch back to the *Pulley* drawing and notice the drawing is also updated.

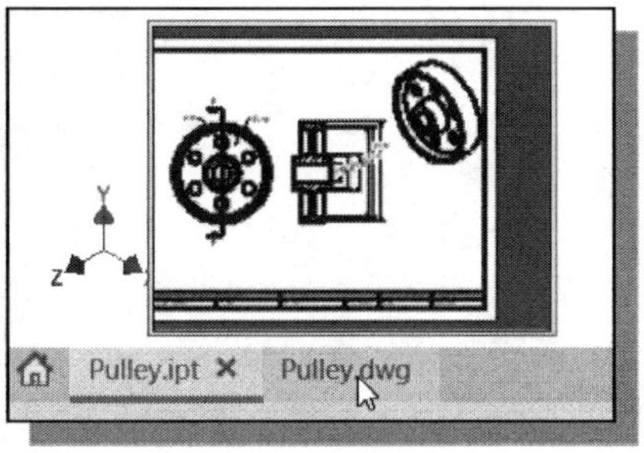

❖ Notice, in the *Pulley* drawing, the circular pattern is also updated automatically in all views.

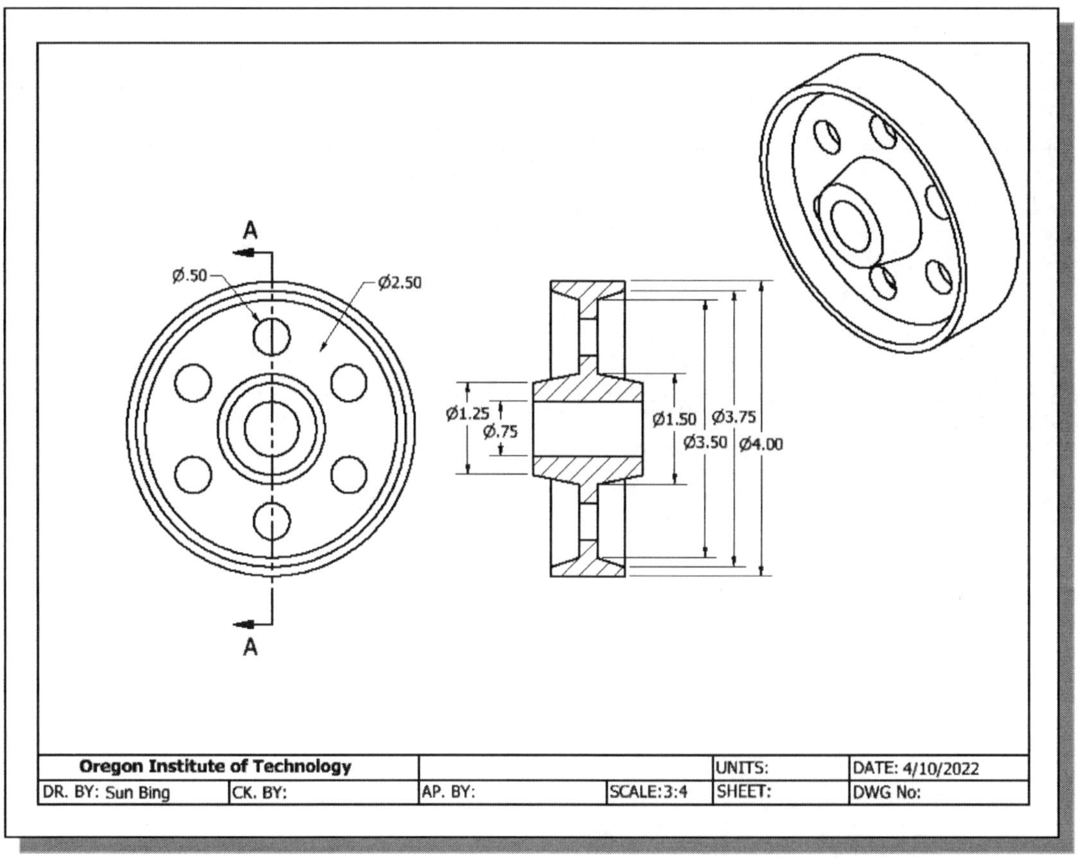

Add Centerlines to the Pattern Feature

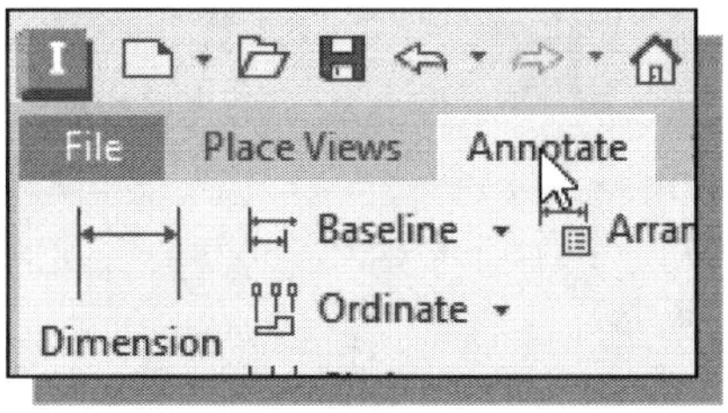

1. On your own, switch to the ***Drawing Annotation*** panel.

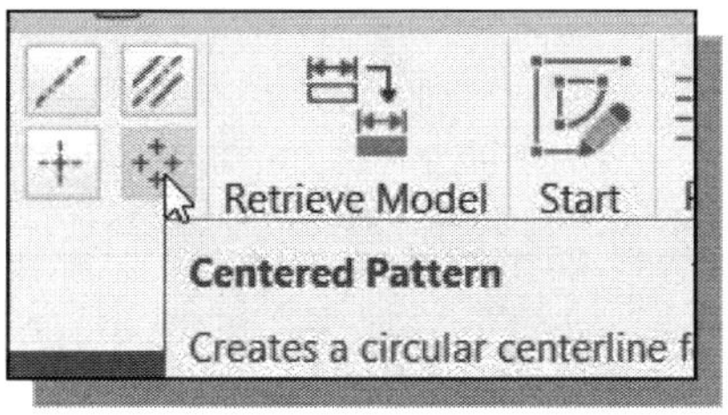

2. Select **Centered Pattern** from the symbol toolbar.

➢ The **Centered Pattern** option allows us to add centerlines to a patterned feature.

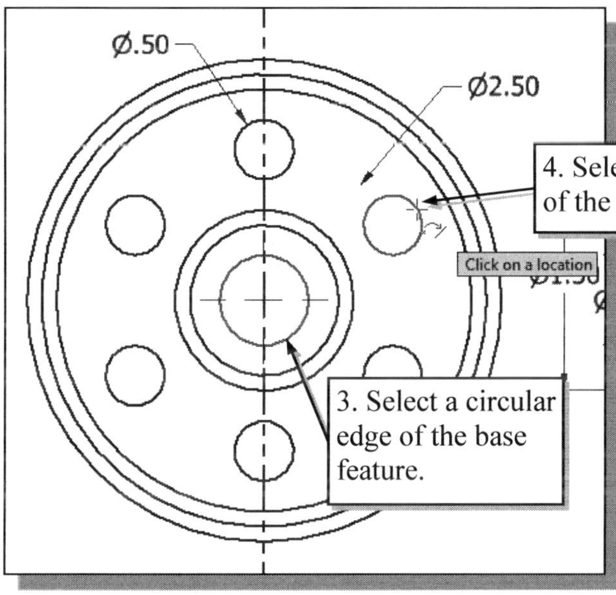

3. Inside the graphics window, click on any **circular edge** of the **base feature**.

4. Select any circular edge that is part of the **patterned feature**.

5. Continue to select the circular edges of the patterned features, in a **counterclockwise** manner, until all patterned items are selected. (Select the **first circle** again as the ending item.)

6. Inside the graphics window, **right-click** once to bring up the option menu.

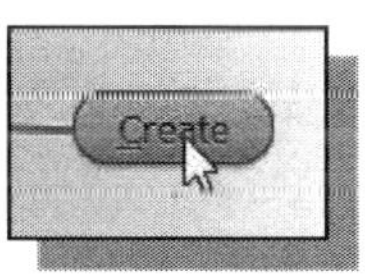

7. Select **Create** to create the centerlines around the selected items.

8. Inside the graphics window, **right-click** once to bring up the option menu.

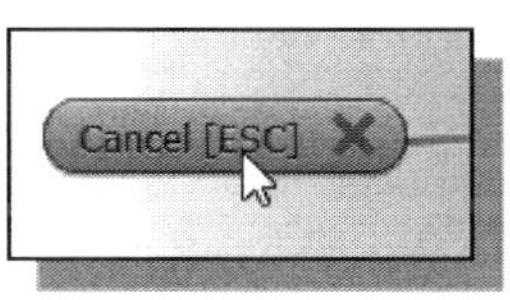

9. Select **Cancel [ESC]** to end the Centered Pattern command.

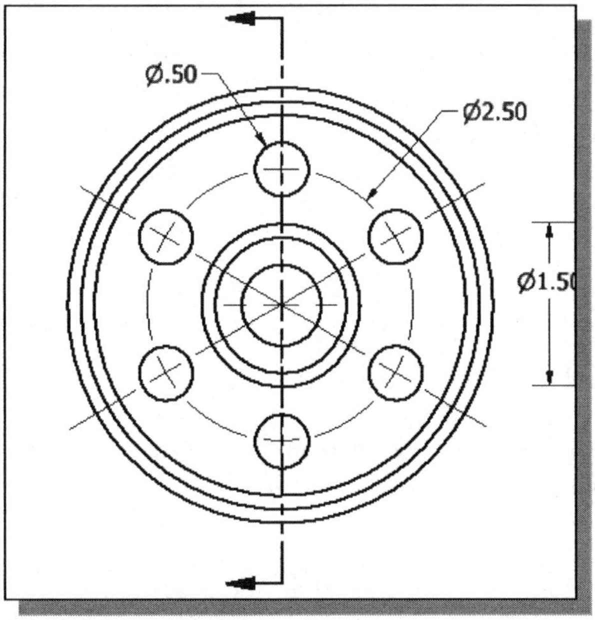

10. On your own, extend the segments of the centerlines so that they pass through the center of the base feature.

Complete the Drawing

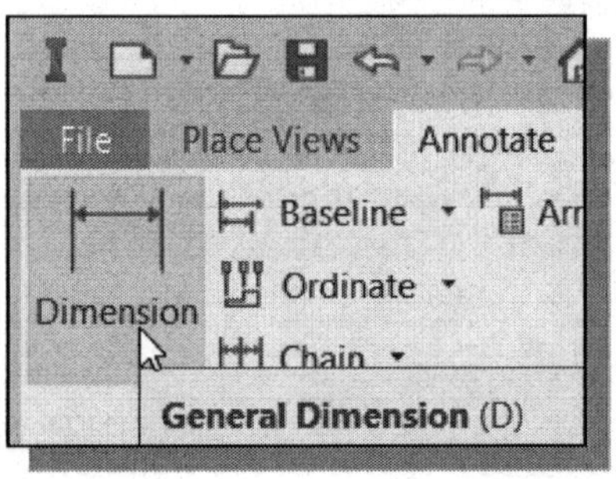

1. On your own, use the **General Dimension** command to create the angle dimension as shown in the figure below.

2. For the diameter of the circular pattern, set the options so that the **Arrowheads Inside** option is switched *ON* and the **Single Dimension Line** option is switched *OFF*.

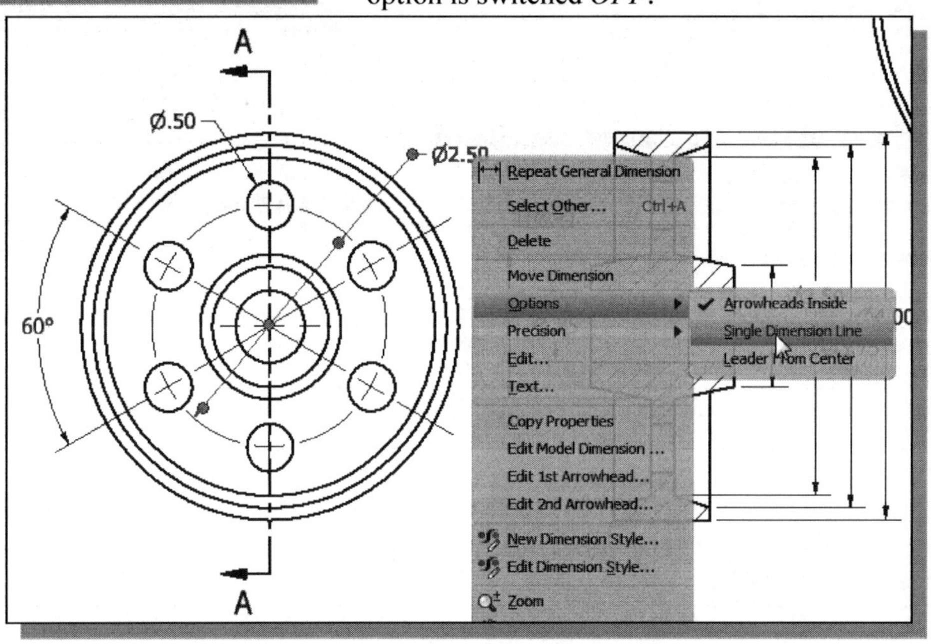

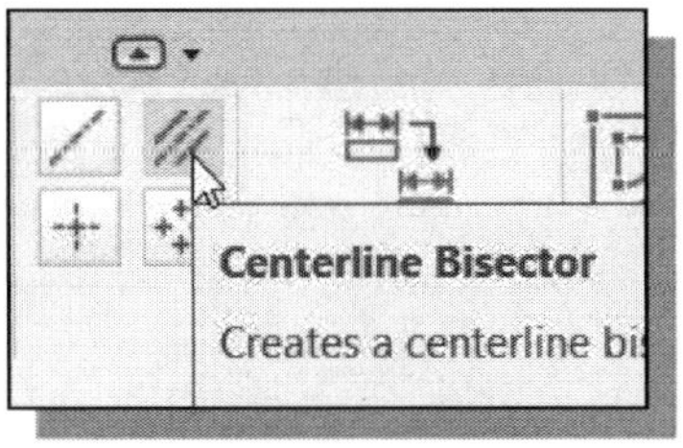

3. Select **Centerline Bisector** from the *Symbols* toolbar.

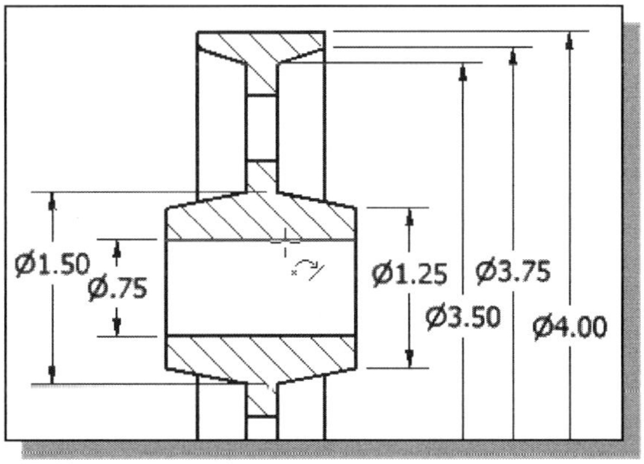

4. Inside the graphics window, click on the **top edge** of the 0.75 diameter hole as shown in the figure.

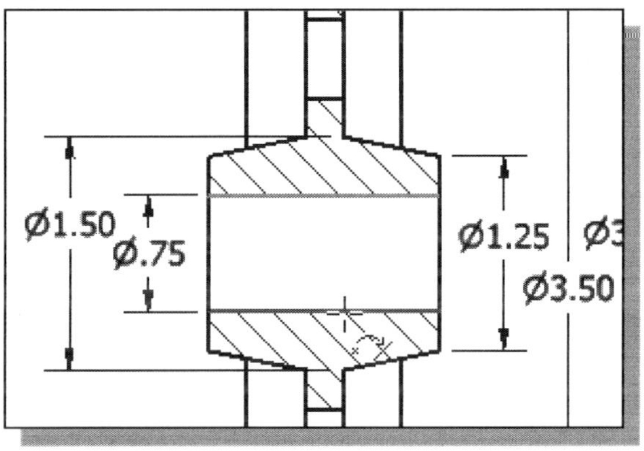

5. Inside the graphics window, click on the **bottom edge** of the 0.75 diameter hole as shown.

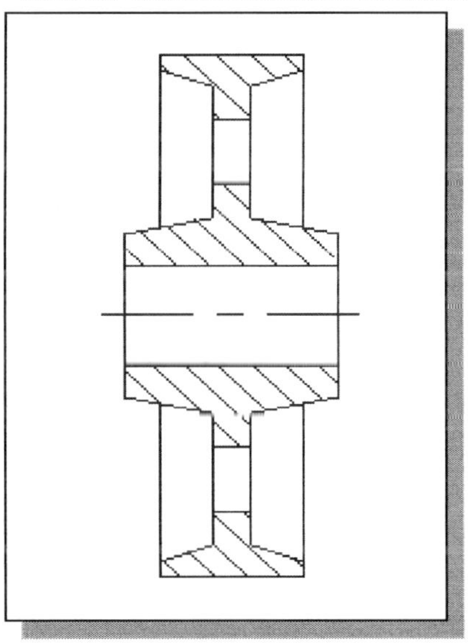

➢ Notice that a centerline is created through the center of the section view as shown in the figure.

6. Repeat the above step and create the centerlines through the other two holes.

7. On your own, complete the drawing and the title block so that the drawing appears as shown on the next page.

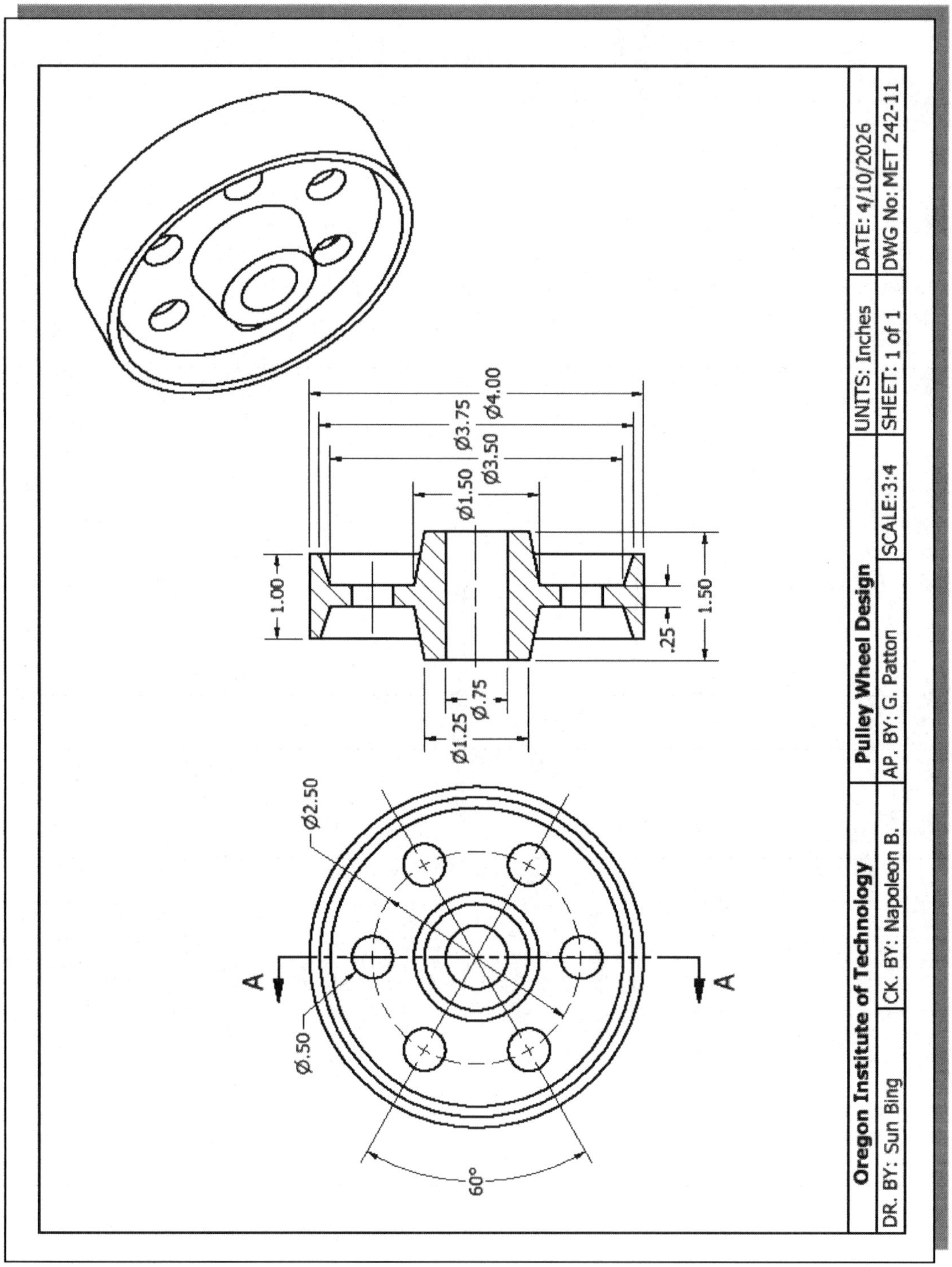
A
A
Ø.50
Ø2.50
60°
Ø1.25
Ø.75
Ø1.50
Ø3.50
Ø3.75
Ø4.00
1.00
.25
1.50
Oregon Institute of Technology
Pulley Wheel Design
UNITS: Inches
DATE: 4/10/2026
DR. BY: Sun Bing
CK. BY: Napoleon B.
AP. BY: G. Patton
SCALE:3:4
SHEET: 1 of 1
DWG No: MET 242-11

Additional Title Blocks

Drawing Paper and Border Sizes
The standard drawing paper sizes are as shown in the below tables. The edges of the title block border are generally 0.5 ~ 1 inches or 10~20 mm from the edges of the paper.

American National Standard	Suggested Border Size
A – 8.5″ X 11.0″	**A – 7.75″ X 10.25″**
B – 11.0″ X 17.0″	**B – 10.0″ X 16.0″**
C – 17.0″ X 22.0″	**C – 16.0″ X 21.0″**
D – 22.0″ X 34.0″	**D – 21.0″ X 33.0″**
E – 34.0″ X 44.0″	**E – 33.0″ X 43.0″**

International Standard	Suggested Border Size
A4 – 210 mm X 297 mm	**A4 – 190 mm X 276 mm**
A3 – 297 mm X 420 mm	**A3 – 275 mm X 400 mm**
A2 – 420 mm X 594 mm	**A2 – 400 mm X 574 mm**
A1 – 594 mm X 841 mm	**A1 – 574 mm X 820 mm**
A0 – 841 mm X 1189 mm	**A0 – 820 mm X 1168 mm**

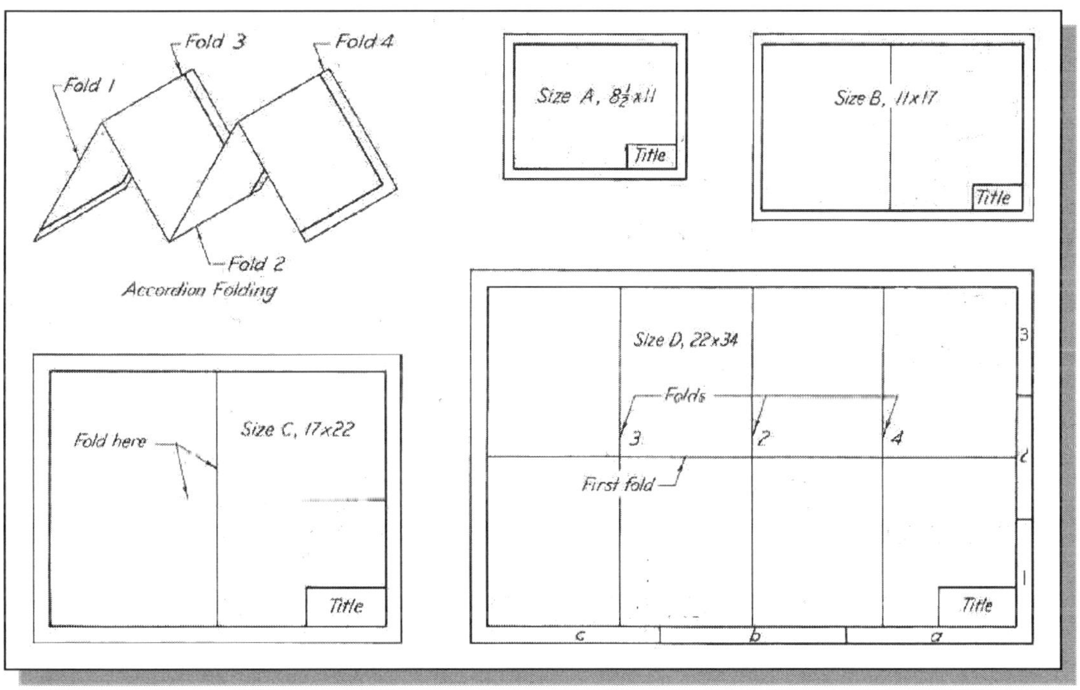

- **English Title Block** (For A size paper, primary dimensions are in inches.)

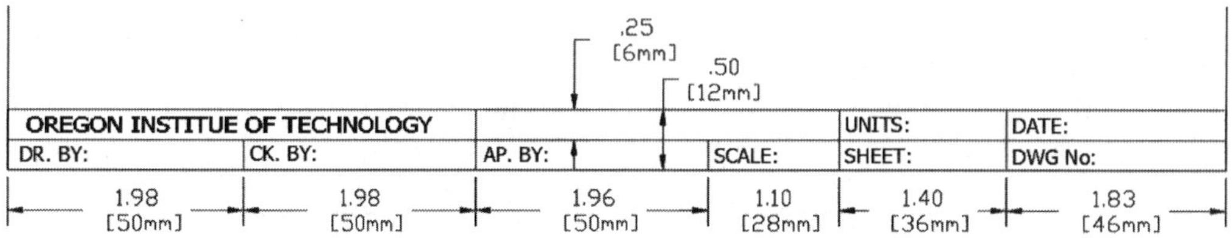

- **Metric Title Block** (For A4 size paper, primary dimensions are in mm.)

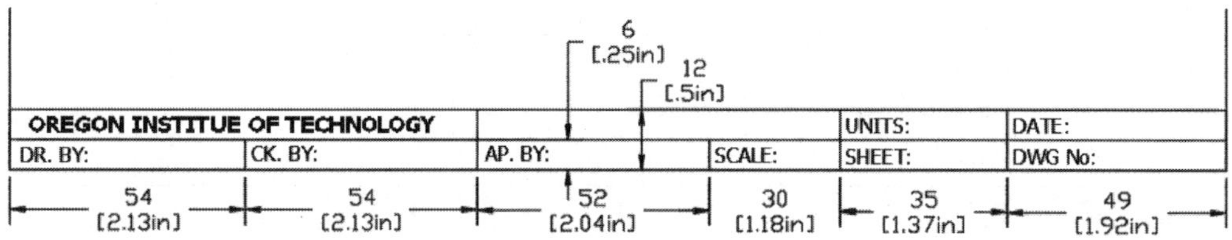

- **English Title Block** (Dimensions are in inches.)

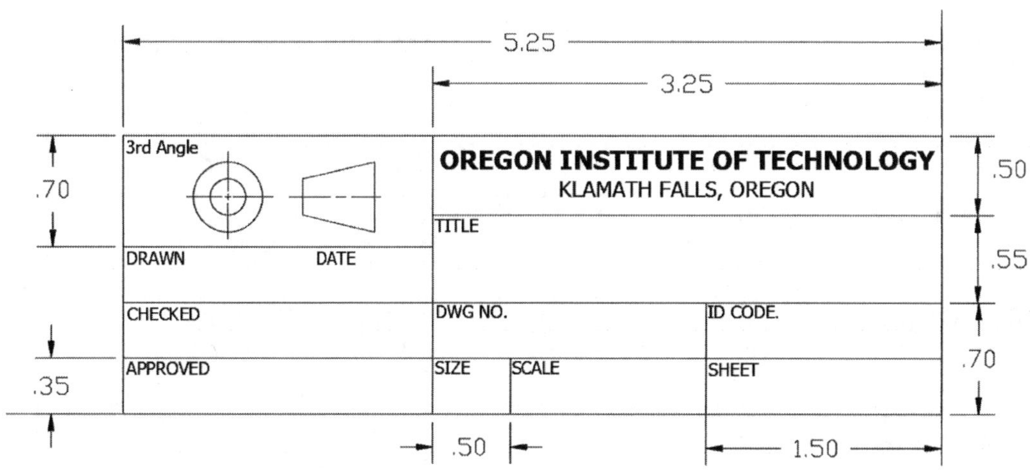

Metric Title Block (Dimensions are in mm.)

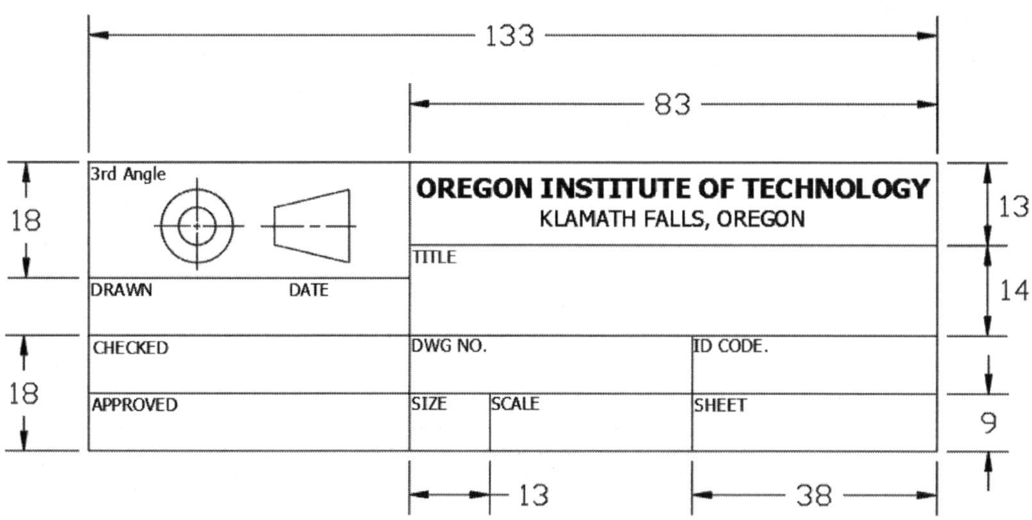

Review Questions:

1. List the different symmetrical features created in the *Pulley* design.

2. What are the advantages of using a *drawing template*?

3. Describe the steps required in using the **Mirror Feature** command.

4. Why is it important to identify symmetrical features in designs?

5. When and why should we use the **Pattern** option?

6. What are the required elements in order to generate a sectional view?

7. How do we create a *Linear Diameter dimension* for a revolved feature?

8. What is the difference between *construction geometry* and *normal geometry*?

9. List and describe the different centerline options available in the *Drawing Annotation* panel.

10. What is the main difference between a sectional view and a projected view?

Exercises: Create the Solid models and the associated 2D drawings.

1. **Shaft Support** (Dimensions are in inches.)

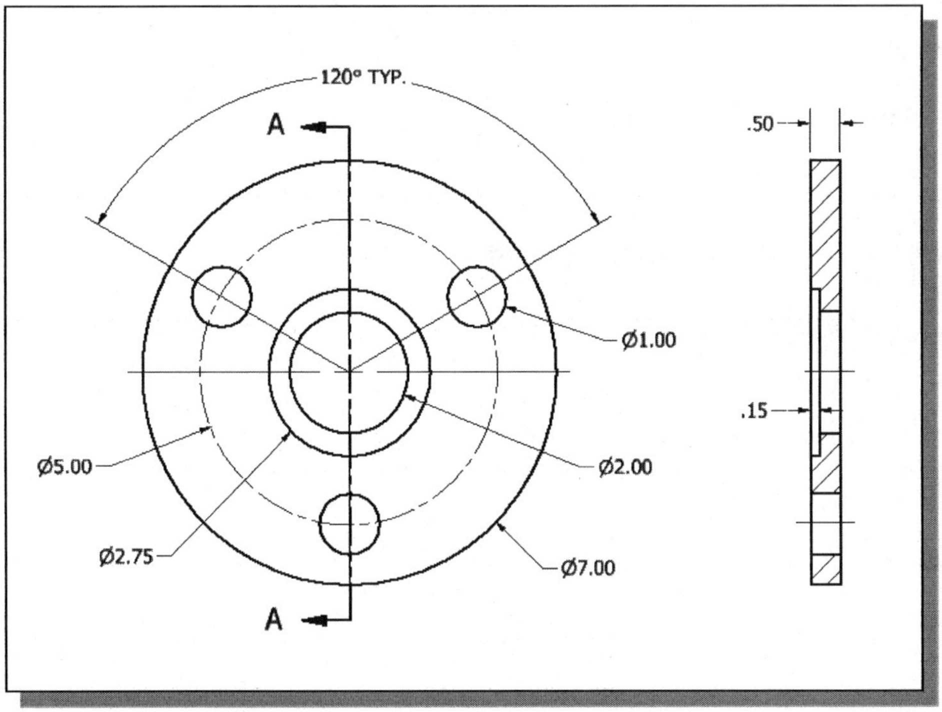

2. **Ratchet Plate** (Dimensions are in inches. Thickness: 0.125 inch.)

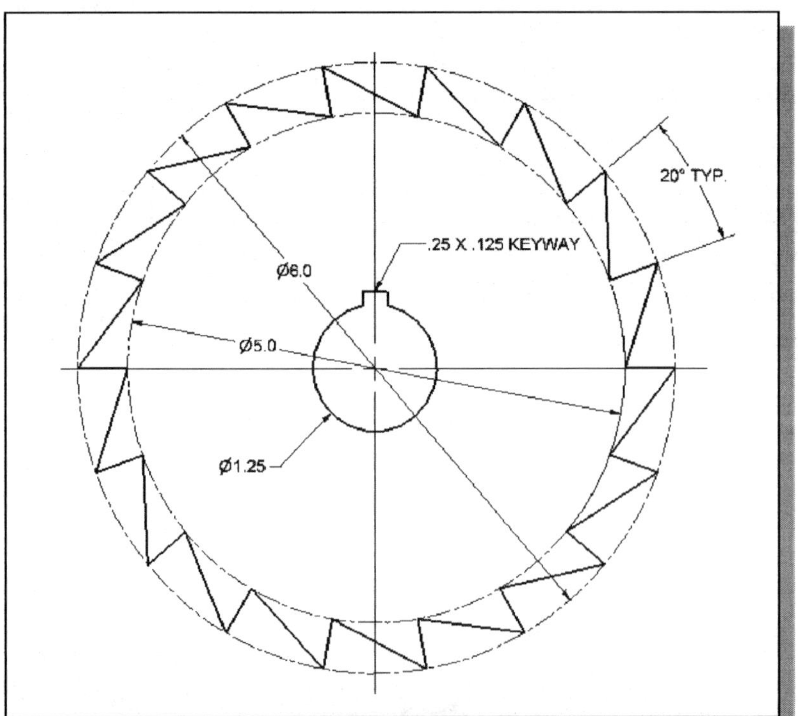

3. **Geneva Wheel** (Dimensions are in inches.)

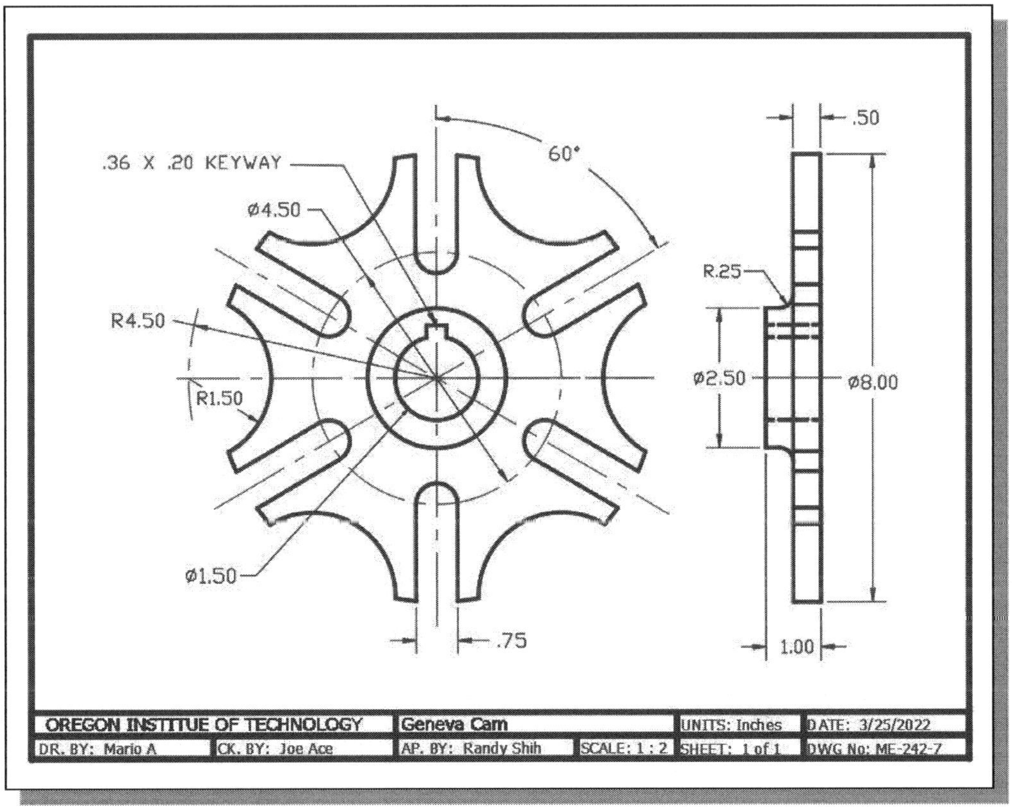

4. **Hub** (Dimensions are in inches.)

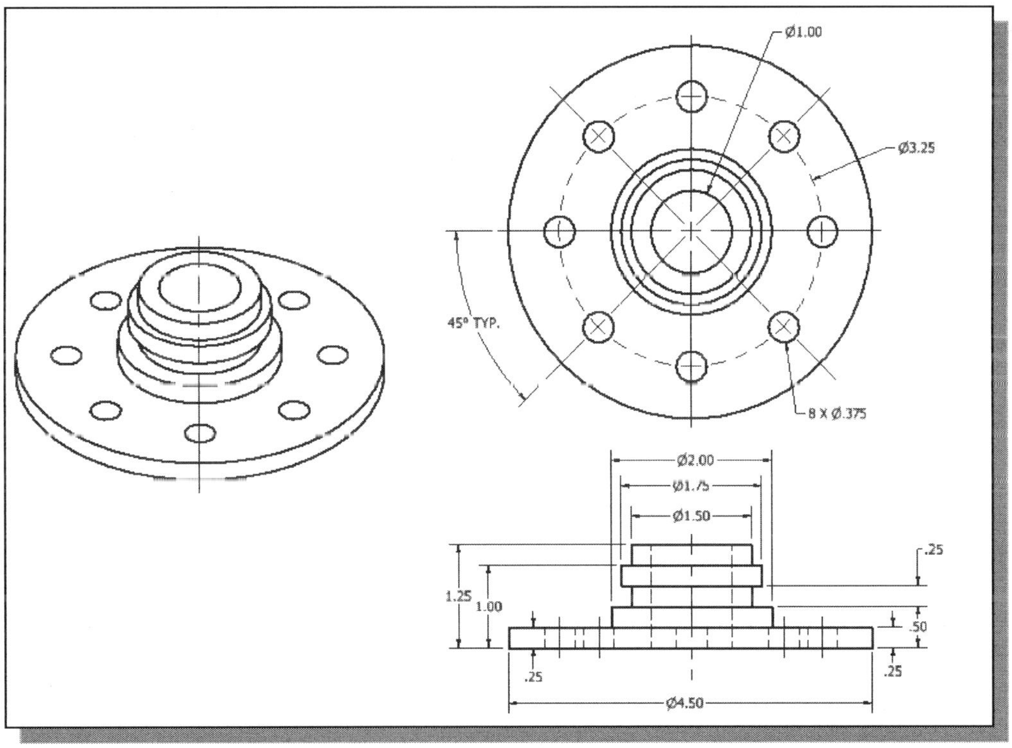

5. **Pulley Wheel** (Dimensions are in inches.)

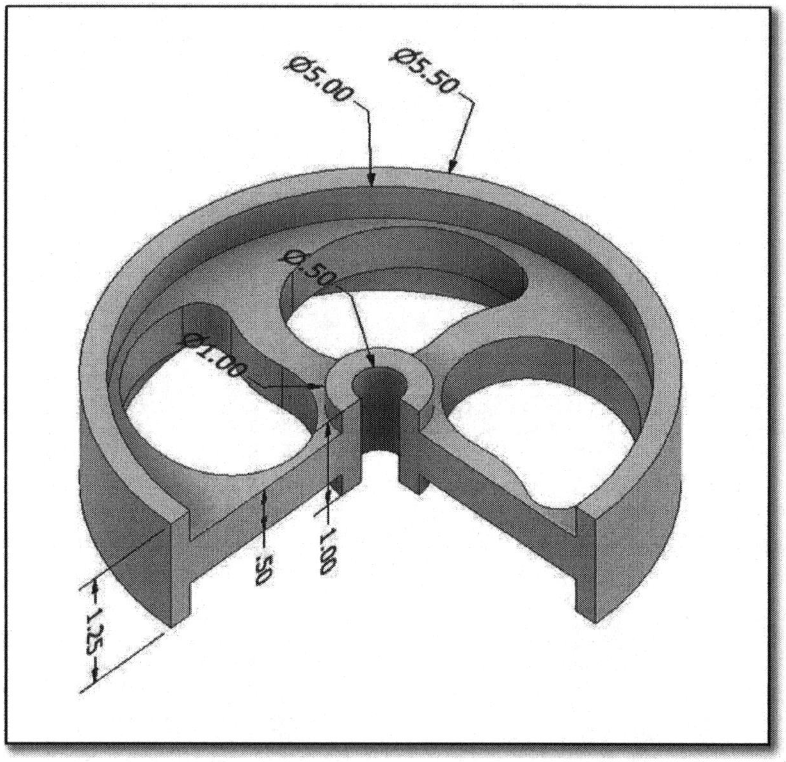

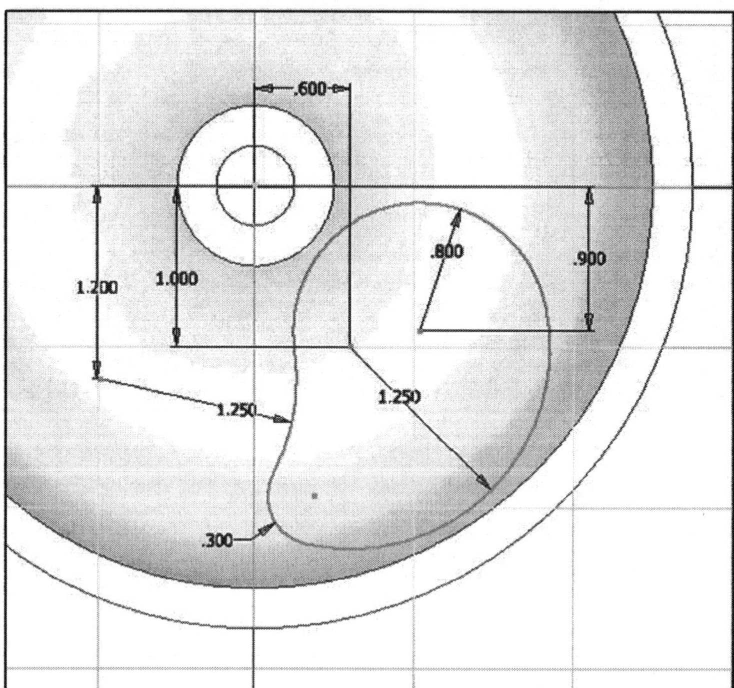

6. **Bearing Seat** (Dimensions are in inches)

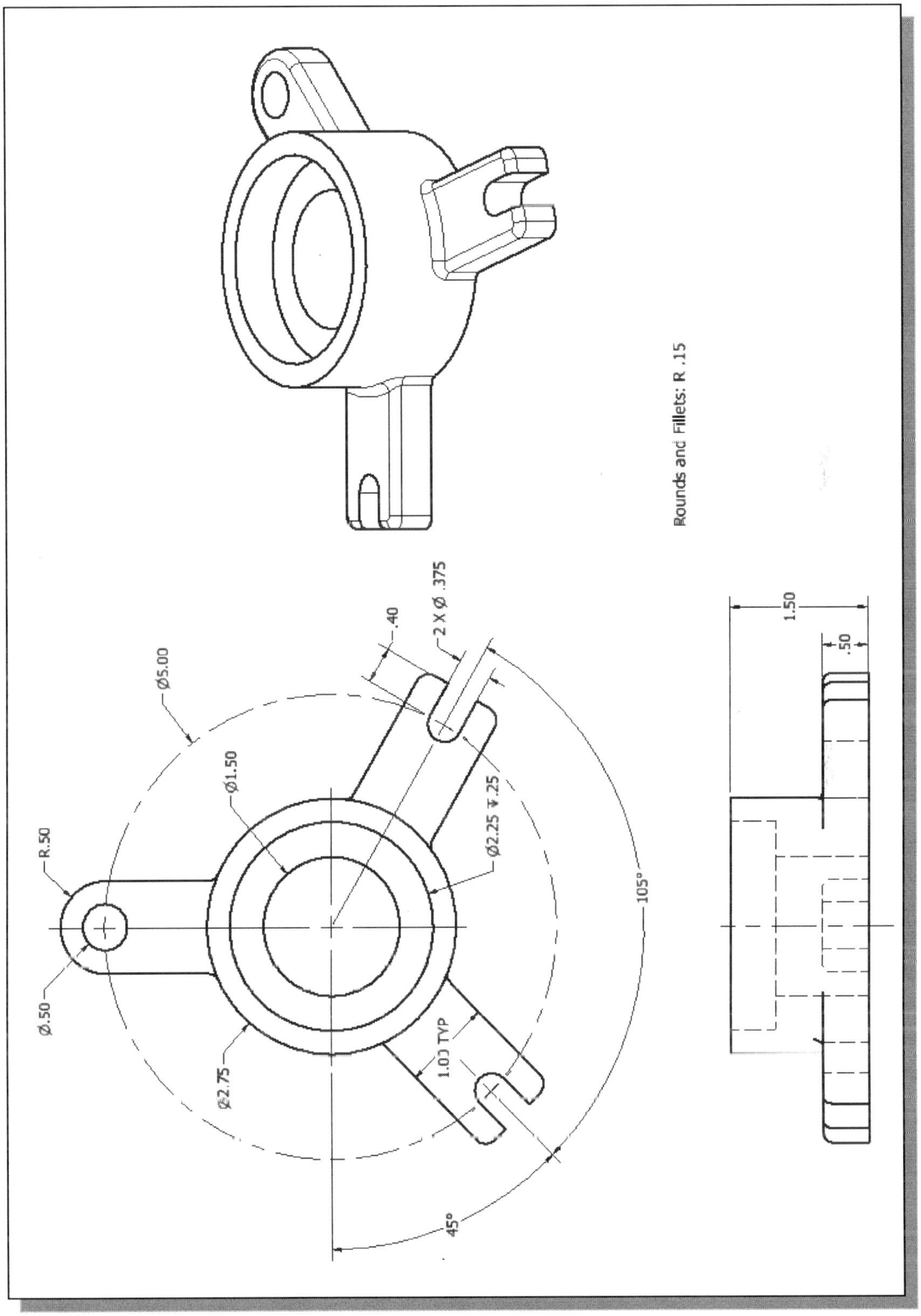

7. **Pivot Arm** (Dimensions are in inches.)

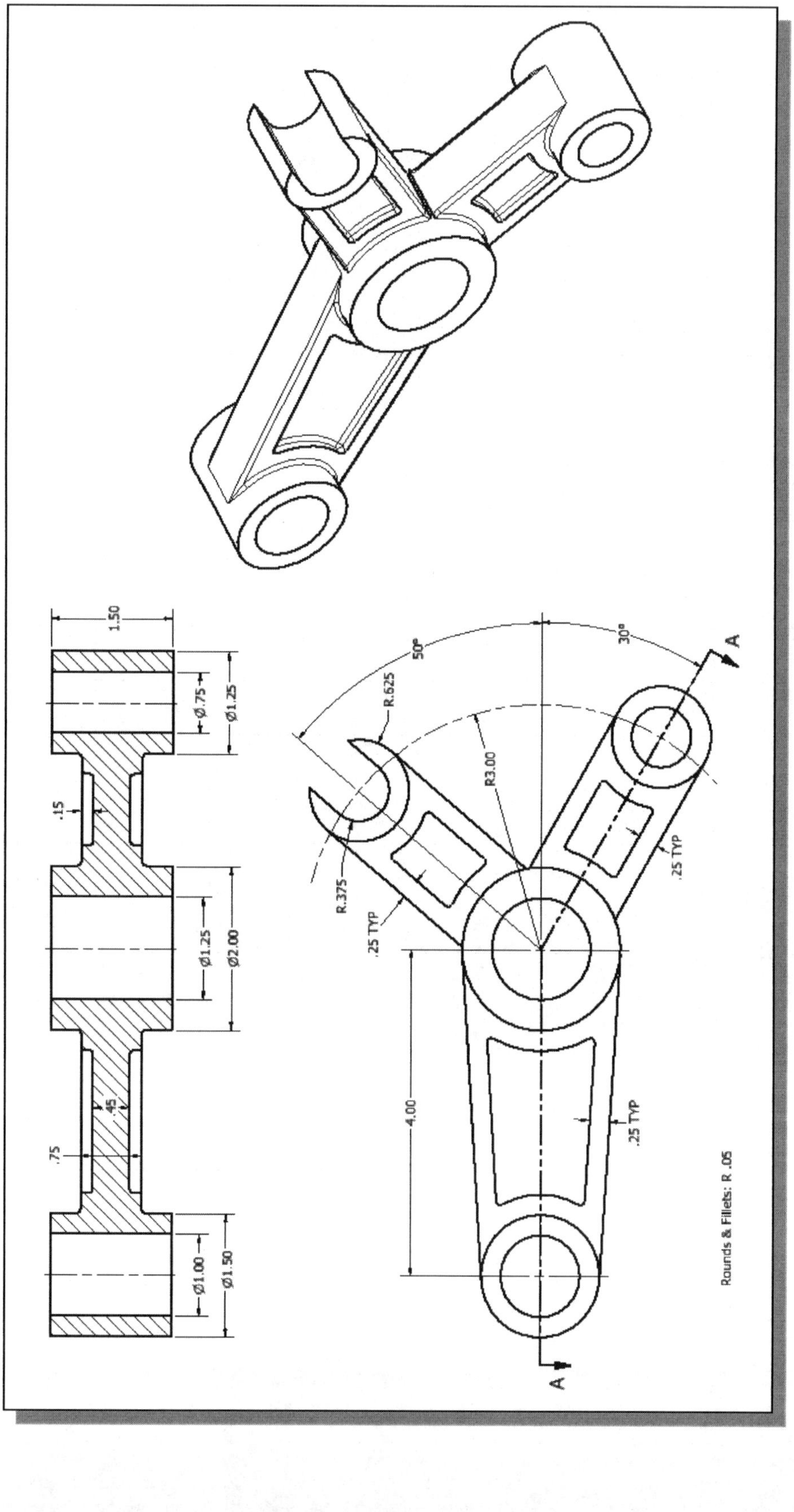

Chapter 15
Design Reuse
Using AutoCAD and Autodesk Inventor

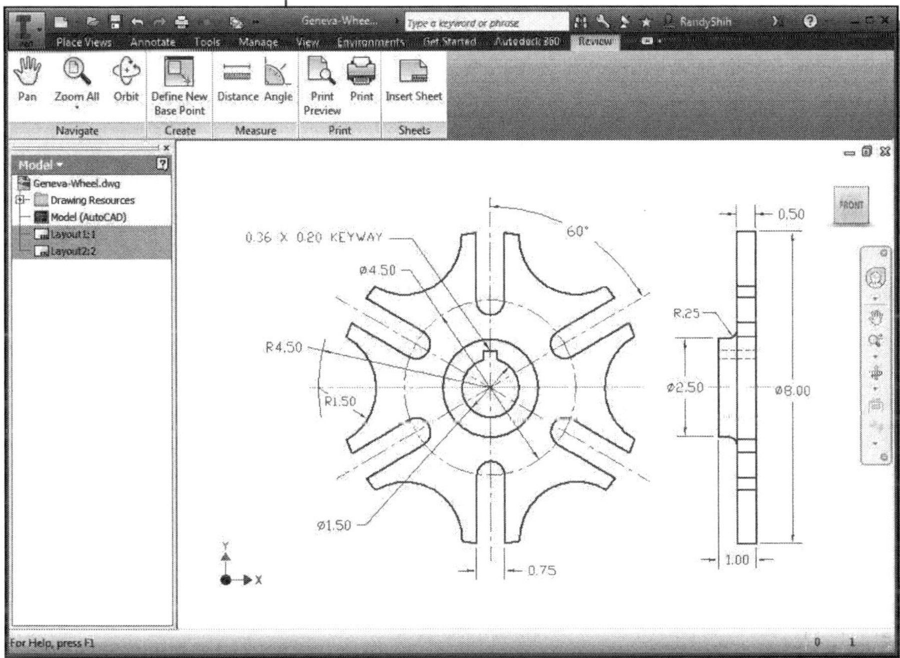

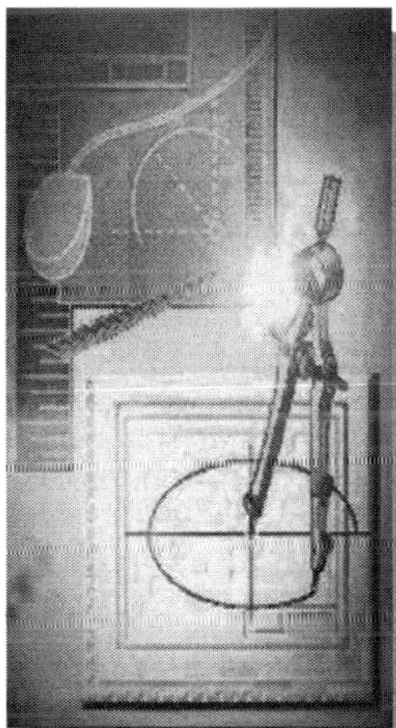

Learning Objectives

- Understand the Design Reuse Concepts
- Open AutoCAD DWG files in Autodesk Inventor
- Measure Distances and Angles
- Reuse 2D AutoCAD Files to Create a Solid Model in Autodesk Inventor
- Reuse Autodesk Inventor Sketches in AutoCAD

Introduction

In this lesson, we will examine the procedures to reuse existing 2D AutoCAD data in Autodesk Inventor. The AutoCAD DWG file format is one of the most commonly used CAD formats in the industry; in 2020, it was estimated that there were over 6 million AutoCAD users worldwide.

In parametric modeling, 2D sketches are commonly used in building 3D features. In Autodesk Inventor, we can use existing 2D AutoCAD data exactly as it is, or as a reference, and thus create the same design in 3D. This process is generally known as **2D Design Reuse**. One of the easiest ways to reuse existing 2D AutoCAD data is to open the AutoCAD DWG file in Autodesk Inventor, and simply Copy and Paste the desired geometry into a new part model sketch. When copying and pasting the 2D geometry, if the associative dimensions are included in the selection, they will be converted into parametric dimensions. The pasted geometry can then be modified and edited as if it were created in Autodesk Inventor.

Here are some guidelines for opening DWG files in Autodesk Inventor:

1. The AutoCAD **Model Space** and **Layouts** are accessible through the ***Inventor Browser*** **window**.

2. The objects that are in *Model Space* are **Read-Only** in Autodesk Inventor. By default, **Read-Only Drawing Review** mode is activated when an AutoCAD DWG file is opened.

3. The layouts are displayed as drawing sheets in Autodesk Inventor and can be **viewed**, **plotted** and **deleted**.

4. The objects that are in *Layouts* can be **deleted**. New geometry can be **added** in *Layouts*, using the Inventor annotation tools and sketching tools.

5. Additional **Views** and **Annotations** can be created on an AutoCAD *Layout* with Inventor sketching tools. The modified file can be saved in Autodesk Inventor, still as an AutoCAD DWG file.

6. The data in the DWG file, either in *Model Space* or *Layouts*, are all viewable in Inventor. The Inventor **viewing** and **measuring** commands are available for determining distances and angles.

7. The data in the DWG file, either in *Model Space* or *Layouts*, can be **selected** to **Copy** and **Paste** into any type of **Inventor sketches** in part, assembly and drawing files.

In this chapter, we will also look at the use of the **Inventor Contact Solver** to detect, and resolve, *collisions* among parts in conjunction with the ***Joint*** tool. The *Inventor Contact Solver* allows us to produce very realistic animations for more complex assemblies.

The Geneva Wheel Design

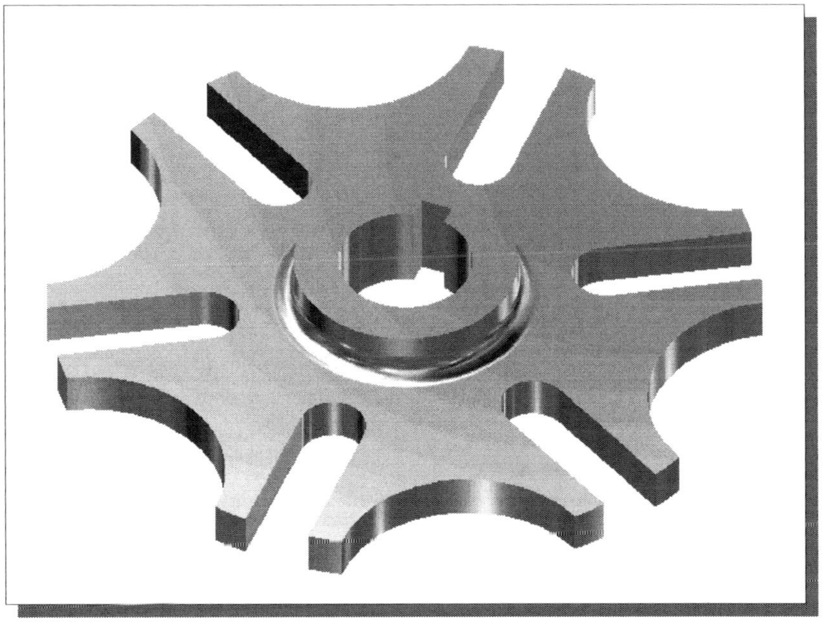

Internet Download the Geneva-Wheel DWG File

To illustrate the concepts and procedures of reusing existing 2D AutoCAD data, we will first download the *Geneva Wheel DWG* drawing from the *SDC Publications* website.

1. Launch your internet browser, such as *MS Edge, Google Chrome* or *Mozilla Firefox.*

2. In the *URL address* box, enter ***http://www.sdcACAD.com/acad2027/Geneva-Wheel.dwg*** as shown in the figure below.

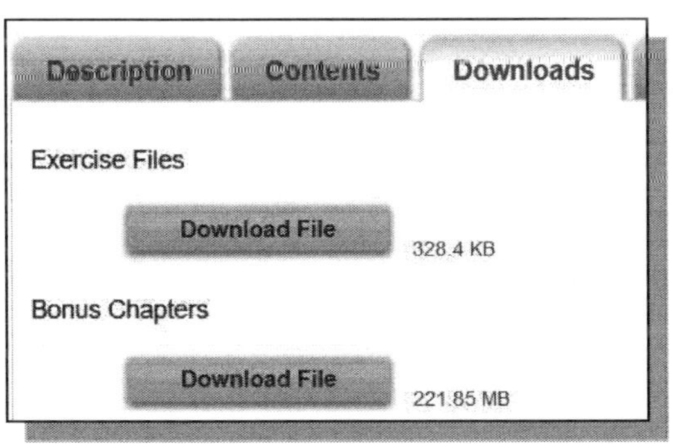

- Visit this book's website through www.SDCPublications.com, and download the **Geneva-Wheel.dwg** file.

3. On your own, save the AutoCAD ***Geneva-Wheel.dwg*** to the Inventor Geneva Project folder.

Opening AutoCAD DWG File in Inventor

1. Select the **Autodesk Inventor** option on the *Start* menu or select the **Autodesk Inventor** icon on the desktop to start Autodesk Inventor. The Autodesk Inventor main window will appear on the screen.

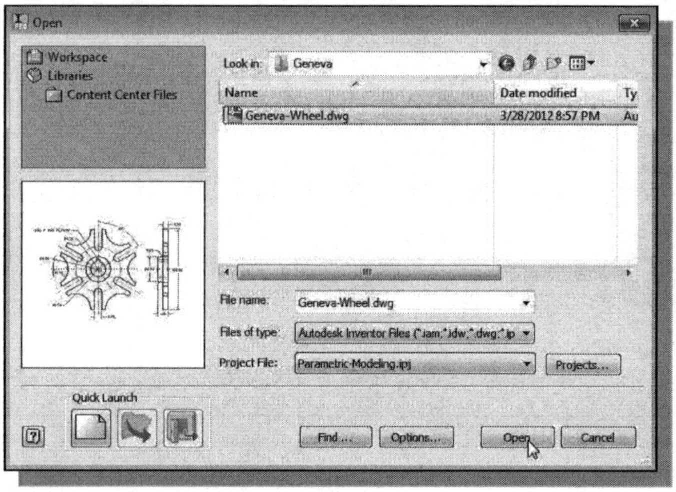

2. Once the program is loaded into memory, select the **Open File** option.

3. Select the **Geneva-Wheel.dwg** file with a single click of the left-mouse-button in the *File name* list box.

4. Click on the **Open** button in the *Open* dialog box to proceed with opening the file.

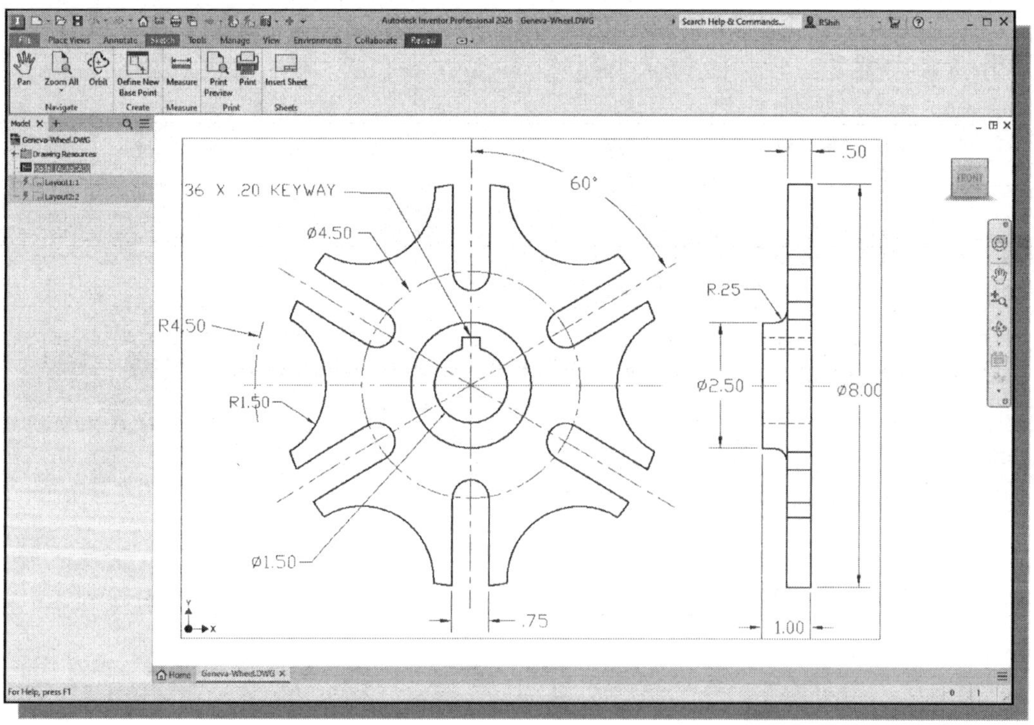

❖ By default, the **Read-Only Drawing Review** mode is activated when an AutoCAD DWG file is opened. Note that objects that are in *Model Space* are also **Read-Only** in Autodesk Inventor.

Switch to the AutoCAD DWG Layout

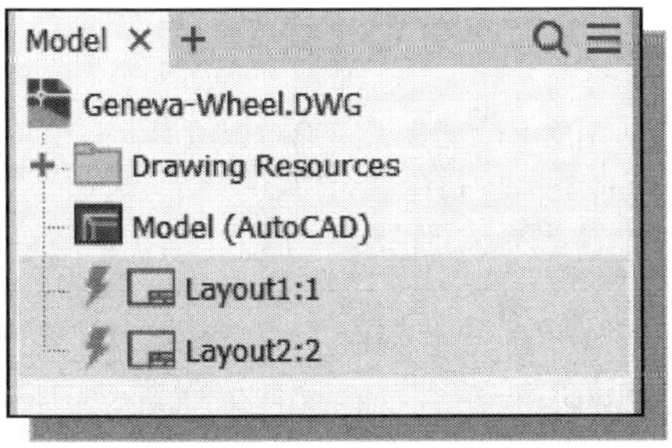

- Note that in the *browser* window, the three items listed are corresponding to the *AutoCAD Model Space* and *Layouts* associated with the *Geneva-Wheel* drawing.

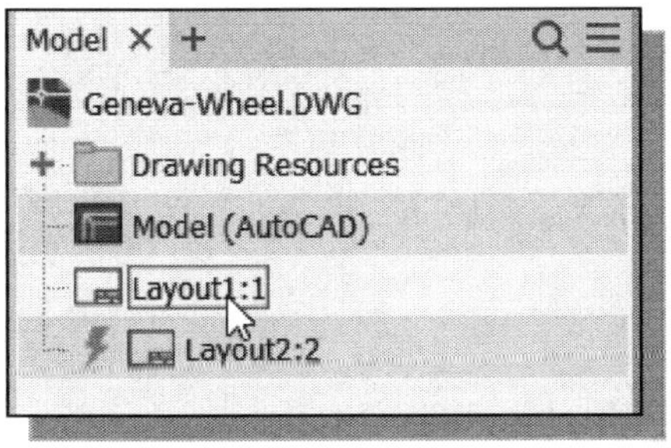

1. In the *browser* window, **double-click** on **Layout1** to open the associated *AutoCAD DWG Layout.*

➢ Inventor now opens the AutoCAD Layout1 in the *Drawing Sheet* mode. Note that the layout contains a title block and one viewport as shown in the below figure. The Layout space is the AutoCAD's Paper Space, which represents a 2D environment.

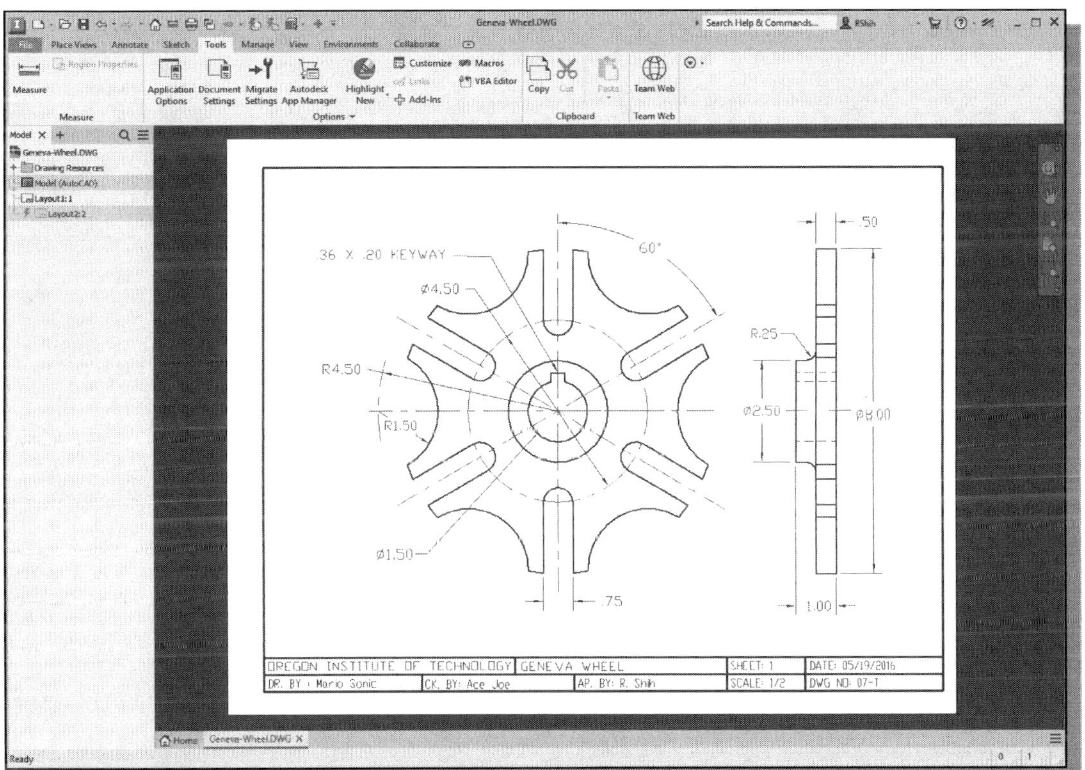

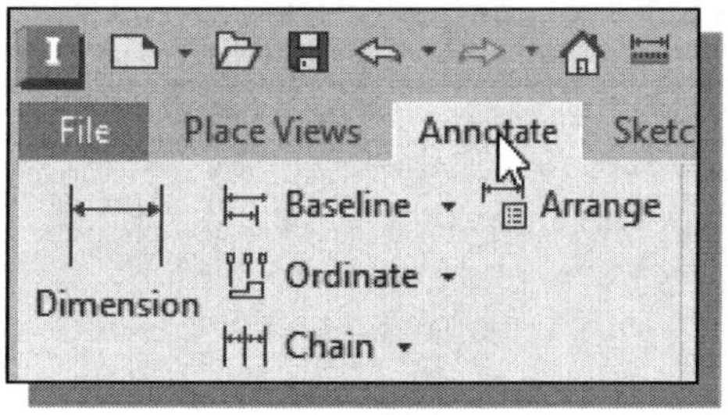

2. Click on the *Annotate* tab to switch to the annotation toolbar panel as shown.

➢ Notice the available **Annotation** commands, such as the **General Dimension** command and the **Center Mark** command.

➢ Note that objects in *Layouts* can be **deleted**. New geometry can also be **added** in *Layouts*, using the Inventor annotation tools and sketching tools.

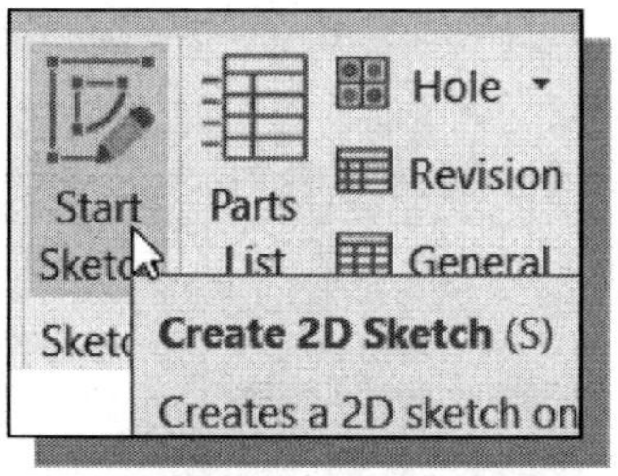

3. In the *Sketch* toolbar, click **Start Sketch** as shown in the figure.

➢ The *2D Drawing Sketch* panel appears above the *browser* window.

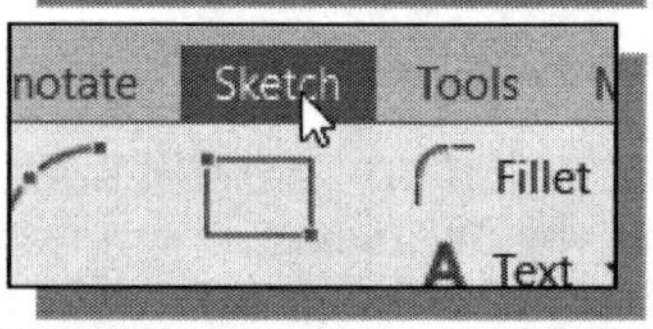

4. If necessary, click on the highlighted *Sketch* tab to switch to the 2D Sketch toolbar panel as shown.

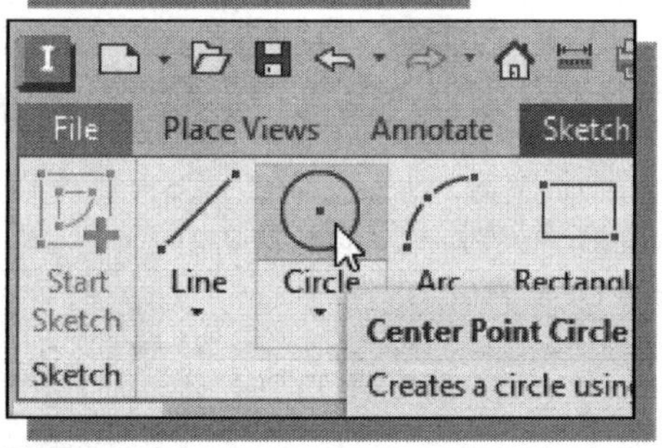

5. Select the **Center Point Circle** icon as shown.

6. Move the cursor near the center of the *front* view and notice that no *SNAP* option is available. Any new entities added will remain only in the *Layout*, not in the *Model Space*.

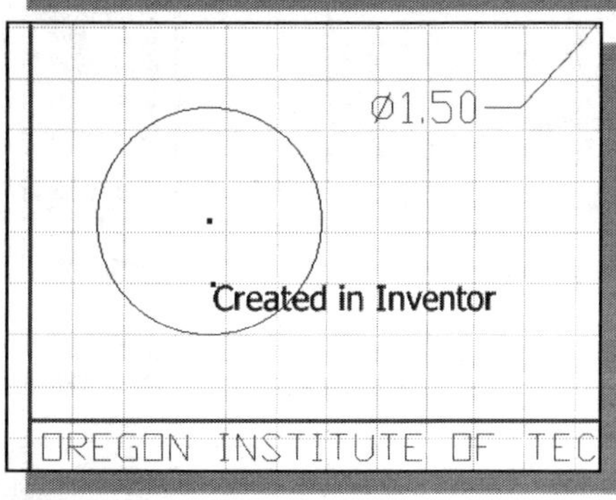

7. On your own, create a circle and some text at the lower left corner of the viewport as shown.

❖ Note that Inventor can be used to create new geometry and annotations in *AutoCAD Layouts*.

8. In the toolbar area, click **Finish Sketch** to exit the Drawing Sketch mode.

2D Design Reuse

The main concept of **2D Design Reuse** is to reuse existing 2D AutoCAD data exactly as it is. One of the easiest ways to reuse existing 2D AutoCAD data is to open the AutoCAD DWG file in Autodesk Inventor, and simply **Copy** and **Paste** the desired geometry into a new part model sketch. When copying and pasting the 2D geometry, if the associative dimensions are included in the selection, they will be converted into parametric dimensions. The pasted geometry can then be modified and edited as if it were created in Autodesk Inventor.

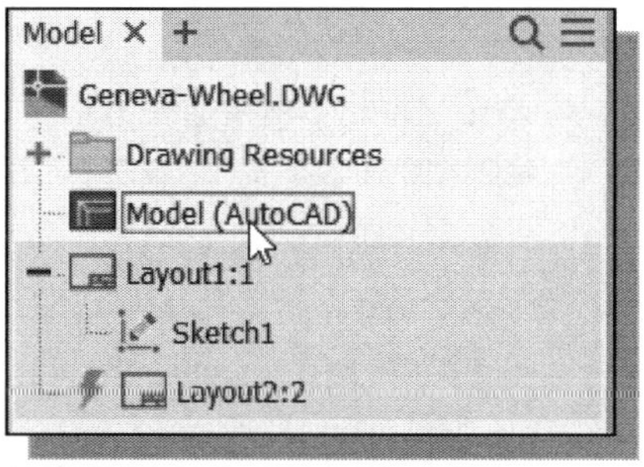

1. In the *browser* window, **double-click** on the **Model (AutoCAD)** icon to switch back to *AutoCAD Model Space*.

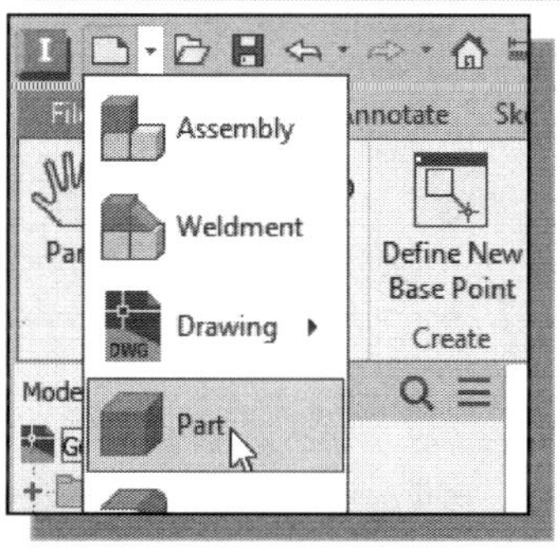

2. Start a new part file by clicking on the **triangle** next to the **New File** icon and choose **Part** as shown.

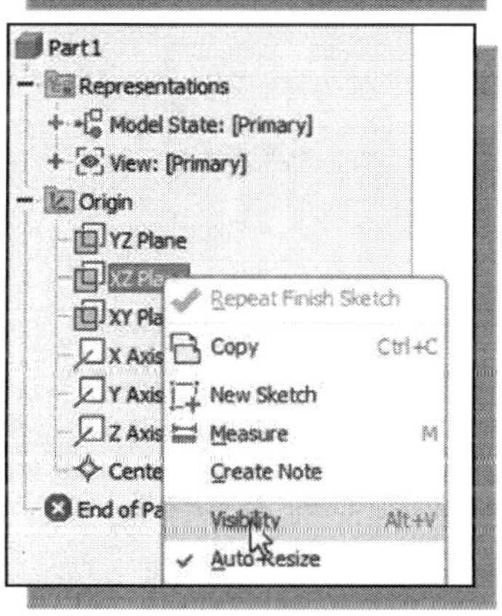

3. On your own, switch *ON* the visibility of the **XZ Plane** as shown.

4. Reset the display to *isometric* view by clicking on the **Home** icon of the **ViewCube** as shown.

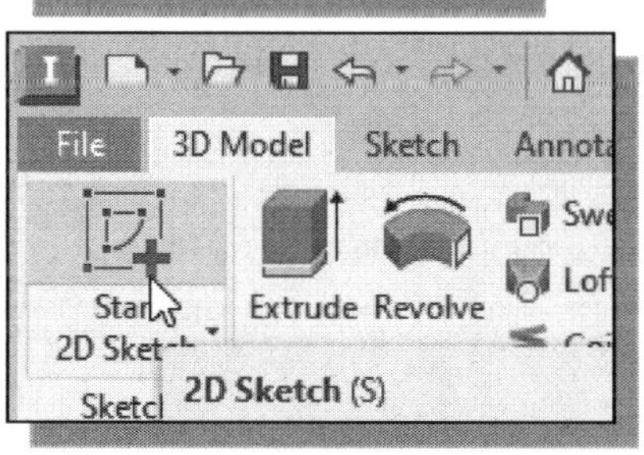

5. Click **Start 2D Sketch** to enter the *2D Sketching* mode.

6. Select the **XZ plane** to align the sketching plane.

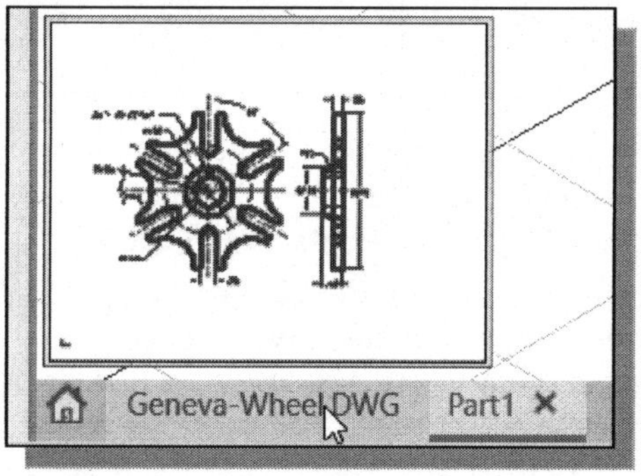

7. Switch to the ***Geneva-Wheel.DWG*** window by clicking on the associated file name tab as shown.

8. Select all the entities in the *front* view by using the Inventor selection window as shown. (Click and drag with the left-mouse-button to enclose all entities inside the window.)

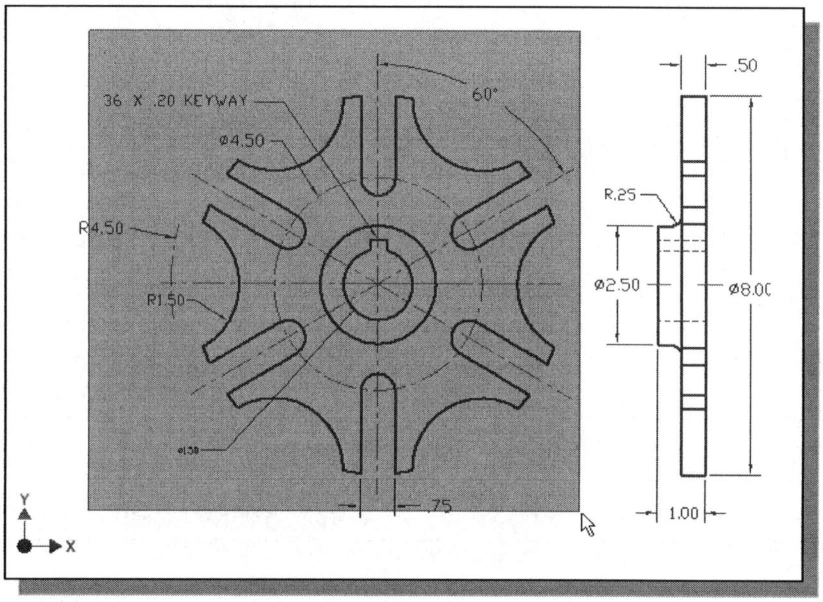

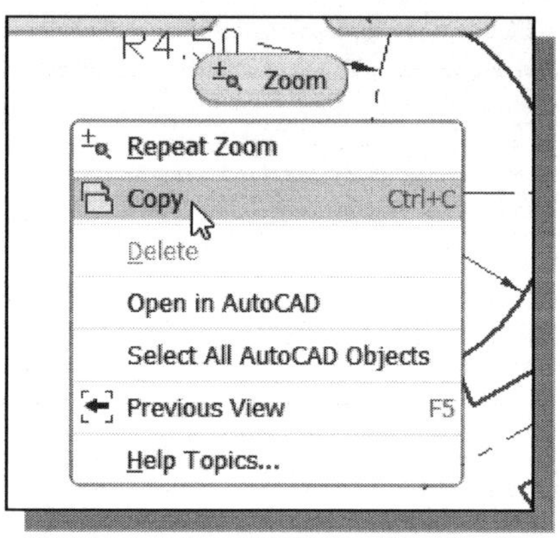

9. Right-mouse click once to bring up the option menu and select **Copy** or use the quick-key option **[Ctrl+C]**.

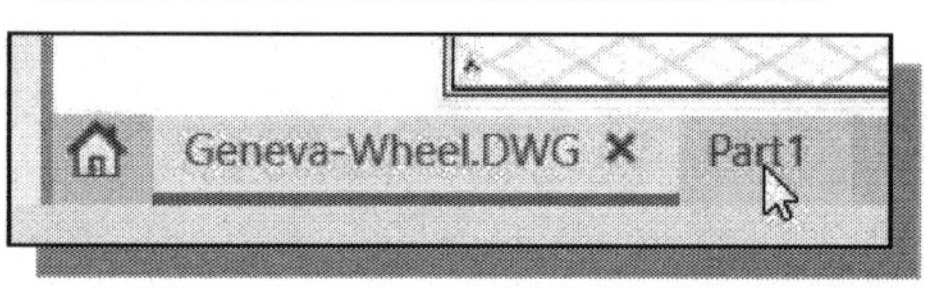

10. Switch to the **Part1** file window by choosing the associated name in the **tabs** as shown.

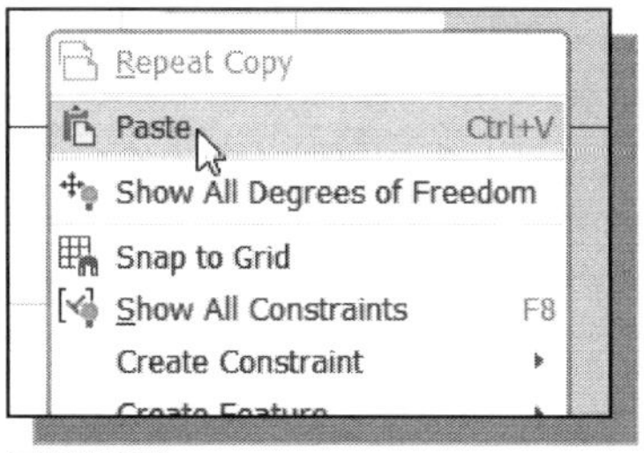

11. Select **Paste** in the **Edit** pull-down menu or use the quick-key option **[Ctrl+V]**.

12. Place the copied entities on the **XZ Plane** by clicking the left-mouse-button at an arbitrary location.

13. Click **Zoom All** in the *Display* toolbar as shown.

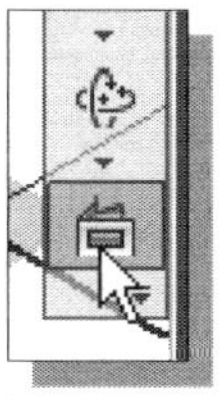

14. Select any of the imported geometry to align the view angle.

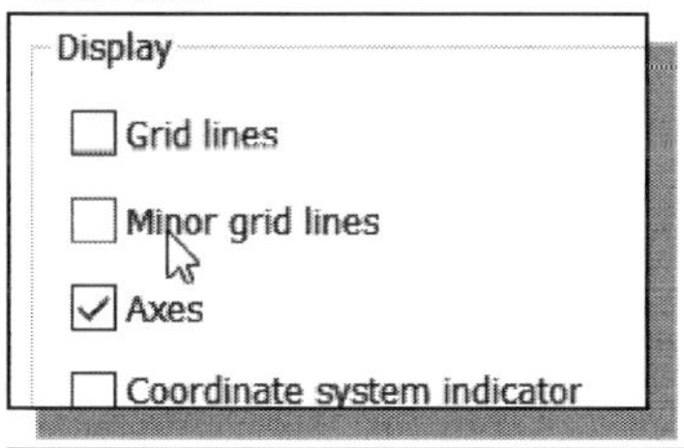

15. On your own, turn *OFF* the **Grid lines** display options as shown.
[Tools → Application Options → Sketch]

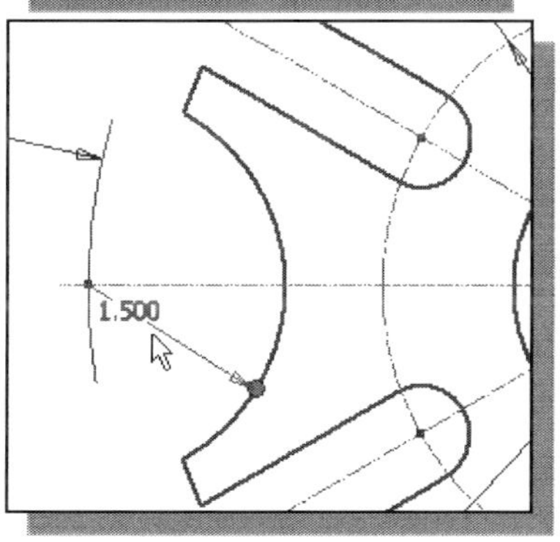

16. Move the cursor on top of the **radius 1.5** dimension and notice that Inventor has converted the radius dimension into a *parametric dimension.*

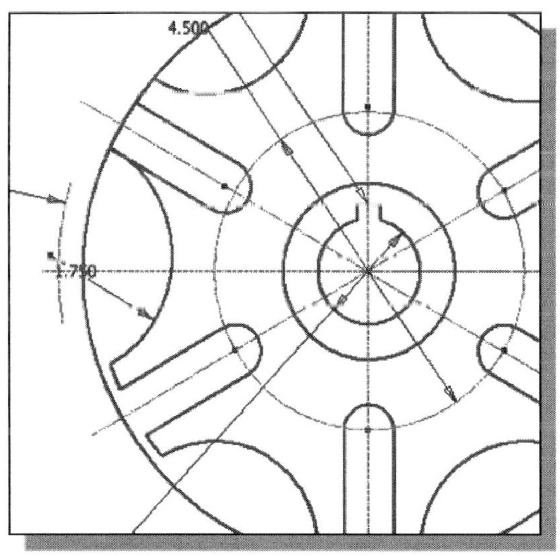

17. On your own, adjust the radius dimension to **1.75** and notice that some of the other geometric entities become distorted when the size of the related arc is updated.

❖ On the *Status Bar* of the Inventor window, Inventor indicates that over 100 additional dimensions are needed to fully define the current geometry.

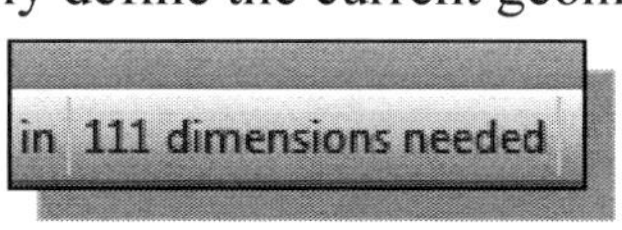

❖ By copying and pasting the entire view, we have extra entities that are not necessary to create the 3D part, such as the note for the keyway and the centerlines. As far as building the 3D model is concerned, we can take advantage of the symmetrical nature of the design and simply copy a relatively small portion of the original geometric entities.

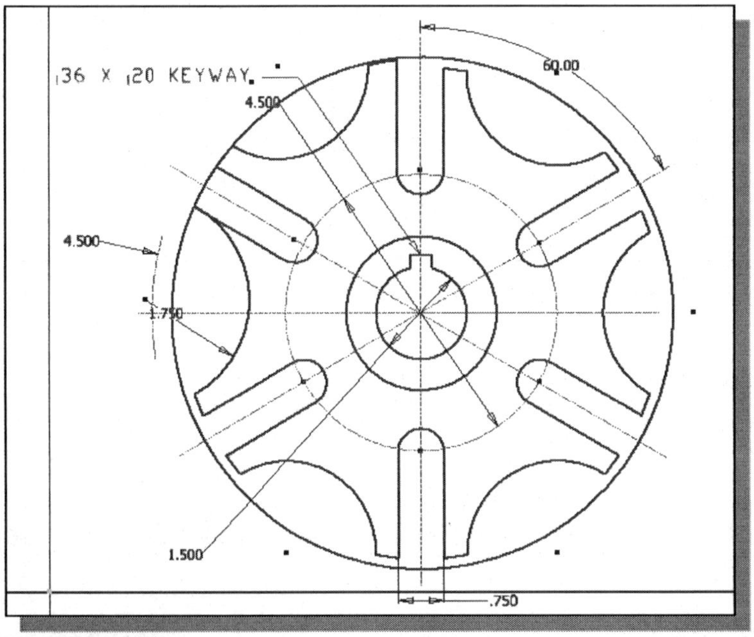

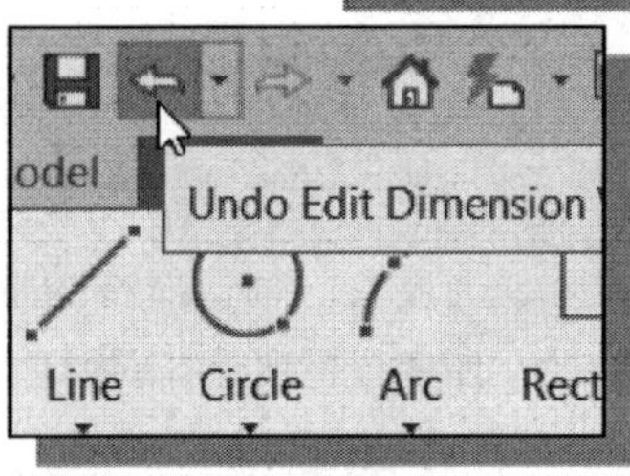

18. In the *Quick Access* toolbar, click **Undo** once to undo the last step.

19. Continue to click **Undo** until all of the pasted geometry entities are removed from the screen.

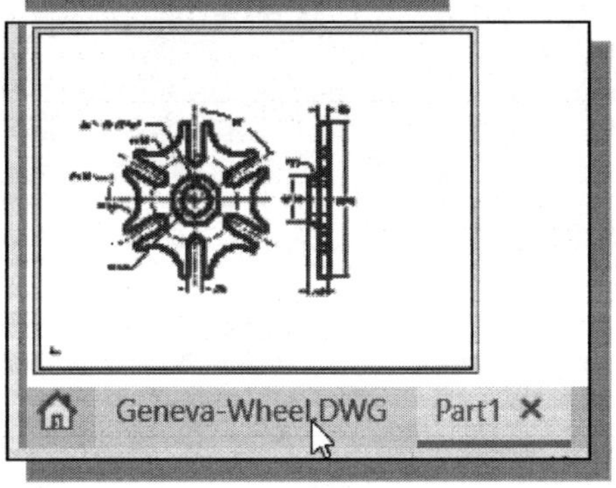

20. Switch to the **Geneva-Wheel.DWG** window by clicking on its *window*, in the toolbar area, or selecting the associated *file tab* as shown.

21. Select any set of four entities that form a 30 degree section as shown. (Hint: Hold down the [**Ctrl**] key while clicking on the entities.)

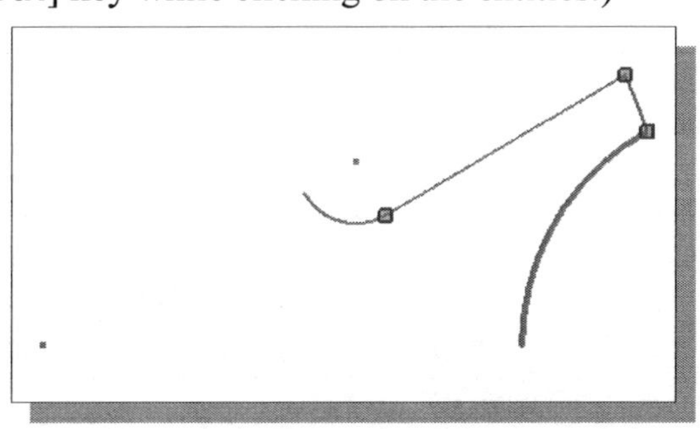

22. Right-mouse click once to bring up the option menu and select **Copy** or use the quick-key option **[Ctrl+C]**.

Complete the Imported Sketch

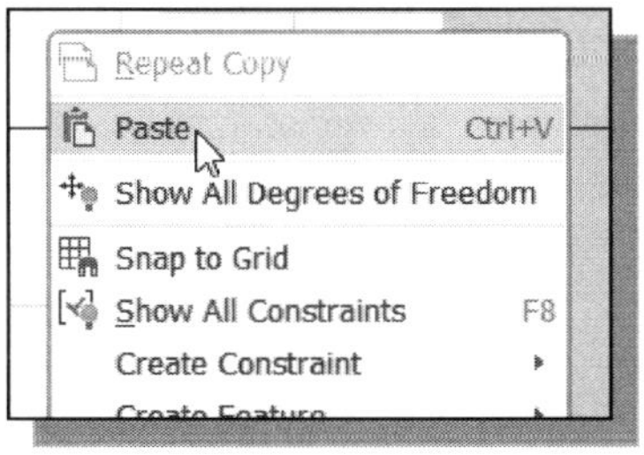

1. On your own, **Copy** and **Paste** the four entities onto the **XZ Plane** of the 2D sketch in the **Part1** file window.

❖ To create an extruded feature, two additional lines are necessary to form a closed region.

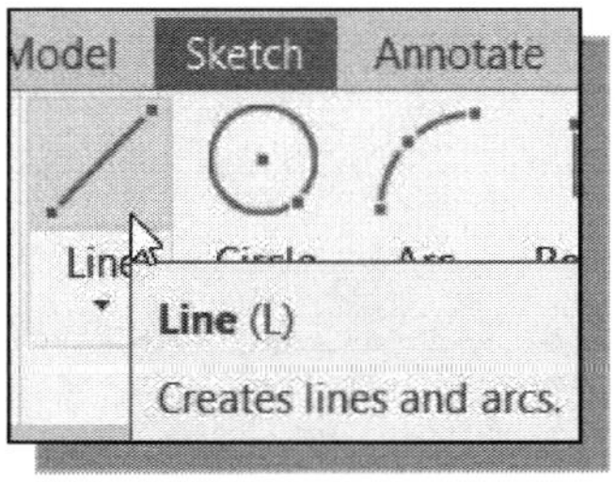

2. Select the **Line** option in the *2D Sketch* panel as shown.

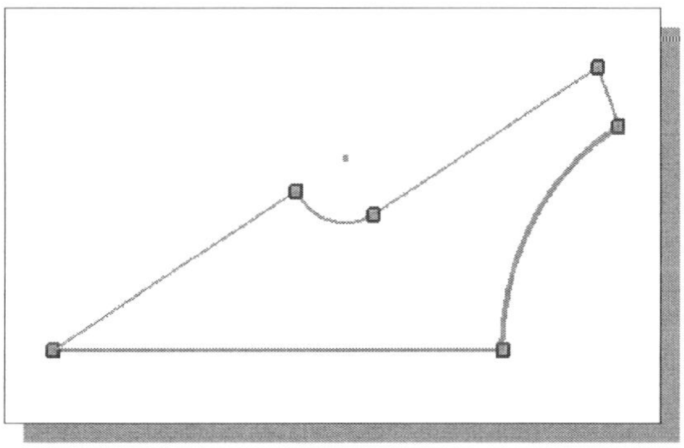

3. Add thc two lincs conncting to thc lower left center point and apply coincident constraint to all corners.

❖ Note that we could simply create the 3D model with the current sketch, without adding any additional dimensions or constraints. However, a fully constrained sketch is more desirable.

4. On your own, create the following six dimensions as shown.

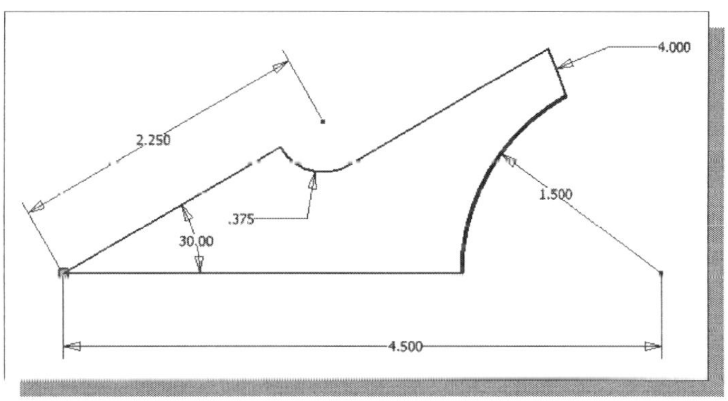

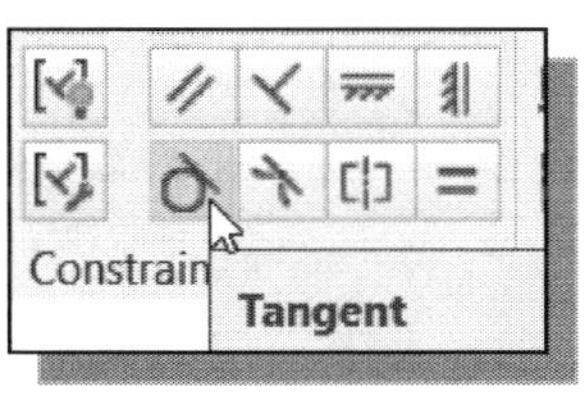

5. Select the **Tangent** constraint in the *Constrain* panel as shown.

6. On your own, apply a tangent constraint between the top-right inclined line and the .375 radius in the above figure.

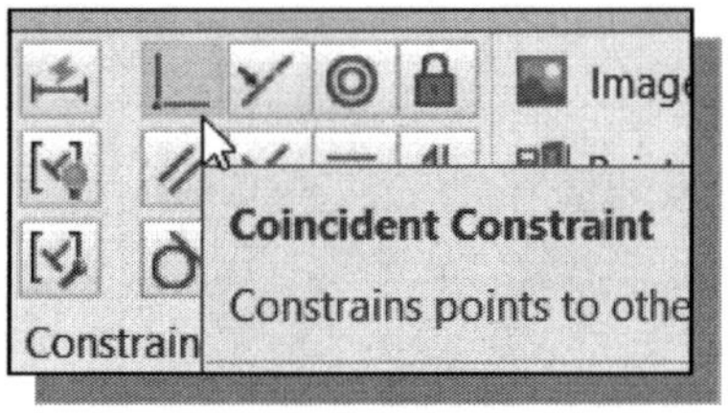

7. Select the **Coincident Constraint** in the *Constrain* panel as shown.

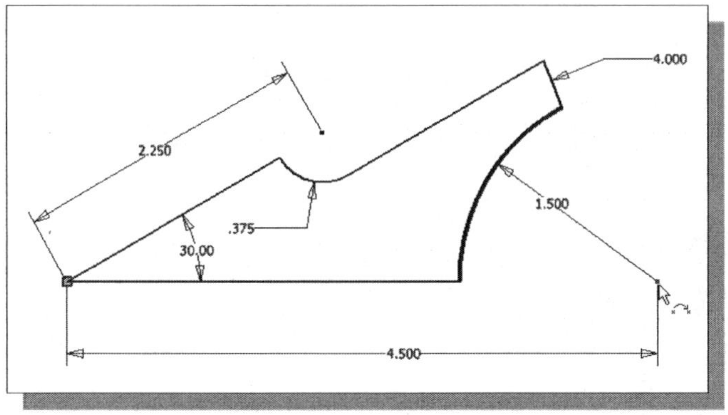

8. Select the center point on the right as shown.

9. Select the bottom horizontal line to align the center of the lower arc to the horizontal line.

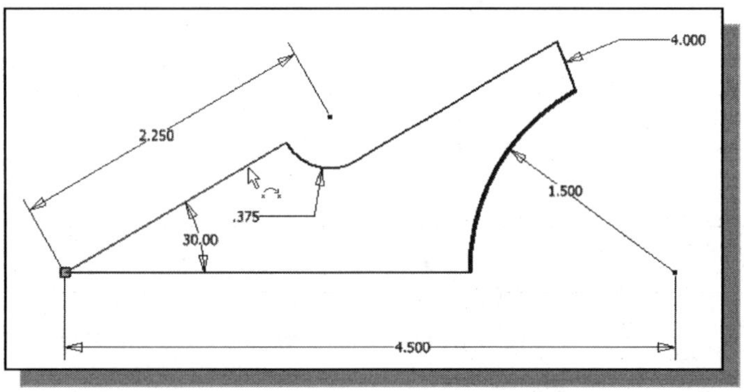

10. Repeat the above steps and align the center point of the radius 0.375 arc to the inclined line as shown.

11. On your own, add a **parallel constraint** to the two parallel inclined lines.

12. On your own, align the lower left corner of the sketch to the origin as shown.

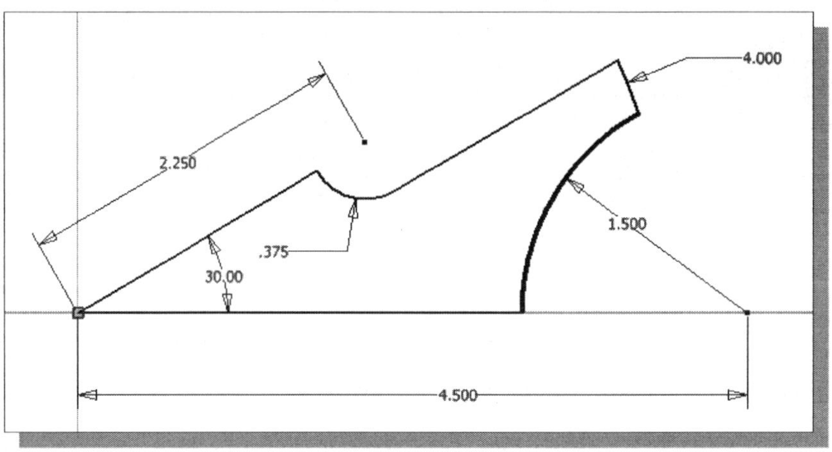

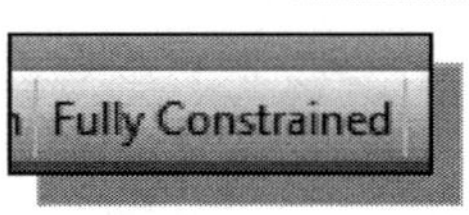

13. Note the sketch is now fully constrained, as indicated in the *Status Bar*.

Create the First Solid Feature

1. In the *Standard* toolbar, select **Finish Sketch**, by left-clicking on the icon, to exit the *2D Sketch Mode*.

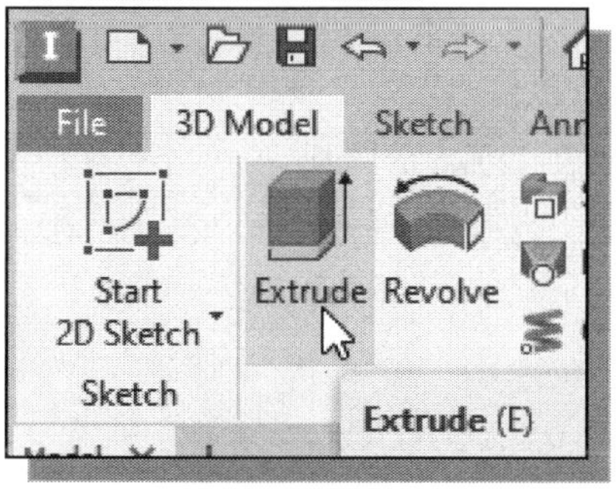

2. In the *3D Model* panel, select the **Extrude** command by left-clicking the icon.

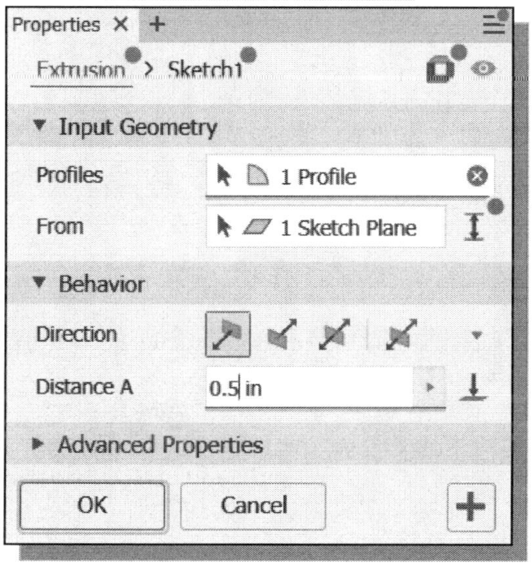

3. Expand the *Extrude* dialog box by clicking on the **down arrow**.

4. In the *Extrude* dialog box, enter **0.5** as the extrusion *Distance* as shown.

5. Click **OK** to accept the settings to create an extruded solid feature as shown.

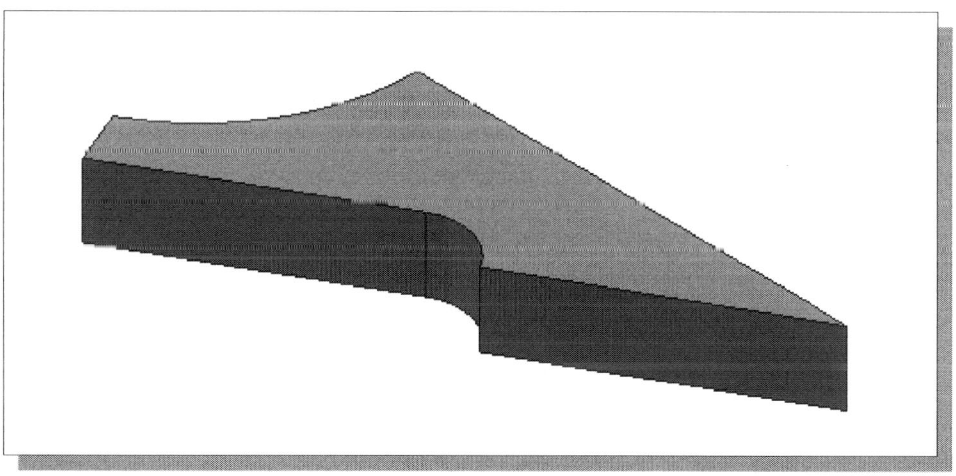

Create a Mirrored Feature

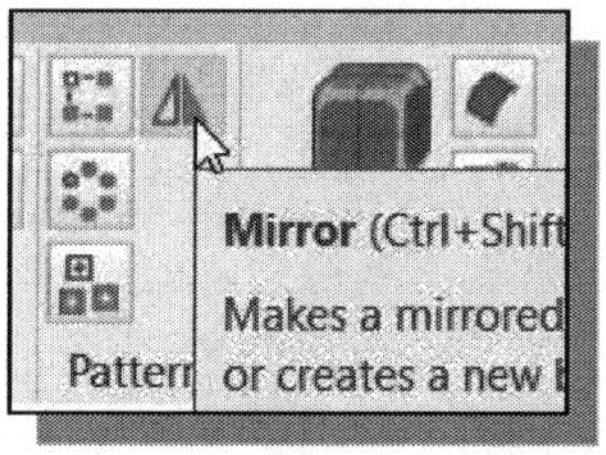

1. In the *Pattern toolbar* panel, select the **Mirror** command by left-clicking the icon.

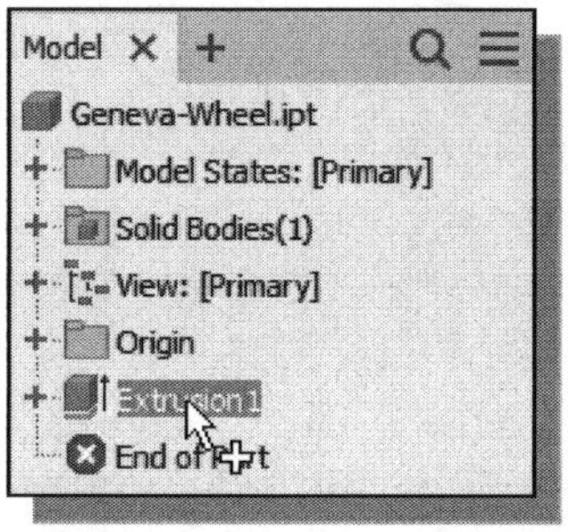

2. Select **Extrusion1** in the *browser* window as shown in the figure.

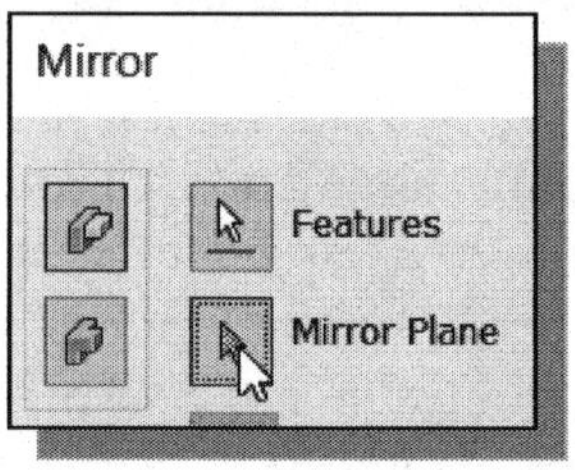

3. Click the **Mirror Plane** button to proceed to the next step, defining the *mirror image plane.*

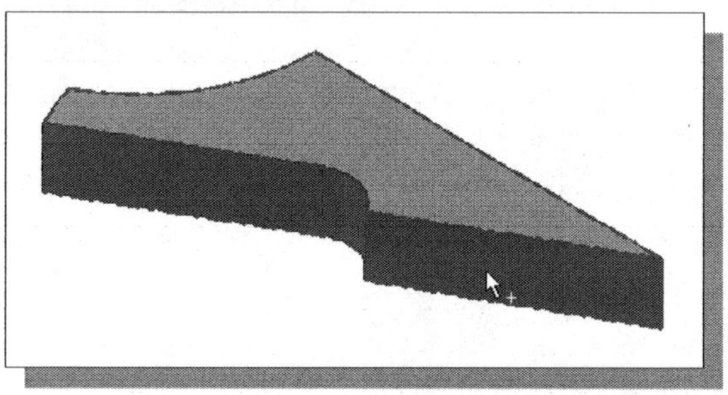

4. Select the small flat plane as shown in the figure.

5. Click **OK** to create the mirror image.

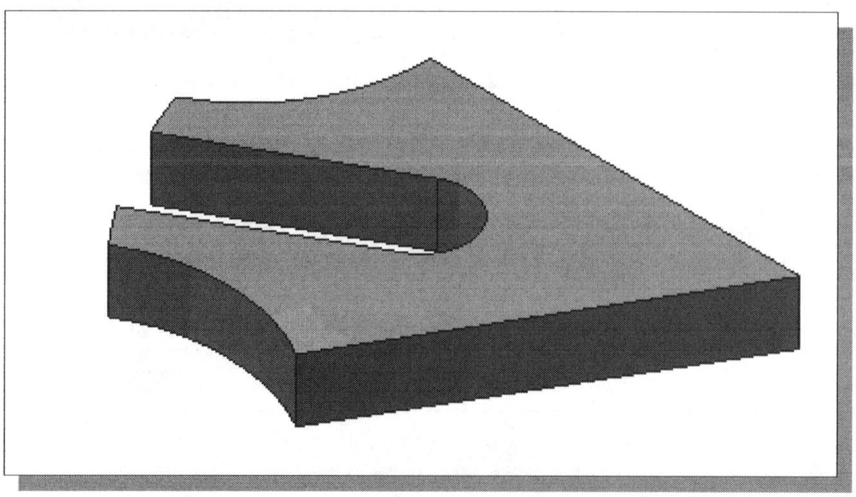

Circular Pattern

In Autodesk Inventor, existing features can be easily duplicated with the **Pattern** command. The patterned features are parametrically linked to the original feature; any modifications to the original feature are also reflected in the arrayed features.

1. In the *3D Model* panel, select the **Circular Pattern** command by left-clicking once on the icon.

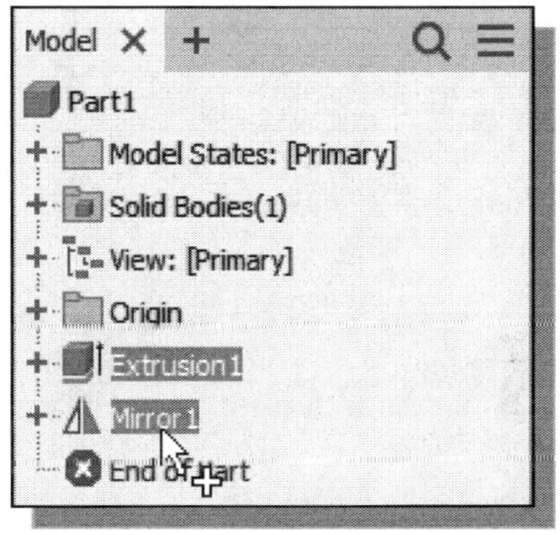

2. The message "*Select Feature to be arrayed*:" is displayed in the command prompt window. Select the **Mirror1** feature in the *browser* window as shown.

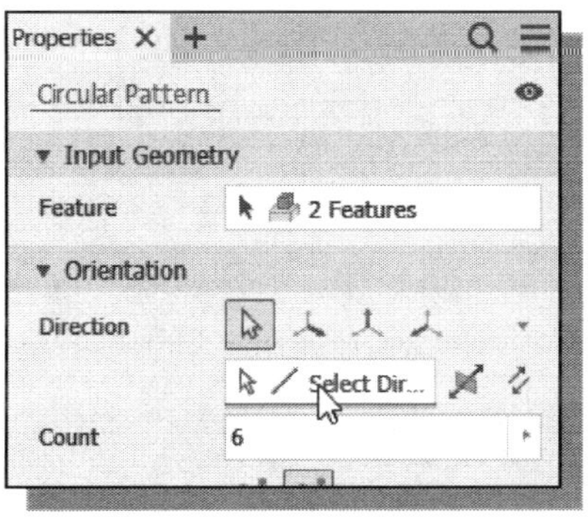

3. Click the **Rotation Axis** button to proceed to the next step, defining the *axis of rotation*.

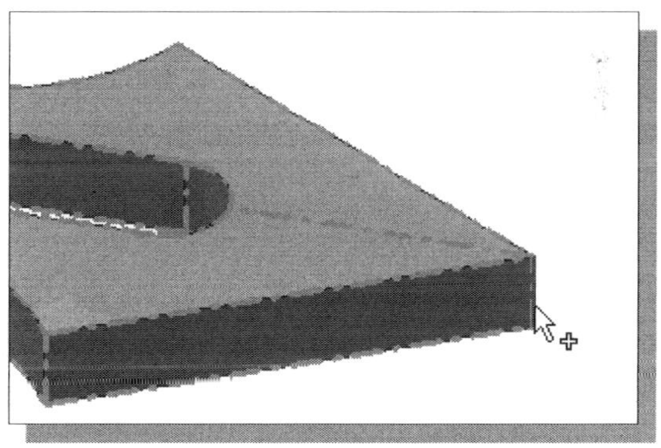

4. Select the sharp edge of the extruded feature as shown.

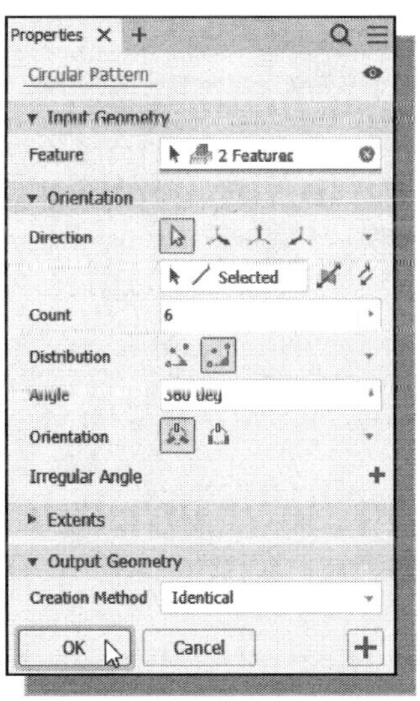

5. Confirm the placement options are set to **6** and **360 deg** as shown.

6. Click **OK** to accept the settings and create the *patterned* feature.

Complete the Geneva Wheel Design

We will now complete the ***Geneva-Wheel*** part by adding a ***revolved*** feature and an ***extruded cut*** feature. The benefits of ***2D design reuse*** are more obvious for designs with complex geometry. The very powerful parametric software, such as Autodesk Inventor, allows us to quickly rebuild 3D models from existing 2D CAD information.

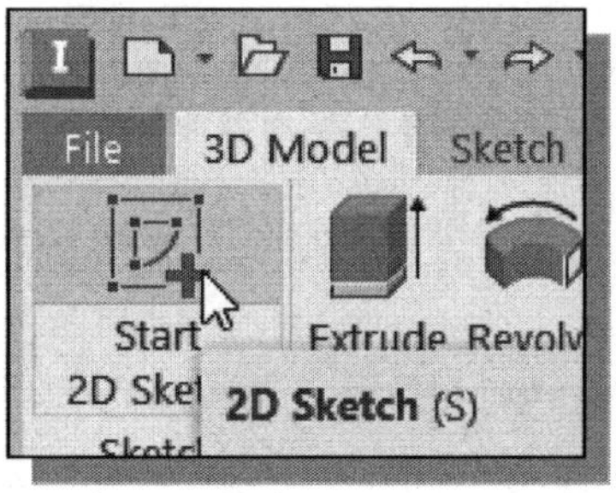

1. Click **2D Sketch** to enter the *2D Sketching* mode.

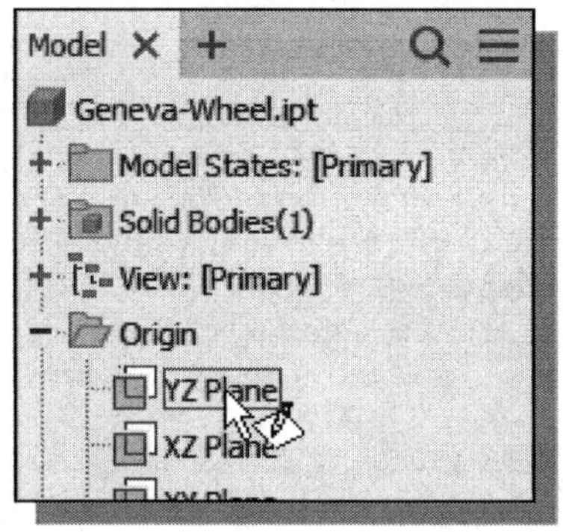

2. Select the **YZ plane** to align the sketching plane.

3. Reset the display to ***right*** **view** by clicking on the corresponding face of the **ViewCube** as shown.

4. Activate the **Project Geometry** command.

5. Select the top edge of the solid model as shown.

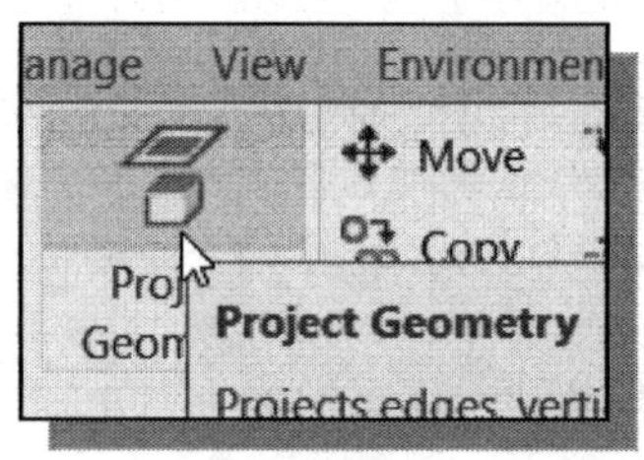

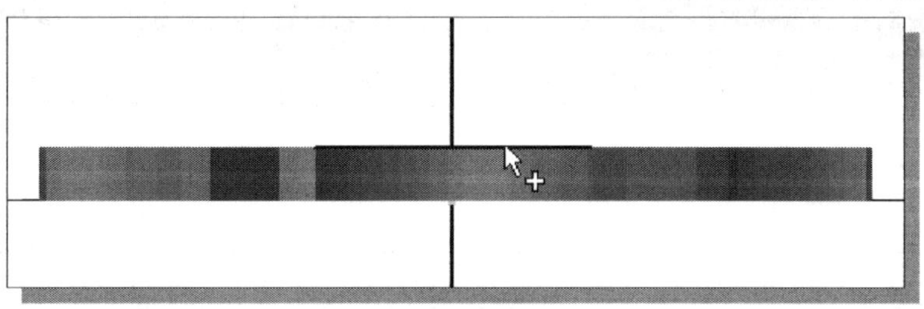

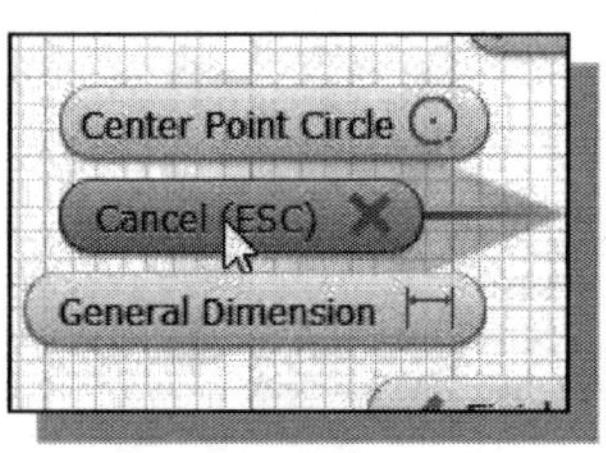

6. **Right-click** once to bring up the option menu and select **Done** as shown.

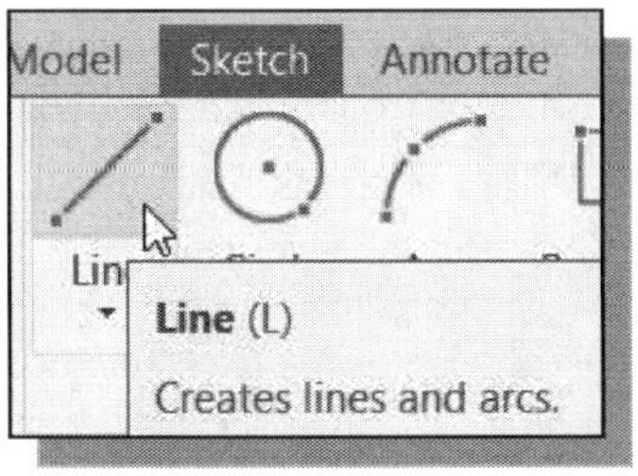

7. In the *Draw* toolbar, click once with the left-mouse-button to select the **Line** command.

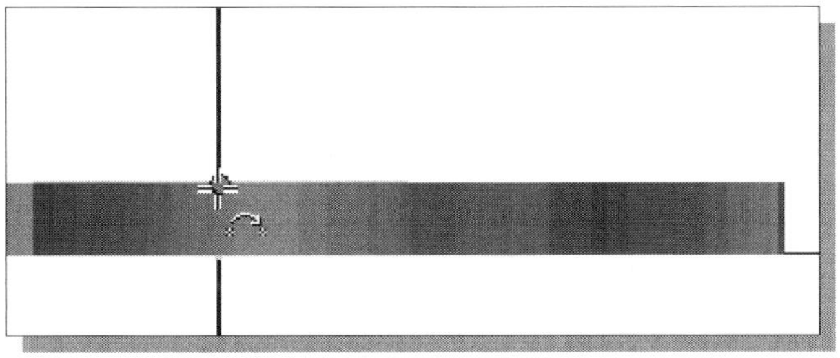

8. Start the line segments at the intersection of the projected edge and the vertical axis as shown.

9. Create three line segments, perpendicular and parallel to each other as shown.

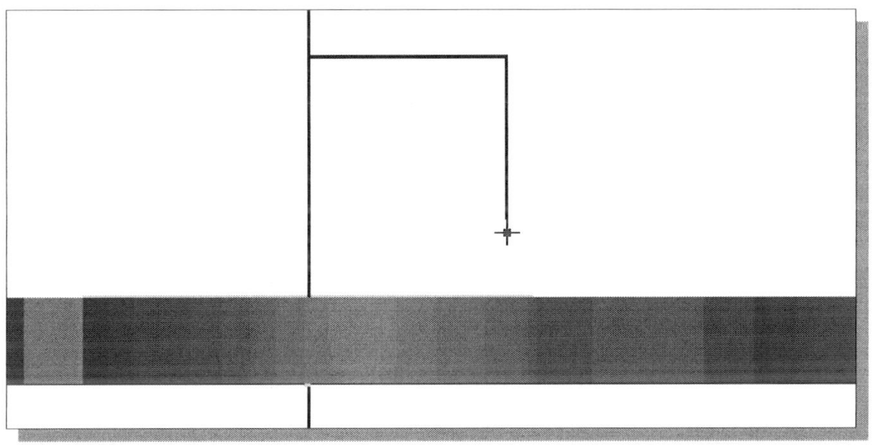

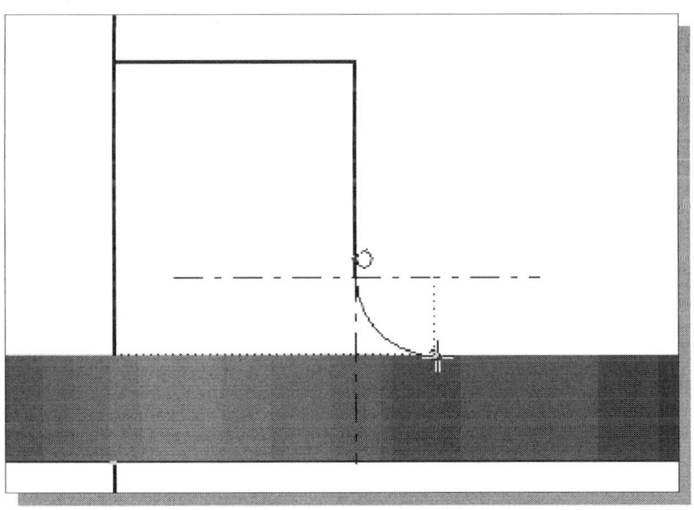

10. With the **left-mouse-button pressed down,** drag the mouse downward to create the ***tangent arc*** as shown.

11. Connect the line segments back to the ***starting point*** to form a closed region.

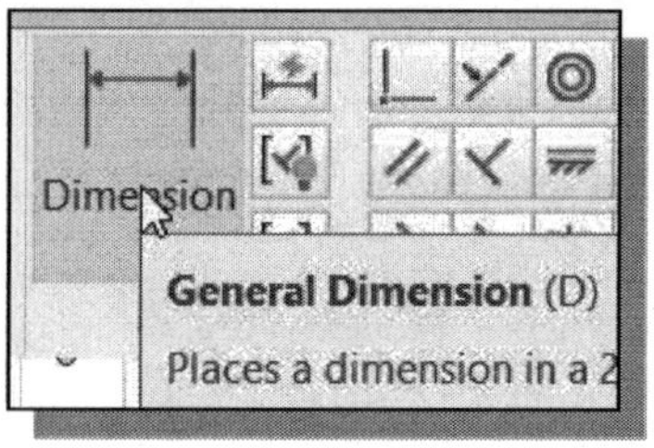

12. In the *Constrain* toolbar, click once with the left-mouse-button to select the **General Dimension** command.

13. On your own, create the three dimensions as shown.

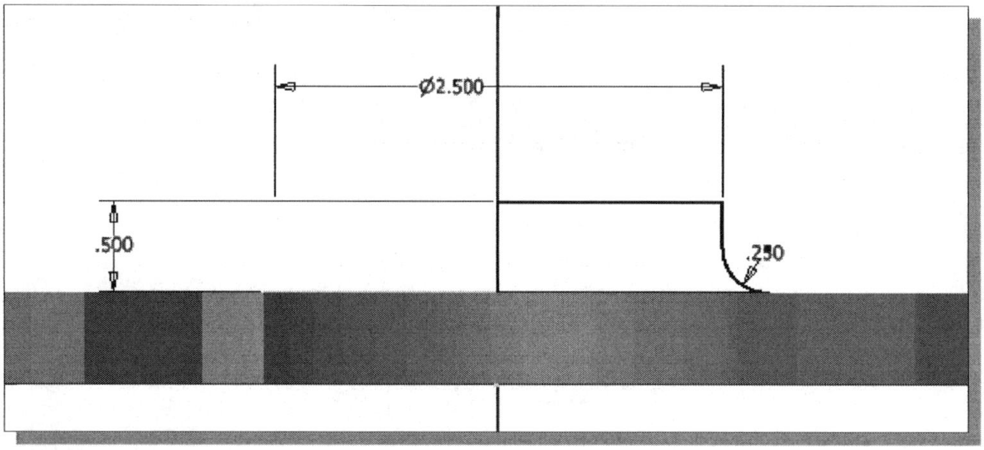

14. In the *Standard* toolbar, select **Finish Sketch**, by left-clicking on the icon, to exit the *2D Sketch Mode.*

15. On your own, create a ***revolved*** feature as shown.

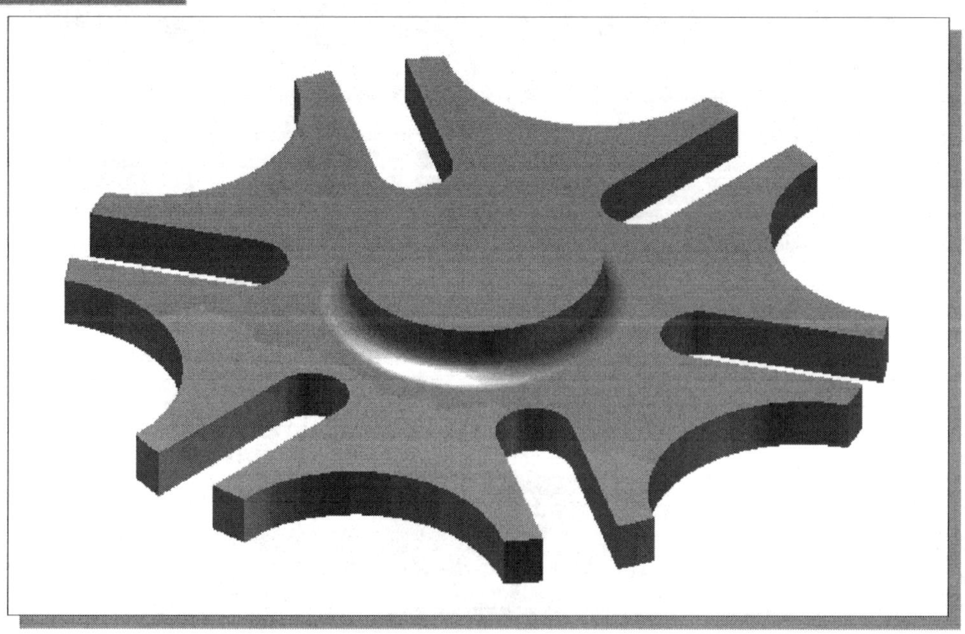

16. On your own, create a 2D sketch (Dimensions: **0.95, 0.36, 1.5**) on the top circular surface as shown.

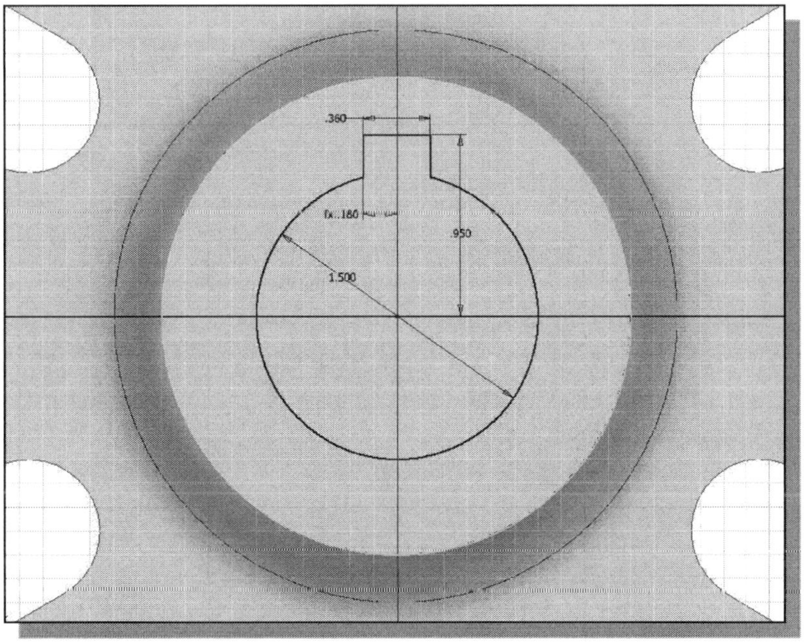

17. Create a cut feature and complete the design as shown.

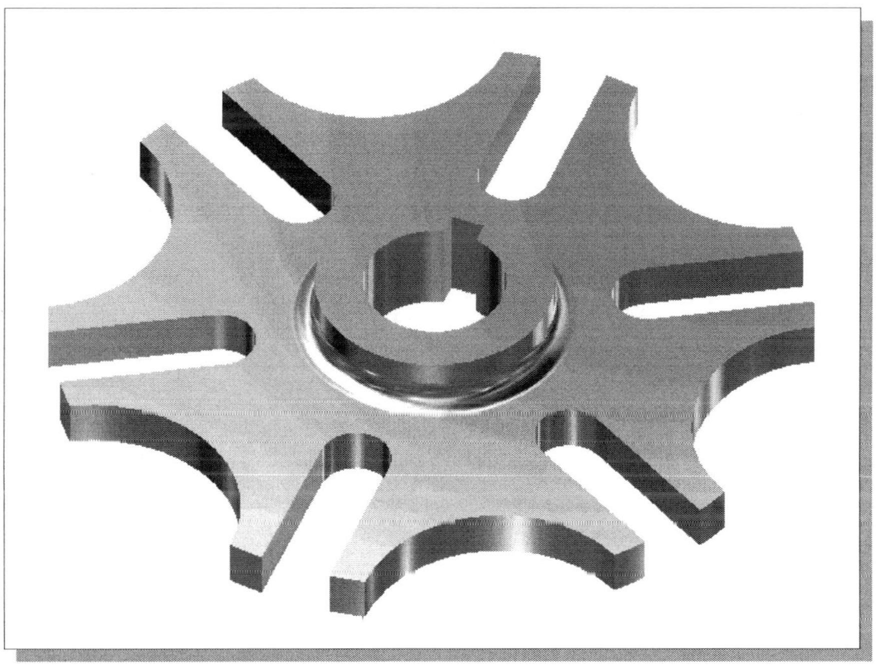

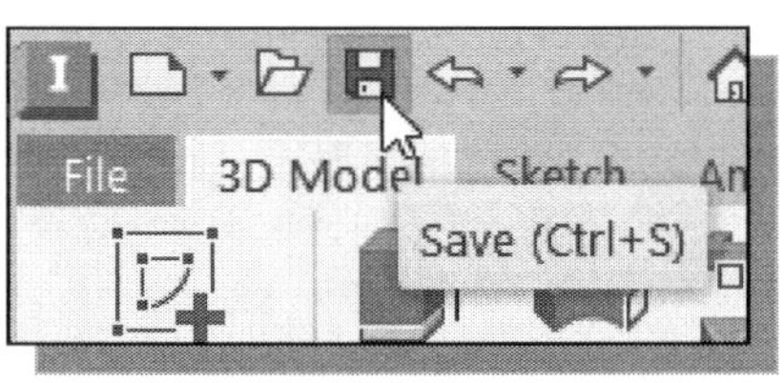

18. Click the **Save** icon and save the model as ***Geneva-Wheel.ipt***.

Export an Inventor 2D Sketch as an AutoCAD Drawing

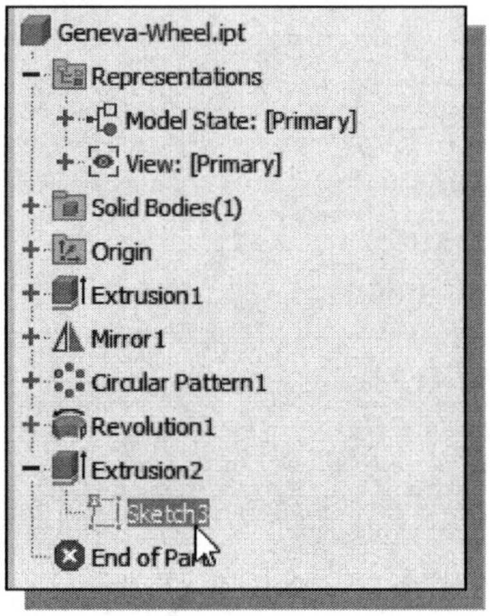

1. In the *Model Tree*, click on the [**+**] sign in front of the last extrusion feature to expand the feature list.

2. **Right-click** once on the **Sketch** item to bring up the option menu and select **Export Sketch As…** as shown.

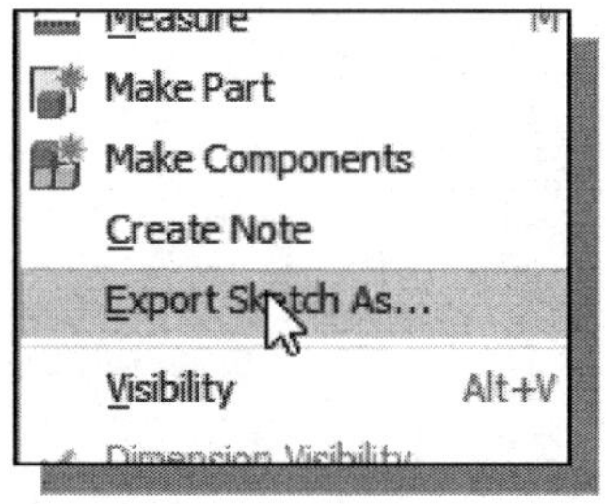

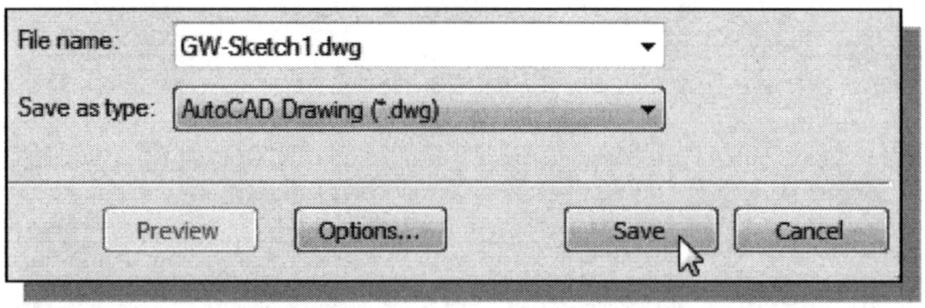

3. On your own, export the 2D sketch as ***GW-Sketch1.dwg*** and open it in Inventor as shown.

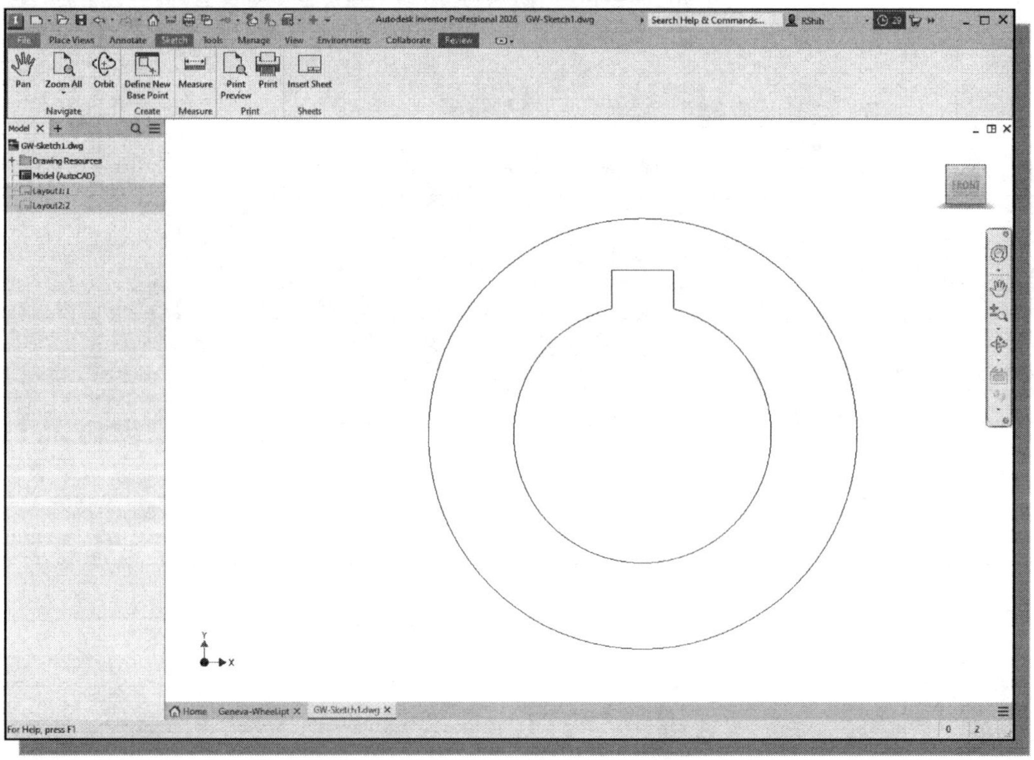

- Note that only the 2D geometry of the sketch is exported.

Design Reuse – Sketch Insert Option

We will next illustrate using the **insert** option to place the *Geneva-Wheel.dwg* directly into the *Sketch* mode.

1. Close the *Geneva-Wheel.dwg* drawing by clicking on the associated tab, as shown in the figure, located near the bottom of the graphics area.

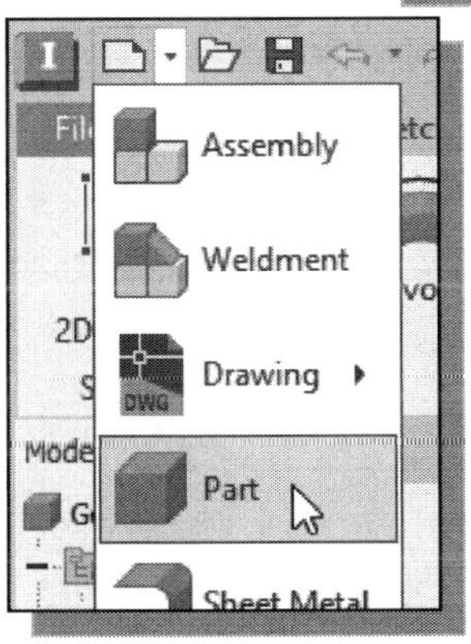

- Note that the associated *DWG* file cannot be in use for the **Insert** command to work.

2. Start a new part file by clicking on the **triangle** next to the **New File** icon and choose **Part** as shown.

3. Reset the display to the *top* view by clicking on the **Top** face of the ViewCube as shown.

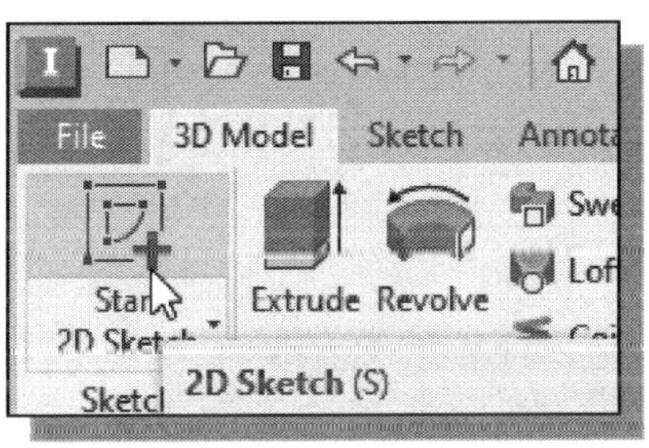

4. Click **2D Sketch** to enter the *2D Sketching* mode.
5. Select the **XZ plane** to align the sketching plane.

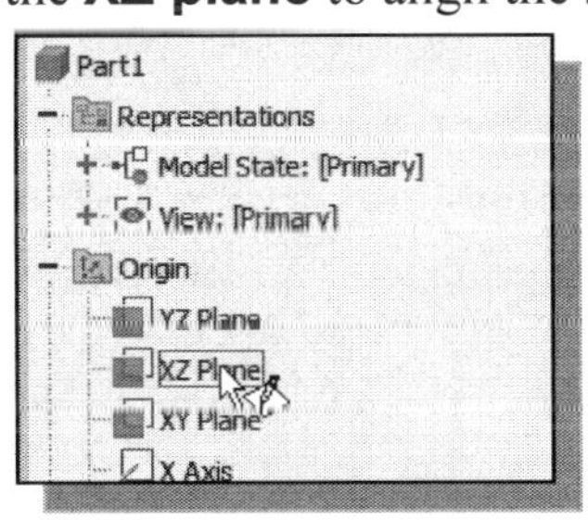

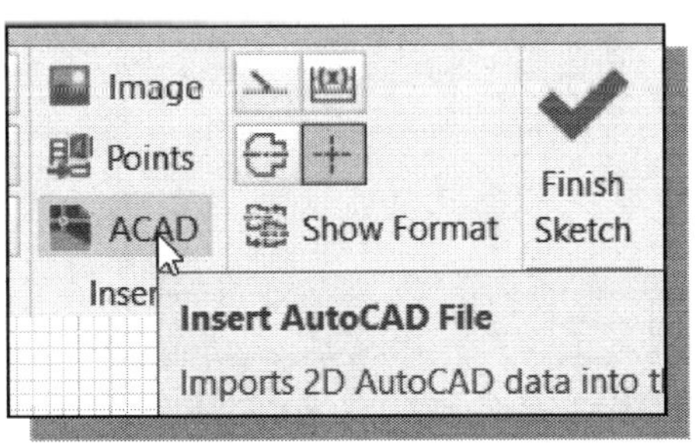

6. In the *Insert* toolbar, click **ACAD** to activate the command to import geometry from an existing AutoCAD drawing.

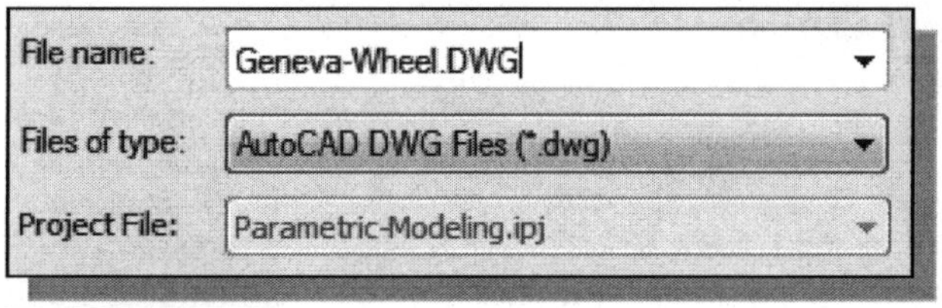

7. In the *Open* dialog box, set the *Files of type* to **AutoCAD Drawings (*.dwg)** and select the ***Geneva-Wheel.dwg*** file as shown.

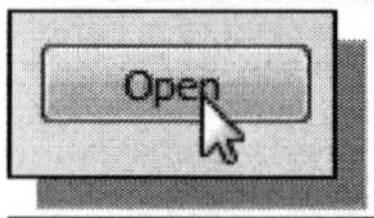

8. Click **Open** to proceed with the Insert AutoCAD command.

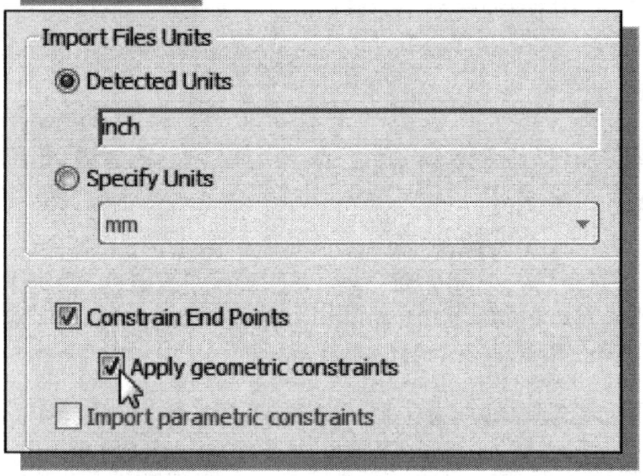

9. Confirm the *Units* is set to **inch** as shown.

10. Switch *ON* the Constrain End Points option and the Apply geometric constraints as shown.

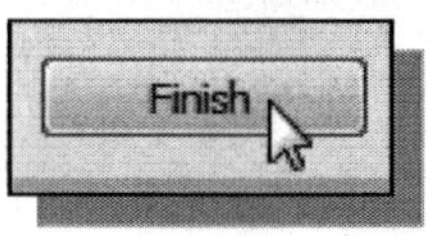

11. Click **Finish** to accept the settings and proceed to importing the *2D* AutoCAD geometry into Inventor.

12. On your own, delete most of the objects keeping only the object lines on the main view as shown.

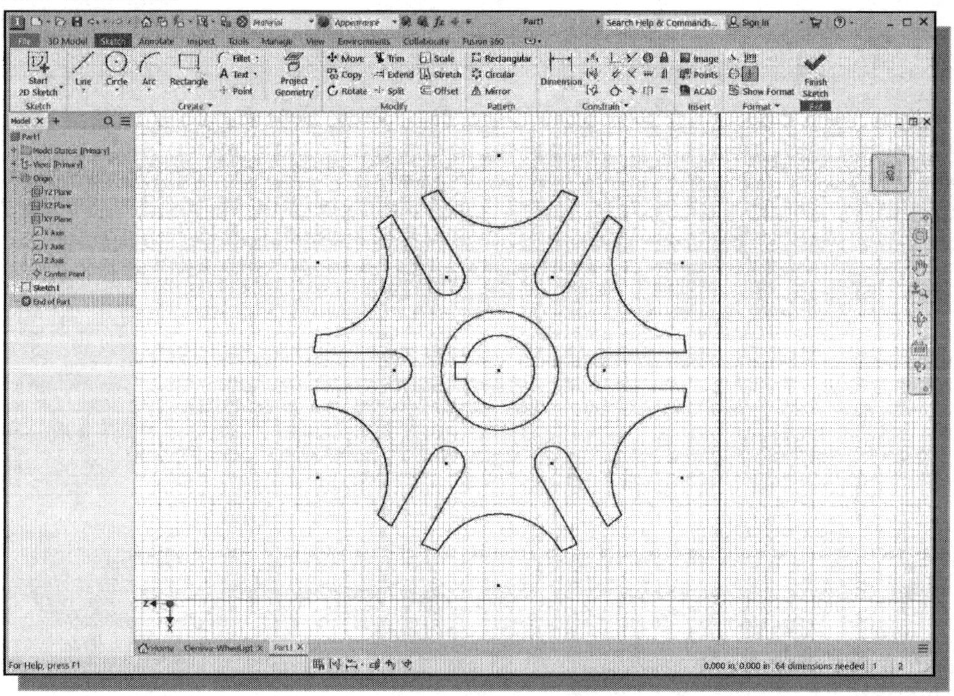

13. In the *Standard* toolbar, select **Finish Sketch**, by left-clicking on the icon, to exit the *2D Sketch Mode*.

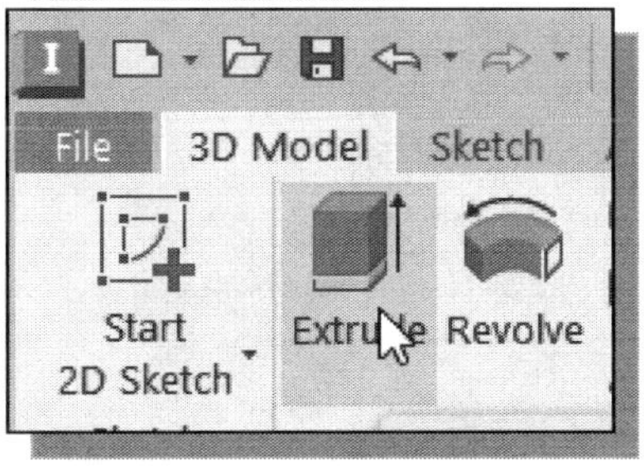

14. In the *Part Features* panel, select the **Extrude** command by left-clicking the icon.

15. Select the **outer region** of the imported sketch as shown.

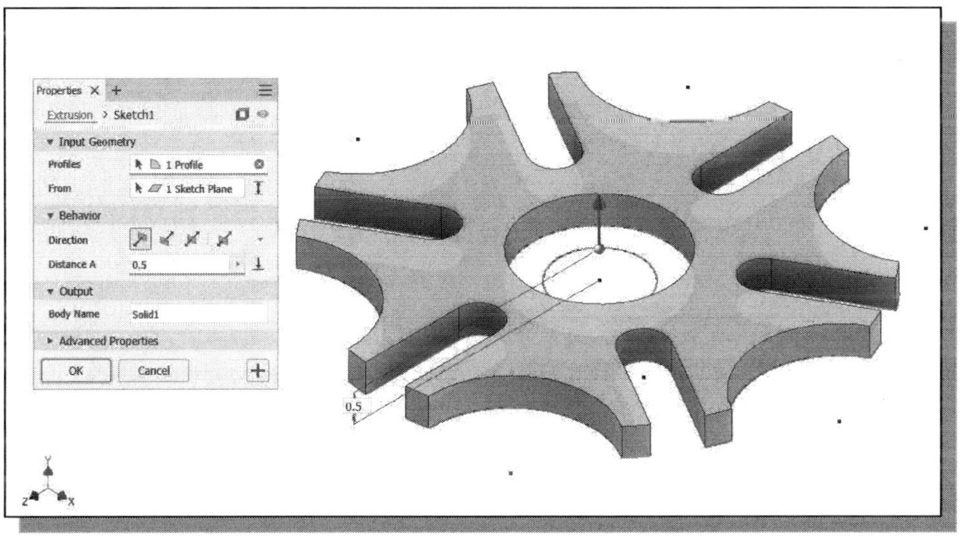

16. In the *Extrude* dialog box, enter ***0.5*** as the extrusion *Distance* as shown.

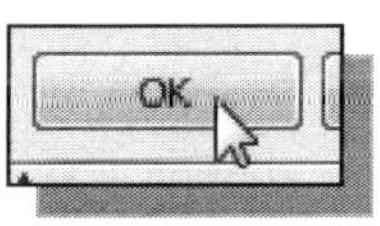

17. Click **OK** to accept the settings to create an extruded solid feature as shown.

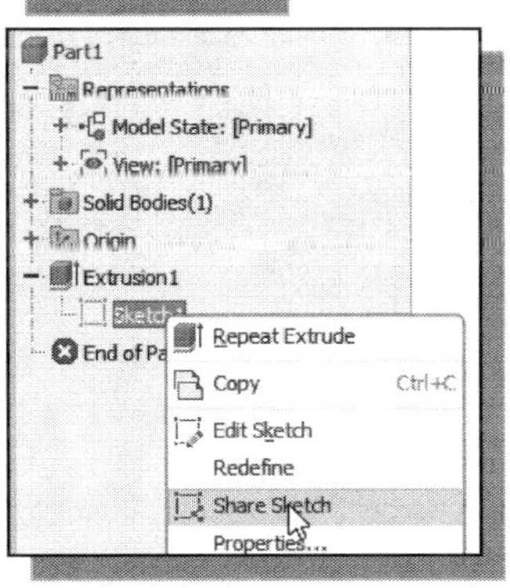

18. In the *Model Tree*, click on the [**+**] sign in front of the extrusion feature to expand the feature list.

19. **Right-click** once on the **Sketch** item to bring up the option menu and select **Share Sketch** as shown.

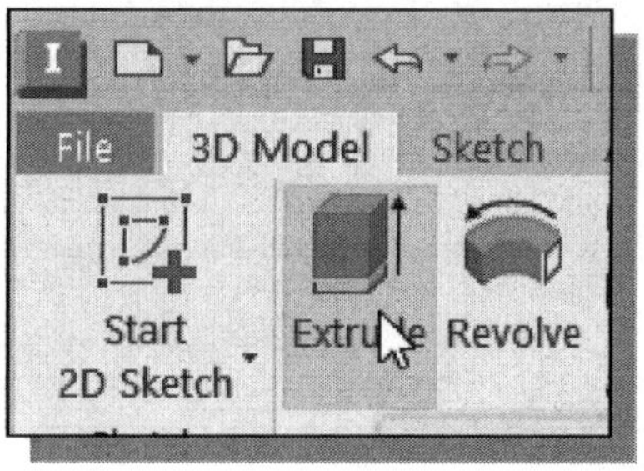

20. In the *Part Features* panel, select the **Extrude** command by left-clicking the icon.

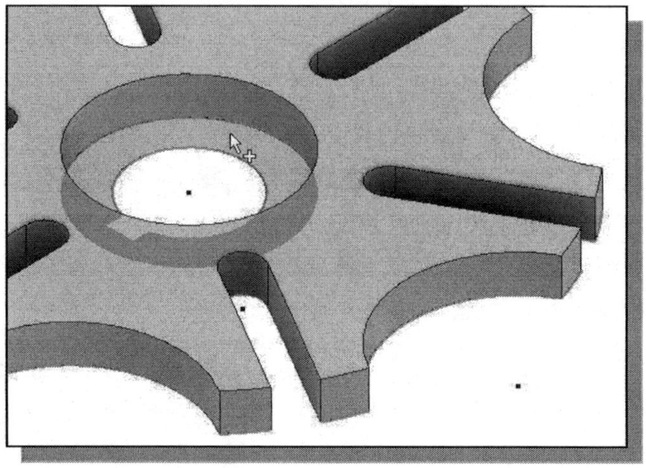

21. Select the **inside region** of the shared sketch as shown.

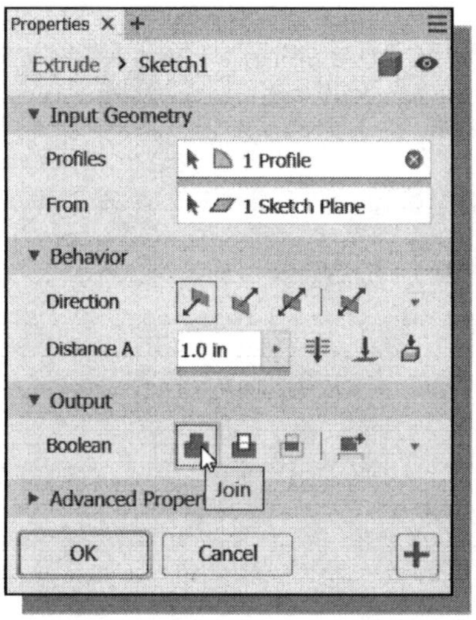

22. In the *Extrude* dialog box, enter ***1.0*** as the extrusion *Distance* as shown.

23. Set the *extrude option* to **Join** as shown.

24. Click **OK** to accept the settings to create an extruded solid feature.

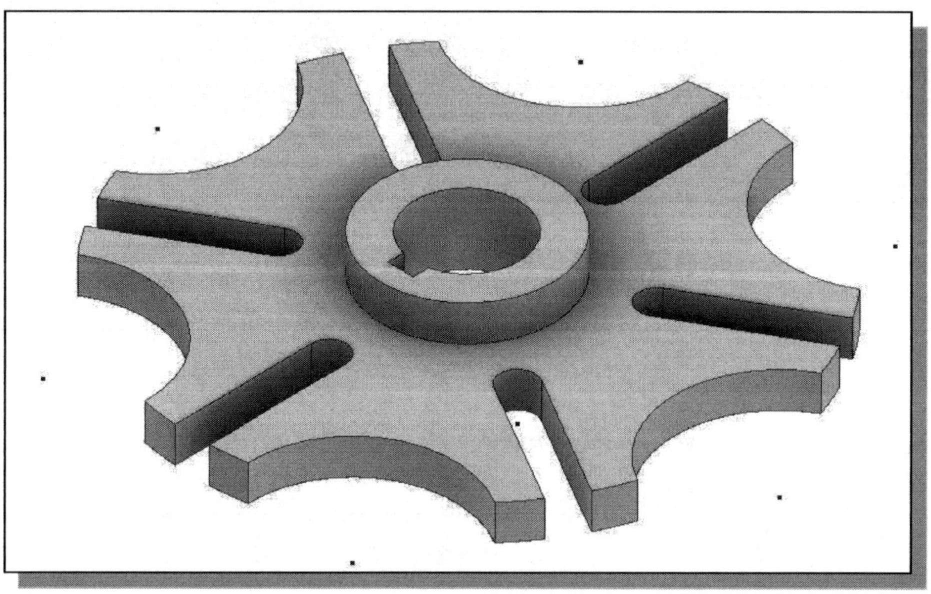

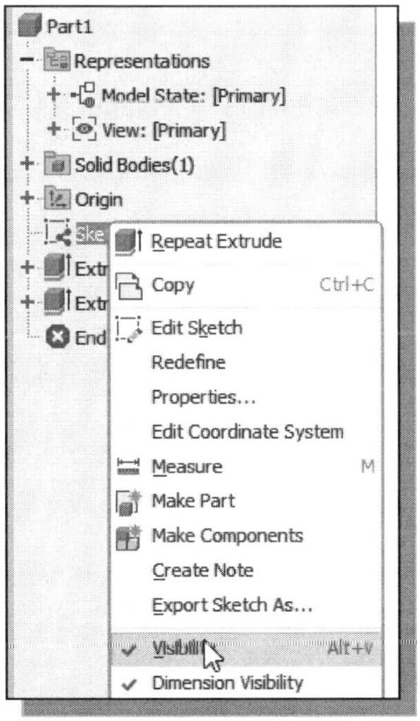

25. Turn ***OFF*** the **Visibility** of the ***shared sketch*** through the option menu as shown.

26. On your own, use the **Fillet** command and create a **radius 0.25** fillet as shown.

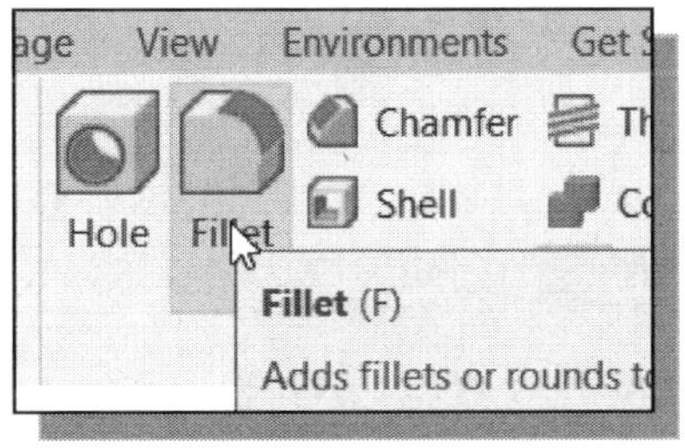

- Note that the solid model was built by taking the 2D AutoCAD geometry information directly, without any modification or alteration. Autodesk Inventor allows us to create designs by using partially constrained or totally unconstrained sketches. The 3D models can be built relatively quickly through the reuse of the existing 2D AutoCAD drawing.

Review Questions:

1. Briefly describe the concept of **2D Design Reuse**. Describe some of the advantages of **2D Design Reuse.**

2. Can AutoCAD DWG files be opened and saved with Autodesk Inventor?

3. Can we edit the AutoCAD DWG entities that are in AutoCAD *Model Space* under Autodesk Inventor?

4. Can we edit the AutoCAD DWG entities that are in AutoCAD Layout under Autodesk Inventor?

5. List and describe three commands available in the *Drawing Review* panel?

6. What does the **Contact Solver** allow us to do?

7. Describe the steps involved in using the Inventor **Contact Solver**.

8. Can we perform a constrained move on fully constrained components?

9. Can Autodesk Inventor calculate the center of gravity of an assembly model? How do you activate this option?

10. When and why would you use the **Collision Detection** option available in Autodesk Inventor?

11. Can Autodesk Inventor calculate the weight of an assembly model? How is this done?

Exercises:

1. Ratchet Plate – Using the design reuse approach, create the associated solid model.

Download the *RatchetPlate.dwg* using the following URL:
http://www.sdcACAD.com/acad2027/RatchetPlate.dwg

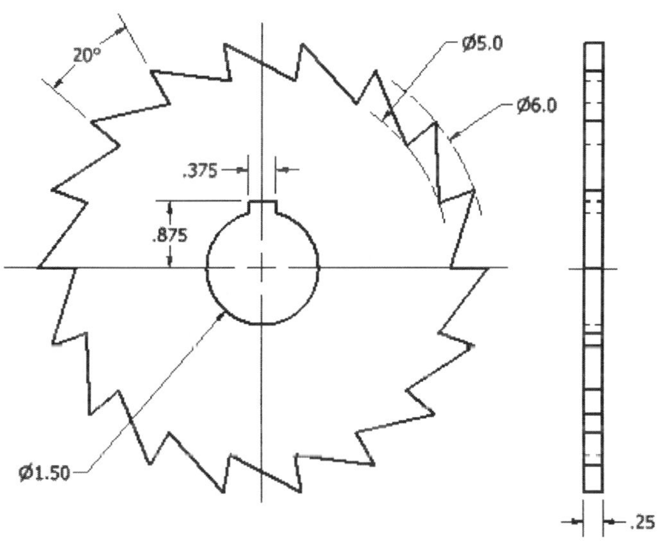

2. Indexing Guide (Construct the 2D views of the design in AutoCAD and use the Design Reuse options to complete the design in Inventor.)

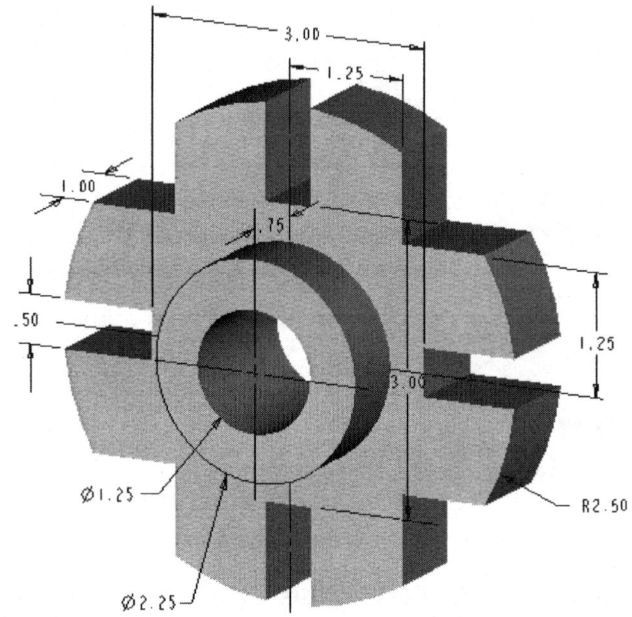

3. Auxiliary Support (Construct the 2D views of the design in AutoCAD and use the Design Reuse options to complete the design in Inventor.)

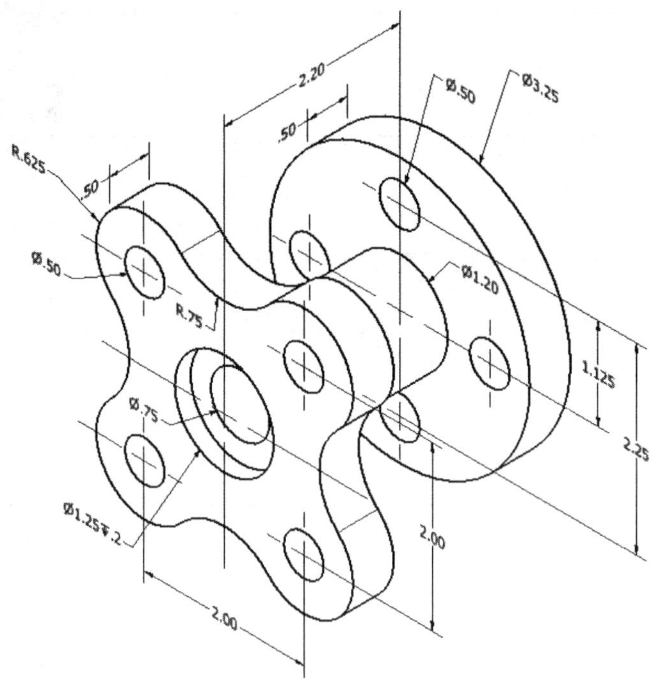

Chapter 16

Assembly Modeling - Putting It All Together - Autodesk Inventor

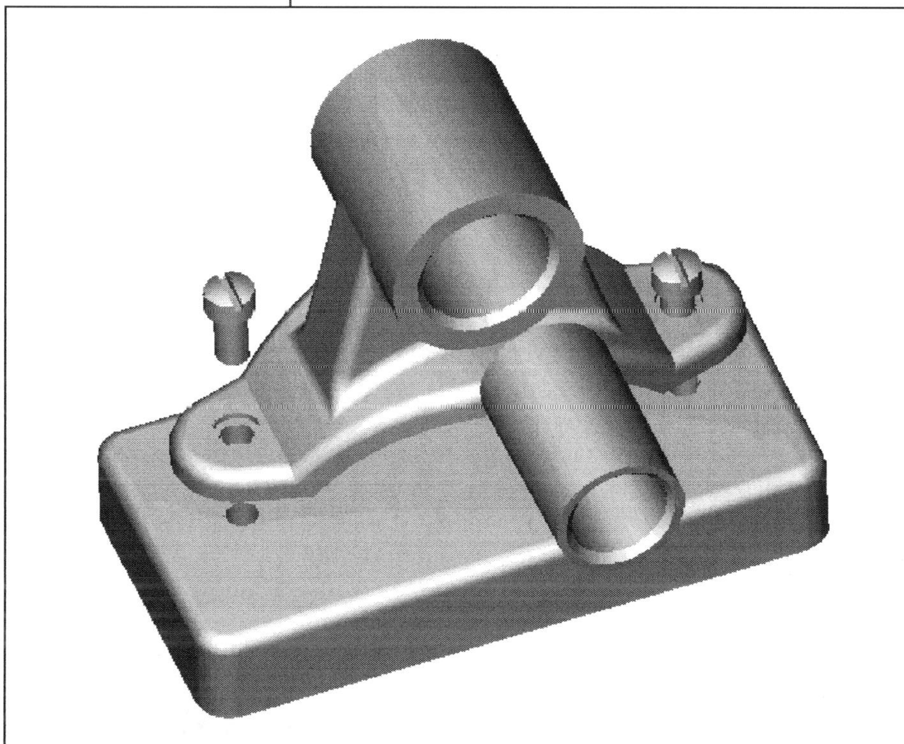

Learning Objectives

- Understand the Assembly Modeling Mcthodology
- Create Parts in the Assembly Modeler Mode
- Understand and Utilize Assembly Constraints
- Understand the Autodesk Inventor DOF Display
- Utilize the Autodesk Inventor Adaptive Design Approach
- Create Exploded Assemblies

Introduction

In the previous lessons, we have gone over the fundamentals of creating basic parts and drawings. In this lesson, we will examine the assembly modeling functionality of Autodesk Inventor. We will start with a demonstration on how to create and modify assembly models. The main task in creating an assembly is establishing the assembly relationships between parts. To assemble parts into an assembly, we will need to consider the assembly relationships between parts. It is good practice to assemble parts based on the way they would be assembled in the actual manufacturing process. We should also consider breaking down the assembly into smaller subassemblies, which helps the management of parts. In Autodesk Inventor, a subassembly is treated the same way as a single part during assembling. Many parallels exist between assembly modeling and part modeling in parametric modeling software such as Autodesk Inventor.

Autodesk Inventor provides full associative functionality in all design modules, including assemblies. When we change a part model, Autodesk Inventor will automatically reflect the changes in all assemblies that use the part. We can also modify a part in an assembly. **Bi-directional full associative functionality** is the main feature of parametric solid modeling software that allows us to increase productivity by reducing design cycle time.

One of the key features of Autodesk Inventor is the use of an assembly-centric paradigm, which enables users to concentrate on the design without depending on the associated parameters or constraints. Users can specify how parts fit together and the Autodesk Inventor *assembly-based fit function* automatically determines the parts' sizes and positions. This unique approach is known as the **Direct Adaptive Assembly** approach, which defines part relationships directly with no order dependency.

In this lesson, we will also illustrate the basic concept of Autodesk Inventor's **Adaptive Design** approach. The key element in doing **Adaptive Design** is to ***under-constrain*** features or parts. The applied *assembly constraints* in the assembly modeler are used to control the sizes, shapes, and positions of ***under-constrained*** sketches, features, and parts. No equations are required, and this approach is extremely flexible when performing modifications and changes to the design. We can modify adaptive assemblies at any point, in any order, regardless of how the parts were originally placed or constrained.

In Autodesk Inventor, features and parts can be made adaptive at any time during the creation or assembly. The features of a part can be defined as adaptive when they are created in the part file. When we place such a part in an assembly, the features will then resize and change shape based on the applied assembly constraints. We can make features and parts adaptive from either the part modeling or assembly modeling environments.

The *Adaptive Design approach* is a unique design methodology that can only be found in Autodesk Inventor. The goal of this methodology is to improve the design process and allows you, the designer, to ***design the way you think***.

Assembly Modeling Methodology

The Autodesk Inventor assembly modeler provides tools and functions that allow us to create 3D parametric assembly models. An assembly model is a 3D model with any combination of multiple part models. *Parametric assembly constraints* can be used to control relationships between parts in an assembly model.

Autodesk Inventor can work with any of the assembly modeling methodologies:

The Bottom Up Approach

The first step in the *bottom up* assembly modeling approach is to create the individual parts. The parts are then pulled together into an assembly. This approach is typically used for smaller projects with very few team members.

The Top Down Approach

The first step in the *top down* assembly modeling approach is to create the assembly model of the project. Initially, individual parts are represented by names or symbols. The details of the individual parts are added as the project gets further along. This approach is typically used for larger projects or during the conceptual design stage. Members of the project team can then concentrate on the particular section of the project to which they are assigned.

The Middle Out Approach

The *middle out* assembly modeling approach is a mixture of the bottom-up and top-down methods. This type of assembly model is usually constructed with most of the parts already created, and additional parts are designed and created using the assembly for construction information. Some requirements are known and some standard components are used, but new designs must also be produced to meet specific objectives. This combined strategy is a very flexible approach for creating assembly models.

The different assembly modeling approaches described above can be used as guidelines to manage design projects. Keep in mind that we can start modeling our assembly using one approach and then switch to a different approach without any problems.

In this lesson, the *bottom up* assembly modeling approach is illustrated. All of the parts (components) required to form the assembly are created first. Autodesk Inventor's assembly modeling tools allow us to create complex assemblies by using components that are created in part files or are placed in assembly files. A component can be a subassembly or a single part, where features and parts can be modified at any time. The sketches and profiles used to build part features can be fully or partially constrained. Partially constrained features may be adaptive, which means the size or shape of the associated parts are adjusted in an assembly when the parts are constrained to other parts. The basic concept and procedure of using the adaptive assembly approach is demonstrated in the tutorial.

The Shaft Support Assembly

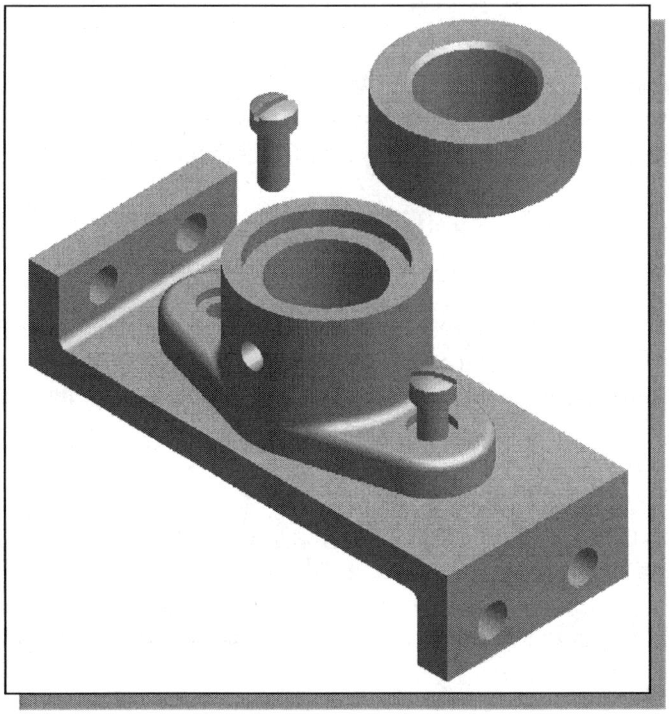

Additional Parts

Four parts are required for the assembly: (1) ***Collar***, (2) ***Bearing***, (3) ***Base-Plate*** and (4) ***Cap-Screw***. On your own, create the four parts as shown below; save the models as separate part files: *Collar, Bearing*, *Base-Plate*, and *Cap-Screw*. (Place all parts in the same folder and close all part files or exit *Autodesk Inventor* after you have created the parts.)

(1) ***Collar***

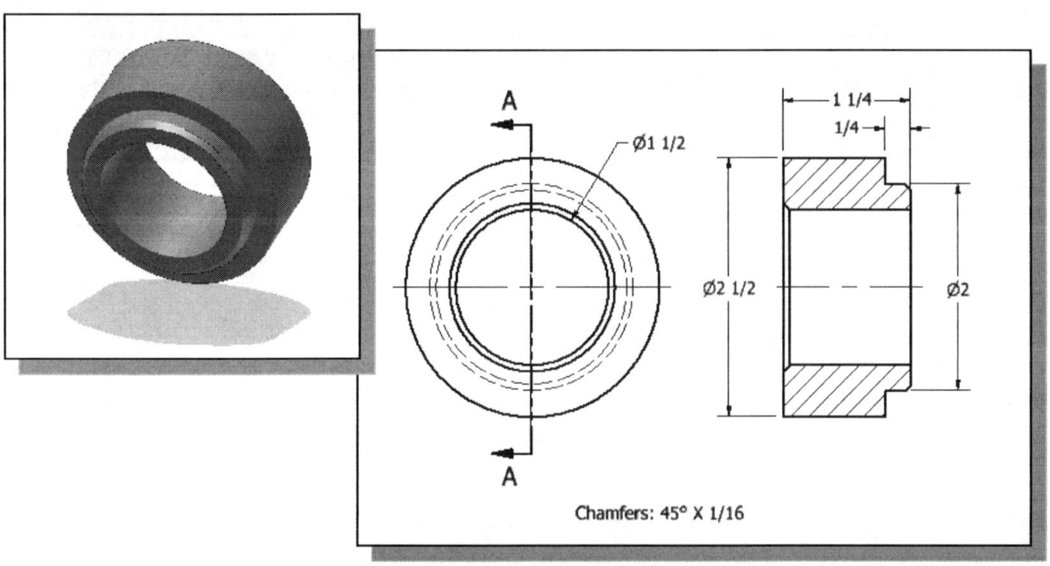

(2) ***Bearing*** (Construct the part with the datum origin aligned to the bottom center.)

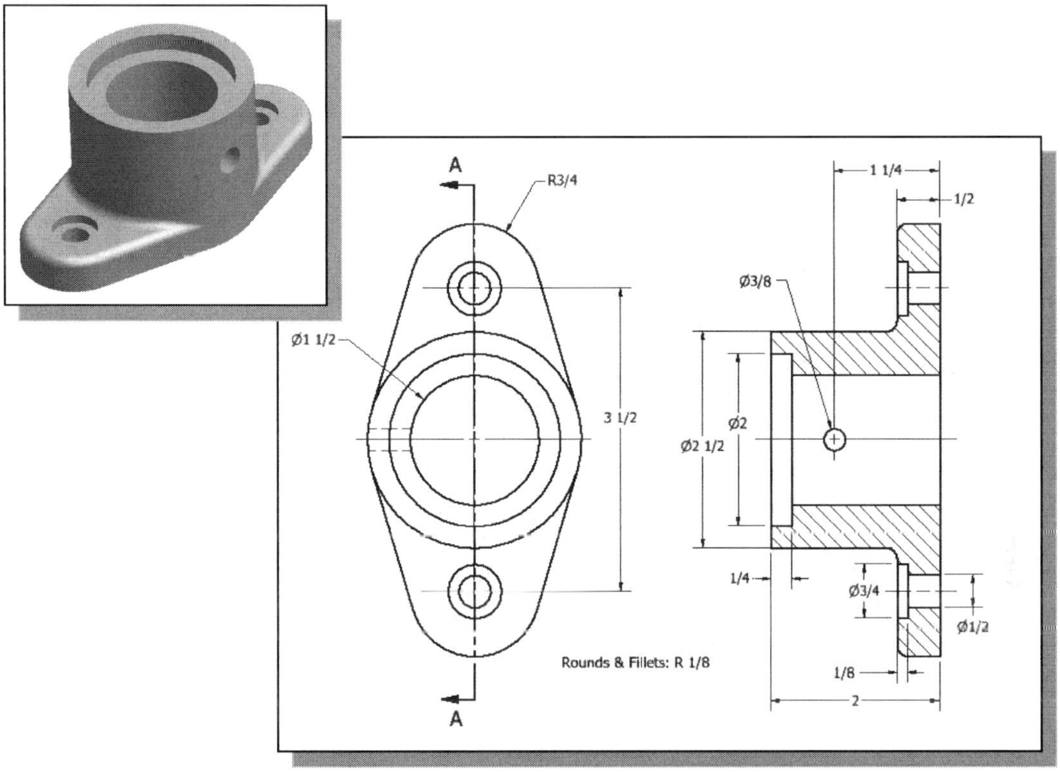

(3) ***Base-Plate*** (Construct the part with the datum origin aligned to the bottom center of the large hole.)

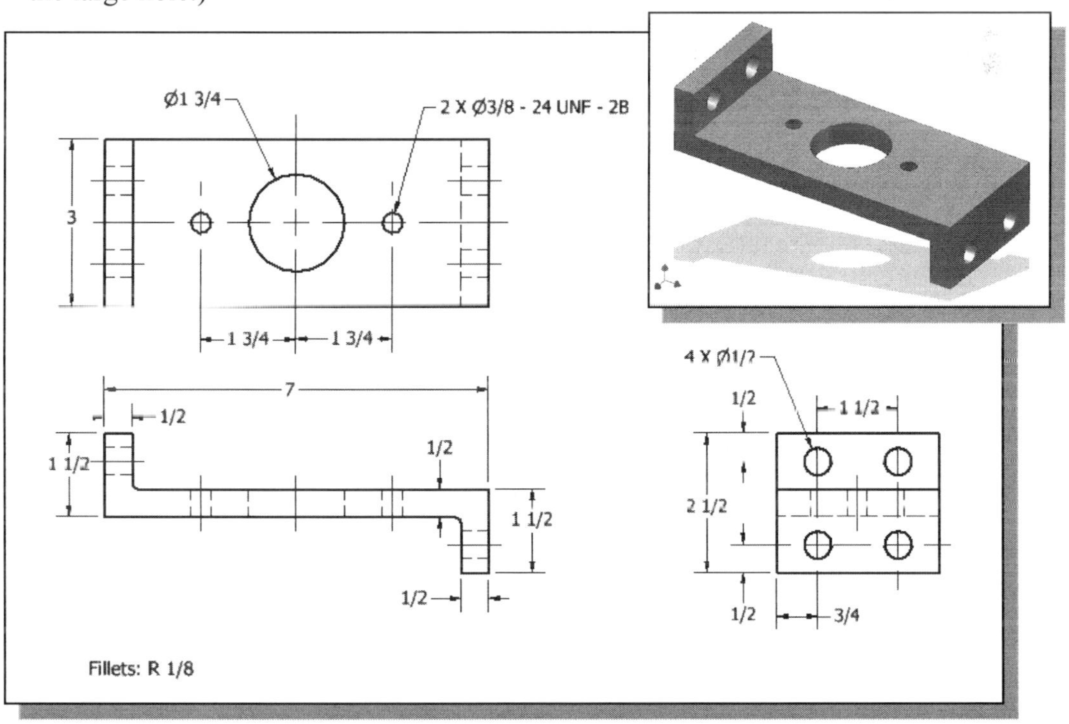

(4) ***Cap-Screw***

- Autodesk Inventor provides two options for creating threads: **Thread** and **Coil**. The **Thread** command does not create true 3D threads; a pre-defined thread image is applied on the selected surface, as shown in the figure. The **Coil** command can be used to create true threads, which contain complex three-dimensional curves and surfaces. You are encouraged to experiment with the **Coil** command and/or the **Thread** command to create threads.

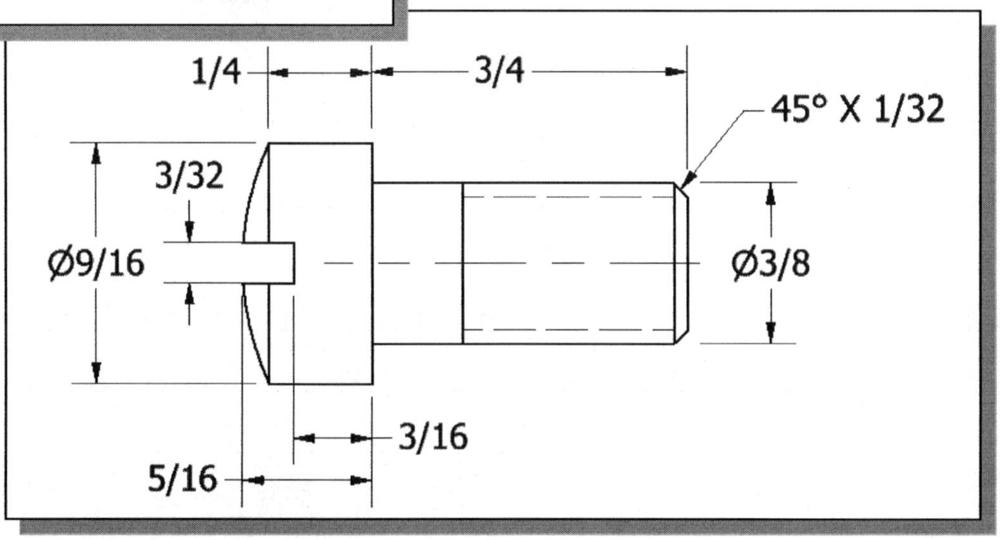

- Hint: First create a revolved feature using the profile shown below.

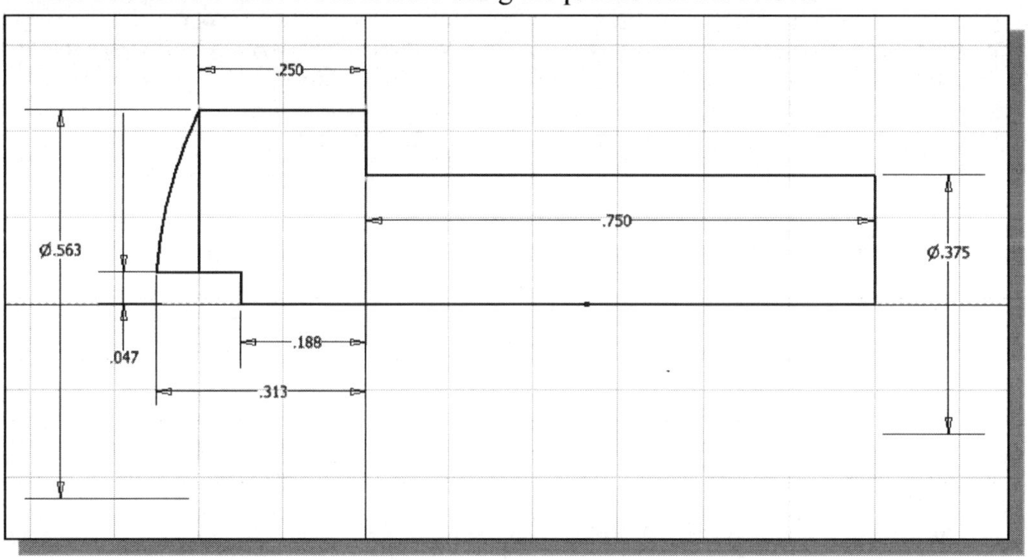

Starting Autodesk Inventor

1. Select the **Autodesk Inventor** option on the *Start* menu or select the **Autodesk Inventor** icon on the desktop to start Autodesk Inventor. The Autodesk Inventor main window will appear on the screen.

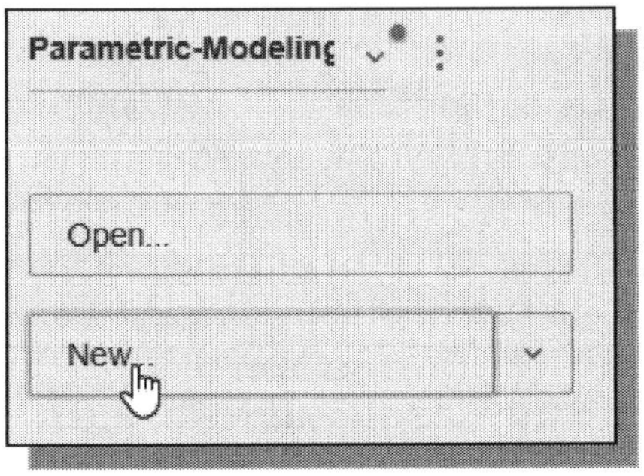

2. Select the **New File** icon with a single click of the left-mouse-button in the *Launch* toolbar as shown.

3. Confirm the ***Parametric-Modeling-Exercises*** project is activated; note the **Projects** button is available to view/modify the active project.

4. Select the **English** tab, and in the *Template* list select **Standard(in).iam** (*Standard Inventor Assembly Model* template file).

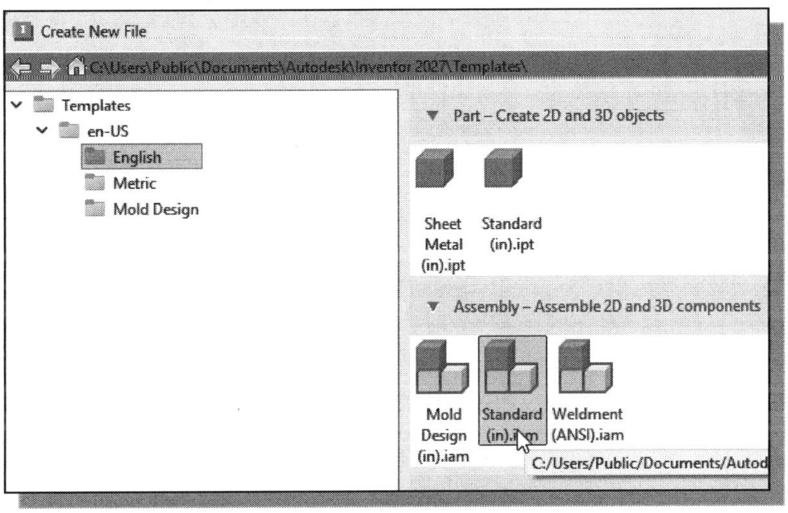

5. Click on the **Create** button in the *New File* dialog box to accept the selected settings.

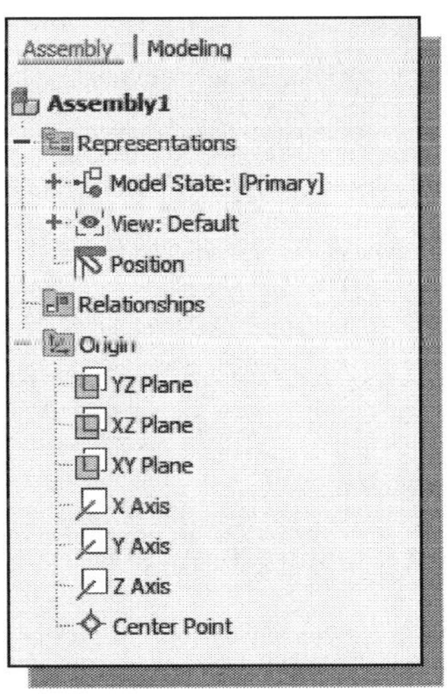

- In the *browser* window, **Assembly1** is displayed with a set of work planes, work axes and a work point. In most aspects, the usage of work planes, work axes and work point is very similar to that of the *Inventor Part Modeler*.

- Notice, in the *Ribbon* toolbar panels, several *component* options are available, such as **Place Component**, **Create Component** and **Place from Content Center**. As the names imply, we can use parts that have been created or create new parts within the *Inventor Assembly Modeler*.

Placing the First Component

The first component placed in an assembly should be a fundamental part or subassembly. The first component in an assembly file sets the orientation of all subsequent parts and subassemblies. The origin of the first component is aligned to the origin of the assembly coordinates, and the part is grounded (all degrees of freedom are removed). The rest of the assembly is built on the first component, the ***base component***. In most cases, this *base component* should be one that is **not likely to be removed** and **preferably a non-moving part** in the design. Note that there is no distinction in an assembly between components; the first component we place is usually considered as the *base component* because it is usually a fundamental component to which others are constrained. We can change the base component to a different base component by placing a new base component, specifying it as grounded, and then re-constraining any components placed earlier, including the first component. For our project, we will use the ***Base-Plate*** as the base component in the assembly.

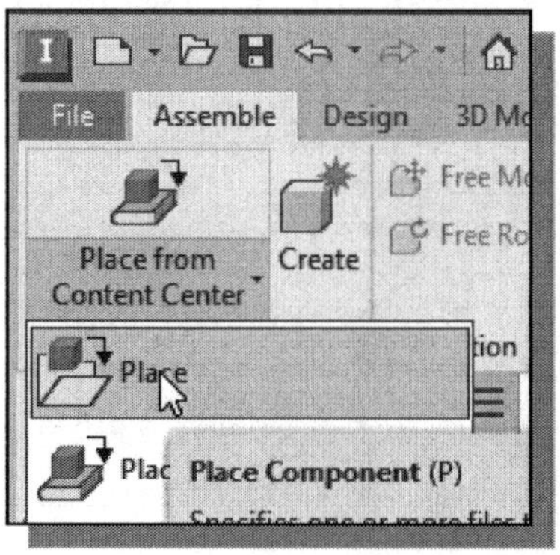

1. In the *Assemble* panel (the toolbar that is located to the left side of the graphics window) select the **Place Component** command by left-clicking the icon.

2. Select the ***Base-Plate*** (part file: ***Base-Plate.ipt***) in the list window.

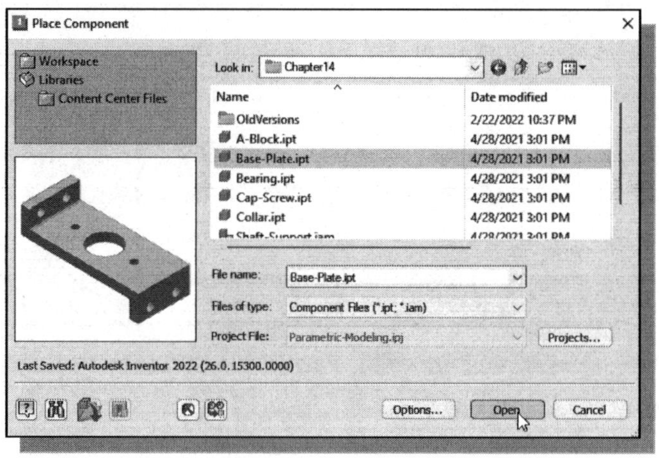

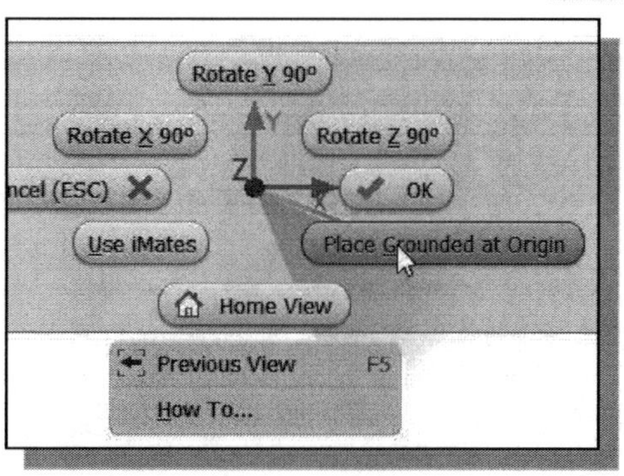

3. Click on the **Open** button to retrieve the model.

4. Right-click once to bring up the option menu and select **Place Grounded at Origin.**

5. Right-click again to bring up the option menu and select **OK** to end the placement of the *Base-Plate* part.

Placing the Second Component

We will retrieve the *Bearing* part as the second component of the assembly model.

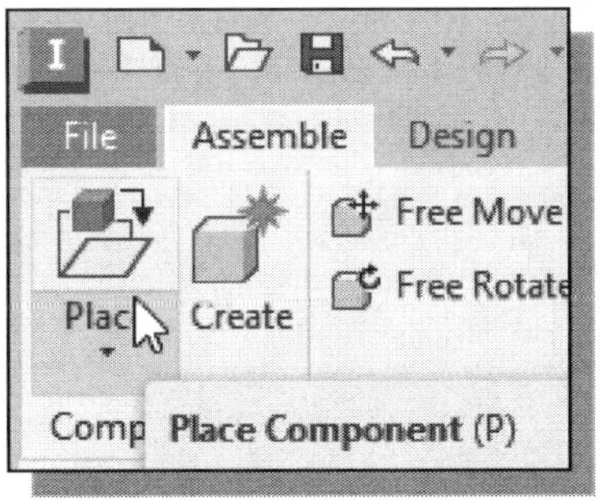

1. In the *Assemble* panel (the toolbar that is located to the left side of the graphics window) select the **Place Component** command by left-clicking the icon.

2. Select the ***Bearing*** design (part file: ***Bearing.ipt***) in the list window. And click on the **Open** button to retrieve the model.

3. Place the *Bearing* toward the upper right corner of the graphics window, as shown in the figure.

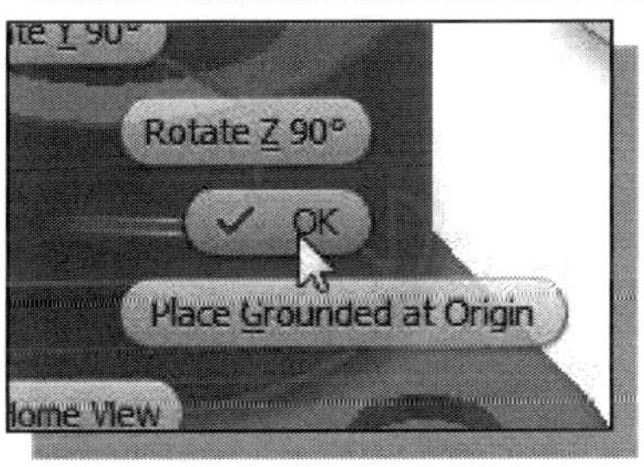

4. Inside the graphics window, right-click once to bring up the option menu and select **OK** to end the placement of the *Bearing* part.

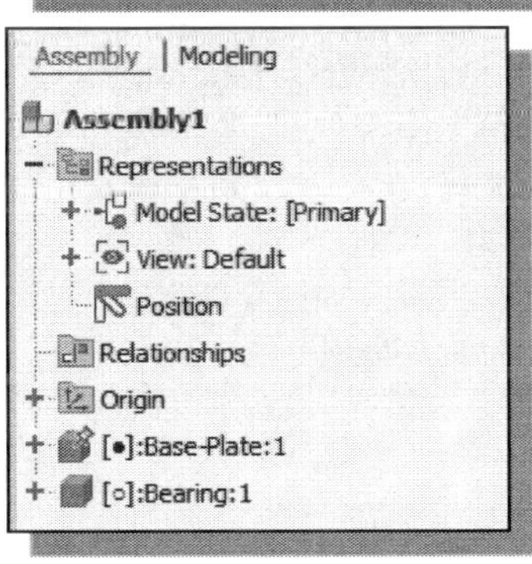

- Inside the *browser* window, the retrieved parts are listed in their corresponding order. The **Pin** icon in front of the *Base-Plate* filename signifies the part is grounded and all ***six degrees of freedom*** are restricted. The number behind the filename is used to identify the number of copies of the same component in the assembly model.

Degrees of Freedom and Constraints

Each component in an assembly has six **degrees of freedom (DOF)**, or ways in which rigid 3D bodies can move: movement along the X, Y, and Z axes (translational freedom), plus rotation around the X, Y, and Z axes (rotational freedom). *Translational DOF*s allow the part to move in the direction of the specified vector. *Rotational DOF*s allow the part to turn about the specified axis.

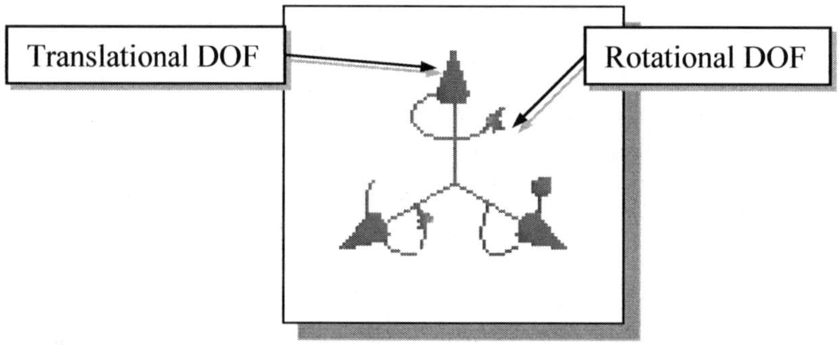

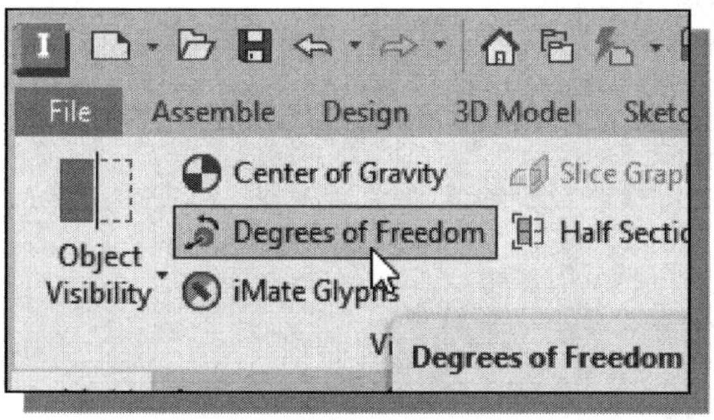

➢ Select the **Degrees of Freedom** option in the **View** tab to display the DOF of the unconstrained component.

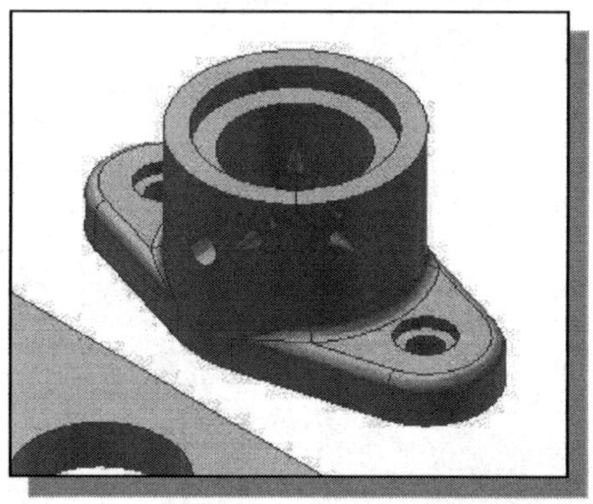

In Autodesk Inventor, the degrees-of-freedom symbol shows the remaining degrees of freedom (both translational and rotational) for one or more components of the active assembly. When a component is fully constrained in an assembly, the component cannot move in any direction. The position of the component is fixed relative to other assembly components. All of its degrees of freedom are removed. When we place an assembly constraint between two selected components, they are positioned relative to one another. Movement is still possible in the unconstrained directions.

It is usually a good idea to fully constrain components so that their behavior is predictable as changes are made to the assembly. Leaving some degrees of freedom open can sometimes help retain design flexibility. As a general rule, we should use only enough constraints to ensure predictable assembly behavior and avoid unnecessary complexity.

Assembly Constraints

We are now ready to assemble the components together. We will start by placing assembly constraints on the ***Bearing*** and the ***Base-Plate***.

To assemble components into an assembly, we need to establish the assembly relationships between components. It is good practice to assemble components the way they would be assembled in the actual manufacturing process. **Assembly constraints** create a parent/child relationship that allows us to capture the design intent of the assembly. Because the component that we are placing actually becomes a child to the already assembled components, we must use caution when choosing constraint types and references to make sure they reflect the intent.

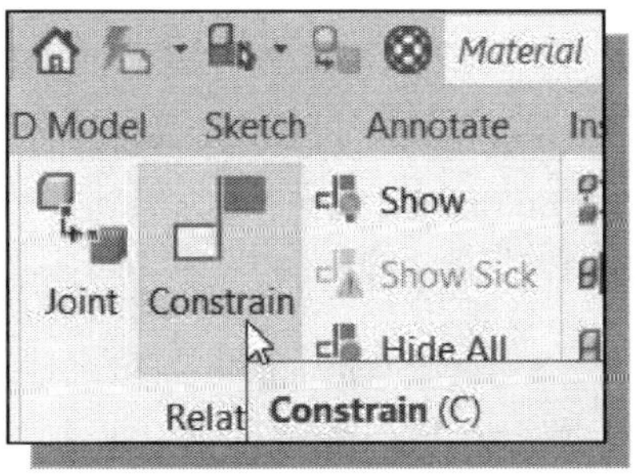

➢ Switch back to the *Assemble* panel; select the **Constrain** command by left-clicking once on the icon.

- The *Place Constraints* dialog box appears on the screen. Five types of assembly constraints are available.

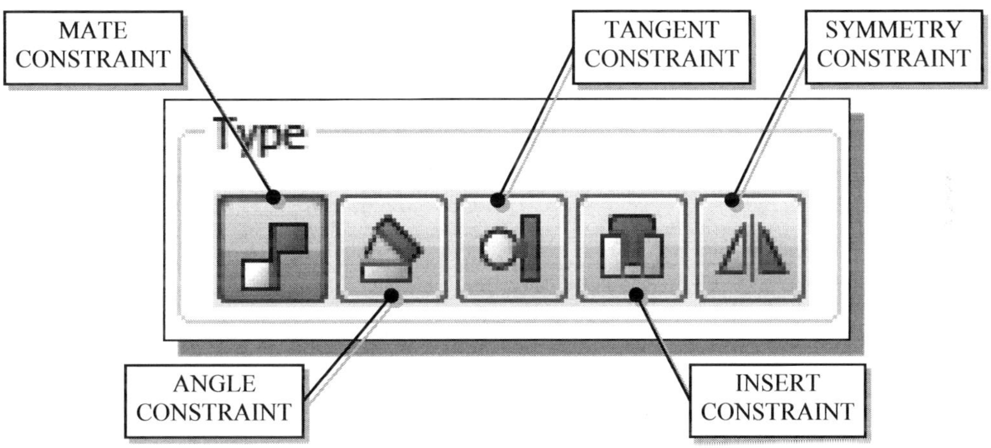

➢ Assembly models are created by applying proper *assembly constraints* to the individual components. The constraints are used to restrict the movement between parts. Constraints eliminate rigid body degrees of freedom (**DOF**). A 3D part has *six degrees of freedom* since the part can rotate and translate relative to the three coordinate axes. Each time we add a constraint between two parts, one or more DOF is eliminated. The movement of a fully constrained part is restricted in all directions. Five basic types of assembly constraints are available in Autodesk Inventor: **Mate**, **Angle**, **Tangent**, **Insert** and **Symmetry**. Each type of constraint removes different combinations of rigid body degrees of freedom. Note that it is possible to apply different constraints and achieve the same results.

- **Mate** – Constraint positions components face-to-face, or adjacent to one another, with faces flush. Removes one degree of linear translation and two degrees of angular rotation between planar surfaces. Selected surfaces point in opposite directions and can be **offset** by a specified distance. **Mate** constraint positions selected faces normal to one another, with faces coincident.

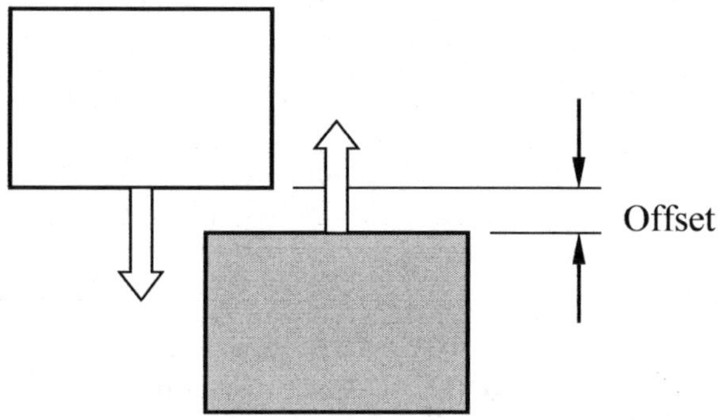

- **Flush** – Makes two planes coplanar with their faces aligned in the same direction. Selected surfaces point in the same direction and are offset by a specified distance. **Flush** constraint aligns components adjacent to one another with faces flush and positions selected faces, curves, or points so that they are aligned with surface normals pointing in the same direction. (Note that the **Flush** constraint is listed as a selectable option in the **Mate** constraint.)

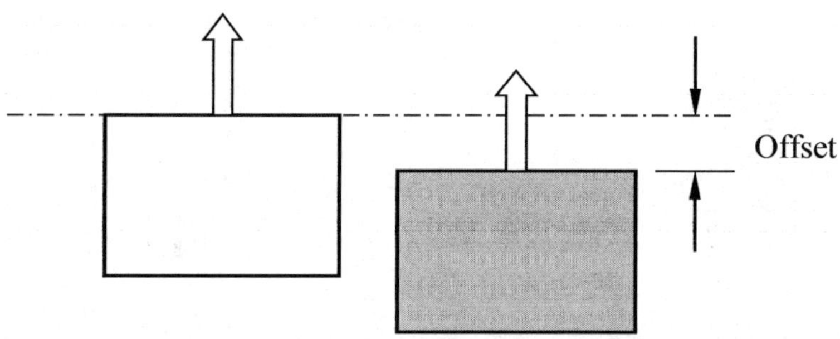

- **Angle** – Creates an angular assembly constraint between parts, subassemblies, or assemblies. Selected surfaces point in the direction specified by the angle.

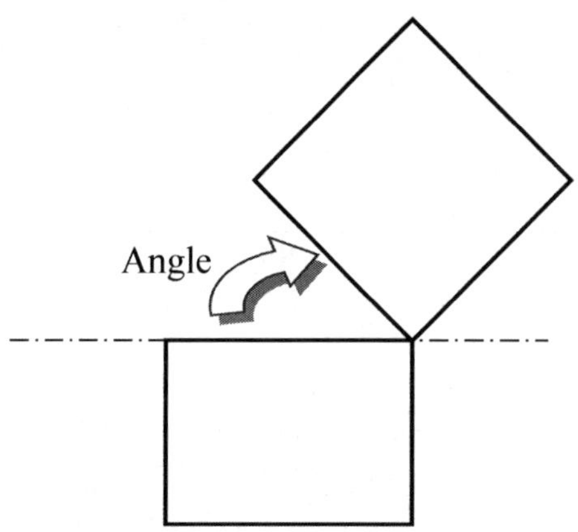

- **Tangent** – Aligns selected faces, planes, cylinders, spheres, and cones to contact at the point of tangency. Tangency may be on the inside or outside of a curve, depending on the selection of the direction of the surface normal. A Tangent constraint removes one degree of translational freedom.

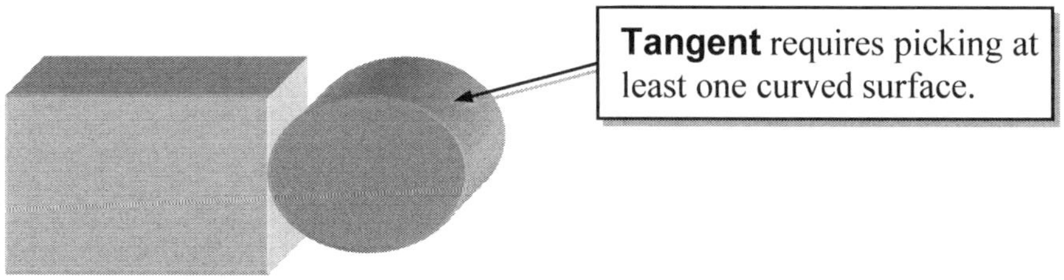

- **Insert** – Aligns two circles, including their center axes and planes. Selected circular surfaces become co-axial. Insert constraint is a combination of a face-to-face Mate constraint between planar faces and a Mate constraint between the axes of the two components. A rotational degree of freedom remains open. The surfaces do not need to be full 360-degree circles. Selected surfaces can point in opposite directions or in the same direction and can be offset by a specified distance.

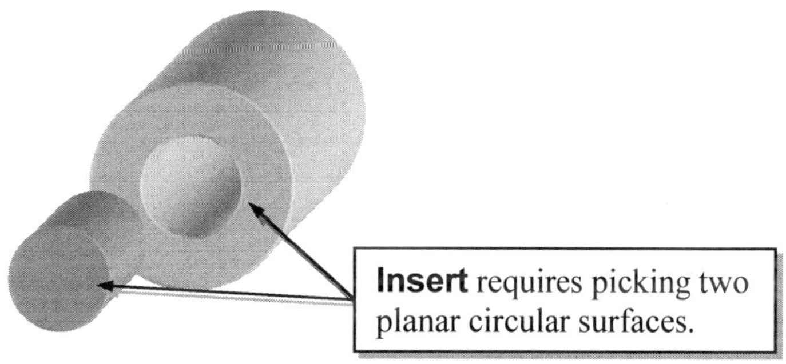

- **Symmetry** – The Symmetry constraint positions two objects symmetrically according to a plane or planar face. The Symmetry constraint is available in the Place Constraint dialog box.

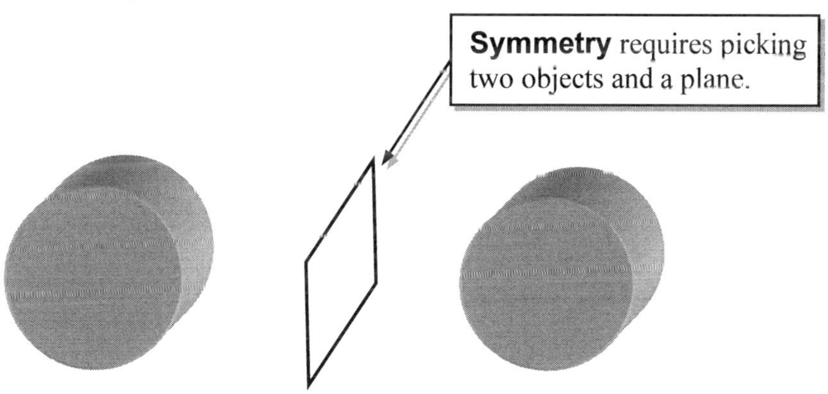

Apply the First Assembly Constraint

1. In the *Place Constraint* dialog box, confirm the constraint type is set to **Mate** constraint and select the **top horizontal surface** of the base part as the first part for the Mate alignment command.

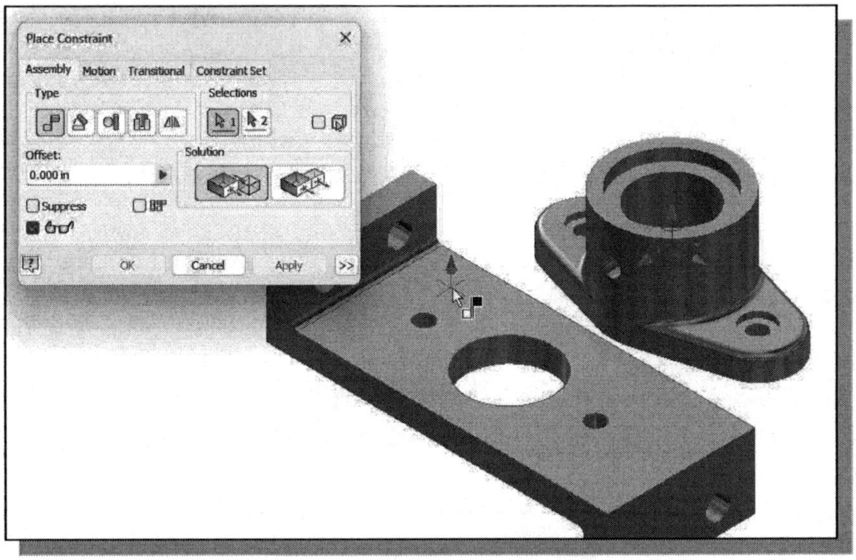

2. On your own, dynamically rotate the displayed model to view the bottom of the *Bearing* part, as shown in the figure below.

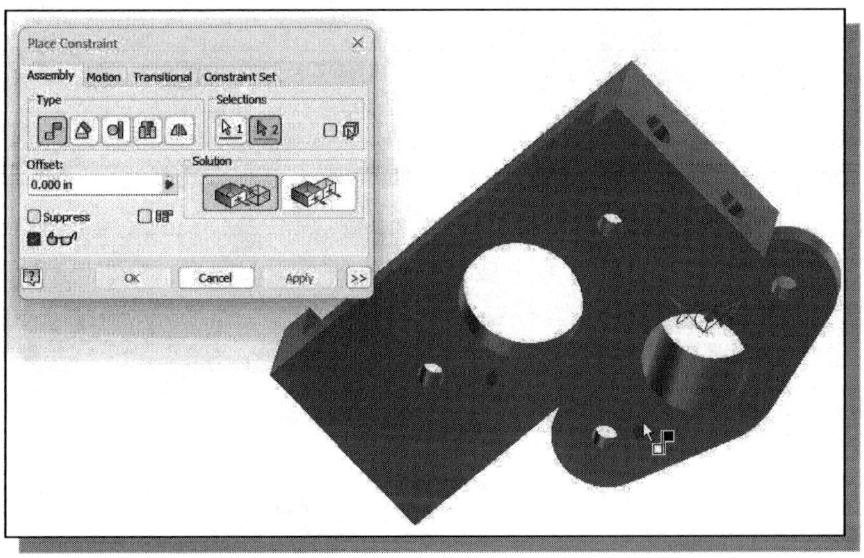

3. Click on the bottom face of the *Bearing* part as the second part selection to apply the constraint. Note the direction normals shown in the figure; the Mate constraint requires the selection of opposite direction of surface normals.

4. Click on the **Apply** button to accept the selection and apply the Mate constraint.

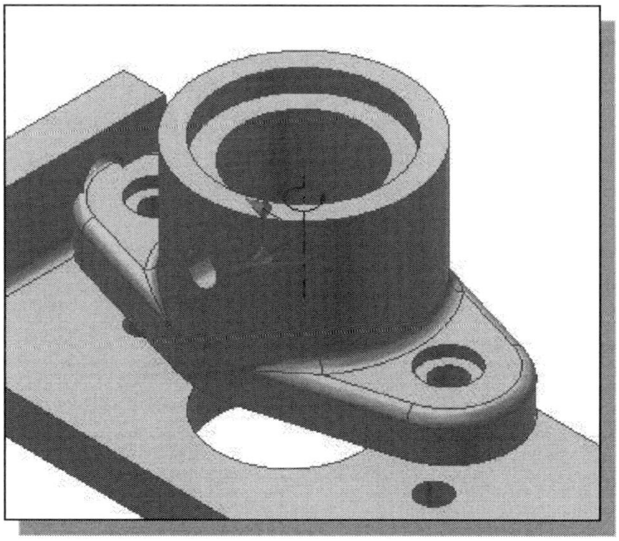

5. On your own, reset the display to **Isometric view** by clicking on the home view in the View Cube.

❖ Notice the DOF symbol is adjusted automatically in the graphics window. The Mate constraint removes one degree of linear translation and two degrees of angular rotation between the selected planar surfaces. The *Bearing* part can still move along two axes and rotate about the third axis.

Apply a Second Mate Constraint

The Mate constraint can also be used to align axes of cylindrical features.

1. In the *Place Constraint* dialog box, confirm the constraint type is set to **Mate** constraint and move the cursor near the cylindrical surface of the right counter bore hole of the *Bearing* part. Select the axis when it is displayed as shown. (Hint: Use the *Dynamic Rotation* option to assist the selection.)

2. Move the cursor near the cylindrical surface of the small hole on the *Base-Plate* part. Select the axis when it is displayed as shown.

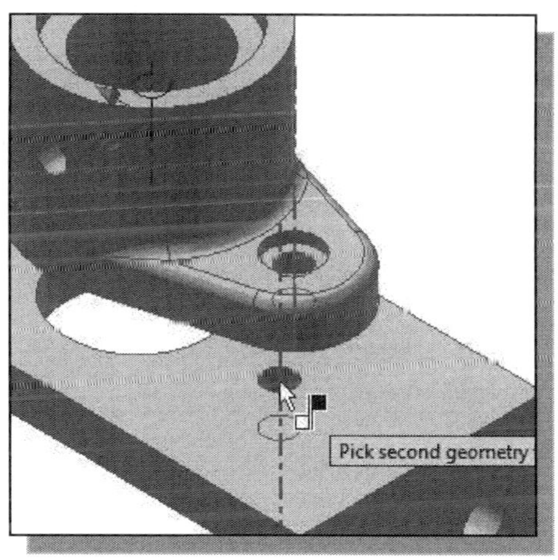

3. In the *Place Constraint* dialog box, set the *Solution* option to **Aligned** (if not aligned) and click on the **Apply** button to accept the selection and apply the Mate constraint.

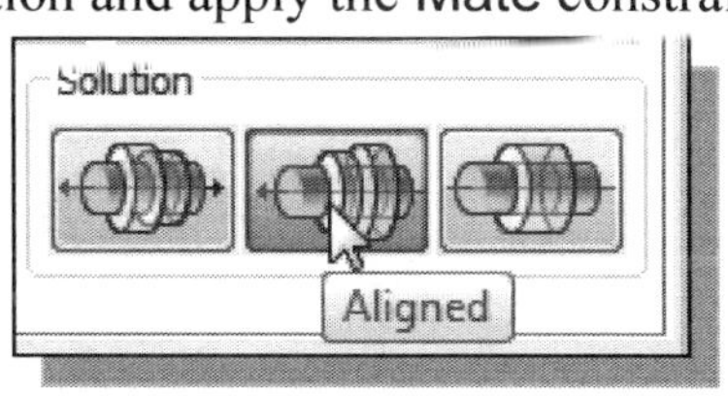

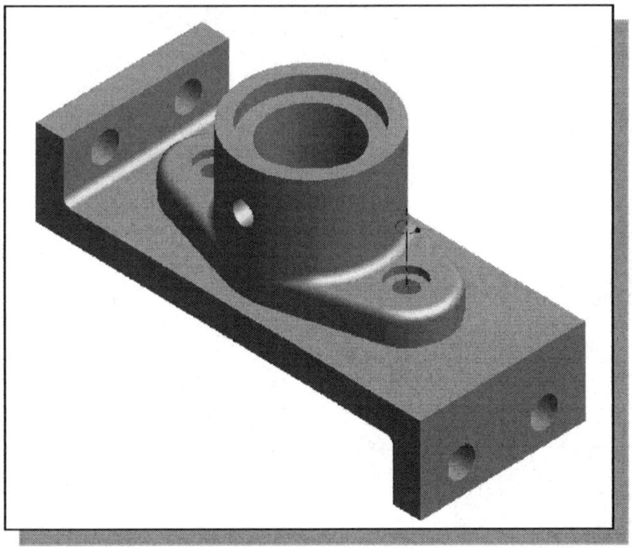

4. In the *Place Constraint* dialog box, click on the **Cancel** button to exit the Place Constraint command.

❖ The *Bearing* part appears to be placed in the correct position. But the DOF symbol indicates that this is not the case; the bearing part can still rotate about the displayed vertical axis.

Constrained Move

To see how well a component is constrained, we can perform a constrained move. A constrained move is done by dragging the component in the graphics window with the left-mouse-button. A constrained move will honor previously applied assembly constraints. That is, the selected component and parts constrained to the component move together in their constrained positions. A grounded component remains grounded during the move.

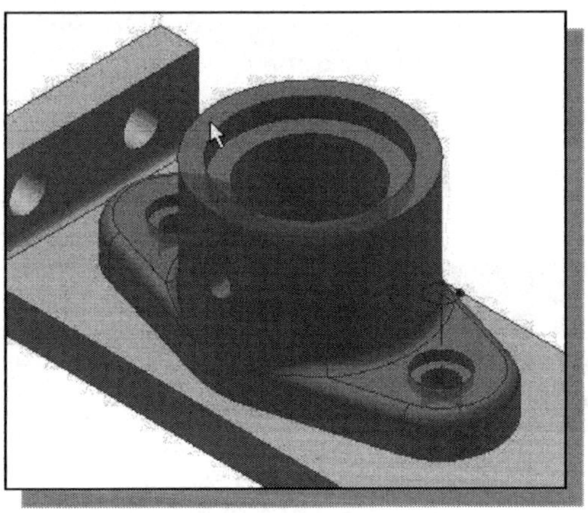

1. Inside the *graphics window*, move the cursor on top of the top surface of the *Bearing* part as shown in the figure.

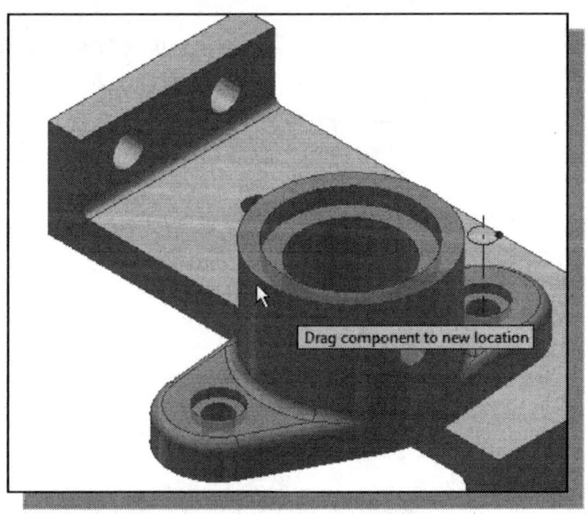

2. Press and hold down the left-mouse-button and drag the *Bearing* part downward.

❖ The *Bearing* part can freely rotate about the displayed axis.

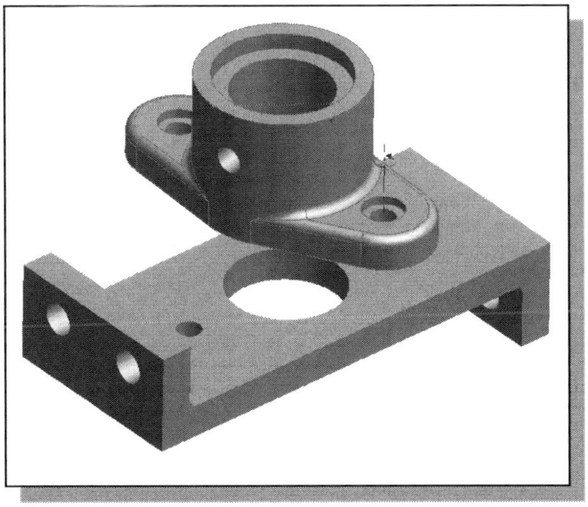

3. On your own, use the dynamic rotation command to view the alignment of the *Bearing* part.

4. Rotate the *Bearing* part and adjust the display roughly as shown in the figure.

Apply a Flush Constraint

Besides selecting the surfaces of solid models to apply constraints, we can also select the established work planes to apply the assembly constraints. This is an additional advantage of using the *BORN technique* in creating part models. For the *Bearing* part, we will apply a **Mate** constraint to two of the work planes and eliminate the last rotational DOF.

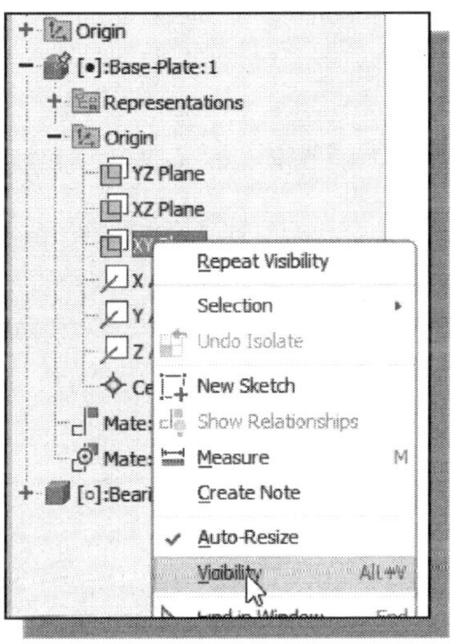

1. On your own, inside the *browser* window toggle *ON* the **Visibility** for the two corresponding work planes, shown on the following page, which will be used for alignment of the *Base-Plate* and the *Bearing* parts.

2. In the *Relationship* panel, select the **Constrain** command by left-clicking once on the icon.

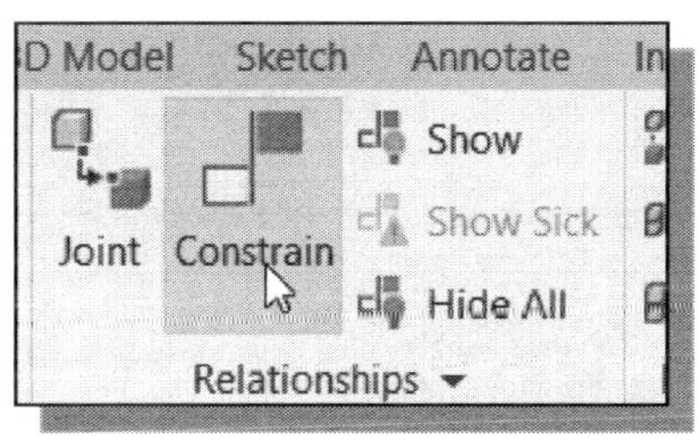

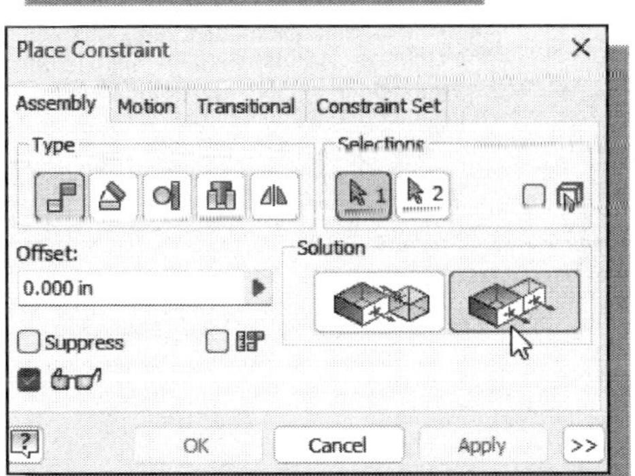

3. In the *Place Constraint* dialog box, switch the *Solution* option to **Flush** as shown.

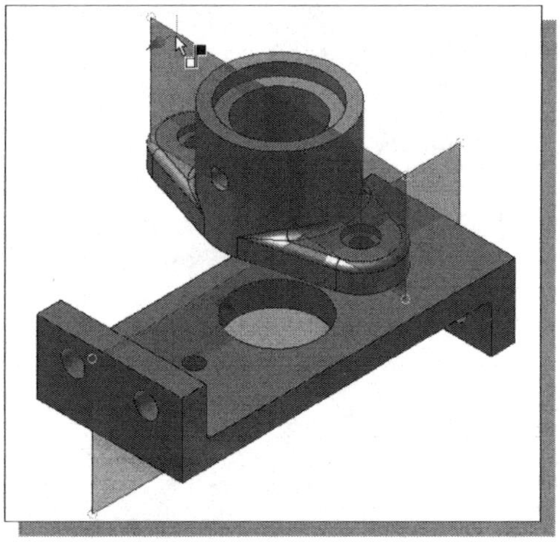

4. Select the *work plane* of the ***Base-Plate*** part as the first part for the **Flush** alignment command.

5. Select the corresponding *work plane* of the ***Bearing*** part as the second part for the **Flush** alignment command.

❖ Note that the **Flush** constraint makes two planes coplanar with their faces aligned in the same direction.

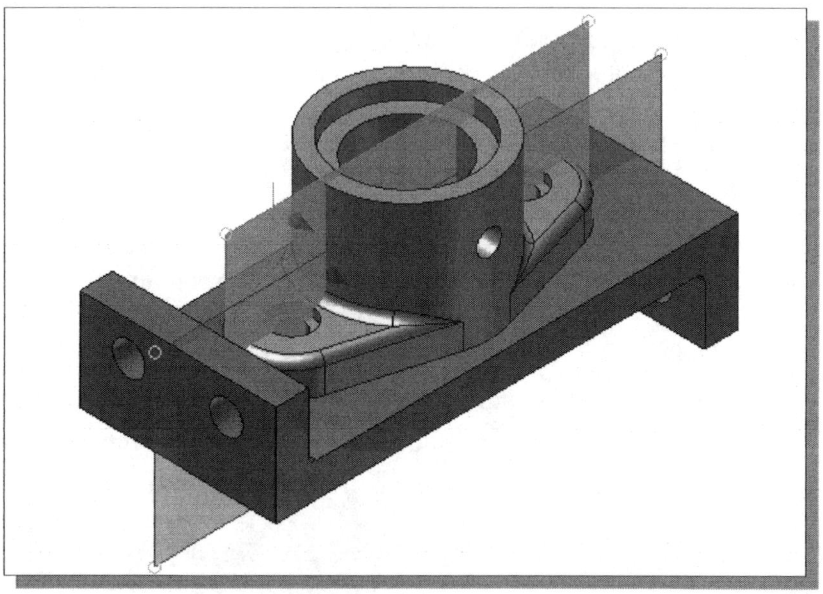

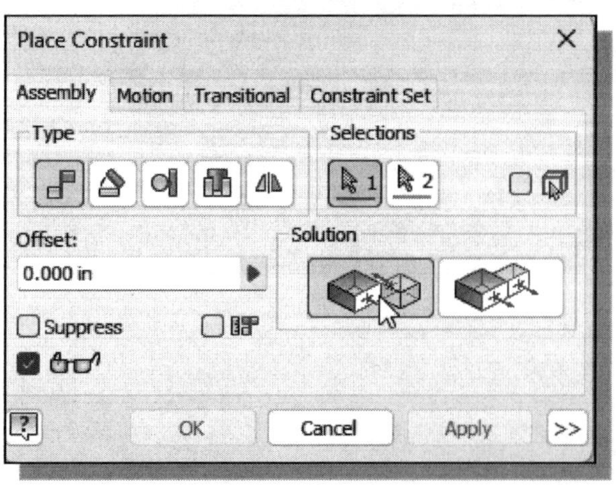

6. In the *Place Constraint* dialog box, switch the *Solution* option to **Mate** and notice the ***Bearing*** part is rotated 180 degrees to satisfy the **Mate** constraint.

❖ Note that the *Show Preview* option allows us to preview the result before accepting the selection.

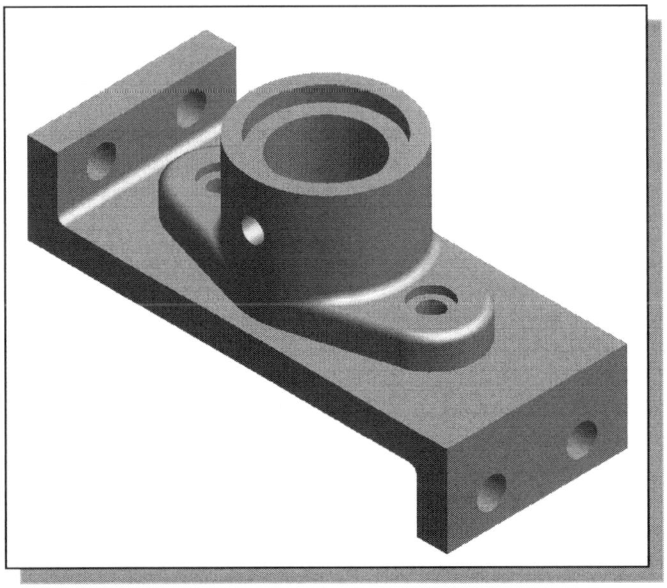

7. On your own, align the two parts as shown and click on the **Apply** button to accept the settings.

8. In the *Place Constraint* dialog box, click on the **Cancel** button to exit the Place Constraint command.

❖ Note the DOF symbol disappears, which indicates the assembly is fully constrained.

Placing the Third Component

We will retrieve the *Collar* part as the third component of the assembly model.

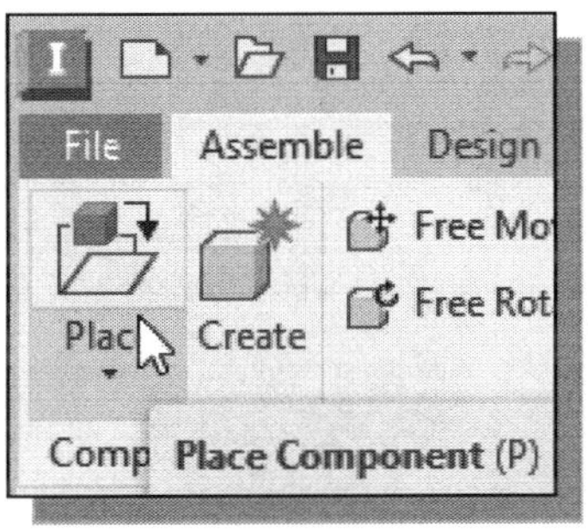

1. In the *Assemble* panel (the toolbar that is located to the left side of the graphics window) select the **Place Component** command by left-clicking the icon.

2. Select the ***Collar*** design (part file: ***Collar.ipt***) in the list window. And click on the **Open** button to retrieve the model.

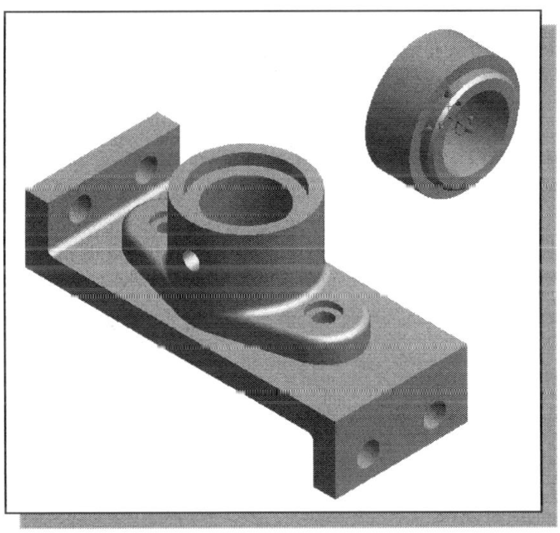

3. Place the *Collar* part toward the upper right corner of the graphics window, as shown in the figure.

4. Inside the *graphics window*, **right-click** once to bring up the option menu and select **OK** to end the placement of the *Collar* part.

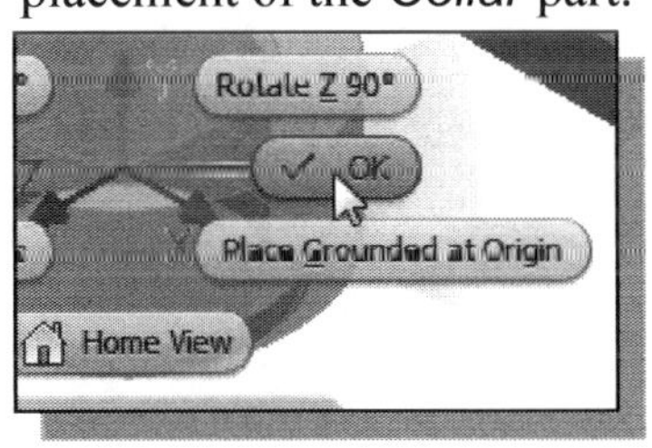

❖ Notice the DOF symbol displayed on the screen. The *Collar* part can move linearly and rotate about the three axes (six degrees of freedom).

Applying an Insert Constraint

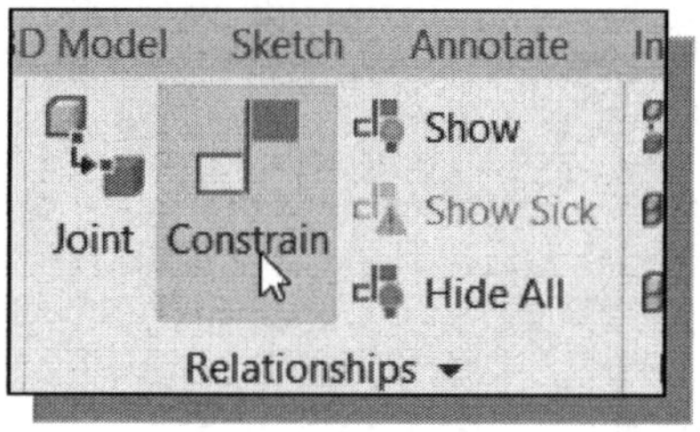

1. In the *Relationships* panel, select the **Constrain** command by left-clicking once on the icon.

2. In the *Place Constraint* dialog box, switch to the **Insert** constraint.

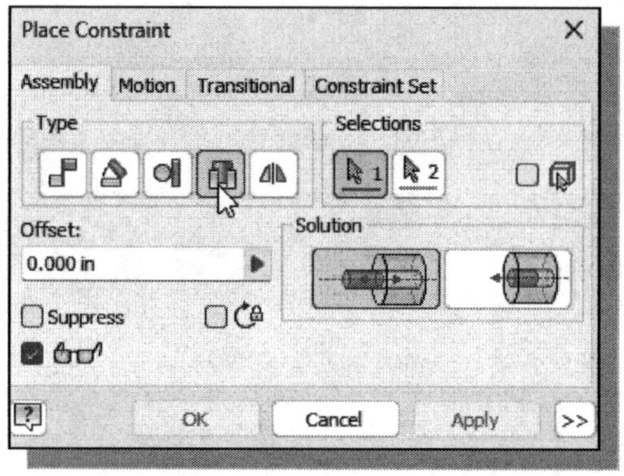

3. Select the inside corner of the *Collar* part as the first surface to apply the **Insert** constraint, as shown in the figure.

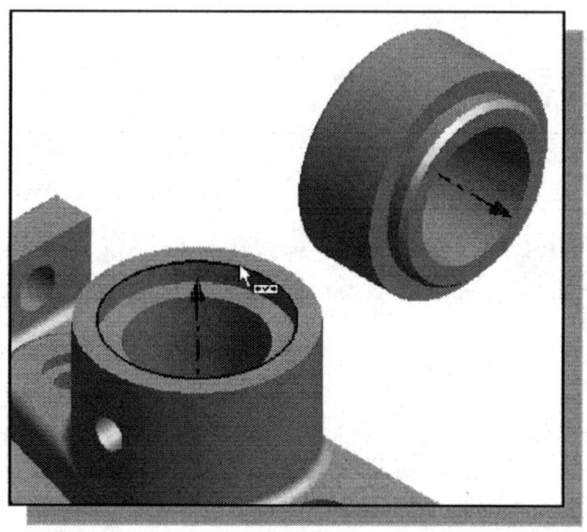

4. Select the inside circle on the top surface of the *Bearing* part as the second surface to apply the **Insert** constraint, as shown in the figure.

5. Click on the **Apply** button to accept the settings.

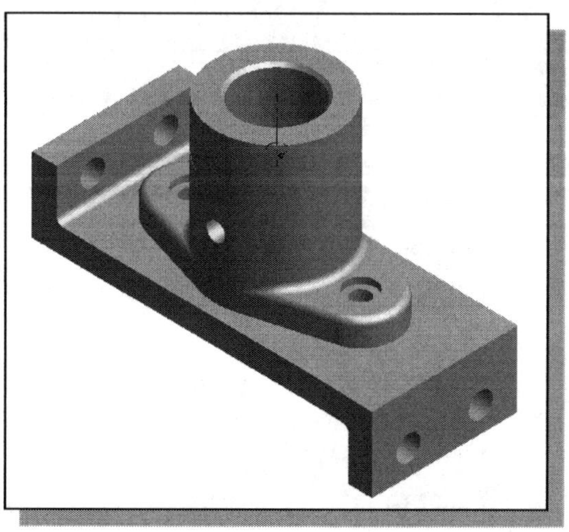

➢ Note that one rotational degree of freedom remains open; the *Collar* part can still freely rotate about the displayed DOF axis.

Assemble the Cap-Screws

We will place two of the *Cap-Screw* parts to complete the assembly model.

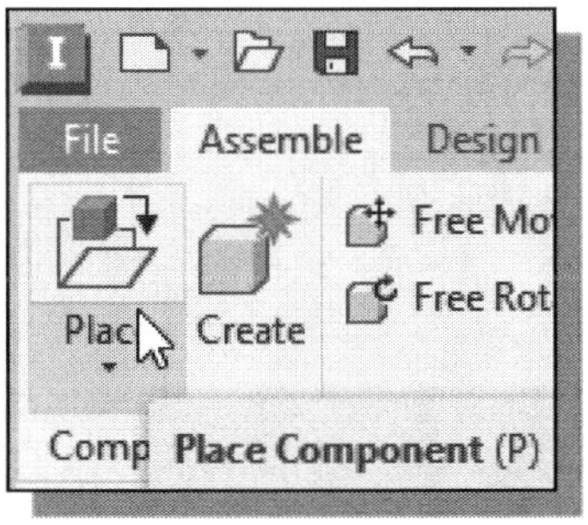

1. In the *Assemble* panel (the toolbar that is located to the left side of the graphics window) select the **Place Component** command by left-clicking once on the icon.

2. Select the ***Cap-Screw*** design (part file: ***Cap-Screw.ipt***) in the list window. And click on the **Open** button to retrieve the model.

3. Place two copies of the *Cap-Screw* part on both sides of the *Collar* by clicking twice on the screen as shown in the figure.

4. Inside the *graphics window*, **right-click** once to bring up the option menu and select **OK** to end the Place Component command.

❖ Notice the DOF symbols displayed on the screen. Each *Cap-Screw* has six degrees of freedom. Both parts are referencing the same external part file, but each can be constrained independently.

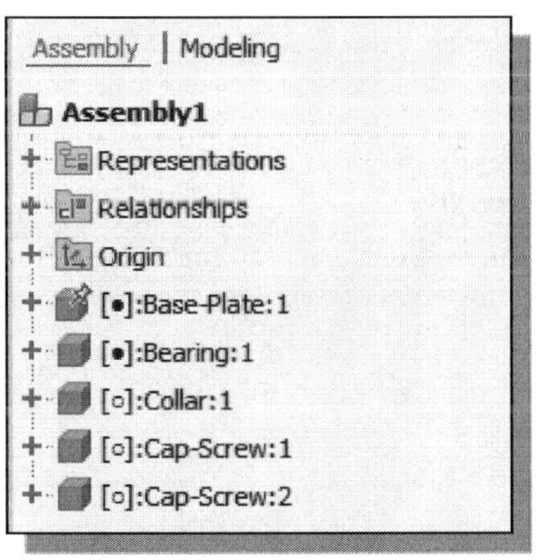

- Inside the *browser* window, the retrieved parts are listed in the order they are placed. The number behind the part name is used to identify the number of copies of the same part in the assembly model. Move the cursor to the last part name and notice the corresponding part is highlighted in the graphics window.

➢ On your own, use the **Place Constraints** command and assemble the *Cap-Screws* in place as shown in the figure below.

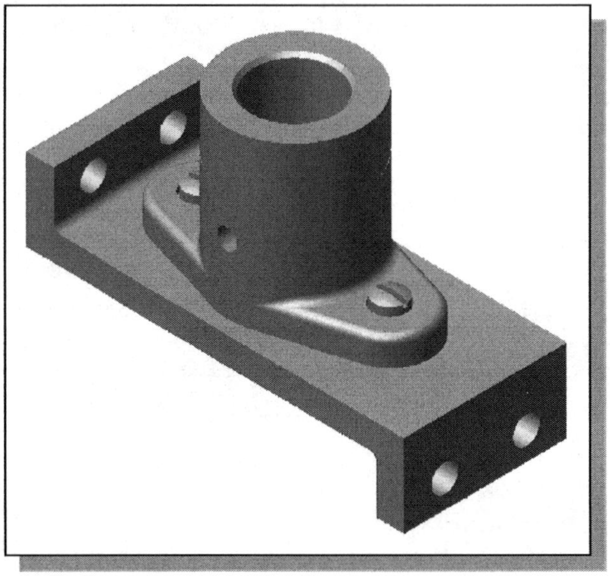

Exploded View of the Assembly

Exploded assemblies are often used in design presentations, catalogs, sales literature, and in the shop to show all of the parts of an assembly and how they fit together. In Autodesk Inventor, an exploded assembly can be created by two methods: (1) using the **Move Component** and **Rotate Component** commands in the *Assembly Modeler*, which contains only limited options for the operation but can be done very quickly; (2) transferring the assembly model into the *Presentation Modeler*. For our example, we will create an exploded assembly by using the **Move Component** command that is available in the *Assembly Modeler.*

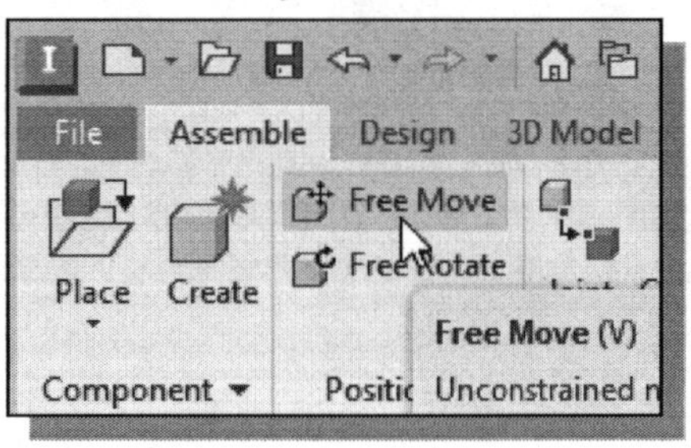

1. In the *Position* toolbar panel, select the **Free Move** command by left-clicking once on the icon.

2. Inside the graphics window, move the cursor on top of the top surface of the *Collar* part as shown in the figure.

3. Press and hold down the left-mouse-button and drag the *Collar* part toward the right side of the assembly as shown.

4. On your own, repeat the above steps and create an exploded assembly by repositioning the components as shown in the figure below.

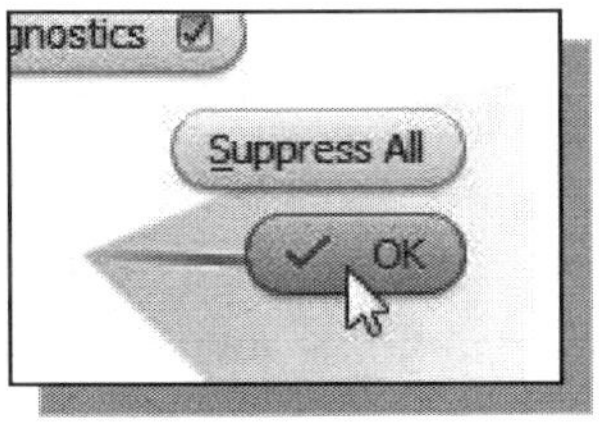

5. Inside the graphics window, right-click once to bring up the option menu and select **OK** to end the **Move Component** command.

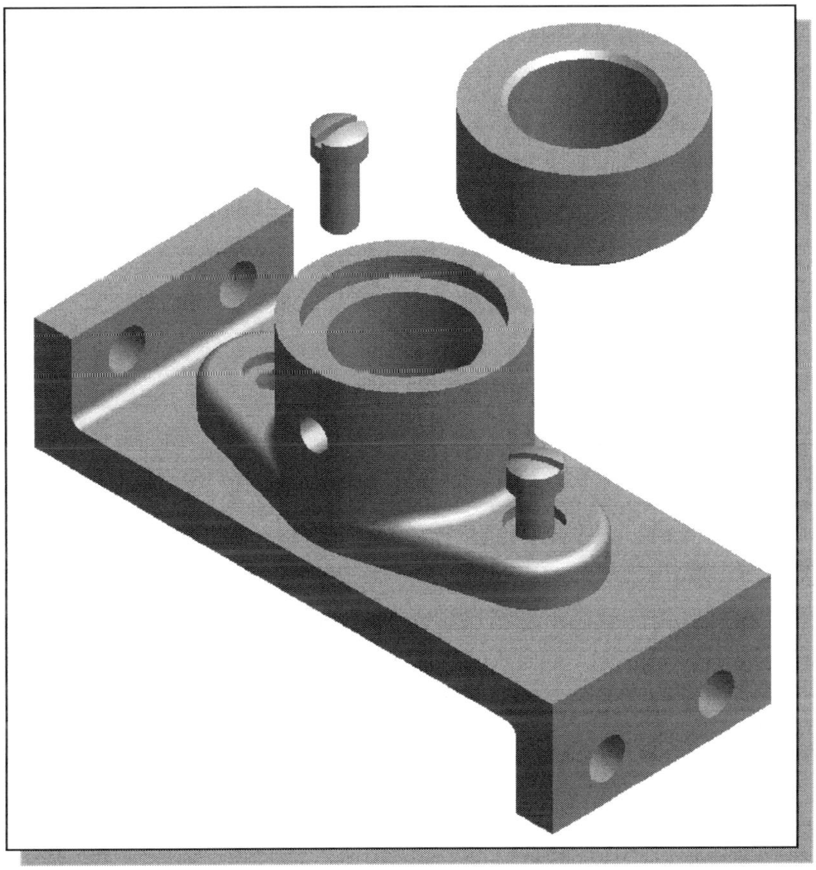

❖ The **Move Component** and **Rotate Component** commands are used to temporarily reposition the components in the graphics window. The displayed image is temporary, but it can be printed with the **Print** command through the pull-down menu.

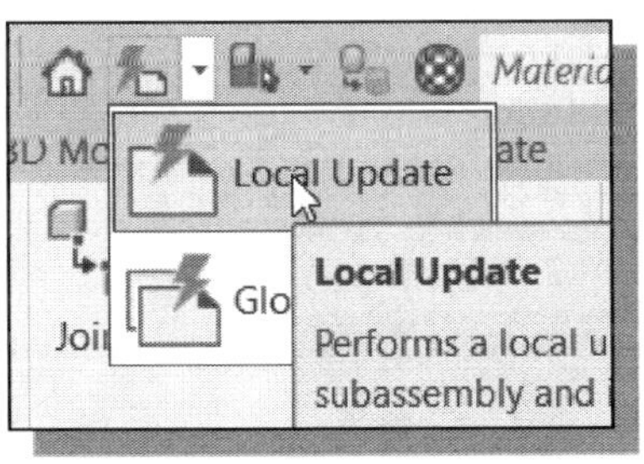

6. Click on the **Update** button in the *Standard* toolbar area.

❖ Note that the components are reset back to their assembled positions, based on the applied assembly constraints.

Editing the Components

The *associative functionality* of Autodesk Inventor allows us to change the design at any level, and the system reflects the changes at all levels automatically.

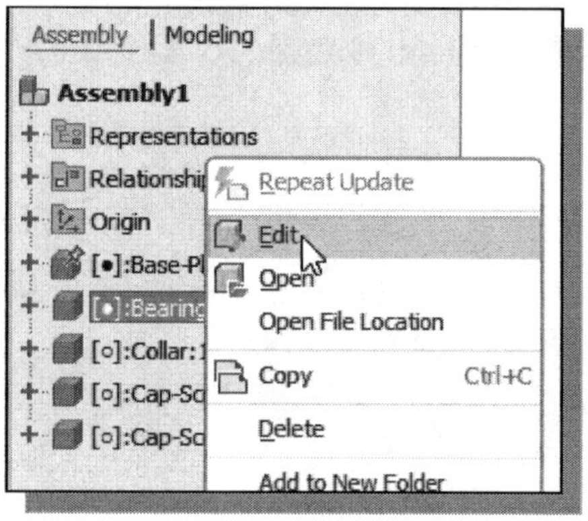

1. Inside the *Desktop Browser*, move the cursor on top of the ***Bearing*** part. Right-click once to bring up the option menu and select **Edit** in the option list.

❖ Note that we are automatically switched back to *Part Editing Mode*.

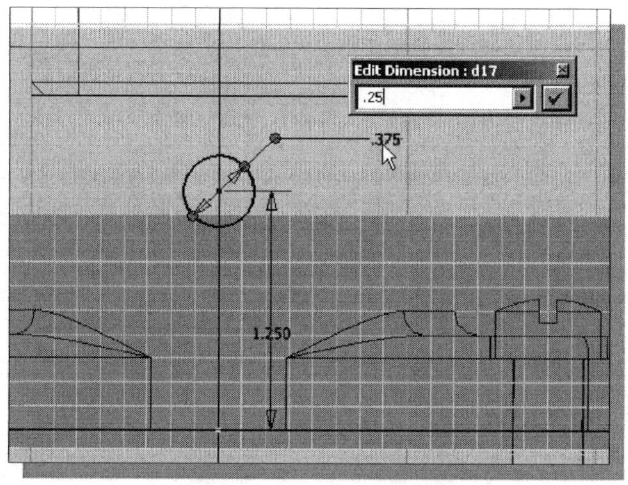

2. On your own, adjust the diameter of the small *Drill Hole* to **0.25** as shown.

3. Click on the **Update** button in the *Standard* toolbar area to proceed with updating the model.

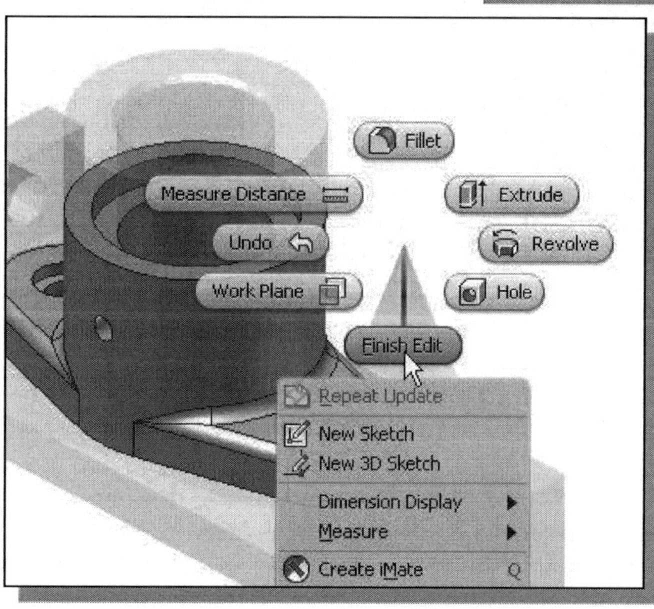

4. Inside the *graphics window*, click once with the **right-mouse-button** to display the *option menu.*

5. Select **Finish Edit** in the pop-up menu to exit *Part Editing Mode* and return to *Assembly Mode.*

➢ Autodesk Inventor has updated the part in all levels and in the current *Assembly Mode*. On your own, open the *Bearing* part file to confirm the modification is performed.

Adaptive Design Approach

Autodesk Inventor's ***Adaptive Design*** approach allows us to use the applied *assembly constraints* to control the sizes, shapes, and positions of ***underconstrained*** sketches, features, and parts. In this section, we will examine the procedure to apply the constraints directly on 3D parts; note that the adaptive design approach is also applicable to 2D sketches.

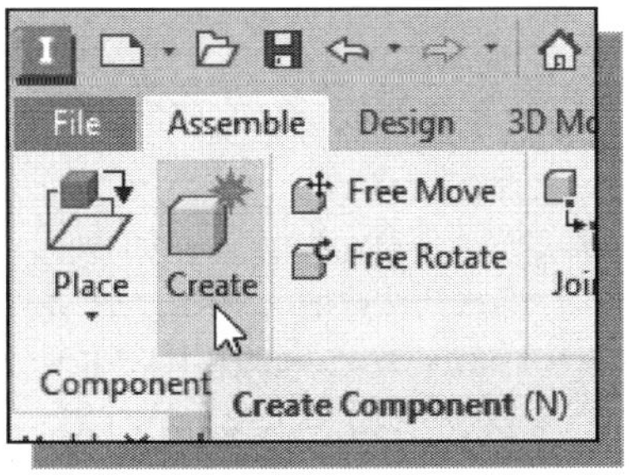

1. In the *Assemble* panel, select the **Create Component** command by left-clicking once on the icon.

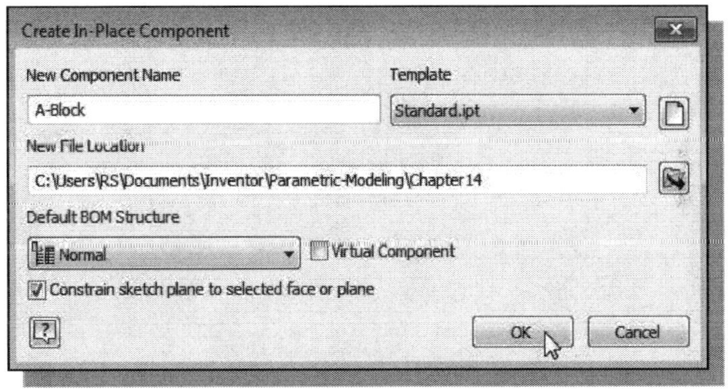

2. In the *Create In-Place Component* dialog box, enter **A-Block** as the new file name.

3. Set the *File Location* to **Chapter16** as shown.

4. Click on the **OK** button to accept the settings.

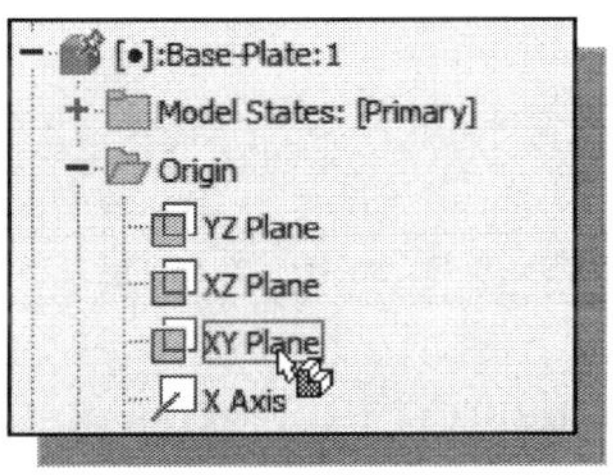

5. Click on the ***XY Plane*** of the *Base-Plate* part, inside the *browser* window, to apply a Flush constraint.

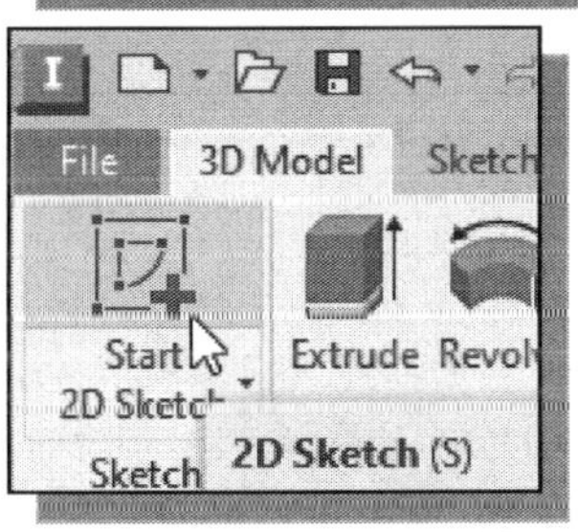

6. Activate the *Model* toolbar and select the **2D Sketch** command by left-clicking once on the icon.

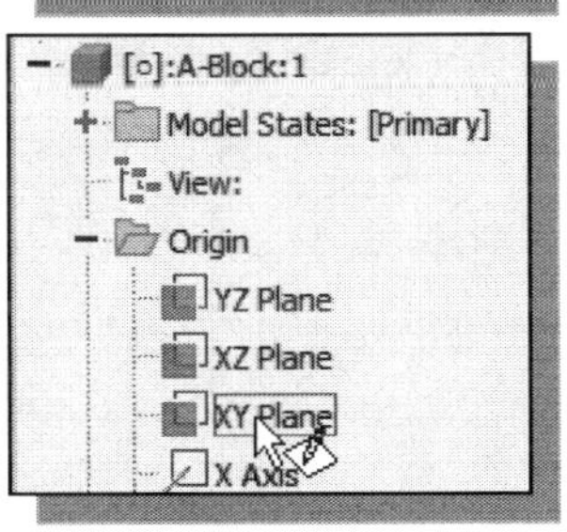

7. Select the ***XY Plane***, in the *browser* window of the *A-Block* part, to align the sketch plane.

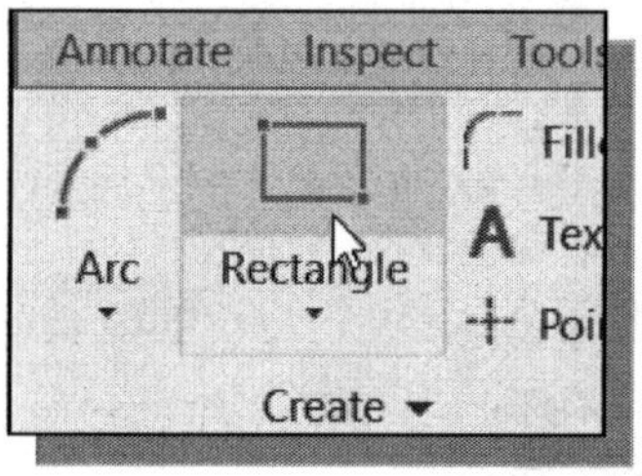

8. Select the **Two point rectangle** command by clicking once with the left-mouse-button on the icon in the *2D Sketch* panel.

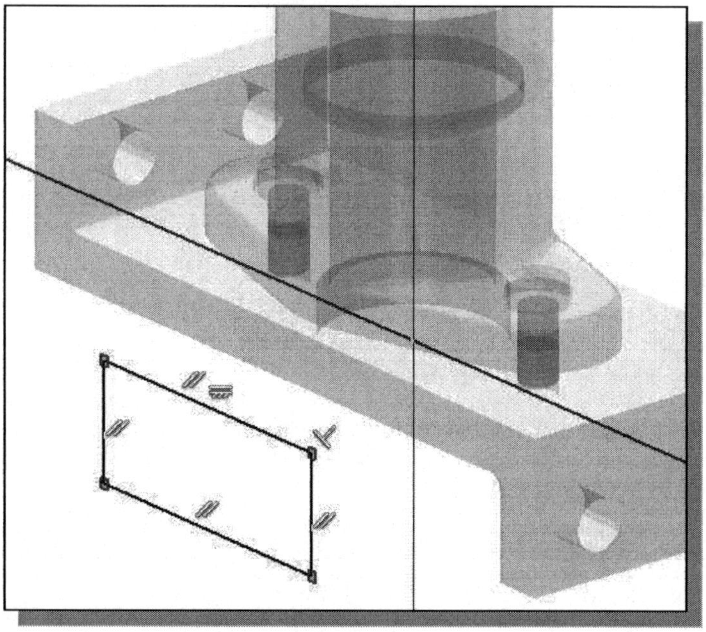

9. On your own, create a rectangle of arbitrary size below the assembly model as shown in the figure.

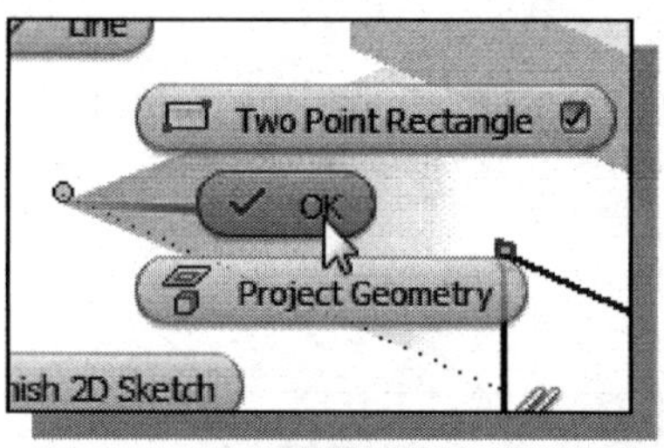

10. Inside the *graphics window*, click once with the **right-mouse-button** to display the option menu and select **OK** to end the Rectangle command.

11. Exit the sketch mode by clicking the **Finish Sketch** button.

12. In the *Ribbon* toolbar panel, select the **Extrude** command in the *Model tab* as shown in the figure below.

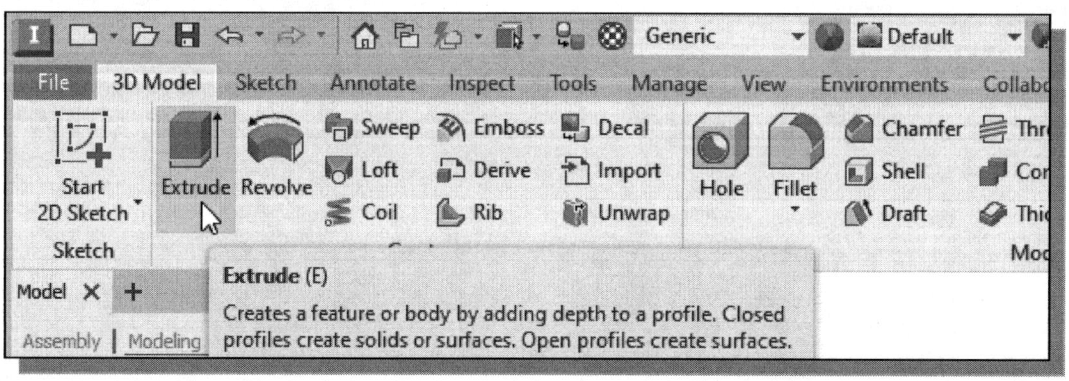

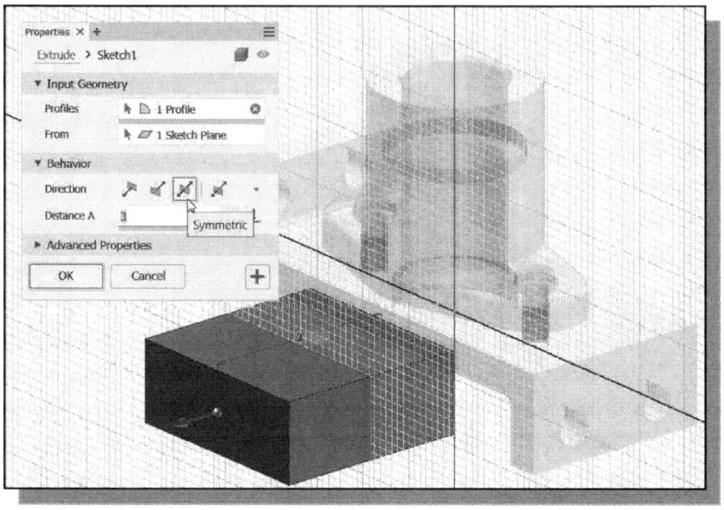

13. Inside the *Extrude* dialog box, select the **Symmetric** option and set the *Extents Distance* to **3 in** as shown.

14. Click on the **OK** button to proceed with creating the feature.

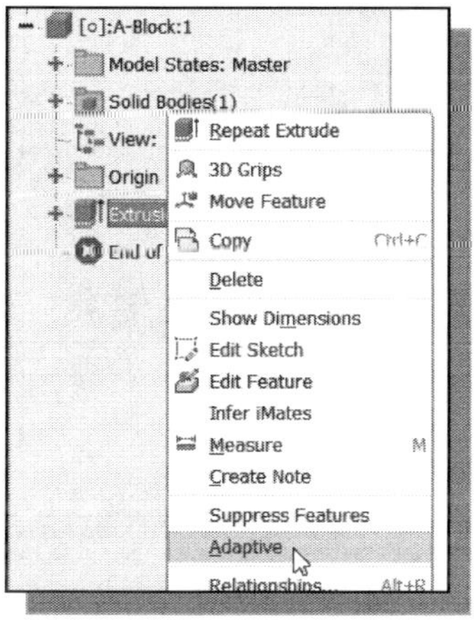

15. Right-click on the ***Extrusion1*** feature of the *A-Block* part, inside the *browser* window, and select **Adaptive** to allow the use of the adaptive design approach.

16. Click inside the graphics window to deselect any part or assembly.

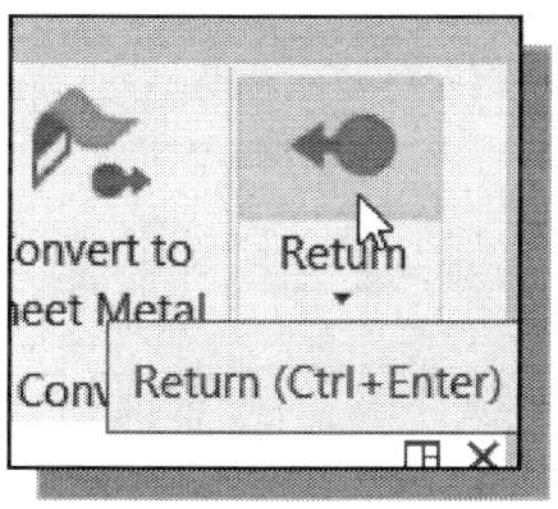

17. Select **Return** in the Ribbon toolbar to exit *Part Editing Mode* and return to *Assembly Modeling Mode*.

- Note that the rectangular block is created with only one dimension, the extrude distance. The 2D sketch of the part is intentionally under-constrained.

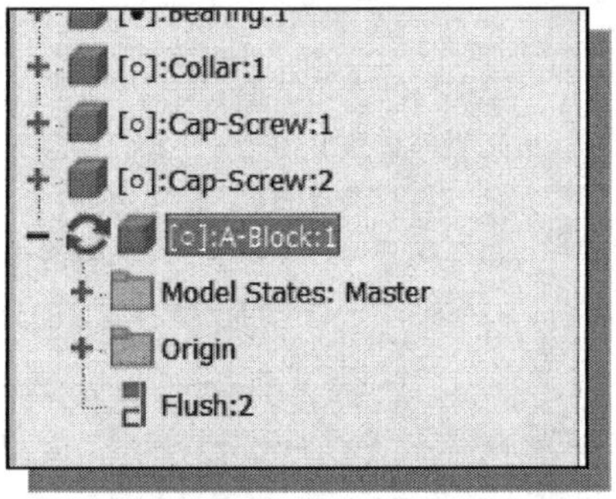

- Note the **Adaptive** icon, the two-rotate-arrows symbol, appears in front of the part name in the *browser* window.

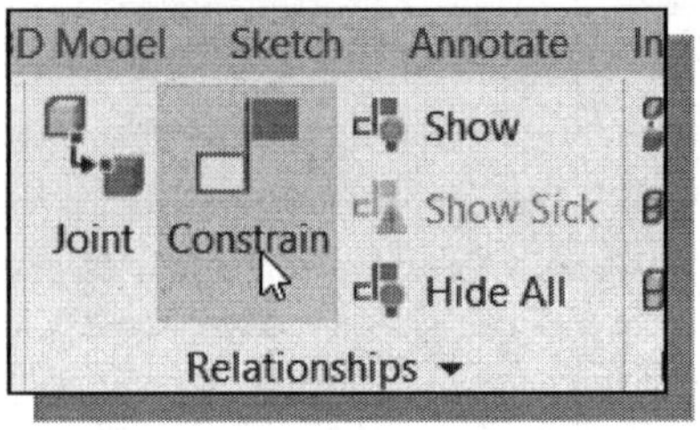

18. In the *Assemble* panel, select the **Constrain** command by left-clicking once on the icon.

19. On your own, use the **Flush** constraint to align the *A-block* to the left-edge of the *Base-Plate* as shown.

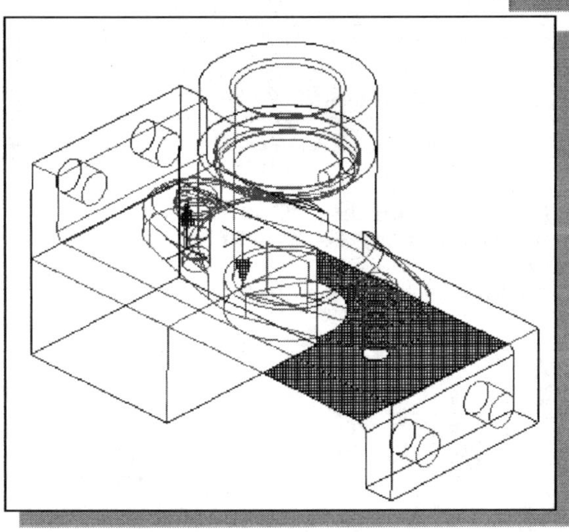

20. Create a **Mate** constraint to align the top of the *A-block* to the bottom of the *Base-Plate* part as shown.

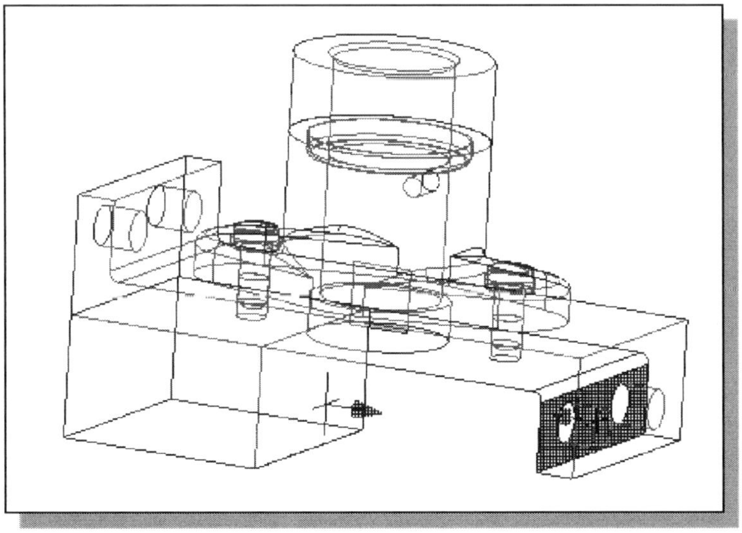

21. Use the **Mate** constraint and align the right surface of the *A-block* to the bottom left surface of the *Base-Plate* part as shown.

- Note that the length of the *A-block* part is adjusted to fit the defined constraint.

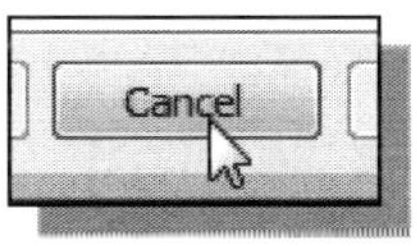

22. In the *Place Constraint* dialog box, click on the **Cancel** button to end the Place Constraint command.

Delete and Re-apply Assembly Constraints

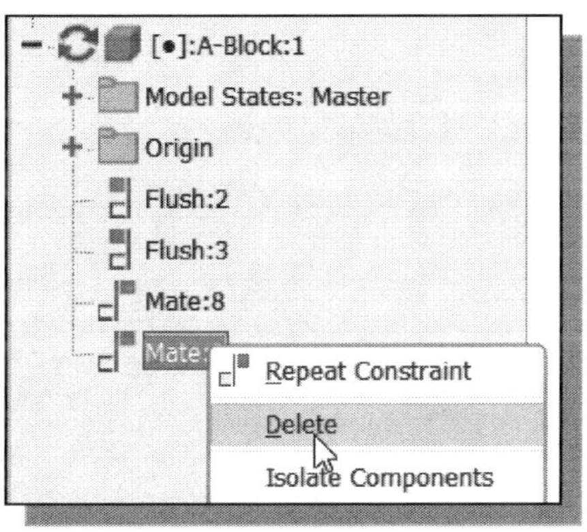

1. Inside the *browser* window, right-click on the last **Mate** constraint of the *A-Block* part to bring up the option menu.

2. Select **Delete** to remove the applied constraint.

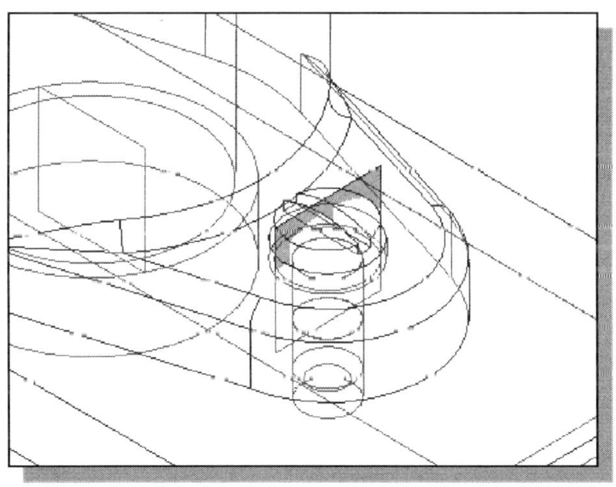

3. On your own, switch ***ON*** the **Visibility** of the vertical work plane of the *Cap-Screw* part, the plane that is perpendicular to the length of the *Base-Plate* part, as shown.

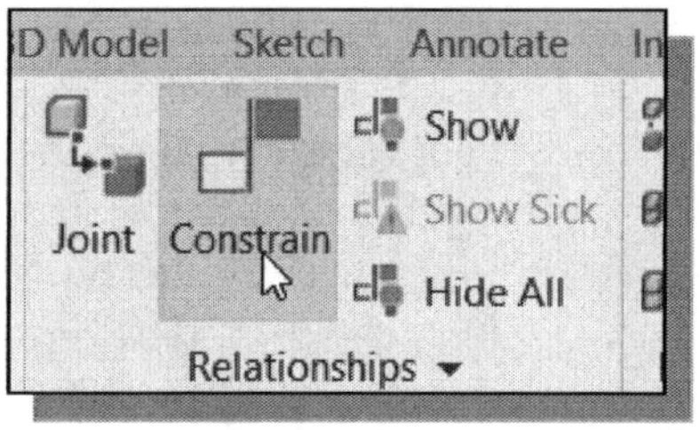

4. In the *Assembly* position panel, select the **Constrain** command by left-clicking once on the icon.

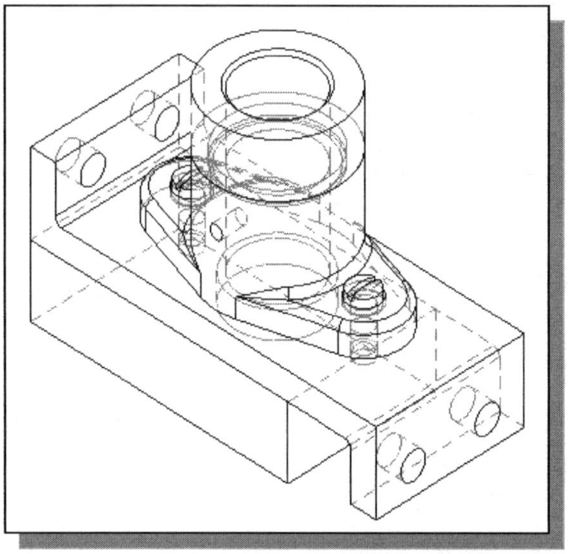

5. On your own, align the right vertical surface of the *A-block* part to the vertical work plane as shown in the figure.

6. On your own, experiment with aligning the right vertical surface of the *A-block* part to other vertical surfaces of the assembly model.

- As can be seen, the length of the *A-block* is adjusted to the newly applied constraint. The ***Adaptive Design*** approach allows us to have greater flexibility and simplifies the design process.

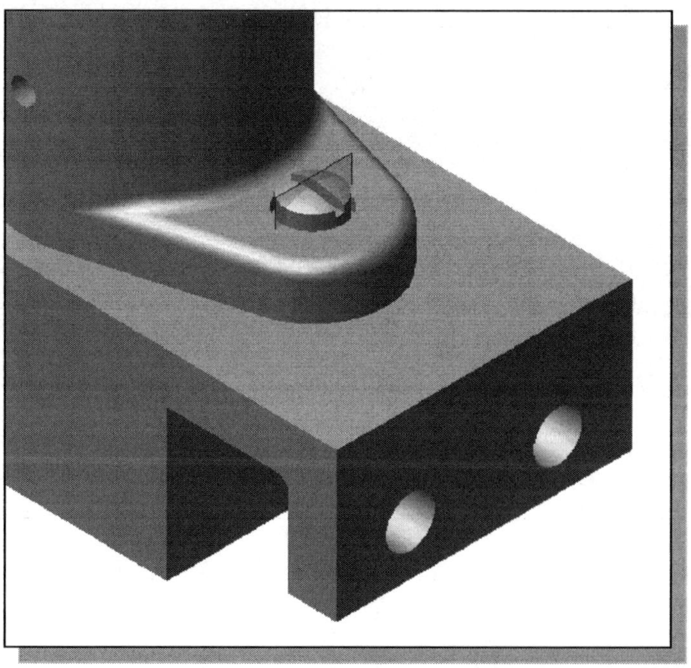

7. On your own, save the assembly model as **Shaft-Support.iam** under the Chapter16 folder.

Set up a Drawing of the Assembly Model

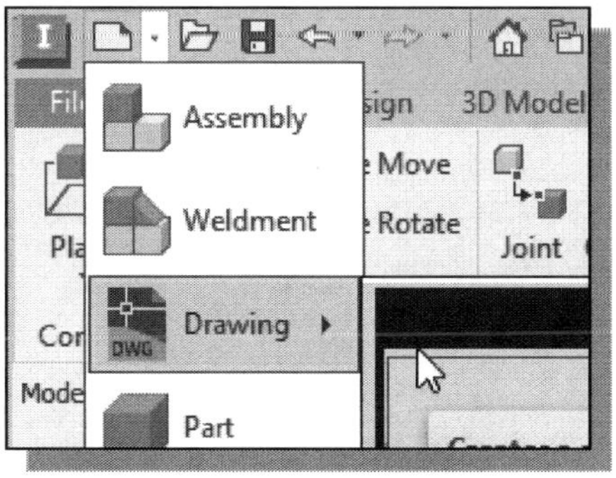

1. Click on the **drop-down arrow** next to the **New File** icon in the *Quick Access* toolbar area to display the available **New File** options.

2. Select **Drawing** from the option list.

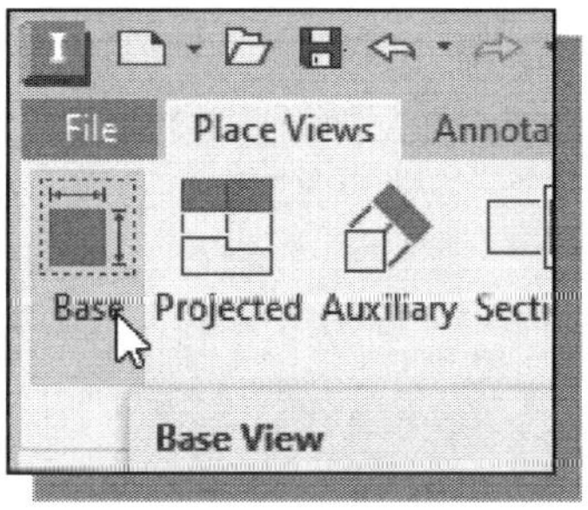

3. Click on the **Base View** in the *Drawing Views* panel to create a base view.

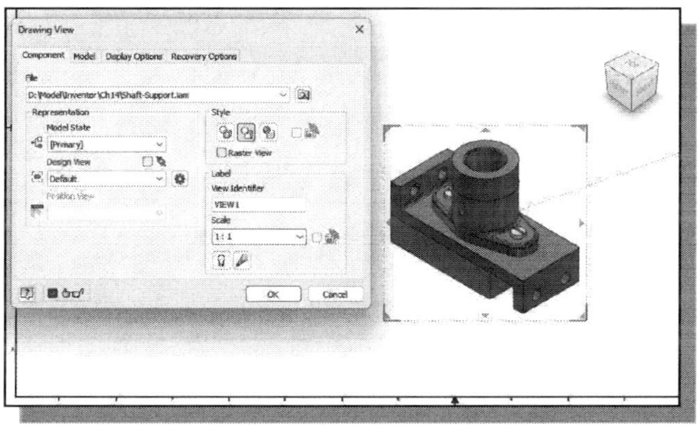

4. In the *Drawing View* dialog box, set *Orientation* to **Iso Top Right View, Scale 1:1** and **Hidden Line Removed** as shown in the figure.

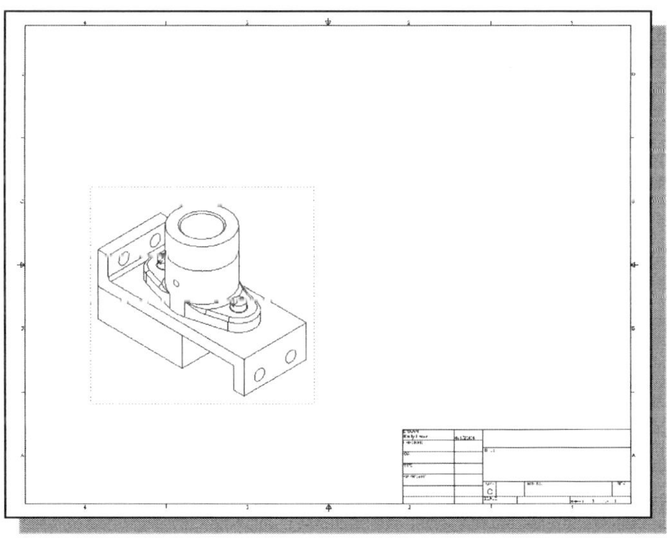

5. Move the cursor inside the graphics window and place the ***base*** view near the lower left side of the *Border* as shown.

6. Click the **OK** button to end the command.

❖ Note that the default sheet size is much bigger than the created view. *Inventor* allows us to adjust the sheet size even when views have been created.

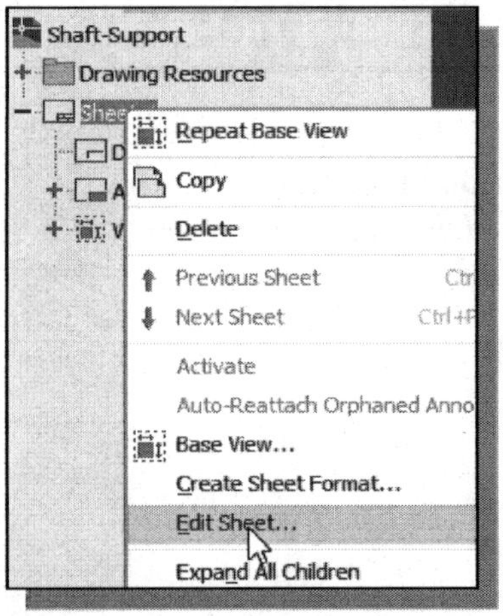

7. Inside the *Drawing Browser* window, right-click on ***Sheet:1*** to display the option menu.

8. Select **Edit Sheet** in the option menu to display the settings for the drawing.

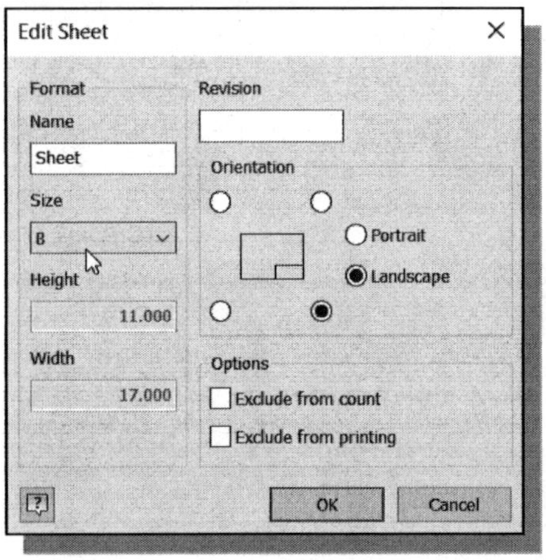

9. Set the sheet size to ***B-size*** as shown.

10. Click on the **OK** button to accept the settings and exit the Edit Sheet command.

11. On your own, reposition the Isometric view as shown in the figure.

❖ Note that the *Border* and *Title Block* are automatically replaced as the sheet size is adjusted.

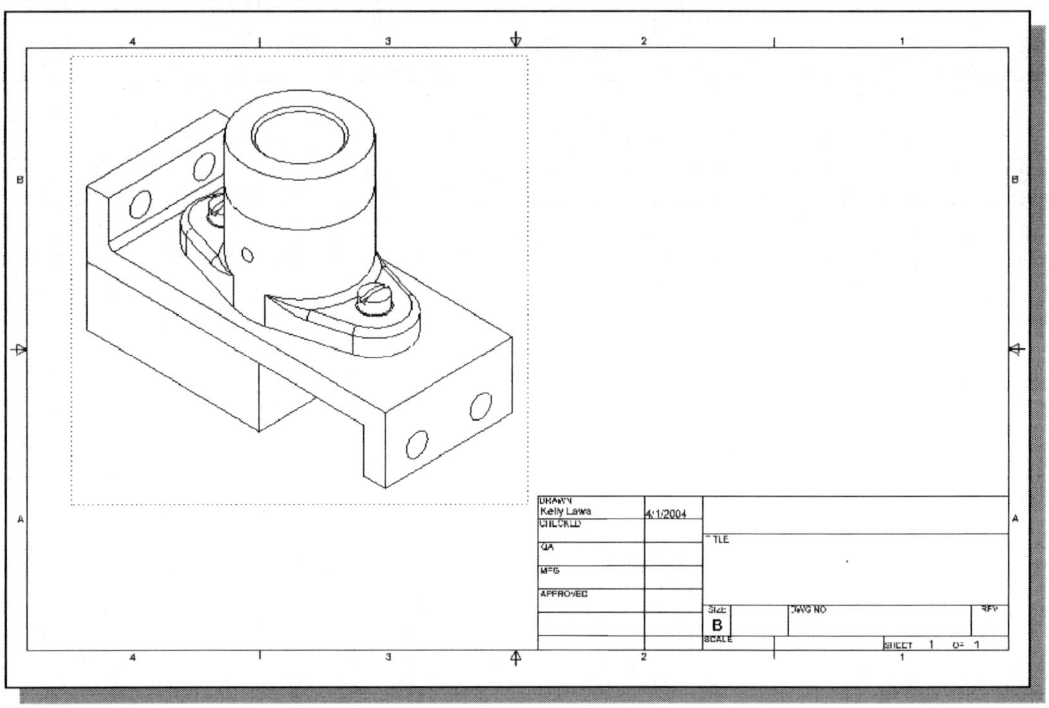

Creating a Parts List

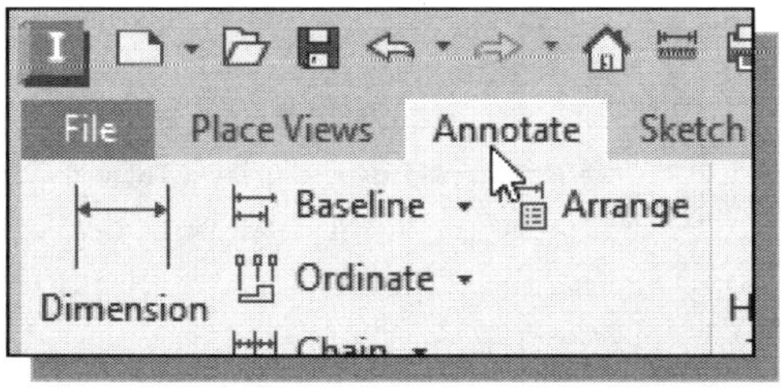

1. In the *Ribbon Toolbar*, click on the **Annotate** tab as shown.

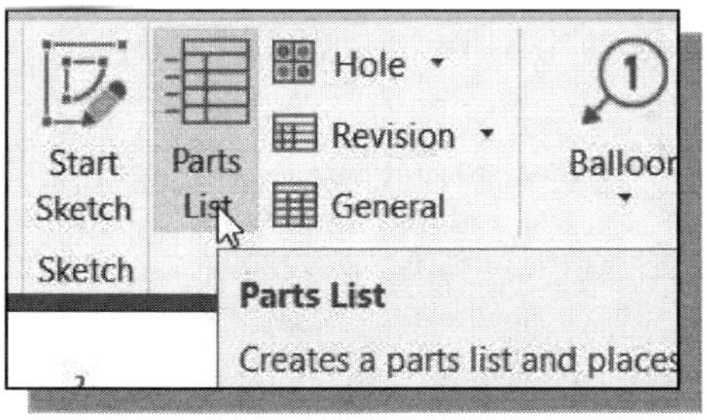

2. In the *Drawing Annotation* window, click on the **Parts List** button.

3. In the *prompt area*, the message "*Select a view*" is displayed. Items in the selected view will be listed in the *Parts List*. Select the **base view**.

❖ The *Parts List* dialog box appears on the screen; options are available to make adjustments to the numbering system and table wrap settings.

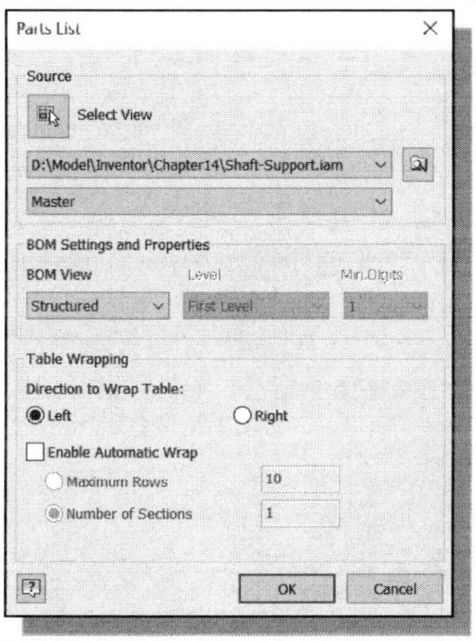

➢ The *Parts List* – BOM options are as follows:

Structured: Creates a parts list in which subassemblies are assigned using a nested numbering system (for example, 1, 1.1, 1.1.1). The nested number extends as many levels as needed for the assembly levels in the model.

Only Parts: Creates a parts list that sequentially numbers all parts in the assembly, including parts that are contained in subassemblies.

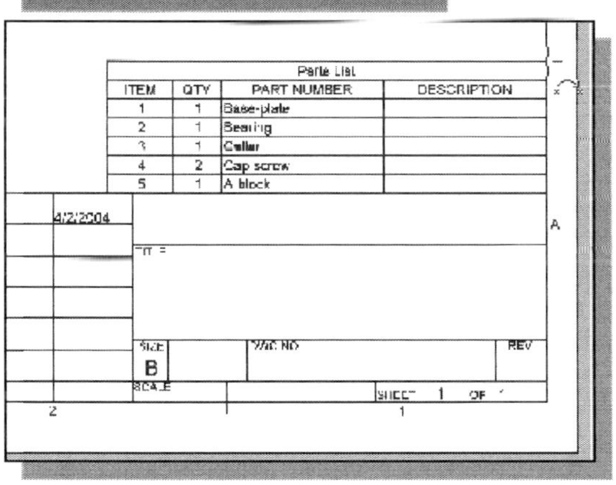

❖ Note that no subassemblies are currently used in the assembly; we will accept the default settings.

4. Click **OK** to accept the default settings and also enable the **BOM View** option.

5. Place the ***Parts List*** above the *Title Block* as shown.

Edit the Parts List

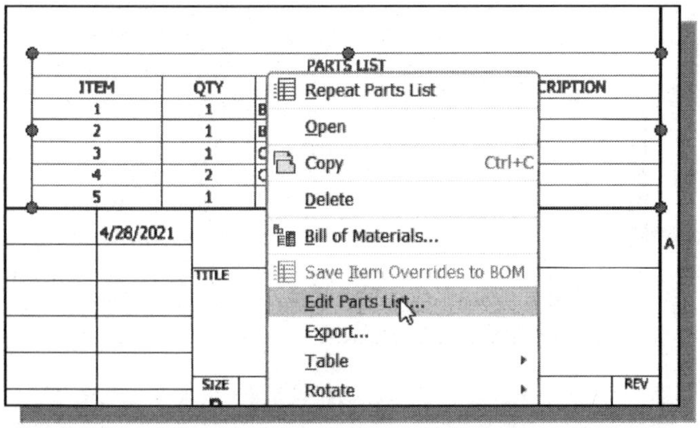

1. Move the cursor on top of the ***Parts List*** and **right-click** once to display the option menu.

2. Choose **Edit Parts List** in the option menu as shown.

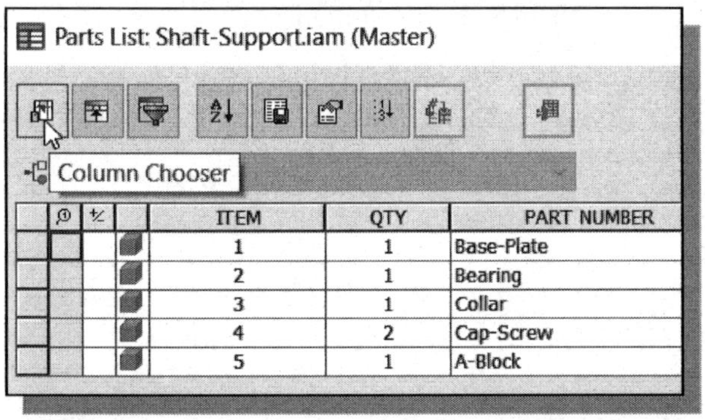

3. Click on the **Column Chooser** button as shown.

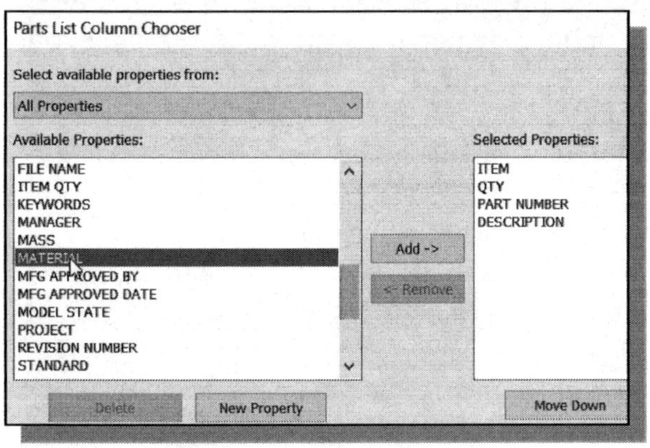

4. Select **MATERIAL** in the *Available Properties* list as shown.

5. Click **Add** to add the selected item to the *Selected Properties* list.

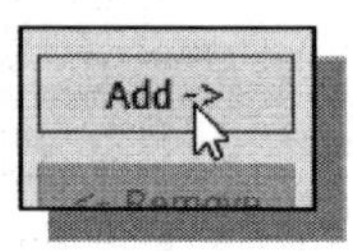

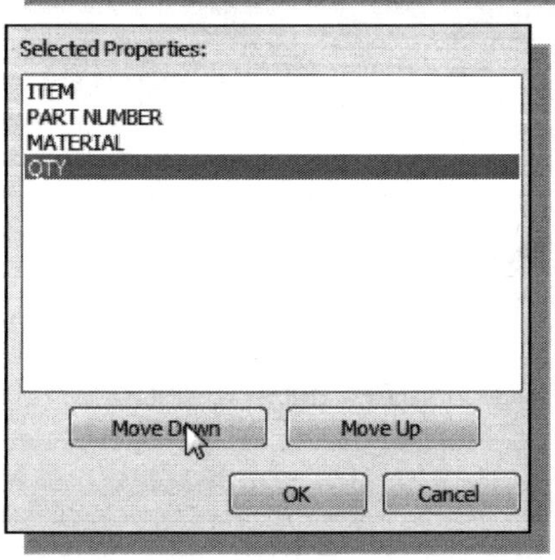

6. On your own, adjust the ***Selected Properties*** list as shown. (Hint: Use the **Move Up** and **Move Down** buttons to arrange the order of the list.)

7. Click **OK** to accept the settings.

❖ The ***Parts List*** is adjusted using the new settings. Note that, currently, all of the parts are using the **Generic** material type.

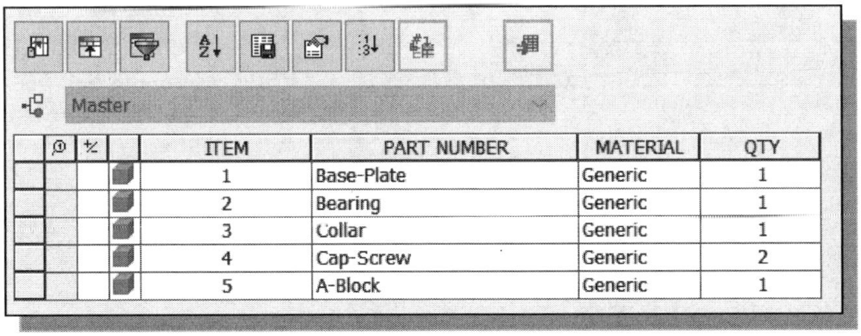

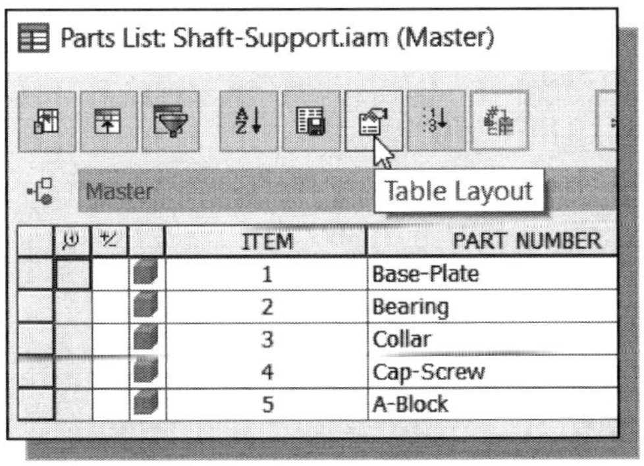

8. Click on the **Table Layout** button as shown.

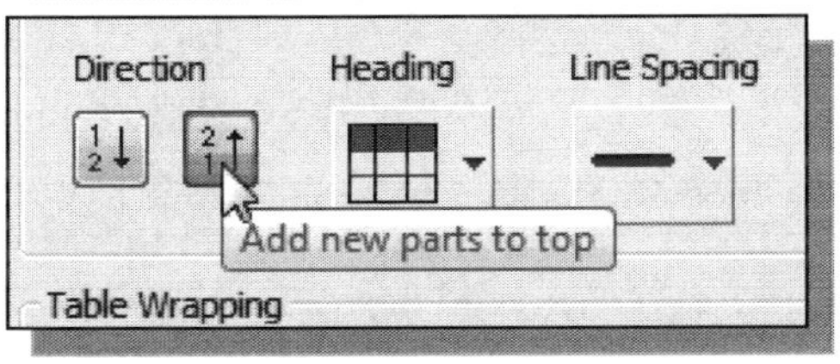

9. Set the ***Table Direction*** to **Add new parts to top** as shown.

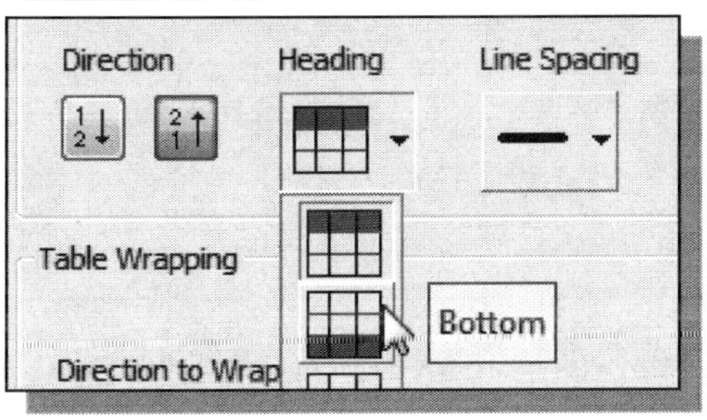

10. Set the ***Heading Placement*** to **Bottom** as shown.

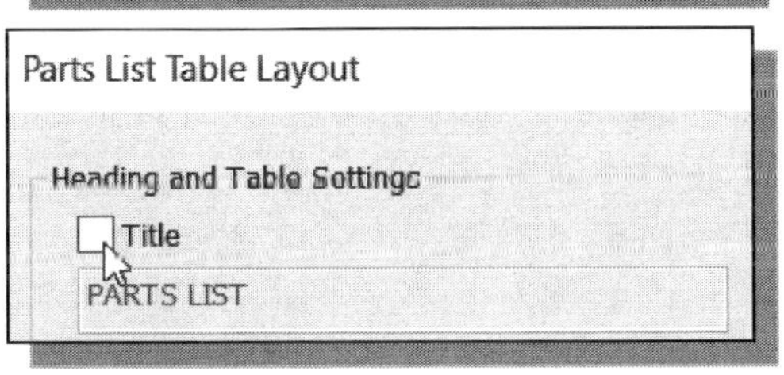

11. Turn **OFF** the ***Parts List Title***.

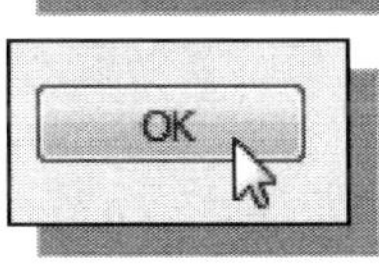

12. Click **OK** twice to accept the ***Parts List*** settings.

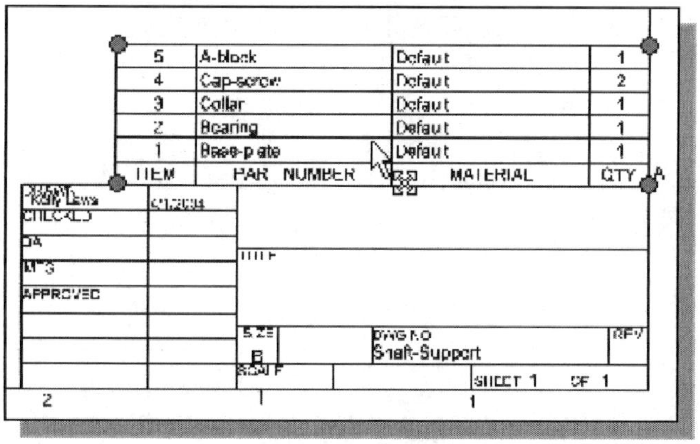

13. On your own, adjust the position of the ***Parts List*** so that it is aligned to the top edge of the *Title Block* as shown. (Hint: Look for the MOVE symbol next to the cursor.)

Change the Material Type

We will switch back to the assembly model to change the assignments of the material type.

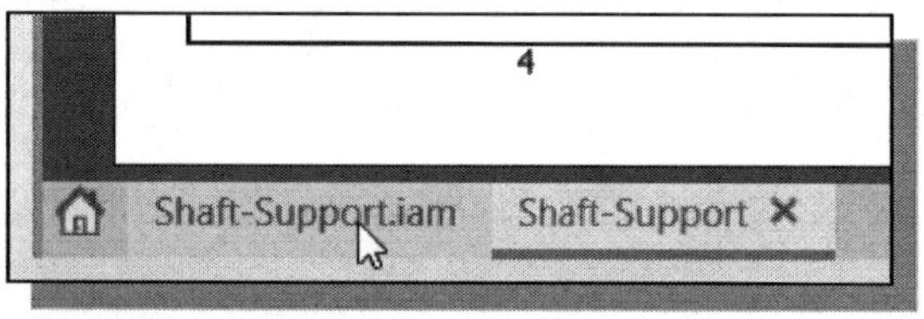

1. Click on the *Shaft-Support.iam* tab to switch back to the assembly model.

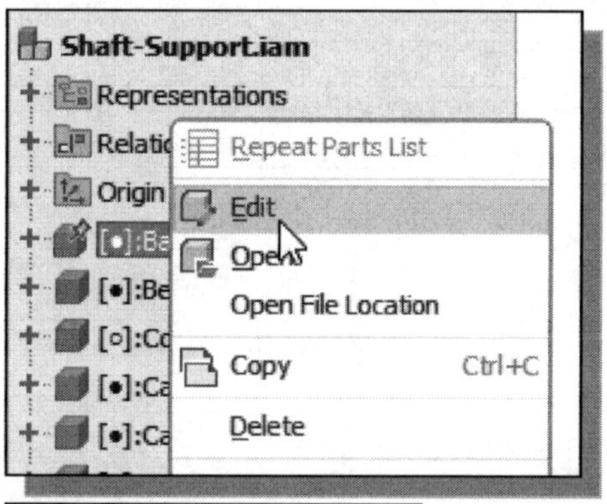

2. Inside the *Model Browser* window, right-click on **Base-Plate:1** to display the option menu.

3. Select **Edit** in the option menu to enter the *Edit Mode* for the selected part.

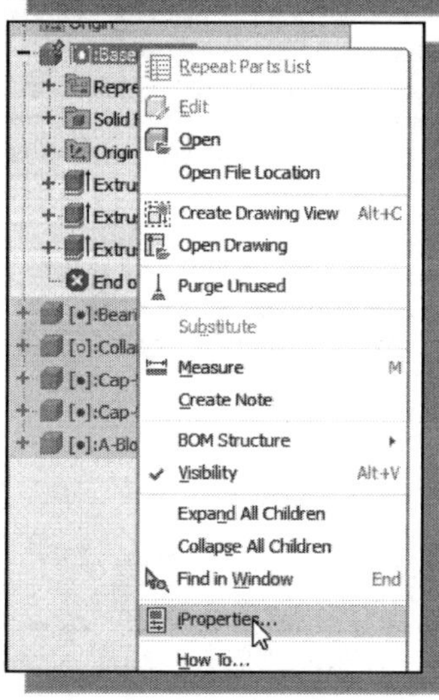

4. Inside the *Model Browser* window, select the **Base-plate** part by clicking once with the left-mouse-button.

5. Right-click on **Base-plate:1** to display the option menu and choose **iProperties** in the options list.

6. Click on the **Physical** tab in the *Base-plate.ipt Properties* window.

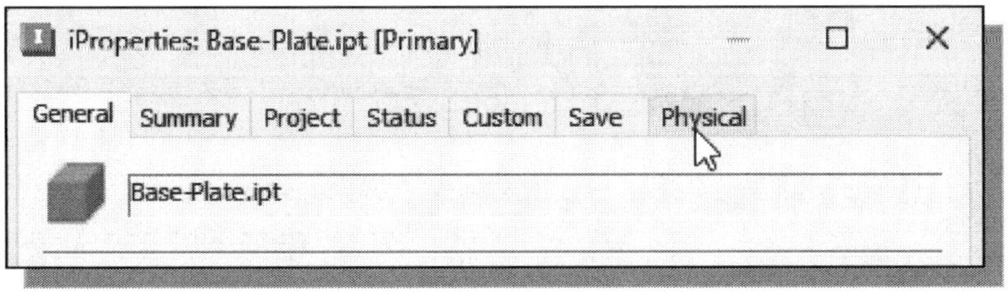

7. Choose the **Steel, Mild** in the *Material* list. Note the properties of the selected material are also displayed in the *Properties* list as shown in the figure.

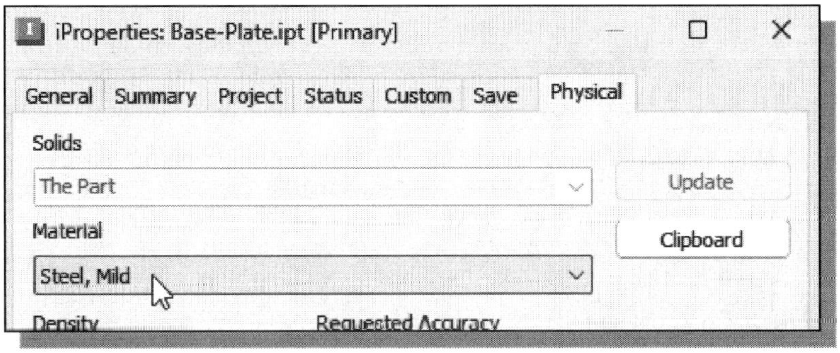

❖ Autodesk Inventor comes with many materials that have pre-entered information; additional material types/properties can also be added/changed as well.

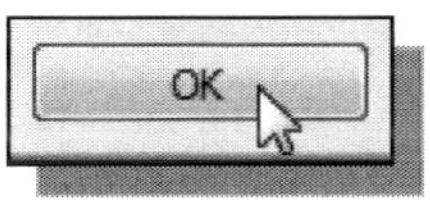

8. Click **OK** to accept the setting and exit the *Materials* dialog box.

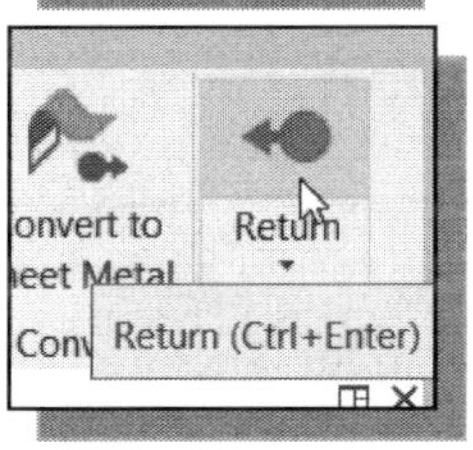

9. Select **Return** in the Standard toolbar to exit the *Part Editing Mode*.

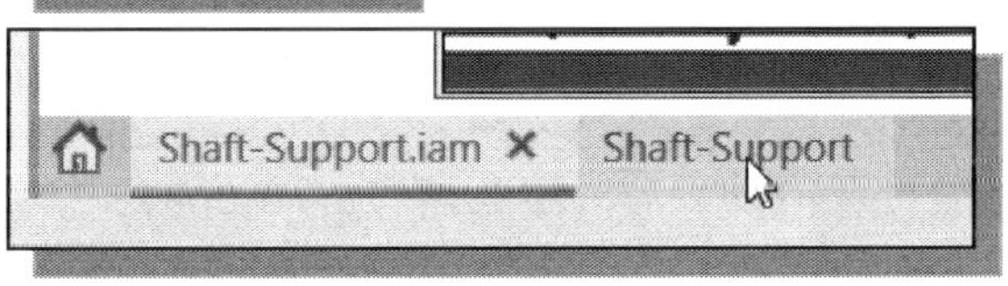

10. On your own, switch back to the *Shaft-Support.idw* window and notice the *Material* information for the ***Base-plate*** part is now updated.

11. On your own, repeat the above steps to change the material information for the other parts as shown in the figure below.

5	A-Block	Aluminum 6061	1
4	Cap-Screw	Steel, Mild	2
3	Collar	Bronze, Soft Tin	1
2	Bearing	Iron, Cast	1
1	Base-Plate	Steel, Mild	1
ITEM	PART NUMBER	MATERIAL	QTY

Add the Balloon Callouts

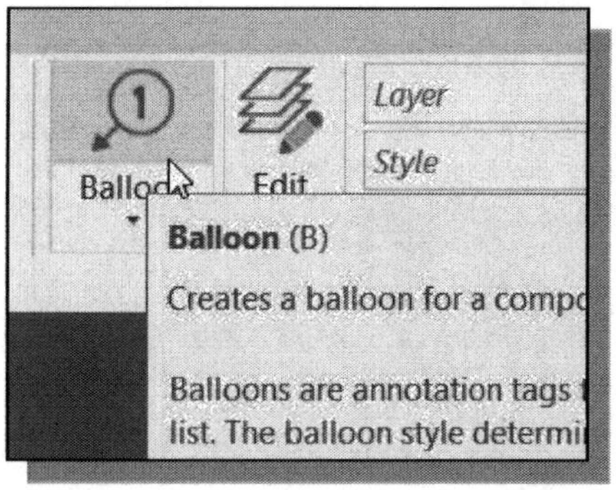

1. In the *Drawing Annotation* window, click on the **Balloon** button.

2. In the prompt area, the message "*Select a location*" is displayed. Click on the ***Collar*** part to attach an arrowhead to the part.

3. Pick another location to **place the balloon** as shown in the figure below.

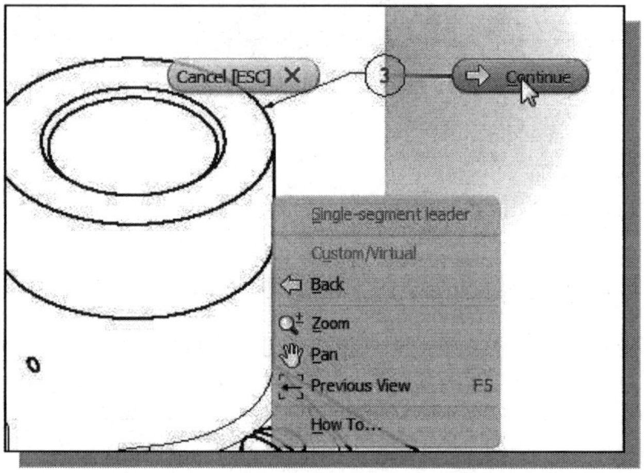

4. Inside the graphics window, click once with the right-mouse-button to display the **option menu**.

5. Select **Continue** in the pop-up menu to proceed with the creation of the balloon.

Completing the Title Block Using the iProperties option

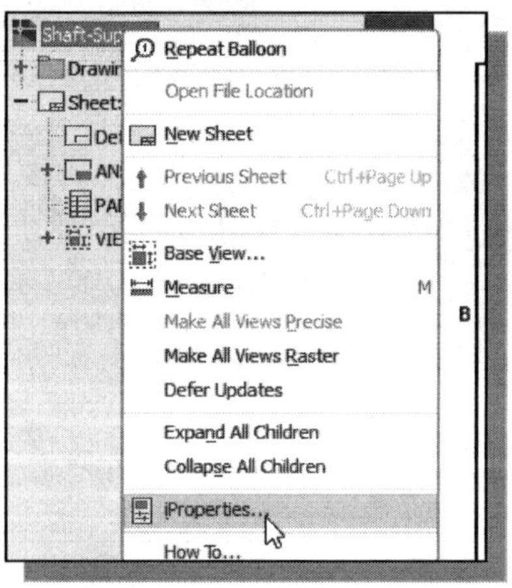

1. Inside the *Model Browser* window, select the **Shaft-Support** drawing by clicking once with the left-mouse-button.

2. Right-click on **Shaft-Support** to display the option menu and choose **iProperties** in the options list.

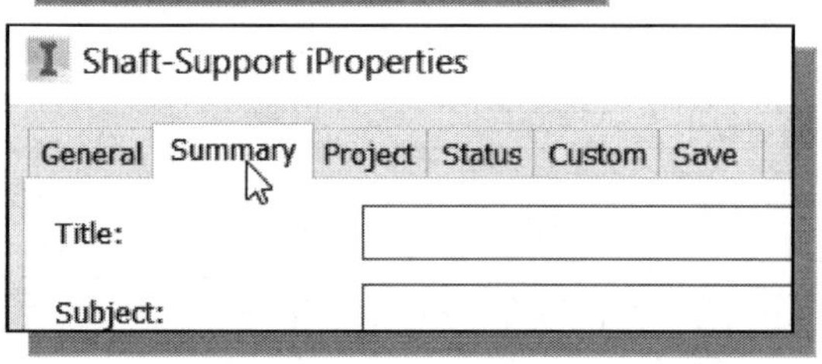

3. Click on the **Summary** tab to view the list of general information regarding the design.

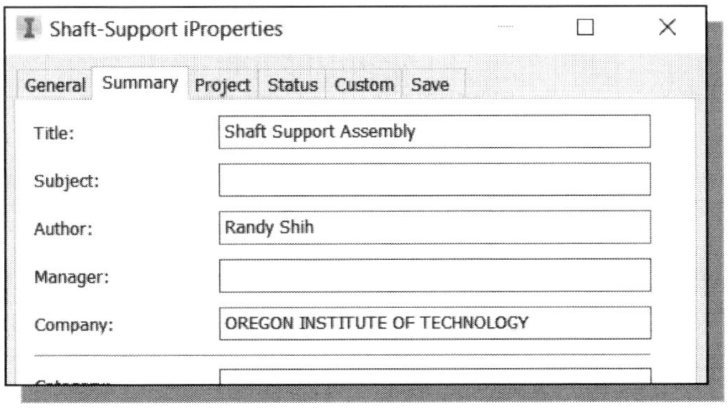

4. Enter the **Title**, **Author** and **Company** information as shown.

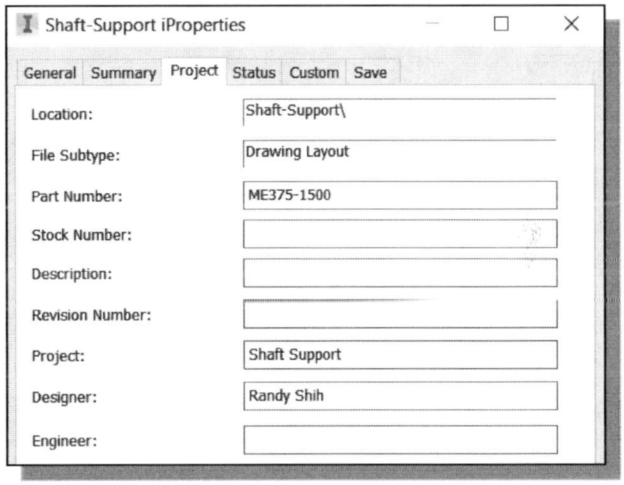

5. Click on the Project tab and enter the Part Number, Project name as shown.

6. Click **OK** to accept the setting and exit the *iProperties* dialog box.

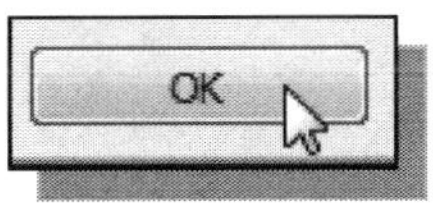

7. On your own, add the additional balloons and complete the drawing as shown.

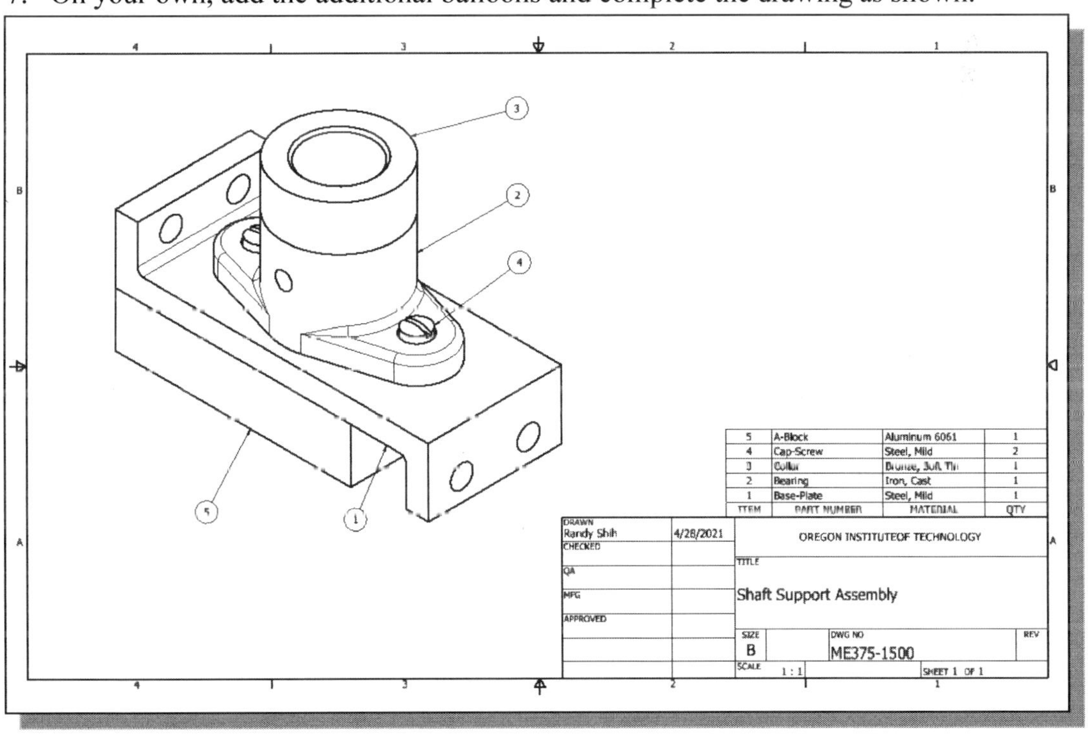

Bill of Materials

A bill of materials (BOM) is a table that contains information about the parts within an assembly. The BOM can include information such as part names, quantities, costs, vendors, and all of the other information related to building the part. The ***parts list***, which is used in an assembly drawing, is usually a partial list of the associated BOM.

In Autodesk Inventor, both the *bill of materials* and *parts list* can be derived directly from data generated by the assembly and the part properties. We can select which properties to be included in the *bill of materials* or *parts list*, in what order the information is presented, and in what format to export the information. The exported file can be used in an application such as a spreadsheet or text editor.

(a) BOM from Parts List

1. Move the cursor on top of the ***Parts List*** and right-click once to display the option menu.

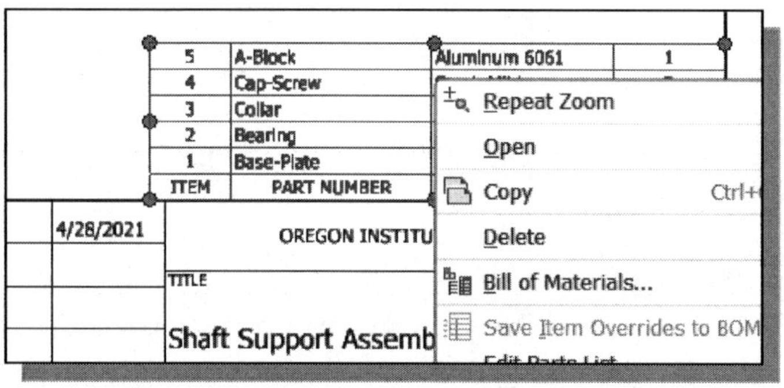

2. Choose **Export...** in the option menu as shown.

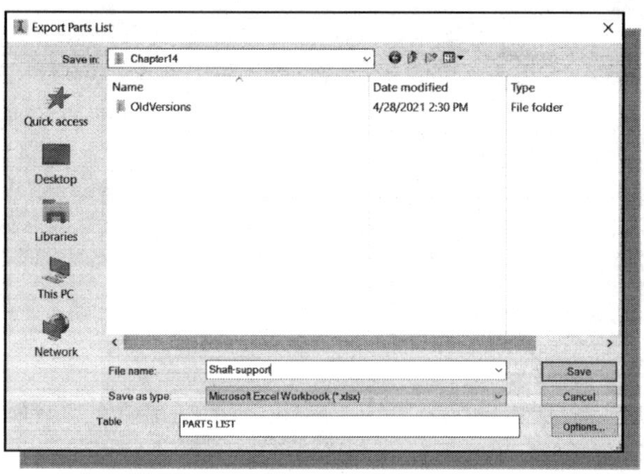

3. Confirm the ***Save as type*** list is set to **Microsoft Excel**.

4. Enter ***Shaft-support*** as the filename and click **Save** to export the BOM.

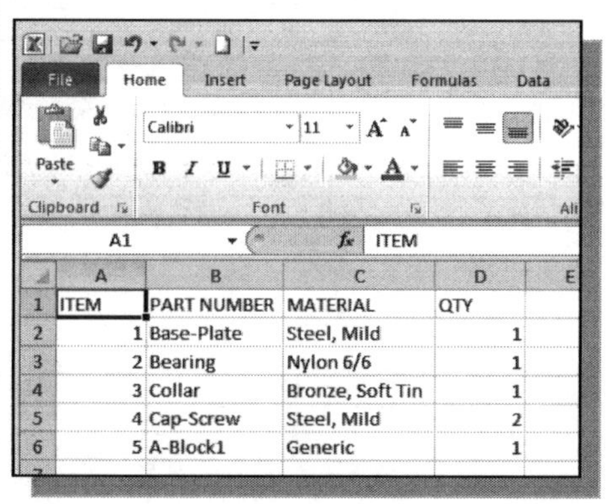

❖ On your own, examine the exported BOM by opening up the file in *Excel*.

(b) BOM from Assembly Model

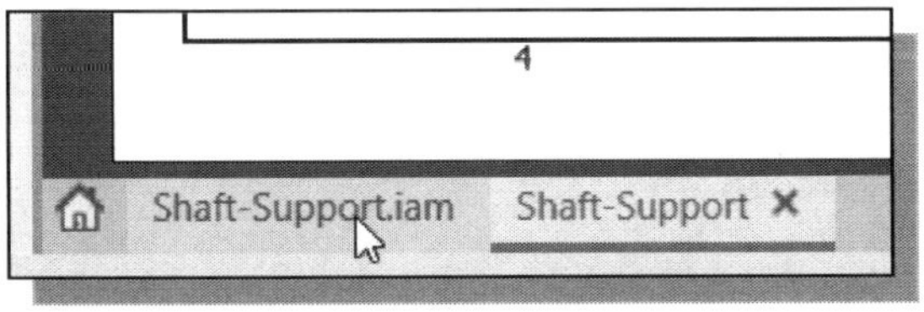

1. Click on the ***Shaft-Support.iam*** tab to switch back to the assembly model.

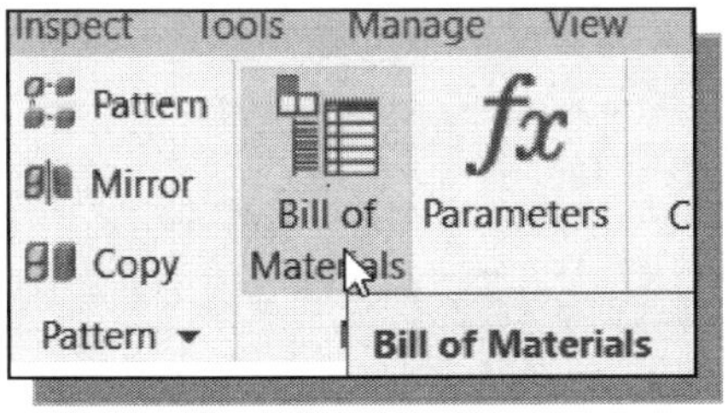

2. Select **Bill of Materials** in the *Manage* tab of the *Ribbon* toolbar panel.

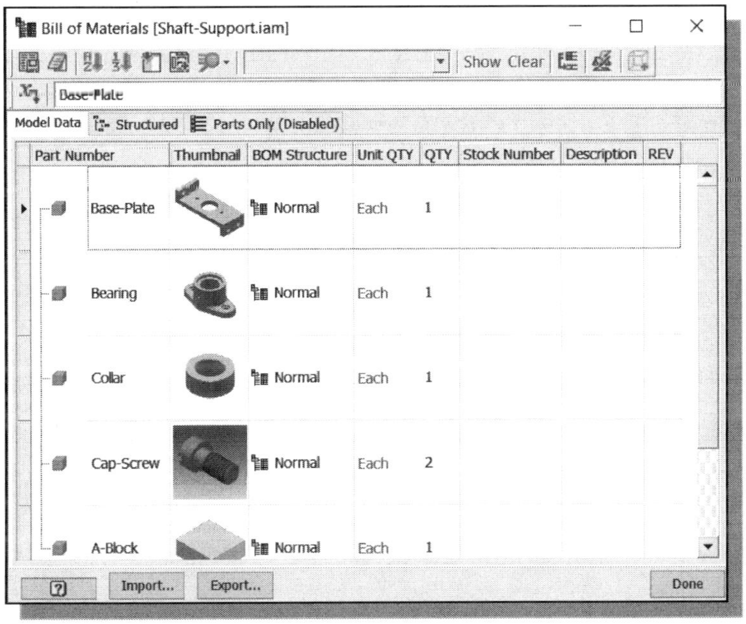

❖ Note that many of the controls and options are similar to those of the **Parts List** command in the *Drawing Mode*.

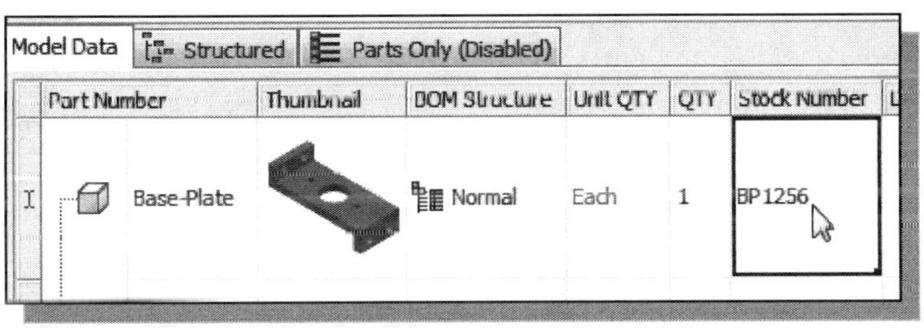

3. Click inside the ***Stock Number*** box to enter the *Edit Mode*.

4. Enter **BP1256** as the new *Stock Number*.

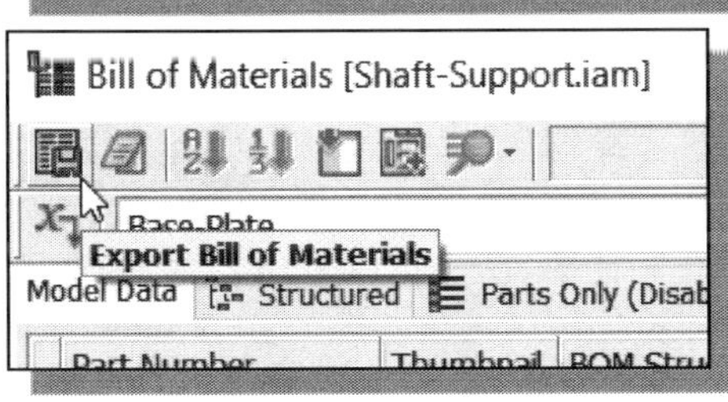

5. Click the **Export Bill of Materials** button.

6. On your own, export using the Microsoft Excel format and examine the *BOM* in Microsoft Excel.

Review Questions:

1. What is the purpose of using ***assembly constraints***?

2. List three of the commonly used ***assembly constraints***.

3. Describe the difference between the **Mate** constraint and the **Flush** constraint.

4. In an assembly, can we place more than one copy of a part? How is it done?

5. How should we determine the assembly order of different parts in an assembly model?

6. How do we adjust the information listed in the **parts list** of an assembly drawing?

7. In Autodesk Inventor, describe the procedure to create a **bill of materials** (BOM).

8. Create sketches showing the steps you plan to use to create the four parts required for the assembly shown on the next page:

Ex.1)

Ex.2)

Ex.3)

Ex.4)

Exercises:

1. **Wheel Assembly** (Create a set of detail and assembly drawings. All dimensions are in mm.)

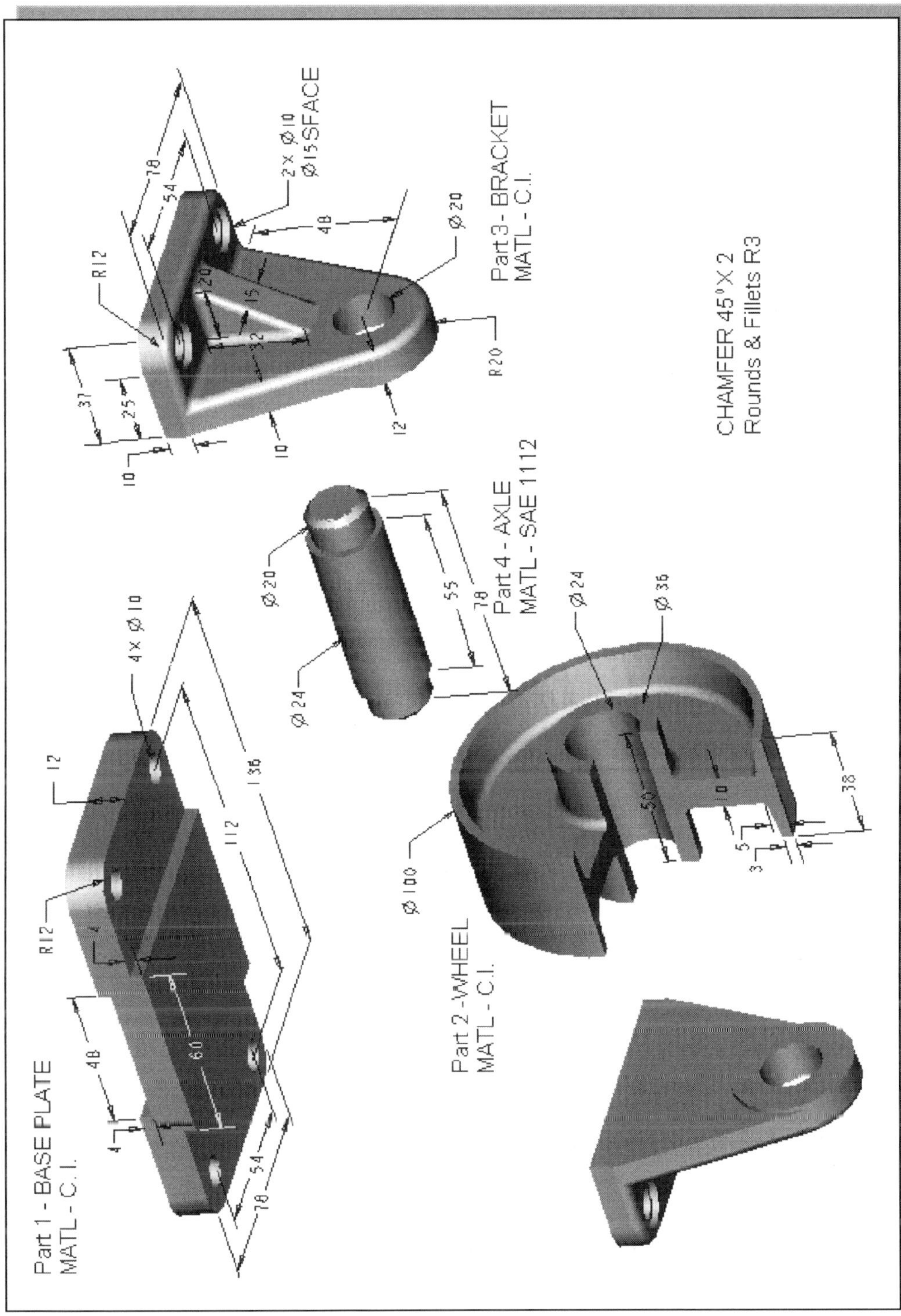

2. **Vise Assembly** (Create a set of detail and assembly drawings. All dimensions are in inches.)

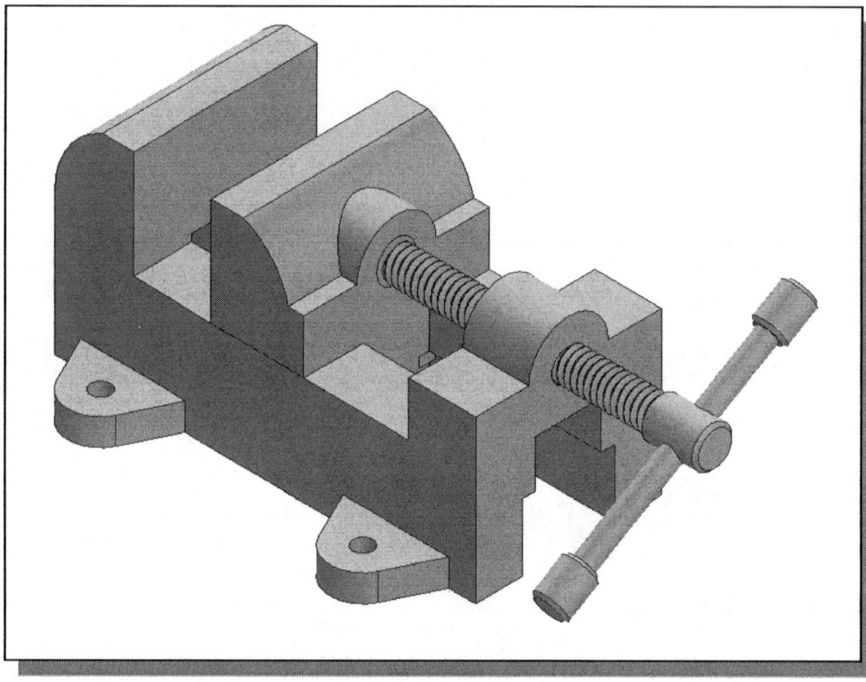

(a) **Base:** The 1.5 inch wide and 1.25 inch wide slots are cut through the entire base. Material: **Gray Cast Iron**. Threads: 5/8”-8-UNC-3B

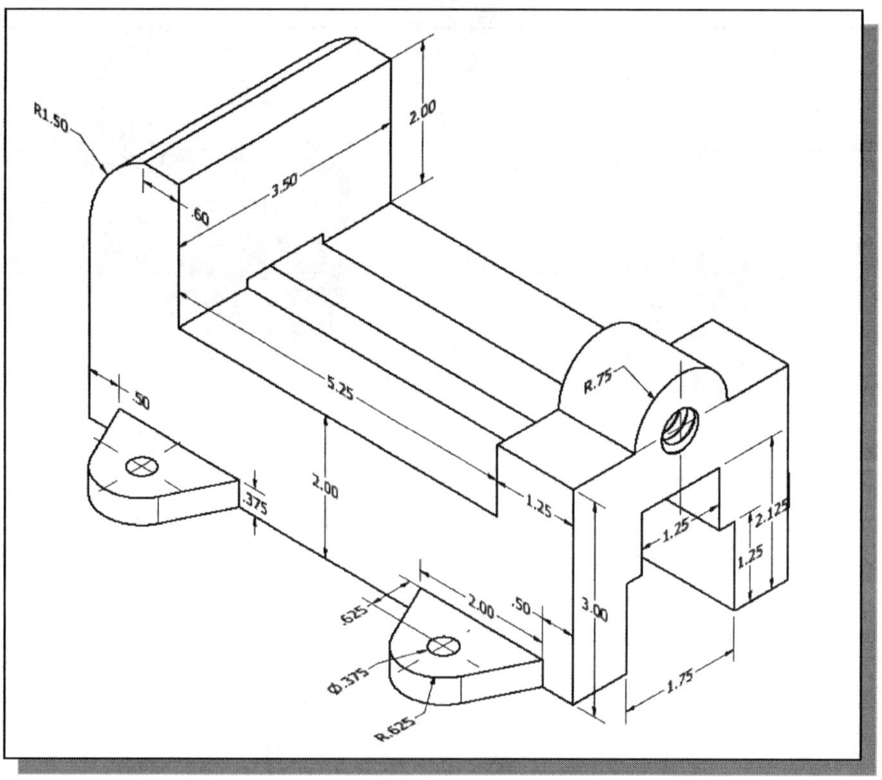

(b) **Jaw:** The shoulder of the jaw rests on the flat surface of the base and the jaw opening is set to 1.5 inches. Material: **Gray Cast Iron**.

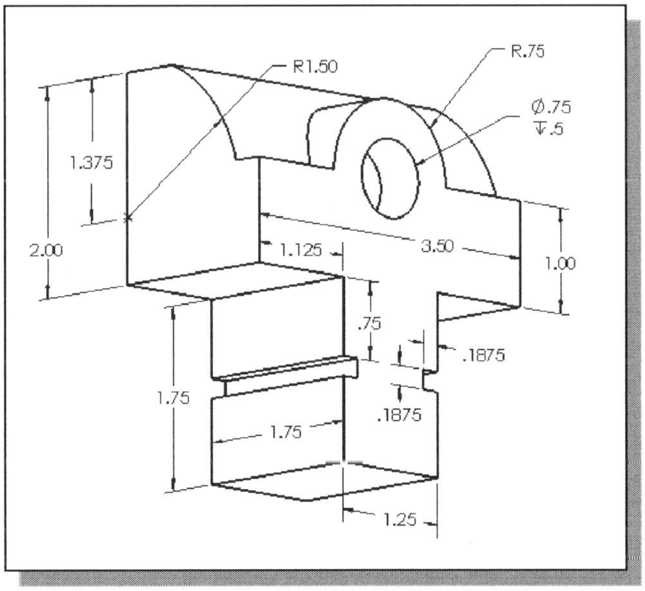

(c) **Key: 0.1875 inch H x 0.3125 inch W x 1.75 inch L**. The keys fit into the slots on the jaw with the edge faces flush as shown in the sub-assembly to the right. Material: **Alloy Steel**.

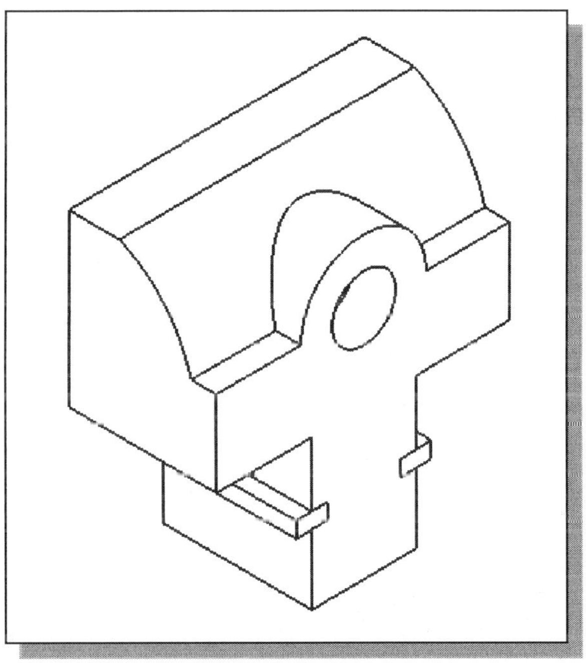

(d) **Screw:** 5/8"-8-UNC-3A There is one chamfered edge (0.0625 inch x 45º). The flat ∅ 0.75″ edge of the screw is flush with the corresponding recessed ∅ 0.75 face on the jaw. Material: **Alloy Steel.**

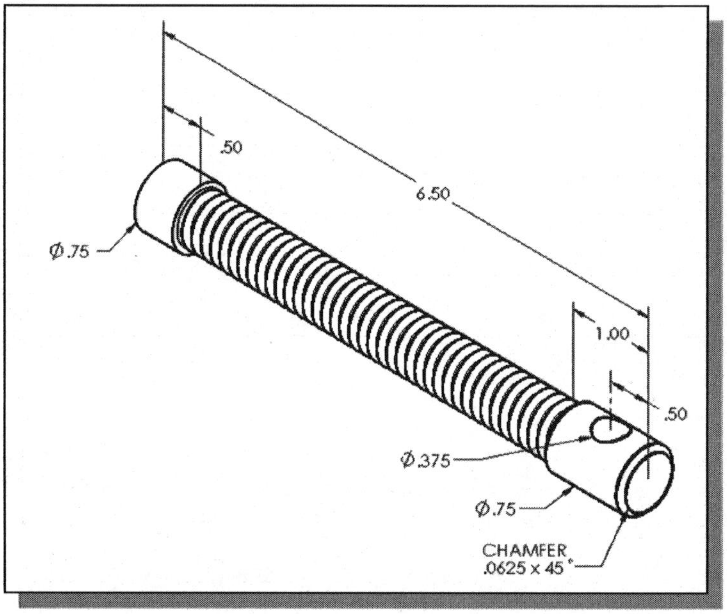

(e) **Handle Rod: ∅ 0.375″ x 5.0″ L**. The handle rod passes through the hole in the screw and is rotated to an angle of 30º with the horizontal as shown in the assembly view. The flat ∅ 0.375″ edges of the handle rod are flush with the corresponding recessed ∅ 0.735 faces on the handle knobs. Material: **Alloy Steel**.

(f) **Handle Knob:** There are two chamfered edges (0.0625 inch x 45º). The handle knobs are attached to each end of the handle rod. The resulting overall length of the handle with knobs is 5.50″. The handle is aligned with the screw so that the outer edge of the upper knob is 2.0″ from the central axis of the screw. Material: **Alloy Steel**.

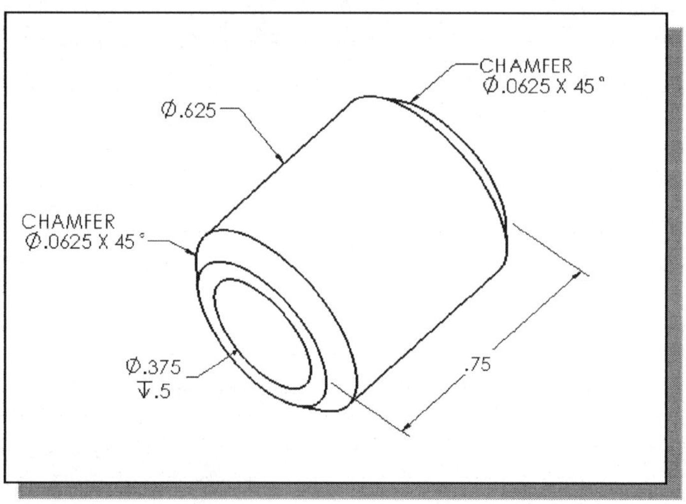

Chapter 17
Design Analysis - Autodesk Inventor Stress Analysis Module

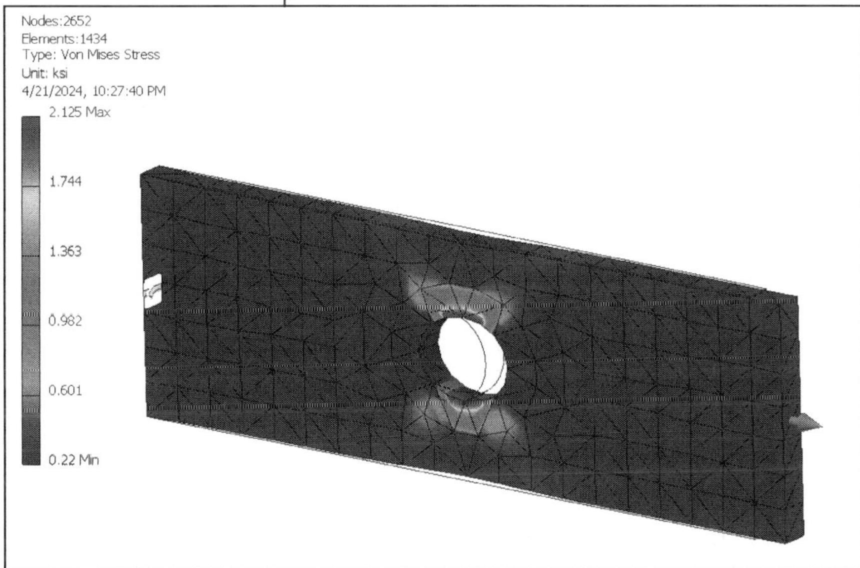

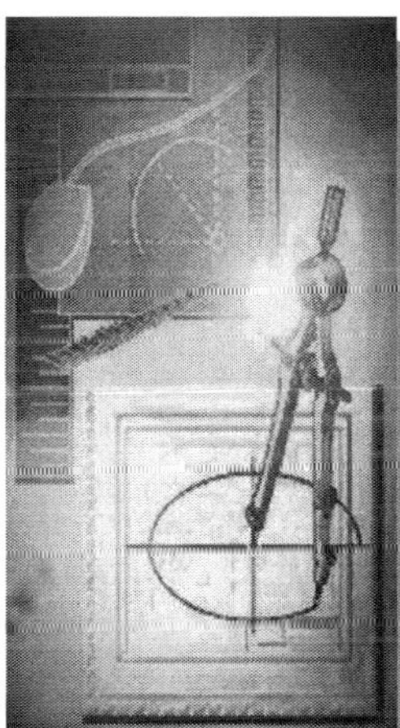

Learning Objectives

- **Create Simulation Study**
- **Apply Fixtures and Loads**
- **Perform Basic Stress Analysis**
- **View Results**
- **Assess Accuracy of Results**
- **Output the Associated Simulation Video File**

Introduction

In this chapter we will explore basic design analysis using the *Inventor Stress Analysis Module*. The *Stress Analysis Module* is a special module available for part, sheet metal, and assembly documents. The *Stress Analysis Module* has commands unique to its purpose. With Autodesk Inventor 2027, *contact analysis*, *frame analysis* and *dynamic analysis* can also be performed.

Inventor Stress Analysis Module provides a tool for basic stress analysis, allowing the user to examine the effects of applied forces on a design. Displacements, strains and stresses in a part are calculated based on material properties, fixtures, and applied loads. Stress results can be compared to material properties, such as yield strength, to perform failure analysis. The results can also be used to identify critical areas, calculate safety factors at various regions, and simulate deformation. *Inventor Stress Analysis Module* provides an easy-to-use method within the Autodesk Inventor's *Stress Analysis Module* to perform an initial stress analysis. The results can be used to improve the design.

In *Inventor Stress Analysis Module*, stresses are calculated using **linear static analysis** based on the **finite element method**. *Linear static analysis* is appropriate if deflections are small and vary only slowly. *Linear static analysis* omits time as a variable. It also excludes plastic action and deflections that change the way loads are applied. The *finite element method (FEM)* is a numerical method for finding approximate solutions to complex systems. The technique is widely used for the solution of complex problems in engineering mechanics. Analysis using the method is called *finite element analysis (FEA)*.

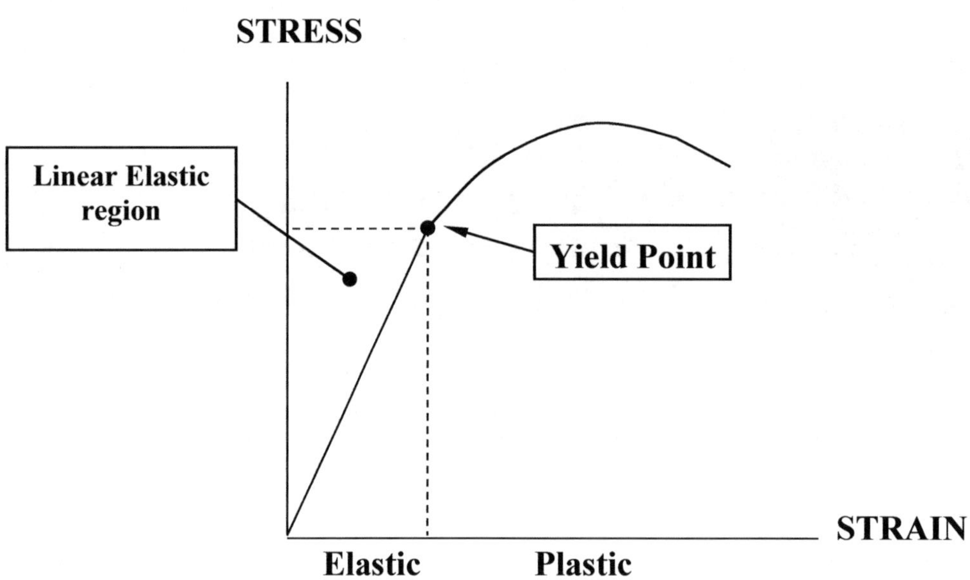

Stress-Strain diagram of typical ductile material

In the finite element method, a complex system is modeled as an equivalent system of smaller bodies of simple shapes, or *elements*, which are interconnected at common points called *nodes*. This process is called *discretization*; an example is shown in the figures below. The mathematical equations for the system are formulated first for each finite element, and the resulting system of equations is solved simultaneously to obtain an approximate solution for the entire system. In general, a better approximation is obtained by increasing the number of elements, which will require more computing time and resources.

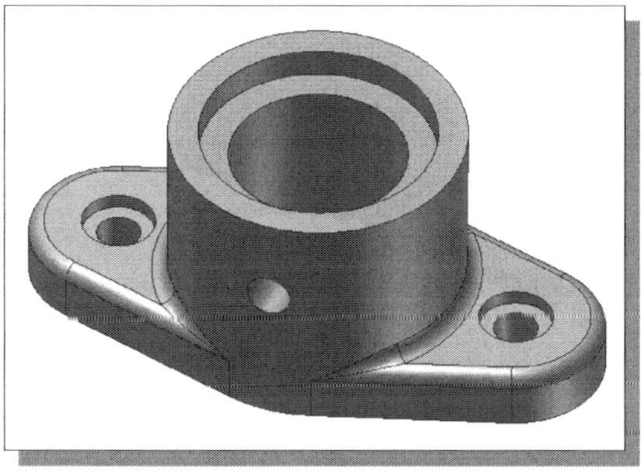

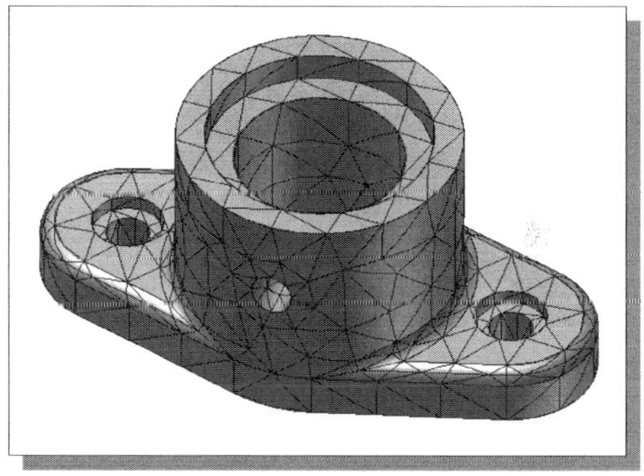

Inventor Stress Analysis Module utilizes tetrahedral elements for which the edges and faces can be curvilinear and which allow the modeling of curved surfaces, as seen in the figure above. The behavior of these elements is analyzed using linear static analysis and the appropriate material properties to relate local coordinate nodal displacements to local forces. The motion of each node is described by displacements in the X, Y, and Z directions, called *degrees of freedom* (DOFs). The equations describing the behavior of each element are assembled into a global system of equations, incorporating compatibility requirements based on connectivity among elements. Using the known material properties, supports, and loads, *Inventor Stress Analysis Module* solves the system of equations for the unknown displacements at each node. These displacements are used in the results stage to calculate strains and stresses.

While *Inventor Stress Analysis Module* is a powerful and easy-to-use tool, it is important to appreciate that it is the designer's responsibility to properly assess the accuracy of the results. A better FEA approximation is generally obtained by increasing the number of elements. An assessment must be made regarding the mesh used to discretize the model to ensure it is adequate. There are other important factors affecting the accuracy of the results. The material properties used in the analysis must accurately characterize the behavior of the material. The supports and loads must be applied in a manner which accurately reflects the actual conditions. Proper meshing and application of boundary conditions often require significant experience in FEA and may require tools and capabilities not available in *Inventor Stress Analysis Module*. *Inventor Stress Analysis Module* is an easy-to-use tool for a quick stress analysis.

Problem Statement

Determine the maximum normal stress that loading produces in the aluminum plate.

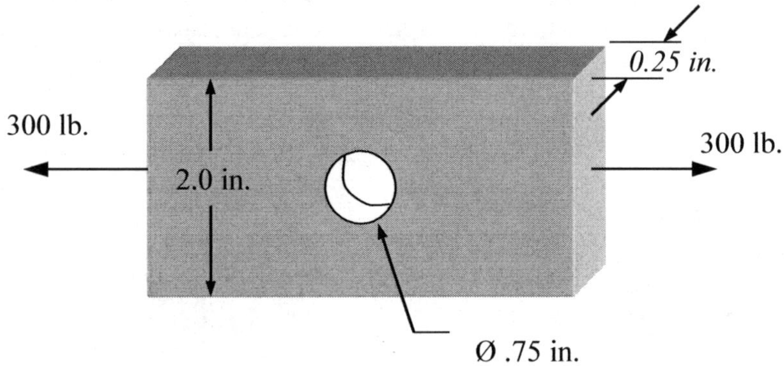

Preliminary Analysis

- **Maximum Normal Stress**
  The nominal normal stress developed at the smallest cross section (through the center of the hole) in the plate is

$$\sigma_{nominal} = \frac{P}{A} = \frac{300}{(2 - 0.75) \times .25} = 960 \text{ psi.}$$

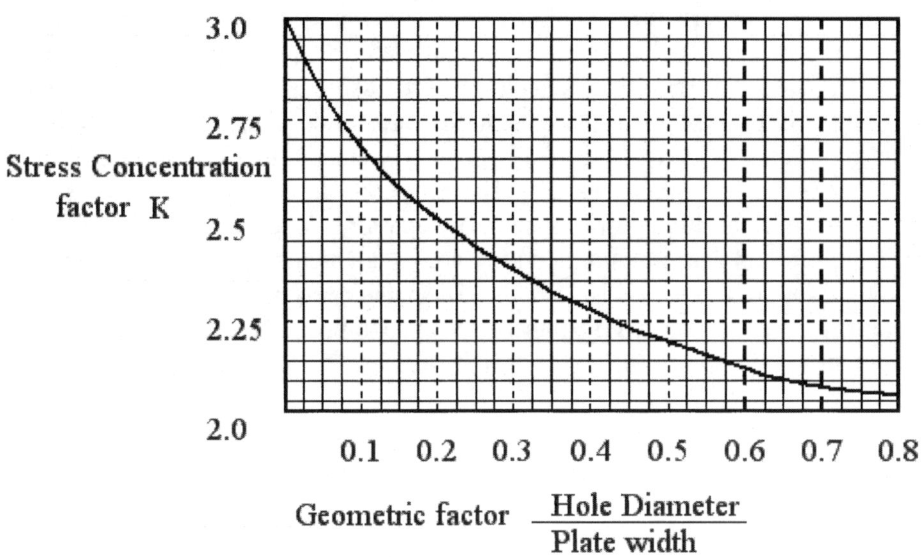

Geometric factor = .75/2 = 0.375
Stress concentration factor K is obtained from the graph, **K = 2.27**

$$\sigma_{MAX} = K\,\sigma_{nominal} = 2.27 \times 960 = 2180 \text{ psi.}$$

- **Maximum Displacement**
  We will also estimate the displacement under the loading condition. For a statically determinant system the stress results depend mainly on the geometry. The material properties can be in error and still the FEA analysis comes up with the same stresses. However, the displacements always depend on the material properties. Thus, it is necessary to always estimate both the stress and displacement prior to a computer FEA analysis.

  The classic one-dimensional displacement can be used to estimate the displacement of the problem:

$$\delta = \frac{PL}{EA}$$

Where P=force, L=length, A=area, E= elastic modulus, and δ = deflection.

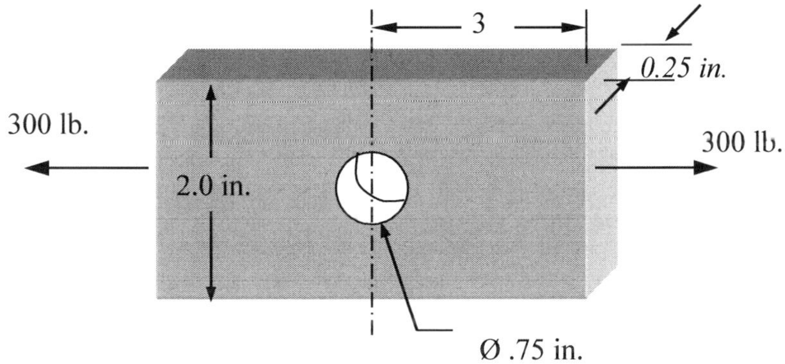

A lower bound of the displacement of the right-edge, measured from the center of the plate, is obtained by using the full area:

$$\delta_{lower} = \frac{PL}{EA} = \frac{300 \times 3}{10E6 \times (2 \times 0.25)} = 1.8E\text{-}4 \text{ in.}$$

and an upper bound of the displacement would come from the reduced section:

$$\delta_{upper} = \frac{PL}{EA} = \frac{300 \times 3}{10E6X(1.25 \times 0.25)} = 2.88E\text{-}4 \text{ in.}$$

but the best estimate is a sum from the two regions:

$$\delta_{average} = \frac{PL}{EA} = \frac{300 \times 0.375}{10E6 \times (1.25 \times 0.25)} + \frac{300 \times 2.625}{10E6 \times (2.0X0.25)}$$

$$= 3.6E\text{-}5 + 1.58E\text{-}4 = 1.94E\text{-}4 \text{ in.}$$

Finite Element Analysis Procedure

In the previous section, an approximate preliminary analysis was performed prior to carrying out the finite element analysis; this will help us to gain some insights into the problem and also serves as a means of checking the finite element analysis results.

For a typical linear static analysis problem, the finite element analysis requires the following steps:

1. Preliminary Analysis.

2. Preparation of the finite element model:
   a. Model the problem into finite elements.
   b. Prescribe the geometric and material information of the system.
   c. Prescribe how the system is supported.
   d. Prescribe how the loads are applied to the system.

3. Perform calculations:
   a. Generate a stiffness matrix of each element.
   b. Assemble the individual stiffness matrices to obtain the overall, or global, stiffness matrix.
   c. Solve the global equations and compute displacements, strains, and stresses.

4. Post-processing of the results:
   a. Viewing the stress contours and the displaced shape.
   b. Checking any discrepancy between the preliminary analysis results and the FEA results.

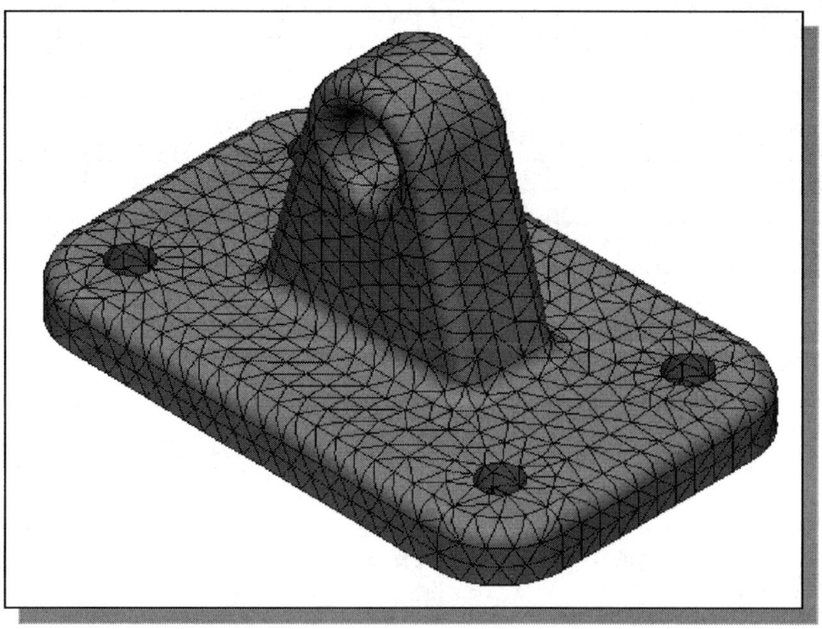

Create the Autodesk Inventor Part

1. Select the **Autodesk Inventor** option on the *Start* menu or select the **Autodesk Inventor** icon on the desktop to start Autodesk Inventor. The Autodesk Inventor main window will appear on the screen.

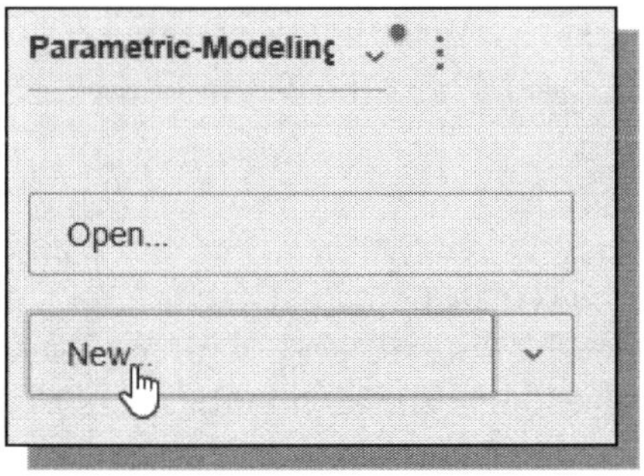

2. Select the **New File** icon with a single click of the left-mouse-button as shown.

3. Select the **English** tab, and in the *New File* area select **Standard(in).ipt**.

4. Pick **Create** in the *New File* dialog box to accept the selected settings.

Create the 2D Sketch for the Plate

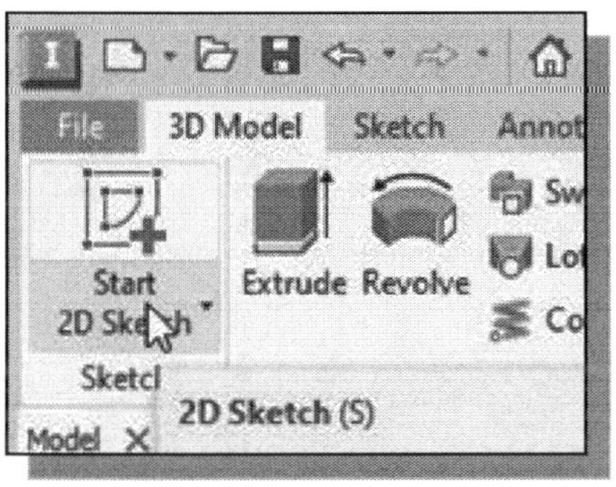

1. In the *3D Model* tab select the **Start 2D Sketch** command by left-clicking once on the icon.

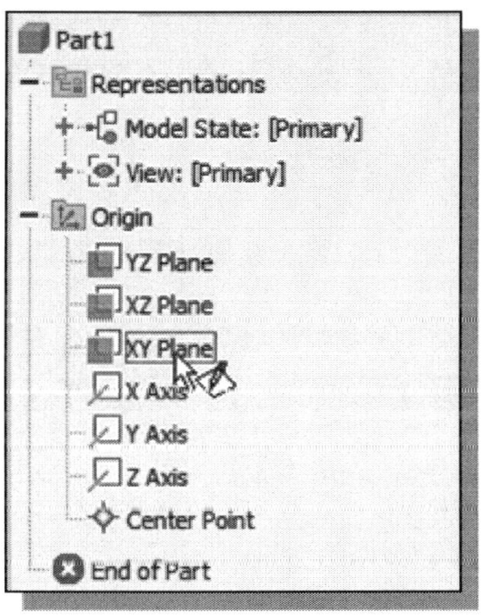

2. In the *Status Bar* area, the message "*Select plane to create sketch or an existing sketch to edit.*" is displayed. Select the **XY Plane** by clicking the associated item in the graphics area or inside the *Model* history tree window or in the graphics window.

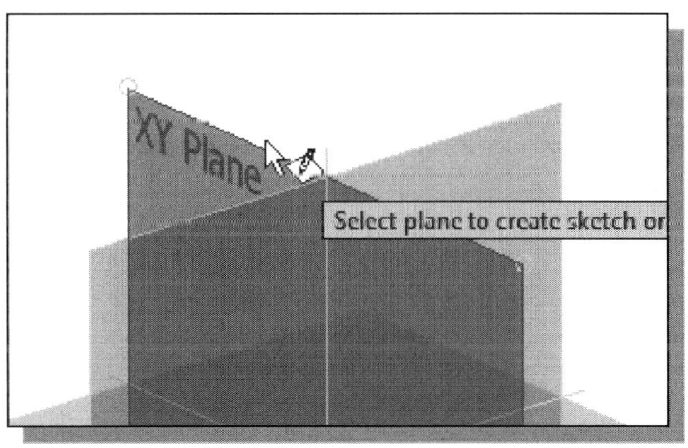

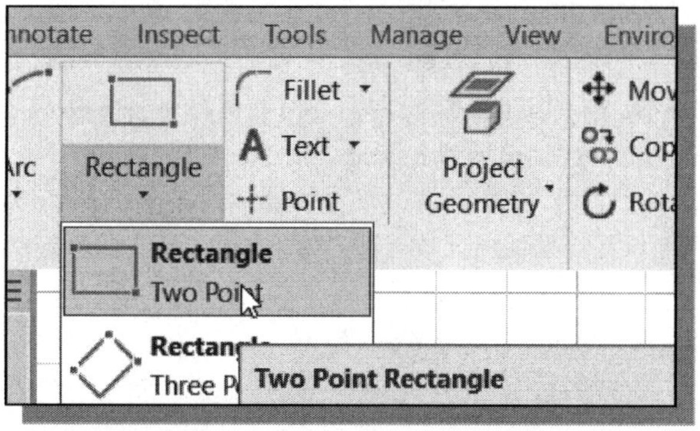

3. Select the **Two point rectangle** command by clicking once with the left-mouse-button on the icon in the *Sketch* toolbar.

4. Create a rectangle of arbitrary size positioned near the center of the screen.

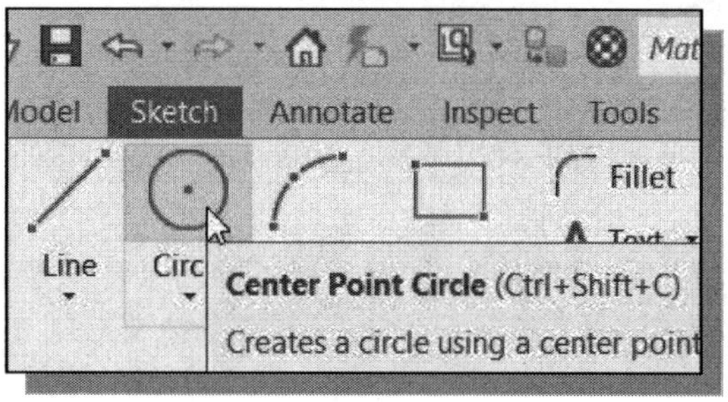

5. Select the **Center Point Circle** command by clicking once with the left-mouse-button on the icon in the *Sketch* toolbar.

6. Create a **circle** of arbitrary size and aligned to the *center point* as shown.

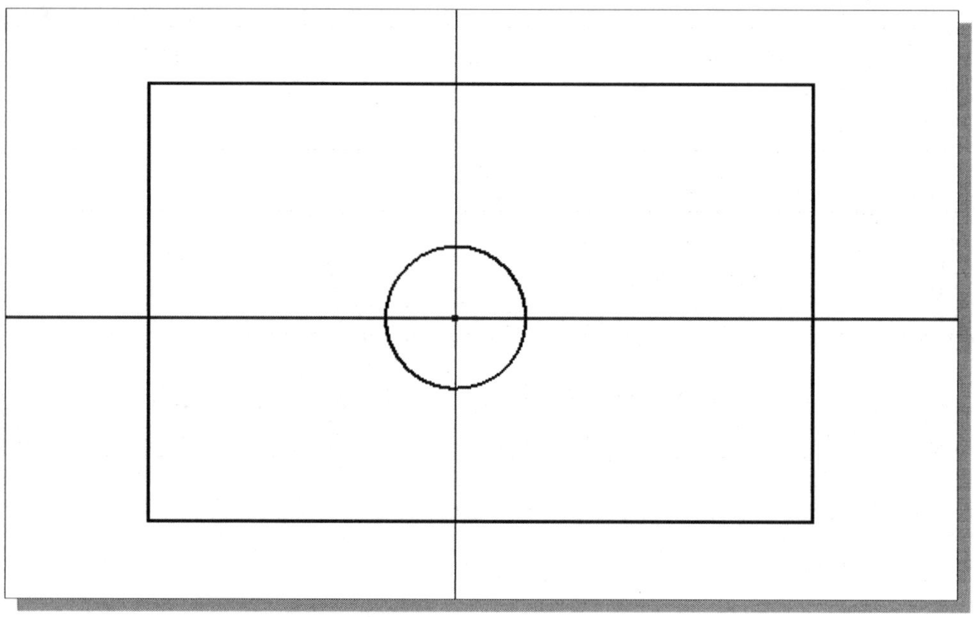

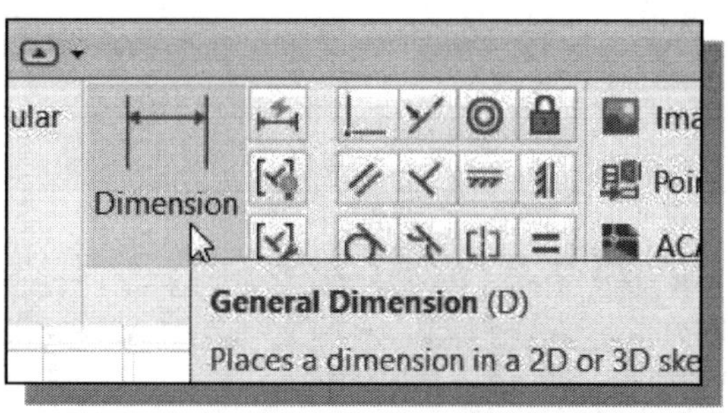

7. Select the **General Dimension** command in the *Constrain* panel.

8. On your own, create and adjust the dimensions of the rectangle and circle as shown. (Hint: Use parametric equations to position the geometry.)

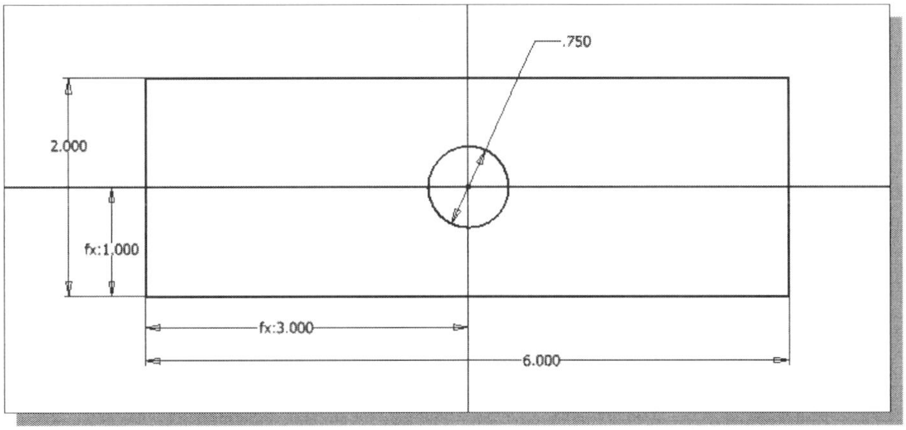

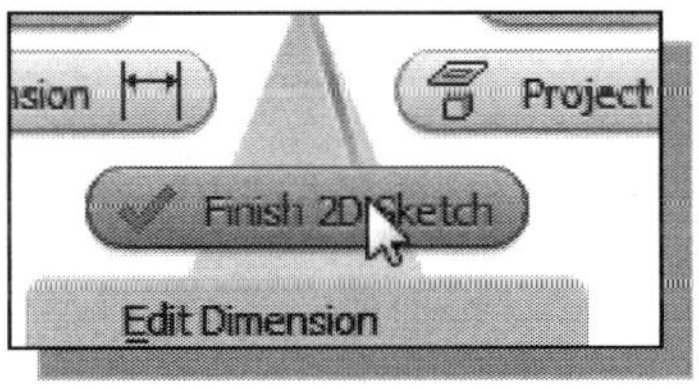

9. Inside the *graphics window*, click once with the right-mouse-button to display the option menu. Select **Finish 2D Sketch** in the pop-up menu to end the Sketch option.

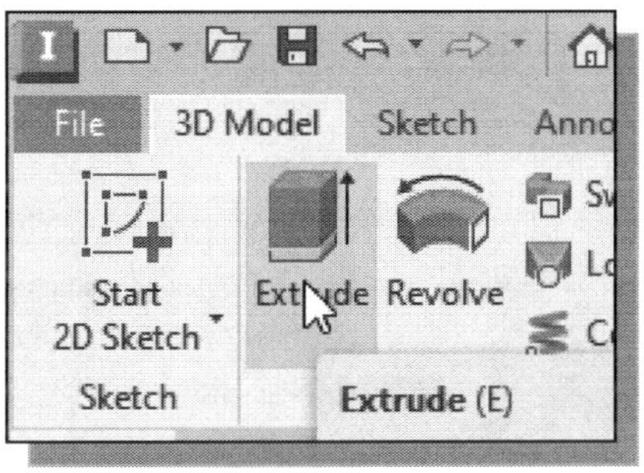

10. In the *3D Model* toolbar, select the **Extrude** command by left-clicking on the icon.

11. On your own, create an **Extruded** feature with a thickness of **0.25 in** as shown.

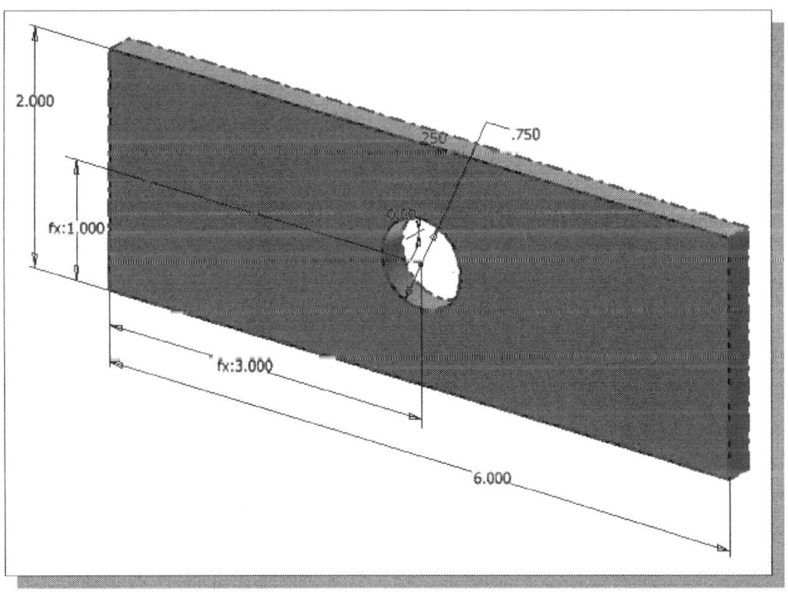

Assigning the Material Properties

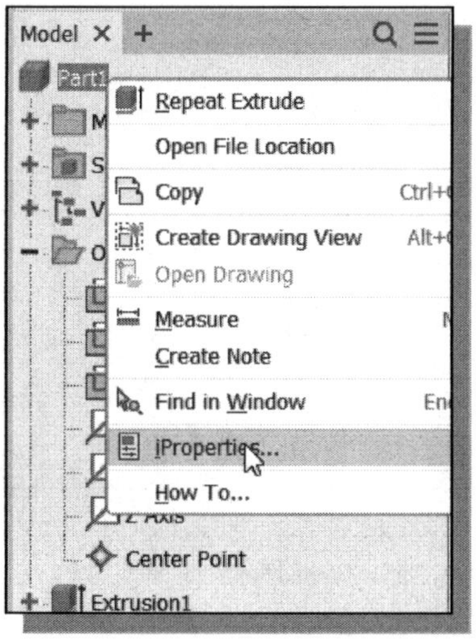

1. In the *browser*, **right-click** once on the ***part name*** to bring up the option menu, and then pick **iProperties** in the *pop-up* menu.

2. On your own, look at the different information listed in the *iProperties* dialog box.

3. Click on the **Physical** tab; this is the page that contains the physical properties of the selected model.

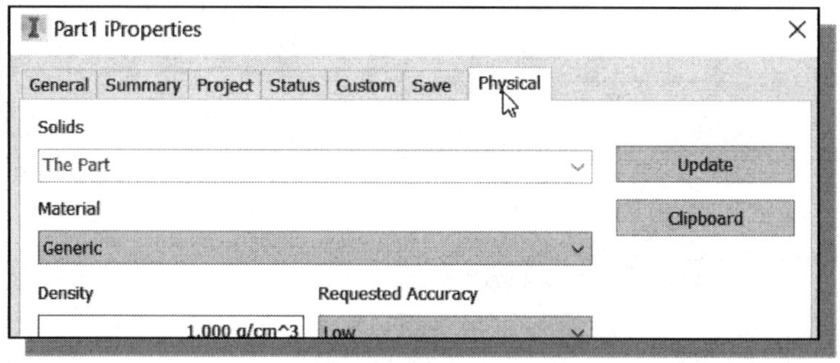

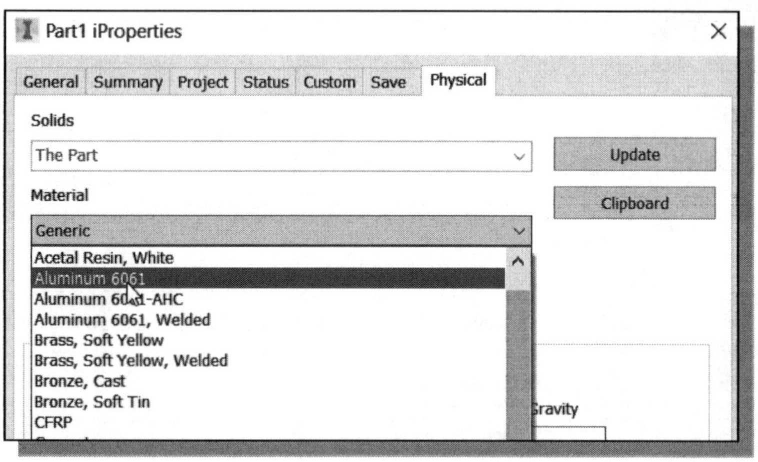

4. Click the down-arrow in the *Material* option to display the material list, and select **Aluminum-6061** as shown.

5. Click **OK** to accept the settings.

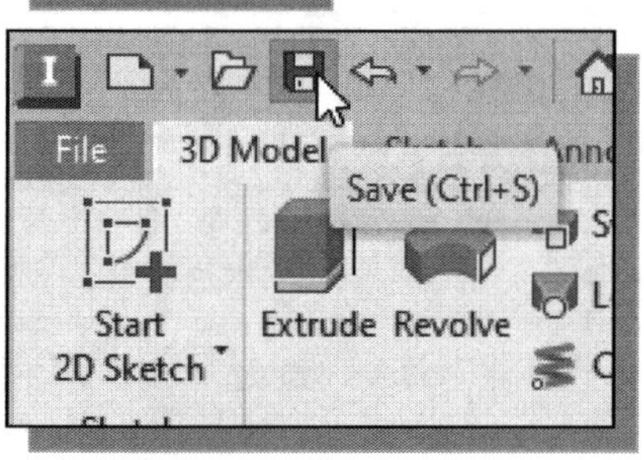

6. On your own, save the part with the filename **FEA_Al_Plate.ipt**.

Switch to the Stress Analysis Module

1. In the *Ribbon* toolbar, select the **Environments** tab as shown.

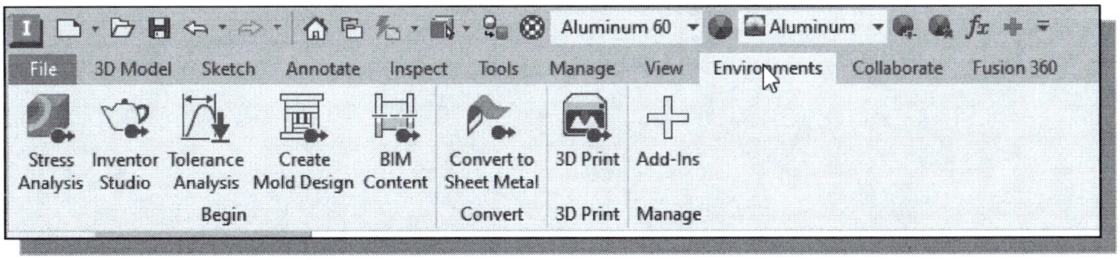

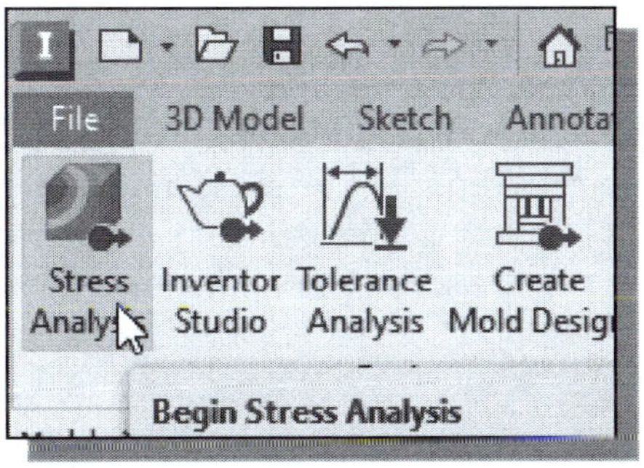

2. Click **Stress Analysis** to enter the *Inventor Stress Analysis Module.*

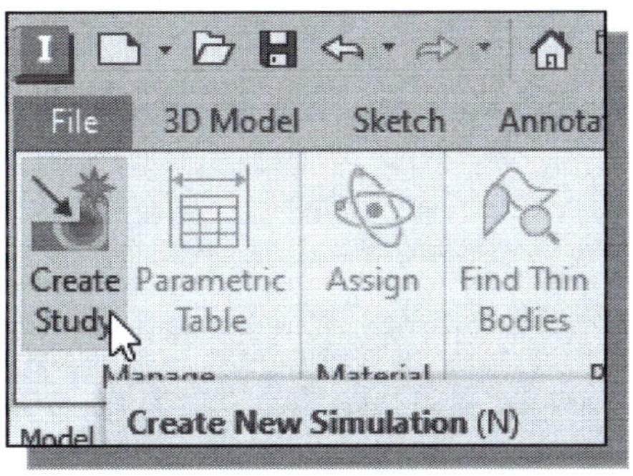

3. Click **Create New Simulation** to start a new simulation.

4. Note the default settings include (1) *Simulation Type* set to perform **Static Analysis** and (2) *Design Objective* set to **Single Point**. These settings are used for basic *linear static analysis.*

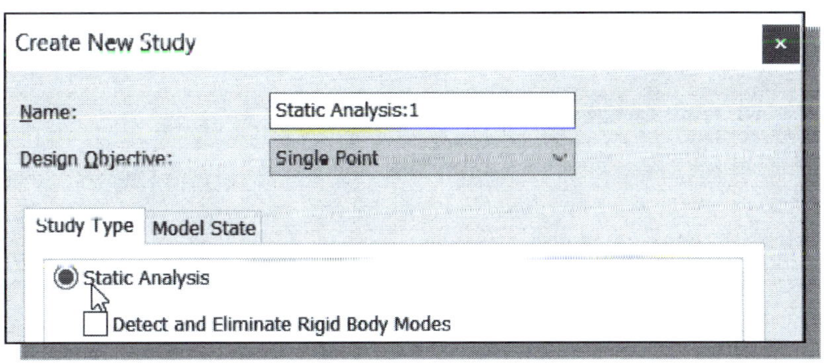

5. Click **OK** to accept the default settings.

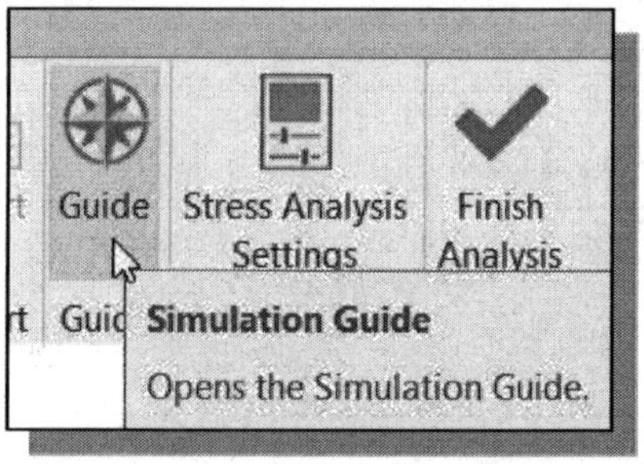

6. In the *Ribbon* toolbar, select the **Simulation Guide** icon as shown.

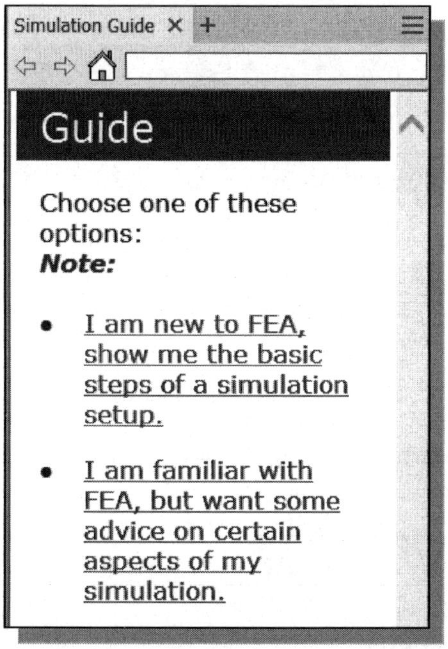

➤ Note the *Simulation Guide* provides an overall view of the Inventor FEA procedure. You are encouraged to read through the *Simulation Guide* to get familiar with the general procedure in performing the Inventor FEA simulation.

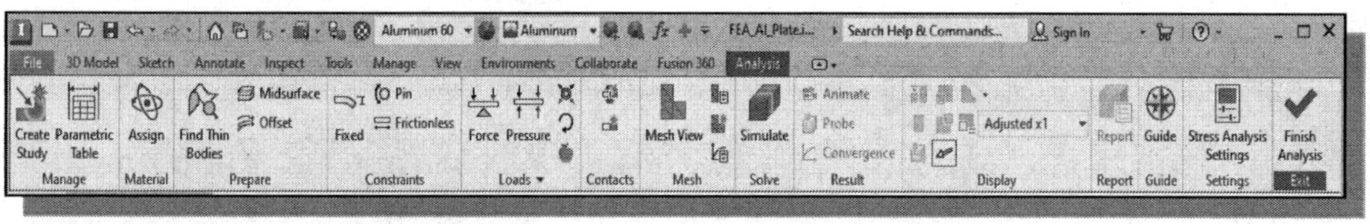

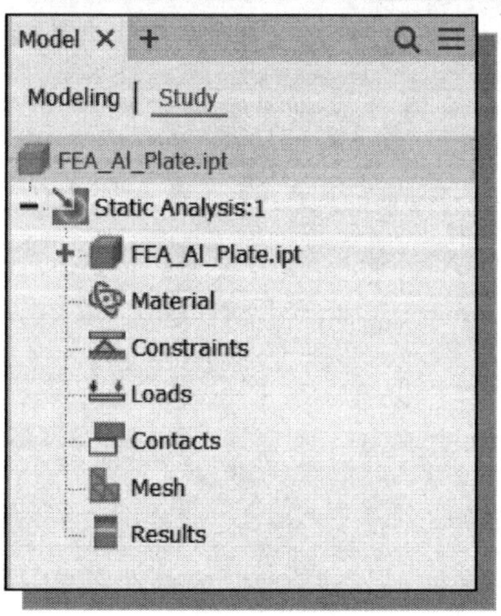

➤ Notice the *Ribbon* toolbar and the *browser* window, to the left side of the graphics area, now display items associated with the *Stress Analysis Simulation Module*. The list in the *browser* window shows the elements necessary to perform the *Finite Element Stress Analysis*.

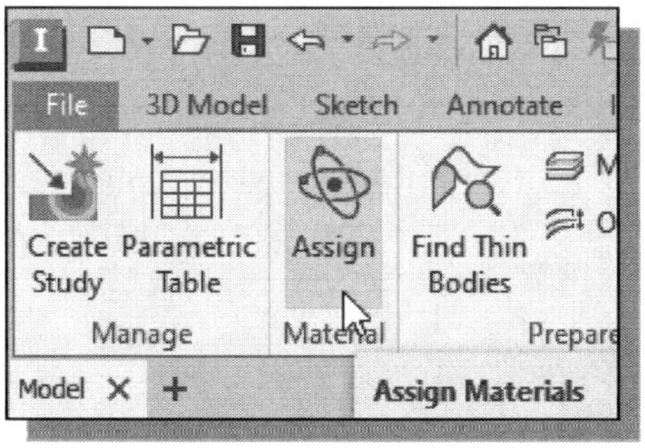

7. In the *Ribbon* toolbar area, select **Assign Materials** to examine the material assignment for the part.

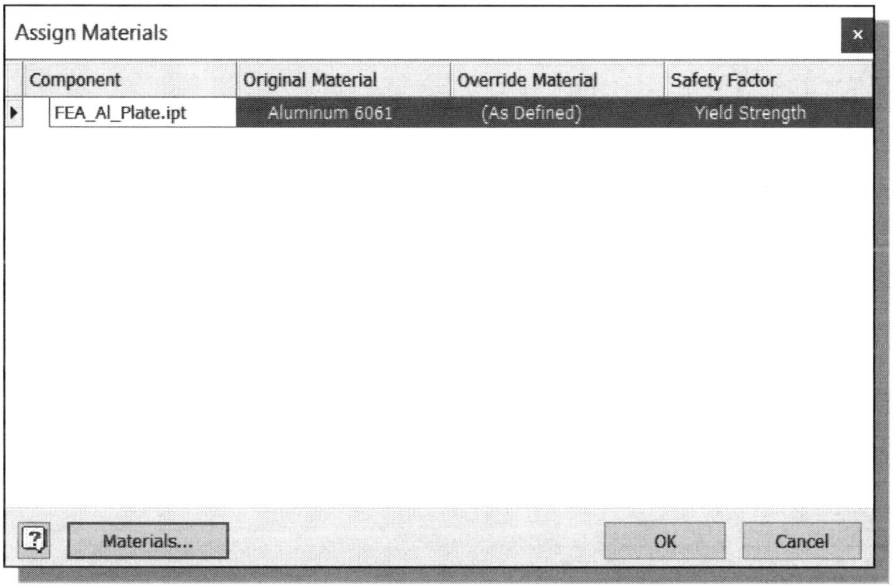

- Note that the assigned material, **Aluminum-6061**, is shown under the *Original Material*; the *Override Material* option is available for us to examine the effects of using different materials.

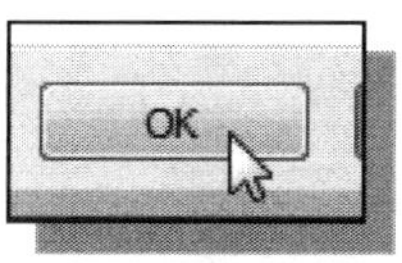

8. Click **OK** to accept the settings.

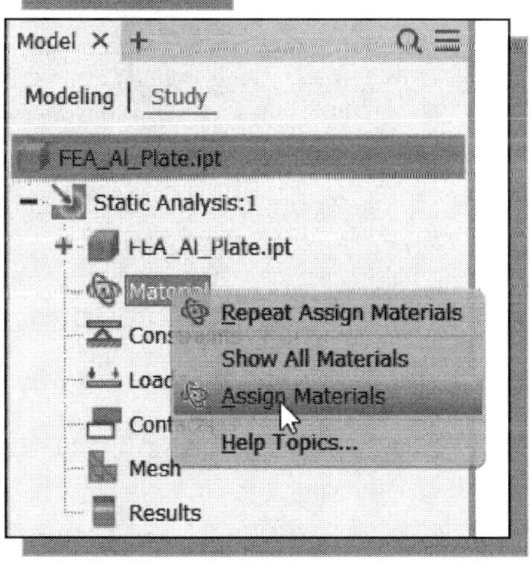

- Note that the same command can also be accessed through the *browser* window.

Apply Constraints and Loads

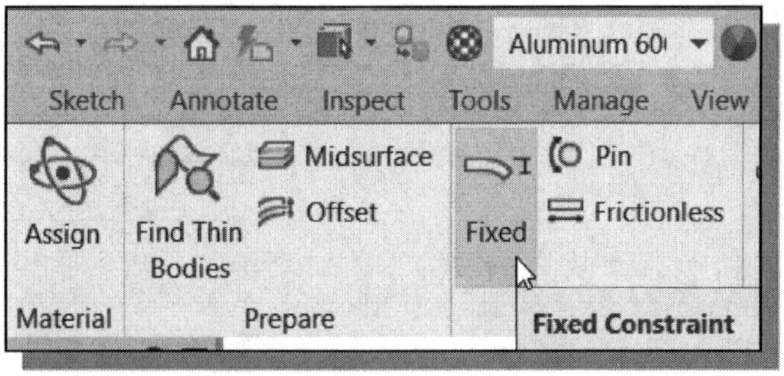

1. In the *Ribbon* toolbar area, select **Fixed Constraint** to assign the support condition of the plate.

2. Click on the **top left corner** of the *ViewCube* to rotate the display; the plate will be rotated 90 degrees showing the left vertical face of the plate.

3. Select the small **vertical surface** of the left-end of the plane as shown.

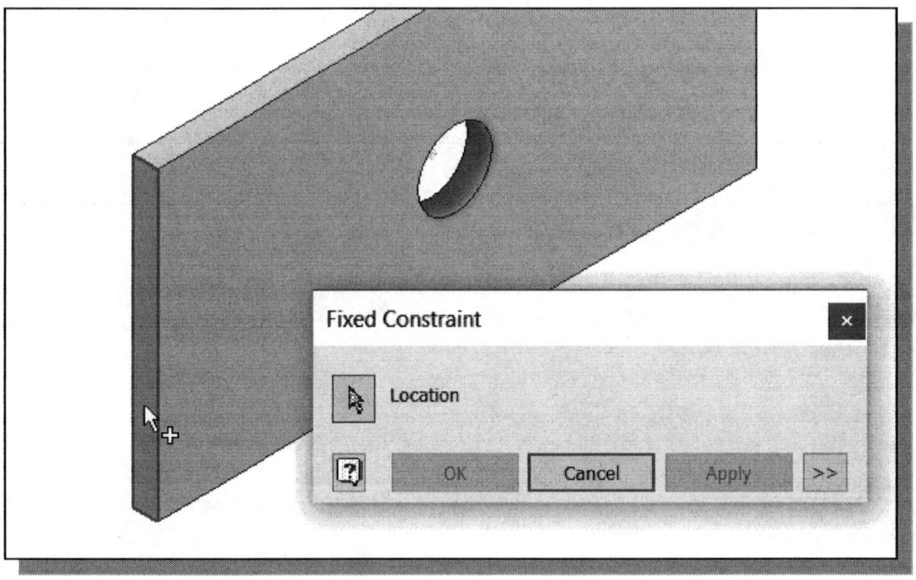

4. Note the selection of the surface is recognized as the selection label is changed to **Faces**. Click **OK** to accept the selection.

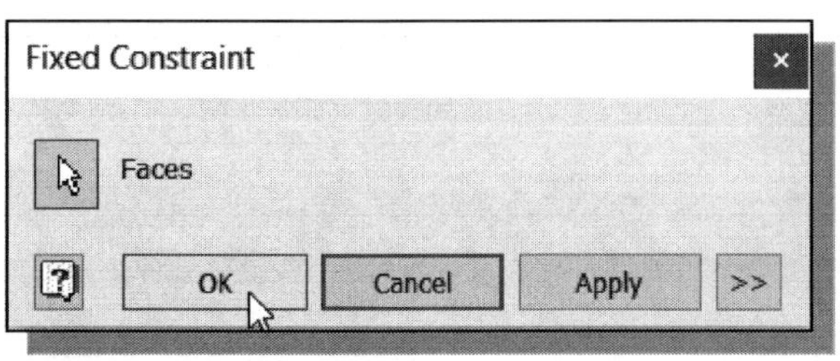

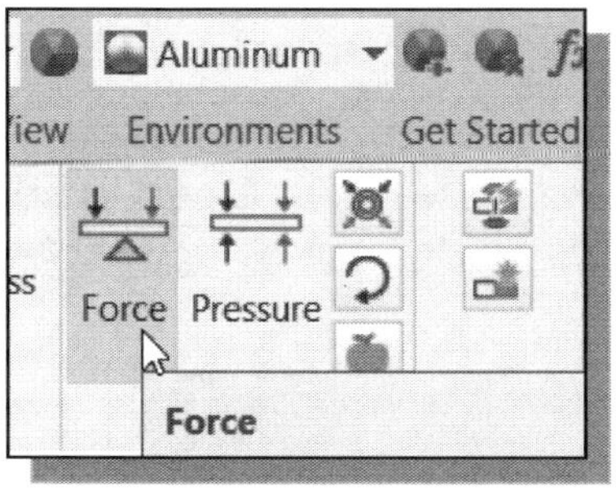

5. In the *Ribbon* toolbar area, select the **Force** command as shown.

6. Click on the **Home** icon above the *ViewCube* to reset the display back to the isometric view.

7. Click on the small vertical surface to the right end of the plate. In the *Force* dialog box, enter **300 lbf** as the force value and check the **Reverse Direction** option box. Notice the direction of the force load is now outward.

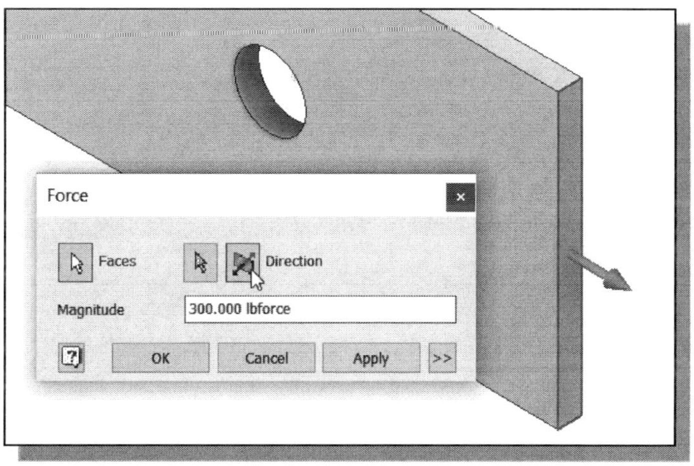

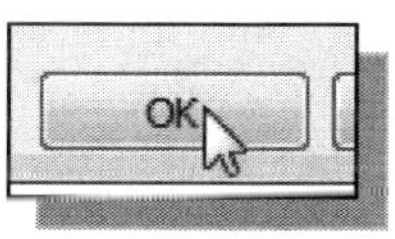

8. Click **OK** to accept the selection and exit the Force command.

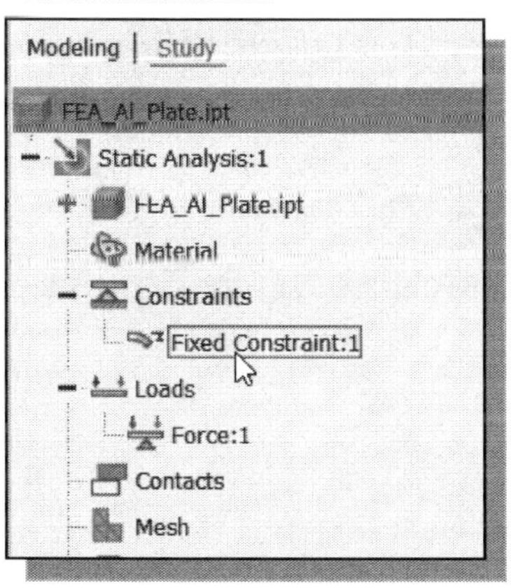

➢ Notice the Fixed constraint and Force load appear in the *browser* window to the left of the graphics area with the default names Constraint:1 and Force:1.

Create a Mesh and Run the Solver

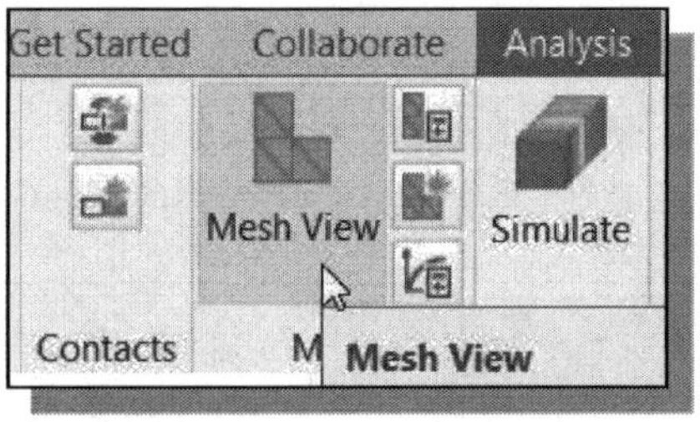

1. In the *Ribbon* toolbar area, select the **Mesh View** command as shown.

- Note that with the default settings, *Inventor Simulation* generated 653 nodes and 291 elements, which is a relatively coarse mesh.

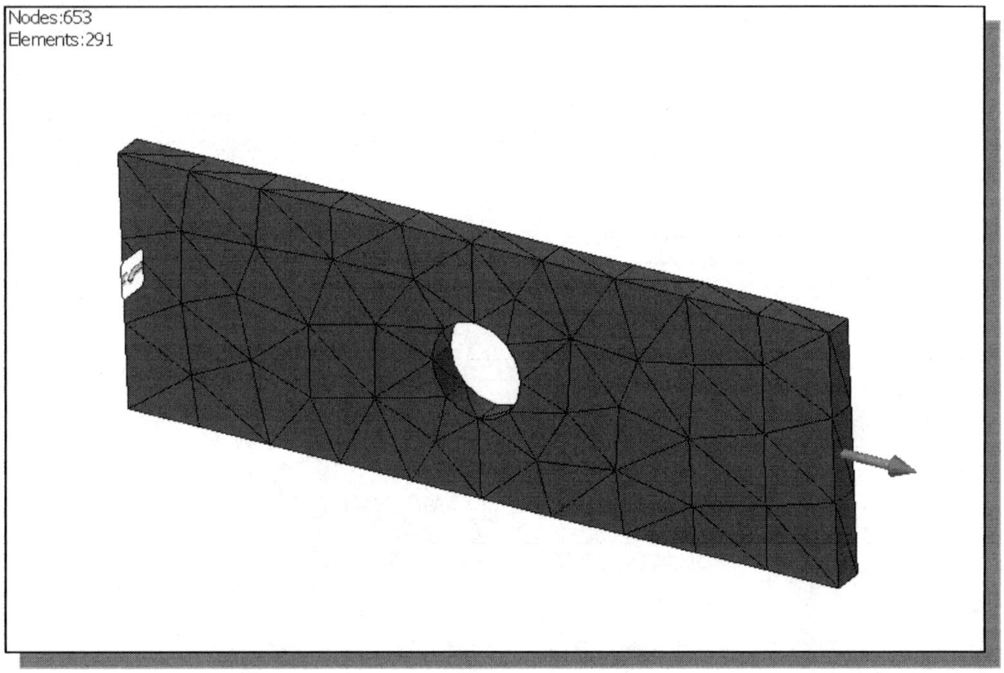

- As a rule in creating the first FEA mesh, start with a relatively small number of elements and progressively move to more refined models. The main objective of the first coarse mesh analysis is to obtain a rough idea of the overall stress distribution. In most cases, use of a complex and/or a very refined FEA model is not justifiable since it most likely provides computational accuracy at the expense of unnecessarily increased processing time.

2. In the *Ribbon* toolbar area, select the **Simulate** command as shown.

3. Click the **Run simulation** button to proceed with the FEA simulation.

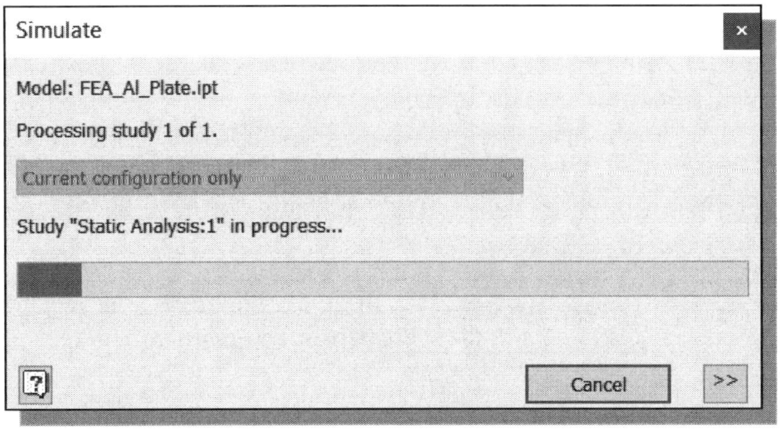

- Note that if the stress display does not look good, you might need to choose a different option of the *Visual Style* to find a better viewing of the stress result. Depending on the computer hardware, some settings might provide better viewing than others.

➢ A plot of equivalent stress (Von Mises stress) is generated and displayed in the graphics area. A color-coded scale is used with the associated scale bar displayed at the right. Red represents the regions of highest stress. The maximum stress is 2074 psi, which is well below the yield strength of the material (3999.3 psi) and is located at the stress concentration points at the upper and lower quadrants of the hole.

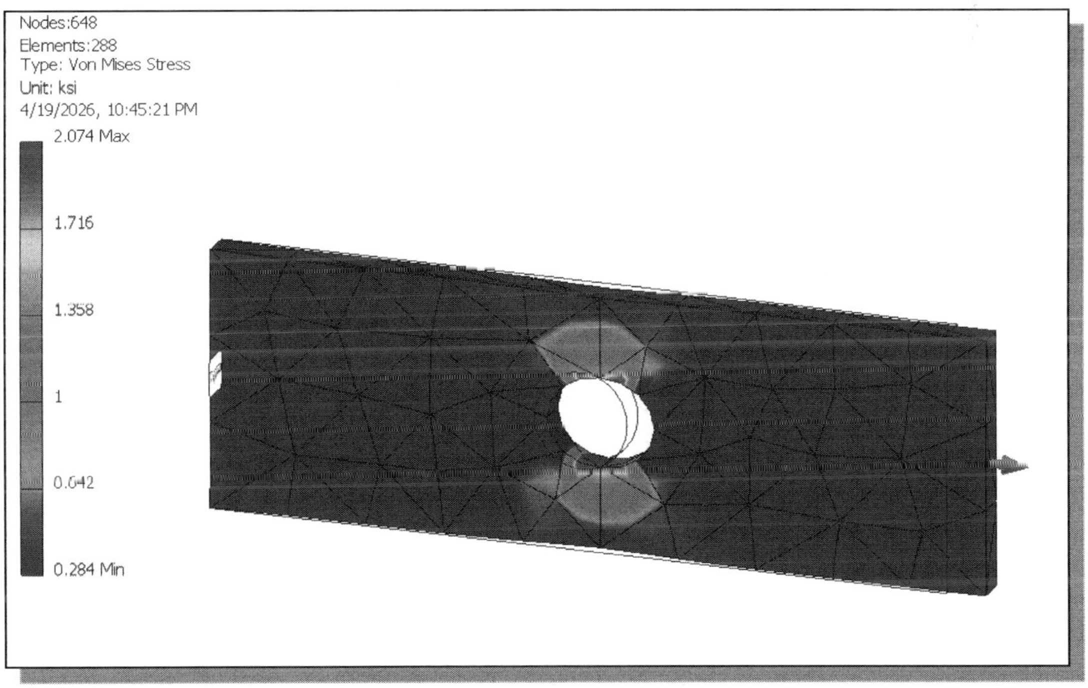

Refinement of the FEA Mesh – Global Element Size

In order to gain accuracy for complex geometries or to represent a highly varying stress distribution, finer elements must be used. The increase in the number of elements will also increase the solution time and computer disk space. This is why the refinement of mesh around the high stress areas is required. The process of mesh refinement is called convergence analysis. As our first analysis confirmed the stress concentration points at the upper and lower quadrants of the hole, we will next refine the mesh to obtain a more accurate FEA result. One way of refinement is simply to adjust the element size to a smaller value. This can be done through adjusting the **Mesh Settings**.

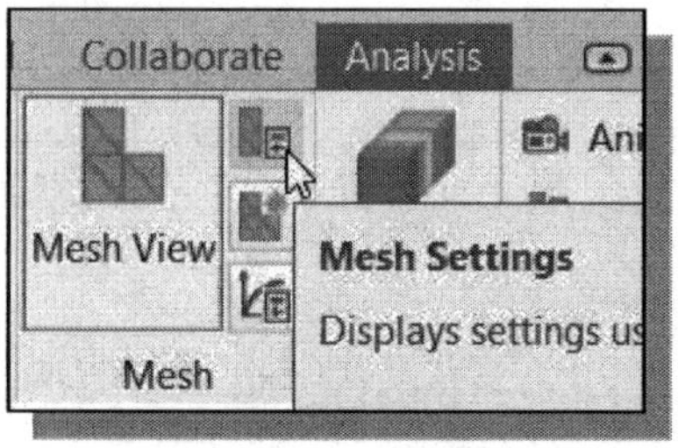

1. In the *Ribbon* toolbar area, select the **Mesh Settings** command as shown.

2. In the *Mesh Settings* dialog box, adjust the *Average Element Size* to **0.05**, which will create twice as many elements. Note the number is a fraction of the length dimension of the plate.

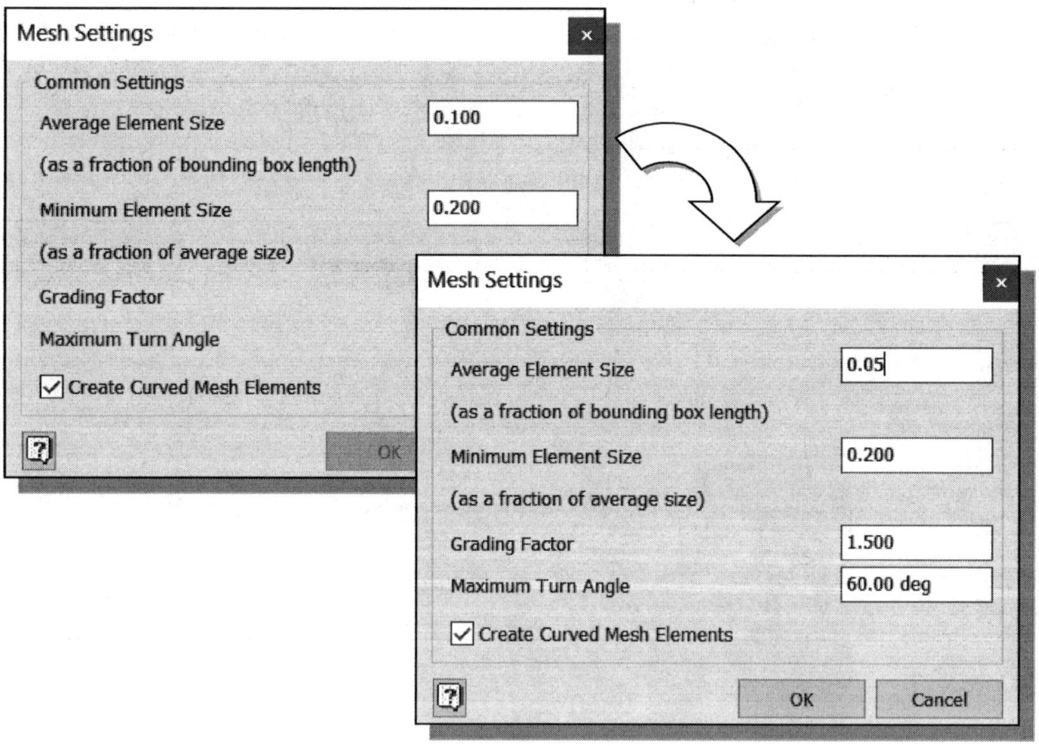

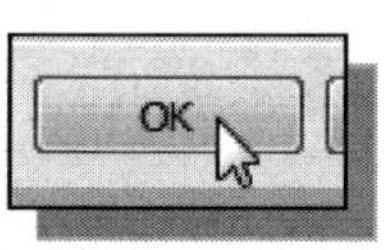

3. Click **OK** to accept the new settings and exit the Mesh Settings command.

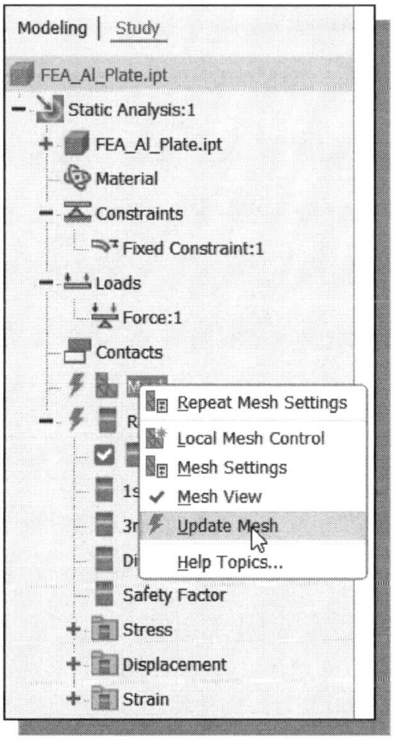

4. It is necessary to update the mesh with the new settings through the *browser* window. Right-click on the **Mesh** item to bring up the **option list**.

5. Select **Update Mesh** in the option list to activate the mesh update.

- Note that with the new settings, *Inventor Simulation* generated 1931 nodes and 907 elements, which is almost three times more than the original coarse mesh.

6. On your own, perform the FEA analysis.

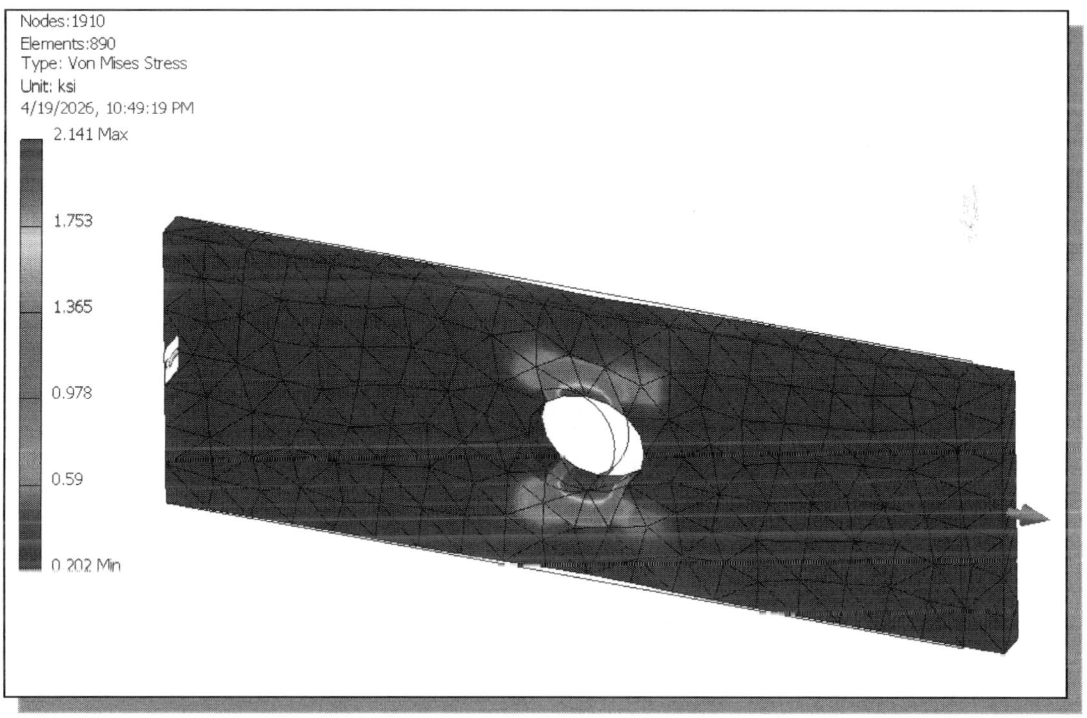

➢ The maximum stress with the refinement is now 2141psi, which is higher than the previous FEA analysis, and very close to the preliminary analysis. Next, we will further refine the mesh in the high stress area.

Refinement of the FEA Mesh – Local Element Size

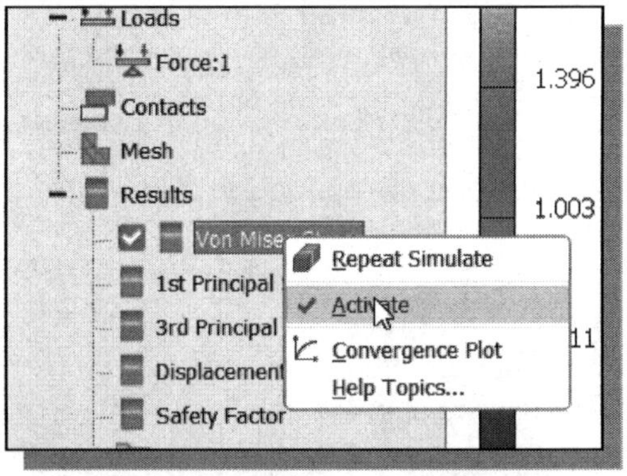

1. In the *browser* window, right-click on the **Von Mises Stress** item to bring up the *option list* and **de-activate** the result as shown.

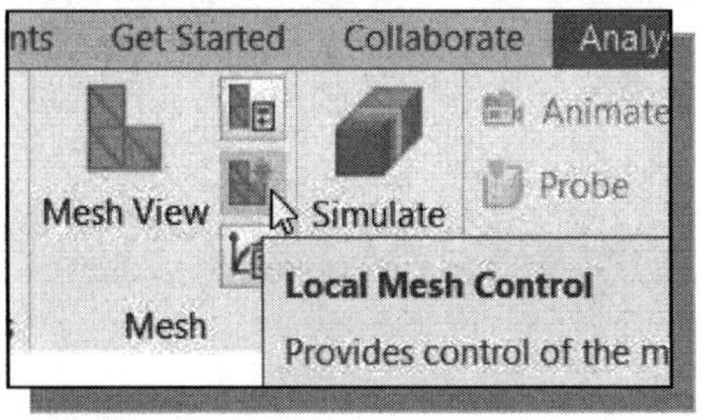

2. In the *Ribbon* toolbar area, select the **Local Mesh Control** command as shown.

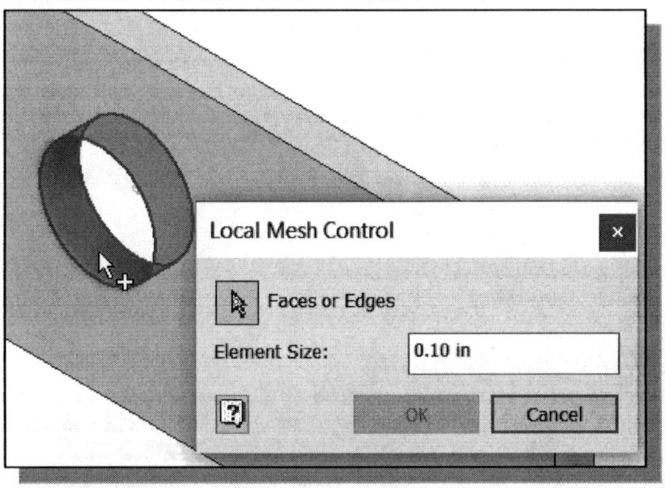

3. Select the **inside cylindrical surface** of the hole as shown.

4. Set the local *Element Size* to **0.1** as shown.

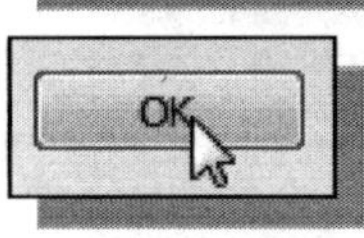

5. Click **OK** to accept the new setting and exit the Local Mesh Control command.

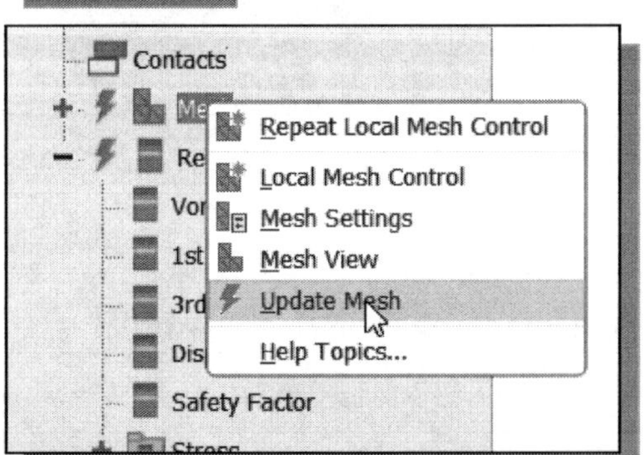

6. On your own, activate the **Update Mesh** command as shown.

- Note that with the new settings, *Inventor Simulation* generated 4378 nodes and 2404 elements, which is about seven times the original coarse mesh.

7. On your own, perform the FEA analysis.

- The maximum stress with the refinement is now 2189 psi, which is just a bit higher than the previous FEA analysis. The refinement caused only a small difference compared to the previous mesh.

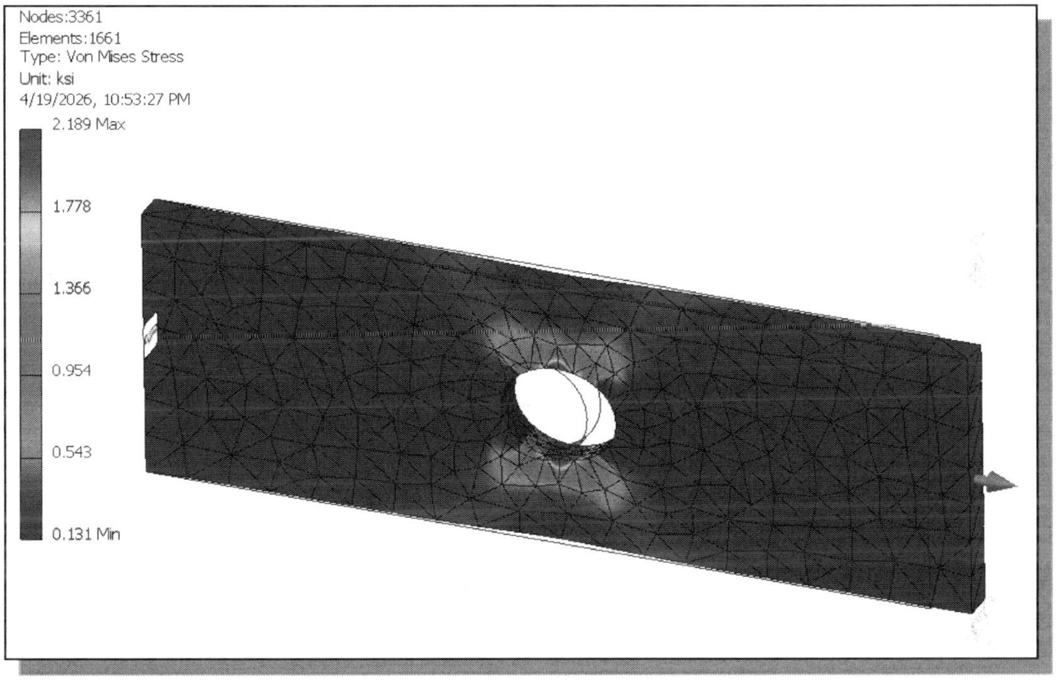

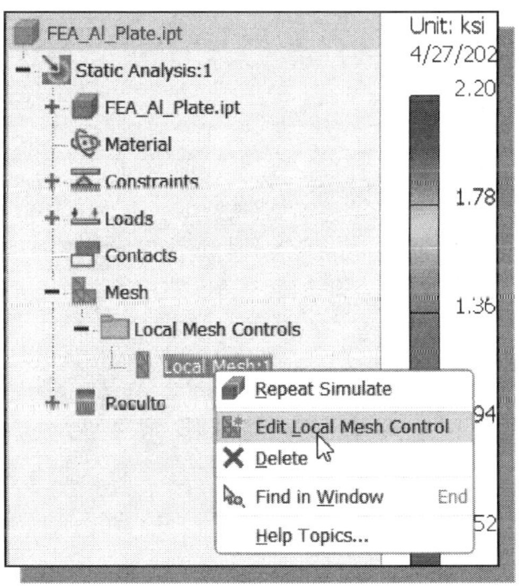

8. On your own, adjust the element size to **0.05** of the **Local Mesh Control** value as shown.

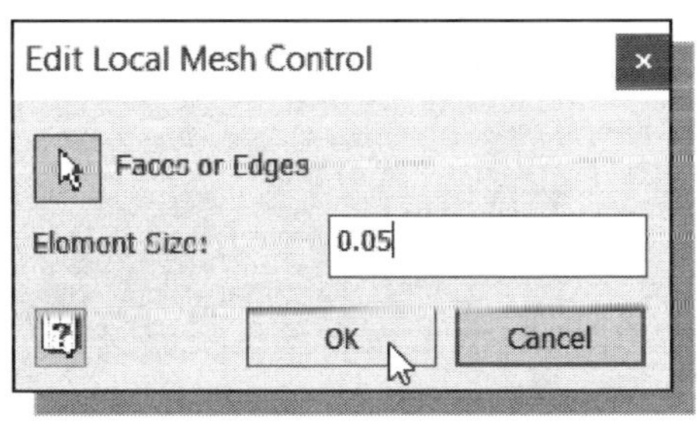

9. On your own, perform another FEA with the current settings.

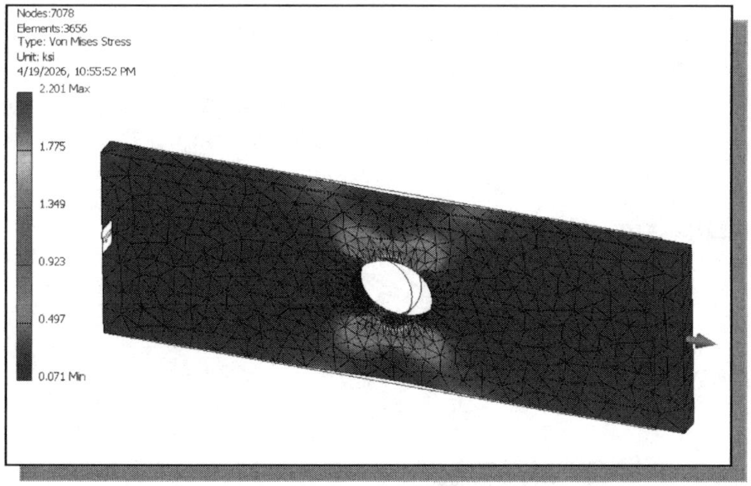

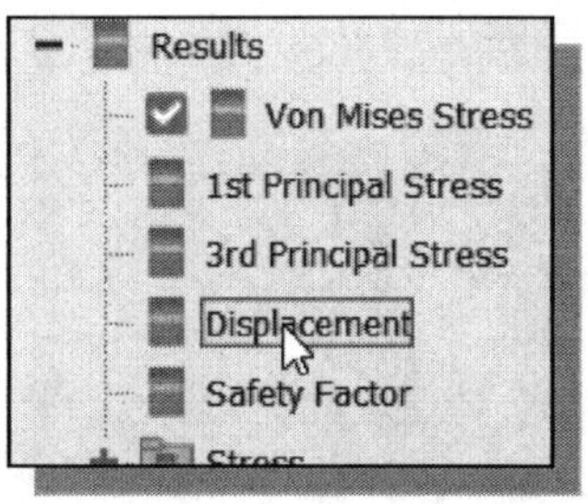

10. Double-click on the **Displacement** item in the *browser* window to display the displacement of the plate.

- The FEA result showed the total displacement of 4.053e-4 inch, which matches quite well with the 3.88e-4 inch preliminary analysis estimate.

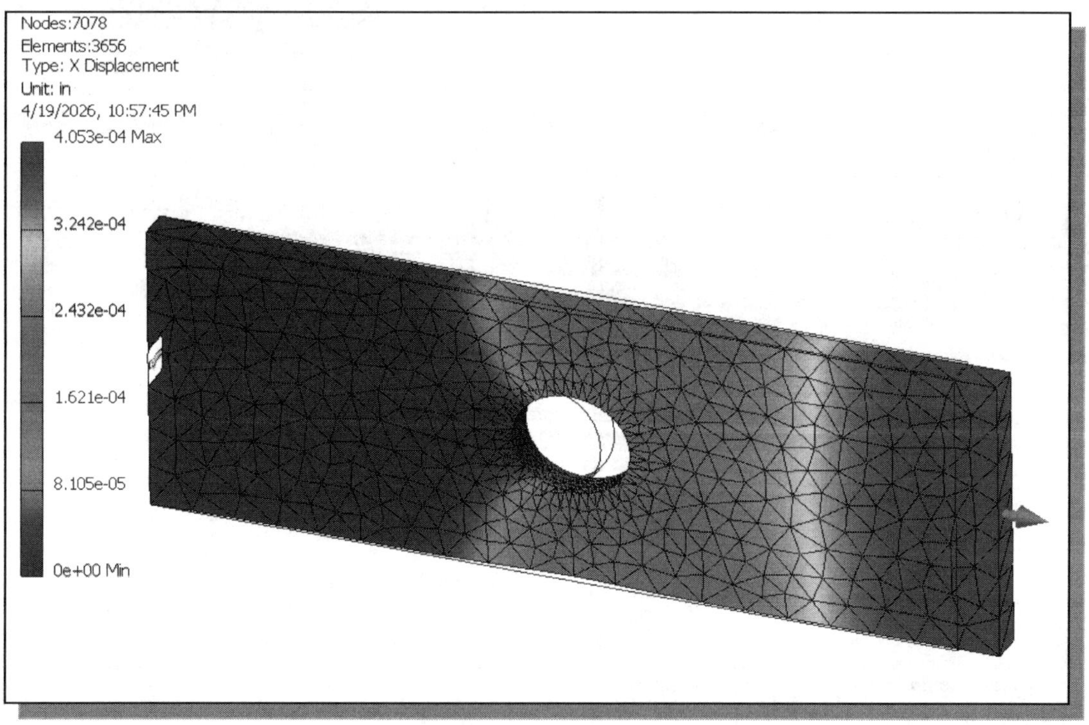

Comparison of Results

The accuracy of the *Inventor Simulation* results for this problem can be checked by comparing them to the analytical results presented earlier. In the **Preliminary Analysis** section, the maximum stress was calculated using a stress concentration factor and the value obtained was **2180 psi**. One should realize the analytical result is obtained through the use of charts from empirical data and therefore involves some degrees of error. The maximum stress obtained by finite element analysis using *Inventor Simulation* ranges from **2074** to **2201 psi**. In the **Preliminary Analysis** section, the maximum displacement was also estimated to be around **1.94E-4 inches**, measured from the center of the hole to one end of the plate. The maximum displacement obtained by finite element analysis using *Inventor Simulation* was around **2.0285E-4 inches**. The agreement between the analytical results and those from *Inventor Simulation* demonstrates the potential of *Inventor Simulation* as a very powerful design tool.

In FEA, the process of mesh refinement is called convergence analysis. For our analysis, the refinement of the mesh does show the FEA results converging near the analytical results. The refinement to the third mesh is quite adequate for our analysis. Any further refinement does not provide any additional insight and is therefore not necessary.

Number of Elements	σ_{max} (psi)	D_{max} (in)
288	2074	2.024e-4
890	2141	2.027e-4
1661	2189	2.028e-4
3656	2201	2.027e-4

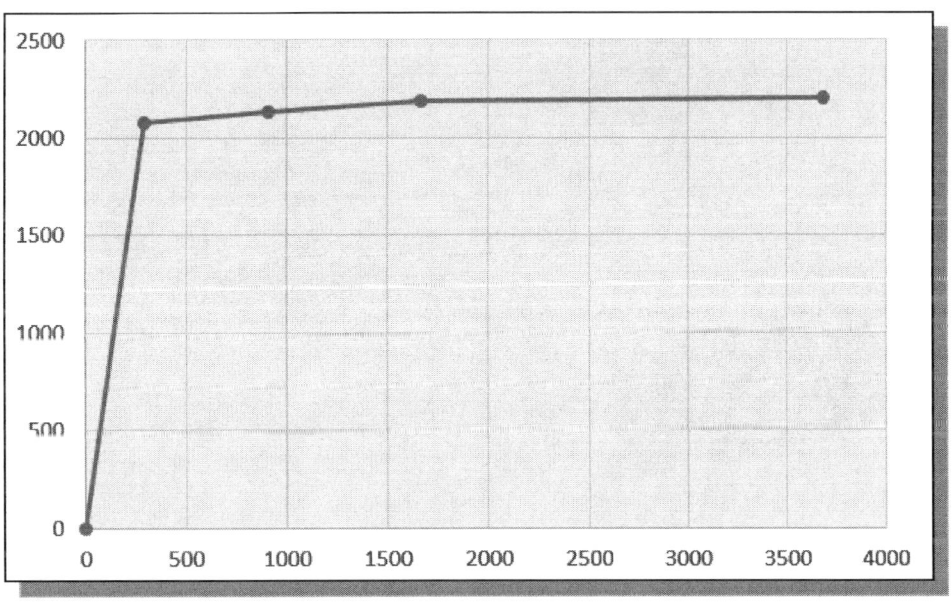

Create an HTML Report

Inventor Stress Analysis Simulation module also includes options to create a report in HTML format which contains data related to the simulation.

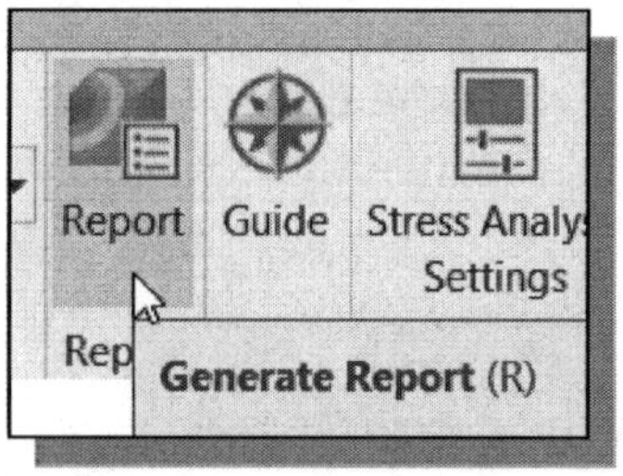

1. Select the **Report** option as shown.

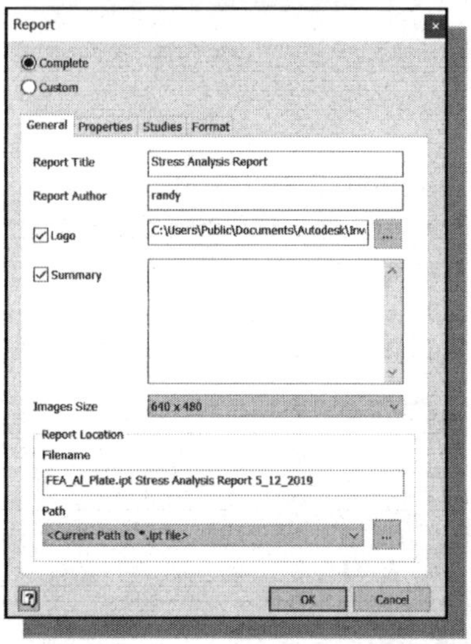

2. On your own, examine the different options available for the report. Click **OK** to generate a report.

➢ *Inventor Stress Analysis Environment* will create an HTML file and automatically open it in your default Web browser. The HTML file is saved in the location shown in the *File Information* section at the beginning of the report.

3. On your own, read through the report. Notice that all the relevant data are recorded.

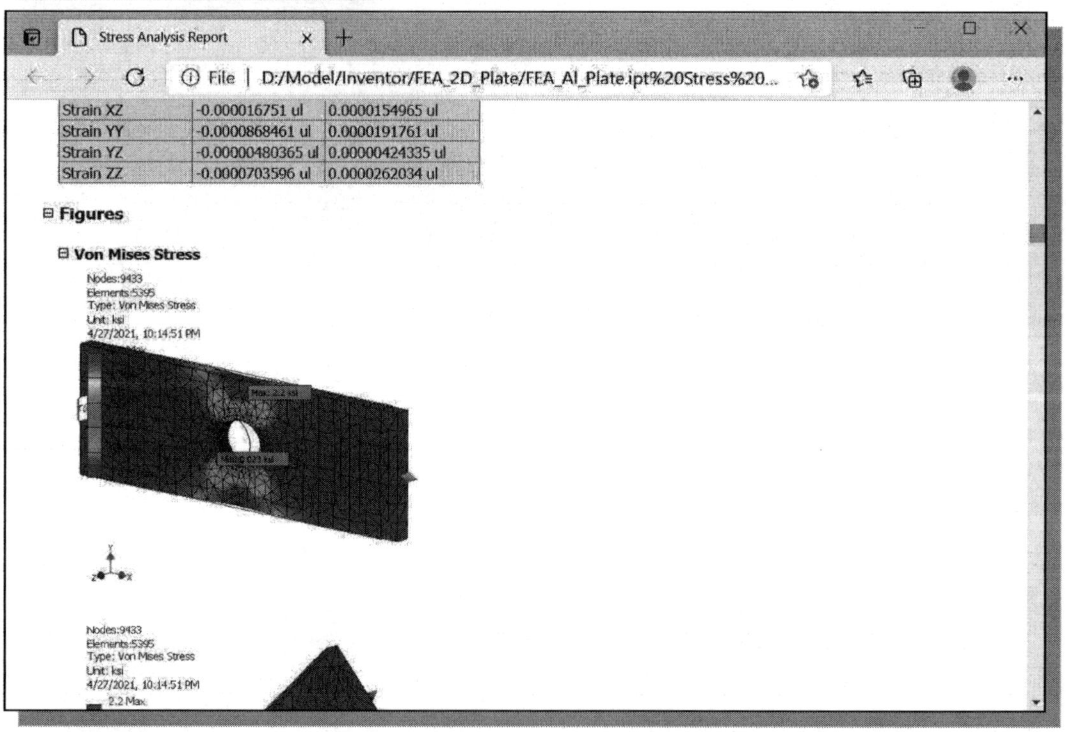

Geometric Considerations of Finite Elements

In the previous sections, the entire plate was created and analyzed, but a closer examination of the associated geometry suggests a more effective approach can be used to analyze the plate.

For *linear statics analysis*, designs with symmetrical features can often be reduced to expedite the analysis.

For our plate problem, there are two planes of symmetry. Thus, we only need to create an FE model that is one-fourth of the actual system. By taking advantage of symmetry, we can use a finer subdivision of elements that will provide more accurate and faster results.

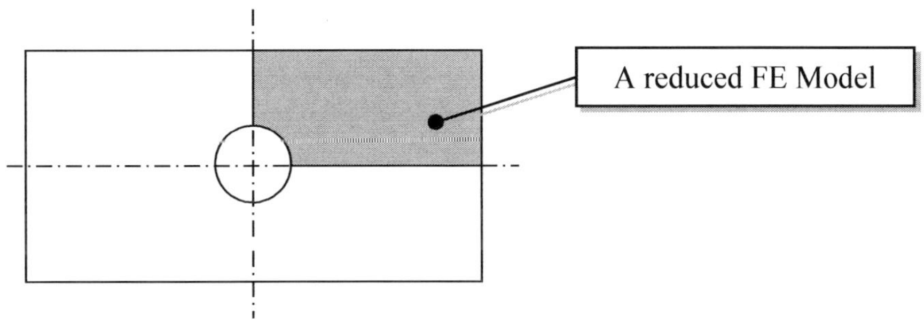

In performing a stress analysis, it is necessary to consider the constraints in all directions. For our plate model, deformations will occur along the axes of symmetry; we will therefore place roller constraints along the two center lines as shown in the figure below. You are encouraged to perform the FEA on this more simplified model and compare the results obtained in the previous sections.

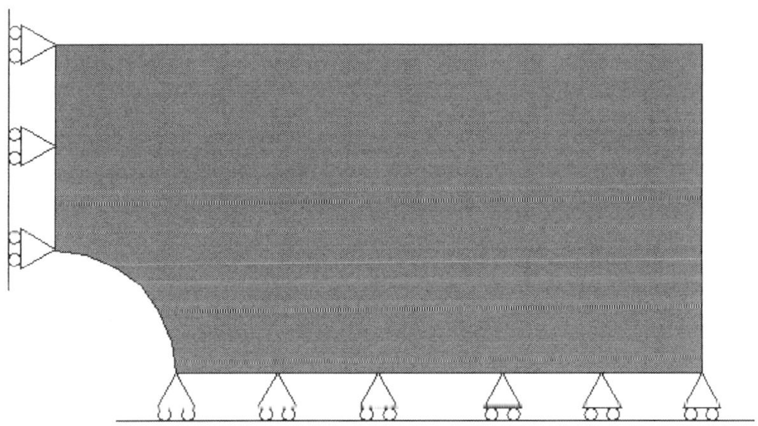

- ❖ One should also be cautious of using symmetrical characteristics in FEA. The symmetry characteristics of boundary conditions and loads should be considered. Also, note the symmetry characteristic that is used in *linear statics analysis* does not imply similar symmetrical results in vibration or buckling modes.

Conclusion

Design includes all activities involved from the original conception to the finished product. Design is the process by which products are created and modified. For many years designers sought ways to describe and analyze three-dimensional designs without building physical models. With advancements in computer technology, the creation of parametric models on computers offers a wide range of benefits. Parametric models are easier to interpret and can be easily altered. Parametric models can be analyzed using finite element analysis software, and simulation of real-life loads can be applied to the models and the results graphically displayed.

Throughout this text, various modeling techniques have been presented. Mastering these techniques will enable you to create intelligent and flexible solid models. The goal is to make use of the tools provided by Autodesk Inventor and to successfully capture the **DESIGN INTENT** of the product. In many instances, only one approach to the modeling tasks was presented; you are encouraged to repeat all of the lessons and develop different ways of accomplishing the same tasks. We have only scratched the surface of Autodesk Inventor's functionality. The more time you spend using the system, the easier it will be to perform parametric modeling with Autodesk Inventor.

Summary of Modeling Considerations

- **Design Intent** – determine the functionality of the design; select features that are central to the design.
- **Order of Features** – consider the parent/child relationships necessary for all features.
- **Dimensional and Geometric Constraints** – the way in which the constraints are applied determines how the components are updated.
- **Relations** – consider the orientation and parametric relationships required between features and in an assembly.

Review Questions:

1. Describe the required steps in performing a stress analysis using *Inventor Stress Analysis Environment*.

2. Describe two ways the material properties can be defined or edited.

3. What is meant by the term *Constraints* in *Inventor Stress Analysis Module*?

4. How do we control whether a load applied to a face is in the *outward* or *inward* direction?

5. Define *degrees of freedom* (DOF).

6. How do we end the *Inventor Stress Analysis Module* and return to the model in Autodesk Inventor?

Exercises:

1. The shaft shown below is fixed at the large end and a 500N force is applied to the small end. Find the maximum stress and maximum deflection in the shaft. The material is AISI 1020. (Dimensions in mm.)

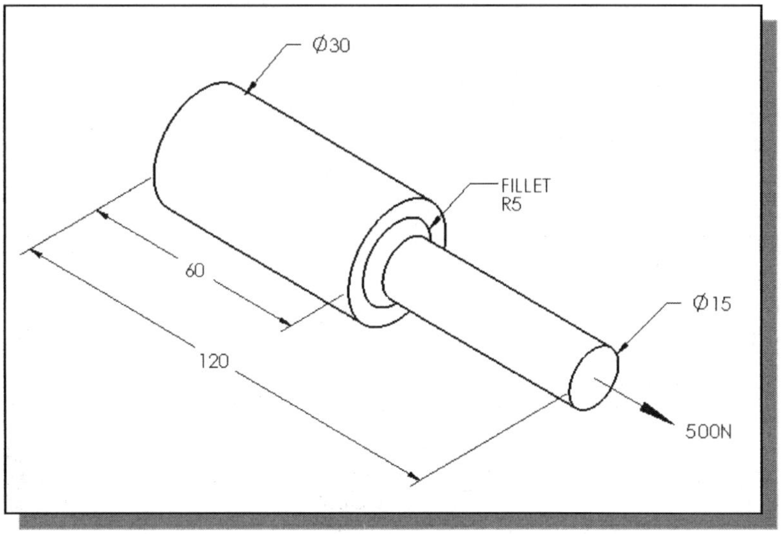

2. For the hanging bracket, the top face is fixed and a 100 psi pressure load is applied to the horizontal surface as shown. Find the maximum stress and maximum deflection in the bracket. The material is Alloy Steel. (Dimensions in inches.)

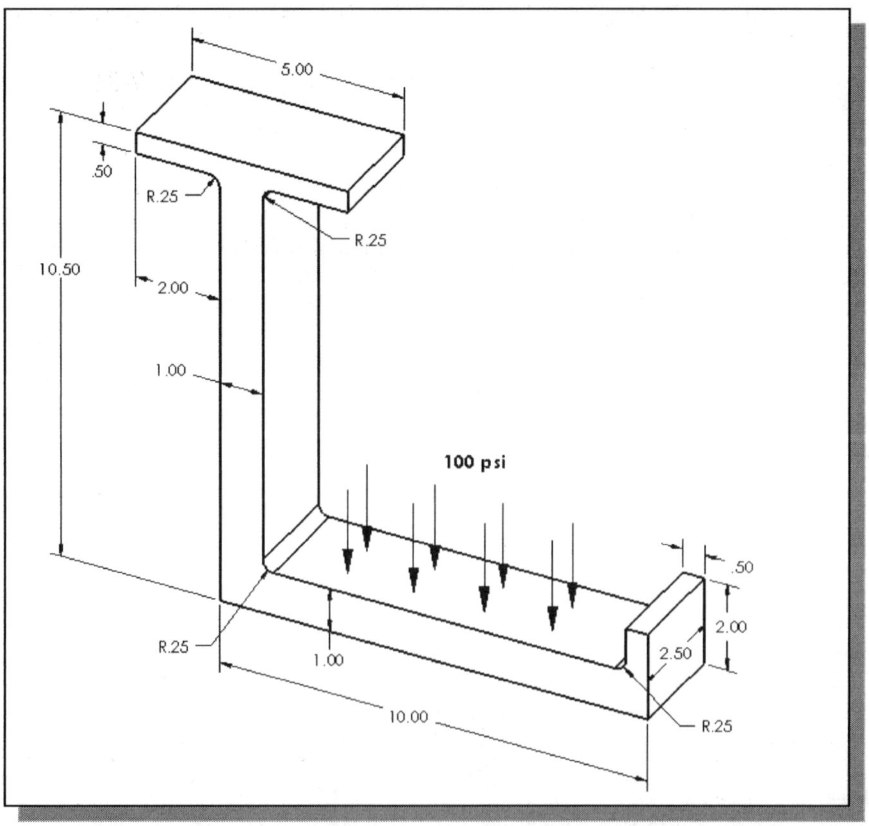

INDEX

A

Absolute Coordinates, AutoCAD, 1-24
Adaptive, 16-2
Adaptive Design approach, 16-2, 16-25
Angle Constraint, 16-12
Annotation Toolbar, 13-29
ANSI Standard, 13-6
Application menu, AutoCAD, 1-3
Application menu, Inventor, 7-14
Arc, AutoCAD, 1-40
Area, AutoCAD, 3-33
Assemble, 16-2
Assembly Modeling Methodology, 16-3
Assembly constraints, 16-11
Associative Functionality, 16-2
Auto Dimension, 10-12
AutoCAD DWG file, 15-4
AutoCAD DWG Layout, 15-7
AutoCAD DWG Model Space, 15-9
AutoCAD Menu Bar, 1-3
AutoSnap and *AutoTrack* AutoCAD, 4-11

B

Balloon, 16-38
Base component, 16-8
Base Feature, 8-7
Base View, 13-11
Base Orphan Reference Node, 12-2
Bill of materials (BOM), 16-40
Binary Tree, 8-3
Block, solids, 8-2
BOM, 16-40
Boolean Intersect, 8-2
Boolean Operations, 8-2
BORN, 12-2
Border, new, 14-19
Bottom Up Approach, 16-3
Boundary representation (B-rep), Intro-4
Browser window, 9-2, 9-5
Buttons, Mouse, AutoCAD, 1-7

C

CAD, Intro-2
CAE, Intro-2
CAM, Intro-2
Canceling commands, AutoCAD, 1-7
Cartesian coordinate system, AutoCAD, 1-22, 1-24
Center Line Bisector, 13-19
Center Mark, 13-19
Center-point Circle, 8-18
Child, 12-2
Circle, AutoCAD, 1-30
CIRCLE, Center point, 8-18
Circular Pattern, 14-17
Close Drawing, AutoCAD, 1-33
Close, LINE command, AutoCAD, 1-28
Coil and Thread, 16-6
Coincident Constraint, 10-6
Collinear Constraint, 10-6
Command Line Area, AutoCAD, 1-3
Command Prompt, AutoCAD, 1-5
Computer Geometric Modeling, Intro-2
Concentric constraint, 10-2, 10-6
Constrained move, 16-16
Constrained Orbit, 7-31
Constraint, Delete, 10-11
Constraints, Geometric, 10-6
Constraints Settings, 10-17
Constraint, Show, 10-4
Constraints Box, Pin, 10-5
Constraints and Load (FEA), 17-14
Construction geometry, 14-14
Construction lines, 14-14
Construction lines, AutoCAD, 4-5
Constructive solid geometry, 8-2
Coordinate systems, 1-22
Create Component, 16-25
Create Feature, Extrude, 16-26
CSG, 8-2
Cursor Coordinates, AutoCAD, 1-5
Cut, All, 7-45
Cut, Boolean, 8-2
Cut, Extrude, 7-45
Cutting Plane Line, 14-2

D

Define Position, AutoCAD, 1-25
Define New Title Block, 14-19
Degrees of freedom (DOF), 16-10
Delete Assembly Constraints, 16-29
Delete Constraints, 10-11
Delete Feature, 12-22
Design Intent, 7-15
Design Reuse, 15-2
  Copy & Paste, 15-2, 15-9
  Sketch Insert, 15-21
  Share Sketch, 15-24
Diameter symbol, AutoCAD, 5-24
Difference, Boolean, 8-2
Dimension, 7-24
Dimensions, AutoCAD, 5-2
Dimensioning, AutoCAD, 5-13
Dimension toolbar, AutoCAD, 5-14
Dimensions, Retrieve, 13-15
Dimension Format, 8-10
Dimension General, 7-24
Dimension Reposition, 8-12
Dimensional Constraints, 10-2
Dimensional Values, 10-20
Dimensional Variables, 10-20
Direct Adaptive Design, 16-25
Display Modes, 7-37
DOF Visibility, 16-10
Drafting settings, AutoCAD, 3-21
Drag Geometry, 11-7
Drawing Annotation, 13-22
Drawing Area, setup, 1-13
Drawing, Assembly Model, 16-31
Drawing Limits, 1-13
Drawing Mode, 13-4
Drawing Resources, 13-8
Drawing Review Panel, 15-5
Drawing Screen, 13-5
Drawing Sheet formats, 13-8
Drawing Sheet formats, Editing, 13-9
Draw toolbar panel, AutoCAD, 1-6
Drawing Template, 14-23
Driven Dimensions, 10-10
Data management, 7-10
DWG files, 15-4
Dynamic Input, 2-3
Dynamic Pan, 7-32
Dynamic Rotation, 7-30
Dynamic Viewing, 7-32
Dynamic Zoom, 7-27

E

Edit Dimension, 7-27
Edit Feature, 11-19
Edit Model Dimension, 13-24
Edit Parts List, 16-34
Edit Sketch, 11-18
Equal constraint, 10-6
Erase, AutoCAD, 1-21
Esc, 1-7
EXIT, AutoCAD, 1-9
EXIT, 7-14
Exit Marker, 7-31
Explode, AutoCAD, 3-35
Exploded view, Assembly, 16-22
Export, 15-20
Extend, AutoCAD, 3-27
Extend, 11-10
Extrude, 7-28
Extrude, Create Feature, 16-26
Extrude, Cut, 7-47
Extrude, Join, 8-19
Extrude, Join, To, 9-10
Extrude, Symmetric, 9-7

F

F2, Pan, 7-32
F3, Zoom, 7-32
F4, 3D Rotate, 7-33
F6, Isometric View, 7-29
Face, 8-17
Feature Based Modeling, 7-15
Feature, Delete, 12-22
Feature Dimensions, Retrieve, 13-15
Feature, Pattern, 13-2
Feature, Rename, 9-11
Feature suppression, 12-21
File Folder, 1-9
FILLET, 2D, AutoCAD, 3-18
FILLET, 2D, 9-18
FILLET, 3D, 15-25
Fillet, Radius, 9-18

Finite Element Analysis (FEA), 17-2
FEA Simulation, 17-12
Solver (FEA), 17-16
Fix constraint, 10-6
Flush constraint, 16-12
Folder create new, 1-9
Format, Units, AutoCAD, 1-12
Free Orbit, 7-30
Fully Constrained Geometry, 10-3

G

General Dimension, 7-24
Geometric Constraint, 7-23, 10-6
Geometric Constraint symbols, 7-23
Geometric Constructions, AutoCAD, 3-4
Global space, 7-19
Graphics Cursor, 1-5, 7-22
Graphics Window, 1-3, 7-7
Grid, 1-18, 1-19
GRID Interval setup, 8-8

H

Help Options, AutoCAD, 1-8
History Access, 9-16
History-Based Modifications, 9-16
History Tree, 9-2
Hole, Placed Feature, 8-24
Home View, 12-23
Horizontal constraint, 10-6
HTML Report, 17-24

I

InfoCenter, AutoCAD, 1-3
Insert Constraint, 16-13
INTERSECT Boolean, 8-2
iProperties, 9-20
Isometric View, 7-29
Isometric Sketching, 6-7

J

JOIN, Boolean, 8-2
Join, Extrude, 8-2

L

Layers Control toolbar, AutoCAD, 1-6
Layers and Object Properties, AutoCAD, 4-4
Layer Properties Manager, AutoCAD, 4-4
Leader, Text, 13-26
LINE command, 7-22
LINE command, AutoCAD, 1-16
LINE Close, AutoCAD, 1-29
Linear diameter, 14-7
List, AutoCAD, 4-24
Local Coordinate System (LCS), 7-19
Local Element Size (FEA), 17-20
Local Update, 9-12
Look At, 11-19

M

Mate constraint, 16-12
Materials, 12-28, 16-36
Measure Angle, AutoCAD, 2-25
Measure Area, 8-13
Measure Distance, AutoCAD, 2-23
Measure Loop, 8-14
Mesh, 17-16
Message area, 7-7
Middle Out approach, 16-3
Mirror Feature, 14-10
Mirror Plane, 15-14
Miter line, AutoCAD, 4-17
Model Dimensions Format, 8-11
Modify Dimensions, 8-11
Modify toolbar panel, AutoCAD, 1-6
Mouse Buttons, AutoCAD, 1-7
Move Component, 16-22
Multiline Text, AutoCAD, 5-23
Multiview drawings, 4-2

N

Navigation Wheel, 7-35
New File, 7-4
New Drawing, AutoCAD, 1-34
New File, 16-7
No new sketch, 12-4

O

Object Snap toolbar, AutoCAD, 2-13
Object Visibility, 12-5

Oblique Sketching, 6-19
Offset, AutoCAD, 3-32
Offset Features, 11-22
Online Help, AutoCAD, 1-8
Online Help, 7-6
Orbit, 3D, 7-30
Orbit, Navigation Wheels, 7-36
Order of features, 8-7
Orientation, Component, 18-7
Ortho, AutoCAD, 3-22
Orthographic View, 7-37
Orthographic vs. Perspective, 7-37
Over-constraining, 10-10

P

Pan Realtime, AutoCAD, 1-27
Pan Realtime, 7-32
Paper Space, 13-4
Parallel Constraint, 10-6
Parent/Child Relations, 12-2, 12-18
Parameters, 10-21
Parametric, Intro-7
Parametric, Benefits, Intro-7
Parametric Equations, 10-21
Parametric Modeling, Intro-6
Parametric Part modeling process, 7-15
Part Browser, 9-5
Parts list, 16-33
Pattern, 14-2
Pattern leader, 14-12
Perpendicular constraint, 10-6
Perspective Sketching, 6-26
  One-point Perspective, 6-27
  Two-point Perspective, 6-28
Perspective View, 7-37
Physical properties, iProperties, 9-20
Pictorials and Sketching, 6-2
Pin icon, Assembly, 16-9
Place Component, 16-9
Place Constraint, 16-11
Placed Feature, 8-24
Point Style, AutoCAD, 3-13
Polar Coordinate System, AutoCAD, 1-24
Polygon, AutoCAD, 2-20
Polyline, AutoCAD, 3-31
Position Define, AutoCAD, 1-25
Profile, 7-43, 11-2
Profile button, 11-20
Project file, 7-10
Project Geometry, 14-13
Projected Views, 13-11
Projects, 7-10
Properties, AutoCAD, 4-25
Purge, AutoCAD, 5-25

Q

Quick Access toolbar, AutoCAD, 1-3
Quick Access toolbar, 7-6
QuickCalc, AutoCAD, 2-23
Quit, AutoCAD, 1-9

R

RECTANGLE command, 8-9
Reference Dimensions, 13-18
Refinement (FEA), 17-18
Region Properties, 8-14
Relations, 10-2, 10-18
Relative Coordinates, AutoCAD, 1-25
Rename, Feature, 9-11
Repeat, AutoCAD, 1-21
Reposition Dimensions, 8-12
Repositioning Views, 13-13
Retrieve Dimensions, 13-15
Revolve, 14-9
Revolve, Full, 14-9
Revolved Feature, 14-9
Ribbon Tabs, AutoCAD, 1-3
Ribbon Tabs, 7-6
Rotate Component, 16-23
Rotation Axis, 14-18
Rough Sketches, 7-21
Running Object Snaps, AutoCAD, 4-7

S

SAVE, AutoCAD, 1-32
SAVE Copy As, 14-23
Save Border, 14-21
Save Title Block, 14-22
Scale, Section View, 13-12
Screen Layout, AutoCAD, 1-3
Screen Layout, 7-5

Section View, 14-24
Selection Window, AutoCAD, 1-21
Settings, Grid, AutoCAD, 1-25
Shaded, Display, 7-37
Share Sketch, 15-23
Show Menu Bar, AutoCAD, 1-3
SIZE and LOCATION, 5-2
Sketch, Command, 7-39
Sketch Plane, 7-38
Sketch plane setting, 12-4
Sketching, 6-2
  Isometric Sketching, 6-7
  Oblique Sketching, 6-19
  Perspective Sketching, 6-26
Snap mode, 1-19
Snap Toolbar, AutoCAD, 2-13
Solid Modeler, Intro-3
Solver (FEA), 17-16
Startup option, AutoCAD, 2-7
Status toolbar, AutoCAD, 1-5
Stress Analysis Module, 17-11
Styles Editor, 13-6
Sub-Assembly, 18-2, 18-5
Suppress Features, 12-21
Surface Modeler, Intro-4
Symmetrical Features, 14-2

T

Table Layout, 16-35
Tangent Constraint, 10-6, 16-13
Template, Drawing, 14-23
Text, Creating, 13-22
Text Leader, 13-26
Thread, 16-6
3D Model-Base Definition, 13-26
Three Dimensional Annotations in Isometric Views, 13-26
Title Block, additional, 14-35
Title Block, new, 14-19
Trim and Extend, 11-10
Trim and Extend, AutoCAD, 2-18
Top Down Approach, 16-3

U

Undo, 10-8
Union, Boolean, 8-2
Units Setup, AutoCAD, 1-12
Units Setup, 7-4
Unsuppress Features, 12-21
Update Part, 9-12, 16-23
User Coordinate System (UCS), AutoCAD, 1-23
User Coordinate System (UCS), 7-19
UCS Icon Display, AutoCAD, 1-23
User parameters, 10-23

V

Vertical constraint, 10-6
View, AutoCAD, 1-27
View, Scale, 13-12
ViewCube, 7-34
Viewing, 7-27
Visibility, 12-5

W

Wireframe Ambiguity, Intro-4
Wireframe, display, 7-37
Wireframe Modeler, Intro-3
Work plane, Visibility, 12-5
World coordinate system (WCS), AutoCAD, 1-22
World space, 7-19

X

XY-Plane, 12-5
XZ-Plane, 12-5

Y

YZ-Plane, 12-5

Z

Zoom All, AutoCAD, 1-14, 1-37
Zoom Extents, AutoCAD, 2-11
ZOOM Realtime, 7-8
Zoom, Navigation Wheel, 7-35
ZX Plane, 12 5

Notes: